Microeconomics

The HarperCollins Series in Economics

Allen
Managerial Economics

Binger/Hoffman
Microeconomics with Calculus

Bowles/Edwards
Understanding Capitalism

Branson
Macroeconomic Theory and Policy

Browning/Browning/Zupan
Microeconomic Theory and Applications

Burgess
The Economics of Regulation

Byrns/Stone
Economics

Caniglia
Statistics for Economics

Canterbery
The Literate Economist: A Brief History of Economics

Carlton/Perloff
Modern Industrial Organization

Caves/Frankel/Jones
World Trade and Payments

Cooter/Ulen
Law and Economics

Ehrenberg/Smith
Modern Labor Economics

Ekelund/Tollison
Economics

Fusfeld
The Age of the Economist

Gordon
Macroeconomics

Gregory/Ruffin
Economics

Gregory
Essentials of Economics

Gregory/Stuart
Soviet and Post-Soviet Economic Structure and Performance

Hamermesh/Rees
The Economics of Work and Pay

Hartwick/Olewiler
The Economics of Natural Resource Use

Hogendorn
Economic Development

Hughes/Cain
American Economic History

Hunt
History of Economic Thought

Hunt
Property and Prophets

Husted/Melvin
International Economics

Kohler
Statistics for Business and Economics

Krugman/Obstfeld
International Economics: Theory and Policy

Kwoka/White
The Antitrust Revolution

Laidler
The Demand for Money

Lardaro
Applied Econometrics

Lipsey/Courant/Purvis/Steiner
Economics

McCafferty
Macroeconomic Theory

McCarty
Dollars and Sense

Melvin
International Money and Finance

Miller
Economics Today

Miller/Benjamin/North
The Economics of Public Issues

Miller/Fishe
Microeconomics: Price Theory in Practice

Mills/Hamilton
Urban Economics

Mishkin
The Economics of Money, Banking, and Financial Markets

Petersen
Business and Government

Phelps
Health Economics

Ritter/Silber
Principles of Money, Banking, and Financial Markets

Ruffin/Gregory
Principles of Economics

Ruffin
Intermediate Microeconomics

Salvatore
Microeconomics

Sargent
Rational Expectations and Inflation

Schotter
Microeconomics: A Modern Approach

Studenmund
Using Econometrics

Tietenberg
Environmental and Natural Resource Economics

Tietenberg
Environmental Economics and Policy

Zerbe/Dively
Benefit—Cost Analysis

Microeconomics

Price Theory in Practice

Roger LeRoy Miller
University of Texas, Arlington

Raymond P.H. Fishe
University of Miami

HarperCollins*CollegePublishers*

For Raburn "Mac" Williams, economist *extrordinaire* and friend.

Thanks,

RLM

For Pat, Jennifer, and Christopher, your encouragement and help was very important.

Thanks,

RPHF

Executive Editor: John Greenman
Developmental Editor: Patricia Nealon
Project Editorial Manager: Melonie Salvati
Design Manager and Cover Design: Lucy Krikorian
Text Design: John Callahan
Cover Photo: David Bishop
Art Studio: Interactive Composition Corporation
Electronic Production Manager: Su Levine
Desktop Administrator: Laura Leever
Manufacturing Manager: Willie Lane
Electronic Page Makeup: Interactive Composition Corporation
Printer and Binder: R.R. Donnelley & Sons Company
Cover Printer: The Lehigh Press Inc.

Microeconomics: Price Theory in Practice

Library of Congress Cataloging-in-Publication Data

Miller, Roger LeRoy.
Microeconomics: price theory practice / Roger LeRoy Miller, Raymond P.H. Fishe
p. cm.—(HarperCollins series in economics)
Includes index.
ISBN 0-06-500526-0
1. Microeconomics. I. Fishe, R. P. H. II. Title. III.Series.
HB172.M645 1995
338.5—dc20 94-21506
CIP

95 96 97 9 8 7 6 5 4 3 2 1

Brief Contents

Detailed Contents

Preface

Imagine the following survey question:

> *What are the most important tools that your students need to learn in order to become good economists?*

We believe that if this survey question were sent out to all teaching economists today, most would answer the following way:

> *The tools of microeconomics are essential.*

We agree that a strong foundation in microeconomic theory is a critical part of a student's understanding of the economic world around us. Our overall goal in writing *Microeconomics: Price Theory in Practice* is straightforward—to provide students with the most solid microtheoretic foundation that they are able to absorb. The key to our technique lies in a judicious blending of modern microeconomic theory with real-world applications and problems. We believe the result is a text with sophisticated core theory, modern topics, and meaningful applications *that work in the classroom.*

As you will see, we focus on theory and look at the most current applications of it, and in addition, we provide a significant series of learning tools that translate the message with meaning. We believe this book offers *more* pedagogical aids than other microeconomics texts today. Finally, students will see mathematical concepts that are presented both intuitively and through algebra and calculus.

Organization and Modern Topics

While we follow a somewhat traditional organization, we add unique treatments. This text started out with several specific content and organizational goals:

- Modernize the treatment of microeconomics with new and current examples.
- Bring the modern theory of the firm—transaction costs, agency problems, asymmetry information, game theory, and bilateral contracting—into the standard discussion of firms and markets.

- Emphasize the constraints individuals face as they make optimal choices, particularly the time constraint.
- Treat pricing issues, auctions, and bargaining as important subjects in an intermediate textbook.
- Incorporate results from the finance literature on how markets adjust to risk and uncertainty.

In tackling these goals, we decided that this book could not become a special interest text. Our sequence of material is standard: introductory material, consumer behavior, theory of the firm, market structures, and general equilibrium. Within this sequence, however, we made a systematic effort to modernize and improve the core material. *Microeconomics: Price Theory in Practice* covers the main core of microeconomic theory and will appeal to a broad range of instructors.

A complete listing of the modern topics we cover would take several pages. Here is a sample: bilateral contracting, search theory, asymmetric information, strategic competition and game theory, bargaining, the agency problem, pricing issues and auctions, and the role of futures and swap markets.

How We Treat Mathematics

There is no one right way to use and teach mathematics in an intermediate microeconomics text. Some students may be comfortable with both algebra and calculus. Others may not be. We researched the development of microeconomics in professional journals and other textbooks. Many texts face an identity crisis: They don't know how to address these preferences in their treatment of mathematics in modern microeconomics. To satisfy all levels of mathematical preparation, we have come up with what we think is an ideal mathematical presentation format.

Most of the mathematical treatment in this text is intuitive. Whenever it is not, we present an intense work-through. Calculus is used in appendices and occasionally in a chapter feature that we call Math Notepad. Math Notepad boxes show students the steps used to derive a particular result, but they are not necessary for the text discussion. Additionally, when necessary and appropriate, we present alternative mathematical treatments in footnotes, sometimes in algebra, sometimes in a calculus format. We also present numerous verbal explanations of the mathematics followed by examples.

Our solution includes a graphical approach to convey *all core concepts.* In addition, we add extra graphs if they are necessary to help explain a particularly difficult concept. There are over 200 graphs in this book. With the help of our many reviewers, we have reworked the graphs to make them crystal clear.

Applications and More Applications

Although some instructors do not believe that it is possible to teach theory through example, most will agree that it is at least possible to excite students about the meaningful scope of intermediate micro theory by providing them with numerous current examples. As emphasized above, our text is strong on theory, but it was developed using a noncalculus approach. Theory is reinforced with example after example. Countless hours were spent researching and developing examples that fit the text material, illustrating both new and traditional concepts. We have gone beyond the occasional brief boxed application so common in today's textbooks. We present two different types of applications—Price Theory in Practice and Policy Applications and Evaluation.

Extensive Pedagogical Teaching Aids within Each Chapter

Solid modern theory does little good to a student who either cannot understand it, retain it, or apply it. To help students learn, we have developed what we believe is the most extensive set of pedagogical features ever presented in an intermediate microeconomics text.

Preview Questions

Four to eight preview questions start every chapter. These questions focus student attention on the key concepts that the chapter addresses. They can be viewed as chapter learning objectives. They are not presented in a vacuum, however. The chapter comes full circle when the student revisits these preview questions in the chapter summary.

Chapter Opening Vignette

Every chapter opens with a real-world vignette that examines a current business situation requiring microeconomic thinking. It can be viewed as your "lecture launcher" to introduce the students to the theory that will follow.

Margin Definitions

Throughout the text, when an important term is first introduced, it is boldfaced and explained. In addition, a glossary definition appears in the margin.

Cartoons

Economics does not always have to be serious. So we have provided a few choice cartoons to lighten the load for your students.

Price Theory in Practice

In addition to examples developed in the text, each chapter includes two or more examples developed as a special feature. These modern examples reinforce the chapter material by applying microeconomic principles to the world at large. They are relevant and current, and they often take a cross-disciplinary stance. Many are international in scope. Topics include the allocation of time in different countries (Chapter 4), the agency problem at the IRS (Chapter 7), production techniques and the building of the tunnel under the English Channel (Chapter 8), rebuilding the U.S. embassy in Moscow (Chapter 9), the Solomon Brothers Treasury auction scandal (Chapter 12), pricing strategies and Disney theme parks (Chapter 12), David Letterman's marginal revenue

(Chapter 14), the future value of television time (Chapter 15), and the gains from trade with Mexico because of NAFTA (Chapter 16).

Learning Exercises

Students use the theory and application from the preceding several pages to solve a Learning Exercise related to each Price Theory in Practice example. These in-chapter questions reinforce student understanding of the concepts just covered. The answers to the Learning Exercises are provided at the end of the text.

Math Notepad

When appropriate, mathematical proofs and mathematical notes are presented in a separate boxed format. Here is where the tools of algebra and calculus are used. The Math Notepad gives the instructor complete flexibility in how much mathematics to use in class. These features offer more detail on mathematical concepts, showing students how to work through the steps of important results.

Policy Application and Evaluation

This teaching feature provides an in-depth examination of some policy application aspect of microeconomics. These boxed features present questions that policymakers currently face. Information is provided on all sides, and students are asked to focus on the economic aspects of the issue. A point-counterpoint format closes with an examination of normative arguments. Critical thinking questions are presented: questions are posed and students are encouraged to draw their own conclusions, because, as the text stresses, ultimately policy positions are normative. For example: Should the purchase and sale of human organs be legal? (Chapter 3) What's happening in the U.S. Postal Service? (Chapter 6) How fairly is executive pay allocated? (Chapter 7) How productive is U.S. labor? (Chapter 8)

Abundance of Chapter-Ending Pedagogy

Beyond the standard chapter-ending format, we have developed an integrated way to make sure that students have understood what they read. We provide the following additional learning tools:

Chapter Summary

This summary addresses each *preview question* linked to its chapter section. We then link that to a brief description of the principle involved. Students will find that by first looking at the chapter preview questions and then revisiting them in the summary, they can better master the major concepts in each chapter.

Trouble Spots

Virtually every discussion of a major topic in intermediate microeconomics will have certain spots that cause trouble for students. Our many years of teaching experience, have allowed us to catalog these trouble spots. They are presented in summary table form. The concept, or trouble spot, is presented with a reminder of how to recognize it. Finally, students are told what to do about each trouble spot.

Review Questions

These questions concentrate on identifying principles and forcing the economic way of thinking.

Price Theory Problems

The problem sets found at the end of each chapter require more rigor than the review questions. They involve application of microeconomic principles.

Writing Exercises

Just because students may want to become economists does not mean that they should not have additional practice in writing. These unique writing assignments require students to apply microeconomic principles to their own real-world situations.

A Complete Learning/Teaching System: The Supplements

Gone are the days when an intermediate price theory book could be sold without a host of supplementary teaching and learning materials. A good text requires an even better supplement package to help instructors present the material effectively and to help students grasp the material quickly. The following supplements are available with *Microeconomics: Price Theory in Practice.*

INSTRUCTOR'S MANUAL

Written by Chris Bell of the University of North Carolina—Asheville. Each chapter of the Instructor's manual contains an outline that provides teaching suggestions and offers theoretical extensions of the chapter content, additional examples for class discussions, and additional short problems with answers. The manual also includes answers to the end-of-chapter questions from the main text.

TEST BANK

We were fortunate to obtain the services of Scott Bloom of North Dakota State University in writing this *Test Bank.* An experienced author in his own right, Professor Bloom has generated almost 1,000 test questions that you can use throughout your course. The test bank is available in both printed and electronic formats.

STUDY GUIDE

A *Study Guide* by Andrew Dane of Angelo State University offers the student a variety of tools to reinforce their understanding of the text. Each chapter contains a review of key points in the chapter, twenty or more multiple-choice questions, two to three solved problems, and ten problems or more for the student to solve. An answer section at the end of each chapter provides answers to that chapter's questions and problems.

TRANSPARENCY MASTERS

A set of 53 transparency masters reproduce key graphs from the text. These visual aids will enhance classroom presentation of each chapter. The masters are contained in the *Instructor's Manual* and are also available in an electronic classroom presentation format.

SOFTWARE

Six software modules are available for the IBM-PC covering elasticity, consumer choice, competition, monopoly, input markets, and game theory. Written by Richard Alston and Wan Fu Chi of Weber State College, the modules encourage students to explore the graphical and analytical relationships described in the text. Numerous problem-solving exercises using the software modules are provided in a new accompanying booklet prepared by Sarah L. Glavin of Boston College.

ACKNOWLEDGMENTS

We cannot claim that we undertook the task of preparing this text alone. There are many who have helped make this project a success. We had the help of numerous kind but critical reviewers. They forced us to increase rigor and expand applications, and they helped us create a much better book for your students. The 34 reviewers have left a permanent imprint on the final form of the text. They offered patient and detailed comments that went far beyond what we had expected. We thank them all many times over for their efforts:

Ted Amato, University of North Carolina at Charlotte
Dale Ballou, University of Massachusetts
Andy Barnett, Auburn University
Chris Bell, University of North Carolina at Asheville
R. Bruce Billings, University of Arizona
Lein-Lein Chen, University of Nevada
John Devereux, University of Miami
Cliff Dobitz, North Dakota State University
David Finifter, College of William and Mary

Ralph Gunderson, University of Wisconsin–Oshkosh
Jonathan Hamilton, University of Florida
Paul Hayashi, University of Texas at Arlington
George Heitman, Pennsylvania State University
Peter Huang, Tulane University
Joyce Jacobsen, Rhodes College
Ed Kittrell, Northern Illinois University
Peter Kressler, Rowan College
Barry Love, Emory and Henry College
Ashley Lyman, University of Idaho
Mark Machina, University of California, San Diego
Warren Matthews, Texas A & I
John McDowell, Arizona State University
Kathryn Nance, Fairfield University
Pascal Ngobuka, University of Wisconsin–River Falls
Jack Osman, San Francisco State University
Edward L. Sattler, Bradley University
Terry Sexton, California State University, Sacramento
David Sisk, San Francisco State University
G. I. Skillman, Brown University
Doug Wakeman, Meredith College
Dale Wasson, Southwest Missouri State University
Frank Wert, Central State University
Anne Winkler, University of Missouri at St. Louis
Larry Wohl, Gustavus Adolphus College

We were also helped by many colleagues and students. University of Miami colleagues John Devereux and Louis De Alessi made many helpful comments during the early stages of the project. Frank Badillo, Pat Conroy, Maritza Peña, and Cigdem Ural helped with the research and development of many examples. Al DeCook provided insightful comments, that helped us develop many applications and problems. Thanks are also owed to literally hundreds of students who responded to our requests to comment on various chapters. We've learned much from their efforts.

Our HarperCollins editor, John Greenman, encouraged us at all phases of the project and kept us on track. For that we are appreciative. A very special debt is owed to Patricia Nealon, our developmental editor, who worked tirelessly through the manuscript many times, always pushing us in the right direction and inspiring us to make the text better and better. We also wish to thank Melanie Salvati, our project editor, and John Callahan, the designer.

As long as most people work to the point at which marginal revenue equals marginal cost, no book will ever be perfect. Ours is no exception. We know that those of you who use it may find points on which you wish to comment. We gladly will accept and acknowledge any comments or criticisms from instructors and students alike. It is with your help that we will continue to make this text better and better in later editions.

Roger LeRoy Miller
Raymond P.H. Fishe

Featured Examples

Microeconomics

1 An Introduction to Microeconomic Reasoning

Preview Questions

When you finish studying this chapter, you should be able to answer the following questions:

How does scarcity affect an individual's choices?

What does the rationality assumption imply about individual behavior?

How does marginal analysis help when making decisions?

What is the principle of comparative advantage and how is it applied?

Why do economists use simplified models to explain behavior?

What is the difference between positive and normative economics?

The headlines in 1993 read:

Markets Breathe a Sigh of Relief Over Inflation

Sharp Rise in the Jobless Rate for Western Germany

U.S. Airlines Clash in Court on Fares

Peasants of China Discover New Way to Weed Out Girls

Andy Warhol Estate's Value Put at $220 Million, a Decline

Long-Distance Big 3 Emerge from Price Wars as Winners

NAFTA Passes, Linking Economies of U.S., Mexico, and Canada

Economics has a part in explaining each of these stories. The power of economic analysis comes from its generality. To develop an understanding of this power and to learn how it is used, read on. . .

The 1990s will go down as the decade that first allowed open-auction bidding for pollution rights. Nicknamed "smog futures," these pollution rights were granted by the Environmental Protection Agency (EPA) and were auctioned by the Chicago Board of Trade on March 30, 1993. Each pollution right allows its owner to emit one ton of sulfur dioxide during a year period. The so-called spot auction was for the year 1995. The EPA offered 50,010 permits. The total quantity bid was for 321,354 permits. The highest bid was $450 and the lowest successful bid was $131. There were 36 successful bids and 70 unsuccessful bids. The total auction proceeds amounted to $7.8 million.

The auction of pollution permits demonstrated the explicit workings of the forces of supply and demand. For the most part, electric utilities were the purchasers of these permits, but brokerage firms, public interest groups, and private investors all put in bids (most of which were unsuccessful). All of the auction participants, however, played a role in helping determining auction prices; that is, they each helped put price theory into practice.

This book is about the price system. We will examine how prices are determined at formal auctions, in formal and informal markets, with bargaining, and by other means. We want to know how goods and services are allocated. For example, how did the EPA come up with its initial quantity of pollution permits? What rights do buyers and sellers have when they transact? Who will monitor the use of the EPA permits? What happens when there are more buyers than sellers, as was the case in the EPA auction? Who is affected by these transactions? Why did environmentalists complain after the auction that the equilibrium price was too low? What determines how much someone will pay for a good or service? How did successful bidders—usually electric utilities—decide what their maximum bid prices would be?

These questions and many more are the backbone of our analysis of virtually every economic phenomenon of any consequence in our society. The approach that we use to answer these questions is to develop the subject of economics from its foundations. We introduce a few of the basic concepts of economics—scarcity, rationality and self-interest, marginal analysis, opportunity cost, and comparative advantage—in this chapter and build on these concepts in subsequent chapters. We also discuss the methodology of economics to give you more insight into the kinds of questions that economics can and cannot answer.

1.1 Economics and Scarcity

Economics as a discipline exists because resources are scarce. Scarcity is the most basic concept in all of economics. **Scarcity** exists when the necessary resources for producing the things that people desire are insufficient to satisfy all wants. Scarcity is not the same thing as poverty. It occurs among the poor and among the rich. The richest person still faces a scarcity of time. Moreover, low income levels do not create more scarcity and high income levels do not create less. The concepts are unrelated. Rather, scarcity is a fact of life, just as is gravity. And just as physicists did not invent gravity, economists did not invent scarcity.

Scarcity The concept that resources are limited compared to wants.

$$$ Price Theory in Practice

Television Commercials and Scarcity

Have you ever thought that television commercials are better than the programs they sponsor? Often we remember a television commercial many days or weeks after it aired. Some commercials have become classics in their own right—the "Where's the Beef?" campaign for Wendy's hamburgers, the "Bo Knows" commercials for Nike shoes starring Bo Jackson, the "Trust Me" commercials for Isuzu featuring Joe Isuzu, and the "It's Pepsi, Uh-Huh" commercials for Pepsi, to name a few. Television commercials have less than sixty seconds to tell a story and convince customers to buy a product. The most critically scarce resource is time.

A standard television program may run for thirty minutes, a miniseries for many hours over several days. Such programs have more time than a commercial to develop the plot, to introduce characters, and to induce the audience to "stay tuned." Some programs are hits while many fail. The same is true for commercials, but they must succeed in less time, so they must be more creative. Commercials must capture our attention quickly. To do so, a commercial must use words with more impact than a television program. Jingles such as "Coke Is It," "It's Cool Whip Time, Baby," and "I Heard It through the Grapevine," sung by Ray Charles, are used in commercials because they are memorable, but they rarely appear in television programs. Scarcity has forced commercials to a creative level above regular television programs. The same can be said for music videos compared to half-hour musical-variety shows.

Learning Exercise 1.1

TV Guide publishes a schedule of upcoming TV programs each week. A scarcity of space on each page limits the discussion of each program. Can you think of other examples in which scarcity of page space affects what magazines or newspapers choose to print?

WANTS VERSUS NEEDS

Wants
Individual consumption when income is not a constraint.

Wants are defined as all the things that individuals would consume if they had unlimited income. Wants are not the same things as needs. The term *need* is objectively indefinable for an economist. When someone says, "I need a new car," there is no way for us to know whether that person is stating a vague wish, a want, or an absolute necessity. People use the term *need* casually in most conversations. What people usually mean is that they want something that they do not currently have. Every individual has competing wants but cannot satisfy all of them, given limited resources. This is the reality of scarcity, for each person must constantly make choices.

You may want to live near the ocean, to own several cars, to retire in twenty years, and to travel frequently. Land near the ocean is available, but there is a limited supply of sites you can build on. You can purchase several cars, but if you do, you may not be able to afford the house near the ocean. If you retire early, you may not have enough resources to support your travel plans. Scarcity forces all of us to choose. Resources—time, income, and land—are scarce, so you must choose which wants you will satisfy. Scarcity and choice go hand in hand and lead us to the basic definition of economics.

DEFINING ECONOMICS

> **Economics is the study of how scarce resources are used to satisfy competing and alternative ends.**

Thus, economics is the discipline charged with the responsibility of telling you that you cannot have everything you want. You must choose between going to class or sleeping late in the morning, between going to the movies or studying for an exam, or between any number of alternatives that offer some benefit to you. Again, it is scarcity that forces you to make a choice. Recognizing that you constantly face scarce resources and are forced to choose will help you understand the principles of economics. You do not have to wonder why resources are scarce but rather how each of these resources find their way to different parts of the economy and in what quantities. After all, everyone—including businesses, governments, the rich, and the poor—faces scarce resources, so you are not alone.

1.2 Rationality and Optimizing Behavior

A basic assumption underlying virtually all analysis in economics is called the **rationality assumption.**

Rationality Assumption
Individuals maximize according to their own self-interest.

> **The rationality assumption states that individual decisions are the result of optimization subject to economic constraints.**

But what is optimization? And what are economic constraints? People optimize if their actions move them closer to accomplishing their goals rather than further away from them. Economic constraints are many. We all have a limited income with which to buy goods and services. Our time is scarce. Income and time are the two most basic economic constraints. Thus, we might say that rational individuals take actions that move them closer toward their goals, subject to income and time constraints.

Still another way to state the rationality assumption is that individuals respond to incentives, and by their response they act in their own *self-interest.* Self-interest does not mean that we are all greedy but rather that we try to do the best we can given our economic constraints. In our choice of goods and services, the rationality assumption implies that we select the goods that offer us the greatest satisfaction without exceeding our budget.

This approach to rationality is different from that in other social sciences. The distinction here is between what people think—the realm of psychology and perhaps sociology—and what they actually do. Economics does not involve itself in analyzing individual or group thought processes. Instead, economics looks at what people actually *do* in life with their scarce resources. It does little good to criticize the rationality assumption by stating, "Nobody acts like they are maximizing," "I never think that way," or "How unrealistic! It's irrational to think that people are rational!" The act of choice is one of optimizing in economics; they are assumed to be one and the same. Economists accept that people can make different choices, however, as long as the choices are the best each person can do with his or her limited resources and other constraints. The idea that individuals act in their own self-interest follows if we assume they optimize behavior when their objective excludes others from consideration.

Although it may appear that self-interest is only a negative concept, it is not. It also explains many of the positive things we do. When we buy lunch at McDonald's, we do so because it is in our self-interest. We may be in a hurry, with little time for lunch, and McDonald's offers us quick service. It is also in McDonald's self-interest to serve us quickly and to make sure that we are satisfied. If we are satisfied we might return again, which increases the company's income. In a general sense, every voluntary exchange—the purchase of lunch or a movie ticket—occurs because it is in the self-interest of *both* parties. If one party did not benefit from the exchange—say, you knew the lunch at McDonald's would make you sick—then it would not occur.

Self-interest is not always centered on an individual. A firm, such as McDonald's, acts for the self-interest of thousands of shareholders. By producing a good product at a price that produces a profit, McDonald's can provide benefits to its shareholders. In a similar vein, parents may compromise on many decisions to achieve peace and harmony. A common example is the decision to eat out. The mother enjoys Chinese food, the father likes French cuisine, and the young children like pizza. The family usually goes to the pizza restaurant because it creates the most "pleasant" meal, even though the narrow self-interest of the mother and father would dictate another choice.

Sometimes self-interest does not seem to be the primary reason for our actions. Many people give anonymously to charities and to people in need that they have read about in the newspaper. Some soldiers have given up their lives to save fellow soldiers by jumping on hand grenades. Many people have risked their lives to rescue trapped motorists who have driven into canals or lakes. Self-interest is a powerful concept, and it is the basis for formal economic models of behavior, but it is sensible to note that this concept alone cannot explain all the behavior we observe.

DECISION MAKING ON THE MARGIN

The rationality assumption implies that we each optimize. To optimize correctly, we must make decisions on the margin. That is to say, individuals in their capacity as consumers, students, managers, employees, and so forth do not look at the whole picture but rather at *changes* in the picture. We therefore use **marginal analysis,** which is an analysis of what happens when small changes take place, to solve our optimization problems.

Marginal Analysis Using incremental changes to make optimal decisions.

Marginal analysis is one of the most often used concepts in economics. For example, Table 1.1 and the graph in Figure 1.1 show the total and marginal benefits and costs of holding a series of fund-raising meetings to ask for campaign contributions. Total benefits are measured by the amount of money raised for your campaign. Marginal benefits are equal to the amount of money raised by each additional fund-raising meeting. Total costs are measured by summing the expenses of each fund-raising meeting. Marginal costs are measured by the expense of each additional fund-raising meeting. We can use marginal analysis to determine how many fund-raising meetings to hold to maximize your net campaign contributions.

TABLE 1.1

Benefits and Costs of Fund-Raising Meetings

Number of Town Meetings	Total Benefits	Marginal Benefits	Total Costs	Marginal Costs	Net Benefit
1	$45,000	–	$5,000	–	$40,000
2	58,000	$13,000	10,000	$5,000	48,000
3	65,000	7,000	15,000	5,000	50,000
4	70,000	5,000	20,000	5,000	50,000
5	73,000	3,000	25,000	5,000	48,000
6	75,000	2,000	30,000	5,000	45,000

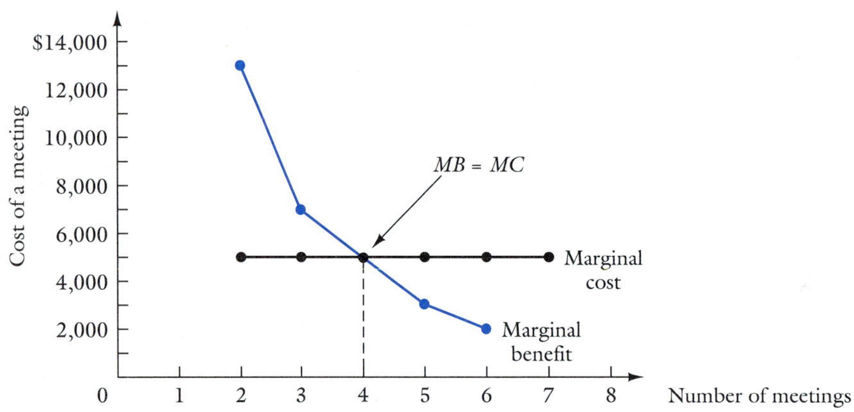

FIGURE 1.1

Marginal Benefits and Marginal Costs of Fund-Raising Meetings

The marginal cost (*MC*) of each fund-raising meeting is constant at $5,000, while marginal benefits (*MB*) decrease with additional fund-raising meetings. Marginal benefit equals marginal cost at four fund-raising meetings. To maximize net campaign contributions, then, four fund-raising meetings should be held.

The amount of campaign contributions produced by each fund-raising meeting varies according to who attends. The first meeting attracts many of your strongest admirers, who contribute a total of \$45,000 to your campaign. The second meeting brings some people who have heard good things about you and also some of the strong supporters who could not attend the first meeting. The second meeting raises an *extra* \$13,000, so your campaign war chest totals \$58,000 after this meeting. The \$13,000 is entered into the *marginal benefit* (MB) column of Table 1.1 because this is the extra amount raised by the second meeting.[1] The term *marginal* always refers to an extra or incremental amount. By the end of the sixth meeting you have met nearly everyone in town who wants to meet you and you have raised \$75,000 for your campaign. Note that the amount raised by each fund-raising meeting decreases as you have more meetings. This is the same as saying that the marginal benefit declines as you have more fund-raising meetings. You would expect this result because at your later meetings you are greeting more citizens who are less enthusiastic about the issues and your campaign.

While these meetings are effective at raising funds for your campaign, they are also expensive. The citizens who attend are treated to snacks, an auditorium must be rented, and promotional material is distributed to the community. Each fund-raising meeting costs \$5,000. We call this amount the *marginal cost* (MC) of a fund-raising meeting.[2] The total cost equals the number of meetings times \$5,000. If you hold five meetings, your cost will be \$25,000.

THE EQUIMARGINAL PRINCIPLE

Again, your problem is to decide how many fund-raising meetings to hold in order to leave your campaign chest with the greatest amount of money after you pay all expenses. That is, you want to maximize the *net* payments to your campaign from these fund-raising meetings. Figure 1.1 shows how you can use marginal analysis to determine a solution to your problem. Net payments to your campaign will be maximized when marginal benefits from a fund-raising meeting are equal to marginal costs, where MB = MC on the graph. This result is known as the **equimarginal principle.**

Equimarginal Principle
The optimum for any problem comparing benefits and costs occurs at the point where marginal benefit (MB) equals marginal cost MC).

We see that if you hold four fund-raising meetings, marginal benefits will be equal to marginal costs. Four meetings will raise \$70,000 at a cost of \$20,000, so you will net \$50,000. How do you know to stop here? If you hold five meetings, you net \$48,000 (\$73,000 minus \$25,000), so you lose \$2,000 by holding the fifth meeting. For five meetings, marginal cost exceeds marginal benefit, so the equimarginal principle tells you that you have gone too far—stop at four meetings.

To apply the equimarginal principle, it is useful to continue to increase output—fund-raising meetings—until you reach a point at which marginal benefit equals marginal cost. Unfortunately, in cases involving integer

[1]Marginal benefit is defined as the change in total benefit (TB) divided by the change in quantity: $\Delta TB/\Delta Q$, where Δ means "change in." For very small changes in quantity, marginal benefit is the derivative of the total benefit function with respect to quantity: dTB/dQ.

[2]By analogy to marginal benefit, marginal cost is defined as the change in total cost (TC) divided by the change in quantity: $\Delta TC/\Delta Q$. For very small changes in quantity, marginal cost is the derivative of the total cost function with respect to quantity: dTC/dQ.

changes—that is, numbers such as 1, 2, 3, . . . ,—there will always be another point at which you receive the same net gain as you receive at the MB = MC point. In the case of the fund-raising meetings, three meetings will also provide a *net* of $50,000. Technically, you are indifferent between holding three or four fund-raising meetings because they offer the same amount of money to your campaign. Practically speaking, however, not all problems will involve integers and two equivalent solutions, so it is better to learn the MB = MC rule and apply it when making your decision.

Marginal analysis is a concept that can help us find the optimal solution—either a maximum or minimum—to a given problem. In this example, we have seen that marginal analysis provides a quick and simple way to determine the optimal number of fund-raising meetings you will hold.

Marginal analysis may not always be so easy to apply. When we are faced with *mutually exclusive* choices, such as whether to change the oil in the car or let a mechanic do the job, marginal analysis states that we compare the marginal benefits and marginal costs of each action. The margin has changed. It is not a quantity, like the number of meetings, but an *action* we select. Because our choices are mutually exclusive, marginal analysis dictates that we compare the *total* benefits and costs of each action. If the mechanic charges $25 to change the oil and your benefit—that is, the cost you face if you do the job yourself—exceeds $25, then the mechanic changes the oil. You simply compare your cost to the price charged by the mechanic to make your decision.

1.3 The Concept of Opportunity Cost

One of the most commonly used terms in the discussion of economic problems is *opportunity cost.* Whenever an alternative has to be selected, there is a cost to the choice that is made. Consider the situation you are in when

1. Your car needs a new set of tires;
2. You have an out-of-town meeting to attend at which you will discuss your raise for next year; and
3. your cupboards are bare, so you need to go grocery shopping.

You have a choice to make from these three alternatives; you cannot do them all at the same time. The choice you make has an opportunity cost, which is determined by what your second choice would have been. For example, suppose that you *rank* these alternatives as follows. Your first choice is to attend the out-of-town meeting to discuss your raise for next year; your second choice is to buy new tires; and your third choice is to go grocery shopping. The opportunity cost of your decision to attend the out-of-town meeting is

- The cost of continued wear and tear on the tires, plus
- The increased cost you may face because an accident is more likely if you have a flat tire while traveling at high speed.

Alternatively, if your first and second choices are reversed (we don't suggest this), the opportunity cost you face is the cost of not attending the important meeting. These costs may include the cost of not receiving a raise next year. The definition of **opportunity cost** follows from this example:

Opportunity Cost
The cost of the next-highest-ranked alternative.

The opportunity cost of each action is the value of what is given up—the next-highest-ranked alternative—because of a choice.

Notice that in this example the cost of not going to the grocery store is omitted. It was not the second-ranked alternative, so its cost does not enter into the opportunity cost of your decision. There may be many alternatives available, but what is important is the one that would be chosen if the present action was not taken.

A word of caution is in order: *Avoid double-counting opportunity costs.* If you attend the out-of-town meeting, you cannot take your car in for a new set of tires *and* go to the grocery store. Your opportunity cost is generated from the *next-highest*-ranked alternative, not from *all* alternatives.

Consider a numerical example. Assume that you earn $10 per hour (after taxes) interviewing customers at the local shopping mall. The mall merchants value your interviews because they provide an economic profile—income, age, sex—of their customers. Your working hours are flexible. Today you are planning to work for six hours, but you become increasingly aware of how beautiful the weather is outside. You begin to think of spending the afternoon in a nearby park or perhaps going swimming. After four hours of interviewing, you find that you cannot resist the need to venture outdoors. You decide to spend two hours in the park. What is the opportunity cost of your decision? It is $20, which is your lost survey income, if your next-highest-ranked alternative was to continue interviewing. If instead the next-highest-ranked alternative was to go swimming, and ranked below swimming was your interviewing job, then the opportunity cost of your picnic is the value you place on swimming, which should be at least $20.

Your actions may also generate out-of-pocket expenses. If the park where you are going has an entrance fee of $10, you must count this expense as part of the opportunity cost of your decision. The reason is that you could have spent the $10 on other items—say, a new CD or a movie—so you are giving up other consumption to gain entrance to the park. Opportunity cost captures the *full price* you pay for your decisions. The full price you pay adds the value of the next-highest-ranked alternative to any out-of-pocket expenses you incur from your actual decision.

$$$ Price Theory in Practice

Drinking in a Drought

A compelling and unfortunate example of opportunity cost occurs regularly in the animal kingdom. During the rainy season in Africa, water holes for zebras and other animals are plentiful. Lions are natural predators for zebras, and when zebras are feeding they are in danger of being trapped and killed by a pride of lions, who try to surround and attack them. But zebras have excellent senses and can often detect lions by their smell or movement in the bushes. Typically, a water hole is surrounded by small bushes, with thick trees and overgrowth some distance away.

During the rainy season, just the appearance of a lion at the edge of the overgrowth causes the zebras to bolt and run to another water hole. Lions must be quick and clever to fool the zebras if they are to catch a meal. When the dry season begins, water holes start to evaporate. If the dry season lasts too long, it turns into a drought and many water holes are without water. Under such circumstances, when a lion appears in the clearing, the zebras take longer to bolt; the lions have a better chance of catching them. The zebras face an opportunity cost of leaving the present water hole, which has water in it, and running to another hole that may be empty. The longer the drought lasts, the longer they will stay at a water hole when a lion appears. In economic terms, as the opportunity cost of running away rises, the zebras chose to wait longer to run away.

Learning Exercise 1.2

Household fires are common. If there were a fire and you had only seconds to leave your house or apartment, what one thing would you try to take with you? Why is this item more valuable than any other?

1.4 Gains from Trade, Specialization, and Comparative Advantage

When individuals work together, the group as a whole gains. When you need to miss class because of a doctor's appointment, a classmate will probably share notes with you, and you will share your notes if he or she must miss class. When you need to change the oil in your car, a garage mechanic will be glad to help if you can pay the fee. There are gains from trade in many different situations.

These examples illustrate an important by-product of the gains from trade: **specialization.** You could probably change the oil in your car—the simplest car maintenance booklet will tell you how to do this—but you benefit by letting a garage mechanic specialize in performing this job. The mechanic will be finished sooner than you would be and has the proper equipment to make the job easier. If you lived in a rural area eighty years ago and owned a car, you probably would have changed the oil and performed many repairs yourself. Eighty years ago there were fewer cars on the road in rural areas, so the market was not big enough for mechanics to open garages in every small town. Times have changed. Nearly every little town you can drive to has a local mechanic because nearly every household either owns or leases a car.

Specialization Developing skills for a limited number of tasks.

While many of us are mechanically inclined, and some of us may be better than the mechanics that we find at our local garage, it is rarely the case that we take such matters into our own hands. The principle of *comparative advantage* offers the best explanation for our behavior. As a college student, you read books, review notes, write papers, attend lectures, and so on, so your time is better spent on college-related activities, even though you might know how to change the oil in your car. The local mechanic has a comparative advantage in changing your oil. In effect, the mechanic has a lower opportunity cost of changing oil than you do. In general, we define **comparative advantage** in terms of relative opportunity costs:

Comparative Advantage The ability to perform a given task at a lower opportunity cost than someone else.

You have a comparative advantage in one activity if you have the lowest opportunity cost of performing that activity.

Comparative advantage is a *relative* concept. When we say that the mechanic has a comparative advantage in changing your oil, we mean that *compared to you,* the mechanic faces a lower opportunity cost of changing oil. We are not saying that you do not know how to change the oil in your car, only that the opportunity cost you face by doing so exceeds the mechanic's opportunity cost. For example, if the mechanic charges $25 to change the oil, which covers his or her opportunity cost, you will accept this offer if the time and effort you expend changing your own oil is worth more than $25.

Whether we consider two individuals, two firms, or two countries, we are comparing the opportunity costs that *two* entities face when producing a specific good or service. We are not comparing the opportunity costs a *single* individual faces when producing different goods or services.

$$$ Price Theory in Practice

COMPARATIVE ADVANTAGE IN THE HOUSEHOLD

Production Process for Cooking a Meal and Cleaning the Kitchen

	Adrianne	*Ken*
Cooking	10 minutes	40 minutes
Cleaning	20 minutes	30 minutes
Total Time	30 minutes	70 minutes

Roommates, husbands and wives, and significant others often share the basic household chores. Comparative advantage helps us understand why. The table above shows the relative time Adrianne and Ken require for cooking and cleaning up when they prepare a meal for themselves. Note that Adrianne spends less time than Ken in both chores. We say that Adrianne has an **absolute advantage** over Ken in cooking and cleaning when her production process requires less time. This does not mean, however, that she should perform both chores. The table below shows the opportunity costs of Adrianne and Ken expressed in terms of the two chores.

Absolute Advantage The ability to produce an output with fewer inputs than someone else.

Opportunity Costs of Cooking and Cleaning

	Adrianne	*Ken*
Cooking	$\frac{1}{2}$ cleaning	$\frac{4}{3}$ cleaning
Cleaning	$\frac{2}{1}$ cooking	$\frac{3}{4}$ cooking

We see that Adrianne's opportunity cost of cooking is $\frac{1}{2}$ the time she spends cleaning. Similarly, her opportunity cost of cleaning is $\frac{2}{1}$ or twice the time she spends cooking. Ken's opportunity cost may be interpreted the same way. Adrianne's opportunity cost of cooking is lower than Ken's, and Ken's opportunity cost of cleaning is lower than Adrianne's. We say that Adrianne has a comparative advantage in cooking, whereas Ken has a comparative advantage in cleaning.

Note that there are gains from trade in this example. If both Adrianne and Ken prepare separate meals, then Adrianne spends 30 minutes cooking and cleaning and Ken spends 70 minutes cooking and cleaning. If they "trade" with each other and specialize in the chore in which they have a comparative advantage, Adrianne will cook and Ken will clean up after every meal. Now if two separate meals are prepared, Adrianne will spend 20 minutes cooking and Ken will spend 60 minutes cleaning. Both Adrianne and Ken save time by working together. There will be other savings too because it is unlikely that they will need to prepare two separate meals. The clear conclusion here is that both Adrianne and Ken gain from voluntary trade when they specialize in the activities in which they have a comparative advantage.

Learning Exercise 1.3

We realize that couples marry because they love each other, but can you also think of economic advantages they receive from living together and sharing household chores?

1.5 Markets, Firms, and Individuals

Microeconomics focuses on the *smallest* unit of economic activity—the individual. The concepts discussed above help explain the choices each individual makes when confronted with scare resources. In the chapters that follow, we build on these decisions to describe how markets and firms operate. Both markets and firms are composed of many individuals, so the concept of the smallest unit of economic activity is blurred when either markets or firms are discussed; try not to lose sight of the individual.

The easiest way to categorize economic agents is as buyers or sellers. Within a market there must be both. Buyers include all consumers, who purchase goods and services, plus all businesses, which purchase production inputs such as labor, capital, and raw materials. These inputs ultimately are used to produce the goods and services that consumers buy. (Some firms produce *intermediate goods* that other firms purchase in order to produce final goods and services.) Almost all individuals act as both buyers and sellers. You may sell your labor services to an employer and buy the product produced by another employer. In any event, it is the interaction of buyers and sellers that forms markets. We can define a **market** as any collection of buyers and sellers that interacts such that exchange is possible. At the beginning of this chapter we gave an example about the market for pollution credits. The buyers and sellers of those credits interacted, and the result was a set of market clearing prices for the right to pollute with sulfur dioxide.

Market
The total collection of buyers and sellers participating in exchange of a given good or service.

Note that markets are not the same thing as industries. An **industry** is typically defined as a group of firms that sell the same or related products. That means that an industry is part of the seller side of a market. Industry studies are

Industry
A group of firms that sell the same or related goods or services.

those that examine groups of firms that are similar. Some of the examples in the following chapters involve the results of industry studies, such as the automobile industry and the diamond industry.

Many, if not all, market issues are issues of individual behavior. For examples, how do so many people, often thousands, interact to determine prices? At the New York Stock Exchange, one of the world's largest markets, individuals do not need to be on the trading floor to determine stock prices. The market for shares of companies traded on the New York Stock Exchange brings together individuals from all over the globe. Although we cannot observe all of the participants in such a market, we can observe the price-making process. When something *big* happens on Wall Street, the evening news shows the trading floor of the New York Stock Exchange. Little pieces of paper are spread out all over the place; some large TV-like machines with digital displays are seen in circular formation on the floor; men and women are huddled together near the machines; and it is very noisy. You are watching the forces of supply and demand in action. Buyers and sellers are brought together through phone communications, amid all the noise and apparent confusion, to determine the prices of over 1,700 stocks each day.

Issues of concern to firms are often issues of individual behavior, too. The goals of a firm, for example, may not be the same as the goals of its individual employees. In a market, the *gains from trade and comparative advantage* provide individuals with an incentive to cooperate and trade. In a firm, the different goals of each individual are aligned with the goals of the firm through wage payments, bonuses, and employment decisions. These three variables affect the *budget constraint* of the individual, expanding or contracting the individual's budget. Because an individual is better off with more income (a larger budget), the firm can offer employment packages that encourage individuals to act in a manner consistent with the firm's goals.

Whether we discuss markets or firms, there will always be individuals whose behavior forms the building blocks of our analysis.

1.6 Economics as a Science

While it is true that economists disagree on a number of issues, economics still qualifies as a science. After all, physicists, biologists, and physiologists disagree about numerous theories, too. Moreover, what economists *dis*agree about makes the news; what virtually all economists actually agree about—probably more than 90 percent of what is in the textbooks you read—just does not make "good press." Finally, if scientists did not disagree, there would be no scientific advancement. Any science worth its salt is based on the examination of evidence. Economists, just like physicists and microbiologists, are constantly examining evidence to see if current theories can be disproved. Remember that the burning debates of one decade become "ho-hum" truths the following decade. No one now believes that the earth is the center of the universe, but for much of our history, everybody did. After World War II, people argued heatedly about the merits of a centralized planned economy, but such debates rarely occur anymore. It is not that one side won the debate; rather, empirical evidence—the collapse of the former Soviet Union and its satellite countries, all of which were centrally planned—settled the question.

THE USE OF MODELS

Economic problems are addressed using models that simplify the world. Models are useful because they provide an efficient approach to economic questions. The simplifications of each model allow us to focus on the important features of the problem rather than extraneous features. Economic models have been applied to an incredibly diverse range of questions, such as how many children are expected to be born to wealthy versus less wealthy families, why people emigrate from one country to another, and what factors affect Euro-Disney's pricing structure.

MODELS, REALISM, AND ASSUMPTIONS

At the outset it must be emphasized that no model in *any* science, and therefore no economic model, is complete in the sense that it captures every detail and interrelationship that exists. Indeed, a model, by definition, is an abstraction from reality. It is conceptually impossible to construct a perfectly complete realistic model. For example, in physics we cannot account, even in theory, for every molecule and its position, and certainly not for every atom and subatomic particle. Such a model would be impossibly expensive to build and impossibly complex to work with. No model of the solar system, for example, could possibly take into account all aspects of the system.

A scientific model should capture only the essential relationships that are sufficient to analyze the particular problem or answer the particular questions with which we are concerned. An economic model cannot be faulted as unrealistic simply because it does not represent every detail of the real world. A map of a city that only shows major streets is not necessarily unrealistic if, in fact, all you need to know is how to pass through the city using major streets. As long as a model is realistic in terms of shedding light on the central issue or the forces at work, it may be useful.

If our goal is to explain observed behavior, then the simplicity or complexity of our model is not important. If a simple model can explain observed behavior in repeated settings as well as a complex model does, then it has some value, and, by definition, it is probably easier to use.

The assumptions that we use in our models can sometimes be thought of as "shorthand" for reality. For example, suppose you are in a large department store and you would like a drink of water. What do you do? You probably ask a sales clerk for directions to the nearest water fountain. The clerk may offer a detailed description of the path you should follow:

> Go up the escalator, turn right, and go past the green-and-yellow display case of Swatch watches; go past the Ninja Turtle clearance sale, which is next to the Star Trek games and videos; keep going until you pass the sofas on sale in the furniture department; go past the display of brass beds

> and antique headboards until you come to a room with patio furniture. In the back of this room there is a large blue sign hanging from the ceiling indicating where the restrooms are. The drinking fountain is next to the restrooms.

This is a fairly complete description of reality—there are few simplifying assumptions in the clerk's description. Unfortunately, by the time the clerk has finished giving you directions and you have repeated the parts that were not clear, your thirst for water may have passed. Consider an alternative approach that offers fewer details but gets to the point:

> Go up the escalator and turn right. Walk straight ahead until you see the large blue sign indicating where the restrooms are. The drinking fountain is next to the restrooms.

With this simple description the clerk has told you what you want to know and has omitted the details that are not important at the moment. Economic models are more often like the second description of how to find the water fountain—they focus on what is important to the problem at hand; other details are omitted because they are not necessary to the present problem.

HOW TO CONSTRUCT MODELS OF ECONOMIC BEHAVIOR

The different points to model building just outlined have often been called the *scientific method*. This method consists of at least five distinct steps:

1. *Define the problem.* It does little good to formulate a model for which the problem is amorphous. You must decide what specific problem you want to address. If you are interested in taxes, for example, you must decide what aspect of taxation is important in your research. You will get much further in your scientific inquiry if you examine, say, the effects of increases in marginal tax rates on total tax revenues collected in the United States over the last 100 years than if you choose to analyze all taxes in all countries since the beginning of civilization. You need to define your problem in such a way that you are examining a specific cause-effect relationship.
2. *Formulate the hypothesis.* In order to formulate a hypothesis, you must find some type of order in the economic phenomenon that you are studying. While it is true that everything depends on everything else, no hypothesis can be tested under such conditions. What are the possible causal variables that might change total tax revenues collected by the U.S. government? Clearly, one variable is the state of the broader economy. Yet another is any changes in marginal tax rates. Your hypothesis might be that holding all other things constant, a given percentage increase in marginal tax rates will lead to a less-than-proportionate increase in total tax revenues collected. As a researcher, your difficult task is to decide which other variables you must account for. Whatever you decide, you will have to accept some level of abstraction. You do this by making a simplifying set of assumptions.

In this particular case you might assume that individuals' work effort is sensitive to changes in the marginal tax rate but not to extraneous items such as global warming, who won the World Series, and the like. Remember here that your assumptions are not necessarily "reality." You use assumptions in order to formulate testable hypotheses. Your assumptions per se cannot be criticized, only the inability of your model to predict well. You might feel better if you use reasonable assumptions, but that is about it.

3. *Deduce your predictions.* Whatever your hypothesis is, or hypotheses are, you should be able to make predictions. If your hypothesis is that individuals work less when their marginal tax rate goes up, one deducable prediction is that an increase in marginal tax rates will yield a less-than-proportionate increase in government tax revenues collected. This is a strong prediction that can be tested.
4. *Test your model.* While no model can be proved in economics, many can be rejected on the basis of empirical evidence. You determine this by testing the predictions of your model with real-world data. If your hypothesis is that individuals work less when marginal tax rates rise and therefore pay less tax than predicted by the government, you can use ample data from the history of this country to test this hypothesis.
5. *Evaluate your results.* You evaluate your results by comparing your predictions with the data that you have collected. You can never prove your theory, but you might find evidence that leads you to reject it. If the last five times the federal government increased marginal tax rates, government-collected tax revenues increased by more than in proportion to the increase in marginal tax rates, then you would begin to doubt your hypothesis and its implications.

Economists use the scientific method to confirm theories. Without confirmation, economic theories do not become widely accepted.

1.7 Positive Versus Normative Economics

There is a distinction between what we can explain with economic models and what behavior we desire to see. When we explain observed behavior, we are applying *positive* economic reasoning to a problem. For example, you may be asked to explain why the price of air travel rises during the end-of-year holiday season. This is a question for positive economics because you are asked to explain what happened in a given situation and why.

Positive economic analysis also includes "what if" questions: *What* will happen to the number of students in college *if* tuition increases 15 percent next year? *What* will happen to the sales of tennis shoes *if* golf becomes more popular? What will happen to the wages of musicians *if* more electronic pianos are installed in hotels and restaurants? Questions like these are the meat and potatoes of economics. Economists and other social scientists have discovered that economic models provide insight and answers to these questions.

There are other questions that our models cannot help us answer. Questions that ask what *should be,* not what *is,* lie outside the domain of economic models. These questions are known as *normative* economic questions. What should be the quota on imported sugar? What should be the minimum wage? What should be the size of government? Each of these questions is a normative economic question. The answers given to normative questions are subjective opinions. These answers are neither right nor wrong; they are just opinions. For example, you may think that a minimum wage of $5 per hour is too low and state this opinion when asked. This is your opinion, and economic models have nothing to say about whether you are right or wrong. No matter how interesting normative questions can be, we will stay away from them because our models offer no help in answering these questions.

Chapter Summary

1. Scarcity makes people choose between alternatives because resources are not plentiful enough to satisfy everyone's needs. Finite resources place limits on everyone.
2. The rationality assumption states that individuals optimize in their own self-interest. Thus, the choices individuals make are assumed to be optimal, given resource constraints.
3. The equimarginal rule states that an optimum is reached at the point where marginal benefit (MB) equals marginal cost (MC). Thus, marginal analysis provides a tool that helps an individual make optimal decisions.
4. One individual has a comparative advantage over another in performing a certain task if he or she has a lower opportunity cost for that task. Comparative advantage explains why people, firms, and nations specialize in various production activities.
5. Economists follow the scientific method by using empirical evidence to support their theories. The simplicity of a theory is not important, except to make it easy to understand. What is important is that the theory is supported by actual data on behavior in the economy.
6. Positive economic reasoning answers "what if" questions. These are questions that examine the empirical evidence to validate theories and draw conclusions. Normative economic reasoning asks for an opinion. Normative economic statements are of the "what should be" type.

Trouble Spots

Concept	Reminder
Wants Versus Need	Although sometimes used as synonyms, these words define two different economic environments. An individual's needs may be limitless and difficult to define, but wants are goods and services that an individual would consume if resources permitted. This is a simple distinction, but it focuses attention on the fact that scarcity of resources limits our ability to satisfy all of our wants.

The Concept of Opportunity Cost	Although we use the term *opportunity cost,* it is somewhat misleading because it makes you think that opportunity costs are just one type of cost. However, nothing could be further from the truth. Costs arise because of forgone opportunities, so all true costs are opportunity costs. Thus, when we compute the opportunity cost of a decision, we must sum the value of the next-highest-ranked use of our time and the value of goods and services we forgo because of the decision.
Economics as a Science	Economics is not a religion, and economists are not ministers delivering a divine message, even if some economists may appear to be spiritually committed to their discipline. But economic analysis is a powerful tool that you can use to guide and improve decisions that you make over your lifetime. The commitment you see in many economists is a commitment to a way of thinking about problems—the economic way of thinking. If you disagree with some economic models, do so using economic analysis and empirical evidence. In this manner you will strengthen your arguments and learn more about the power of economic analysis.

1.8 Review Questions

1. It is often said that air is not a scarce resource. Do you agree with this claim? Is the claim so imprecise that you cannot answer the question? Is it a certain mix of air (i.e., the amount of nitrogen, oxygen, hydrogen) that is scarce?
2. Explain how my "need" for a college degree is different from my "want" for a college degree. How do limited income and wealth affect the definition of needs and wants?
3. Explain why economists often use simplifying assumptions to explain behavior. What is gained from such simplicity? What is lost?
4. The mathematics of passing a car with another car is very complicated, yet motorists pass other cars frequently. Can we say that they are acting *as though* they can solve a complex mathematical equation? If so, can we use the equation to predict whether a motorist will successfully pass another car?
5. How do you use marginal analysis to solve a problem? What is the equimarginal principle?
6. What is the opportunity cost of attending college? Is the price of meals part of the opportunity cost of attending college? Why or why not?
7. How has the development of timesaving devices such as microwave ovens affected the gains from marriage?
8. How can a business firm align the goals of an individual with the goals of the firm?
9. What is the basic difference between positive and normative economic questions? Give two examples of each type of questions.

1.9 Price Theory Problems

1. *TV Guide* does not publish a list of the commercials to be aired along with programs. Why? How does scarcity affect *TV Guide*'s decision?
2. If there is no way to test a theory with real-world data, can we determine whether it is a good theory? Why is empirical evidence used to validate a theory?
3. Which of the following are part of the opportunity cost of going to a movie instead of renting a video to watch at home? Are any of these items omitted from the opportunity cost calculation? If so, why?

    a. The expense of a baby-sitter for your children.
    b. The expense of a restaurant meal before the movie.
    c. The rental expense of the video.
    d. The value of one hour of sleep lost because of a traffic jam at the theater.
    e. The prorated share of the rent that you pay for your home while you are at the movies.

4. If your economics and marketing exams are scheduled for the same day, how do you determine how much time you will spend studying for each exam? How does your current course grade affect your decision?
5. Suppose that you enjoy your drive to and from work because it gives you time to reflect on your day ahead when you go to work and the events of the day just past when you travel home. You value the time spent commuting according to the following schedule:

Time Spent Commuting	Personal Value
10 minutes	$100
10 to 20 minutes	70
20 to 30 minutes	50
30 to 40 minutes	35
40 to 50 minutes	25
50 to 60 minutes	20

   If you earn $20 per hour at your job, how long will you desire to spend commuting to work?
6. Identify which of the following statements use positive economic analysis and which use normative economic analysis.

    a. The government should not regulate the banking system. After all, the savings and loan mess has shown that they don't know what they are doing.
    b. Eliminating barriers to emigration between European countries caused wages to equalize in many industries.
    c. Paying members of Congress more gives them less incentive to commit wrongful acts, such as bouncing checks at the House bank.
    d. We need more restrictions on industrial polluters because air pollution is killing the planet.

1.10 Writing Exercise

Carefully keep track of your activities over the course of a week. Create a diary of how you spend your time and what items you purchase. When you have completed the diary, write a description of the various decisions you made during the week—to study, attend class, go out to lunch, go to a party, and so on—focusing on the opportunity cost of each decision. In other words, what was the next-highest-ranked alternative action for each decision? Try to compute the actual opportunity cost of some of your decisions. If applicable, use the principle of comparative advantage to explain some of your actions.

2

Demand and Supply: A Review

Preview Questions

When you finish studying this chapter, you should be able to answer the following questions:

- What is the difference between relative and absolute prices?
- How are stocks different from flows?
- What are five factors that affect demand?
- How is the market demand curve determined?
- What does the price elasticity of demand measure?
- How is the market supply curve determined?
- What condition is necessary for a market equilibrium?
- How does price elasticity of demand help predict changes in total revenue?
- Why do you bargain for some goods and not others?

At the flower market in Amsterdam, tulips, roses, and many other flower varieties are auctioned early in the morning to wholesalers and retailers. A lot of tulips, for example, is shown to bidders and then the auctioneer, with the help of a mechanism called a bid clock, begins the bidding process. As the clocklike device ticks down, each new tick represents a lower price. The bidders are silent until one among them signals a sale. The lot of tulips is sold, and no other buyer has a chance to bid because the winner is the first bidder. Flowers are a perishable good, so they must be sold quickly, and the bid-clock mechanism facilitates a quick sale.

At the Pike Place fish market in Seattle, vendors sell salmon, Dungeness crab, and other fresh seafood to tourists and local customers. Prices can change daily and sometimes hourly for these products. In contrast, Coldwell Banker Company and many other firms sell real estate throughout the United States. Asking prices are set by sellers and often remain unchanged for months even though no buyers have made offers. A typical home takes nearly five months to sell, and some homes take two or three years to find a buyer. Why? What explains the behavior of prices in these markets? We can sum up the answer in three words—supply and demand.

In open markets, demand and supply determine prices and the allocation of resources. Because the analysis of many problems facing us involves an application of demand and supply analysis, it is important to provide a review of this mechanism. Together, demand and supply determine the market price of most goods and services. Before reviewing demand and supply analysis, we must make two important distinctions: (1) the difference between relative and absolute prices and (2) the difference between stocks and flows.

2.1 Relative and Absolute Prices

When we discuss prices it is important to distinguish between the absolute level of prices and the relative prices of specific goods and services. For example, lunch in an average restaurant in Italy these days costs over 10,000 lira. Does that sound expensive? At 1994 exchange rates, it represented about \$6.25. How do we know if something is expensive? Price numbers, which we call the **absolute price** or *nominal price,* mean little by themselves. We measure whether a good is expensive by its **relative price,** that is, its price compared to the prices of other goods.

Absolute Price
Pure numbers measured in current dollar values.

Relative Price
The price of one good compared to another.

A basic prediction of price theory is that individuals respond to relative prices rather than absolute prices; it is relative prices that convey important information to the marketplace. For buyers, the relative price of a good indicates what they must give up in terms of other goods in order to purchase that good. For example, if lunch costs \$7.50 and a movie costs \$7.50, then one lunch will cost the equivalent of one movie. The opportunity cost of one good in terms of the other good is revealed by relative prices. Thus, individuals and firms focus on relative prices—which measure opportunity costs—when making decisions.

Relative prices do not have to involve two specific goods. They can be measured relative to an index of the prices of several goods. For example, we could ask about the relative price of your labor services in terms of all goods in general. If you were paid \$20,000 in 1985 and you are paid the same amount in 1995, we would say that your nominal income is unchanged, but your real income has fallen. **Nominal income** is the money income you receive, whereas **real income** measures the value of your money income in terms of goods and services, that is, things that you buy. Typically, real income equals your nominal income divided by an index of absolute prices, such as the Consumer Price Index (CPI), which in shown Table 2.1 under the heading "All Consumer Items." From 1982–1984 to 1994, the CPI rose 47 percent, so relative to 1982–1984 the prices of goods were 47 percent higher at the beginning of 1994. Your real income has fallen to \$13,633 (\$20,000 divided by 1.467 from Table 2.1) in 1983 dollars. How did such a change in real income affect your behavior? You could not afford to buy as many goods in 1994 as you did in 1982–1984 with the same nominal income.

Nominal Income
The flow of money income received in a given period.

Real Income
Nominal income divided by an index of absolute prices.

What happened to the *relative* prices of different goods between 1982–1984 and 1994? In Table 2.1, relative prices are computed using the price index of all consumer items as the base of comparison. That is, we divide the price of a particular good by the price index of all consumer items to compute the relative price of that good. The relative price of food was little

TABLE 2.1

Comparing Absolute and Relative Prices 1982–1984 Versus 1994

Good	1982–1984	1994	Changes in Absolute Price	Change in Price Relative to "All Consumer Items"
All Consumer Items	100.0	146.7	47%	—
Food	100.0	142.9	43%	–3%
Apparel	100.0	129.4	29%	–12%
Medical Care	100.0	207.7	108%	+42%

Source: U.S. Department of Labor, Bureau of Labor Statistics, Summary Data from the Consumer Price Index News Release, 1994.

changed over this period, while the relative price of clothing declined by 12 percent. The biggest change in relative prices is in medical care. The relative price of medical care *increased* 42 percent over this period.

Often there is confusion between relative and absolute prices. Table 2.1 shows that absolute prices are increasing for *all of these goods* between 1982–1984 and 1994; that is, there is general inflation. Relative prices tell a different story. Food and clothing are becoming less expensive relative to all consumer items, whereas medical care is becoming more expensive. Although the movement of absolute prices is important for measuring inflation, remember that microeconomics focuses on relative prices. Relative prices tell us what something costs compared to other goods. Thus, the opportunity costs of your choices in the marketplace are revealed by relative prices.

LEARNING EXERCISE 2.1

From an index cost of 100 in 1982–1984, private college tuition has increased to an index cost of 170 in 1994. Compute the absolute change in college costs over this period. How did college costs change relative to the cost of all consumer items in Table 2.1?

2.2 STOCKS AND FLOWS

Stock
The quantity of a resource available at a given point in time.

Flow
The change in the stock of a resource between two points in time.

A distinction exists between stocks and flows of a good. A **stock** of books on your bookshelf, for example, is defined as a quantity of books that exists on your bookshelf at a moment in time. How many books are on your bookshelf right now? If there are 22 books, then 22 books is your stock of books at the present point in time. Over time the stock of a good will change. A **flow** of a good is defined as the change in the stock over a certain period of time. If you buy a new book each week, then the flow of your consumption of books is one book *per week*. Notice that a flow is always measured relative to units of time—per day, per week, or per year—but a stock is measured at a point in time—at 4 P.M. on February 12, 1995, you found 22 books on your bookshelf.

A good example of the difference between a stock and a flow involves nominal income versus wealth. Nominal income is a flow concept. **Wealth** is the stock of nominal income and other assets that you hold at a given point in time. You have to know the time period over which the income flows in order to understand a person's income. If you are told that someone is making $100, you don't know if that person is making very little or a huge amount. If the $100 refers to one month, then we are looking at someone making a small amount of income. In contrast, if the $100 of income is earned per hour, then this is someone who is making over $200,000 per year and is in the top 2 percent of all income earners in the United States.

Wealth
A stock of assets at a given point in time.

2.3 Individual Demand

What influences your decision to purchase a good? Think about a common good, say, apples. It is reasonable to say that the price of apples affects how many apples you will buy. We know that there is some price at which you will not buy apples—$10 each probably qualifies as such a price. But how many apples will you buy when the price is, say, 10 cents per apple? The decision is yours to make, but you probably will buy more than one. A **demand curve** for a good shows how much a consumer will buy at different prices of that good. Your decision to buy more apples when the price falls is called the **law of demand.**

Demand Curve
The relationship between quantity purchased and price.

Law of Demand
An inverse relationship exists between quantity demanded and price.

> **The *law of demand* states that a larger quantity will be purchased when price decreases (other things equal). Similarly, a smaller quantity will be purchased when price increases (other things equal).**

The law of demand applies to all goods and services. It is true because you and other consumers make it true. Economists observe that more is purchased when prices fall. The law of demand is thus a law because we have observed no (or very few) counterexamples. We can actually show that an exception to the law exists in theory (see Chapter 6), but the exception does not appear to be relevant in practice.

The law of demand is illustrated in Figure 2.1, which shows how many apples you will buy each week at various prices. Note that at prices *above* $2 per apple, you do not buy any apples. At these prices, you are not a direct participant in the apple market. When the price of apples reaches $2, you are willing to purchase one apple each week. At a price of $1.75, you are willing to buy two apples per week; at $1.50, three apples per week; and so on. The quantity demanded increases as price decreases. What you actually buy depends on the market price, a factor that we will determine a little later in this chapter.

Note that demand is a flow concept. In Figure 2.1, we describe quantity demanded as the number of apples you are willing to buy *per week* at each price. Supply, which we discuss below, is also a flow concept.

There is always a qualification added to the law of demand. The qualification is that other variables are held constant; that is, price can change but nothing else can change. The Latin expression *ceteris paribus* is used to state

Demand Schedule

Price	Quantity
$2.25	0
2.00	1
1.75	2
1.50	3
1.25	4
1.00	5
.75	6
.50	7
.25	8

(a)

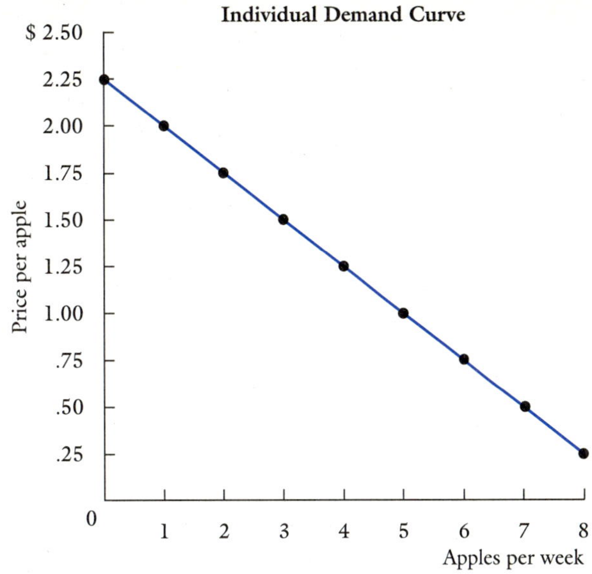

(b)

FIGURE 2.1

Demand for Apples

Panel (a) describes how the quantity of apples demanded responds to the price of apples, holding all other factors constant. When the price of an apple is $2, the quantity demanded is 1 apple. When the price of an apple is $.25, the quantity demanded is 8 apples. Using the data in panel (a), a downward-sloping demand curve is plotted in panel (b). The demand curve shows the number of apples you are willing to buy at different prices. Price and quantity demanded are negatively related.

Ceteris paribus
Other things being the same.

this qualification. ***Ceteris paribus*** means "other things being the same, or equal." The "other things" we are referring to here are any variables *other than* the price of the good itself that may affect demand. This qualification is very important to our analysis because it allows us to focus on the effects of a single variable. Obviously, if other variables that affect demand are changing along with price, we may have a difficult time sorting out the effects of a price change. The *ceteris paribus* assumption resolves this problem by holding these other variables constant.

WHAT VARIABLES SHIFT (OR AFFECT) DEMAND?

To affect demand implies that the demand curve shifts, either to the right or to the left. There are numerous variables that can cause the demand curve to shift if they change. Changes in the following variables stand out and are most often used by economists to explain observed behavior:

- Income
- Prices of substitutes
- Prices of complements
- Changes in your knowledge about the good or bad effects of the good or service
- Expectations
- Tastes

Consider the variables that affect your demand for apples. If you want to buy an apple, even a 25-cent apple, you must have some income. If you have more income, you can buy more apples. Similarly, if you like bananas, you might consider them a substitute for apples. A **substitute good** is one whose price has a positive effect on consumption of another good. If bananas and apples are substitutes, the price of bananas will affect how many apples you buy. If bananas cost 5 cents apiece, you may buy only bananas and avoid apples for the time being. Alternatively, if bananas cost 50 cents, you may avoid bananas and buy only apples. Thus, as the price of bananas increases, the quantity of apples you buy also increases—a positive relationship. You may buy both apples and bananas, but as the price of one changes you will tend to consume more of the good that has become relatively cheaper.

Substitute Good
Good A is a substitute for good B if the demand for good A varies directly with the price of good B.

Demand is also affected by the price of complements. A **complement** is a good whose price has a negative effect on consumption of another good. If you like apples dipped in hot caramel, which we will call caramel-coated apples, then the quantity of apples you purchase is affected by the price of caramel. If caramel and apples are complements, then, as the price of caramel increases, it becomes more costly for you to consume caramel-coated apples, so you buy fewer apples—a negative relationship. Alternatively, if the price of caramel decreases, caramel-coated apples become cheaper, so you buy more apples.

Complement
Good A is a complement to good B if the demand for good A varies inversely with the price of good B.

Other variables may affect your demand for apples. *Knowledge or information* about a good can affect demand. For example, if you thought that apples were bad for you because they were sprayed with Alar, a chemical that helps preserve and redden them, you might avoid apples altogether. Many consumers did just that during the Alar scare of 1989. Newspapers and TV broadcasts carried stories about the possibility that Alar causes cancer. Apple growers responded by stopping the use of Alar, and consumers began to buy apples again. Similarly, suppose you find out that apples are not a nutritious food but oranges are. Thus, your demand for apples is expected to decrease (shift to the left) and your demand for oranges will likely increase.

Another important variable that determines your demand for goods and services concerns the concept of expectations. An **expectation** is a view or belief you hold about the future behavior of a variable. In keeping with the apple example, assume that you are a fruit merchant who knows a pilot flying to Alaska for a commercial airline. She has to fly over the state of Washington. When she does so her instruments register the most extreme low-pressure area she has ever seen. She tells you this information and you determine that there is going to be a severe freeze in the state of Washington, particularly where apples are growing. Your expectations are that the apple crop will be less than normal and therefore the price of apples will rise. Consequently, your present

Expectation
A belief about the future.

demand for apples will increase; that is, you will buy now before prices increase. The expectation that the market price will rise causes your demand for apples to change.

Tastes A description of the goods and services that you like and dislike.

Your **tastes** or preferences also affect demand. Tastes describe the goods and services that you prefer. Obviously, if you don't like apples, then you will buy fewer apples at a given price than someone who does like apples, *ceteris paribus.* If you once liked apples and then changed your preferences so that you don't like them, we would say that your tastes have changed. A change in tastes causes demand to shift.

QUANTITY DEMANDED VERSUS DEMAND

Our discussion of the factors that affect demand has identified seven variables that influence your demand for a good: price, income, the price of substitutes, the price of complements, changes in knowledge or information, expectations, and tastes. Of these variables, only price can cause a movement *along* the demand curve. Look at panel (a) in Figure 2.2. The price variable is shown on

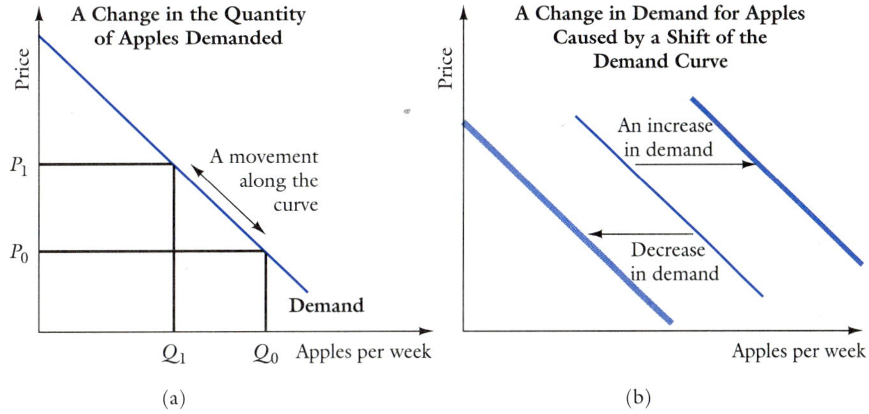

FIGURE 2.2

Change in Demand versus a Change in Quantity Demanded

Panel (a) depicts a typical demand curve with price on the vertical axis and quantity demanded on the horizontal axis. If price changes from P_0 to P_1, quantity demanded will decrease from Q_0 to Q_1. This price change causes a movement along the demand curve. Panel (b) shows what happens to demand when there is a change in income, the price of complements, the price of substitutes, or expectations. These variables cause the demand curve to shift, either to the right or the left. When the demand curve shifts to the right, you are willing to purchase more of the good at each price. This shift represents an increase in demand. When the demand curve shifts to the left, you are willing to purchase less at each price. A shift to the left indicates a decrease in demand. Note that a shift in demand can be interpreted as a willingness to pay either a higher or lower price for a given quantity of the good.

the vertical axis, with quantity demanded on the horizontal axis. If price changes from P_0 to P_1, quantity demanded will change from Q_0 to Q_1. We see that the price change has caused a movement along the demand curve as claimed. We refer to such a movement as a change in **quantity demanded,** which is a change in the number of units demanded.

Quantity Demanded The number of units purchased at a given price.

We also claimed, however, that only a change in the good's price can cause a movement on the demand curve. This is true because our graph in panel (a) shows only the relationship between price and quantity demanded. Income, the price of substitutes, the price of complements, changes in knowledge or information, expectations, and tastes do not appear on either the vertical or horizontal axes. These "shift" variables cannot cause a movement *along* the given demand curve.

Panel (b) in Figure 2.2 shows what happens to demand when there is a change in income, the price of substitutes, the price of complements, or variables measuring expectations. These variables cause the demand curve to shift either to the left or right. These variables do not appear on either axis, so they must cause the demand curve to shift if they have any influence on demand. We call such movements a *shift,* or *change,* in demand.

$$$ Price Theory in Practice

Steinway Tunes in on the Competition

The Steinway Co. has been making pianos since 1853. Other piano makers come and go, but Steinway stays; its mystique and preeminent position with concert artists helps bolster sales and its reputation. There is a saying often heard at piano stores: "You are in the market either for a piano or a Steinway." Because of this reputation, you do not expect a Steinway piano to be cheap. The least expensive model, an upright, costs over $10,000, and the most popular model, a 9-foot concert grand, costs about $40,000. The most expensive model sells for more than $60,000, about half the price of an average home in an urban area.

The past fifteen years have been tough for piano makers; even Steinway has been affected. The heyday of pianos occurred in the 1920s, when there were fewer ways to provide in-home entertainment. Advances in technology brought stereos and television into many homes. These goods became viable substitutes for pianos, offering cheaper in-home entertainment to consumers. The price and availability of these substitutes steadily reduced the demand for pianos (shifted the demand curve to the left).

Technology has also lowered the cost of substitutes. Since the mid-1970s, other substitutes, such as VCRs, CDs, and electronic keyboards, have fallen in price. The price of electronic keyboards, for example, fell from about $3,000 in the mid-1970s to less than $300 today (for a keyboard of equivalent quality). Piano sales declined rapidly after VCRs, CDs, and electronic keyboards were introduced. In 1976, 250,000 pianos were sold in the United States; in 1982, about 200,000 were sold; and in 1991, fewer than 125,000 were sold. Over the same period, the number of electronic keyboards sold increased from a few hundred to over 1 million units.

To understand the important role substitutes play in the piano market, consider how the relative price of pianos and electronic keyboards has changed since the mid-1970s. The average price of a piano was $1,300 in 1976, compared to about $5,000 today. So, in the mid-1970s, an average piano cost about 43 percent as much as an electronic keyboard. Today, the average piano costs 17 times as much as an electronic keyboard. In other words, today you can buy 1 piano or 17 electronic keyboards for the same amount of money. Such large changes in relative price encourage consumers to substitute to the cheaper good, which is what has happened.

Steinway has begun to respond to the threat posed by less expensive in-home entertainment products. The company has designed a line of "midpriced" pianos, to be built by a low-cost Japanese manufacturer. These pianos will carry the Steinway name and guarantee. In addition, Steinway has automated some of the piano assembly process at its plants in New York. (Some of the assembly equipment in these plants is over a hundred years old.) Lower production cost and lower piano prices are expected to increase profits and sales.

These changes may backfire, though. The Steinway piano is known for its unique playing characteristics; no two Steinways play exactly alike. In addition, Steinway has traditionally used high-quality woods, and each piano represents many hours of work. Some of the recent changes signal a shift away from tradition. In response, some concert pianists have begun using a near-perfect substitute for a new Steinway: an old Steinway that has been reconditioned. A 50-year-old Steinway that has been reconditioned may actually sell for more than a new Steinway. While other piano manufacturers compete with substitutes, such as VCRs, CDs, and electronic keyboards, Steinway must compete with a market-tested, proven competitor: Steinway.

LEARNING EXERCISE 2.2

What effect does the price of a used Steinway have on the demand for a new Steinway?

2.4 MARKET DEMAND

Market Demand
The (horizontal) sum of the demand curves of all participants in the market.

We can describe the market demand for a product in much the same way as we have discussed an individual's demand. The difference is that the **market demand** is the total quantity demanded by all individuals at each price. Thus, we must somehow aggregate the demand curves of all individuals to find the market demand curve. We combine individual demand curves by summing up the quantity demanded by each individual at different prices:

> **The market demand curve is a schedule that shows the quantities of a particular commodity that will be purchased by a particular group of customers per period of time at different prices. It is therefore the (horizontal) sum of the demand curves of all participants in the market.**

Figure 2.3 illustrates how we sum up individual demand curves. Panel (a) shows the demand for apples by you and Susan, a friend and apple aficionado. As you can see from panel (a), your demand for apples is less than Susan's demand. Specifically, Susan will buy six apples a week to your one when the price is $2. At a price of $1.25, Susan will buy nine apples to your four, and so on.

There are clearly others in the market for apples. To put everyone's demand curve in the graph would unnecessarily clutter the diagram. In fact, it would become a complete mess. To overcome this problem and to allow others to enter the market for apples, we will use the representative consumer concept. A **representative consumer** is someone whose demand is just like other peoples' demand. Assume that you are the representative consumer. Then your demand curve is also the demand curve for the other participants in

Representative Consumer
A consumer whose demand is like the demand of many other consumers.

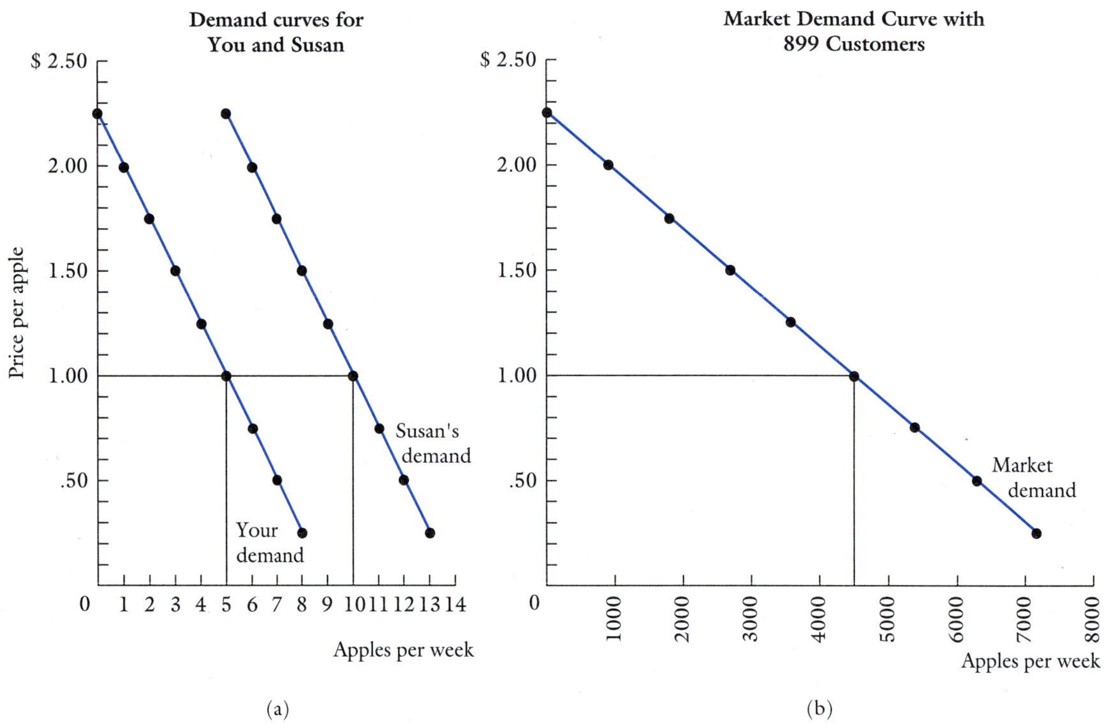

FIGURE 2.3

Deriving the Market Demand for Apples

The market demand curve is the horizontal sum of the demand curves of all individuals in the market. Panel (a) shows the demand curves of two consumers: you and Susan. When the price of apples is $2, you will buy 1 apple, whereas Susan will buy 6 apples. To find the market demand for all 899 apple consumers, we add the quantity demanded by each person at each price. Panel (b) shows the market demand curve for all 899 apple consumers. At a price of $1, these customers will buy a total of 4,500 apples per week.

the market—except for Susan, of course. Let's assume that there are 899 people in the market for apples, including Susan and yourself.

To find the market demand curve for all 899 apple consumers, we must add the quantity demanded by each person at each price. To begin, if the price is 25 cents, Susan will demand 13 apples, you will demand 8 apples, and the other 897 people—who are just like you—will demand 7,176 apples (8 × 897). Total market demand at a price of 25 cents is 7,197 apples (13 + 8 + 7,176). Alternatively, if the price is $1 per apple, you will demand 5 apples, Susan will demand 10 apples, and the other 897 people will demand 4,485 apples (5 × 897). Total market demand at a price of $1 is 4,500 apples (5 + 10 + 4,485). We can compute the market demand at other prices in the same manner.

Panel (b) in Figure 2.3 shows the market demand curve for all 899 apple consumers at various prices. Note that the market demand curve is much flatter than either yours or Susan's. As more people enter the market and more is purchased at lower prices, the market demand curve becomes flatter. Thus, as more people enter the market, for any given change in price, there is a greater absolute response in quantity demanded.

Now, if there are more than 899 people who want to buy apples, the demand curves of these other people must be combined with yours, Susan's, and those of the other current consumers in order to find the market demand curve. The demand curves of *all* participants in the market are added together to form the market demand curve. Thus, the number of buyers is an important determinant of the market demand curve.

Learning Exercise 2.3

What is the market demand of apples at a price of 25 cents if there are only 400 people in the market, that is, you, Susan, and 398 others?

CONSUMPTION DECISIONS ARE INDEPENDENT

Note that when we add individual demand curves together to define the market demand curve, we assume that there is *no interaction* between the purchase decisions of different individuals. Another way of saying this is that your consumption of apples is not affected by Susan's or anyone else's. Consumption decisions are independent.

Suppose this was not the case. Suppose that when you find out that Susan is consuming nine apples at a price of $1.25, you decide to buy something else to be different. So you decide to drop out of the market when Susan's consumption is nine apples. What has happened is that your demand for apples equals zero at prices below $1.25; instead of consuming four apples at $1.25, you now consume zero apples. You can see immediately the problem this creates for the market demand curve. In Figure 2.3 a price of $1.25 creates a market demand for 3,601 apples. Now if your demand for four apples at this price is set equal to zero, the market demand is for 3,597 apples. A hole develops in the market demand curve—not a very big one, but a hole nonetheless.

Moreover, if Susan is affected by your decision, the simple notion of summing up the individual demand curves is greatly complicated. How do we add together demand curves across individuals if these demand curves are shifting? It is not easy to do this. Because of this difficulty, we assume that each individual's demand for a good is *independent* of the demand of other individuals.

2.5 Price Elasticity of Demand

Of general interest is how the quantity demanded is affected by price changes. The **price elasticity of demand** is a measure of how responsive quantity demanded is to changes in price. It is reasonable to ask why such a measure is useful; after all, our graphs of demand offer a fairly clear picture of the relationship between price and quantity demanded. There are three reasons why we use price elasticity of demand:

Price Elasticity of Demand
The ratio of the percentage change in quantity demanded to the percentage change in price.

1. Graphs of demand curves may be misleading. If we change the units in which quantity of price are measured—for example, from pounds of apples to ounces of apples purchased per week—the shape and appearance of the demand curve will change, and it may seem that the effect of price on quantity demanded is different. The price elasticity of demand does not depend on the units we use to measure quantity or price, so if these units change, *ceteris paribus*, price elasticity does not change.
2. A given percentage price change for one good—for example, milk—may cause only a small change in quantity demanded, but the same percentage price change for another good—for example, VCRs—may cause a veritable explosion in quantity demanded. Price elasticity provides a simple and direct way of identifying how *different* goods respond to similar percentage price changes.
3. The price elasticity of demand can be used to predict how sales revenue will change when price changes. Sales revenue is one part of a firm's profit function; the other part is cost. By predicting how sales revenue will change when price changes, price elasticity of demand helps firms predict how profits will change.

As we discuss the concept of price elasticity of demand, keep in mind that it is a measure of how you and others react to price changes. As such, it is not fixed; it may change as your behavior changes.

Defining the Price Elasticity of Demand

The price elasticity of demand is a measure of how responsive quantity demanded is to a change in price. The price elasticity of demand is defined as follows:

$$\text{Price Elasticity of Demand } (\eta) = \frac{\text{Percentage Change in Quantity Demanded}}{\text{Percentage Change in Price}}$$

where eta, or η, is the Greek letter used to symbolize the price elasticity of demand. We can rewrite this equation as

$$\eta = \frac{\% \Delta Q_{\text{demanded}}}{\% \Delta P} \tag{2.1}$$

where % Δ means "percentage change in."

This measure of responsiveness is independent of how we measure price or quantity. Changing our price axis in Figure 2.1 to measure the price of apples in pennies or the quantity axis to measure apples in dozens will not affect the number we compute for the price elasticity of demand. Because our elasticity measure is not affected by the units we use, it is dimensionless, or a pure number.

The price elasticity of demand is a negative number.

When price increases, quantity demanded decreases—an inverse, or negative, relationship. We usually take the *absolute value* of the price elasticity of demand for purposes of analysis. For example, we say demand for apples is **elastic** if the price elasticity of demand is greater than 1 in absolute value. In this case, a 1 percent change in price causes a greater than 1 percent change in quantity demanded. Similarly, demand is **inelastic** if a 1 percent change in price causes a less than 1 percent change in quantity demanded. Finally, demand is **unitary elastic** if a 1 percent change in price causes a 1 percent change in quantity demanded. Note that we are changing only price in the price elasticity equation; variables such as income, the price of substitutes, and the price of complements are held constant.

Elastic
Price elasticity of demand greater than 1 in absolute value.

Inelastic
Price elasticity of demand less than 1 in absolute value.

Unitary Elastic
Price elasticity of demand equal to 1 in absolute value.

COMPUTING THE PRICE ELASTICITY OF DEMAND

Equation (2.1) defines the price elasticity of demand. The formula is stated in terms of percentage changes in both price and quantity. However, this is not what the real world presents to us. Rather, we observe discrete changes that may be large or small, and from these changes we must compute percentage changes. When your local electronics store has a sale, for example, the price of camcorders usually drops by \$200 to \$300. Such a large price change is invariably discrete. A general problem develops when we compute percentage changes from discrete changes in any variable, either price or quantity. To understand this problem, we need to study the algebraic representation of equation (2.1):

$$\eta = \frac{\Delta Q/Q}{\Delta P/P} = \frac{\Delta Q}{\Delta P}\frac{P}{Q} \tag{2.2}$$

Equation (2.2) is the formula for the **point elasticity of demand.** It is referred to as the point elasticity formula because it applies to very small price and quantity changes on the demand curve—small changes from a given point. For small price and quantity changes, we can use the initial values of P in the denominator of $\Delta P/P$ and the initial value of Q in the denominator of $\Delta Q/Q$ when we calculate η. For large price changes, however, using the initial values of P and Q to calculate equation (2.2) may produce an answer quite different

Point Elasticity of Demand
Price elasticity of demand measured at a single point on a demand curve.

from the answer we will find if we use the *new* values of P and Q. Because the results differ when we use the new and old values of P and Q, it creates a general problem for our calculation of the price elasticity of demand; that is, which numbers do we use?

The way out of this difficulty is to take the average of the initial and new prices and quantities. Using averages, the estimate of price elasticity of demand is at the midpoint of an arc drawn between the new and initial points on the demand curve. This approach gives the **arc price elasticity of demand.** The formula for computing arc price elasticity is written as follows:

Arc Price Elasticity of Demand
Price elasticity of demand measured between any two points on a demand curve rather than at a single point.

$$\eta_{arc} = \frac{\Delta Q/[(Q_1 + Q_2)/2]}{\Delta P/[(P_1 + P_2)/2]} = \frac{\Delta Q}{\Delta P} \times \frac{(P_1 + P_2)}{(Q_1 + Q_2)} \quad (2.3)$$

where the subscripts $_1$ and $_2$ refer to the two different points on the demand curve. Note that the 2s cancel out in equation (2.3), so for all practical purposes they can be ignored.

Figure 2.4 shows a graphic interpretation of the arc price elasticity formula as compared to the point price elasticity formula when price falls from P_1 to

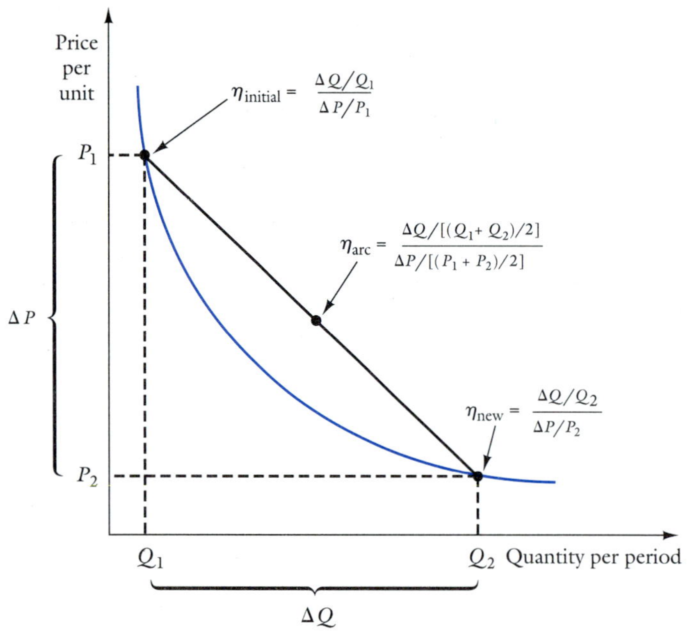

FIGURE 2.4

Comparing Arc and Point Elasticities

The arc price elasticity computes the elasticity at the midpoint of a line segment drawn between two points on the demand curve. The arc price elasticity uses an average of the price and quantity demanded at the two points to compute percentage changes. By using an average, the arc price elasticity does not vary with the initial starting point.

P_2. Note that the arc price elasticity formula is simply the point elasticity formula with the average of the two Q's substituted for Q and the average of the two P's substituted for P. In effect, the arc price elasticity is the point elasticity computed at the midpoint of a straight line connecting the two points on the demand curve.

LEARNING EXERCISE 2.4

Compute the arc price elasticity for *all* the adjacent points on the following demand schedule, which shows the quantity of lunches per week demanded at Le Bistro restaurant:

Price	*Quantity*
$20	0
15	1
12	2
9	3
6	4
3	6

PRICE ELASTICITIES FOR SOME ORDINARY GOODS

We often classify goods according to the price elasticity of demand. Table 2.2 shows estimates of the price elasticities of several commonly consumed goods. As may be seen, commodities that are likely to have many substitutes, such as public transportation services and green peas, tend to have more elastic demand. Goods that have fewer substitutes, such as water and electricity, have less elastic demand.

TABLE 2.2

Price Elasticities of Demand for Selected Products

Good or Service	Estimated Price Elasticity
Public Transportation	–3.5
Green Peas	–2.8
Boats and Recreational Vehicles	–2.4
Beer	–1.2
Movies	–0.9
Newspapers and Magazines	–0.5
Electricity	–0.3
Water	–0.2

Source: Houthakker and Taylor, 1970; Elzinga, "The Beer Industry," in *The Structure of American Industry,* Walter Adams (ed.). New York: Macmillan, 1977.

SLOPE DOES NOT EQUAL ELASTICITY

Strictly speaking, price elasticity of demand and the slope of the demand curve are two different concepts and should not be confused with one another. Let's go back to the point elasticity of demand formula—equation (2.2). We know that $\Delta Q/\Delta P$ is the reciprocal of the slope of the demand curve, and we also know that P/Q is the ratio of price to quantity. The slope of a demand curve—that is, its flatness or steepness—is based on the total changes in price and quantity. Price elasticity of demand, however, is concerned with *total change relative to price and quantity,* that is, the change in quantity relative to Q and the change in price relative to P. Therefore, the slope of the demand curve and the price elasticity of demand are different concepts. Do not confuse, for example, the flatness or steepness in a demand curve with its price elasticity. Figure 2.5 illustrates this caveat.

In Figure 2.5, two demand curves are presented. Demand curve D_a is flatter than demand curve D_b. It follows then that demand curve D_a has a smaller slope—in absolute value—than demand curve D_b. The slope of demand curve D_a is –.25. The slope of demand curve D_b is –.5, which confirms our claim. Because demand curve D_a is flatter, a comparison of slopes alone might suggest that the individual with demand curve D_a is more responsive to a price change than the individual with demand curve D_b. This is incorrect; appearances can be deceiving. For the price change shown—a decrease in price from

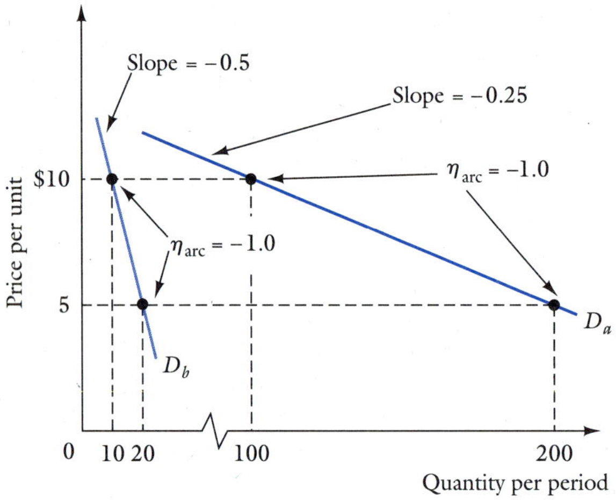

FIGURE 2.5

Don't Confuse Slope and Elasticity

Even though demand curve D_b is steeper than demand curve D_a—that is, the slope of D_b is greater than the slope of D_a in absolute value—it is shown to be more elastic for prices between \$5 and \$10. This figure illustrates the point that slope and elasticity are two different concepts: the relationship between the slopes of two demand curves may not imply the same relationship between the elasticities of two demand curves.

\$10 to \$5—the arc price elasticities of both demand curve D_b and demand curve D_a are -1.0 and -0.2 respectively. Looking only at the slopes of the two curves, then, does not tell us how responsive demand is to a price change.

A visual comparison of elasticities is possible, however, if the two demand curves intersect and the comparison is made only at the point of intersection. Figure 2.6 shows two demand curves that intersect at point *Z*. For price changes relative to this point, we can say that the flatter demand curve is more elastic.

\$\$\$ Price Theory in Practice

CHRYSLER MINIVAN SALES

During 1991, Chrysler cut prices on its popular minivans. The firm acted to fend off competition from other auto companies that were making inroads into the minivan market that Chrysler created in the early 1980s and has dominated ever since. Chrysler's action can also help illustrate the concept of price elasticity of demand.

Recall that the arc price elasticity formula is used to compute the price elasticity between two points on the demand curve. The arc price elasticity formula, as given by equation (2.3), uses the average change in price and the average change in quantity to calculate percentage changes.

For example, Chrysler dropped the price of its minivans from \$14,111 (P_1) to \$13,811 (P_2) for its basic model. Before Chrysler cut minivan prices, it was selling about 31,000 minivans per month (Q_1). After the price cut, the automaker was selling an estimated 32,240 minivans per month (Q_2). The arc

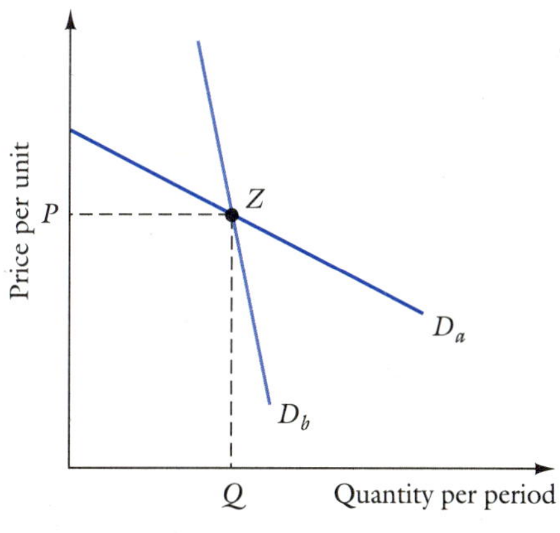

FIGURE 2.6

Comparing Elasticities at a Point of Intersection

When two demand curves intersect, it is possible to determine their relative price elasticities at the point of intersection. In the neighborhood of the intersection point *Z*, demand curve D_a is more elastic than demand curve D_b. We can determine this because D_a is flatter than D_b for points near the intersection point.

price elasticity measures the price elasticity for the segment of the demand curve between 31,000 and 32,240 minivans. That means the arc price elasticity can be computed as follows:

$$\eta_{arc} = \frac{\Delta Q}{\Delta P}\,\frac{(P_1 + P_2)/2}{(Q_1 + Q_2)/2} = \frac{1{,}240}{-\,300}\,\frac{(14{,}111 + 13{,}811)/2}{(31{,}000 + 32{,}240)/2} = -1.8$$

The elasticity of −1.8 is consistent with other findings that show that demand for big-ticket items, such as boats and recreation vehicles, is fairly price elastic. In addition, monthly revenue from minivan sales increased from $437.4 million to $445.3 million. This result shows that Chrysler's decision paid off in terms of increased sales revenue, which will always occur when demand is price-elastic over the range of the price change.

LEARNING EXERCISE 2.5

If Chrysler lowered minivan prices to $13,500 from $13,811, how many additional vans would you expect the company to sell each month?

SOME SPECIAL CASES OF PRICE ELASTICITY

Some special cases of price elasticities will be important to our later discussion of competitive firms and industry structure. In particular, a perfectly competitive industry structure is composed of firms that are presumed to face a horizontal demand curve, while a firm that has a monopoly faces a negatively sloped demand curve.

Figure 2.7 shows two demand curves, one vertical and one horizontal. The horizontal demand curve is called **perfectly elastic,** or infinitely elastic, because the price elasticity is infinite ($\eta = -\infty$) for all points on the demand curve. A horizontal demand curve can arise if the product has many close substitutes or even just one perfect substitute. Narrowly defined services or products, such as those of Sam & Bill's Dry Cleaning Shop, Alice Hasting's Travel-by-Air Agency, and Royal Crown Cola, may have many close substitutes; thus, their demand curves are expected to be horizontal or nearly horizontal.

Perfectly Elastic
A demand curve that has a price elasticity equal to $-\infty$.

Figure 2.7 also shows a vertical demand curve. On such a demand curve, you will pay almost any price for the same fixed quantity of the good in question (given the limit of your budget). A vertical demand curve is called **perfectly inelastic** to indicate that you are not responsive to changes in price. Obviously, there may be some price that exhausts your wealth, but up to that point demand may be vertical. The price elasticity of a vertical demand curve is zero ($\eta = 0$). Vertical demand curves arise when a product is highly preferred and there are no close substitutes. A diabetic's demand for insulin might give rise to a vertical demand curve; without a fixed quantity of insulin per period, a diabetic will almost surely die. A kidney transplant patient must take immunosuppressant drugs, primarily cyclosporine, to prevent organ rejection. As is the case with insulin, the demand curve for cyclosporine is expected to be nearly vertical,

Perfectly Inelastic
A demand curve that has a price elasticity equal to 0. Quantity demanded is not affected by price changes.

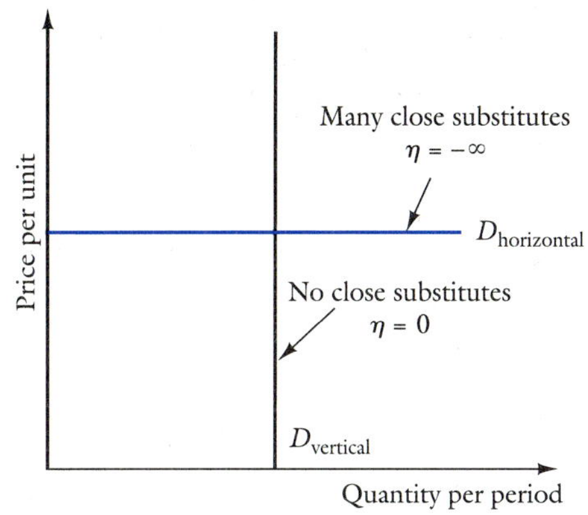

FIGURE 2.7

Horizontal and Vertical Demand Curves

Goods where demand is infinitely price elastic have horizontal demand curves. Such goods are expected to have many close substitutes. Goods where demand is perfectly price inelastic have vertical demand curves. These goods are expected to have no close substitutes.

which is also expected to be the case for the drug AZT that is used to treat AIDS patients. As substitutes become available, the demand curve becomes more responsive to price changes and its price elasticity moves away from being perfectly inelastic.

$$$ Price Theory in Practice

SUMMER DISCOUNTS FOR AIRLINE PASSENGERS

The domestic airline business has become notoriously competitive since deregulation in 1978, and the summer months are generally the most competitive time period. The summer of 1992 was no exception.

Price cutting on most domestic routes began on April 9 when American Airlines announced new fare structures for first-class, coach, and advance purchase passengers. These new fares offered discounts that averaged about 38 percent but did not significantly help vacation travelers, who usually buy 14-day advance purchase tickets. The prices of 14-day advance purchase tickets fell only about 10 percent in American's new fare structure. All the other major airlines—United, Delta, Northwest, and USAir—matched American's new fares within a few days.

The lower fare structure held in place until May 26, when Northwest Airlines announced a two-for-one fare discount: A parent and a child could fly for the same price as the parent alone. Northwest was trying to lure summer vacation travelers with its offer. The next day American Airlines responded by cutting its advance purchase fares by 50 percent for all passengers—those with and those without children. The new fares were in effect until June 5 and applied to domestic travel through September 13.

Passenger response to the new fares was immediate. May 28 and 29 were two of the busiest days of the year for long-distance and local phone companies; normally such call volume occurs only on such special days as Mother's Day and Christmas. When the discount fare time period had ended, the airlines found that the number of advance purchase tickets sold for the summer months was up over 140 percent relative to the number they were issuing before the 50 percent discount. As a result, both United and American Airlines flew over 10 billion revenue passenger miles in August, which had never happened before.[1] Using these results, we can estimate that the price elasticity of demand for 14-day advance tickets during the summer months is approximately −2.8 (140% / −50%). Such a high price elasticity (in absolute value) indicates a very responsive demand curve for air travel by summer passengers. We might expect this result because other forms of travel can easily be substituted for air travel. Car travel, for example, is the most popular form of transportation during a summer vacation.

Even though the airlines were successful in attracting passengers with the 50-percent-off fares, profitability did not improve. For most airlines total revenue increased, but total cost increased more as additional flights were added on some routes and temporary personnel were hired to handle the extra passengers. Thus, while the airlines made many vacation travelers happy, their shareholders did not enjoy the summer months. In addition, several airlines sought relief in the courts for their financial losses. A lawsuit was filed against American Airlines alleging that it tried to drive competitors out of business with its discount pricing scheme. In 1993, the courts found American Airlines innocent of these charges.

Learning Exercise 2.6

If the airlines had cut fares 70 percent, how much would ticket sales have increased?

2.6 Supply

Who produces the goods that you desire to consume? How is production related to price, and what other factors affect production? These are all issues that we will address in discussing supply.

In the simplest of terms, quantity supplied is a function of price, just as in the simplest of terms, quantity demanded is a function of price. There is a basic relationship between price and what is supplied, and we call this relationship the **law of supply:**

Law of Supply A positive relationship exists between quantity supplied and price.

> **The law of supply states that, generally, a larger quantity will be offered for sale when price increases (other things equal). Similarly, a smaller quantity will be offered for sale when price decreases (other things equal).**

[1] Revenue passenger miles are the number of miles flown by paying passengers.

The law of supply states that there is a positive relationship between the quantity supplied and price. Recall that the law of demand stated that there is a negative relationship between quantity demanded and price. The quantity supplied and the quantity demanded respond differently to a change in price. The law of supply tends to hold in general for almost all goods. It may not hold perfectly for a few goods, particularly for the supply of labor, but these goods are an exception.

Let us continue with our apple example to illustrate the supply schedule for apples by an apple grower. Figure 2.8 shows the quantity of apples that RoundTree Growers is willing to supply at various prices. Note that RoundTree is a small grower of apples with only 50 acres of apple trees. Figure 2.8 confirms the law of supply: there is a positive relationship between price and the quantity supplied.

In Figure 2.8, we see that RoundTree is willing and able to supply 1,000 apples per week when the price is 25 cents. The amount the company is willing to supply increases steadily until it is supplying 4,500 apples per week at a price of $2. How can the company supply more apples when price increases if the number of apple trees is fixed during the harvesting season? After all, there are only so many apples in the orchard. The answer is simple: At lower prices it

Supply Schedule

Price	Quantity
$ .25	1,000
.50	1,500
.75	2,000
1.00	2,500
1.25	3,000
1.50	3,500
1.75	4,000
2.00	4,500

(a)

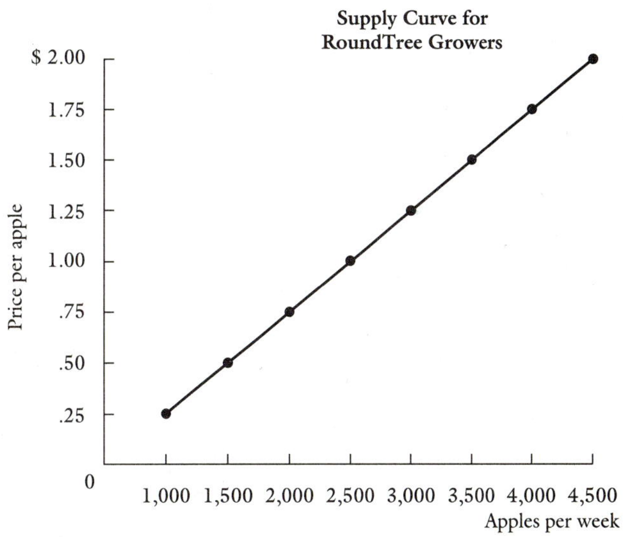

(b)

FIGURE 2.8

Supply of Apples

The price of apples affects the quantity supplied. When the price per apple is $2, RoundTree Growers supplies 4,500 apples. When the price is $.25, Roundtree Growers supplies only 1,000 apples. Using the data in panel (a), panel (b) plots a supply curve, which shows a positive relationship between price and quantity supplied.

does not pay for RoundTree to pick every apple on every tree; hard-to-reach apples remain on the tree because they are more expensive—requiring more time and effort—to pick. At higher prices, the grower spends more time picking each tree and picks more of the hard-to-reach apples.

PRICE ELASTICITY OF SUPPLY

As with demand, we can define an elasticity measure to judge how responsive quantity supplied is to a change in price. The **price elasticity of supply** is defined as follows:

Price Elasticity of Supply
The ratio of the percentage change in quantity supplied to the percentage change in price.

$$\textit{Price Elasticity of Supply} = \frac{\textit{Percentage Change in Quantity Supplied}}{\textit{Percentage Change in Price}}$$

Just as with the price elasticity of demand, the price elasticity of supply is the ratio of two percentage changes. In this case, though, the percentage change in quantity is computed using quantity supplied. In addition, the price elasticity of supply is independent of how we measure price or quantity. The price elasticity of supply is always a positive (or nonzero) number. When price increases, quantity supplied increases, a direct or positive relationship. We say that supply of apples is *elastic* if the price elasticity of supply is greater than 1. Similarly, supply is *inelastic* if a 1 percent change in price causes a less than 1 percent change in quantity supplied. Finally, supply is *unitary elastic* if a 1 percent change in price causes a 1 percent change in quantity supplied.

Learning Exercise 2.7

If quantity supplied increases by 8 percent when price increases by 4 percent, what is the price elasticity of supply? What is the percentage change in quantity supplied if price changes by 12 percent and the elasticity of supply is 1.5?

WHAT VARIABLES SHIFT (OR AFFECT) SUPPLY?

What are some of the factors that can affect supply? That is, what factors can cause the supply curve to shift to the right or left? Changes in any of the following variables are the most important:

- Prices of resources
- Prices of related outputs
- Technology
- Taxes and subsidies
- Expectations

First, let's consider the *prices of resources* (also called inputs or factors) used to produce the product. If what RoundTree Growers pays each of its workers per hour to pick apples decreases, the supply curve will shift to the right; that is, more apples will be supplied at each and every price because it will be cheaper to have some workers pick the hard-to-reach apples. The opposite will be true if wages of workers increase; the supply curve will shift to the left.

Closely related to the price of inputs is the *price of related outputs* that the firm can produce. For example, suppose that the land RoundTree owns is suitable for growing pears as well as apples. Pears and apples are **substitutes in production** if the price of pears has a negative effect on the quantity of apples produced. If the price of pears increases sufficiently, for example, it will be profitable for RoundTree to convert (over time) some apple-growing acreage into pear-growing acreage. Thus, the quantity of apples produced varies inversely with the price of pears.

Substitutes in Production
Output A is a substitute for output B if the production of output A varies directly with the price of output B.

Sometimes goods are **complements in production;** that is, they are both produced together, and changes in the price of one good have a positive impact on the production of the other good. For example, oil wells often produce natural gas as well as crude oil. If the price of oil increases, more oil is produced, which increases the supply of natural gas. Similarly, beef and leather are both produced from cattle. As the price of leather increases, the supply of beef increases, too.

Complements in Production
Output A is a complement to output B if the production of output A varies inversely with the price of output B.

Technology can also affect supply. Supply curves are drawn assuming a given technology, or "state of the art." Over time, the technology available may change. If the change involves technology that is less costly, the supply curve shifts rightward. In other words, if a better production technique becomes available, the supply curve shifts to the right; a larger quantity is produced at each and every price.

Taxes and subsidies affect supply, as we will show in Chapter 3. It turns out that certain taxes, such as excise taxes, are effectively an addition to production costs because they must be paid in the production and marketing of the product. They therefore decrease supply (i.e., shift the supply curve). A subsidy, which we can think of as a negative tax, does the opposite and shifts the supply curve to the right. In general, taxes reduce supply and subsidies increase supply.

As with demand, *expectations* can affect supply. Expectations of the future price of a product can affect producers' current willingness to supply, just as price expectations affect consumers' willingness to purchase. For example, consider what you would have done if you owned a gasoline station during the 1990–1991 Persian Gulf crisis. Initially, there was a significant threat that world oil supplies would be disrupted. A disruption of this order would increase the price of gasoline. As a producer, you might have decided to withhold some gasoline in your storage tanks because you believed you would receive a higher price for these gallons if you waited a while to sell them. Such an action would decrease the quantity of gasoline you supplied at each and every price; that is, the supply curve would have shifted to the left during the crisis.

QUANTITY SUPPLIED VERSUS SUPPLY

Just as we must be careful in our distinction between quantity demanded and demand, we have to be careful in our distinction between quantity supplied and supply. **Quantity supplied** is a number that tells us the amount supplied at a given price. A change in the price of the product changes the quantity sup-

Quantity Supplied
The amount offered for sale at a given price.

plied. A change in supply, however, is a shift in the supply curve. The factors discussed above—price of resources, technology, taxes and subsidies, and expectations—cause the supply curve to shift.

2.7 Market Supply

Analogous to market demand, **market supply** is the supply by all firms in the marketplace at each price. The relevant question is, how do we combine the supply of different firms? We combine the supply curves of each individual firm by summing them together as long as each firm is acting independently of the others. The independence assumption is valid if the firms are competing against each other for customers and not trying to collude to set price or output in any way. Under these circumstances, independent behavior by firms allows us to define market supply as follows:

Market Supply The (horizontal) sum of the supply curves of each firm in the market.

> **The market supply curve is a schedule that shows the quantities of a particular commodity that will be supplied by a particular group of suppliers per period of time at different prices. It is therefore the (horizontal) sum of the supply curves of each firm in the market.**

Figure 2.9 shows how the market supply curve is determined for the apple market. There are two producers in the apple market: RoundTree Growers and

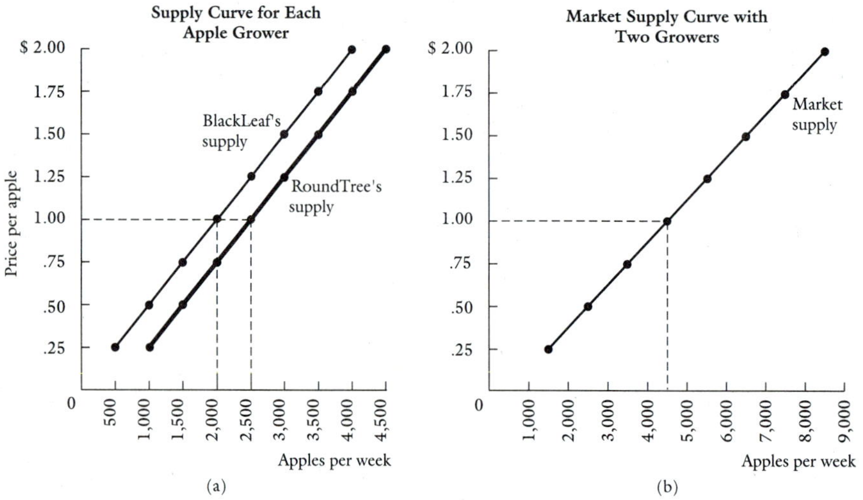

FIGURE 2.9

Deriving the Market Supply of Apples

There are two producers in the apple market, RoundTree Growers and BlackLeaf Apples. Because of higher costs, BlackLeaf requires a higher price at every output level than RoundTree. If the price is $2 per apple, RoundTree will produce 4,500 apples and BlackLeaf will produce 4,000 apples. The market supply curve in panel (b) shows that at a price of $2 per apple the two growers will supply 8,500 apples.

BlackLeaf Apples. The supply curve for RoundTree shown in panel (a) is the same one shown in Figure 2.8. BlackLeaf is new to us. It is competing with RoundTree for apple customers.

BlackLeaf has a problem that RoundTree does not have. Its orchards are constantly bothered by insects and fungus, so its yield is lower. BlackLeaf has adopted a pesticide and antifungal spraying program to solve its problems, but this program increases BlackLeaf's costs. Because of these problems, BlackLeaf can supply only 500 apples per week when the price is 25 cents. At higher prices, it pays BlackLeaf to harvest some of its hard-to-reach apples, just as it did for RoundTree, but BlackLeaf's yield will always be less than RoundTree's. Note that at any given output level, BlackLeaf requires a higher price than RoundTree to produce that output. BlackLeaf's higher expenses create this situation.

We will assume that these two growers are the only apple producers in the market. The market supply curve is thus shown in panel (b) of Figure 2.9. The market supply curve adds together the production of each grower at a given price. For example, if the price is 25 cents per apple, RoundTree will produce 1,000 apples and BlackLeaf will produce 500 apples, so the market supply is 1,500 apples per week. At a price of $1 per apple, RoundTree produces 2,500 apples and BlackLeaf produces 2,000 apples, so the quantity supplied to the market is 4,500 apples per week.

Learning Exercise 2.8

Draw the market supply curve for apples if another grower, identical to RoundTree, entered the market. What is the quantity of apples supplied at a price of $1?

2.8 Market Equilibrium

The price system acts to equate both quantity demanded and quantity supplied in the market. In equilibrium, consumers find that they are able to buy exactly the amount that they are demanding at the prevailing price, and producers are able to sell exactly the amount that they are supplying at the prevailing price. In effect, neither consumers nor producers have any incentive to change their behavior in equilibrium. Generally, a **market equilibrium** is defined by the following statement:

Market Equilibrium
A situation in which, at the prevailing price, quantity supplied equals quantity demanded.

A market equilibrium occurs when the prevailing price equates quantity demanded to quantity supplied.

To understand how to apply this statement, let us return to the market demand and supply of apples. Figure 2.10 (page 46) re-creates the market demand and supply curves on one graph. Note that at prices above $1, quantity demanded is less than quantity supplied, and at prices below $1, quantity demanded is greater than quantity supplied. The market equilibrium price is thus $1 per apple; only at this price will quantity demanded equal quantity supplied. The equilibrium quantity transacted by the market is 4,500 apples per week.

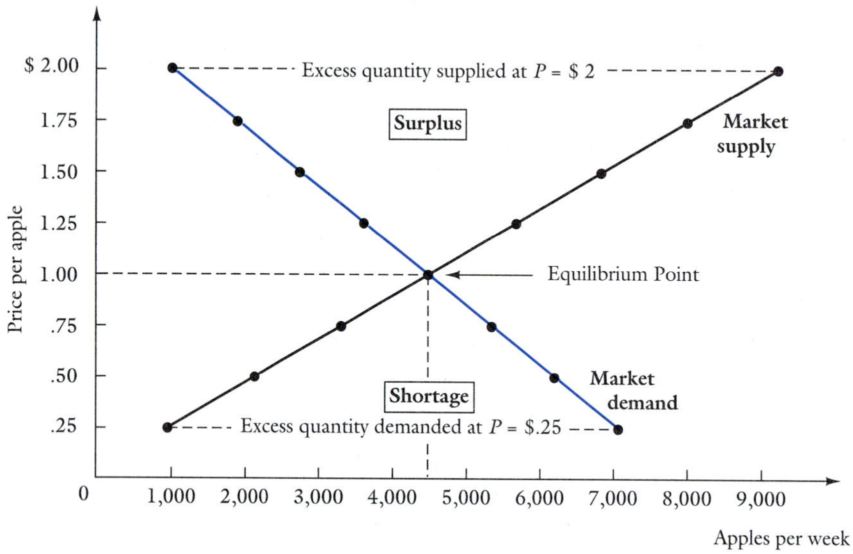

FIGURE 2.10

Equilibrium in the Market for Apples

To graph an apple market equilibrium, we combine market demand from Figure 2.3 with market supply from Figure 2.9. An equilibrium between supply and demand is reached when the price is $1 per apple and 4,500 apples are purchased. At prices above $1, there is a surplus of apples. At prices below $1, there is a shortage of apples.

In contrast, the apple market is not in equilibrium but is in disequilibrium whenever price is not equal to $1 per apple. In **disequilibrium,** quantity demanded is not equal to quantity supplied at the current price. Either consumers or producers are encouraged to change their behavior. For example, suppose the price is $2 per apple; now the quantity demanded is 904 apples per week and the quantity supplied is 8,500 apples per week. Producers will soon find that they have 7,596 rotting apples on their hands each week (the smell will be impressive). We call this a **surplus** of goods; there is an excess quantity of apples supplied compared to the quantity demanded at a price of $2. What will producers do to solve the surplus problem? Clearly, they can reduce the number of rotting apples if they reduce their price. If price decreases to $1.50 per apple, quantity supplied decreases to 6,500 apples and quantity demanded increases to 2,702 apples. Now the excess quantity of apples supplied equals 3,798. There are fewer rotting apples at a price of $1.50 than at a price of $2. When will there be no incentive to reduce price further? The answer is when the apple market reaches the equilibrium price. With an excess supply of apples, there is a strong tendency for producers to reduce price toward the equilibrium price.

Disequilibrium
A situation in which, at prevailing prices, quantity demanded does not equal quantity supplied.

Surplus
Quantity supplied exceeds quantity demanded at a given price.

Shortage
Quantity demanded exceeds quantity supplied at a given price.

The market is also in disequilibrium when price is below its equilibrium level. For example, suppose price is 25 cents per apple; now quantity demanded is 7,197 apples per week and the quantity supplied is 1,500 apples per week. Consumers have a problem—a **shortage** of goods, with an excess quantity of apples demanded compared to the quantity supplied at a price of 25 cents. Consumers cannot buy all the apples they want at the prevailing price. They must wait in lines until a new shipment of apples arrives, but even waiting in lines will not provide the quantity of apples they demand because producers are not supplying 7,197 apples per week. Consumers, who are denied apples, will begin to offer producers higher prices for some of their scarce apples. At higher prices, producers are willing to increase the quantity supplied—it now pays to pick some of the hard-to-reach apples. Market price stops increasing only when the equilibrium price is reached. With a shortage of apples, there is a strong tendency for consumers to bid price to the equilibrium level.

EQUILIBRIUM ADJUSTMENTS

The apple market we have described is in equilibrium at a price of $1 per apple so long as the market supply and demand curves do not change. A shift of either market supply or demand will change the equilibrium point. Figure 2.11, on page 48, shows how the equilibrium price and quantity are affected by shifts in supply and demand. The four panels in this figure document four possibilities: an increase in demand, a decrease in demand, an increase in supply, and a decrease in supply. Note that the old and new equilibrium points are marked in each panel.

If the market demand curve shifts to the right, an increase in demand, then, as shown in panel (a) of Figure 2.11, both the equilibrium price and quantity increase. Alternatively, if market demand decreases, which is a shift to the left as shown in panel (b), then both equilibrium price and quantity decrease. A shift in market supply will have the opposite effect on the equilibrium point. If supply shifts to the right, which is an increase in supply as shown in panel (c), then equilibrium price decreases but equilibrium quantity increases. Finally, if supply decreases as shown in panel (d), then equilibrium price increases and equilibrium quantity decreases.

The variables that cause market demand and supply to shift are the same as those that cause these curves to shift for the individual and the firm. We have seen in Figure 2.2(b) that the price of substitutes and complements, income, and expectations can cause an individual's demand curve to shift. Similarly, resource or factor costs, technology, taxes and subsidies, and expectations can cause a firm's supply curve to shift. When one of these variables changes—say the price of a substitute increases—then each individual demand curve shifts to the right, and the total of all these individual shifts is the shift we observe in the market demand curve. An analogous statement can be made for variables that shift an individual firm's supply curve. That is, if factor costs increase, for example, the supply curve of each firm shifts to the left (a decrease in supply), and the total shift in market supply is the sum of these individual shifts.

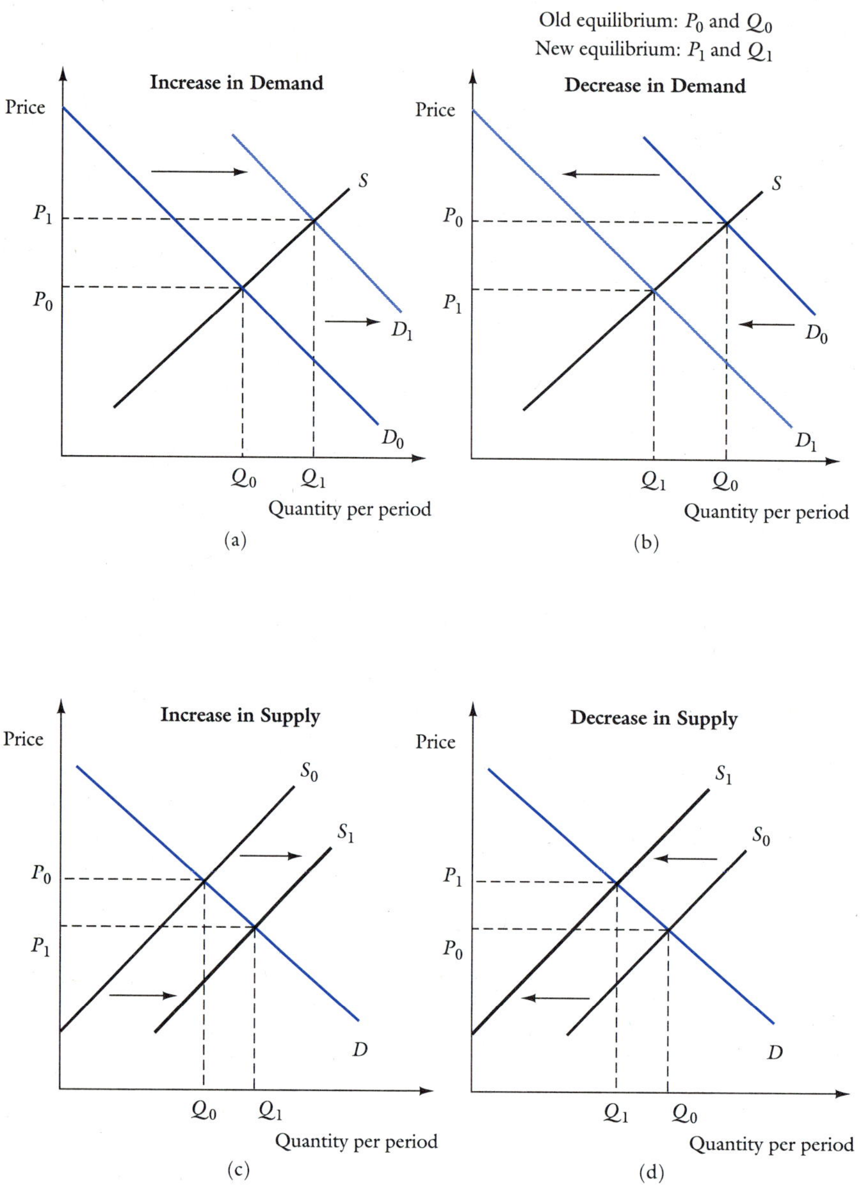

FIGURE 2.11

Effects of Shifts in the Demand and Supply Curves

The apple market that we have described is in equilibrium at a price of $1 per apple as long as the market supply and demand curves do not change. A shift in either market supply or market demand will change the equilibrium price. In panel (a), market demand increases, shifting the demand curve to the right and causing both equilibrium price and quantity to increase. In panel (b), market demand decreases, shifting the demand curve to the left, which decreases both the equilibrium price and quantity. An increase in supply, shown in panel (c) as a shift in supply to the right, causes equilibrium price to decrease but causes equilibrium quantity to increase. In panel (d), if supply decreases, then equilibrium price increases and equilibrium quantity decreases.

LEARNING EXERCISE 2.9

How do equilibrium price and quantity change when demand decreases and supply increases? Show that when *both* demand and supply curves shift, there will be one variable (either price or quantity) whose direction of response can be predicted and one variable whose direction of response will be ambiguous (i.e., it could rise, fall, or remain constant).

2.9 SOLVING FOR THE MARKET EQUILIBRIUM

Another way to express the market equilibrium is to represent both market supply and demand curves algebraically and then to solve these equations for the equilibrium price and quantity. Generally, we write quantity demanded and supplied as a function of price.

Define $D(P)$ as the demand equation and $S(P)$ as the supply equation. Both are a function of price, P. The market equilibrium price, denoted by P^*, is the price that sets quantity demanded equal to quantity supplied:

$$D(P^*) = S(P^*) \tag{2.4}$$

at the equilibrium price P^*. To solve for P^* we need a specific expression for both demand and supply equations. Suppose that these equations are straight lines:

$$D(P) = a - bP \tag{2.5}$$

$$S(P) = c + dP \tag{2.6}$$

where a and c are parameters that define the intercepts along the vertical axis and b and d are parameters that define the slopes of these equations. You can determine the equilibrium price by setting these two equations equal to each other:

$$D(P) = S(P)$$

or

$$a - bP = c + dP$$

The equilibrium price is solved by rearranging the above expression to place P on the left-hand side and the parameters on the right-hand side of the equation:

$$P^* = \frac{a - c}{b + d} \tag{2.7}$$

The equilibrium quantity is solved by substituting the solution for price in equation (2.7) into either the demand or supply equation. Substituting P^* into the supply equation gives

$$S(P^*) = c + dP^*$$

$$= c + d\left(\frac{a - c}{b + d}\right)$$

$$= \frac{cb + da}{b + d} \tag{2.8}$$

A numerical example will help you understand these equations. Consider the demand and supply for apples discussed above. The demand curve is composed of Susan's demand, your demand, and the demand of 897 others whose demand is the same as yours. A careful analysis of Figure 2.3 shows that Susan's demand equation is $D_{Susan} = 14 - 4P$ and your demand equation is $D_{you} = 9 - 4P$. Multiplying your demand equation by 898—you plus 897 others—and adding the result to Susan's demand equation gives the market demand equation. Similarly, RoundTree's supply equation is $S_{RoundTree} = 500 + 2000P$ and BlackLeaf's supply equation is $S_{BlackLeaf} = 2000P$. Adding these two equations gives the market supply equation. The market demand and supply equations follow from these results:

$$D(P) = 8{,}096 - 3{,}596P \tag{2.9}$$

$$S(P) = 500 + 4{,}000P \tag{2.10}$$

where in terms of the parameters in equations (2.5) and (2.6), $a = 8{,}096$, $b = 3{,}596$, $c = 500$, and $d = 4{,}000$. These values can be substituted into equation (2.7), the expression for the equilibrium price, to give

$$P^* = \frac{a - c}{b + d} = \frac{8{,}096 - 500}{3{,}596 + 4{,}000} = \$1$$

Similarly, these parameter values can be substituted into equation (2.8), the expression for the equilibrium quantity, to give

$$Q^* = \frac{cb + da}{b + d} = \frac{500(3{,}596) + 4{,}000(8{,}096)}{3{,}596 + 4{,}000} = 4{,}500$$

These equations confirm what we already know about our apple example, but they also represent another way of finding the market equilibrium price and quantity. This analytical approach is particularly helpful when demand and supply equations are estimated with statistical methods because these methods often use linear equations.

MATH NOTEPAD

Market Equilibrium Using the Inverse Equations

It is also possible to solve for the market equilibrium price and quantity using *inverse supply* and *inverse demand* equations. The inverse demand equation specifies price as a function of quantity demanded—just the reverse of what we did above. Similarly, the inverse supply equation specifies price as a function of quantity supplied. Let's define $P(Q_{demand})$ as the inverse demand equation and $P(Q_{supply})$ as the inverse supply equation. Then as straight lines we have the following equations:

$$P(Q_{demand}) = e - fQ_{demand}$$

$$P(Q_{supply}) = g + hQ_{supply}$$

where e and g are parameters that define the intercepts along the vertical axis and f and h are parameters that define the slopes of these equations. In equilibrium, $Q_{demand} = Q_{supply}$, so we can substitute Q^* for Q_{demand} and Q_{supply} in the above equations in order to determine the market equilibrium. The market equilibrium quantity, Q^*, is found by setting the two inverse equations equal to each other:

$$P(Q_{demand}) = P(Q_{supply})$$

or

$$e - fQ^* = g + hQ^*$$

The solution here is solved by rearranging the above expression to place Q^* on the left-hand side and the parameters on the right-hand side of the equation. The answer is

$$Q^* = \frac{e - g}{h + f}$$

The equilibrium price is solved by substituting the solution for Q^* into either the inverse demand or inverse supply equation. The final result is

$$P^* = \frac{eh + fg}{h + f}$$

This approach represents an alternative method of computing the market equilibrium. The results are always the same as those found using the (normal) supply and demand equations, so it does not matter which method is used. Because inverse equations are often presented—indeed, our graphs of supply and demand show inverse equations because price is on the vertical axis—it may be more convenient to remember these solutions.

ELASTICITY OF DEMAND FOR THE LINEAR DEMAND CURVE

It is often useful to understand how the price elasticity of demand can change, even when demand is defined in a simple linear form. The slope of a linear demand curve is constant, equal to –b in equation (2.5), but its elasticity changes at every point. Look at Figure 2.12. In this figure we have plotted the demand relationship $Q = a - bP$ in its inverse form; that is, $P = a/b - Q/b$.[2]

[2] Using the parameters from equation (2.8), $e = a/b$ and $f = 1/b$.

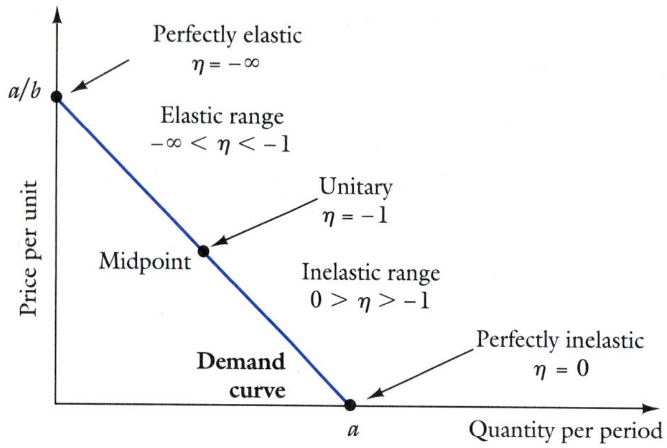

FIGURE 2.12

Price Elasticity Changes

The price elasticity of demand changes continuously along a linear demand curve. At the midpoint of the demand curve, price elasticity of demand equals −1, or unitary elastic. At points to the left of the midpoint, the demand curve is price-elastic. At points to the right of the midpoint, the demand curve is price-inelastic.

In Figure 2.12, we see that the price elasticity of demand begins at $-\infty$ on the vertical axis and increases to 0 when demand intersects the horizontal axis. The algebra that generates this result can be developed using the point elasticity formula given in equation (2.2). The slope of the linear demand curve, $\Delta Q/\Delta P$, is $-b$. Substituting this result into equation (2.2) yields

$$\eta = \frac{\Delta Q}{\Delta P}\frac{P}{Q} = -b\frac{P}{Q} \qquad (2.11)$$

Equation (2.11) shows why the price elasticity of demand varies in Figure 2.12; that is, it varies because P and Q change as we move along the demand curve. When $P = 0$, then $\eta = 0$, which occurs at the point where the demand curve intersects the quantity, or horizontal, axis. Similarly, when Q approaches zero, η approaches $-\infty$, so we say that $\eta = -\infty$ at the point at where the demand curve intersects the price, or vertical, axis. Between these two extremes, η changes continuously. At points near the point at which the demand curve intersects the price axis, η is a large negative number. As we move down the demand curve towards its midpoint, η approaches -1. Over this range, demand is price-elastic. At the midpoint of the demand curve, $\eta = -1$, which we call unitary elastic. Below the midpoint, $\eta > -1$, which we call price-inelastic.

Sometimes the concepts of elastic, unitary, and inelastic demand are defined in absolute terms. In such cases, we say demand is elastic if $|\eta| > 1$, demand is unitary elastic if $|\eta| = 1$, and demand is inelastic if $|\eta| < 1$.[3] We can see that for the linear demand curve, there are prices for which demand is

[3] The vertical bars, $|\eta|$, around η indicate that we are computing the absolute value of η.

price-elastic and price-inelastic, with the division between these prices occurring at the midpoint of the demand curve.

2.10 Total Revenue and Price Elasticity

During the first six months of 1993, about 40,000 Macintosh Powerbook computers were sold by Apple Computer. At an average retail price of $1,500 per computer, total revenues were $60 million. What will happen to total revenues from the sale of Macintosh Powerbook computers if Apple cuts their price by 10 percent? One reason we gave for studying the concept of price elasticity was that it can be used to predict how total revenue changes when price changes. To develop this point, we define **total revenue (TR)** as the quantity purchased, Q, times the price per unit, P:

Total Revenue
Price per unit times quantity sold for a given time period.

$$\text{Total Revenue} = P \times Q \tag{2.12}$$

Equation (2.12) shows that decreasing P *appears* to lower total revenue. When P falls, however, Q is expected to increase—by the law of demand—so the change in total revenue, $P \times Q$, is uncertain when P decreases. Figure 2.13 shows this result for the case of the Macintosh Powerbook computer.

In Figure 2.13, the price of a Macintosh Powerbook computer falls from P_1 to P_2 and quantity demanded increases from Q_1 to Q_2. Total revenue is $P_1 \times Q_1$ at the initial price level, which is equal to the sum of the area in

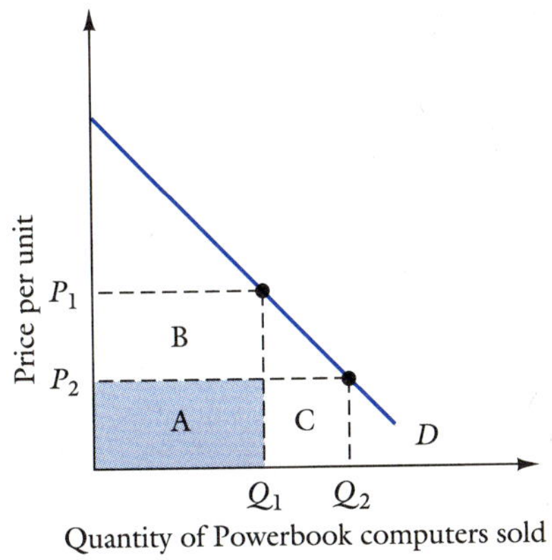

FIGURE 2.13

Effects of a Price Change on Total Revenue

When price changes, an individual buys more units, but the price paid per unit decreases. The effect of a price change on total revenue depends on whether price is changing more or less (in relative terms) than quantity demanded. If quantity is increasing more than price is decreasing, then area **C** is larger than area **B** and total revenue is increasing. Otherwise, area **B** is larger than area **C** and total revenue is decreasing or area **B** equals area **C** and total revenue is constant as price falls.

rectangles A and B. When price decreases, total revenue changes to $P_2 \times Q_2$, which is the sum of the area in rectangles A and C. The change in total revenue is $P_2 \times Q_2$ minus $P_1 \times Q_1$, which is equivalent to the difference between the area in rectangle C minus the area in rectangle B. If rectangle C is larger than rectangle B, then total revenues increase when price falls from P_1 to P_2; otherwise, they decrease or remain the same.

The price elasticity of demand can be used to determine which of the rectangles in Figure 2.13, B or C, is larger or whether they are the same size. To show this result, we must first define the concept of marginal revenue. **Marginal revenue (MR)** is defined as the change in total revenue associated with a small change in the quantity sold:

Marginal Revenue
Change in total revenue associated with a small (or one-unit) change in the quantity sold.

$$\text{MR} = \frac{\Delta \text{TR}}{\Delta Q} \tag{2.13}$$

The price elasticity of demand influences total revenue through its effect on marginal revenue. Let's use the case of the linear demand curve discussed above to show how η is related to MR. Recall that the *inverse* linear demand function is $P = a/b - Q/b$, with its elasticity given by $\eta = -b(P/Q)$. Total revenue is equal to $P \times Q$, so for the linear demand function we multiply it by Q to obtain

$$\text{TR} = PQ = \frac{a}{b}Q - \frac{1}{b}Q^2 \tag{2.14}$$

Marginal revenue is equal to the change in total revenue for a one-unit change in the quantity sold. This is another way of saying that MR is the slope of the total revenue function at a given output level. Using the power rule of calculus, marginal revenue for a linear demand function is[4]

$$\begin{aligned} \text{MR} &= \frac{a}{b} - \frac{2}{b}Q \\ &= \frac{a}{b} - \frac{1}{b}Q - \frac{1}{b}Q \end{aligned} \tag{2.15}$$

but $P = (a/b) - Q/b$, so that

$$\text{MR} = P - \frac{1}{b}Q \tag{2.16}$$

where we have substituted the inverse linear demand function, $P = 5\,a/b - Q/b$, into the second step to arrive at the third expression for MR.

Using $\eta = -b(P/Q)$ for the linear demand function and solving for Q gives $Q = -b(P/\eta)$. Substituting this result into equation (2.16) gives

$$\text{MR} = P(1 + \frac{1}{\eta}) \tag{2.17}$$

where b cancels with $1/b$ and P factors out of the equation.

[4] The power rule of calculus states that if $Y = X^n$, then $\Delta Y/\Delta X = nX^{n-1}$ for small changes in X.

Equation (2.17) is derived for a linear demand function, but, as an expression of the relationship between MR and η, it applies to all demand functions. In general, then, equation (2.17) shows that MR is equal to price times the quantity 1 plus the inverse of the price elasticity of demand. When $\eta = -1$, demand is unitary elastic and MR = 0. Because MR is the slope of the total revenue curve, when MR = 0, total revenue is at an extreme point. This situation is illustrated in Figure 2.14 using the linear demand function to compute total revenue.

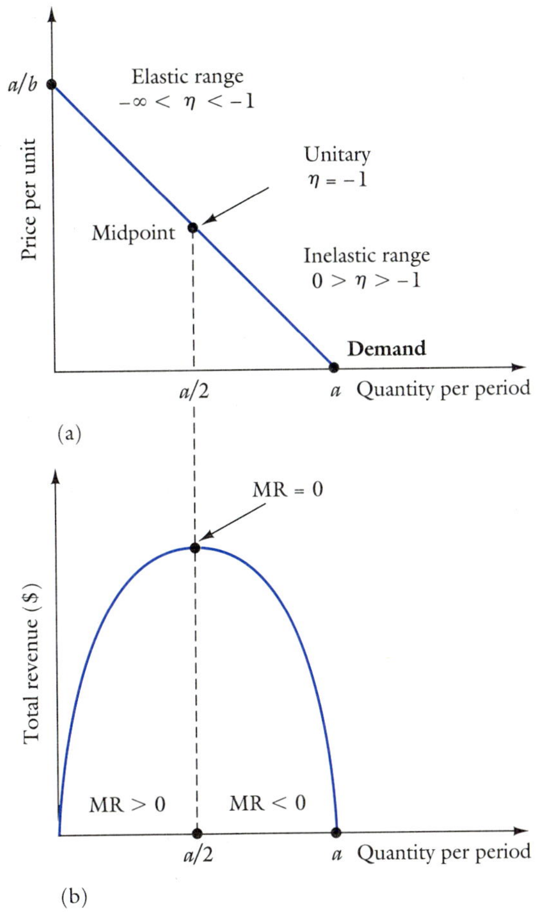

FIGURE 2.14

The Relationship Between Total Revenue and Elasticity

Panel (a) shows how price elasticity changes along a linear demand curve. Panel (b) shows how total revenue changes as price falls on a linear demand curve. In the elastic region of demand, price decreases cause total revenue to increase. Total revenue reaches a peak at the point where the elasticity of demand is unitary. After this point, demand is price inelastic and price decreases cause total revenue to decrease.

In panel (a) of Figure 2.14, the linear demand function is plotted. We see that $\eta = -1$ at the midpoint of the demand function; above the midpoint, demand is price-elastic; and below the midpoint, demand is price-inelastic. Panel (b) shows a graph of the total revenue curve for the linear demand function. In effect, this is a graph of equation (2.14). At the peak of the total revenue curve, MR is zero. The peak of the total revenue curve occurs at the point $Q = a/2$, which is also where $\eta = -1$.[5] At quantities less than $a/2$, the slope of the total revenue curve is positive, so $\text{MR} > 0$ for these quantities. Along the demand curve, marginal revenue is positive for all points that are price-elastic, that is, where $\eta < -1$. At quantities greater than $a/2$, the slope of the total revenue curve is negative, so $\text{MR} < 0$ for these quantities. Marginal revenue is negative for the points along the demand curve that are price-inelastic, that is, when $\eta > -1$.

Figure 2.13 also illustrates the relationship between η and total revenue. When demand is price-elastic ($\eta < -1$), a decrease in price causes quantity demanded to increase, which causes total revenue to increase because $\text{MR} > 0$ for these levels of Q. Similarly, when demand is price-inelastic ($\eta > -1$), a decrease in price causes quantity demanded to increase, which causes total revenue to decrease because $\text{MR} < 0$ for these levels of Q.

These findings provide an answer to our question about which rectangle in Figure 2.13 is larger, rectangle B or C. If demand is price-elastic between P_1 and P_2, then the area of rectangle C is larger than the area of rectangle B because reducing price will increase total revenue (we will move up the total revenue function in Figure 2.14). In contrast, if demand is price-inelastic over this range, then the area of rectangle B will be larger than the area of rectangle C because total revenue will decrease as price decreases. Only in the case in which demand is unitary elastic will total revenue remain unchanged, and then the area of rectangle B will equal the area of rectangle C.

We must note one last point about the relationship between total revenue and price elasticity. Total revenue is equal to the payments made to producers for their products. If there are no taxes or subsidies to consider, then payments made to producers are equal to the total expenditures of consumers. Therefore, the relationship between total revenue and price elasticity defined above applies to total expenditures, too.

2.11 Retail Pricing

We have discussed supply and demand equilibrium for a few particular cases to illustrate how a market achieves an equilibrium. When you go shopping in a department store, a grocery store, or even a restaurant, you typically do not see this equilibrium mechanism at work in exactly the way that our diagrams have indicated. For example, if you go into a restaurant and only a few people are there eating dinner, you might say, "Well, it looks as if the quantity of seats supplied exceeds the quantity demanded, so meal prices should fall." When

[5] Substitute $Q = a/2$ into equation (2.15) to see that $\text{MR} = 0$ at the peak of the total revenue curve.

you sit down to eat your meal and the waiter brings you a menu, it doesn't look as if meal prices have changed since the last time you were there. At that time, the place was filled with people and you had to wait thirty minutes for a table. So what's going on here? Is our model inadequate to explain this common situation?

The answer to this question requires a little more development of the equilibrium of supply and demand for restaurant services. For example, it might be a Tuesday night when you find many empty seats. Tuesday is a slow night for all restaurants, not just the one you have chosen. When you were here last it was a Friday night, which is a busy time for restaurants, and you had to wait. Our supply-and-demand model suggests that prices will be lower on Tuesday than Friday. You have looked at the menu carefully, and unfortunately, there is no difference in prices. When the waiter visits your table again to announce the evening's "specials," you begin to notice a difference. The specials this time are less expensive than they were when you visited on a Friday night. So prices have changed a little—for the specials, at least, but not for anything else on the menu. In effect, the demand curve for restaurant meals shifts to the left during weekdays and also during the early evening hours before most people want to have a restaurant meal. At the same time, though, the supply curve has not really shifted.

Is there something wrong with supply and demand because only the price of specials has changed? We think not. The simple fact is that it's costly to change prices. Typically, you find meal prices printed on menus, so a restaurant has to reprint the menus to adjust price. To reprint a menu because demand varies by the day of the week, season of the year, and so on can become very costly. Some restaurants, particularly those in resort areas with seasonal visitors, may adopt such a policy, but most restaurants do not reprint menus very often. Instead, they adjust to changing demand conditions by offering specials whose price reflects the current demand or by offering "early bird" pricing so that if you come early on a weekday, you can order items on the menu at reduced prices, typically from 20 to 30 percent off the regular price. So, there is a way in which restaurants adjust to a change in demand, but it may not always be that they reprint the menu to change prices.[6]

Let's pursue this situation a little further. When you find a grocery store with only a few customers or a clothing store almost empty, do you see clerks running around marking down prices? Well, not typically. The prices are usually posted on the items that you see when you walk into the store. We call this **posted-offer pricing.** The reason that restaurants, grocery stores, clothing stores, and other retail outlets use this pricing system is that there is a cost to changing prices, particular when the retailer doesn't know whether the change in demand is temporary or permanent. On the one hand, if the change in demand is *temporary*, retailers do not usually want to incur the cost of changing prices, up and down, as demand shifts back and forth. A restaurant, for example, will set prices that leaves some tables empty on Tuesday night while

Posted-Offer Pricing
The practice of labeling goods with prices before demand is known.

[6] Many restaurants have explicit "early bird" menus that offer complete meals at considerable savings compared to à la carte purchases of the same items. The "kicker" is that such menus are only passed out between the hours of, say, 5 and 7 P.M.

some patrons wait on Friday night. On the other hand, if the change in demand is *permanent*, it will probably be worthwhile for the restaurant to reprint the menu with lower prices if demand has decreased or with higher prices if demand has increased.

2.12 Bargaining

Bargaining The process of negotiating the price of a product.

Although most retail firms use posted-offer pricing to price their goods and services, there are other ways to price a product. An automobile dealer may post a "sticker" price on the window of a car, but every customer realizes that this is a starting price—the actual price will be found by **bargaining** with the dealer. The sticker price is the dealer's first offer; you are expected to counter with an offer of your own. The offer and counteroffer process is called bargaining. Bargaining is a way of changing prices immediately. It is costly to bargain in the same way that it is costly for a restaurant to reprint a menu. Bargaining requires time, information, and effort.

An interesting aspect of bargaining is the type of goods that people bargain for and the characteristics of the individuals who bargain. For example, suppose you go to buy a pair of shoes at a department store in the United States and find that the posted price of the shoes is $45. Do you say to the clerk, "OK, I found a pair that fit me, but $45 is too much; I'll give you $35"? Probably not. If you go to another country, such as Bolivia, however, you will find many stores that will bargain on the price of a pair of shoes. Why is the pricing process different in Bolivia and elsewhere? One reason is the opportunity cost of bargaining. Bolivians on average receive a lower wage rate compared to U.S. workers, so the time cost of bargaining is less for many Bolivians.

To see how lower wages affect bargaining, consider the shoe example again. Lower wages in Bolivia imply that a $45 pair of shoes represents a larger share of an average Bolivian's income than of your average income. Because shoes represent a larger share of income, a lower price affects the consumption of other goods more in Bolivia than in the United States. For example, suppose the average annual income in Bolivia is $1,000 and the average annual income in the United States is $25,000. If you bargain over the price of shoes and reduce their price from $45 to $35 you save $10, or roughly .04 percent of your annual income. In Bolivia, the same $10 represents 1 percent of annual income, so the effect on the budget of a Bolivian is many times larger.

There are many goods—such as cars and houses—that you will bargain for because they represent a significant portion of your income. For example, the $10 you might save on a $45 pair of shoes is a 22 percent reduction in their price. If you bargain over the price of a $14,000 automobile and reduce its price by 22 percent, you will save $3,080, which represents 12 percent of your annual income. Clearly, successful bargaining over the price of a car affects your budget constraint more than successful bargaining for a pair of shoes.

Our analysis of bargaining suggests that more bargaining will occur when time costs are low and when the potential savings are high relative to income. This is another way of saying that bargaining over price is more likely when the total benefits from bargaining exceed the opportunity cost of bargaining.

Chapter Summary

1. Relative prices measure the opportunity cost of purchasing one good or service in terms of another good or service. Absolute prices measure the money income required to buy a good. Price theory predicts that individuals respond to relative prices, not absolute prices, because relative prices measure the changing value of the various alternative consumption choices.
2. Stocks are a sum total of flows (minus any losses). Flows are measured in terms of rates, such as income per month or gallons per hour. Stocks are measured at a point in time, such as investor wealth after the October 1987 stock market crash or the gallons of water in a bathtub.
3. For most goods and services, income, the price of substitutes, the price of complements, expectations, and changes in information are factors that can affect demand, causing it to shift.
4. When individuals act independently, the market demand curve equals the sum of all the individual demand curves. The sum is across quantity demanded at each price, which is called a horizontal sum.
5. Price elasticity of demand is a measure of the responsiveness of quantity demanded to changes in price. Demand is *elastic* if quantity responds by a greater percentage than the percentage change in price and *inelastic* if it responds by a lower percentage. If the percentages are the same, demand is *unitary* elastic.
6. As long as each firm's output decision is independently determined, the market supply curve equals the sum of each firm's supply curve. The sum is across quantity supplied at each price.
7. Market equilibrium occurs when quantity supplied equals quantity demanded at the existing market price.
8. Total revenue is related to the price elasticity of demand through marginal revenue. When demand is price-elastic ($-\infty < \eta < -1$), marginal revenue is positive, so there is a negative relationship between changes in total revenue and changes in price. When demand is price-inelastic ($0 > \eta > -1$), marginal revenue is negative, so there is a positive relationship between changes in total revenue and changes in price.
9. When the expected gain from bargaining exceeds your opportunity cost, you have an incentive to bargain. Because bargaining often requires a large amount of time, it does not occur for relatively lower-priced goods; that is, the expected savings are less than the opportunity cost of your time spent bargaining.

Trouble Spots

Concept	*Reminder*
Relative and Absolute Prices	The *absolute* price of a commodity is the current price in most circumstances. The sticker or advertised price is an absolute price. The *relative* price, however, must be interpreted with reference to another good or another period of time. When we interpret the relative price for the same good in another period of time, we have the *real* price of the good in constant dollar terms. Often real prices and relative prices are considered distinct concepts, but they are not distinct; the real price is a special type of relative price.
Stocks and Flows	We always measure the demand for *flows* of goods and services, not the *stock* of goods and services. Thus, the horizontal axes in our supply and demand diagrams always have a time unit.
Price Elasticity of Demand	Use the arc price elasticity of demand formula for all of your elasticity calculations that involve two prices and two quantities. Remember that the formula for the arc price elasticity uses the *average* of the two prices and the *average* of the two quantities to compute percentage changes.
Total Revenue and Price Elasticity	The relationship between total revenue and price elasticity is indirect, as it involves the relationship between marginal revenue and price elasticity and then the relationship between marginal revenue and total revenue. The relationship is most easily remembered by committing Figure 2.14 to memory.
Retail Pricing	Although there may appear to be many examples in which price is not adjusting to changes in either demand or supply conditions, these cases can often be explained by the cost of actually adjusting price. Such transaction costs are not highlighted in our graphs describing market equilibrium, but they are present and they do affect the speed at which the market can adjust price to changes in either supply or demand, as the restaurant example illustrates.

2.13 Review Questions

1. If we do not have scarce resources, will we have a law of demand? Will we observe price rationing for goods?
2. Explain the difference between real income and nominal income. If the prices of all goods double and your nominal income doubles, does your real income increase? Why or why not?

3. List three examples that distinguish between stocks and flows of goods or services.
4. Suppose you are shopping at the mall and it begins to rain. How will this event affect your demand for umbrellas? What factors are important to your decision to buy an umbrella?
5. What is the difference between an increase in demand and an increase in quantity demanded?
6. How does the increase in the price of a substitute affect demand? Is the effect the same as that observed when the price of a complement decreases?
7. How does rapid population growth affect the market demand for housing in a given locality? How do you compute the new market demand curve after an influx of population?
8. Define the point and arc price elasticities of demand. Explain why the *point* price elasticity estimate may differ between two points on the demand curve.
9. Does the estimated price elasticity of demand change when the units used to measure either axis are changed?
10. Construct on the same graph two straight-line demand curves with the same intercept on the vertical axis, with one curve flatter than the other. Can you make a general statement about which one is the more elastic curve? If so, what is it?
11. What is the difference between a quantity shortage and a quantity surplus? How does market price adjust in each case?
12. How do new entrants—new firms—affect the market supply curve? If demand is unchanged, what happens to the market price when new firms enter the market?
13. How are total and marginal revenue related to the price elasticity of demand? If demand is price-elastic and price falls, what happens to total revenue?
14. How does the value of one's time affect the incentive to bargain over the price of a good?

2.14 Price Theory Problems

1. Suppose that it is August 1990 and you have just heard the news that Iraq has invaded Kuwait. How does this information change your expectations regarding the future price of gasoline? How does your change in expectations affect your present behavior? How are gasoline companies likely to respond to this information—that is, how do their expectations and production plans change?
2. Suppose that the price elasticity of demand for movies equals −2 for students and −1 for senior citizens. How do these two groups respond to a 10 percent increase in the price of movies? Can you say from this information which group has the greatest (absolute) change in quantity demanded?
3. Using the following demand schedule to compute the arc price elasticity of demand between every adjacent price:

Point	*Price*	*Quantity*
a.	\$75	0
b.	60	20
c.	50	29
d.	45	36
e.	40	40

How does total revenue change as price decreases from \$75 to \$40?

4. Like the perfectly elastic ($\eta = -\infty$) and perfectly inelastic ($\eta = 0$) demand curves, the unitary elastic demand curve is somewhat of a curiosity. Give a general formula for a unitary elastic demand curve. Look at that equation; why is it impossible for the curve ever to intersect either axis? Suppose you were the only owner on earth of Martian chocolate bars, a perishable good, the demand for which is unitary elastic at all prices. What price would you charge if you wanted to make the most revenue possible?
5. Explain how a stepwise demand curve for certain (durable) commodities helps explain why individuals do not buy more when market price changes by a small amount. What is the shape of the market demand curve when individual demand is stepwise if all individuals are the same? Under what circumstances will the market demand curve smooth out across individuals?
6. In medieval times, alchemists tried unsuccessfully to turn lead into gold. Gold was used as money during this period. If the alchemists had been successful, they would have developed a money machine. An ounce of gold in medieval Europe was worth 30 times more than an ounce of lead. Suppose that a way to turn lead into gold had been invented. Answer the following questions using supply-and-demand analysis:
   a. How does such an invention affect the market supply and demand curves for lead and gold?
   b. If the process is virtually costless to implement, what are the new equilibrium prices of lead and gold?
7. Use supply-and-demand analysis to explain how the following events affect the market for air travel:
   a. A decrease in the price of jet fuel
   b. An increase in the number of terrorist attacks on airlines
   c. A rise in the real income of households
   d. Spring break for college students
   e. A new discount price plan for round-trip bus service
8. The market for roses adjusts frequently to changes in market demand and supply. During each week in the year, except the week containing February 14 (Valentine's Day), the typical *individual's* demand for roses is given by the following demand equation:

$$Q_d = 14 - P$$

During each of these weeks—that is, non-Valentine's Day weeks—there are 1000 individuals in the market for roses. The weekly *market* supply of roses during non-Valentine's Day weeks is given by the following equation:

$$Q_{Market\ supply} = 10{,}000 + 1{,}000P$$

a. Find the weekly market demand curve for roses during the non–Valentine's Day weeks.
b. What are the weekly market equilibrium price and quantity of roses sold?
c. During the Valentine's Day week, the number of buyers of roses triples and the number of sellers of roses doubles. Find the new market supply and demand equations.
d. Given your answer to part (c), find the equilibrium price and quantity of roses sold during the Valentine's Day week.

9. Consider the market for apartments near a major university. Because of zoning laws, there are only two areas where students can live. One is within walking distance of the university and the other is 10 miles away. The area near the university is completely built out (i.e., no more apartments may be built), but there is room for many more apartment buildings in the more distant location. The zoning code has also standardized apartments so that they all have two bedrooms and two baths, with comparable views. At the present equilibrium, the rent paid for nearby apartments is 2 times the rent paid for the distant apartments.
   a. Draw the supply and demand curves for the nearby and more distant apartment markets. Be sure to illustrate the two equilibrium prices.
   b. Assume that the university experiences a surge in enrollment so that the demand for both nearby and distant apartments increases by 25 percent. The builders in the area were told of the higher enrollments many months earlier so that they could plan and complete any new construction before the new school year. Draw two graphs illustrating the new equilibrium price for apartments in these two markets. If the equilibrium price of distant apartments increases by 10 percent, will the price of nearby apartments increase by more or less than 10 percent? What factors affect the answer to this question?

10. An encyclopedia sales representative faces the following demand for encyclopedias in his sales territory: $Q = 5{,}800 - 5P$, where P is price and Q is quantity demanded per year.

a. If the sales representative has been selling 800 encyclopedias per year, what is the market price of encyclopedias?
b. What is the price elasticity of demand at the market price? If the market price increases, will total revenue increase or decrease?
c. What price should the sales representative charge in order to maximize total revenues?

11. After Hurricane Andrew devastated the southern tip of Florida, more than 50,000 people were left homeless and nearly 1 million lost electricity for over a week. Bags of ice became a relatively scarce commodity as the population tried to remain cool in the sweltering heat of summer. Before Hurricane Andrew, ice sold for 50 cents per bag at nearly every convenience and grocery store. After the hurricane, entrepreneurs drove trucks carrying bags of ice into the damaged areas. Some came from as far away as Tennessee and South Carolina. On the first day after the hurricane, a bag of ice sold for \$6; on the second day, the price had fallen to \$4; on the third day, it was \$2; and on the fourth day, price had fallen to 50 cents.
    a. Analyze how supply and demand changed after the hurricane, assuming that these are equilibrium prices.
    b. Compute the price elasticity of demand between day 1 and day 3 and between day 3 and day 4, assuming that ice bag sales increased from 50,000 bags on day 2 to 80,000 bags on day 3 and 140,000 bags on day 4.
    c. If out-of-state trucks were kept out of the damaged area, what do you think would have happened to the price of ice bags on days 2 through 4?

12. Which of the following items are likely to be purchased in the United States using bargaining to determine price? Explain your reasoning.
    a. Single-family homes
    b. College education
    c. Textbooks
    d. Legal services
    e. Computer software
    f. Hamburgers
    g. Milk
    h. Carpentry services

2.15 Writing Exercise

Supply and demand forces operate in all markets. Select the market for a particular good or service and determine the factors that affect market demand

and supply. Interview local suppliers of the product to determine the importance of each factor. When possible, collect specific evidence about how demand and/or supply responds to changes in the various factors you have identified. For example, you might monitor the quantity sold during a weekend promotional sales campaign and compare this to sales during a normal weekend. Then, compute the price elasticity of demand from your data. Do the same for supply when you can isolate changes in the factors that affect quantity supplied.

3 Taxes and Restrictions on Price and Quantity

PREVIEW QUESTIONS

When you finish studying this chapter, you should be able to answer the following questions:

- What is the effect of an excise tax on market equilibrium?
- How is the per unit burden of a tax shared between consumers and producers?
- What is measured by consumers' and producers' surpluses?
- How do quantity restrictions, such as import quotas, affect the market equilibrium price?
- How do price ceilings and price floors affect the market equilibrium?
- How do externalities affect market participants?

Taxes will not go away. Thirteen states raised personal income tax rates and nine raised corporate income taxes in 1993. About the same number of states increased gasoline and sin taxes, that is, taxes on alcoholic beverages and tobacco products. Between 1992 and 1993, states raised taxes by $18 billion. Federal taxes have also increased. Although taxes will not go away, it is discouraging to most individuals to discover how complicated tax compliance has become. In 1913, the first year of constitutional individual income taxes, the 1040 tax form included eight lines of information and the normal tax rate was 1 percent after deductions with 6 percent being the highest tax rate. Today, the 1040 form includes 65 lines, and the highest tax rate is 39.6 percent.

What effects do taxes (or subsidies) have on the operation of markets? In general, taxes raise the cost of production, which causes the supply curve to shift. If consumers are directly assessed the tax, the amount they are willing to pay for a good or service decreases proportionately, which shifts the demand curve. Thus, taxes (or subsidies) have the effect of shifting supply and/or demand curves, which changes the market equilibrium price and quantity.

Government policy sets taxes. However, governments may use measures other than taxes to affect markets. Federal, state, and local governments may pass laws that restrict price, quantity, or some combination of both price and quantity. If the government determines that less industrial pollution is desirable, then industrial polluters may need special permits to pollute. Such permits may be expensive or very difficult to obtain. An antipollution law limits the quantity of output of polluting firms, which affects the market equilibrium price and quantity of the product produced by polluting firms. Similarly, minimum wage laws limit a firm's wage structure because firms cannot pay employees less than the minimum wage.

This chapter analyzes the effects of taxes (and subsidies) and price and quantity restrictions on the market equilibrium. The government also plays a role in defining property rights in a market, particularly when externalities, such as pollution, are present. Without a system of well-defined property rights, transactions are more costly because participants may not know who owns the goods being sold. We also examine how externalities affect the behavior of market participants.

3.1 Taxes and Subsidies

Suppose the headlines read, "U.S. Congress Passes the 'Alar' Tax." In this new law, a 10-cent excise tax is to be collected on each apple sold in the United States. An **excise tax** is a tax levied on each unit transacted. The intent may be to discourage farmers from using the chemical Alar to redden their apples. In fact, some recent studies have shown that Alar may cause cancer in laboratory mice, although the implications that scientists have drawn from these studies are debatable.

Excise (or Unit) Tax A tax per unit of the good sold.

How would an Alar tax affect the equilibrium price and quantity of apples? How do we introduce a tax into our supply-and-demand analysis? The answers to these questions are shown in Figure 3.1, where we have redrawn the market supply and demand curves from Figure 2.10. Apple growers must pay the government 10 cents for each apple they sell. The tax thus has the effect of *shifting* the supply curve up by 10 cents; that is, because of the tax, growers' outlays have increased by 10 cents for each apple produced. To understand this result, think of what you would do if you were an apple grower and the government required you to pay a tax of 10 cents on every apple sold. After you finished complaining, you would reevaluate your production plans. The tax increases the cost of selling apples so you reduce your apple output at each price level. This is exactly what the shift of the supply curve in Figure 3.1 shows. Note that at a price of $1, quantity supplied *with the tax* is 4,100 apples, which is less than the 4,500 apples supplied *without the tax.*

The market equilibrium changes because of the tax. The new equilibrium price of apples increases to P^{**}, which is greater than the old equilibrium price (P^{*}) of $1. As we show below, the new equilibrium price is not $1.10 (old price plus the tax) but $1.05. In addition, the number of apples sold per week decreases to 4,320 (Q^{**}) from 4,500 (Q^{*}). Thus, the tax has the effect

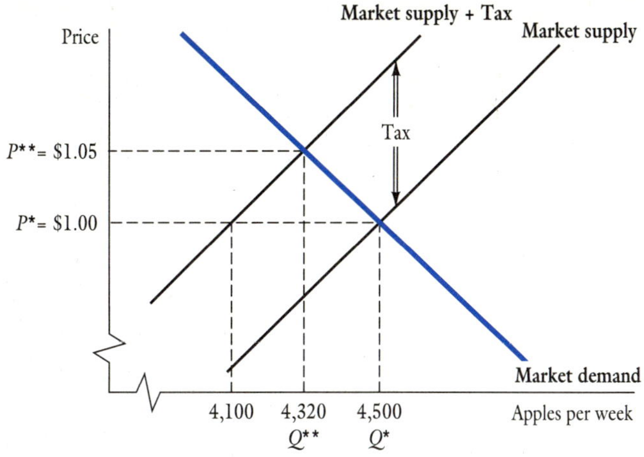

FIGURE 3.1

Unit Tax and the Apple Market

Market supply shifts to the left when the \$.10 Alar tax is instituted. The vertical distance between the new and old supply curves equals \$.10, the excise tax. The horizontal distance between the new and old supply curves measures how quantity supplied is affected by the tax. Because of the tax, the new equilibrium price paid by consumers increases to \$1.05 from \$1.00 and equilibrium quantity decreases to 4,320 from 4,500 apples per week.

of raising the equilibrium price and reducing the equilibrium quantity of apples sold.

The logic that unit taxes raise costs and cause supply to shift upward also applies to other factors that increase costs. If wages increase, firms face higher costs and supply shifts up. Thus, the results of our analysis of taxes extend to other issues.

SOLVING FOR THE EXCISE TAX EQUILIBRIUM

The 10-cents-per-unit tax has changed both equilibrium price and quantity and has changed the price received by apple growers. Before the tax, consumers paid \$1 for each apple, and growers received \$1. Now, consumers pay price P^{**}, but growers receive 10 cents *less* than this price. If we label what consumers pay as P_{demand} and what growers receive as P_{supply}, then the 10-cent tax drives a "wedge" between these two prices. We can show this by noting that the total expenditure of consumers equals the total revenue of firms plus the total tax payments:

$$P_{demand} \times Q = (P_{supply} \times Q) + (\text{tax} \times Q)$$

which after dividing both sides by Q becomes

$$P_{demand} = P_{supply} + \text{tax} \tag{3.1}$$

In other words, the difference between the price paid by consumers and that received by growers is the per unit tax; that is, $P_{demand} - tax = P_{supply}$. The intuition behind this result is that the price paid by consumers must cover both the minimum price producers will accept and the added cost of the excise tax.

The new equilibrium price, P^{**}, is the price paid by consumers, P_{demand}. To find this price, we substitute the above relationship into our demand and supply equations. The demand and supply equations for the apple market were given as equations (2.9) and (2.10):

$$D(P_{demand}) = 8{,}096 - 3{,}596P_{demand} \tag{2.9}$$

$$S(P_{supply}) = 500 + 4{,}000P_{supply} \tag{2.10}$$

Substituting for P_{supply} from equation (3.1), $P_{supply} = P_{demand} - tax$, and setting quantity supplied equal to quantity demanded, we find

$$\begin{aligned}
8{,}096 - 3{,}596P_{demand} &= 500 + 4{,}000(P_{demand} - tax) \\
8{,}096 - 500 &= 3{,}596P_{demand} + 4{,}000P_{demand} - 4{,}000tax \\
7{,}596 + 4{,}000tax &= 7{,}596P_{demand} \\
\text{or } P_{demand} &= 1 + (4{,}000/7{,}596)tax \qquad (3.2)
\end{aligned}$$

Substituting the 10-cent tax into the above equation gives P_{demand} = \$1.05 (approximately).[1] The new equilibrium price means that growers receive 95 cents for each apple, that is, the price paid by consumers *minus* the tax. The equilibrium quantity may be found by substituting P_{demand} = \$1.05 into demand equation (2.9): $Q^{**} = D(P_{demand}) = 8{,}096 - 3{,}596(1.05)$, which implies that $Q^{**} = 4{,}320$ apples. The old equilibrium quantity was 4,500 apples, so the 10-cent tax reduces sales by 180 apples.

LEARNING EXERCISE 3.1

If the tax is raised to 20 cents per apple, what are the new equilibrium price and quantity? What is the price received by apple growers? Draw the *new* supply and demand curves.

MATH NOTEPAD

Solving for the Effects of a Unit Tax

Using the general form of the linear supply and demand equations 2.5 and 2.6, we have

$$D(P_{demand}) = a - bP_{demand}$$

$$S(P_{supply}) = c + dP_{supply}$$

[1] The exact answer is P_{demand} = \$1.0527.

Substituting the relationship $P_{demand} - tax = P_{supply}$ into the supply function and setting quantity demanded equal to quantity supplied gives

$$D(P_{demand}) = S(P_{demand} - \text{tax})$$

$$a - bP_{demand} = c + d(P_{demand} - tax)$$

$$P_{demand} = (a - c)/(b + d) + (\text{tax})[d/(b + d)]$$

Recall from equation (2.7) that the (no-tax) equilibrium price (P^*) equals $(a - c)/(b + d)$. Thus, we can write the price paid by consumers as

$$P_{demand} = P^* + (\text{tax})[d/(b + d)]$$

In other words, the excise tax increases the price paid by consumers (relative to the no-tax price) by an amount equal to (tax)[$d/(b + d)$].

SALES TAX

Sales Tax
A percentage tax placed on the total receipts of a transaction.

A sales tax is different from an excise tax, but its effects on market prices are very similar. A **sales tax** or *ad valorem tax* is a tax on the dollar value of a transaction, whereas an excise tax is a tax on each unit sold. If you pay a 10-cent excise tax on apples and buy 5 apples at $1 each, you pay 50 cents in excise taxes. An apple sales tax of 6 percent, instead of an excise tax, implies that you pay an extra 6 percent in taxes. In this case, if you buy 10 apples, you pay 60 cents (6 percent of the posted price) in sales tax.

A sales tax affects the equilibrium price in a multiplicative manner. Analogous to equation (3.1), the price paid by the consumer is related to the price received by the seller according to the following equation:

$$P_{demand} = (1 + \text{sales tax})P_{supply} \tag{3.3}$$

The sales tax also drives a wedge between what consumers pay and what producers receive for a good. Unlike the excise tax, the wedge becomes increasingly larger as the price increases. Recall that with an excise tax, the wedge between what consumers pay and what producers receive was the tax, which was constant. Now, with the sales tax, the size of the wedge depends on the price paid. At higher prices, the wedge is larger than at lower prices. With a 6 percent sales tax, for example, the wedge equals 6 cents if the price is $1 but increases to 60 cents if the price is $10.

Figure 3.2 on page 72 compares the effects of a 10-cent unit tax and a 6 percent sales tax. Both of these taxes are collected by the apple grower, so the supply curve is affected in each case. The unit tax causes the supply curve to shift vertically by the amount of the tax, just as was shown in Figure 3.1. Consumers pay $1.05 per apple at the new equilibrium price. In contrast, the sales tax causes the supply curve to shift upward along an ever-increasing path because it is multiplied by (1 + sales tax), which gives

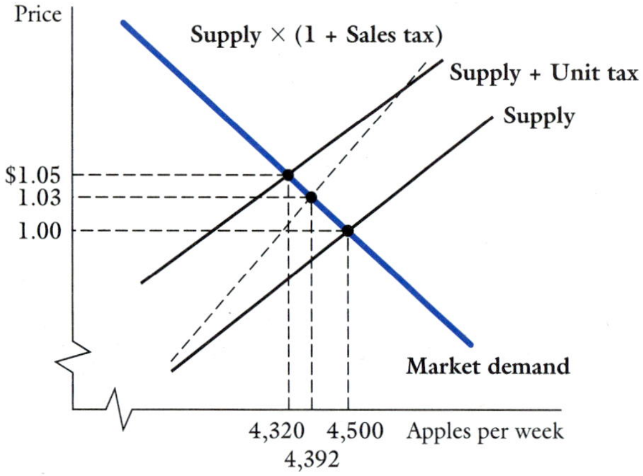

FIGURE 3.2

Comparing a 6-Percent Sales Tax to a 10-cent Unit Tax

An excise tax equal to \$.10 per apple causes the supply curve to shift up by \$.10 to Supply + Unit tax. A sales tax levied on suppliers also causes supply to shift up, but in a multiplicative manner. With a sales tax of 6 percent, the new supply curve equals Supply × (1 + Sales tax) represented by the dashed curve.

a larger shift for higher prices. The new equilibrium price paid by consumers is found by substituting equation (3.3) into equation (2.9)—shown above—and setting quantity demanded equal to quantity supplied. This gives $P_{demand} = \$1.03$, and the suppliers receive approximately 96 cents after paying 6 cents in taxes.

In Figure 3.2, the 6 percent sales tax causes a smaller increase in market price than the unit tax. This is not a general result but depends on the size of the sales tax. Obviously, if we had increased the sales tax to 15 percent, the resulting market price for consumers would exceed that found using a unit tax of 10 cents.

Whether a unit tax or a sales tax is used is not a simple issue. There are different costs of implementing and enforcing these taxes, for example, that affect the relative desirability of each tax in a given situation. A unit tax on many items may be impossible to impose. Balloons, for example, are sold in packages. Store clerks might be required to count the number of balloons in each package—a very time-consuming activity—to determine the proper tax. A sales tax is less costly to implement on items that may be sold in packages. In contrast, gasoline is sold by the gallon at service stations that use pumps to carefully measure how much is sold. A unit tax is imposed on gasoline partly because it is less costly to implement and enforce. Tax agents can inspect the pumps at service stations to determine the number of gallons sold, but they would have a difficult time determining how many balloons were sold at a toy store.

MATH NOTEPAD

Solving for the Effects of a Sales Tax

Using the general form of the linear supply and demand equations shown in Chapter 2, we have

$$D(P_{demand}) = a - bP_{demand}$$

$$S(P_{supply}) = c + dP_{supply}$$

Substituting the relationship $P_{demand} = P_{supply}(1 + \text{sales tax})$ into the demand function and setting quantity supplied equal to quantity demanded gives

$$D(P_{supply}) = D[P_{supply}(1 + \text{sales tax})]$$

$$c + dP_{supply} = a - b[P_{supply}(1 + \text{sales tax})]$$

$$P_{supply} = (a - c)/[d + b(1 + \text{sales tax})]$$

Using equation (3.3) gives

$$P_{demand} = [(1 + \text{sales tax})(a - c)]/[d + b(1 + \text{sales tax})]$$

Substituting for the parameters a, b, c, and d gives $P_{demand} = \$1.03$.

THE BURDEN OF TAXES

Who bears the burden of the tax? Is it true, as many popular news articles might have you believe, that a tax is just "passed on" to consumers? The answer depends on what is meant by the word *burden*. In both the excise and sales tax examples, consumers and producers are affected by the tax. In the excise tax case, consumers pay more, but not 10 cents more, and producers receive less per unit than before the tax. So, if burden is measured by the change in price, then the burden of the tax is *not completely passed on* to consumers; it is shared by both consumers and producers. The sharing occurs primarily because

> **A tax is not really a tax on consumers or a tax on producers but a tax on the *transactions* between consumers and producers.**

Who bears the burden of a tax will then depend on how the *new* equilibrium compares to the *old* equilibrium and on how we define the burden.

Figure 3.3 on page 74 shows how the price paid by consumers and the price received by firms has changed with the 10-cent excise tax. At the new equilibrium price of \$1.05, consumers pay 5 cents *more* per unit than before the tax. Similarly, firms receive 95 cents for each apple, which is 5 cents *less* than before the tax. In this case the per-unit burden of the tax is split equally between the consumer and producer. In general, we define per-unit tax burden as follows:

- Consumers' per unit burden is equal to the new equilibrium price minus the old equilibrium price. Algebraically, consumers' per-unit burden equals $P_{\text{demand}} - P^*$.
- Producers' per unit burden is equal to the old equilibrium price minus the price received by producers after paying the tax. Algebraically, producers' per-unit burden equals $P^* - P_{\text{supply}}$.

Note that the consumers' per-unit burden plus producers' per unit burden equals the total unit tax. Thus, the amount of per-unit burden imposed is fixed; again, the issue is, who bears it? Although it is split equally in our example, the split will rarely if ever be equal in the real world. In general, the relative shape of the demand and supply curves determines the way the per-unit burden is distributed between consumers and producers. As the demand curve flattens—that is, its slope approaches zero—the consumer tends to shift more of the burden to the producer. In other words, the consumer shifts the per-unit burden to the producer by a greater response in quantity demanded when the demand curve is flat than when it is steep. Alternatively, if the supply curve flattens—that is, its slope approaches zero—the producer can shift more of the per-unit burden to the consumer. Analogously, the producer shifts the per-unit burden to the consumer by a showing a greater response in quantity supplied when the supply curve is flat than when it is steep. In general, the more

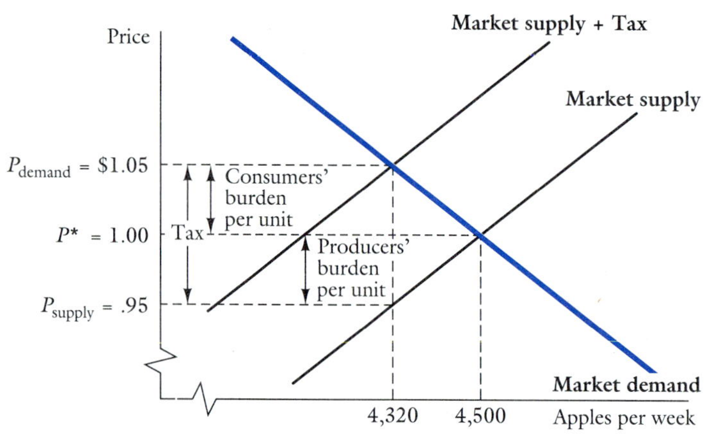

FIGURE 3.3

The Per Unit Burden of an Excise Tax

The consumers' tax burden equals the difference between the price paid with the tax and the price paid without the tax. The producers' burden equals the difference between the price received without the tax and the price received with the tax. The consumers' and producers' burdens add to equal the $.10 tax. The degree to which consumers or producers bear the burden of a tax depends on the price elasticities of demand and supply.

responsive in terms of quantity either the consumer or producer is to a price change, the more that party can escape the per-unit burden of a tax.

LEARNING EXERCISE 3.2

How is the per-unit burden of a 10-cent tax shared between consumers and producers if the demand curve is a horizontal line at $P^* = \$1$? How is the burden shared when the supply curve is vertical at the old equilibrium quantity?

SUBSIDIES

Subsidy
A payment made to either buyers or sellers for each transaction.

Suppose that instead of imposing an excise tax, the U.S. Congress decided to help apple producers, by subsidizing the sale of apples with a 10-cent subsidy per apple. A per-unit **subsidy** is a payment for each unit transacted. What happens in this case to the supply curve? The answer is that the supply curve of apples *shifts to the right* as more apples are produced at each price. Effectively, the subsidy has lowered the per-unit cost of production to apple growers. Figure 3.4 shows the effect of a subsidy on the market equilibrium price and quantity. Equilibrium price decreases to 95 cents and equilibrium quantity increases to 4,680. Again, the *change* in equilibrium price is less than the amount of the subsidy.

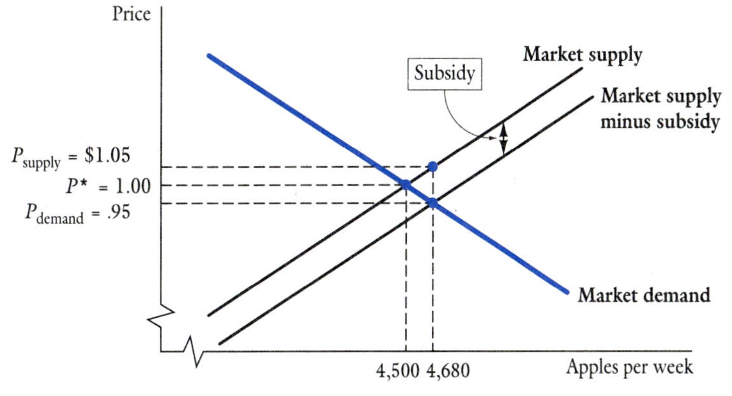

FIGURE 3.4

A Per-Unit Subsidy and the Apple Market

A subsidy of \$.10 per apple paid to producers shifts the supply curve to the right. The vertical distance between the old and new supply curves equals the \$.10 subsidy. The price paid by consumers (P_{demand}) decreases to \$.95 and the price received by producers (P_{supply}) increases to \$1.05, compared to the old equilibrium price (P^*) of \$1.00. The subsidy causes the equilibrium quantity of apples sold to increase from 4,500 to 4,680 per week.

To compute the change in the equilibrium price, we follow a procedure similar to that used to compute the tax equilibrium. First, we note that the subsidy increases the price received by producers:

$$P_{\text{demand}} = P_{\text{supply}} - \text{subsidy} \tag{3.4}$$

Next, we substitute for P_{supply} in equation (2.10) after rearranging equation (3.4) to state $P_{\text{supply}} = P_{\text{demand}} + \text{subsidy}$. By setting quantity supplied equal to quantity demanded, we solve for P_{demand}. Again, P_{demand} is equal to the new market equilibrium price. As shown in Figure 3.4, the new equilibrium price is 95 cents. Producers receive this price plus the subsidy, which implies that producers receive $1.05 for each apple sold.

There is symmetry between a subsidy and a tax in our example. The equilibrium quantity *decreases* by 180 apples with a tax and *increases* by 180 apples with a subsidy. Similarly, equilibrium price increases by 5 cents with a tax and decreases by 5 cents with a subsidy. The symmetry occurs because we have *straight-line* market demand and supply curves. If they are not straight, the symmetry between taxes and subsidies may not arise. Note that we will find the same result whether we place the administrative responsibility of collecting and paying the tax on the producer or the consumer. This claim applies for a subsidy, too.

LEARNING EXERCISE 3.3

What would happen to equilibrium price and quantity if a 10-cent subsidy per apple is paid directly to consumers? How do P_{demand} and P_{supply} differ from the values shown in Figure 3.4? Is the equilibrium quantity different from that shown in Figure 3.4?

3.2 Consumers' and Producers' Surpluses

We can measure the effects of government policy using changes in equilibrium price and quantity, which is useful if we are trying to measure effects on a *per unit* basis, such as the per unit burden of a unit tax, or we can measure changes in the *aggregate* gains and losses in the market from a particular policy. If we use changes in the aggregate gains and losses, the relevant approach is to compute the *net benefits*—that is, total benefits minus total costs—for both consumers and producers. To this end, we use the concepts of consumers' surplus and producers' surplus.

DEFINING CONSUMERS' AND PRODUCERS' SURPLUSES

Consumers and producers transact at the market equilibrium price, so all units are traded at this price. With the market demand curve negatively sloped, however, some consumers are willing to pay more than the market equilibrium price. Because consumers do not pay more but rather pay the equilibrium price for all units, they generally receive a "surplus" for each unit bought, which for the whole market is called consumers' surplus. Technically,

Consumers' Surplus
The net benefit to consumers from purchasing a given quantity of a good; it equals the difference between the value placed on each unit and its price summed over all purchases.

consumers' surplus equals the total benefits received by all consumers (the area under the market demand curve up to Q^*) minus the total amount paid for the actual quantity purchased in the market. Thus, we can think of consumers' surplus as the *net benefit to consumers* from a given output rate.

Figure 3.5 illustrates how consumers' surplus is defined for a particular market equilibrium. This market is in equilibrium at a price of \$10 per unit with Q^* units sold. The market demand curve is composed of a large number of people, many of whom value the good at more than \$10. Let's consider two particular cases: Mary and William. Mary values one unit of this good at \$18 and William values one unit at \$15. Because they each can purchase one unit at \$10, they both receive some consumers' surplus for the units that they buy. Mary's surplus equals \$8 (\$18 – \$10), and William's surplus equals \$5 (\$15 – \$10). When we compute the surpluses for all the participants who bought some of the good and add them together, we have the consumers' surplus for the whole market, which is shown as area *A* in the figure. (Note that some people may buy more than one unit, so in this case we must compute their surplus for *each* unit bought.)

Producers' surplus is analogous to consumers' surplus, but it is for producers. The cost of producing additional units generally increases for producers. Although the cost of producing some units may equal market price, the cost of other units is expected to be less. These other units will still sell for the market price in equilibrium, even though they do not cost this much to produce. Thus, the firm receives a "surplus" equal to the difference between the

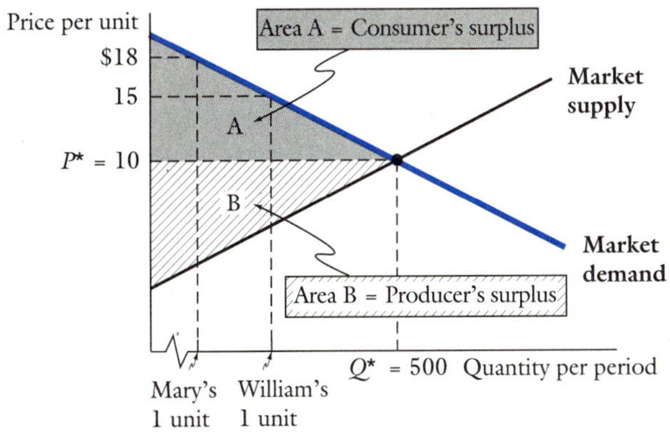

FIGURE 3.5

Defining Consumer and Producer Surpluses

Consumers' surplus is equal to area **A,** the area under the market demand curve and above the market price of P^*. Consumers' surplus for Mary equals \$8, which is the difference between the maximum she is willing to pay (\$18) and what she actually pays (\$10). Similarly, consumers' surplus for William equals \$5. Area **A** is the sum of all of the surplus for every consumer buying a product in this market. Producers' surplus, area **B,** is the analogous concept for firms. Producers' surplus equals the difference between the market price and the marginal cost of each unit summed over all units sold.

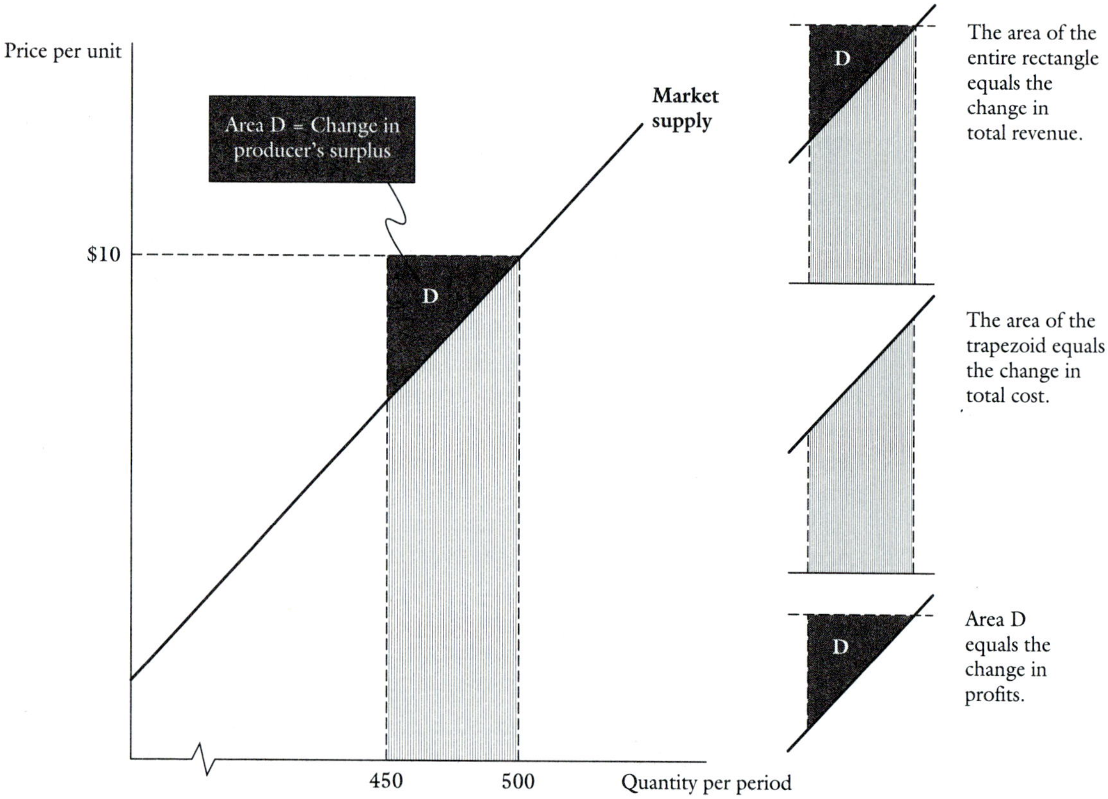

FIGURE 3.6

The Change in Producers' Surplus Equals the Change in Profits

The change in producers' surplus equals the change in profits for the market as a whole. If firms increase total output from 450 to 500 units—holding market price at $10—revenues increase by the size of the rectangle and costs increase by the size of the trapezoid formed below the supply curve. The difference between these two areas—area **D**—equals the change in profits and also the change in producers' surplus.

cost of producing a given unit and the market price of that unit. If we add up this surplus across all firms for all units sold at the market equilibrium price, we have the **producers' surplus.** Producers' surplus is shown as area *B* in Figure 3.5. It is the area above the market supply curve and below the market price. (Note that the market supply curve measures the marginal cost of each unit produced.)

Producers' Surplus
The benefit to firms from producing a given output rate; it equals the difference between the price and marginal cost summed over all units sold.

Producers' surplus can be used to determine how profits *change* when the market equilibrium changes. **Profit** for a firm equals the difference between total revenue and total cost. Producers' surplus and profit are not the same, unless the firm has no fixed production costs. But producers' surplus can be used to measure the *change* in profits. In Figure 3.6, quantity supplied increases from 450 to 500 units while market price is held constant at $10 per unit. The vertical bars beneath the market supply curve represent the marginal

Profit
The difference between total revenue and total cost.

cost of each unit produced. The marginal cost of producing the five hundredth unit, for example, equals \$10 because this is the height of the vertical bar beneath the supply curve at 500 units. Adding all these vertical bars together gives the *increase* in total costs when market output increases by 50 units, from 450 to 500. In other words, the area under the supply curve between 450 and 500 units equals the *change* in total costs.

The total revenues for firms in this market increase from \$4,500 to \$5,000, which is measured by the area of the rectangle formed below the price of \$10 and between 450 and 500 units. Note that we are holding price constant at \$10 between 450 and 500 units for this example. Now, producers' surplus equals the triangular area below the market price and above the market supply curve, so the *change* in producers' surplus equals area D as quantity supplied increases from 450 to 500 units. This is equivalent to the *change* in profits because the change in profits equals the change in total revenue (the large rectangle) minus the change in total cost (the trapezoid). Because the change in producers' surplus can be used to measure the change in profits, we can interpret it as the *net benefit to firms* from a change in the equilibrium output rate.

Note that we will focus on the change in producers' and consumers' surpluses, not their total values, to measure the effects of government policy. Changes in producers' and consumers' surplus form an anchor for our analyses because we are making a relative comparison with these changes; that is, we are comparing the *before* and *after* equilibrium conditions. This type of comparison allows us to see who is gaining and who is losing from policy changes.

LEARNING EXERCISE 3.4

Assuming that the supply curve is a straight line between 450 and 500 units in Figure 3.6, what is the change in profits?

AN APPLICATION TO EXCISE TAXES

We can illustrate how to use changes in consumers' and producers' surplus to determine the effects of the 10-cent excise (or unit) tax on apples described in Figure 3.3. Figure 3.7 on page 80 illustrates these effects.

The area between the demand and supply curves in Figure 3.7 is divided into six pieces labeled A, B, C, X, Y, and Z. The following table describes how these pieces are combined to compute consumers' and producers' surpluses before and after the tax and the resulting change in these surpluses.

	Consumers' Surplus	Producers' Surplus	Total Tax Revenue
Before the Tax	$A + B + C$	$X + Y + Z$	None
After the Tax	A	Z	$B + X$
Net Change	$-(B + C)$	$-(X + Y)$	$(B + X)$

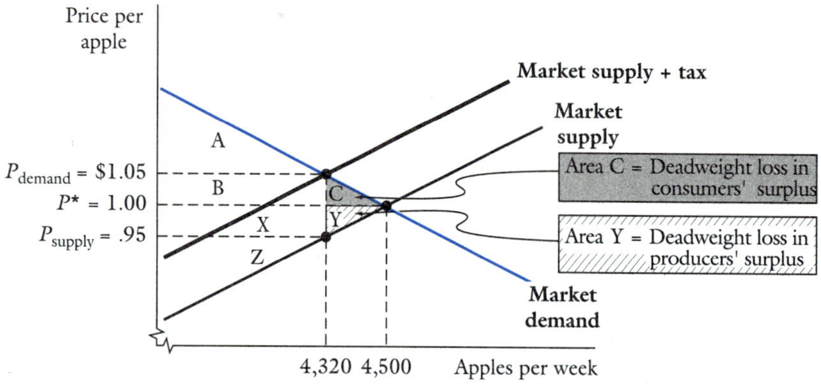

FIGURE 3.7

Effects of a Unit Tax on Consumers' and Producers' Surpluses

The burden of a unit tax can also be measured using consumers' and producers' surpluses. The unit tax decreases the equilibrium output rate to 4,320 apples from 4,500 apples per week. Consumers' surplus decreases by area **C** and producer's surplus decreases by area **Y** as a result. These changes in surplus are called deadweight losses because they are benefits that are removed from the market due to the tax.

Generally, we use the increase in total tax revenue, $B + X$, as an offset to the losses in consumers' and producers' surplus because these dollars end up with consumers and/or firms once the government spends the tax revenue. Allowing for this offset, we find that the unit tax on apples causes a net loss of benefits equal to areas $C + Y$; that is, the sum of the net changes is $-(B + C) - (X + Y) + (B + X)$, which equals a loss of $C + Y$. These areas represent a **deadweight loss** in consumers' surplus (area C) and producers' surplus (area Y); that is, these surpluses have been removed from the market by introduction of the tax. Generally, the larger the deadweight loss from a tax, the more market participants will organize to oppose a tax; that is, the more market participants stand to lose, the more incentive they have to prevent these losses.

Deadweight Loss
The permanent loss in consumers' and producers' surpluses from a change in the market environment, for example, a new government program.

3.3 Restrictions on Price and Quantity

Governments sometimes impose restrictions on a market. Quotas on the importation of foreign goods and services are a form of *quantity* restriction. For example, tobacco, sugar, and immigrant labor are all subject to import quotas. An import quota is a U.S. law, or a trade agreement between the United States and other countries, that specifies the maximum amount of a good that can be imported in a given year. In contrast, minimum wages are a restriction placed on the price paid for labor services. Similarly, the prices of natural gas, oil, and trucking services have been regulated in the past. In each instance, government regulations imposed a price restriction on the market for these goods and services. There are also cases in which market participants regulate price movements without government direction. The futures markets are one prominent example. Let's examine how quantity and price restrictions affect markets using three examples: U.S. sugar quotas policy to illustrate quantity restrictions, minimum wage laws to illustrate price restrictions, and Treasury bond futures contracts to illustrate market-imposed price restrictions.

QUANTITY RESTRICTIONS: SUGAR QUOTAS

The U.S. government imposes quotas on sugar imports to maintain the domestic price of sugar in the range of 20 to 22 cents per pound.[2] The price of sugar outside the United States, called the world price, is typically less than one-half the U.S.-supported price. Figure 3.8 shows the prices of both U.S. sugar (called domestic sugar) and world sugar on April 17, 1994.

SUGAR – WORLD (CSCE) – 112,000 lbs.; cents per lb.

May	11.15	11.28	11.03	11.28	+ .23	12.47	8.65	39,441
July	11.53	11.62	11.42	11.60	+ .15	12.50	9.15	41,254
Oct	11.17	11.29	11.07	11.27	+ .10	11.98	9.42	30,909
Mr95	10.98	11.08	10.88	11.06	+ .18	11.52	10.56	14,519
May	11.00	11.02	10.94	11.06	+ .14	11.48	10.57	1,946
July	10.98	11.02	10.99	11.06	+ .14	11.43	10.57	1,065
Oct	10.99	11.00	10.99	11.02	+ .14	11.40	10.57	356

Est vol 27,113; vol Tues 64,932; open int 129,495, – 8,546.

SUGAR – DOMESTIC (CSCE) – 112,000 lbs.; cents per lb.

May	21.95	21.95	21.93	21.93	– .03	22.11	21.35	648
July	22.08	22.08	22.05	22.07	– .02	22.16	21.55	2,141
Sept		....	....	22.07	– .02	22.16	21.80	1,952
Nov		....	....	21.95	– .04	22.03	21.82	2,141
Ja95		....	....	21.90	– .06	22.02	21.86	387
Mar		....	....	21.90	– .06	21.98	21.82	203

Est vol 900; vol Tues 198; open int 7,523, – 46

FIGURE 3.8

World Sugar Futures Prices

The high, low, and closing prices for world and domestic sugar futures contracts are shown for various delivery months. Contract prices differ across months and between world and domestic sugar. The U.S. sugar quota program maintains domestic prices between between \$.20 and \$.22 per pound. In contrast, world sugar prices are less than one-half domestic prices. (Source: *The Wall Street Journal*, Thursday, April 7, 1994.)

[2] U.S. sugar policy is described by Ralph Ives and John Hurley, "United States Sugar Policy: An Analysis," International Trade Administration, U.S. Department of Commerce, 1988.

Sugar contracts are traded on the New York Coffee, Sugar, and Cocoa Exchange (NYCSCE). A sugar contract is an agreement between a buyer and seller to exchange 112,000 pounds—not the amount you usually find in the grocery store—of sugar at the agreed contract price. Sugar contracts are traded for delivery several months into the future—in April 1994, they were for May 1994, July 1994, September 1994, October 1994, November 1994, March 1995, May 1995, July 1995, and October 1995—so there are many prices for sugar depending on when one desires to take delivery.

Sales of world sugar contracts for all delivery months totaled about 6,269 on this particular day. In contrast, only 900 domestic sugar contracts were sold. Sales are different from the number of outstanding contracts, which is called **open interest** in Figure 3.8. There are 129,495 contracts outstanding for world sugar and only 7,523 outstanding for domestic sugar. (Note that sugar sales are a *flow* of contracts and open interest is a *stock* of contracts.)

Open Interest The number of futures contracts outstanding.

As can be seen from Figure 3.8, the *primary* effect of sugar quotas is that they raise domestic sugar prices. We do not need a complicated graph or argument to show this result; it is clear from the newspaper clipping. Generally speaking, quantity restrictions raise equilibrium prices.

To see exactly how the sugar quotas work, look at Figure 3.9, which shows the domestic supply and demand of sugar. Because quotas are set annually, we have drawn yearly supply and demand curves. Note that we must add the import quota to the domestic supply curve to determine the total supply of sugar in the domestic market. Annual consumption of sugar in the United States is about 16 billion pounds at the current price of 21.4 cents per pound. Annual production in the United States is about 15.4 billion pounds. The difference between production and consumption is the amount of imports sold in the United States.[3]

By restricting imports to 0.6 billion pounds of sugar per year, the United States can maintain the price of sugar in the support range of 20 to 22 cents per pound. In contrast, the price in the world market—determined by world demand without the United States and world supply minus exports to the United States—is about 9.3 cents per pound. At this price approximately 242 billion pounds of sugar are sold each year.[4]

Now, if the United States relaxes its import quota restrictions, foreign suppliers will quickly enter the U.S. market because its price exceeds that in the world market. This action causes the domestic-supply-plus-imports curve to shift to the right, which causes the domestic equilibrium price to fall. Simultaneously, as exports to the United States increase, the world-supply-minus-exports curve shifts to the left, which causes the world price to rise to the free market price. An increase in imports is shown in Figure 3.9 by a shift to the right in the market supply curve. Perversely, if the United States opens its sugar market to the world, the world price rises, making sugar a relatively more expensive source of calories for many poor countries.

---

[3] Actually, the difference shown in the graph is the net imports—all imports minus all exports—of sugar. Some domestically produced sugar is sold on the world market.

[4] Ron Lord and Robert Barry, *The World Sugar Market—Government Intervention and Multilateral Policy Reform,* U.S. Department of Agriculture, September 1990.

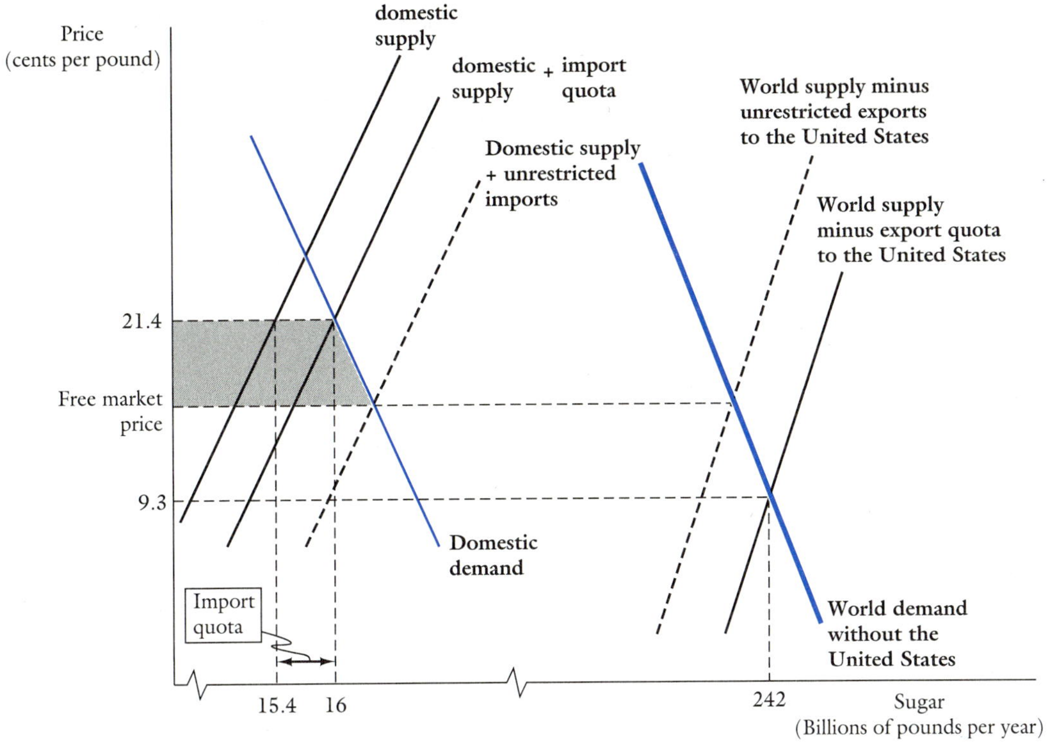

FIGURE 3.9

The Effects of U.S. Sugar Import Quotas

The import quota on sugar has the effect of raising the domestic price of sugar relative to the world price. The quota is set to maintain domestic prices between 20 and 22 cents per pound. The world price is free to fluctuate with the forces of supply and demand. If the quota program is abolished, unrestricted sugar imports will increase domestic supply and cut domestic production greatly, reducing the domestic price and slightly increasing the world price.

One way to measure the cost to consumers of the sugar quota program is to compute the consumers' surplus that is lost because the market does not operate without restrictions. If there were no restrictions on sugar imports to the United States, for example, the free market price of sugar—both world and domestic—might be approximately 14 cents per pound. We would call this the free market price. In this case, the shaded area in Figure 3.9 would represent the *loss* in consumers' surplus because of the government's sugar quota program. The bigger this area, the more consumers in the United States gain from the elimination of sugar quotas.

There are also *secondary* effects of the sugar quota program. If the government adjusts the import quota to keep prices around 20 to 22 cents per pound, then any increase in domestic supply will reduce the import quota. Domestic supply will increase—a shift to the right—if costs of production fall or if yield per acre increases. Sugar growers (like any other firm) have an incentive to invest in cost-reducing production techniques if their profits will increase as a result. The question here is whether sugar growers have an added incentive to invest in cost-saving techniques because the import quotas keep domestic prices higher than world prices. The answer is yes if there are start-up costs associated with cost-reducing research that can be recovered at the higher domestic price but not at the lower world price. Because domestic yield per acre has increased over the last decade, the evidence suggests that growers have invested in cost-saving production techniques.

In addition, high domestic sugar prices create incentives for consumers to find substitutes for sugar. Substitutes, such as artificial sweeteners—Equal, Sugar Twin, and Sweet 'N Low—and high-fructose corn syrup, have been developed in recent years to compete with sugar. Consumption of high-fructose corn syrup has been increasing rapidly, from 1 billion pounds in 1975 to over 12 billion pounds today. Although health-consciousness trends encouraged manufacturers to develop sugar substitutes, the lower level of use of such substitutes in other countries suggests that high sugar prices in the United States are an important factor.

Events during 1985 made it clear that manufacturers are affected by sugar quotas. During 1985, world sugar prices fell to less than 3 cents per pound. At these low prices it became profitable for large domestic buyers to try to evade sugar quotas. Some firms began importing products such as Canadian cake mix that contained a high proportion of sugar but were not subject to the sugar quota. The sugar was extracted from these products and sold at domestic sugar prices for a profit. Such perverse behavior would not occur if firms could import sugar directly from world markets.

Sugar quotas show how market prices are increased by government-imposed quantity restrictions. Compared to the world price, the higher domestic price adds about $20 to the average household's annual food costs. In effect, the quota program costs each household two haircuts at SuperCuts, six videos rented from Blockbuster Video, or a meal for two at a moderately priced restaurant. The net effect of the program on the economy is more difficult to compute. We must determine how much producers' surplus decreases when we move to a free market price. Certainly, these losses will be substantial, but under normal demand and supply conditions they are less than the gain in consumers' surplus, so the net effect of moving to a free market price is positive.

LEARNING EXERCISE 3.5

How do you compute the change in consumers' surplus in the world market when the sugar quota program is initiated?

PRICE RESTRICTIONS

Price restrictions usually act as a constraint on the equilibrium price. There are typically three types of price restrictions:

1. Price floors
2. Price ceilings
3. Restrictions on price changes over time

Price Floor
A minimum price for market transactions, for example, the minimum wage.

Price Ceilings
A maximum price for market transactions, for example, rent controls in some cities.

A **price floor** is a minimum price below which the market is not allowed to go. Minimum wage laws create a price floor in the labor market. We analyze the effects of minimum wages below. Price floors are effective (in the current period) only if they are set *above* the market equilibrium price, thereby preventing the market from reaching the lower equilibrium price. **Price ceilings** set a limit on how high the price can go. Usury laws in most states, for example, restrict the interest rates that banks can charge customers. The usury ceiling is 18 percent per year in many states. Price ceilings are effective (in the current period) only if they are set *below* the market equilibrium price, thereby preventing the market from reaching the higher equilibrium price. Finally, price restrictions may hold price changes within a certain bound—for example, up or down by at most 1 percent each day. Although it is not required by a government body, futures markets restrict price changes to a daily limit. We will discuss the price restrictions in futures markets below.

PRICE FLOORS: THE MINIMUM WAGE EXAMPLE

The federal minimum wage is a floor on hourly wages paid in the United States. If you are an employer paying less than the minimum wage and you are not exempt (very few jobs are exempt), you face significant fines and may be required to make up for past differences between what you paid employees and the minimum wage. The minimum wage increased from 25 cents in 1938, when it was first instituted, to $4.25 in 1991, or an average of 5.5 percent per year. It is currently about 35 percent of the average wage paid in manufacturing and about 60 percent of the average wage paid in retailing. Because the minimum is less than the average wage paid in most sectors of the economy, supporters of the minimum wage argue that it has little or no effect on the labor market. Opponents of the minimum wage argue that it does have an effect: it hurts exactly those people it is trying to help, that is, the poor and less skilled workers.

Note that the minimum wage issue is intertwined with both *positive* and *normative* arguments by both supporters and opponents. Supporters often make the normative claim that a minimum wage is a fair wage that guarantees a decent standard of living. Similarly, opponents make the normative claim that the government should not tell businesses what to pay workers. Although these claims are certainly worthy of debate, they cannot be resolved here (if at all). We will focus on the positive aspects of the minimum wage question, which looks at the effects of the minimum wage on employment of labor, not its social merits or drawbacks.

Now, whether you are an opponent or supporter of the minimum wage is likely to depend on your position in the labor market. If you are earning the minimum wage and Congress passes legislation to increase it, you receive a pay raise *if you can keep your job.* If you do keep your job, you may support the increased minimum wage; if you lose it, you may be against the change and the minimum wage law. Whether you or anyone else will lose a job, however, depends on where the minimum wage is set relative to the market equilibrium wage.

Figure 3.10 shows the supply and demand for labor in two labor markets: the unskilled and the highly skilled. The equilibrium wage in the unskilled market is less than the equilibrium wage in the highly skilled market. Note that the equilibrium wage is the real wage rate; that is, it is divided by the general price index. As noted in Chapter 2, individuals work for *real wages,* not nominal wages, so movements in real wages affect the willingness of individuals to supply labor services.

Figure 3.10 shows the initial effect of increasing the minimum wage in both the skilled and unskilled labor markets. In the skilled labor market, changing the minimum wage has no apparent effect on real wages because the equilibrium real wage exceeds the new minimum wage. In the unskilled labor market, the new minimum wage has created a surplus of labor—read "unemployment." The size of the surplus is the subject of much debate. When Congress considered raising the minimum wage to $4.25 from $3.35 in 1989, economists estimated that between 50,000 and 400,000 people would become unemployed. In a work force of 125 million people, this is a small fraction. But these people are unskilled workers, and unskilled workers are mostly teenagers and first-time job seekers, many of whom are members of minority groups. There are about 6 million unskilled workers in the United States. Using 225,000 unemployed as the average estimate of the surplus, about 1 out of every 26 unskilled workers are expected to lose their jobs when the minimum wage increases. Recognizing this problem, Congress decided to implement the new minimum wage law in phases, with the $4.25 wage going into effect in April 1991. In addition, Congress adopted a "training" wage for inexperienced teenagers equal to 85 percent of the minimum wage. Employers were permitted to pay the training wage for the first three months on the job. In 1993, the training wage was dropped. The argument given was that firms had had time to adapt to the new minimum wage and that the training wage was not being used by many firms.

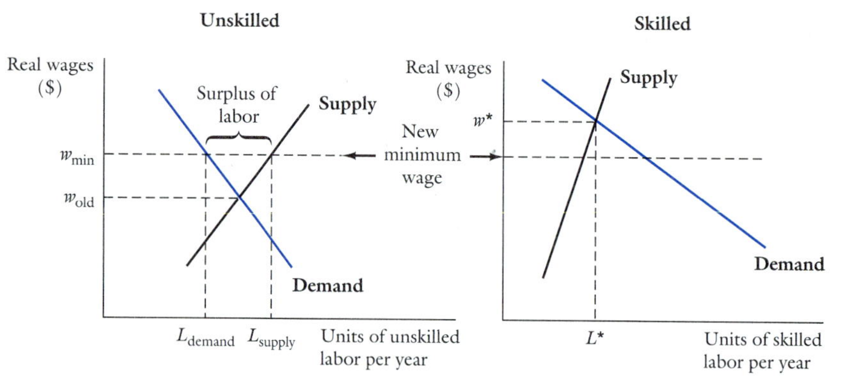

FIGURE 3.10

Minimum Wage Effects in Unskilled and Skilled Labor Markets

The new minimum wage (w_{min}) causes a surplus of labor in the unskilled labor market if it is set above the market-clearing equilibrium real wage (w_{old}). Initially, w_{min} does not affect the wages paid to skilled labor because it is below the equilibrium wage (w^*) for skilled labor.

Even with the precautions taken by Congress, some unskilled workers have become unemployed because of the minimum wage. Those who lose their jobs are caught in a vicious cycle. They are laid off because they have fewer skills than those remaining employed. When they do find a job, primarily because demand has increased or inflation has lowered the real value of the minimum wage, they may be the first fired the next time the minimum wage increases because they have had less time to acquire job skills. The cycle can lead to prolonged poverty for workers who lose their jobs when the minimum wage increases. Additionally, the existence of a minimum wage above a market clearing wage makes entry into the labor market more difficult for teenagers and others with low productivity, such as some unskilled senior citizens.

On-the-Job Training

Although Figure 3.10 does not show it, minimum wages may indirectly affect the market for skilled workers. Today's unskilled workers may be the skilled workers of tomorrow. Through on-the-job training, unskilled workers may acquire the skills necessary to become skilled workers. As more unskilled workers acquire skills, the supply curve of skilled workers increases (shifts to the right). An increase in supply lowers the equilibrium real wage of skilled workers. Higher minimum wages can slow down this process. By decreasing the number of unskilled workers, minimum wage laws reduce the number of unskilled workers who eventually enter the skilled labor market. With fewer people entering the skilled labor market, the supply of skilled labor increases by a smaller amount than would otherwise be the case. Thus, the real wages paid to highly skilled workers are higher than they would be otherwise.

Skilled Labor Demand

Minimum wage laws may also affect the *demand* for skilled labor. In many businesses, skilled labor and unskilled labor are substitutes in production. That is, a skilled worker can accomplish the assigned task in less time than an unskilled worker. A skilled worker, for example, may hang 20 strips of wallpaper in an hour, whereas an unskilled worker may hang only 10 strips of wallpaper in an hour. One skilled worker can be substituted for two unskilled workers in this example. By changing the *relative* wage cost of skilled and unskilled workers, minimum wage laws encourage firms to substitute toward skilled workers in their production process. This effect causes the demand for highly skilled labor to increase (shift to the right), which increases employment and wages of highly skilled workers.

Foreign Manufacturing

Finally, a generally unmeasured effect of the minimum wage is the incentive it provides to U.S. firms to manufacture products in foreign countries. The Smith-Corona Company, the last U.S.-based manufacturer of typewriters, announced in 1992 that it was moving its operations to Mexico from Cortland, New York. One of the reasons for the move was that the company could not compete effectively against Japanese-made typewriters because of its higher labor costs. Another may have been the North American Free Trade

Agreement, which lowered or phased out tariffs on most goods imported from Canada and Mexico. In Mexico, the company found a ready supply of workers available for a fraction of the price it paid in New York. Smith-Corona is not alone in its decision to move. Many companies in various industries—furniture, textiles, automobiles, machinery—have opened manufacturing plants in Mexico and other countries to take advantage of the lower relative labor costs. Thus, the full effects of the minimum wage law cannot be judged by unemployment data in the United States but must also include an estimate of the losses created when firms "export" jobs to other countries.

LEARNING EXERCISE 3.6

Redraw Figure 3.10 to show how increasing the minimum wage affects the demand for skilled workers.

OTHER PRICE RESTRICTIONS

Price ceilings are more common in countries other than the United States, although the United States has imposed its share of price ceilings at one time or another. For example, during World Wars I and II, price ceilings were common on goods essential for military production—tires and gasoline. More recently, some cities have placed price ceilings on rental apartments—Santa Monica and Berkeley, California, are prominent examples, as New York City has long been. In rental housing, price ceilings lead to deteriorating structures because owners reduce upkeep and maintenance investments. Owners of rent-controlled apartment buildings sooner or later find that the rate of return on their investment is lower than what they could make elsewhere. In an attempt to match rates of return on other investments, landlords will therefore attempt to reduce costs, because they are prohibited from raising prices. One way to reduce costs is, of course, to reduce repair expenses. In some instances, price ceilings are circumvented by landlords who (illegally) charge up-front fees to new residents of rent-controlled apartments. The up-front fees are designed to capture the rent the landlord would receive if a market price were charged. Such fees can range into the tens of thousands of dollars in cities like New York, where noncontrolled rents have appreciated significantly since rent controls were first imposed.

Futures markets impose price restrictions by their own trading rules, not by government action. Exchanges are member-sponsored organizations that are formed to officiate trading in futures contracts and to provide a meeting place for traders. A futures contract for Treasury bonds, for example, provides its holder with $100,000 in bonds, delivered at a known date in the future, at a price that is set when the contract is sold. The exchanges impose limits on how much the price of a Treasury bond futures contract can change each day. The limit can fluctuate, but it is typically $3,000. That is, the price of a Treasury bond futures contract cannot move up or down more than $3,000 each day. Figure 3.11 shows the effects of these limits on the futures market in Treasury bond futures contracts.

Figure 3.11 shows the price restrictions as upper and lower limits on the change in equilibrium price based on the previous day's closing price ($P_{yesterday}$). If bad news arrives—say, the Federal Reserve announces that it will

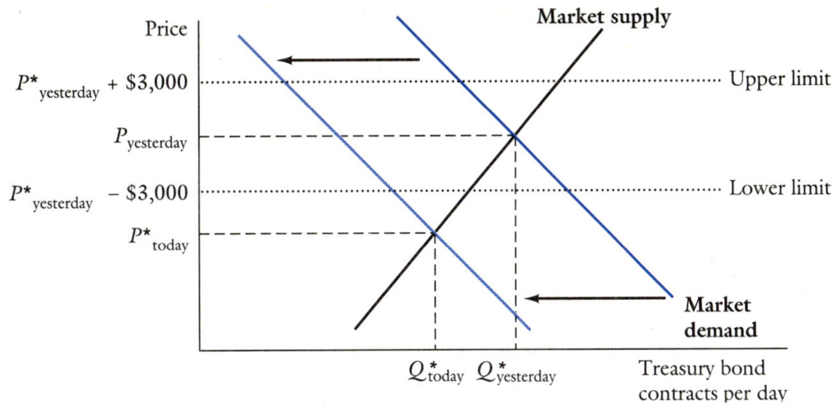

FIGURE 3.11

Price Limits on Treasury Bond Futures Contracts

Both upper and lower limits are imposed on price changes for Treasury bond futures contracts. The limits are commonly set at $3,000 per contract. If $P_{yesterday}$ is yesterday's closing price, the limits restrict today's prices to the range $P_{yesterday}$ ± $3,000. A significant decrease in market demand can produce an equilibrium price (P_{today}) below the lower limit. Trading ceases when this occurs, resuming the next day with the closing price reset to the lower limit, $P_{yesterday}$ – $3,000. When trading resumes the next day, there is a new price band of ± $3,000 around $P_{yesterday}$ – $3,000.

support the government's deficits by printing money, thereby generating inflation worries—the demand for Treasury bond futures contracts may decrease. If the news is bad enough, the new equilibrium price (P_{today}) may be below the lower price limit, as shown here. In this case, the exchange stops trading in Treasury bond futures contracts. Trading does not resume until the next day. On the next day, the lower limit, $P_{yesterday}$ – $3,000, is considered the previous day's closing price. New limits are set to a $3,000 range about this price. In our example, the limits allow the market to reach the new equilibrium price in two days.

Why do exchange members impose price limits on themselves voluntarily? Financial economist Michael Brennan has argued that price limits reduce the number of contract defaults.[5] Fewer defaults ensure the continuity of the market process. If a default occurs, the exchange's clearinghouse pays the trader who would have gained and may hire a lawyer to pursue the trader who defaulted. If there were many defaults, the clearinghouse would not have enough funds to pay the winning traders. In such an event, the futures market would break down, with traders doubting they would receive their profits. Brennan argues that defaults are less likely with price limits because such limits restrict information about the true equilibrium price. Those who have lost money because of price decreases are more willing to pay the "limited" losses

[5] Michael J. Brennan, "A Theory of Price Limits in Futures Markets," *Journal of Financial Economics* 16 (June 1986), 213–233.

than the true losses.[6] In futures markets, traders must settle their accounts with their brokers each day; that is, profits and losses are paid daily. This practice is called *marked-to-market* because the value of all accounts are updated using market prices each day. When brokers call with the bad news, traders can fulfill their obligation to pay $3,000 (the limit) more easily than they could pay a larger amount. In addition, the news on the next day may be better, so traders may regain some of their losses in the next day's trading.

While most price restrictions represent externally imposed barriers, price limits in futures markets are an example where internal market forces have imposed restrictions to benefit all market participants. Without such limits, futures markets might serve fewer traders—those with more collateral—or might stop trading some commodity or financial futures contracts whose prices are highly volatile. In both cases, the services provided by futures markets would decrease.

LEARNING EXERCISE 3.7

How would you test whether price limits decrease the number of defaults in futures markets? State the information you would need to conduct your test.

Policy Application and Evaluation

HUMAN ORGANS

Issue—*Should the purchase and sale of human organs be illegal?*

Background

The National Organ Transplant Act of 1984 makes it illegal to buy and sell human organs and establishes funds to help match needy patients with potential donors. In effect, government policy has "killed" the human organ market. The organs that are legally available for transplant today are the result of donations. For example, someone who dies unexpectedly or is brain dead may have made a provision to donate his or her organs, or the surviving family may decide to donate the organs. *The donors are not paid for the organs.* The supply-and-demand model suggests that at a price of zero fewer organs will be supplied than demanded; more transplant operations would be feasible if only there were an organ to be had.

Advances in medical science have made the shortage of organs worse over time. For example, genetic screening and new drugs have substantially reduced rejection rates, making an organ transplant a less risky alternative for more people. There were 33,581 people waiting for a kidney, heart, liver, pancreas, lung, or heart and lung transplant as of January 31, 1994, a 13 percent increase over

[6] Exchanges and brokers impose margin requirements on traders in futures markets. Contract losses are paid from a trader's margin account.

the previous two years.[7] Moreover, the number of people dying while waiting for an organ has increased. In 1993, 2,887 people died while awaiting transplants, a 31 percent increase from 1990. This situation is expected to worsen further as the general population ages, causing increased demand for organ transplants.

Figure 3.12 shows the estimated market supply and demand curves for kidney transplants at the beginning of this decade. The supply curve intersects the horizontal axis at 10,800 transplants. The fact that there are so many voluntary donations of kidneys at a zero price is a tribute to several nonprice factors. For example, many doctors and hospitals appeal directly to the family of the deceased to "save another life" with their donation of a kidney. In addition, about 20 percent of these transplants come from relatives of the recipient, so family considerations affect the supply of organs. In effect, these nonprice factors have shifted the supply curve to the right; without them, the quantity of kidneys supplied might be zero at a price of zero.

How are organs allocated? Approximately 20 percent of kidneys are donated by relatives for specific recipients. For organs donated by surviving family members, the allocation is determined by a waiting list, with hospitals having a high degree of flexibility in the disposition of an organ. Many hospitals belong to both national and regional networks for organ "sharing." These networks keep track of how long patients have been waiting for an organ, where the patients are located, and their physical characteristics. Those who have been on the list longer are given a higher priority if an organ becomes available. Hospitals have some discretion, however, to offer organs they receive to local patients first.

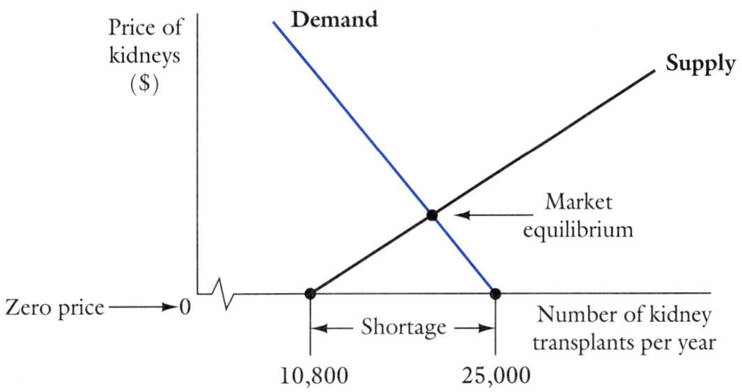

FIGURE 3.12

The Market for Kidney Transplants

The National Organ Transplant Act of 1984 prohibits the sale of organs, which implies that kidney donors are paid nothing for their donation. At a zero price, there is a shortage of 14,200 kidneys (25,000 minus 10,800) in the U.S. kidney transplant market.

[7] *UNOS Update,* published by United Network for Organ Sharing, Richmond, VA, Vol. 10, No. 2, February 1994.

The Case for a Free Market

The demand curve for kidneys indicates that about 25,000 people desired a kidney transplant in 1993. Note that if you need a kidney transplant, your alternatives are limited. A kidney dialysis machine is an alternative for some people, but it is generally not a permanent solution and it may not work well for everyone. As indicated by Figure 3.12, there was a *shortage* of 14,200 kidneys in 1993 and the price of kidneys was zero. The shortage could be eliminated in three ways:

1. Shift the supply curve to the right.
2. Shift the demand curve to the left.
3. Let the price rise.

The factors that caused the supply curve to shift from zero to 10,800, such as family appeals, are continuously used, so it is probably not possible to shift the supply curve much further to the right from domestic sources. The supply curve would be expected to increase substantially, however, if organs could be bought and imported from other countries. Under current laws, such purchases are illegal. Shifting the demand curve to the left is a solution if the cause of the shift is a substitute for a transplanted kidney. Medical science may develop such a substitute in the future, but it is not available as yet. The last alternative is to raise price. Remove the restrictions on the sale of organs so that more people contribute organs in their wills and more families "sell" the organs of their deceased loved ones to save others.

Some have considered a mix of these solutions. One idea is to let organ recipients pay funeral expenses for donors. Such in-kind payments are not as simple as paying cash, but they are still expected to have a positive effect on organ supply.

The Case for the Current Policy

First, paying for organs might reduce the number of altruistic donations because some people may be less willing to donate if a payment is made. While it is hard to evaluate this claim, there exists some evidence that such an effect may occur, because motivation to help others is believed to be the strongest reason for donating organs, and altruists resist coercion.[8] Second, patients may fear that the quality of health care will decrease if they agree to sell their organs. Physicians may act to preserve the patient's organs rather than preserve the patient, according to this argument. While this appears to be a logical argument, the degree to which it is a problem is unknown. Finally, if the price of organs were high enough, some people might kill others if they could somehow benefit from selling their victims' organs.

Questions for Evaluation

Should hospitals have discretion in the allocation of organs? Is there a need for a national waiting list to prevent local discretion? What would be the effects of

[8] W. Upton, "Altruism, Attribution and Intrinsic Motivation in the Recruitment of Blood Donors," in *Selected Readings in Donor Motivation and Recruitment*, Vol. 2, American Red Cross, 1973.

a national waiting list on those currently waiting for an organ on a local waiting list? Should we repeal the National Organ Transplantation Act to make buying and selling organs legal? Would kidney dialysis companies support or oppose the repeal of this act?

3.4 Externalities and the Market for Pollution Credits

Up to this point we have discussed the reaction of individuals, firms, and the marketplace to changes in incentives created by government policies. We have studied how each individual's or firm's actions can alter the costs and benefits accruing to that particular individual or firm. Many transactions, however, involve third parties who gain or lose from the transaction. Such a situation involves externalities, which generally change the role played by the government.

THE THEORY BEHIND EXTERNALITIES

Externality
A cost or benefit imposed on others who are not party to creating the cost or benefit.

An **externality** is present when the actions of an individual or firm produce benefits or costs that affect another individual or firm. An externality arises because of actions that occur outside of a normal market setting. When parents send a sick child to school, they create an externality for the other children in the class. The other children may catch the illness. Those who do may require a visit to a physician and bed rest, all of which is a cost that is imposed on these children and their parents. The action of sending a sick child to school creates a *negative* externality because it imposes a cost on the other children. Similarly, people who bring a cellular phone to a symphony concert impose a negative externality on the other patrons if the phone rings during the concert. Many concert halls ban cellular phones for this reason (and beepers, too). A baby crying during a movie is also a negative externality. Similarly, pollutants from a Cremora factory (Cremora is a nondairy creamer made by Borden) in the town of Chester, South Carolina, have been staining streets and sidewalks and causing residents to wash their house windows and cars more often. The Cremora product—a combination of sodium silicoaluminate and corn syrup—hardens when it dries, making it more difficult to wash a car or window. The residents of Chester are faced with a negative externality because the making of Cremora affects their production of clean cars and houses.

Externalities are not always negative. A farmer who is victimized by a fox in the henhouse may stay up the entire night to catch or kill the bothersome fox. If successful, the farmer will have undoubtedly provided a *positive* externality to other farmers in the area who have been victimized by the same fox. If you are vaccinated against mumps and rubella as a child, you provide a positive externality to your school and neighborhood playmates because you will not spread these diseases. If your roommate is clean and tidy, you are lucky and you benefit from such behavior.

The Coase Theorem

When we address the problem of externalities in Chapter 17, it will become apparent that there are two sides to the coin called externalities. For example, say it is Sunday and you want to study for an important test on Monday, but your neighbor is mowing the lawn. You face a negative externality. You might ask your neighbor to mow the lawn later, but it may be difficult for your neighbor to comply if it is already late in the day. The other side of the coin is that your neighbor desires to have a nice, well-kept lawn. If it is not mowed today, it may not be mowed for another week. If the neighbor complies with your request, he bears the cost of waiting a week before the lawn is mowed. If he does not comply, you bear the cost of not studying while he is mowing the lawn.

Ronald H. Coase was the first to observe that both parties to an externality are affected by costs.[9] Coase's great contribution to economics was that he saw a solution to such problems that was independent of the legal system if the parties involved could negotiate cheaply with one another. For example,

The dam bursts

[9] The article that Coase wrote, called "The Problem of Social Cost" [*Journal of Law and Economics* 3 (1960), 1–44], is one of the most widely cited papers in economics.

suppose that it is illegal to mow lawns on Sunday (because of the loud noise thereby created) without your neighbor's permission. You can now call the police and have them stop your neighbor from mowing the lawn, and then you can go back to studying for your exam. Alternatively, you can approach your neighbor with a simple proposition: You tell him that you will give him your permission to mow if he can compensate you for your lost study time (you must choose your words carefully here). Let us suppose that your neighbor will finish mowing in one hour. He realizes that you cannot study while he mows, but he is close to finishing, so he does not want to stop and start again next week. Your neighbor might indicate that he will offer you \$20 if you let him finish mowing.[10] Is this offer worth it? It is worth it if your study time is worth less than \$20; otherwise, no.

How is this result independent of the legal system? It is independent only in the sense that you and your neighbor can negotiate a solution that is not determined by who has the legal rights to mow or prevent mowing. Suppose that your neighbor does not need your permission to mow on Sunday. Now you must make an offer to your neighbor for him to stop mowing. Let us say that the test on Monday is *really* important and that you must receive a good grade. You offer to pay your neighbor \$30 if he stops mowing. Given that his \$20 offer is less than your \$30 offer, he should stop mowing. Note that this is also the case above—when it was illegal to mow lawns on Sunday—because you would refuse his offer and ask the police to stop the mowing. So it does not matter whether your permission is or is not needed to mow on Sunday; your neighbor will stop mowing.

The law does not affect mowing activity, but it does affect who bears the cost. When it is illegal, no money or in-kind payments occur, but your neighbor bears a \$20 cost because he cannot mow. When it is legal, you pay \$30 to your neighbor, so he nets \$10 in the transaction. The law affects the distribution of income, not the actual amount of the externality-producing activity, when the costs of negotiating are low.

Internalizing Externalities

It is useful to note again that externalities arise because of actions that occur *outside* of a market setting. If the externality can be priced by the market, so that its costs can be *internalized,* it is no longer an externality. For example, suppose there is a vacant lot next to your house that is used as a local dump by the community at large. The dump is unsightly, and it smells when the weather is warm. You bear the cost of the smell and visual pollution because you live next door. You have asked the local municipality to clean up the lot, but nothing has been done. You have talked to the owner, who is unwilling to pay anything to clean up the lot. It turns out that the lot is too small to build a house on, so the owner has little interest in maintaining it. One way to internalize the cost of the pollution generated by the lot is to buy it. Assuming that you and the owner can agree on a price (which should not be

[10] The offer might be made in kind. For example, your neighbor might offer to wash and wax your car, which would be worth \$20 to you.

too difficult), you can clean up the lot and erect a fence to keep away polluters. This option is not cheap, but if you carry it out, it must be cheaper to you than continuing to incur the external costs of pollution.

LEARNING EXERCISE 3.8

In the lawn mowing example, if the police charge you $50 each time they enforce the no-mowing-on-Sunday law, will you call them for help if your neighbor refuses your offer? Will your neighbor stop mowing if there is a $75 fine for mowing on Sunday?

THE MARKET FOR POLLUTION RIGHTS

In 1992, the Tennessee Valley Authority (TVA), one of the country's largest producers of electric power, purchased the rights to generate more pollution. Specifically, the TVA bought 10,000 tons of pollution allowances from the Wisconsin Power and Light Company. This transaction was made possible by the Clean Air Act of 1990, which requires power companies to reduce their emissions of sulfur dioxide (SO_2) and other pollutants but provides some flexibility in how they may accomplish these reductions. This flexibility allows the TVA to fail to meet the required reductions in its plants if it purchases allowances from another company that exceeds the requirements in its plants—in other words, the TVA can pollute more because Wisconsin Power and Light agreed to pollute less for a price. On balance, all firms must meet the required reductions in pollution.

The Clean Air Act allows power companies to reduce emissions in phases, with phase I beginning in 1995 and phase II beginning in 2000. Table 3.1 summarizes the required reductions by phase.[11]

To meet the required SO_2 pollution reductions, power companies may install pollution abatement equipment, close plants, or purchase pollution allowances from firms that exceed the required reductions in emissions. In effect, the Clean Air Act allows the marketplace to determine the least-cost

TABLE 3.1

The Clean Air Act's Pollution Reduction Requirements for SO_2 Emissions

	Phase I	Phase II
Number of power companies affected	261	1107
Current SO_2 emissions (million tons)	8.3	15.1
Allowable SO_2 emissions (million tons)	5.6	8.9
Reduction needed to meet allowable SO_2 emissions	33%	41%

[11] Donald A. Hanson, "The 1990 Clean Air Act: A Tougher Regulatory Challenge Facing Midwest Industry," *Economic Perspectives* (May/June 1992), 2–18.

approach to reducing pollution emissions. Previously, firms had to comply individually with the government's overall pollution goals; that is, if the goal was to reduce SO_2 emissions by 33 percent (as phase I mandates), *each firm* had to reduce its SO_2 emissions by 33 percent. With pollution allowances tradable, however, firms that reduce emissions more than the 33 percent requirement can sell allowances to other firms that do not find it profitable to meet the 33 percent requirement. The allowances that these firms buy must exactly offset the firms' decision not to meet the 33 percent requirement. In other words, firms may meet the 33 percent requirement by reducing their own emissions or by buying allowances from a firm that has reduced its emissions beyond the requirement. Because the only firms that will sell allowances are those that exceed the 33 percent requirement and the only ones likely to buy the allowances are firms that fail to meet the requirement, the total amount of pollution across *all firms* will be reduced by at least 33 percent. The value of using the marketplace approach is that any *single* firm has more flexibility in how it will meet these requirements; that is, it may exceed the requirements and sell allowances, or it may not meet them and may instead buy allowances to make up the difference.

An Example with a 30 Percent Reduction in SO_2 Emissions

To see why the marketplace approach is less costly than a mandatory reduction for every single firm, let's develop a simple example. Suppose that there are three types of power firms: A, B, and C. A Type A firm produces more SO_2 emissions than Type B, and Type B produces more emissions than Type C. Each type of firm faces a different cost of abating (reducing) its SO_2 emissions, so the firms that face the least cost of abatement have an incentive to reduce the greatest amount if they can profitably sell allowances to firms that face the greatest cost of abatement. These characteristics are summarized in Table 3.2.

According to the data in Table 3.2, Type A firms must reduce SO_2 emissions by 1.2 million tons (4.0 – 2.8), which will cost a total of $960 million (1,200,000 × $800) if each firm must meet the reduction requirement individually. Similarly, Type B firms will spend $450 million to reduce emissions

TABLE 3.2

SO_2 Emissions and Abatement Costs for Three Types of Power Companies

	Type A	Type B	Type C	Total
Number of Firms	100	90	70	260
Current SO_2 Emissions (million tons)	4.0	3.0	1.0	8.0
Allowable SO_2 Emissions (million tons)	2.8	2.1	0.7	5.6
Reduction Needed to Meet Allowable SO_2 Emissions	30%	30%	30%	30%
Abatement Cost (per ton)	$800	$500	$300	

by 0.9 million tons (3.0 – 2.1), and Type C firms will spend $90 million to reduce emissions by 0.3 million tons (1.0 – 0.7). Again, these figures assume that each firm must reduce its emissions by 30 percent and that no trading is allowed, which was the case *before* the Clean Air Act of 1990. Thus, the total cost of reducing SO_2 emissions by 30 percent is $1,500 million when trading pollution allowances is prohibited.

Trading Pollution Allowances

When trading allowances is permitted, the total cost of meeting the 30 percent emission reduction requirement decreases. To see why, we must first describe the market for emission allowances to determine the equilibrium price. Figure 3.13 describes the supply and demand curves for SO_2 emissions allowances.

The supply and demand curves in Figure 3.13 are stepwise because we have grouped firms into three types, which causes discrete jumps in these curves. The demand curve is derived by first plotting the amount of allowances that Type A firms are willing to buy, followed by Type B firms, and then by Type C firms. Because Type A firms can reduce SO_2 emissions for $800 per ton, they will not demand any allowance if the price exceeds $800. Once the price drops below $800, however, Type A firms will demand the entire required reduction of 1.2 million tons; that is, it is cheaper to buy allowances than to reduce SO_2 pollutants for $800 per ton. If the price of allowances falls to $500 per ton or below, Type B firms enter the market, so we add their required reduction of 0.9 million tons to the quantity demanded by Type A firms. Finally, when price drops to $300 per ton or below, Type C firms enter the market and demand their required reduction of 0.3 million tons.

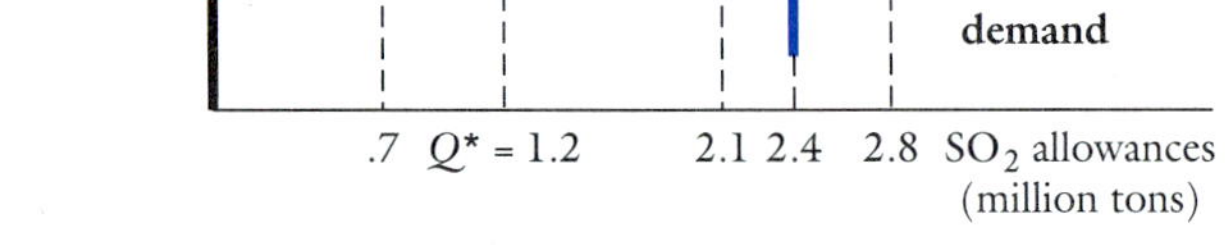

FIGURE 3.13

Market Equilibrium for SO_2 Pollution Allowances

Stepwise supply and demand curves are shown for pollution allowances. Power companies have an incentive to trade such allowances because abatement costs vary by type of firm. The market reaches an equilibrium at Q^* = 1.2 million tons of allowances, selling for $500 per ton.

The supply curve is derived from the allowances firms generate when they reduce emissions by ***more than*** the 30 percent requirement. Type C firms have an incentive to reduce SO_2 pollutants to zero when the allowances sell for more than \$300 per ton.[12] In this case, Type C firms can supply 0.7 million tons of allowances when price exceeds \$300, which is shown by the vertical segment of the supply curve above 0.7 million tons. When price reaches or exceeds \$500 per ton, type B firms will begin to exceed the reduction requirement. If all these firms reduce emissions to zero (hypothetically), then they can supply the market with 2.1 million tons of allowances, which brings the total supply to 2.8 million tons of allowances (0.7 + 2.1). Once price reaches \$800 per ton, then Type A firms will find it profitable to reduce emissions by more than the requirement, but this situation will not arise because the market reaches an equilibrium at a price of \$500 per ton. Thus, the potential supply from Type A firms does not enter into determining the equilibrium price.

At an equilibrium price of \$500 per ton, Type A firms will find it advantageous to buy allowances rather than to reduce emissions at a cost of \$800 per ton. Thus, quantity demanded is 1.2 million tons of allowances.[13] To meet this demand, Type C firms provide 0.7 million tons and Type B firms supply 0.5 million tons of allowances.

Comparing Compliance Costs

We can now compute the cost of meeting the SO_2 emissions requirements. Type A firms pay \$500 per ton to purchase 1.2 million tons of allowances, so they spend \$600 million. Type B firms reduce emissions by 1.4 million tons (0.9 required plus 0.5 extra for the sale of allowances), which costs \$700 million. Offsetting part of this cost is the \$250 million (0.5 million tons × \$500) received by Type B firms from selling allowances, so their *net cost* of meeting the requirements is \$450 million. Type C firms reduce 100 percent of their SO_2 pollutants at a cost of \$300 million (1 million tons × \$300), which is more than offset by their sales of 0.7 million tons of allowances for \$350 million (0.7 million tons × \$500). Thus, Type C firms end up with a net gain of \$50 million from the new pollution requirements. Now, with allowances tradable, the net cost of meeting the new requirements equals \$1,000 million (\$600 + \$450 – \$50), which is only two-thirds of the cost when trading is prohibited. In short, the trading of allowances allows for an efficient sorting of firms in terms of those that face a lower cost of abating pollution and those that face relatively higher costs of abatement. Thus, resources are more efficiently utilized when trading of allowances is possible.

---

[12] Technically, it is not possible to reduce SO_2 emissions to zero, but we are using this assumption to simplify the presentation of the market equilibrium price for allowances.

[13] Note that Type B firms are indifferent to reducing SO_2 pollution themselves and buying allowances at a price of \$500 per ton. We assume that they reduce pollution themselves, so that no allowances are traded between two Type B firms.

LEARNING EXERCISE 3.9

Reconstruct the example above assuming that Type C firms face an abatement cost of $800 and Type A firms face an abatement cost of $300. What is the new equilibrium price of allowances? How much is saved when allowances are tradable compared to the situation in which they cannot be traded?

3.5 THE GOVERNMENT AND PROPERTY RIGHTS

The American movie producer Samuel Goldwyn (1882–1974) once said, "A verbal agreement isn't worth the paper it's written on." He had a point. What makes contracts or agreements valuable? When you buy a product, the seller's rights of ownership are transferred to you. But how is the assignment made? The exchange of money is normally sufficient under contract and sales law to transfer these rights. The courts in the United States act to enforce your rights to the product if the transfer is made in good faith. Through the court system, the government plays a significant role in each transaction you make. When the government enters a market to define property rights, transactions are usually made easier.

Suppose you are approached by a stranger who is trying to sell a car. How do you know the stranger owns the car to begin with? Maybe it was stolen. But the owner of a car receives a title certificate from the state where the car was bought. If the stranger owns the car, he or she will have the title certificate. Without a title certificate, ownership is uncertain. What you will pay for a car when ownership is uncertain is *less* than what you will pay if ownership is known. By documenting who owns a car, the state has increased the market price the car commands because the buyer no longer bears the risk that the car was stolen.

In Peru and other Latin American countries, there are many examples in which property rights are not clearly defined. Peruvian economist Hernando de Soto has documented some examples in his discussion of the informal housing market in Peru.[14] De Soto shows that the Peruvian bureaucracy has made transferring title to a home very costly to the average Peruvian. There are often delays of several months and thousands of dollars in legal and bureaucratic costs to pay. The poor of Peru cannot afford to pay such costs. Some poor people have taken the drastic step of invading government-owned property to build housing. Such settlements start small but can grow to hundreds of dwellings if the government fails to evict the invaders. In a large invasion, the government may tolerate the invaders indefinitely.

Housing on invaded property is difficult to sell because its title is in doubt. It is occasionally sold, although no formal title is transferred. The community of invaders typically reviews the credentials of the buyer before a sale and may veto a potential buyer if they think it necessary. The invasion is

[14] Hernando de Soto, *The Other Path: The Invisible Revolution in the Third World,* HarperCollins: New York, 1989.

viable when the invaders stick together against the government—act en masse. A new buyer must demonstrate a willingness to help the group oppose the government if it should try to evict them. Because of this screening and the lack of clear title, such housing has a lower value than equivalent but properly titled housing.

The Instituto de Libertad y Democracia (ILD), a nonprofit research institute in Lima, Peru, headed by Hernando de Soto, has compared property values for two invasion settlements: Mariscal Castilla and Daniel Alcides Carrión, both settlements on the outskirts of Lima. They were built next to one another and are populated by people with very similar socioeconomic characteristics. The main difference between these settlements is that the government of Peru has classified the Mariscal Castilla invasion as permanent, thereby giving its residents legal status. The Daniel Alcides Carrión invasion is classified as removable, which means that the government retains the option to evict the settlers. The ILD found that dwellings in Mariscal Castilla are worth 12 times more than similar dwellings in Daniel Alcides Carrión. Using a larger sample of 37 settlements, the ILD found that property in legally recognized settlements is worth, on average, 9 times more than nonrecognized property.

There are many examples in which clearly defined property rights improve the operation of the price system. The examples here show that the government's role in the marketplace is not always one of interfering with equilibrium price and quantity. In fact, when property rights are clearly defined, exchange of goods and services is less costly. Thus, the efficiency of the marketplace depends on how well property rights are defined and enforced.

Chapter Summary

1. An excise tax that is levied on suppliers causes the market supply curve to shift upward by the amount of the (per unit) tax. The market equilibrium price increases and quantity transacted decreases.
2. The degree to which market price increases and equilibrium quantity decreases is determined by the elasticities of supply and demand. The more elastic the market demand curve, the less the price increases and the more the per-unit burden is shifted to producers. The more elastic the market supply curve, the more price increases and the more the per-unit burden is shifted to consumers.
3. Consumers' surplus measures the total benefits to market participants from purchasing units at less than the maximum they are willing to pay. Producers' surplus measures the total benefits to firms from selling units for more than their marginal production costs.
4. Restrictions on the quantity supplied are generally equivalent to shifting the market supply curve to the left by the amount of the restriction, thereby increasing the price. An import quota, for example, limits the total quantity of imports, which causes the import portion of the market supply curve to decrease to the quota level.

5. Price ceilings restrict the market price when they are set below the current market equilibrium price. Analogously, price floors affect the market price when they are set above the current market equilibrium price.
6. An externality can increase or decrease the satisfaction consumers receive from particular goods. Equivalently, an externality can increase or decrease production costs for firms. The important point is that an externality is caused by some other individual's or firm's actions.

Trouble Spots

Concept	Reminder
Taxes and Subsidies	To understand how a tax affects the market equilibrium, it is necessary to realize that the tax (or subsidy) affects transactions, that is, both the buyer and the seller, not just one or the other. In short, taxes generally decrease output rates and subsidies generally increase output rates.
Consumers' and Producers' Surpluses	A change in producers' surplus is easy to measure because it equals the change in profits for firms in the market. A change in consumers' surplus, however, is not easy to measure because consumers' surplus is based on the difference between what consumers are willing to pay and what they actually pay. Because we cannot generally measure what consumers are willing to pay, consumers' surplus is not generally observable. Even so, a change in consumers' surplus is just as real as a change in profits.

3.6 Review Questions

1. Explain the difference between a unit tax and a unit subsidy. Is the after-tax equilibrium affected by who collects the tax?
2. What is the relationship between the demand price (P_{demand}) and the supply price (P_{supply}) for a unit tax and also for a sales tax?
3. Explain how the per-unit burden of a tax is affected by the price elasticity of the demand and supply curves.
4. Explain how producers' surplus and profits are related to each other.
5. Compare the per-unit burden of a tax to the deadweight loss measure of the effects of a tax. What are the differences between these two measures?
6. Explain what would happen to the world sugar market if the United States abandoned its sugar import quota program.
7. Explain how price ceilings and price floors cause quantity rationing. Give an example of each type of price restriction.
8. Explain why price restrictions in futures markets are different from rent controls or minimum wage restrictions. What is the purpose of such restrictions in futures markets?

9. Give two examples of both a positive and a negative externality. Explain how the Coase theorem helps resolve the problem posed by externalities.
10. Briefly explain why it costs less to meet a given pollution reduction standard using an approach in which pollution allowances are tradable instead of an approach in which each firm must achieve the standard individually.

3.7 Price Theory Problems

1. Suppose a tax of $1 per ride is placed on taxi rides to the local airport, which is to be collected by the taxi companies. Explain how this tax affects the market equilibrium price of taxi rides to the local airport. How do people who previously rode taxis to the airport, but have dropped out of this market due to the higher price, get to the airport?
2. Assume that the following supply and demand functions apply to the weekly market for gasoline in a small town:

$$D_b(P) = 200 - 10P \quad \text{if } P \leq \$20$$

$$D_c(P) = 200 - 25P \quad \text{if } P \leq \$8$$

$$S(P) = 45P$$

where D_b is the demand function for Mercedes-Benz owners and D_c is the demand for Chrysler owners.

   a. What is the equation for the total market demand for gasoline? Draw a graph illustrating the market demand function.
   b. What are the market equilibrium price and quantity?
   c. If a tax of $6 per gallon is levied on the supplier, what are the new equilibrium price and quantity? Show all of your work for partial credit.
   d. Relative to the market equilibrium in part (c), what fraction of the tax burden is shared by the consumers?

3. How do you determine the unit tax that maximizes tax revenues? Show the problem graphically by indicating what area you are trying to maximize in a supply and demand graph; then discuss the factors that affect the determination of the optimum tax rate.
4. The Santa Monica Rent Control Board has estimated that the market demand for one-bedroom apartments is $Q_{demand} = 45{,}000 - 50P$, where price and quantity are measured in monthly units. It has also determined that the market supply is given by $Q_{supply} = 5{,}000 + 50P$.

   a. What is the free market equilibrium price and quantity of one-bedroom apartments?
   b. Suppose the Rent Control Board establishes that the maximum rent is $300 for a one-bedroom apartment. How will the quantity supplied change? What is the deadweight loss

in consumers' and producers' surpluses? (Assume that apartments are allocated by ranking individuals according to their willingness to pay.)

5. Who benefits and who loses from the law against the sale of human organs, and why? Does this restriction encourage the use of substitutes, such as livers from baboons? Describe how the market for kidney dialysis machines would be affected if it becomes legal to buy and sell human organs.
6. Unskilled workers may be affected by minimum wages, but who are the unskilled workers in the economy? What are some of the ways an employer can avoid paying minimum wage?
7. It is possible to set a limit on the number of workers that raises wages to the same level set by the minimum wage. Show what happens to employment when demand increases under a quota policy versus a minimum wage policy. Which policy results in the greatest unemployment?
8. During periods of gasoline rationing in the late 1970s, long lines formed at many gasoline service stations because prices were regulated. To ration available supply, some service stations limited the quantity of gallons each customer could purchase. Explain the effect this had on consumers' surplus in the gasoline market. Under what conditions would you expect to find consumers waiting in a second line for additional gasoline?
9. Education and good health are often cited as examples of a positive externality. Explain why these goods generate a positive externality. How are the externality-producing benefits of these goods different from the external costs generated by pollution?
10. Explain why there is no externality "problem" in a market in which the costs of negotiating with another party (individual or firm) are very low or nonexistent. How is the distribution of income affected by the definition of property rights to create the externality in such a situation?

3.8 Writing Exercise

Develop an essay that addresses whether the government is a necessary institution for the purpose of establishing and enforcing property rights. In your essay, consider whether markets can maintain themselves without known property rights arrangements and whether the private sector can establish such arrangements at a lower cost than the government. Also, distinguish between the roles currently played by the different levels of government—federal, state, and local—in the establishment and enforcement of property rights.

4

Budget and Time Constraints

Preview Questions

When you finish studying this chapter, you should be able to answer the following questions:

- What makes one bundle of goods different from another?
- What factors constrain your purchases of goods?
- How does your consumption of one good affect your consumption of other goods?
- What is a composite good?
- What is the trade-off you face between income and leisure?

How do you feel when you lose something around your house or apartment? You're probably a little upset, troubled that you can't remember where the item is, and discouraged because you must spend time to look for it. And, if it's not found, then perhaps you must buy another item to replace it. What have you really lost here? If you can't find it and must replace it, you've lost the income that you must spend. These funds have an opportunity cost, which might represent a nice winter coat, a new software program, repairs on your home or apartment, a Hawaiian vacation, or literally thousands of other goods that you might have purchased if you could somehow retrieve the item that is now gone. In addition, you've lost the time you spent looking for the item, time that could have been used for another purpose. Potentially, you've lost time and the other goods that you might have bought had you found the misplaced item. These loses may be the ultimate reason why you are discouraged when you lose something.

This chapter has two purposes. First, it examines the relationship between income and the goods you can buy. The more income you have, the more goods you can buy. Equivalently, the lower the prices of goods, the more you can buy with a fixed income. So when you use income (say, because you choose to replace a misplaced item), you are really losing the opportunity to purchase some other goods. We summarize the relationship between income and the goods you can buy as your *budget constraint.* Anything that affects prices and income affects your budget constraint. Taxes and subsidies, for example, affect individual behavior through their effect on the budget constraint.

There is another fundamental constraint on behavior that we cannot forget: your time constraint. Both time and budget constraints limit what we can do. How much time you have to study for an economics test depends on how long you sleep, how much time you spend eating, how much time you spend commuting, and how much time you spend studying for other tests. Time constrains all our activities, including our search for misplaced items. The limited amount of time available to each of us restricts how long we work and thus puts a constraint on how much income we can earn. The second purpose of this chapter is to examine the effects of the time constraint on purchases of goods by illustrating the trade-offs you face between leisure and work time.

4.1 The Budget Constraint

The **budget constraint** limits the set of commodities, or *bundles,* that you can purchase with a given amount of income. Our discussion of the budget constraint explains how prices, specifically relative prices, affect your choices. We also explain how government policy—reflected in the food stamp program—affects your budget constraint and thus what you can purchase.

Budget Constraint
An equation showing the maximum combination of different goods a consumer can purchase with a given income.

Bundles

A specific collection of goods is called a **bundle.** You may buy three loaves of bread and five liters of Coca-Cola every week. These quantities form a particular bundle. The bread and Coca-Cola bundle is written as {three loaves of bread, five liters of Coca-Cola}, or {3, 5} in numerical form. A bundle refers to a single *point* on a graph with loaves of bread on one axis and liters of Coca-Cola on the other axis. Figure 4.1 shows this commodity bundle as point *A.*

Bundle
A specific collection of goods.

If you buy two more liters of Coca-Cola each week, you will own a different bundle. This bundle is {three loaves of bread, seven liters of Coca-Cola}, or {3, 7}, which is point *B* in Figure 4.1. Similarly, point *C* represents the bundle containing six loaves of bread and two liters of Coca-Cola. Each of the points in Figure 4.1 represents a specific commodity bundle. Although not labeled, all the other combinations in the graph are commodity bundles, too; commodity bundles cover the entire graph in Figure 4.1.

Income and Relative Prices

Your income and prices of goods determine what you *can* buy. To illustrate, consider the choice between pay-per-view TV programs and video rentals. Let us suppose that your income allows you to spend \$80 per week on enter-

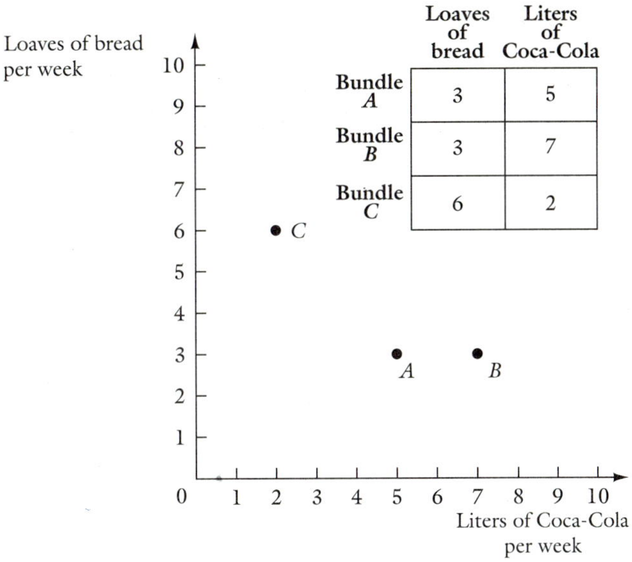

FIGURE 4.1

Three Commodity Bundles

Each of three commodity bundles, *A, B,* and *C,* contains a given quantity of two goods: loaves of bread per week and liters of Coca-Cola per week. Bundle *A,* for example, contains 3 loaves of bread and 5 liters of Coca-Cola.

tainment.[1] The price of pay-per-view TV is \$8 per program, and the price of each video rental is \$4. Your options are now defined by prices and income. You can buy 10 pay-per-view TV programs (\$80/\$8); 20 video rentals (\$80/\$4); or any other bundle, such as 5 pay-per-view TV programs and 10 video rentals, that exhausts your weekly entertainment budget.

A comment is in order before we continue. The \$80 is your entertainment budget, not your income. The analysis, though, is the same whether we are discussing your entertainment budget or income, so we use these terms interchangeably. In fact, we could be describing your food budget or your budget for travel and the approach would be the same. The only difference between analyzing your entertainment budget and analyzing your income is that you spend your income on more than just two goods. We can discuss your consumption of many commodities, but it is much simpler, at first, to illustrate a budget constraint using only two goods. We do not lose any generality by doing this, and it makes the graphical analysis possible.

[1]How much you decide to spend on entertainment—either video rentals or pay-per-view TV programs—versus what you spend on other goods is a decision you have already made, so it is taken as given. We will consider how you make this decision in Chapter 5 when we discuss your optimal choices.

The example using pay-per-view TV programs and video rentals illustrates the concept of opportunity cost from the market's point of view. Prices are determined by supply and demand in a market, so the price ratio of the two goods represents the market's assessment of the opportunity costs that you face. That is, one price divided by the other equals the market-determined rate at which you can exchange these goods. The price ratio or *relative price* of pay-per-view TV programs to video rentals is equal to 2 ($8/$4). Your decision to buy another pay-per-view TV program for $8 will cost you two video rentals. Alternatively, one video rental will cost you one-half of a pay-per-view TV program. The market-determined opportunity cost is defined by how much of the other good you must give up to obtain another unit of the good in question.

FEASIBLE BUNDLES

The various combinations of pay-per-view TV programs and video rentals you can buy with $80 make up what is called your **feasible set.** To see what bundles are feasible, let us define the following terms:

Feasible Set
The various combinations of bundles that you can buy with your budget or income.

TV = the number of pay-per-view TV programs per week

VCR = the number of video rentals per week

P_{TV} = the price of a pay-per-view TV program

P_{VCR} = the price of a video rental

M = your weekly budget for entertainment

Your entertainment budget is spent on pay-per-view TV programs and video rentals, so your purchases must conform to your budget. Algebraically, the budget constraint relationship is written as

$$M = (P_{TV} \times TV) + (P_{VCR} \times VCR) \tag{4.1}$$

The first term on the right-hand side ($P_{TV} \times TV$) of equation (4.1) is your expenditure on pay-per-view TV programs, that is, price times how much you buy. The second term ($P_{VCR} \times VCR$) is your expenditure on video rentals. Together, these expenditures exhaust your entertainment budget (M).

Substituting your $80 entertainment budget and the two market prices into the budget constraint determines what bundles are feasible:

$$\$80 = (\$8 \times TV) + (\$4 \times VCR) \tag{4.2}$$

All feasible bundles of pay-per-view TV programs and video rentals must satisfy equation (4.2) if you plan to spend your entire entertainment budget. This equation is your budget constraint for weekly entertainment purchases.

We can rearrange terms in your budget constraint to show the trade-offs you face between the quantity of each good purchased. With a fixed income or entertainment budget, spending more on one good implies that you must spend less on the other good. Subtracting your expenditure on video rentals

Budget Line
Algebraic rearrangement of the budget constraint to show the trade-off between two goods when income and prices are fixed.

$(P_{VCR} \times VCR)$ from your budget (M) in equation (4.1) and then dividing both sides by the price of a pay-per-view TV program (P_{TV}) gives your **budget line:**

$$TV = M/P_{TV} - (P_{VCR}/P_{TV}) \times VCR \tag{4.3}$$

The budget line is an algebraic statement of the trade-off between pay-per-view TV programs and video rentals. As video rentals increase—*VCR* on the right-hand side of equation (4.3)—the number of pay-per-view TV programs you can buy decreases. Alternatively, if *VCR* decreases, then *TV* increases. Substituting the price and income amounts from equation (4.2) into equation (4.3) yields the relationship between pay-per-view TV programs and the number of VCRs you can buy as given by the budget line:

$$TV = 80/8 - (4/8) \times VCR$$

$$= 10 - (1/2) \times VCR \tag{4.4}$$

Figure 4.2 shows a graph of the budget line as given by equation (4.4). The vertical axis measures the number of pay-per-view TV programs, and the horizontal axis measures the number of video rentals purchased each week. The trade-off here is linear. In other words, the budget line equation represents a straight line, with its intercept on the TV axis equal to M/P_{TV} and a slope

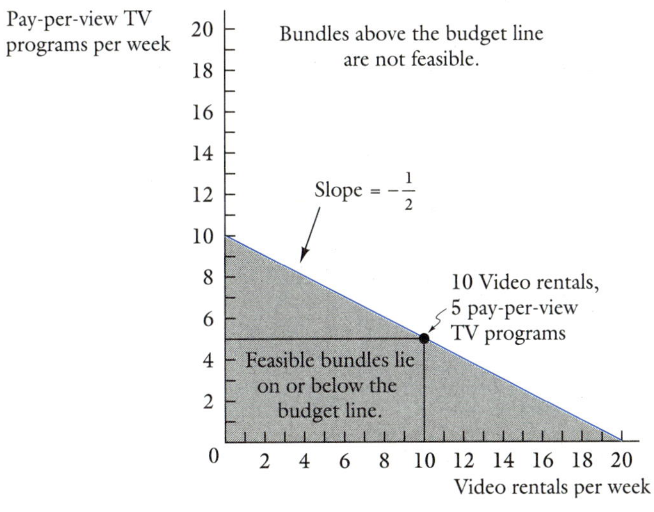

FIGURE 4.2

The Budget Line

Given an entertainment budget of \$80 per week, the budget line shows what bundles can be purchased when pay-per-view TV programs cost \$8 each and video rentals cost \$4 each. All bundles on and below the budget line are within the consumer's budget; that is, they are in the feasible set. The slope of the budget line (equal to –½) shows the trade-off between pay-per-view TV programs and an extra video rental. Purchasing an extra video rental implies that the consumer gives up one-half of a pay-per-view TV program.

equal to $-P_{VCR}/P_{TV}$. Because the budget line is straight, it may be drawn by locating two points, one on each axis. On the vertical axis, we find the quantity of pay-per-view TV programs you can buy if you spend *all* of your entertainment budget on pay-per-view TV programs and none of it on video rentals, which is given by the ratio $M/P_{TV} = 10$. On the horizontal axis, we find the quantity of video rentals you can purchase if you spend *all* of your entertainment budget on video rentals and none of it on pay-per-view TV programs, which is given by the ratio $M/P_{VCR} = 20$. These quantities form the end points of the budget line, and the straight line connecting them is the budget line.

The shaded area below the budget line and the points on the line form the *feasible region* of pay-per-view TV programs and video rentals. The feasible region represents all the commodity bundles you can buy given your current budget and the prices you face. You are expected to buy a bundle that is *on* the budget line, not below it. All the bundles below your budget line cost less than \$80, so you do not spend all of your entertainment budget if you buy one of these bundles. Having money left over is not terrible, but in our example you have nothing else to spend it on, so you might as well spend all of your entertainment budget on the two goods, which places you *on* the budget line.[2]

The slope of the budget line is determined by the relative price of video rentals and pay-per-view TV programs.[3] The relative price (P_{VCR}/P_{TV}) equals \$4/\$8, or $^1/_2$. On the graph in Figure 4.2, the slope of the budget line is negative even though relative prices are positive. The negative sign indicates that you face a trade-off along the budget line. If you want one more video rental, you must *give up* $^1/_2$ of a pay-per-view TV program. The negative sign is a reminder that we will lose some of one good when we want more of another with a limited budget. Our market-determined opportunity cost or market rate of trade—what we give up—is thus equal to the slope of the budget line.

LEARNING EXERCISE 4.1

Reverse the two axes in Figure 4.2—place video rentals on the vertical axis and pay-per-view TV programs on the horizontal axis—and redraw the graph. What is the slope of the new budget line, and how do you interpret it?

PRICE CHANGES

Let us assume that you are one of many, many consumers. When you decide to buy more pay-per-view TV programs or video rentals, there is a very tiny, really imperceptible change in the market demand for these goods. Under such circumstances, market prices are not affected by your consumption decisions.

[2] Chapter 15 develops a model in which you can save income for consumption at a later date so you need not spend all of your current income on current consumption.

[3] The slope of the budget line can also be determined by computing the *rise* over the *run*. The rise is a given distance along the vertical axis that corresponds to the run, which is a given distance along the horizontal axis. The ratio of the rise over the run, again with a negative sign in front, is the slope of the budget line.

Price Taker
Your situation when market prices are not affected by your consumption decisions.

Accordingly, you act as a **price taker.**[4] The prices at the local video store or cable TV company are market prices in our economy, and you will accept them as given because your actions cannot change them.

As a price taker, you react to price changes that affect your budget line. A price change affects the slope of your budget line and its overall position. Panel (a) in Figure 4.3 on page 112 shows the effect of *increasing* the price of video rentals from $4 to $5. There are two points to note about the effects of this price change:

1. The relative price of video rentals has changed, so in response, the slope of the budget line has changed from $-\frac{1}{2}$ to $-\frac{5}{8}$. The opportunity cost of one extra video rental has risen to equal $\frac{5}{8}$ of a pay-per-view TV program.
2. The budget line intersects the horizontal axis at a new point. The intersection point has moved from 20 to 16 video rentals.

The first effect changes the relative price (P_{VCR}/P_{TV}), and the second effect changes the *potential* number of video rentals you can buy. Given your budget, the largest number of video rentals you can buy equals M/P_{VCR}, or $\$80/P_{VCR}$. When the price of video rentals (P_{VCR}) increases, the ratio M/P_{VCR} falls, so the number of video rentals you can buy falls. The effect of the price increase is to decrease the size of your feasible set. The shaded area of panel (a) in Figure 4.3 represents the bundles of pay-per-view TV programs and video rentals you *cannot* purchase now that the price of video rentals has increased.

Panel (b) in Figure 4.3 shows the effect of a *decrease* in the price of pay-per-view TV programs on the budget line, starting from the original prices. In this panel, the price of pay-per-view TV programs falls to $5 from $8, possibly because a discount coupon in the newspaper offers a lower price, while the price of video rentals remains at $4. The price decrease affects the slope and overall position of the budget line. The difference between this situation and panel (a) is that the intersection point between the budget line and the vertical axis is changing and the feasible set is expanding, not contracting. The new slope of the budget line equals $-\frac{4}{5}$, which implies that $\frac{4}{5}$ of a pay-per-view TV program is required to buy one more video rental. More pay-per-view TV programs are required than before because pay-per-view TV programs have become cheaper relative to video rentals. Now, more of the relatively cheaper good is required to buy one unit of the other good.

INCOME CHANGES

Figure 4.4 shows the effects of an increase in income or, in our context, your entertainment budget on the budget line. Holding prices at their original levels, your entertainment budget increases from $80 per week to $112 per week in Figure 4.4. The intersection point on both axes changes when your entertainment budget increases. If you spend all of your budget on video rentals,

[4]If you are buying an item that represents a larger share of your income, you have incentive to bargain, as noted in Chapter 2. In this case, you are less likely to act as a price taker.

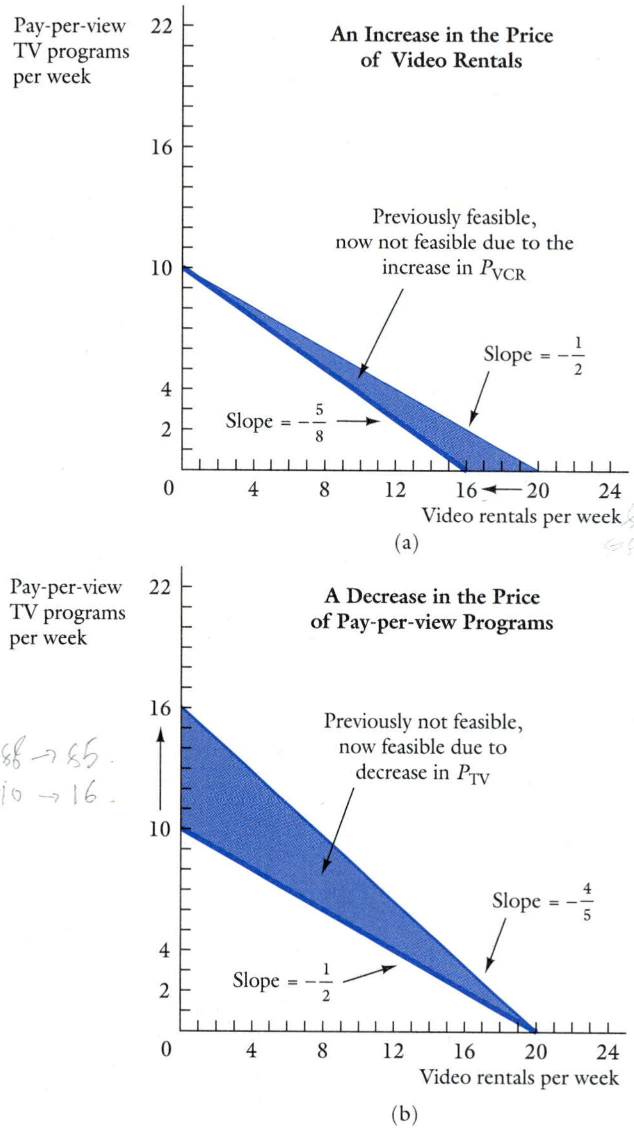

FIGURE 4.3

How Do Price Changes Affect the Budget Line?

Panel (a) shows the effect on the budget line when the price of a video rental increases from \$4 to \$5. The intersection point between the budget line and the horizontal axis moves toward the origin. The shaded area represents bundles that are no longer in the feasible set. Panel (b) shows the effect when the price of a pay-per-view TV program decreases from \$8 to \$5. The shaded area represents new bundles that are now in the feasible set.

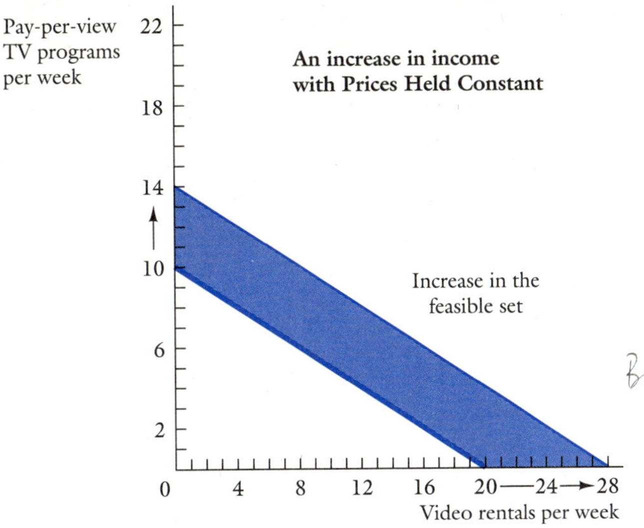

FIGURE 4.4

The Effect of Income Changes on the Budget Line

When the entertainment budget increases from \$80 to \$112 per week, the budget line shifts outward, away from the origin. The new budget line is parallel to the old budget line. The shaded area represents new bundles that are now in the feasible set.

you can buy 28 rentals each week. Alternatively, if you spend all of your budget on pay-per-view TV programs, you can buy 14 pay-per-view TV programs each week. Your feasible set of bundles increases along *both* axes. A change in income with prices unchanged causes a *parallel* shift of the budget line. The slope of the budget line is unchanged because income or budget changes do not affect relative prices. The change in your feasible set follows the direction of change in your income: More income implies a larger feasible set; less income implies a smaller feasible set.

LEARNING EXERCISE 4.2

Draw the new budget line as if the two price changes in Figure 4.3 occurred simultaneously; that is, P_{VCR} = \$5 and P_{TV} = \$5. Using the new prices, show how the budget line changes if your entertainment budget decreases to \$60 per week.

Money Illusion
A situation in which consumers think the feasible set has changed just because income and all prices change proportionately.

NO MONEY ILLUSION

Money illusion exists if you think the feasible set has changed when income and all prices change proportionately. Suppose entertainment prices double, so that each pay-per-view TV program costs \$16 and a video rental costs \$8 and, at the same time, your income or entertainment budget doubles to \$160.

What happens to the budget line? What happens to the feasible set? The answer is nothing! If you spend all of your budget on pay-per-view TV programs, the most you can buy is 10 pay-per-view TV programs, the same as before. Similarly, if you spend all of your income on video rentals, the most you can buy is 20 video rentals, the same as before. The slope of the budget line has not changed—it is still equal to −½. In short, the budget line has not moved, so your feasible set of bundles has not changed.

There is no money illusion in our analysis of a consumer's budget constraint. In other words, consumers are not fooled into believing the feasible set has changed when both income and prices change proportionately.

MORE THAN TWO GOODS

We can extend our discussion to more than two goods. If CDs are entertaining and the price of CDs (P_{CD}) is \$5, then you can buy 16 CDs (\$80/\$5) if you spend all of your entertainment budget on CDs. Your entertainment budget will allow you to buy 4 CDs, 2 pay-per-view TV programs, and 11 video rentals, as well as many other combinations of these three goods.

With three goods, there are *two* relative prices for each good that represent the market's assessment of your opportunity costs: the price of video rentals relative to the price of pay-per-view TV programs (P_{VCR}/P_{TV} = \$4/\$8) and the price of video rentals relative to the price of CDs (P_{VCR}/P_{CD} = \$4/\$5). Now, when you decide on entertainment for the week, these two relative prices influence your decision. Similarly, if there are four entertainment choices, there are three relative prices to consider when making your decision.

The budget constraint formula can be expanded to include many goods. The expenditure on these other goods is added to the expenditure on existing goods to form the new budget constraint. The budget constraint for three goods—pay-per-view TV programs, video rentals, and CDs—can be written as follows:

$$M = (P_{TV} \times TV) + (P_{VCR} \times VCR) + (P_{CD} \times CD) \quad (4.5)$$

The only difference between this budget constraint formula and the one shown in equation (4.1) is that the expenditure on CDs, ($P_{CD} \times CD$), has been added to the right-hand side. If there are more than the three goods shown, the expenditure on each of these new goods is added to the right-hand side of equation (4.5) to form the new budget constraint.

COMPOSITE GOODS

When you buy textbooks, paper, pens, and pencils, you buy a collection of goods broadly referred to as *school supplies*. Similarly, when you buy shirts, shoes, socks, blouses, and pants, you buy articles of *clothing*. *Clothing* and *school supplies* are composite terms that refer to groups of goods. When you buy more clothing, you buy more units of the group of goods that we call clothing. Composite terms, such as clothing, appliances, food, and school supplies, provide a convenient way to summarize spending. For example, we might find that the average household in the United States spent 12 percent of its after-tax income on food last year. Rather than keep track of the thousands of separate items or goods that can be eaten, we keep track of a **composite good**—food—that represents all of these other goods.

Composite Good
Combines the purchases of all but one good. The combined goods are called "all other goods."

Using composite goods in the budget constraint is called the *composite good convention*. The composite good convention lets us focus on how one specific good—not the composite good—affects the budget constraint. The budget constraint is reformulated with the specific good—say, video rentals—on one axis and the composite good, usually given by *expenditures* on all other goods, on the other axis. The composite good convention lets us examine the budget trade-offs between the specific good and all other goods, which are lumped together to form a composite good. We must remember, however, that when we use the composite good convention, the relative prices of goods in the bundle are held constant. This is done so that we avoid the problem that arises when the consumer has an incentive to rearrange purchases of the goods in the bundle as their relative prices change. In this case, the bundle is no longer the same composite good that we started with.

To illustrate how we can use the composite good convention, let's consider the three goods described above—video rentals, pay-per-view TV programs, and CDs. Assume that the prices of these goods have not changed; that is, pay-per-view TV programs cost \$8, video rentals cost \$4, and CDs cost \$5. Using equation (4.5), the budget constraint may be written as:

$$M=(\$8 \times TV)+(\$4 \times VCR)+(\$5 \times CD)$$

The composite good convention rearranges the budget constraint to show expenditure on all other goods on the left-hand side and the remaining variables on the right-hand side of the equation. Using video rentals as our specific good, the budget line becomes:

$$(P_{TV} \times TV) + (P_{CD} \times CD) = M - (P_{VCR} \times VCR)$$

$$\text{Expenditure on all other goods} = M - (P_{VCR} \times VCR) \qquad (4.6)$$

A graph of the budget line now places expenditure on all other goods on the vertical axis and video rentals—the good we are interested in—on the horizontal axis. Note that the vertical axis measures dollars spent on the composite good, not quantities purchased. Figure 4.5, on page 116, shows the budget line for the video rentals case, which assumes that the weekly entertainment budget (M) is \$80, the same as before.

Notice that the slope of the budget line is −4, which is the price of video rentals with a negative sign in front. The slope may again be interpreted as a trade-off between goods. In this case, though, it measures the trade-off between *expenditure* on all other goods and an extra video rental. The slope tells us that an extra video rental will cost \$4 of expenditure on all other goods. What we give up when we consume another video is any of the other goods that \$4 will buy.

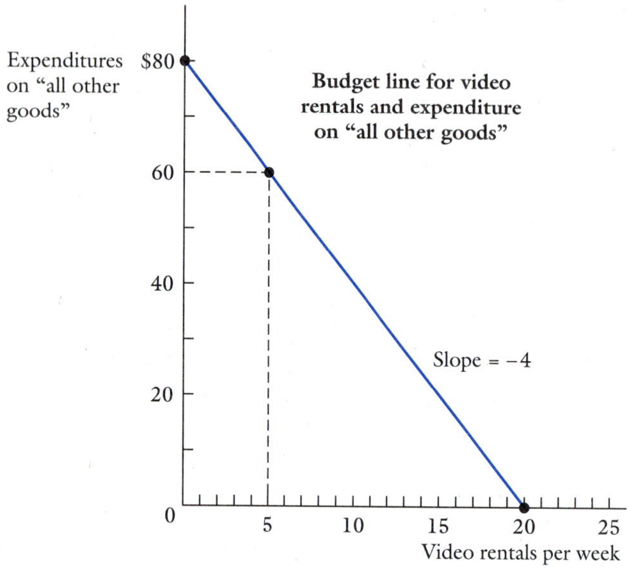

FIGURE 4.5

Video Rentals and the Composite Good Convention

Using the composite good convention, expenditures on all other goods is measured on the vertical axis and the number of video rentals is measured on the horizontal axis. The consumer can purchase $80 worth of all other goods or 20 video rentals each week. The slope of the budget constraint (equal to −4) measures the trade-off between an extra video rental and expenditures on all other goods. An extra video rental will reduce expenditures on all other goods by $4.

The effects of income and price changes on the budget line drawn using the composite good convention are similar to the effects on the regular budget line. An increase in income, with prices constant, causes a parallel shift to the right of the budget line. More of the specific good—video rentals—and more of all other goods can be purchased when income increases. If the price of the specific good changes, the budget line pivots on the vertical axis, which shows expenditures on all other goods. An increase in the price of video rentals, for example, implies that the budget line pivots inward, toward the origin. A decrease in price implies that the budget line pivots outward, away from the origin. In both cases, the intercept along the horizontal axis changes.

LEARNING EXERCISE 4.3

Draw the budget line for video rentals using the composite good convention when your entertainment budget is $120 per week and the price of each video rental is $6. Show how the budget line changes when the price of a video rental decreases to $4.

4.2 Curved and Kinked Budget Constraints

The budget lines illustrated in Figures 4.2 to 4.5 are *straight lines,* which is the same as saying that the equation we use to graph these budget lines is a *linear* equation. The budget line is linear for two reasons:

1. Prices do not change when you change your purchases. As we have stated, you are a price taker, so the market determines the prices you pay. With prices fixed, the slope of the budget line is constant.
2. Your purchases are limited by (fixed) prices and your income; there are no other restrictions on how much you can buy.

The following discussion relaxes both of these assumptions. With quantity discounts, prices can change as you purchase more of a good. Quantity discounts are commonplace and available even to price takers, so their affect on your budget constraint is important. In addition, we show how spending restrictions affect your budget constraint. Specifically, we discuss how subsidies in the form of the government food stamp program affect the shape of your budget constraint. With both quantity discounts and spending restrictions, your budget constraint is curved and kinked; it is no longer a straight line.

Quantity Discounts

Quantity Discounts
A price discount received when a consumer buys more than a specified quantity of a good.

If you call a travel agent to book a cruise from Miami to the Bahamas, you will find a wide range of prices and accommodations. If you are traveling alone, you will pay one price for the cruise. If you are traveling with someone else or a group, you will find that the group price is far less than the price of going it alone. We call such pricing an example of a **quantity discount**. Many other goods—computers, hotel rooms, pizza, and automobiles—can often be purchased for less if you buy large quantities.

Quantity discounts transform the budget line into a curve with kinks. The kinks occur at points at which an extra unit lowers price. To illustrate, consider the prices you face when you take a document to the copy center. Suppose you are trying to sell your car and you want to place "Car For Sale" announcements around the campus. The copy center posts a schedule of prices, such as those shown in panel (a) of Figure 4.6 on page 118. The price starts at 25 cents per page for the first five copies of a document; the next ten copies cost 15 cents per page; and any copies after that cost 5 cents per page.

Assume that your budget for supplies and copies is \$5 per week and that if you do not buy copies you buy items such as notepads, pens, pencils, and computer disks. Using the *composite good convention,* we can lump together your expenditure on these other items. The graph in Figure 4.6 shows your budget line. Your expenditure on all other goods is placed on the vertical axis (just as in Figure 4.5) and the number of copies you buy is shown on the horizontal axis. Your budget line shows the trade-off you face between extra copies of your announcement and expenditures on other supplies.

Copies	Price per Page
First 5	25¢
Next 10	15¢
Any extra	5¢

(a)

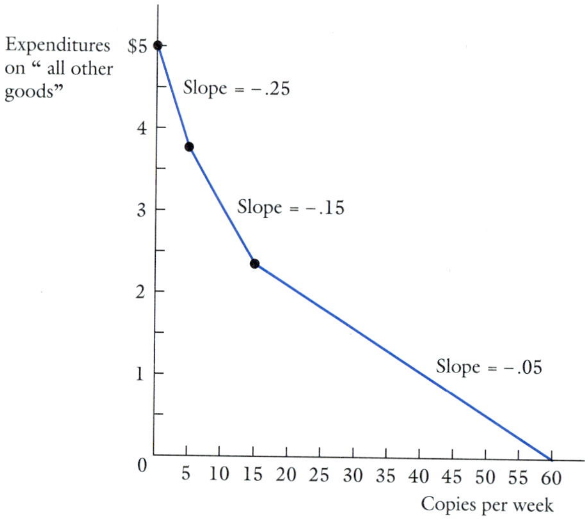

(b)

FIGURE 4.6

The Budget Constraint with Quantity Discounts at the Copy Center

Panel (a) shows the price schedule for photocopies at the Copy Center. The charge for the first five copies is $.25 each; cost per copy decreases as additional copies are purchased. The price schedule reflects quantity discounts for copying. Quantity discounts create kinks in the budget constraint, as shown in panel (b), which uses the composite good convention to plot the relationship between copies per week and expenditures on all other goods. At the points where price decreases, the slope of the budget constraints changes, causing a kink in an otherwise straight budget line.

The budget line is not straight; it has two kinks. Each kink occurs at the point at which the price per copy changes and hence where the slope of the budget line changes. For example, your first 5 copies cost 25 cents each, and after that you pay 15 cents each for the next 10 copies. On the graph, there is a kink in the budget line at 5 copies. The budget line becomes flatter at this point because you are paying less for each of the next 10 than you paid for each of the first 5 copies. The second kink occurs at 15 copies for the same reason: price changes after this quantity of copies is purchased.

Learning Exercise 4.4

Using the data in Figure 4.6, show how your feasible set is higher when there are quantity discounts compared to the case when the price per page is 25 cents no matter how many copies you make.

$$$ Price Theory in Practice

Food Stamps

During the 1960s, the United States began many programs to help the poor. The Food Stamp Act of 1964 provided poor families with a means to purchase more food than their budget allowed. Food stamps are equivalent to cash at grocery stores. They are printed in \$1, \$5, \$10, and \$20 amounts. Initially, qualified individuals purchased food stamps for less than their face value; that is, \$20 in food stamps could have been bought for \$10 in cash. The food stamp program changed after 1979, so that qualified individuals did not pay at all for the food stamps they received. Those who qualify receive a certain amount of food stamps each month.

The effects of the food stamp program depend on whether food stamps can be converted into money. It is illegal to sell food stamps, but many recipients sell their stamps anyway. Let us first examine the situation in which food stamps *cannot* be resold.

Assume that an individual receives \$250 in food stamps each month and that *M* represents monthly income. Without resale, the effect of the food stamp program on an individual's budget constraint is shown in panel (a) of Figure 4.7.

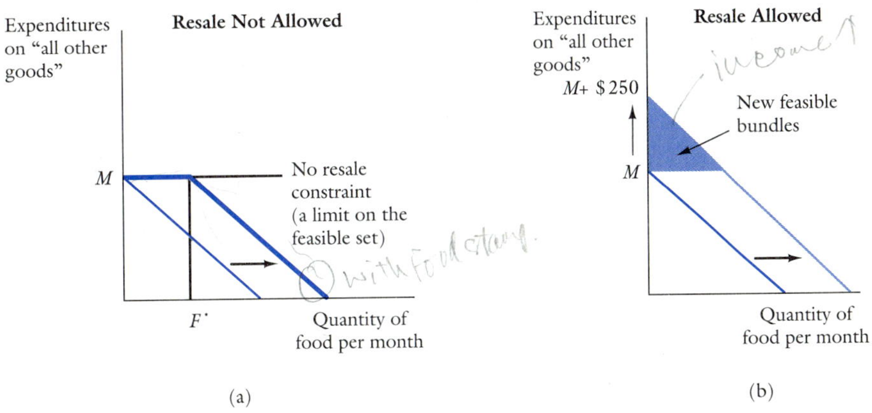

FIGURE 4.7

Food Stamp Program and the Budget Constraint

The food stamp program imposes a no-resale constraint on food stamp recipients. As shown in panel (a), the no-resale constraint is a horizontal line extending out from *M*, the consumer's total income. Food stamps shift a consumer's budget line away from the origin, but the no-resale constraint limits the bundles that can be purchased. In effect, the no-resale constraint creates a kink in the budget line. Panel (b) shows how the set of feasible bundles increases when the no-resale constraint is removed. In this case, food stamps are equivalent to an increase in income.

The food stamp program causes the budget line to shift outward in panel (a). The \$250 in food stamps acts like an increase in income. The difference is that the food stamps cannot be used to buy other goods—those shown on the vertical axis. The no-resale constraint is a horizontal line extending out from income (M) on the vertical axis. The no-resale constraint restricts the food stamp recipient to spending at most M dollars on all other goods. That is, the food stamps cannot be sold and the money received used to increase income.

The no-resale restriction creates a ***kink*** in the budget constraint. The new budget constraint moves along the no-resale constraint until \$250 worth of food is bought—point F^* on the graph equals the amount of food that \$250 can buy. At F^*, the budget constraint is kinked. Food purchases beyond F^* are restricted by the new budget line, which is parallel to the old budget line.

Panel (b) shows the effects of the food stamp program *without* the no-resale constraint. If food stamps can be sold for their face value, the food stamp program increases monthly income by \$250, no matter what commodity bundle is purchased. The triangular area in the upper portion of the graph shows the bundles that can now be purchased. Removing the no-resale constraint has the effect of including these bundles in the feasible set of bundles.

Note that the actual increase in the feasible region is *less* than the shaded area shown in panel (b) of Figure 4.7 because food stamps cannot be sold for their full face value. Because the resale of food stamps is illegal, buyers and sellers face the risk of prosecution, so food stamps sell for less than their full face value. Typically, they are sold for about 80 percent of their face value. The effect of an 80 percent resale value on the budget line is shown in Figure 4.8.

The upper part of the budget line pivots down when food stamps sell for 80 percent of their face value. Compare the budget line in Figure 4.8 to the one in panel (b) of Figure 4.7. Some of the bundles that were gained by relaxing the resale constraint have been lost. The new budget line has a kink in it above F^*, the amount of food the \$250 in food stamps can purchase. The size of the feasible set has decreased in Figure 4.8. If the resale value declines further, the budget line will pivot toward M on the vertical axis. A resale value of 0 percent, for example, creates a budget line identical to the no-resale budget line. In general, resale of food stamps at less than 100 percent of face value reduces the size of the feasible set.

It is reasonable to ask whether food stamps make recipients better off, worse off, or no different than before they were issued. The full answer to this question must wait until we develop the concept of satisfaction and preferences in Chapter 5, but we can make some initial observations here. First, food stamps increase the size of the feasible region, so there are more bundles available for purchase than without food stamps. With more bundles available for purchase than before, the individual cannot be worse off, so food stamps make recipients better off, or at least no different than before.

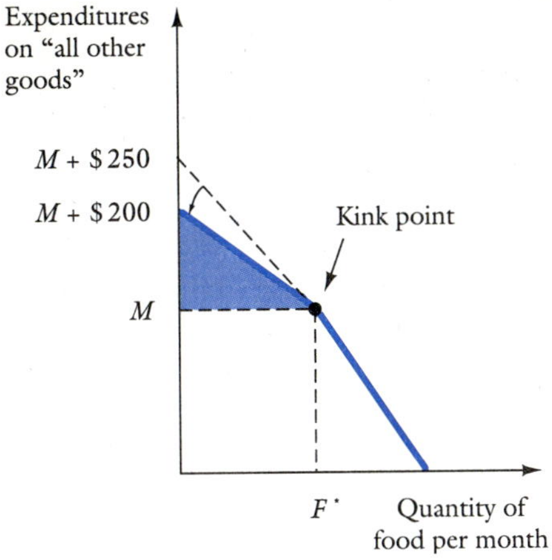

FIGURE 4.8

The Budget Constraint When Food Stamps Are Resold for 80 Percent

Food stamps are typically illegally sold for less than their face value. This figure shows the effect of food stamps on an eligible consumer's budget if food stamps are sold for 80 percent of their face value. The budget line pivots for all quantities of food below F^*, the amount of food the consumer's food stamps will purchase. The pivoting reduces the point of intersection between the vertical axis and the budget line. With resale at 100 percent of face value, the intersection point occurs at $M + \$250$. With resale at only 80 percent of face value, the intersection point occurs at $M + \$200$. The pivoting creates a kink in the budget line.

LEARNING EXERCISE 4.5

Show how the budget constraint changes when the price of food decreases, assuming no resale first and then 80 percent resale value for food stamps. Does the original kink point change?

Price Theory in Practice

CLIP 'N SAVE — COUPON MANIA

During a recession, consumers watch their spending carefully, real income generally falls, and the potential for losing one's job increases. Consumers respond by using their time and effort to relax the tightening they face in their household budget constraint. The recession of 1990–1991, for example, put 2 million people out of work. Actual job loss for some and worry about job loss for others led consumers to use retail discount coupons in increasing numbers. During 1990, for example, over 300 billion coupons were printed by manufacturers—more than 1,200 coupons for every man, woman, and child in the United

States. This was a 17 percent increase over the number of coupons printed in 1989, when the economy was still growing.

Typically, coupons are distributed in newspapers or through the mail. They offer consumers a price discount on a particular product, averaging about 50 cents. The average coupon clipper is middle-aged, married, and living in a home with a household income of about $30,000 before taxes. The average clipper saves about $6 from a weekly grocery bill of $74, or about 8.1 percent. Assuming that it takes about fifteen minutes to find and clip coupons and fiddle with them at the check-out counter, the average clipper earns about $24 per hour for the effort, which is tax-free. Dividing the household income of the average clipper by 2,000 hours, the usual number of hours worked in a year, reveals that the clipper's household time is worth about $15 per hour ($30,000/2,000) before taxes. At an average tax rate of 20 percent, the average household earns $12 per hour after taxes. Clipping coupons then offers a *net* return after taxes of about $12 per hour ($24 − $12).

If every coupon was redeemed, it would cost manufacturers about $150 billion. Because only about 4 percent of all coupons are redeemed, coupons cost manufacturers about $6 billion in 1990.[5] Although there is a cost, both coupon clippers and manufacturers benefit from redemption of coupons. Manufacturers benefit because they sell goods that might not otherwise be bought. That is, the *law of demand* applies: As price decreases, more of the good is sold. In addition, they benefit if coupon-discounted goods are complementary to other goods the manufacturer sells that may not be discounted. Coupon discounts may increase the demand for complements. Coupon clippers benefit because they pay a lower price for the good, which increases the feasible set of commodities they can purchase. A recession threatens consumers' budget constraints, so coupons help alleviate the effects of a recession.

Learning Exercise 4.6

How does the budget constraint in Figure 4.5 change if a coupon is available that reduces the cost of a pay-per-view TV program by $2? Redraw the constraint again to show how it is affected by a discount coupon for video rentals that offers $5 off the rental of two videos.

4.3 Time Constraint

What is the source of the income that you spend on goods? When you are in college, you may receive some or all of your income from your parents. When you leave college, you will most likely take a job and work to support yourself. The income will then come from your work. The income you earn working is affected by many factors—your career choice, your ambition, your boss, other employees, the success of your company, and your skills. We investigate the effects of wages and the time you spend working, holding all these other factors constant. Our

[5]The cost to manufacturers increases somewhat when the cost of printing, advertising, and processing coupon reimbursements is included.

interest is to show how time, which is scarce, limits the amount of income you earn and thereby restricts your purchases of goods.

WORK OR LEISURE

There are 168 hours in a week. If you sleep 8 hours per night, you have 112 hours left for work, play, and household chores. For simplicity, we will combine household chores and play together and call this your *leisure time.* So, each week, you have 112 hours to divide between leisure and work time. The time constraint can be represented by the following equation:

$$T_{\text{total}} = T_{\text{work}} + T_{\text{leisure}} \tag{4.7}$$

where T_{total} is the total time available (112 hours each week), T_{work} is the time you spend working, and T_{leisure} is the time you spend in leisure activities.[6]

Note that you face a time trade-off. You can spend more time in leisure activities (T_{leisure}), but this reduces the time you have to spend working (T_{work}). If you spend more time in leisure, the time constraint shows that your income is reduced. To illustrate, suppose that you work 40 hours each week. If your wage rate is $10 per hour, you earn $400 each week before taxes (tax effects are investigated below). During the week, you spend 72 hours in leisure activities. If you decide to work an extra hour each week, you earn an extra $10, but you must give up an hour of leisure. The time trade-off you face forces you to give up leisure in exchange for income or, equivalently, to give up income in exchange for leisure.

FULL INCOME

Suppose that, like most people, you derive all your income from work; that is, you are not a multimillionaire sitting back watching the stock market and earning dividends on your investments for income. If you don't work, you don't eat. If your hourly wage rate is denoted by w, then your income (M) is equal to your wage rate times the amount of time you spend working:

$$M = w \times T_{\text{work}} = w \times (T_{\text{total}} - T_{\text{leisure}}) \tag{4.8}$$

where the term in parentheses is equal to T_{work}. In effect, your income (M) is equal to the total wages you could earn if you worked *all* the time ($w \times T_{\text{total}}$) minus the wages lost due to leisure activities ($w \times T_{\text{leisure}}$). Economist and Nobel laureate Gary Becker calls $w \times T_{\text{total}}$ your full income.[7] **Full income** is

Full Income
The amount of income a consumer can earn if all available time is spent working.

[6]Leisure time includes all nonmarket activities. The constraint can be generalized to partition other uses of your time that you would not choose to call leisure, but such generality does not improve the present discussion. The model is expanded to separate shopping time from other time activities, for example, in the study by Howard Marmorstein, Dhruv Grewal, and Raymond P. H. Fishe, "The Value of Time Spent in Price-Comparison Shopping: Survey and Experimental Evidence," *Journal of Consumer Research* 19 (June 1992), 52–61.

[7]Becker's article, "A Theory of the Allocation of Time" [*Economic Journal* 75 (September 1965), 493–517], includes nonlabor income in full income. Nonlabor income includes investment earnings, welfare payments, and other cash receipts. If V represents nonlabor income, then full income is equal to $w \times T + V$.

the amount of money you could earn if you were paid a market wage for the total time you have available to you. Using the illustration above, if $T_{total} = 112$ hours and your wage rate is \$10 per hour, the most you can earn in a week is \$1,120 before taxes. Spending 72 hours in leisure activities reduces your full income by \$720. The difference of \$400 is your work-related income.

Your budget and time constraints can be combined into one equation:

$$w \times (T_{total} - T_{leisure}) = \text{Expenditure on Goods}$$

$$w \times T_{total} = \text{Expenditure on Goods} + (w \times T_{leisure}) \tag{4.9}$$

This says that your full income is divided between the goods you purchase—video rentals, pay-per-view TV programs, CDs—and the "cost" of your leisure activities ($w \times T_{leisure}$). We call this relationship your **full-income constraint.**

Full-Income Constraint An equation showing how a consumer's full income is allocated to the "purchase" of both goods and leisure.

Combining the time and budget constraints provides another view of the trade-off you face. The goods you buy are paid for with income from work. Time spent working competes with leisure time. You can buy more goods if you work more, but if you work more, you have less leisure time. Figure 4.9 shows the trade-off you face between expenditures on goods (or work income) and leisure time.

The trade-off between expenditures on goods (or income) and leisure time is a straight line with a negative slope. The slope is equal to the wage rate with a negative sign in front, which indicates that an extra hour of leisure reduces income by the hourly wage rate. These results should be fairly intu-

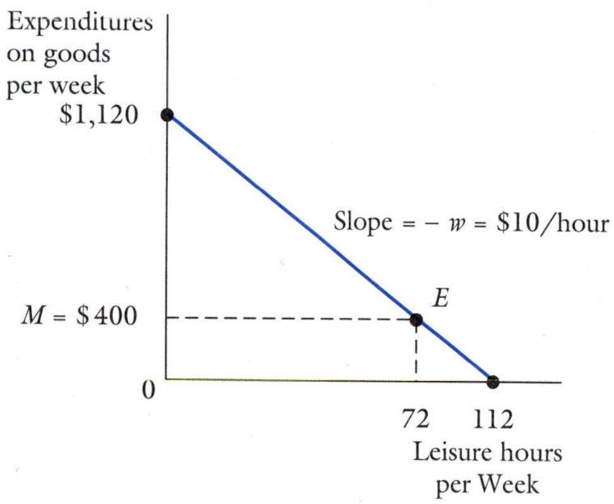

FIGURE 4.9

The Trade-off Between Income and Leisure Time

The full-income constraint shows the trade-off between expenditures on goods and leisure time. Expenditures on goods equal the income earned from working. Work time reduces the time spent in leisure; higher expenditures on goods implies less leisure and vice versa. The rate of trade-off is measured by the slope of the full-income constraint. The slope equals minus the wage rate ($-w$). An additional hour of leisure implies expenditures are reduced by \$$w$. At point E, the consumer spends 72 hours in leisure and 40 hours working, earning \$400 each week.

itive: your time is valuable, and it is valued at the wage rate you can earn in the labor market. If you spend an extra hour in leisure, you give up one hour of earnings—your hourly wage for the extra hour of leisure. The trade-off is a straight line because your wage is assumed to be constant for all hours that you work; that is, no overtime pay is available.[8] In Figure 4.9, point E on the full income constraint represents the case in which 72 hours of leisure are consumed each week, leaving 40 hours (112 – 72) for work at $10 per hour, which produces $400 of income.

Note that the vertical axis in Figure 4.9 measures expenditures on *all* goods. In contrast, the vertical axis in Figure 4.5—composite goods—measures expenditures on *all other goods.* The difference is that for composite goods we have isolated one good from all other goods, while our full income constraint isolates leisure time (horizontal axis) from money expenditures on *all goods.* In both cases, we are isolating a variable of interest; in one case it is a specific good, and in the other case it is leisure time.

WAGE CHANGES AND INCOME TAXES

What happens to the trade-off between income and leisure when your wage rate changes? From Figure 4.9, we know that the slope of the full income constraint equals the wage rate with a minus sign in front. If the wage rate changes, then the slope of the full income constraint changes, too; in effect, an increase in the wage rate increases the cost of leisure time. Let us assume that your boss gives you a nice raise. Panel (a) in Figure 4.10 on page 126 shows the effect of increasing the wage rate from $10 to $15 per hour. At $15 per hour, you can earn $1,680 per week if you work *all* the time. If you continue to work 40 hours per week, which means that you spend 72 hours in leisure activities, then you earn $600 per week.[9] The new wage rate produces a new slope and, accordingly, a new trade-off between income and leisure. Now, if you spend another hour in leisure, you will give up $15 of expenditure on goods.

Wage changes can be happy occasions, such as the raise described in panel (a), or they can prove disappointing, as when your first paycheck arrives and you see how much you paid in income taxes. Income taxes effectively lower wage rates. Panel (b) in Figure 4.10 shows how a 20 percent proportional tax rate changes the full income constraint. The change occurs through the wage rate. If you are earning $10 per hour without any taxes, you can earn $400 per week. If you must pay a 20 percent proportional income tax, your wage is reduced to $8 per hour after taxes. At $8 per hour, your after-tax income is $320 per week. Algebraically, if τ represents the tax rate, then your after-tax wage rate equals $(1 - \tau) \times w$, or 1 minus the tax rate times your before-tax wage rate.

---

[8]See Price Theory Problem 10 in this chapter for an example of how overtime affects the full income constraint.

[9]It is unlikely that you will continue to work the same number of hours. Chapter 5 shows how wage changes affect the number of hours you *choose* to work.

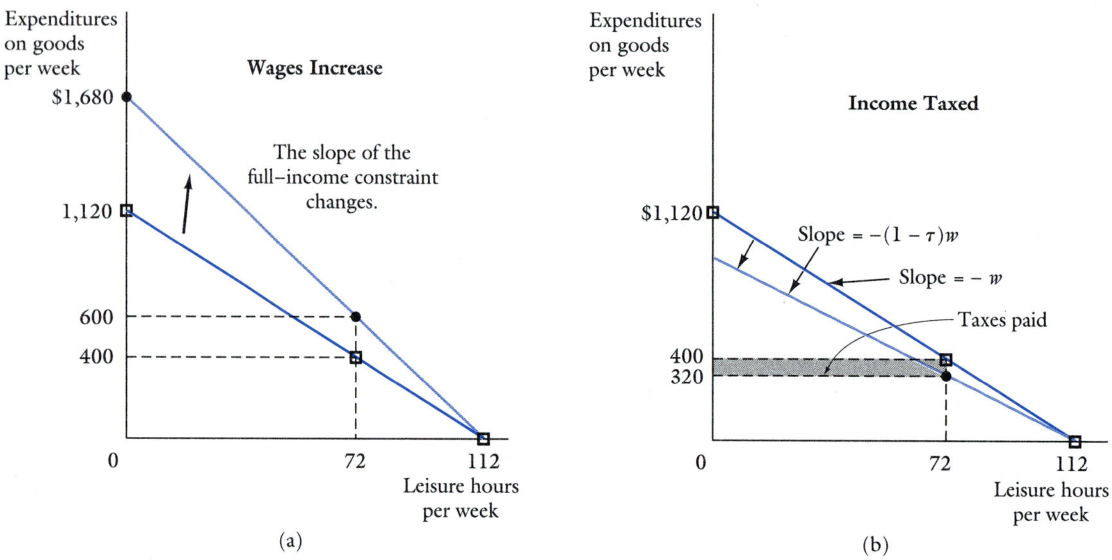

FIGURE 4.10

The Effect of a Wage Increase on the Full-Income Constraint

Panel (a) shows the effect of an increase in wages on the full-income constraint. A wage increase changes the slope of the full-income constraint and raises the point at which the full-income constraint intersects the vertical axis; in effect, an increase in the wage rate increases the cost of leisure time. With wages increasing to $15 from $10 per hour, the consumer earns $600 by working 40 hours and spending 72 hours in leisure. Panel (b) shows the effect of income taxes on earnings and the full-income constraint. A 20 percent tax on wages of $10 per hour implies that a consumer earns $8 per hour after taxes. Working 40 hours produces $400 in before-tax and $320 in after-tax earnings. In effect, taxes lower the point at which the full-income constraint intersects the vertical axis.

Proportional income taxes cause the full income constraint to pivot down, thereby reducing your trade-off opportunities between income and leisure. As shown in panel (b), if you continue to work 40 hours, which implies you spend 72 hours in leisure activities, your weekly earnings decrease from $400 to $320. You pay $80 in income taxes at a tax rate of 20 percent.

Learning Exercise 4.7

How does the full income constraint change if you receive a subsidy for each hour you work? Using the assumptions in Figure 4.9, draw the full income constraint when you are paid a government subsidy of $2 per hour.

NONLABOR INCOME

Have you ever wondered what you would do if you won $1 million in a state lottery? It is nice once in a while to fantasize about such events, no matter how unlikely they are. Let's suppose you did win a million dollars. If you put this money in a safe investment that paid 8 percent interest annually, you would earn $80,000 a year (again, we are ignoring income taxes). The $80,000 is about $1,538 each week. How does the extra income affect your full income constraint? In effect, you can spend $1,538 each week without any work effort. Your full income is increased by $1,538. Using our earlier notation, your full income now equals $w \times T_{total}$ + $1,538. The new full income constraint is shown in Figure 4.11.

The interest earnings on the lottery prize pushes your full income constraint up in our graph. The whole constraint shifts up by $1,538. If you decide to keep working 40 hours per week at $10 per hour, you can increase your weekly income—before taxes—to $1,938 ($1,538 + $400). Alternatively, if you spend all your time—112 hours—in leisure activities, you will earn $1,538 per week. Winning the lottery represents nearly a 400 percent increase in your income, which greatly increases the leisure and goods combinations you can select. Without any work effort, for example, the lottery earnings allow you to purchase more goods than if you spent all of your time working. It is probably no wonder that many lottery winners leave their jobs.

Note that the trade-off between expenditures on goods and leisure time is still defined by your wage rate *if* you are working. When you work, an extra hour of leisure (again) costs you one hour of wage earnings. If you are *not* working, however, there is no trade-off. With no work, you are spending all of

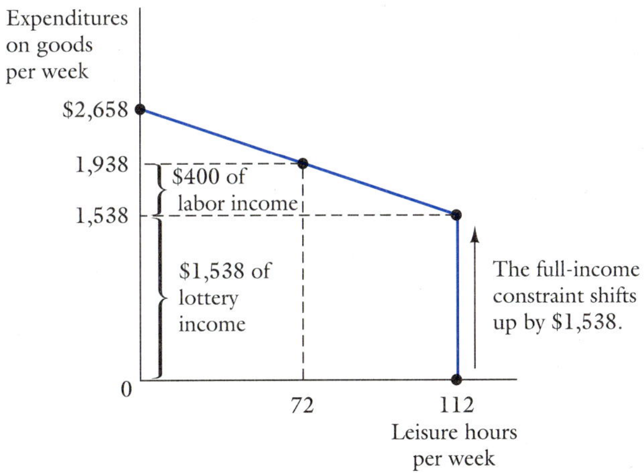

FIGURE 4.11

How Lottery Income Affects the Full-Income Constraint

Winning the lottery and investing the proceeds provides a weekly income of $1,538. The lottery income shifts the full-income constraint up the vertical axis by $1,538. Working 40 hours at $10 per hour earns $400. Adding the lottery income to this amount gives a weekly income of $1,938 (before taxes).

your time in leisure and there is no way to increase your leisure time—you're at the limit.

LEARNING EXERCISE 4.8

If you win the lottery and work all the time—112 hours per week—what is your weekly income? What is your wage rate if you work 40 hours per week and earn $1,538?

$$$ Price Theory in Practice

THE ALLOCATION OF TIME ACROSS COUNTRIES

Ultimately, time may be our scarcest resource. Goods are scarce partly because our income is limited, and income is limited because we have only a certain amount of time to devote to work. Thus, how we allocate our time reflects a decision of great significance.

There have been several studies of how men and women allocate their time in households across different countries. In one such study, two economists, F. Thomas Juster and Frank P. Stafford, both of the University of Michigan, provided a detailed summary of the results of several time allocation studies.[10] Their findings are reported in Table 4.1 for Japan, the former Soviet Union, and the United States.

Although the latest study period for the United States is 1981 and the latest study period for Japan and the former Soviet Union is 1985, we can still make several observations about these data:

1. Men spend more time in market work and less time in household work than women. Although this situation is changing in all three countries, it is doing so at a slow pace.
2. Men in the United States and Japan show the greatest changes in market work and leisure activities between the two study periods. Men in the United States decreased market work by an average of 7.6 hours per week, while men in Japan decreased market work by an average of 5.7 hours per week. In contrast, men in the (former) Soviet Union decreased market work by an average of only 0.8 hours per week.
3. Women in the United States are moving against the trend away from market work observed in Japan and the (former) Soviet Union. Women in the United States increased market work by an average of 5 hours per week, while women in Japan decreased market work by 8.6 hours per week and women in the (former) Soviet Union decreased market work by 4.5 hours per week.
4. It is a myth to think that the United States is a nation of couch potatoes, spending leisure time watching television. More time is spent

[10]See F. Thomas Juster and Frank P. Stafford, "The Allocation of Time: Empirical Findings, Behavioral Models, and Problems of Measurement," *Journal of Economic Literature* 29 (June 1991), 471–522.

TABLE 4.1

Weekly Time Allocation for Men and Women in Japan, the Former Soviet Union, and the United States, 1965–1985

	Japan				Former Soviet Union				United States			
	Men		Women		Men		Women		Men		Women	
Activity	**1965**	**1985**	**1965**	**1985**	**1965**	**1985**	**1965**	**1985**	**1965**	**1981**	**1965**	**1981**
Market work	57.7	52.0	33.2	24.6	54.6	53.8	43.8	39.3	51.6	44.0	18.9	23.9
Commuting	3.6	4.5	1.0	1.2	4.9	5.2	3.7	3.4	4.8	3.5	1.6	2.0
Housework	2.8	3.5	31.5	31.0	9.8	11.9	31.5	27.0	11.5	13.8	41.8	30.5
Leisure	34.4	40.3	32.7	40.3	36.9	34.6	26.1	32.0	36.7	41.8	35.4	41.9
TV	16.8	17.3	19.4	21.4	5.6	14.5	3.9	11.2	13.4	12.7	9.3	11.5
Personal care	73.0	72.4	70.6	72.1	66.6	67.8	66.4	69.8	68.2	68.2	71.9	71.6
Sleep and rest	63.8	60.0	59.6	57.0	56.0	56.9	55.5	58.2	58.7	57.9	59.9	58.9
Total hours	168.0	168.0	168.0	168.0	168.0	168.0	168.0	168.0	168.0	168.0	168.0	168.0

Source: F. Thomas Juster and Frank P. Stafford, "The Allocation of Time. Empirical Findings, Behavioral Models, and Problems of Measurement," *Journal of Economic Literature* 29 (June 1991), 471–523. Reprinted by permission of the American Economic Association.

watching television each week in Japan than in the United States or the (former) Soviet Union.

These findings are a reflection of choices made by individuals subject to a full income constraint. The question and challenge is to use differences in the full income constraint across countries and consumers to explain the differences we observe in these time studies. Specifically, the economies of Japan and the United States were growing in real terms between the two study periods, so real wages and wealth were increasing. The net effect of these changes is to relax the full income constraint, which makes more income and leisure bundles available. These events may help explain the findings in item 2 above for the United States and Japan. In contrast, for much of the period between the two studies, the economy of the former Soviet Union was stagnant or growing only slightly. Thus, fewer opportunities for substitution toward leisure and away from work arose, which is consistent with an unchanging full income constraint.

Changes in tax rates and other tax laws may also have influenced time allocation among men and women. In some countries, such as Japan and the United States, income of married couples is taxed at a single (uniform) marginal tax rate. In other countries, such as Norway and Sweden, the earnings of each individual are taxed at separate rates. In the countries with separate tax rates, men and women show a stronger tendency to change the amount of time spent in household and market work when tax rates change than is observed in single-tax (uniform) rate countries. The reason for this is that the cost of leisure time equals the after-tax wage rate for each individual separately in separate-tax-rate countries, so if tax rates change, each person is affected separately. But in single-tax countries, the couple is affected jointly, so there is less incentive to change the mix of market and household work hours.

LEARNING EXERCISE 4.9

How can you use the full income constraint to help explain the increased participation of women in market work in the United States?

Chapter Summary

1. A consumer may select different amounts of any good. A bundle of goods is a set with a certain quantity of each good. A bundle of potato chips and hot dogs, for example, may include one hot dog and one bag of potato chips. Another bundle may include three hot dogs and two bags of potato chips.

2. With a fixed budget you can buy only a certain amount of goods. The prices of each good determine how much the fixed budget can buy. The budget constraints is an equation that describes this relationship. The budget constraint for two goods, X and Y, is written as $M = P_x \times X + P_y \times Y$, where M is the budget (or income), P_x is the price of X, P_y is the price of Y, and X and Y are quantities of each good.

3. The slope of the budget line is equal to the price ratio of two goods, with a negative sign in front. If good X is on the horizontal

axis and good Y is on the vertical axis, the slope of the budget line equals $-P_x/P_y$. The slope indicates the market-determined trade-off each consumer faces. An extra unit of good X will cost (P_x/P_y) units of good Y.

4. The composite good convention allows us to show the budget constraint when more than two goods are consumed. Consumption of the composite good is measured by expenditures. The composite good is called "all other goods." The trade-off between the composite good and the specific good omitted is equal to the price of the omitted good. One more unit of the omitted good will reduce expenditure on the composite good by an amount equal to the price of the omitted good.
5. The full income constraint combines the time and budget constraints. The full income constraint shows how your full income—what you would earn if you worked all of the time—is divided between purchases of goods and leisure. In the full income constraint, the opportunity cost of leisure time is the wage rate. You buy leisure time at your wage rate because it reduces your full income.

Trouble Spots

Concept	Reminder
Price Ratio, Slope	The price ratio, or slope, shows the price of the good shown on the horizontal axis in the numerator and the price of the good shown on the vertical axis in the denominator. Thus, if good Y is on the vertical axis and good X is on the horizontal axis, we compute the price ratio as P_x/P_y, not as P_y/P_x.
Price Changes and the Budget Constraint	When the price of a good *decreases,* the budget line pivots *out,* away from the origin. When the price of a good *increases,* the budget line pivots *in,* toward the origin. (The move *in* and the word *in*crease are paired with each other.)
Kinked Budget Constraints	A kinked budget constraint has a slope that changes at the point at which there is a kink.
Resale Constraint	The resale constraint is represented by a separate line on a graph showing the budget line. Removing the resale constraint is the same as removing the line from the graph.
Composite Good versus Full Income Graphs	There is a difference between the vertical axes when the full income constraint and budget line are graphed using the composite good convention. With the full income constraint the vertical axis shows expenditure on *all* goods, whereas the composite good convention shows expenditure on *all other* goods.

4.4 Review Questions

1. If two different bundles cost the same amount of income, do they lie on the same budget line?
2. Interpret the price ratio of two goods. How do changes in the price ratio affect the budget line?
3. What determines whether a bundle is feasible?
4. If income decreases, what happens to the size of the feasible set? What happens to the feasible set if the price of one good (in a two-good graph) decreases?
5. Suppose your money income triples and so do prices. Explain why your feasible set has not changed.
6. What is a composite good? How do you interpret the price ratio between a composite good and the "omitted" good? If income increases, how does the budget line change when you are using the composite good convention to describe the budget constraint?
7. How do quantity discounts affect the budget constraint? If there are three price discounts, how many kinks will the budget constraint have?
8. How does the no-resale constraint affect the feasible set for consumers receiving food stamps? How will the feasible set change if one-half of the food stamps received are allowed to be resold?
9. What is the time constraint? What trade-off is present when the time constraint is combined with the budget constraint?
10. How is a consumer's full income determined? How does full income change when wages increase?
11. In the full income constraint, what is the "cost" of leisure? How is expenditure on goods affected when a consumer decides to spend more time in leisure activities?
12. How does nonlabor income affect the full income constraint?

4.5 Price Theory Problems

1. Plot the following bundles of Tootsie Rolls and M&M's: A = {3, 2}, B = {7, 2}, C = {2, 3}, D = {5, 1}, E = {6, 1}, where the order is {Tootsie Rolls, M&M's}. Given that the price of Tootsie Rolls is 50 cents, the price of M&M's is $1, and your sweet-tooth budget is $4 per week, show which of these bundles are in your feasible set.
2. Assume that you like both pizza and tuna salad sandwiches. The price of each pizza is $8 and the price of each tuna salad sandwich is $4. Your food budget is $80 per week.
    a. What is the equation for the budget constraint? What is the equation for the budget line? Graph the budget line.
    b. What is the market-determined trade-off between pizza and tuna salad sandwiches? How does this trade-off affect the budget line?
    c. If you spend all of your budget on pizzas, how many can you buy? Show this point on your graph. How many tuna salad sandwiches can you buy if you spend all of your budget on tuna salad sandwiches? Show this point on your graph.

3. True or false:
    a. If you know the slope of the budget line, you know the absolute price of each good.
    b. If you know the intersection point on one axis and the slope of the budget line, you know the consumer's budget.
    c. If you know the intersection point on both axes and the slope of the budget line, you know the budget and the absolute price of the two goods.
4. If the price of frozen yogurt is \$2 per cup, the price of ice cream is \$1.50 per cone, and your dessert budget is \$12 per week, draw the budget line for these two goods. Show the feasible set of bundles.
    a. Show how the budget line changes if the price of ice cream increases to \$3 per cone.
    b. Starting from the higher price of ice cream, show how the budget line changes when your dessert budget increases to \$18 per week.
    c. With the increase in your dessert budget in part (b), can you purchase all of the bundles in your original feasible set? What bundles are still excluded?
5. If you earn \$2,000 per month (after taxes) and a round-trip airline ticket costs an average of \$250, show the feasible set of airline tickets you can purchase, using the composite good convention to represent expenditures on all other goods. What is the trade-off between airline tickets and expenditures on all other goods? How does your budget line change if your income increases to \$3,000 per month (after taxes)?
6. Suppose you enjoy going to movies. You buy a VCR to watch some movies at home. Your expenditure on the VCR, though, has reduced the income you have available for movies. Show how your budget line is affected by your purchase of a VCR, using the composite good convention.
7. A local hotel offers discounts on the room rate if five or more rooms are reserved. The rate charged for the first four rooms is \$100 per night; the fifth and any extra rooms cost \$75 per night. If your income is \$900 per week, show how your budget constraint is affected by the hotel's discount policy. Use the composite good convention.
8. A local boat dealer is giving coupons to customers, one coupon to each customer. The coupons entitle customers to free admission to the upcoming boat show. Normally, the admission fee is \$15. You generally go to the show with six friends and pay for everyone's admission.
    a. Using the composite good convention, show how the discount coupon has affected your budget constraint.
    b. Show how your budget constraint is affected if you can resell each coupon for \$10.
9. Suppose that you have 4,000 hours in a year to divide between work and leisure. Your wage rate is \$15 per hour and you have no other source of income.

a. What is your full income constraint?
b. How much time do you work if you spend $27,000 per year on goods? At this point, how much time do you spend in leisure?
c. If you receive a raise to $20 per hour and continue to work the same number of hours as in part (b), how much do you spend on goods? (Assume that there is no savings.)
d. Draw the full income constraint to illustrate the situation in cases (b) and (c).

10. Assume that you can spend time in leisure or work for $10 per hour. If you work more than 40 hours per week, you earn overtime pay of $15 per hour. If you can spend 112 hours per week in leisure or work, draw the full income constraint for this situation.
    a. Show how a 20 percent income tax affects the full income constraint.
    b. Show how the feasible set changes if overtime pay starts at 50 hours per week, not 40 hours.
11. Rewrite the time constraint when your time is divided between work (T_{work}), leisure ($T_{leisure}$), and household activities ($T_{household}$). How is the full income constraint changed by this specification? What is the cost of spending your time in household activities?
12. Assume you win the Publisher's Clearinghouse sweepstakes. Mr. Ed McMahon presents you with your first check for $10,000. You will receive a check for this amount each year for the next 20 years. Assume that your wage rate is $25 per hour and you can spend up to 4,000 hours per year in work or leisure. Show how the sweepstakes award affects your full income constraint this year. If you reduced the time you spend working to 1,500 hours from 2,000 after winning the sweepstakes, do you have more or less income to spend on goods?

4.6 Writing Exercise

Time constraints are often affected by the goods that you purchase. Microwave ovens, for example, reduce the time you spend preparing food, which gives you more time for other activities. Prepare a list of goods that you have bought that have the effect of changing your time constraint—either increasing or decreasing it. Estimate how much time you have saved (or lost) from the purchase of these goods. What is the value that you place on these savings (losses)? Did you include a computer on the list?

5

Individual Preferences and Optimal Choice

Preview Questions

When you finish studying this chapter, you should be able to answer the following questions:

- What three characteristics hold true for everyone's preferences?
- What are indifference curves?
- What are the four properties of an indifference curve?
- How do you interpret the marginal rate of substitution between two goods?
- What is the problem of choice for an individual?
- What is the solution to the problem of choice?
- What is the difference between an interior and a corner solution?
- What is the equilibrium solution for the case of many goods?
- How do you solve the problem of choice with a full income constraint?

Comedian Buddy Hackett once said, "As a child, my family's menu consisted of two choices: take it or leave it." As children many choices are made for us, but as adults we are expected to make our own choices. In fact, nearly every day you decide how to allocate your time and income by buying goods and services that offer you satisfaction. Do you ever stop to think about how you make your choices? What factors do you consider, for example, in your decision about where to eat lunch? How many greeting cards do you send and phone calls do you make during the end-of-the-year holidays? How many pairs of shoes do you own? How many hours do you work during the year? The answer to each of these questions combines the discussion of budget and/or time constraints in Chapter 4 with a discussion of preferences, or tastes, presented below.

Let's think about tastes, or preferences, for goods. Your tastes define the satisfaction you receive from different bundles of goods. Do you like chocolate milkshakes, tofu in your soup, or gold watches? Your tastes, or preferences, define what you like and the satisfaction you receive when you consume different goods. In contrast, your income and the prices of goods define what and how much you can buy. By combining your preferences with information about what bundles you can buy, we can explain your consumption choices. By explaining consumption choices, we can define your demand for different goods.

In this chapter, we analyze your preferences for goods. With preferences defined, we then show how you choose a bundle of goods that offers the most satisfaction without violating your budget constraint. In addition, we show how you solve the problem of allocating time between leisure and work—the work/leisure choice—and show how overtime pay affects the amount of time you choose to spend working.

5.1 Tastes, or Preferences

Your tastes, or preferences, are what make you truly unique. You may like yellow shirts, blue cars, and green curtains while others prefer different colors. You may prefer to eat frozen yogurt while others eat ice cream. Your preferences describe which goods or bundles of goods give you satisfaction and how much satisfaction they offer. We accept that your preferences are different from others. We accept that different preferences may explain why you purchase some goods and not others. But, instead of relying on changing preferences to explain your choices, as economists we typically model your behavior with your preferences fixed. We are not saying that tastes don't differ across people, but instead we assume that they don't change rapidly or very much over time.

One reason that we hold tastes constant is because they cannot be observed or measured objectively. When you change your purchasing habits, we cannot read your mind to determine if your tastes have changed, and if we could, what units would we use to measure your tastes? We can, however, observe changes in income and relative prices, and these changes can be measured in objective units, such as dollars. Typically, economists have found that changes in these variables alone explain a large percentage of the changes in your choices. In other words, changes in taste appear to be less important than changes in income and relative prices.

THE ASSUMPTION OF RATIONAL PREFERENCES

We make three basic assumptions that define rational preferences: (1) completeness, (2) nonsatiation, and (3) transitivity. We will address each of these assumptions individually.

Completeness

Completeness is the assumption that says you can *rank* bundles. Your preferences are *complete* if you can say that one bundle is preferred to another or that you are indifferent between the two bundles. Preferred means that you will choose one bundle over the other, other things being equal. Indifferent means that both bundles give you the same satisfaction.

Completeness
A property of preferences that implies bundles of goods can be ranked as preferred, indifferent, or less preferred to one another.

Your preferences are properly defined over *bundles,* not over the goods individually. To understand this point, recall that a bundle represents a set containing a certain amount of each good you consume. Suppose that you prefer a bundle of 6 ounces of hot tea, one-fourth of a lemon, and no cream to a bundle with 6 ounces of tea, no lemon, and 1 ounce of cream. In addition, you prefer a bundle of 6 ounces of coffee, no lemons, and 1 ounce of cream to a bundle containing 6 ounces of coffee, one-fourth of a lemon, and no cream. (We don't know anyone who consumes lemon with their coffee.) Now, can you determine whether you prefer lemon to cream or vice versa? The answer is no. These goods are not preferred or less preferred individually; they give satisfaction when combined with other goods in a bundle, so it is the bundle that you compare to define your preferences.

Nonsatiation

Nonsatiation
The "more is better" property of preferences. A bundle with more of one good and no less of any other is preferred or indifferent to an otherwise equivalent bundle.

Nonsatiation means that you always receive satisfaction from more of a good, even when you have many goods. It is another way to say, "More is better." You prefer a bundle of eight computer disks to an otherwise equivalent bundle with only seven computer disks. You prefer a bundle containing three Rolex watches to a bundle containing only two Rolex watches, particularly if you plan to give one to each of your three children.

The "more is better" assumption applies to bundles that have an unambiguous ordering of goods. When there are three rolls of toilet paper and one computer disk in one bundle and two rolls of toilet paper and three computer disks in another bundle, the comparison is ambiguous. The first bundle has more toilet paper but fewer computer disks, so the "more is better" assumption does not apply. When bundles have varying quantities of each good, so that some bundles have more of some goods but less of the other goods, we cannot say which bundles a consumer might prefer.

Figure 5.1, on page 138, shows several bundles of mystery novels and popular magazines. We assume that these bundles give you satisfaction, so if you read more mystery novels or popular magazines, you are better off.

Our reference bundle is bundle *Z*, which contains five mystery novels and five popular magazines. As Figure 5.1 shows, bundles above and to the right of *Z*, such as bundle *D*, offer you more satisfaction than *Z*. Our nonsatiation or "more is better" assumption guarantees this result. Look at bundle *D*. It contains seven mystery novels and seven popular magazines, which is more of both goods than bundle *Z* contains. Similarly, you prefer bundle *Z* to bundles to the left and below it, such as bundle *A*.

Consider bundle *B*, which contains two magazines and five mystery novels. Because bundle *Z* has three more magazines than bundle *B*, you prefer bundle *Z* to bundle *B* by the nonsatiation assumption. We must be careful, though, with bundle *B*. There can be unusual examples in which more of one good, without increasing the other good, will not increase your satisfaction. Our discussion of perfect complements below illustrates this point. If the two goods are right-handed gloves and left-handed gloves, for example, more right-handed gloves without additional left-handed gloves will not increase satisfaction. When comparing two bundles that differ only with respect to the quantity of *one* good, such as bundle *Z* and bundle *B*, we say that you prefer bundle *Z* over bundle *B* *or* you are indifferent between bundle *Z* and bundle *B*. By qualifying our statements this way, we allow for unusual examples, such as right- and left-handed gloves.

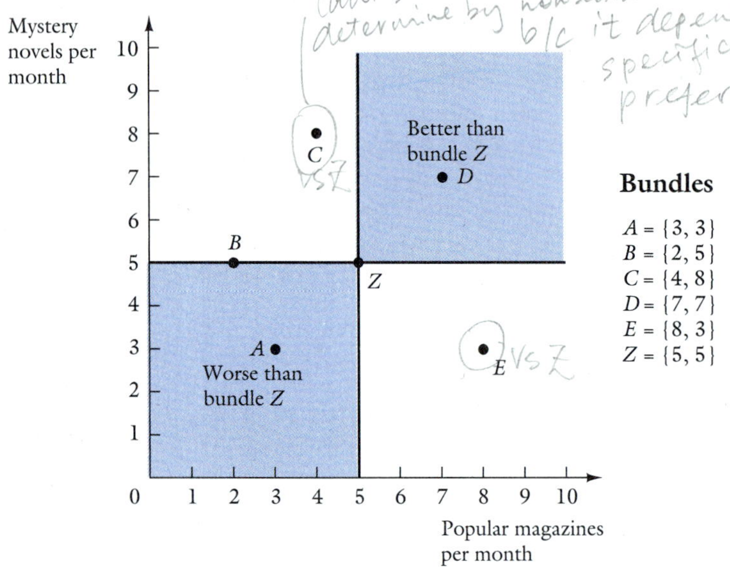

FIGURE 5.1

Ranking Commodity Bundles—"More Is Better"

According to the "more is better" or nonsatiation assumption, you prefer bundle *D* to bundle *Z*. Similarly, you prefer bundle *Z* to bundle *A* or bundle *B*. The nonsatiation assumption does not tell us your preferences regarding bundle *C* or bundle *E* when compared to bundle *Z*.

The nonsatiation assumption does not allow us to rank all the bundles in Figure 5.1. For example, we do not know if bundle *C* is preferred, indifferent, or less preferred to you than bundle *Z*. We know that bundle *C* contains eight mystery novels and four popular magazines. Bundle *C* has more mystery novels than bundle *Z* but fewer popular magazines. The individual's ranking of bundles *Z* versus *C* (and *Z* versus *E*) cannot be determined from the nonsatiation property; rather, it depends upon the specifics of the individual's preferences.

There are a few obvious instances in which the nonsatiation assumption may be misleading. Overeating or drinking too much may make many of us worse off, so in these instances we would limit the application of the nonsatiation assumption.

Transitivity

Transitivity implies that our preferences for different bundles are consistent. Thus, if you first indicate a preference for an Apple PowerPC computer over an IBM 486 computer and then indicate a preference for a Compaq computer over an Apple PowerPC, to be consistent, you must also indicate a definite preference for a Compaq computer over an IBM 486 computer.

Turning back to Figure 5.1, if you prefer bundle *E* to bundle *Z* and bundle *Z* to bundle *A*, then transitivity implies that you prefer bundle *E* to bundle

Transitivity The logical consistency property of preferences. If bundle *A* is preferred to bundle *B* and bundle *B* is preferred to bundle *C*, then transitivity implies that bundle *A* is preferred to bundle *C*.

A. Transitivity also applies to the "indifferent" relation as well. Let's say you are indifferent between bundle *E* and bundle *Z* and between bundle *C* and bundle *Z*. The property of transitivity implies that you are indifferent between bundle *E* and bundle *C*.

Transitivity appears to be an application of simple logic, but there are cases in which such logic may not apply. For example, if the New York Yankees defeat the Los Angeles Dodgers and the Dodgers defeat the Minnesota Twins, then transitivity, if it held in this situation, would imply that the Yankees would defeat the Twins. Followers of baseball can attest that such logic fails quite often. The assumption of transitivity does not apply here because the *outcome* of a baseball game is the product of skill and luck on the playing field. Transitivity applies to the comparison of bundles of goods, not the outcome of an event that you cannot choose. In short, transitivity cannot be used to predict a future outcome.

Learning Exercise 5.1

In Figure 5.1, what do our assumptions say about the preference relationships between bundle *E* and bundle *A*; bundle *C* and bundle *B*; and bundle *D* and bundle *C*?

5.2 Indifference Curves

Indifference Curve
A collection of bundles that offer the same level of satisfaction.

Your preferences and the three assumptions above give rise to indifference curves.[1] An **indifference curve** is a graphical description of the bundles that offer the same level of satisfaction. The purpose of developing indifference curve analysis is that it lets us link your preferences to your budget (or full income) constraint. As such, indifference curve analysis will show us how you make choices under constraints. To see how we find the bundles that make up an indifference curve, refer to Figure 5.2 on page 140.

Figure 5.2 shows bundles *A, Z,* and *D* from Figure 5.1. We know from the nonsatiation assumption that you prefer bundle *D* to bundle *Z* and that you prefer bundle *Z* to bundle *A*. Now, look at the two curved paths connecting bundles *A* and *D*. We have drawn these paths between bundles *A* and *D* because we are moving from a bundle that is less preferred than bundle *Z* to one that is more preferred than bundle *Z*. These two curves pass through many bundles. You will prefer bundles that are close to bundle *D* along these curves to bundle *Z*. In addition, you will prefer bundle *Z* to bundles that are close to bundle *A* along these curves. As we travel along the two curved paths, moving from bundle *A* to bundle *D*, we pass from bundles that you find are less preferred than bundle *Z* to bundles that you find are more preferred than bundle *Z*. *Somewhere on each path there is a*

[1]There is one additional technical assumption needed to generate indifference curves: continuity. Continuity implies that there are no discrete changes in your preference ordering; that is, minuscule changes in the quantity of a good in a bundle give rise to a smooth change in your preference for the new bundle compared to the old bundle.

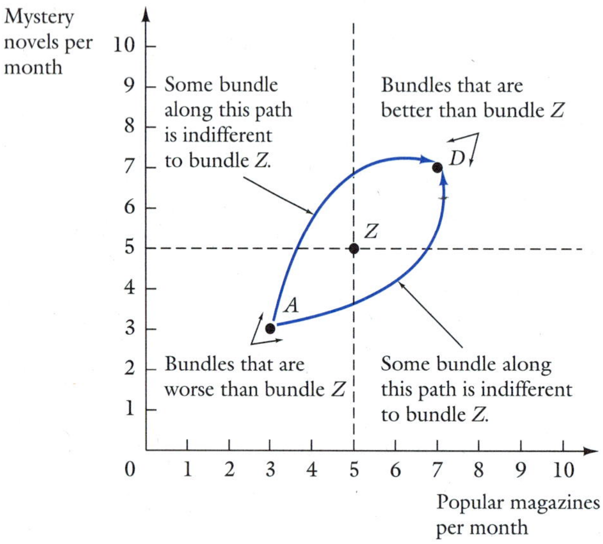

FIGURE 5.2

Where Are the Indifferent Bundles?

The bundles that you view as indifferent to bundle *Z* are found in the northwest and southeast quadrants. As you move along either of the two curves shown, you encounter a bundle that you view as indifferent to bundle *Z*.

bundle that provides the same satisfaction as bundle Z; that is, you are indifferent between this bundle and bundle *Z*. The bundles to which you are indifferent must lie in the regions shown in Figure 5.2—the upper left and lower right quadrants of the graph.

If we can draw two paths connecting bundle *A* to bundle *D*, then we can draw other lines through other bundles and make the same argument. In other words, there must be one bundle on each of the new lines that gives you the same satisfaction as bundle *Z*. The indifferent bundles must lie in the specified regions shown on Figure 5.2. If we perform this exercise several times, we will find many bundles that you view as indifferent to bundle *Z*. Figure 5.3 shows a set of four bundles that you view as indifferent to bundle *Z*. Bundles *X*, *Υ*, *V*, and *W* provide the same satisfaction as bundle *Z*, so we say that they lie on the same indifference curve.

The quantity of popular magazines and mystery novels in bundles *V*, *W*, *X*, *Υ*, and *Z* is shown in Figure 5.3. We can see one thing immediately: For you to remain indifferent among the various bundles, fewer mystery novels must be offset by more popular magazines or vice versa. This result follows from the "more is better" assumption. Both of these goods give you satisfaction. Therefore, if some of one good is given up, the only way that you can remain equally satisfied is by being compensated with more of the other.

Bundle	Mystery Novels per Month	Popular Magazines per Month
X	3	8
Y	4	6
Z	5	5
V	6	4
W	8	3

(a)

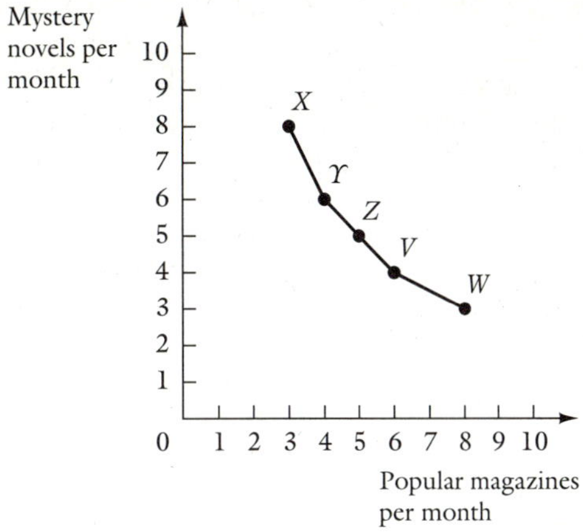

(b)

FIGURE 5.3

An Indifference Curve

The indifference curve is generated by connecting the bundles that offer the same level of satisfaction. Bundles *X* and *Y* lie to the northwest of bundle *Z*, while bundles *V* and *W* lie to the southeast of bundle *Z*.

PROPERTIES OF INDIFFERENCE CURVES

We can identify four properties of indifference curves:

1. ***Satisfaction is constant along an indifference curve.***
2. ***Every bundle lies on an indifference curve.***
3. ***Indifference curves have a negative slope for goods that provide satisfaction.***
4. ***Indifference curves do not intersect.***

Each property reflects an important aspect of your preferences and, ultimately, your choice of a consumption bundle. These properties provide certain limits to your behavior. Let's explore what these limits mean.

Satisfaction Is Constant Along an Indifference Curve

The first property follows from the definition of an indifference curve. If you are indifferent to all the bundles on an indifference curve, they must offer you the same satisfaction.

Every Bundle Lies on an Indifference Curve

Every bundle lies on an indifference curve because we can pick any bundle and apply the logic of Figure 5.2 to that bundle. By partitioning the graph into four quadrants, we can isolate the bundles that you view as better and worse than the bundle we pick. Somewhere in the northwest and southeast quadrants, there will be bundles to which you are indifferent as to the bundle we pick. So when we pick a bundle—any bundle—we can always find other bundles that you think are indifferent to it. Such reasoning implies that there are many indifference curves, each with a given level of satisfaction. Figure 5.4 shows three indifference curves for mystery novels and popular magazines.

Figure 5.4 shows that indifference curves offer more satisfaction when they are farther from the origin (the zero point of intersection for the two axes). The nonsatiation or "more is better" assumption gives us this result. Indifference curves that are farther from the origin generally have more of both commodities than those closer to the origin, so they offer more satisfaction.

Indifference Curves Have a Negative Slope for Desirable Goods

The property that indifference curves have a negative slope follows only if the two goods are desirable; that is, your satisfaction increases when you consume more of either good. Looking back to Figure 5.3, the nonsatiation or "more is better" assumption forces you into a trade-off. When you give up some mystery novels, you will be indifferent only if you have more popular magazines, another desirable good. An upward-sloping indifference curve, then, will violate the nonsatiation assumption for two goods if both goods are desirable.

Suppose that instead of "goods," we consider the trade-off between a desirable good and an undesirable good, or a "bad." The desirable good provides satisfaction, but the bad is undesirable and lowers satisfaction. Bads are important to consider because they show that our analysis extends to com-

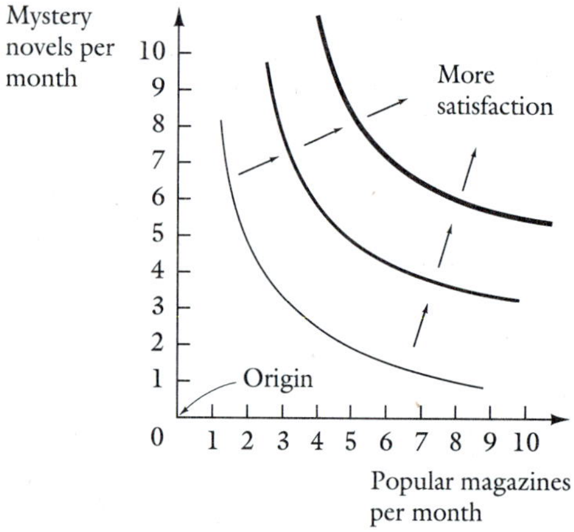

FIGURE 5.4

Higher Indifference Curves Representing More Satisfaction for the Case of Two Goods

Indifference curves that are farther away from the origin represent a higher level of satisfaction when bundles are formed for desirable goods. Note that indifference curves are not necessarily symmetric.

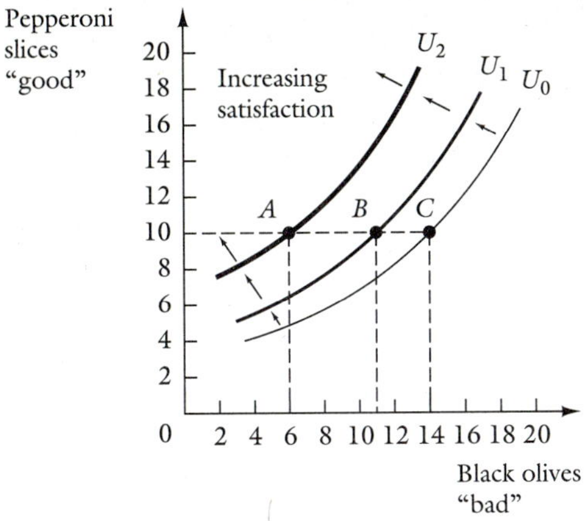

FIGURE 5.5

Indifference Curve for Toppings on a Medium-Sized Pizza

Indifference curves may have a positive slope when one good in the bundle is a "bad." Indifference curves that are farther away from the axis that measures the "bad" represent higher levels of satisfaction. For example, bundle *A* offers you more satisfaction than bundle *B* or bundle *C*.

modities that you don't prefer. Consider your preference for pizza toppings. Suppose that you like pepperoni but you don't care for black olives on your pizza.[2] Pepperoni is good and black olives are bad in terms of the satisfaction they provide. More black olives will decrease the satisfaction you receive from eating a pizza. Three indifference curves for pepperoni and black olive toppings are shown in Figure 5.5.

The three indifference curves for pepperoni and black olives are upward-sloping. When you find more black olives on your pizza, you require more pepperoni to achieve the same level of satisfaction. In effect, the extra pepperoni disguises the taste of the black olives. *Now, a higher level of satisfaction is represented by a shift of the indifference curves up and to the left.* Moving up in the direction of the pepperoni axis implies that there are more pepperoni slices on your pizza for any given number of black olives. Bundles *A, B,* and *C* illustrate this relationship. Each of these bundles contains 10 pepperoni slices, but the number of black olives differs. Bundle *A* contains 6 black olives, bundle *B* contains 11 black olives, and bundle *C* contains 14 black olives. Because black olives are a "bad" good, more black olives reduce the satisfaction you receive from a given bundle. In this example, bundle *A* provides you with the most satisfaction, bundle *B* the next most satisfaction, and bundle *C* the least satisfaction. Bundle *A* offers the most satisfaction because it contains the least amount of the undesirable good. In general, the nonsatiation or "more is better" assumption works in reverse for undesirable goods. For undesirable goods, we say that "less is better."

[2]If you happen to like black olives on your pizza, think of the "bad" topping as anchovies. If you like anchovies, change the example to high test grades (a good) and study time (a bad).

LEARNING EXERCISE 5.2

Some goods may be neutral goods; that is, your satisfaction doesn't change when you consume more of a neutral good. Redraw Figure 5.5 with the assumption that black olives are a neutral good, not a "bad" good.

Indifference Curves Do Not Intersect

The last property of indifference curves follows from the nonsatiation and transitivity assumptions. These two assumptions imply that *indifference curves cannot intersect.* To show this result, assume that it is *not* true.

Look at the two intersecting indifference curves in Figure 5.6. The two indifference curves intersect at bundle *X*. Bundle *X* contains five oranges and five bananas. Because bundle *X* is on the same indifference curve as bundle *Y*, both bundles provide you with the same level of satisfaction. Bundle *X* is also on another indifference curve with bundle *Z*, so bundle *X* and bundle *Z* offer you the same level of satisfaction. In short, you are indifferent between bundle *Y* and bundle *X*, and you are indifferent between bundle *X* and bundle *Z*. Transitivity implies that you are indifferent between bundle *Y* and bundle *Z*. Now, look at bundles *Y* and *Z*. Bundle *Y* contains seven oranges and four bananas, and bundle *Z* contains six oranges and three bananas. The "more is better" assumption implies that you prefer bundle *Y* to bundle *Z*; that is, bundle *Y* offers you more satisfaction than bundle *Z*. This *contradicts* our previous claim that you are indifferent between bundles *Y* and *Z*. Our assumptions do not allow contradictions, so we cannot allow indifference curves to intersect.

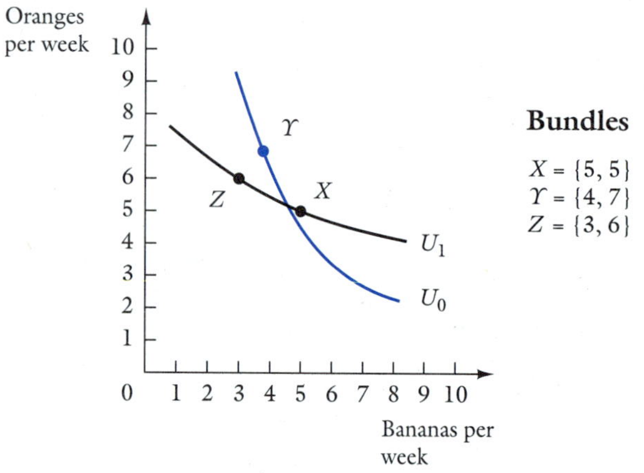

FIGURE 5.6

Indifference Curves Cannot Intersect

Indifference curves that intersect violate the assumption of transitivity. Two intersecting indifference curves imply that you are indifferent between bundles *Y* and *Z*. But the nonsatiation assumption implies that you view bundle *Y* as preferred to bundle *Z*.

Note that the property that indifference curves do not intersect does not imply that they are always symmetric curves. As Figure 5.4 shows, nonsymmetric indifference curves may be drawn that do not intersect.

LEARNING EXERCISE 5.3

Can indifference curves intersect if one good is a "good" and one good is a "bad," as in the pepperoni and black olive example? Using the logic above, show why they cannot intersect.

$$$ Price Theory in Practice

SOME FAMOUS PREFERENCES

- President Bill Clinton likes hamburgers at McDonald's and rock-and-roll music from the 1960s.
- Former President George Bush does not like broccoli. In 1990, President Bush proclaimed, "I'm President, so no more broccoli!" Broccoli farmers were greatly upset by President Bush's preferences.
- Former President Ronald Reagan likes jelly beans. He kept a jar full of jelly beans in the Oval Office for visitors.
- Queen Elizabeth II likes horses; in fact, she is an excellent rider. She likes fruit salad, tea (she is English), carnations, and chocolate mints. She dislikes cats, oysters, garlic, cigars, and tennis.
- The eighteenth president of the United States, Ulysses S. Grant, liked cucumbers and cigars.
- Fashion designer Giorgio Armani prefers eating at La Briciola in Milan, Italy, rather than at home. He prefers vegetables, very little meat, and no sauces. He says, "I hate sauces."
- A cheesedog in paradise? Singer Jimmy Buffett's favorite fast food is a chili cheese hot dog from JB's drive-in in Thomasville, Georgia.

LEARNING EXERCISE 5.4

Do the completeness, nonsatiation, and transitivity assumptions distinguish famous people from everyone else? Why or why not?

MARGINAL RATE OF SUBSTITUTION

The slope of an indifference curve measures the trade-off you choose to make between two goods.[3] As you move down an indifference curve for two "good" commodities—see Figure 5.3—you require more of one good to offset the satisfaction you lose from the good you give up. This trade-off, or substitution, is called the marginal rate of substitution (MRS). Consider, for example, your

[3]Remember, the slope is computed as the "rise" divided by the "run." Algebraically, we write the slope as $\Delta Y/\Delta X$, where Y is the good on the vertical axis, X is the good on the horizontal axis, and Δ is the change operator.

choice between concerts and movies. If concerts attended are plotted on the vertical axis and movies attended are plotted on the horizontal axis, then the MRS measures the trade-off between movies and concerts, written as $MRS_{movies,concerts}$. The **marginal rate of substitution (MRS)** is defined as follows:

Marginal Rate of Substitution (MRS) Measures the trade-off between an additional unit of good X (horizontal axis) and good Y (vertical axis), holding satisfaction constant.

> **$MRS_{x,y}$ is equal to the amount of good Y (vertical axis) that is given up for each unit of good X (horizontal axis) gained to stay indifferent. The marginal rate of substitution is the absolute value of the slope of the indifference curve at a specific point.**

The MRS is more than just a technical term; it is a summary of your willingness to substitute one good for the other, *without giving up any satisfaction*. That is, you are comparing bundles on the same indifference curve. As such, the MRS reflects your preferences for the two goods.

Look at Figure 5.7, which shows an indifference curve for movies and concerts attended each year. As we move down the indifference curve, we attend more movies and fewer concerts. Bundle *A* contains 30 concerts and 15 movies, and bundle *B* contains 15 concerts and 25 movies. If you start at bundle *A* and add 1 movie, you give up 3 concerts to stay on the indifference curve. The $MRS_{movies,concerts}$ equals 3 (3 concerts divided by 1 movie) at bundle *A*. The $MRS_{movies,concerts}$ indicates that you are willing to trade 3 concerts for 1 more movie when you are at bundle *A*. Alternatively, if you are at bundle *B*, you are willing to give up 1 concert for 1 extra movie. The $MRS_{movies,concerts}$ equals 1 at bundle *B*.

As noted above, the marginal rate of substitution equals the absolute value of the slope of the indifference curve evaluated at a specific point. If *Y* denotes

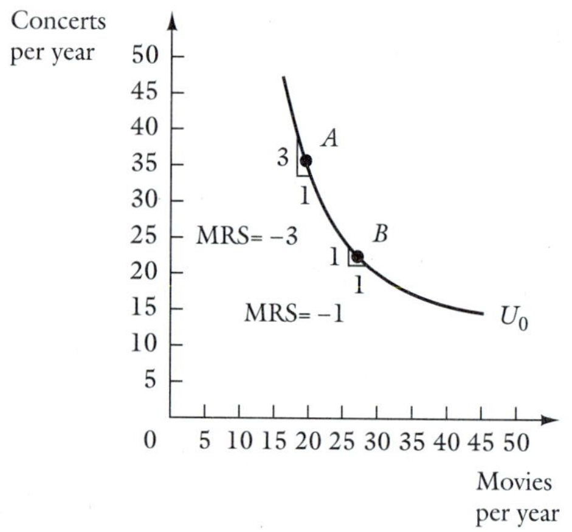

FIGURE 5.7

Marginal Rate of Substitution of Movies for Concerts

The marginal rate of substitution (MRS) of movies for concerts decreases as you move down the indifference curve. In absolute value, the slope of the indifference curve at bundle *B* is less than the slope at bundle *A*.

the good on the vertical axis and X denotes the good on the horizontal axis, then $\Delta Y/\Delta X$ is the slope of the indifference curve. At bundle A in Figure 5.7, the change in the vertical axis equals a loss of 3 concerts for a gain of 1 movie on the horizontal axis. Algebraically, $\Delta Y = -3$ and $\Delta X = 1$. The slope at bundle A, $\Delta Y/\Delta X$, equals $-3/1 = -3$. Because the marginal rate of substitution is the absolute value of the slope, at bundle A, $MRS_{movies,concerts} = 3$, which is the result we found above.

DIMINISHING MARGINAL RATE OF SUBSTITUTION

We can see from Figure 5.7 that the MRS changes between bundle A and bundle B. In effect, your willingness to trade concerts for movies depends on where you are on the indifference curve. When you consume 30 concerts and 15 movies, concerts are relatively abundant. Your willingness to give up 3 concerts for 1 extra movie is partly a reflection of the abundance of concerts in bundle A. Bundle B is different. In bundle B, you consume 15 concerts and 25 movies. Movies are relatively more abundant than concerts in bundle B. Your willingness to give up concerts for an extra movie—$MRS_{movies,concerts}$—is less at bundle B than at bundle A.

Diminishing MRS The property that $MRS_{x,y}$ decreases as the amount of good X increases and the amount of good Y decreases on a given indifference curve.

If your willingness to substitute one good for the other declines along the indifference curve, you have a **diminishing marginal rate of substitution.** In effect, when you have many concerts and few movies in your bundle, such as at bundle A, movies may be thought of as relatively scarce, so the $MRS_{movies,concerts}$ is higher. When movies are relatively abundant compared to concerts in your consumption bundle, such as at bundle B, then your $MRS_{movies,concerts}$ is correspondingly lower. A diminishing marginal rate of substitution is a property of all indifference curves that are convex to the origin. A downward-sloping indifference curve is convex to the origin if it lies on or below a straight line (chord) drawn between any two points on the curve. When we are investigating your preferences for desirable commodities as opposed to "bads," the indifference curves are assumed to be convex to the origin.

LEARNING EXERCISE 5.5

Return to the pizza toppings example shown in Figure 5.5. Redraw these indifference curves to show a diminishing marginal rate of substitution between pepperoni and black olives.

5.3 OTHER TYPES OF INDIFFERENCE CURVES

There are cases when two goods have a particular relationship that affects the shape of indifference curves. We develop two such cases below: perfect complements and perfect substitutes. In addition, we develop the indifference curve relationship for two complex consumption goods. Drawing on the discussion of the full income constraint in Chapter 4, we show that indifference curves exist for bundles containing expenditures on all goods as one consumption item and leisure as the other consumption item. There is really no difference between indifference curves for these complex consumption goods, except that the time constraint in equation (4.7) limits how much leisure time a bundle can contain.

PERFECT COMPLEMENTS

Some goods have a special relationship to each other. Your left shoe and your right shoe are paired together; coffee and coffee cups make a pair, and so do tennis rackets and tennis balls. There is no realistic way to substitute a right shoe for a left shoe. In terms of your preferences, if you have three right shoes and one left shoe, you are no better off than if you have one right shoe and one left shoe. Right shoes and left shoes are an example of two goods that are **perfect complements**—they provide additional satisfaction when they are increased in the same proportion. For instance, two right shoes and two left shoes offer more satisfaction than one right shoe and one left shoe. Additional satisfaction from shoes is achieved when right shoes and left shoes are increased to maintain a one-to-one ratio (1:1). As one might expect, goods that are perfect complements are generally sold as a package—you do not buy them separately.

Perfect Complements Goods that generate right-angled indifference curves.

Figure 5.8 shows two indifference curves for tennis sneakers and shoelaces, two goods that are perfect complements. Laces and tennis sneak-

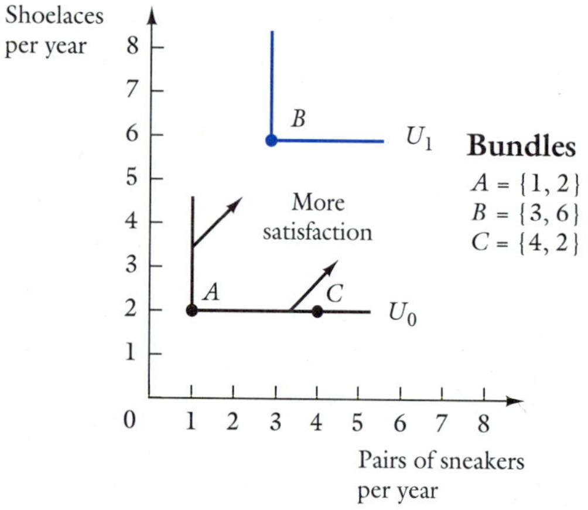

FIGURE 5.8

Indifference Curves for Perfect Complements Form Right-Angled Curves

Two goods that are perfect complements are consumed in fixed proportions. For example, one pair of sneakers requires two shoelaces. The 2:1 ratio is the proportion that must be maintained to increase satisfaction. Bundle *C* contains 2 shoelaces and 4 pairs of sneakers, a ratio of 2:4, or simplified, 1:2. Thus, bundle *C* does not offer you any more satisfaction than bundle *A*.

ers are paired together in consumption. A pair of sneakers requires two laces, so the ratio is one pair of sneakers to two laces (1:2). The first indifference curve, U_0, shows the bundles that you view as indifferent to bundle *A*, which contains one pair of sneakers and two laces. Bundle *C*, for example, offers you the same level of satisfaction as bundle *A*. Bundle *C* contains four pairs of sneakers and two laces. The ratio of pairs of sneakers to laces in bundle *C* is 4:2, which is not the same as the 1:2 ratio found in bundle *A*. The two laces can be matched with one pair of sneakers, leaving the other three sneakers without laces. Without laces, the other shoes are not usable, so bundle *C* does not offer you any more satisfaction than bundle *A*. (It's hard to play tennis in shoes without laces.)

You achieve a higher level of satisfaction at bundle *B* on indifference curve U_1. Bundle *B* contains three pairs of tennis sneakers and six laces. The ratio between pairs of sneakers and laces is 1:2 in bundle *B*, the same as found in bundle *A*. Now, there are enough laces for the three pairs of tennis sneakers; each pair is usable to the consumer. Your satisfaction increases because there are now more goods in bundle *B* than in bundle *A* and the goods are both usable.

PERFECT SUBSTITUTES

Perfect Substitutes Goods that generate straight-line indifference curves.

In contrast to perfect complements, some goods can perform exactly the same function for a consumer. These goods are called **perfect substitutes.** This situation is common for branded products: medium-point pens made by Write Bros. and medium-point pens made by Bic Pen Co. are probably perfect substitutes for most consumers. Tylenol (acetominophen) and its generic counterparts may be perfect substitutes, too. For all practical purposes, goods that are perfect substitutes are considered *identical* by a consumer. For example, both Publix Supermarkets, Inc. and Winn-Dixie Stores, Inc. sell milk under their own brand names in Florida. Many consumers view a gallon of Publix brand milk as identical to a gallon of Winn-Dixie brand milk. For these consumers, the two brands of milk are perfect substitutes.

Two indifference curves for garbage bags made by Hefty and garbage bags made by Glad, two goods that are perfect substitutes, are shown in Figure 5.9 on page 150. Indifference curves for perfect substitutes are straight lines. The marginal rate of substitution, $MRS_{Hefty,Glad}$, is constant along these indifference curves. In Figure 5.9, the marginal rate of substitution is unity ($MRS_{Hefty,Glad} = 1$) because one Hefty garbage bag is equivalent to one Glad garbage bag from the consumer's point of view. Note that this is a special case; the MRS could be constant at a number different from unity in other examples.

Bundles *D* and *E* in Figure 5.9 illustrate the perfect substitute relationship. Bundle *D* contains three Hefty garbage bags and three Glad garbage bags, a total of six garbage bags. Bundle *E* contains one Hefty garbage bag and five Glad garbage bags, a total of six garbage bags, too. Because the consumer views one Hefty bag as equivalent to one Glad bag, the total number of bags in the two bundles is all that is important. The total number of garbage bags is

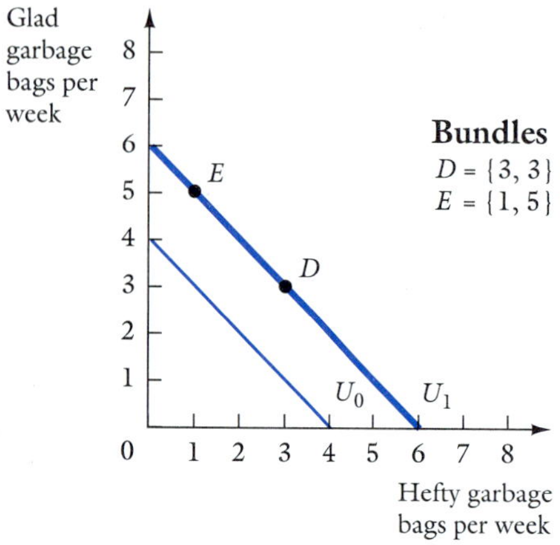

FIGURE 5.9

Indifference Curves for Perfect Substitutes Are Straight Lines

Indifference curves for perfect substitutes are parallel straight lines. The marginal rate of substitution is the same for every bundle on these lines. In this case, the marginal rate of substitution is 1 because you are willing to give up one Glad garbage bag for one Hefty garbage bag at any point on the indifference curve. Note that the marginal rate of substitution does not have to equal unity for perfect substitutes; it must be a constant, but not necessarily 1.

the same in the two bundles, so the consumer is indifferent between bundle *D* and bundle *E*.[4]

Perfect substitutes and perfect complements are two ends of the spectrum of a consumer's preferences. Most goods are neither perfect substitutes nor perfect complements for other goods. Assuming that these goods are "good" goods, their indifference curves lie somewhere between the shapes shown in Figures 5.8 and 5.9. The closer two goods are to being perfect substitutes, the closer their indifference curves will be to a straight line. The marginal rate of substitution for these near-perfect substitutes will not change much over the indifference curve. In contrast, the closer two goods are to being perfect complements, the closer their indifference curves will be to right angles. The marginal rate of substitution for near-perfect complements will change significantly over the indifference curve. One can then judge—although imperfectly—by the appearance of the indifference curves and the marginal rate of substitution whether two goods are likely to be substitutes or complements. In Chapter 6, we develop this thought further to define complements and substitutes by the use of elasticities.

[4]This is true because the $MRS_{Hefty,Glad}$ equals unity. If we had perfect substitutes and the $MRS_{Hefty,Glad}$ was equal to another number, then we would adjust our sum based on the new marginal rate of substitution.

LEARNING EXERCISE 5.6

Draw two indifference curves for your consumption of banana splits, which require bananas and scoops of ice cream to make. Assume that you like two bananas for every three scoops of ice cream on your banana split. Are bananas and scoops of ice cream perfect complements?

INCOME AND LEISURE TRADE-OFFS

We know from your full income constraint that you face a choice between leisure and work time. Additional time spent in leisure reduces work time, which decreases your income and thus your expenditures on goods. The trade-off you face is between income and leisure or, equivalently, expenditure on all goods and leisure. Your choice between expenditure on all goods and leisure is affected by your preference for these two consumption items. According to the nonsatiation assumption, more goods are better, so the more income you have, the more goods you can purchase, and the better off you are. Leisure is a consumption good for most people, too. Holding consumption of other goods equal, more leisure is better than less leisure. An indifference curve can be derived for alternative combinations of expenditure on all goods and leisure, just as it can be derived for any two goods, such as mystery novels and popular magazines. Figure 5.10 shows a typical indifference curve for expenditure on all goods and leisure.

Five bundles are identified on indifference curve U_0 in Figure 5.10. By definition, each of these bundles offers the same satisfaction to the consumer. For example, bundle *A*, which contains 30 hours of leisure and \$800 of expenditures on all goods, is indifferent to bundle *D*, which contains 75 hours of leisure and \$340 of expenditures on all goods. A trade-off is clearly present along this curve, as bundles *B* and *D* indicate. The marginal rate of substitution at bundle *B* is 15, so the consumer is willing to give up \$15 of consumption for 1 extra hour of leisure, holding satisfaction constant. In contrast, at bundle *D*, the marginal rate of substitution is 4.5. At bundle *D*, the consumer is willing to give up only \$4.50 of consumption to obtain an extra hour of leisure, holding satisfaction constant.

A decreasing $MRS_{leisure,consumption}$ follows because the indifference curve in Figure 5.10 is convex to the origin. That the indifference curve is convex may be expected for pragmatic reasons. If there are 112 hours available for work or leisure in a week, then bundle *B* implies that the consumer works 72 hours each week. Working 72 hours is unusual and exhausting, so extra leisure time may have considerable value at this point. In contrast, the consumer works 37 hours in bundle *D*, which is close to the length of a typical work week. It may be expected that leisure is less valuable at bundle *D* than at bundle *A*, a view that is the same as saying the $MRS_{leisure,consumption}$ decreases when more leisure is added to the consumption bundle.

Note that it is unreasonable for the indifference curve in Figure 5.10 to extend too far along the leisure axis. For example, it cannot go beyond 168 hours because the horizontal axis measures leisure time per week, and there are

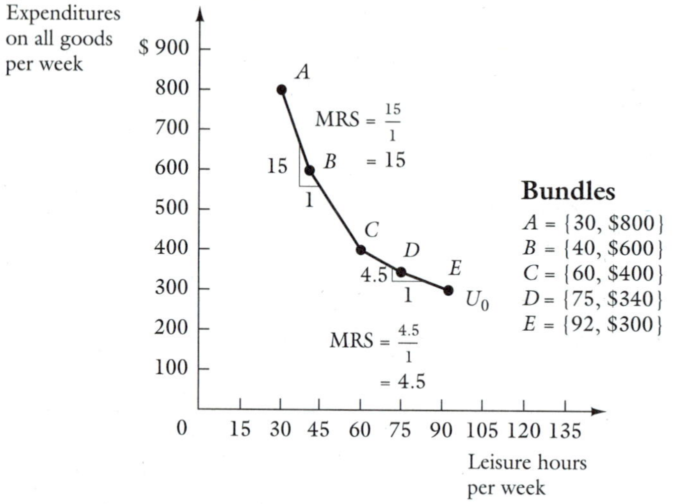

FIGURE 5.10

Indifference Curve Showing the Trade-Off Between Expenditures on All Goods and Leisure

Indifference curves may be drawn for your choice of expenditures on all goods and leisure. Bundles of these two "goods" are composed of hours of leisure and dollar expenditures on goods. At bundle *B*, for example, you are willing to give up $15 of expenditures to receive 1 extra hour of leisure, holding satisfaction constant. On the indifference curve shown, the marginal rate of substitution (MRS) decreases from 15 to 4.5 as you move from bundle *B* to bundle *D*.

only 168 hours in a week. Typically, it will not go beyond 112 hours, because sleeping 8 hours each night leaves only 112 hours available for leisure. The time limit along the leisure time axis is the only difference between an indifference curve for expenditures on all goods and leisure and an indifference curve for two goods—say, mystery novels and popular magazines. It does not matter that expenditures on all goods includes a variety of different goods. If the consumer's preferences are complete, then the different bundles of expenditures and leisure can be ranked. And completeness combined with the nonsatiation assumption generates indifference curves.

5.4 The Problem of Choice

Your preferences show how you rank different bundles in terms of the satisfaction they offer. Your budget constraint shows the bundles that you can actually purchase, given your income and the prices of goods. The problem of choice is to find a bundle that offers the greatest satisfaction without violating your budget constraint. We can restate the problem of choice as follows:

The problem of choice is solved by finding a bundle that offers the greatest level of satisfaction the consumer can purchase with his or her income.

OPTIMAL SOLUTION: THE BUDGET CONSTRAINT

To illustrate how you solve the problem of choice, let's consider your choice of where to eat lunch. Let's assume that sometimes you skip lunch during the week, but most of the time you go out to eat. When you go out, you eat lunch at either McDonald's or Le Bistro, a fancy French restaurant. At McDonald's, you always buy the McLean Deluxe hamburger, large french fries, and a large Coke, all of which costs \$6. At Le Bistro, you order the chef's special, which varies over the week but always costs \$12. Generally speaking, you like the lunches at Le Bistro better than the lunches at McDonald's, but they also cost more at Le Bistro, and you have only a limited budget for lunches. Specifically, your weekly lunch budget is \$48, which implies that your budget constraint is as follows:

$$M = (P_{\text{McDonald's}} \times X_{\text{McDonald's}}) + (P_{\text{Le Bistro}} \times X_{\text{Le Bistro}})$$
$$\$48 = (\$6 \times X_{\text{McDonald's}}) + (\$12 \times X_{\text{Le Bistro}}) \qquad (5.1)$$

or, so that we can graph the constraint easily,

$$X_{\text{Le Bistro}} = 48/12 - (6/12) \times X_{\text{McDonald's}}$$
$$= 4 - (1/2) \times X_{\text{McDonald's}}$$

where $X_{\text{McDonald's}}$ is the number of lunches eaten at McDonald's each week and $X_{\text{Le Bistro}}$ is the number of lunches eaten at Le Bistro each week. The budget line corresponding to equation (5.1) is plotted in Figure 5.11 on page 154. (Note that any fractional lunches on the budget line may be thought of as partial meals: You had french fries and a Coke, for example, and did not purchase a hamburger at McDonald's.)

Note the points where the budget line intersects the vertical and horizontal axes. If you spend all of your lunch budget at Le Bistro (vertical axis), you can afford to eat there four times per week. On the other three days you will have to skip lunch. In contrast, if you spend all of your lunch budget at McDonald's (horizontal axis), you can afford to eat there eight times per week. In effect, on one day, you can eat lunch twice at McDonald's if you want to spend *all* of your weekly lunch budget there. The slope of the budget line is equal to $-P_{\text{McDonald's}}/P_{\text{Le Bistro}}$, which equals $-\frac{1}{2}$ after substituting the actual prices. As we noted in Chapter 4, the slope measures the market-determined trade-off between two consumption goods. The slope here implies that an extra lunch at McDonald's will cost you one-half of a lunch at Le Bistro. Equivalently, the *opportunity cost* of a lunch at Le Bistro is two lunches at McDonald's.

Figure 5.11 also shows three indifference curves for lunches at McDonald's and Le Bistro. Satisfaction is increasing as these curves move away

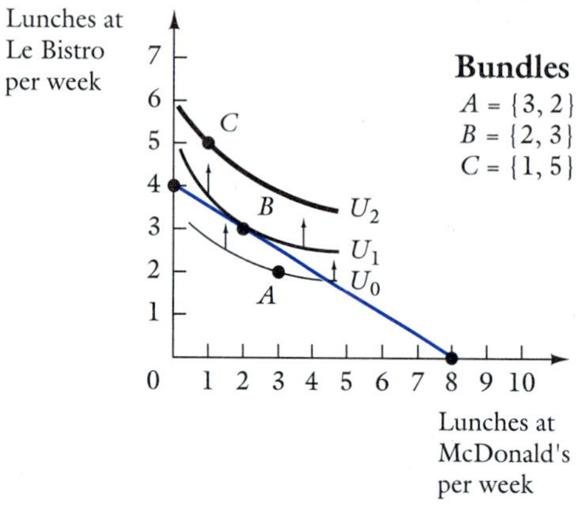

FIGURE 5.11

Solving the Problem of Choice—Where to Eat Lunch?

Bundle *B* is the optimal bundle. Bundle *B* lies on the budget line, so it can be bought, and it offers more satisfaction than any other bundle on the budget line. Bundle *C* cannot be bought with your income. Bundle *A* can be bought, but it offers less satisfaction than bundle *B*.

from the origin. The bundles on indifference curve U_0 offer less satisfaction than the bundles on indifference curve U_1, which offer less satisfaction than the bundles on indifference curve U_2. Note that these indifference curves are relatively flat; that is, the $MRS_{\text{McDonald's, Le Bistro}}$ is a small number that decreases slowly as you eat more lunches at McDonald's. The low $MRS_{\text{McDonald's, Le Bistro}}$ implies that relatively few lunches at Le Bistro will be given up to gain an extra lunch at McDonald's, holding satisfaction constant. The small value of the $MRS_{\text{McDonald's, Le Bistro}}$ indicates a preference for lunches at Le Bistro as compared to lunches at McDonald's. (This result makes sense: most adults prefer a lunch at a French restaurant to a lunch at McDonald's, other factors held constant.)

Three bundles are identified in Figure 5.11. Bundle *A* is on indifference curve U_0 and contains 3 lunches at McDonald's and 2 lunches at Le Bistro. Bundle *A* costs $42 to purchase ($6 times 3, plus $12 times 2). Your lunch budget is $48 per week, so you have money left over at bundle *A*. The money left over is not providing you with satisfaction. By changing your eating habits, you can increase your satisfaction and spend your entire lunch budget. At bundle *B*, you eat 3 lunches at Le Bistro and 2 lunches at McDonald's. This bundle is on indifference curve U_1, which offers more satisfaction than indifference curve U_0. It costs $48 to purchase bundle *B* (2 times $6, plus 3 times $12), so you spend your entire budget at bundle *B*. At bundle *C*, you eat 5 lunches at Le Bistro and 1 lunch at McDonald's. Bundle *C* costs $66. You cannot purchase bundle *C* with your current budget. In fact, you cannot purchase any bundle on indifference curve U_2 because all of these bundles lie above the budget line. The question is, what bundle do you purchase to maximize your satisfaction without violating your budget constraint? Bundle *B* looks like the solution to this problem, but let's take a closer look.

Figure 5.12 offers a close-up view of the budget line, indifference curve U_1, and bundle *B*. If bundle *B* is the solution to the problem of choice, then we should not be able to find another bundle that is both affordable and offers more satisfaction than bundle *B*. Confining our attention to the feasible set—the bundles on and below the budget line—we see that bundle *A* can be purchased, as noted above, but that it lies on an indifference curve offering less satisfaction than indifference curve U_1. Bundle *A* is therefore not a viable alternative to bundle *B*. Bundles that offer more satisfaction than bundle *B* must lie on indifference curves that are above—that is, farther away from the origin than—indifference curve U_1. These indifference curves could not intersect the budget line unless they first crossed indifference curve U_1. But we know that indifference curves cannot cross one another, so there are no affordable bundles that offer a higher level of satisfaction than bundle *B*.

We have backed into the result that bundle *B* is the best choice for you. But how do we find bundle *B* directly?

We find the optimal bundle by looking for a point of tangency between the budget line and an indifference curve.

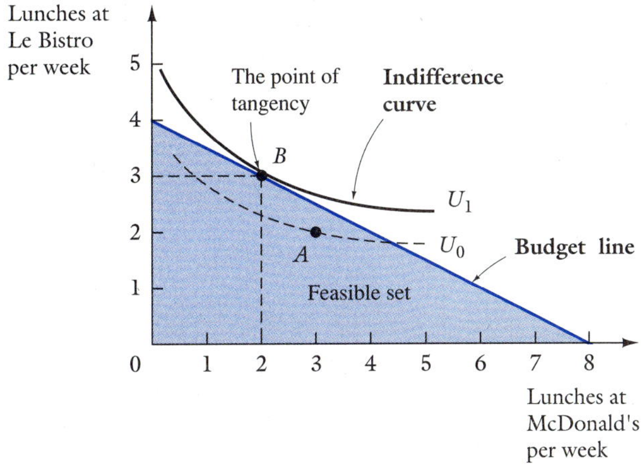

FIGURE 5.12

Solving the Problem of Choice—A Close-up View of the Point of Tangency

Bundle *B* is a point of tangency between the budget line and indifference curve U_1. Bundle *A* is not at a point of tangency. If the solution to the problem of choice lies along the budget line—not at either end—then it will occur at a point of tangency.

At bundle *B*, the budget line—a straight line—is tangent to indifference curve U_1. (Because the budget line is a straight line that intersects indifference curve U_1 at only one point, bundle *B*, it is tangent to indifference curve U_1 at bundle *B*.) Because bundle *B* is a point of tangency between the budget line and indifference curve U_1, we can conclude that there are no other bundles you can purchase with your income, given existing prices, that offer more satisfaction than bundle *B*.

LEARNING EXERCISE 5.7

Can an indifference curve that is convex to the origin have more than one point of tangency with the budget line?

DESCRIBING THE OPTIMAL CONSUMPTION BUNDLE

The point of tangency we have identified in Figure 5.12 represents more than just an algebraic statement. At a point of tangency, the slope of the tangent line equals the slope of the curve. The budget line is the tangent line. The slope of the budget line is $-P_{\text{McDonald's}}/P_{\text{Le Bistro}}$. The slope of the indifference curve is $\Delta X_{\text{Le Bistro}}/\Delta X_{\text{McDonald's}}$, which is a negative number. The marginal rate of substitution ($\text{MRS}_{\text{McDonald's,Le Bistro}}$) equals the absolute value of the slope of an indifference curve. If we multiply the $\text{MRS}_{\text{McDonald's, Le Bistro}}$ by −1, it is a negative number equal to $\Delta X_{\text{Le Bistro}}/\Delta X_{\text{McDonald's}}$. The property of tangency thus implies

$$\frac{\Delta X_{\text{Le Bistro}}}{\Delta X_{\text{McDonald's}}} = -\text{MRS}_{\text{McDonald's, Le Bistro}} = \frac{-P_{\text{McDonald's}}}{P_{\text{Le Bistro}}} \tag{5.2}$$

which simplifies to the following equation after eliminating the minus sign on both sides of equation (5.2):

$$\text{MRS}_{\text{McDonald's, Le Bistro}} = \frac{P_{\text{McDonald's}}}{P_{\text{Le Bistro}}} \tag{5.3}$$

Equation (5.3) states that the problem of choice reduces to finding a bundle *on the budget line* that has a MRS equal to the price ratio. The problem of choice is greatly simplified by this result. First, only bundles on the budget line matter, so the bundles below the budget line can be ignored; and second, the best bundle on the budget line is the one that satisfies equation (5.3). The problem of choice is thus solved by equation (5.3), which is another way of saying that you have reached an optimum when equation (5.3) is satisfied by a bundle on the budget line.

THE MRS AND THE PRICE RATIO

Let's discuss the solution identified by equation (5.3) in more detail. The marginal rate of substitution is the trade-off *you* assign to the goods in a given bundle. The *price ratio* is the trade-off assigned by the marketplace to the goods in the bundle. The optimum defined by equation (5.3) implies the following:

> **Your subjectively determined trade-off equals the market-determined trade-off at the bundle on the budget line that offers the greatest satisfaction.**

To elaborate, look at Figure 5.13, which shows three bundles—*B*, *W*, and *Z*—at which the trade-offs are compared. Bundle *B* satisfies equation (5.3), so it is the bundle that offers the most satisfaction given your limited budget. Other bundles on the budget line, to the left and right of bundle *B*, offer less satisfaction than bundle *B*. Bundle *W*—to the left of bundle *B*—lies on indifference curve U_0, which is below indifference curve U_1. At bundle *W*, the $MRS_{\text{McDonald's, Le Bistro}}$ is greater than the price ratio. We know this result because an imaginary line tangent to indifference curve U_0 at bundle *W* is steeper than the budget line, so its slope (in absolute value) is larger than the slope of the budget line (in absolute value). At bundle *W*, the lunches (maybe fractions of a lunch) you are willing to give up at Le Bistro for an extra lunch at McDonald's, staying on indifference curve U_0, reduce your lunch costs so much that you do not spend all of your lunch budget. Thus, the result that $MRS_{\text{McDonald's, Le Bistro}} > P_{\text{McDonald's}}/P_{\text{Le Bistro}}$ at bundle *W* is telling you that you can rearrange your lunch budget and increase your satisfaction. At bundle *Z*, the inequality between the marginal rate of substitution and the price ratio is

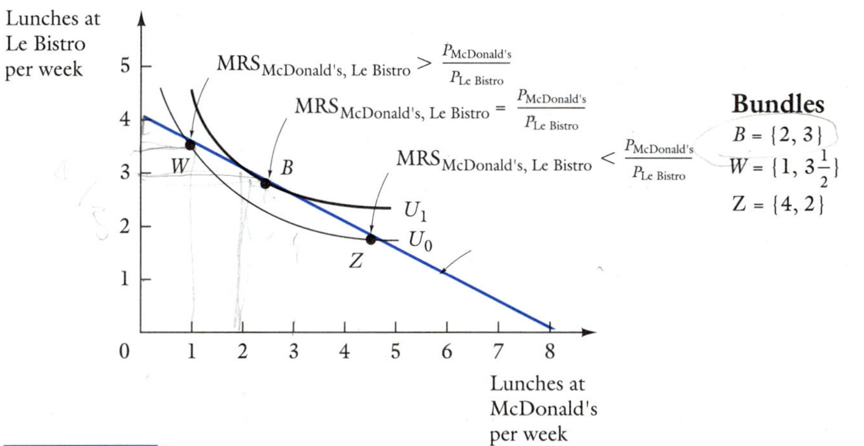

FIGURE 5.13

Comparing the Marginal Rate of Substitution (*MRS*) to the Price Ratio for Bundles on the Budget Line

The marginal rate of substitution is equal to the price ratio at the point of tangency between the budget line and an indifference curve. At bundle W, the $MRS_{\text{McDonald's, Le Bistro}}$ is greater than the price ratio. Here you should eat more lunches at McDonald's and fewer at Le Bistro to increase satisfaction. At bundle *Z*, you should do just the opposite to increase satisfaction.

reversed, but the conclusion is the same; that is, if you rearrange your lunch budget, you can increase your satisfaction.

In Figure 5.13, we can see that you want to move toward bundle *B* when you rearrange your budget. If you are at bundle *W*, you want to increase the number of lunches at McDonald's and decrease the number of lunches at Le Bistro to increase satisfaction. If you are at bundle *Z*, you want to increase the number of lunches at Le Bistro and decrease the number of lunches at McDonald's to increase satisfaction. If you don't have a graph such as the one shown in Figure 5.13, how do you know what to do? Recall that the MRS measures the trade-off between the good on the vertical axis for an extra unit of the good on the horizontal axis, holding satisfaction constant. Because the MRS is referring to an extra unit on the horizontal axis, if the MRS is ***greater than*** the price ratio, you will gain by ***adding*** "extra units" of the good on the horizontal axis. In contrast, if the MRS is less than the price ratio, you gain by ***subtracting*** extra units of the good on the horizontal axis.

The solution identified by equation (5.3) applies to each individual, separately. Equation (5.3) implies that the MRS is equal to the price ratio when an individual maximizes satisfaction subject to a budget constraint. The price ratio applies to, or is constant across, everyone because it is market-determined. For a given bundle, however, the MRS may change across people if each person has a different set of indifference curves; that is, their preferences are different. Strictly speaking, then, bundle *B* in Figure 5.13 is the optimal bundle for one particular person—you—who has a lunch budget of $48 per week and preferences that are given by indifference curves U_0 and U_1.

The individual-specific nature of equation (5.3) implies that we cannot determine whether someone is behaving optimally just from knowing the bundle of goods they purchase. For example, if preferences differ *across* people, two people with the same budget, facing the same prices, may select different bundles. With different preferences, they will have different indifference curves, so both people may satisfy equation (5.3) and be acting optimally even though they select different bundles.

Learning Exercise 5.8

In Figure 5.13, there is a bundle between bundles *W* and *Z* on indifference curve U_0 that has an MRS equal to ½, which is the price ratio. Explain why this is not an optimal bundle even though it satisfies equation (5.3).

INTERIOR VERSUS CORNER SOLUTIONS

The solution we have described above is an interior solution to the problem of choice. An **interior solution** is one in which all commodities are consumed in positive amounts. Called a tangency condition, an interior solution satisfies equation (5.3). For example, bundle *B* in Figure 5.13 is an interior solution to the problem of choosing where to eat lunch during the week because it lies on the budget line at a point where the budget line is tangent to the indifference curve. It is possible that the best bundle in the feasible set may not satisfy the

Interior Solution
A bundle on the budget line at which the MRS equals the price ratio.

Corner Solution
A bundle that lies on one end of the budget line and provides more satisfaction than any other bundle on the budget line.

tangency condition. The best bundle may be one at which the MRS is either greater or less than the price ratio of the two goods. When this occurs we have a **corner solution;** one of the two bundles that lie on the axes is the solution. A corner solution typically occurs when the two goods are perfect—or near-perfect—substitutes. Figure 5.14 illustrates a corner solution for Pepsi and Coca-Cola, which we assume are perfect substitutes.

The indifference curves between Pepsi and Coca-Cola are straight lines. The $MRS_{Coca\text{-}Cola,\ Pepsi}$ equals 2; that is, you are willing to give up 2 ounces of Pepsi to gain 1 extra ounce of Coca-Cola, holding satisfaction constant. The budget line indicates that the price of Pepsi equals the price of Coca-Cola, so the price ratio equals 1. With the $MRS_{Coca\text{-}Cola,\ Pepsi}$ constant, and equal to 2 for all bundles on a given indifference curve (and across indifference curves, for this example), it is not possible for the $MRS_{Coca\text{-}Cola,\ Pepsi}$ to equal the price ratio. As may be seen from Figure 5.14, when you move to higher indifference curves, seeking to maximize satisfaction and remain within your budget, you move to a corner solution. The corner solution implies that you consume only Coca-Cola. In particular, your budget lets you purchase 30 ounces of Coca-Cola each day at the optimal solution. The corner solution occurs on the Coca-Cola axis (horizontal axis) because the $MRS_{Coca\text{-}Cola,\ Pepsi}$ is *greater than* the price ratio. If the $MRS_{Coca\text{-}Cola,\ Pepsi}$ is *less than* the price ratio, then the corner solution occurs on the Pepsi axis (vertical axis), and you consume only Pepsi at the optimum.

Corner solutions have important implications for the behavior of firms in the marketplace. For example, the consumer in Figure 5.14 consumes only Coca-Cola because the $MRS_{Coca\text{-}Cola,\ Pepsi}$ is greater than the price ratio. Now,

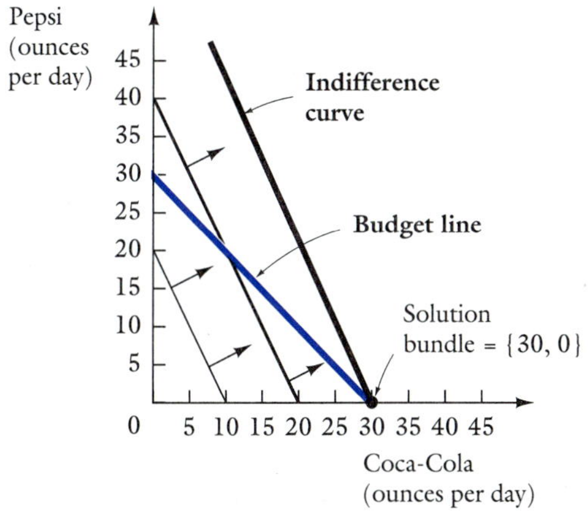

FIGURE 5.14

A Corner Solution for Two Perfect Substitutes: Pepsi and Coca-Cola

A corner solution is expected to be optimal when two goods are perfect substitutes, such as Pepsi and Coca-Cola (for a particular consumer).

if the price of Pepsi is decreased, some consumers are expected to switch from consuming only Coca-Cola to consuming only Pepsi. As a strategy issue, if PepsiCo lowers its price, Coca-Cola will lose sales, possibly a dramatic loss of sales. We would thus expect the Coca-Cola Company (and PepsiCo) to monitor prices closely. Moreover, we would expect these companies to adopt practices and procedures that allow them to change their prices rapidly. For instance, both the Coca-Cola and Pepsi companies provide grocery stores with "hang tags" that slip over the neck of their products. Groceries can change prices quickly by writing new prices on these "hang tags." Without the ability to change prices rapidly, soft-drink companies could not counter the change in the price ratio caused by their competitors.

A corner solution may also occur when indifference curves are not convex to the origin. Figure 5.15 illustrates this situation.

In Figure 5.15, we have placed addicting drugs on the horizontal axis and all other goods on the vertical axis—so we are using the composite goods convention (see Chapter 4). We are not trying to be profound, but it is reasonable to say that at least some individuals who consume addicting drugs eventually become addicts. An addict develops an increasing preference for a drug as the body develops higher and higher levels of tolerance. The result is that the addict has an *increasing* marginal rate of substitution for addicting drugs; the more drugs consumed, the more of all other goods the addict is willing to give up to gain additional drugs. An increasing marginal rate of substitution is a property of *concave* indifference curves, such as U_0 and U_1 in Figure 5.15. Concave indifference curves look like convex indifference curves that have flipped over. The concave shape of the indifference curves leads to a corner

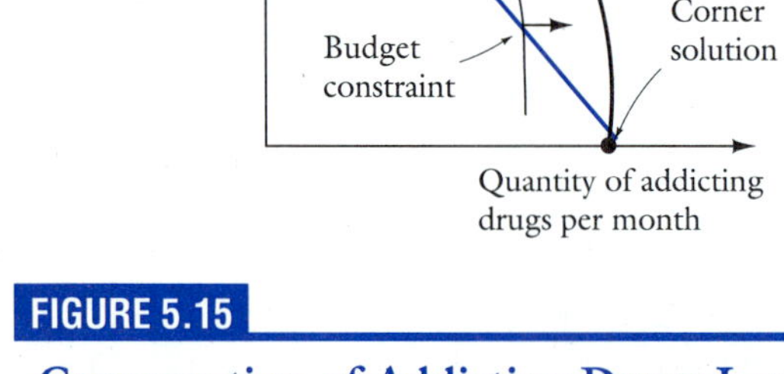

FIGURE 5.15

Consumption of Addicting Drugs Leading to Concave Indifference Curves and a Corner Solution

A corner solution may arise when indifference curves are concave; that is, the marginal rate of substitution is increasing, rather than decreasing, as you increase your consumption of the good on the horizontal axis. The case of addicting drugs is one example of an increasing marginal rate of substitution.

solution at which the addict consumes only drugs—a hard-core user, so to speak. In the world of drug addiction, corner solutions are not uncommon.[5] Hard-core addicts may spend all of their disposable income on drugs and may borrow or steal to consume even more than their budget constraint allows; that is, they may steal to shift their present budget constraint to the right.

LEARNING EXERCISE 5.9

Suppose the $MRS_{\text{Coca-Cola, Pepsi}}$ equals 1 for all bundles on any indifference curve in Figure 5.14. What is the optimal bundle? Is the optimal bundle unique?

OPTIMAL SOLUTION FOR MANY GOODS

We have solved the problem of choice for the case of two goods. What is the solution when there are many goods from which to choose? The results above extend to the case of three, four, five, or any number of goods. For an interior solution, we can say that the consumer is maximizing satisfaction subject to a many-good budget constraint when the following two conditions hold:

1. The bundle selected exhausts the consumer's budget; that is, there is no income left over for the purchase of other goods at the optimal solution.
2. For any two goods in the bundle—say, good X and good Y—the $MRS_{x,y}$ equals the price ratio, P_x/P_y.[6]

The first condition is clear: the consumer must spend the entire budget on the optimal bundle of goods. The second condition applies to *any* combination of two goods in the optimal bundle. In effect, if there are three goods—say, tea, coffee, and milk—then there are three MRS conditions: $MRS_{\text{tea, coffee}} = P_{\text{tea}}/P_{\text{coffee}}$; $MRS_{\text{coffee, milk}} = P_{\text{coffee}}/P_{\text{milk}}$; and $MRS_{\text{milk, tea}} = P_{\text{milk}}/P_{\text{tea}}$. Each of these three conditions must be satisfied for the bundle to be an optimal choice for the consumer. As it so happens, if any two of the three MRS conditions are satisfied, the third condition will also be satisfied. This finding reduces the number of calculations to 1 less than the number of goods.

For choices among many goods, corner solutions are also possible. A corner solution implies that the second condition above may not hold for all of the MRS combinations. It may not be possible to find a bundle at which the MRS for one (or more) combination of two goods equals the price ratio of the two goods. For example, some consumers own CDs, cassette tapes, and LP records—an interior solution—but many have chosen only one of these three types of music media—a corner solution. At a corner solution, the MRS may be either greater or less than the price ratio, so there is no simple condition that confirms whether a corner is the optimal solution.

[5]We do not want to overemphasize concave preferences; they seem to be more of an exception than the rule. They drive an individual to a corner solution, which, in a practical sense, does not appear to be that common.

[6]Technically, when two goods are perfect complements, this second condition does not hold, but an interior solution still arises.

5.5 Income and Leisure Choices

The full income constraint combines your budget and time constraints into one constraint. It defines the trade-off you face between income and leisure or, equivalently, expenditures on all goods and leisure. As we show above, indifference curves can be used to represent your preferences for expenditure on all goods and leisure time. With your preferences for these consumption items and your full income constraint defined, you face another problem of choice, namely, how much leisure to consume. The answer to this question generates a certain amount of work time, which produces a certain amount of income that can be used to purchase goods. As you will see below, the solution to the problem of choice with a full income constraint is not too different in appearance from the solution with a simple budget constraint.

Optimal Solution: Full Income Constraint

The problem of choice with a full income constraint can be solved following the steps used to solve the problem of choice with a simple budget constraint. The steps are defined as follows:

1. **Plot the full income constraint.**
2. **Find the indifference curve that offers the most satisfaction and does not violate the full income constraint.**
3. **Solve either for the point of tangency between the full income constraint and the highest indifference curve or for a corner solution.**

Figure 5.16 shows an interior solution to the problem of choice when you face a full income constraint in a world with no taxes. The full income constraint assumes that you have 112 hours per week available for leisure time. The time you do not spend in leisure is spent working. Your wage rate is \$10 per hour. The indifference curve, U_0, offers the most satisfaction without violating the full income constraint. The optimal solution in Figure 5.16 indicates that you spend 72 hours per week in leisure and 40 hours (112 – 72) in work. At \$10 per hour, you receive \$400 in money income. To repeat, we assume that there are no taxes. Without taxes, the amount you can spend on consumption equals your weekly income; that is, expenditure on all goods equals \$400 per week.

The equilibrium shown in Figure 5.16 equates the marginal rate of substitution between leisure and expenditures to the market-determined trade-off between income and leisure. The market-determined trade-off equals the wage rate, which is the absolute value of the slope of the full income constraint. An extra hour of leisure will cost you \$10 in income or, equivalently, \$10 in expenditures on all goods.

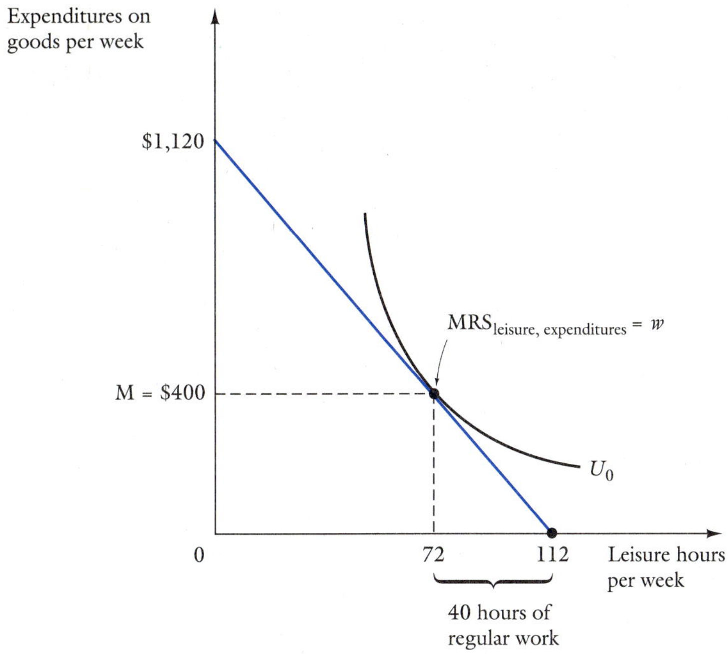

FIGURE 5.16

Solving the Problem of Choice with the Full-Income Constraint

The problem of choice between expenditures on goods and leisure may be solved by finding the bundle for which $MRS_{\text{leisure, expenditures}}$ equals the wage rate, w. Here, the optimal bundel contains 72 hours of leisure per week and $400 of income to purchase goods.

In general, then, $MRS_{\text{leisure,expenditures}} = w$ at an interior solution to the problem of choice with a full income constraint.

Remember that in this example, the marginal rate of substitution is the subjective trade-off between expenditures on goods, or income, and consumption of leisure. You achieve an optimum only when the subjective trade-off is equal to the market-determined, or objective, trade-off. If $MRS_{\text{leisure, expenditures}} \neq w$, then you can rearrange your choice of leisure to increase your satisfaction, or total utility, which makes you better off.

A corner solution may also arise with the full income constraint. At a corner solution, you typically do not work; that is, you specialize in nonmarket activities, which we call leisure. If this case arises, then $MRS_{\text{leisure, expenditures}} > w$ because the wage rate you could earn in market activities is not high enough to induce you to enter the workforce. In many households with only one member in the workforce, corner solutions arise for the nonworking spouse. In other words, it takes the potential of higher wages to move the affected spouse into the workforce, which is a partial explanation for why many women left the household to enter the labor market in the 1970s and 1980s.

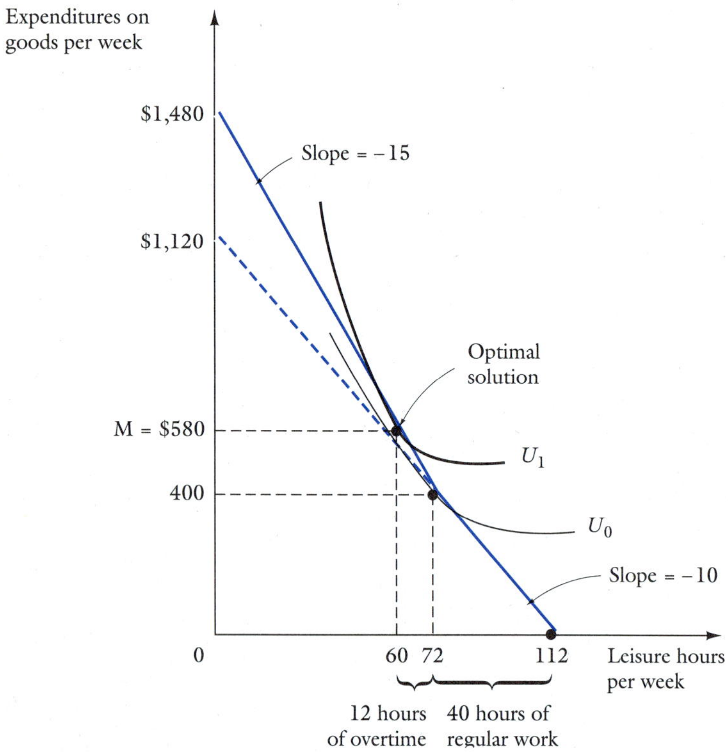

FIGURE 5.17

Effect of Overtime Pay on the Time Spent Working

Overtime pay causes a kink in the full-income constraint at the point at which the overtime pay begins. The slope of the full-income constraint changes at the kink. It is optimal to consume 72 hours per week of leisure—that is, 40 hours of work—before overtime pay is offered. When overtime pay is offered, it is optimal to increase work effort, spending 52 hours per week working and 60 hours per week in leisure activities.

$$$ Price Theory in Practice

OVERTIME PAY

About 60 percent of the workforce has a job in which overtime pay is available.[7] Overtime pay is generally available at 1.5 times regular pay, after 40 hours of work at regular pay. In the example above, regular pay equals $10 per hour, so overtime pay equals $15 per hour. Overtime pay causes a kink in the full income constraint at the point where overtime pay begins. Figure 5.17 illustrates how overtime pay affects the full income constraint described in Figure 5.16.

[7]Ronald G. Ehrenberg and Robert S. Smith, *Modern Labor Economics*, New York, NY: HarperCollins, 1991.

Looking at Figure 5.17, we can see that the kink in the full income constraint occurs when you consume 72 hours of leisure, which is equivalent to 40 hours of work. If you work more, which means that you consume less leisure (move to the left on the leisure axis), you are paid $15 for each additional hour. Overtime pay changes the slope of the full income constraint if you work more than 40 hours. It is apparent that the overtime pay segment of the full income constraint allows you to achieve a higher level of satisfaction. Many of the bundles on indifference curve U_0 now lie below the overtime segment of the full income constraint. The optimal solution here implies that you work a total of 52 hours per week: 40 hours of work at regular pay and 12 hours of work at the overtime wage rate. Your income equals $580 at the optimal solution. Again, assuming no taxes, you have $580 to spend on goods that provide satisfaction.

Learning Exercise 5.10

Some companies offer overtime pay in two parts: You can earn 1.5 times your regular pay for up to 8 hours of overtime and 2 times your regular pay per week for any overtime work beyond 8 hours. Show how the two-part pay scale affects the full income constraint in Figure 5.17.

$$$ Price Theory in Practice

Paying for Study Time

As a student, you are probably not married, but there is a high likelihood that you will be married someday. There is also a good chance that you will raise a family. If this happens, you will face many joys and problems as your children grow older. One problem that you are likely to face is how to encourage your children to study instead of watching television. An economic solution to this problem is to "tie" your child's allowance to the time spent studying. Figure 5.18, on page 166, compares the behavior of a child whose allowance is tied to study time with the case in which the allowance is "untied."

In Figure 5.18, the "tied" approach pays $1 per hour for study time. (The minimum wage laws do not apply here.) Assuming that there are at most 50 hours available for study time or watching TV during the week, the child's full income constraint is a straight line connecting $50 on the vertical axis to 50 hours on the horizontal axis. Indifference curve U_0 is the highest satisfaction the child can achieve without violating the full income constraint. The "tied" solution shows that the child spends 40 hours per week watching TV and 10 hours per week studying. The 10 hours of study time produce an allowance of $10.

It may be expensive for the parents to monitor the "tied" approach. After all, do you really know if children are studying when their workbooks are open and they are looking at each page? They may just be daydreaming. An "untied" approach is the case in which an allowance is given regardless of the time spent studying. An "untied" approach may be motivated by the difficulty of monitoring study time. In Figure 5.18, the "untied" approach pays an allowance of $8 per week. Because the child likes to watch TV and does not like to study, the "untied" approach results in a corner solution, which achieves a higher level of

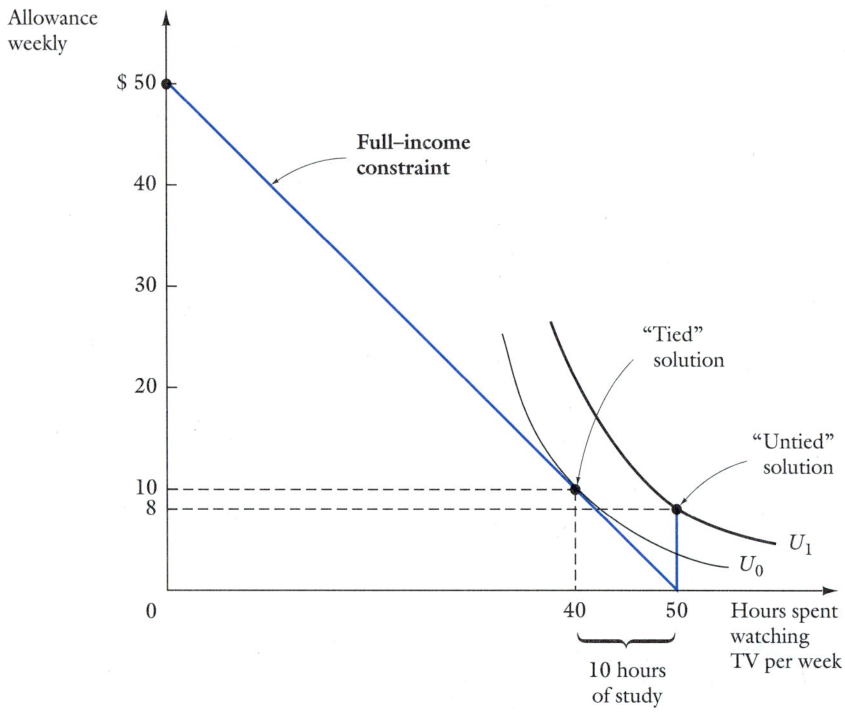

FIGURE 5.18

Comparing an Allowance "Tied" to Study Time with an "Untied" Allowance

Economic constraints affect optimal behavior. When the allowance is "tied" to study time, a child spends 10 hours per week studying and 40 hours per week watching TV. When the allowance is "untied," the child spends 50 hours per week watching TV and 0 hours studying.

satisfaction than the "tied" approach. At the "untied" solution, the child spends 50 hours per week watching TV and zero hours studying. If you were the parent of the child shown in Figure 5.18, which solution would you desire to see—"tied" or "untied?" Economic incentives can have an effect on everyone's behavior, even the behavior of children.

Learning Exercise 5.11

Some parents combine the "tied" and "untied" allowances into one. For example, you might offer \$5 per week as an "untied" allowance and \$1 per week for each hour spent studying. Show how this scheme affects the full income constraint in Figure 5.18.

Chapter Summary

1. All preferences are complete and satisfy nonsatiation and transitivity. Completeness implies that bundles can be ranked. Nonsatiation implies that "more is better" in any bundle. Transitivity implies that comparisons between bundles are consistent; that is, if bundle *A* is preferred to bundle *B* and bundle *B* is preferred to bundle *C*, then bundle *A* is preferred to bundle *C*.
2. An indifference curve is a collection of bundles that offer the same level of satisfaction. A consumer is indifferent between any two bundles on the same indifference curve.
3. The four properties of an indifference curve are: (1) Satisfaction is held constant across bundles on the same indifference curve; (2) Every bundle lies on an indifference curve; (3) An indifference curve for two "good" goods has a negative slope; and (4) Indifference curves do not intersect.
4. The marginal rate of substitution between good X (horizontal axis) and good Y (vertical axis) is the amount of good Y a consumer is willing to give up in exchange for an extra unit of good X, holding satisfaction constant.
5. The problem of choice is to find a bundle that offers the greatest satisfaction but does not violate your budget constraint.
6. You have solved the problem of choice when you find a bundle on the budget line that offers more satisfaction than any other bundle on the budget line. An interior solution requires that the MRS_{X_1,X_2} equal the price ratio, P_1/P_2.
7. An interior solution solves the problem of choice with a bundle that is *not* at either end of the budget line. For an interior solution, the MRS_{X_1,X_2} equals the price ratio, P_1/P_2. At a corner solution, one of the two bundles at either end of the budget line offers the highest level of satisfaction. At the corner solution, the MRS_{X_1,X_2} does not necessarily equal the price ratio, P_1/P_2.
8. With many goods, an interior solution requires that the MRS_{X_i,X_j} equal the price ratio, P_i/P_j, for all two-good combinations, *i* and *j*, in the consumption bundle. In addition, all income must be spent at the optimal solution.
9. Plot the full income constraint and find the bundle of expenditures on goods and leisure lying on the constraint that offers the highest level of satisfaction. At an interior solution, the $MRS_{\text{leisure, expenditures}}$ is equal to the wage rate, *w*.

Trouble Spots

Concept	Reminder
Tastes, or Preferences	Your tastes make you unique. Your tastes differ from the tastes of other people, but we hold tastes constant for each person, separately, over time.

Transitivity	Transitivity applies to all variations of your preferences. We have focused on the "preferred" case: Bundle *A* is preferred to bundle *B* and bundle *B* is preferred to bundle *C*, so bundle *A* is preferred to bundle *C*. The logic applies to the "indifferent" and "less preferred" cases, too.
Indifferences Curve	When two desirable goods are compared, indifference curves have a negative slope. When one good is a "bad," indifference curves have a positive slope.
Diminishing Marginal Rate of Substitution	Diminishing $MRS_{x,y}$ implies that the value of $MRS_{x,y}$ is smaller as you increase good X and decrease good Y, remaining on the same indifference curve. The $MRS_{x,y}$ and the slope of the indifference curve are not interchangable terms. The $MRS_{x,y}$ is the ***absolute value*** of the slope of the indifference curve. Because the slope is negative, a diminishing $MRS_{x,y}$ implies that the slope *increases*. For example, a slope of −8 may increased to −3 as good X is increased along the indifference curve.
The Problem of Choice	When you choose an optimal bundle, you may not "think" that you are maximizing satisfaction subject to a budget constraint as economists suggest, but the theory is still correct if you reveal that you are acting in that manner. By analogy, when an astronomer writes the orbital equation for a planet, the planet may not "think" in terms of the equation—because planets don't think—but the actions of the planet reveal that the equation is correct. Do not believe the solution is wrong because you do not think in the manner specified; all that is required is that you act in the manner specified.
The MRS and the Price Ratio	With X_1 on the horizontal axis and X_2 on the vertical axis, $MRS_{X_1,X_2} = P_1/P_2$ defines an equilibrium bundle. If $MRS_{X_1,X_2} > P_1/P_2$, you increase the amount consumed of X_1, the good on the horizontal axis. If $MRS_{X_1,X_2} < P_1/P_2$, you increase consumption of X_2, the good on the vertical axis. To remember this result, remember that the letter *g* in "greater than" comes before the letter *l* in "less than," so the greater-than inequality refers to increasing X_1, whereas the less-than inequality refers to increasing X_2.

5.6 Review Questions

1. Why are tastes, or preferences, held constant in models of economic behavior?
2. What are the three assumptions that apply to everyone's preferences?
3. What assumption is violated in the following situation: Bundle *A* is less preferred than bundle *B* and bundle *B* is less preferred than bundle *C*, but bundle *C* is more preferred than bundle *A*.

4. Explain why an indifference curve for two desirable goods cannot slope upward.
5. What does "convex to the origin" imply about the trade-off between two goods along the same indifference curve?
6. Explain why two indifference curves cannot intersect.
7. What is the marginal rate of substitution? Is it defined between two indifference curves or along one indifference curve?
8. How do we interpret a diminishing marginal rate of substitution?
9. What is the shape of an indifference curve for two goods that are perfect complements? Perfect substitutes?
10. What is the only conceptual difference between an indifference curve showing the preference trade-off between expenditures on goods and leisure and an indifference curve showing the preference trade-off between two desirable goods?
11. What is the problem of choice? What are the three steps involved in solving the problem of choice?
12. Explain why the solution to the problem of choice can be interpreted as finding a bundle of goods that offers the "biggest bang for your buck."
13. Explain relationship between the MRS and the price ratio for two goods when the consumer is at the optimum solution.
14. Explain how a consumer can prefer one bundle of goods yet actually purchase a different bundle.
15. When does a corner solution to the problem of choice arise? Is a corner solution more likely in the case of perfect substitutes or perfect complements?
16. If the $MRS_{beer,\ wine} > P_{beer}/P_{wine}$, should you buy more beer or more wine?
17. Explain how overtime pay at 2 times the regular rate affects the full income constraint if overtime begins after 40 hours of regular work.
18. Explain how nonlabor income (winning the lottery) makes a corner solution at which only leisure is consumed more likely for a typical individual.

5.7 Price Theory Problems

1. Which of the following statements are consistent with our assumptions about consumer preferences?
   a. I can't decide whether to go to Europe this summer or stay at home.
   b. It's mine. You can't have it. And there is nothing you can do to make me change my mind.
   c. I love hot dogs at football games. If I had my way, I'd never stop eating them.
   d. My American Express card? I never leave home without it.
2. What does an indifference curve that is parallel to the horizontal axis imply about preferences for the good on the horizontal axis? Can the

same statement be made about the good on the vertical axis if the indifference curve is parallel to the vertical axis?

3. What is the relationship between the following goods—are they substitutes, complements, perfect substitutes, or perfect complements? Do these relationships change with the setting they are in, such as in an office or at home?

    a. Knife and fork in a dinner setting
    b. Staples and paper clips
    c. Nickels and quarters
    d. Shoes and socks
    e. Beer and wine
    f. Paint and paint brushes

4. Draw the indifference curve relationship implied by the following statements:

    a. Mazola margarine is just as good as butter.
    b. Grey Poupon mustard—why, of course, I'll have no other.
    c. He wears only Brooks Brothers suits, no others will do.
    d. Ranch-style Doritos are addictive—if you eat one, you must eat another, and another, and another . . .

5. "The more I listen to jazz, the more I like it."

    a. Sketch an indifference curve between jazz (horizontal axis) and your consumption of all other goods (vertical axis).
    b. How does the marginal rate of substitution between jazz and all other goods change when you consume more jazz?

6. "The new pain reliever, Nuprin, really works. One 250-milligram tablet of Nuprin offers the same pain relief as two 500-milligram tablets of Tylenol."

    a. Draw an indifference curve between Nuprin and Tylenol.
    b. If Tylenol is available only in 1,000-milligram tablets, how does your indifference curve change?

7. Sketch the indifference curves for the following:

    a. Assuming that meat and potatoes are desirable goods for a typical person, draw an indifference curve for meat and potatoes.
    b. Draw a vegetarian's indifference curve for meat and potatoes. (Remember that the potato is a vegetable.)
    c. Draw a fruitatarian's indifference curve for meat and potatoes. (Note that a fruitatarian consumes only fruit and water.)

8. Marge likes ginger ale better than Coke and likes Coke better than root beer. She likes water better than Coke and is indifferent between milk and water. What is the relationship between the following goods?

    a. Milk and root beer
    b. Water and ginger ale

9. True or false:

   a. Even though two people may select different bundles of the same two goods, when each person selects an optimal bundle, their marginal rates of substitution between the two goods are equal.
   b. If $MRS_{fish,chips} < P_{fish}/P_{chips}$, you should buy more chips and less fish.

10. Suppose you are standing in the check-out line at a grocery store. You have \$20 to spend on food. You have eight Lean Cuisine dinners and six ears of corn in your grocery cart, a bundle that exhausts your budget and maximizes your satisfaction. Along comes your sister, who tries to convince you to buy more corn and fewer Lean Cuisine dinners. Show the relationship between your optimal choice of food and your sister's optimal choice. What is the relationship between the $MRS_{corn,dinners}$ and the price ratio, $P_{corn}/P_{dinners}$, for your sister at the bundle you plan to purchase?
11. Ali is an advertising executive. She refuses to wear any blouse that is not 100 percent cotton. Her closet is filled with 50 cotton blouses; no cotton-polyester blends can be found there. What is the relationship between the $MRS_{cotton,\ cotton\text{-}polyester}$ and the price ratio, $P_{cotton}/P_{cotton\text{-}polyester}$, at Ali's equilibrium bundle?
12. Suppose that your food and exercise preferences lead you to consume only salads (S) and exercise at a nearby gym club (G). Each salad costs \$4 and each visit to the gym club costs \$8. Given your food and exercise budget, you consume 15 salads and 5 visits to the gym each week. One day the price of salads falls to \$3 and the price of gym visits increases to \$10. Now, you buy 20 salads and 4 gym visits each week.

    a. Draw the old and new budget constraints and show the two optimal bundles. What is your weekly budget for food and exercise?
    b. Is it possible to say whether you are better or worse off after the price changes?

13. Return to the McDonald's and Le Bistro example. Your weekly lunch budget is \$48; the price of a meal at McDonald's is \$6; and the price of a lunch at Le Bistro is \$12. The optimal bundle is two lunches at McDonald's and three lunches at Le Bistro.

    a. Suppose McDonald's offers a deal: "Buy two lunches during the week, get the rest during the same week for half price." Draw the new budget constraint. Has the optimal solution changed because of this offer?
    b. Not to be outdone by McDonald's, Le Bistro announces a new policy: "Buy two lunches, get the third lunch free." Redraw the budget constraint in part (a) above to include the Le Bistro offer. If you don't change your consumption after this offer, what segment of the budget line are you on?

14. Maria is a corporate frequent flyer whose fares are reduced when she reaches certain mileage levels. If she travels 20,000 miles in a year, her fares on subsequent flights are reduced 30 percent. If she travels 50,000 miles, her fares on subsequent flights are reduced 60 percent below the original fares. Assuming her average fare is $250, without any discounts, draw her budget line for air miles traveled and expenditures on all other goods, the composite good.
15. Suppose that you consume food (F) and the composite commodity, all other goods. Your weekly income is $500 and the price of food is $5 per pound consumed.
    a. Draw your budget line and select an optimal bundle.
    b. Now suppose the government offers to subsidize your food purchases with a 50 percent rebate program; that is, they send you a check equal to one-half of your expenditures on food. How does this program affect the budget line? Select a new optimal bundle.
    c. Show on your diagram the *minimum* amount of income supplement you would need to achieve the utility of the subsidy solution, starting from the optimal bundle in part (a) above.
16. Suppose the tax code requires individuals to pay 15 percent income tax on the first $30,000 of adjusted gross income, 28 percent on each additional dollar up to $80,000, 33 percent on each dollar between $80,001 and $125,000, and 28 percent on each dollar above $125,000. Suppose that you earn $150 per hour as an attorney and you bill your clients for 1,200 hours each year.
    a. Assume that the most you can work is 2,000 hours per year. Show your full income constraint before and after taxes.
    b. How much do you pay in taxes at the optimum solution? How much do you spend on goods?

5.8 Writing Exercise

Choose a friend with whom you can spend a day. During the day, keep careful track of your friend's purchases and activities. Make a note of any clear choices that are made (i.e., to study for class versus go to a party). After a few days, follow up with a survey of your friend's preferences. For example, if your friend went to a mystery movie, ask whether he or she prefers a comedy to a mystery movie if the price is the same. Make this sort of comparison for various goods or services that were consumed during the day you kept track of your friend's activities. Write an analysis of your friend's responses and activities. Does your friend's stated preferences match his or her actual behavior?

Appendix 5A
Utility Theory

Utility theory is another way to show the structure of an individual's preferences. The term *utility* is a synonym for satisfaction; more utility means more satisfaction, and less utility means less satisfaction. Our discussion of preferences has ignored the functional relationship that underlies indifference curves. Utility theory develops the equations to show this functional relationship and shows how the analysis can be extended to more than two goods, which is difficult to show using two-dimensional graphs.

Ordinal Versus Cardinal Utility

Ordinal Utility
A summary measure of satisfaction that ranks bundles of goods but does not assign a numerical value to utility.

Cardinal Utility
A summary measure of satisfaction that places a numerical value on the satisfaction received from a bundle of goods.

Indifference curves presume that people can rank each bundle according to their preferences. An analysis that involves only a *ranking* of goods is called an **ordinal utility** analysis. In contrast, an analysis of preferences that uses definite numbers—going beyond a simple ranking—is called **cardinal utility** analysis.

The difference between ordinal and cardinal analysis can be illustrated as follows. Recall that *first*, *second*, and *third* are ordinal numbers; they imply a rank, or order. Of course, numbers such as 1, 2, and 3 are cardinal. We know that 2 is exactly twice as many as 1; 3 is exactly three times as many as 1. A tennis tournament, for example, ranks players as first, second, third, and so on, to determine who plays whom in the initial round of play. With tennis rankings, we cannot say whether the player ranked first is two times (or ten times) better than the player ranked second. We can only comment about their importance relative to one another; that is, the player ranked first is expected to defeat the player ranked second, the player ranked second is expected to defeat the player ranked third, and so on.

The analysis of indifference curves is an ordinal analysis because it does not require that people know how much more or less preferred one bundle is to other bundles. We do not expect, for example, that a consumer can say, "Bundle *A* provides 3.25 times the satisfaction (or utility) of bundle *B*." In fact, there is no attempt to show how much satisfaction a bundle provides or how much satisfaction an indifference curve represents. We have presented the analysis this way because the level of someone's satisfaction does not matter;

we care only about whether satisfaction is increasing, remaining constant, or decreasing across commodity bundles.

Utility theory allows for either cardinal or ordinal analysis. Its first use in the 1800s was as cardinal analysis. The term *util* was developed by economists as the unit of measurement of satisfaction, or utility. Thus, consuming your first chocolate bar of the week might yield 4 utils of satisfaction, the first soda, 6 utils. The use of *utils* in this form implies a quantitative exactness to differences in and levels of utility. As we develop utility theory below, you will see that the cardinal interpretation is not necessary to support our statements. So, if we say that bundle *A* offers 100 more utils than bundle *B*, it is only a pedagogical statement that provides a clearer way to show the ordinal truth that bundle *A* provides more satisfaction than bundle *B*. The results derived in this appendix depend only on the ordinal—not the cardinal—relationship between bundles.

Utility Functions

Utility theory represents preferences using a formula that links utility to the quantity of goods consumed. A utility function is specified by the following relationship:

$$U = u(X_1, X_2, X_3, \ldots X_n), \tag{5A.1}$$

where U is the total utility received for consuming goods $X_1, X_2, X_3, \ldots, X_n$ and u represents the functional relationship between goods consumed and satisfaction. The X's may represent the quantities of any goods consumed over any specific time period. For example, X_1 may represent the number of mystery novels read each month, X_2 may represent the number of popular magazines read each month, X_3 may represent the number of apples eaten each month, and so on. The last good, X_n, also represents a good and signifies that there are many goods that individuals consume; that is, the subscript n may be a very large number.

When we focus on only two goods—for example, mystery novels and popular magazines—our analysis *holds the quantity consumed of all other goods constant.* In effect, we are looking at only a slice of the utility surface, that part that shows how utility is affected by the two goods we are examining. The utility function for two goods may be written as follows:

$$U = u(X_{\text{novels}}, X_{\text{magazines}}; \text{all other goods are held constant}) \tag{5A.2}$$

which is shortened to

$$U = u(X_{\text{novels}}, X_{\text{magazines}}) \tag{5A.3}$$

to conserve space. Remember that individuals consume more than just two goods, so in a discussion with two goods, the quantity consumed of all other goods is held constant.

Utility analysis also generates indifference curves. For any given level of utility, U_0, we can can solve for all of the various combinations of X_{novels} and

$X_{magazines}$ that produce this level of satisfaction. Thus, the utility function approach generates indifference curves that are indistinguishable from those we generated using the more direct indifference curve approach. Basically, when describing preferences, we can start directly with indifference curves (the indifference curve approach) or start with a utility function (the utility theory approach) that generates indifference curves, too. The two approaches are equivalent.

Although the two approaches are equivalent, there is still an important difference between them. If we start with a utility function, we can generate a unique set of indifference curves. *However, if we start with a set of indifference curves, we cannot go back and find a unique utility function.* If we try to go backwards from a set of indifference curves, we will find that there are an infinite number of utility functions that can generate the same set of indifference curves. This result is similar to the problem students face if they find an incomplete reference in a textbook. Suppose you wish to properly cite a quotation, but all you have is the page number—page 20—of the book in which the quote appears. Imagine asking a librarian for the book with page 20. There are literally thousands of books that have a page numbered 20. A given utility function is analogous to having the correct book with the quote on page 20. In contrast, a particular set of indifference curves is analogous to the information "page 20," which gives you thousands of books to choose from. What we are saying is that page 20 is not unique to any particular book, but if you have a given book it will have only one page 20. A given utility function (book) produces a unique set of indifference curves (page 20), but a set of indifference curves (page 20) does not produce a unique utility function (book).

Marginal Utility and the $MRS_{x,y}$

Marginal Utility
Measures the change in total utility generated from consuming an extra unit of one good.

Marginal utility measures how much total utility changes when an extra unit of one good is consumed. If X_1 is increasing by one unit, its effect on total utility is measured by the marginal utility of X_1, denoted MU_{X_1}. Marginal utility is defined specifically for the good that is changing at the quantity level being changed. For example, suppose X_1 represents tuna salad sandwiches, and you are currently consuming three tuna salad sandwiches each week, which gives you 100 utils of satisfaction. If your total utility increases to 120 utils when you consume another tuna salad sandwich, then the marginal utility of the *fourth* tuna salad sandwich is 20 utils (120 – 100). Marginal utility in this example is identified with the fourth unit of the good consumed, which emphasizes that it measures the utility gained from consuming an extra tuna salad sandwich.

Law of Diminishing Marginal Utility
An assumption that marginal utility decreases as you consume more of a good.

The **law of diminishing marginal utility** states that marginal utility decreases as you consume more of a good. Continuing with the tuna salad sandwich discussion, if you consume a fifth tuna salad sandwich, your total utility may increase from 120 utils to 135 utils. The marginal utility of the fifth sandwich is 15 utils (135 – 120). In contrast, the marginal utility of the fourth sandwich was 20 utils. We find that as you consume more sandwiches, your extra satisfaction decreases—from 20 utils down to 15 utils—which is the claim made by the law of diminishing marginal utility. Do not confuse marginal and total utility. The total utility you receive from consuming five sandwiches is higher and will continue to increase as you consume more sandwiches. *Marginal*, not total, utility is decreasing as you consume more sandwiches.

There is an algebraic relationship between marginal utility and the marginal rate of substitution. As noted above, the marginal rate of substitution is the absolute value of the slope of an indifference curve evaluated at a particular bundle. The relationship between marginal utility and marginal rate of substitution can be shown by developing the relationship between marginal utility and the slope of an indifference curve. For the case of two goods, changes in utility may be expressed as follows:

$$\Delta U = \text{MU}_{X_1} \times \Delta X_1 + \text{MU}_{X_2} \times \Delta X_2 \qquad (5A.4)$$

Equation (5A.4) is interpreted as follows. A change in total utility, ΔU, may be caused by changes in X_1 and X_2. When X_1 changes by one unit (ΔX_1), it affects utility by an amount equal to the marginal utility of X_1 (MU_{X_1}) times the amount of the change in X_1. Similarly, when X_2 changes by one unit (ΔX_2), it affects utility by an amount equal to the marginal utility of X_2 (MU_{X_2}) time the amount of the change in X_2. The total change in utility is the sum of the changes caused by X_1 and X_2.

The slope of an indifference curve can be found from equation (5A.4) if ΔU is set equal to zero. We set ΔU equal to zero because utility is not changing along an indifference curve. Equation (5A.4) is now written as $0 = \text{MU}_{X_1} \times \Delta X_1 + \text{MU}_{X_2} \times \Delta X_2$. Subtracting $\text{MU}_{X_2} \times \Delta X_2$ from both sides gives $-\text{MU}_{X_2} \times \Delta X_2 = \text{MU}_{X_1} \times \Delta X_1$. Dividing both sides of this expression by $-\text{MU}_{X_2} \times \Delta X_1$ yields

$$\frac{\Delta X_2}{\Delta X_1} = \frac{-\text{MU}_{X1}}{\text{MU}_{X_2}} \qquad (5A.5)$$

Equation (5A.5) shows that the slope of an indifference curve between two goods equals the ratio of the marginal utilities of the two goods with a minus sign in front.

The marginal rate of substitution is equal to the ratio $\text{MU}_{X_1}/\text{MU}_{X_2}$, dropping the minus sign.

Utility Maximization

The problem of choice is to find a bundle you can purchase with your income that offers the most satisfaction. This statement implies that you are maximizing your satisfaction, or total utility, subject to a budget constraint. Using a utility function, the problem of choice becomes a problem of constrained optimization. Mathematically, the two-good problem is written as follows:

Maximize $U(X_1, X_2)$

Subject to $M = (P_1 \times X_1) + (P_2 \times X_2) \qquad (5A.6)$

Generally, equation (5A.6) states that you try to find the values of X_1 and X_2 that maximize utility without violating the budget constraint. You choose quantities X_1 and X_2 to solve this problem. There are three *explicit* parameters in equation (5A.6): the two prices, P_1 and P_2, and income, M. These parameters are fixed and are not affected by your choices. Your choice of X_1 and X_2 will be a function of these three parameters. Generally, if any of these parameters change, causing the budget constraint to change, your optimal choice will change, too.

There is also an *implicit* parameter: your tastes. Imbedded in the utility function are parameters that define your tastes. The solution to equation (5A.6) will also be a function of these parameters, which we have assumed to be fixed over time.

There are different ways to solve the problem of choice as represented by equation (5A.6). One approach is called the *Lagrange multiplier method*. It is a general approach that can be applied to many problems, not just utility maximization subject to a budget constraint. The *Lagrange multiplier method* is illustrated in the Math Notepad on page 178. Another approach that can be used for fairly simple problems is to substitute the constraint into the objective function (when the constraint is an equality) and to then maximize the objective function. To apply this second approach, we can rearrange the budget constraint to place X_2 on the left-hand side and X_1, P_1, P_2, and M on the right-hand side of the constraint. Then, the equation that defines the budget line [equation (4.3)] is substituted into the utility function in place of X_2. Specifically, the two-good budget line from Chapter 4 can be written as follows:

$$X_2 = M/P_2 - (P_1/P_2) \times X_1 \qquad (5A.7)$$

Using equation (5A.7)—to substitute for X_2 in the utility function—transforms the problem of choice into the following optimization problem:

$$\text{Maximize } U(X_1, M/P_2 - (P_1/P_2) \times X_1) \qquad (5A.8)$$

which you can solve by choosing an appropriate value for X_1. The optimal value of X_2 can be found by substituting the optimal X_1 into equation (5A.7).

The optimal solution is found when you have reached a peak on the utility surface. At the peak, the slope of the utility function is zero; that is, utility is not changing with small changes in X_1. This implies that the following equation holds at the optimal solution:

$$\frac{\Delta U}{\Delta X_1} = \text{MU}_1 - (P_1/P_2) \times \text{MU}_2 = 0 \qquad (5A.9)$$

where MU_1 and MU_2 are the marginal utilities of X_1 and X_2, respectively. (*Note:* Do not confuse MU_1 or MU_2 with income, M. Income and marginal utility are two different terms. Marginal utility is *not* income multiplied by utility.)

The right-hand side of equation (5A.9) may be rearranged to reveal that the solution to the utility maximization problem is the same as the solution found using indifference curves:

$$\text{MRS}_{X_1,X_2} = \frac{\text{MU}_1}{\text{MU}_2} = \frac{P_1}{P_2} \tag{5A.10}$$

where the middle term, MU_1/MU_2, is the absolute value of the slope of an indifference curve, so it is equal to the MRS_{X_1,X_2}.

The optimal solution shown in equation (5A.10) implies that the ratio of the marginal utility of X_1 to the marginal utility of X_2 equals the price ratio. We can gain insight into the meaning of equation (5A.10) by cross-multiplying to rearrange terms:

$$\frac{\text{MU}_1}{P_1} = \frac{\text{MU}_2}{P_2} \tag{5A.11}$$

which says that the extra utility received from the last dollar spent on X_1 must equal the extra utility gained from the last dollar spent on X_2. This condition implies that you cannot rearrange your expenditures on X_1 and X_2 and gain more utility. To understand that this is true, suppose that equation (5A.11) is not satisfied; that is, suppose that $(\text{MU}_1/P_1) > (\text{MU}_2/P_2)$. In this situation, the last dollar spent on X_1 offers more extra utility than the last dollar spent on X_2. Are you at an optimal solution? No. If you rearrange your purchases so that you purchase more X_1 and less X_2, you will gain more satisfaction without violating your budget constraint. It is only when the marginal terms are equal in equation (5A.11) that you cannot rearrange your spending to make yourself better off.

We can generalize equation (5A.11) to the case of many goods. With many goods, utility maximization implies that the extra utility gained from the last dollar spent on each good is equated across all goods. In terms of equation (5A.11), the many goods solution is achieved when $(\text{MU}_1/P_1) = (\text{MU}_2/P_2) = (\text{MU}_3/P_3) = \ldots = (\text{MU}_n/P_n)$ for all n goods. The intuition is the same as the case of two goods. If one of these ratios is not equal to all the others, then it is possible to rearrange your purchases without violating your budget constraint and to increase your utility, or satisfaction.

MATH NOTEPAD

The Lagrangian Utility Maximization Problem

The Lagrangian expression for maximizing utility subject to a budget constraint is

$$£ = U(X_1, X_2) + \lambda(M - P_1X_1 + P_2X_2)$$

Setting the partial derivatives of £ (with respect to X_1, X_2, and λ) equal to zero yields three equations that are the necessary conditions for an interior maximum:

$$\frac{\partial £}{\partial X_1} = \frac{\partial U}{\partial X_1} - \lambda P_1 = 0$$

$$\frac{\partial \pounds}{\partial X_2} = \frac{\partial U}{\partial X_2} - \lambda P_2 = 0$$

$$\frac{\partial \pounds}{\partial \lambda} = M - P_1X_1 - P_2X_2 = 0$$

These three equations can be used to solve for X_1, X_2, and λ, given a specific functional form for U. The solution is equivalent to that implied by equation (5A.10). We can show this by dividing the second partial derivative equation into the first after placing the λP terms on the right-hand side of the equals sign. Note that $\partial U/\partial X_1 = MU_1$ and that $\partial U/\partial X_2 = MU_2$ by definition.

An Example Using the Cobb-Douglas Utility Function

The Cobb-Douglas utility function can be used to illustrate how to solve the problem of choice for an individual. For the case of two goods, the Cobb-Douglas utility function is written as follows:

$$U = X_1^{\alpha}X_2^{\beta} \tag{5A.12}$$

where α and β are positive exponents that may be considered as taste parameters. Different values of α and β indicate that the consumer places different weights on good X_1 versus good X_2, reflecting the consumer's preferences for one good versus the other. The taste parameters, α and β, are assumed to remain constant over time.

Using the Cobb-Douglas utility function, the problem of choice can be written as follows:

$$\text{Maximize } U = X_1^{\alpha}X_2^{\beta}$$

$$\text{Subject to } M = P_1X_1 + P_2X_2 \tag{5A.13}$$

Substituting for X_2 from the budget constraint implies that equation (5A.13) can be written as

$$\text{Maximize } U = X_1^{\alpha}[M/P_2 - (P_1/P_2)X_1]^{\beta} \tag{5A.14}$$

Using the product, power, and chain rules of calculus, the change in utility with respect to X_1 can be written as follows:

$$\frac{\Delta U}{\Delta X_1} = \alpha X_1^{\alpha-1}[M/P_2 - (P_1/P_2)X_1]^{\beta} - \beta(P_1/P_2)X_1^{\alpha}[M/P_2 - (P_1/P_2)X_1]^{\beta-1} = 0 \tag{5A.15}$$

which can be simplified by dividing both terms on the right-hand side by $X_1^{\alpha-1} \times [M/P_2 - (P_1/P_2) \times X_1]^{\beta-1}$ and rearranging:

$$\frac{\Delta U}{\Delta X_1} = \alpha[M/P_2 - (P_1/P_2)X_1] - \beta(P_1/P_2)X_1 = 0 \tag{5A.16}$$

We can use equation (5A.16) to solve for the optimal X_1. Manipulating terms to place X_1 on the left-hand side and the other terms on the right-hand side reveals the optimal solution for X_1:

$$X_1 = \frac{\alpha M}{(\alpha + \beta)\, P_1} \tag{5A.17}$$

Similarly, substituting the solution for X_1 into equation (5A.7) gives the optimal solution for X_2:

$$X_2 = \frac{\beta M}{(\alpha + \beta)\, P_2} \tag{5A.18}$$

The solutions specified by equations (5A.17) and (5A.18) are a general solution to the problem of choice when preferences are represented by a Cobb-Douglas utility function. These equations are demand functions. The quantity demanded of X_1 and X_2 can be determined using these equations; the only elements missing from these equations are parameter values for M, P_1, P_2, α, and β.

Suppose, for example, that we return to the problem of where to eat lunch during the week. Remember that either you eat at McDonald's or Le Bistro or you skip lunch altogether. You also have a preference for lunch at Le Bistro, ceteris paribus, over lunch at McDonald's. Let's say that X_1 represents lunches at McDonald's and X_2 represents lunches at Le Bistro. Your preference for lunches at Le Bistro can be modeled using the taste parameters α and β. Let's say that $\alpha = 1/4$ and $\beta = 3/4$ for purposes of illustration. These values make the indifference curves generated by the Cobb-Douglas utility function "flatter," which is how they are represented in Figures 5.12 and 5.13 to show your preference for lunches at Le Bistro.[8] Your weekly lunch budget, M, is equal to \$48. The price of lunch at McDonald's, P_1, is equal to \$6, and the price of lunch at Le Bistro, P_2, is equal to \$12. Given these values for the parameters, we can use equations (5A.17) and (5A.18) to solve for the quantities demanded of X_1 (lunches at McDonald's) and X_2 (lunches at Le Bistro). Substitution reveals that $X_1 = 2$ and that $X_2 = 3$, which, coincidentally, is the solution we called bundle B in Figures 5.12 and 5.13.

5A.1 Questions and Problems

A1. *True or false?*

a. A diminishing marginal rate of substitution implies that indifference curves have a negative slope.

b. Given a set of indifference curves, we can find a unique utility function that generates these curves.

c. A monotonic transformation of the utility function always changes the marginal rate of substitution.

[8] They are flatter because the exponent on X_2 (i.e., $\beta = 3/4$) exceeds the exponent on X_1 (i.e., $\alpha = 1/4$).

A2. You consume movies (M) and concerts (C) during the year, and you have a Cobb-Douglas utility function for movies and concerts, $U = M^{1/2}C^{1/2}$. (You may need a calculator here.)

a. Draw the indifference curve for combinations of movies and concerts that provide 12 utils of satisfaction.

b. What is the $MRS_{movies,concerts}$ for the bundle containing 16 movies and 9 concerts? What is the $MRS_{movies,concerts}$ for the bundle containing 36 movies and 4 concerts?

A3. Every week you play a low-stakes poker game for fun. As the deal rotates, you and your friends play either five-card draw (D) or seven-card stud (S) poker. The utility you receive from consuming each type of poker game is $U = D + 2S$.

a. Draw the indifference curve for combinations of draw (D) and stud (S) poker that provide 10 utils of satisfaction. Draw another indifference curve for 20 utils of satisfaction.

b. What is the equation that generates the indifference curves in part (a)? What is the $MRS_{draw,stud}$?

c. Are draw and stud poker complements or substitutes? Perfect or imperfect?

A4. In contrast to the case in which work time lowers satisfaction, suppose that you receive utility from both leisure and work time. Your utility function is $U = (T_{leisure})(T_{work})(C)$, where $T_{leisure}$ represents the time spent in leisure, T_{work} represents the time spent in work, and C represents expenditures on goods. The total time available is restricted to 100 hours, so $100 = T_{leisure} + T_{work}$. Find four bundles of leisure, work, and expenditures that generates 1,200,000 utils of satisfaction.

6

How Price and Income Changes Affect Demand

PREVIEW QUESTIONS

When you finish studying this chapter, you should be able to answer the following questions:

How do you derive a demand curve from a price-consumption curve?

How do you derive an Engel curve from an income-consumption curve?

What are income and substitution effects?

What is a Giffen good?

What is the relationship between an ordinary demand curve and a compensated demand curve?

How do you measure changes in the cost of living?

It has often been said, "The cost of living is going up, but it's still worth it." Of course this is true, but truth is of little comfort when we find that tuition costs are increasing or our food and electricity bills are rising faster than our income. The price of medical care, for example, increased by 7.1 percent per year over the past ten years. In contrast, the price of gasoline and other energy costs remained virtually unchanged. Average weekly earnings rose by 2.9 percent over this period. Some prices increased faster than income and some prices did not, so how do we know if we are actually worse off or better off when several prices change? Because you adjust your consumption pattern when relative prices and income change, you may be better off or worse off than before. We need a systematic approach to sort out whether you have benefited from these adjustments.

In this chapter, we will explore how price and income changes influence your choice of an optimal consumption bundle. We will focus on the details of how you adjust to price changes and how your adjustments give rise to a demand curve. We will show how every price change can be decomposed into two parts: a *substitution effect,* caused by a change in relative prices, and an *income effect,* caused by a change in your purchasing power, or real income. In addition, we will show you how to calculate a price index—such as the Consumer Price Index (CPI)—

and explain how this index can be used to measure whether price changes have made consumers better off or worse off over time.

Three examples of how price changes affect choice are highlighted in this chapter: transportation costs and the relative price of juicy oranges, the effects of a luxury tax on boat sales, and the effects of income taxes on work effort.

6.1 Changes in the Relative Price of One Good

How do you react to a change in one price relative to other prices? In general, you purchase more of a good when its relative price falls and less when its relative price rises, holding other variables constant. We have called this the *law of demand*. This relationship can be derived by using indifference curve analysis.

Price-Consumption Curve

Initially, assume that your income, or budget, of $60 per month is allocated to greeting cards and phone calls. The price of greeting cards, P_{cards}, is $2 per card (including postage), and the price of phone calls, P_{calls}, is $1 per minute. Let us assume that income and the price of phone calls are constant while we change the price of greeting cards, P_{cards}. By changing the price of greeting cards, we are changing both the absolute and the relative price when compared to the price of phone calls, $P_{\text{cards}}/P_{\text{calls}}$. This analysis is shown in panel (a) in Figure 6.1.

In panel (a) in Figure 6.1, the price of greeting cards falls from $2 on budget line L_1 to $1.50 on budget line L_2 and then to $1.00 on budget line L_3 while income and the price of phone calls remain constant. Recall from Chapter 4 that we can find the corner points for the budget line (that is, points where the budget line cuts the greeting cards axis and the phone calls axis) by asking how much of a commodity could be purchased at the existing prices if none of the other commodity were purchased. Consider movements on the horizontal axis first. When the price of greeting cards is $2 per card, the amount that can be purchased is determined by dividing $2 into total income, $M = \$60$, which implies that 30 greeting cards can be bought. When the price of greeting cards falls to $1.50, the maximum amount of greeting cards that can be purchased increases to 40; and when the price falls to $1 per card, it increases again to 60 greeting cards. These points are shown along the horizontal axis in panel (a) in Figure 6.1. Thus, even though income does not change, the amount of greeting cards that can be purchased increases. (Remember: $-P_{\text{cards}}/P_{\text{calls}}$ equals the slope of the budget line. The slope becomes flatter or smaller as P_{cards} falls while P_{calls} remains constant.)

Each time the budget line changes, you will select a new optimal bundle. At first it is bundle *A*, then bundle *B*, and then bundle *C*. The curve we create by varying the price continuously and connecting all such optimal points is called the **price-consumption curve.**

Price-Consumption Curve
The set of equilibrium bundles generated from successive changes in the price of one good, holding income and other prices constant.

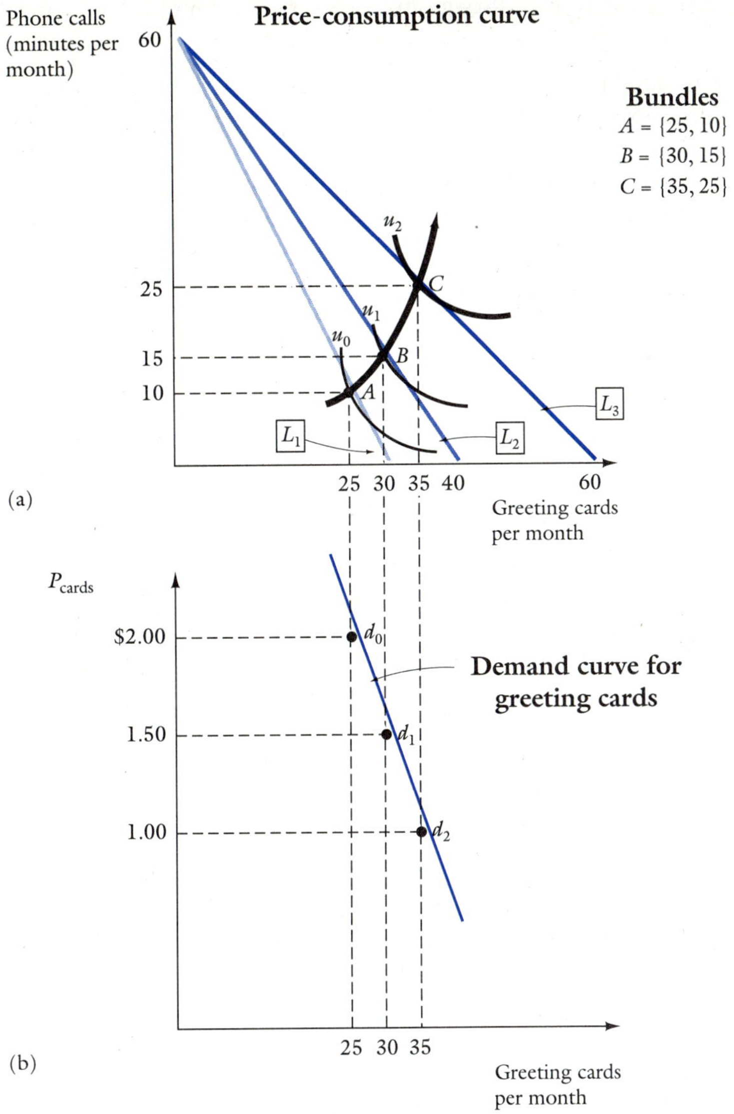

FIGURE 6.1

Deriving a Demand Curve From a Price-Consumption Curve

Reducing the price of greeting cards, with income and the price of phone calls constant, causes the budget line to pivot and generates a set of new equilibrium bundles. The price-consumption curve connects these equilibrium bundles. Price falls from \$2.00 to \$1.50, and then to \$1.00. Optimal consumption of greeting cards increases from 25 to 30 cards per month, and then to 35 cards per month, respectively. In panel (b), a demand curve for greeting cards is derived from the price-consumption curve.

The price-consumption curve is defined as the collection of optimal bundles that result from a change in one price, holding income and other prices constant.

We cannot stress enough that the price-consumption curve is the collection of *optimal* bundles. Thus, the individual has chosen an optimal quantity of each good to consume at every relative price that the price-consumption curve represents. In addition, for the case shown, the price-consumption curve is positively sloped. Generally, though, we cannot say anything a priori about the shape of the price-consumption curve.

DERIVING AN INDIVIDUAL DEMAND CURVE

Equilibrium bundles *A, B,* and *C* in Figure 6.1 implicitly define the relationship between relative prices and the quantity of greeting cards purchased. Panel (b) explicitly illustrates this relationship. The price of greeting cards, P_{cards}, is plotted on the vertical axis, and the quantity of greeting cards is plotted on the horizontal axis. Note that these horizontal axes are the same in the top and bottom panels; they both plot the quantity of greeting cards. Points d_0, d_1, and d_2 are extracted from the optimal bundles along the price-consumption curve. Point d_0, for example, shows that 25 greeting cards are purchased in bundle *A* when the price of greeting cards is \$2 per card and income is \$60. Similarly, point d_1 shows that 30 greeting cards are purchased in bundle *B* when the price of greeting cards is \$1.50 per card. At bundle *C*, 35 greeting cards are purchased when the price is \$1 per card. In panel (b), the curve connecting the three optimal points is a *demand curve* for greeting cards.

The demand curve is drawn with only one parameter of the budget constraint changing: P_{cards}. Income, *M*, and the price of phone calls, P_{calls}, are held constant at every point along the demand curve and at every bundle along the price-consumption curve. By changing P_{cards} alone, we are changing the relative price of greeting cards and phone calls. The relative price is \$2/\$1 on budget line L_1; it is \$1.50/\$1 on budget line L_2; and it is \$1/\$1 on budget line L_3. We see that the relative price of greeting cards has fallen as we move from budget line L_1 to budget line L_2 and then to budget line L_3. In effect, the decline in the relative price of greeting cards causes you to purchase more greeting cards. In our analysis of demand, it is the changing relative price, not just the change in nominal prices, that causes optimal behavior to change.

The shape of the demand curve depicted in Figure 6.1 is a graphic representation of the law of demand. We expect the law of demand to apply for all commodities. It so happens, though, that the law of demand can have exceptions. Our discussion of income and substitution effects below highlights both the standard case, for which the law of demand holds, and the exceptional case, for which the law of demand does not hold.

LEARNING EXERCISE 6.1

Redraw the price-consumption and demand curves in Figure 6.1 under the assumption that income, *M*, equals \$80; the price of greeting cards changes as before; and the equilibrium bundles are $A = \{33, 14\}$, $B = \{40, 20\}$, and $C = \{55, 35\}$.

6.2 Changes in Income

What happens to your consumption when income changes? Let us continue with our example of greeting cards and phone calls. If income doubles, holding the prices of greeting cards (P_{cards}) and phone calls (P_{calls}) constant, you *could* purchase twice as many greeting cards and phone calls as before. An increase in income, *ceteris paribus*, shifts the budget line away from the origin while it remains parallel to the original budget line. Similarly, a decrease in income shifts the budget line toward the origin while it remains parallel to the original line. These shifts are shown in panel (a) of Figure 6.2 on page 189.

The changes in income in Figure 6.2 can be measured in terms of different goods, greeting cards or phone calls, or in dollars. For example, if budget line L_1—the same as in Figure 6.1—represents \$60 of income and greeting cards cost \$2 each (including postage), your income, in terms of greeting cards, is equal to \$60/\$2, or 30 greeting cards. If income increases such that you are on budget line L_2, which represents \$80 in income, we can say that there has been a \$20 increase in income, or an increase in income equal to 10 greeting cards. We can do the same thing for phone calls. Suppose phone calls cost \$1 per minute. On budget line L_1, your income in terms of phone calls is 60 phone calls; on budget line L_2, it is 80 phone calls. Recall that the slope of the budget line is equal to the *negative* of the ratio of the prices of the two commodities. In Figure 6.2, the slope of each budget line is $-P_{\text{cards}}/P_{\text{calls}}$, which equals $-\$2/\$1$. If these prices remain constant, the slope of the budget line will be fixed no matter how income changes.

Now we would like to find out how your consumption changes with successive increases in income, holding prices constant. Let's look again at panel (a) in Figure 6.2. On budget line L_1, your equilibrium is point A, at which you receive the highest level of satisfaction, denoted by indifference curve U_0. The bundle at point A contains 25 greeting cards and 10 one-minute phone calls: $A = \{25, 10\}$. So far, the analysis is the same as in Figure 6.1. At point A, the rate at which you are *willing to* substitute greeting cards for phone calls (the slope of the indifference curve at that point) is equal to the rate at which you are *able to* substitute greeting cards for phone calls in the marketplace (the slope of the budget line), which is −2. Now let income increase to \$80, which is budget line L_2. Budget line L_2 is parallel to budget line L_1 because relative prices have not changed. A new optimum is established when the highest attainable indifference curve, U_1, is tangent to budget line L_2, which occurs at point B. Here we find that bundle B contains 33 greeting cards and 14 phone calls. Let's assume that income is again increased, to \$100, which is budget line L_3. With this income, your optimum is obtained at bundle C. (Note that commodity bundles B and C in Figure 6.2 are *not* the same as commodity bundles B and C in Figure 6.1. In general, commodity bundles on different graphs are different even though the notation is the same.)

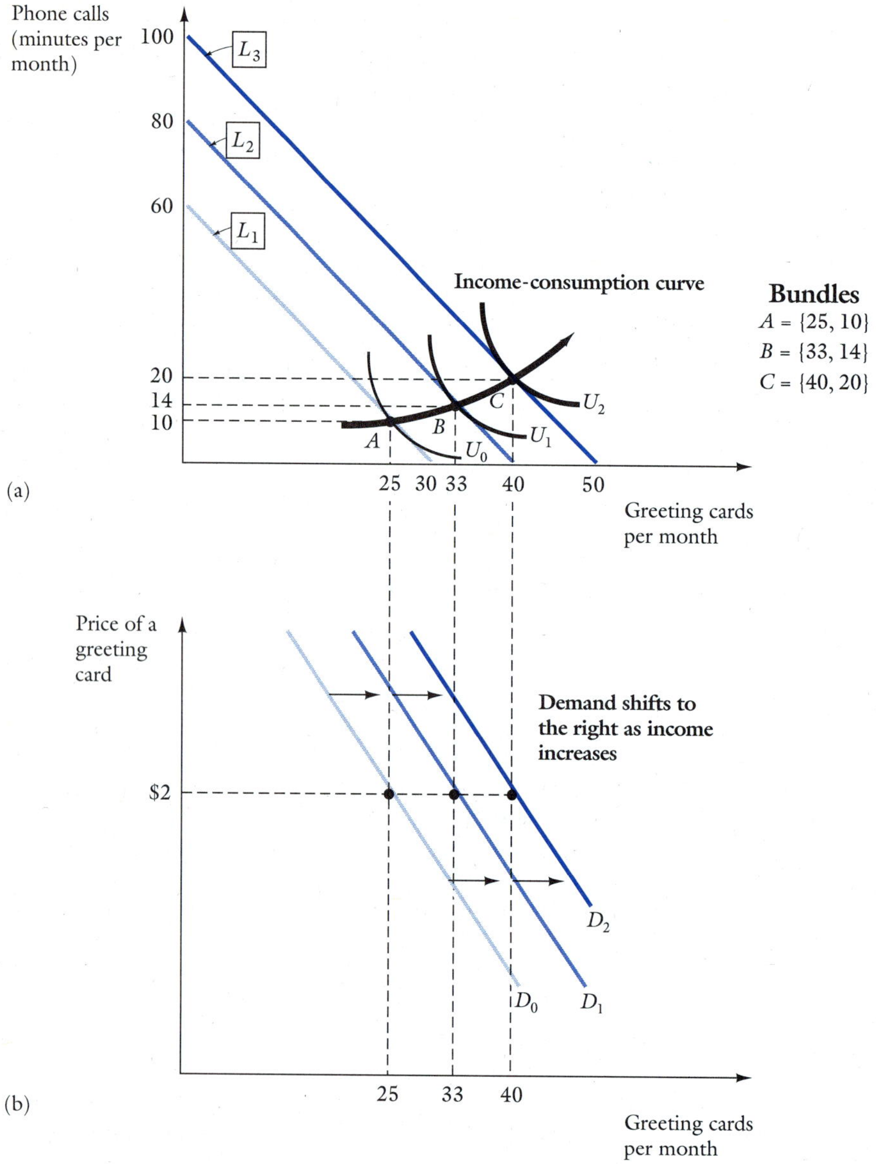

FIGURE 6.2

Drawing the Income-Consumption Curve

Increasing income, holding the prices of greeting cards and phone calls constant, causes parallel shifts of the budget line and generates a set of new equilibrium bundles. The income-consumption curve connects these equilibrium bundles. Optimal consumption of greeting cards increases from 25 to 33 cards per month, and then to 40 cards per month as income increases. In panel (b), changes in income cause the demand curve for greeting cards to shift to the right, holding the price of greeting cards at $2 per card.

Income-Consumption Curve
The set of equilibrium bundles generated from successive increases in income, holding nominal and relative prices constant.

If we connect the three equilibrium points, *A*, *B*, and *C*, we have a curve that is called the **income-consumption curve.** We define an income-consumption curve as follows:

The income-consumption curve is the collection of the equilibrium bundles that you select as income increases continuously, holding nominal and relative prices of the two goods in question constant.

Panel (b) in Figure 6.2 shows how increasing income affects your demand for greeting cards. Increases in income cause the demand for greeting cards to shift to the right, from D_0 to D_1 and then to D_2, holding prices constant. Contrast these changes with those in Figure 6.1. In Figure 6.1, the price of greeting cards is changing, so you move along a *given* demand curve; in this figure, however, income is changing, so the demand curve *shifts*. With an upward-sloping income-consumption curve, the demand for greeting cards shifts to the right. Your optimal consumption path moves along a horizontal line, drawn from the point at which P_{cards} = \$2.

NORMAL AND INFERIOR GOODS

Normal Good
A good for which purchases increase as income increases and decrease as income decreases.

We can classify commodities in terms of how optimal purchases change when income changes. The income-consumption curve in Figure 6.2 portrays a typical response to changes in income. It shows that the quantities consumed of both greeting cards and phone calls increase as income increases. Because this occurs, we call greeting cards and phone calls **normal goods.** We define a normal good as a good that an individual buys more of as his or her income increases and buys less of as his or her income decreases.

Look at Figure 6.3 (page 190). Here we have drawn a graph that shows two budget lines for consumption of good X and good Y (two arbitrary goods). We use goods X and Y here to emphasize that the concept of normal and inferior goods is general and not specific to a particular example, such as phone calls and greeting cards. Income starts out at *M*, with prices equal to P_x and P_y for good X and good Y, respectively. The consumer equilibrium is depicted by point *A*. Income is then doubled to 2*M*. (Note that we could discuss any increase in income; we doubled income just for simplicity.) The budget line shifts outward and parallel to the former budget line. We do not know where the new optimal bundle will be unless we draw additional indifference curves. We can, however, determine the bundles at which goods X and Y are normal goods. If the new optimal bundle lies along the budget line, between points *E* and *F*, then both X and Y are normal goods.[1] We know that if the optimal bundle is along this segment of the budget line, the consumer is purchasing more of both goods, which, by definition, makes both goods normal.

In contrast, if the new equilibrium bundle occurs at a point to the left of the vertical dashed line through point *E*, we know that less of good X and

[1] By convention, if you consume exactly the same amount of a good as income increases, we call the good a normal good.

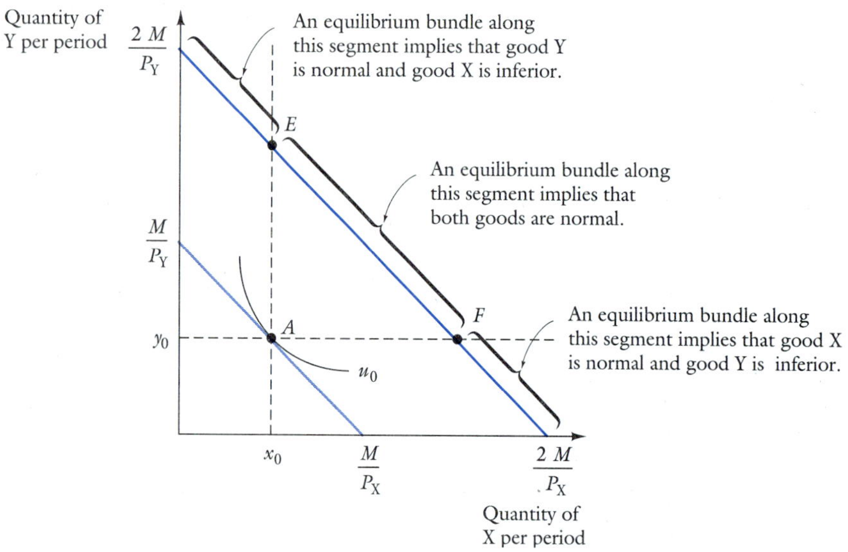

FIGURE 6.3

Normal and Inferior Goods

As income increases, consumption of normal goods increases while consumption of inferior goods decreases. If the new equilibrium bundle lies between bundles *E* and *F*, both goods X and Y are normal. If the new equilibrium bundle lies to the right of bundle *F*, good X is normal and good Y is inferior. If the new equilibrium bundle lies to the left of bundle *E*, good X is inferior and good Y is normal.

more of good Y is purchased after income doubles. In this situation, we say that good X is an **inferior good.** A consumer's purchases of an inferior good move in the opposite direction to changes in income. A consumer will purchase less of an inferior good when his or her income rises and more of an inferior good when his or her income falls. The vinyl shoes you see in discount shoe stores are an inferior good for most people. Leather shoes are a normal good. Generic beer is another example of an inferior good. If the new point of consumer optimum is below the horizontal dashed line through point *F*, less of good Y and more of good X is purchased as income increases, which implies that good X is a normal good and good Y is an inferior good.

Inferior Good A good for which purchases decrease as income increases and increase as income decreases.

The use of the terms *normal* and *inferior* is arbitrary. We are not trying to make any value judgments about particular goods with these terms; they are only descriptive. A normal good for one person may be an appalling commodity for someone else. Moreover, one consumer may find a particular commodity to be an inferior good and another may find it to be a normal good. How you solve the problem of choice when income changes will determine what goods you view as normal and inferior. In general, though, empirical studies of demand find that most goods are normal goods.

LEARNING EXERCISE 6.2

In Figure 6.3, both commodities can be normal goods, but both commodities cannot be inferior goods. Why?

ENGEL CURVES

We can use the income-consumption curve to derive the relationship between the level of income and the optimal quantity purchased of each good. A nineteenth-century German economist, Ernst Engel, was the first to relate expenditures on particular commodities to income. It is fitting, therefore, that curves showing this relationship are named after Engel. Here we use quantities purchased, rather than expenditures, to show the relationship Engel investigated.[2]

Engel Curve
The set of points showing the various quantities of a commodity purchased at different levels of income.

Let's derive the **Engel curve** for greeting cards. We do this by transferring the various combinations of income and the quantity of greeting cards purchased from Figure 6.2 to Figure 6.4. Note that greeting cards are now placed on the vertical axis. This is done to emphasize that greeting card consumption is functionally determined by income, not the other way

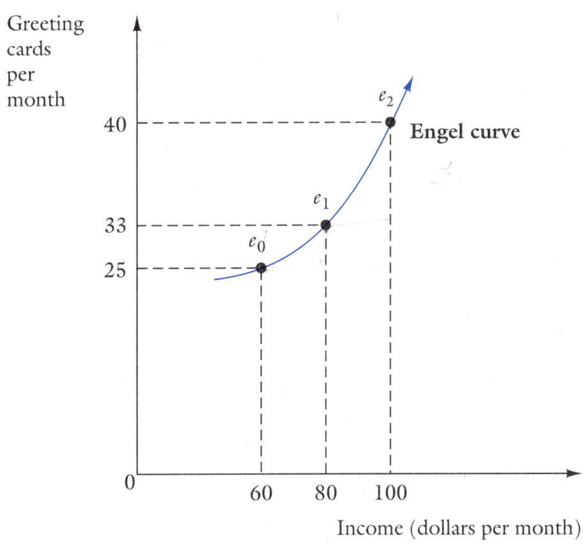

FIGURE 6.4

Deriving an Engel Curve for Greeting Cards

The Engel curve shows the relationship between the quantity of greeting cards purchased and income. The Engel curve for greeting cards has a positive slope because greeting cards are a normal good.

[2] The relationship between the quantity of a good purchased and income is called an *Engel curve;* the relationship between money expenditures on a commodity and income is called an *Engel expenditure curve.*

around. Thus, we find point e_0, representing income of $60 per month and the purchase of 25 greeting cards; point e_1, representing income of $80 per month and the purchase of 33 greeting cards; and point e_2, representing income of $100 per month and the purchase of 40 greeting cards in equilibrium. By connecting these three points, we construct an Engel curve. (Note that the nominal price, P_{cards}, and relative price, $P_{\text{cards}}/P_{\text{calls}}$, of greeting cards to phone calls remains constant throughout the analysis.) The income-consumption curve in Figure 6.2 and the Engel curve in Figure 6.4 appear similar in shape, but they are not identical curves; *the axes on the two diagrams measure different variables.* In Figure 6.2, the vertical axis measures the quantity of phone calls purchased per month; in Figure 6.4, the horizontal axis measures income per month, so these two figures do not capture the same relationships.

Now look at Figure 6.5. We have drawn a hypothetical Engel curve for the commodity X. We find that for increases in income up to income level M_1, the optimal quantity of good X purchased per unit time period also increases. At income level M_1, though, the Engel curve starts to bend downward. For example, above income level M_1, the optimal quantity of greeting cards purchased per unit time period falls as income rises, perhaps because you make more phone calls to your friends. Thus, we say that for incomes

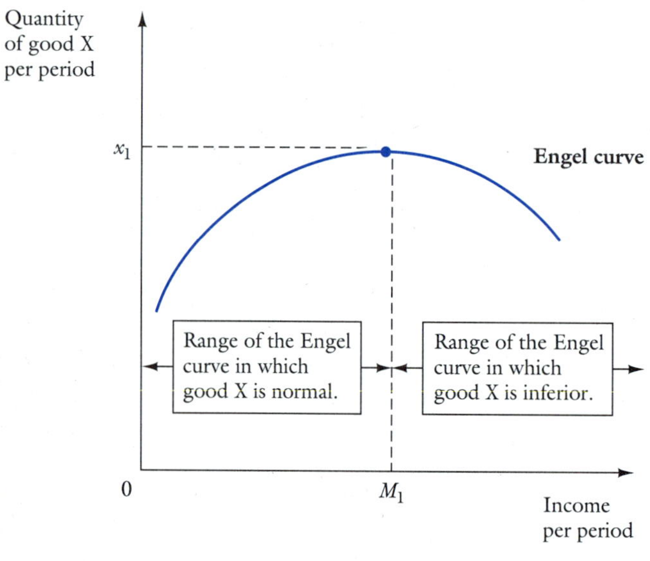

FIGURE 6.5

Normal and Inferior Goods and the Engel Curve

A positively sloped Engel curve shows that good X is normal; a negatively sloped Engel curve shows that good X is inferior. The graph shows that it is possible for a normal good to become inferior as income increases. If income exceeds M_1, then good X is inferior; otherwise, it is normal.

from zero to M_1, good X is *normal;* for incomes above M_1, good X is *inferior*. The slope of the Engel curve can then be used to determine whether a good is normal or inferior. For the range of income at which the Engel curve has a positive slope, the good is normal. If there is a range of income at which the Engel curve has a negative slope, the good is inferior over this range.

It is not hard to find real-world examples of goods whose Engel curves can be represented by the one depicted in Figure 6.5. Consider how an individual would react to a rise in income in terms of purchases of bus transportation. At very low income levels, a motorcycle or automobile is too expensive, so buses are used for travel around town. As income increases, more bus trips are taken, but at some point bus travel become too time-intensive, so individuals substitute a motorcycle or an inexpensive automobile for transportation. At this point, the use of bus transportation declines as income increases. Thus, the backward-bending Engel curve would seem an appropriate description of this behavior.

Alternatively, consider your purchase of seats at a music concert. On a student's limited income, you may tend to purchase the less expensive seats, which are farther away from the performance. As your income increases, say due to an increase in part-time work or to an increase in stipends from the university, you will be able to purchase more of these "distant" seats. For example, your higher income will let you buy seats for a friend who likes the same music as you do. The more distant seats are a normal good over this income range. If for some reason, however, you suddenly have an increase in income of, say, \$2,000 per month (perhaps a monthly gift from a rich uncle or aunt), we can imagine that the amount of distant seats purchased will decrease and that you will purchase the more expensive seats, which are closer to the performance. Again, the backward-bending Engel curve in Figure 6.5 describes this behavior.

On a practical level, the information in Engel curves can be used by market research firms to target goods to particular income groups. Suppose a good, such as a fast-food lunch at Wendy's, has a steep Engel curve for low income levels, say less than \$25,000, but becomes very flat after income increases beyond \$25,000. What does this information tell Wendy's? Certainly, the steeper the Engel curve, the greater the response in quantity demanded when income changes. What should Wendy's do? While it has many choices in how to market its product, it can use this information to target local areas in which to place new stores. The U.S. Census provides information on income levels by locality. By monitoring income growth patterns—that is, finding those areas that have more income growth at lower income levels—Wendy's can place new stores in areas in which they are likely to succeed.

INCOME ELASTICITY OF DEMAND

The effects of income on quantity demanded can also be shown using the concept of elasticity discussed in Chapter 2. Elasticity is the ratio of two percentage changes. The dependent variable—that is, the variable responding to the change—is in the numerator, and the independent variable—that is, the variable causing the change in quantity—is in the denominator. In this instance, income is the independent variable. Making this adjustment, we can write the **income elasticity of demand** as follows:

Income Elasticity of Demand
The responsiveness of quantity demanded to changes in income; the percentage change in the quantity demanded of a good divided by the percentage change in income.

$$\epsilon = \frac{\% \Delta Q_{\text{demand}}}{\% \Delta M} \tag{6.1}$$

where $\% \Delta M$ represents the percentage change in income and the Greek letter epsilon (ϵ) is used to represent the income elasticity of demand.

Unlike the price elasticity of demand, the income elasticity of demand can be either positive or negative. A positive income elasticity of demand ($\epsilon > 0$) implies that the good is normal. A negative income elasticity of demand ($\epsilon < 0$) implies that the good is inferior. Sometimes normal goods are divided into necessities and luxury goods. A **necessity good** is one whose income elasticity is positive but less than 1 ($0 < \epsilon < 1$). A **luxury good** is one whose income elasticity is positive but greater than 1 ($\epsilon > 1$). These terms may not be the most accurate description of the actual goods that are luxuries and necessities.

Necessity Good
A good whose income elasticity is positive but less than 1.

Luxury Good
A good whose income elasticity is greater than 1.

For example, Table 6.1 shows estimates of the income elasticities for various goods. Furniture is a luxury according to this table, although every home and apartment probably has some furniture. Furniture is classified as a luxury because $\epsilon > 1$ implies that consumers spend a greater fraction of their income on furniture as income increases. Let's say that the average price of furniture is $100 per piece and that you buy 10 new pieces per year for a total expenditure of $1,000. According to this table, a 10 percent increase in income is expected to cause a 26 percent increase in the quantity demanded of furniture, so you are expected to buy 2.6 additional pieces of furniture for a total of 12.6 pieces per year. Thus, you are expected to spend $1,260 per year on furniture. If your income is $20,000 per year, a 10 percent increase in income is equal to $2,000. Before the change in income you spent 5 per-

TABLE 6.1

Selected Income Elasticities of Demand

Good or Service	Income Elasticity
Furniture	2.6
Automobiles	2.5
Restaurant meals	1.6
Water	1.4
Movies	0.8
Tobacco	0.6
Electricity	0.2
Margarine	–0.2
Public transportation	–0.4

Source: Hendrick S. Houthakker and Lester Taylor, *Consumer Demand in the United States: Analyses and Predictions*, 2nd edition (Cambridge, MA.: Harvard University Press, 1970.)

cent ($1,000/$20,000) of your annual income on furniture. After the change in income, you spend 5.7 percent ($1,260/$22,000) of your annual income on furniture. In contrast, goods that are necessities, such as food, represent a smaller share of your budget as income increases.

Income changes and the concept of income elasticity can go a long way toward explaining much of the behavior we observe. One of the more common purchases that we observe students make after they have graduated and begun their first job is a new car. Because new cars have an income elasticity greater than 1 (see Table 6.1), we expect a greater share of income to be spent on new cars as income increases. While attending college, many students do not own a car or own a used car, often handed down from their parents. Typically, the first job represents a substantial change in income relative to the budget a student is living on while attending college, so many students respond by purchasing a new car when income increases.

LEARNING EXERCISE 6.3:

If $\epsilon = 1.5$ and income decreases by 8 percent, by what percent does quantity demanded change?

HOW INCOME ELASTICITIES ARE RELATED ACROSS GOODS

The income elasticities of demand are not independent of each other. When we say that furniture has an income elasticity of demand equal to 2.6, we are indirectly commenting on the income elasticities of the other goods that a consumer purchases. The reason is simple: When income changes, the total change is spent on goods, so income spent on one good is income that cannot be spent on another good. If furniture's share of income is increasing as income rises, then the share of income spent on all other goods must be falling. The relationship between the share of income spent on each good and the budget constraint creates a relationship between the income elasticities of all goods. This relationship is depicted in the following equation, which uses furniture and all other goods as an example:

$$1 = (\alpha_{\text{furniture}} \times \epsilon_{\text{furniture}}) + (\alpha_{\text{all other goods}} \times \epsilon_{\text{all other goods}}) \tag{6.2}$$

where the weights are the α terms, which represent the share of income spent on the good—in other words, $\alpha_{\text{furniture}} = P_{\text{furniture}} \times X_{\text{furniture}}/M$, where $X_{\text{furniture}}$ equals the quantity of furniture purchases—and the ϵ terms are the income elasticities of demand. Note that the summation of the α terms must equal 1; that is, by summing to 1, the equation ensures that all income is spent on goods.

Equation (6.2) makes sense in light of our discussion above. If we assume that all income is spent, then on average, a 1 percent increase in income will yield a 1 percent increase in purchases. Some goods, such as furniture, will change by a larger fraction, but this means that all other goods must change by a smaller fraction, so that the total is 1 percent. To get the appropriate total, we weight the income elasticities of demand by the share of income spent on each good. While we illustrate this result for furniture relative to all other goods, we could have just as well written equation (6.2) showing the income elasticity for each good separately. Equation (6.2) would become quite long, but the implication would be the same. The weighted average of income elasticities for all goods consumed must add up to 1.

LEARNING EXERCISE 6.4

Suppose that you spend 50 percent of your income on food, whose income elasticity is .7. What is the income elasticity of all other goods? Can you make any general comments about the relationship between necessities and luxuries from your answer?

6.3 Income and Substitution Effects

When the relative price of a good decreases, you choose a new equilibrium bundle. We can observe the old and new bundles, but underlying the adjustment process are two effects that we cannot readily observe. First, as relative price decreases, one good becomes cheaper, and so you have an incentive to substitute to the relatively cheaper good in your new bundle. Greeting cards

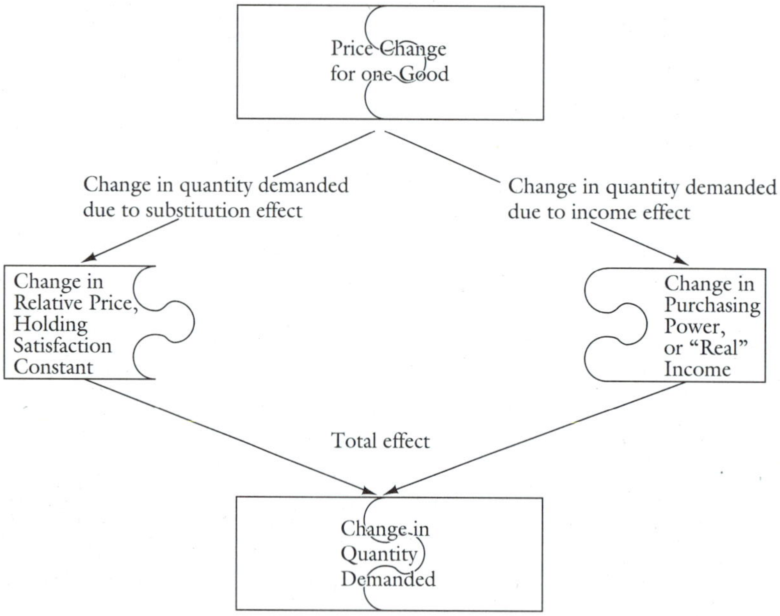

FIGURE 6.6

Income and Substitution Effects

Just like pieces of a puzzle, the change in quantity demanded caused by a price change can be separated into two parts: substitution and income effects. The sum of these parts is the total effect of a price change on quantity demanded.

become relatively cheaper compared to phone calls when the price of greeting cards falls from \$2 to \$1. Second, as price falls, consumers enjoy an increase in the *purchasing power* of their income, or an increase in *real income*. Let's return to the example of greeting cards and phone calls in Figure 6.1, when income is \$60. As the price of greeting cards falls from \$2 to \$1, your income in terms of greeting cards increases to 60 (\$60/\$1) greeting cards from 30 (\$60/\$2) greeting cards. In terms of purchasing power, you are better off when relative price falls because you can purchase the same bundle as before and have money left over to purchase other goods.

The separation of these two effects is shown in Figure 6.6. The depiction of these effects—a change in relative prices and a change in purchasing power, or real income—depends on whether the good whose price is changing is normal or inferior. We will consider both cases below.

INCOME AND SUBSTITUTION EFFECTS: NORMAL GOODS

Look at Figure 6.7 on page 198. Here we show the effect of a decrease in the price of greeting cards on the quantity of greeting cards consumed. Budget line L_1 is the original budget line. On budget line L_1, the price of greeting cards is \$2 per card; the price of phone calls is \$1 per minute, income is \$60; and the initial equilibrium bundle is *A*, in which you consume 25 greeting cards per month. Budget line L_2 is the new budget line. The only difference between budget lines L_2 and L_1 is that the price of greeting cards has decreased to \$1 on budget line L_2. The lower price of greeting cards generates a new optimal bundle, *C*, in which you consume 35 greeting cards per month. Note that at bundle *C* you have increased consumption of greeting cards and also increased satisfaction.

Substitution Effect
When the price of one good changes, the part of the change in quantity demanded that is due to a change in relative prices.

Income Effect
When the price of one good changes, the part of the change in quantity demanded that is due to a change in purchasing power, or real income.

Now we want to try to isolate each of the two effects that occur when the price of greeting cards falls. One effect is due to the substitution of a good that becomes relatively less expensive for a good that becomes relatively more expensive. This is called the **substitution effect.** The substitution effect is always negative; that is, a decrease in relative price causes an increase in quantity demanded or, equivalently, an increase in relative prices causes a decrease in quantity demanded. The other effect is the result of the increase in purchasing power (or real income, M/P_{cards}, expressed in terms of the quantity of greeting cards that can be purchased) that occurs as greeting cards become cheaper and income remains unchanged. This is called the **income effect.** For normal goods, as income goes up, more of the good is purchased. Therefore, the income effect is positive; that is, the relationship between changes in income and in quantity demanded is a direct one. For inferior goods, the income effect is negative; that is, the relationship between changes in income and in quantity demanded is an inverse one. We'll show the income effect for normal goods first and for inferior goods next.

Look at Figure 6.7 again. Moving from bundle *A* to the new optimal bundle *C* increases consumption of greeting cards from 25 to 35 cards per month, a change of 10 cards per month. The change of 10 greeting cards—shown on

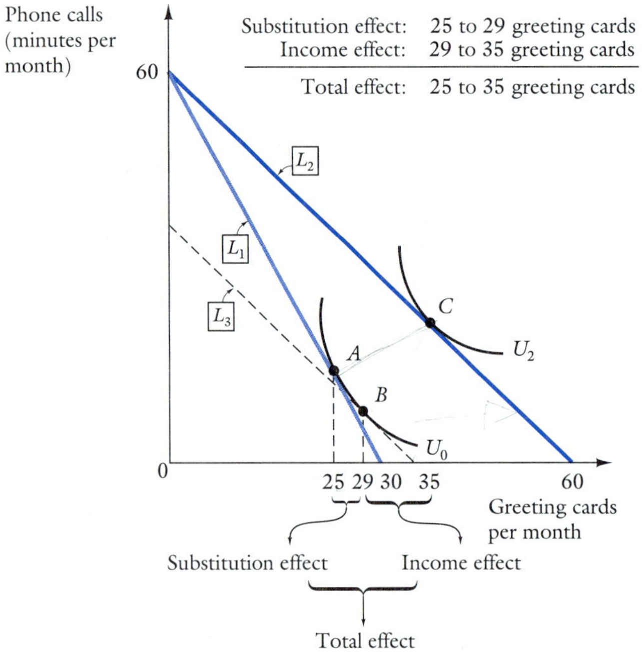

FIGURE 6.7

Income and Substitution Effects for a Normal Good

The decrease in the price of greeting cards causes budget line L_1 to pivot to budget line L_2. You move from the original equilibrium bundle *A* to the new equilibrium bundle *C*. The substitution effect is represented by the move to bundle *B*—the point of tangency between the original indifference curve and budget line L_3—at which point you consume 4 extra greeting cards. The income effect is represented by the move from bundle *B* to bundle *C*, representing the purchase of an additional 6 greeting cards. Greeting cards are a normal good here because the income effect is positive. The total effect is an increase in quantity demanded of 10 greeting cards.

the horizontal axis in Figure 6.7—is the *total effect* of a price change. It includes *both* substitution and income effects.

SEPARATING THE INCOME AND SUBSTITUTION EFFECTS

Now let's separate these two different effects. We can do so by constructing a hypothetical budget line tangent to the original indifference curve, U_0, but parallel to the new budget line, L_2. Denote the hypothetical budget line as budget line L_3. In this exercise, we are changing the relative price, but we are also keeping you at the original level of utility.

Another way of looking at this experiment is to impose an imaginary lump-sum tax. A *lump-sum tax* is a tax of a fixed amount that does not vary over time or with other factors. The purpose of the lump-sum tax is to eliminate the income effect in order to isolate the substitution effect. Thus, relative prices have changed so that the new budget line is L_2, but we impose an imaginary lump-sum tax so that you are just tangent to your original indifference curve, U_0. The size of the imaginary lump-sum tax in Figure 6.7 is the vertical distance between budget line L_3 and budget line L_2 (all times \$1).

The hypothetical budget line is tangent to the original indifference curve at bundle *B*. Because this bundle is on the original indifference curve, it offers the same satisfaction as bundle *A*. The effect of the hypothetical budget line, then, is to change the relative price of greeting cards without changing utility, or satisfaction. Note that the hypothetical budget line represents both lower relative prices *and* lower real income (lower because of the imaginary lump-sum tax). Your optimal response, bundle *B,* may be thought of as the optimal response to a change in relative prices, holding satisfaction constant. Given the convexity of indifference curves, you substitute greeting cards for phone calls when you move from bundle *A* to bundle *B*. We see that on the horizontal axis, bundle *B* contains more greeting cards and fewer phone calls per month than bundle *A*. This is the substitution effect at work. The size of the substitution effect here is 4 greeting cards (29 – 25).

Now if we give back the purchasing power we took away when we moved from budget line L_2 to budget line L_3, you will move from bundle *B* to the new optimal bundle, *C*. That is, we give back the lump-sum tax we just took away in our hypothetical exercise, which effectively increases your real income. Your consumption of greeting cards now changes from 29 greeting cards to 35 greeting cards per month. The increase of 6 greeting cards (35 – 29) per month is called the income effect. Note that the income effect is reflected by a parallel shift in the hypothetical budget line, so that relative prices do not change. Because greeting cards are a normal good, a change in real income leads to an increase in the quantity of greeting cards demanded.

TOTAL EFFECT OF A PRICE CHANGE

The total effect of changing the price of greeting cards is the sum of the substitution and income effects.

The substitution effect is equal to an increase of 4 greeting cards demanded. The income effect is equal to an increase of 6 greeting cards demanded. Thus, the total effect is equal to an increase of 10 greeting cards demanded. Because greeting cards are a normal good, the income and substitution effects move consumption in the same direction; that is, they increase consumption of greeting cards when the price of greeting cards falls. With inferior goods, however, the two effects move consumption in opposite directions, which we show below.

\$\$\$ Price Theory in Practice

TRANSPORTATION COSTS AND THE RELATIVE PRICE OF JUICY ORANGES

Most oranges sold in grocery stores are grown in either Florida or California. You might think, then, that the juiciest, most seedless oranges are for sale in these states. You are likely to be wrong if you think this because the juiciest oranges are hard to find in grocery stores in these states. Instead, these juicy oranges are sold in grocery stores in Chicago, New York, and other large cities that are a long distance away from the orange groves in Florida and California. While this observation may seem like a paradox, it is not; it is an example of the so-called Alchian and Allen theorem.

The Alchian and Allen theorem states that the relative price of a high-quality good compared to a low-quality good falls when a fixed transportation cost is added to both prices.[3] We can illustrate this theorem with our oranges example. Suppose that a high-quality orange—real juicy with few seeds—costs 20 cents and a lower-quality orange—green on the bottom and with many seeds—costs 10 cents in California. The relative price of the high-quality to the low-quality orange is 20 cents/10 cents, or 2, in California. Now, if it costs 5 cents per orange to ship oranges from California to New York, the high-quality orange will cost 25 cents and the low-quality orange will cost 15 cents. The relative price of high-quality to low-quality oranges is now equal to 25 cents/15 cents, or $5/3$. Because $5/3 < 2$, we can say that high-quality oranges are relatively cheaper in New York than they are in California. Because the relative price is lower in New York, we would expect fruit customers in New York to demand a *higher quantity* of high-quality oranges than fruit customers in California, *ceteris paribus.* For this reason, high-quality oranges are relatively scarce in California grocery stores but are more easily found in New York grocery stores.

The Alchian and Allen theorem can apply to many goods, and it does not matter whether the good or the consumer carries the fixed cost. For example, if you are traveling on vacation, you probably expect to dine at relatively more higher-quality restaurants than when you dine out at home. You have incurred the fixed cost of traveling, so dining out at higher-quality restaurants is relatively cheaper. In summary, it does not matter whether the good or the consumer is shipped; a fixed cost of transportation on both high- and low-quality goods increases the quantity demanded of the high-quality good, *ceteris paribus.*

Learning Exercise 6.5

Where would you expect to find higher-quality managers, at home or at offices abroad, if the offices abroad are staffed with managers sent overseas?

INCOME AND SUBSTITUTION EFFECTS: INFERIOR GOODS

When there is an inferior good whose price is changing, the income effect is, by definition, negative: changes in income are associated with changes in the opposite direction in quantity demanded. This can be seen in Figure 6.8, which is like Figure 6.7 except that your preferences make greeting cards an inferior good. We start off at bundle *A*, the same point we started at in Figure 6.7. The

[3] For a more formal treatment of the Alchian and Allen theorem, including all of the caveats, see Eugene Silberberg, *The Structure of Economics—A Mathematical Analysis,* McGraw-Hill: New York, 1990, pp. 384–389.

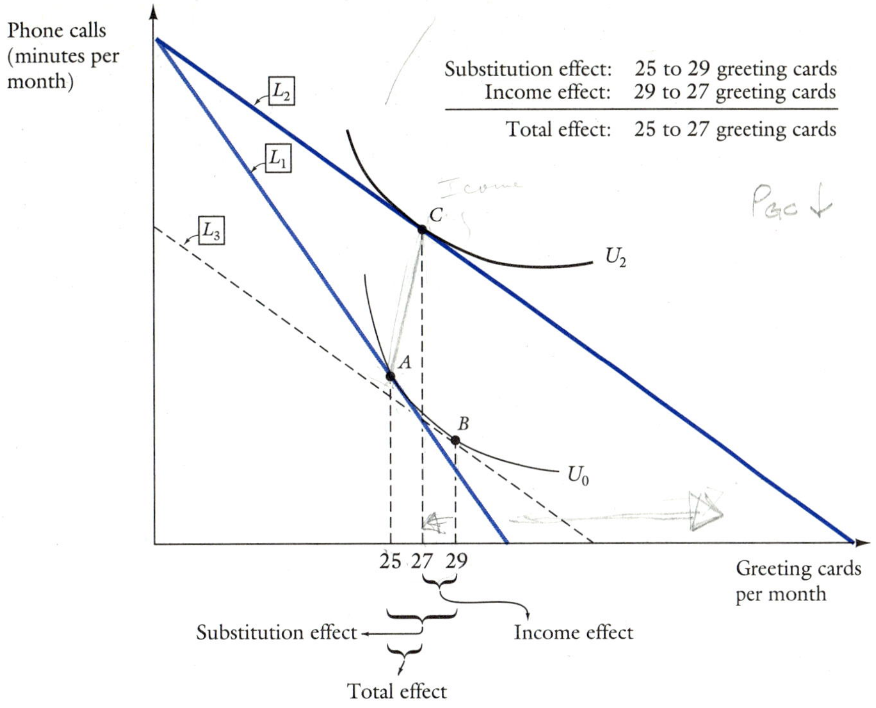

FIGURE 6.8

Income and Substitution Effects for an Inferior Good

The decrease in the price of greeting cards causes budget line L_1 to pivot to budget line L_2. You move from the original equilibrium bundle *A* to the new equilibrium bundle *C*. The substitution effect is represented by the move from bundle *A* to bundle *B* on the original indifference curve, at which point you consume 4 extra greeting cards. The income effect is represented by the move from bundle *B* to bundle *C*, representing a 2-unit decrease in the consumption of greeting cards. Greeting cards are an inferior good here because the income effect is negative. The total effect is an increase in quantity demanded of 2 greeting cards.

price of greeting cards, P_{cards}, declines from \$2 to \$1 per card; the optimal bundle moves from *A* to *C*; and the quantity of greeting cards purchased increases from 25 to 27 per month. Now we wish to sort out how much of the increase in quantity demanded is due to the income effect and how much is due to the substitution effect.

We find the substitution effect by shifting budget line L_2 back until it is just tangent to indifference curve U_0. This is the hypothetical budget line that we discussed in Figure 6.7. It is denoted as budget line L_3 in Figure 6.8. Budget line L_3 is just tangent to the original indifference curve at bundle *B*. We can see that the substitution effect always involves an inverse relationship between price changes and the associated changes in quantity demanded. The substitution effect here is the change in quantity demanded from 25 to 29 greeting cards per month, or 4 greeting cards per month.

Now we can find the income effect. If we shift the hypothetical budget line—budget line L_3—out to a point of tangency with indifference curve U_2, the resulting change in consumption of greeting cards is the income effect. In Figure 6.8, we see that moving budget line L_3 out to budget line L_2 causes you to move from bundle B to bundle C. In this case, consumption of greeting cards decreases from 29 to 27 cards per month. The increase in real income causes you to purchase fewer greeting cards. Thus, the income effect is negative; it is equal to −2 greeting cards per month. In this example, greeting cards are an *inferior* good. The substitution effect, however, is larger (in absolute value) than the negative income effect, and, consequently, the law of demand still holds; that is, you purchase more greeting cards as their relative price declines.

Notice an important point. The substitution effect always generates an inverse relationship between a change in the price of a good and a change in the quantity demanded of that good. The income effect, however, allows for either a positive or negative relationship between changes in your purchasing power, or real income, and changes in the quantity demanded of a good, depending on whether the good is normal or inferior. When P_{cards} falls, the consumer buys more greeting cards due to the substitution effect. The fall in P_{cards}, however, also increases real income. The consumer buys more greeting cards due to the increase in real income if greeting cards are a normal good and fewer greeting cards if greeting cards are an inferior good. Thus, for all normal goods, the income effect of a price change reinforces the substitution effect, whereas for inferior goods, the income effect works against the substitution effect.

Learning Exercise 6.6

Draw a graph, similar to Figure 6.7, that shows the income and substitution effects for a normal good when the price of greeting cards increases.

WHEN THE LAW OF DEMAND FAILS: GIFFEN'S PARADOX

When we have a strongly inferior good, it is conceivable—although unlikely—that the demand for that good will be positively sloped. Such goods are called **Giffen goods.**[4] This situation, illustrated by Figure 6.9, is due to the negative relationship between income and the quantity of goods purchased. Your initial equilibrium bundle is A. Now, assume that the price of good X decreases. Your new equilibrium bundle is C, which contains less X than bundle A contains. To see how this can happen, let's decompose the price change into substitution and income effects. The substitution effect is shown as the move from bundle A to bundle B in Figure 6.9. Here the fall in the relative price of good X increases consumption of good X. The income effect, however, implies that good X is an inferior good. The income effect reduces consumption of good X from x_1 to x_2.

Giffen Good
A good that is so inferior that a fall in price causes quantity demanded to decrease; that is, the demand curve slopes upward.

[4] The Giffen good is named after Sir Robert Giffen (1837–1910), a British statistician and economist.

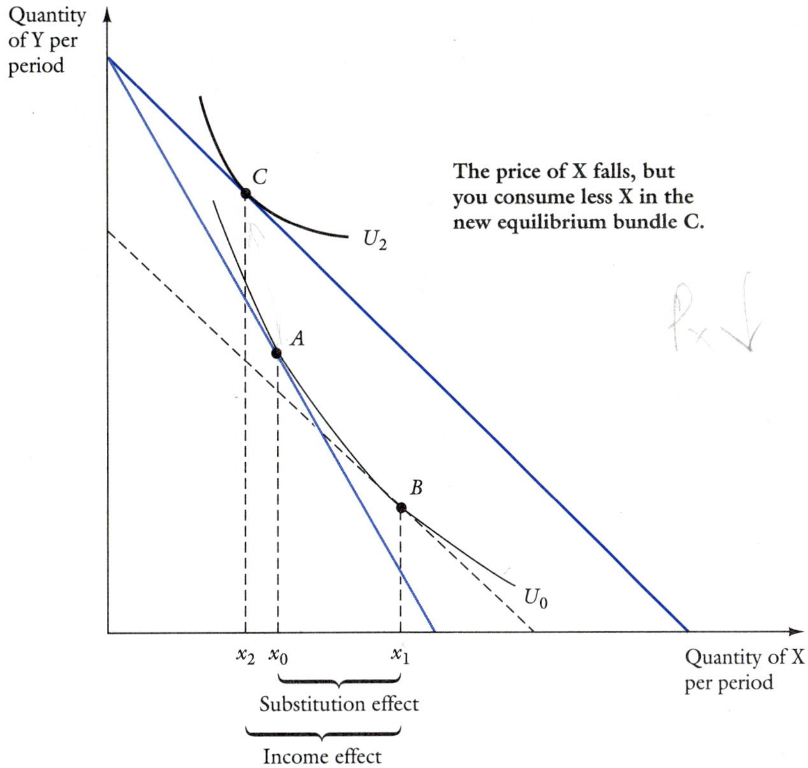

FIGURE 6.9

Income and Substitution Effects for a Giffen Good

For a Giffen good, the income effect more than offsets the substitution effect when price decreases. You consume x_0 of good X at the initial equilibrium bundle *A*. After the price of X falls, you consume x_2 in the new equilibrium bundle *C*. The substitution effect increases consumption of good X to x_1 from x_0. The negative income effect more than offsets the substitution effect, causing consumption of good X to decrease to x_2 from x_1. The total effect is the move from x_0 to x_2.

In this instance, the income effect is larger (in absolute terms) than the substitution effect. In other words, the fall in consumption of good X due to the income effect offsets the increase in consumption due to the substitution effect when the price of good X decreases. The final result is that less of good X is consumed.

If we plot the demand curve for a Giffen good, we find that it has a positive slope, which violates the law of demand. This situation is unlikely because it requires that expenditures on the Giffen good be a large proportion of the consumer's total budget and that the change in the price of this good be a large proportion of its original price. Very few, if any, goods can meet these two requirements. In any case, what may be true for some particular consumers is seldom true for the market as a whole.

CROSS-PRICE ELASTICITY OF DEMAND

As we noted in Chapter 2, the effects of a change in the price of a good on quantity demanded can be measured using the price elasticity of demand. The income and substitution effects decompose this result into its subcomponents for an own-price change. What we have not yet discussed is that we can measure price effects for other goods as well. For example, we can measure the effects of a change in the price of a substitute or complement on quantity demanded of a good. We have defined substitutes and complements in terms of whether a reduction in the price of one good causes a shift leftward or rightward, respectively, in the demand curve of the related good. Alternatively, we can develop this relationship using the elasticity concept.

Specifically, we can use the cross-price elasticity of demand to show how complements and substitutes affect the demand for a good. The **cross-price elasticity of demand** is defined as follows:

Cross-Price Elasticity of Demand
The percentage change in the quantity demanded of good X divided by the percentage change in the price of good Y; to be contrasted with price elasticity of demand.

$$\epsilon_{xy} = \frac{\%\,\Delta Q_x}{\%\,\Delta P_y} \tag{6.3}$$

where the subscripts refer to two commodities, X and Y; Q_x is the quantity demanded of good X; and P_y is the price of good Y. The cross-price elasticity can be used to classify goods as either complements or substitutes:

> **When ϵ_{xy} is positive, the two commodities X and Y are substitutes.**
> **When ϵ_{xy} is negative, the two commodities X and Y are complements.**

We can use the cross-price elasticity of demand to predict changes in quantity demanded. By rearranging equation (6.3), we can express the percentage change in quantity demanded as a function of the percentage change in price and the cross-price elasticity of demand. Specifically, we have $\%\Delta Q_x = \%\Delta P_y \times \epsilon_{xy}$. By multiplying the percentage change in the price of good Y by the cross-price elasticity of demand, we can forecast how the quantity demanded of good X is expected to change.

We must be careful in our treatment of substitutes and complements. Substitution is primarily a matter of relative price. A common example of substitutes involves margarine and butter because they have similar physical characteristics. If butter cost $100 per pound and margarine $1 per pound, however, we would undoubtedly find out empirically that they were not good substitutes in the market. Even if the price of margarine went up by a large percentage, few consumers could be induced to switch to butter. We wouldn't, therefore, call them substitutes at these relative prices. But if butter cost $100 a pound and margarine cost $80 a pound, they would be likely to be substitutes. In short, the degree of substitutability and complementarity are dependent on the relative price of two commodities.

Learning Exercise 6.7

Suppose that the cross-price elasticity between toast and crackers is 2 and the cross-price elasticity between toast and butter is –.4. By how much will the quantities demanded of crackers and butter change when the price of toast increases by 15 percent?

$$$ Price Theory in Practice

Luxury Tax on Boats—Repealed

Sailboat enthusiasts looking to buy their dream boats were discussing something other than crosswinds and crosscurrents from 1991 to 1993. They may not have realized it, but they were talking about the cross-price elasticity of demand.

Congress adopted a luxury goods tax effective January 1, 1991, and partially repealed it in the summer of 1993. The tax levied a 10 percent charge on the purchase of new boats, as well as other luxury goods such as jewelry, furs, expensive new cars, and new aircraft. It was repealed for boats. The tax applied when the price paid for a new boat exceeded $100,000. The price of a typical 45-foot ocean-cruising sailboat, for example, was $285,000. The luxury tax applied to the amount in excess of $100,000, or $185,000 ($285,000 – $100,000). The luxury tax would be $18,500, which is 10 percent of the $185,000 difference. The luxury tax raised the total price of a new sailboat to $303,500, or an increase of about 6.5 percent.

The luxury tax led many prospective boat buyers to consider substitutes for new boats. Used boats that are not too old are close substitutes for new boats. Used boats became relatively cheaper when the tax was in effect.

The effect of the luxury tax on used boat sales between 1991 and 1993 can be measured by the cross-price elasticity of demand between used and new luxury boats. Boating industry officials indicated that boat buyers view new and nearly new luxury boats as almost identical products. In this case, the cross-price elasticity of demand is expected to be fairly high. If we assume that $\epsilon_{\text{used, new}} = 2.5$, then the 6.5 percent increase in the price of new luxury boats increased the quantity demanded of used luxury boats by 16.25 percent. In addition, using an estimated own-price elasticity of new boats of –2.4 implies that the 6.5 percent increase in new boat prices caused a 15.6 percent decrease in the quantity of new luxury boats demanded. Given these results, it is no wonder that boating industry officials and manufacturers of new luxury boats lobbied hard to repeal the new tax.

Learning Exercise 6.8

The luxury tax directly affected new-boat manufacturers, but did any companies in the boating industry benefit from the tax? Who are these companies? Why did they benefit?

Policy Application and Evaluation

The U.S. Postal Service

Issue *Should the U.S. Postal Service be protected from private competition?*

Background

The U.S. Postal Service delivers over 160 billion pieces of mail annually, with revenues of approximately $42 billion. By law, known as the Private Express Statutes, it is granted an exclusive right to deliver first-class mail—letters and postcards—but this right does not extend to all forms of mail. The Postal Service delivers less than 6 percent of fourth-class mail, which includes parcels and books, and has watched its 100 percent share of the overnight express mail market drop to less than 12 percent today. Approximately 88 percent of the mail delivered by the Postal Service originates from businesses, with the other 12 percent coming from households. Recently, its relatively exclusive control of the third-class mail market—mainly businesses mailing advertising materials, brochures, and fliers—has come under attack. Publishers Express, Inc., a subsidiary of Time-Warner, Inc., has started to deliver magazines and mail-order catalogs in six major cities. In addition, Alternative Postal Delivery, Inc., offers a similar service in 31 cities, serving 4.5 million households.

According to the Postal Reorganization Act of 1970, Postal Service customers have some input into the process of determining postal rates. The Postal Service must file any rate changes with the Postal Service Commission, an independent agency, which holds public hearings in order to form an opinion about the proposed changes. Even with an independent agency, postal rates increased significantly in the 1980s, with substantial rate increases occurring after 1988.

The Case for a Free Market

The basic case for a freer market in mail delivery states that with competition, postal rates would not continue to increase so fast and that customers would receive better service. First-class mail delivery is protected from entry by the Private Express Statutes. The Postal Service has increased the rate charged for first-class mail delivery an average of 6.5 percent per year since 1971. In contrast, consumer prices, as measured by the Consumer Price Index, have increased at a rate of 4.9 percent over this period. Importantly, the rates charged on all classes of mail have not increased as fast, particularly for fourth-class mail. In fourth-class mail delivery—large boxes and packages—the Postal Service faces stiff competition from such firms as United Parcel Service and Roadway Express. While the volume of fourth-class mail delivery has grown significantly for private firms over the past twenty years, it has declined by 29.5 percent for the Postal Service. In effect, the Postal Service has not been able to compete with private firms in the areas in which competition is allowed.

The effects of the Private Express Statutes on the mail delivery market can be seen from estimates of own- and cross-price elasticities of demand. Economist George S. Tolley of the University of Chicago generated elasticity estimates for both first- and third-class mail delivery, which together represent about 83 percent of the Postal Service's business.[5] Tolley's model used quarterly data from

[5] Tolley's results are reported in *Pricing Postal Services in a Competitive Environment,* United States General Accounting Service, GAO/GGD-92-49, March 1992.

TABLE 6.2

Price Elasticity Estimates for First- and Third-Class Mail

Mail Type	Elasticity Estimate
Volume of First-Class Letters	
Own-Price Elasticities	
Current Quarter	−.105
Lagged 1 Quarter	−.056
Lagged 2 Quarters	−.043
Lagged 3 Quarters	−.041
Total	*−.245*
Cross-Price: First-Class Postcards	
Current Quarter	.002
Lagged 1 Quarter	.003
Lagged 2 Quarters	.002
Lagged 3 Quarters	.000
Total	*.006*
Cross-Price: Third-Class Bulk Mail	
Current Quarter	.006
Lagged 1 Quarter	.020
Lagged 2 Quarters	.016
Lagged 3 Quarters	.000
Total	*.043*
Volume of Third-Class Bulk Mail	
Own-Price Elasticities	
Current Quarter	−.252
Lagged 1 Quarter	−.134
Lagged 2 Quarters	−.126
Lagged 3 Quarters	−.113
Total	*−.624*
Cross-Price: First-Class Letters	
Current Quarter	.041
Lagged 1 Quarter	.066
Lagged 2 Quarters	.065
Lagged 3 Quarters	.041
Total	*.212*
Cross-Price: Third-Class Postcards	
Current Quarter	.004
Lagged 1 Quarter	.006
Lagged 2 Quarters	.006
Lagged 3 Quarters	.004
Total	*.020*

Source: George S. Tolley, *Pricing Postal Services in a Competitive Environment,* General Accounting Office, GAO/GGD-92-49, March 1992.

1970 to 1989 on mail volume and average price by mail class to estimate own- and cross-price elasticities.[6] His results are reported in Table 6.2 on page 207.

As shown in Table 6.2, Tolley's model provides elasticity estimates for current quarter price changes as well as price changes lagged back each of the previous three quarters. That is, some consumers of mail services may adjust more slowly to a change in mail prices, so their response is captured by these lag variables. The total effect of a price change is measured by summing these elasticity estimates. For purposes of analysis, the total effects are the relevant ones because they show the overall impact of a price change on mail volume.

Tolley's results are consistent with current stylized facts about the Postal Service. First-class mail delivery is relatively price inelastic, with a total price elasticity of −.245 and almost no cross-price effect with first-class postcards or third-class bulk mail. With direct competition prevented by law, this is an expected result. Unfortunately, the price of faxes and E-mail was not included in Tolley's model, so we don't know how these recent, alternative forms of mail delivery affect first-class mail volume. In contrast, third-class mail volume, which is facing increased competition from private mail carriers (although it is still partially protected by the Private Express Statutes), shows more responsiveness to price changes. The total own-price elasticity for third-class mail equals −.624, with the cross-price elasticity for first-class letters equal to .212 (a substitute). What appears fairly clear is that the Postal Service has been able to use its exclusive control of first-class mail delivery to increase these rates faster than rates for other, more competitive mail classes.

The Case for the Current Policy

The Postal Service recognizes that it has a problem controlling costs, particularly labor costs. Labor costs amounted to $34.2 billion in 1990, which represents about 85 percent of total operating costs. The Postal Service has responded to this problem. The four-year labor contract signed in June 1991, which covers 560,000 workers, resulted in wage increases of about 3.3 percent per year, which is less than the rate of inflation. In addition, this contract allows the Postal Service to hire new workers at 10 percent lower pay and to use more temporary and part-time workers. The contract also allows the Postal Service to lay off workers who have less than six years of service.

Another aspect of the Postal Service's strategy for improving its services and controlling cost growth was its plan to invest $5.3 billion by 1995 in mail-processing automation. The expectation was that automation would reduce the Postal Service's labor force by 84,000 workers over this period. In addition, the Postal Service plans to offer volume discounts to its larger customers in an attempt to remain more competitive and serve its customers better.

Lastly, it is argued that if competition were allowed into the first-class mail delivery market, the private sector would service the large urban areas, leaving the rural areas, which are most costly to service, to the Postal Service. Thus, the Postal Service would face higher costs as it lost market share to competition in the urban areas. These changes might lead to a public bailout of the Postal Service to keep mail delivery available to rural areas.

[6] The price charged by the Postal Service varies by weight, shape, drop-off location, and whether the items are presorted. Tolley used a weighted average of prices charged for mail pieces within a given postage class.

Questions for Evaluation

Does the Postal Service have an incentive to solve its labor cost problems if there is no threat of private competition? Should urban customers subsidize the cost of delivering mail to rural customers? Given the price elasticity estimates for first-class and third-class mail, do you expect that volume discounts will increase or decrease revenue generated from these mail classes?

6.4 The Compensated Demand Curve

Individual demand curves include both income and substitution effects of a price change. They are appropriate for analyzing responses to price changes when income and other prices are not similarly changing. On occasion, though, price changes are tied to changes in income. For example, it has been proposed that Medicare premiums be increased to help cover the spiraling cost of health care, while at the same time an extra tax deduction be given to the elderly to help offset the higher premiums. In some cases, the credit would completely offset the higher Medicare premium. Under such legislation, the government would increase the price paid for Medicare insurance and simultaneously increase the incomes—through lower taxes—of the elderly who receive Medicare. In this example, then, we must use a demand curve that *compensates* for the change in income to analyze the effect of price changes.

From our analysis of income and substitution effects, we can define two types of demand curves:

Ordinary Demand Curve
A demand curve generated by changing the price of one good, holding nominal income and all other prices constant.

Compensated Demand Curve
A demand curve generated by changing the price of one good and compensating (or taxing) the individual to keep him or her on the original indifference curve.

1. An **ordinary demand curve,** such as that shown in panel (a) of Figure 6.1 (page 185), where we plot the relationship between quantity purchased and price, holding income and other prices constant.
2. A **compensated demand curve,** where we plot the relationship between quantity purchased and price after compensating (or taxing) the individual with income to keep him or her on the original indifference curve.

Figure 6.10 (page 210) shows the difference between an ordinary and a compensated demand curve. This figure shows how your purchases of Pouilly-Fuissé wine change when its price increases. Initially, you are buying 15 bottles of Pouilly-Fuissé per month at a price of P_{low}. Bundle *A* represents your initial equilibrium bundle. Note that we are using the composite good convention in this example; the vertical axis measures your expenditures on all other goods. The price of wine increases to P_{high}, which causes your budget constraint to pivot inward along the horizontal axis. Bundle *B* is the equilibrium bundle on the new budget constraint. In bundle *B*, you purchase 8 bottles of Pouilly-Fuissé per month.

It is possible to compensate you for the effect of the higher price of wine on your utility, or satisfaction. The compensated budget line, shown in panel (a) of Figure 6.10, has the same slope as the new budget line—that is, the new relative price applies—but it represents a higher income. The extra income in the compensated budget line is *just enough* so that you can purchase one bundle on the original indifference curve, U_0. This is bundle *C*. In bundle *C*, you buy

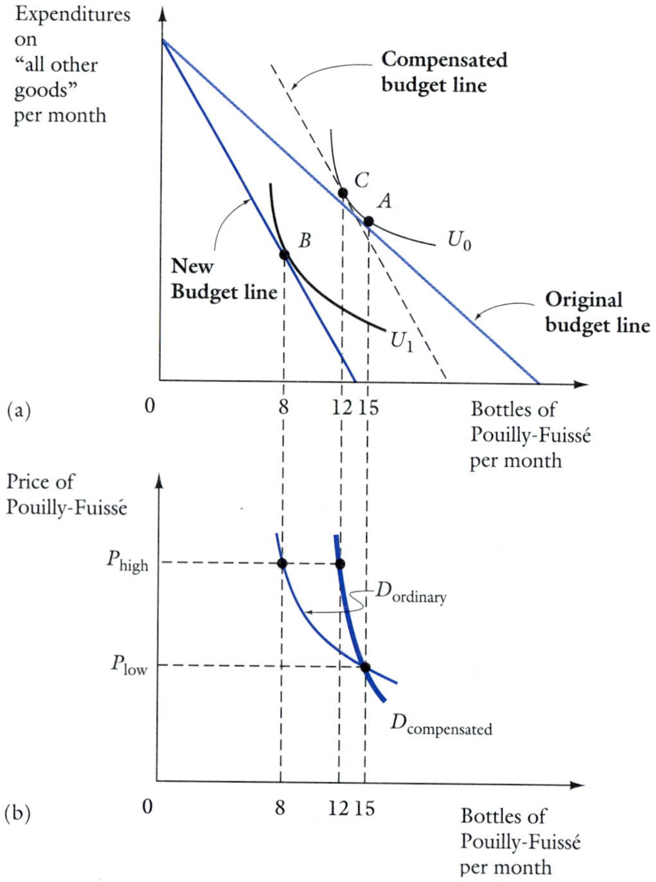

FIGURE 6.10

Deriving a Compensated Demand Curve for Pouilly-Fuissé Wine—A Normal Good

When the individual is compensated for the price increase in Pouilly-Fuissé wine, the equilibrium bundle moves from *A* to *C*. Consumption of Pouilly-Fuissé wine decreases to 12 from 15 bottles per month. Without compensation, consumption falls to 8 from 15 bottles per month. Panel (b) shows the relationship between an ordinary (uncompensated) demand curve and a compensated demand curve. For a normal good, when price rises, quantity demanded is greater on the compensated demand than the ordinary demand curve. The opposite is true when price falls.

12 bottles of Pouilly-Fuissé per month. In terms of income and substitution effects, the change from 15 to 12 bottles is the substitution effect and the change from 12 to 8 bottles is the income effect. The total effect is the change from 15 to 8 bottles of wine.

Your purchases of wine before and after the price change are plotted on the graph in panel (b) of Figure 6.10. The curve connecting 8 bottles and 15 bottles of wine is an ordinary demand curve, $D_{ordinary}$, just like the one shown in Figure 6.1. On this demand curve you face the entire brunt of the price rise; you do not receive any offsetting compensation. The curve connecting 12 bottles to 15 bottles of wine is a compensated demand curve. On this curve, you are given enough income at the new relative prices to hold your satisfaction at the original level. Note that these curves cross at price P_{low}, the original price. If price is raised above this level, you are compensated for the price change—that is, your income increases—which increases the quantity you purchase relative to the ordinary demand curve. At prices below P_{low}, however, quantity demanded on the compensated demand curve is less than on the ordinary demand curve. This is because you are taxed—that is, income is taken away—when prices fall. The "tax" reduces your purchases of wine relative to your purchases on the ordinary demand curve. Note that each point of the ordinary demand curve has a corresponding compensated demand curve passing through it. Thus, we can define the income (or tax) necessary for you to remain as well off as your current quantity demanded reflects, no matter where you are on the ordinary demand curve when price changes.

LEARNING EXERCISE 6.9

The analysis in Figure 6.10 assumes that Pouilly-Fuissé is a normal good. Redraw the diagram for the case when Pouilly-Fuissé is an inferior good.

$$$ Price Theory in Practice

INCOME TAXES AND WORK EFFORT

We can use indifference curves and the full income constraint to analyze the effect of an income tax on the quantity of work effort supplied. At the same time we can also determine the income and substitution effects of a change in the rate of income taxation. This analysis follows from our discussion of expenditures on goods and choice of time spent in leisure presented in Chapter 5.

We will make two simplifying assumptions:

1. We begin from a situation in which there are no income taxes.
2. The income tax imposed is a proportional one, that is, a constant percentage levied on each dollar earned.

In Figure 6.11 on page 212, the initial full income constraint facing the worker is full income constraint F_1. Given the worker's indifference curve U_1, the quantity of leisure demanded will be L_1, which is determined at point A, where curve U_1 is tangent to the full income constraint. Note that if the worker took no leisure and devoted all his or her time to working during the time period, the take-home income would be M_1.

Now we impose an income tax. What does the income tax do? To answer that, let's first consider that the price of leisure is the *opportunity cost* of not working. Without a tax, the opportunity cost of not working for exactly one hour is equal to a worker's wages for that hour (assuming that there are no deductions for other things, e.g., pension and Social Security). With an income tax, the per hour cost of not working is equal to the *after-tax* wage rate. Because

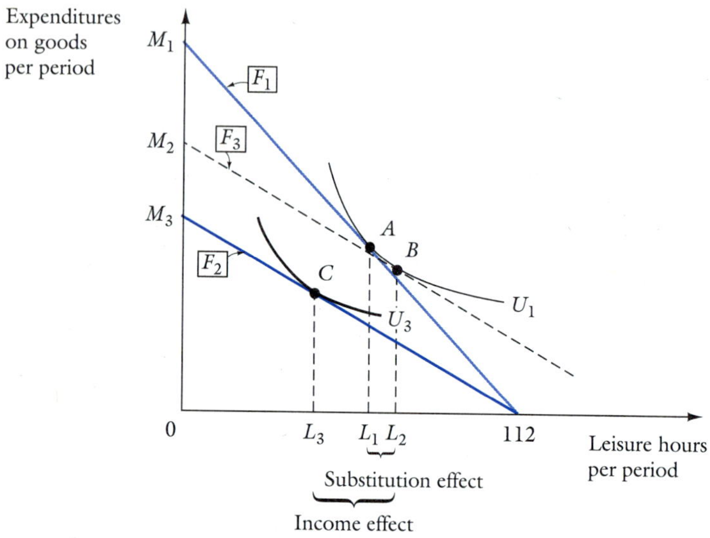

FIGURE 6.11

Income and Substitution Effects for a Proportionate Income Tax on Work Effort

Bundle A is the initial equilibrium bundle. A proportionate income tax reduces the full income constraint from F_1 to F_2, with the new equilibrium at bundle C. The substitution effect is found by using the point of tangency, B, between the full income constraint, line F_3, and the original indifferent curve, U_1. The substitution effect causes leisure to increase to L_2 from L_1. The income effect causes leisure to decrease to L_3 from L_2. The total effect of the proportionate tax on leisure is given by the move from L_1 to L_3.

the income tax reduces wages, the opportunity cost of not working is lower; this is the same as saying that the income tax lowers the relative price of leisure. Now, if the worker took no leisure and devoted all of his or her time to working during the time period, the take-home income would be M_3, which is less than M_1 by the amount of taxes deducted from income. In effect, an income tax rotates full income constraint F_1 counterclockwise to full income constraint F_2, the after-tax full income constraint. This means that income taxes reduce the opportunity cost of leisure time.

What happens when the worker is faced with a proportional income tax? In our example, the worker will go to a new optimum at point C, at which he or she consumes a new quantity of leisure, L_3. Because leisure is measured on the horizontal axis, L_3 represents a reduction in the quantity of leisure demanded and therefore an increase in the total number of hours worked. Why does this individual work more? Because the income effect outweighs the substitution effect. Note that the income and substitution effects move work effort in opposite directions. In other words, the income tax reduces income by so much that, even though leisure has become cheaper in this case, the individual works more to try to make up for some of the lost income that went into taxes.

We can find the substitution effect by drawing in a hypothetical budget constraint that leaves the worker on the same indifference curve, U_1, but presents him or her with the new lower relative price of leisure. This is the hypothetical full income constraint F_3, which has the same slope as full income constraint F_2 and is tangent to indifference curve U_1. Along this full income constraint F_3, the worker equilibrium is at B. A larger quantity of leisure, L_2, is consumed relative to bundle A. The substitution effect $(L_1 - L_2)$ is always negative. The lower price of leisure leads to a larger quantity demanded; it costs less not to work. The income effect, however, is measured by the reduction in leisure from L_2 to L_3. The income effect is positive because a reduction in income leads to a reduction in the quantity of leisure demanded. In other words, leisure is a *normal* good. The normal nature of leisure is verified by experience. For example, windfall gains, such as those acquired by winning the Irish Sweepstakes or the Florida lottery, usually result in more, rather than less, leisure consumed.

LEARNING EXERCISE 6.10

What is the shape of the labor supply curve, given the behavior described in Figure 6.11?

6.5 PRICE INDICES AND THE COST OF LIVING

When we read about prices in newspapers or magazines, we rarely see that one price has changed while other prices are held constant. We usually read reports about price indices, such as the Consumer Price Index (CPI) or the Producer Price Index (PPI), that have increased or decreased. These indices summarize changes observed in many prices, not just one price, between two points in time. With many prices changing, it is important to ask whether you are better or worse off as a result of the various price changes. In some situations, we can offer a definitive answer to this question; in others, we simply do not know the answer.

To begin, let us examine the relationship between an index of prices and your equilibrium consumption bundle. Figure 6.12 on page 214 shows your monthly consumption of food and clothing—both composite goods—during 1994 and 1995. In 1994, the prices of food, P^{94}_{food}, and clothing, P^{94}_{clothing}, place you at equilibrium bundle e_{94}, on budget line L_1 , at which you consume

Reprinted by permission: Tribune Media Service.

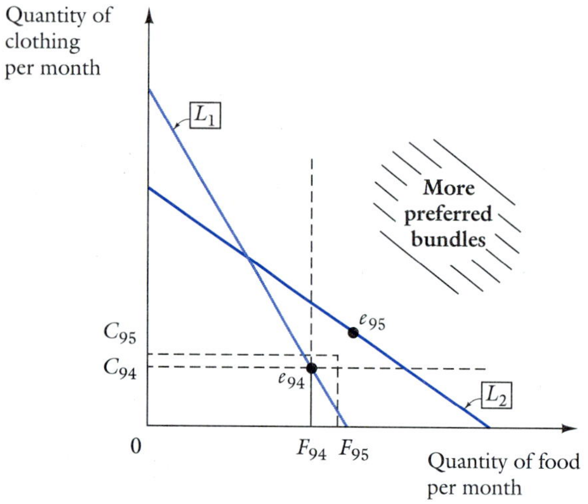

FIGURE 6.12

Comparing Equilibrium Bundles When Both Prices and Income Change Between 1994 and 1995

Prices and income place the consumer on budget line L_1 in 1994. Prices and income change in 1995 as represented by budget line L_2. Bundle e_{94} is the 1994 equilibrium bundle, and bundle e_{95} is the 1995 equilibrium bundle. The nonsatiation assumption shows that the consumer is better off in 1995 and in 1994 because consumption of both food and clothing increases.

F_{94} units of food and C_{94} units of clothing. (Our notation is very general, so that we could be referring to price and consumption changes of any two goods.) The prices of food and clothing change to P^{95}_{food} and P^{95}_{clothing}, respectively, in 1995. Your new equilibrium bundle, e_{95}, is found on budget line L_2, at which you consume F_{95} units of food and C_{95} units of clothing per month. Are you better off or worse off as a result of these price changes? Does an index of these price changes answer this question?

As to the first question (Are you better off?), we can say without any ambiguity that your level of satisfaction, or utility, has increased between 1994 and 1995. We know this because bundle e_{95} contains more of both food and clothing than bundle e_{94}. Using our nonsatiation assumption (see Chapter 5), we know that bundle e_{95} offers more satisfaction that bundle e_{94}. For this example, we can also show that you are better off using a price index.

First, let's define the **expenditure index** as the ratio of expenditures on food and clothing between 1994 and 1995:

Expenditure Index
The ratio of expenditures in one time period to expenditures in another—usually previous—time period, computed using the prices and quantities observed in these periods.

$$E = \frac{P^{95}_{\text{food}}F_{95} + P^{95}_{\text{clothing}}C_{95}}{P^{94}_{\text{food}}F_{94} + P^{94}_{\text{clothing}}C_{94}} \tag{6.4}$$

where the numerator measures the cost of bundle e_{95} and the denominator measures the cost of bundle e_{94}. The expenditure index serves as a reference point to how your income is changing. Because we assume that you spend all of your income on food and clothing, an expenditure index that is greater than 1 implies that income is increasing between 1994 and 1995. Income is falling between these two years if the expenditure index is less than 1, and (nominal) income is constant if the expenditure index is equal to 1. What we must determine is whether your income has increased faster than food and clothing prices. Intuitively, we can see you will be better off if your income is rising faster than prices and worse off if your income is rising slower than prices.

Laspeyres Index The ratio of expenditures in one time period to expenditures in another—usually previous—time period, computed using the prices observed in these periods, while holding quantities at their initial levels.

The most common index that is used to measure price changes is called the **Laspeyres index.** Both the Laspeyres and expenditure indices are ratios of the money value of the two bundles. The difference between these indices is in the choice of consumption bundles. The expenditure index is the ratio of expenditures on the new bundle to expenditures on the old bundle. In contrast, the Laspeyres index is the ratio of expenditures on the old bundle, *evaluated at new prices,* to expenditures on the old bundle, *evaluated at the old prices.* We can write the Laspeyres index as follows:

$$L = \frac{P^{95}_{\text{food}}F_{94} + P^{95}_{\text{clothing}}C_{94}}{P^{94}_{\text{food}}F_{94} + P^{94}_{\text{clothing}}C_{94}} \tag{6.5}$$

The consumer and producer price indices—CPI and PPI—are Laspeyres indices. They are computed assuming that your consumption bundle does not change when prices change.

Let's return to the question of whether you are better or worse off when prices change. The Laspeyres index holds your consumption bundle fixed and allows prices to change. In a sense, this index is measuring how fast prices are changing, because we are using the same consumption bundle in both the numerator and denominator. As we have noted, the expenditure index measures how your income is changing. Now, let's figure out the relationship between L and E for bundles e_{94} and e_{95}. Suppose that $L < E$ for these two bundles. What does this inequality imply? It implies that your expenditure on bundle e_{94} at the 1995 prices (the numerator of L) is less than your expenditure on e_{95} at the 1995 prices (the numerator of E). In effect, this inequality implies that it takes less income than you have in 1995 to purchase your 1994 equilibrium bundle. We can see from Figure 6.13 (page 216) that this is a true claim.

In Figure 6.13, budget line L_3 represents the income required to purchase bundle e_{94} at the 1995 prices. Because budget line L_3 is below budget line L_2, we know that it takes *less* income to purchase bundle e_{94} at the 1995 prices than the income required to purchase bundle e_{95} at the 1995 prices. In effect, the finding that $L < E$ implies that prices increased less than income between 1994 and 1995. When this occurs, you are better off at the new equilibrium bundle (a result that we already knew because of the nonsatiation assumption).

Although we can conclude that you are better off when $L < E$, we cannot reverse the inequality and similarly reverse our conclusion. If $L > E$, it will take more income to purchase the old bundle at the 1995 prices than it takes to purchase the new bundle at the 1995 prices. As shown in Figure 6.13, if the old equilibrium bundle lies on the segment of budget line L_1 above bundle $e_{\text{intersect}}$, then more income is required at the 1995 prices to buy this bundle. Our assumptions about your preferences do not tell us whether you view bun-

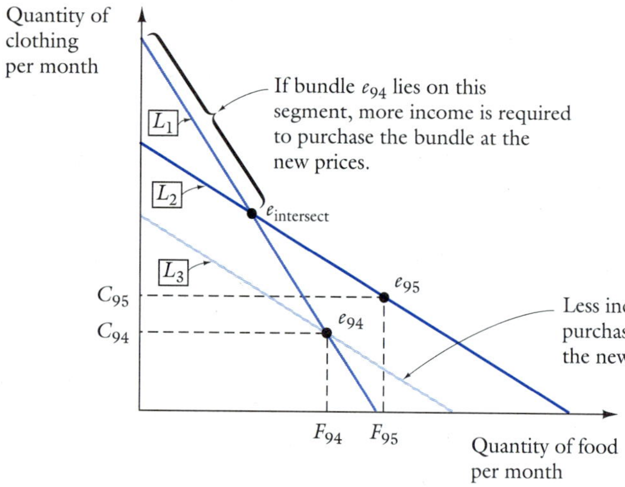

FIGURE 6.13

Comparing the Laspeyres and Expenditure Indices

The Laspeyres and expenditure indexes may be used to show that the consumer is better off in 1995 than in 1994. Budget line L_3 shows that it takes less income to purchase the original bundle, e_{94}, at the 1995 prices than to buy the new bundle, e_{95}. This result implies that the Laspeyres index is less than the expenditure index, so the consumer is better off. Alternatively, if the Laspeyres index is greater than the expenditure index, then the original bundle will lie on budget line L_1 above bundle $e_{intersect}$ and we do not know if the consumer is better off.

dles along this segment as preferred, indifferent, or less preferred to bundle e_{95}. So, when $L > E$, we cannot say whether you are better or worse off at the new level of prices and income.[7]

Learning Exercise 6.11

Compute the Laspeyres and expenditure indices using the following information:

	1994	*1995*
Quantity of food	50	70
Quantity of clothing	25	20
Price of food	5	6
Price of clothing	30	40

Can we say whether you are better or worse off in 1995 than in 1994?

[7] An alternative to the Laspeyres index is the Paasche index, which substitutes the current period's (year 1995) consumption of food and clothing into equation (6.5) instead of the previous period's consumption. Using this substitution, we can show that if the Paasche index is greater than the expenditure index, the consumer is better off in the current period. That is, the inequality relationship found for the Laspeyres index reverses when the Paasche index is used.

Chapter Summary

1. The price-consumption curve shows the equilibrium bundles purchased when the price of one good changes, holding income and the price of other goods constant. The demand curve is the graph of the equilibrium quantity of the good, whose price is changing, against its price.
2. An income-consumption curve shows the equilibrium bundles purchased when income changes, holding prices constant. The Engel curve plots the equilibrium consumption of any one good against income.
3. When the price of one good changes, its effect on quantity demanded can be decomposed into income and substitution effects. The income effect is the part that is caused by a change in purchasing power, or real income, when price changes. The substitution effect is the part that is caused by a change in relative prices, holding satisfaction, or real income, constant.
4. A Giffen good has a positively sloped demand curve. This situation may occur when the good in question is inferior and the income effect is sufficiently large (in absolute value) to fully offset the substitution effect. Such a good is thought to be rare or nonexistent when we look at the market demand curve.
5. An ordinary demand curve is derived from a price-consumption curve, holding nominal income and other prices constant. A compensated demand curve shows the relationship between quantity purchased and price after compensating (or taxing) the individual to keep him or her on the original indifference curve. (When the good is normal, the relationship between these two demand curves is shown on Figure 6.11.)
6. The Laspeyres index can be used to measure changes in the cost of living. It equals the ratio of your expenditures on your original bundle at the new prices to your expenditures at the original prices. If the Laspeyres index is less than the expenditure index, then price and income changes have made you better off. If the Laspeyres index is greater than the expenditure index, then we do not know if you are better or worse off when prices and income change.

Trouble Spots

Concept	Reminder
Price-Consumption Curve	Only one price is changing when we derive the price-consumption curve and subsequently an individual's demand curve. Other prices and nominal income are held constant.
Engel Curves	An Engel curve is not the same as an income-consumption curve. The Engel curve plots changes in quantity purchased of one good against income.

	A good is inferior over the income range at which the Engel curve has a negative slope; it is normal over the income range at which the Engel curve has a positive slope. The income-consumption curve plots the various equilibrium *bundles* purchased as income changes.
Income and Substitution Effects	First, we generally do not observe the intermediate step that is used to define the income and substitution effects. The intermediate budget line that is shown in our graphs is a hypothetical budget line. (For example, when price changes, equilibrium consumption changes from bundle *A* to bundle *C* in Figure 6.7. The intermediate bundle *B* is never observed.) Second, income and substitution effects are both caused by a change in the price of one good; nominal income is *not* changing in our analysis of these effects.
Giffen Goods	A normal good cannot be a Giffen good; only an inferior good can be a Giffen good.
The Compensated Demand Curve	On a compensated demand curve, if price increases, you are compensated for the increase with extra income. If price decreases, however, you are taxed to keep you on the original indifference curve. For the former, you have the bad—higher price—with the good—extra income. For the latter, you have the good—lower price—with the bad—a tax. On the compensated demand curve, we always mix the good with the bad.

6.6 Review Questions

1. In deriving a price-consumption curve, which variables are held constant and which are allowed to change?
2. Explain how you derive a demand curve from a price-consumption curve.
3. Suppose that your income and all prices double. Does this situation give you another point on your income-consumption curve? Why or why not?
4. Suppose that as nominal income changes, the price of one good also changes. How will this situation affect your efforts to trace out the income-consumption curve?
5. Define an inferior and a normal good. Can a good be inferior for some people and normal for others?
6. All goods cannot be inferior, but does that mean that all goods cannot be normal, too?
7. When a good's price changes, there are two effects: substitution effect and income effect. Explain why the substitution effect is always negative but the income effect can be negative or positive.

8. "Rice in Asia" is often asserted to be an example of a Giffen good that defies the law of demand. Assuming for the moment that the assertion is correct, what is the reasoning underlying it?
9. Define income and cross-price elasticity of demand. Explain how the income elasticities across goods are related in the budget of a given consumer.
10. Is a compensated demand curve more or less elastic than an ordinary demand curve for a normal good? (Evaluate the price elasticity at the intersection point of these two curves.)
11. How do you determine how much income to take away (or give) to permit the individual to purchase the original bundle after a price change?
12. Under what circumstances will you decrease your leisure consumption if your income tax rate increases?
13. If you find that the expenditure index is equal to 1 and the Laspeyres index is less than 1 after prices have changed, are you better off or worse off? Can you tell from this information?

6.7 Price Theory Problems

1. Suppose that you consume two goods: cassette books and food. After the end-of-the-year holidays, the price of cassette books increases. At the same time you receive a holiday bonus, which is of sufficient size to keep your *satisfaction* constant.
    a. Show this situation using both budget and indifference curves. How has your consumption of cassette books changed?
    b. After the holidays, can you still purchase the bundle of cassette books and food that you bought before the holidays? Explain.

2. True or false:
    a. The compensated demand curve for a Giffen good is negatively sloped.
    b. Satisfaction increases as you move up the price-consumption curve.
    c. The price-consumption curve for two commodities that are perfect substitutes is a straight line.

3. True or false: If the price of an inferior good increases, you will increase consumption of at least one other good, but not all other goods. Explain.
4. Analyze each of the following statements:
    a. The best French wine is for sale in the United States.
    b. Only the most expensive diamonds are registered with the Gemological Society of America and issued certificates attesting to their quality.

5. Suppose that last year you spent half your income on food and half on rent. This year your nominal income has gone up 10 percent, the price of food has increased 20 percent, and rental rates have not changed. Are you able to determine whether your real income went up, went down, or remained the same? Why or why not? Explain.
6. True or false: Food stamps increase the quantity of food consumed by all households, including those who do not receive them.
7. Suppose you are examining the income elasticity of clothing and all other goods. The income elasticity of clothing equals .8 and its share in your budget equals 20 percent. What is the income elasticity of all other goods? What is the share of all other goods in your budget?
8. Derive the price-consumption curve for good X when good X and good Y are perfect substitutes. Derive the price-consumption curve when good X and good Y are perfect complements.
9. Which of the following cross-price elasticities of demand would you expect to be positive and which to be negative?
   a. Tennis balls and tennis racquets
   b. Tennis balls and golf balls
   c. Fax machines and first-class mail
   d. Dental services and candy
   e. Kites and string
   f. Bicycles and skateboards
10. Compare the following three systems of welfare payments:

System	Payment
1.	\$100 per family per week, regardless of whether any family members earn any income on their own
2.	\$100 per family per week, reduced by \$1 for every \$3 earned by family members on their own
3.	\$100 per family per week, reduced by \$1 for every \$1 earned by family members on their own

   a. At what level of weekly earnings would a family leave welfare under each of the three systems?
   b. Which system appears to have greater incentives for a family to work and to become at least partially self-supporting?
11. Suppose that you purchase gasoline and a composite good that represents expenditures on all other goods. The government imposes an excise tax on gasoline and rebates the tax collected back to each individual; that is, it gives back the taxes you have paid. Does such a rebate scheme allow you to achieve the satisfaction you received before the tax? Explain.
12. Suppose you spend all of your income on two goods, X and Y. In 1994, the price of good X was \$2, the price of good Y was \$4, and your income was \$200. In 1995, the price of good X is \$3, the price of good Y is \$3.40, and your income is \$250. In 1994, you consumed 60 units of X and 20 units of Y in equilibrium. In 1995, you consume 55 units of X and 25 units of Y in equilibrium.

a. Calculate the expenditure and Laspeyres indices for this situation.
b. Are you better or worse off in 1995 than you were in 1994? Can you actually tell? Why or why not?

13. In 1994, your monthly budget constraint was given by $100X_1 + 50X_2 = \$2000$. In 1995, the government decides to impose a ***unit tax*** on good X_1 of \$60; that is, for every X_1 consumed you must pay a tax of \$60. To help reduce the effect of the tax, the government gives you \$400 in extra income each month.
    a. What is the formula for the new budget line? Graph the new and old budget lines, carefully labeling the intersection points on each axis.
    b. Assume that the optimal solution for X_1 is 8 units and for X_2 is 24 units in 1994. In 1995, the optimal solution for X_1 is 5 units and for X_2 is 32 units. Using this information, calculate the Laspeyres and expenditure indices.
    c. Are you better or worse off in 1995 when compared to 1994?

6.8 Writing Exercise

Price indices can be computed between any two points in time—years, months, weeks, or days—or between any two stores offering the same merchandise. Collect the advertising sections of your local newspaper for two consecutive weekends. Choose any two commodities that you are likely to purchase in the future (or have just purchased), and compute the Laspeyres and expenditure indices for your planned expenditures on these commodities between the two weeks. Have the observed price changes made you better or worse off? Can you tell? Also, compute these two indices for two goods offered by competing firms. Can you determine which firm is the best place to shop? Write up your results, presenting a detailed discussion of your calculations.

7

Organization and Management of the Firm

Preview Questions

When you finish studying this chapter, you should be able to answer the following questions:

- What is a firm?
- Why do we have production organized in firms?
- What is the goal of the shareholders (owners) of a firm?
- What rule does a firm follow to maximize profits?
- What are the problems created by team production?
- How do agency costs affect the structure of contracts in a firm?
- What is the difference between a moral hazard and an adverse selection problem?
- Why do investments in specific assets cause the holdup problem?

In February 1990, Forbes *magazine reviewed the potential for growth in the shipping industry and shipping stocks. At the time,* Forbes *thought that the economic fundamentals looked good. Demand for cargo ships was growing faster than existing capacity, so cargo rates were increasing. The potential for higher profits was excellent. But in June 1993,* Forbes *admitted that its analysis hadn't worked out as planned. Higher insurance rates, costly new regulations following the Exxon Valdez oil spill in Alaska, and the 1990–1991 recession worked against its forecast. Investors who bought the shipping stocks mentioned in the first article lost an average of 28 percent. Investors who bought stock in some self-liquidating firms—firms formed to buy secondhand vessels for sale in the future—lost almost 90 percent. Particularly annoying to* Forbes *was the likelihood that the managers of these self-liquidating firms were paying themselves fat fees from cash flow while investors suffered huge losses. How can management do this? If it is true, can it be prevented? What is it about the structure of the modern business firm that occasionally leads to tales such as this?*

Our exposure to modern business firms is multifaceted: We are customers when we purchase goods and services; we are employees in the workplace; and we are investors when we purchase bonds or shares of stock. Each of these activities casts a different light on business firms, but each activity is an integral part of the structure of the organization we call a firm. Generally, these activities are managed within the firm to increase the wealth of the firm's owners. We begin our analysis of firms and their behavior with the view that the present structure—rules, contracts, and procedures—increases the wealth of the firm's owners.

But not every activity within a firm is consistent with maximizing the wealth of the firm's owners. Mistakes are sometimes made, which can be very costly. A newly recruited manager may not work out, for example, and valuable time has been lost in the process of sorting out this fact. To better understand the problems that can arise, we explore several aspects of the business firm, including its generally accepted objective of profit maximization; behavioral problems that arise as a firm tries to manage its business activities; and situations that affect how managers of a firm interact with employees, customers, and suppliers. We focus on several fundamental questions: Why is most production organized in firms? (The answer here helps explain why firms exist in the first place.) Why do owners choose the profit-maximizing goal? How can owners align the goals of managers with the goal of maximizing profit? We also discuss many agency problems, including problems of shirking, moral hazard, adverse selection, and end-of-period contracts, and we explain how firms adjust to these problems. Finally, we consider other forms of organizations, particularly nonprofit firms, and explain how many nonprofit firms are organized and operated.

7.1 What Is a Firm?

As a practical matter, the modern business **firm** is a legal entity formed by charter with a state government. The charter and federal and state laws determine much of what a firm can and cannot do. In economic terms, however, a business firm takes on much more meaning and shape than simply a legal entity subject to state and federal laws. For example, it may or may not have a charter from the state. More generally, it is an organization formed to produce goods and services to sell for a profit. The firm hires workers, hires or buys capital and other resources, applies management skills, and takes risks to pursue its goals. If a business firm survives over time as an independent organization, then it is at least one efficient means of providing goods and services. To an economist, a firm is more than a legal entity; it is an integral part of the marketplace, playing an important role by supplying goods and services at least cost to consumers.

Firm
An organization in which there is more than one employee working as part of a team to produce a good or service. The team is linked together by explicit and implicit contracts.

WHY DO FIRMS EXIST?

In economic terms, firms exist because they can provide goods and services to customers at less cost than the customers can produce the items themselves. Some consumers make their own ice cream, for example, but the vast majority buy it at grocery stores or franchise outlets. Many companies have lawyers and accountants on their payrolls while others buy these services from other firms.

Some consumers choose to mow their lawns and clean their own gardens while others use professional help for these activities. Some firms own their own delivery trucks (United Parcel Service is an example) while other firms rent delivery trucks from trucking companies such as Ryder System, Inc. Although it may be tempting to suggest that the size of a firm explains how firms are organized, this would be incorrect. These examples make a distinction between firms that have organized production of certain activities within their own structure and those who rely on the *marketplace* for certain inputs. Essentially, the question "Why do firms exist?" becomes "What determines the extent to which a firm chooses to make or to buy the goods and services that it uses in production?"

Consider what would happen if production activities were not integrated within firms, but instead *all* production activity relied on the marketplace. Individuals would contract with each other for goods and services. In effect, all production activity would be in the form of a "cottage industry." There would be no managers and employees, just entrepreneurs creating products without the assistance of others. But in contemporary terms, this is not how most production is organized. Most production is organized in business firms, some with few and some with many employees, who acquire *some* inputs to the production process from the marketplace, *but not all.*

IN-HOUSE OR MARKET-BASED PRODUCTION

To determine whether to use the marketplace to acquire inputs, a firm acts in its self-interest. As a consequence, a firm compares the cost of using the marketplace to the cost incurred from its own production. When a firm uses the marketplace to supply inputs, there are **transaction costs.** These costs arise for at least four important reasons:[1]

Transaction Costs
Costs that arise from negotiating and completing a transaction with another firm or independent party.

1. Monitoring the quality of production or delivery of services is costly.
2. Negotiating price and delivery schedules is costly.
3. Monitoring contract performance is costly.
4. It is costly to enforce contracts; that is, the use of the court system is costly.

When a firm produces within its own structure, or in-house, as opposed to relying on the marketplace, it incurs **managerial costs.** Managerial costs include the costs of monitoring production to ensure quality, contracting costs, and other costs of coordinating production activities within the firm. It should be clear that managerial costs include some of the same costs incurred when a firm uses the marketplace. Monitoring to ensure quality, for example, is a cost that arises in both cases. The difference is that the size of the monitor-

Managerial Costs
The costs of organizing, monitoring, and coordinating production within the firm.

[1] The transaction cost approach to the existence of firms has a host of contributors. The first article to develop the idea was by 1991 Nobel laureate Ronald Coase: "The Nature of the Firm," *Economica* 4 (1937), 386–405. Many of the subsequent contributions, including a discussion of teamwork, are summarized in Armen A. Alchian and Susan Woodward, "Reflections on the Theory of the Firm," *Journal of Institutional and Theoretical Economics* 143 (March 1987), 110–136.

ing cost may vary depending on whether the firm uses the market or produces in-house. In addition, the remedies a firm may seek differ between the two approaches, which affects their relative cost. In-house production lets a firm single out specific individuals or parts of the organization to discipline if the production process is not operating correctly, whereas using the market does not generally allow this flexibility. If the firm uses the market and is not satisfied, then it may renegotiate, end its relationship with the other party, or use the courts to seek a remedy, but it cannot tell the other party how to run its business—how to reorganize its production process or who to fire—primarily because it does not have the information necessary to solve the other firm's problem.

A firm compares the cost of using the marketplace to the managerial cost of in-house production to determine how to organize its production process. If the cost of purchasing a given input to the production process from the marketplace is less than the managerial cost of producing it in-house, then the firm purchases this input from the marketplace. If the reverse is true, then the firm produces in-house. These arguments allow us to make the following observation about why firms exist:

> **The parts of the production process are organized and managed within a firm when this is less costly than using the market to supply these parts of the production process.**

Clearly, in many cases, the frequency of use tips the scale in favor of in-house production. A firm that regularly prints and mails promotional material often will find it advantageous to develop an in-house printing service. Firms that print brochures only once a year will probably purchase these services from the marketplace. A well-organized firm makes a comparison between the costs of using the market and the costs of in-house production on a regular basis, so that it can produce its output at least cost, making it a strong competitor in its output market.

7.2 The Profit-Maximizing Goal

Given that firms exist, what goal do they try to accomplish? Do firms try to maximize profits? A firm could conceivably maximize its sales, employment, growth rate, or any number of possible variables. Let's explore why firms are assumed to maximize profits and in later sections discuss the many practical problems that affect the attainment of the profit-maximizing goal.

Shareholder
An owner of shares in a corporation; shareholders own the rights to the firm's residual payments.

Residual
The residual of a firm is its profits, that is, the difference between total revenues and total costs, including the opportunity cost of all resources used.

Why Maximize Profits?

One compelling reason why managers are given the goal of maximizing profits is to provide the firm's owners with the greatest increase in their wealth. A **shareholder,** who is an owner of the firm's profits (profits are also called the **residual** after paying prior claims, which makes shareholders

Residual Claimants The owners of a firm's profits. If the firm is a corporation, then the owners are the shareholders.

residual claimants), finds that his or her budget constraint is relaxed, so that bundles containing more goods can be purchased, when income increases. The change in the budget constraint allows the shareholder to choose a more preferred bundle of goods. Goals other than profit maximization may increase shareholders' income, *but not by as much as the profit-maximizing goal.* Thus, by offering the *greatest* increase in wealth, the profit-maximizing goal offers the greatest potential increase in shareholders' satisfaction.[2]

SELECTING THE OPTIMAL OUTPUT

Assuming that managers wish to maximize profits, how do they decide on the optimal output rate? If there is a simple rule to follow, then everyone—employees, managers, and owners—will gain when the rule is known to all. There is a general rule: marginal revenue equals marginal cost. Let's see how it works.

Let Q denote the firm's output rate; $R(Q)$ the total revenue generated from an output rate of Q units per period; and $C(Q)$ the costs of producing Q units of output, where costs include the direct expenses plus the opportunity costs of all resources used in production. Both total revenue and total cost are a function of the output rate, so profits are also a function of the output rate. Thus, profits of a firm, denoted by $\pi(Q)$, may be written as

$$\pi(Q) = R(Q) - C(Q) \tag{7.1}$$

Note that $C(Q)$ is the cost function of the firm *given its present organizational structure.* Costs may be higher or lower than those of similar firms in the industry, depending on how successful the firm's structure is in aligning the behavior of employees, managers, and outside vendors with the profit-maximizing goal of its owners.

THE MARGINAL-REVENUE-EQUALS-MARGINAL-COST RULE

Because owners desire to maximize profits, they seek to follow a rule or procedure that will maximize equation (7.1). This problem is solved using the *equimarginal principle* first discussed in Chapter 1. To apply this principle, we want to find the output rate at which marginal benefits are equal to marginal costs. Using equation (7.1), we see that the marginal benefits to the firm arise from changes in total revenue. Similarly, marginal costs arise from changes in total cost. Analytically, the slope of the revenue function at a given output rate, $\Delta R(Q)/\Delta Q$, is called the marginal revenue of the firm, and the slope of the cost function, $\Delta C(Q)/\Delta Q$, is called the marginal cost of the firm at a

[2] Shareholders may consider other goals for a firm, such as maximizing the utility of wealth, not just maximizing wealth. Louis Makowski's research entitled "Competitive Stock Markets" [*Review of Economic Studies* 50 (April 1983), 305–330] has shown that shareholders unanimously prefer wealth maximization as a goal, even if they are individually averse to risk.

given output rate. In effect, **marginal revenue** is the change in total revenue for a small change in output, and **marginal cost** is the change in total cost for a small change in output. From equation (7.1), we can see that the marginal change in profit, $\Delta\pi(Q)/\Delta Q$, equals the difference between marginal revenue and marginal cost:

Marginal Revenue The amount by which total revenue changes when output changes by a small amount—usually by one unit.

Marginal Cost The amount by which total cost changes when output changes by a small amount—usually by one unit.

$$\frac{\Delta\pi(Q)}{\Delta Q} = \frac{\Delta R(Q)}{\Delta Q} - \frac{\Delta C(Q)}{\Delta Q} = 0 \tag{7.2}$$

Equation (7.2) offers a general rule for profit maximization:

> **A firm continues to increase production until it finds an output rate at which marginal revenue is equal to marginal cost:**

That is,

$$\text{MR}(Q) = \text{MC}(Q) \tag{7.3}$$

Why must equation (7.3) hold? We can think of a firm's managers as operating in steps to maximize profits. They are always asking themselves whether the next step will increase or decrease profits. The steps here are the additional output the firm produces. To determine whether an addition to the output rate increases profits, we must compare the increase in total revenue to the resulting increase in costs. If the change in total revenue exceeds the change in total costs, then the additional output increases profit, and the managers should produce the extra output. But where does this process stop? There will be some point at which an increase in the output rate raises total revenue and total cost by the same amount. In this circumstance, the firm breaks even on the additional output. It should stop here, because if it goes further, it will find that the increase in total costs exceeds the increase in total revenue, which implies that profit is falling. This result is exactly what is implied by condition (7.3). Marginal revenue is the change in total revenue for a small change in output, and marginal cost is the change in total cost for a small change in output. Thus, by finding the output rate at which marginal revenue equals marginal cost, the firm's managers have exhausted all opportunities to increase profits by increasing the output rate. This condition is telling the managers not to go further; that is, they should stop while they are breaking even with the last units added to output.

There is a technical condition that is also required to hold if equation (7.3) is to define maximum profits instead of minimum profits:

> **The slope of the marginal cost curve must exceed the slope of the marginal revenue curve.**

In most all cases this condition will hold, but you must keep it in mind because there are unusual cases in which the condition is not satisfied.

In summary, we can say that if the managers of a firm follow the rule that marginal revenue equals marginal cost, specified in equation (7.3), they will produce an output rate that fulfills the owners' goal of maximizing profits. It cannot be overemphasized, however, that the organizational structure of a firm affects its costs. In poorly managed firms, a rule or procedure change that changes employee incentives may lower costs, which then affects marginal cost and, consequently, the firm's optimal output rate and corresponding maximum attainable level of profits.

LEARNING EXERCISE 7.1

Assume that $MR(Q) = 50$ and that $MC(Q) = 20 + 0.2Q$. Solve for the profit-maximizing level of output.

MATH NOTEPAD

A Numerical Example of Profit Maximization

To see how to use the profit-maximizing rule, let's consider a numerical example. Suppose the firm can sell its output at the market price of \$10 per unit; then $R(Q) = 10Q$. Let's also say that costs can be approximated by a quadratic equation, $C(Q) = 10 + 5Q + 0.1Q^2$. Marginal revenue is equal to the change in total revenue when output changes by a small amount. If the output rate changes by 1 unit, say, then marginal revenue is equal to \$10, that is, $MR(Q) = \$10$. Similarly, marginal cost for this cost function may be written as $MC(Q) = 5 + 0.2Q$. Technically, $MC(Q) = [C(Q + \Delta Q) - C(Q)]/\Delta Q$ as ΔQ approaches zero. Substituting for the cost function gives $MC(Q) = [10 + 5(Q + \Delta Q) + 0.1(Q + \Delta Q)^2 - 10 - 5Q - 0.1Q^2]/\Delta Q$. Canceling terms and assuming that $(\Delta Q)^2$ is infinitesimally small as ΔQ approaches zero yields $MC(Q) = 5 + 0.2Q$. The marginal-revenue-equals-marginal-cost rule in equation (7.3) implies that the profit-maximizing output is the solution to $10 = 5 + 0.2Q$. Rearranging terms yields $Q^* = (5/0.2) = 25$. At 25 units of output, profits are given by

$$\pi(Q) = (10 \times 25) - 10 - (5 \times 25) - (0.1 \times 25^2) = \$52.50$$

The firm earns \$52.50 per period by producing 25 units of output. No other output rate offers as high a profit rate. We know this from checking the second-order conditions. That is, the slope of the marginal cost function equals 0.2 and the slope of the marginal revenue function equals 0, so the second-order condition is satisfied. We can also derive this result by trying any other output rate in the profit expression; the profit rate you calculate will be less than \$52.50 per period. As a final exercise, you should compute the output rate at which profits are zero (or nearly zero). You should find that the answer is between 2 and 3 units of output.

7.3 THE CONTRACT-BASED APPROACH TO FIRM STRUCTURE

We've developed a simple rule for managers to follow to maximize profits, but why would managers act this way? If they don't work hard, they gain more leisure time. Employees could follow the managers' example and gain more leisure time, too. Fairly soon, the output rate of the firm would be lower than its profit-maximizing rate. The managers and employees would be better off, but, of course, the owners of the firm would be worse off. Thus, the simple rule developed above ignores a basic problem that owners face: How do they align the goals of managers and employees with their own goal of maximizing profits?

The contract-based approach to firm structure and organization is one way that firms address this issue. Using this approach, we can determine whether managers and employees have or don't have incentive to maximize profits. We can also investigate which contracts provide optimal incentives and which ones create problems, and we can discuss some problems that cannot be solved with simple contractual arrangements. Let's explore the implications of this approach further, starting with a discussion of team behavior.

THE BEHAVIOR OF TEAMS

Most, if not all, of the output that is produced within a firm is the result of teamwork. Employees and managers alike are part of a **team** that works together to produce the firm's output. A team will stay in existence if it can produce more output than the sum of the output that team members can produce when they work independently. If this is not true, the managers of the firm have an incentive to disband the team to allow its members to work independently.

Team
A collection of individuals working jointly to produce a product or service, or a specific part of a product or service.

A team does not come by its output advantage magically but rather through a combination of the production technology and the contracts that are agreed to between team members and the firm. The production technology dictates what is possible with team production versus individual production. In a simple case, two individuals can move furniture for a moving company much more quickly and with less damage than a single individual. Some furniture pieces, in fact, may not be movable by a single individual. So, team production dominates in the furniture-moving industry.

The contracts between the firm and team members define the benefits of team production as well as the restrictions the firm places on individual team members. The benefits include a paycheck if output is produced in a timely manner and, generally, an implicit understanding that the paycheck will continue as long as team production within the firm is cheaper than using the marketplace. These contracts may also specify restrictions on the behavior of team members. Some restrictions include firing only for cause, the hours during which the team must work and limits on each member's ability to contract with others for similar services—for example, an employee cannot also work for a competing firm.

LEARNING EXERCISE 7.2

Team production also occurs in a household, particularly for the raising of children. Yet, there has been an enormous increase in the purchase of market-produced child-care services in the past two decades. What are some of the reasons why households have substituted market services for "in-house" services?

THE INCENTIVE TO SHIRK

Shirking
Changing work effort in a manner that imposes a cost on other team members.

Team production generally increases output relative to individual production, but it also creates costs that are not present in individual production. One cost is the possibility of **shirking:** members of a team have an incentive to perform less than expected, or shirk, if their behavior may not be detected. Shirking can take many forms, from not completing an assignment on time to failing to vigorously block a pass rusher in a football game. Because the output of a team cannot be attributed to an individual member, the costs of shirking by one member are spread across all other members. In contrast, when output is produced individually, the cost of shirking is born by the person who shirks.

The incentive to shirk is shown in Figure 7.1. This diagram is similar to the labor versus leisure trade-off we discussed in Chapter 5. We have assumed that output is produced using five team members. For simplicity, let's assume that these five individuals design, assemble, and market Hawaiian kites. The reward line labeled R_1 shows the relationship between leisure (or more work effort) for a single team member and a team member's share of output *under the assumption that* no one *in the team shirks.* Basically, we can interpret reward

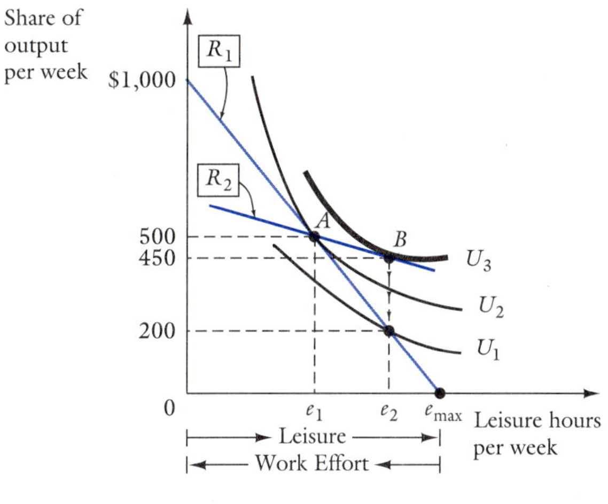

FIGURE 7.1

The Incentive for an Individual Team Member to Shirk

Reward line R_1 shows the trade-off between leisure and income for a single team member when all team members share equally in the output and work equally hard. Initially, the individual selects bundle A as the optimal bundle. This bundle contains e_1 units of leisure and $500 per week of income. Reward line R_2 is available to the individual if he or she alone changes consumption of leisure; the other team members must continue to consume e_1 units of leisure per week. Bundle B on reward line R_2 is optimal; it offers more satisfaction than bundle A. This individual consumes e_2 units of leisure per week in bundle A. Income for *all* team members is reduced to $450 per week. Because shirking increases satisfaction for one team member, all team members have an incentive to shirk, thereby destroying the viability of the team.

line R_1 as the trade-off a single team member faces when all team members supply the *same* amount of effort to the job. We will assume that team members share equally in the value of the kites produced. In effect, then, reward line R_1 splits the output of the team equally among all five team members.

Optimizing Behavior

For simplicity, we also assume that team members have identical preferences, so they will have identically shaped indifference curves. Three indifference curves are shown in Figure 7.1: U_1, U_2, and U_3. The absolute value of the slope of these curves at any point is a measure of the marginal rate of substitution between leisure and income produced from working with the other team members. Recall that a consumer is optimizing in his or her choice of leisure and income when the marginal rate of substitution is equal to the wage rate. In this case, the wage paid per period is determined by the output produced by all five team members. The absolute value of the slope of reward line R_1 is equivalent to the wage rate for the individual we are analyzing. So, optimal behavior requires the individual to select the amount of leisure (or equivalently, work effort) at which the reward line is tangent to an indifference curve. At the point of tangency, the marginal rate of substitution between leisure and work equals the absolute value of the slope of the reward line.

If all five team members choose to work all the time—a zero level of leisure—then *each* team member will receive \$1,000 per week, which is equal to the total value of kites produced divided by 5 (\$5,000/5). With *no shirking*—that is, we are on reward line R_1—the marginal rate of substitution equals the absolute value of the slope of the reward line at point A. In this optimal bundle, each team member selects e_1 units of leisure per week, which produces \$2,500 in total output value that pays \$500 in weekly income to each team member.

Shirking Allowed

Now, if we allow shirking, reward line R_1 will no longer be the relevant one for the shirking team member. Shirking occurs when one team member increases his or her leisure while the other team members do not change their leisure consumption. If one member of the team shirks, then output will fall, but the shirking team member will not bear the full cost of the decrease in output because it is shared equally with the other members of the team. If the shirking team member selects a leisure rate equal to e_2 units—holding the effort of the other team members at e_1—then total output value will fall by \$250, reducing each team member's weekly pay to \$450. The shirking team member is moving along reward line R_2 while the other team members remain at point A on reward line R_1. Reward line R_2 offers more income at each leisure rate for leisure rates to the right of e_1. In effect, the other team members are paying for four-fifths of the cost of the extra leisure consumed by the shirking member. The shirking team member now finds that bundle B is optimal. The satisfaction achieved by the shirking member at bundle B—given by indifference curve U_3—has increased relative to the satisfaction received at the no-shirking bundle, A. The shirking team member is better off by shirking *if none of the other team members change their behavior.*

The other team members are not likely to enthusiastically accept the shirking by one member. If all team members change their leisure rate to e_2, then they are no longer subsidizing the shirking team member. Total output of kites falls as a result, which decreases the weekly pay of each team member to \$200. The level of satisfaction also declines—U_2 and U_3 compared to U_1. So shirking by one team member reduces the incentive of the whole team to work, which makes *all* team members worse off.

MANAGING A TEAM TO PREVENT SHIRKING

You may reason, of course, that there may be no end to the shirking created by the example in Figure 7.1. Team members may continue to shirk until there is no output produced, that is, until the leisure rate is equal to e_{max}, the maximum leisure that can be consumed in a week. Obviously, if this occurs, the team is no longer a team. Two aspects of the problem may create this result.[3] First, team production leads to a sharing of kite output, so the full cost of shirking is not borne by the shirking team member. Second, the team stays together until the bitter end. If members can be "fired" by other team members and new members "hired" to replace them, then there may exist a sufficient threat to prevent the shirking cycle from reaching a point at which the team falls apart. The threat of firing causes individual team members to shirk less than if there was no possibility of firing. Although kite output is still reduced by shirking when firing is possible, the threat of firing makes the team itself viable.

Because shirking behavior decreases output, it is likely to decrease a firm's profits, so shareholders have an incentive to reduce such behavior. We can see a clear role for managers in such situations. Managers monitor the team for shirking behavior and implement appropriate penalties if it is detected. The nonshirking team members are made better off if the managers can effectively perform this task. By monitoring and possibly firing shirking employees, managers can generally reduce the quantity of shirking, but they cannot totally eliminate it. In effect, firms try to internalize the cost of shirking to those who are shirking. The use of profit sharing contracts is one way firms try to internalize the losses caused by shirking. Various other approaches are used, too, and many of these are discussed below.

LEARNING EXERCISE 7.3

In Figure 7.1, why is the share of output on the shirking reward line, R_2, below the share of output on the no-shirking reward line, R_1, when the leisure rate is below e_1?

[3] The 100 percent leisure solution may not occur if the individual indifference curves are relatively flat at e_{max}. If four workers shirk and provide no work effort, the fifth worker receives only one-fifth of any output he or she chooses to produce. This worker may choose to work if the slope of indifference curve is less than (in absolute value) one-fifth the slope of reward line R_1.

CONTRACTING FOR PROFIT-MAXIMIZING BEHAVIOR

Because a firm is composed of many parts, contracts are necessary to define the relationship between these parts. The contract-based approach to the theory of a firm explains the behavior of a firm as influenced by the incentives created by the contracts it adopts. According to this approach, the firm's employment rules, debt contracts, contracts with outside vendors, contracts with customers, and all other contracts can be interpreted in light of how they help to maximize profits.

Poor performance of a firm, relative to other firms in the same industry, may be attributed to poorly designed contracts. In such a case, the existing contracts in a firm do not provide some part of the firm—often it is the managers—with an incentive to maximize profits. Poor performance may lead shareholders to change the firm's contracts, which can be accomplished in various ways. Mergers with other firms, leveraged buyouts by management groups, and hostile takeovers can often be viewed as an attempt to restructure a firm's contracts so that they provide *all* parts of a firm with an incentive to maximize profits.

7.4 Coordinating and Monitoring Production

As owners, shareholders face numerous problems when they try to align the incentives of others with their own profit-maximizing objective. In this section, we review some of these problems, emphasizing the agency problem, the high cost of coordinating production when the firm has many owners, the problems of moral hazard and adverse selection, and the problem of end-of-period incentives. In retrospect, we will find that much of the organizational structure of a firm is designed to reduce shirking as well as mitigate these many other problems in order to maximize profits for shareholders.

THE AGENCY PROBLEM

The agency problem is a permanent fixture on the corporate landscape, but it also permeates nearly all economic transactions in one way or another. To illustrate the problem, suppose you contract with a builder to construct an addition to your house. The addition is of a simple design—four sides and a roof, three windows, one outside door, two interior walls, and electrical connections—that does not require complicated construction techniques. You sign a contract with JustRite Builders to construct the addition. As the structure is nearing completion, you notice—entirely by accident—that the interior walls have a hollow sound when you tap on them. A closer inspection reveals that the studs used to frame these walls are too far apart. The contractor assures you that the walls are structurally sound, but you are still doubtful. What has happened here? The contractor has saved some money and time by building substandard interior walls. The contractor's incentive is to cut cost to increase profits when cost-cutting measures cannot normally be detected; your goal is to purchase a durable structure. These two goals conflict with one another, as tapping the interior walls has revealed.

Principal
The individual or party who initiates some action.

Agent
The individual or party responsible for performing the action requested by the principal.

Agency Costs
Costs the principal incurs because of some action by an agent.

In this example, you are the **principal,** because you initiated the project, and the contractor is the **agent,** the one charged with carrying out your goals. Legally, the agent is one who is authorized to act for, or in place of, another. In this case, the agent is acting for the principal.

The agency problem arises because the goals of the agent are not always aligned with the goals of the principal.

When the two goals diverge, there are **agency costs** that the principal may incur because of some action the agent takes. In the house addition example, the agency costs are the monitoring costs to detect the problem plus the costs you may incur in the future to fix the problem if it goes undetected during construction.

THE MANY FORMS OF AGENCY

In a firm, principal and agent relationships exist on many levels. These levels are described in Figure 7.2. The two most common agency problems in a firm are:

1. The divergence in goals between the owners or shareholders and the managers, which may represent itself as a conflict between the shareholders and the board of directors and then, possibly, the board of directors and the managers

PRINCIPAL	AGENT
Shareholders/Owners	Board of Directors/Managers
Board of Directors	Managers
Managers	Employees
Managers	Outside Suppliers
Banks and Debtholders	Shareholders/Owners
Internal Revenue Service	The Firm/Accountants

FIGURE 7.2

The Agency Relationships in a Firm

Six typical principal-agent relationships are described. The first four are internal to the firm and its organizational structure. The last two are principal-agent relationships that arise between the firm and outsiders.

2. The incentive of shareholders to transfer wealth from bondholders or, collectively, debtholders

Note that the **board of directors** is the governing body of a company; its members are elected by a vote of the company's shareholders.

Board of Directors
A group elected by the shareholders to represent their interests with the firm's managers. The board of directors has the fiduciary responsibility to monitor the firm's managers.

In the first instance, the conflict arises because managers own less than 100 percent of the firm, so they may have an incentive to shirk or otherwise increase their satisfaction at the expense of shareholders. Executive perks, such as first-class travel, posh offices, art galleries in the executive suites, and country club memberships, are a few of the purported examples of how managers increase their satisfaction (or benefits) at the expense of shareholders. Managers may also work relatively slowly to find new investments that offer a positive net present value if the return on these investments accrues only to shareholders.

Although shareholder/manager conflict surely exists, shareholders can anticipate such problems, and they can adjust management contracts and the value they place on ownership in the firm to allow for such problems. Consider, for example, how a firm typically evolves over time. Initially, firms are small, with only a few owners, limited capital funds, and an innovative idea or product. The owners are nearly always the managers of such small firms—called owner-manager firms. These firms grow if their idea or product is successful in the marketplace. The now classic example is Apple Computer, which started in a garage and grew to become a multibillion-dollar company in less than ten years. At some point in the firm's development, the owner-managers find that they need additional funds to continue the firm's growth. It is usually at this point that the owner-manager firm becomes a shareholder-*and*-manager firm, with the managers now owning less than 100 percent of the firm. If the agency problem between shareholders and managers is *fully anticipated,* then the price that the new investors (shareholders) offer the owner-managers for shares in the firm reflects a discount for the agency costs the managers are expected to impose on shareholders.

The original owner-managers bear all of the agency costs resulting from anticipated conflicts between shareholders and managers.

CONFLICTS BETWEEN SHAREHOLDERS AND DEBTHOLDERS

The agency problem that arises between shareholders and debtholders can take many forms, but all instances involve an attempt to transfer wealth from debtholders to shareholders. When a debt contract is written, it will specify, at a minimum, the interest rate the firm must pay and a repayment schedule. The interest rate on the debt presumably represents the opportunity cost of the funds borrowed plus a premium for the riskiness of the firm. The riskiness of the firm is usually determined by the planned use of the funds, the likelihood of bankruptcy, and the variability of returns on the firm's past investments. A more risky firm is charged a higher interest rate because there is a higher probability that the debtholders will not receive all of their investment back. Once the interest rate is set, however, shareholders may encourage managers to find and invest in riskier projects. Such projects would normally carry a higher interest charge from debtholders, but, because shareholders have locked in the interest rate, debtholders are stuck with a lower-than-market interest rate. In effect, debtholders are subsidizing shareholders by not charging them enough for the funds they have borrowed.

To prevent such behavior by shareholders, many debt contracts contain covenants that specify how the funds are to be used, restrictions on the riskiness of the firm's future investments, restrictions on the firm's ability to change its financial structure, and other restrictions. The Trust Indenture Act of 1939 contains a host of such "boilerplate" restrictions that debtholders typically incorporate in their contracts with firms.[4]

One benefit to shareholders of leverage, or debt, is that such contracts may help reduce the agency costs caused by managers. When a firm obligates itself to a debtholder, it guarantees a minimum level of performance in the contract. Interest and principal payments are scheduled on a regular basis, which means that managers must produce enough earnings to make these payments. If the payments are not made, the debtholders may become the owners of the firm through bankruptcy proceedings. Managers are then likely to lose their jobs and to find other employment more difficult to obtain—they are tainted by their own failure. Because of the consequences of bankruptcy, a large debt burden may cause managers to work harder to maximize profits, thereby reducing some—but never all—of the agency costs present between shareholders and managers.

UNANTICIPATED AGENCY COSTS

It is possible that shareholder and manager conflicts, shareholder and debtholder conflicts, and other agency conflicts may be mitigated by the contracts initiated when these relationships are first formed, but this view does not allow for *unanticipated* agency costs. Shirking by managers may be cleverly disguised and can change over time. Shareholders at the turn of the century worried about managers riding in private railroad cars or sleeping in luxurious suites on ocean liners crossing the Atlantic, but they surely did not anticipate the growth of air travel or the likely increasing value of the artwork found in some executive suites. So, while anticipated perks and shirking can be used to discount a stock's price, unanticipated perks and shirking continue to pose a problem.

For debtholders, new financial instruments seem to be the greatest worry. Interest rate swaps—contracts in which two parties exchange different interest payments on the same size principal amount—were a nearly nonexistent market in the early 1970s, for example, and are a multitrillion dollar market today. Such transactions may change the riskiness of the firm, which may increase the likelihood of default on debt contracts, thus costing the debtholder a bankruptcy expense that was not fully anticipated.

[4] For an extensive analysis of bond covenants—that is, the clauses that restrict a firm's behavior after bonds are issued—see Clifford W. Smith and Jerold B. Warner, "On Financial Contracting: An Analysis of Bond Covenants," *Journal of Financial Economics* 7 (1979), 117–161.

$$$ Price Theory in Practice

The Agency Problem at the IRS

The problem a government faces as it tries to collect taxes from its citizens is a principal-agent problem. The problem arises from the implicit contract that exists between the government and taxpayers. The government—the principal—provides public services, and in return, citizens—the agents—pay the taxes necessary to provide these services. The problem is that many of the government's services are public goods; that is, they are produced for the benefit of all, without the ability to exclude anyone (e.g., national defense, interstate highways, law enforcement). In addition, nearly one-half of government expenditures are transfer payments that, in effect, take from one group and give to another. With public goods and transfer payments, each individual has an incentive to make someone else pay the cost while he or she still receives the benefits.

The Internal Revenue Service (IRS) is charged with the job of collecting the taxes owed by citizens. The task is complicated because it is difficult to discover tax cheating. Cheating behavior is often not observable—in other words, the government does not always know whether an individual purposely failed to report income or has simply made a mistake preparing a tax return. To fulfill its implicit contract, the government must monitor taxpayers, thereby providing an incentive for them to live up to their part of the implicit contract and pay their taxes.

Each year, the IRS audits over 100,000 taxpayer and corporate returns. Even with this effort, the IRS estimates that substantial income is not reported. The IRS estimated, for example, that $9 billion in taxes was not paid in 1991 because individuals did not file tax returns and over $50 billion was not paid because individuals underreported their income.

When the IRS does conduct an audit, however, the amount recovered is substantial. In 1990, for example, the IRS handled 4,322,000 delinquent returns at a cost of $2.52 billion. Errors, cheating, or omissions led to the recovery of $24.2 billion in taxes owed for a return of 860 percent on the IRS's investment.[5]

The IRS is fairly well organized in its program of audits. It is less expensive to catch an error (or cheating) on a simple return than on a complicated return. So, the average taxpayer is more likely to be caught than the wealthy individual or corporation. Because of the more than 1 billion W-2 and 1099 forms that businesses must file each year with the IRS, the actual income of the average taxpayer is partly observable. Those forms make it possible for the IRS to compute tax returns for nearly 40 percent of the country's taxpayers, primarily those with incomes under $100,000.

In 1990, for example, the IRS billed a Connecticut college student $125 in back taxes and another $125 in penalties and interest. The student had worked several part-time jobs as a student during 1987 but did not file a tax return

[5] *IRS Annual Report* Commissioner of the Internal Revenue Service, U.S. Treasury, GPO Publication 55, 1992.

because she believed she was exempt. The IRS computers used the information from W-2 forms to compile a tax return and send her a bill.

In contrast, IRS computers are not yet sophisticated enough to compute the exact taxes owed by wealthy taxpayers and corporations; they can only estimate taxes owed for these groups, and the estimates are often incorrect. To collect taxes on complicated tax returns, the IRS must devote significant labor resources to an audit. Budget constraints at the IRS limit its ability to conduct such audits; hence, sophisticated taxpayers and many firms have less incentive to reveal all their income.

As a result, there are differences in how the IRS monitors taxpayers. The IRS does not investigate nearly one-half of the people with incomes *over* $100,000 who they think have failed to file tax returns. When some of those nonfilers file a return for a later year, nearly 11 percent receive refund checks even though they might actually owe money from a previous year. In contrast, IRS computers compile a tax bill for every person with income *under* $100,000 who fails to file a return. No one in that group who files a return in a subsequent year receives a refund until the amount previously owed is paid. Although the monitoring approach of the IRS is discriminatory, it may be optimal given the cost of auditing sophisticated tax returns.

LEARNING EXERCISE 7.4

Under present laws, fines and prison terms may be imposed on individuals who are convicted of criminal tax fraud. Yet, there is still substantial underreporting of income. How would an increase in fines for cheating affect the amount of cheating? Does your answer depend on the IRS continuing its current monitoring policies? What do you think will happen to the amount of cheating if the individual tax rate is decreased?

END-OF-PERIOD PROBLEMS

The end-of-period problem is a special type of agency problem that arises when there is a terminal period specified in a contract. As the terminal period approaches, the incentive to perform under the contract changes. A worker who is about to retire, for example, may not work as hard as another worker who is many years from retirement. The last few airplanes produced under a government contract that is to be transferred to another firm may be of lower quality than airplanes produced before the firm discovered the contract was not to be renewed. In a corporate restructuring, key managers who expect to lose their jobs may spend their time looking for new employment instead of continuing to work productively in their present firm.

The end-of-period problem has an *unraveling* characteristic that must be taken into account in contracts. Suppose that you are a trusted bank teller and you are told that you will be fired in 30 days. On the thirtieth day, you have little incentive to remain trustworthy—for simplicity, let's say that there are no moral issues here and that the bank cannot pursue you after you leave the company—so you might dip into the cash box for a little extra money. But if this is true on the thirtieth day, then it is at least partly true on the twenty-ninth day, so you will be less trustworthy on this day, too. What is partly true for the twenty-ninth day is again in some part true for the twenty-eighth day, and so forth. The problem unravels back to the day you are informed that you will be fired. From that day forward, your trustworthiness changes.

To help overcome the unraveling aspect of end-of-period problems, firms adopt contingent contracts. A worker nearing retirement, for example, may receive retirement benefits based on wages paid during each of the last five years, so workers have an incentive to be productive in the five-year period before retirement to keep their wages high. In the trustworthy employee case, workers may receive a severance package that is forfeited if they are caught cheating. The dollar value of the severance package is expected to be high enough to deter cheating activity. In other cases, such as the firing of a radio disc jockey, firms frequently give no notice that the employee is to be dismissed. On the day the person is fired, locks may be rekeyed and the employee may be "locked out" of the building. Such drastic action occurs when an employee has the potential to impose a large cost on the firm by his or her actions. By using obscenities over the airwaves, a radio disc jockey could cause a firm to be fined or to lose its FCC license.

The end-of-period problem often affects the design of a firm's contracts. The firm attempts to overcome the problem by specifying contingencies that prevent contracts and incentives from unraveling.

LEARNING EXERCISE 7.5

What will happen to class attendance in your economics course if the final exam is made optional two weeks before the end of the semester?

7.5 THE SEPARATION OF OWNERSHIP AND CONTROL

Because there are typically many shareholders, there are potentially many "bosses" in a firm. If each "boss" tried to manage the firm's production activities, there would be chaos. Shareholders of the modern business firm avoid such chaos by delegating or contracting with others to perform certain tasks within the firm, such as the coordination of production activities and the selection and planning of future investments. In effect, shareholders have set up a structure in which the *control* of most of a firm's activities is transferred to others for a limited time period. In spite of the resulting agency problems—which include shirking by managers—most organizations are characterized by a *separation of ownership and control.*

BOARD OF DIRECTORS

Shareholders provide the capital a firm needs for its investment plans while also giving up a great deal of the control over how such funds are invested. In exchange for such control, managers set performance goals and reveal how well the firm's investments are expected to perform. Given such information, shareholders can decide whether to invest in the firm's future. Of course, managers could always lie about their expectations and paint a rosy scenario to seduce shareholders to invest. To prevent such opportunistic behavior, shareholders elect a small group from their number to monitor the firm's top management. This group, called the board of directors, transfers managerial control to top managers for only a limited time period.

Generally, the board of directors consists of both outsiders and insiders, that is, people who do not work for the firm and people who do. Usually, the outsiders are individuals who have extensive business or academic experience and/or individuals who own large amounts of the firm's stock. The insiders are the managers the board interacts with most often, usually the president and the chief executive officer (CEO) of the firm.

Managers present their expectations of future investment returns to the board on a regular basis—at least quarterly in most companies. If the top managers acted opportunistically to misrepresent their expectations or they are simply wrong (and it is costly to be wrong), then the board of directors is charged with the duty to dismiss the top managers of the firm when the facts are known and to find top managers to replace those dismissed. So, in exchange for control over the use of shareholder's funds, top managers accept the consequences that follow when their expectations are not realized—they are fired.

WHO MONITORS THE MONITORS?

A board of directors appears to represent a sensible solution to the problem of too many "bosses"; that is, shareholders choose a small number of "bosses" to monitor their investments. But is it really a workable solution? For example, who monitors the board of directors to ensure that they are really acting on the behalf of the broader shareholder population? It is quite possible that the board of directors may be susceptible to nonpecuniary bribes from the firm's top managers. In other words, to keep their positions and the perks of board membership, the board may cast a positive light on the firm's financial performance, even if it is abysmal and top management is completely responsible for the bad performance. The broader shareholder population then has a really *big* problem—whom can it trust?

Generally, no single shareholder has much incentive to monitor the performance of a firm for all the other shareholders.

> **A shareholder who spends resources to monitor incurs all of the expense but enjoys only part of the gain; the rest of the shareholders share in the gain but not in the cost.**

So, each shareholder will underinvest in monitoring, and the total monitoring effort will be less than that found in a firm owned by a single individual. The board of directors is expected to perform the monitoring function, but how can the board be trusted? Because of the agency problem, top managers may not always act to maximize profits; if they can coerce the board of directors into believing that what is being done is acceptable, then the board is no longer acting as an effective monitoring body.

Three solutions have evolved to help solve the problem of who monitors the monitors. The first is that members of the board of directors are legally fiduciary agents of the shareholders, so they can be sued if they misrepresent the truth. In fact, they may be personally liable under certain circumstances for any fraud that they knowingly perpetrate as board members, and it is unlikely that so-called director's insurance will cover them in such situations. So, board members must think carefully about their actions if they could possibly misrepresent the truth by what they do.

The second solution is for the shareholders to transfer the monitoring function to individual board members for only a limited time. If a director is acting inappropriately, shareholders may choose to vote for another nominee to fill that director's place on the board when his or her term expires.

The third and most important solution involves a market for corporate control that greatly limits the discretion of the board of directors and top management.[6] Suppose the agency problem begins to manifest itself in a way that lowers the value of ownership in the firm—that is, the price of a share of stock falls. Then, among the investing public, some individual or group of individuals may think there is a profit opportunity to be had by correcting the agency problem. The profit opportunity will appear if the investors can buy *all or nearly all* of the shares of the firm. By buying all or nearly all of the firm's shares, these investors will solve the problem of underinvesting in monitoring, because they will reap the entire return from this activity. A corporate takeover solves the existing agency problem and eliminates, for a while, the problem of who monitors the monitors. Thus, the market for corporate control—the threat of a takeover—may be the ultimate limit on the behavior of managers and the board of directors.

POISON PILL CONTRACTS

Partly in response to the wave of merger activity in the 1980s, many firms adopted antitakeover provisions to fight off attempts by other firms, called suitors, to take over or buy the firm outright. Table 7.1 shows the merger trend from 1970 to 1990. There was a notable increase in merger activity in the 1980s, particularly for mergers worth over $100 million (in nominal terms). As activity increased in the market for corporate control, many top managers requested and received special provisions—called **poison pills**—to fight the takeovers they deemed undesirable. These provisions are designed to impose extra costs on a potential suitor. For example, Knight-Ridder, Inc., which owns newspapers in several major cities in the United States, adopted a poison pill provision that requires potential suitors, in effect, to pass a "journalistic ethics and morality test" before the board of directors approves a

Poison Pills
Special provisions adopted by a firm, often without the vote of shareholders, that make a corporate takeover more costly for the acquiring company.

[6] For an early discussion of the market for corporate control, see Henry G. Manne, "Mergers and the Market for Corporate Control," *Journal of Political Economy* 73 (1965), 110–120.

TABLE 7.1

Merger Activity in the United States, 1970–1990

Year	Value of Mergers (billions)	Constant Dollar Value of Mergers (billions)	Number of Mergers	Number of Mergers Valued at $100 Million or More	Number of Mergers Valued at $1,000 Million or More
1970	$16.4	$39.0	5,152	10	1
1971	12.6	28.4	4,608	7	0
1972	16.7	35.9	4,801	15	0
1973	16.7	33.7	4,040	28	0
1974	12.5	23.0	2,861	15	0
1975	11.8	19.9	2,297	14	1
1976	20.0	31.7	2,276	39	1
1977	21.9	32.5	2,224	41	0
1978	34.2	47.4	2,106	80	1
1979	43.5	55.3	2,128	83	3
1980	44.3	51.7	1,889	94	4
1981	82.6	87.9	2,395	113	12
1982	53.8	53.8	2,346	116	6
1983	73.1	70.4	2,533	138	11
1984	122.2	113.5	2,543	200	18
1985	179.7	161.9	3,001	270	36
1986	173.1	152.0	3,336	346	27
1987	163.7	139.1	2,032	301	36
1988	246.9	203.5	2,258	369	45
1989	221.1	175.1	2,366	328	35
1990	108.2	82.3	2,074	181	21

Notes: This data is collected by Merrill Lynch Business Advisory Services; Merrill Lynch reports the value of mergers that disclose transaction price; the number of mergers is based on announced transactions in a given year—canceled mergers are subtracted from the total in the year they are announced; the constant dollar value of the merger series is based on 1982 dollars.

merger or takeover. The consequences of not passing the test and continuing with the takeover are many, including the dilution of the suitor's investment with a new stock issue and expensive payments—"golden parachutes"—to top managers who lose their jobs in the process.

Some shareholders have tried to fight back, realizing that even if there is no actual takeover, the threat of one may help to reduce agency costs and, consequently, to increase profits. To fight back, shareholder groups have sought to repeal many of the more onerous poison pill provisions. For example, the California State Teachers' Retirement System, with over $20 billion in investments, has in several instances proposed the repeal of board-adopted poison pill provisions.

Table 7.2 reprints the California State Teachers' 1987 proposal to the shareholders of Colgate-Palmolive Company and the position of Colgate's

TABLE 7.2

Shareholder Proposal on Rights Plan for Colgate-Palmolive Co., 1987 Proxy Statement

Management has been advised that the California State Teachers' Retirement System, P.O. Box 15275-C, Sacramento, CA 95851, owner of 137,126 shares, intends to submit the following proposal at the meeting and that the California Public Employees' Retirement System, Lincoln Plaza-400 P Street, Sacramento, CA, owner of 298,999 shares, intends to co-sponsor the proposal.

RESOLVED, that it is recommended that the Board of Directors of Colgate-Palmolive rescind or submit for shareholder approval, at the earliest possible date, the Common Share Rights Plan adopted on October 11, 1984.

Shareholder Supporting Statement

On October 11, 1984, the Board of Directors unilaterally and without shareholder participation or approval, adopted the Common Share Purchase Rights Plan. These "Rights" when distributed to holders of the Corporation would, in our view, significantly deter a non-negotiated takeover of the Corporation. The "Rights" more commonly known as "poison pills," will be "triggered" by (i) the acquisition of 20% or more of the Company's outstanding common stock, or (ii) a tender offer for 30% or more of the Company's outstanding shares of common stock.

In our opinion, this "poison pill" will not only deter non-negotiated takeovers of the Corporation, but would serve to entrench current management, all to the detriment of the shareholders.

We as a $20 billion public school teachers' fund, become concerned when we see corporations such as Colgate-Palmolive, enacting "poisoning pills."

And we are not alone.

In commenting on "poison pill" proposals the SEC stated: "Tender Offers can benefit shareholders by offering them an opportunity to sell their shares at a premium and by guarding against management entrenchment. However, because poison pills are intended to deter non-negotiated tender offers, and because they have this potential effect without stockholder consent, poison pill plans can effectively prevent shareholders from even considering the merits of a takeover that is opposed by the board." SEC Release No. 34-23486 (July 31, 1986).

Your Board recommends a vote AGAINST this proposal.

This proposal is similar to others that these two organizations have submitted to a number of other companies. It appears to the Board that they intend a general campaign against plans like our Rights Plan without regard to the particular corporation adopting the plan.

During the past few years, takeover activity has markedly increased. Even though a third party may offer a premium over the current market price of a corporation's stock, that premium may not necessarily recognize the inherent value of that corporation. In some cases, these third parties make substantial open market purchases of a corporation's stock from professional investors who have acquired that stock with the sole objective of selling out at a quick profit. A third party, of course, can be expected to act only in its own self interest, with little or no regard for the interests of the stockholders or other constituencies of a corporation. Your directors, on the other hand, are obligated as fiduciaries to exercise their business judgment and act in

TABLE 7.2

Shareholder Proposal on Rights Plan for Colgate-Palmolive Co., 1987 Proxy Statement (Continued)

what they reasonably determine in good faith to be in all stockholders' best interests and in the best interests of all constituencies of the Company.

The Delaware Supreme Court has held that adoption of a rights plan is a valid exercise of a board's business judgment in that a rights plan helps a board to fulfill its fiduciary responsibilities. While redeeming the Rights Plan may enable some investors to reap quick profits in the event of a non-negotiated offer for the Company's stock, the Board does not believe that stockholder value is enhanced through Strategic Initiatives of the type undertaken since 1984 when the Rights Plan was adopted. The Board believes that the implementation of the Strategic Initiatives—the business restructuring, the divestment of non-core businesses, the emphasis on new products, the corporate reorganization and the common stock repurchase—have greatly influenced Company results and attendant stockholder value.

The Rights Plan does not prevent the making of an acquisition proposal or the acceptance of an acquisition proposal that the Board finds to be in the interests of stockholders. Rather, it is designed to strengthen the ability of the Board, in the event of such an offer, to negotiate and maximize stockholder value. Experience shows that there have been acquisition offers made to many corporations that have adopted rights plans as well as many situations in which the board of directors of a corporation has determined to redeem its rights plan in connection with the acquisition of that corporation. Indeed, there have been a number of instances where, with a rights plan in place, directors have been able to improve stockholder returns even in the face of an initial, above-market offer. This confirms our belief that the question of whether to redeem the Rights Plan should only be answered in the context of a specific acquisition proposal. In determining whether to redeem our Rights Plan in the context of a specific proposal, your Board has an obligation to meet its fiduciary duties and exercise its business judgment.

board regarding the proposal. The board recommended that shareholders "vote AGAINST this proposal." As you can see, Colgate's board claimed that its poison pill was "designed to strengthen the ability of the Board, in the event of such an offer, to negotiate and maximize stockholder value." The California Teachers' position was just the reverse: "In our opinion, this 'poison pill' will not only deter non-negotiated takeovers of the Corporation, but would serve to entrench current management, all to the detriment of the shareholders." In effect, the poison pill would dilute the value of ownership in Colgate-Palmolive Company. In this instance, the Board's position prevailed; only 18 percent of the votes cast supported the California Teachers' proposal.

Poison pills have had the effect of making a takeover more costly to potential suitors. As a result, the ability of the market for corporate control to limit opportunistic behavior by managers (and the board of directors) and to reduce agency costs has been restricted.

$$$ Price Theory in Practice

Thelma Gibson and the Separation of Ownership and Control

Do managers act in their self-interest or in the interest of shareholders? Instead of asking an economist or a business executive, it might be informative to ask someone you might expect to be your next-door neighbor, Thelma Gibson, a retired registered nurse from Miami.

Gibson was on the board of directors of the Miami savings and loan CenTrust when it failed in 1990 under a mountain of bad loans. As federal regulators looked beneath the rubble, they found that CenTrust's managers had engaged in questionable business practices, practices not necessarily intended to maximize profits for shareholders.

While leading CenTrust to large losses, managers—headed by Chairman David Paul—spent $175 million to build a corporate office tower that the government later sold for $44 million. CenTrust's offices in the tower were adorned with gold-plated bathroom fixtures and multimillion-dollar "old masters" paintings, including Rubens's "Portrait of a Man as the God Mars," purchased with depositors' money in 1988 for $29 million. For a time, some of these paintings had hung in Chairman Paul's private residence.

In the aftermath of the thrift's failure, Gibson and the other directors became the target of a federal lawsuit that charged them with failing to fulfill their fiduciary duty to monitor the firm's managers on behalf of the shareholders. The directors say they acted only on the advice of lawyers, accountants, and consultants. Nevertheless, the federal government sought $245 million in damages.

The CenTrust case illustrates the hazard of serving as a director of a company and the problem created by agency costs. Directors, such as Thelma Gibson, are expected to represent the shareholders and ensure that top managers, such as David Paul, are operating the firm for the benefit of the shareholders, not themselves. Paul, for example, has been accused by the government of spending $15.8 million of CenTrust's money on himself, which the government is trying to recover. Paul has also been accused of using CenTrust to help convicted junk bond wizard Michael Milken manipulate the junk bond market during the 1980s. Paul was named in a $6.8 billion government lawsuit against Milken and the firm he worked for, the now defunct Drexel Burnham Lambert. The suit charges that Milken, Paul, and several others conspired to inflate junk bond prices artificially. CenTrust fell into receivership when the government forced it to reduce the value of its junk bond portfolio to its market value.

The government's action against CenTrust's directors and its chairman may not end with its claims in civil court. As Table 7.3 shows, many executives of failed savings and loans have been accused, convicted, and sentenced for criminal behavior.

TABLE 7.3

Prison Sentences Related to Savings and Loan Failures

Name and Position	Institution	Prison Term
William R. Runnells, Jr. Founder	Landbank Equity Co. Norfolk, VA	40 Years
Wailen H. York Borrower/Developer	Empire Savings and Loan Mesquite, TX	35 Years
Marika Runnells President	Landbank Equity Co. Norfolk, VA	31 Years
Woody F. Lemons Chairman	Vernon Savings and Loan Dallas, TX	30 Years
Paul Sau-ki Cheng Co-owner	Guaranty Savings Dallas, TX	30 Years
Simon Edward Heath Co-owner	Guaranty Savings Dallas, TX	20 Years
Janet Faye McKenzie Consultant	North American Savings and Loan Santa Ann, CA	20 Years
Ralph Strader Borrower/Developer	Sunbelt Savings Dallas, TX	10 Years
Lowell Rosenthal Borrower/Developer	Sunbelt Savings Dallas, TX	10 Years
Charles Keating Chairman	Lincoln Savings and Loans Phoenix, AZ	12 Years
Don R. Dixon Owner	Vernon Savings and Loan Dallas, TX	5 Years

The CenTrust case is not just an example of the problems directors face monitoring managers; it also illustrates the problem created by the U.S. deposit insurance system. The deposit insurance system encourages bank and savings and loan executives to take risks, such as investing in junk bonds, because the insurance fund will bail out depositors if those investments do not pay off. Shareholders may receive large dividends from banks and savings and loans before these risky investments fail. Chairman Paul, for example, owned a large fraction of CenTrust's stock, and he received substantial compensation in the form of dividends. The deposit insurance system, then, tends to magnify the problems created by the separation of ownership and control in banks and savings and loans.

Learning Exercise 7.6

If Chairman David Paul had owned 100 percent of CenTrust, do you think the firm's investment behavior (e.g., junk bonds, gold-plated bathrooms, art) would have been any different? How would your answer change if there was no deposit insurance?

Policy Application and Evaluation

Executive Pay

Issue *Are corporate executives overpaid?*

Background

Executive salaries at American corporations were the subject of critical news articles over several years. Invariably, when total cash compensation is revealed, usually in the first quarter of the year, some executive at a major corporation is reported to have earned tens of millions of dollars. In 1992, Thomas Frist, the chief executive of HCA Hospital Corporation of America, reported cash compensation of $126 million. In the same year, Sanford Weill, CEO at Primerica Corporation, earned $64 million. Nearly all these earnings are from stock options. Stock options offer an executive the option to purchase company stock at a price established, generally, several years before the options are exercised. If the company's profits improve and the stock price increases, the options increase in value. The United States is the leader in the use of stock options for corporate executives. Even without stock options, however, executives in the United States appear to earn more than their overseas counterparts. In 1992, the 20 highest-paid executives in the United States earned on average $4.8 million in salary and bonuses.[7] In Germany the comparable average was $1.8 million, and in Japan the average was $530,000.

The Case for Shareholder Concern

Should shareholders worry about the relative pay of chief executive officers? The success that some German and Japanese firms have had competing head-to-head with American companies suggests that executive pay needs a careful review. If the governance structure of a corporation favors existing management—poison pill provisions and golden parachutes for executives—shareholders can lose wealth to managers over time. Before the development of poison pills, shareholders could rely on corporate raiders or the market discipline imposed by a falling share price to signal that managers were not performing up to expectations. But with poison pills, the threat of a hostile takeover is diminished, so a greater opportunity exists for management to extract some wealth from shareholders, which the relative pay comparisons may reflect.

The "Much Ado About Nothing" View

Absolute and relative pay comparisons are seriously incomplete as commonly reported. Thomas Frist earned the stock options that resulted in $126 million compensation over 25 years. He just chose to exercise them in a single year, which vastly overstates his annual pay. In addition, when an executive's options are issued, they are priced at the current market price, so there is no gain to be had from exercising them immediately; only if the stock price increases will the

[7] See *Forbes,* "The Global Boss' Pay: Where (and How) the Money Is," June 7, 1993.

executive gain. But if the executive gains, so do the shareholders as their holdings become more valuable. Comparisons with Germany and Japan are also incomplete. The United States has strict laws on what information corporations must report about executive compensation. Germany and Japan operate under different rules, which allow corporations to report less information about executive compensation. All comparisons are therefore based on estimates and educated guesses. What we know is that these countries have higher tax rates for high-income individuals, so corporations offer a "mix" of benefits to their executives. Cars, housing allowances, vacation packages, country club memberships, education allowances, and board memberships at related companies are just a few of the in-kind payments companies provide in order to avoid the higher tax rates on income. In addition, many multinational companies in Japan and Germany issue several checks to each of their top executives. These checks are from accounts in their overseas subsidiaries, which makes them subject to the overseas tax rate on income. Because the information is not available to correctly measure executive pay in Japan and Germany, it is unclear whether the relative pay comparisons frequently made are correct.

Questions for Evaluation

In 1993, IBM searched for a new CEO and had trouble finding a prominent executive who would accept the job. If CEOs are overpaid, why did IBM have trouble finding someone for the top spot? Should the government do anything about the pay to corporate executives? If the CEO's pay is cut, what signal does that action send to lower-level managers in the company? Will these lower-level managers work harder to move up the corporate ladder?

7.6 Moral Hazard and Adverse Selection Problems

Moral Hazard
A problem arising when agents discover information that is valuable to the principal *after* the principal has contracted for their services.

Contributing to the agency costs of a firm are two special problems that shareholders (and individuals) face because they have limited information and because monitoring is costly. The **moral hazard** problem arises when the agent (managers) takes some action that the principal (shareholders) cannot observe or that would be costly to observe.[8] The action taken advances the interests of the agent at the expense of the principal. The problem is referred to as a *moral* hazard because the behavior creates a moral conflict. Morally speaking, the agent should inform the principal about the situation and renegotiate, if necessary. But the agent gains from taking the action, so a moral hazard for the principal arises.

[8] Technically, moral hazard problems can be divided into two subcategories: hidden action and hidden information problems. With the hidden action problem, the agent takes some action that is unobservable or costly to observe. With the hidden information problem, the agent has information that cannot be observed. The hidden action problem formally subsumes the hidden information problem because the information is not generally of any consequence unless some action is taken.

The adverse selection problem is slightly different. In **adverse selection,** managers have information that shareholders do not know at the time the principal-agent contract is formed. The knowledge is valuable to shareholders and may or may not be valuable to managers, but in any event it is withheld from those who would use it. With the information, the principal might select or contract differently with the agent. Thus, without the information the principal may make an adverse selection. In contrast, the moral hazard problem assumes that the principal and agent have identical information at the time the contractual arrangement is formed. Each of these problems is developed below.

Adverse Selection
A problem arising when agents possess information that is valuable to the principal *before* the principal has contracted for their services.

THE MORAL HAZARD PROBLEM

We can return to the previous renovation example to illustrate the moral hazard problem, this time with more information. Recall that you accidently discovered that there were too few studs in the interior walls. Now you have another problem. What neither you nor the builder knew was that your house rests on soft ground, so the addition will require more reinforcing steel in its concrete footings, which are poured during the first few days of construction as part of the foundation. If the extra steel is not added to the footings, the soft ground will make the addition structurally weak, causing it to gradually sink. Such sinking or settling causes cracks and other problems in the structure that appear over several years. In short, you have a much bigger problem than the lack of studs in interior walls.

What action the builder takes in this situation depends on a number of factors. First are the terms of your contract. If you can make the builder pay for the extra steel rods, the builder may have an incentive to remain silent about the soft ground if he discovers it first. If the contract allows for renegotiation after the fact, with you paying to solve the problem, the builder may tell you the unfortunate news and outline the costs of a solution. And, if you can discover the problem in the near future may affect the builder's behavior.

The moral hazard problem just described has two key elements:

1. You—the principal—have contracted with the builder—the agent—*before* the information is known to either of you.
2. The builder's gain (or loss) from any action taken may be different from what you lose (or gain) from such actions.

The first element highlights the role played by **asymmetric information.** Information about the problem is symmetric *before* you sign the contract—that is, neither of you knows about the problem—but asymmetric afterwards. Because both you and the builder are "in the dark" about the soft ground before you sign the contract, you cannot adjust the initial contract price for the addition to cover the problem. Information about the problem is asymmetric after the fact because the builder discovers the problem but you do not.

Asymmetric Information
Information that is known to one party to a contract or transaction but is not known to the other party.

The second element of the problem provides information about the likelihood that any detrimental action will be taken. Suppose that the cost of monitoring the agent is higher than the present value of the *anticipated* losses—which are equal to zero here because you are uninformed, which is why you face this problem. Then you will not monitor, so you will not discover the problem unless the builder reveals it. In this case, the builder decides what to do on the basis of the existing contract and the gains or losses that will result from revealing the information. If the contract calls for the builder to pay to correct the problem—a fixed-price contract—then there is little or no incentive to reveal it.[9] If the contract calls for you to pay to fix *unforeseen* problems, then the builder may reveal the problem in order to avoid any difficulties that might arise later when you complain about cracks in the new addition.

In general, if the builder faces a cost when information is *not* revealed, you can design a contract that provides an incentive to reveal such information. Suppose, for example, that the cost to the builder to add the extra steel in the footings is $1,000. The cost and headache you will suffer from cracks and correcting the problem later has a present value of $5,000. Your complaints to neighbors about the lousy builder who did not fix the problem to begin with are expected to cost the builder, in present value, $600 in lost business. One can clearly see that if the builder must pay all the costs to correct the problem, the information will not be revealed ($1,000 > $600). And if you pay all the costs, the information will be revealed ($600 > 0).

But the information will also be revealed if you do not pay all the costs. Suppose the contract calls for you and the builder to each pay *one-half* the costs of correcting the problem. You will be glad to pay $500 now rather than the present value of $5,000 in costs. The builder will be glad to pay $500 now rather than the present value of $600 in costs. You are still both better off, even with a contract that shares the costs. What this example shows is that you do not (always) bear *all* of the costs of correcting a moral hazard problem if the contract is designed with the proper incentive structure.

LEARNING EXERCISE 7.7

Let's change the numbers in the moral hazard problem you face building a house addition. Suppose that you split the costs 50/50 with the builder and it costs $2,000 to correct the situation. Will the builder reveal the problem to you?

THE ADVERSE SELECTION PROBLEM

A growing problem in companies today is employee theft. Estimates of annual losses due to employee theft range between $40 and $120 billion, with the large variation due to differences in how theft is measured.[10] When such theft is discovered, employees are typically fired. The previous employer can greatly limit a larceny-prone employee's chances of finding a new job by revealing

[9] We assume that there are no external costs to the builder from withholding the information, such as a loss of reputation capital when the building begins to crack many years later or costs arising from a possible negligence lawsuit. Such costs, of course, may affect the builder's decision to reveal such information.

[10] For example, some researchers measure tangible losses due to theft, and others measure intangibles—such as late arrivals or fake illness—when preparing estimates of losses. For a discussion of these differences, see Neil Snyder, Karen Blair, and Tina Arndt, "Breaking the Bad Habits Behind Time Theft," *Personnel Management* 40 (October-December 1990), 31–33.

what occurred at the previous job. Because of this possibility, potential employees are unlikely to reveal to future employers the name of a previous employer. This implies that employers face an adverse selection problem when they hire new workers. These workers have information about their past employment history and behavior that employers do not have and may not be able to obtain at low cost. The adverse selection problem is caused by asymmetric information, but unlike the moral hazard problem, the asymmetric information exists *before* the principal and agent enter a contractual relationship, not after.

Some Examples

The lack of information on the part of employers in the above example is potentially costly. A larceny-prone employee is likely to lower profits instead of raise them if the opportunity exists for such activity. In another example, banks face an adverse selection problem when they make loans. Suppose that the current interest rate on real estate debt is 10 percent. An applicant for a real estate development loan appears to qualify, but the loan officer has some doubt about the viability of the project and the applicant's intent; that is, the applicant might run away with the money. Because the project is more risky than the standard commercial loan, the bank may want to charge a higher-than-market interest rate—say, 15 percent. If the applicant intends to cheat the bank anyway, however, a higher interest rate will not deter him or her. The bank faces an adverse selection problem; it does not truly know the applicant's intent.

Some Solutions

Employers and banks understand the costly dilemma posed by adverse selection problems, and there is typically no costless solution to these problems. Employers worried about employee theft invest in monitoring equipment in offices and at job sites, such as the cameras that gambling casinos use to monitor their employees. Employers may also delve into a potential employee's past history, looking for information that might be highly correlated with an employee's tendency to steal. A past history of credit card delinquency could indicate financial hardship and a need for extra income that may lead to on-the-job theft. An employer may thus use (imperfect) signals to help decide whether a potential employee is likely to steal. A bank approaches the problem somewhat differently. In a typical real estate loan, a bank limits the withdrawal of loan funds to match actual construction expenses. For a large real estate project, banks require that some fraction of the project be "presold" before any money is released. These practices are costly to the bank, but they help lower the costs imposed by the adverse selection problem.

As is the case with moral hazard, adverse selection causes companies to adopt business practices and contracts to protect them from information that they do not know but that could potentially affect their profits.

Learning Exercise 7.8

List three cases in which the moral hazard problem arises and three cases in which the adverse selection problem arises. Remember that they differ on the basis of whether information is known before or after the contract is agreed to.

7.7 Specificity and the Holdup Problem

A firm's choice between using the marketplace to purchase goods and services for its production process or producing these inputs itself may also be influenced by the investments it makes to produce these products. Some of these investments may be specific to the firm itself because they are more valuable to the firm than to the general marketplace. When a firm (or individual) makes specific investments as part of a contract, the *holdup problem* arises. In the holdup problem, one party to the contract may take advantage of the other because of the presence of a specific investment in the relationship. In other words, one party may hold up the activities—production, distribution, or marketing—of the other party, thus imposing a cost on the other party. To understand the holdup problem in more detail, let's consider several examples.

Specific Assets

Specific Asset
A good, service, or intangible that is more valuable in its present use than in any alternative use. Some specific assets have no alternative use, making them a sunk cost.

A **specific asset** is a good, a service, or an intangible that is worth more in its present use inside the firm than it would be worth if it were sold in the market. For example, a company may invest in signs bearing its name in large, bold letters. Signs help customers find the location of the company, but they have little or no resale value in the marketplace. (What would you pay for a sign that says "Mike Gordon's Seafood Bazaar"?) Companies that have patents or exclusive rights on products may acquire special machines to make these products. Boat companies, for example, copyright the design of the boats they build, so the molds they own to make these boats are specific to the particular boat design. The molds have no value in the market by themselves; they are valuable only when the copyright is sold or licensed with the mold, so that the acquirer can legally produce the boat.

An investment in a specific asset is often necessary to fulfill the terms of a contract. The classic example is the case of an electric plant with coal-fired generators locating next to a coal mine. The electric company has agreed to locate next to the mine in return for a long-term contract that fixes the price of coal (correcting for inflation). As part of the contract, a railroad line is to be constructed between the coal mine and the electric plant. The rail line is specific to the long-term supply contract between the two firms and has little value in the market without such a contract. The Fisher Body Company, now a part of General Motors, had a long-term contract to supply the bodies for many of GM's cars. Under this contract, Fisher Body invested significant funds in the dies and molds used to make these car bodies. These investments had little value to anyone other than GM.

Often, specific assets are created from human capital investments. A harbor pilot, for example, invests in learning the safest method of navigating into a given port or harbor. Because tides and weather change, such knowledge is acquired only after years of work experience. Ship owners pay harbor pilots to bring their vessels safely into port. In part because of the responsibility they have, harbor pilots earn above-average incomes. Much of the knowledge they have of a given port or harbor, however, is not transferable to another port or harbor. Such knowledge is a specific asset. When a firm installs a new computer system to keep track of its sales and inventory, certain employees must learn to use the system. An investment of this sort is transferable only to firms that use the same computer system. If there are no other firms using the system, then the investment is a specific asset.

THE HOLDUP PROBLEM

Investments in specific assets generally have a large sunk cost component. **Sunk cost** is the monies that cannot be recovered by subsequent resale of an asset. After the investment is made, sunk costs are ignored for profit-maximizing decisions. But before the investment is made, a firm expects to earn a return on its investment—it is not sunk until it is actually made. Because of the before and after difference in value of a specific asset, firms making such investments are subject to the **holdup problem.**

Sunk Cost
An investment that has a zero opportunity cost.

Holdup Problem
When one party takes an action that prevents another party from fully earning the normal return on its investment in a specific asset.

Suppose your firm buys a new computer system and the company that installed the system offers to train you for $1,500. Note that this is a system that no one else owns. If you pay for the training, you have invested $1,500 in a specific asset, that is, knowledge of your firm's new (and unique) computer system. But you would like your firm to reimburse you for your investment. What is the firm's incentive to pay you for your specific investment *after* you have made it? Certainly a firm wants happy and loyal employees, but its incentive to pay for the full cost of your training is less than before you undertook the training. Your investment is a sunk cost to you; the firm does not have to pay you, after the fact, for the specific investment. You are likely, however, to anticipate this problem and to ask the firm to pay the $1,500 for your investment and to pay you your current hourly wage while you are in training. Without such an arrangement, you have little or no incentive to learn the new computer system.

The holdup problem may materialize in many settings, all of which involve a specific asset to some degree. Children who organize an informal game of baseball may have been exposed to the holdup problem at one time or another. One child invariably owns the baseball. If it is the only baseball readily available, this child has a specific asset. The other children may accede to this child's demand that he or she be the pitcher (even if he or she is not a good pitcher) in order to use the child's baseball. If the child's demands are not met, he or she may simply leave and there will be no game.

The holdup problem offers a partial explanation for why many secretaries were initially reluctant to switch from their typewriters to word processing in the early 1980s. Secretaries may have noticed that innovation occurs rapidly in the computer industry, so investing in a word-processing system that may be obsolete in the near future is potentially a poor investment. The incentive to learn word-processing skills overcame any such drawbacks, however, when it became clear that enormous productivity gains were to be had and that word-processing software and skills were at least partially transferable to newer computers, as well as an asset in the job market.

What does the holdup problem imply about the decision to use the market versus in-house production? If two firms, such as GM and Fisher Body, contract through the marketplace for goods and services that are produced using large, specific investments, one firm is dependent on the other for a return on its specific investment. GM, for example, may offer a lower price to Fisher Body after Fisher has invested in the assets necessary to build GM car bodies. Because Fisher Body's investment is (partly) specific, it is a sunk cost. Looking forward, then, Fisher Body may accept the lower price GM offers *after the fact.* Because Fisher Body is subject to holdup by GM, this is a *unilateral* holdup problem; that is, only one firm can holdup the other. If Fisher Body can retaliate by delaying delivery of car bodies, which holds up GM's assembly line process, then we have a *bilateral* holdup problem, which implies that both firms have investments that are specific to their contractual arrangement. Both unilateral and bilateral holdup problems make it expensive for firms to use the marketplace to purchase inputs. The fact that GM bought Fisher Body is partly a sign that in-house production is cheaper than trying to cope with market-determined contracts that require investments in specific assets.

Generally, then, when a large investment in specific assets is necessary for a production relationship to exist, a firm may find it advantageous to use in-house production—for example, through a merger or takeover—instead of the marketplace to avoid the holdup problem.

LEARNING EXERCISE 7.9

Suppose you invest $50 in paint brushes, rollers, and painting equipment that you will use during the summer to earn income. A friend thinks you have a good idea and wants to work with you. She will use the roller while you use the paint brush. She wants to split the earnings equally with you. Is there a potential holdup problem here? How would you split the earnings with your friend if she refuses to repay you for the rollers?

7.8 SIGNALING AND MARKET FRAUD

Firms may try to tell customers and suppliers that they will not act opportunistically when they produce a product or service. If they are believable, such signals—often in the form of advertising—may lead to long-term relationships that help avoid agency costs and holdup problems. Firms have an incentive to invest in such signals when they are the least-cost method of providing information inside and outside the firm and particularly when they produce a product that others might copy or counterfeit. Let's investigate signaling and the potential for fraud in the marketplace.

THE ROLE OF SIGNALING

Credible Signal
An action taken or message sent by an individual or firm that is believed by the marketplace.

One way firms can show that they are legitimate and that their products will work as claimed is to send a **credible signal** to consumers. A fuse or circuit breaker, for example, is an item that you install in an electric panel in a household or in appliances and electronic equipment, such as computers, VCRs, and stereos. Both a fuse and a circuit breaker protect equipment from a surge of electricity, but these items are unusual because they do not work until they are needed to work. If they are defective when they are needed, the consequences may be very costly to correct. Many house fires, for example, are caused by faulty wiring. If they operate correctly, fuses or circuit breakers can shut off electricity to a circuit that is defective, possibly preventing a fire.

The firms that manufacture fuses and circuit breakers understand that consumers need assurance that their products will work when they are needed. Independent testing laboratories, such as Underwriters Laboratory and Consumers Union, test various products for reliability and durability. Firms making high-quality products welcome such tests because they provide a signal to the market that their products will work as claimed.

Firms typically use signals to indicate a product's quality or to reveal information about the firm's future profitability. Quality signals abound in the market for many products. The Gemological Society of America offers a rating service to jewelers who want to confirm the color, clarity, and perfection of diamonds and other gemstones. High-power microscopes are used to rate "certificate" diamonds, so there is little room for debate about the quality of the gemstone. Such diamonds are frequently sold sight unseen (subject to a liberal return policy) because customers know exactly what they are buying. On a different level, firms often screen applicants for jobs on the basis of academic credentials. These firms use school reputation, class rank, and test scores as a signal of the candidate's quality and expected ability.

A firm's directors use ***dividends*** as a signaling tool. Shareholders find it expensive to individually monitor a firm's performance, particularly if the process involves an analysis of quarterly and annual financial statements. Management may use dividends to signal to shareholders (and bondholders) that they are meeting their profitability objectives. By paying dividends on a frequent basis, a firm signals its ongoing success.

SCAMS AND FRAUD

Scams are illegal. But they are also quite profitable if the perpetrators are not caught. Most scams offer you some way to make a million dollars with some ridiculous rate of return on your investment, say, double your money in two months. One of the more interesting scams we know of is a stock market scam. This particular scam seemed to start out innocently enough. The perpetrator mailed 10,000 letters to subscribers of a popular financial newspaper. The letters introduced the perpetrator as an expert (or, should we say, wizard) on the stock market. The letters also contained a prediction on the direction of the market—up or down—on the following Monday. As the weeks went by, more letters were mailed with similar predictions.

Below the surface an elaborate scheme was developing. In the initial mailing, 5,000 letters said "The market will go up next Monday" and 5,000 letters said "The market will go down next Monday." As the weeks went by, the perpetrator repeated the mailing, but each time the letter was sent to only the group who received the correct prediction. So in the second round, only 5,000 letters were sent: 2,500 saying "up" and 2,500 saying "down" to those who had received an accurate prediction the preceding week. After three weeks, a letter was sent to the remaining individuals who had received three accurate predictions, asking them to send $5 for the next week's prediction. A large majority sent the $5.

The "split prediction" mailings continued, and the amounts requested for the next week's prediction increased. Eventually, only a handful of individuals remained who had received accurate predictions, but these predictions were "perfect"—there were no misses over many, many weeks of letters. Some of these individuals were willing to pay hundreds of dollars for the next prediction letter.

We hope you can see that this is a scam. The perpetrator did not know any more about the future direction of the market than the man in the moon might know. The successes recorded were the result of chance and the split mailings. In effect, the perpetrator was right half the time, but to the individuals receiving the "correct" predictions it looked like he was right all the time.

COUNTERFEIT GOODS AND CRIMINALS

Scams and fraud make consumers and others wary of the intentions of many firms, particularly those who offer products that are priced significantly below the competition. Such products are often found to be of lower quality. To relieve consumers' anxiety, a firm might invest in a credible signal, which is usually some asset that is specific to the firm or the claims made about the product. As we show in Chapter 10, the firm receives a higher price for a higher-quality product only when it invests in specific assets (or signals) that indicate its product is of high quality. In effect, investments in specific assets act as *collateral* or a guarantee to consumers, increasing the chance that firms will perform according to their claims. With the higher price, however, comes a risk that someone will disobey the laws of the land for short-term gain. Counterfeiting high-quality products is a very profitable enterprise if a counterfeiter can get away with the crime. Counterfeit designer blue jeans, computers, and drugs are frequently discovered by legitimate manufacturers.

If consumers cannot tell the genuine product from the counterfeit product, then there is an incentive to counterfeit. To help prevent counterfeiters from devaluing their investments in credible signals, firms may enter into exclusive marketing arrangements. Under these arrangements, their products are initially sold only by certain retailers. Consumers buying the product elsewhere are wary—they may not be buying the genuine product. Rolex watches are sold in this manner. There are factory-authorized dealers for these watches, who charge more than unauthorized retailers. The higher price at the authorized dealer allows the dealer to earn a return on the signal and specific assets it has purchased. Because on these investments, consumers are almost certain that authorized dealers do not sell counterfeit Rolex watches.

Sometimes firms must adjust to the behavior of criminals. The Tylenol poisoning scare in 1982 led Johnson & Johnson Company, the manufacturer of Tylenol, to develop a new packaging system for its pain relief drug.

Someone had tampered with the Tylenol capsules, substituting cyanide for acetaminophen (the pain relief drug), and placed the altered capsules back in stores for sale to the public. Several people died as a result. To eliminate the tampering problem, Johnson & Johnson initially placed special seals on Tylenol boxes and on the bottles inside. The public was reassured and Tylenol began to reclaim lost sales, but the company remained concerned that a clever criminal could still find a way to tamper with the capsules. In 1986, Johnson & Johnson stopped the sale of capsules and introduced Tylenol in gelcaps. Like capsules, gelcaps are easy to swallow and leave no aftertaste, but unlike capsules, they are solid and thus are highly tamper-resistant.

Firms and consumers exist in an environment in which there are scams, criminals, and counterfeit goods. Specific assets, acting as collateral, send a signal to consumers and others that the firm making such investments is not likely to act opportunistically by misrepresenting product quality.

$$$ Price Theory in Practice

Telemarketing Fraud

In 1991, more than 8,000 consumers who fell for a phony telephone sales pitch from three oil and gas companies got back nearly all the money they lost, thanks to the efforts of the U.S. Federal Trade Commission (FTC). The $47 million in refunds obtained by the FTC was its biggest fraud settlement that involved telemarketing.

When a firm sells a product or a service to a consumer, it is usually assumed that both parties to the transaction are acting in good faith, but, as this FTC case shows, that is not always the case. One party may lack information or may be unable to observe all the actions of the other party. With asymmetric information, the buyer or the seller may take actions to defraud or otherwise harm the other, as did the firms in the FTC case.

The fraudulent scheme in the FTC case was run by three South Florida firms: U.S. Oil & Gas Corporation, Eagle Oil & Gas Corporation, and the Stratford Company. The firms' telephone solicitors sold consumers a service that filed applications in their name for a federal lottery that awarded the rights to oil and gas resources on federal land.

The companies charged several thousand dollars to file several applications, but only a fraction of that money was used for filing fees. The companies falsely claimed that they had exclusive knowledge of the most valuable land parcels and the chance of winning a lease. The firms also offered investors an insurance plan that would return their original investments after seven years whether or not they won a lease. The companies used investors' money to buy the insurance; however, the investors were not made beneficiaries of the policies.

In all, consumers invested more than $51 million in the scheme, with the average investment between $5,000 and $10,000. Under the settlement, investors received about 90 cents of each dollar they lost.

The FTC was able to arrange the $47 million in refunds by adopting a new tactic. Instead of just prosecuting the firms that masterminded the fraud, the FTC took action against a number of other firms that had allegedly helped the principal firms. These secondary firms agreed to out-of-court settlements totaling $47 million. These secondary firms included the Better Business Bureau of South Florida, which had allowed the three oil and gas companies to use it as a reference. The South Florida Bureau and its national council paid $4.5 million.

The action against the secondary participants in the fraud became possible when a Federal district court in Miami froze $12 million of the assets of the three oil and gas companies in 1983. At the request of the FTC, the court then authorized the lawyers acting as receiver of the companies to sue any other firms and individuals who allegedly helped make the scam possible. The actions of the receiver allowed the FTC to take action against banks, insurance companies, and nonprofit groups allegedly involved in the fraud, even though the commission does not have jurisdiction over them.

The new thrust, which was highly touted by FTC officials, may greatly affect such organizations as the Better Business Bureau, in addition to accountants and lawyers. Such organizations will now be required to know their customers' or members' businesses in much more detail than in the past.

Learning Exercise 7.10

How do you think the Better Business Bureaus across the nation will change their practices as a result of the FTC's successful action? Will it be more expensive to join the Better Business Bureau?

7.9 Nonprofit Organizations

Our discussion has focused on the incentives within a firm that chooses to maximize profits for the benefit of its owners. Using the profit-maximizing goal, we can explain many characteristics of the modern business firm, such as profit sharing contracts that align the incentives of managers with those of the owners, pension contracts that determine payments based on productivity in the last few years of employment, and the role of managers in monitoring the output of team members. Not all firms, however, are purportedly in business to maximize profits. Many firms, such as churches, hospitals, schools and universities, museums, and foundations, are chartered with the expressed goal of being a nonprofit firm. All the revenues of a **nonprofit firm** are spent within that firm, usually for the purpose of furthering the cause of the organization. These organizations operate with the intention of making zero annual profits; they have no shareholders and they pay no dividends.

Nonprofit Firm
An organization that has no shareholders, restricts the distribution of its assets, and tends to equate annual revenues to annual costs.

The American Cancer Society, for example, is a nonprofit firm. This organization raises money to help find a cure for cancer. The Muscular Dystrophy Foundation operates in a similar manner, raising funds to find a cure for muscular dystrophy. Nearly every college and university is chartered as a nonprofit firm. Private universities charge students tuition, but these charges and research grants cover only part of the costs of education; the remaining cost is paid for by donations. Universities try to cover their annual costs, but they don't seem to strive to earn more than their costs. Churches are also nonprofit firms. Some church revenues come from services, such as bingo games and carnivals, but most revenues are earned from donations.

OPERATING STRUCTURE OF NONPROFIT FIRMS

The operation of a nonprofit firm is expected to be different from that of a for-profit firm. There are no shares for sale in a market, so there is no formal market for control of such organizations. Takeovers or leveraged buyouts cannot occur in the same manner as in for-profit firms. Top managers are thus not subject to the same degree of *external* control as they are in for-profit firms. The actions of the managers of a nonprofit firm will then depend on the *internal* incentives such organizations adopt.

A board of directors is usually responsible for setting policies and defining incentives in a nonprofit firm. The board is restricted by a set of by-laws that provide guidance on the goals and activities of the firm. The by-laws, for example, provide a method of electing new members to replace retiring members of the board so that the organization can continue its activities. The by-laws may also restrict the investment activities of the nonprofit organization, such as preventing the organization from investing outside the United States.

The actions taken by the board of directors, including the incentive structure it adopts, are largely determined by how the board of directors is elected or chosen. Those who sit on nonprofit boards owe their allegiance to those who voted for or chose them. If it is valuable to sit on the board of a nonprofit firm, then we would expect board members to adopt policies that cater to the very group that elected them. In this respect, a nonprofit firm is similar to the local, state, and federal government because elected officials, if they value reelection, cater to the groups that voted them into office.

Sometimes the existing board of directors is the same body that votes on the election of new members, which is usually the case for museums. This election scheme is likely to lead to a board of directors composed of mutual friends and acquaintances. The policies that such a board adopts are expected to reflect the individual preferences of its members. With members electing their friends, one might expect to find fairly homogeneous preferences on such a board. A museum may thus tend to exhibit works of art that are liked by the members of the board of directors, which may or may not be a practice that attracts the most visitors or the best art.

In other cases, the board of directors is elected by a broader group, such as the election to the board of overseers for Harvard University, which is voted on by the alumni of Harvard. The board of overseers at Harvard is expected to implement policies favored by existing alumni. We would expect the board of overseers to oppose any decline in the admissions standards at Harvard because such changes could depreciate the value of Harvard's degree programs and its outstanding degrees. For the same reason, the board of overseers may oppose deleting an existing degree program, even though it currently has only a few students enrolled, if such a program once produced many graduates.

DO NONPROFITS MAXIMIZE PROFIT?

Our discussion of nonprofit firms suggests that there is wide variety in organizational structures and incentives. Certainly, there is more room for individual preferences to affect the behavior of nonprofit organizations than for-profit organizations. When individual preferences conflict with the profit maximizing goal of for-profit firms, we have noted above that these organizations adopt rules and incentive structures to eliminate or reduce such conflicts. We cannot say the same for nonprofit firms. When individual preferences cause a conflict, such as in the choice of art for a museum to purchase, the members of the board of a nonprofit firm may simply argue and scream at one another. They are likely to resolve the conflict only when new members are elected to the board or existing members retire or quit.

On occasion, the profit motive pushes itself into the decision-making process in nonprofit organizations. Many nonprofit firms solicit funds from wealthy patrons to help support program and operational expenses. Obviously, the preferences of these patrons—toward art in museums, for example—affects the decisions made by nonprofits. By offering programs and activities that donors are willing to support, a nonprofit can increase revenues. If it can control costs in these programs, its behavior may appear consistent with the goal of profit maximization.

WHY DO NONPROFIT FIRMS EXIST?

As is the case with for-profit firms, it is reasonable to ask why nonprofit firms exist. There is no simple answer here. Many nonprofit foundations—for example, the Ford Foundation, the Rockefeller Foundation, and the Carnegie Foundation—were first chartered and operated according to the goals of a single individual. Clearly, the desire of these individuals to continue to pursue certain goals, even posthumously, gave these foundations a reason to exist.

In other cases, such as churches and universities, nonprofit status may actually produce more revenue than a for-profit charter. Contributions to nonprofit organizations are tax-deductible, which provides a revenue source that is typically not available to for-profit firms. In addition, a nonprofit organization cannot distribute its assets in the form of dividends, so all contributions stay within the firm.

The restriction that a nonprofit firm cannot distribute its assets—except to other nonprofit firms—may also help explain why some nonprofits exist. Churches and universities produce products whose quality is difficult to judge. We would thus expect such firms to invest in specific assets to send a signal to consumers that they will not act opportunistically, that is, that they will not suddenly lower the quality of their product. If such organizations could distribute assets, there would be a gain, to someone, from opportunistic behavior. With the restriction that assets cannot be distributed, because there are no shareholders, these organizations further restrict their ability to act opportunistically, which tends to perpetuate their existence. In fact, churches and universities have typically outlived for-profit firms. Harvard University, for example, began operations in 1636.

Nonprofit firms are not as simple to analyze as for-profit firms. They may exist for various reasons, and they may have widely differing goals and incentive structures. In some instances, though, their organizational structure, such as a restriction on the distribution of assets, may be necessary for them to attract customers and to remain viable over time.

Chapter Summary

1. A firm is a set of contracts, explicit and implicit, that link employees, managers, owners, and outside suppliers together for the purpose of producing an output.
2. Production is organized in firms when it is the least-cost method of creating a good or service, that is, when the cost of using the marketplace exceeds the managerial cost of in-house production.
3. To choose an output rate that maximizes profits, a firm finds the output rate at which marginal revenue is equal to marginal cost. The marginal revenue curve is determined by the demand for the firm's product, and the marginal cost curve is determined by the production process and the price paid for inputs, which includes monitoring and agency costs.
4. Team production may be costly to monitor, and individual team members have an incentive to shirk. Shirking reduces the effort a team member expends, without making that individual pay the full cost of shirking. Output will fall with shirking, but the cost imposed on the firm is spread across all team members.
5. The shareholders (owners) ask the managers of a firm to design contracts to maximize profits. This goal expands the shareholders' feasiable set of goods, thereby increasing shareholders' satisfaction.
6. Agency costs arise because the goals of the principal are not always aligned with the goals of the agent. When it is costly to observe an agent's actions, it is costly to develop schemes or incentives to align the goals of the agent with those of the principal. To reduce agency costs, firms monitor performance and adopt contracts that offer agents a part of the return paid to the principal.
7. Moral hazard arises when a principal and agent (for example, a shareholder and manager) contract with each other for goods or services and valuable information is revealed to the agent *after* the contract is made. The incentive to use the valuable information to benefit the agent at the partial or full expense of the principal causes the moral hazard problem. Adverse selection arises when the valuable information is known to the agent *before* the contract is made. Again, the information may be costly to the principal.
8. Specific assets are more valuable to the firm or a given contract than they are to the broader marketplace. If a firm invests in specific assets as part of a contractual relationship, the investment becomes a fixed cost after it is made. The other party to the contract may then try to

"hold up" the firm by renegotiating the contract so that the firm does not earn a return on its specific investment.

Trouble Spots

Concept	Reminder
The Contract-Based Approach to Firm Structure	The concepts of teamwork, costly monitoring, and shirking go hand in hand. Output efficiency in teams creates a benefit to teamwork. Against this benefit is the cost of determining what each team member actually contributes to the production process. Shirking may arise when it is costly to monitor such activities and when the shirker does not bear the full cost of his or her actions. Shirking does not arise because some team member is of low character but rather because there is a gain to such activities that exceeds their cost.
The Profit-Maximizing Goal	Firms are not endowed with the goal of maximizing profits; rather, managers and employees are given an incentive to behave this way by the owners of the firm—that is, the shareholders. One reason the owners prefer this goal over other goals is that it provides owners with more income than other goals—that is, any other goal to which all of the owners can agree. More income relaxes the owners' budget constraints, thereby increasing the size of the feasible set of goods and services they can consume and increasing their satisfaction.
Moral Hazard and Adverse Selection Problems	Sometimes moral hazard is thought to be a problem faced just by insurance companies. When an insurance policy is written, the policyholder may change his or her behavior as a result of the insurance. Although insurance is an example of the moral hazard problem, the problem itself is much broader than just insurance, as our discussion of insider trading suggests. Remember, the key to identifying a moral hazard problem is that information is known *after* a contract or agreement between two parties; the information was not known before the agreement. For the case of auto insurance, the past driving record may be known when the policy is written, but the unknown information is the degree to which the driver is less careful when an insurance company—instead of the driver—will pay for an accident.
Specificity and the Holdup Problem	Specific assets can take many different forms. They may be a human capital investment, such as a computer training program; they may be a site investment, such as the railroad tracks leading to an electric plant; and they may be a firm or contract investment, such as a sign on a building. The one feature these investments have in common is that their highest and best use is as planned; the market value is much

less for other uses. The specific nature of the investment combined with the fact that there is a difference between the actual investment and market value creates the holdup problem.

7.10 Review Questions

1. What does a firm do? How are teams important to the notion of a firm?
2. State and explain four factors that produce transaction costs.
3. How does a profit-maximizing firm choose its optimal output?
4. How should a manager change output if marginal ravenue exceeds marginal cost at the present operating position?
5. Is a firm really a collection of contracts? Is there anything that a firm does to produce that does not involve contracts with one party or another?
6. Why is there a shirking problem? Will going to church eliminate such a problem?
7. Explain why the owners of a firm benefit when the top managers act to maximize profits.
8. Why is the profit-maximizing goal preferred to a sales-maximizing goal?
9. Give two examples of the agency problem inside a firm.
10. Why do firms separate the ownership or capital investment function from the control or managerial function?
11. What is the difference between a moral hazard and an adverse selection problem?
12. Explain the relationship between the holdup problem and investments in specific assets.
13. How do credible signals help prevent fraud and counterfeiting?
14. Who benefits from shirking? What if it is anticipated before the contractual arrangement is made?

7.11 Price Theory Problems

1. "The way to have the best of both worlds (low transaction costs and low managerial costs) is to have employees and suppliers working on piecework and to pay them according to just how much they produce." If this statement were accurate, we would expect to see few, if any, workers paid according to their time input. Yet the vast majority of employees are paid by the hour, week, or month. The evidence is in conflict with the assertion. What do you think has been overlooked here?
2. "Because 'proxy fights'—the attempted takeover of a corporation by a united block of stockholders—are partly a phenomenon of the 1980s, they obviously cannot be a very important factor in

keeping inefficient managements in line." Is this statement true or false? Why?

3. We speak of transaction costs as the costs of using the market to purchase goods and services, but, except for flea markets, where you pay an entrance fee, most markets do not charge a fee for their use. What are the transaction costs of using these no-entrance-fee markets?
4. Complete the table below, and then find the profit maximizing output rate and the optimal level of profits.

Output (Units/wk.)	Price ($/Unit)	Total Revenue ($/wk.)	Total Cost ($/wk.)	Marginal Cost ($/wk.)	Marginal Revenue ($/wk.)
0	100	0	200	–	–
1	100	100	250	50	100
2	100	?	?	30	100
3	?	300	300	20	?
4	?	400	330	?	100
5	100	500	380	50	?
6	100	600	460	?	100
7	100	?	560	100	?
8	100	800	?	140	100
9	100	?	900	?	100

5. Assume that the firm can sell all of its output at $1,000 per unit, so its total revenues are then $R(Q) = \$1{,}000Q$. Its costs are given by the relationship $C(Q) = 100 + 50Q - Q^2$, where $MC(Q) = 50 + 2Q$. Find the profit maximizing output rate and the optimal level of profits for this firm.
6. Redraw the shirking diagram, Figure 7.1, to show the indifference curve that the nonshirking team members are on when a single team member shirks. Do they receive more or less satisfaction than prior to the shirking by a single team member?
7. In the shirking diagram, Figure 7.1, how does the solution change if monitoring by other team members can immediately detect any change in effort by a single team member? Does your answer depend on the consequences from shirking?
8. Every major corporation has its financial statements audited by an independent accounting firm. Why don't corporations audit their own books? In addition, large companies are audited by large (not small) accounting firms, that is, firms who have many customers, so that a single customer is not a significant portion of its business. Why do large corporations choose large accounting firms to audit their financial statements?
9. "Golden parachutes" for corporate executives are often thought of as antitakeover measures. Can you think of another explanation for such contingent compensation packages based on the specific investments that corporate executives make in their businesses?

10. In some firms, employees and shareholders are one and the same. How will such an arrangement affect the management structure of these firms? Under what conditions will such firms adopt the profit maximizing goal? How is your answer to these questions affected if the shares can be sold to outsiders?
11. Determine whether a moral hazard or adverse selection problem could arise in the following situations:
    a. Using a doctor for minor aches and pains after but not before you have purchased health insurance
    b. Complaining to a professor after finding out your grade that you were sick during an exam
    c. Buying beef wrapped in an opaque plastic container at the grocery store
    d. Dealing with Monty Hall on *Let's Make a Deal,* a syndicated TV game show
    e. Seeking a second opinion from another doctor before you submit to exploratory surgery
    f. Revealing to some of your friends exactly where you caught a 9-pound bass
    g. The purchase of a used car
12. Explain which of the following items you believe represent an investment in a specific asset. Is the investment in these assets sunk, or is part of it recoverable?
    a. Monogrammed ties
    b. A cherry-red automobile
    c. A brown UPS truck
    d. A warehouse
    e. A television advertisement
    f. A business card
    g. A pair of tennis shoes
13. Most insurance companies charge a "deductible" of several hundred dollars for each accident claim under an auto insurance policy. The policyholder must pay any charges up to the amount of the deductible, after which the insurance company pays. What is the purpose of such a charge? If a law is passed to eliminate the deductible, what will happen to insurance premiums? Will the number of claims increase or decrease without the deductible?
14. Suppose a "lemon law" is passed that requires used car dealers to refund a customer's money if he or she is not satisfied with a used car. Before the law, customers faced a(n) ____________________ problem. After the law is passed, dealers face a(n) ____________________ problem. (Fill in the blanks with either *moral hazard* or *adverse selection.*) How will the market price of used cars change as a result of the new law? What will be the price paid for "returned" cars if the dealer is required to inform potential buyers that a car has been returned?

7.12 Writing Exercise

Look at the Yellow Pages for a type of business with which you are familiar. Select two or more firms for analysis. Contact these firms and report on their organizational structure. What do they produce? How many managers and employees do they have? How are these individuals compensated? Use the many concepts developed in this chapter to explain the organizational structure of these two (or more) firms. Explain how these firms differ in their structure and why you think they are organized differently.

8

Production

Preview Questions

When you finish studying this chapter, you should be able to answer the following questions:

- What is the economic meaning of production, and what is a production function?
- How are fixed and variable inputs different from each other?
- What is an isoquant?
- How are the average and marginal products of an input related in the short run?
- What is the law of diminishing returns, and is it really a law?
- How does technological progress affect the average product of an input?
- What are returns to scale?

If you ever find yourself in Winston-Salem, North Carolina, make a point to visit the Stroh's brewery where Stroh's, Schlitz, and Old Milwaukee beers are produced. What you will see is a good example of modern production technology. The first stop on the tour is an enormous room in which the beer is canned, pasteurized, and packaged. The process runs almost continuously, closing down only for maintenance and repairs at night. The cans are partially assembled by large, noisy machines; conveyor belts carry the various components from one machine to the next. After assembly, beer is injected and lids are attached. Then, in the pasteurization process, the cans are cooked to kill the yeast. After cooking, the beer cans are labeled and packaged for shipment, which is also fully mechanized. Trucks wait behind the building to deliver the beer to large retailers and regional distributors. The grocery store shelf and purchase by the final consumer are the next and last stops.

The Stroh's brewery in Winston-Salem is a production process at work. Factors of production, such as labor, capital, energy, and materials, come in one door, and canned beer goes out another. This chapter describes how a typical production process actually works. The discussion provides an economic blueprint of production, focusing on the way in which factors interact to produce a product. Concepts that apply to all production processes are developed and illustrated with specific examples. We discuss the economic characteristics of production, substitution possibilities, short- and long-run production, and measures of labor productivity, which we use to compare living standards between the United States and Japan.

8.1 Production Technology

Why is production technology important? The simple answer is that production is what firms do. Decisions about what, how much, and when to produce are the essential questions faced by managers trying to maximize profits. Production technology consists of the engineering and physical relationships that define what is possible between inputs and the output. A manager looking to cut costs, for example, may decide to eliminate jobs he or she views as nonessential—say, maintenance and repair positions—but when equipment starts to fail because of lack of maintenance, it will become clear that maintenance and repair are a necessary part of the production process; that is, machines will not continue to run if they are not maintained properly. A decision that initially might save some costs creates additional costs later on as the engineering and physical relationships of production impose restrictions on how output is produced.

Production technology is also important because it affects our everyday lives. Twenty years ago, if you wanted to withdraw money from your bank, you had to go to the bank between the hours of 9 A.M. and 2 P.M. Some banks had drive-through tellers that were open a little later, but only a few banks offered this service. Today, bankers' hours have changed and technology has permanently changed the way banks interact with their customers. Automatic teller machines (ATMs) now offer withdrawal and deposit services 24 hours a day. Many ATMs are linked together in regional and nationwide networks to permit withdrawals and deposits from distant cities. Twenty years ago, there were no ATMs. In 1994, there were over 350,000 ATMs operating throughout the world, and, according to the *Nilson Report* (a credit card industry newsletter), this amount is expected to double by the year 2000.

Other advances in production have changed our lives and the way we conduct business. Perhaps nowhere has technology had a greater effect than in the medical profession. Drugstores carry kits for pregnancy testing and blood sugar testing; thermometers are electronic; flu shots are injected painlessly by a "flu gun"; prescription eyeglasses have been replaced by contact lenses for many with poor vision; and now contact lenses can be worn for extended periods without daily cleaning. Doctors and hospitals use computers to monitor the condition of patients before, during, and after operations. Even your blood pressure can be taken on a regular basis by a computer.

In short, production technology has affected nearly every aspect of economic life.

$$$ Price Theory in Practice

CDs and New Technology

The power of new technology to create and change markets is vividly illustrated by the continuing story of the compact disc (CD). When CDs were introduced in the early 1980s, they were slow to catch on, but eventually their scratch-free, hiss-free sound caught the attention of music fans. Compact discs now account for over 44 percent of all recorded-music sales. Since the introduction of the compact disc, total sales in the recorded-music industry have doubled.

The music industry is now bracing for the changes that will follow the newest technology: A mini-CD that can record music or information. Sony Corporation is developing what it calls a minidisc (MD) that is only 2½ inches in diameter, about half the size of a regular CD. Ultimately, the new technology may have more impact than the first CDs because of its computer applications. MDs can store more data than the magnetic hard disks that most computers use. MDs, for example, may allow laptop computers to handle tasks that would otherwise require the larger storage capacity of desktop personal computers.

Sony began production in 1992 of a player-recorder that initially cost about $500. Sony's approach is to quickly place technology in a popular consumer product, whose large volume means lower production costs. Sony is not the only company marketing the new technology: Toshiba and IBM are also competing to set the standard in MD technology. Sony, however, appears to be ahead of the others.

The MD is not the only technology vying to appeal to consumers. Philips Electronics developed a digital compact cassette player that plays digital audiotape and conventional tapes. Sony entered the digital audiotape market recently, but with little success.

The winner among new and old technologies will be determined by market forces. Whichever technology wins, it is nearly certain that music consumers will gain by these advances in the production of music.

Learning Exercise 8.1

Explain the economic reasons why the cassette tape player replaced the 8-track tape player in automobiles during the mid-1970s. Explain why current CDs have not replaced cassette players.

THE MEANING OF PRODUCTION

Production
Any use of resources that converts one commodity into a different commodity; production therefore includes storing, wholesaling, transporting, and repackaging services as well as manufacturing.

We can define **production** in its broadest sense as any use of resources that transforms one commodity into a different commodity. Production includes both goods and services, and the term *commodity* refers to both. Indeed, there is rarely any difference between goods and services from an economic point of view. Both are generally produced using some labor and some capital. Commodities can be defined in terms of what they are, in terms of when or where they are located, or in terms of what the consumer can do with the commodity. Pepsi-Cola, for example, is a soft drink with a well-defined set of ingredients that does not vary. A Pepsi available for sale by a vendor on a sunny beach, however, may be thought of as a different product than a Pepsi available for sale at a restaurant that is opening for business in two weeks. Production, therefore, includes not only manufacturing but storing, wholesaling, transporting, retailing, and repackaging as well as business services such as banking, tax accounting, and personnel management.

In addition, *production is a flow concept.* It is an activity that is measured as a rate of output per unit time, where output is expressed in constant-quality units, or units that are similar in durability and function. Thus, when we talk of increasing production, we mean increasing the rate of output, with all other dimensions of production held constant. Similarly, the use of resources in a production process is measured in terms of flows. Capital is measured in machine-hours, not in numbers of machines. Labor is measured as person-hours; materials are measured in units per week or units per hour; energy is measured in kilowatts per hour or per week; and any other inputs are measured as a flow per unit of time.

THE PRODUCTION FUNCTION

To maximize profits, a firm combines certain types of inputs such that an output results. We call the relationship between physical output and physical inputs the **production function.** It is defined as the schedule or mathematical equation that gives the maximum quantity of output that can be produced from a specific set of inputs. In fairly broad terms, a production function is described by the equation

Production Function The mathematical expression of the technical relation between output and one or more inputs.

$$Q = f(K, L, E, M) \tag{8.1}$$

where Q is the rate of output per unit time period, K is the service flow from the stock of capital, L is the service flow from the firm's laborers, E is the flow of energy into the production process, and M represents the flow of materials into the production process.

Equation (8.1) tells us that the *physical* quantity of output is some function of the *physical* quantities of the inputs: capital, labor, energy, and materials. We have not specified the exact relationship; rather, we have left it as a general relationship, capable of defining many different production processes. It is important to note, however, that all production functions are statements of mechanical or other physical transformations of inputs into outputs.

A production function, by itself, does not say anything about the worth or value of the inputs or the outputs.

It is also noteworthy that the output produced by the production process is of constant quality and physical characteristics. Higher- or lower-quality products may be produced, but they require a different mix of inputs and a slightly different production technology.

There may be other inputs to a production process besides those discussed here. In agriculture, for example, land is an important factor of production. We can add or subtract factors in many examples when it will help to simplify or improve our understanding of production. Typically, we simplify the production function shown in equation (8.1) to include only labor and capital as inputs. Rewriting equation (8.1), we have

$$Q = f(K, L) \tag{8.2}$$

We drop materials and energy (and all other inputs) because capital and labor dominate the production process and because we can explain some important production concepts easily if we have only two inputs. In this specification, capital may include the skills that a laborer has gained by investing his or her time and other resources. Thus, even services that may seem to involve only the use of labor probably are produced using what has come to be called *human capital.*

We can illustrate the concept of a production function with an example of a sport that you may have experienced, kite flying. We can think of kite flying as a production relationship with two inputs: you running along the ground pulling the kite up by a string *and* the speed of the wind. The output is the altitude the kite achieves. Table 8.1 shows how high your kite is likely to fly based on the relationship between these two inputs.

As you can see from Table 8.1, if you run faster, the kite is expected to fly at a higher altitude, holding the wind speed constant. If the wind speed is constant at 7 mph, for example, running at 4 mph causes the kite to reach an altitude of 69 feet; at 5 mph it reaches an altitude of 84 feet; at 6 mph it reaches 96 feet; at 7 mph it reaches 105 feet; and at 8 mph it reaches 113 feet. Alternatively, if the wind speed increases, you do not need to run as fast to reach the higher altitudes. This table is called a **production schedule.** It shows the output—kite altitude—you can achieve for varying rates of your inputs—running and wind speed. A typical firm's production function works the same way; it transforms inputs into an output.

Production Schedule A table or chart showing the relationship between input and output quantities.

FIXED AND VARIABLE INPUTS

In any production relationship there will be inputs that are less costly to change than other inputs. Labor is generally less costly to change than capital. You can hire or fire new employees more quickly and generally at a lower

TABLE 8.1

Flying a Kite: An Example of Production With Two Variable Inputs

		Running Speed (mph)				
		4	5	6	7	8
Wind Speed (mph)	4	30	45	63	80	92
	5	46	66	83	97	100
	6	58	76	91	102	112
	7	69	84	96	105	113
	8	80	93	102	109	115
	9	91	101	108	114	118
	10	100	107	112	116	119

Note: Figures in the table are the kite's altitude in feet.

transaction cost than you can construct or destroy a building or machine. We can distinguish inputs by whether it is feasible to change them in the production process. Thus, we define two types of inputs: fixed and variable. A **fixed input** is fixed if under the time horizon presently being considered it is not feasible to change the input. A **variable input** can change under the current time horizon. This is not to say that the firm must change a variable input but that if a change in output will increase profits, the firm will alter the variable input, not the fixed input, to change output. By doing so, the firm changes output in the most cost-effective—that is, profitable—manner.

Fixed Input
An input that does not change under the present planning horizon.

Variable Input
An input that may be changed under the present planning horizon in order to change output.

The **planning horizon,** or time period a firm uses to define fixed and variable inputs, may be identified as either the short or long run. In the **short run,** there will always be some input, usually capital, that is fixed. The **long run** is the planning horizon under which it is possible to change *all* inputs. In the long run, then, there are no fixed inputs; all inputs are variable.

Planning Horizon
The length of time associated with the profit-maximizing decision to change one or more inputs.

Note that there is no magical length of time associated with the transition between the short and long run. The short run can be very short for some firms and long for others. An electric utility company, for example, faces a short run that is from five to ten years long. This is the length of time required to design a new plant, obtain the necessary permits, and finish construction. A service firm, such as a law firm, requires a short run of only one or two months, enough time to find and move to a new office. If the firm has a multiyear lease in its present location, it could be longer. In such a case, the short run is the length of time required to profitably sublet or break the existing lease.

Short Run
The planning horizon for which at least one, but not all, inputs are fixed.

Long Run
The planning horizon for which all inputs are variable.

Learning Exercise 8.2

Identify the fixed and variable inputs in the following statements:

a. The dinner guests are about to arrive, and I don't have enough glasses to serve wine to everyone at the dinner table.
b. The hard disk in my computer is full, and I need to load in a new software program for data analysis.
c. We have three phone lines in our travel agency, and we are continually losing customers because they can't get through to a travel agent.

8.2 Isoquants

The kite-flying example in Table 8.1 illustrates a feature that is common to many production relationships—that is, it is possible to generate the same output with different combinations of inputs. An altitude of 100 feet may be reached when the wind is blowing at 5 mph and you are running at 8 mph or when the wind is blowing at 10 mph and you are running at 4 mph. Either combination produces the same output. In technical terms, we say that these two input combinations *lie on the same isoquant.* An **isoquant** is a curve that shows all the possible combinations of inputs that produce a given rate of output.

Isoquant
The locus of points showing all the combinations of capital and labor that will yield the same output level.

Using the simplified production function, equation (8.2), we will analyze isoquants using only two inputs: labor and capital.

DEFINING AN ISOQUANT

Figure 8.1 shows three isoquants for a typical production process. The horizontal axis measures physical amounts of labor, expressed in service flows per week; the vertical axis depicts physical amounts of capital, expressed in service flows per week. The isoquants are drawn for three different output rates: Q_1 = 100 units per week, Q_2 = 200 units per week, and Q_3 = 300 units per week.

On isoquant Q_1, for example, any combination of capital and labor given by a point along the isoquant will yield exactly 100 units per week of output. At point a_1, we are using 5 units of capital and 2 units of labor to produce 100 units of output per week. Alternatively, we could produce 100 units of output per week with 3 units of capital and 4 units of labor, as given by point b_1. As we move along isoquant Q_1, we vary the proportions in which capital and labor are used to hold the output rate constant.

CHOICE OF INPUTS IN THE SHORT RUN

Figure 8.1 provides a way to distinguish between short- and long-run production. In the short run, if capital is fixed, output can be increased only by increasing labor. Note that for simplicity, energy and materials are assumed to be fixed or simply not inputs to the production process. Points a_1, a_2, and a_3 lie on three different isoquants, but at each point the amount of capital used in the production process is constant at 5 units per week. Thus, capital is a fixed

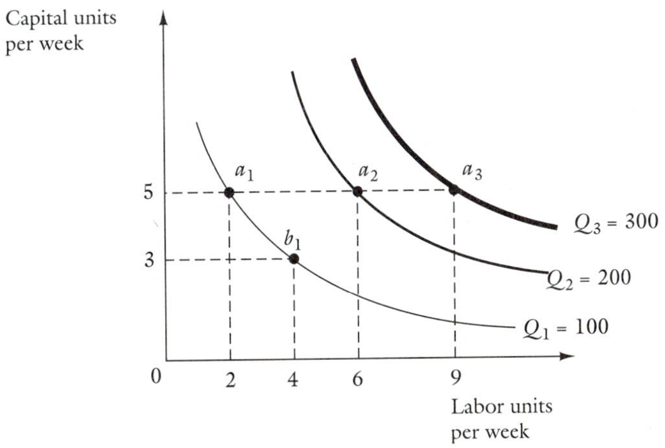

FIGURE 8.1

Isoquants for a Typical Production Technology

Here we show convex isoquants for varying rates of production, 100, 200, and 300. Points a_1, a_2, a_3 all correspond to five units of capital per week, but because those points are on different isoquants, they represent different rates of output. Each point also requires an increasing amount of labor in order to allow for the increase in the rate of production.

input as we expand production between these three points. Our choice of input combinations is, therefore, *limited* in the short run; we must expand production using the input combinations that lie on the straight line connecting points a_1, a_2, and a_3. In the long run, as we show below, we can choose any combination of capital and labor, because both inputs are variable.

Note that although our choice of inputs is limited because we must expand production along the horizontal line connecting points a_1, a_2, and a_3, we choose the optimal mix of inputs according to which combination is profit-maximizing.

FIXED AND VARIABLE PROPORTIONS PRODUCTION

The isoquants shown in Figure 8.1 allow for substitution between capital and labor. That is, along a given isoquant, the ratio of capital to labor can be varied while the same output is produced. At point a_1, for example, the ratio of capital to labor is ⅚, while at point b_1 it is ¾. Both of these points produce 100 units of output per week, but the ratio of capital to labor varies to accomplish this objective. This result gives rise to the following definition:

> **If a production technology permits the ratio of inputs to vary while output remains constant, it is called a *variable proportions* production technology.**

Variable Proportions
A production technology that permits the ratio of inputs to vary along an isoquant.

Fixed Proportions
A production technology that holds the ratio of inputs constant as output increases.

It is possible, however, that the production technology requires inputs to be used in **fixed proportions.** A fixed-proportions production technology holds the ratio of inputs constant while output increases. The business of court reporting offers an example of fixed-proportions production. A record of legal proceedings generally requires a court reporter and a transcribing machine. To record more proceedings, you must keep the ratio of reporters to machines constant at unity. More machines without more reporters, for example, does not allow you to record more proceedings.

We can show what the isoquants look like in the case of a fixed-proportions production technology. The *ratio* of capital to labor is fixed as output increases in Figure 8.2. The ratio is equal to the slope of the ray (the straight line drawn out from the origin). The isoquants are necessarily right angles. For output Q_1, it is necessary to use capital and labor in the proportion K_1/L_1. In other words, given the amount of labor L_1, the use of more capital than K_1 does not make a difference. The maximum output available is Q_1 using L_1 of labor. Conversely, given the amount of capital K_1, it does not matter if more labor than L_1 is used; output cannot be expanded beyond Q_1. At output level Q_2, the amount of labor necessary is L_2 and the amount of capital is K_2. The proportion K_2/L_2 is equal to the proportion K_1/L_1. In other words, $K_2/L_2 = K_1/L_1$. While there are not many examples of fixed-proportions production technologies, there are many production processes that are nearly fixed proportions, so this assumption may be fairly commonly used. When the isoquants are perpendicular, as in Figure 8.2, we say that the inputs are *perfectly complementary,* which is another way to say that they must be used in fixed proportions.

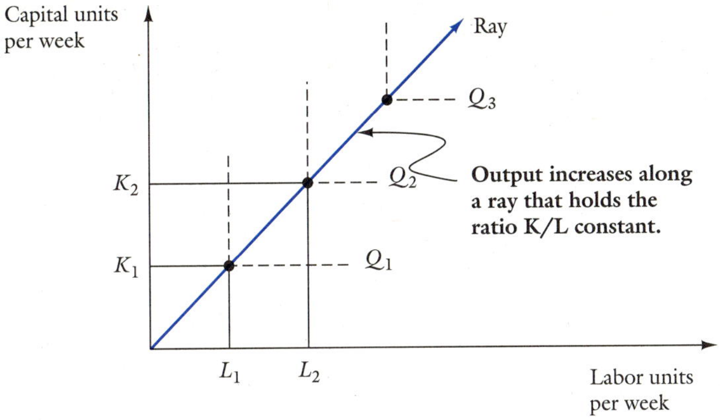

FIGURE 8.2

A Fixed-Proportions Production Technology

A fixed-proportions production technology generates right-angled isoquants. The output rate can increase only if the quantity of both inputs is increased in proportion to each other. Thus we find that the ratio K_1/L_1 is equal to the ratio K_2/L_2 as output increases from Q_1 to Q_2.

LEARNING EXERCISE 8.3

Using the production function $Q = 2K + 3L$, graph the isoquant curve for $Q = 90$ and $Q = 120$. What does the shape of these isoquants imply about your ability to substitute capital for labor in the production process? (Hint: Solve for several K and L combinations that can produce these output levels, and approximate the isoquants using these points.)

8.3 Production in the Short Run

We can increase our understanding of a typical production function by examining how output changes when one or more (but not all) inputs are fixed. Let's assume that capital is fixed and, in order to increase output, we must increase our use of the labor input. To make the analysis more concrete, suppose you are producing in-line skates—"ice skates with wheels." Your capital equipment is in place, and you must decide how much labor to hire to assemble and package the in-line skates. To make this decision, you will need to know how much each worker adds to output.

Table 8.2 (page 278) provides the necessary information. It shows how output changes when the number of employees increases, holding the amount of capital fixed at five machines. When you do not have any employees, your output is zero. (Although it is not shown, this result also arises if you do not have any capital.) To make in-line skates, then, you must have both capital *and* labor in the production function. As you hire more labor, output increases until you have 10 employees. After this point, adding more employees is

TABLE 8.2

A Production Schedule with the Capital Input Fixed and the Labor Input Variable for In-line Skates

Labor Units (L)	Capital Units (K)	Total Product (Q)	Average Product (Q/L)	Marginal Product ($\Delta Q/\Delta L$)
0	5	0	—	—
1	5	15	15	15
2	5	50	25	35
3	5	99	33	49
4	5	164	41	65
5	5	225	45	61
6	5	270	45	45
7	5	301	43	31
8	5	320	40	19
9	5	333	37	13
10	5	340	34	7
11	5	330	30	−10
12	5	300	25	−30

actually counterproductive. What happens is that employees begin to interfere with each other's work; tools become harder to find because they are misplaced, which delays production; and general congestion at the machines slows output.

The relationship between labor and output shown in Table 8.2 is a *short-run production schedule* because capital is fixed. We show this relationship graphically in panel (a) of Figure 8.3. In this graph, we have approximated the production schedule with a curve called the **total product curve.** The term *total product* is just a synonym for output. Note that the total product curve increases as labor increases up to 10 employees, after which it begins to decrease. In addition, note that at point c_1, the slope of the total product curve is no longer rising at an increasing rate; it is rising, but at a decreasing rate. Technically, point c_1 is called an **inflection point.** This point will be important to the following discussion of the marginal product of labor.

Total Product Curve
A curve showing the physical output that results from the production process.

Inflection Point
A point where the total product curve changes from increasing at an increasing rate to increasing at a decreasing rate.

AVERAGE AND MARGINAL PRODUCTS

The effect of labor on output can also be described in terms of the average and marginal products of labor. The last two columns in Table 8.2 show the average and marginal product of labor at the different levels of employment. The **average product** of labor (AP_L) is defined as output divided by the quantity of labor employed; this is written as Q/L. It is total product per time period divided by the number of employees. Changes in the average product are an indicator of the productivity of *newly hired* workers. If average product increases when a new employee is hired, then the new employee is helping increase output more than the average of the previously hired employees. If the average product declines when a new employee is hired, then the new employee is not

Average Product
Total output divided by the number of units of the variable input used.

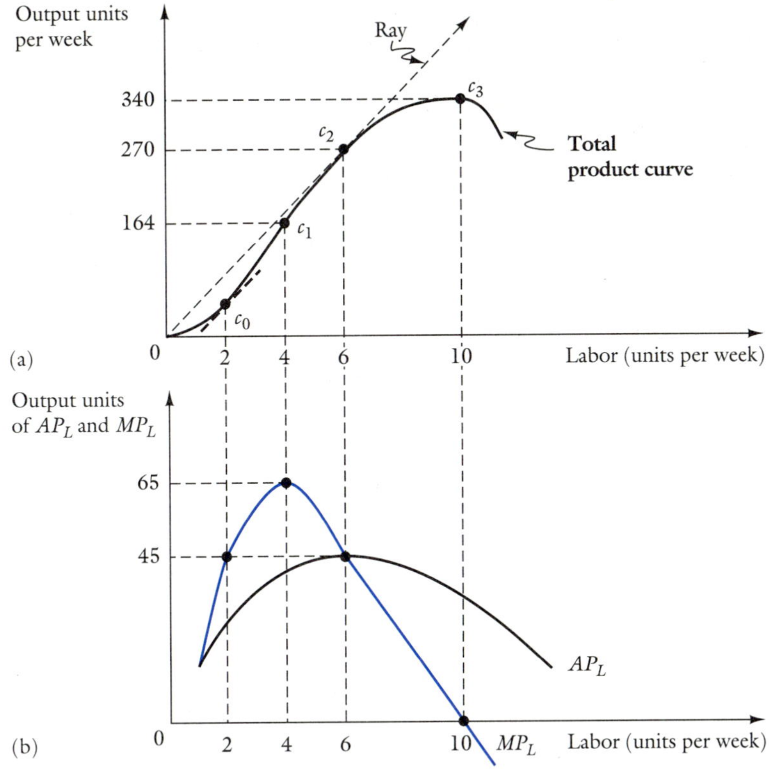

FIGURE 8.3

Total, Average, and Marginal Product Curves

Panel (a) shows the typical behavior of the total product curve (or output) as labor changes. Panel (b) shows the behavior of the average product of labor (AP_L) and the marginal product of labor (MP_L) for this total product curve. The AP_L curve is equal to the slope of a ray that intersects the total product curve. At c_2, for example, AP_L equals 270/6 (rise over the run), or 45. The MP_L equals the slope of the total product curve. At c_0, MP_L equals 45 because the tangent line at c_0 is parallel to the ray shown in panel (a) and they have the same slope.

as productive as the average of the previously hired employees. Average product is shown in panel (b) of Figure 8.3. The average product curve first rises, reaching a peak at six workers, and then falls. So, each new employee up to the sixth employee caused output to increase more than the average productivity of the previously hired employees.

Marginal Product
The change in output due to a small change (i.e., a 1-unit change) in a variable input, all other inputs held constant.

The **marginal product** of labor (MP_L) is defined as the change in total product caused by a change in labor. This would be a 1-unit change in the in-line skates example. In effect, the marginal product of labor is equal to the slope of the total product curve at a given point; the relationship is written as $\Delta Q/\Delta L$. The marginal product of labor for the production of in-line skates is shown in the last column of Table 8.2. Numerically, the marginal product of labor is equal to the change in the total output in column 3 divided by the change in labor in column 1 of Table 8.2.

The marginal product of labor is shown graphically in panel (b) of Figure 8.3. Note that the marginal product of labor curve increases when up to 4 employees are present, at point c_1 on the total product curve, and after this point marginal product declines. As an inflection point, c_1 shows where the marginal product of labor reaches a peak. After this point, a new employee does not add as much to the change in output as the last employee hired. Marginal product becomes negative after 10 employees have been hired; after this point any new employees actually lower total output.

THE RELATIONSHIP BETWEEN MARGINAL AND AVERAGE PRODUCTS

The relationship between the average and marginal products of labor or any variable input is determined by whether the marginal product of the input exceeds or is less than the average product. We can state this relationship as follows:

- Marginal product exceeds average product when average product is increasing.
- Marginal product equals average product at the maximum of the average product curve.
- Marginal product is less than average product when average product is decreasing.

An easy way to remember the relationship between marginal and average products is to think of how the weight in an elevator changes when another person steps in. Suppose that there are two people in an elevator and they each weigh 150 pounds. The average weight in the elevator is then 150 pounds. If a 300-pound person steps in, the average weight increases to 200 pounds [equal to (150 + 150 + 300)/3]. The marginal person weighs more than the existing average, so the average is increased. Analogously, if a child weighing 75 pounds is the third person to step in, then the average weight decreases to 125 pounds [equal to (150 + 150 + 75)/3]. Generally speaking, as long as the marginal value is greater than the average value, the average value will increase; when the marginal value is less than the average value, the average value will decrease. These two observations combined imply that the average and marginal values must be equal when the average reaches its maximum.

LEARNING EXERCISE 8.4

Using the short-run production function $Q = \sqrt{K}\sqrt{L}$, find the marginal and average products of labor for $L = 4$ and $L = 16$, holding K constant at 9 units. Note that $MP_L = 0.5\sqrt{K}/\sqrt{L}$.

MATH NOTEPAD

Deriving the Average and Marginal Product Relationship

The marginal and average products of labor intersect at the point at which the average product of labor reaches a maximum. This result can be seen from a comparison of the average product of the last employee hired (AP_L) to the average product of a new employee ($AP_{L+\Delta L}$). (Note that $L + \Delta L$ represents the number of employees after a new employee is hired.) First, we are interested in whether a new employee increases the average product of labor, that is, whether $AP_{L+\Delta L} > AP_L$. Let's examine the conditions in which this inequality holds. We can restate this question analytically as follows:

$$AP_{L+\Delta L} > AP_L$$

By substituting the definition of the average product of labor, the equation above implies that

$$\frac{Q + \Delta Q}{L + \Delta L} > \frac{Q}{L}$$

which, after cross-multiplying by $(L + \Delta L)$ and L, gives the inequality $(Q + \Delta Q) \times L > Q \times (L + \Delta L)$. The $Q \times L$ terms on each side cancel out, leaving $\Delta Q \times L > Q \times \Delta L$. Dividing both sides by $L \times \Delta L$ gives

$$\frac{\Delta Q}{\Delta L} > \frac{Q}{L}$$

or, rewriting this expression in terms of average and marginal products,

$$MP_L > AP_L$$

This equation shows that a new employee increases the average product of labor if the marginal product of that employee exceeds the average product of the previously hired employees. Panel (b) in Figure 8.3 shows this result for the production of in-line skates. The marginal product of labor curve is above the average product of labor curve up to 6 employees. Correspondingly, the average product of labor is increasing up to 6 employees. Beyond 6 employees, the marginal product of labor curve is below the average product of labor curve, so the average product of labor is decreasing. Because the marginal product of labor curve is *above* the average product of labor curve when AP_L is increasing and then below AP_L when AP_L is decreasing, MP_L must intersect AP_L at its maximum point. So, in general, we can say that marginal and average products of labor (or any input) are equal at the maximum of the average product curve.[1]

[1] All these relationships apply only when it is possible to produce different levels of output with different proportions of capital and labor inputs. It would have been impossible for us to draw these curves if capital and labor had to be used in fixed proportions. Thus, we say that the above results apply only to *variable proportions* production functions.

THE GEOMETRY OF MARGINAL AND AVERAGE PRODUCTS

There is a geometric way to see the relationship between the marginal and average product curves. Look at panel (a) in Figure 8.3 again. The slope of the total product curve at any point is equal to the marginal product of labor. The dashed line just tangent to point c_0, for example, reveals the slope of the total product curve at point c_0 (that is, the marginal product of labor when 2 units of labor are employed). In contrast, the average product of labor can be determined by finding the slope of a ray that extends out from the origin, as long as the ray intersects the total product curve. The slope of the ray that intersects point c_2, for example, gives the average product of labor for 6 employees. Note that when the ray is just tangent to the total product curve, as is the case at point c_2, the slope of the ray and the slope of the total product curve are equal. At this point, then, the average and marginal product curves will also be equal.

At point c_3 in panel (a), the total product curve has reached its maximum at 10 employees. Notice on panel (b) that this is exactly where marginal product equals zero.

THE LAW OF (EVENTUALLY) DIMINISHING RETURNS

The shape of the total product curve in panel (a) of Figure 8.3 and the corresponding average and marginal product curves in panel (b) are not accidental. These curves show a relationship based on the **law of diminishing returns,** or diminishing marginal product. Actually, in the way we have set up our example, the marginal product from an additional employee first rises, going from 15 units of output when the first labor unit is employed to 65 units of output for the fourth labor unit, and then falls. At the point at which the marginal product of labor falls, we say that diminishing returns have set in. In Figure 8.3, diminishing returns begin after the fourth employee is hired.

Law of Diminishing Returns
With a given technology and at least one fixed input, the marginal product of a variable input will eventually decrease.

It is relatively easy to understand why the law of diminishing marginal returns (or marginal product) would apply to a typical production technology. After all, we are holding the amount of capital constant while we add more workers. Each worker is thus working with a proportionately smaller and smaller share of capital stock. The last worker hired is not more lazy or inefficient; it's just that this worker reduces the amount of capital available per worker. Think of this situation in terms of the in-line skate manufacturing problem. There are only five machines in the short run to complete the assembly of in-line skates. After some point, the assembly process will slow down as workers wait for others to complete their work on these machines. At that point, diminishing marginal returns will set in. We should mention that if diminishing returns did not set in after some point, unusual and unbelievable results are conceptually possible. The world's total supply of wheat, for example, could be produced in a flowerpot if there were no diminishing returns in agricultural production.

Let us formally state the law of diminishing returns:

Increasing a variable input, holding one or more other inputs constant, will eventually cause the marginal product of the variable input to decrease.

The law of diminishing returns holds if

1. Only one variable input is changed and all others are held strictly constant, and
2. Technology does not change.

These conditions allow us to isolate the effects that a single input has on the production process. If technology or other inputs are changing at the same time as a single input changes, then we cannot say from observing output alone that there are diminishing (or nondiminishing) returns to a specific input.

The law of diminishing returns is *an empirical assertion* about reality. It is not a theorem or logical proposition derived from a set of assumptions, and hence susceptible to mathematical proof or refutation. It is merely a statement concerning physical relationships that has been observed to hold in actual firms. One of the reasons we accept this "law" is that we would otherwise find it difficult to explain why firms stop adding inputs (additional labor in our example) at certain points in the production process. In other words, profits would increase without bound if marginal product increased as more of an input is used when input and output prices are constant.

THREE STAGES OF PRODUCTION

In Figure 8.4 (page 284), we have redrawn the average and marginal product of labor curves from panel (b) in Figure 8.3 to highlight three stages of production. In what we define as stage I of production, the average product of labor is increasing. In stage II, the average *and* marginal products of labor are decreasing, but the marginal product of labor is positive. In stage III, the average and marginal products of labor continue to decrease, but the marginal product of labor is negative.

The three stages of production are important because they help define the quantity of labor (or any variable input) that a profit-maximizing firm will employ. You will not maximize profits in the short run, for example, by hiring more than 10 employees to manufacture in-line skates because this places you in stage III. Stage III lowers profits because additional workers add to costs but simultaneously lower revenues by reducing output. Thus, revenue goes down and costs go up, so profit is decreasing as output increases in stage III.

Profit-maximizing incentives will also move production out of stage I. To illustrate this result, suppose that you can sell all of your output at a single price. In stage I, your average product of labor is increasing, which implies that your *average* cost of production is declining as you increase output.[2] (We will discuss this result in Chapter 9.) Total revenue increases as output increases

[2]Note that in the two-input case, stage I of production for one input corresponds to stage III for the other input.

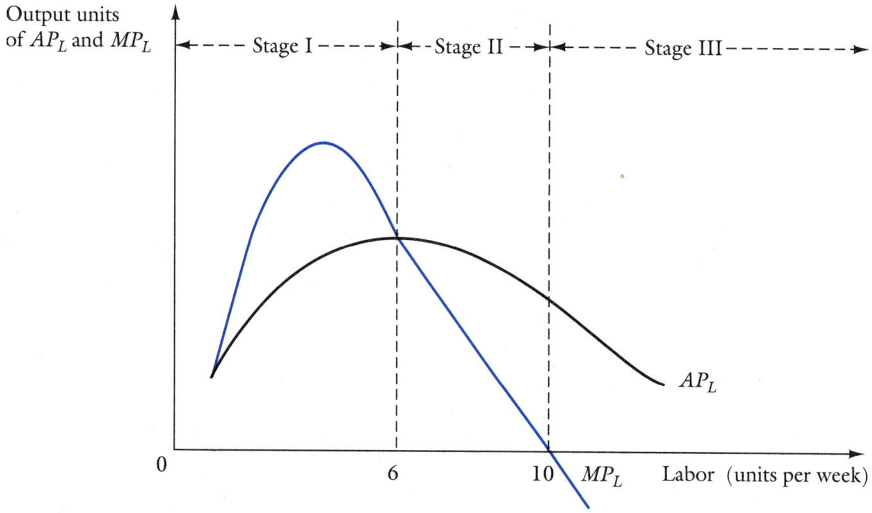

FIGURE 8.4

The Three Stages of Production

There are three stages of production in the short run. In stage I, the AP_L curve is increasing, so the MP_L exceeds the AP_L. In stage II, both the MP_L and AP_L curves are declining, but the MP_L is positive. In stage III, the MP_L is negative. A firm will find that it maximizes profits by choosing a quantity of labor that places it in stage II.

because you can sell all of your output at one price. Thus, revenue is increasing and costs are decreasing, so profits are increasing in stage I. In this situation, you will continue to increase output as long as short-run *average* costs are declining. As such, you cannot maximize profits in stage I because if you increase your output rate you will always increase profits. These results imply that you maximize profits by selecting an amount of labor and thus output that places your manufacturing process somewhere in stage II. If in-line skates are sold at a given market price, then you will employ between 6 and 10 workers to maximize profits in the short run.

LEARNING EXERCISE 8.5

Using an isoquant diagram, show the marginal product of labor diminishing when capital is held fixed. On the same diagram, show how the marginal product of capital diminishes when labor is held fixed.

Policy Application and Evaluation

PRODUCTIVITY OF LABOR IN THE UNITED STATES

Issue *Has the U.S. productivity growth rate fallen behind that of other countries? If true, will this affect the standard of living in the United States?*

Background

In empirical studies, labor productivity is usually measured by the average product of labor and *productivity growth* is measured by increases in the average product of labor. For the economy as a whole, the average product of labor is generally estimated by dividing the value of total domestic output (gross domestic product, or GDP) by the number of workers or by population. Such an aggregate measure of labor productivity is related to the average standard of living shared by all people in the economy.

To understand the relationship, note that all payments for goods and services are equal to the payments made to inputs in the production process; that is, payments to labor, capital, materials, and the residual (called profits, which is paid to firms' owners) are equal to input payments. But payments to factors of production eventually end up in the hands of individuals, as it is individuals who ultimately own the factors used by firms. Because productivity affects the rate of output, it affects the total payments that individuals eventually receive. If labor productivity improves—say because of an advance in technology—the rate of output increases without the need for additional labor. The dollar value of all goods increases as a result, and this implies that consumers will (ultimately) receive more income. A higher income, holding the economy-wide price level constant, implies an increase in the standard of living. In simple terms, increasing productivity causes an increase in the income and wealth of consumers, *ceteris paribus.* Similarly, a decline in productivity, as measured by the average product of labor, implies that consumers' standard of living will (eventually) fall.

The Case for Concern

Now the question is, has labor productivity in the United States fallen behind other countries? If so, will the standard of living in the United States fall in the future when compared to these other countries? Table 8.3 on page 286 shows the rate of growth in U.S. labor productivity compared to some developed and undeveloped countries for the period 1950–1988. In this table, labor productivity is measured as GDP divided by population.[3]

Labor productivity growth in the United States has averaged about 2 percent per year over the period 1950–1988, a lower rate than in all other countries except Chile and Peru. For the same period, labor productivity growth in Japan has averaged 6.13 percent per year, leading many economists to warn that the Japanese are quickly catching up to the U.S. standard of living. Clearly, the data show reason for concern about the future standard of living in the United States.

A Closer Look at the Issue

On the surface, there is reason to worry about relative living standards in the United States, but below the surface there is much more to be said about the data reported in Table 8.3. First, the growth of labor productivity is sensitive to

[3]Dividing GDP by the number of workers or by an estimate of hours worked (when hours worked can be computed) produces nearly identical results, so our statements are not sensitive to our measure of labor productivity.

TABLE 8.3

Growth in Labor Productivity and Investment per Capita in Developing and Developed Countries, 1950–1988

	Developing Countries				Developed Countries			
	Labor Productivity Growth Rates for Selected Periods (percent per year)							
YEARS	Chile	Egypt	Mexico	Peru	Japan	West Germany	United Kingdom	USA
1950–88	1.18	3.31	2.15	1.46	6.13	3.74	2.34	1.99
1973–88	0.29	4.65	0.77	–0.55	2.88	1.95	1.94	1.72
1950–73	1.77	2.45	3.06	2.79	8.30	4.92	2.60	2.17
1973–83	–0.90	7.01	1.74	–1.13	2.56	1.66	1.17	0.85
1983–88	2.71	0.08	–1.14	0.63	3.53	2.52	3.49	3.50
	Growth in Investment per Capita for Selected Periods (percent per year)							
1950–88	0.86	4.31	2.74	1.57	8.33	3.47	4.20	2.03
1973–88	2.80	6.11	–0.69	–0.81	1.68	0.89	1.74	1.82
1950–73	–0.38	3.15	5.05	3.16	12.90	5.19	5.84	2.16
1973–83	–4.21	11.95	–0.44	–2.32	–0.59	–0.34	–1.01	–0.55
1983–88	18.39	–4.68	–1.19	2.29	6.36	3.39	7.49	6.73

Source: Robert Summers and Alan Heston, "The Penn World Tables (Mark 5): An Expanded Set of International Comparisons, 1950–1988," *Quarterly Journal of Economics* (May 1991), 327–368.

the period used. Often, data on labor productivity are divided at two points, 1973 and 1983. The 1973 point marks the rise of the Organization of Petroleum Exporting Countries (OPEC) and the 1973 oil embargo against the United States and other developed nations. The 1983 point marks the end of a major postwar recession and the beginning of a worldwide acceleration of economic activity. Table 8.3 shows that labor productivity growth rates for the United States and other countries vary when measured between these different periods. Nearly every country experienced slower growth between 1973 and 1983. More important, while the United States seems to have recovered from the 1973–1983 slowdown, growing at 3.5 percent per year, which is faster than the pre-1973 rate, many other countries—most notably Japan—have not yet recovered to their pre-1973 growth pattern.

Second, the United States has averaged about 2 percent productivity growth since 1870, with significant slowdowns occurring during the Great Depression in the 1930s and in the 1973–1983 period cited above.[4] Thus, the

[4]See Jeffery G. Williamson, "Productivity and American Leadership: A Review Article," *Journal of Economic Literature* 24 (March 1991), 51–68.

fact that the United States has averaged about 2 percent between 1950 and 1988, including the 1973–1983 period, indicates that the United States is likely moving along in its 120-year-old growth pattern.

The United States Versus Japan

What is unusual is not productivity growth in the United States but the productivity behavior of other countries, particularly Japan. Figure 8.5 shows the 5-year moving average growth rate of productivity in Japan and the United States. Japan experienced high rates of productivity growth before 1973, averaging 8.3

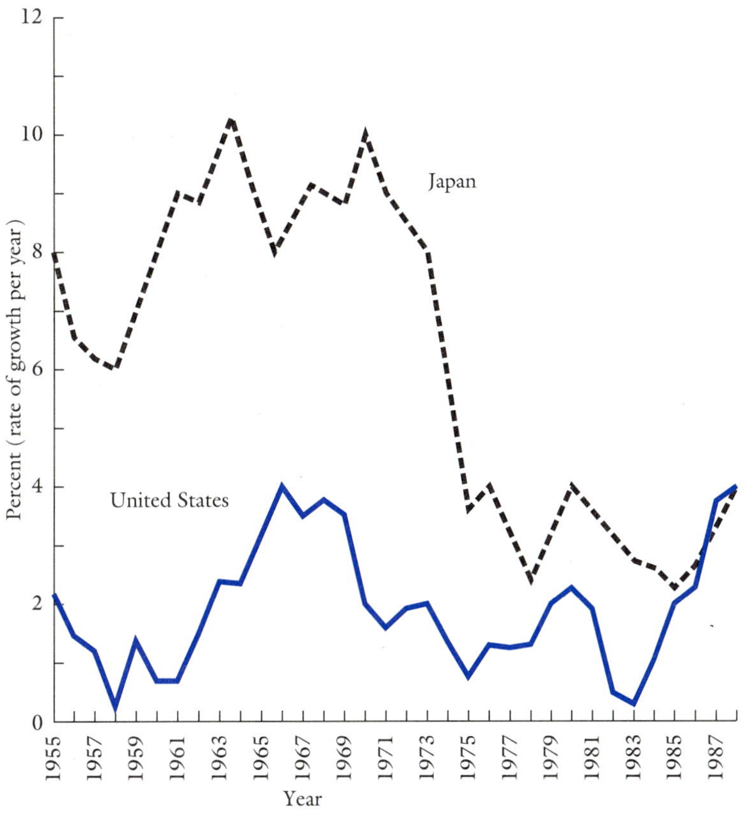

FIGURE 8.5

Five-Year Moving Average Growth Rate of Real Gross Domestic Product (RGDP) per Capita—United States and Japan, 1955–1988

The five-year average growth rate of real gross domestic product (RGDP) shows that Japan has experienced higher rates of RGDP growth than the United States for most of the period 1955–1988. A significant decline in RGDP growth occurred in Japan after 1972, and Japan has not yet recovered to its pre-1973 growth pattern. In addition, since 1983, RGDP growth rates in the United States have risen sharply, exceeding RGDP growth in Japan during 1988.

percent per year, but these rates dropped rapidly in the 1970s and have returned to only 3.53 percent per year during the economic boom period of 1983–1988, which is nearly identical to the U.S. rate for this period. While there may be reason for some concern about the U.S. standard of living, Japan and other countries must also be concerned, because they seem to have moved to a slower growth path in the post-1973 period. Undoubtedly, the OPEC oil embargo and subsequent rise in world oil prices had a more lasting effect on Japan—which imports nearly 100 percent of its oil—and other countries than on the United States.

Figure 8.6 illustrates the reason for Japanese concern by graphing the time path of per capita GDP in Japan and the United States between 1950 and 1988. Note the decline that occurred in both series immediately following 1973. Note, too, that the United States enjoyed an advantage in annual per capita domestic product of over $6,000 in 1988. With Japan's post-1973 productivity slow-

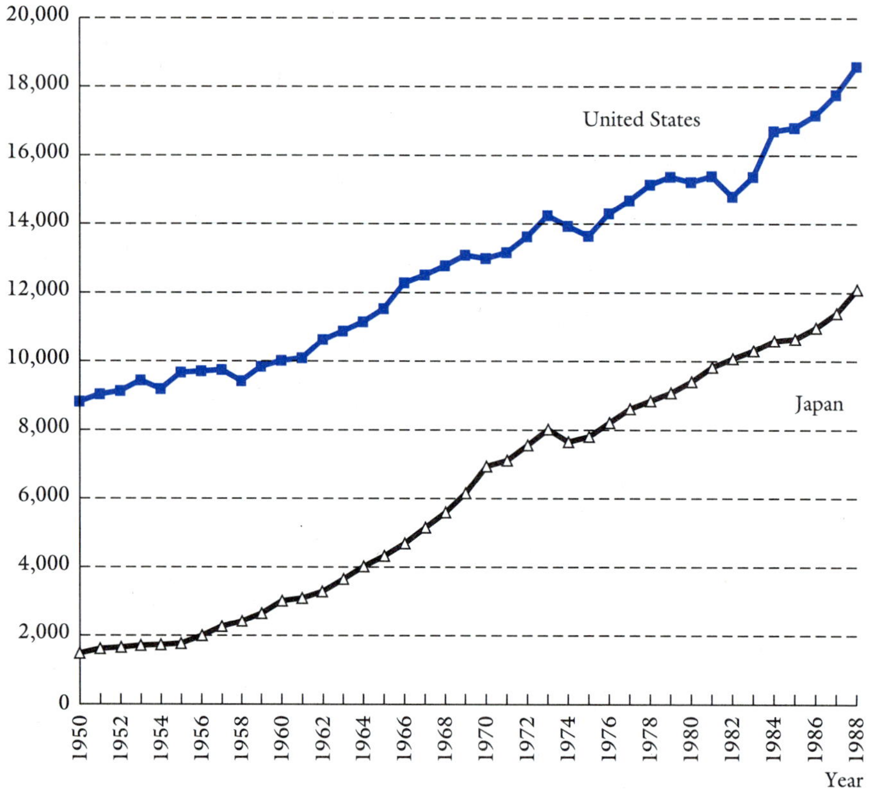

FIGURE 8.6

Real Domestic Product per Capita—United States and Japan, 1950–1988

Although Japan has had substantially higher real gross domestic product (RGDP) growth, its real domestic product *per capita* has lagged behind that of the United States. In 1988, for example, real domestic product per capita in the United States exceeded real domestic product per capita in Japan by over $6,000.

down, it will be a very long time indeed before its standard of living overtakes that of the United States, as measured by annual per capita GDP.

Explanations for the Changes in Productivity Growth Rates

What besides OPEC might explain the changes we observe in productivity growth in the United States and other countries? Growth in capital investment slowed in the post-1973 period, as shown in the lower half of Table 8.3 (page 286). A larger capital stock increases the average product of labor, usually by increasing output for the same level of effort—an efficiency effect. Sometimes the average product of labor increases when capital stock makes each worker's job easier, thereby increasing a worker's endurance. In the United States, investment per capita grew at a rate of 2.16 percent per year between 1950 and 1973, then became −0.55 percent per year between 1973 and 1983, only to grow at an extraordinary annual rate of 6.73 percent since 1983. Generally speaking, U.S. capital investment growth recovered significantly from the decade of disinvestment, 1973–1983. As noted above, labor productivity in the United States also recovered, so the changes in the U.S. capital stock since 1983 probably have helped the recovery greatly in labor productivity.

Again, it is the other countries shown in Table 8.3 that have not recovered to their pre-1973 investment levels. Japan, for instance, experienced per capita investment growth of 12.9 percent per year between 1950 and 1973, only to have investment growth slow to 6.36 percent per year between 1983 and 1988, a rate slower than that of the United States for the latter period. Most other countries, except Egypt (which was helped by the oil embargo and the Camp David accords) and the United Kingdom, tell a similar story.

The growth of the service sector worldwide may also help explain the slowdown in labor productivity, particularly in other countries. Productivity growth is less in the services than in manufacturing, so a shift toward more service sector jobs implies a shift toward lower-productivity growth rates. While the service sector has grown in the United States, it has grown more in other countries. Service sector growth—as measured by labor employment shares—has been higher in all other *industrialized* countries, so the lower productivity of the services may help explain why these other countries—except the United Kingdom—have not experienced a post-1983 recovery similar to the U.S. recovery.

A Final Thought

We must make a general observation about the importance of productivity growth. It is true that more rapid productivity growth in other countries implies that their standard of living (ultimately) will increase faster than that in the United States, but the United States also benefits from foreign productivity growth. Consumers in the United States can import goods more cheaply, *ceteris paribus,* when productivity growth increases abroad. The emergence of a low-cost, high-quality electronics industry in Japan has benefited U.S. consumers. Productivity growth—in the United States or abroad—is good, not bad, for economies all around the globe.

Questions for Evaluation

Should the United States government develop a policy that favors investments to increase labor productivity, for example, job training and continuing education subsidies? How would such a policy affect the incentive to invest in physical capital if it was successful? Even if U.S. productivity growth rates did not change, would a slowdown in Japan's rate of productivity growth help or hurt economic activity in the United States?

8.4 Production in the Long Run

In the short run, the firm is constrained to use only its variable inputs to expand production. In the long run, however, the profit goal implies that the firm should consider how *all* inputs interact in the production process. In the long run, then, the firm can move to any output combination along an isoquant. The degree of substitution—capital for labor—along an isoquant determines how much flexibility a firm can employ to escape the effects of an increase in the relative price of one of these inputs. Let's explore the concept of input substitution further.

SUBSTITUTION AMONG INPUTS

The isoquants we drew in Figure 8.1 implicitly assumed that substitution among inputs is feasible. It turns out that the shape of an isoquant indicates the degree of substitution that is technically feasible between inputs. The basic shape of an isoquant is determined by how its slope changes as we move along the isoquant. To see this result, let's investigate how slope changes for a particular isoquant.

In Figure 8.7, we have drawn a single isoquant ($Q_1 = 100$). The slope of isoquant Q_1 is equal to $\Delta K/\Delta L$ at any point. As we move down the isoquant, we increase the usage of the labor input ($\Delta L > 0$) and decrease the usage of the capital input ($\Delta K \leq 0$), keeping output constant. Thus, the slope of the isoquant, $\Delta K/\Delta L$, is negative. For example, if we measure the slope of isoquant Q_1 at point a_1, we find that $\Delta K = -3$ and $\Delta L = 1$, so the slope at this point equals $-3/1$ or -3. The same reasoning shows that the slope of the isoquant is equal to $-1/2$ at point b_1.

The decrease in the slope (in absolute value) between points a_1 and b_1 in Figure 8.7 gives the isoquant its convex shape. The convex shape of the isoquant implies that the rate at which labor may be substituted for capital *varies* along the isoquant. The rate of substitution depends on the existing mix of capital and labor in the production process. In other words, the rate depends on where you are on the isoquant. The existing mix at point a_1 is capital-intensive because it is uses relatively more capital than labor to produce 100 units of output. The slope is -3 at this point, indicating that 3 units of capital can be sold (or given up) while an additional employee is hired and output will remain constant. In contrast, at point b_1, the substitution possibilities are more limited. At

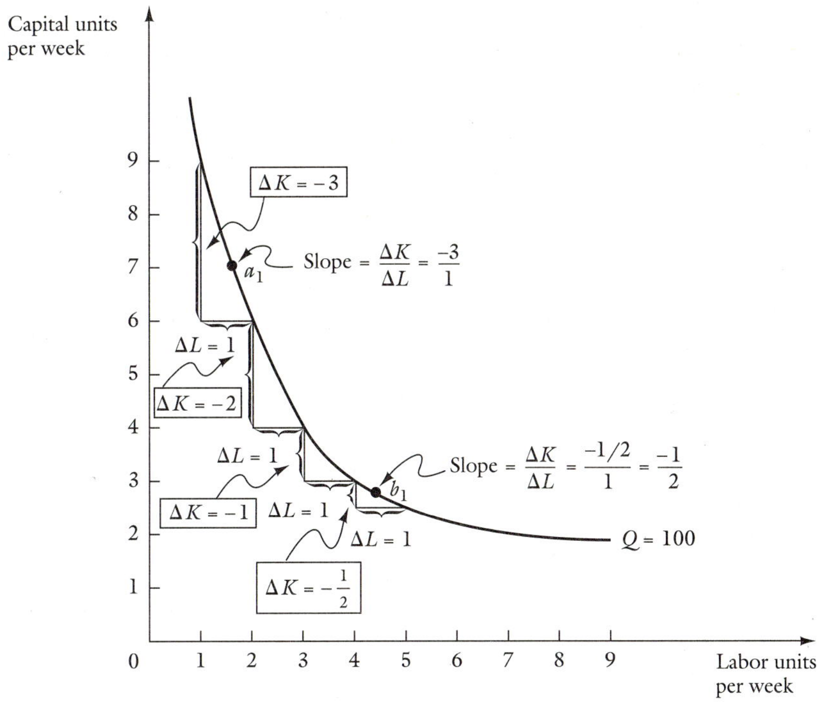

FIGURE 8.7

Substituting Labor for Capital along the Isoquant

The slope of any isoquant is equal to the change in capital divided by the change in labor. The basic shape of an isoquant is determined by how this slope changes as we move along it. Here we have drawn a single isoquant in which $Q_1 = 100$. As we move down the isoquant, labor input increases while the capital input decreases, keeping output constant at Q_1 at all times. The slope of the isoquant is negative. The slope decreases in absolute terms as we move from point a_1 to b_1. The isoquant is convex.

point b_1, the slope of the isoquant equals − ½. Here we have less capital than at point a_1. The production technology is more restrictive as we substitute capital for one additional employee at point a_1.

> **By definition, with convex isoquants, the rate at which we can substitute capital for labor *decreases* as we move down an isoquant.**

We can relate the slope of an isoquant to the marginal product of labor and the marginal product of capital. Remember from our discussion of Table 8.2 that MP_L is defined as $\Delta Q/\Delta L$, keeping the capital input fixed. Similarly, the marginal product of capital MP_K is defined as $\Delta Q/\Delta K$, holding the labor input constant. As we move down an isoquant, we are changing both labor and capital. If we were to change only labor, the effect on output would be equal to $MP_L \Delta L$; that is, the marginal product of labor times the change in labor equals the change in output (ΔQ) when labor changes by ΔL. Analogously, if we were to change only capital, the change in output would be equal to $MP_K \Delta K$. If we change *both* labor and capital at the same time, which is what occurs as we move down an isoquant, then the resulting change in output is equal to the sum of the two separate changes, or

$$\Delta Q = MP_L \times \Delta L + MP_K \times \Delta K \tag{8.3}$$

Because output does not change along an isoquant, $\Delta Q = 0$ for all points on a *given* isoquant. Equation (8.3), then, implies that $MP_L \times \Delta L + MP_K \times \Delta K = 0$ on an isoquant, or, after rearranging terms, $MP_L \times \Delta L = - MP_K \times \Delta K$. The definition of an isoquant forces this result: Each term on the right-hand side of equation (8.3) measures how output is changing when only one input changes. For output to remain constant when *both* inputs change, each input's separate effect on output must cancel out the other. So, to remain on an isoquant, we find that the effect of labor on output, $MP_L \times \Delta L$, equals −1 times the effect of capital on output, that is, $-MP_K \times \Delta K$. Rearranging this result still further, we find the following relationship:

$$\frac{\Delta K}{\Delta L} = -\frac{MP_L}{MP_K} \tag{8.4}$$

Equation (8.4) shows that the slope of an isoquant equals −1 times the ratio of the marginal product of labor to the marginal product of capital. Because the slope of an isoquant is a measure of a firm's technical ability to substitute capital for labor in the production process, equation (8.4) shows that the *ratio of marginal products* is a measure of the capital-labor substitution possibilities. We generally drop the minus sign when we use the ratio of marginal products to discuss substitution possibilities. Without the minus sign, we call the ratio MP_L/MP_K the **marginal rate of technical substitution (MRTS).**

Marginal Rate of Technical Substitution (MRTS)
The rate at which labor can be substituted for capital, holding output constant; or the ratio of the marginal product of labor to the marginal product of capital (i.e., $MRTS = MP_L/MP_K$).

From our discussion of Figure 8.7, we know that the MRTS is declining as we move down an isoquant. When capital decreases and labor increases along an isoquant, the ratio of their marginal products declines. When we discussed the law of diminishing returns, we examined how the marginal product of an input changes, holding all other inputs constant. Along an isoquant, we have the long-run analog to the law of diminishing returns. Instead of focusing on the change in the level of the marginal product of a single input, we examine how the *ratio of marginal products* changes as we substitute one input for another. The profit-maximizing interpretation of a diminishing MRTS is that the marginal product of labor is decreasing (stage II, moving toward stage III) and the marginal product of capital is increasing (stage II again, but moving toward stage I) as capital decreases and labor increases along an isoquant. Conceptually, then, long-run adjustments generate a *relative productivity effect,* because we observe the ratio of marginal products changing, not just changes in their individual levels when the other inputs are held constant.

LEARNING EXERCISE 8.6

Find the marginal rate of technical substitution for the production function $Q = \sqrt{K}\sqrt{L}$ when $K = 8$ and $L = 8$ and when $K = 1$ and $L = 8$. Are these points on the same isoquant?

$$$ Price Theory in Practice

ENGLISH (AND FRENCH) CHUNNEL

For more than 100 years the English and French have thought of building a tunnel that would allow them to cross the 23-mile-wide English Channel that separates the two countries.

A magazine article in 1882 reported that one of the first attempts on the English side excavated at a rate of 100 yards per week. The author speculated with a healthy dose of optimism that if digging also were started on the French side, work could be completed in less than $3^1/_2$ years.

It was not until December 1990 that French and English miners were able to push aside the last dirt and shake hands 300 feet beneath the surface of the English Channel. A train through the tunnel began operating intermittently in summer 1994.

The huge scale of the project is another reason it took so long before anyone could build the tunnel. Because the channel crossing is believed to be the world's biggest civil engineering project, it would have greatly taxed the management capabilities and financial resources of any single firm.

The current tunnel project did not begin until 1986, when a group of 10 contractors and 5 banks won the rights to build the tunnel and run it for 55 years. Financing the project, estimated to cost $15.2 billion in 1991 dollars, required an extensive network of banks and investors. More than 200 banks provided the first $10 billion in loans. Another $1.5 billion was raised by selling stock.

The case of the English Chunnel (*ch*annel t*unnel*), as it is sometimes called, illustrates the importance of technology and substitution possibilities in production. Although the demand for a tunnel existed long ago, the technology necessary to produce it did not exist until recently. The technology used by the miners during those first efforts in the late 1800s was labor-intensive. Much of the digging was done by men wielding picks and shovels and by steam-driven earthmovers, generally the most advanced equipment at the time. The task was not completed with that technology.

With today's capital-intensive technology, labor-intensive picks and shovels take a backseat to machines. Huge machines, with rotating cutting edges up to 27 feet wide, drilled their way into the ground as fast as 1,900 feet per week. Some technicians monitored complex electronic controls on their drilling machines while others operated a system of railways, conveyor belts, and pumps to haul the dirt and muck the drilling machines produced.

Although the differences in technology over time are significant, the French and British engineers also used different technology. These differences show how alternative combinations of labor and capital can achieve the same output (an isoquant), even when the task is as complex as digging beneath the English Channel.

The tunneling by the French, for example, tended to be more capital-intensive than the British effort. One of the reasons for the different mix of inputs is that the ground on the French side is softer and water-soaked, requiring a more sophisticated boring machine that can withstand water pressure of 145 pounds per square inch. The French, however, also chose a system for removing soil that crushes it, mixes it with water, and pumps the material out of the tunnel. The British, meanwhile, built a complex rail system that hauls the dirt on rail cars. The differences may be explained by a lower British wage rate for the workers who run the rail system, which enabled the British to use existing mining equipment and techniques more cheaply.

Even with the capital-intensive technology available on both sides, it still took about the $3^1/_2$ years that the early tunnel watchers speculated it would take to dig the first tunnel.

LEARNING EXERCISE 8.7

Given that the input mix is different on the English and French sides of the channel, do you expect the marginal product of labor to be equal between the two production technologies? Why or why not?

TECHNOLOGICAL PROGRESS AND R & D

Many firms find it valuable to invest in improving their production technology. The many billions of dollars spent annually by U.S. firms on research and development attest to the significance of improved technology. Such improvements have a direct effect on the relationship between inputs and outputs in a production function, which is illustrated in Figure 8.8.

Figure 8.8 shows how the productivity of labor can increase through technological improvement. Improved technology shifts the total product curve upward from $Q_{\text{year 1}}$ to $Q_{\text{year 2}}$. Without changing the amount of labor hired, the average product of all workers increases—from $AP_L = 30$ to $AP_L = 36$—because of the improved technology. (Note that each total product curve still exhibits diminishing returns; technological improvements may retard, but cannot eliminate, the eventual onset of the law of diminishing marginal returns.)

Technological progress can affect inputs individually or jointly. When there are joint effects, we find that output increases as a result of a new technology. The development of the computer had such an effect on the manufacturing and service sectors in the United States during the 1960s and 1970s. To some extent, the computer revolution continues today, but the productivity effect tends to be biased toward improving the average product of labor. Technological change can also have indirect effects on productivity—effects that were not planned for initially. The development of safety devices, such as seat belts and air bags, has made it possible to use lighter-weight metals and plastics in the construction of automobiles without greatly reducing the chances of surviving an automobile accident. Plastics and lightweight metals

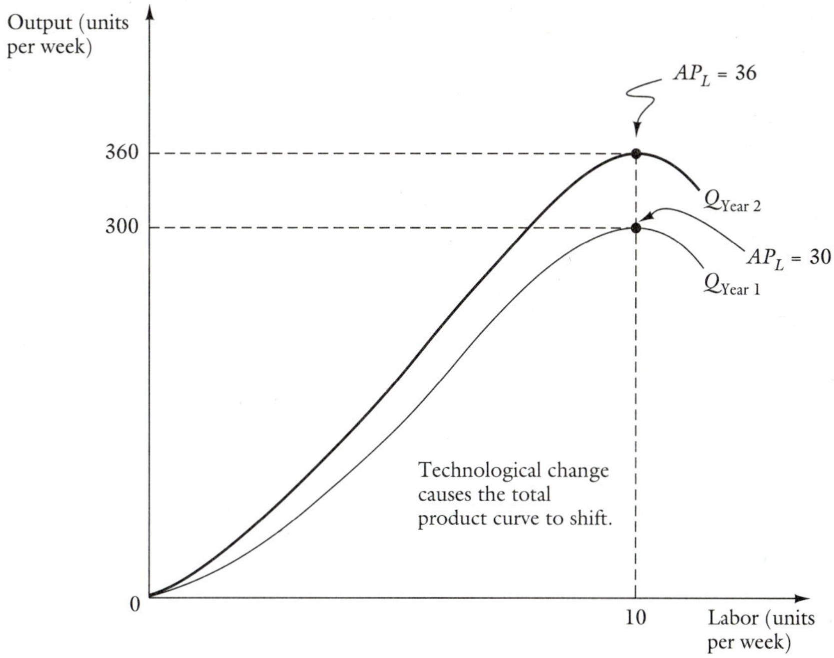

FIGURE 8.8

The Effect of Technological Progress on Labor Productivity

A change in technology causes the total product curve to shift. The use of 10 units of labor in year 1 generates an output rate of 300 units per week and an AP_L equal to 30. In year 2, a new technology is introduced that increases the productivity of labor. Now 10 units of labor produces 360 units of output per week for an AP_L equal to 36.

are easier to mold and install on vehicles, which increases the productivity of an automobile assembly line.

In short, technological progress acts like a shift factor in the production process, shifting the productivity of either a single input—such as labor—or many inputs. The net result is more output without changing the levels of the existing inputs.

RETURNS TO SCALE

Increasing Returns to Scale
The long-run characteristic that a change in all inputs by a fixed percentage causes output to change by more than the fixed percentage.

Production processes may differ in terms of their scale. But bigger is not always better. The important question we consider here is, does a large plant—more capital, labor, and other inputs—lead to proportionately more output? This question focuses on the returns to scale of the production technology.

Technically, there are three types of returns to scale. First, a production technology exhibits **increasing returns to scale** if the output produced more than doubles when all inputs used are doubled. Second, the production process exhibits **constant returns to scale** if the output produced doubles when all inputs used are doubled. Finally, the production technology exhibits **decreasing returns to scale** if the output less than doubles when all inputs used are doubled.

Constant Returns to Scale
The long-run characteristic that a change in all inputs by a fixed percentage causes output to change by the same fixed percentage.

Decreasing Returns to Scale
The long-run characteristic that a change in all inputs by a fixed percentage causes output to change by less than the fixed percentage.

Each of the three types of returns to scale has a different implication for the efficient size or scale of a plant. With increasing returns to scale, there are efficiency gains from a large plant. If the doubling of inputs also doubles costs and at the same time output more than doubles, then average cost (the ratio of total costs to output) declines. A falling average cost of production encourages competitive firms to become larger to realize these lower unit costs. In contrast, with decreasing returns to scale, a doubling of inputs leads to an increasing average cost of production, which eventually discourages expansion of the scale of operations. Constant returns to scale falls in the middle, with average costs remaining constant when the scale increases.

Usually, the returns to scale will vary over the possible plant sizes that can be built. So, a given production technology may experience increasing returns to scale at the outset of production, moving to a scale in which there are constant returns and then to a scale in which there are decreasing returns. A production technology that displays all three types of scale contains a built-in limit to the efficient size of a firm. A production technology that displays the three types of returns to scale is shown in Figure 8.9.

In Figure 8.9, a map of isoquants is shown for varying output rates. This particular production process first exhibits increasing returns, then constant returns, and lastly decreasing returns to scale. Changing the use of inputs from point *A* to point *B* represents a doubling of both capital and labor that causes the output rate to more than double—from 100 to 300 units of output. Over this range of inputs, then, the production process exhibits increasing returns to scale. Changing the use of inputs from point *B* to point *C* also represents a doubling of inputs. In this case, output doubles too, so between points *B* and *C,* the production process exhibits constant returns to scale. Finally, doubling the inputs again by moving from point *C* to point *D* causes output to change by less than double. Between points *C* and *D,* then, the production process exhibits decreasing returns to scale.

Because the returns to scale of a production process are important to the efficient size of a firm, it is valuable to review some of the reasons why there are both increasing and decreasing returns to scale.

Specialization

As a firm's scale of operation increases, the opportunities for specialization in the use of resource inputs also increase, which may cause increasing returns to scale. This is sometimes called increased division of tasks or operations, or an increased division of labor among tasks. Gains from increasing the division of labor, or increased specialization, are well known, as we suggested in our discussion of comparative advantage in Chapter 1. In terms of managerial personnel, we also find that larger enterprises may be able to put together more highly specialized staffs. Larger enterprises may have the ability to tap better managerial skills.

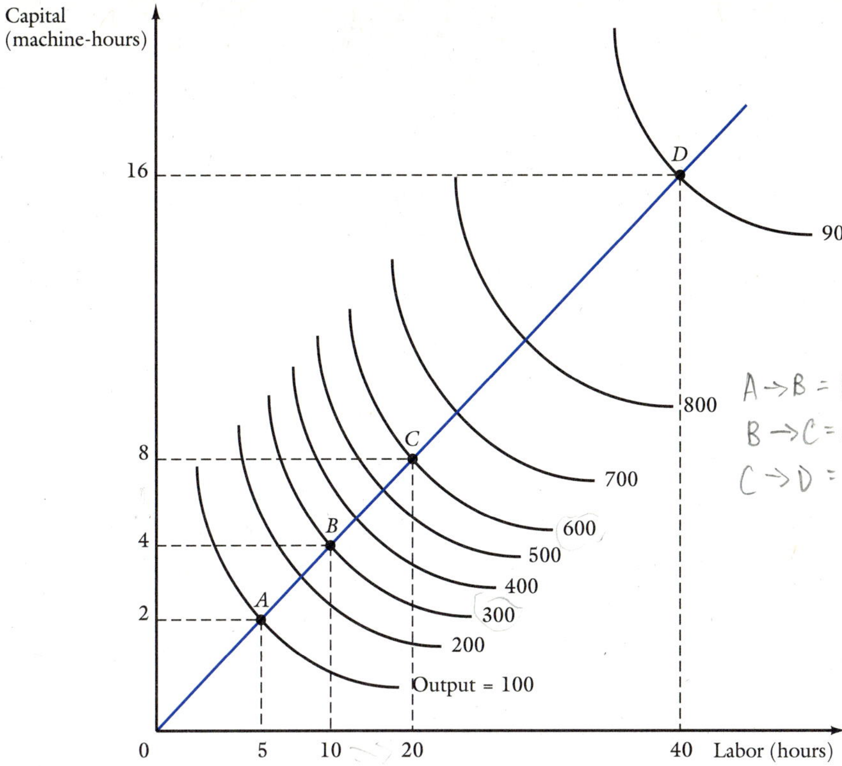

FIGURE 8.9

An Example of Increasing, Constant, and Decreasing Returns to Scale in a Production Process

Improved Productive Equipment

The larger the scale of the enterprise, the more it is able to take advantage of larger-volume or specially "tailored" types of machinery, which may give rise to increasing returns to scale. Small-scale operations may not lend themselves to machines that require a large volume of output to be used profitably, and such operations seldom find it profitable to have a machine built or modified to the details of their particular production situations.

Monitoring and Shirking Problems

One of the basic reasons we can eventually expect to observe decreasing returns to scale is that there are limits to the efficient functioning of management. As more workers are hired, for example, a more-than-proportionate increase in managers may be needed, and this can cause increased cost per unit. It may be possible to hire from zero to ten workers and give them each a shovel to dig ditches; however, as soon as ten workers are hired, it may also be necessary to hire an overseer to coordinate their ditch-digging efforts. Thus, perhaps increasing or constant returns to scale will take place until ten workers and ten shovels are employed; then decreasing returns to scale set in. As the layers of supervision grow, the cost of information and communication often grows more rapidly.

Physical Constraints

Some inputs are subject to physical constraints that cause decreasing returns to scale. For example, a firm can double the number of machines while it doubles the use of all other inputs and not necessarily double the machines' contribution to output. Consider the possibility of the machines generating excessive noise and heat, thus requiring a larger space (that is, more than double the working space) in order to keep the machines physically efficient. There are numerous other examples of such physical problems that can cause decreasing returns to scale.

$$$ Price Theory in Practice

HOUSEHOLD PRODUCTION IN EARLY NEW ENGLAND AND RETURNS TO SCALE

Although we have discussed the concept of returns of scale as it applies to firms in a market setting, it is equally applicable to production activities that take place in a household. Members of a household cook meals, clean and repair simple appliances, wash clothes, and perform many other chores that we may call production. The extent to which households participate in productive activities has evolved over time, particularly because returns to scale are possible as markets grow in size.

Settlers in seventeenth-century New England, for example, not only prepared their own meals but grew the fruits and vegetables and maintained the livestock used to produce a meal. These settlers did not use a real estate agent to find a home; they built their own homes. Their children were not initially educated in a community school but were taught to read and write (if they were taught at all) in the household.

As more settlers arrived from England and elsewhere in Europe, the nature of household production changed. A larger population allowed the New England settlers to realize increasing returns to scale in the production of certain goods and services. It therefore became *cheaper* to let others produce some goods and to trade with these "specialists" in a market setting. Some settlers specialized in producing corn, others potatoes, and still others raised livestock. A farmers' market developed to facilitate trade. As the population grew, other specialized trades developed, such as schoolteachers, who specialized in education; constables, who specialized in law enforcement; and wagon drivers, who specialized in hauling products.

Today, returns to scale have led to even more specialization and less household production. Meals are frequently prepared at restaurants for take-out or home delivery. Entertainment is produced by home videos or CD players, whereas it was once produced by families singing and dancing. Children attend many after-school events, whereas before they played at home with their siblings or neighbors' children.

As specialized as we have become, it is still likely that returns to scale exist in some aspects of household production, so the role of families and the marketplace will continue to evolve as population grows (and technology changes).

LEARNING EXERCISE 8.8

Can you identify any returns to scale in the production of a college education that were not possible before the computer revolution of the past twenty years?

ESTIMATING A PRODUCTION FUNCTION

Many researchers have investigated the nature of real-world production functions. A variety of techniques have been developed to estimate these functions. Researchers have analyzed data from a long period of time to show the various inputs used and the amount of output produced in each period in the past. For example, a researcher could obtain information on the amount of labor and capital used in the primary aluminum industry during each year from, say, 1950 to 1994. The researcher would then have 45 observations from which to estimate the relation between inputs and the resulting output.

An alternative technique involves analyzing data either from a large number of firms or from different sectors of the same industry at a particular time. Information on the amount of capital and labor used by firms in the tire manufacturing industry can be obtained for a particular year, say, 1994. The number of observations would be equal to the number of firms from which data are obtained. From such data, an estimate of the relationship between inputs and the resulting output may be obtained using statistical methods.

Statisticians dealing with the data used to estimate production functions run into many problems. It is often difficult to measure the capital input because at any point in time, the stock of capital is composed of equipment that is not of the same type or of the same age and productivity. Even the measurement of the labor input is difficult because the labor in any one firm is of varying quality. A complete list of the problems in the measurement of production functions could fill an entire book.

The Cobb-Douglas Production Function

The exact mathematical form of the production function must also be chosen. When we defined a production function by equation (8.1), we did not specify the form but rather left it implicit. Researchers in this area have often simply assumed that a production function was of the Cobb-Douglas form (see Appendix 5A). This class of production functions has the following appearance:

$$Q = AK^{\alpha}L^{\beta}E^{\gamma}M^{\delta} \tag{8.5}$$

where Q represents output, L represents labor, K represents capital, E represents energy, M represents materials, and α, β, γ, and δ are parameters that vary from firm to firm and from industry to industry. The constant term, A, represents a shift parameter, which may change as technology changes.

The exponent parameters of equation (8.5) help define the effect of a given input on output and the returns to scale of the production technology. The coefficient of labor, β, from the Cobb-Douglas production function in equation (8.5) is the percentage increase in output that would result from a 1 percent increase in labor, the quantity of capital, materials, and energy being held constant. Similarly, α is the percentage increase in output that would result from a 1 percent increase in capital, the quantity of labor, materials, and energy being held constant. This observation applies to the other exponents as well. In other words α, β, γ, and δ are the elasticities of output with respect to each input.

The sum of the exponents of the Cobb-Douglas production function reveal the returns to scale of the production process. To see this result, multiply all the inputs in equation (8.5) by 2:

$$Q_{\text{new}} = A(2K)^{\alpha}(2L)^{\beta}(2E)^{\gamma}(2M)^{\delta} \tag{8.6}$$

or, after factoring out the multiplicative constant,

$$Q_{\text{new}} = (2^{\alpha + \beta + \gamma + \delta})AK^{\alpha}L^{\beta}E^{\gamma}M^{\delta} \tag{8.7}$$

From equation (8.7), it is clear that the new output level created by doubling all inputs is equal to $2^{\alpha + \beta + \gamma + \delta}$ times the old output level; that is, $Q_{\text{new}} = (2^{\alpha + \beta + \gamma + \delta})Q$. If the sum of the exponents equals unity ($\alpha + \beta + \gamma + \delta = 1$), then the production process exhibits constant returns to scale because a doubling of all inputs changes output by 2^1 times its original level. If $\alpha + \beta + \gamma + \delta > 1$, then the production function exhibits increasing returns to scale because output changes by more than 2 times its original level. Similarly, if $\alpha + \beta + \gamma + \delta < 1$, then the Cobb-Douglas production function exhibits decreasing returns to scale.

An important feature of the Cobb-Douglas production function is that it can be transformed into a linear-in-parameters equation by taking the natural logarithm of each element of equation (8.5):

$$\ln Q = \ln A + \alpha \ln K + \beta \ln L + \gamma \ln E + \delta \ln M \tag{8.8}$$

where the ln term is the operator for the natural logarithm transformation.

The value of this transformation is that some relatively simple statistical procedures, such as regression analysis, can be used to estimate the parameters of the production process. In contrast, production functions that are not linear in parameters or cannot be easily transformed to this specification require more complex and time-intensive statistical estimation techniques.

Generally, the Cobb-Douglas production function is viewed as a good place to start modeling the production process, but it is by no means the best place to stop. Other functional forms, such as the constant elasticity of substitution (CES) and the trans-log production function, offer more flexibility to economists studying the production process.[5] The more general the produc-

---

[5]For a discussion of the specification and estimation of CES and trans-log production functions, see Ernst R. Berndt, *The Practice of Econometrics: Classic and Contemporary*, New York: Addison-Wesley, 1991.

tion function, the more likely it is to be useful in many different firms. The Cobb-Douglas production function lacks such generality; for example, it cannot model the real possibility that the returns to scale change as the plant size increases. It is likely, as noted above, that firms experience increasing returns to scale for their initial production levels, then a range of constant returns to scale, and finally decreasing returns to scale. The Cobb-Douglas functional form does not allow for such changes.

Chapter Summary

1. Production is the creation of a commodity or service using inputs. Production may be specialized to different tasks a firm performs. Wholesale, retail, and manufacturing are all forms of production. A production function is a mathematical expression describing the relationship between inputs and the product or output they produce.
2. Fixed and variable inputs are related to each other through a firm's production process and its planning horizon. It is not feasible to change a fixed input for a given planning horizon, but it is feasible to change the variable input.
3. An isoquant is a curve that shows the various combinations of capital and labor that produce a given output level. Isoquants may change as the production technology changes.
4. Average and marginal products of a variable input are both computed from a short-run total product curve. When marginal product exceeds average product, the average product curve increases. When marginal product is less than average product, the average product curve decreases.
5. The law of diminishing returns states that when one input is fixed, increasing amounts of a variable input will (eventually) cause the marginal product of the variable input to diminish. It is not a law in the legal sense, but it is an empirical phenomenon confirmed in many case studies of production processes.
6. Technological progress can affect the average and marginal products of an input. A technological advance may increase both the average and marginal products of each input hired, enabling the firm to produce more without using more inputs.
7. Returns to scale are a measure of how the firm's output is affected when all inputs are changed. Increasing returns to scale imply that output is changing faster than the given proportionate change in all inputs; constant returns to scale imply the same rate of change for output and inputs; and decreasing returns to scale imply that output is changing at a slower rate than the proportionate change in all inputs.

Trouble Spots

Concept	Reminder
Production Technology	Production is a relationship between physical units: inputs and outputs. A production function does not define the relationship between the dollar value of inputs and the output produced.

Fixed and Variable Inputs	There is no preset period of time that we can use to define a fixed input. As a manager of a firm, you must constantly determine the least-cost method of changing output. In many cases, it is too costly to change output by changing capital, for example, so capital is fixed until the planning horizon suggests that it is profitable to change this input.
Average and Marginal Products	Average and marginal products are defined for each level of an input. There is an average product of labor for two employees, for three employees, for four employees, and so on. Similarly, there is a marginal product of labor for the second employee, for the third employee, for the fourth employee, and so on. Remember, the term *marginal* applies to the last unit while the term *average* applies to all existing units.
Returns to Scale	The returns to scale of a production process have *nothing* to do with the law of diminishing returns. Returns to scale apply when we change *all* inputs by a fixed amount and observe how output changes. The law of diminishing returns holds at least one input (but not all) constant, so it necessarily refers to a short-run setting, whereas returns to scale apply only to the long run. In addition, diminishing returns refers to marginal changes, whereas returns to scale measure an average or total change in output.

8.5 Review Questions

1. What is the economic meaning of a production function? How are short- and long-run production functions different from one another?
2. When a new academic year begins, restaurants near campus sell more meals. Would you accommodate the increase in demand by hiring more employees or by expanding the size of your restaurant? Why?
3. Why do the marginal and average products of labor increase and then decrease in the short run?
4. In terms of isoquants, what is the difference between fixed and variable proportions production functions?
5. An isoquant and an indifference curve look very much alike. What are the differences between these two concepts?
6. What is the general shape of the short-run expansion path if capital is fixed and labor is variable? What if labor is fixed and capital is variable?
7. Is it possible to have both diminishing returns and constant returns to scale in the same production function?
8. Define the essential features of all three stages of production in the short run.
9. Explain how and why the marginal rate of technical substitution changes along an isoquant in a variable proportions production function.

10. Why would a profit-maximizing firm avoid both stage I and stage III of its production function when it chooses its output rate?

8.6 Price Theory Problems

1. Fill in the omitted values for marginal, average, and total products in the following table. (Note: Capital and labor are the only two inputs in the production function, and capital is held fixed.)

Units of Labor	Total Product	Marginal Product	Average Product
6	120	Unknown	20
?	147	?	21
8	?	23	?
9	?	?	20

2. In the short-run production function, marginal product begins to decline before average product, and average product declines before total product. Explain why this occurs, using your knowledge of marginal, average, and total product relationships.
3. Graph the short-run total, marginal, and average product curves for the following production functions if capital is fixed at $K = 5$.
   a. $Q = 5K + 4L$
   b. $Q = K \times L^2$
   c. $Q = \min\{K,L\}$

   where the *min* function returns the lowest value from the two variables inside the brackets.
4. What is the difference between the short run and the long run? How are these two concepts related to a firm's fixed and variable inputs? Why is it difficult to define the length of time implied by the short and long run?
5. Using the definition of production, examine the following two statements to determine whether any production took place:
   a. Five minutes after buying a used car for $500, and without so much as washing it, the dealer turns around and sells it to someone else for $600.
   b. A ton of pitted apricots, with a market value of $300, is exposed to the sun's rays for a week and then sold (only half a ton now that much of the water has evaporated) for $400.
6. Determine whether the following production functions exhibit increasing, decreasing, or constant returns to scale:
   a. $Q = 50K^{.3}L^{.5}$
   b. $Q = 14K^{.5}L^{.5}$
   c. $Q = 300K + 25L$
   d. $Q = 2K^{.4}L^{.5}E^{.15}M^{.1}$
7. What information is shown by a single isoquant? What is signified by a move to the northwest along an isoquant, and what might induce a firm to make such a move?

8. For the Cobb-Douglas production function, $Q = AK^{\alpha}L^{\beta}$, the marginal products are given by

$$MP_L = AK^{\alpha}L^{\beta - 1}$$

$$\text{and } MP_K = AK^{\alpha - 1}L^{\beta}$$

Explain how these marginal products change when there are increasing, constant, or decreasing returns to scale, that is, when $\alpha + \beta > 1$, when $\alpha + \beta = 1$, and when $\alpha + \beta < 1$.

8.7 Writing Exercise

Select a production process that is of interest to you and describe, in detail, the steps necessary to create the product or service. You should explain the product(s) first and then document the inputs necessary for production. Estimate the proportions used and explain whether these proportions have changed over time and whether they change if there is seasonal fluctuation in demand. Try to estimate the relative cost of the inputs. When describing the production process, note how the inputs are used and any intermediate outputs that are produced. Finally, discuss how the firm finances its production: Does it borrow, does it use internally generated cash, or does it issue new equity?

9 Costs

Preview Questions

When you finish studying this chapter, you should be able to answer the following questions:

- When do accounting costs differ from economic costs?
- What is the relationship between marginal cost and marginal product in the short run?
- How do you choose the least-cost combination of inputs in the long run?
- How does a profit-maximizing firm choose inputs?
- What is the relationship between long-run and short-run cost curves?
- How do economies and diseconomies of scale affect the average total cost curve?
- What are economies of scope?

The movie business is changing rapidly. Films such as Jurassic Park and Terminator II demonstrated the value of advanced computer technology. Terminator II cost $80 million and Jurassic Park cost $70 million to produce. Both were smash hits. Jurassic Park set a new opening record, grossing over $100 million in its first ten days at theaters. One factor that made Jurassic Park enjoyable was the realism of the dinosaurs. Such realism is costly; reportedly each Velociraptor *cost $1 million to make, and the* Tyrannosaurus rex *is reported to have cost many times this amount. Because of the high cost of technical effects, movie studios face tough choices when they select films. Do they produce a film with higher-quality and better-paid actors and actresses, or do they spend their limited resources on technical and special effects? Essentially, movie studios must decide on the mix of inputs for a film—more capital with special effects or more labor with higher-quality actors and actresses. How studios and other firms in general sort out the answer to this and other questions requires an analysis of the cost structure of production.*

The act of production generates costs. More labor and capital will add to total cost. Thus, firms can be persuaded to increase output only if they are offered a higher price. That is, the benefit offered to suppliers must exceed the change in costs if they are to be persuaded to increase output. Suppliers must worry, however, because the market will not pay for just any change in costs. Inefficient production methods that generate unnecessary costs are not rewarded by markets. The marketplace forces firms to control their costs of production in order to find the *least-cost method* of expanding output. In this chapter, we will explore how a firm's costs are related to its production process and then show how a profit-maximizing firm selects a least-cost input combination for a given output rate. In addition, we will explain how firms, including movie studios, choose a least-cost mix of inputs, and we will show how the mix can change if the relative price of the inputs changes.

9.1 Cost and Production

Cost has a special meaning in economics, but it is the same meaning whether we are referring to a firm's actions or to a consumer's problem of choice. Cost in economics means one and only one thing: *opportunity cost.* Recall from Chapter 1 that opportunity cost is defined as the value of a resource in its next-best or highest-ranked alternative use. In this definition, opportunity cost does not depend on who is using the resource.

To make use of the opportunity cost concept, we must explicitly state what a firm's opportunity costs are and how to measure them. Specifically, to define profits we must know a firm's costs; but what are the firm's costs? Some costs that a firm faces are easy to identify: its wages, the cost of materials, energy costs, and the rent it pays for capital. These payments compensate the owners of these inputs for the opportunity costs they incur producing and marketing these inputs. But what if a firm owns its current office building and does not pay itself any rent? There is no *explicit* transfer of money, so how does a manager know the opportunity cost of space in the office building? We will investigate these questions from the profit-maximizing perspective; that is, the answers we offer are consistent with the firm attempting to generate the highest profits.

Measurement Problems: Accounting Versus Economic Costs

The measurement of costs is typically done by accountants, but accounting records may not properly define the *current* opportunity costs of a firm. This occurs because accounting records are generally retrospective; that is, they record payments for resources when they are made, but they do not adjust these payments as opportunity costs change. The accounting profession follows this practice partly to conform to IRS rules and partly because it is the standard measurement practice in the profession. In contrast, economists focus on measuring current and future costs because it is these costs that affect the firm's profitability. A manager of a firm, for example, can do nothing to change a firm's sales last year but can make decisions that affect the firm's future sales, which affects future profitability.

Fortunately, not all the information provided by accounting statements is inconsistent with an economist's notion of opportunity cost. Let's look at both the circumstances in which accountants and economists agree and the circumstances in which they disagree.

When Accounting Statements Reveal Opportunity Costs

Nondurable Resource
An input to production that is transformed or otherwise used up during the production process.

The historical costs provided in accounting statements reflect current opportunity costs when the accounting statements record recent expenditures for nondurable resources. A **nondurable resource** is one that is used up in production; it cannot be stored for later use. If you decide to hire another worker in your firm, what you pay that worker reflects the opportunity cost of the service he or she provides. The worker provides a flow of services that the firm cannot store for later use, so a recently prepared accounting statement will show such payments at their current cost, which will be their opportunity cost. Inputs such as materials, tax preparation services, and energy cannot easily be stored, so accounting costs reflect the opportunity costs of using these resources if the accounting statements are current.

When Accounting Statements Disguise Opportunity Costs

There are three important ways in which accounting statements disguise the actual opportunity costs faced by a firm:

1. Computing the tax-based depreciation of durable resources
2. Assigning a zero cost to inputs that are not directly purchased
3. Improperly valuing inventories

Durable Resource
An input, such as capital, that provides a flow of services over time to the firm.

A **durable resource** is one that provides a flow of services to the production process and is not completely used up during production. A firm's office or manufacturing building and the machines used to assemble its product are durable resources. These inputs may be purchased in one year and provide a service flow to the production process for many subsequent years. The value of a durable resource at any point in time is defined as follows:

> **The opportunity cost of a durable resource equals the interest cost of the funds paid plus the change in its market value.**

Economic Depreciation
The change in market value (adjusted for inflation) of an asset between two points in time.

The change in *market* value, measured between two points in time, is called **economic depreciation.** Because the IRS specifies the rate at which durable resources can be depreciated, an accounting approach to depreciation is likely to differ from a market-based approach. For example, suppose RapidExpress Co. purchases a new truck on January 1 for $100,000 in cash. Over the course of the first year, IRS rules allow RapidExpress to charge off 20 percent of the purchase price as depreciation, so an accounting statement will show the cost of the truck's service flow at $20,000. The economic depreciation of the truck, however, depends on the change in the market value of the truck over the year. If the truck fetches $85,000 in the used truck market, then its *economic depreciation* is $15,000, not $20,000.

The opportunity cost of the truck also includes an allowance for the cost of the funds used to purchase the truck. If RapidExpress Co. can invest $100,000 in a one-year certificate of deposit yielding 10 percent, then it must forgo $10,000 in interest over the year because it has purchased a new truck.

To an economist, the (opportunity) cost of purchasing the new truck is equal to $25,000 ($15,000 plus $10,000), not the $20,000 that an accounting statement shows. This calculation is illustrated in Table 9.1 (last two rows).

Table 9.1 also illustrates how a firm can understate its opportunity costs when it uses resources for which it does not explicitly pay. The owner of RapidExpress Co. loaned the company $50,000 at the beginning of the year to pay expenses but did not charge interest on the loan. The accounting statement shows $0 paid in interest cost, but the economic statement shows that the opportunity cost of these funds is $5,000 (calculated by assuming a 10 percent rate on a one-year certificate of deposit). Even though the firm does not pay any *explicit* interest, its use of the loan proceeds carries an *implicit* opportunity cost. Similarly, the accounting statement in Table 9.1 shows that the firm pays no rent on its current office space. The owner of RapidExpress owns the office building and does not charge the firm rent. The economic statement shows that the space would rent for $40,000 per year based on current square footage costs. Simply put, if the firm does not pay for a resource that it uses as part of its production process, its accounting statement will not show a charge for the resource. But there is always a cost, which the economic statement will show.

In total, the accounting and economic statements differ by $50,000. Thus, relying on the accounting statement may lead RapidExpress to make an incorrect choice of its profit-maximizing output rate. The firm may appear to be earning a profit when, in fact, it is not earning a profit after opportunity costs are properly included in the profit calculation.

Inventories can also drive a wedge between accounting and economic statements of costs. A firm's **inventory** is the stock of materials and finished or semifinished goods it has on hand. There are different methods of valuing inventories on an accounting statement. One method shows the value of inventories as determined by the cost of the last item added to the inventory—called the last-in–first-out or LIFO method; another values inventories based on the cost of the first item added to the inventory—called the first-in–first-out or FIFO method; and still another computes a weighted average of the

Inventory
The stock of output or resource inputs that is available to the firm at a given point in time.

TABLE 9.1

Comparing Accounting and Economic Statements of RapidExpress Co.'s Costs

Cost Category		Accounting Statement	Economic Statement
Wages		$250,000	$250,000
Materials		28,000	28,000
Utilities		7,000	7,000
Office Rent		0	40,000
Personal Loan (forgone interest)		0	5,000
Truck Purchase (forgone interest)		0	10,000
Truck Depreciation		20,000	15,000
	Total Cost	$305,000	$355,000

cost of the items in inventory. Each of these methods may value inventory at a price that *does not reflect true opportunity costs.* Although the LIFO method is less accurate for items that are sold infrequently, it tends to reduce the differences between accounting and economic cost statements because it uses more recent data on market prices. Each method, though, tends to place a value on a firm's inventory that differs from replacement costs—its opportunity cost—and this causes an accounting statement to disguise a firm's true opportunity costs.

LEARNING EXERCISE 9.1

For the following items on a balance sheet, explain whether an accountant's statement of costs may differ from an economist's statement of costs:

a. Cash
b. Accounts payable
c. Marketable securities
d. Long-term debt

The Incentive to Measure Opportunity Costs Carefully

Strictly speaking, for opportunity costs to be measured accurately, managers of a firm must spend time collecting information about the market price of resources used by the firm. Such an investment is worthwhile only if it increases the firm's profits. The question is whether an economic statement, such as that shown in Table 9.1, is a valuable guide to making profit-maximizing decisions. The answer is a qualified yes: An economic statement is a better guide to making profit-maximizing decisions because all costs are correctly computed.

If RapidExpress Co. ignores the opportunity cost of renting, it will underestimate its production cost and unwittingly make an unprofitable choice of its output rate. In effect, it will be ignoring $40,000 per year in costs. The question RapidExpress must answer, however, is whether the cost of collecting information on office rents exceeds the cost resulting from not knowing about the $40,000. If it does, collecting such information will harm the firm more than not collecting it. Because there are collection costs, it may not always be profitable for a firm to compute its opportunity costs accurately. In such cases, a firm may rely on an imperfect measure of opportunity costs—such as shown on an accounting statement—to compute profits and make pricing decisions.

In general, then, better profit-maximizing decisions are made using opportunity costs, not accounting costs, but the decision to collect such information depends on collection costs compared to the losses incurred by using an incorrect measure of opportunity costs.

SUNK COSTS AND FIXED COSTS

Although it may be expensive to measure opportunity costs correctly, if the measurement of such costs is profitable, then they should always be taken into account for decision making. There are some costs that should not be used by decision makers.

There are *sunk costs,* which have an opportunity cost of zero for *all* decisions the firm may make. Recall from Chapter 7 that sunk costs arise when an investment in an asset cannot be recovered by subsequent resale:

An investment is a *sunk cost* when its opportunity cost is zero.

Specific assets, such as signs used by retailers, generate sunk costs. What is the market value of signs announcing "Pete and Linda's Raw Bar" or the "Sam's Starving Student Copy Center"? Unless someone in the marketplace wants to name their raw bar after Pete and Linda or fancies the "Sam's Starving Student" label, these signs have zero resale value. The investment made in signs is a sunk cost; it cannot be recovered and must be ignored when making profit-maximizing decisions.

There are also fixed costs, but these costs do not necessarily have a zero opportunity cost for all decisions. **Fixed costs** (FC) are those unavoidable contractual costs the firm pays regardless of its output rate. In the long run, there are no unavoidable contractual costs, so fixed costs are zero. In the short run, however, the situation is different. Some inputs that are held constant in the short run, such as capital, generate fixed costs—for example, office rent or a car lease. Recall that the short run is a period of time when it is not profitable to change all inputs in order to adjust output. Fixed costs *are* ignored when managers make short-run profit-maximizing decisions, but they *are not* ignored in the long run. Basically, fixed costs have a zero opportunity cost in the short run but a positive opportunity cost in the long run.

Fixed Costs (FC) Costs that are not avoidable in the present planning horizon, usually due to a fixed input.

To conclude, asset costs are ignored for profit-maximizing decisions if they have zero opportunity costs in the present planning horizon—that is, either the short or long run. This implies that sunk costs are always ignored, but fixed costs are ignored only in the short run.

Learning Exercise 9.2

Explain which of the following are sunk and/or fixed costs in an investment decision and why:

a. A concert piano for a symphony orchestra
b. Monthly bank fees for a checking account
c. Investment in a dry oil well
d. New-car insurance

$$$ Price Theory in Practice

Rebuilding the U.S. Embassy in Moscow

In 1979, the U.S. government began construction of an eight-story embassy building near the Moskva River in Moscow. In August 1985, because of "security concerns," the U.S. government locked out the Soviet construction workers who had been helping build the embassy. Subsequent inspection of the building indicated that it was filled with bugs, that is, Soviet eavesdropping devices. The building was about 65 percent completed when work was stopped, and about $30 million had been spent on the project by American taxpayers.

Since the bugs were discovered, the State Department has been asking Congress to fund construction of a new building, arguing that nothing can be done about the bugs in the existing structure. Most of the bugs were embedded in walls made of poured concrete. To remove them, the United States would need to repour the entire structure, which is the same as building a new building. In essence, the State Department is arguing that the past expenditures on the building are a sunk cost, so they can be ignored for the purpose of making future decisions.

Although many members of Congress disagree with this assessment, the State Department is correct: past investments are sunk costs *if* they have zero recovery value. The question for Congress to consider is whether or not the existing structure has a zero recovery value. Specialists who have studied the problem suggest that the existing structure has some recovery value; it is not totally necessary to tear it down and start again. One suggestion is that the building be torn down to the fourth floor, keeping the bugs from the fourth floor down to the basement. New bug-free floors would then be built on top of the fourth floor. This proposal implies that the total investment in the building is not all sunk cost. Some part of the building investment is recoverable and could be used for general office clerical work, presumably without any diminution in security. Other alternatives, such as turning it into an apartment building, also indicate that the existing structure has some positive recovery value.

Officials in the State Department argue that these alternatives are not workable, that there is no recovery value, and so a new building must be built. Even with the new democratic structure in the former Soviet Union, it is clear that the U.S. embassy should be bug-free, at least in some parts of the structure. The question the Congress must sort out is the true cost of building a new embassy in Moscow. It is estimated that construction costs of the new embassy will be $300 million. If the existing investment is a sunk cost, then Congress's decision to tear down the existing building and build a new one will cost $300 million. If, however, the building has some recovery value, say $3.75 million per floor (equal to $30 million for all 8 floors), then Congress's decision carries a much higher true cost.

Learning Exercise 9.3

The government charges itself for the full price of many durable assets, such as weapons systems, at the time of purchase; it does not allocate these costs over several years as do private firms. Can you explain this practice in light of our discussion of sunk costs?

SOCIAL COSTS AND PRIVATE COSTS

Private Costs All costs explicitly or implicitly incurred by individuals or firms.

The opportunity costs discussed above are costs of resources that the firm owns. These costs may be thought of as the **private costs** of the firm. The process of production (or consumption), however, may generate costs (or benefits) that are not recorded on a firm's profit statement; that is, they are *not* private costs. A paper mill pays the cost of raw materials, labor, and capital, which are the private costs of producing paper pulp. The milling process also produces by-products, such as foul odors and liquid and solid wastes (called effluents) that may harm those in the vicinity of the mill. These effluents are a *negative externality* generated from the production of paper pulp: The costs that the effluents impose on others are not part of the firm's profit statement. That is, they are costs external to a firm's decision-making process. If we add together the private costs of production of paper pulp and the economic damages (negative externalities) imposed upon others, we come up with what are called social costs. **Social costs** are the total costs to society for a given production activity. When social costs differ from private costs, governments may (but do not always) adopt rules and regulations to reduce the firm's affect on others.

Social Costs
Private costs plus costs imposed on other members of society who are not parties to the transaction, that is, third parties.

We will develop the distinction between private and social costs more fully in Chapter 17 when we examine the problems of market failure and externalities. Suffice it to say here that the total cost of any activity—production or consumption—equals the total social cost, not just the private cost.

9.2 Short-Run Costs

In the short run, a firm's total costs can be divided into two components: total fixed costs and variable costs. Associated with these two components are the firm's average fixed costs and average variable costs. In addition, the firm incurs incremental or marginal costs when it changes it output rate by a small amount. The short-run behavior of these costs is determined by the firm's production process. Let's explore the definition of each of these costs and their relationship to the firm's rate of output.

DEFINING AND MEASURING COSTS

The data in Table 9.2 show the cost structure of a typical firm. (A typical firm is one whose production process can be described by a production function that relates physical inputs to physical outputs as described in Chapter 8.) For simplicity, the production process underlying Table 9.2 uses only labor and capital as inputs, and capital is fixed in the short run. In this table, total and average costs are divided into their short-run components.

Total Fixed Costs

Total fixed costs (FC) are equal to the costs of the inputs that are fixed in the short run. In Table 9.2, the capital input is fixed and generates a cost of $100 per week, which is shown in column 1. Notice that the costs of the fixed input do not change when the rate of output changes. By definition, these costs are fixed for the short run; they do not change with output or any other variable.

Total Fixed Costs (TFC)
The costs of the inputs that are fixed in the short run.

TABLE 9.2

A Typical Firm's Short-Run Cost Structure

Rate of Output (units/hr)	Fixed Cost (FC) (1)	Variable Cost (TVC) (2)	Total Cost (TC) (3)	Marginal Cost (MC) (4)	Average Fixed Cost (AFC) (5)	Average Variable Cost (AVC) (6)	Average Total Cost (ATC) (7)	Labor Units (*L*) (8)	Marginal Product of Labor (MP_L) (9)	Average Product of Labor (AP_L) (10)
0	100	0	100	–	–	–	–	–	–	–
1	100	50	150	50	100	50	150	3	0.40	0.40
2	100	95	195	45	50	48	98	5	0.44	0.42
3	100	135	235	40	33	45	78	7	0.50	0.44
4	100	170	270	35	25	43	68	9	0.57	0.47
5	100	200	300	30	20	40	60	10	0.67	0.50
6	100	240	340	40	17	40	57	12	0.50	0.50
7	100	300	400	60	14	43	57	15	0.33	0.47
8	100	380	480	80	13	48	60	19	0.25	0.42
9	100	500	600	120	11	56	67	25	0.17	0.36
10	100	660	760	160	10	66	76	33	0.13	0.30

Note: In column 8, the labor units figures are rounded to the nearest whole number.

Total Variable Costs

Total variable costs (TVC) are those costs incurred by the use of variable inputs in the production process. In other words, variable costs are affected by changes in the rate of output because variable inputs are changed to affect the rate of output. In Table 9.2, labor is the variable input, so labor generates the variable costs. In this table, variable costs are shown in column 2.

Total Variable Costs (TVC) The total cost caused by the variable inputs to the production process; this cost varies as the output rate changes.

Total Cost

Total cost (TC) is defined as the sum of total variable costs and total fixed costs. The formula for this result is TC = TVC + FC. Total costs are shown in column 3 of Table 9.2.

Total Cost (TC) The sum of total variable and fixed costs.

Marginal Cost

Marginal cost (MC) is defined as the change in total cost when there is a 1-unit change in the rate of production. Stated otherwise, marginal cost is equal to the change in total cost per unit change in output:

Marginal Cost (MC) The change in total cost (or in variable cost) due to a 1-unit change in the rate of output.

$$\text{MC} = \frac{\Delta \text{TC}}{\Delta Q} = \frac{\Delta \text{TVC}}{\Delta Q} \tag{9.1}$$

where $\Delta Q = 1$ for most examples. As equation (9.1) shows, marginal cost may be defined in terms of how total cost changes (ΔTC) or how total variable cost changes (ΔTVC). We can make this claim because total variable costs are the only costs that change in the short run, so they completely describe how total costs are changing when output increases by 1 unit.

We present marginal cost for our example in column 4 of Table 9.2. Note that marginal cost is the difference between successive total cost amounts. This is because we are changing the output rate by 1 unit at each new row of Table 9.2.

Average Fixed Cost

An average is the total divided by the number of units over which the total is spread; thus, **average fixed cost (AFC)** equals total fixed cost divided by the number of units of output, or AFC = FC/Q. Average fixed cost is shown in column 5 of Table 9.2.

Average Fixed Cost (AFC) Total fixed cost divided by output.

Average Variable Cost

Average variable cost (AVC) is defined as total variable cost divided by output, or AVC = TVC/Q. We find AVC in our example in column 6 of Table 9.2.

Average Variable Cost (AVC) Total variable cost divided by output.

Average Total Cost

Average total cost (ATC) is defined as total cost divided by output, or ATC = TC/Q. Because TC = TVC + FC, we can also state that ATC = AVC + AFC, which says that the average of total costs equals the sum of average variable and average fixed costs. We find ATC in our example in column 7 of Table 9.2.

Average Total Cost (ATC) The total of all fixed and variable costs divided by output.

TABLE 9.3

A Glossary of Cost Relationships

Term	Symbol	Equation	Other Relationships
Total Cost	TC	TC = FC + TVC	$TC = Q \times (AFC + AVC)$ TC = area in the rectangle whose (opposite) corners are given by the origin and the point on the ATC curve at the existing output rate (Figure 9.3)
Variable Cost	TVC	TVC = TC − FC	$TVC = Q \times AVC$ TVC = area in the rectangle whose (opposite) corners are given by the origin and the point on the AVC curve at the existing output rate (Figure 9.3) TVC = area under the MC curve up to the existing output rate (Figure 9.4)
Fixed Cost	FC	FC = TC − TVC	$FC = Q \times AFC$ FC = area in the rectangle whose (opposite) corners are given by the origin and the point on the AFC curve at the existing output rate (Figure 9.3)
Average Total Cost	ATC	$ATC = TC/Q$	
Average Variable Cost	AVC	$AVC = TVC/Q$	AVC = ATC − AFC
Average Fixed Cost	AFC	$AFC = FC/Q$	AFC = ATC − AVC
Marginal Cost	MC	$MC = \Delta TC/\Delta Q$	$MC = \Delta TVC/\Delta Q$

A Summary of Costs

Table 9.3 presents a summary of the algebraic relationships between the different measures of cost. This table is a good reference tool to use when you review this chapter or when you answer the review questions and problems.

Learning Exercise 9.4

Given that average total cost (ATC) is given by $ATC = Q + 10 + 16/Q$, find the expression for total cost (TC), average variable cost (AVC), and fixed cost (FC). Find the marginal cost (MC) of producing the sixth unit of output.

HOW THE PRODUCTION PROCESS AFFECTS SHORT-RUN COSTS

In the short run, a profit-maximizing firm finds that its variable inputs exhibit diminishing returns.[1] In our example above, labor is the variable input, so the marginal product of labor (MP_L) will actually fall as the firm expands output in the short run. Because marginal product reflects output changes when there is

[1]In this discussion, we are assuming a competitive market for all inputs to the production process and a competitive market for the firm's output. Relaxing either or both of these assumptions will necessarily complicate the discussion.

a 1-unit change in labor, it has a direct impact on the firm's incremental, or marginal, cost structure. If the marginal product of labor declines rapidly, for example, the extra output generated from each additional unit of labor also declines rapidly. Correspondingly, a firm's marginal cost will increase rapidly.

Let's look at the link between marginal product and marginal cost in more detail. Suppose that the firm pays a weekly wage of w to each unit of labor it hires. Then the firm's wage bill will change by $w \times \Delta L$ if the firm hires ΔL more employees. Because labor is the firm's only variable input (in this example), $w \times \Delta L$ equals the change in total cost when the firm hires ΔL units of labor; that is, $w \times \Delta L = \Delta \text{TC}$. Recall from equation (9.1) that marginal cost (MC) is equal to $\Delta \text{TC}/\Delta Q$. Substituting for ΔTC in this equation gives

$$\text{MC} = \frac{w \times \Delta L}{\Delta Q} \tag{9.2}$$

Now recall that the marginal product of labor is defined as $\Delta Q / \Delta L$, holding all other inputs constant. Dividing the top and bottom of the right-hand side of equation (9.2) by ΔL gives

$$\text{MC} = \frac{w}{\text{MP}_L} \tag{9.3}$$

Equation (9.3) shows that marginal cost is *inversely* related to the marginal product of labor when labor is the only variable input.[2] Columns 8 and 9 of Table 9.2 show how many units of labor are used in the short run and the corresponding marginal product of labor. In this example, the firm pays \$20 per hour for each labor unit it hires. At 6 units of output per hour, for example, the firm pays \$240 per hour for a total of 12 labor units. The marginal product of the twelfth unit of labor is 0.5; that is, the last unit of labor hired produces one-half unit of output. (Note that the labor unit figures in Table 9.2 are rounded to the nearest whole number, so the variable cost figures may not be exactly consistent with the labor unit figures.)

We can see how diminishing returns influence marginal costs in the short run. The marginal product of labor increases until the tenth unit of labor is hired, after which diminishing returns set in and the marginal product of labor declines. The marginal cost figures reveal this effect too. Marginal cost is declining up to the tenth unit of labor, after which it increases. This result is exactly what equation (9.3) predicts: an inverse relationship between marginal cost and marginal product of the variable input.

There is also a simple relationship between average variable cost and the average product of the variable input. Given that labor is the variable input, we can write average variable cost as

$$\text{AVC} = \frac{\text{TVC}}{Q} = \frac{w \times L}{Q} \tag{9.4}$$

where the last equality holds because labor is the *only* variable input, so total labor cost is the same as total variable cost.

[2]When there is more than one variable input the relationship is more complicated, but it is still true that when marginal product rises with additional units of an input, marginal cost tends to decrease as output increases.

Recall that the average product of labor is equal to total product divided by the quantity of labor used in production, or $AP_L = Q/L$. Dividing the top and bottom of the right-hand side of equation (9.4) by L gives

$$AVC = \frac{w}{AP_L} \tag{9.5}$$

With the wage rate fixed, there is an inverse relationship between the average product of labor and average variable costs. From column 10 in Table 9.2, we can see the inverse relationship with actual numbers. We see that the average product of labor increases initially, reaching a peak somewhere between 10 and 12 units of labor, and then falls. Correspondingly, average variable costs decline initially, reaching a minimum somewhere between 10 and 12 units of labor, after which they increase. Allowing for rounding error, these figures for the relationship between average cost and average product are exactly those suggested by equation (9.5).

Because there is a link between the production process and a firm's cost structure, the law of diminishing returns has a well-defined, direct effect on short-run costs. Marginal costs are inversely related to the marginal productivity of the variable input, and average variable costs are inversely related to the average product of the variable input. Thus, a change in the marginal productivity of labor—say that a new voice recognition computer technology eliminates the need for many typing services—causes the firm's marginal cost to decrease in direct proportion to the change in marginal product.

Learning Exercise 9.5

If $AVC = 20$ and $AP_L = 2$, then if labor is the only variable cost in the short run, find the wage rate.

9.3 Short-Run Cost Curves

The data provided in Table 9.2 can be used to show the shapes of a typical firm's cost curves. We consider fixed, variable, and total cost curves first; then we show how marginal, average fixed, average variable, and average total costs change with output.

Fixed, Variable, and Total Cost Curves

In Figure 9.1, on page 318, we have plotted the fixed, variable, and total cost data shown in Table 9.2. A continuous curve has been drawn through these points to illustrate the general behavior of each curve. Note that both the variable and total cost curves increase as output increases. To increase output, the firm must increase its use of labor, which adds to both variable and total costs. The fixed cost curve, however, does not change as output increases. Fixed costs are just that, fixed; they do not change as the level of output changes.

The algebraic relationship between these costs (discussed above) implies that the total and variable cost curves are separated by the amount of fixed

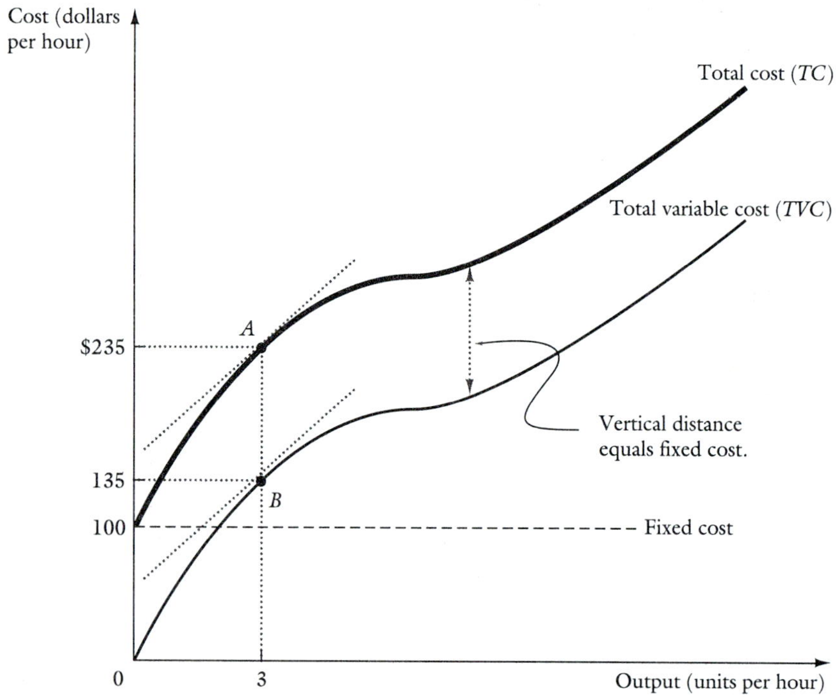

Rate of Output (units per hour)	Fixed Cost [1]	Variable Cost [2]	Total Cost [3]	Marginal Cost (MC) [4]	Average Fixed Cost (AFC) [5]	Average Variable Cost (AVC) [6]	Average Total Cost (ATC) [7]
0	100	0	100	—	—	—	—
1	100	50	150	50	100	50	150
2	100	95	195	45	50	48	98
3	100	135	235	40	33	45	78
4	100	170	270	35	25	43	68
5	100	200	300	30	20	40	60
6	100	240	340	40	17	40	57
7	100	300	400	60	14	43	57
8	100	380	480	80	13	48	60
9	100	500	600	120	11	56	67
10	100	660	760	160	10	66	76

FIGURE 9.1

Short-Run Total, Variable, and Fixed Cost Curves for the Typical Firm

The data from Table 9.2 yield typical total, variable, and fixed cost curves. Fixed cost is $100 per hour, so this curve is horizontal. The total and variable cost curves have the same shape, differing only by the amount of fixed cost. At 3 units of output per hour, total costs are equal to $235 (point *A*) and variable costs are equal to $135 (point *B*). In addition, because the total and variable cost curves have the same shape, their slopes are the same at any given output rate, as illustrated by the two parallel lines just tangent to these curves at points *A* and *B*.

cost. When output is 6 units per hour, for example, total cost is $340 per hour and variable cost is $240 per hour, with the difference of $100 equal to fixed cost. In other words, FC = TC − TVC. The geometric representation of this result implies that there is a fixed (vertical) distance between the total and variable cost curves at all output rates.

MARGINAL, AVERAGE FIXED, AVERAGE VARIABLE, AND AVERAGE TOTAL COST CURVES

Figure 9.2 on page 320 shows the graphical relationship between the marginal, average fixed, average variable, and average total cost curves using the data provided in Table 9.2. As with Figure 9.1, these curves are drawn to smoothly approximate the behavior of costs as output increases. The curve that has the simplest shape is the average fixed cost curve. Fixed costs are $100 at all output rates, so as output increases, average fixed costs (FC/Q) decline. This curve starts at $100 when the output rate is 1 unit per hour and decreases to $10 when the output rate is 10 units per hour.

In contrast to the average fixed cost curve, the marginal, average variable, and average total cost curves are typically U-shaped. These costs first decline as output increases, then reach a minimum, and then increase. It is important to note that the marginal cost curve is affecting the behavior of the average variable and average total cost curves. Just as in the elevator example in Chapter 8, when an extra unit of output results in extra or marginal change that is less than the existing average, the new average will fall. When the marginal change is above the existing average, the new average will rise. This fact implies that the marginal cost curve lies below the average variable and average fixed cost curves when they are declining and above them when they are increasing. When the output rate is 4 units per hour, for example, marginal cost equals $35, average variable cost equals $43, and average total cost equals $68. The average variable and average fixed cost curves are declining at 4 units of output per hour, so the MC curve is below the two average cost curves. In contrast, when the output rate is 8 units per hour, marginal cost equals $80, average variable cost equals $48, and average total cost equals $60. At 8 units of output, the average variable and average fixed cost curves are increasing, so the MC curve is above the two average cost curves.

As implied by equation (9.3), the behavior of the marginal cost curve is determined by the behavior of the marginal product of the variable input. The law of diminishing returns is an important factor in this short-run relationship. Recall that the law of diminishing returns states that the marginal product of the variable input must eventually decrease as the firm hires more of this input, holding all other inputs constant. Thus, the short-run marginal cost curve must eventually slope up, which means that the two average cost curves must eventually increase. Because the marginal product of the variable input may increase initially, all these cost curves may decline for some output rates, but eventually the law of diminishing returns causes these curves to turn upward, which gives them their U-shaped appearance.

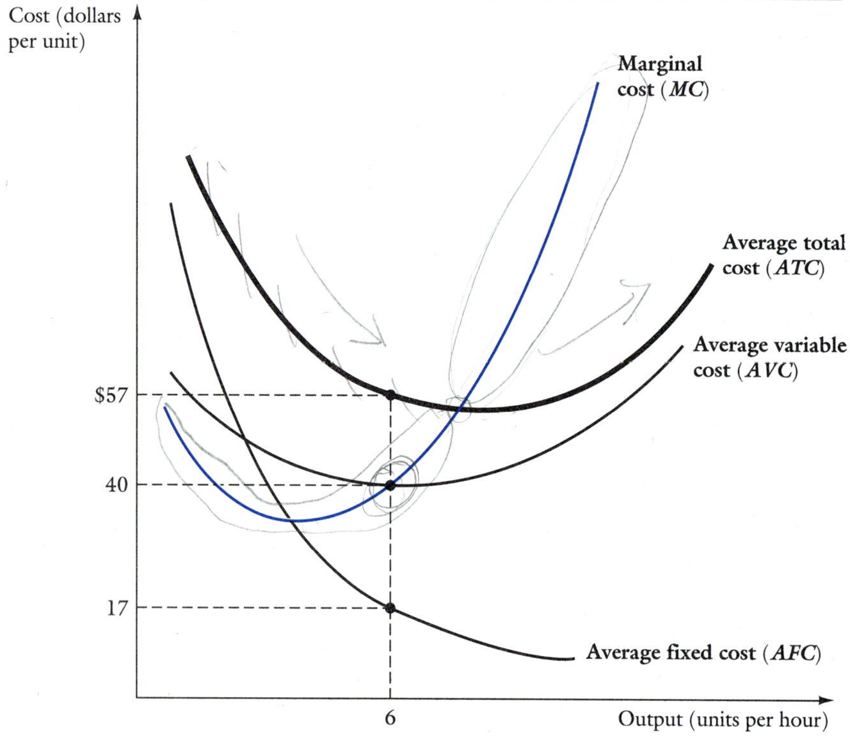

Rate of Output (units per hour)	Fixed Cost [1]	Variable Cost [2]	Total Cost [3]	Marginal Cost (MC) [4]	Average Fixed Cost (AFC) [5]	Average Variable Cost (AVC) [6]	Average Total Cost (ATC) [7]
0	100	0	100	—	—	—	—
1	100	50	150	50	100	50	150
2	100	95	195	45	50	48	98
3	100	135	235	40	33	45	78
4	100	170	270	35	25	43	68
5	100	200	300	30	20	40	60
6	100	240	340	40	17	40	57
7	100	300	400	60	14	43	57
8	100	380	480	80	13	48	60
9	100	500	600	120	11	56	67
10	100	660	760	160	10	66	76

FIGURE 9.2

Short-Run Marginal, Average Total, Average Variable, and Average Fixed Cost Curves for the Typical Firm

The data from Table 9.2 yield typical marginal, average total, average variable, and average fixed cost curves. Average fixed cost declines as output increases, while the other curves are U-shaped. The marginal cost curve intersects the average variable and the average total cost curves at their respective minimum values.

The relationship between the marginal cost curve and the two average cost curves implies that the marginal cost curve intersects the two average cost curves at their minimum values. In Figure 9.2, we see that the marginal cost curve intersects the average variable cost curve at 6 units of output per hour, the rate for which average variable cost equals \$40. Marginal cost intersects the average total cost curve somewhere between 6 and 7 units of output per hour, which is also the minimum of the average total cost curve. This result is important because the minimum point of the average variable cost curve will be a critical value that helps determine whether a firm continues to operate (or shuts down) in the short run.

MATH NOTEPAD

Where Do MC and ATC Intersect?

We know that $MC = \Delta TC/\Delta Q$ by definition. Because $ATC = TC/Q$ implies that $TC = ATC \times Q$, we can rewrite the definition of MC as $MC = \Delta(ATC \times Q)/\Delta Q$, which can be expanded to $MC = ATC + Q(\Delta ATC/\Delta Q)$. The ATC curve reaches a minimum when its slope, $\Delta ATC/\Delta Q$, is zero. If $\Delta ATC/\Delta Q = 0$, then MC = ATC at this point.

A final comment on the marginal cost curve: As equation (9.1) on page 314 shows, $MC = \Delta TC/\Delta Q$ and $MC = \Delta TVC/\Delta Q$. Now, what does this result imply about the shape of these cost curves? In effect, the marginal cost curve is the common slope of the total cost curve and the total variable cost curve at a given output rate. Look at the two parallel dashed lines in Figure 9.1 on page 318. The top line is tangent to the total cost curve at point *A*, so its slope is equal to the slope of the total cost curve at this point. The bottom line is tangent to the total variable cost curve at point *B*, so its slope is equal to the slope of the variable cost curve at this point. Because these lines are parallel, the slopes of the two curves are equal; hence, either curve can be used to measure marginal costs. Geometrically, then, the marginal cost curve can be drawn by plotting the slope of either the total cost curve or the total variable cost curve.

LEARNING EXERCISE 9.6

Draw a graph of the ATC, AVC, and FC curves, using the expressions you derived in Learning Exercise 9.4.

DEFINING THE AREAS UNDER COST CURVES

It is frequently convenient to work with average and marginal cost curves when analyzing how firms are affected by output and price decisions. The areas under these curves provide a direct link to the corresponding total cost curves. Figure 9.3 illustrates this link for the average variable and average total cost curves.

Figure 9.3 reproduces the average variable and average total cost curves from Figure 9.2. At 5 units of output, average total cost is \$60 and average variable cost is \$50. From the definition of average total cost, we have ATC = TC/*Q*, or TC = ATC × *Q*. Multiplying \$60 by 5 units implies that TC = \$300. The same multiplication defines the rectangular area bordered on the vertical axis by \$60 and on the horizontal axis by 5 units. The shaded region in Figure 9.3, area *A* plus area *B*, is equal to ATC × *Q* (or \$300), which is the total cost of producing 5 units. Similarly, total variable cost (TVC) is equal to AVC × *Q*. At 5 units of output, TVC = \$60 × 5 = \$300, represented by area *B* alone in Figure 9.3.

To find the fixed cost of production, we use the relationship FC = TC − TVC. Applying this result to Figure 9.3 shows that fixed cost is equal to areas *A* plus *B* minus area *B*, which leaves area *A* as the result. So a firm's fixed cost is always given by the rectangular area between its average variable and average total cost curves.

Sometimes we will use the area under the marginal cost curve to define total variable costs instead of using the area of the rectangle defined from a point on the average variable cost curve. Let's examine the intuitive reason for this. We know that marginal cost measures how costs are

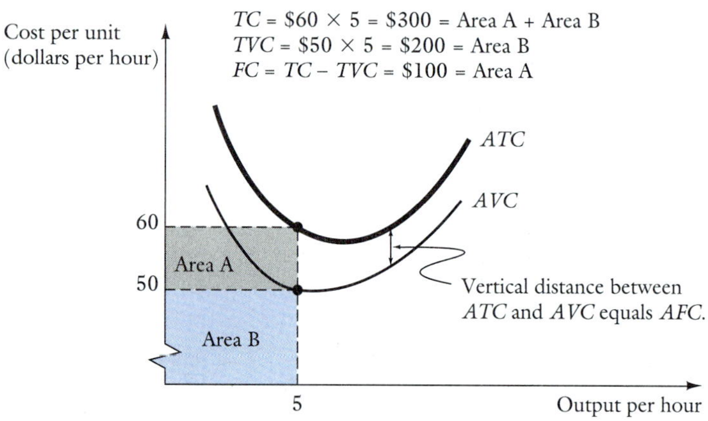

FIGURE 9.3

Using the Areas Under the Average Cost Curves to Define Total, Variable, and Fixed Costs

The area in the rectangle under the average total cost curve (area A) equals total cost, and the area in the rectangle under the average variable cost curve (area B) equals variable cost up to a given output rate. At 5 units of output, average total cost equals \$60 and average variable cost equals \$50. Area A plus area B then equals the total cost of producing 5 units (\$60 × 5), and area B alone equals the variable cost of producing 5 units (\$50 × 5).

changing for each new output rate and that fixed costs don't change with changes in the output rate. Because variable inputs are used to change the output rate, they generate the change in cost that is captured by marginal cost. So if we add up the maginal cost of each new output rate up to a given output rate, the total will give us the total variable cost of producing that given output rate. Figure 9.4 illustrates this situation. The area under the MC curve up to Q_0 represents the total variable cost of producing Q_0 units of output. If we know the level of fixed cost, then we can add this amount to the area under the marginal cost curve to compute the total cost of Q_0. In the long run, for example, fixed cost is zero, so the area under the marginal cost curve is equal to total cost (and TVC because all costs are variable).

In summary, the areas under the average and marginal cost curves can be used to define the costs—total, variable, and fixed—of producing specific output rates.

Learning Exercise 9.7

Given that TC = $500 + 10Q - 0.5Q^2$, find the expression for ATC, AVC, and FC. Draw these curves and use the area formula to find the total cost, total variable cost, and fixed cost of producing 10 units of output.

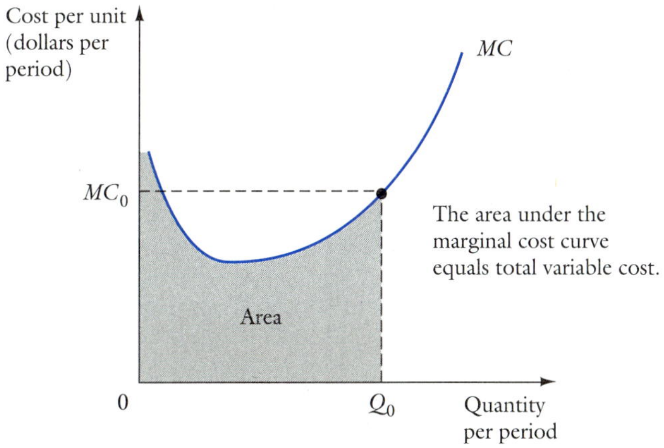

FIGURE 9.4

Using the Area Under the Marginal Cost Curve to Define Total Variable Cost

The area under the marginal cost curve equals the total variable cost of producing a given output rate. The area shown equals the total variable cost of producing Q_0 units of output per period. If fixed costs are zero, the area under the marginal cost curve equals the total cost of producing a given output rate.

$$$ Price Theory in Practice

Product Liability Costs

Payments to employ labor and capital are two costs commonly considered in the analysis of the production costs of a firm. In reality, firms face a variety of costs. Among them, firms sometimes encounter costs when their products malfunction, causing harm or damage to consumers. These are product liability costs.

Firms usually buy insurance to protect themselves from potential product liability costs. During the 1980s, however, firms found that liability insurance was becoming too costly or completely unavailable. Firms and insurers believed that the U.S. legal system was to blame. They argued that the system creates too much uncertainty about the way liability for product-related injuries is determined; they viewed jury awards as excessive, particularly for punitive damages and noneconomic damages such as pain and suffering; and they believed that firms were being held liable regardless of whether the firm could have prevented the product's danger.

While consumer groups argued that the liability insurance crisis was caused by temporary economic factors, firms and the insurance industry lobbied legislators to limit award amounts and make other changes. In response, Congress asked the General Accounting Office (GAO) to determine whether the legal system was the cause of the liability insurance crisis and to analyze the potential effects of proposed changes.

The GAO review produced some interesting numbers on the potential liability costs faced by firms. The agency reviewed court records of 305 product liability cases that went to trial from 1983 to 1985 in five states: Arizona, Massachusetts, Missouri, North Dakota, and South Carolina. These results are shown in Table 9.4. Overall, the consumers injured by products won 45 percent of the cases and were awarded an average of $845,000 by the courts.

TABLE 9.4

Cases Plaintiffs Won and Damage Awards, by State

State	Total Cases	Won by Plaintiffs: Cases	Percent	Average Award
Arizona	59	28	48	$1,462,000
Massachusetts	66	22	33	709,000
Missouri	108	50	46	780,000
North Dakota	16	12	75	880,000
South Carolina	56	24	43	369,000
Summary	305	136	45	$ 845,000

Source: "Product Liability, Verdicts and Case Resolution in Five States," United States General Accounting Office, September 1989.

The analysis by the GAO found that, in general, the legal system was not producing erratic and excessive damage awards. Firms were found negligent in about two-thirds of the verdicts for plaintiffs—a higher rate than had been assumed previously. In addition, firms were found to be liable even though they were not negligent in another 27 percent of the verdicts for plaintiffs. In those cases, according to the GAO, juries and judges were allowed by law to determine that firms could have foreseen or prevented harm to the consumers.

The GAO found that a large award by a trial court does not necessarily represent the final cost to firms and insurers. Large awards are usually reduced during appeals and posttrial settlement negotiations. In the 11 cases in which trial courts awarded plaintiffs more than $1 million in total damages, the consumers ultimately received only 39 percent of the initial award. Overall, appeals and posttrial settlement negotiations reduced total award amounts by 43 percent. Awards were reduced in half the cases won by plaintiffs and in 71 percent of the cases with total awards of $1 million or more. All 12 punitive damage awards were reversed or sent back for retrial.

The GAO also found that most of the proposed reforms would have had little or no effect of the cases tried in the five states. Some states, for example, have limited the size of punitive damages awards, but few punitive damage awards in the cases studied by the GAO would have exceeded the limits. Two proposals would have affected the awards more than others. One would reduce awards according to the degree to which the plaintiff was responsible for the injury. The other would reduce awards by the amount covered by workers' compensation insurance.

One proposed change could have potentially major effects. Recognizing that punitive damages are often thrown out upon appeal, the proposal would make it more difficult for trial courts to award punitive damages. That would be accomplished by raising the standard of evidence required to award punitive damages. Critics caution, however, that making it more difficult to award punitive damages will eliminate the powerful role they play in deterring firms from producing faulty products. In other words, a firm that spends a certain amount each year to detect faulty products has an incentive to spend less when the penalty for product failure decreases. That would mean more faulty products on the market and more product liability lawsuits.

While firms might differ with the results, the GAO report overall found little—in spite of the liability insurance crisis of the 1980s—to support the belief that the product liability costs faced by firms are excessive. Nor did the GAO find that the proposed legal changes would do much to lower the production costs firms face in the form of liability costs.

Learning Exercise 9.8

How do product liability costs change with a firm's output rate? In other words, if the firm produces more in a given period, is it likely to face higher costs as a result of product liability suits?

9.4 Production Costs in the Long Run

Recall that the long run is defined as a situation in which full adjustment can be made to any and all changes in the economic environment. Thus, in the long run, all factors of production are variable, which implies that there are no fixed costs. Because the firm can choose any amount of any input, it is important to consider how a firm determines its mix of inputs in the long run. We examine this question by identifying the least-cost mix of inputs for each possible output rate, keeping in mind, of course, that the firm's goal is to maximize profits, not to minimize costs.

We continue our analysis of the long run by illustrating the shape of the firm's long-run cost curves, with particular attention given to the effect of scale economies on the shape of the average cost curves.

CAUTION: MINIMIZING COST IS NOT THE FIRM'S OBJECTIVE

Before we go any further, it's valuable to mention that a firm does not have the objective of minimizing the costs of production for a given output rate. The firm's goal is to maximize profits, and as part of doing this, it determines an optimal output rate. What we will show is that the profit-maximizing firm chooses a least-cost method of production.

CHOICE OF INPUTS IN THE LONG RUN

The choice of input mix in the long run is not constrained in the way that it is in the short run. Although any combination of labor and capital could conceivably be chosen in the long run, the profit-maximizing firm will confine its interest to a specific set of input combinations. That specific set includes those combinations that represent the least-cost way of producing a given rate of output. To find the least-cost input combinations, we must introduce the cost of inputs into the discussion.

Isocost Lines

To simplify the analysis, let's assume that input prices are taken as given by the firm and are determined by the forces of supply and demand in the input market. The firm is a small part of the input market and can buy as much or as little as it wants at the current market price.

We use the letter w to denote the unit price of labor services and the letter r to denote the unit price of capital services, where r is *not* an interest rate. Sometimes r is called the implicit rental value per unit of capital. If, for example, a firm is able to rent a dump truck for \$1,000 per week, the weekly price for the services of the dump truck, r, is equal to \$1,000. If the firm owns the dump truck for which it paid \$200,000, the unit price of services from the dump truck does not change to \$200,000. Rather, it implicitly would stay the same: \$1,000 per week, if that continues to be the going weekly price at which dump trucks can be rented. Remember that the only true or choice-relevant costs for economists are opportunity costs. Sunk costs are, by definition, unrecoverable and are thus irrelevant for decision making. Now, the total cost of production (TC) may be written as

$$TC = (w \times L) + (r \times K) \tag{9.6}$$

Isocost Line
The line along which total costs are constant in a graph with inputs on both axes. The isocost line shows the combinations of labor and capital that produce the same total cost.

The straight line formed from equation (9.6) when total costs are held constant is called an isocost line. The **isocost line** shows the various combinations of capital and labor that can be hired for a given level of total costs. It is similar to the budget line along which a consumer's budget is held constant. The equation for an isocost line can be found by rearranging equation (9.6) to write capital as a function of labor. Subtracting $w \times L$ from both sides gives $TC - w \times L = r \times K$. Dividing both sides of this result by r gives the following expression for an isocost line:

$$K = \frac{TC}{r} - \frac{w}{r}L \tag{9.7}$$

Figure 9.5 plots the isocost line on a graph that has capital on the vertical axis and labor on the horizontal axis, which are the same axes used to graph isoquants. On the horizontal axis, if we do not hire any of the capital input, we can hire TC/w units of the labor input. Similarly, on the vertical axis, if we do not hire any of the labor input, we can hire TC/r units of the capital input.

The slope of the isocost line in Figure 9.5 is equal to $-w/r$. The slope measures the market rate at which the two inputs can be exchanged, holding total costs constant. Suppose, for example, that labor costs $10 per hour and that capital rents for $20 per hour in a production process; then the slope of

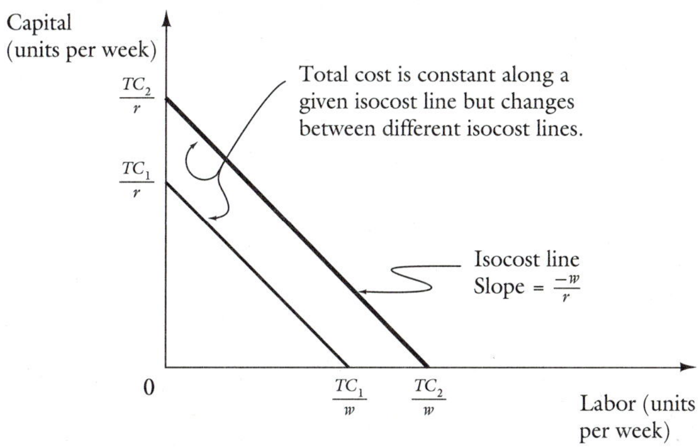

FIGURE 9.5

the isocost line is –\$10/\$20, or –½. In this instance, the slope implies that an extra hour of labor can be hired, holding total costs constant, if ½ hour of capital is not purchased.

If input prices remain constant, an increase in total cost will shift the isocost line. The line in Figure 9.5 closer to the origin represents an isocost line with lower total costs than the heavier isocost line to the right. With input prices fixed, an infinite number of isocost lines can be drawn in the input graph. These lines will be parallel; the only difference between them will be the costs they represent.

Finding the Least-Cost Mix of Inputs

It is now possible to combine isocost lines with isoquants to find the input combination that minimizes the cost of producing a *given rate of output.* In other words, suppose it is desirable—for profit-maximizing reasons—to produce 100 units of output. Your problem, then, is to find the combination of inputs that can produce 100 units of output at the least cost.

In Figure 9.6, we present the least-cost problem using an isoquant to represent the various ways to produce 100 units of output. Two isocost lines are shown in this figure. The heavier line represents \$1,000 in total costs, and the lighter isocost line represents \$800 in total cost. Notice that

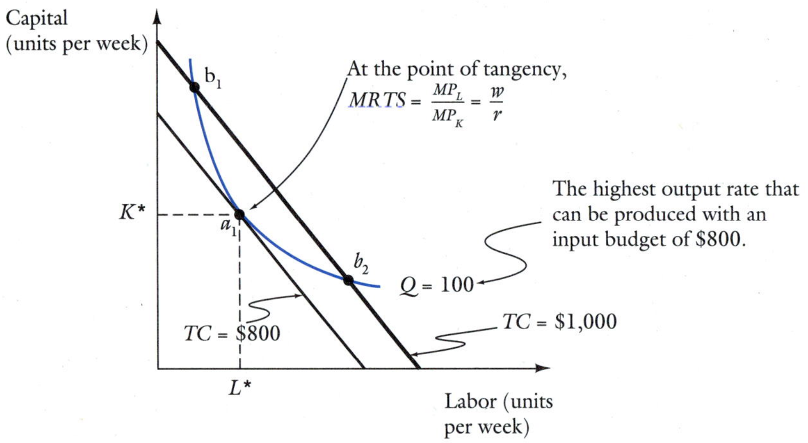

FIGURE 9.6

Finding the Least-Cost Combination of Capital and Labor to Produce a Given Output Rate

Finding the least-cost input combination requires the firm to find the point at which the isocost line is just tangent to the desired isoquant. Point a_1 represents the least-cost combination of capital and labor for 100 units of output. At this point, L^* units of labor and K^* units of capital are purchased for a total cost of \$800. The marginal rate of technical substitution (MP_L/MP_K) is equal to the input price ratio (w/r) at a_1. In contrast, the input mix at either b_1 or b_2 can produce 100 units of output, but it will cost the firm \$1,000 to purchase the inputs at either of these points.

both isocost lines intersect at least one point on the isoquant curve. Thus, it is possible to produce 100 units of output by spending \$1,000—at points b_1 or b_2—or by spending \$800—at point a_1. The least-cost combination of capital and labor is given by point a_1, where $K = K^*$ and $L = L^*$. This is because there are no isocost lines below the TC = \$800 isocost line that also intersect the isoquant curve. In other words, there are cheaper combinations of capital and labor, but none of them can be combined to produce the desired output rate.

The least-cost point occurs where the isocost line is tangent to the isoquant curve, which is point a_1 in Figure 9.6. The slopes of these two curves are, by definition, equal at a point of tangency. The slope of the isocost line is equal to $-(w/r)$, and the slope of the isoquant curve at any point is equal to $-MP_L/MP_K$ [from equation (8.4)]. Setting these two slopes equal to each other and canceling out the minus sign gives the result that the least-cost input mix satisfies:

$$\frac{MP_L}{MP_K} = \frac{w}{r} \tag{9.8}$$

or, using the definition of the *marginal rate of technical substitution (MRTS)* from Chapter 8, $MRTS = MP_L/MP_K$, the least-cost input mix requires that

$$MRTS = \frac{w}{r} \tag{9.9}$$

Equation (9.9) helps explain why a diminishing MRTS is important. If isoquants were not convex to the origin—as a diminishing MRTS implies—but rather concave to the origin, we would end up with a corner solution to the least-cost problem. The reasoning behind this result is analogous to the corner solution result that we found using indifference curve analysis. Concavity of the isoquant implies that a corner solution produces the greatest output for the least cost. At a corner solution, the firm would find that it chooses only one input to use in its production process. In other words, concave-to-the-origin isoquants (increasing MRTS) imply specialization in input usage. Because we do not observe such specialization in most firms, we believe that convex- rather than concave-to-the-origin isoquants are more realistic.

LEARNING EXERCISE 9.9

Using the short-run production function $Q = \sqrt{K}\sqrt{L}$, find the least-cost combination of K and L to produce 100 units of output if $w = \$10$ and $r = \$20$. How does the solution change if $w = \$20$ and $r = \$20$?

The Long-Run Expansion Path

How does a firm minimize its input costs when other outputs are produced? Figure 9.6 identifies the least-cost input combination—K^* and L^*—when the firm desires to produce 100 units of output. What is the least-cost solution, though, when the firm desires to produce an output rate different from 100 units? Figure 9.7, on page 330, shows how the least-cost input combination is found for the entire range of output rates.

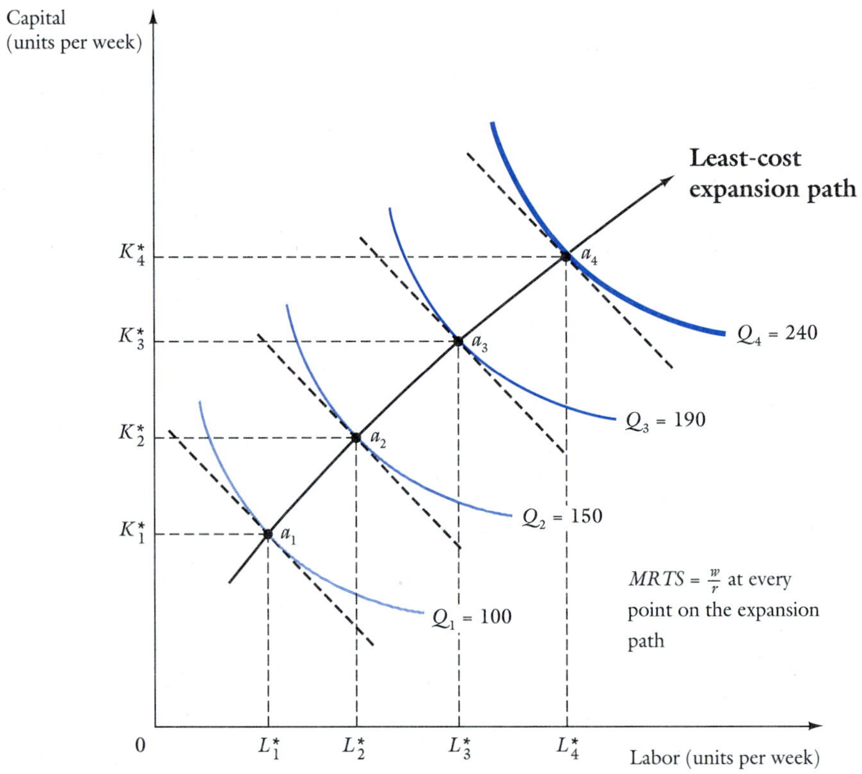

FIGURE 9.7

Deriving a Least-Cost Expansion Path

The expansion path shows the least-cost sequence of input combinations to produce any output rate. At point a_1, the firm uses L_1* units of labor and K_1* units of capital to produce 100 units of output at least cost. Similarly, points a_2, a_3, and a_4 show the least-cost method of producing 150, 190, and 240 units of output, respectively. These points have one common feature: they are selected by finding the various input combinations for which the marginal rate of substitution (MP_L/MP_K) equals the input price ratio (w/r).

The general solution involves the repeated application of equation (9.8) for all possible isoquants, that is, for all possible output rates. Figure 9.7 shows the solutions for four isoquants, $Q_1 = 100$, $Q_2 = 150$, $Q_3 = 190$, and $Q_4 = 240$. The optimal input combinations for these output rates are given by points a_1, a_2, a_3, and a_4, respectively. At each of these points, the ratio of the marginal product of labor to the marginal product of capital, MP_L/MP_K, equals the ratio of input prices, w/r. The line drawn through these points is called the **least-cost expansion path.** At every point on the expansion path, equation (9.8) on page 329 is satisfied, so each point represents the least-cost method of producing some particular output rate.

Least-Cost Expansion Path
The set of input combinations that produce each level of output at least cost.

LEARNING EXERCISE 9.10

What is the expansion path for a firm in the short run when capital is fixed? (Use an isoquant diagram to illustrate your answer.)

PROFIT-MAXIMIZING FIRMS ARE COST MINIMIZERS, *TOO*

The expansion path is important because a profit-maximizing firm will select an input combination from the expansion path—no other combinations are considered by a profit-maximizing firm in the long run.

To see this result, recall the output condition, established in Chapter 7, to maximize profits. That is, the profit-maximizing output rate is the one at which

$$MR(Q) = MC(Q) \tag{9.10}$$

where $MR(Q) = \Delta TR/\Delta Q$ and $MC(Q) = \Delta TC/\Delta Q$.

Equation (9.10) applies to the problem of selecting an output rate to maximize profits, but with some modification, we can apply this equation to the problem of selecting an input combination to maximize profits. Let's consider the case of two inputs, for simplicity, labor and capital. A profit-maximizing firm will continue to hire more inputs until the extra revenue generated by the last input hired is exactly equal to that input's extra cost. This statement is a slight variation of equation (9.10). Instead of finding the output rate at which MR equals MC, the firm now sets marginal revenue equal to marginal cost for each input it employs.

The marginal revenue of a specific input can be computed by determining the change in output caused by that input and multiplying this change by the value of the firm's output. From our analysis of production, we know that the marginal product of an input measures how output changes when an extra unit of the input is utilized. Now, if we are describing a competitive firm, then it can sell its output at a fixed price (P) in the market. Thus, the marginal revenue of a specific input is equal to its marginal product times the output price ($MP \times P$), which is called the **value of the marginal product,** or, in the more general case in which price is not constant, the **marginal revenue product** of an input.

Value of Marginal Product (Marginal Revenue Product) This equals marginal revenue times marginal product. In competitive firms, it is equal to price of output times marginal product.

The marginal cost of a specific input is the cost of hiring an extra unit of the input. If the firm is small, it is not likely to affect these costs by its hiring decision, so it can employ as much of the input as it wants without the input's price changing. For example, if the firm desires to hire another worker, we assume that there is a worker willing to accept the job at the wage rate of w per hour. Similarly, if the firm desires to hire still another worker, we assume that there is someone else who will accept the job at w per hour, too. The marginal cost of a specific input is thus equal to the unit cost of the input, that is, w in the case of labor and r in the case of capital.

Applying equation (9.10) to labor and capital separately gives

$$MP_L \times P = w \tag{9.11}$$

$$MP_K \times P = r \tag{9.12}$$

Using equations (9.11) and (9.12), the profit-maximizing firm hires inputs up to the point at which their marginal revenue product equals their extra cost. By following this rule, the profit-maximizing firm selects an input combination that lies on the firm's long-run expansion path. We can see this result by dividing equation (9.11) by equation (9.12), which gives $MP_L/MP_K = w/r$. This is the same as the expression in equation (9.8), the equation that must be satisfied by all input combinations that lie on the firm's long-run expansion path. We can now state

The profit-maximizing firm selects an input combination that lies on the least-cost expansion path in the long run.

Although the profit-maximizing firm does not have the goal of minimizing costs, it acts to satisfy this goal when it chooses a profit-maximizing combination of inputs.

$$$ Price Theory in Practice

The Silver Price Bubble and the Photoprocessing Industry

Between 1979 and 1980, silver prices rose from a low of $6.25 per troy ounce to a high of $48 per troy ounce, a nearly 670 percent increase. The major users of silver had to adjust to a very rapid increase in their production costs. These users began to look for substitutes for silver. The case of the photography industry is illustrative of the reaction of many major silver users.

The United States consumes about 120 million troy ounces of silver each year, with about 40 percent of this total used in the photoprocessing industry. The extraordinary sensitivity of silver halide compounds to light has made them a near-perfect material to use in photoprocessing. As the price of silver increases, however, film processors, such as Kodak and Fuji Film, have an incentive to substitute to other methods of processing film. Figure 9.8 shows the basic response of these firms to the dramatic increase in the price of silver during 1979–1980.

As Figure 9.8 shows, photoprocessing companies had a readily available, although imperfect, substitute for silver in photopolymers. Photopolymers are light-sensitive plastics that are transformed into long-chain molecules when exposed to light. The properties of photopolymers—just like silver halides—allow solvents to dissolve unexposed parts of a photograph, thereby leaving an exposed image. Photopolymeration has traditionally been a more expensive film processing technique, limited to larger plate images instead of mass-produced film rolls.

The increase in silver prices lowered the relative price of photopolymers. This is shown as a change in the slope of the isocost line in Figure 9.8. Film processors were initially operating at point a_1, producing Q_1 units of processed film in 1979. As silver prices increased, the slope of the isocost line changed, making the line steeper in Figure 9.8. The quantity of film consumed decreased to Q_0 in 1980, and film processors used less silver and more photopolymers in their production process.

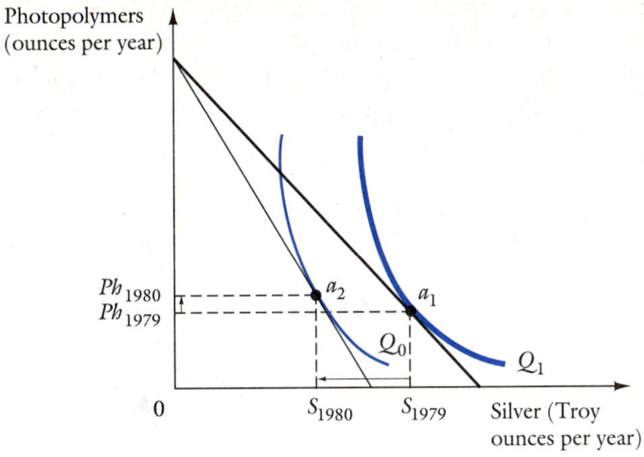

FIGURE 9.8

The Change in the Isocost Line for Photoprocessors During 1979–1980

As the price of silver increased in 1979 and 1980, photoprocessors substituted towards photopolymers to process film. In 1979, point a_1 represented the least-cost mix of inputs, using S_{1979} units of silver and Ph_{1979} units of photopolymers. After silver prices increased, point a_2 became the least-cost input mix, using S_{1980} units of silver and Ph_{1980} units of photopolymers to process film.

A postscript is in order here. Silver prices plunged to between $4 and $6 per troy ounce in recent years and the use of silver in the photoprocessing industry increased steadily. The use of silver substitutes, such as photopolymers, was only a small-scale, temporary response to the unusual change in silver prices between 1979 and 1980.

LEARNING EXERCISE 9.11

Using a graph similar to Figure 9.8, show how the degree of substitutability between silver and photopolymers affects the size of the decrease in silver usage.

TECHNICAL AND ECONOMIC EFFICIENCY

Technical Efficiency The technical relation between output and inputs as defined by the production function.

There is a distinction in economics between technical and economic efficiency. **Technical efficiency** implies that the production process is operating correctly. To understand this, consider the production function $Q = 8L + 2K$. If you hire 4 units of labor and 2 units of capital, the production function is expected to produce 36 units of output per period. If this occurs, your production process is *technically efficient.* If you produce less than 36 units of output for this combination of labor and capital, then your production process is *technically* *inefficient;* under the circumstances, it was expected to produce 36 units of output but did not. Technical efficiency is a statement about the production process, not about the choice of inputs to the process.

In contrast, **economic efficiency** is a statement about the choice of inputs. A firm that selects an input combination along the short- or long-run expansion path chooses a least-cost input mix for its given planning horizon. Firms that choose input combinations from either the short- or long-run expansion path are *economically efficient.* These firms are minimizing the cost of producing a given output rate; they do not waste resources. If the firm does not select the least-cost input mix for the output produced (given either a short- or long-run horizon), then the firm is *economically inefficient.* Economic inefficiency implies that resources are wasted compared to their opportunity costs. The firm (and society) will be better off if the firm rearranges its input mix so that there are no wasted resources.

Economic Efficiency Selecting an input along the least-cost expansion path.

9.5 Comparing Long-Run and Short-Run Cost Curves

The long-run cost structure of a firm is derived from its least-cost expansion path. In this section, we discuss the shape of the average and marginal cost curves in the long run and compare these curves to their short-run counterparts. In addition, we explain how returns to scale affect costs and generalize this concept to allow the ratio of inputs to change when output changes.

OPTIMAL EXPANSION PATHS IN THE SHORT AND LONG RUN

Because a firm's managers choose to hold at least one input fixed in the short run, the long- and short-run expansion paths tend to diverge as output increases. This situation is illustrated in Figure 9.9 for the case of two inputs.

Figure 9.9 shows both the long- and short-run expansion paths for three output rates: $Q_0 = 50$, $Q_1 = 75$, and $Q_2 = 100$ units per week. To make the short- and long-run paths comparable, we start our analysis at an input combination, K_1 and L_1, where the short- and long-run paths intersect. This input mix produces 75 units of output for the firm. On the short-run path, capital is fixed at K_1, so input utilization expands along the horizontal line extending out from K_1. To produce 100 units of output per week in the short run, the firm must increase its use of labor to L_3. In the long run, the firm can adjust capital, so it can produce 100 units of output per week using less of the labor input. The firm selects L_2 units of labor ($L_2 < L_3$) in the long run to produce 100 units of output per week.

Linking Expansion Paths and Cost Curves

The important difference between the short- and long-run expansion paths is that the costs of production are greater on the short-run expansion path at all points except the one at which the short- and long-run paths intersect. At this point, both the short- and long-run paths choose the same input mix, so total and average costs must be the same. The average total cost of producing 75

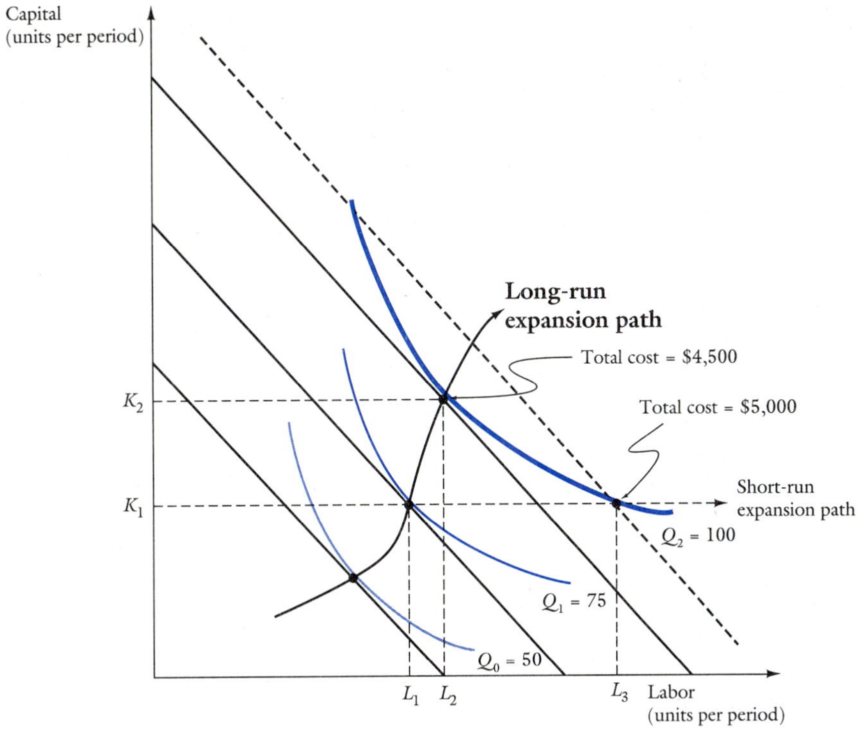

FIGURE 9.9

Comparing Long-Run and Short-Run Expansion Paths

The short-run expansion path holds at least one input fixed, while in the long run all inputs may change. Suppose that the firm is initially using L_1 units of labor and K_1 units of capital to produce 75 units of output per period. An increase in demand to 100 units of output per period requires L_3 units of labor, holding capital fixed in the short run. The short-run total cost of production equals $5,000 per period. In contrast, in the long run, the firm chooses L_2 units of labor and K_2 units of capital to produce 100 units of output, which may be purchased for a total cost of only $4,500 per period.

units per week, for example, is $40 per unit for both the long- and short-run paths. As the firm expands output, however, short-run average total costs (SATC) increase faster than long-run average total costs (LATC). When the firm produces 100 units per week, its long-run average total cost is $45 per unit (LATC = $4,500/100), but its short-run average total cost is $50 per unit (SATC = $5,000/100). This situation is illustrated in Figure 9.10.

Figure 9.10 shows the short- and long-run average total cost curves for the firm described in Figure 9.9. Both curves have the familiar U-shaped appearance. As discussed above, the law of diminishing returns explains the appearance of a U-shaped cost curve in the short run. In the long run, however, the U-shaped curve is generated because of scale economies, which we discuss below.

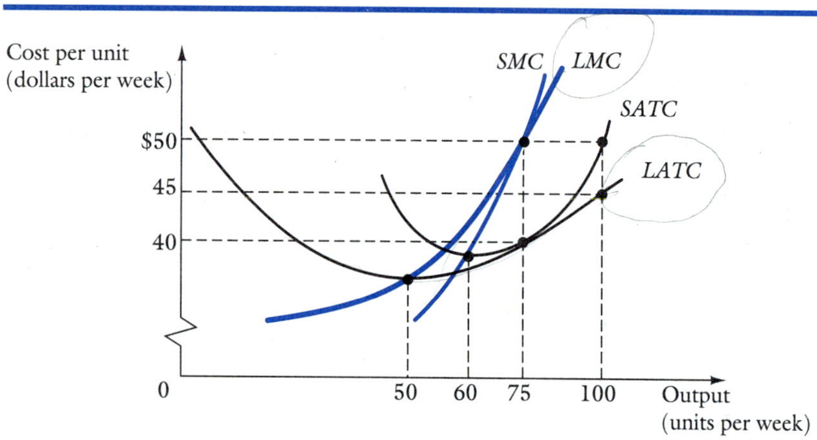

FIGURE 9.10

Comparing Short-Run and Long-Run Average Total Cost Curves

The short-run average and marginal cost curves intersect their long-run counterparts at only one point. As shown in Figure 9.9, this is the point at which the short- and long-run expansion paths intersect. At 75 units of output, for example, the short- and long-run average total cost equals $40 per period and the short- and long-run marginal cost equals $50 per period. At output rates greater or less than 75 units, the *LATC* curve lies below the *SATC* curve.

The short- and long-run average cost curves are derived directly from the short- and long-run expansion paths of the firm. Figure 9.9 shows that the long-run cost of producing 100 units per week equals $4,500. Dividing this amount by 100 gives the average total cost of $45 per unit shown in Figure 9.10. The short-run average cost of producing 100 units exceeds this amount. In Figure 9.9, the short-run expansion path implies a total cost of $5,000 for producing 100 units, which gives a short-run average cost of $50 per unit. All the points along the average costs curves are computed in this manner, that is, using the cost derived from the appropriate expansion path.

Figure 9.10 shows that the short-run cost curve reaches a minimum at 60 units of output per week. In comparison, the long-run cost curve reaches a minimum at an output rate of 50 units per week. Note that the short- and long-run cost curves are tangent at 75 units of output per week, the output rate at which the short- and long-run expansion paths cross. In addition, note that the short-run average total cost curve lies above the long-run average total cost curve for all output rates to the right *or* left of 75 units per week. It is more costly, then, to expand *or* contract output in the short run than in the long run, a result that the isoquant diagram in Figure 9.9 also shows.

Short- and Long-Run Profits

Although we can compare short- and long-run cost curves and show that costs are generally higher in the short run, we should not make a similar comparison with short- and long-run profits. Recall that the firm has chosen to hold capital fixed in the short run and to expand output using only the labor input. This was a profit-maximizing decision, based on the cost of adjusting capital relative to the profits that such a decision may produce. If it is optimal for the firm to hold capital fixed, then this decision, by definition, produces the greatest profits. If capital is changed when it is not optimal to do so, profits are reduced because of adjustment or transaction costs. The situation we are describing in Figures 9.9 and 9.10, then, is a comparison between the long run, when it is optimal to change capital, and the short run, when it is optimal to hold capital fixed.

The Long-Run Marginal Cost Curve

Figure 9.10 also shows the general shape of the long-run marginal cost curve (LMC). The LMC is U-shaped and intersects the short-run marginal cost curve (SMC) at one output rate, which is the output rate at which the LATC intersects the SATC. At output rates to the right of the intersection point, short-run marginal costs exceed long-run marginal costs; at points to the left of the intersection point, short-run marginal costs are less than long-run marginal costs. In effect, there are some *changes* in output that produce fewer additional costs in the short run than in the long run. Even so, the average cost of production is always less (or equal) in the long run than the short run.

It is important to note that the SMC curve has a steeper slope than the LMC curve for output rates at which both of these curves are increasing. This is because the firm is constrained in its choice of inputs in the short run, so marginal costs tend to increase more rapidly in the short run than in the long run.

The LATC Curve Envelops the SATC Curves

The LATC always represents the lowest average cost of producing any output rate. This is true because the firm can adjust all inputs to find the absolute lowest-cost input mix for any output rate it chooses to produce. The LATC must lie beneath the many short-run average total cost curves, with a tangent point occurring when a short-run expansion path crosses the long-run expansion path. This situation is shown in Figure 9.9.

Figure 9.11 shows three short-run average total cost curves: $SATC_1$, $SATC_2$, and $SATC_3$. Each of these curves intersects the long-run average total cost curve at only one output rate. At this output rate, the short-run expansion path for each curve crosses the long-run expansion path, just as shown in Figures 9.9 and 9.10.

Note the geometric relationship between the LATC curve and the three SATC curves. The minimum of the LATC curve occurs at output rate Q_2; thus, long-run average total costs are higher to the left or right of this output rate. The short-run curve $SATC_2$, which is tangent to the LATC curve at output rate Q_2, is tangent at its minimum point. Thus, the minimum of the LATC curve is also a minimum point on one specific SATC curve. At Q_3, which is to the right of Q_2, the tangent point between the long- and short-run curves is to the right of the minimum of the SATC curve. Analogously, at Q_1 (which is to the left of Q_2), the tangent point between the long- and short-run curves is to the left of the minimum of the SATC curve. In effect, the LATC curve is an *envelope* that surrounds these SATC curves from below; thus, the LATC curve always represents the lowest average cost (and total cost) of producing any output rate.

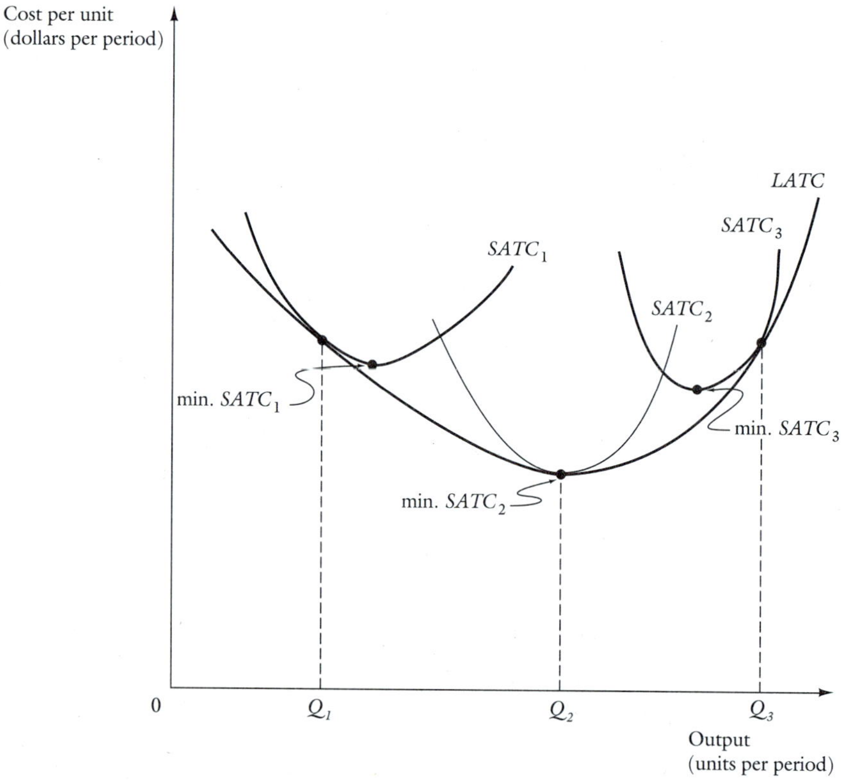

FIGURE 9.11

The Long-Run Average Total Cost Curve is an Envelope of Many Short-Run Average Total Cost Curves

The *LATC* curve is an envelope of the many *SATC* curves. To the left of the minimum of the *LATC* curve, at output rate Q_2, the *SATC* curves are tangent to the *LATC* at a point that is to the left of the minimum of the *SATC* curve. This situation is illustrated by the $SATC_1$ curve that is tangent to the *LATC* curve at output rate Q_1. As shown, however, the minimum of the $SATC_1$ curve occurs at an output rate that exceeds Q_1. For output rates that exceed Q_2—the minimum of the *LATC* curve—the tangencies between the *SATC* curves and the *LATC* curve occurs to the right of the minimum of the *SATC* curves. The $SATC_3$ curve illustrates this situation.

Learning Exercise 9.12

Explain why the LATC curve *cannot* be constructed as a curve that connects the minimum point on each SATC curve.[3]

[3]This is a famous problem in economics, called Viner's dilemma after economist Jacob Viner (1892–1970), who "incorrectly" thought that the LATC curve could be drawn as a curve that connects the minimum of the SATC curves. The problem that Viner faced was that such a drawing must imply that the LATC crosses the SATC curves, so it lies above the SATC curves for some output rates. This result contradicts the concept that the LATC is the lowest possible cost structure.

ECONOMIES OF SCALE AND COST CURVES

How does changing the size of the firm affect the firm's long-run cost structure? One determinant of the shape of the long-run cost curves is the returns to scale of the production process. Recall from Chapter 8 that with *decreasing returns to scale,* a doubling of all inputs results in a less than doubling of output. If costs double when inputs double, then average costs increase if the production process exhibits decreasing returns to scale. The payoff for increasing plant or firm size with decreasing returns to scale then diminishes as the firm grows.

Suppose, instead, that the production process exhibits *increasing returns to scale.* A doubling of inputs causes output to more than double, so long-run average costs are falling. The payoff here to expanding output, *ceteris paribus,* is increasing as the firm grows.

The concept of returns to scale is restrictive because it holds the ratio of inputs constant as output expands. As we can see from Figure 9.9, it may not be optimal to hold the ratio of inputs constant in the long run. A straight-line long-run expansion path, extending out from the origin, holds the ratio of inputs constant. In Figure 9.9, the long-run expansion path is curved, so the ratio of inputs is changing as the firm expands output. Thus, the notion that we must increase or decrease all inputs by the same proportion has limited use. Because we can vary the ratio of inputs to minimize costs, we discuss *scale effects* by looking directly at how average costs change. We focus on output changes, taking for granted the changes occurring on the input side.

Economies of Scale
The situation when output increases more than in proportion to the change in inputs causing average total cost to decrease; this may result from increasing returns to scale or from such external-to-the-firm changes as falling factor prices.

Constant Economies of Scale
The situation when output increases in proportion to the change in inputs, causing average total cost to remain constant; this may result from constant returns to scale or from such external-to-the-firm changes as fixed factor prices.

Diseconomies of Scale
The situation when output rises less than in proportion to a change in inputs, causing average total cost to increase; this may result from decreasing returns to scale or from such external changes as an increase in the price of inputs.

Economies of scale occur when a doubling of output causes costs to *less* than double. With economies of scale, long-run average costs are falling. Note that we do not restrict a firm's use of inputs with this definition, which was restricted when we defined returns to scale in Chapter 8, nor do we necessarily hold input prices constant as output changes. Often, for example, input prices increase as more inputs are purchased, which in turn affects the behavior of total costs. **Constant economies of scale** occur when a doubling of output causes costs to double. With constant economies of scale, a firm's long-run average costs are constant (or flat). Finally, **diseconomies of scale** occur when a doubling of output causes costs to *more* than double. With diseconomies of scale, a firm's long-run average costs are increasing.

The concepts of economies, constant economies, and diseconomies of scale include increasing, constant, and decreasing returns to scale (in production) as special cases because the ratio of inputs may be held fixed as the output rate changes. In other words, a state of increasing returns to scale implies that we have economies of scale over some range of output, but we cannot reverse this claim. The same may be said for constant returns to scale and constant economies and decreasing returns to scale and diseconomies. Thus, the production concepts of increasing, constant, and decreasing returns to scale are not a complete guide to the efficient size of a firm.

The concepts of economies, constant economies, and diseconomies of scale are more general also because they allow other factors to affect a firm's cost structure. Technology and changes in factor prices may also affect scale economies. If an input industry innovates because a user of its services expands production, for example, the subsequent fall in input prices may result in economies of scale. Alternatively, if an increase in the output rate causes input prices to rise, then diseconomies of scale may develop.

Figure 9.12 shows the effects of economies, constant economies, and diseconomies of scale on the long-run average cost curve. There are economies of scale for all output rates up to Q_1, which implies that the LATC curve is declining. Between Q_1 and Q_2, there are constant economies of scale, so a given percentage increase in the output rate causes total cost to increase by the same percentage, which keeps LATC constant. Note that the LMC curve overlaps the LATC curve when the LATC curve is horizontal. Because costs are changing in direct proportion to output when there are constant economies of scale, the LMC is constant and equal to the LATC. Lastly, there are diseconomies of scale for all output rates greater than Q_2. For these output rates, the LATC is increasing and the LMC curve is above the LATC curve.

Although it may be tempting to suggest that the optimal firm size (or capacity) is given by the capital and labor combination that produces output

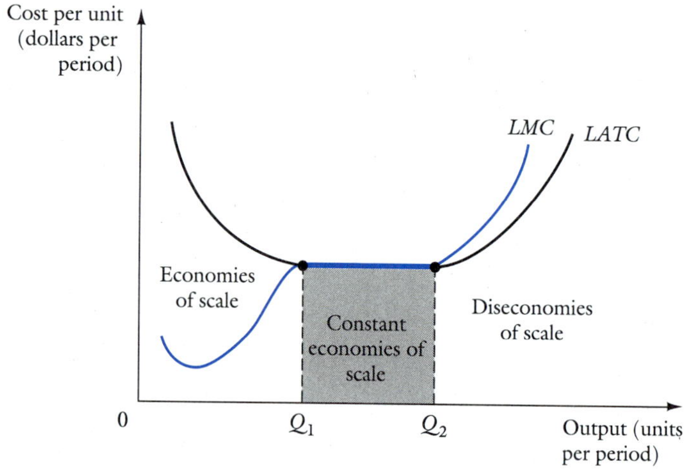

FIGURE 9.12

Economies, Constant Economies, and Diseconomies of Scale and the Long-Run Average Total Cost Curve

Scale economies affect the shape of the average total cost curve. Economies of scale occur up to output rate Q_1, at which point the *LATC* stops its decline. Between output rates Q_1 and Q_2, the firm experiences constant economies of scale. Over this output range, the *LATC* curve is flat. Diseconomies of scale occur at output rates greater than Q_2. The *LATC* curve increases as output expands beyond Q_2.

rate Q_2 in Figure 9.11—that is, where the firm produces at the minimum of the LATC curve—such a conclusion is not warranted without further information about the market structure and output price. Firms operating in competitive markets (see Chapter 10), for example, are typically forced to select the minimum-LATC-curve input combination in the long run, but they may deviate from this choice in the short run as market price changes. In contrast, firms that have some market power may select an input combination that produces nearly any output rate on the LATC curve, so they may not tend toward the combination implied by the minimum of the LATC curve. In general, then, the optimal input mix—or capacity decision—depends on the structure of the market—competitive or otherwise—and the planning horizon—short run or long run.

$$$ Price Theory in Practice

Scale Economies and Internationalization of the Beer Brewing Industry

Slowly but consistently over the past twenty-five years, beer brewing has become an international industry. The value of world trade in beer increased from \$149 million in 1965 to \$2.08 billion in 1987, a 14-fold increase. In comparison, world trade in all goods increased only 12.5 times over the same period. In constant dollar terms, there was about a 3.5-fold increase in world trade in beer and about a 3-fold increase in all world trade. When measured in unit sales, world trade in beer has increased at an annual rate of 6.5 percent since 1965. The largest exporters are the Netherlands, Germany, Czechoslovakia, Belgium, and Canada. The largest importers are the United States, Great Britain, France, Italy, and Germany.

To accommodate the growth in world demand for beer, many beer companies have signed agreements with foreign manufacturers to produce their beers. Such license agreements can be explained by several factors. First, they often allow manufacturers to avoid trade barriers and tariffs that the other beer exporters must pay. Second, they reduce transportation and distribution costs because manufacturers can use raw materials in the foreign country to make its beers rather than ship the final product. Because beer is 90 percent water, there can be significant savings when shipping costs are reduced. Third, beer has a shelf life of about three to four months, and shipping beer, either overland or by boat, may take up to three weeks, which significantly reduces the shelf life in the foreign country. Finally, economies of scale in the beer industry promote the use of license agreements so that beer can be produced at the lowest possible unit cost.

Table 9.5 on page 342 provides a representative sample of some recent licensing arrangements between major beer manufacturers in the United States and abroad. As this table illustrates, beer manufacturers have significantly expanded their reach into world markets by the use of licensing accords. In Canada alone, it is estimated that the volume of licensed beer sold is 17 times greater than the amount of beer directly imported. Licensed beer was estimated to account for 15 percent of Canadian beer consumption in 1986, compared to

TABLE 9.5

Foreign Licensing Agreements for Selected Major Beer Brewers

Brewer	Licensee	Agreement
Anheuser-Busch	*Guinness*	Guinness brews Budweiser in Ireland.
	Labatt	Labatt brews Budweiser and Michelob in Canada.
	Oriental	Oriental brews Budweiser in Korea.
	Suntory	Suntory brews Budweiser in Japan.
	Watney Mann	Watney Mann brews Budweiser in Great Britain.
Carlton & United	*Carling O'Keefe*	Carling brews Foster's in Canada.
	Courage	Courage brews Foster's in Great Britain.
	Watney Mann	Watney Mann brews Foster's in Great Britain.
Coors	*Asahi*	Asahi brews Coors in Japan.
	Molson	Molson brews Coors in Canada.
United	*Beamish & Crawford*	B&C brews Carlsberg in Ireland.
	Labatt	Labatt brews Carlsberg in Canada.
	Falken	Falken brews Carlsberg in Sweden.
	Heileman	Heileman brews Carlsberg in the United States.
	Suntory	Suntory brews Carlsberg in Japan.
Lowenbrau	*Asahi*	Asahi brews Lowenbrau in Japan.
	Miller	Miller brews Lowenbrau in the United States.
Heineken	*Kirin*	Kirin brews Heineken in Japan.
	Whitehead	Whitehead brews Heineken in Great Britain.

Source: Modern Brewery Age, July 13, 1987.

the 2.1 percent of consumption accounted for by imports.[4] Although data are difficult to obtain, it is believed that a similar imbalance between licensed and imported beer exists in Japan, Great Britain, and France.

The role that economies of scale play in the decision to license versus export can be analyzed using the long-run average total cost curve for a typical beer manufacturer. Panel (a) in Figure 9.13 shows the long-run average total cost curve, $LATC_{US}$, for Coors beer production in the United States. The current quantity demanded of Coors is equal to Q_{US}. At this output rate, Coors is manufactured and distributed in the United States at a unit cost of C_2. Now the Coors beer company must decide whether to manufacture and export Coors or to license a Japanese company to produce Coors in Japan.

Panel (b) in Figure 9.13 shows the long-run average total cost curve, $LATC_{Japan}$, for a Japanese company to manufacture and distribute Coors in

[4]See Jeffery D. Karrenbrock, "The Internationalization of the Beer Brewing Industry," Federal Reserve Bank of St. Louis *Review* 72 (November/December 1990), 3–19.

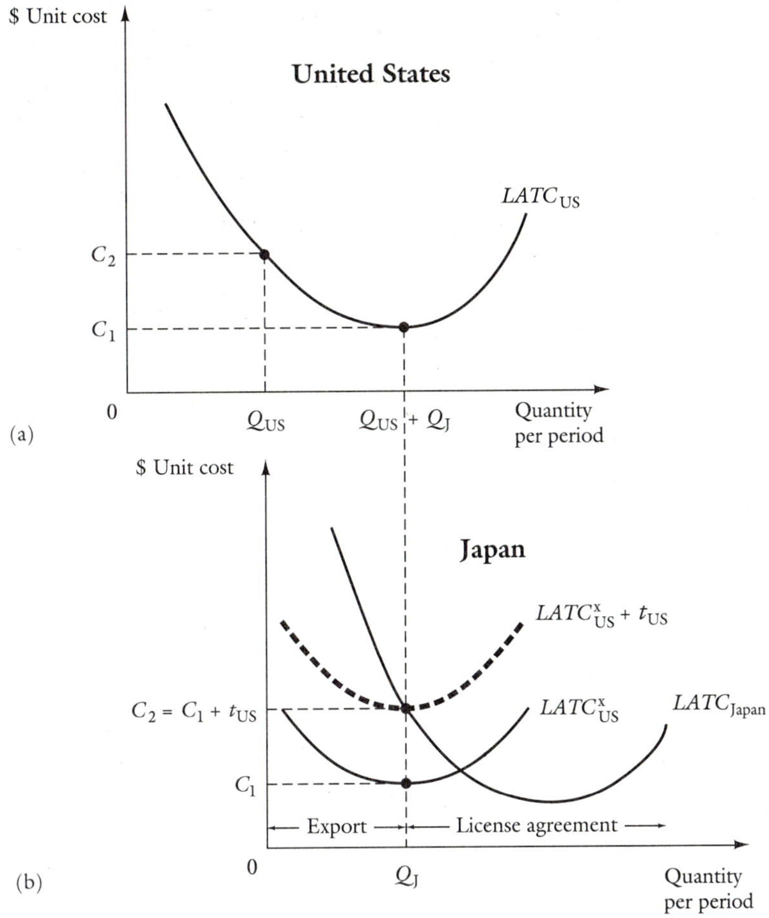

FIGURE 9.13

Determining Whether to Export or License the Production of Coors Beer

Panel (a) shows the shape of the *LATC* curve for the Coors brewing company in the United States. U.S. demand for Coors is Q_{US} units per period. To decide whether to export or license production to a Japanese brewer, Coors compares the average total cost of exporting to the average total cost of a licensing arrangement. In panel (b), $LATC^{X}_{US}$ is the average cost of producing Coors for export, $LATC^{X}_{US} + t_{US}$ is the average export cost plus the required tariffs and transportations charges, and $LATC_{Japan}$ is the average total cost of producing Coors using a Japanese brewer. If the demand for Coors in Japan equals Q_J per period, the average total cost of exporting (including tariffs and transportation charges) equals the average total cost of Japanese production. Thus, for output rates less than Q_J, Coors will be produced in the United States and exported to Japan. For output rates greater than Q_J, Coors will be produced in Japan under a license agreement.

Japan. (Note that the two long-run average total cost curves, $LATC_{US}$ and $LATC_{Japan}$, are identical. We are assuming that manufacturing and distribution costs are identical in these two countries to simplify the analysis.) Also in panel (b), we have projected the part of the $LATC_{US}$ curve that lies beyond current quantity demanded (Q_{US}) in the United States. If the U.S. firm manufactures Coors for export, its production and (internal) distribution costs are determined by this portion of the $LATC_{US}$ curve, so we call this curve the average cost of exporting curve, $LATC^X_{US}$. In addition, though, exporting beer to Japan adds a tariff and transportation cost of t_{US} per unit to the long-run average total cost curve. Adding these costs to $LATC^X_{US}$ gives the effective long-run average total cost of exporting, which is shown as $LATC^X_{US} + t_{US}$ in panel (b) of Figure 9.13.

If the quantity demanded of Coors in Japan equals Q_J, the Coors company can produce this beer in the United States at a unit cost of C_1. Exporting this quantity to demand adds t_{US} per unit to the cost, so the total unit cost of exporting beer is $C_1 + t_{US}$. Alternatively, if a license agreement is signed with a Japanese company, the quantity Q_J may be produced for a unit cost of C_J, which is exactly equal to $C_1 + t_{US}$. At this output rate, the Coors company is indifferent between domestic production for export and a foreign license agreement. This suggests that the size of the Japanese market may be the important issue in deciding whether to export or license. We can see that for output rates to the left of Q_J, average costs for a Japanese producer, $LATC_{Japan}$, exceed those of the U.S. firm, $LATC^X_{US} + t_{US}$, even when tariffs and transportation costs are included. Thus, we can state that for output rates *less than* Q_J per period, it is less costly to manufacture Coors in the United States and export to Japan.[5] If the output rate is *more than* Q_J per period, however, it is less costly to license production of Coors to a Japanese company.

In short, the decision to export or license beer is largely dependent on the size of the market. If a large quantity is demanded for a particular brand of beer in a country, it is likely that licensing will offer lower unit costs. Alternatively, if a small quantity is demanded, exporting is probably cheaper.

LEARNING EXERCISE 9.13

Using a diagram similar to Figure 9.13, show how a per unit *subsidy* to U.S. beer exports affects the decision to license production of beer to a Japanese firm. Show how an increase in Japanese tariffs can offset the effects of such a subsidy.

ONE PLANT OR TWO? COORDINATING MULTIPLANT PRODUCTION

We usually show a single marginal cost curve for a firm because we assume a single production process. Of course, some firms have more than one production facility, and because the costs of operating the facilities may be different, the firm's managers must decide when to use only one plant or expand pro-

[5]We are assuming that the decision to license production to a Japanese beer producer does not raise unit costs in the United States.

duction to two plants. There is a general rule that managers can follow when faced with this problem:

To minimize production costs, output is allocated to the different plants to equate the marginal cost of production across plants.

The intuition behind this result is that firms have an incentive to rearrange their output between plants if the marginal costs differ. The plant with the lowest marginal cost will be given more output to produce; it can do so at a lower cost than the other plants. The shifting of output now increases this plant's marginal cost. The process of shifting output around stops when marginal cost is equated across plants.

Suppose a firm has plant New and plant Old. Let's further suppose that the firm desires to produce 100 units of output per period. The managers of the firm must find the output rates for each plant such that the following two equations are jointly satisfied:

(a) $MC_N(Q_N) = MC_O(Q_O)$

(b) $Q_N + Q_O = 100$

where $MC_N(Q_N)$ is the marginal cost of plant New, $MC_O(Q_O)$ is the marginal cost of plant Old, Q_N is the output of plant New, and Q_O is the output of plant Old.

Figure 9.14 shows such a situation. In panel (a) we see the marginal cost curves for the two plants. Notice that plant New has a lower marginal cost at a

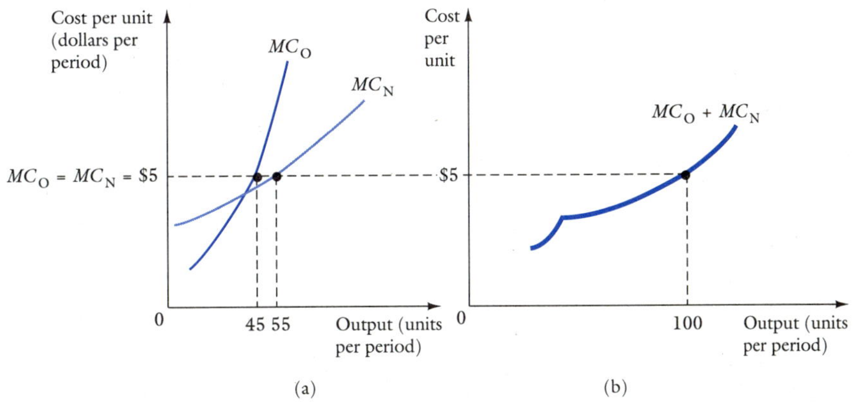

FIGURE 9.14

The Cost-Minimizing Allocation of Output Between Two Plants

A firm that operates both Old and New plants allocates production between them to equate marginal costs of production. Total demand is 100 units, as shown in panel (b). The *combined* marginal cost of producing 100 units is $5 per period. In panel (a), the firm allocates the total output to each plant by finding the output rate at which marginal cost is equal to $5. The marginal cost for the Old plant (MC_O) equals $5 at 45 units of output; the marginal cost for the New plant (MC_N) equals $5 at 55 units.

higher rate of output than plant Old. In panel (b) we have constructed the sum of the plant Old and plant New marginal cost curves. We add these two curves together to illustrate a simple, graphical solution to the problem of selecting the cost-minimizing allocation of output. Because the managers of the firm desire to produce 100 units of output per period, the solution can be found by locating the combined marginal cost of producing 100 units in panel (b). As may be seen, the combined marginal cost of producing 100 units is equal to \$5. Carrying this cost back to panel (a), we see that the *optimal* allocation is for plant Old to produce 45 units per period and plant New to produce 55 units per period.

Note that it may not always be optimal to use both plants to produce some of the total output. If the managers desire to produce a total output less than Q_{cutoff}, then it will be optimal to use only plant Old because it has a lower marginal cost for producing low output rates than plant New.

These curves show us that the optimal allocation problem can be solved by looking at the *combined* marginal cost curve. This is true whether we are describing two plants or fifty plants, so the solution technique may be generalized to other situations. Note, too, that we compare the marginal cost curves, not the average variable or average total cost curves. These curves play no role in the cost-minimizing allocation decision.

LEARNING EXERCISE 9.14

Suppose that $MC_N(Q_N) = 15 + 2Q_N$ and $MC_O(Q_O) = 5 + 8Q_O$. If the managers desire to produce 100 units of output, $Q_N + Q_O = 100$, then find the cost-minimizing allocation of output.

9.6 MULTIPRODUCT FIRMS AND DYNAMIC CHANGES IN COSTS

The firm that we have described produces only one product, but many firms we can think of produce more than one product. Food companies, such as Quaker Oats, Kellogg's, and General Mills, offer consumers a variety of products. Computer firms produce both desktop and laptop computers. Universities produce both teaching and research, and hospitals offer both diagnostic and surgical services. Often such output combinations exist because there is a cost advantage to producing multiple products compared to the cost of producing a single product.

Similarly, both multiproduct and single-product firms can save money as they gain experience with the production process. The first time you try to find your classes at the beginning of a school year takes longer than the second time. For firms, it is often the case that the first unit or first batch of output is more costly than subsequent batches of output. Such learning tends to lower costs over time.

In this section, we will describe the cost structure of multiproduct firms and explain how learning over time tends to affect costs.

ECONOMIES OF SCOPE

Economies of Scope
The situation when production of multiple outputs in one firm is less expensive than the costs of producing the same outputs in separate firms (or plants).

If a firm saves costs when producing more than one output, then it is said that there are **economies of scope** in multiproduct firms. Consider the case of two outputs, Q_1 and Q_2. If we define $C(Q_1, Q_2)$ as the total cost of producing these outputs, then economies of scope exist if

$$C(Q_1, Q_2) < C(0, Q_2) + C(Q_1, 0) \tag{9.13}$$

where $C(0, Q_2)$ is the cost of producing output Q_2 alone and $C(Q_1, 0)$ is the cost of producing output Q_1 alone. In other words, equation (9.13) states that economies of scope exist if the cost of producing both outputs, Q_1 and Q_2, is less than the sum of the costs of producing each output alone.

Economies of scope may arise from specialization in managerial tasks, from inventory savings when the goods require the same or similar inputs (e.g., shoes and boots), from better utilization of production equipment, from technological changes that favor joint production (e.g., R & D in drug companies may produce many different products), or from any aspect of the production process that becomes cheaper when multiple products are manufactured. The banking industry is commonly cited as an example of scope economies. Banks offer many products to consumers, such as checking deposits, loan services, and currency exchange, that can be offered separately or jointly. Economies of scope give banks a cost advantage when these products are produced jointly.

Diseconomies of Scope
The situation when production of multiple outputs in one firm is more expensive than the costs of producing the same outputs in separate firms (or plants).

In contrast, **diseconomies of scope** arise when it is more costly to try to produce two different outputs in a single firm than to produce these outputs in two separate firms. Many of the conglomerates that were formed in the late 1960s and early 1970s, such as LTV Company, which was an integrated metals producer, found that there were more costs, not less, when their managers tried to run many different businesses. Some of these companies—including LTV Company—fell into bankruptcy, while others sold those businesses that did not have economies of scope with their primary product. Recently, Quaker Oats, known as a food product company, sold Fisher-Price Company, a manufacturer of children's toys, primarily because it was a business unrelated to Quaker's primary product(s). Diseconomies of scope can help to explain some or all of these decisions.

The total cost curve is affected by economies of scope as shown in Figure 9.15 on page 348. Instead of increasing in one dimension, as shown in Figure 9.1, the total cost curve is defined for both the Q_1 and Q_2 axes. Its general curvature is the same as Figure 9.1 on either output axis—that is, it has a shoe-like appearance—but when both outputs are produced, the total cost curve dips in the middle like a funnel that is cut in half. The dip defines the area of output for which economies of scope exist. As we have drawn the cost structure, economies of scope exist for all output rates.

Note that economies of scope are not related to returns to scale in the way that economies of scale are; that is, economies (or diseconomies) of scale include the returns to scale concept as a special case, but the concept of economies (or diseconomies) of scope does not imply a particular form—

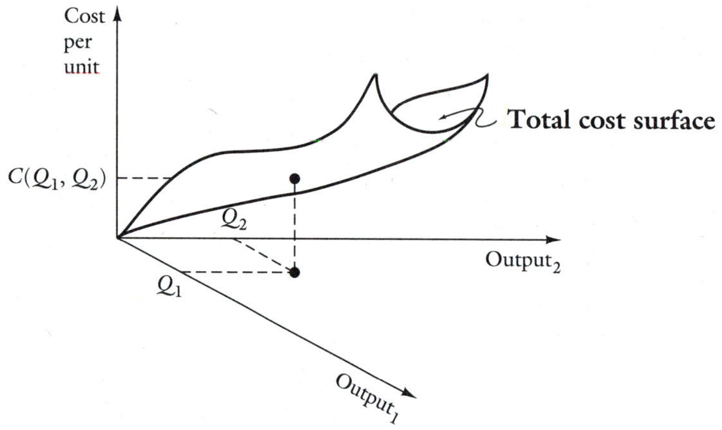

FIGURE 9.15

The Shape of the Total Cost Curve with Economies of Scope

The figure shows a total cost curve for a firm that produces two outputs with economies of scope. The cost curve is actually a three-dimensional surface, shaped much like a funnel that is cut in half. Economies of scope imply that the firm may produce both output rates, Q_1 and Q_2, at a lower cost than either output can be produced separately.

increasing, constant, or decreasing—of returns to scale. A firm that produces high-quality china may find its marketing costs lower if it is part of a company that makes silverware. Because of the skilled labor involved, the china company may operate on a small scale, but the silverware company may use machines to produce on a much larger scale. Thus, the marketing cost savings generate economies of scope for the two firms combined, but individually they realize different returns to scale.

Economies of scope are one explanation for mergers. Firms may find that they can save administrative or other costs by operating as one company instead of two. Such mergers are economically efficient because the resulting firm can produce both products at lower cost, which often translates into lower prices for consumers.

LEARNING CURVES

Some manufacturing processes are like puzzles: your first attempt to put the pieces together takes much longer than any subsequent attempt because you *learn* where some pieces belong on the first attempt. In addition, you will probably continue to learn on subsequent attempts as you refine your understanding of the puzzle pieces. When manufacturing involves the assembly of many parts to make a product, learning usually occurs over time as workers gain more knowledge of the relationships among all of the parts of the product. In addition, suppliers of raw materials may learn more about the produc-

TABLE 9.6

Average Unit Costs for Manufacturing Diodes

Production Activity	Initial Average Unit Cost	Average Unit Cost After Output Doubled	Average Unit Cost Change (percent)
Photolithography	$0.06	$0.05	16.67%
Diffusion	0.17	0.14	17.65%
Contact Plating	0.11	0.08	27.27%
Scribing	0.42	0.34	19.05%
Furnace Sealing	2.00	1.70	15.00%
Totals	$2.76	$2.31	16.30%

Source: Adapted by permission of *Harvard Business Review*. An exhibit from "Building Strategy on the Experience Curve," by Pankaj Ghemawat, March–April 1985, 143–149.

tion schedule as more units are produced, resulting in time and cost savings because of fewer delays.

The effects of learning on average unit costs in the production of diodes—semiconductors found in nearly every electronic device—is described in Table 9.6. Diode production is divided into several parts, and the costs of each part of the process can be measured fairly accurately. Initially, average unit costs of manufacturing—excluding overhead, marketing, and other nonmanufacturing costs—are $2.76 per unit. After output has doubled, however, these costs fall to $2.31 per unit for a savings of 16.3 percent. These savings are due to learning effects.

The relationship between learning and production costs was first observed in 1936 in the aircraft industry.[6] It was observed that labor costs per plane declined as the cumulative total number of airplanes produced increased. An aircraft frame requires the assembly of thousands of parts in more or less a predetermined sequence. It is no wonder, then, that learning occurs in this industry. Workers gain knowledge of the time it takes for glue to dry, for metal to be formed and reformed, and for errors to be repaired. Over time, the planes are produced with many fewer mistakes and in much less time than the first aircraft. When the U.S. Defense Department procures a new airplane, it is aware of the cost savings from learning. The Defense Department almost always awards the contract to a single firm so that it receives the lowest price possible, as this firm now has the opportunity to realize all the cost savings from learning.

The effects of learning on the average total cost of production are shown in Figure 9.16 on page 350. In this figure, two average total cost curves are shown. The average cost of production without any learning effects is shown

[6] See T. P. Wright, "Factors Affecting the Cost of Airplanes," *Journal of Aeronautical Sciences* 3 (1936), 122–128.

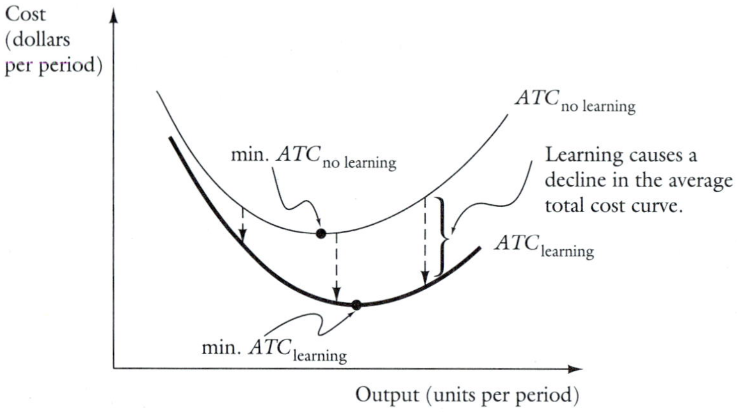

FIGURE 9.16

The Effects of Learning on the Average Total Cost Curve

Firms that learn about the production process as more output is produced find that the *ATC* curve declines with learning. Learning is usually modeled as a cumulative volume effect. When a greater volume is produced, the *ATC* curve shifts down to reflect the valuable information gained.

as $ATC_{no\ learning}$. The average cost curve with learning is shown as $ATC_{learning}$. Learning causes a *cumulative* change in the firm's cost structure. So the $ATC_{learning}$ curve is nearly equal to the $ATC_{no\ learning}$ curve for very low output rates. As more output has been produced—a cumulative total—the $ATC_{learning}$ curve tends to diverge from the $ATC_{no\ learning}$ curve. In the figure, this divergence is shown as an increasing distance between the $ATC_{no\ learning}$ and the $ATC_{learning}$ curves.

Even though learning causes significant cost savings, these savings may not be enough to reverse the effect of diseconomies of scale. We know that the $ATC_{learning}$ curve may thus turn upward at some output rate. This output rate will be to the right of the output rate at which diseconomies of scale begin on the $ATC_{no\ learning}$ curve. So, learning has the effect of extending the region in which economies of scale are realized.

Cost savings due to learning are important to recognize when a firm plans its pricing policy. Higher prices result in fewer sales and lower output rates, so any cost savings due to learning takes longer to realize than if a lower price policy is adopted. The pricing problem is now tricky. If there are significant learning effects, it may be advantageous to price the product below the ATC of low-volume production, causing losses for a short period, to achieve the cost savings from learning quickly. Managers must then trade off present losses for higher profits in the future.

Chapter Summary

1. Accounting costs are historical in nature and measure costs as recorded for actual transactions. Economic costs measure the opportunity

cost associated with the use of resources, which may not always generate a transaction, or paper trail, that can be counted. Costs for items such as office rent provided for free because the company's owner also owns the building are not included in an accounting statement but are included in an economic statement of costs.

2. The short run holds one or more inputs fixed, but not all. If there is only one variable input in the short run, then changes in total cost are directly related to changes in the variable input. In this case, marginal cost is equal to the unit cost of the variable input divided by the marginal product of the variable input.
3. The least-cost combination of inputs is found by identifying the point of tangency between a given isoquant and an isocost line. For the case of two inputs—capital and labor—the point of tangency occurs where the ratio of the two input prices, w/r, equals the ratio of the two marginal products, MP_L/MP_K.
4. The profit-maximizing firm equates marginal revenue to marginal cost to find an optimal output rate. To find its optimal choice of inputs, the profit-maximizing firm equates the marginal revenue product of an input to the input's marginal cost. For labor and capital inputs, we find that the profit-maximizing firm solves $MP_L \times P = w$ and $MP_K \times P = r$, respectively.
5. The long-run cost curves of a firm are derived allowing all inputs to vary, whereas the short-run cost curves hold at least one input fixed. The long-run cost curves always represent the lowest possible costs of producing any output rate. The short-run costs will thus be greater than (or equal to) the long run cost curves. For average cost curves, this relationship implies that the long-run average total cost curve forms an envelope around the short-run average total cost curves.
6. Economies of scale arise when a doubling of output causes average total costs to decrease. Diseconomies of scale arise when a doubling of output causes average total costs to increase. Constant economies of scale arise when average total costs remain unchanged when output doubles.
7. Economies of scope arise in multiproduct firms when the total cost of producing multiple outputs is less than the sum of the costs of producing each output separately.

Trouble Spots

Concept	Reminder
Finding the Least-Cost Mix of Inputs	The least-cost input combination is the one at which w/r equals MP_L/MP_K. Note that the inputs are referred to consistently in these ratios. The numerator of both ratios refers to labor and the denominator of both ratios refers to capital. This consistency is important. We can invert both terms and find the least-cost mix, because we will keep the numerator and denominator referring to the same input, but we cannot invert only one term and find the least-cost input mix.

Comparing Long-Run and Short-Run Cost Curves	Short- and long-run cost curves should not be confused with short-and long-run expansion paths; for the latter are used to derive the former. The expansion paths show the least-cost mix of inputs given the planning horizon of the firm, either short- or long-run. The cost curves are the by-product of choosing the optimal mix of inputs to produce a given output rate. Thus, the cost curves are plotted with cost and output on the axes, while the expansion paths are shown with the inputs on the axes.
Economies of Scale and Cost Curves	Economies and diseconomies of scale are not the same as increasing and decreasing returns to scale. Economies and diseconomies of scale explain the behavior of the average total cost curve as output changes, whereas increasing and decreasing returns to scale explain the behavior of output as inputs change proportionately. Economies and diseconomies of scale include the concepts of increasing and decreasing returns to scale as special cases, but the reverse is not true.
Learning Curves	Learning curve effects are generally measured by showing a negative relationship between cost and the cumulative total output produced. The learning curve effect is necessarily temporal because output is cumulated over time.

9.7 Review Questions

1. How would you compute the opportunity cost of attending college from September until June? Who bears this cost? Would you include the cost of meals in this calculation?
2. How do durable resources affect an economist's and accountant's statements of a firm's costs?
3. How do sunk costs differ from fixed costs? Is a building, such as the U.S. embassy in Moscow, normally a sunk or fixed cost? Explain?
4. "I know that the 'short run' for my gas station won't end for at least 10 more years, because that's how long my lease runs." Assuming that this person does not have the right to sublet, do you agree or disagree? Why?
5. Is a fixed cost ever a function of output in the short run? Why or why not? What is the formula for average fixed cost?
6. Define marginal cost. Does your definition refer to a change in total cost or in variable cost? Does it matter? Why or why not?
7. Explain how average product is related to average variable cost when there is only one variable input in the short run. Explain how marginal product is related to marginal cost in the same situation.
8. Explain how you can use the areas under the average and marginal cost curves to compute total, total variable, and fixed costs.
9. Suppose you are producing a rate of output Q, employing a combination of inputs such that the marginal product of capital is 8 times that of labor. If the rental price per unit of capital is 10 times as much as

the wage rate per unit of labor, are you minimizing your costs for that output? Why or why not? What change in inputs will lower your cost of producing output Q? Explain.

10. Define the long-run average total cost of production. In light of the fact that businesses are operated day to day in the short run, of what use is the concept of long-run average total cost to the owner or manager?
11. Explain why there can be only one long-run expansion path.
12. What is the difference between technical and economic efficiency?
13. Why is it that a significant expansion of an entire industry, particularly a fairly rapid one, will often shift the marginal cost curve of each individual firm leftward?
14. Why do you think the federal government allows taxpayers using their own personal cars in their work (other than just in commuting) to deduct as an expense an amount (about 26 cents per mile at this writing) that is approximately equal to the ATC of the vast majority of car owners? Why doesn't Congress limit the deduction to marginal cost?
15. How do economies of scope and learning effects change the cost structure of a firm?
16. Suppose that the U.S. Congress changed the tax laws so that stock dividends became a tax-deductible "expense" for corporations. What impact would such a move have on the relative attractiveness of debt financing (issuing new bonds or borrowing from a bank to raise capital) and equity financing (issuing new shares of stock to raise capital)? Why? (Hint: Consider these two types of financing as inputs to the production process.)

9.8 Price Theory Problems

1. "We seldom use that old machine, but it doesn't cost us anything to keep it because it's been completely depreciated on the company books." Criticize this statement.
2. "There are periods in the production cycle when I must wait for another employee to complete his job before I can continue with my work." Does this describe a case in which opportunity costs are zero? Would you change your answer if the idle employee is paid a piece wage, that is, is paid on the basis of the number of units produced?
3. Your accountant has quit suddenly because she won the California lottery. You are left with an incomplete summary of last month's production costs. Please complete the cost table.

Units	Total Cost	Fixed Cost	Variable Cost	ATC	AVC	AFC	MC
0	$400			–	–	–	–
1	?	?	?	?	?	?	$40
2	?	?	$100	?	?	?	?
3	?	?	$200	?	?	?	?
4	$750	?	?	?	?	?	?

4. Assume that a bicycle manufacturer has a constant marginal cost of production of $100, with fixed costs of $1,000 per month.
   a. Draw a diagram showing the average variable, average total, and average fixed cost curves for this firm.
   b. Is there an output rate that minimizes the average total cost of production for this firm?
5. Economic costs measure the cost of all resources used by a firm. If the government imposed a lump-sum tax of $100 per year—that is, a tax that is fixed for one year—on all firms, will this tax affect the shape of the short-run average total cost and marginal cost curves? How are these cost curves affected if the tax is equal to $2 per unit produced?
6. *True or False:* If there are diminishing marginal returns to labor and labor is the only variable input, the marginal cost curve must be increasing in the short run.
7. Suppose a firm finds that it always minimizes its long-run production costs for a given output rate when it uses twice as many labor units as capital units. Draw this firm's long-run expansion path.
8. "Despite all the developments in power gardening equipment that have occurred in recent years, the typical home gardening service consists of a single gardener, sometimes two, and a pickup truck full of equipment. One of these days, one of them is going to get smart and increase the scale of operations to six or eight workers and operate with a very large truck full of highly specialized equipment. The result will be lower costs, and the smaller traditional operators who are unable to purchase the larger-scale equipment will be driven out of business." Criticize this statement.
9. Suppose you are an industrial engineer charged with keeping your firm's production costs at a minimum. (You are not asked to make decisions as to the rate of output of the firm; such decisions are made for you by the firm's managers.) In order to do your job well, what information do you need to know besides that given by the production function? Why?
10. Assume that the production function for computer disks is $Q = 500\sqrt{K} \cdot \sqrt{L}$. In addition, assume that the price of labor is $10 per unit per period and the price of capital is $20 per unit per period.
    a. Find the cost-minimizing combinations of capital and labor for $Q = 10{,}000$ and $Q = 50{,}000$. What are the total costs of producing these output rates?
    b. If profit maximization tells you to produce 25,000 unit per period, how much capital and labor will you hire?
    c. Holding capital fixed at 10 units, what is the cost-minimizing amount of labor you will hire to produce $Q = 25{,}000$ units per period. What is the total cost of this input combination?

How do these costs compare to the cost of production in part (b)?

11. A watch manufacturer recently developed a new time movement. As its output rate increased, the manufacturer found that average total costs were given by

$$ATC = 1{,}000/Q + 10Q - 0.2C_Q$$

where C_Q is the cumulative output.

   a. Is there a positive or negative learning effect for this firm?
   b. Find the output rate at which decreasing returns begin, setting C_Q equal to zero. (Hint: Find the minimum of the ATC curve.)
   c. Assuming that $C_Q = 200 + Q$, where Q is the present output rate, find the output rate at the minimum of the ATC curve. How does this output rate compare to your answer to part (b)?

12. Consider a three-plant firm. At present output Q, each plant is producing one-third ($Q/3$) of the total. You are hired as the company's new industrial engineer. The first thing you do is ascertain the marginal cost of each plant at the present output rate of $Q/3$. Your figures show the marginal cost of plant 1 to be \$10 and that of plants 2 and 3 to be \$8. Further, you realize that the marginal cost curve of each plant is positively sloped. Assuming that you wish to continue output at the same level Q, how should you rearrange production shares so as to decrease costs? Does it make any difference to your decision if all sales occur at the location of plant 1 and the outputs of plants 2 and 3 must be shipped to plant 1 in order to be sold?
13. Pizza stores often issue coupons that offer price discounts for pizza. One coupon might offer two medium pizzas for \$9.99 with eight toppings included. If you don't like all eight toppings, you will probably find that you cannot use the discount coupon. In other words, you can't say, "I want two medium pizzas—take off six toppings, give me sausage and ham on one pizza and pepperoni and mushrooms on the other pizza and omit the other toppings." Why do the stores have such a policy? After all, it would seem that fewer toppings would be cheaper to produce.
14. NewData, Inc., is a small publishing company that collects and distributes economic data on CD-ROM disks. The company is planning to collect data on stock and bond prices since 1890. The costs of collection are estimated to equal \$100,000 and the cost of distribution is estimated to be \$5 per CD-ROM disk. Assuming that these are the only costs involved, draw the long-run marginal and average cost curves for this project. What is the equation that defines the long-run total and average costs of this project?

9.9 Writing Exercise

Economies of scale and scope are important concepts that help explain the organization of firms, but can these concepts help explain how various local, state, and federal government bodies are organized? Write an essay that either supports or refutes the idea that there are economies of scale and/or scope in government. You may choose to focus on only local government, for example, to keep the essay tractable. Support your reasoning with historical evidence that describes how government services have changed over time. Explain how at least one government service is produced, outlining where there are economies of scale and/or scope if they are present.

Appendix 9A
An Analytical Treatment of Cost Minimization

This appendix presents an algebraic formulation of cost and production theory, using optimization methods and calculus to derive the basic results. A review of the mathematical appendix at the back of the text may be helpful if you are unfamiliar with the Lagrangian multiplier approach.

The Cost Minimization Problem

A firm that maximizes profits may divide its problem into two parts. First, it defines the input combinations that produce any given output rate at least cost, and second, it decides what output rate maximizes profits. The first part is called the cost minimization problem. To describe this problem, assume that output is produced with only two inputs, capital (K) and labor (L). The firm utilizes a variable proportions production function defined by $f(K, L)$. The price of the service flow of capital is denoted by r per unit and the price of the service flow of labor is w per unit. In a competitive market, firms take these prices as fixed, so the cost minimization problem can be written as

$$\text{Minimize TC} = wL + rK \tag{A9.1}$$

where TC represents the total cost of production, subject to the requirement that a fixed amount of output, Q_0, be produced each period:

$$f(K, L) = Q_0 \tag{A9.2}$$

To determine the optimal input combination that solves the cost minimization problem, we first restate the problem using the Lagrangian multiplier method:

$$\text{Minimize } L = wL + rK + \lambda[Q_0 - F(K, L)] \tag{A9.3}$$

where λ is called the Lagrangian multiplier.

The first-order conditions for a minimum are given by

$$\frac{\partial \pounds}{\partial L} = w - \lambda \frac{\partial F}{\partial L} = 0 \tag{A9.4}$$

$$\frac{\partial \pounds}{\partial K} = r - \lambda \frac{\partial F}{\partial K} = 0 \tag{A9.5}$$

$$\frac{\partial \pounds}{\partial \lambda} = Q_0 - F(K, L) = 0 \tag{A9.6}$$

where the term $\partial F/\partial L$ is the marginal product of labor and the term $\partial F/\partial K$ is the marginal product of capital.

Dividing equation (A9.4) and equation (A9.5), after substituting the MP_L and MP_K notation used in the chapter, gives

$$\frac{\mathrm{MP}_L}{\mathrm{MP}_K} = \frac{w}{r} \tag{A9.7}$$

This is the result that we derived as equation (9.8). Thus, restating our earlier result, the firm has found the least-cost combination of K and L to produce output rate Q_0 when equation (A9.7) is satisfied.

The Dual to the Cost Minimization Problem

The problem of finding the least-cost combination of K and L can be restated in its **dual form.** The dual form requires the firm to find the combination of K and L that produces the greatest output for a given amount of costs. The dual can be written as

Dual Form An equivalent form of a given optimization problem.

$$\text{Maximize } Q = f(K, L) \tag{A9.8}$$

subject to the requirement that a fixed amount of costs, TC_0, be spent on the purchase of the two inputs:

$$wL + rK = \mathrm{TC}_0 \tag{A9.9}$$

To determine the optimal input combination that solves the dual problem, we again restate the problem in Lagrangian form:

$$\text{Maximize } \pounds = f(K, L) + \mu[TC_0 - wL - rK] \tag{A9.10}$$

where μ is the Lagrangian multiplier for the dual problem.

The first-order conditions for a maximum are given by

$$\frac{\partial \pounds}{\partial L} = \frac{\partial f}{\partial L} - \mu w = 0 \tag{A9.11}$$

$$\frac{\partial \pounds}{\partial K} = \frac{\partial f}{\partial K} - \mu r = 0 \tag{A9.12}$$

$$\frac{\partial \pounds}{\partial \mu} = TC_0 - wL - rK = 0 \tag{A9.13}$$

where again the term $\partial F/\partial L$ is the marginal product of labor and the term $\partial F/\partial K$ is the marginal product of capital.

Dividing equation (A9.11) and equation (A9.12) gives the same result we derived in equation (A9.7), $\mathrm{MP}_L/\mathrm{MP}_K = w/r$, so the dual approach generates the same optimal input combinations as the standard cost minimization problem.

The Cost Function for the Cobb-Douglas Case

An algebraic solution to the cost minimization problem can be found using a specific functional form for the production process. Let's assume that the production process can be described by the Cobb-Douglas production function $Q = AK^{\alpha}L^{\beta}$, where α and β are elasticities of output for capital and labor, respectively, and A is a parameter that embodies technology and any of the effects of learning on the production process. Recall from Chapter 8 that the sum of the exponents, $\alpha + \beta = s$, measures the returns to scale (s) of the production process, so $s > 1$ implies increasing returns to scale, $s = 1$ implies constant returns to scale, and $s < 1$ implies decreasing returns to scale.

Substituting the Cobb-Douglas production function into the Lagrangian form of the cost minimization problem gives:

$$\text{Minimize } \pounds = wL + rK + \lambda[Q_0 - AK^{\alpha}L^{\beta}] \tag{A9.14}$$

The first-order conditions for a minimum now become

$$\frac{\partial \pounds}{\partial L} = w - \lambda(\beta AK^{\alpha}L^{\beta - 1}) = 0 \tag{A9.15}$$

$$\frac{\partial \pounds}{\partial K} = r - \lambda(\alpha AK^{\alpha - 1}L^{\beta}) = 0 \tag{A9.16}$$

$$\frac{\partial \pounds}{\partial \lambda} = Q_0\ AK^{\alpha}L^{\beta} = 0 \tag{A9.17}$$

where the $MP_L = \beta AK^{\alpha}L^{\beta - 1}$ and the $MP_K = \alpha AK^{\alpha - 1}L^{\beta}$. Note that if α and β are both less than 1, then the MP_L varies inversely with L and the MP_K varies inversely with K.

As an exercise (a somewhat tedious one), you may use equation (A9.7) and equation (A9.17) to show that the optimal amounts of K and L are given as

$$L^* = \left(\frac{\beta r}{\alpha w}\right)^{\alpha/s}\left(\frac{Q_0}{A}\right)^{1/s} \tag{A9.18}$$

$$K^* = \left(\frac{\alpha w}{\beta r}\right)^{\beta/s}\left(\frac{Q_0}{A}\right)^{1/s} \tag{A9.19}$$

where $s = \alpha + \beta$ as defined above.

Note that as the relative cost of labor (w/r) increases, the amount of labor used decreases and the amount of capital used increases. Similarly, as the relative cost of capital (r/w) increases, the use of capital decreases and the use of labor increases. Note, too, that an increase in technology (or learning) as measured by an increase in the parameter A causes the firm to use less of both capital and labor in the long run.

We can substitute equations (A9.18) and (A9.19) into the firm's total cost equation, $TC = wL + rK$, to show how a firm's total costs change on the optimal expansion path in the long run. After simplification, the firm's long-run cost function is given by:

$$TC = \left[w\left(\frac{\beta r}{\alpha w}\right)^{\alpha/s} + r\left(\frac{\alpha w}{\beta r}\right)^{\beta/s}\right]\left(\frac{Q_0}{A}\right)^{1/s} \qquad \text{(A9.20)}$$

Equation (A9.20) is also known as the **indirect objective function** to the cost minimization problem. This equation shows how costs change when the firm can optimally respond to changes in both market parameters, w and r, and production parameters, α, β, and A. Note that if the firm's production process exhibits *constant returns to scale*, $s = 1$, then the last term in equation (A9.20) becomes (Q_0/A), so a doubling of output (Q_0) causes costs to double.

Indirect Objective Function
The form of the objective function after substituting the expression that defines the optimal choice of each variable.

Estimation of the Cost Function

Economists who use the Cobb-Douglas approach to the production process estimate the response of a firm's cost to changes in market parameters using a simple transformation of equation (A9.20). First, the terms in this equation can be rearranged so that the cost function is written as

$$TC = \underbrace{\left[\left(\frac{\alpha}{\beta}\right)^{\beta/s} + \left(\frac{\alpha}{\beta}\right)^{-\alpha/s}\right]}_{H} A^{-1/s} w^{\beta/s} r^{\alpha/s} Q_0^{\ 1/s} \qquad \text{(A9.21)}$$

With data on the firm's past history of total costs, output, and input prices, this function can be estimated using regression analysis after taking the logarithmic transformation of both sides of equation (A9.21):

$$\ln TC_t = [\ln H - (1/s)\ln A] + (\beta/s)\ln w_t + (\alpha/s)\ln r_t + (1/s)\ln Q_t \qquad \text{(A9.22)}$$

where ln is the logarithmic operator, the t subscript is added to denote the time series nature of the data that an economist has on the behavior of a given firm, and the H term equals the constant term within the brackets in equation (A9.21).

As can be seen, the logarithmic transformation simplifies the form of the cost function. The exponent terms for input prices and the firm's output are now just linear coefficients of the logarithm of these terms. A regression analysis provides estimates of these terms plus the bracketed constant term. From these estimates, the cost function is fully specified.

The logarithmic form of the cost function also facilitates the analysis of the effects of learning on total costs. If allowed to change over time, the term $(-1/s)\ln A$ may embody the effects of learning and technological change on the firm's total costs. For example, a common specification of learning effects is

$$A_t = \left(\sum_{j=1}^{t} Q_j\right)^{\gamma} \qquad \text{(A9.23)}$$

where the sum term is cumulative to the current time period; that is, A_t measures the firm's cumulative output, $Q_1 + Q_2 + \ldots + Q_j$, up to any given time period, $j = t$.

The learning or technology term in equation (A9.23) now becomes equal to $(-\gamma/s)\ln A_t$, where $-\gamma$ measures the elasticity of costs with respect to the learning variable, A_t. If there are cost savings due to learning, then $\gamma > 0$, so $-\gamma$ is expected to be negative. We require actual data on a firm's cost structure and output to confirm the size and significance of learning effects.

Problems

A1. Find the cost-minimizing solution when the production function is given by $f(K, L) = K^2 + L^2 + KL$. Write the dual form of this problem.

A2. Solve for the cost-minimizing solution in the Cobb-Douglas production function when neutral technological change is introduced in the form $A = de^{rt}$, where d is a constant, r is the rate of technical change, and t is a time index.

10

Price-Taking Firms in Competitive Markets

Preview Questions

When you finish studying this chapter, you should be able to answer the following questions:

- What assumptions are used to define perfectly competitive markets?
- What is marginal revenue to a price-taking firm?
- When does a firm shut down its operations?
- What is the short-run supply curve for a perfectly competitive firm?
- What is the short-run supply curve for a perfectly competitive market?
- What conditions determine the long-run equilibrium for a perfectly competitive market?
- Does the perfectly competitive market exhaust all gains from trade?
- How do competitive markets adjust to asymmetric information about product quality?

The changing political landscape of Eastern Europe in the 1990s has opened new markets to firms from around the world. Countries whose names are fairly difficult to pronounce are still struggling to build new markets. Black market goods, such as consumer electronic products, are sold for many times their price in the West. The black market is a response to former communist decision making. Many goods that were once rationed under a communist system are now provided by profit-maximizing firms and entrepreneurs. Stories of new Russian and Eastern European millionaires also are common. The changes experienced in these new countries has raised many questions about how firms and consumers compete for goods. What does it mean when we say that a market is competitive? How do firms react when other firms enter the market? Do new entrants to a market make consumers better off? To answer these questions, we must first understand the market structure in which firms and consumers interact.

In this chapter, we show how firms and consumers interact in so-called perfectly competitive markets. We will see that perfectly competitive firms act independently; they do not collude or "gang up" on new entrants, but rather change prices in response to changes in the cost of production and market demand. We will show that the profit motive and the lack of government restrictions encourages such firms to enter new markets when there is sufficient demand to make such ventures profitable. We will show that the perfectly competitive market structure is efficient in that all profitable trades are made when the market is in equilibrium. We also will show that consumers receive all of the benefits accruing from the perfectly competitive market structure.

10.1 Perfectly Competitive Markets

Perfect competition is a *process* that describes how profit-maximizing firms and consumers interact in a market. The exact nature of the competitive process is governed by a set of assumptions. These assumptions specify how both firms and consumers interact. As such, they are assumptions about both supply and demand in the market. Let's now turn to the four key assumptions of perfect competition:

Perfect Competition
A market structure in which firms are price takers, entry and exit are unrestricted in the long run, information is known by both buyers and sellers, and a homogeneous product is sold.

1. **Firms sell a homogeneous product.**
2. **Firms and consumers are price takers.**
3. **Entry and exit of firms is unrestricted in the long run.**
4. **Information is symmetrically distributed to buyers and sellers.**

These assumptions define the constraints—or the lack of constraints—affecting both firms and consumers in a perfectly competitive industry. Let's examine these four assumptions in more detail.

Assumption 1: Firms Sell a Homogeneous Product

Consumers in a perfectly competitive industry view the products sold by different firms as perfect substitutes for each other. Thus, the **homogeneous product** is the set of all products that are perfect substitutes. If the physical characteristics of a product are all that matter to consumers, then this assumption is rarely satisfied. A blue shirt and a red shirt made by two different firms are different products because they have different physical characteristics. But physical characteristics are not the determining factor. The consumers' satisfaction and preferences determine whether two products are homogeneous. A red shirt and a blue shirt are physically different from each other, but if consumers in the market for shirts are *indifferent* between these two colors, then these products are homogeneous, or equivalent, for the purpose of computing market demand.

Homogeneous Products
The collection of all products that consumers view as perfect substitutes for each other.

The assumption that red shirts and blue shirts are homogeneous products allows us to add different consumers' demand curves for these shirts in order to derive the market demand curve for shirts. As we saw in Chapter 2, the market demand curve is equal to the (horizontal) sum of each individual demand curve, where the sum is across quantity demanded at a given price. Thus, the homogeneous product assumption narrows our discussion of perfect competition to a market or segment of a market in which the products are perfectly substitutable.

LEARNING EXERCISE 10.1

What is the value of the cross-price elasticity of demand between two firms that produce goods that are perfect substitutes? (Hint: See Chapter 6 for the cross-price elasticity formula.)

ASSUMPTION 2: FIRMS AND CONSUMERS ARE PRICE TAKERS

Price Taker
A firm that cannot affect market price by its output decision.

Price Maker
A firm that can affect the market price by its output decision.

To be a price taker implies that you are not a price maker. A **price taker** is a firm or consumer that *cannot* influence the market price of a product. In contrast, a **price maker** sets or can affect the market price of a product. Most consumers do not believe that they can set or affect the market price of a product. Most firms, however, believe that they can set the price of their products, so how can we make sense of the price-taker assumption?

Firms do set prices for their products, but these may not be the prices that will produce the sales they desire in order to maximize profits. If there are many firms in the market, a firm that sets a price above the prices set by competitors will find its inventories increasing as its sales decline. When this occurs, the firm has an incentive to lower price to clear out excess inventories. Similarly, a firm that sets too low a price will find that it does not have enough merchandise on hand to satisfy all of its customers' requests. In this situation, the firm is likely to set a higher price to ration its scarce inventories. Firms will thus iterate or search in their price-setting activity; they will work their way to the so-called right price. This *price-setting* activity is different from *price-making* activity in which the firm can set or affect the price for the *entire* market. A firm that searches for the right price cannot set or change prices for the entire market. This firm is responding to competitive forces, so it is a price taker. Usually, the presence of many competitive firms with small market shares is enough to ensure that firms are price takers.

The presence of many firms is one way to justify the price-taker assumption, but it is not the only approach. Firms may have large market shares and still act like price takers if they anticipate rapid entry from firms not currently in the market. Potential entrants pose a constant threat to existing firms in perfectly competitive markets. Suppose a large firm sets a price that attracts entry. With entry, total quantity supplied increases and market price falls. So the price set by a large firm in a perfectly competitive industry is not sustainable if it is above the no-entry market price. In effect, existing firms become price takers at the no-entry price.

Alternatively, firms with large market shares may operate as price takers if the other firms in the industry act *strategically* to offset the effects of a single firm's output decision on market price. Suppose, for example, that there are three firms in an industry, each with one-third of the industry output. If one firm has a fire at its manufacturing site that reduces its production (temporarily), what will the other firms do? If the other firms can attract the unfortunate firm's customers, so that they now supply the quantity demanded by these customers, then the total quantity supplied in the market does not change. If the total quantity supplied is constant, then market price will not change (assuming demand is constant, too). In effect, the self-serving, strategic actions of these other firms can fully offset the loss in supply caused by the fire, keeping market price constant. These firms are thus operating as price takers because their strategic actions leave market price unchanged.

MATH NOTEPAD

Relating Firm and Market Elasticities of Demand

The actual influence that a single firm has over the market price depends on how big the firm is relative to the size of the market. We can show this relationship using the price elasticity of demand. First, let's hold the output supplied by all other firms constant. Define Q_{market} to be the total output in the market and Q_f to be the output of a single firm. The price elasticity of demand for the market as a whole is given by $\eta_{market} = (P/Q_{market})/(\Delta P/\Delta Q_{market})$, where $\Delta P/\Delta Q_{market}$ measures how market price, P, is affected by a change in total industry output, ΔQ_{market}. Similarly, the price elasticity of demand for a single firm in the market is given by $\eta_{firm} = (P/Q_f)/(\Delta P/\Delta Q_f)$, where $\Delta P/\Delta Q_f$ measures how market price, P, is affected by a change in the output of the single firm, ΔQ_f. The slope terms, $\Delta P/\Delta Q_{market}$ and $\Delta P/\Delta Q_f$, are equal to each other because changing industry output by one unit may be accomplished by changing the output of a single firm by one unit. Because of this result, we may relate the price elasticity of demand for a single firm to the price elasticity of demand for the industry. Using the definition of η_{firm} and η_{market} and dividing gives $\eta_{firm}/\eta_{market} = Q_{market}/Q_f$. Cross-multiplying by η_{market} and rewriting Q_{market}/Q_f as $1/(Q_f/Q_{market})$ gives the result

$$\eta_{firm} = \frac{\eta_{market}}{(Q_f/Q_{market})}$$

Now, if the quantity supplied by all other firms is not constant, then there is an output response by the other firms as price changes in the elasticity of demand formulas. The effect of the change in output by the other firms on a given firm's output is proportional to how that firm's output rate compares to the total output rate of the other firms. To show this result, define the output of a given firm as the difference between the total market output and the output of all other firms (Q_O):

$$Q_f = Q_{market} - Q_O$$

Differencing both sides of the above equation gives

$$\Delta Q_f = \Delta Q_{market} - \Delta Q_O$$

Dividing this expression by $\Delta P/P$ and Q_f and multiplying the terms on the right-hand side by Q_{market}/Q_{market} and Q_O/Q_O gives

$$\eta_{firm} = [\eta_{market}/(Q_f/Q_{market})] + [\epsilon_O/(Q_f/Q_O)],$$

where ε_O is the elasticity of supply of all other firms and Q_o is the output of all other firms.

In both cases, as market share increases, the firm's price elasticity of demand decreases in absolute value. This result is important because the greater a firm's price elasticity of demand (in absolute value), the less effect that firm has on market price, and thus the more likely that the firm is a price taker.

LEARNING EXERCISE 10.2

Solve the following problems.

a. If $\eta_{market} = -1$ and the firm's market share is 10 percent at the current equilibrium, find η_{firm}.
b. If $\eta_{market} = -1$ and $\eta_{firm} = -5$ at the current equilibrium, find the firm's market share.
c. If $\eta_{firm} = -5$ and the firm's market share is 2 percent at the current equilibrium, find η_{market}.

ASSUMPTION 3: ENTRY AND EXIT OF FIRMS IS UNRESTRICTED IN THE LONG RUN

This assumption implies that firms in a perfectly competitive industry are not hampered in their ability to mobilize and relocate resources in the long run. Firms may move from one business venture to another, moving labor and capital in pursuit of profit-making opportunities. As one venture becomes unprofitable, factors of production are sold or dismissed without consequence to the firm's owners. Although this assumption is probably satisfied in most industries, it may be unrealistic in some industries. Both the federal government and state governments impose restrictions on a firm's ability to enter certain businesses and its ability to dismiss its labor force. Firing without cause, for example, may lead to lawsuits, charges of discrimination, and damage payments by firms to dismissed employees. In addition, government restrictions in some industries, such as cable television and radio, limit the entry of new firms.

It is important to note that this is an assumption that applies to the *long run,* not the short run. In the short run, it is profitable to hold at least one factor of production fixed, so a firm is restricted from changing some of its inputs. Such a restriction implies that new firms will not enter this industry in the short run because entry requires new capital and capital (or another factor) is fixed. In the long run, however, no inputs are fixed, so entry and exit of new firms is not restricted by limits on the mobility of resources.

ASSUMPTION 4: INFORMATION IS SYMMETRICALLY DISTRIBUTED AMONG BUYERS AND SELLERS

This assumption implies that buyers and sellers have the same information. Without identical information, for example, a firm may not seek to increase its profits by adopting a cost-saving innovation used by a competitor. In addition, to take advantage of profitable opportunities in other markets, a firm must know about their existence. Consumers, too, require information to make rational choices. Without information about lower prices charged by competing firms, consumers may not substitute to competing products as relative prices change.

There are some cases in which information is not symmetrically distributed. Doctors, for example, may know more about the chances of survival from an operation than patients. Automobile mechanics may know more than customers about the operation of car engines. If the mechanic says that a tune-up is required, even though an oil change is all that is necessary, the consumer may consent to a tune-up rather than invest time and money to discover the truth. As we discussed in Chapter 7, asymmetric information between buyers and sellers is costly to the uninformed party.

A COMMENT ON THE ASSUMPTIONS OF PERFECT COMPETITION

Although we have been careful not to go overboard by claiming that these assumptions apply to all markets, the behavior they predict appears to be found in several different markets. We judge the validity of the model by seeing how accurately these assumptions predict the behavior of buyers and sellers and the market equilibrium, not whether every assumption is satisfied exactly as stated.

We may compare our interest in the perfectly competitive market structure to the interest that a physicist has in the equations defining the motion of planets. A physics teacher uses mathematically sophisticated equations to describe the motion of the planets in our solar system. To derive these equations, the physicist makes certain assumptions about the gravitational pull of the sun, the various planets, and the rest of the galaxy. Careful measurement by astronomers has shown that these assumptions are not exactly correct. Strictly speaking, the math does not *exactly* correspond with reality. But the orbits of the planets are very, very close to the orbits predicted by these equations, even with the errors that are known to exist. Because accurate predictions are what is important for satellite and space travel, these equations are used by NASA and taught to physics students.

By analogy, then, what is important is the accuracy of the predictions of the perfectly competitive model. Because these predictions help to explain reality in several different markets, the model is used by economists and taught to students studying economics.

10.2 The Perfectly Competitive Firm

In this section, we use the price-taking assumption to determine the conditions under which a firm will operate in the short run and to calculate its profit-maximizing output rate. With this information, we derive the firm's short- and long-run supply curves.

PROFIT-MAXIMIZING CONDITIONS

A perfectly competitive firm is a price taker, so it sells its output at the prevailing market price, *P*, and has the same as the cost structure as other firms. As a consequence, a perfectly competitive firm's profits can be written as

$$\pi(Q) = P \times Q - C(Q) \tag{10.1}$$

where $C(Q)$ is the firm's cost function and $P \times Q$ is the firm's total revenue.

Recall that the rule derived in Chapter 7 for profit maximization requires that managers select an output rate, Q^*, at which marginal revenue equals marginal cost: $MR(Q^*) = MC(Q^*)$. At this output rate, the difference between total revenue and total cost is largest. For the perfectly competitive firm, marginal revenue equals the market price. Marginal cost, however, may vary with output, as we saw in Chapter 9. The profit-maximizing rule for a perfectly competitive firm may thus be written as

$$P = MC(Q) \quad . \tag{10.2}$$

In the equation, *P* is the market price (or marginal revenue). The firm now tries to find an optimal output rate, Q^*, such that $P = MC(Q^*)$, in order to maximize profits.

Note that this profit-maximizing rule applies when the firm finds it optimal to operate. If it is optimal to shut down operations, we must modify the rule, which is explained below.

There is a second, technical condition that must hold if the rule that marginal revenue equals marginal cost defines a maximum instead of a minimum profit position. The second condition is that the slope of the marginal cost curve exceeds the slope of the marginal revenue curve:

$$\frac{\Delta MC(Q)}{\Delta Q} > \frac{\Delta MR(Q)}{\Delta Q} \tag{10.3}$$

For the perfectly competitive firm, $MR(Q) = P$ because of the price-taker assumption. Thus, the slope of the marginal revenue curve is zero because market price is not changing as the firm changes its output; that is, $\Delta P/\Delta Q = 0$. With a U-shaped cost curve, the marginal cost curve is expected to be positively sloped, so the condition given in equation (10.3) is generally satisfied. However, if the marginal cost curve is not upward-sloping at the output rate satisfying equation (10.2)—say because of economies of scale or increasing marginal returns—we must check to see if the second condition for profit maximization holds.

LEARNING EXERCISE 10.3

Suppose the marginal cost curve for a perfectly competitive firm is $MC(Q) = 10 + 2Q$ and the market price is \$30. What is the profit-maximizing output rate for this firm?

SHORT-RUN BEHAVIOR OF A PERFECTLY COMPETITIVE FIRM

In the short run, a profit-maximizing firm has fixed costs. Fixed costs are ignored in the calculation of marginal cost but are not ignored in the decision of whether the firm will actually produce. Let's investigate the short-run profit maximization decision with special reference to whether the firm will continue operations.

Short-Run Operating Position

Consider the QuickDisk Manufacturing Company, a firm operating in the computer disk industry, which is assumed to be perfectly competitive. The monthly cost and revenue structure of the QuickDisk Manufacturing Company is shown in panel (a) of Figure 10.1. The company has a fixed cost—mostly from equipment and building leases—of \$6,000 per month. Its short-run total cost curve, TC(Q), follows the classic shape described in Chapter 9: first, increasing marginal returns cause short-run total costs to increase at a decreasing rate; then, decreasing marginal returns cause short-run total costs to increase at an increasing rate. The short-run total cost curve thus has the familiar shoe-shaped profile.

The QuickDisk product, a rapid-access $3^1/_2$-inch formatted disk, competes for sales with rapid-access disk products sold by many other firms. The prevailing market price of a rapid-access disk is 50 cents. The total revenue curve, TR(Q), is a straight line extending out from the origin, with its slope, $\Delta TR(Q)/\Delta Q$, equal to market price, 50 cents.

The monthly profit curve, $\pi(Q)$, for the QuickDisk Manufacturing Company is shown in panel (b) of Figure 10.1. The firm maximizes monthly profits at the output rate of 90,000 disks per month. This output rate generates \$45,000 per month in total revenue at a total cost of \$36,000 per month, which produces a profit of \$9,000 per month for the firm's owners. Profit maximization requires that marginal revenue equal marginal cost at the optimal output rate. Because marginal revenue is the slope of the total revenue curve and marginal cost is the slope of the total cost curve, these two slopes must be equal at 90,000 units per month. Panel (a) in Figure 10.1 confirms this result. The slope of the total revenue curve is equal to market price, P, at all points along the curve. The dashed line that is tangent to the short-run total cost curve at 90,000 units is parallel to the total revenue curve, so we can claim that the slopes of these two curves are equal at this output rate. This result is equivalent to satisfying the condition in equation (10.2), which implies that the firm sets an output rate such that marginal cost equals the market price.

Even though we have not yet shown the marginal revenue and marginal cost curves, there is no doubt that 90,000 units per month is a maximum profit position because panel (a) in Figure 10.1 shows that total revenue lies above total cost at this output rate. The second, technical, condition for profit maximization is therefore satisfied.

Panel (b) in Figure 10.1 also shows that the QuickDisk Manufacturing Company first breaks even—profits are zero—on its operations at the output rate of 50,000 units per month. This is also true for the output rate of 110,000 units per month. As the graph shows, the firm is profitable for all output rates between 50,000 and 110,000 units per month, that is, for output rates between the two break-even points.

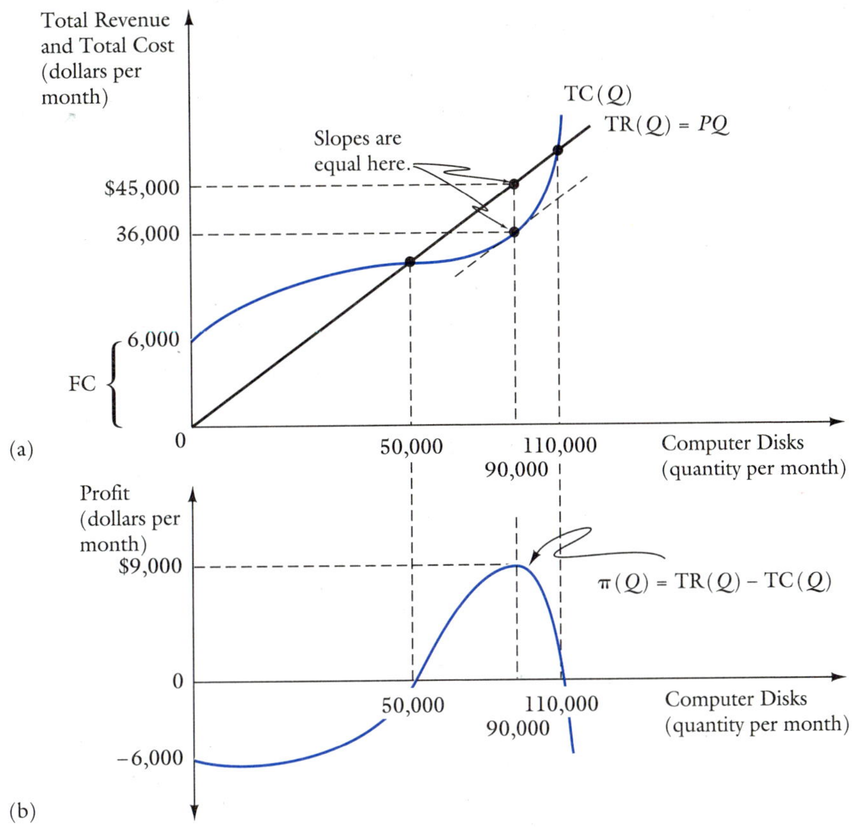

FIGURE 10.1

Total Revenue, Total Cost, and Profits for a Perfectly Competitive Firm in the Short Run

Panel (a) shows the typical shape of the short-run total cost and total revenue curves for QuickDisk Manufacturing Company, a perfectly competitive firm. The total revenue curve is a straight line because the firm is a price taker, so market price does not change with the firm's output rate. Panel (b) shows the profit function corresponding to these total revenue and total cost curves. QuickDisk breaks even at two output rates: 50,000 and 110,00 disks per month. At these output rates, total revenue equals total cost. Profits are maximized for QuickDisk at 90,000 disks per month. At these output rates, total revenue equals total cost. Profits are maximized for QuickDisk at 90,000 disks per month. At the profit-maximizing output rate, total revenue equals $45,000 and total cost equals $36,000 per month, so profit equals $9,000 per month.

Figure 10.2 shows the structure of marginal cost, marginal revenue, and average costs for the QuickDisk Manufacturing Company. The marginal and average cost curves have the familiar U-shaped appearance. In contrast, the marginal revenue curve is a straight line extending out from vertical axis at the level of market price. Because of the rule that price equals marginal cost at optimal output rates, the firm must find the output rate at which marginal cost equals 50 cents. As we have seen in Figure 10.1, this is an output rate of 90,000 units per month. For this output rate, short-run average total cost equals 40 cents per unit. The difference between price and average total cost is the profit per unit, which equals 10 cents. Short-run profits, shown as the shaded rectangular area in Figure 10.2, are computed by multiplying the profit per unit by the output rate.

The Incentive to Change Output Rates

Figure 10.2 helps us understand the incentive that the QuickDisk Manufacturing Company has to change output rates when it is not at the optimum position. Suppose that the firm is operating at the break-even rate of 50,000 units per month. At this output rate, marginal revenue, *P*, exceeds the

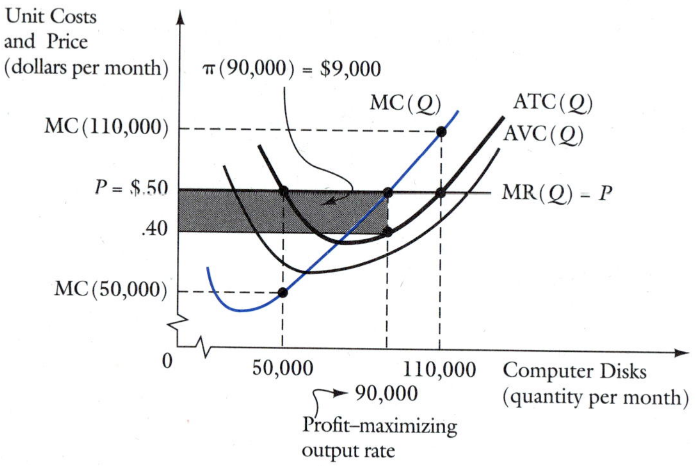

FIGURE 10.2

Short-Run Marginal Cost, Marginal Revenue, and Average Costs for a Perfectly Competitive Firm

The revenue and cost profile of QuickDisk Manufacturing Company may be seen from its average and marginal cost curves and its marginal revenue curve. Market price, *P*, equals marginal revenue for QuickDisk because it is a perfectly competitive firm. The firm maximizes profits at 90,000 disks per month, the output rate at which price equals marginal cost [$P = MC(Q)$]. Profits of \$9,000 per month are given by the shaded rectangle, which is equal to [$P - ATC(90{,}000)$] × 90,000. On sales of 50,000 and 110,000 disks per month, QuickDisk breaks even because market price equals average total cost at these output rates.

firm's marginal cost, MC(50,000).[1] Such a situation tells the firm's managers than an increase in the output rate adds *P* dollars to total revenue and MC(50,000) dollars to total costs. Thus, a one-unit change in the output rate causes profits to increase by *P* – MC(50,000) dollars, a positive amount. Increasing the output rate from this position will then make the firm's owners wealthier, which is expected to be rewarding to managers.

Consider the other break-even point, *Q* = 110,000 units per month. At this output rate, marginal cost, MC(110,000), exceeds marginal revenue, *P*, so an extra unit of output adds more to total cost than to total revenue. If a manager increases output from this position, total profits will decrease. But a *decrease* in the output rate will reverse this situation. A decrease in the output rate by one unit will lower total cost by MC(110,000) dollars, which is more than the loss in total revenue, *P*. The profit-maximizing manager will then decrease the output rate whenever marginal cost exceeds marginal revenue.

We can see that the process of increasing or decreasing the output rate stops at only one operating position: the position at which the firm's marginal revenue is equal to its marginal cost. This iterative story is the basic reason that equation (10.2) is a necessary condition for profit maximization by perfectly competitive firms. If these firms do not operate at the output rate for which price equals marginal cost, then there will be a continuing incentive to change the output rate to increase the wealth of the firm's owners.

Shutdown Decision

It is clear that the QuickDisk Manufacturing Company is in a desirable position if it is earning $9,000 per month from its operations. We can say this because the $9,000 represents economic profits, not accounting profits. Recall that the cost curve includes all opportunity costs, not just paid expenses. This firm is earning profits after all opportunity costs are taken into account, so its owners are earning more than they could earn elsewhere.

Although the present operating position is desirable, market demand may change for the disks that the QuickDisk Manufacturing Company produces, causing the firm's managers to change their operating strategy. Figure 10.3, on page 374, considers two such possibilities.

In panel (a) of Figure 10.3, the prospect of a new high-density disk coming on the market in the near future decreased market demand, thus reducing market price to 35 cents per disk. Even though this price is below its average total cost of production, the QuickDisk Manufacturing Company will continue to operate in the short run. Let's find out why. Marginal cost is equal to the new market price when the firm produces 40,000 units per month. The average total cost is $.38 and the average variable cost is $.23 at this output rate. Total revenues are equal to $14,000 per month ($.35 × 40,000) and total costs are equal to $15,200 per month ($.38 × 40,000). The firm is thus losing $1,200 per month from its operations. Now, if the owners close the company down and suspend all sales, they must continue to pay the fixed costs of the

[1] Note that MC(50,000) is the marginal cost of producing the fifty thousandth unit; it is not MC times 50,000.

firm, which are equal to \$6,000 per month. Logically, then, the owners prefer to lose \$1,200 per month in the short run by continuing to operate than to lose \$6,000 per month by closing down.

Panel (b) in Figure 10.3 shows market price for disks after a large Japanese company announced that all its computers will be made solely compatible with a new high-density disk that the QuickDisk Manufacturing Company *does not* produce. The market price for the QuickDisk product decreases to \$.15 per disk. Price is equal to the firm's marginal cost at an output rate of 30,000 units per month. For this output rate, average total cost is equal to \$.42 and average variable cost is equal to \$.22. Total revenue equals \$4,500 per month (\$.15 × 30,000) and total cost equals \$12,600 per month (\$.42 × 30,000). The firm is now losing \$8,100 per month from its operations. It is now optimal for the firm to close its doors. The firm will continue to lose the \$6,000 per month of fixed cost in the short run, but this is less than the \$8,100 per month it loses by operating.

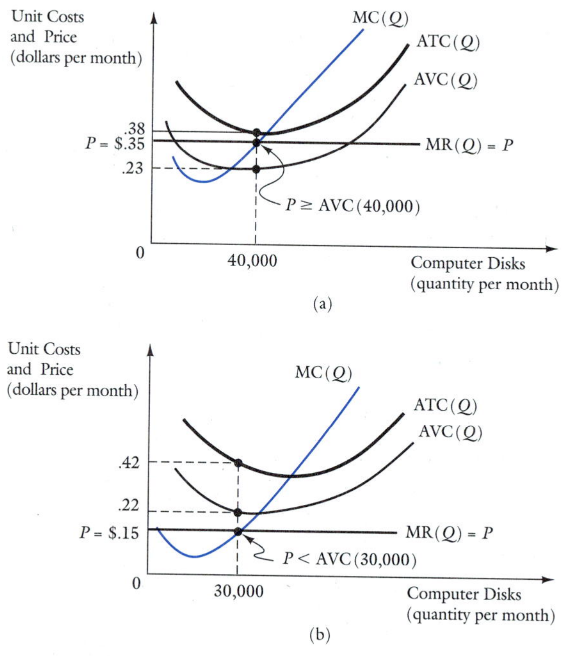

FIGURE 10.3

The Shutdown Decision in the Short Run

Average revenue to a perfectly competitive firm equals market price. As shown in panel (a), if market price equals or exceeds average variable cost, QuickDisk continues to operate in the short run. In this position, it loses less by operating—selling only 40,000 disks per month—than by shutting down. As panel (b) shows, if price falls below the average variable cost of production, the firm shuts down in the short run; its loss of fixed costs during shutdown is less than its operating losses at a market price of 15 cents per disk.

Shutdown Rule
A firm ceases operating if its average revenue is less than its average variable costs.

There is a basic rule, called the **shutdown rule,** that determines whether a firm shuts down in the short run.

If a firm's average revenue from operations is *less than* the minimum of its average variable cost curve, then the firm closes down.

A firm's average revenue is equal to total revenue divided by the number of units sold: $TR(Q)/Q$. For perfectly competitive firms, average revenue equals market price, P, a constant. So, the shutdown rule requires owners to compare market price to average variable cost:

$$\text{Shut down if } P < \text{minimum of the AVC}(Q) \text{ curve} \qquad (10.4)$$

This is a short-run rule; its corollary is that the owners of the firm should stay in business if $P \geq$ minimum of the AVC curve in the short run. (The firm is actually indifferent if P equals the minimum of AVC.)

The shutdown rule can be applied to the operations of the whole company or to parts of a company. Suppose, for example, that the QuickDisk Manufacturing Company owned two manufacturing plants, one in the United States and one overseas. Suppose further that the U.S. plant has higher labor costs than the overseas plant, so its average variable cost curve lies above the average variable costs curve for the overseas plant. As market price falls, the company will close down the U.S. plant first because the rule that P is less than the minimum of the AVC(Q) curve will apply to this plant before it applies to the overseas plant. This rule, then, explains why companies systematically close their older manufacturing plants during economic downturns—these plants have higher average variable costs.

Learning Exercise 10.4

The following table shows the short-run cost structure for a typical firm. Below what price will this firm shut down? (Hint: You must compute the AVC for each output rate.)

Output	*TC*	*TVC*
0	$100	$ 0
1	150	50
2	180	80
3	205	105
4	260	160
5	325	225

$$$ Price Theory in Practice

Fixed Costs in a Recession

At the worst point in of the 1990–1991 recession, retail stores across the United States filed for bankruptcy at the rate of about 100 per month. The performance of the $160 billion retail industry during that economic slowdown provides an interesting picture of the shutdown decision faced by firms.

We know from our discussion of the shutdown decision that a firm continues to operate if its average revenue exceeds its average variable cost. Now, in a recession the prices paid for nearly all goods tend to fall. Relative prices may also change, but it is the decline in the general level of prices that affects firms equally. If firms begin the recession by breaking even on their sales, then, as prices fall, firms with low fixed costs are likely be the first to shut down because it is more profitable to shut down rather than continue to operate.

The high rate of bankruptcy among retail stores can be partly explained by the shutdown model. Retail stores—in contrast to manufacturing firms—have relatively low fixed costs. Costs in retail stores are dominated by merchandise charges and sales and promotional payments. This means that the gap between the average variable and average total cost curves is small for most retail stores. As a result, retail stores operating near the minimum of the average total cost curve cannot absorb a very large drop in merchandise prices, which is what happens as the demand for retail goods declines during a recession.

Bankruptcies during the 1990–1991 recession occurred, as the shutdown model predicted, among the small to medium-sized retail outlets, generally with annual sales of less than $50 million. The experience of Abrahams Brothers in New York is typical of many small retailers. The medium-sized family-owned firm had been in the retail business since 1911. In early 1991, though, it found that bankruptcy was preferred to the ongoing losses caused by the recession. In contrast, Jamesway Corporation, a retailer with most of its stores in the Northeast, had revenues of $855 million in 1991 and lost $22 million during the recession, but it continued to operate. Jamesway had approximately $110 million in long-term debt to service—its fixed cost—so shutting down in the short run was not a profitable option.

Firms sometimes adopt a conscious strategy of accepting a mix of large and small fixed-cost plants with the thought that the large fixed-cost operation can continue to operate while the small fixed-cost operation shuts down (temporarily) in the short run. Electrical utility companies use this strategy when they produce electricity. The large fixed-cost plants—often nuclear plants—operate continuously, while the smaller fixed cost plants—called peakers—come on line when demand increases significantly. Many electrical utilities can charge customers (industrial and commercial) more during the peak periods, which allows them to adopt a pricing strategy that is consistent with the shutdown model.

LEARNING EXERCISE 10.5

Test the predictions of the shutdown model yourself. Compare 1991 and 1992 editions of the Yellow Pages for your region of the country. Do you find more small (i.e., low-fixed-cost) firms out of business in 1992?

SHORT-RUN SUPPLY FOR A PERFECTLY COMPETITIVE FIRM

Short-Run Supply Curve
The curve that shows the output rate of a firm in the short run at various market prices.

The **short-run supply curve** for the perfectly competitive firm is derived from the answer to the question "At a market price of P, what will you produce?"

The answer is found in our analysis of the firm's shutdown decision. If the firm continues to operate, it produces the output rate that equates price and marginal cost.

> **The segment of the marginal cost curve above (and equal to) the minimum of the AVC curve is then the firm's supply curve.**

If the market price is such that $P < \text{AVC}(Q)$, at the output rate where market price equals marginal cost the firm does not operate, so output is zero. Figure 10.4 describes this situation.

In Figure 10.4, we see that if the firm operates, the supply curve equals the segment of the marginal cost curve that lies on or above the minimum of the average variable cost curve. If market price falls *below* the minimum of the average variable cost curve, then the supply curve jumps to the small segment on the vertical axis at which there is zero output. These two discontinuous pieces define the short-run supply curve for the perfectly competitive firm.

LEARNING EXERCISE 10.6

Suppose a new government regulation requires egg distributors to test one out of every 500 eggs for bacterial growth. How does the new regulation affect the average and marginal cost curves in the egg industry? How is the supply curve of a perfectly competitive egg distributor affected in the short run?

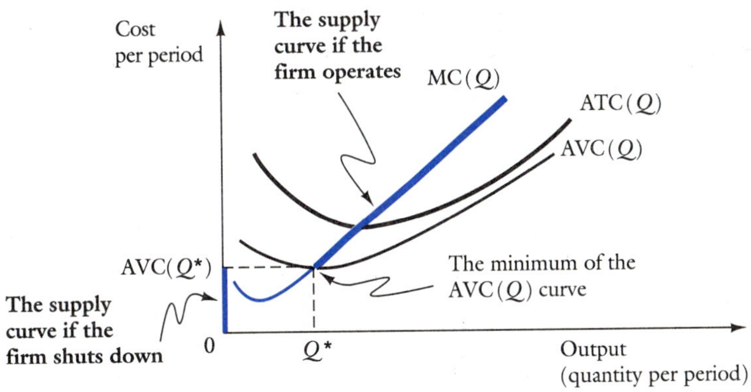

FIGURE 10.4

The Short-Run Supply Curve for a Perfectly Competitive Firm

The supply curve of a perfectly competitive firm in the short run equals its short-run marginal cost curve for all market prices that equal or exceed the minimum of its average variable cost curve, AVC(Q^*). The firm enters the market producing an output rate of at least Q^*. At market prices below AVC(Q^*), the firm shuts down, so its supply is zero.

LONG-RUN SUPPLY FOR A PERFECTLY COMPETITIVE FIRM

The **long-run supply curve** for the perfectly competitive firm is derived from the answer to the same question that generates the short-run supply curve. The difference is that the firm does not face any fixed costs in the long run. Without fixed costs, the shutdown decision is simplified:

Long-Run Supply Curve
The curve that shows the output rate of a firm in the long run at various market prices.

> **In the long run, a firm will shut down operations if *P* is less than the minimum of the long-run average total cost (LATC) curve.**

In contrast, the firm will operate in the long run if *P* is greater than or equal to the minimum of the LATC curve. Figure 10.5 describes this situation.

To maximize profits, the firm's managers continue to select an output rate at which market price equals marginal cost, except that in the long run, marginal cost is defined by the long-run marginal cost curve (LMC). In Figure 10.5, we see that the supply curve equals the vertical axis when firms shut down, and it equals the segment of the LMC curve that lies equal to or above the minimum of the LATC curve when firms operate.

It is informative to compare the short- and long-run supply curves for a perfectly competitive firm. Recall from Chapter 9 that all short-run marginal cost curves intersect the long-run marginal cost curve at the output rate at which the long-run average total cost curve intersects the short-run average total cost curve. Near these intersection points, long-run average total cost is *less than* the short-run average total cost, so short-run marginal cost increases faster than long-run marginal cost. Marginal cost increases faster in the short run because the firm is constrained in its choice of inputs. This implies that the

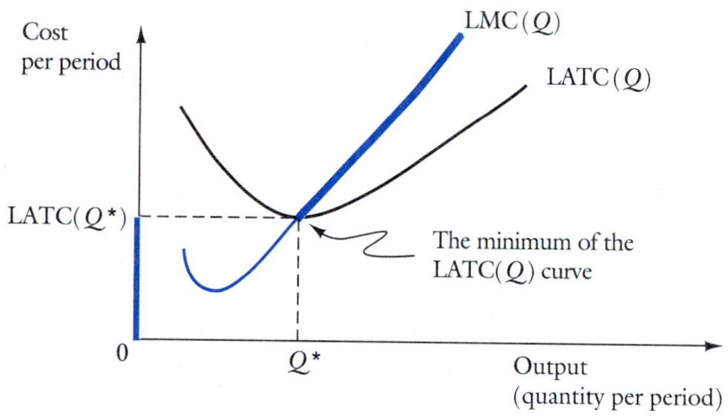

FIGURE 10.5

The Long-Run Supply Curve for a Perfectly Competitive Firm

The long-run supply curve for a perfectly competitive firm equals the segment of its long-run marginal cost curve (LMC) that equals or exceeds the minimum of its long-run average total cost curve (LATC). In the figure, the minimum of the LATC curve occurs at an output rate of Q^*. Thus, market prices below LATC(Q^*) cause the firm to withdraw from the market; that is, it is no longer in this industry. This is shown as the segment of the long-run supply curve that lies on the vertical axis.

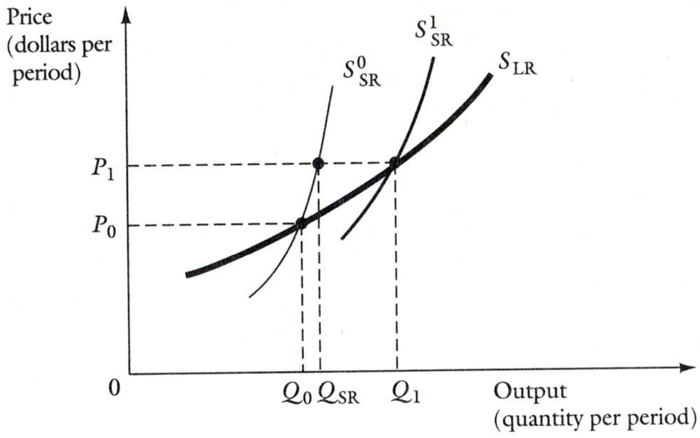

FIGURE 10.6

Comparing the Short- and Long-Run Supply Curves for a Perfectly Competitive Firm

The long-run supply curve for a perfectly competitive firm is more elastic than any of its short-run supply curves. A market price increase from P_0 to P_1 causes quantity supplied in the short run to increase from Q_0 to Q_{SR} along supply curve S^0_{SR}. In contrast, quantity supplied in the long run increases from Q_0 to Q_1 for the same price change.

short-run marginal cost curves are steeper than the long-run marginal cost curve, which implies that the short-run supply curve—when the firm operates—is steeper than the long-run marginal cost curve. This situation is shown in Figure 10.6.

The two short-run supply curves shown in Figure 10.6, S^0_{SR} and S^1_{SR}, reveal that the firm has more flexibility to change its costs and output in the long run than in the short run. For a given price change, for example, the output response is greater in the long run than in the short run. If the firm is operating on the short-run supply curve, S^0_{SR}, and market price increases from P_0 to P_1, the firm's response is to increase the output rate from Q_0 to Q_{SR}. In the long run, however, the firm increases the output rate from Q_0 to Q_1. We can conclude that the long-run supply curve of a perfectly competitive firm is more elastic than any given short-run supply curve for the same firm.

10.3 The Perfectly Competitive Market in the Short Run

We have shown how a competitive firm responds to short-run changes in market price. Our task now is to describe how the short-run responses of each individual firm combine to form a market response to changes in price. The short-run market supply curve is the representation of these combined responses. By linking this curve with the market demand curve, we can define the market equilibrium price and quantity for the perfectly competitive market in the short run.

TEMPORARY ASSUMPTIONS: NUMBER OF FIRMS AND INPUT PRICES

Our analysis uses two additional assumptions. *The first assumption is that the number of firms in the industry is fixed in the short run.* We are holding at least one input fixed in the short run; usually it is the amount of capital. If this restriction is optimal for one firm, then it is optimal for all other firms, both those in the market and those that might consider entering the industry. Those that are not in the market are constrained to stay out of the market in the short run because it is not profitable for them to begin production without using the input that is fixed. When we discuss the long run, we will drop this assumption.

The second assumption is that the industry has no effect *on input prices or the opportunity cost of any resources used in the production process.* By "no effect" we mean that a change in the output of all firms in the market, which requires the use of more variable inputs, will not change the per unit price paid for these inputs. If you can hire labor for $10 per hour to work in your manufacturing plant and then decide to increase output, we are assuming that you can hire additional labor for $10 per hour. Your wage bill will increase, but the price you pay per hour will not.

This fixed-cost-of-inputs assumption allows us to add together the individual firm's supply curves without worrying that they may be shifting up or down because factor prices are changing. We will relax this assumption after we have shown how to derive the market supply curve for a perfectly competitive market.

SHORT-RUN SUPPLY FOR THE PERFECTLY COMPETITIVE MARKET

The symmetry-of-information assumption gives each firm access to the most efficient—that is, least-cost—production process. Thus, the short-run market supply curve can be defined by summing the short-run firm supply curves. In effect, we are asking, "At a given price, what is the quantity supplied by *all* firms in the market?" The answer is the sum of the individual supply curves, as we first explained in Chapter 2. Figure 10.7 illustrates this situation.

Figure 10.7 shows three firms—firm A, firm B, and firm C—operating in the industry. Each firm is assumed to have an identical supply curve, which is indicated by the equality $S_A = S_B = S_C$. The shutdown output rate for each of these firms is denoted by Q. The market supply curve, S_{market}, is equal to the sum of the three supply curves, $S_A + S_B + S_C$. Note two characteristics about the market supply curve: It begins at the output rate $3Q$, and it is flatter than the supply curve of each firm. The beginning output rate is a consequence of the shutdown output rate for each individual firm. In effect, with the cost structure the same for all firms, the whole industry will shut down if the market price falls below the minimum of the average variable cost curve of any firm. The flatness of the market supply curve is caused by our summation across quantity, holding price fixed. Note that even though market supply is flatter than each firm's supply curve, it has the same elasticity because the firm supply curves are identical.

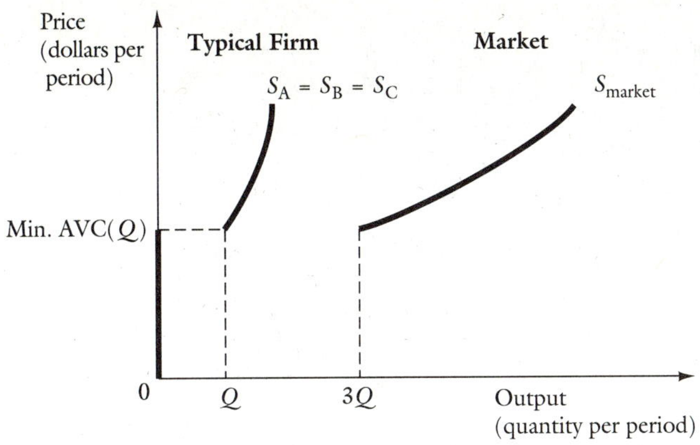

FIGURE 10.7

The Short-Run Market Supply Curve

Suppose that there are three identical firms, A, B, and C, in a perfectly competitive market. The supply curve of each firm is the same: $S_A = S_B = S_C$. The supply curve for the industry, S_{market}, equals the (horizontal) sum of the three individual supply curves. If each firm enters the market producing Q at a price equal to the minimum of the AVC curve, then the industry supply curve starts at the output rate of $3Q$ at this price. (Note that the industry supply curve is more elastic than any individual firm's supply curve.)

The Factor Price Effect

Factor Price Effect
The effect the change in output for the whole industry has on factor prices, causing average and marginal cost curves to shift.

Suppose that we relax our assumption that the industry can purchase any quantity of inputs at a fixed per unit price in the short run. Instead, suppose the price paid for inputs *increases* if all firms try to expand output at the same time. We call this the **factor price effect.** (Note that we may continue to assume that a *single* firm cannot influence factor prices.) How will the factor price effect change the shape of the market supply curve? Figure 10.8 on page 382 shows the answer to this question.

Each firm must pay more for its variable factors of production when it—and every other firm—expands output. Thus, the marginal cost curve of each firm shifts upward. The firm requires a higher price to supply a given quantity of output than previously. In effect, the supply curve of each firm shifts up to S_{all}.[2] Summing this curve over all three firms gives a new aggregate supply curve for the industry, $S_{total\ all}$, which lies above the market supply curve derived when there was no factor price effect.

The $S_{total\ all}$ curve is not the new market supply curve. It is simply the sum of the individual firm's supply curves when they all face a higher factor cost. The new market supply curve shows us how the industry responds as factor costs increase from the old to the new level, or to any level beyond the new or

[2] If only one firm changes output, however, the supply curve would remain the same; that is, it would equal the $S_A = S_B = S_C$ curve.

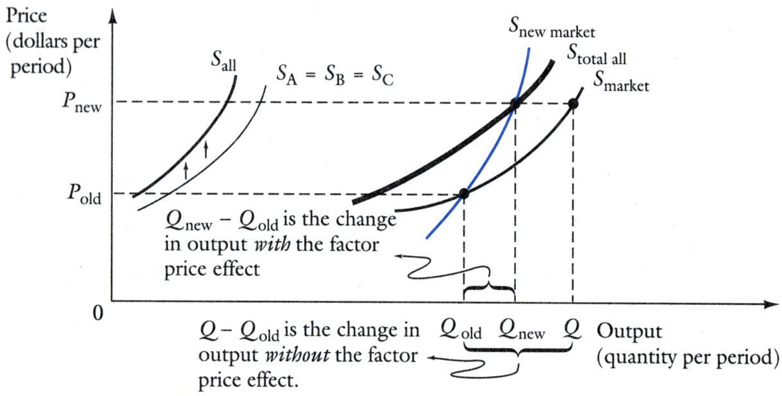

FIGURE 10.8

The Effects of Increasing Factor Prices on Industry Supply

Increasing factor costs cause the average and marginal cost curves to shift up as industry output increases and thus cause a firm's supply curve to shift up. The curve $S_A = S_B = S_C$ is the supply curve for three of the firms in the industry *without* the increasing-factor-cost effect. The market price without the increasing-factor-cost effect is P_{old}. The curve S_{all} is the supply curve for the typical firm *with* the increasing-factor-cost effect *given* that the market price is P_{new}. The S_{market} curve is the supply curve for the industry *without* the increasing-factor-cost effect. The $S_{total\ all}$ curve is the sum of the S_{all} curves across all firms. This is not the industry supply curve. The $S_{new\ market}$ curve shows the industry supply curve with the factor price effect. The $S_{new\ market}$ curve intersects S_{market} and $S_{total\ all}$ curves at the point where market price also intersects these curves. A given price change, P_{old} to P_{new}, causes a smaller change in quantity supplied with the increasing factor cost effect than without it: $Q_{new} - Q_{old}$ compared to $Q - Q_{old}$.

below the old. The $S_{total\ all}$ curve can help us derive the new market supply curve because they share one point in common: the new equilibrium output rate for the industry.

If P_{new} is the new equilibrium price, then Q_{new} is the new output rate for the industry. Similarly, if P_{old} is the equilibrium price before an increase in industry output caused factor prices to change, then Q_{old} is the previous equilibrium output rate. The new market supply curve, $S_{new\ market}$, includes both of these points as shown in Figure 10.8.

We can see that the factor price effect causes the new market supply curve to become less elastic, or less responsive to market price changes. In Figure 10.8, as price increases from P_{old} to P_{new}, the change in quantity supplied by the industry *without* the factor price effect is given by $Q - Q_{old}$ from market supply curve S_{market}. The change in quantity supplied *with* the factor price effect, however, is only $Q_{new} - Q_{old}$, which is from market supply curve $S_{new\ market}$. As Figure 10.8 shows, $(Q_{new} - Q_{old}) < (Q - Q_{old})$, so the factor price effect causes quantity supplied by the industry to be less responsive to changes in the market price.

LEARNING EXERCISE 10.7

Suppose that input prices decrease as the industry expands its output rate. How does this affect the elasticity of the market supply curve?

The Effects of More Efficient Firms

The symmetry-of-information assumption implies that perfectly competitive firms have the same cost structure. When we relax this assumption, we can still define a market supply curve following the steps above. We do not want to toss out the whole assumption, however, because it implies more than just identical costs across firms. For example, it implies that firms have information on profitable ventures in other industries. But let's relax the requirement that all firms' marginal and average costs are the same. Figure 10.9 illustrates the effects that a varying cost structure has on the market supply curve in the short run.

Figure 10.9 shows three firms, firm A, firm B, and firm C, with differential costs. Firm A is the most cost-efficient, so its supply curve, S_A, lies below the supply curve of firm B, S_B, and the supply curve of firm C, S_C. Firm B is the next-most cost efficient, so its supply curve lies below that of firm C. Each of these firms will shut down at a different market price. Firm A will shut down if the market price is below P_0, firm B will shut down if the market price is below

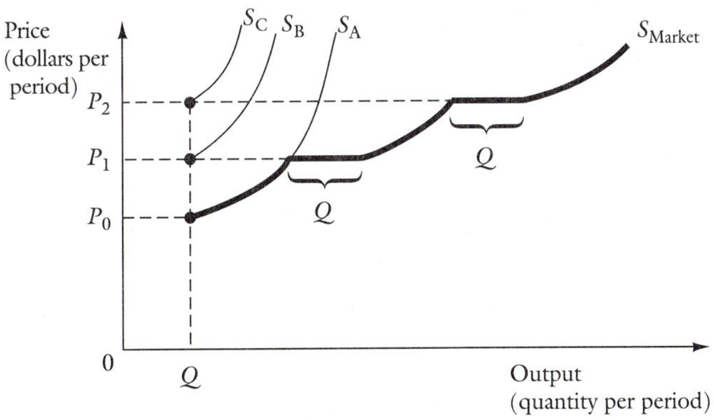

FIGURE 10.9

The Short-Run Supply Curve When There Are More Efficient Firms

When firms vary in their level of costs, they may enter the market at different market prices. In the figure, firm A is the most cost efficient, firm B the next-most cost efficient, and firm C the least cost efficient. The market supply curve begins at an output rate of Q when market price is P_0. It moves along the supply curve of firm A, S_A, until firm B enters the market at a price of P_1. It then takes a horizontal jump of length Q and continues to increase until firm C enters the market at a price of P_2. The entry of firm C causes another horizontal jump of length Q, after which the supply curve increases continuously.

P_1, and firm C will shut down if the market price is below P_2. Analogously, the different shutdown prices represent different entry prices. For simplicity, each firm produces Q at its entry price.

The market supply curve is again the sum of the individual firm's supply curves. In contrast to Figure 10.7, the market supply curve is identical to firm A's supply curve for market prices between P_0 and P_1. At prices above P_1, the market supply curve includes the supply of firm B; then, at prices above P_2, it includes the supply of firm C. So, short-run market supply flattens out and moves away from the individual firm supply curves when market price rises above P_1.

It is important to note that in a perfectly competitive market, varying levels of efficiency are sustainable in the short run but not in the long run. In the long run, the symmetry-of-information assumption, entry, and the mobility of inputs all act to drive inefficient firms out of the market. Thus, if firm B and firm C desire to remain in this industry in the long run, they must learn the efficient practices of firm A.

SHORT-RUN MARKET EQUILIBRIUM

The equilibrium price in a perfectly competitive market is the one that equates quantity demanded to quantity supplied for the entire market. We have shown how the market supply curve is derived under three scenarios, so now all we need in order to define the equilibrium price and quantity is a market demand curve. Figure 10.10 introduces a market demand curve to the perfectly competitive industry described in our first scenario (represented by Figure 10.7).

To make the analysis more specific, however, we use the video rental industry in Pembroke Pines, Florida, as our example. In this town, there are three competitive video stores. Three stores is a small number, but entry is costless, so these stores act like perfectly competitive firms. Each firm has the same marginal and average cost structure in the short run. These cost curves are shown for the typical firm (TF) on the left side of Figure 10.10.

The supply curve of the typical firm is shown as S_{TF}. The three firms will each shut down if the market price falls *below* \$2.25 per video rental, so the firm supply curve jumps to the vertical axis—where zero is produced—for prices less than \$2.25. At a market price of \$2.25, all three firms operate in the short run, each supplying 500 video rentals per day. Market supply, then, begins at 1,500 video rentals per day (3 × 500) when the market price is \$2.25.

The daily market demand in Pembroke Pines, Florida, is given by D_{market}. The market reaches an equilibrium at a price (P^*) of \$4 per video rental. At this price, the three video stores rent 1,800 videos per day. In turn, each store rents $Q^* = 600$ videos per day at the market equilibrium price. The typical firm's average total cost is \$3 per video rental per day at this output rate. The profit per video rental per day equals market price minus average total cost, (P^* – ATC*). Substituting for P^* and ATC* gives \$4 – \$3 = \$1 as the profit per video rental per day. The *total* profit per day for the typical firm equals the

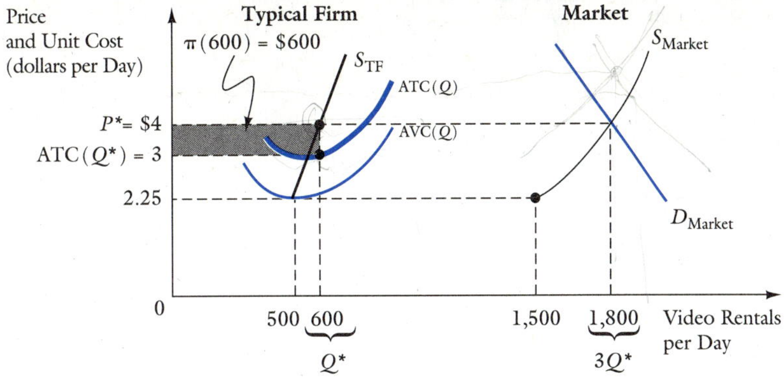

FIGURE 10.10

The Market for Video Rentals in Pembroke Pines, Florida

The market for video rentals in Pembroke Pines has three perfectly competitive firms. The supply curve of the typical firm is given by S_{TF}. The market supply and demand curves are shown on the right-hand side of the figure. In the *short run*, the market is in equilibrium at a price of P^* = \$4 per video rental. Each firm maximizes profits by renting 600 videos per day at an average total cost, ATC, of \$3 per video rental. The three firms supply a total of 1,800 video rentals daily at the market clearing price. Daily profit for the typical firm equals \$600 [(\$4 – \$3) × 600 rentals]. Note that the daily profit is an economic profit; these firms are receiving more than the opportunity cost of the resources they are using to rent videos.

profit per video rental per day times the number of daily video rentals: $(P^* - \text{ATC}^*) \times Q^*$. Substituting the appropriate amounts into this expression gives profit per day of \$600 for the typical store, which is represented by the shaded area in Figure 10.10.

These profits are economic profits because our cost curves include *all* opportunity costs these video firms incur when they operate. In this light, the owners of these three video firms are delighted with the current market equilibrium, because it offers a return that exceeds what they could earn elsewhere on the resources they have invested in these stores. The number of firms is fixed in the short run, but as we move to the long run, the existence of economic profits will attract firms to this business and location. In a sense, then, the owners of these three firms can expect more competition in the future.

LEARNING EXERCISE 10.8

Answer the following questions from Figure 10.10 assuming that the three firms operate 365 days each year and that the AVC of 600 video rentals equals \$2.35.

a. What is the annual fixed cost of the typical video firm?
b. What are the annual profits of the typical firm?
c. What is the average total cost of renting 500 videos per day in the typical firm?

10.4 Perfect Competition in the Long Run

Our analysis of the short-run behavior of perfectly competitive firms holds the number of firms fixed. With a fixed number of firms, we can add together the individual firm supply curves to define the market supply curve; a fixed number of firms tells us when to stop adding. In the long run, however, the number of firms in the industry is variable, with economic profits acting to cause entry and economic losses acting to cause exit. Our summation of supply curves, holding the number of firms fixed, is no longer a valid approach to determining the market supply curve. To explain how we compute the long-run market supply curve, we first develop the effects of economic profits and losses on entry, exit, and industry equilibrium.

Economic Profits and Losses Will Cause Entry and Exit

Economic profit equals total revenue minus total cost, but what is important is that total cost includes the opportunity costs of all resources used in production. If economic profits are positive, the owners of a firm earn more than they could earn if they invest in any other—not just the next-best-alternative investment. The symmetry-of-information assumption guarantees that others will learn about positive economic profits if they exist. With this information and information about how existing businesses operate, new entry is assured. New entrants can make the same calculation that existing entrants make, so a new entrant's investment earns more in an industry with positive economic profits than in any other industry.

Entry will continue until the increased supply has reduced market price to a point at which there are zero economic profits.

Similarly, economic losses cause firms to leave an industry as they find that they are not covering all of their opportunity costs. From this analysis, we can conclude that

All firms earn zero economic profits in the long run.

Although we have made the point elsewhere, you should remember that it is economic profits, not accounting profits, that matter here. Accounting profits may disguise economic profits, so an accounting statement is not a reliable guide to whether a firm is expected to enter or exit an industry.

Long-Run Equilibrium

The information that all firms earn zero economic profits in the long run reveals the exact operating position of each firm. Because all firms maximize profits, they find an output rate at which market price equals marginal cost: $P = MC(Q^*)$.[3] But the zero-profit condition requires that market price equals

[3] Assuming, of course, that the second condition for profit maximization is satisfied at this output rate.

the long-run average total cost of producing the optimal output rate: $P = \text{LATC}(Q^*)$. Because long-run economic profits, $\pi(Q)$, can be written as $\pi(Q) = [P - \text{LATC}(Q)] \times Q$, the firm earns zero economic profits only when $P = \text{LATC}(Q^*)$. These two conditions, profit maximization and zero profits, require that marginal cost equal average total cost at the optimal output rate: $\text{MC}(Q^*) = \text{LATC}(Q^*)$. Our analysis of costs in Chapter 9 shows that if the average cost curves are U-shaped, then the marginal cost curve equals the average total cost curve at the minimum of the average total cost curve. Combining these results, we can now define the firm's long-run operating position:

> **Entry and exit forces perfectly competitive firms to a long-run output rate, Q^*, at which market price equals the minimum of the long-run average total cost curve.**

Although this statement represents an equilibrium for each firm *and* for the total number of firms, it is an equilibrium for the industry, too, if the resulting market price equates quantity demanded to quantity supplied for the whole market. With the additional caveat that the market must clear at the price that is equal to the minimum of the long-run average total cost curve, the above statement represents the condition for long-run equilibrium in a perfectly competitive industry.

> **This condition implies that a perfectly competitive firm produces its output rate at the lowest possible cost in the long run.**

This situation is illustrated in Figure 10.11 on page 388.

The left-hand side of Figure 10.11 shows the long-run average total cost and marginal cost curves and the long-run supply curve for the typical firm. The supply curve for the typical firm, S_{TF}, is equal to the segment of the long-run marginal cost curve, $\text{LMC}(Q)$, that is equal to or above the minimum of the $\text{LATC}(Q)$ curve. We use the long-run marginal cost curve to define a typical firm's supply response because firms can adjust the use of all inputs in the long run. Although the number of firms is *not fixed* in the long run, we assume that the entry of new firms is not immediate, so we use the $\text{LMC}(Q)$ curve to locate a profit-maximizing output rate.

To begin, let's assume that the industry is initially not in a long-run equilibrium. There are currently 45 firms in the industry. Each firm can adjust along its long-run marginal and average cost curves in response to a change in price, but eventually economic profits will lead to entry of other firms. The supply curve, $S_{45\text{ firms}}$, represents the sum of a typical firm's supply curve—that is, the $\text{LMC}(Q)$ curve—for all 45 firms. The market demand curve is given by D_{market}, so the present market clearing price equals P_0. At this price, the typical firm produces Q_0 per period and earns an economic profit of $\pi(Q_0) > 0$.

Positive economic profits attract new firms to this industry in the long run. Within an appropriate period of time, 5 new firms enter the industry, which increases the total quantity supplied to the market. The supply curve $S_{50\text{ firms}}$ represents the sum of the typical firm's supply curve—again, the $\text{LMC}(Q)$ curve—for all 50 firms. The new market clearing price is P^*, which is also

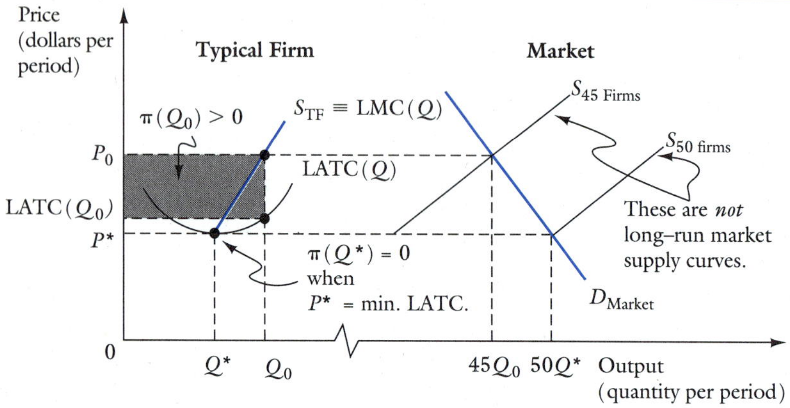

FIGURE 10.11

The Long-Run Equilibrium Price and Quantity for a Perfectly Competitive Market

In the long run, economic profits attract entry. The market is in short-run equilibrium with 45 firms, each producing Q_0 per period, for a total market output of $45Q_0$ at the market clearing price of P_0. Profits for the typical firm are positive, $\pi(Q_0)$, at this price. Entry of 5 firms causes an increase in the quantity supplied to the market. Each firm produces Q^* which is less than Q_0 at the new market clearing price of P^*. At the new market clearing price, profits for the typical firm are zero, $\pi(Q^*) = 0$, so there is no incentive for additional firms to enter the market. The market is in long-run equilibrium at a price of P^* and a total output rate of $50Q^*$.

equal to the *minimum* of the typical firm's long-run average total cost curve. At this price, the typical firm produces Q^* per period and earns zero economic profits. With zero economic profits, there is no incentive for new firms to enter or existing firms to exit this industry.[4] The industry and all firms are now in long-run equilibrium. The long-run equilibrium is characterized by a market clearing price of P^*, a quantity transacted by the market of $50Q^*$, and a total of 50 firms operating in the industry.

Table 10.1 summarizes the results of both the long-run and short-run behavior of a perfectly competitive firm. As you may deduce, the no-entry and profit-maximizing conditions imply that $P = LMC$ = minimum of LATC if the firm operates, which is the result we found earlier.

LEARNING EXERCISE 10.9

If the market demand curve decreases in the long run, what is the adjustment mechanism? Does the output rate of each firm change, do the number of firms change, or both?

[4] Technically, the incentive to exit depends on the economic profits in other industries. If opportunity costs are computed correctly, zero economic profits implies that there are no known positive economic profits that the owners of these firms can capture in other industries.

TABLE 10.1

Short- and Long-Run Equilibrium Conditions for the Perfectly Competitive Firm

	Short Run	Long Run
Profit Maximization Rule: If firms operate, they select quantity using this rule.	$P = \text{MC}$	$P = \text{LMC}$
Shutdown Rule: A firm will shut down operations if this condition exists at the profit-maximizing output rate.	$P <$ min. AVC	$P <$ min. LATC
New Entry Condition: New firms will enter if this condition exists at the present market price.	Assumed that no entry is possible	$P >$ min. LATC
No Entry Condition: Entry stops when this condition exists.	Assumed that no entry is possible	$P \leq$ min. LATC

INDUSTRY SUPPLY IN THE LONG RUN

The long-run equilibrium analysis in Figure 10.11 holds the number of firms fixed when market supply is calculated. The two supply curves, $S_{45 \text{ firms}}$ and $S_{50 \text{ firms}}$, define the quantity supplied by 45 and 50 firms, respectively. In the long run, as we have indicated, the number of firms is variable, not fixed, so these curves *do not* represent long-run market supply curves. In other words, the long-run supply curve for the perfectly competitive industry is not equal to the sum of the individual long-run marginal cost curves for prices above the minimum of the LATC curve.

To find the long-run market supply curve for a perfectly competitive industry, we must answer the following question: *What is the total quantity supplied as market demand changes?* When we stated the same question for the firm, we referred to market price, not market demand. We can refer to market price for an individual firm because each firm is a price taker. For the whole industry, however, market price is determined by the interaction of market supply and market demand, so market price cannot function as a given when we discuss *industry* supply. We let market demand change, then, to determine how industry supply responds in the long run.

The answer to the question of how to determine the long-run industry supply depends on the *factor price effect;* that is, do factor prices change as the industry output changes, or do they remain fixed? If factor prices change, do these changes affect firms average and marginal cost curves? There are three possibilities to consider here.

Constant-Cost Industry
An industry in which average and marginal cost curves remain unchanged as the output of all firms changes.

Possibility 1: Constant Costs

A **constant-cost industry** is one in which factor prices do not change as industry output changes. In an industry with constant (factor) costs, then, average and marginal cost curves *do not shift* when industry output changes. As we show below, the long-run supply curve for a constant-factor-cost industry is a horizontal line equal to the minimum of the LATC curve. Figure 10.12 illustrates this result.

Figure 10.12 shows the effects of shifting the market demand curve from D_0 to D_1. Initially, there are 50 firms in the industry, each producing Q^* units in response to a market price of P^*, which is equal to the minimum of the LATC curve for the typical firm. Initially, then, the industry is in long-run equilibrium because economic profits are zero for each firm. The increase in market demand from D_0 to D_1 causes the existing 50 firms to expand output along their marginal cost curves, LMC(Q), in response to the new market clearing price, P_0. At this price, the typical firm produces Q_0 units, earning economic profits of $\pi(Q_0) > 0$.

The existence of positive economic profits attracts new firms to the industry, a condition which drives down the market clearing price. The industry reaches a *new* long-run equilibrium when there are 60 firms, each producing Q^* units in response to a market price of P^* = minimum of the LATC curve, and all firms earn zero economic profits. The new equilibrium output of the industry is $60Q^*$. Thus, the new long-run equilibrium differs

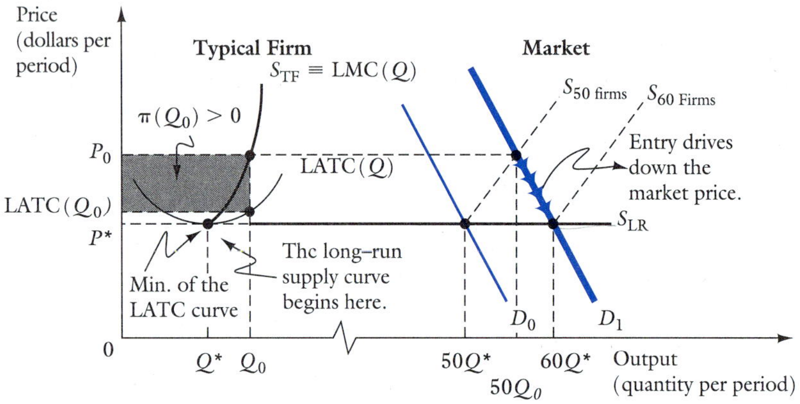

FIGURE 10.12

The Long-Run Supply Curve for a Constant-Cost Industry

In a constant-cost industry, a change in the total output of the industry has no effect on the price paid for inputs. Thus, the long-run supply curve for a constant-cost industry is horizontal at the market price (P^*) that generates zero economic profits. The zero-profit price equals the minimum of the long-run average total cost curve (LATC). Initially, there are 50 firms producing a total output of $50Q^*$, where each firm produces Q^*. As market demand increases from D_0 to D_1, the perfectly competitive industry adjusts by increasing the output rate of each firm to Q_0. Every firm earns economic profits at the market price of P_0, which causes firms to enter the industry. In the long run, the market reaches an equilibrium at which there are 60 firms producing a total output of $60Q^*$. The equilibrium price returns to its previous level of P^*. The long-run adjustment takes place in the number of firms, not in the output rate of a typical firm or in the market clearing price, for a constant-cost industry.

from the initial equilibrium only in terms of the number of firms and total output; the market clearing price remains the same.

This exercise can be repeated again and again, with market demand either increasing or decreasing, and the result will be the same: in the long run, under the constant-factor-cost assumption, the perfectly competitive industry supplies any quantity (above Q^*) at the market price of P^* = minimum of the LATC curve. The market supply curve, S_{LR}, is therefore horizontal.

Possibility 2: Increasing-Cost Industry

Increasing-Cost Industry
An industry in which average and marginal cost curves shift up as the output of all firms changes.

The constant-factor-cost assumption may be reasonable in an industry whose inputs are used by many other industries, such as hardware stores, because they are a small part of the overall retail sales industry. Other businesses, however, are **increasing-cost industries.** This implies that an expansion of industry output causes factor costs to increase, which causes average and marginal cost curves to shift upward. As we showed in our analysis of the factor price effect in the short run, both the firm and market supply curves are affected by shifts in the marginal cost curve. The firm and market supply curves become less price-elastic when factor prices increase in response to an increase in industry output.

Shifts of the long-run average total cost curve provide the key to determining how the increasing-factor-cost assumption affects long-run industry supply. As the LATC curve shifts up, its minimum value shifts up, too, which increases the market clearing price that generates zero economic profits. Long-run equilibrium in the industry requires zero economic profits, so the long-run supply curve must increase to follow increases in the long-run equilibrium price. We can now conclude that the long-run supply curve in an increasing-factor-cost industry is positively sloped.

Possibility 3: Decreasing-Cost Industry

Decreasing-Cost Industry
An industry in which average and marginal cost curves shift down as the output of all firms changes.

Although somewhat unusual, a **decreasing-cost industry** is one in which changes in factor prices cause average and marginal cost curves to shift down when industry output increases. The effect on the long-run industry supply is just the opposite of the effect of increasing factor costs on long-run supply. A decline in the LATC curve causes its minimum value to fall, so the market price that generates zero economic profits declines as industry output expands. In addition, as industry output increases, new firms enter at successively lower market prices. The long-run supply curve is thus negatively sloped.

Decreasing-cost industries potentially pose a problem for perfectly competitive markets. Larger firms may have some influence over the price paid for inputs. If this is the case, these firms may have a cost advantage over new entrants, which enables them to earn economic profits even when entry is not restricted. The perfectly competitive model does not operate perfectly in this instance because entering firms are at a disadvantage compared to large existing firms.

Summary of Industry Cost Effects

Figure 10.13 summarizes the relationship between the various factor cost assumptions and the shape of the long-run market supply curve. As you look at this figure, remember that each point on a supply curve, for whichever of the three curves is appropriate, implies a price at which all firms earn zero economic profits in the long run. In other words, there is no level of industry supply that offers positive economic profits in the long run.

The three possible supply curves shown in Figure 10.13 predict very different patterns for market price as demand changes. Market price increases with increases in demand for the increasing-cost industry, remains constant for the constant-cost industry, and decreases for the decreasing-cost industry. Although a decreasing-cost industry is generally the exception, in one industry—electronics—it tends to be more the rule. The electronics industry has consistently offered consumers products at lower prices (holding quality constant) as market demand increased over time. Part of this phenomenon is due to technological improvements and learning curve effects that reduce cost, but a larger part is due to the entry of foreign firms—particularly the Japanese—as the market has expanded. As more firms entered the industry, the cost paid for

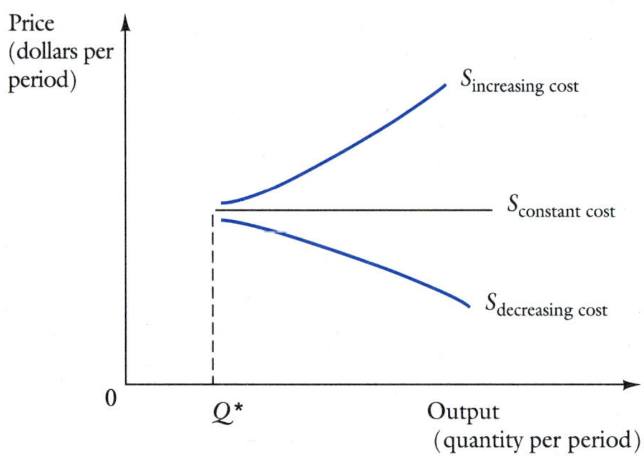

FIGURE 10.13

Comparing the Long-Run Supply Curve for Increasing-, Constant-, and Decreasing-Cost Industries

The long-run supply curves for increasing-, constant-, and decreasing-cost industries are shown. In an increasing-cost industry, an increase in the output of the industry causes some (or all) input prices to increase, which causes average and marginal cost curves to shift up. Thus, the zero-profit price increases as industry output expands, causing the long-run supply curve to have a positive slope. The opposite effect occurs for a decreasing-cost industry. An increase in industry output causes some (or all) input prices to fall, which has the effect of reducing the average and marginal cost curves. Thus, the zero-profit price falls as industry output increases, causing the long-run supply curve to have a negative slope. With the constant-cost industry, there is no change in input prices as industry output changes, so the long-run supply curve is horizontal.

raw materials declined, leading to lower production costs per unit for all firms and lower market prices.

LEARNING EXERCISE 10.10

How do entry and exit prices change as market demand increases in constant-, increasing-, and decreasing-factor-cost industries?

10.5 EFFICIENCY OF PERFECT COMPETITION

One characteristic of the perfectly competitive equilibrium is that there is no incentive for firms or consumers to change their behavior in the short run; that is, all gains from trade between buyers and sellers are realized. In this section, we demonstrate this result.

ALLOCATIVE EFFICIENCY

Allocative Efficiency A situation in which all gains from voluntary trade are realized.

Allocative efficiency means that the market structure exhausts all gains from trade. The perfectly competitive market does this by operating at the $P = MC$ point. To illustrate that all gains from trade are realized at this operating position, consider the equilibrium described in Figure 10.14.

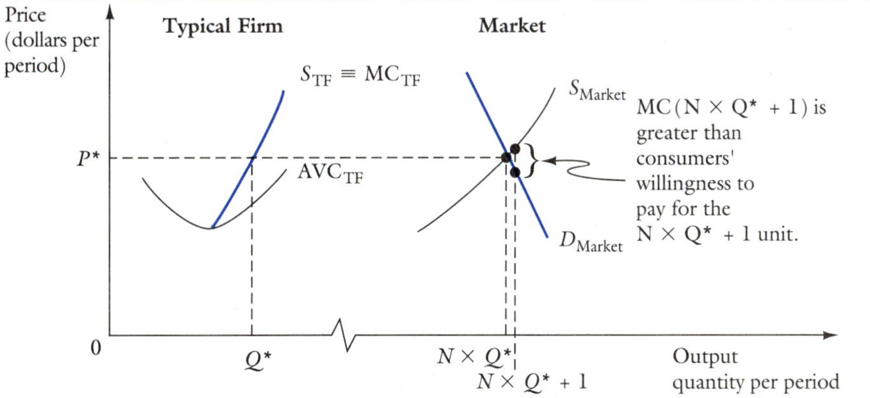

FIGURE 10.14

The Short-Run Competitive Equilibrium Exhausts All Gains from Trade

There are no gains from additional, voluntary trade at the short-run perfectly competitive equilibrium. Suppose there are N firms in the market, each producing Q^* in equilibrium. Thus, total quantity supplied is $N \times Q^*$. If one firm tries to sell another unit, the output rate increases to $(N \times Q^*) + 1$. But the marginal cost of this extra unit, MC($N \times Q^* + 1$), exceeds the willingness of the marginal consumer to pay for an extra unit. A firm will not accept less than MC($N \times Q^* + 1$) for the extra unit, but the marginal consumer will not pay this amount, so this unit will not be sold.

There are a total of N identical firms in the industry in the short run. The marginal and average cost structure for the typical firm are shown on the left-hand side of Figure 10.14. The market demand and supply are shown on the right-hand side of this figure. The equilibrium price is P^* and the equilibrium quantity is $N \times Q^*$, where Q^* is the profit-maximizing output for each firm.

To say that all gains from trade are realized implies that no buyer and seller can agree on a price that induces a buyer to buy and a seller to sell one more unit of a product. We see that $N \times Q^*$ is presently sold by producers and bought by consumers. The question, then, is whether the $N \times Q^* + 1$ unit will be voluntarily sold to a consumer by a producer. At the present equilibrium, each firm faces a marginal cost equal to market price, P^*. Another unit may be produced, but only at a cost—marginal cost—that is *higher than* P^*. Analogously, the present consumers are paying P^* per unit for $N \times Q^*$ units. More units may be sold to consumers, but only if the price is *less than* P^* per unit. Under these conditions, there is no room to maneuver. Producers will not voluntarily sell another unit for an amount less than P^* and consumers are not willing to pay the marginal cost of an extra unit, which is slightly higher than P^*. We can conclude that no additional trade will take place, so the competitive equilibrium is *allocatively efficient*—that is, it has exhausted all gains from trade.

LEARNING EXERCISE 10.11

Using a graph similar to Figure 10.14, explain why the output rate $N \times Q - 1$ is not allocatively efficient.

ALLOCATIVE EFFICIENCY USING PRODUCERS' AND CONSUMERS' SURPLUSES

Another way to interpret allocative efficiency is to say that a competitive equilibrium maximizes the net benefits to consumers and producers. We define the net benefits to consumers and producers as the sum of producers' and consumers' surpluses. These two concepts were introduced in Chapter 3. Let's review each of them briefly before we demonstrate (again) the allocative efficiency of the perfectly competitive market.

Reviewing Consumers' and Producers' Surpluses

The net benefits to all consumers is called *consumers' surplus.* Consumer surplus for a given consumer equals the amount the consumer is willing to pay minus what he or she actually pays for the units purchased. When a consumer pays a single price for all purchases, consumer surplus equals the area under the demand curve extended out to the quantity purchased minus total expenditures.

The net benefit from trade to all producers is called *producers' surplus.* Analogous to consumers' surplus, producers' surplus measures the producers' net gain from all units sold. It is tempting to claim that producer surplus for a single firm is equal to economic profits. This claim is correct in the long run, but because fixed costs are ignored when we choose the short-run operating position, we define producer surplus for a single firm as

Producer surplus (PS) equals total revenue (TR) minus total variable cost (TVC).

MATH NOTEPAD

Producer Surplus Equals TR – TVC

Total revenue minus total variable cost is the same as economic profits plus fixed cost. Thus, an equivalent statement is that producer surplus equals economic profits plus fixed cost. To show this result, define $PS(Q) = TR(Q) - TVC(Q)$ as the producer surplus generated from the sale of Q units. The firm's profit is given by $\pi(Q) = TR(Q) - TVC(Q) - FC$, where FC is the fixed cost. Rearranging the profit equation gives $\pi(Q) + FC = TR(Q) - TVC(Q)$, or $\pi(Q) + FC = PS(Q)$.

In Figure 10.15, we show two ways to calculate producer surplus for a typical firm in a perfectly competitive market. The market price is P^* in equilibrium, so total revenue is $P^* \times Q^*$, where Q^* is the profit-maximizing output rate. Total variable cost equals average variable cost, $AVC(Q^*)$, times quantity, or $AVC(Q^*) \times Q^*$. Thus, producer surplus is represented by the shaded rectangular area in panel (a), which is the difference between total revenue and total variable cost: $PS(Q^*) = [P^* - AVC(Q^*)] \times Q^*$.

In panel (b), producer surplus is computed as the area above the firm's supply curve out to the optimal output rate but below the market price. We can show that this approach gives the same answer as that found in panel (a) by splitting the calculation into two pieces. Area A in panel (b) equals the difference between total revenue and total variable cost when Q_{min} is produced, where Q_{min} is the output rate at the minimum of the average variable cost curve. Taken by itself, area A equals producer surplus if Q_{min} is the optimal output rate. For the analysis in panel (b) to be correct, then, area B must measure the change in producer surplus as the output rate increases from Q_{min} to Q^*. In fact, this is the case, because the area under the marginal cost curve between Q_{min} and Q^* is equal to the change in total variable costs. We know this result from Chapter 9. The change in total revenue is equal to $(Q^* \times Q_{min}) \times P^*$. Subtracting the change in total variable costs from the change in total revenue gives area B, which is thus equal to the change in producer surplus as the output rate increases from Q_{min} to Q^*.

The *total* surplus for producers—also called producers' surplus—in the market is equal to the producer surplus for the typical firm (all firms are identical) times the number of firms, N, in the market. Recall that $PS(Q^*) = [P^* - AVC(Q^*)] \times Q^*$ is the producer surplus for a typical firm. Algebraically, then, producers' surplus in a perfectly competitive market equals $PS(Q^*) \times N$.

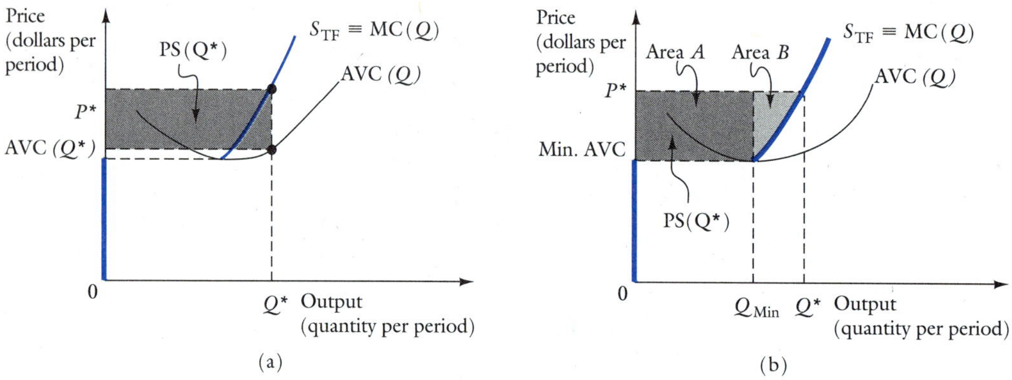

FIGURE 10.15

Two Equivalent Methods of Computing Producer Surplus for the Typical Firm

The surplus for a given producer in the short run equals its profits plus fixed cost. Panel (a) shows that producer surplus can be computed by multiplying quantity supplied by the difference between price and average variable cost. If the market price is P^*, for example, the firm supplies Q^* in the short run. Producer surplus, denoted by PS(Q^*), equals the shaded rectangle in panel (a). Panel (b) shows another method of computing producer surplus. Area *A* computes producer surplus up to output rate Q_{min} using the method described in panel (a). Area *B* computes producer surplus between the optimal output rate, Q^*, and Q_{min}. Area *B* equals the difference between the total revenue and total variable cost generated from the output between Q_{min} and Q^*. Total revenue equals $P^* \times Q^* - Q_{min}$. Total variable costs, however, equal the area under the marginal cost curve between Q^* and Q_{min}. Producer surplus in panel (b) equals the sum of areas *A* and *B*.

Showing Allocativc Efficicncy

To show that the net benefits to consumers and producers are maximized at the competitive equilibrium, we must show that the *total surplus* in the market is lowered if the market price is different from P^*. The **total market surplus** equals the sum of consumers' and producers' surpluses. First, consider the effect of a higher market price, $P_H > P^*$, on the output and total surplus of a perfectly competitive industry, which causes both total revenue and total cost to decrease. This situation is shown in panel (a) in Figure 10.16.

Total Market Surplus The sum of consumers' and producers' surpluses.

In panel (a), we see that the initial perfectly competitive equilibrium is at a market price of P^* with $N \times Q^*$ units sold, where N is the number of (identical) firms. When price increases to P_H, the equilibrium quantity sold decreases to $N \times Q_H$. The effect of this change on the total market surplus is described as follows:

	Market Price of P^*	Market Price of P_H
Consumers' Surplus	$A + B + C$	A
Producers' Surplus	$D + E$	$B + D$
Total Market Surplus	$A + B + C + D + E$	$A + B + D$

As market price increases to P_H, the total market surplus *decreases* by an amount equal to area C + area E, which is the difference between the two total

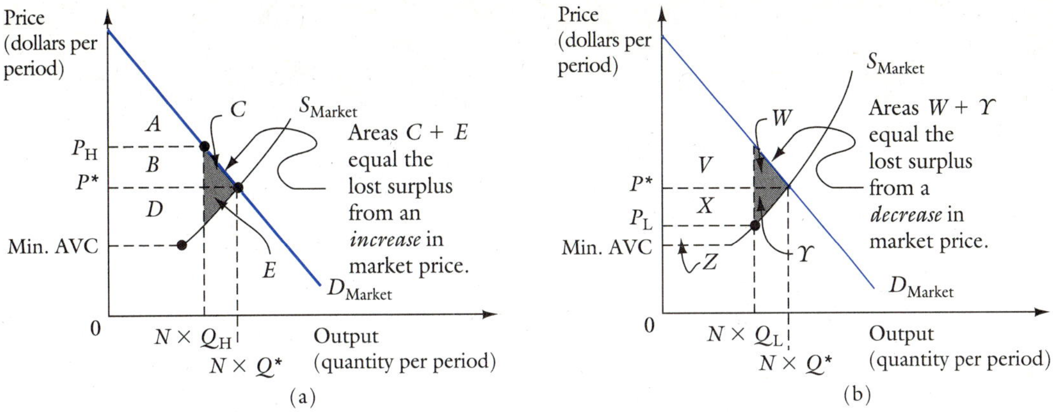

FIGURE 10.16

Raising or Lowering Price Away from the Equilibrium Price Reduces the Total Surplus

Moving away from the market clearing price lowers the total surplus in a perfectly competitive market. In panel (a), market price is increased to P_H from P^*. The equilibrium quantity purchased decreases from $N \times Q^*$ to $N \times Q_H$, where N equals the number of firms in the industry, Q^* is the output rate of the typical firm before the price increase, and Q_H is the output rate of the typical firm after the price increase. The lost surplus for the market—both producers' and consumers' surplus—equals areas $C + E$. In panel (b), market price is lowered to P_L from P^*. In this case, quantity supplied decreases from $N \times Q^*$ to $N \times Q_L$ for the market. The lost surplus for the market—again, both producers' and consumers' surplus—equals areas $W + Y$ in panel (b).

market surpluses shown above. We can now state that raising price above the perfectly competitive equilibrium reduces the total surplus in the market. What happens, however, when price is lowered? Panel (b) in Figure 10.16 works through this situation.

As price decreases to P_L in panel (b), firms reduce their output rates, so that a total of $N \times Q_L$ is sold in the market at the lower price. Note that this is less than the quantity demanded at this new price, so some consumers who are willing to pay P_L per unit do not receive all the units they wish to purchase. The effect of this change on the total surplus in the market can be described in a manner similar to that followed for a price increase:

	Market Price of P^*	**Market Price of P_L**
Consumers' Surplus	$V + W$	$V + X$
Producers' Surplus	$X + Y + Z$	Z
Total Market Surplus	$V + W + X + Y + Z$	$V + X + Z$

As market price decreases to P_L, the total market surplus *decreases* by an amount equal to area W + area Y, which is the difference between the two total market surpluses shown above. Now we can conclude that lowering price below the perfectly competitive equilibrium reduces the total market surplus. Because both raising price and lowering price reduce the total market surplus, the net benefits must be at a maximum at the perfectly competitive equilibrium.

LONG-RUN EFFICIENCY AND THE INVISIBLE HAND

Over two centuries ago, Adam Smith wrote *An Inquiry into the Nature and Causes of the Wealth of Nations.* In this remarkable book, Smith observed that

> As every individual . . . endeavours as much as he can . . . to maximize his own economic well-being, every individual necessarily labors to render the annual revenue of the society as great as he can. He generally, indeed, neither intends to promote the public interest, nor knows how much he is promoting it . . . he intends only his own gain, and he is in this . . . led as if by an *invisible hand* to promote an end which was no part of his intention. [Emphasis added.]

The self-interest of both buyers and sellers is the "invisible hand" that leads to a perfectly competitive market equilibrium. The invisible hand also ensures that all gains from trade are exhausted, so the perfectly competitive market is allocatively efficient in the long run, too. Buyers receive a good for a price less than they are willing to pay; only the marginal or last buyer pays an amount equal to his or her valuation of the good. Sellers maximize profits for their own benefit. Perfect competition, then, maximizes total market surplus in the long run as well as the short run.

> **What is impressive about perfect competition in the long run, compared to the short run, is that consumers receive *all* of the surplus because producers earn zero economic profits.**

This means the firms' owners earn a normal rate of return on their investment. The total market surplus, which is equal to the sum of producers' and consumers' surpluses, is equal to consumers' surplus because producers' surplus is zero; that is, there are no fixed costs in the long run, so producers' surplus equals economic profits. This result is not caused by collusion among buyers but rather by the entry of new firms that compete away positive economic profits.

10.6 Competitive Markets with Asymmetric Information

An important assumption of the perfectly competitive market structure is that the same information is available to both buyers and sellers. This assumption implies that buyers and sellers can clearly discern a product's characteristics before a transaction is made. As we noted earlier, the validity of this assumption is questionable if quality is an important attribute of the product. The clothes we see in a retail store, for example, vary on the basis of quality. The materials in some clothes are more durable, so they last longer; some clothes are assembled, or stitched, in a more careful manner, which also makes them last longer. In addition, some garments are easier to clean because of the high-quality dyes that are used. Generally, it is costly for consumers to determine the quality of clothes before a purchase. Quality is generally determined after the purchase. When consumers wear and wash (or dry-clean) clothes, this process reveals quality differences among garments. If quality is determined after a purchase, asymmetric information creates an incentive for firms to misrepresent the true quality of their products. Let's explore the implications of this problem for the perfectly competitive market structure.

ASYMMETRIC INFORMATION CREATES TWO PERVERSE INCENTIVES

It is reasonable to claim that higher-quality clothes are more expensive to produce. This claim is probably true for all higher-quality products. If higher quality is more expensive to produce, then firms that make high-quality products must receive a higher price than firms that make low-quality products.[5] But this simple fact creates an enormous problem for consumers. If quality is not fully known before a purchase, two perverse incentives exist for firms:[6]

1. Firms making low-quality products may try to represent their merchandise as of higher quality in order to receive a higher price.
2. Firms making high-quality products may switch to producing low-quality products, continuing to charge the high-quality price until consumers discover the switch.

Figure 10.17, on page 400, illustrates why these two incentives exist for profit-maximizing firms. Two sets of cost curves are shown in this figure, which refer to two types of quality: high or low. The LMC_H and LATC_H curves are for a firm that produces a high-quality product and the LMC_L and LATC_L curves are for a firm that produces a low-quality product.

Now, *if there is no asymmetric information,* so that consumers can distinguish between high- and low-quality products, then both high- and low-quality products are expected to be produced. In the long run, entry and exit of firms creates zero economic profits. The long-run market clearing price for the high-quality product is P_H, which is equal to the minimum of the LATC_H curve. At this price, the typical firm produces Q_H units of the high-quality product per period. The market clearing price for the low-quality product is P_L, which is equal to the minimum of the LATC_L curve. At this price, the typical firm produces Q_L units of the low-quality product. With asymmetric information, however, we have the two perverse incentives noted above, so it is not clear that a high-quality product will be produced and sold for a price above P_L.

The two perverse incentives show that either firm may cheat the consumer. In Figure 10.17, we see that if a firm producing a low-quality product is paid the high-quality price of P_H, then it maximizes profits at the output rate Q_X. This action creates *positive* economic profits: $\pi_\text{L}(Q_X) = [P_\text{H} - \text{LATC}_\text{L}(Q_X)] \times Q_X > 0$. Positive economic profits are preferred to zero economic profits, so the firm making the low-quality product is expected to try to misrepresent the quality of its product to consumers.

---

[5] The high-quality and low-quality products we discuss here are imperfect substitutes.

[6] This discussion is based on a paper by Benjamin Klein and Keith B. Leffler, "The Role of Market Forces in Assuring Contractual Performance," *Journal of Political Economy* 89 (August 1981), 615–641.

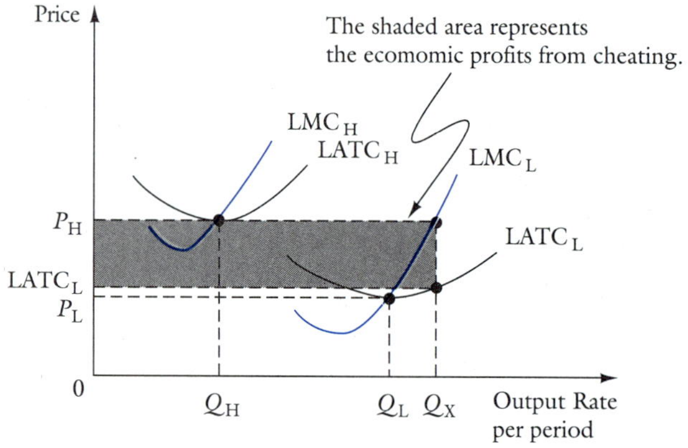

FIGURE 10.17

Cost Curves for the Production of High- and Low-Quality Products

The long-run marginal (LMC_H) and average ($LATC_H$) cost curves for a firm producing a high-quality product generally lie above the long-run marginal (LMC_L) and average ($LATC_L$) cost curves for a firm producing a low-quality product. At the zero-profit price (P_H) for a high-quality product, the firm producing the high-quality product has an incentive to cheat by producing the low-quality product while charging the high-quality price. With cheating, the profit-maximizing output rate is Q_X and the profit received is shown as the shaded rectangle in the figure.

The firm making the high-quality product faces a similar incentive. If this firm switches to making the low-quality product, its cost curves become those for the typical firm making a low-quality product. The (formerly) high-quality producer chooses to produce Q_X units of the low-quality product, expecting to sell these units at the high-quality price. Again, this action generates positive economic profits, compared to the zero-profit equilibrium before the switch, so we expect the firm making a high-quality product to switch to a low-quality product and to cheat its customers in the process.

As things stand now, the two perverse incentives imply that both types of firms will try to cheat consumers. Consumers may be uninformed about product quality, but they cannot be systematically fooled; they can reason through this problem just as we have. Without any further assurances that a product is really of high quality, consumers will not pay more than the low-quality price for *any* product in this market. This is called the **lemons problem** because consumers act as if the low-quality product—a lemon—is all that is sold in the marketplace.[7] The market for used cars is one often-cited example of the lemons problem. There may be both high- and low-quality used cars, but without a costly inspection it is hard for car buyers to tell the difference.

Lemons Problem
A phenomenon in which consumers will pay at most the low-quality price for products because they cannot determine quality before a purchase.

[7] The lemons problem is discussed by George Akerlof, "The Market for Lemons: Qualitative Uncertainty and the Market Mechanism," *Quarterly Journal of Economics* 84 (1970), 484–500. Formally speaking, the lemons problem is an example of *adverse selection* because the sellers have information that buyers do not have before a purchase is made.

Consumers are right to be wary of the lemons problem. Firms will not produce high-quality products if they sell for the low-quality price, P_L. We know this because P_L is below the minimum of the $LATC_H$ curve, which implies that firms producing a high-quality product will shut down in the long run.

IS THERE A QUALITY-ASSURING PRICE?

Quality-Assuring Price A price that will induce firms to produce a high-quality product and not to cheat consumers by switching to the low-quality product in some period in the future.

An important question to ask is whether there is a price that induces firms to produce the high-quality product *without* giving them an incentive to cheat customers. Such a price, if it exists, is called a **quality-assuring price.** The quality-assuring price offers positive economic profits to the firm producing a high-quality product. These profits must exceed (or equal) the profits the firm receives from cheating by switching to the low-quality product. The quality-assuring price must exceed P_H, which is the zero-profit price.

There are different methods of determining if a quality-assuring price exists. We observe, for example, that most markets are characterized by customer referrals and repeat purchases from current customers. A firm producing a high-quality product gains new customers from these referrals. Its profits from producing the high-quality product will thus multiply over time as its business grows. In contrast, if it cheats, it gains extra profits for *only one period* as customers discover they have been fooled and therefore refuse to pay a price greater than P_L for the firm's products. Repeat purchases accrue to firms that continue to perform as they have claimed, so a firm that sells a high-quality product continues to attract existing customers in future periods. In this setting, the quality-assuring price must be high enough to make the *present value* of the stream of profits from customer referrals and repeat purchases greater than or equal to the one-period gain from cheating.[8]

To develop this idea, let's hold the customer base constant. There may be referrals from present consumers, but there may also be customer losses to competitors for reasons that do not involve cheating—such as relocation from the area, income changes, and changes in the price of substitutes. The referrals and customer losses offset each other, *so the firm enjoys a constant number of customers each period.* In addition, let's assume that the market for the high-quality good exists for the indefinite future. The *longer* the stream of positive profits from producing the high-quality product, the more likely it is that the *present value* of such a stream exceeds the onetime gain a firm receives from cheating. Now, the lowest possible quality-assuring price, P^*, is the one that equates the present value of profits for the typical firm producing a high-quality product to the *single-period* profits for the cheating firm. Analytically, the *minimum* possible quality-assuring price satisfies the following three equations:

$$\frac{[P^* - LATC_H(Q_H^*)] \times Q_H^*}{r} = [P^* - LATC_L(Q_C)] \times Q_C \quad (10.5)$$

$$P^* = LMC_H(Q_H^*) \quad (10.6)$$

$$P^* = LMC_L(Q_C) \quad (10.7)$$

[8] Present value is the value of the stream of income expressed in today's dollars. Present value is discussed fully in Chapter 15.

where r is the per period rate of interest, Q_C is the low-quality output if price is P^* and the firm cheats, and Q_H^* is the optimal output rate for the high-quality product. (Note that $Q_H \neq Q_H^*$.)

The logic behind equation (10.5) can be explained as follows. The firm receives $[P^* - LATC_H(Q_H^*)] \times Q_H^*$ in profits each period from producing the high-quality product. Dividing this term by the interest rate gives the *present value* of profits if this profit stream continues indefinitely. The term $[P^* - LATC_L(Q_C)] \times Q_C$, on the right-hand side of equation (10.5), is the profit the firm receives from cheating. The minimum possible quality-assuring price must equate these two profit terms to make the firm's owners *indifferent* between producing the high-quality product and cheating.

The next two equations solve for a typical firm's output rate. Equation (10.6) gives the solution for the profit-maximizing output rate of the typical firm producing a high-quality product, and equation (10.7) gives the profit-maximizing solution for the firm that decides to cheat and produce a low-quality product that is sold at the quality-assuring price, P^*, for one period.

If there is a P^* that solves all three equations, we are assured that both high- and low-quality products can be produced in the market. If there is no solution, then only the low-quality product is expected to be produced because the lemons problem implies that consumers will not pay more than the low-quality price under asymmetric information.

LEARNING EXERCISE 10.12

Given the structure of the cost curves shown in Figure 10.17, is it possible for a quality-assuring price to exist if the market dissolves itself after one period, that is, there are no future sales periods?

MARKET EQUILIBRIUM WITH SPECIFIC ASSETS

If a quality-assuring price exists, then firms that produce the high-quality product earn positive economic profits. But we know that positive economic profits attract new entrants in a perfectly competitive market. New entrants will increase market supply and thereby reduce market price. A lower market price, however, is not sustainable because the solution to the above equations produces the *minimum* quality-assuring price. Entry of new firms that reduce the market price below the quality-assuring price causes the model to collapse. In order for the perfectly competitive model to work, there must be a way for competition between firms to reach a zero-profit market equilibrium. Specific assets may cause this result.

In order to compete for new and existing customers and share in the positive economic profits, firms may invest specific assets. Specific assets, such as advertising expenditures, signs, brand names, product logos, or trademarks, are investments with zero recovery value; that is, they are *sunk costs.* As sunk costs, they do not affect the operating position of the firm. To represent to customers that they are producing a high-quality product, firms may invest in myriad specific assets. These assets may be firm-specific or specific to the high-quality product line. As a valid signal to consumers, specific assets have the characteristic that their value inside the firm is lost if the firm cheats by producing the low-quality product. In other words, cheating the customer causes the firm's specific assets to lose value. Product logos and slogans are specific assets that frequently present the image of a high-quality product; they often say "*Best grade,*" "Certified to be of the highest quality," or something similar. If the firm cheats, the value of these investments goes rapidly to zero.

Although investments in specific assets are worthless to others, they are valuable to the firm. By showing customers that it is investing in specific assets, the firm is revealing that it is receiving positive economic profits at the current market price. Consumers take this as a signal that the firm is producing a high-quality product.

Investments in specific assets are a nonprice form of competition that can result in zero economic profits. Any firm tempted to enter the high-quality market must compute the full cost of entry. This cost includes the operating profit, which is positive, plus the cost of the specific assets that it must purchase.

The market is in equilibrium when the investment in specific assets exactly offsets the present value of the operating profits for a firm.

From equation (10.5) on page 401, we find that the present value of operating profits is $(1/r)[P^* - \text{LATC}_H(Q_H^*)] \times Q_H^*$. If A_s represents the firm's investment in specific assets, then

$$A_s = (1/r)[P^* - \text{LATC}_H(Q_H^*)] \times Q_H^*$$

if the market is in long-run equilibrium. Rearranging this equation, we see that the quality-assuring price can be written as $P^* = \text{LATC}_H(Q_H^*) + (rA_s/Q_H^*)$. This situation is described in Figure 10.18 on page 404.

Figure 10.18 shows that the firm producing the high-quality product charges P^*, produces Q_H^* units, and earns profits per period of $\pi(Q_H^*)$, equal to the cost per period of its investment in specific assets, rA. On net, competition forces it to the zero-economic-profits position. Note that the output of the high-quality product is greater than what would be produced if the firm operated at the minimum of the LATC_H curve, which is where it would operate if there was no asymmetric information. Because the quality-assuring price is higher than the perfectly competitive price—that is, the minimum of the LATC_H curve—fewer units must be sold in the total market than under perfect competition. But because each firm produces more, fewer firms must be producing the high-quality product when there is asymmetric information than when information is symmetric. A relative scarcity of firms producing the high-quality product is one of the predictions of this model.

The firm producing the low-quality product does not invest in specific assets—it does not need a quality signal—so it earns zero economic profits each period by selling Q_L units at a price, P_L, equal to the minimum of its average variable cost curve. At prices P^* and P_L and with an investment of A_s in specific assets by each firm producing a high-quality product, there is no incentive for new firms to enter this business, so the market is in long-run equilibrium.

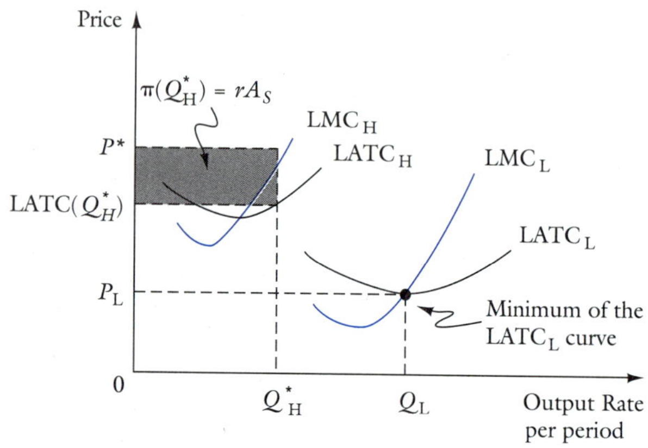

FIGURE 10.18

The Perfectly Competitive Market Equilibrium at the Quality-Assuring Price

The high-quality product may be produced if there is a quality-assuring price (P^*) that offers economic profits that exceed those received from cheating. The high-quality market reaches a long-run equilibrium when the economic profits received at the quality-assuring price, $\pi(Q^*_H)$, are exactly offset by investments in specific assets, rA_s, where A_s is the total investment in specific assets and r is the interest rate each period.

This model makes sense out of much that firms do. There is a role for advertising beyond its simple informative role in the perfectly competitive model. Advertising shows consumers that firms are making investments in specific assets, which is a signal that their products are of higher quality. Some types of advertising are particularly indicative of specific investments. Celebrity endorsements (which are not very informative), charitable contributions, and sponsorship of athletic events draw particular attention to a firm's purchase of assets that become sunk costs. In addition, firms advertise that they have advertised in the past—for example, "As seen on TV"—to further indicate their investment in assets that generate sunk costs.

In summary, this model implies that the long-run zero-profit condition of the perfectly competitive model may not be affected by changing the symmetric information assumption. It also shows that firms can adjust along nonprice dimensions—that is, by competing using specific assets—to reach a market equilibrium. Finally, it is tempting to say that price may be used as an indicator of a product's quality. The high-quality product is, after all, more expensive than the low-quality product. Although this indicator may work for any single consumer, it cannot work for all consumers. If all consumers look at price alone and ignore whether a firm has specific assets, we are back to the problem posed by the two perverse incentives mentioned above. So price itself *is not* a reliable indicator of quality for all consumers; rather, price *combined with* knowledge of a firm's specific investments normally is an indicator of quality.

$$$ Price Theory in Practice

Textbook Supplements Are Specific Assets

Nearly every basic textbook that you can buy for a college course includes supplementary material. You can get instructor's manuals, study guides, computer software to help students with concepts and problems, laser disks for fancy classroom presentations, acetates for overhead projectors, annotated texts for instructors, newsletters, and much more. A recently published textbook on the principles of economics, for example, listed 11 supplements for instructors and 12 supplements for students. Some of these items are used frequently, such as the instructor's manual and the study guide for students, but many go unused or are used at only a few schools.

With such dubious demand, why do publishing companies continue to produce more and more supplements? The answer can be found in our discussion of perfect competition under asymmetric information. Textbooks are adopted by instructors, so the primary customer for publishers is the course instructor. Instructors want a book that is modern in its coverage of topics, comprehensive, readable, and *error-free.* Because there are several major publishers, there are many books from which to choose for nearly every course, so the market is competitive. Time constraints limit the ability of an instructor to thoroughly review a book before the course is taught. Instructors do not have the time, for example, to check to see if all of the questions are answered correctly and whether every graph is drawn right (they do some spot-checking, however). There is certainly not enough time to do this for every textbook on the market. This type of review is generally done as the course progresses, but a book must be chosen before the course begins. Thus, asymmetric information is present in the textbook market when books are adopted (the point of purchase).

To send a signal to instructors that the books they produce are of high quality—error-free, modern, and comprehensive—publishers invest in specific assets. The supplements produced by publishers serve this purpose; in fact, they are product-specific assets. An instructor's manual and a study guide, for example, cannot be used with another book and cannot be sold if the text is not adopted. These supplements serve as a signal to instructors that the questions are answered correctly, the graphs are drawn right, and so on. If the signal is misleading, an instructor will discover the book's errors as the course progresses and will very likely discontinue the use of the text in the next term. If all instructors act similarly, then the textbook will have a very short life. The publisher's specific investment in supplements will be worthless because no one will adopt the textbook in the future, and subsequent editing will generally not produce more revenue for the publisher and author.

As the use of supplements increases, the quality-assuring price for new textbooks probably increases, too. More supplements imply a larger investment in specific assets, which implies that there are economic profits available to pay for such investments. Higher economic profits follow from higher market prices or lower production costs. Unfortunately for students, it is probably higher market prices for new textbooks, not lower production costs, that are generating the increased profits to pay for the extra supplements.

LEARNING EXERCISE 10.13

Given the asymmetric information problem that instructors face, is it likely that a low-cost textbook will be successful in the future—that is, a generic textbook that covers all the key concepts, has only the most popular supplements, and is sold for a low price?

Chapter Summary

1. Four assumptions are necessary for the perfectly competitive market structure: all firms sell a homogeneous product, firms are price takers, entry and exit of firms and factors of production are unrestricted in the long run, and information is symmetrically distributed to buyers and sellers. These assumptions imply that competitive firms earn zero economic profits in the long run.
2. Because the perfectly competitive firm acts as a price taker, it cannot influence the market price of its product by changing its output rate. Each additional unit will sell for the market price, so the firm's marginal revenue is equal to the market price: MR = P.
3. A perfectly competitive firm will shut down its operations in the short run if average revenue is less than the minimum of its average variable cost curve. Because average revenue equals market price for the perfectly competitive firm, the firm shuts down if $P <$ minimum of the AVC curve. The long-run shutdown condition is $P <$ minimum of the LATC curve because all costs are variable in the long run.
4. When market price is below the minimum of the average variable cost curve, the firm shuts down, so quantity supplied is zero over this price range. When price is greater than or equal to the minimum of the average variable cost curve, the firm selects its optimal output rate by equating market price to marginal cost. Thus, the supply curve for a perfectly competitive firm over this price range is equal to the marginal cost curve.
5. In a perfectly competitive market in the short run, some inputs are held fixed, so the number of firms is fixed because potential entrants cannot begin production without some of the fixed input. With the number of firms fixed, the short-run supply curve for the industry is the sum of the supply curves for all firms.
6. In a perfectly competitive market, all factors of production are variable in the long run, so new firms may enter the industry under these circumstances. Firms have an incentive to enter if the existing firms are earning positive economic profits. Thus, new entry continues until there are zero economic profits, or, analytically, until $P =$ minimum of the LATC curve.
7. The perfectly competitive industry reaches an allocatively efficient equilibrium at which no additional trade between buyers and sellers is

voluntarily forthcoming. Producers' plus consumers' surplus is maximized at this equilibrium, so the perfectly competitive market exhausts all gains from trade.

8. Asymmetric information about product quality gives rise to a lemons problem, which implies that consumers will not pay more than the low-quality price for any product. If a quality-assuring price exists, it offers firms producing the high-quality product positive economic profits. The market reaches a long-run equilibrium not by entry of new firms to drive down economic profits but by investments in specific assets.

Trouble Spots

Concept	Reminder
Assumption 2: Firms Are Price Takers	Perfectly competitive firms are price takers; they cannot affect the *market* price by their actions. Either a small market share for all firms or strategic behavior by all other firms to offset the changes in output by a single firm will produce this type of market structure. Firms may engage in price-*setting* behavior, but such behavior does not affect the market price.
Assumption 4: Information Is Symmetrically Distributed Among Buyers and Sellers	The assumption that information is symmetrically distributed does not mean that buyers and sellers know everything about everything. They know information that all market participants know; there are no secrets about costs, quality, or prices under this assumption.
Shutdown Decision	The shutdown decision determines whether firms will operate or not in the short run. If a firm shuts down, it is still in the industry because it is servicing its fixed costs. In the long run, however, when a firm shuts down, it exits the industry.
Short-Run Supply for a Perfectly Competitive Firm	Although the short-run supply curve for the perfectly competitive firm equals its marginal cost curve, the two curves are conceptually different. For marginal cost, the firm selects an output rate (horizontal axis) and the marginal cost curve gives a dollar cost. For supply, the firm is given a price (vertical axis) and the supply curve gives an output rate.
The Factor Price Effect	The factor price effect causes marginal and average cost curves to shift when the output of the *whole industry* changes. Changing the output of a single firm does not cause the factor price effect.

Perfect Competition in the Long Run	The long-run equilibrium for the perfectly competitive industry implies that all firms earn zero economic profits. This is not the same as zero accounting profits because accounting statements exclude some opportunity costs. A firm that earns zero economic profits receives an income stream that covers all opportunity costs, so it is compensated exactly for its decision to continue production.

10.7 Review Questions

1. What assumption do we make so that firms know whether it is profitable to invest in other industries?
2. What are the two arguments we use to rationalize the price-taker assumption?
3. What assumption do we use to add together the short-run supply curves so that we can call the result the short-run market supply curve?
4. What conditions must hold at the short-run market equilibrium? How do these compare to the long-run market equilibrium?
5. Explain when and why the marginal cost curve is the same as the supply curve for a perfectly competitive firm.
6. If a competitive firm cannot pay its fixed costs, will it shut down in the short run? If it operates, what will it say to its creditors?
7. Explain why a competitive firm operates at the minimum of its long-run average cost curve over time.
8. Explain why the perfectly competitive market is allocatively efficient in the short and long run.
9. Is it a contradiction of our model if some firms enter a perfectly competitive industry while others are exiting the industry?
10. Why must the quality-assuring price offer firms that produce a high-quality product positive economic profits from their operations (excluding their investment in specific assets)?

10.8 Price Theory Problems

1. Firms may earn positive profits in the short run, but they will shut down if their average revenue is less than their average variable cost of production. Because positive profits are unlimited and fixed costs are given, it would seem that firms may on *average* earn positive profits over time. Analyze this claim. Is it true?
2. *True or False:* A more efficient firm will drive less efficient firms from a perfectly competitive industry in the long run.
3. The price elasticity of demand for the market is –.5, the market output rate is 1,000 units per month, and there are 20 firms in the market. Assuming that each firm has an equal market share, what is the price elasticity of demand for a typical firm? Suppose that two firms merge. What is the price elasticity of demand for the new combined firm?

4. Suppose the marginal and average variable cost curves for a perfectly competitive firm are given by $SMC(Q) = 4 + 16Q$ and $AVC(Q) = 4 + 8Q + (3{,}200/Q)$. What is the profit-maximizing output rate if market price equals \$260? Will the firm shut down or continue to operate in the short run? What is the minimum market price at which the firm will operate? How much will it produce at the minimum price?
5. Suppose that IBM-compatible computers are produced in a perfectly competitive market. In each of the following situations, determine the effect on market price and quantity of computers sold, both for the whole industry and for the typical firm. Perform your analysis for both the short run and the long run.

    a. A trade embargo is placed on the import of Japanese computers. Before the embargo, the Japanese had a 55 percent share of the total market.
    b. Space-based production of computer memory chips begins and lowers the price of memory chips by 20 percent.
    c. A new software program is written for IBM-compatible computers that allows them to understand human speech and all of its subtle meanings.

6. Suppose that the population of video renters in Pembroke Pines, Florida, doubles overnight. Explain how the industry adjusts to the new demand for video rentals in the short and long run. Draw a diagram showing the path of adjustment for the typical firm and for the industry. What can you say about the nature of costs for the industry if market price increases in the long run?
7. All manufacturers in the cellular phone business have a long-run average total cost curve given by $LATC(Q) = (1{,}000{,}000/Q) + Q + 10$. What is the industry's long-run equilibrium price? What will be the long-run output level of a typical firm? If there are 50 manufacturers of cellular phones, what is the equilibrium output in the industry?
8. *True or False:* A unit tax imposed on a constant-cost industry will not affect the output rate of the typical firm. (Note: It could be a very large tax.)
9. Lump-sum taxes are taxes that are not related to sales or output of a firm; rather, they are paid because a firm exists (legally) over a given period of time. City and county occupational licenses, for example, are lump-sum taxes. Because such taxes are fixed, they become part of a firm's fixed costs. Draw a diagram to show how lump-sum taxes affect the shutdown decision of a firm. If they affect the shutdown decision, do they affect the firm's supply curve in the short run?
10. Business cards are typically sold in packages of 500 cards. The weekly market demand curve for packages of business cards is given by $Q = 100 - .5P$, where Q is the total number of packages demanded at price P. Assume that there are 5 firms in the market. The marginal cost of producing business cards is constant and equal to \$100 per package.

    a. How many packages of business cards are sold in equilibrium? What is the market clearing price?

b. If each firm sells an equal share, how much does the typical firm produce?
c. Assume now that the state government places a $10 unit tax on the sale of business card packages. What are the new equilibrium price and quantity sold?
d. What is the amount of the deadweight loss due to the tax? Are both consumers' and producers' surpluses part of the deadweight loss, or is it just consumers' surplus?

11. Frisbees are produced in a perfectly competitive market. There are currently 10 firms in the market. Each firm's long-run average and marginal costs are given by

$$LATC = .5Q_f + 1 + (8/Q_f)$$

and

$$LMC = Q_f + 1$$

a. If the market is in long-run equilibrium, what are the market clearing price and quantity?
b. The (inverse) market demand curve is $P = 85 - 2Q_{market}$, where Q_{market} is the total quantity sold in the market. What is the total surplus at the market clearing price?
c. Suppose demand increases to $P = 170 - 2Q_{market}$ and firms adjust along their LMC curves to meet the new demand before there are new entrants. What are the new market clearing price and quantity without entry? After there is entry, how many firms are there at the long-run market equilibrium?

12. Suppose that the total cost structure for the typical firm producing a high- or low-quality product is given by

$$C_H = F_H + \beta_H Q_H^2$$
$$C_L = F_L + \beta_L Q_L^2$$

where C_L is the total cost, F_L is fixed cost, and Q_L is the output rate of the firm producing the low-quality product, and C_H is the total cost, F_H is fixed cost, and Q_H is the output rate of the firm producing the high-quality product. Using equations (10.5), (10.6), and (10.7) in the text, show that the quality-assuring price is given by

$$P^* = \left\{ \frac{1 - \left(\frac{F_L}{F_H}\right)\frac{r}{1+r}}{1 - \frac{r}{1+r}\left(\frac{\beta_L}{\beta_H}\right)} \right\}^{1/2}$$

10.9 Writing Exercise

Unrestricted entry and exit to and from an industry is the key that drives perfectly competitive firms to a zero-profit equilibrium in the long run. Choose a product that you are familiar with and investigate the costs of beginning a new business to manufacture and produce this product. Carefully document the costs that are unique to the product you have chosen—such as a license to dispose of hazardous waste—versus those costs that any new firm must pay—such as rent for an office. Investigate whether all existing firms were required to pay the product-specific costs that you must pay; that is, are there rules that apply to you as a new entrant but not to existing firms? Document the turnover rate in firms producing this product over the past five years. Write a report that describes your findings.

11

Monopoly and Market Power

Preview Questions

When you finish studying this chapter, you should be able to answer the following questions:

- What is the meaning of market, or monopoly, power?
- How does a single-price monopolist choose output to maximize profits?
- What is the profit-maximizing price markup for a monopoly?
- What are the four barriers to entry that can create market power?
- Why is there an incentive to cheat in a cartel?
- How are consumers' and producers' surpluses affected by a monopoly?
- How is federal antitrust law used to combat the effects of a monopoly?

Those who have acquired immune deficiency syndrome (AIDS) are certain to live a shorter life, although there are drug treatments available that can help slow the progress of the disease. One of these is the drug AZT. The Burroughs Wellcome Co. holds six patents on the use of AZT for treating AIDS patients. These patents give Burroughs the exclusive right to market AZT in the United States until the year 2005. In effect, Burroughs is a monopoly; it is the sole seller of AZT. One might think that Burroughs can charge whatever it likes for AZT. After all, what would one pay to prolong one's life? But there are limits to what one will pay. We know that income and wealth are limited, so a very high price for AZT brings only a few buyers. Alternatively, a very low price provides the drug to more customers, who will demand it for a longer period of time, but this may not make the most economic profits. Burroughs must look for the price that maximizes its profits. The problem Burroughs faces as a monopoly is more difficult than that of a competitive firm. Burroughs does not react to market price like competitive firms do; it must set the market price.

In the perfectly competitive market structure, a firm's output decision has no effect on market price, but a monopoly can affect the market price of its product by its output decision. In effect, monopolies are price makers, not price takers. The entry of new firms plays a key role in the perfectly competitive model because entry eliminates economic profits in the long run. With a monopoly, however, either there is no entry or entry is restricted, so economic profits can persist over time.

This chapter analyzes the effects of a firm with monopoly power on price, output, and profits. We discuss how monopolies develop, how they act to maximize profits, and what they do to maintain themselves. We examine government policy toward monopolies and the possible ways to detect whether a firm has monopoly power in a market. We also show how a monopoly can be regulated to increase consumers' surplus. After this chapter has developed the basic behavior of a monopolist, Chapter 12 will present more general ways for firms with market power to price their products.

11.1 Price and Output Decisions for a Monopoly

Technically, a **pure monopoly** exists when there is only *one* seller of a good or service—that is, a monopoly is the only firm in the industry. A situation that fits this definition is often difficult to identify in the real world. For example, only the Apple Computer Company may sell the Macintosh computer, but does that make Apple Computer a monopolist? Probably not, because many people find other computers to be substitutes for the Macintosh. The important question is, how *close* are these other computers to substituting for the Macintosh? Before the development of Microsoft Windows software, no other desktop computers that sold for under $3,000 offered the screen presentation software found on the Macintosh. Before the development of Microsoft Windows, then, Apple Computer Company had some market power. **Market power** (also called *monopoly power*) is present when a firm is a price maker, not a price taker. Market power implies that the demand curve for the firm's product or service is negatively sloped. The firm is a **price maker** because its output decision directly affects the market price. The current widespread use of the Windows software allows IBM-compatible computers to represent an alternative to the Macintosh computer. Thus, Apple's market power has eroded over time. Let's explore how market power affects the profit-maximizing decision of a firm.

Pure Monopoly
A single seller or supplier of a well-defined commodity for which there are no close substitutes.

Market Power
The ability to affect the market price by changing the firm's output rate.

Price Maker
A firm with market power.

The Demand Curve for a Monopolist

If the firm is a pure monopoly, then its demand curve is the *market* demand curve because it is the only firm in the industry. To help develop the analysis, assume that the Picasso Jewelry Company has some market power. The company makes a very stylish pair of earrings that customers find highly desirable. No other company offers this distinctive design. The annual demand curve for this product is given by the following equation:

$$Q = 20{,}000 - 100P \qquad (11.1)$$

where Q is the annual quantity of pairs of earrings demanded and P is the price charged per pair. Notice that the demand curve is negatively sloped: Each $1 increase in price causes quantity demanded to decrease by 100 pairs of earrings. We can rearrange equation (11.1) to show the inverse demand curve. The inverse demand curve places price on the left-hand side and quantity on the right-hand side of the equation:

$$P = 200 - \frac{Q}{100} \tag{11.2}$$

The inverse demand curve shows the direct effect that a change in quantity has on the market price of earrings. By choosing Q optimally, the monopolist is also determining the price of its product; that is, the monopolist is a price maker. If 10,000 pairs of earrings are currently produced, for example, then the market clearing price is \$100 per pair (i.e., \$100 = 200 – 10,000/100). To sell one more pair of earrings, the firm must reduce price. The slope of the inverse demand function, –1/100, represents the amount by which price must fall to sell another pair of earrings; that is, the monopolist must reduce price by 1 cent to sell another pair of earrings. Alternatively, if one less pair of earrings is produced, the firm is expected to raise price 1 cent to establish a new market clearing price. In contrast, if this was a perfectly competitive firm, it would expect to sell another pair of earrings without any change in market price.

In short, the inverse demand curve shows how a firm with market power can and does affect the price of its product.

LEARNING EXERCISE 11.1

Find and graph the inverse demand equation—that is, P as a function of Q—when $Q = 500 - 10P$ and $Q = 100/P$. In both instances, find how much price will fall if Q increases from 100 to 110 units.

MARGINAL REVENUE FOR A SINGLE-PRICE MONOPOLY

Single-Price Monopoly A monopolist that charges the same price for all units sold.

Now, let's assume for simplicity that the Picasso Jewelry Company adopts a strategy of setting a single price for its earrings. A firm that adopts such a strategy is called a **single-price monopoly.** This strategy implies that all buyers pay the same price, regardless of the quantity bought. A single price for all buyers is the likely result when resale of the monopoly product is possible. Different prices to different customers will quickly be eliminated by arbitrage trading in the resale market.

To maximize profits, the firm finds the output rate at which marginal revenue equals marginal cost. You will remember that marginal revenue is defined as the change in total revenue due to a one-unit change in quantity sold: $\Delta TR(Q)/\Delta Q$. Total revenue for the Picasso Jewelry Company is written as $TR(Q) = P \times Q$. Substituting for P from equation (11.2) gives $TR(Q) = 200Q - Q^2/100$. Now, we saw in Chapter 2 that for a linear demand equation, defined as $Q = a - bP$, where a and b are constants, marginal revenue equals $(a/b) - (2/b)Q$. In terms of equation (11.1), $a = 20{,}000$ and $b = 100$, so marginal revenue for the Picasso Jewelry Company can be written as

$$MR(Q) = 200 - \frac{2}{100}Q \tag{11.3}$$

Equation (11.3) shows that a monopolist can affect marginal revenue by its choice of output. If the Picasso Jewelry Company produces 1,000 pairs of earrings, for example, its marginal revenue is \$180 (i.e., 200 – 2,000/100). If the firm increases its output, then marginal revenue decreases. If the firm produces 3,000 pairs of earrings, for example, then its marginal revenue equals \$140 (i.e., 200 – 6,000/100). These calculations and others are shown in the table accompanying Figure 11.1. In contrast, a perfectly competitive firm has no control over the marginal revenue it receives as its output changes. The perfectly competitive firm is a price taker, so marginal revenue is fixed and equal to the market price.

Figure 11.1 shows the demand curve for earrings sold by the Picasso Jewelry Company and its marginal revenue curve. The demand curve—equation (11.2)—intersects the vertical axis at a price of \$200 per pair and intersects the horizontal axis at a quantity of 20,000 pairs of earrings. The marginal revenue curve, too, intersects the vertical axis at \$200, but it intersects the horizontal axis at a quantity of 10,000. The marginal revenue curve declines faster than the (inverse) demand curve because each change in price applies to *all* buyers, so for existing buyers there is a loss in total revenue.

MATH NOTEPAD

Show That $P \geq$ MR for a Single-Price Monopolist

We can show that $P \geq \text{MR}$ by examining how total revenue, $\text{TR}(Q) = PQ$, changes for a monopolist. Taking the total differential of both sides of the total revenue equation gives

$$\Delta\text{TR}(Q) = P\Delta Q + Q\Delta P$$

Dividing this equation by ΔQ gives

$$\Delta\text{TR}(Q)/\Delta Q = P + Q(\Delta P/\Delta Q)$$

where the last term on the right-hand side, $(\Delta P/\Delta Q)$, equals the slope of the inverse demand curve, which is *negative*. By definition, $\text{MR}(Q) = \Delta\text{TR}(Q)/\Delta Q$, so marginal revenue is less than or equal to P for negatively sloped demand curves. Note that $\text{MR}(Q)$ equals P when output equals zero.

The table shown at the bottom of Figure 11.1 provides a numerical summary of the behavior of marginal revenue and quantity demanded. As can be seen from this table, marginal revenue is also related to the price elasticity of demand, denoted by η. In Figure 11.1, we see that when marginal revenue is zero at $Q = 10{,}000$, the price elasticity of demand equals –1. The relationship between marginal revenue and the price elasticity of demand can be shown using the results developed in Chapter 2. There it was shown that:

$$\text{MR}(Q) = P\left(1 + \frac{1}{\eta}\right) \tag{11.4}$$

is a general result when a single price is charged to all customers.

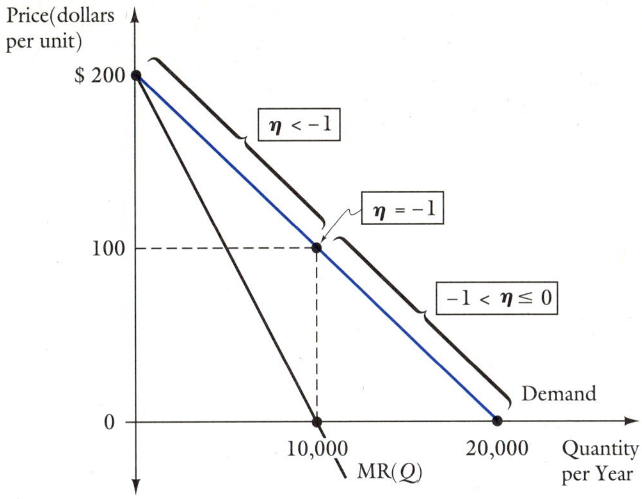

Quantity	Price	MR	Price Elasticity
0	$200.00	$200.00	
1	199.99	199.98	
2	199.98	199.96	
⋮	⋮	⋮	
1,000	190.00	180.00	$\eta < -1$
⋮	⋮	⋮	
3,000	170.00	140.00	
⋮	⋮	⋮	
9,999	100.01	0.02	
10,000	100.00	0.00	$\eta = -1$
10,001	99.99	−0.02	
⋮	⋮	⋮	$-1 < \eta \leq 0$
19,999	0.01	−199.98	
20,000	0.00	−200.00	

FIGURE 11.1

The Demand Curve for Earrings Made by the Picasso Jewelry Company

The demand curve for earrings made by the Picasso Jewelry Company intersects the vertical, or price, axis at $200 per pair of earrings. As price decreases, quantity demanded increased until the demand curve intersects the horizontal, or quantity, axis at 20,000 pairs of earrings. The marginal revenue curve (MR) bisects the distance between the demand curve and the price axis, reaching zero at 10,000 pairs of earrings. At this quantity, the price elasticity of demand equals –1. The table illustrates the relationship between price elasticity and marginal revenue for various output rates.

Equations (11.4) and (11.3) are consistent with each other. The price elasticity of demand for the Picasso Jewelry Company is given by $\eta = -100(P/Q)$.[1] Substituting this expression into equation (11.4) gives $MR(Q) = P - 100Q$. We can substitute for P in this equation using the inverse demand function, $P = 200 - Q/100$, from equation (11.2). This gives $MR(Q) = 200 - 2Q/100$, which is the same as the expression shown in equation (11.3).

For the case of perfect competition, we found that marginal revenue equals price; that is, when the firm is a price taker, $MR(Q) = P$. Demand is horizontal or perfectly elastic ($\eta = -\infty$) for a price-taking firm. The monopolist, however, does not face a horizontal demand curve, so $\eta \neq -\infty$. To maximize profits, the monopolist would never operate at a point at which marginal revenue is negative. If it did, it could reduce output and thereby increase revenues, lower total costs, and consequently increase profits. This result implies that a monopolist will never operate in that portion of the demand curve for which demand is price *inelastic*. Using Figure 11.1, then, we see that the Picasso Jewelry Company will never produce more than 10,000 pairs of earrings to satisfy its goal of maximizing profits.

LEARNING EXERCISE 11.2

Find and graph the marginal revenue equations for the two demand functions given in Learning Exercise 11.1.

MAXIMIZING PROFITS FOR A SINGLE-PRICE MONOPOLIST

We now know that the firm will not operate in the inelastic region of its demand curve if it has market power, but we have not found exactly where it does operate. As noted above and many times in Chapter 10, profit is maximized at the output rate at which marginal revenue equals marginal cost.[2] If the firm goes past this output rate, total profits will be less because, for each additional unit sold, cost increases more than revenue. If the firm does not produce the output rate at which marginal revenue equals marginal cost, total profits will be less than they could be, because an additional unit sold increases revenues by more than it increases costs.

Given the marginal revenue structure above, all we need is a marginal cost curve to solve for Picasso Jewelry Company's profit-maximizing output rate. In Figure 11.2, we have redrawn both the marginal revenue and demand curves in Figure 11.1, and we have included the firm's short-run average and marginal cost curves. These cost curves are generated directly from the firm's short-run total cost curve. We will assume that the short-run total cost of producing earrings, STC(Q), is described by the following equation:

$$STC(Q) = 250{,}000 + 40Q + .01Q^2 \tag{11.5}$$

[1] From Chapter 2, we know that $\eta = -b(P/Q)$ for a linear demand equation of the form $Q = a - bP$. Substituting $b = 100$ from equation (11.1) gives $\eta = -100(P/Q)$.

[2] This statement assumes that the $MR = MC$ position also satisfies the second condition for profit maximization, which is that the slope of the marginal cost curve is greater than the slope of the marginal revenue curve at the chosen output rate.

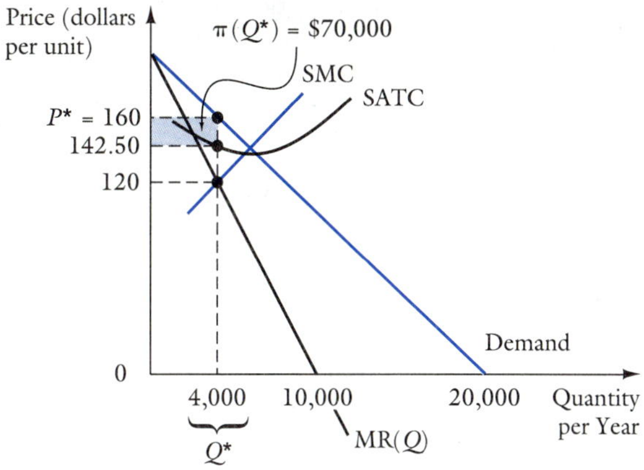

FIGURE 11.2

The Profit-Maximizing Output Rate for the Picasso Jewelry Company

The Picasso Jewelry Company maximizes short-run profits at the output rate at which marginal revenue, MR(Q), equals short-run marginal cost, SMC. The firm produces 4,000 pairs of earrings, which cost an average of $142.50 per pair to produce and sell for $160 per pair. Short-run profits, $\pi(Q^*)$, equal $70,000.

Equation (11.5) implies that the firm incurs $250,000 in fixed cost in the short run. The firm's average total cost equals its total cost divided by output: SATC(Q) = (250,000/Q) + 40 + .01Q. The firm's marginal cost, SMC(Q), is equal to the change in total cost when output changes by one unit. Algebraically we can write the Picasso Jewelry Company's short-run marginal cost as[3]

$$\text{SMC}(Q) = 40 + .02Q \tag{11.6}$$

Setting marginal revenue equal to marginal cost, MR(Q) = SMC(Q), solves for the profit-maximizing output rate. Using equation (11.3) for marginal revenue and equation (11.6) for marginal cost gives

$$200 - \frac{2}{100}Q = 40 + .02Q$$

or

$$Q^* = \frac{160}{.04} = 4{,}000$$

where Q^* is the optimal output rate. Substituting Q^* = 4,000 into either the marginal revenue or marginal cost equation shows that MR(4,000) = SMC(4,000) = $120.

[3] For any cost equation with the form TC(Q) = $d + eQ + fQ^2$, the marginal cost equation is always MC(Q) = $e + 2fQ$. In equation (14.5), d = 250,000, e = 40, and f = .01. Substituting for e and f in the MC(Q) formula gives the result in the text.

The firm charges a market clearing price of \$160 per pair of earrings. This price is found after substituting $Q^* = 4{,}000$ into equation (11.2), the equation that defines the (inverse) demand curve (i.e., $160 = 200 - 4{,}000/100$). Similarly, the firm's average total cost at Q^* equals its total cost from equation (11.5) divided by 4,000, which is \$142.50. Multiplying the difference between price and average total cost by quantity gives the firm's profits. The shaded region in Figure 11.2, on page 419, shows the annual profits from earring sales using this calculation. The Picasso Jewelry Company earns \$70,000 in profits each year; that is, $(\$160 - \$142.50) \times 4{,}000 = \$70{,}000$.

The \$70,000 per year represents the short-run *economic* profits that the firm earns. The circumstances that give rise to its market power—that is, its negatively sloped demand curve—determine whether these short-run economic profits will persist into the long run. If entry is not allowed, say, because the firm has a government-granted patent on its earring design (discussed below), then other firms cannot copy its product. So the development and sale of perfect or near-perfect substitutes may not occur in the immediate future. In this case, these short-run economic profits will persist as long as the demand and cost curves remain as specified; there is nothing that other firms can do to extract these economic profits.

In a sense, a monopolist behaves much like a perfectly competitive firm does in the way that it chooses its optimal output rate. Both firms, for example, compare the added revenue from an extra unit of output to its added cost to decide whether the unit should be produced. In general, if marginal revenue exceeds marginal costs, both a perfectly competitive firm and a monopolist will expand output. Similarly, if marginal revenue is less than marginal cost, then both of these firms will contract output. The difference is that price is fixed for a perfectly competitive firm, so marginal revenue equals price, but the monopolist affects prices because it faces a negatively sloped demand curve for its product or service. The monopolist is thus a price maker. In addition, the negatively sloped demand curve implies that marginal revenue is less than price if the monopolist charges a single price—that is, all customers pay the same price—for its product or service. Because marginal revenue is less than price, the monopolist chooses a lower output rate to maximize profits than that chosen by a comparable perfectly competitive firm. This last point is important, and we will develop its implications for consumer welfare in section 11.4 below.

Learning Exercise 11.3

Suppose the cost function for the Picasso Jewelry Company is $STC(Q) = 200{,}000 + 80Q + .01Q^2$. What are the new profit-maximizing output rate, market clearing price, and total profits of the firm?

MARKUP PRICING FOR A SINGLE-PRICE MONOPOLIST

There is another way to look at the profit-maximizing solution that we have just derived for the Picasso Jewelry Company. Suppose we combine the $MR(Q) = SMC(Q)$ condition with equation (11.4) on page 417, the equation for marginal revenue. Substituting for MR(Q) from equation (11.4) gives:

$$P(1 + \frac{1}{\eta}) = \text{SMC}(Q).$$

Price Markup
The fractional difference between price and marginal cost.

Subtracting P/η and SMC(Q) from each side gives $P - \text{SMC}(Q) = -P/\eta$. Dividing both sides by P gives the **price markup** formula for maximizing profits:

$$\frac{P - \text{SMC}(Q)}{P} = \frac{-1}{\eta} \qquad (11.8)$$

Equation (11.8) states that to maximize profits, the firm should follow a price markup rule that is inversely proportional to the firm's price elasticity of demand. The markup here is relative to the firm's marginal cost. For example, using a linear demand curve, $Q = a - bP$, we know from Chapter 7 that $\eta = -b(P/Q)$, where $b =$ 100 for the Picasso Jewelry Company. If the firm produces 4,000 pairs of earrings, then its price elasticity of demand equals −4 (i.e., $\eta = -100 \times 160/4{,}000$). From equation (11.8), we find that price exceeds marginal cost by 25 percent ($.25 = -1/-4$) at the profit-maximizing output rate.

The markup pricing rule is illustrated in Figure 11.3 for the Picasso Jewelry Company. The price elasticity of demand is computed using the formula

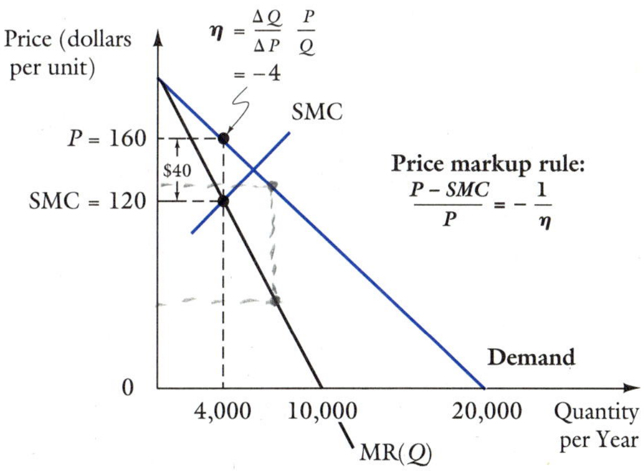

FIGURE 11.3

The Price Markup Rule Applied to the Picasso Jewelry Company

The price markup rule is another way to determine the profit-maximizing output rate. At the optimal output rate, the ratio $(P - \text{SMC})/P$ equals negative one divided by the price elasticity of demand, $-1/\eta$. For the Picasso Jewelry Company, $P =$ \$160 and SMC = \$120 at the output rate of 4,000 pairs of earrings. Thus, the ratio $(P - \text{SMC})/P = 4$, which is also equal to $-1/\eta$.

$\eta = \frac{\Delta Q}{\Delta P}\frac{P}{Q}$. Substituting $P = 160$, $Q = 4{,}000$, and $\frac{\Delta Q}{\Delta P} = -100$ from equation (11.1) gives $\eta = -4$. The implied optimal markup is thus equal to $-1/\eta$, or 25 percent. Given that SMC = \$120 and P = \$160 at the output rate of 4,000 pairs of earrings per year, we find that the firm is actually marking up its product correctly, that is, .25 = (160 – 120)/160.

The price markup formula is more than just descriptive; it is proscriptive. The two sides of equation (11.8) *must* equal each other if the firm is operating at an output rate that maximizes profits. If this equation is out of balance, then the firm is not at the profit-maximizing output rate. Suppose that the price markup equals 20 percent at the current output rate, the market clears at the price the firm is charging, and the price elasticity of demand equals –2. At $\eta = -2$, the optimal markup is 50 percent (.50 = –1/–2), so the firm *is not* in equilibrium at its current output rate because its markup is too low relative to that implied by equation (11.8). The firm is actually producing too much and charging too low a price compared to its profit-maximizing output rate.

SHUTDOWN RULE FOR A SINGLE-PRICE MONOPOLIST

For the perfectly competitive market structure, we found that it was optimal for the firm to shut down in the short run if price was less than the minimum of the firm's average variable cost curve.

> **For any firm with market power that charges a single price, it is optimal for the firm to shut down in the short run if there is no output rate at which its demand curve exceeds its average variable cost curve.**

When this situation occurs, there is no price that the firm can charge that exceeds its average variable cost of production, so operating causes more losses than shutting down.

We can state this result in another form. The demand curve is the average revenue curve because average revenue is always equal to price. Average revenue, AR(Q), equals total revenue divided by Q. Because TR(Q) = PQ, we see that AR(Q) = P for any output rate. A monopolist shuts down when there is no output rate at which average revenue exceeds average variable cost. In other words, by shutting down, the monopolist loses its fixed costs, but these are less than its losses from continuing operations in the short run. This is equivalent to the statement made in Chapter 10 for the perfectly competitive firm; it is thus a general claim that applies to any firm that charges a single price for all units.

In Figure 11.4, we show a situation in which a firm will shut down in the short run. As you can see, the short-run average variable cost curve, SAVC, lies above the demand curve for the monopolist at all output rates. There is no output rate that is more profitable than the zero output rate in the short run.

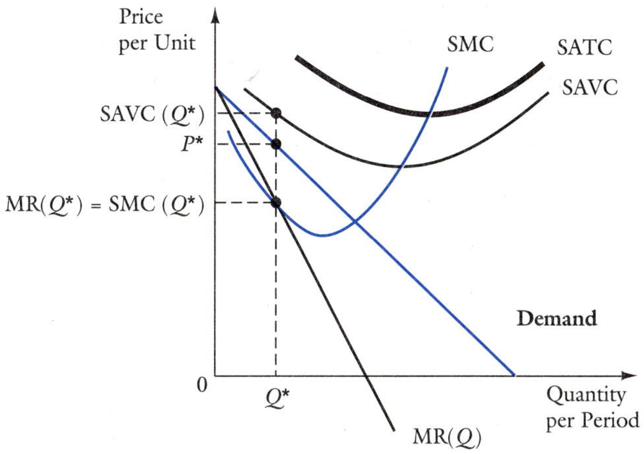

FIGURE 11.4

An Example Where the Monopolist Should Shut Down in the Short Run

The firm should shut down operations in the short run if average revenue, which equals price, P^*, is less than short-run average cost, SAVC(Q^*), at the optimal *operating* output rate.

A MONOPOLIST HAS NO SUPPLY CURVE

We found that the firm's supply curve in a perfectly competitive market is derived from its marginal cost curve. The short-run industry supply curve was shown to equal the (horizontal) sum of all individual firms' marginal cost curves above average variable cost. It may appear logical, then, that the monopolist's supply curve would also be its marginal cost curve.

Even though this thought may seem logical, it is not correct.

The monopolist has no supply curve.

A supply curve is defined by the answers to a sequence of questions: "How much do you produce at a price of $100?" "How much do you produce at a price of $101?" "How much do you produce at a price of $102?" and so on. For a monopolist, though, there is no *unique* relationship between price and the quantity supplied, so it is not possible to determine the exact quantity that it will produce at a given price or even at various prices. We illustrate this result in Figure 11.5.

Panel (a) in Figure 11.5 shows two demand curves, D_0 and D_1, and their corresponding marginal revenue curves, MR_1 and MR_1. The marginal cost curve, MC, for the monopolist is also shown. If the firm faces demand curve D_0, then the profit-maximizing output rate equals Q^* and the market clearing price equals P_0. Alternatively, if the firm faces demand curve D_1, the profit-maximizing output rate is again Q^*, but the market clearing price is now P_1. This panel shows that it may be optimal for the monopolist to

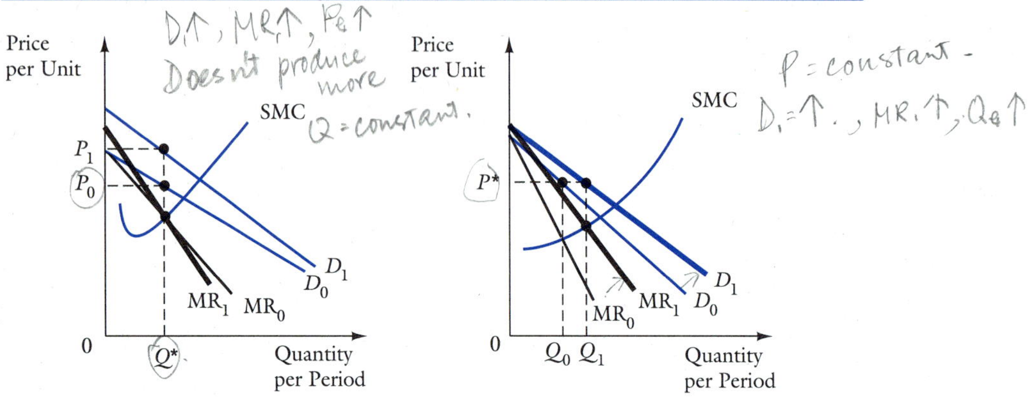

FIGURE 11.5

There is No Unique Relationship Between Price and Quantity for a Monopolist

For a monopolist, there is no unique relationship between price and quantity, so there is no supply curve. Panel (a) shows that a shift in demand from D_0 to D_1 causes the optimal price to increase from P_0 to P_1 but does not change the optimal quantity, Q^*. Similarly, panel (b) shows that a shift in demand from D_0 to D_1 causes the optimal quantity to increase from Q_0 to Q_1 but does not change the optimal price, P^*.

charge different prices when demand changes, even though its output does not change.

Panel (b) in Figure 11.5 also shows two demand curves and their associated marginal revenue curves. If demand is given by D_0, then it is optimal for the monopolist to produce Q_0 and to charge a market clearing price of P^*. In contrast, if demand is given by D_1 , then it is optimal to increase the output rate to Q_1, but the market clearing price remains at P^*. In this situation, to maximize profits, the monopolist changes its output rate but not its market clearing price. A shift in demand is the only way to make the monopolist reevaluate its optimal output and price decision. But when we shift the demand curve, we cannot find a unique relationship between price and quantity supplied. Thus, there is no supply curve for a monopolist.

An alternative interpretation of this result is that the monopolist is just not a price taker; it is a price maker. So, the monopolist cannot sensibly answer the question that we pose to define a supply curve ("What quantity will you produce at various given prices?"). The question cannot be answered because the monopolist does not take any price as given; it determines price by its output decision. Because it cannot answer the question, it cannot have a supply curve.

EFFECTS OF A TAX ON A SINGLE-PRICE MONOPOLIST

The effects of a tax on a monopolist may be very different from what one might expect. Generally, a unit tax will cause market price to rise by less than the full amount of the tax. The per unit burden of a unit tax is typically shared between both consumers and producers. For a monopolist, however, market price may rise by more than the tax, so the per unit burden may actually exceed the tax.

To develop this point, suppose that a unit tax of amount $T = \$10$ is imposed on a monopolist. The tax increases the monopolist's marginal cost curve by \$10. If the original marginal cost curve is $\text{SMC}(Q)$ and the marginal revenue curve is $\text{MR}(Q)$, then the new profit-maximizing solution is given by

$$\text{SMC}(Q) + T = \text{MR}(Q) \tag{11.9}$$

Notice that the tax drives a wedge between marginal revenue and marginal cost, so some *deadweight loss* in total market surplus for a monopoly structure is expected, just as it was in the perfectly competitive market structure.

In Figure 11.6, we show how the new tax affects the optimal output rate and price for the monopolist. The monopolist is originally maximizing profits at Q_0 and charging a market clearing price of P_0 to each customer. With the tax, the marginal cost curve shifts upward to SMC + T. The new profit-maximizing output rate is Q_1. The monopolist charges P_1 at this new output rate. Although we do not show the monopolist's profits, we know that they cannot increase with the tax and that they probably fall. If they do increase, the monopolist will have made an error, for example, by choosing output rate Q_0 initially when there was no tax to pay. Thus, we know that profits decrease or, at best, remain the same.

The question is whether the *change in price*, ΔP, is more or less than the tax, T. The general answer is that we do not know. The change in price for a monopolist may be greater than or less than the unit tax. In a perfectly competitive market, however, the change in price must always be less than (or equal to) the unit tax. In Figure 11.6, $\Delta P < T$ as drawn.

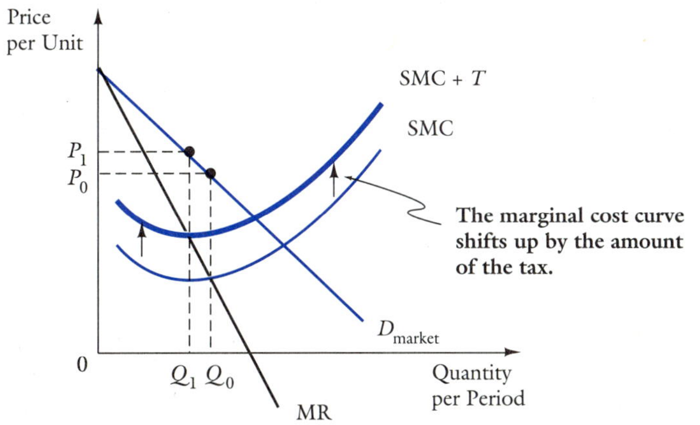

FIGURE 11.6

The Effect of a Unit Tax on a Single-Price Monopolist

A per unit tax of T causes the short-run marginal cost curve, SMC, of a monopolist to shift upward by the amount of the tax. The profit-maximizing output rate decreases from Q_0 to Q_1, and the market clearing price increases from P_0 to P_1.

We can create the opposite result, that the change in price exceeds the tax, in a simple example. Suppose that the demand curve has a constant price elasticity of -2. The markup pricing rule in equation (11.8) on page 421 tells us that the optimal markup is *always* 50 percent. Suppose that the marginal cost curve is constant, such that SMC = \$50. In addition, assume that $P = \$100$ *before* the tax is imposed. We see that the markup rule is satisfied at these prices; that is, $.5 = (100 - 50)/100$. Now, if a unit tax of \$10 is imposed, SMC + $T = \$60$. To maintain the 50 percent markup, the firm must move to an output rate at which $P = \$120$. In this case, then, price increases by \$20 even though the unit tax is only \$10.

LEARNING EXERCISE 11.4

Suppose a \$20 unit tax is imposed on the Picasso Jewelry Company. What are the new optimal output and price? How have profits changed because of the tax? How much money is paid in taxes?

THE LONG-RUN BEHAVIOR OF A MONOPOLIST

The analysis of the Picasso Jewelry Company uses short-run average and marginal cost curves. If we move to the long run, the analysis can be repeated using the long-run average and marginal cost curves. The decision rule for maximizing profits is the same, except that long-run cost curves replace the short-run curves. The monopolist maximizes profit, for example, by finding the output rate at which marginal revenue equals long-run marginal cost. In addition, it is optimal for the monopolist to shut down—and leave the industry—if its demand curve lies *below* its long-run average total cost curve. (Remember that all costs are variable in the long run, so the long-run average total cost curve is really an average variable cost curve.) In short, the monopolist acts the same in the long run as it does in the short run, except that its cost curves are different.

There is a more general question, however, that a long-run analysis presents: Can the economic profits earned by a monopolist persist in the long run? Some economists will answer no to this question, not because the monopoly loses its monopoly power but because a monopoly's economic profits are capitalized and thus will be included in its average total cost curve. In other words, if a monopoly is earning economic profits and the firm changes ownership, the new owner is expected to pay a price that reflects the (discounted) present value of those economic profits. The new average total cost curve is thus higher than the average total cost curve that the original owner of the monopoly faced. Thus, the new average total cost curve effectively eliminates the economic profits *for the new owner*. Even without a change in ownership, the source of the monopoly profits may represent an opportunity cost that the firm must account for in its cost structure. If the source is a government arrangement, such as an exclusive license, then the ongoing investment made to secure the arrangement may dissipate all monopoly profits.

Alternatively, new technology can have a major effect on the market power of a monopolist. New technology allows other firms to produce close substitutes for the monopolist's product—without violating patent laws—which reduces the demand for the monopolist's product. Synthetic diamonds, for example, are now more difficult to distinguish from actual diamonds, making them closer substitutes than in the past and thereby reducing the influence that the De Beers Company has on the diamond market.

Either a transfer of ownership or the entry of firms producing close substitutes changes the profitability of a monopolist in the long run.

11.2 Origins of Monopolies and Market Power

Now, let's consider the question of how a firm with market power can develop and maintain itself over time. There are several ways to create market power, but the difficult part is to maintain it over time. As our discussion of perfect competition shows, entry of new firms eliminates economic profits in the long run, so barriers to entry are of foremost importance to maintaining market power. We discuss four barriers to entry: ownership of resources with no close substitutes; economies of scale; government licenses, franchises, and certificates of need; and patents. In addition, we examine the circumstances under which mergers are likely to give the combined firm some market power and discuss how informal collusion by existing firms creates a monopoly-like result.

Barriers to Entry

For market power and monopoly profits to exist in the long run, there must be some way in which the market is closed to entry. Either legal means or certain aspects of the industry's technical or cost structure may prevent entry. We will discuss four **barriers to entry** that have allowed firms to develop and maintain market power in the long run.

Barriers to Entry
Any impediments to entry into an industry that give existing firms market power.

1. Ownership of Resources with No Close Substitutes

Preventing a newcomer from entering an industry is often difficult. Indeed, there are some economists who contend that no monopoly, acting without government support, has been able to prevent entry into its industry unless that monopoly has control of some natural resource essential to production. Suppose one firm owns the entire supply of a raw material that is essential in the production of a particular commodity. This exclusive ownership of a vital resource serves as a barrier to entry until an alternative source of the raw material is found or an alternative technology, not requiring the raw material in question, is developed. A good example of this is the Aluminum Company of America (Alcoa), a firm that, prior to World War II, controlled the world's supply of bauxite, the essential raw material used in the production of aluminum. Alcoa could maintain market power, even when there were competitors, such as Reynolds Aluminum, because the competitors had to buy bauxite from mines controlled by Alcoa.

In the best-selling novel *Gorky Park,* author Martin Cruz Smith describes how a small group of smugglers try to break the monopoly on Russian sables by smuggling live sables out of the former Soviet Union. The smugglers plan to breed the sables for furs to compete with the Russian government's monopoly on sable furs. Some of the smugglers paid dearly—with their lives—for their crimes. In the book and in real life, the Russian government benefits from its monopoly control of live sables. The Russian sable produces the world's highest-quality fur, surpassing even the mink, which is regarded as a substitute, but not too close a substitute, for many consumers. Because Russian sable fur is softer and warmer than mink, the sable is an exclusive resource. Until the Russian sable is successfully exported and bred outside Russia, the government of Russia will have exclusive ownership and thus a monopoly on this product.

The De Beers Company operating from London and South Africa has enjoyed a similar monopoly over the production of uncut diamonds. For nearly fifty years, De Beers has controlled approximately 80 percent of the world's supply of raw diamonds because it either owns the diamond mines or has an exclusive marketing contract with other mine owners. As noted above, De Beers's exclusive control and monopoly pricing has fostered the development of close substitutes. Synthetic diamonds were once viewed as inferior to the real product by most consumers—they had a glassy appearance that tended to reveal their laboratory origin—but technology has made synthetic diamonds nearly indistinguishable from real ones. This has eroded the monopoly position and market power exercised by De Beers. Because monopoly pricing encourages technological advances, ownership of an exclusive resource today may produce a close substitute tomorrow.

LEARNING EXERCISE 11.5

Some economists maintain that the U.S. government has a monopoly in the production of paper money, but this claim assumes that the U.S. dollar has no close substitutes. Are there any close substitutes for the U.S. dollar? If so, what are they?

2. Economies of Scale

Sometimes it is not feasible for more than one firm to exist in an industry because costs are too high for more than one firm to make a normal rate of return. This can occur when the demand curve is such that two (or more) firms sharing the market cannot cover average total costs individually. Only when a single firm engages in the production of the product can average total costs be covered, because the producing firm realizes greater economies of scale than when two or more firms try to operate simultaneously in this market. The perfectly competitive model breaks down in this situation.

Consider the situation depicted in Figure 11.7. Here the industry demand curve is D_{industry}, the corresponding marginal revenue curve is MR, the long-run average total cost curve is LATC, and the long-run marginal cost curve is LMC. Notice that long-run average total costs are falling over a wide range of output. The profit-maximizing output rate (Q_m) for the single

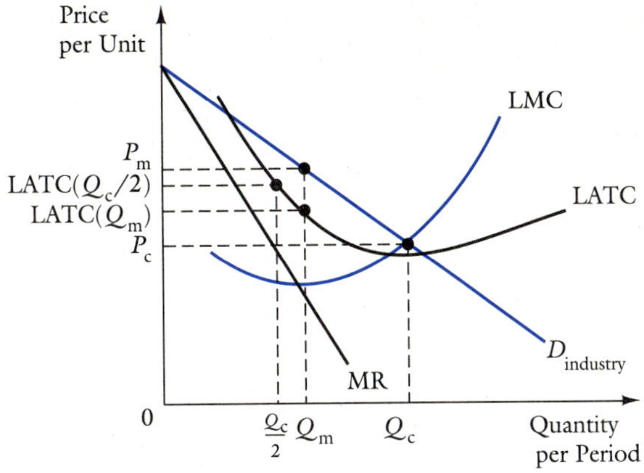

FIGURE 11.7

Economies of Scale Can Create a Natural Monopoly

A natural monopoly arises when economies of scale give one large firm a cost advantage over any greater number of small firms. If two firms share the competitive output rate, Q_c, equally, they will both produce $Q_c/2$ at a long-run average total cost of LATC ($Q_c/2$). But the market clearing price, P_c, is less than LATC($Q_c/2$), so both firms cannot survive in the long run. A monopoly, however, can operate profitably in the long run, producing Q_m at an average cost of LATC(Q_m) that is less than the monopoly price, P_m.

firm is determined by the intersection of the long-run marginal cost curve, LMC, and the industry's marginal revenue curve, MR. This firm can successfully operate in the industry at the output rate of Q_m, making a profit per unit equal to $[P_m - \text{LATC}(Q_m)]$.

Now consider what would happen if the industry demand is split equally between two firms. Suppose the combined output of the two firms is Q_c and the market clearing price is P_c. Each firm produces $Q_c/2$. The long-run average total cost for each firm is LATC($Q_c/2$), which exceeds the market clearing price, P_c. Each firm loses $[\text{LATC}(Q_c/2) - P_c]$ on every unit produced. Our discussion of the shutdown rule above tells us that each firm ceases operating in this situation. But if they both stop operating, it is then optimal for one of them to reenter the market and produce at the monopoly output rate of Q_m. In effect, we have a situation in which economies of scale are so great relative to demand that only one firm can successfully exist in this market. This is a case of **natural monopoly.**

Natural Monopoly
A case in which only one firm can successfully compete in the market because economies of scale are so large relative to demand that this firm has an absolute cost advantage over other firms.

Natural monopolies are believed to exist in only a few industries. The distribution of local phone and cable television services are frequently cited examples. The average cost of providing these services decreases as more and more customers are connected to a common distribution system. In such cases, local and state governments often try to regulate market price to prevent these natural monopolies from earning monopoly profits. We will discuss how such regulation is designed in more detail below.

3. Government Licenses, Franchises, and Certificates of Need

It is illegal to enter some industries without a government-provided license, franchise, or certificate of need. For example, in some states, you cannot open a hospital without first obtaining a certificate of need from the appropriate authority, which is usually the state's health and human services agency. These certificates are sometimes difficult to obtain because existing hospitals file papers and motions opposing any new entrants. The new entrant's case must be strong and significant funds must be spent lobbying government officials to obtain a certificate of need.

In order to enter the television or radio broadcast business, it is necessary to obtain a license from the federal government. This license grants the owner exclusive rights to transmit on a certain frequency. Broadcasting licenses are renewable and are rarely revoked. To revoke a license, the federal government must show that the owner is not acting in the public interest, which is difficult to prove unless the license is used for criminal gain. Because new licenses are granted infrequently, monopoly profits are likely to accrue to existing license holders over time.

The various local and state governments also issue franchises to some firms. Ambulance service in many localities is granted as a franchise. Cable television and garbage collection are also common franchises. The logic behind issuing these franchises to one or two firms is twofold: Either economies of scale are argued to exist in these businesses, or the general public is better served with fewer firms because it is less costly to monitor their actions. The economies of scale argument makes competition unsustainable, as we have noted above. The service efficiency argument, which is often applied to ambulance franchises, is that the local government can monitor the *on-time* service of one or two firms better than, say, twenty firms. If a firm cannot meet the performance standards set by the local government, it will lose its franchise.

One problem created by government-granted licenses or franchises is **rent-seeking behavior.** Firms and individuals may invest significant funds in an attempt to persuade public officials to grant them an exclusive monopoly, even in goods that the government is not currently regulating. Such investments are viewed as wasteful if a competitive market is a viable alternative to government regulation.

Rent-Seeking Behavior An attempt to secure monopoly profits by investing resources to influence public policy.

In short, a franchise to a single firm creates a pure monopoly and the incentive to price accordingly. A franchise to two or more firms restricts entry, which may or may not create market power, but it does allow economic profits to persist over time.

4. Patents

Closely related to an entry franchise is a **patent.** A patent is issued to protect an inventor from having his or her invention copied for a period of 17 years. Suppose that you discover a new, inexpensive compound that makes fabric and metal ten times more resistant to fire and heat than any other product now on the market. Your compound is clear, flexible, and easy to apply to either fabric or metal. There is a ready market for it in airplanes, cars, baby cribs, and many other products. If you are successful (or your attorneys are) in obtaining a

Patent A government-granted right to the exclusive use of an invention, which expires after 17 years.

patent for this discovery, you can legally prevent other individuals from copying it. Note, however, that you may need to expend resources to prevent others from imitating your compound even if you do have a legally "watertight" patent.

A patent provides you with the right to sue others who violate the right to exclusive production or assignment. It is not a criminal law or regulatory rule that is enforced by public prosecution; you must enforce your own rights to the patent. Many resources are devoted by patent owners to enforcing their exclusive rights. Indeed, you can have a patent on a particular commodity or production process and end up with no economic profits at all; the costs of policing can be so high that you don't bother to protect your patent or, if you do, you end up spending so much on attorney's fees and other policing costs that you spend all of your economic profits.

It is argued that patents are necessary for defining and enforcing the property rights to new ideas. Granted, this is a reasonable claim, but there is little theoretical justification for a patent's life extending to 17 years. Why not 10, 20, or 50 years, or infinity? Economists do not have any simple answers to this question. There is a trade-off involved with a longer patent life. The longer an individual can anticipate having a property right or monopoly in a specific invention, the more resources will go into inventing patentable items, so more new technologies will be discovered. The longer a patent exists, however, the longer the monopoly exists, and presumably the longer the price will remain at a monopoly level rather than a competitive one. To find the socially optimal length of a patent, we must weigh the benefits of more research and creative efforts going into patentable products against the higher price that those products will carry during the length of the patent.

$$$ Price Theory in Practice

Enforcing the Intermittent Windshield Wiper Patent

In 1969, Robert W. Kearns, an engineer by training, was granted a patent for the intermittent windshield wiper. Kearns's invention allows windshield wipers to cycle on and off at varying rates—a simple idea that gained rapid acceptance from car and truck buyers. The patent expired in 1986. Long before the patent expired, however, nearly every domestic and foreign-made car used the device. Kearns's problem was that he did not authorize manufacturers to use his patent. In simple terms, these companies infringed on his patent.

But knowing that a misdeed has occurred and proving it to the satisfaction of the courts are two different matters. Initially, Kearns did not seek the court's help. The Ford Motor Company, for example, began negotiations with Kearns that lasted into the early 1970s. No agreement was reached, but Ford decided to use intermittent windshield wipers anyway. With no hope for a mutually acceptable deal, Kearns filed suit against Ford, Chrysler, and 15 other car manufacturers in 1978. These were large corporations Kearns chose to fight, and they had the money to prolong the battle. Ford's attorneys, for example, delayed final action in Kearns's lawsuit until 1990, *four years after his patent had expired.* Kearns won the lawsuit and Ford agreed to pay him $10.2 million to settle his patent claims. In 1991, he won the same battle against the Chrysler Corporation. His suit against the other car manufacturers continues.

For Kearns, court victories cannot make up for the time he lost. His court fight outlasted his patent, so he was not able to exercise the right to the *exclusive use* of his invention that a patent is supposed to grant. Moreover, Kearns argues that had he been granted the exclusive use of his patent by the courts before it had expired, he would have started to manufacture his invention. Undoubtedly, he would have sold it to the major automobile companies at a monopoly price, thus earning monopoly profits. His current, court-determined awards may compensate him for these lost monopoly profits, but they cannot replace what Kearns describes as his forgone opportunities to invest these profits in new research and new ventures that may lead to new inventions. Mr. Kearns is over 70 years old. His most productive and inventive years have been spent in a courtroom, trying to enforce his rights.

But Kearns has not given up. He is seeking a remedy that, if accepted by the courts, may greatly affect whether companies infringe on and challenge patents. Kearns has asked the court to issue an injunction against automobile manufacturers for 12 years, which is the time it took to win his suit. For the next 12 years, these companies would not be allowed to manufacture intermittent windshield wipers. Kearns, or others authorized by him, would be given the *exclusive* right to production during this period. The courts have typically issued such injunctions when a patent is still in effect, but they have yet to rule in this manner when a patent has expired. In effect, Kearns is asking the court to extend the life of his patent as compensation for courtroom delays.

What are Kearns's chances of a patent extension? It would appear that the court could grant such an extension under present patent law. Moreover, the court may find that past public policy suggests such an action. The U.S. Congress, for example, recently passed legislation to extend the patent terms for certain drugs to compensate for the years that drug companies spend getting approval to market their drugs from the Food and Drug Administration. For a man of Kearns's age, though, such an extension is truly bittersweet.

Learning Exercise 11.6

How will the number of patent applications and patent challenges change if Kearns wins an extension of his patent? How will the price of a new car change if he is granted an extension?

MERGERS MAY CREATE MARKET POWER

The four barriers to entry described above may both produce and maintain market power. In addition to these barriers, a merger may be an alternative way to obtain market power. A **merger** is the joining of two or more firms under a single ownership or control. There are two types of mergers: vertical and horizontal. *Horizontal mergers* combine firms in the same line of business or the same market and are the ones that have the greatest likelihood of creating market power. The case for market power from *vertical mergers,* which combine firms in different lines of business and are often called nonhorizontal

Merger
The joining of two or more firms together under a single ownership.

mergers, is tenuous unless market power exists before the merger takes place or such integration creates an effective barrier to entry.

Even though we are discussing mergers in terms of increasing market power, we must note that not all mergers have the goal of enhancing market power or creating a monopoly. Many mergers take place for efficiency reasons; that is, costs of production are lower in the merged firm. Furthermore, even if a merger is desired to enhance market power, the end result may nonetheless do little to increase the merging firms' market power.

Horizontal Integration

Horizontal Integration
A merger that involves firms selling commodities that are close substitutes.

Horizontal integration involves mergers among firms selling a similar commodity. If two video rental firms merge, that is horizontal integration. If a group of banks merge into one bank, that also is horizontal integration. The horizontal merger of NCNB and C&S/Sovran banks in 1991, for example, created the NationsBank, the fourth-largest bank in the United States at that time. A horizontal merger can create market power only if it gives the combined firm some control over market price and/or a negatively sloped demand curve for its product.

Suppose, for example, that a horizontal merger gives one firm 40 percent of a market. The remaining four firms in the industry each have 15 percent of the market. Suppose, too, that the shutdown point for all firms is at 10 percent of the current total market output rate. Each of the four smaller firms can decrease its output rate by 5 percent of the market rate before shutting down. Now, if the merged firm decides to increase its output rate by 25 percent of the current quantity sold in the market, its action will have an effect on the market clearing price because the other firms, as a whole, cannot *offset* this change in output. The other four firms cannot jointly decrease total market output by 25 percent without one or more of them dropping out of the market. One may ask why the merged firm would do this, but the answer is irrelevant to the point: the merged firm in this situation can affect the market price by its output decision.

Mergers that may result in a so-called unreasonable restraint of trade—such as that just described—are usually prevented or prosecuted by the U.S. Justice Department and/or the Federal Trade Commission under existing antitrust statutes. We will discuss such laws and how they are implemented below.

Vertical Integration: An Efficiency Argument

Vertical Integration
A merger that involves one firm buying either a seller of one of its inputs or a purchaser of its outputs.

Vertical integration occurs when one firm merges either with a firm from which it purchases an input or with a firm to which it sells its output. Vertical integration occurs, for example, when an electric utility with a coal-fired generator purchases a coal-mining firm or when a shoe manufacturer purchases retail shoe outlets.

It seems that most vertical integration is for efficiency gains, not for the purpose of creating or adding to market power. Professors Benjamin Klein, Robert Crawford, and Armen Alchian have argued that vertical mergers reduce the costs arising from postcontractual opportunistic behavior.[4] Suppose that the Unique Watch Company buys its crystals from HardRock Crystals, Inc. The two-year deal between these companies calls for delivery of 300 finished and rounded sapphire crystals per month at a price of $25 per crystal. The arrangement works well for the first four months but then starts to deteriorate. HardRock is late delivering the order in the fifth month, which delays Unique Watch's shipment to its customers. Some of HardRock's crystals are not fully rounded and must be returned for new crystals. These problems add to Unique Watch's cost structure. Unique Watch may seek many remedies to this problem, such as using another firm or suing HardRock for nonperformance. Alternatively, Unique Watch may enter the crystal-making business by purchasing HardRock. By vertically integrating, Unique Watch may implement its own production controls and monitoring techniques to ensure that HardRock's crystals are made correctly. Thus, vertical integration may increase efficiency by reducing the incentive for postcontractual opportunistic behavior.

Note that correctly defined opportunity costs make it difficult for a monopoly to gain market power from a vertical merger. Consider the case of a monopoly purchasing its inputs in a competitive market. This means that the monopolist is but one of many firms purchasing the inputs from suppliers. These inputs are used to make the monopolist's product. The question is, how much will the monopolist benefit by a merger with a supplier that operates in a competitive market?

To answer this question we must determine the appropriate *internal* transfer price that should be charged for the input. The appropriate internal transfer price of an input is its opportunity cost, which the monopolist can easily determine from the competitive market price. If a transfer price, other than the opportunity cost of the input, is built into the monopolist's cost structure, the monopolist's marginal cost curve is incorrectly defined and a non-profit-maximizing price and rate of output will result. In other words, it makes no difference to the monopolist whether the input supplier is independent or part of the firm.[5] The price of the input remains the same, whether it be implicit or explicit, so there is no gain in market power from such a merger.

Monopoly power at one particular place in the production and distribution chain does not necessarily confer monopoly power to any other point in that chain. If you own the only supply of a critical raw material in the production of computer chips, for example, all you need to do is set the monopoly profit-maximizing price on the critical input that you own; you do not need to merge with a computer manufacturer.

Vertical Integration: A Market Power Argument

It is alleged that, in some instances, a *powerful* firm will be able to squeeze out independent and nonintegrated firms. Assume, for example, that the integrat-

[4] See B. Klein, R. G. Crawford, and A. A. Alchian, "Vertical Integration, Appropriable Rents, and the Competitive Contracting Process," *Journal of Law and Economics* 21 (1978), 297–326.

[5] We are assuming, of course, that the reason for the merger is to gain market power, not to lower costs or reduce the transaction costs of using the marketplace as discussed in Chapter 7.

ed firm has a monopoly in an input that it uses to produce a final product. The integrated (monopoly) firm can raise the price it charges for the input to a nonintegrated firm; then the integrated firm can lower the price of the final product that it produces. The nonintegrated and independent firm has to buy the unfinished input at the monopoly price but is forced to be competitive in selling its final product. Nonintegrated firms can be forced out of business in the final output market by this kind of "squeeze play."

As logical as this may seem, this type of behavior is not without cost for the vertically integrated firm. The integrated firm must forgo monopoly profits during the period in which the price of the final product is kept lower than it would be otherwise. Whether such behavior is rational in terms of net worth maximization of the firm's owners is certainly not obvious. It can be shown, for example, that it is less costly to buy rivals outright—at the competitive market price—if antitrust laws make this option legal. In addition, driving a competitor out of business offers little gain if there is free entry into the market. Another firm may enter as soon as the price of the final good is raised to generate additional monopoly profits. Ultimately, some type of barrier to entry is necessary for the squeeze play to work.

Alternatively, vertical integration may be used as a way to prevent entry. The manufacturer of aluminum products can prevent entry into that industry, for example, by purchasing the entire supply of all the ingredients that go into making aluminum. In this case, vertical integration establishes exclusive ownership of a resource. Again, by creating a barrier to entry by merger, the firm can gain some market power.

INFORMAL COLLUSION

A merger is one way to combine firms to control the output decision of a competitor. However, if achieving market power is the goal, the players must be prepared to be scrutinized carefully by government officials, who may challenge the merger's merits. To avoid the immediate attention of government officials, firms may make *informal* agreements between themselves to restrict output and charge higher prices. We call such informal agreements **informal collusion** between firms. Such agreements can have the same effect as a merger but are less likely to be noticed by government officials.

Informal Collusion Informal agreements between two or more firms designed to affect market price and output.

The now-infamous electrical equipment conspiracy of the 1960s is one example of informal collusion. A number of electrical firms in the United States got together regularly to fix prices and market shares for electrical equipment. Although officials of these companies met, they never signed a formal agreement to fixed prices. This informal collusion had its greatest effect on the price charged to electric utilities for equipment that was sold using sealed bids. In a sealed-bid arrangement, at a specified hour on a specified date all the bids are opened at once. Generally, the lowest bid is awarded the contract. This arrangement made it easy for firms to collude because any firm that violated the collusive agreement became known immediately to all other firms. Thus, penalties and other harm could be imposed on the violator. The conspiracy broke up when it was revealed to government officials by one of the co-conspirators, who was dissatisfied with how the arrangement operated.

Learning Exercise 11.7

Of the following business practices, which might indicate some type of tacit collusion in order to gain market power, and why?

a. Sharing a list of customers with a competitor
b. Following a competitor's lead in lowering prices but not in raising prices
c. Sharing a new technology with a competitor
d. Co-sponsoring a charity event with a competitor

$$$ Price Theory in Practice

Flying the Colluded Skies

Firms probably *attempt* to collude more often than they actually do collude. One party or another, for example, may decide that the potential criminal penalties are less than the potential economic profits from collusion. One remarkable instance of an attempt to collude occurred on February 1, 1982, in a phone conversation between Howard Putman, president and CEO of the now-defunct Braniff Airline Company, and Robert Crandall, president and CEO of American Airlines. These two companies were in direct competition on a number of routes both into and out of Dallas-Fort Worth airport and were continually trying to undercut each other's fares. Mr. Crandall called Mr. Putman to discuss the problem, and after a few brief comments, Mr. Crandall got to the point:[6]

Mr. Crandall: I think it's dumb as [expletive] for Christ's sake, all right, to sit here and pound the [expletive] out of each other and neither one of us making a [expletive] dime.

Mr. Putman: Well . . .

Mr. Crandall: I mean, you know, [expletive], what the [expletive] is the point of it?

Mr. Putman: Nobody asked American to serve Harlingen, nobody asked American to serve Kansas City, and there were low fares in there, you know, before. So . . .

Mr. Crandall: You better believe it, Howard. But, you . . . you . . . you know, the complex is here—ain't gonna change a [expletive] thing, all right. We can . . . we can both live here and there ain't no room for Delta. But there's, ah, no reason that I can see, all right, to put both companies out of business.

---

[6] As reported in *The New York Times,* February 24, 1983.

Mr. Putman:	But if you're going to overlay every route of American on top of, over, on top of every route that Braniff has—I can't just sit here and allow you to bury us without giving our best effort.
Mr. Crandall:	Oh sure, but Eastern and Delta do the same thing in Atlanta and have for years.
Mr. Putman:	Do you have a suggestion for me?
Mr. Crandall:	Yes, I have a suggestion for you. Raise your [expletive] fares 20 percent. I'll raise mine the next morning.
Mr. Putman:	Robert, we . . .
Mr. Crandall:	You'll make more money and I will, too.
Mr. Putman:	We can't talk about pricing!
Mr. Crandall:	Oh [expletive], Howard. We can talk about any [expletive] thing we want to talk about.

Unknown to Mr. Crandall at the time, the phone call was recorded by Mr. Putman. Without this tape recording, we would probably never know what had happened between Mr. Crandall and Mr. Putman. The U.S. Department of Justice sought to have Mr. Crandall barred from the airline business for two years, but the courts later ruled that no collusion occurred because Mr. Putman refused to cooperate. Even so, American Airlines and Mr. Crandall agreed never to make such a proposal again. The irony here is that Braniff was not able to effectively compete with American Airlines and eventually went out of business.

Learning Exercise 11.8

Following the disclosure of Mr. Crandall's phone call to Mr. Putman, William Baxter, then chief of the Justice Department's antitrust division, suggested that all CEOs record their phone conversations. Do you expect the conversations of CEOs to change if they are recorded? Why?

11.3 Cartels

Cartel
A group of firms that have agreed to coordinate price and output decisions in an attempt to gain market power.

A **cartel** is a group of firms that have organized themselves in an attempt to gain market power and thereby act like a monopoly. The most famous and successful cartel has been the Organization of Petroleum Exporting Countries (OPEC), which was formed in 1960. OPEC had little influence on world oil prices until after the 1973 Arab oil embargo. In the 11-month period following the oil embargo, the price of crude oil rose from about \$3 per barrel to more than \$15 per barrel. Prices fluctuated in the mid-1970s; during 1979 prices averaged \$30 per barrel, which was probably the peak of OPEC's power to influence oil prices. Since 1979, OPEC has struggled to maintain unity among its members, as many member countries find it in their best interest to cheat on OPEC's price and production agreements.

The National Collegiate Athletic Association (NCAA) is also a well-known cartel.[7] The member colleges of the NCAA conspire regularly to fix the wages paid to college athletes. Outside of scholarship funds and limited in-kind transfers, the wages paid by colleges are set at zero by the NCAA. Unlike OPEC, however, the NCAA has effectively convinced many people that its actions are *good* for the athletes involved and *good* for sports in general. The NCAA maintains that its rules ensure sports fans that amateur athletics is not vitiated by the large sums of money earned in professional sports. Of course, the NCAA also ensures that many athletes—actually, the vast majority—who do not make it in the "pros" are not compensated for their efforts while in college, thereby reducing their lifetime income for the benefit of NCAA member colleges.

To be effective, each member in a cartel must agree to produce less than it would under perfect competition. The reduction in total output causes market price and profits to increase. In the next section we discuss how individual firms can gain by collusion and also the reasons why cheating causes collusive agreements to break down.

THE INCENTIVE TO CREATE A CARTEL

To start the analysis, consider the initial situation as perfectly competitive with 20 firms in the industry. Each firm is equally efficient. The price at which each firm sells its output equals the market clearing price for all firms. The market clearing price, P_0, is set by the interaction of the industry supply curve, which is the (horizontal) sum of 20 identical marginal cost curves, and the industry demand curve. The profit-maximizing output rate for each firm solves the equation $P_0 = \text{SMC}(Q)$. Because the cost structure is the same for all firms, each firm produces exactly one-twentieth of the total industry output. If Q_0 is the total industry output, then each firm produces $Q_0/20$.

The basic setup is illustrated in Figure 11.8. Each firm earns zero economic profits at the current market clearing price because $P_0 = \text{SATC}(Q_0/20)$. If these 20 firms agree to form a cartel, they must agree to reduce their current rate of output. In Figure 11.8, the optimal price for a cartel to charge is determined by equating MR and $\sum_{i=1}^{20} \text{SMC}_i$ in the market; that is, a cartel acts as a group, so the marginal cost curve for the group as a whole equals the sum of all 20 individual marginal cost curves.[8] The total output in the market is Q_m and the market clearing price is P_m at this position. Each firm is assumed to reduce its competitively determined output rate by $(Q_0/20 - Q_m/20)$ as a result of the cartel agreement. Assuming that all firms obey these quotas, they will all produce the same reduced output. Thus, we know that if each firm increases output by 1 unit, the industry will increase

[7] Technically, the NCAA is a buyers' cartel, or monopsony, because it sets the price paid for some input by buyers. We will discuss monopsony in more detail in Chapter 14.

[8] Recall that Σ is the summation operator. The term following this operator is added over successive values of the index, *i*, until the terminal value of 20 of the index is reached.

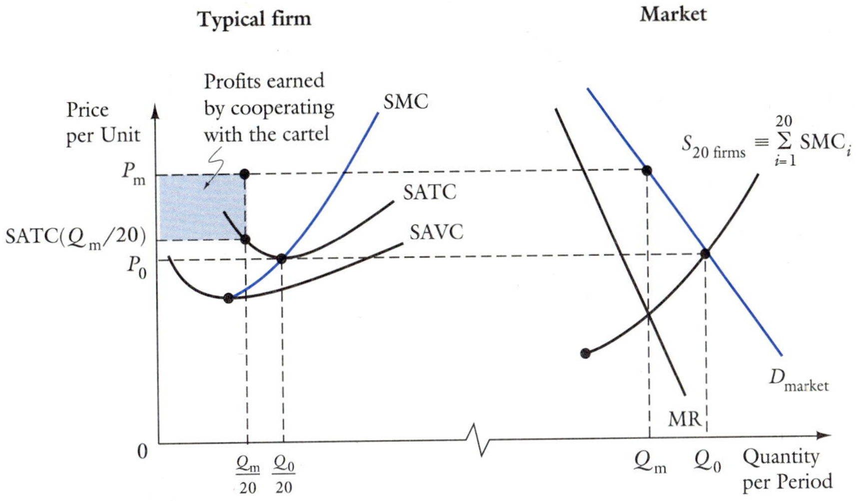

FIGURE 11.8

The Incentive to Create a Cartel

The incentive to form a cartel exists because each firm enjoys some share of the monopoly profits a cartel generates. If 20 identical firms sell output in a long-run competitive market, the market clearing price is P_0 and each firm produces $Q_0/20$ units per period. No firm earns economic profits. Alternatively, if these firms form a cartel with each firm reducing its output rate to $Q_m/20$, then the market clearing price increases to P_m and each firm earns positive economic profits given by the shaded area.

output by 20 units. Now, it is no longer true that the individual firm can sell all it wants at the market clearing price. The market price depends on the rate of output of each firm, because all the firms are acting in unison. The shaded region in Figure 11.8 shows the profits that each firm earns by cooperating with the cartel. These profits clearly exceed those offered at the perfectly competitive solution.

We can now see that the incentive to form a cartel is simple: It offers more profits to firms than a competitive market. Formation of cartels is not desired for *unethical* purposes; rather, it is a phenomenon consistent with profit maximization. Unfortunately for most cartels, the goal of profit maximization also gives each firm an incentive to renege on its agreement to curtail output.

Learning Exercise 11.9

Suppose that the (inverse) demand function is $P = 500 - Q/100$ and that there are four firms in the industry, each with a marginal cost structure given by $SMC_i = 50 + .02Q_i$. If these are perfectly competitive firms, what are industry output and profits in the short run? If these firms form a cartel, what are industry output and profits, and how much does each firm produce? [Note: SMC(4 firms) = $50 + .005Q$.]

THE INCENTIVE TO CHEAT

There is a significant incentive for a single firm to cheat on the other firms in a cartel. Similarly, the incentive not to join an existing cartel is also great. We can see this in Figure 11.9. The cost structure of a typical cartel member is redrawn from Figure 11.8. At the cartel output rate of $Q_m/20$, the typical cartel member earns economic profits given by area *A*. If the typical firm acts *independently* of the cartel, it can view itself as a price taker; that is, it may regard P_m as fixed as long as the other cartel members do not cheat. The firm must then find the output rate that maximizes profits given that the price equals P_m. The optimal output rate is the one that equates P_m to SMC. This is shown as Q_{cheat} in Figure 11.9. The cheating firm produces more than a cartel member does. Because P_m > SMC at the cartel solution, the cheating firm has an incentive to increase its output rate. As the figure shows, the optimal output for the cheating firm is $Q_{cheat} > Q_m/20$. At Q_{cheat}, the firm earns economic profits equal to area *A plus* the shaded region labeled area *B*. Cheating on the other firms in the cartel is thus more profitable than the cartel arrangement.

Because every firm has an incentive to cheat, there is a strong likelihood that cartels will fall apart over time. As members act independently, they increase total market output, which decreases the market clearing price. Higher output and lower prices reduce economic profits. In effect, with cheating, the members of the cartel begin to act like perfectly competitive firms. To prevent the total collapse of the cartel, its organizers may invest funds to

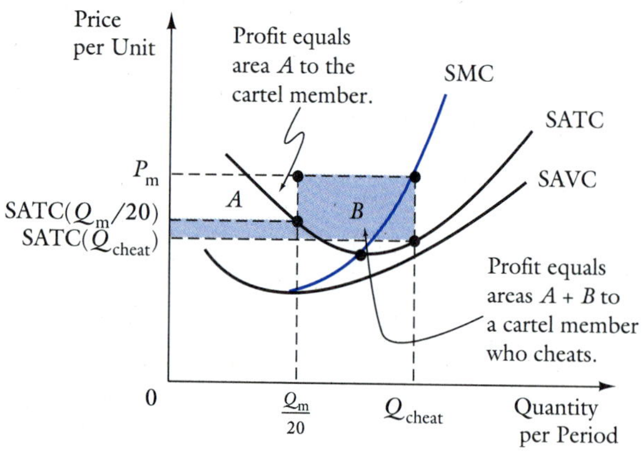

FIGURE 11.9

The Incentive to Cheat on Other Cartel Members

Cheating a cartel agreement is profitable to the firm that cheats if the other members do not change their output rates. If one firm operates at the output rate Q_{cheat}, at which the monopoly price (P_m) equals its short-run marginal cost (SMC), then it earns economic profits equal to areas *A* plus *B*. The profit it receives from not cheating equals only area *A*, so there is a gain from cheating.

enforce the cartel output restrictions. The OPEC cartel, for example, regularly threatens to punish members who cheat on its output quotas. OPEC's punishment is generally output-related. Saudi Arabia, which is OPEC's largest producer of oil, often increases its oil production to drive down the world price so that the cheating members do not benefit from their opportunistic behavior. When profits have fallen sufficiently, the cheating members ask to be forgiven and then ask for new output quotas so that the world price will increase to cartel levels.

$$$ Price Theory in Practice

THE MATZO CARTEL

Apparently nothing is sacred when it involves the lure of monopoly profits. At least that was the case for three makers of matzo, the unleavened bread commonly eaten during Passover.

The U.S. Justice Department found that three New York-area matzo makers conspired during the 1980s to reduce production and increase prices of matzo bread, which symbolizes the day Jewish people fled in haste from Egypt and could not wait for their bread to rise.

The cartel agreement was struck over a meal at a small restaurant on the Lower East side of Manhattan, according to the government. The offenders were among the oldest names in the matzo-making business: Horowitz Bros. & Margareten, B. Manischewitz Co., and Aron Streit, Inc.

In 1991, Manischewitz was fined $1 million after it pleaded "no contest" to price-fixing charges. Horowitz and Streit had been named as unindicted co-conspirators.

Although it is unclear exactly how much the three firms were able to increase the price of matzo bread, the price of matzo bread rose faster than other food prices during the time period. In 1991, distributors in Chicago paid about $33 for a 30-pound case of Manischewitz matzo. That is about 37.5 percent more than the $24 they paid in 1983. By comparison, producer prices for food increased 24.6 percent during the same time period.

The downfall of the matzo cartel was caused by a problem that arises with many cartels: They require the cooperation and silence of everyone in the industry in order to work successfully. In this case, Chicago matzo bread distributor Irwin Ashkanazy refused to go along with the arrangement. Mr. Ashkanazy, an independent distributor of Horowitz matzo bread, was steadfast in his resistance to the cartel despite threats and acts of sabotage to his product displays at retailers.

The irony of the case is that despite the government's action and the $1 million fine, the monopoly power the three matzo makers sought to accumulate may have developed anyway. Since the price fixing occurred, Manischewitz has purchased Horowitz Brothers as well as the rights to make matzo bread under the name of matzo maker A. Goodman & Sons. This means that Manischewitz now makes three of the four major matzo brands—Streit is the exception—and controls about 90 percent of matzo bread sales during Passover.

LEARNING EXERCISE 11.10

What is the relationship between the price elasticity of demand for matzo bread during Passover compared with other days that are not holidays? Is your answer the same for the price elasticity of demand for roses on Valentine's Day compared to other days?

SHARING OUTPUT WITH MORE EFFICIENT FIRMS: THE MULTIPLANT MONOPOLY SOLUTION

We initially assumed that all firms are equally efficient. The output quota for each firm is thus the total industry output divided by the number of firms—that is, an equal share of output to each firm. If firms have different cost curves, however, the appropriate quota for each firm must be based on its true costs. This poses a problem because costs may not be easily observable. The incentive to cheat on the cartel may materialize in how a firm represents its costs to the other cartel members. By misrepresenting costs, a cartel member may receive a higher output quota than its cost structure warrants, which generates more economic profits.

To maximize profits for the cartel as a whole, output allocation must be based on marginal costs. Suppose that there are only two firms in the cartel; a high-cost and a low-cost firm. The short-run marginal cost structure for these two firms is shown in Figure 11.10. The marginal cost curve for the high-cost firm is SMC_H, and the marginal cost curve for the low-cost firm is SMC_L. The

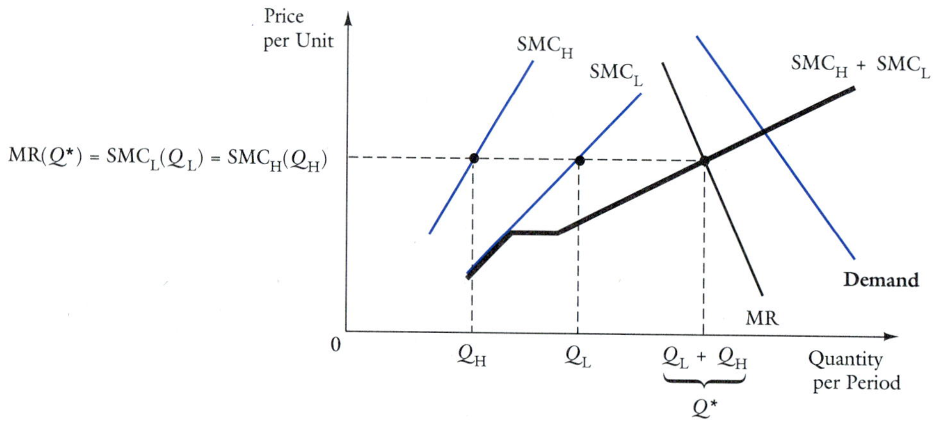

FIGURE 11.10

Allocating Costs to Less Efficient Firms in a Cartel

When members of a cartel are of varying levels of efficiency, the cartel allocates output by equating marginal revenue, $MR(Q^*)$, to the short-run marginal cost, SMC, of each member firm. In the case of two firms, one with high costs and one with low costs, the cartel allocates a larger output rate to the low-cost firm, Q_L, than to the high-cost firm, Q_H. The total $Q_L + Q_H$ equals the industry output rate, Q^*.

marginal cost curve for the cartel is the sum of the two separate marginal cost curves, $SMC_H + SMC_L$. The profit-maximizing output rate for the cartel is found by equating $SMC_H + SMC_L$ to the industry marginal revenue curve, MR. As shown in the figure, the optimal output rate for the cartel is Q^*.

The optimal output rate is allocated between the two firms by setting each firm's marginal cost equal to the marginal revenue of the optimal output rate. In other words, if $MR(Q^*)$ is the marginal revenue of the optimal output rate, then the output rate of the low-cost firm (Q_L) is the solution to $SMC_L(Q_L) = MR(Q^*)$, and the output rate of the high-cost firm is the solution to $SMC_H(Q_H) = MR(Q^*)$. In general, we can state that

$$MR(Q^*) = SMC_L(Q_L) = SMC_H(Q_H) \tag{11.10}$$

at the profit-maximizing output rate for both firms in the cartel.[9] If there are more than two firms in the cartel, we can extend this rule: $MR(Q^*) = SMC_1(Q_1) = SMC_2(Q_2) = \ldots = SMC_n(Q_n)$, where there are n firms in the cartel. In effect, the output rate of each firm is determined by setting marginal cost for all firms equal to marginal revenue at the market output rate.

As can be seen from Figure 11.10, equation (11.10) implies that the relatively less efficient firm produces less, which implies that its profits will be less, *ceteris paribus.* With its profit less than that of its partners, the high-cost firm may be more likely to cheat. If the low-cost firm realizes this, it may offer to transfer some of its profits to the high-cost firm to maintain the stability of the cartel. Such transfers sometimes occur within OPEC in its effort to prevent members from cheating.

Note that the situation described here—two firms with different cost structures in a cartel—is identical to the situation of a monopoly with two plants, the so-called multiplant monopoly, each having a different cost structure. Thus, for the monopoly to allocate output optimally to its different plants, it must follow the rule stated in equation (11.10) or its generalization if there are more than two plants.

LEARNING EXERCISE 11.11

Is it possible that some less efficient firms will produce zero output in a cartel? Under what conditions will this situation arise? Is there a price range over which the other firms do not have to pay the no-output firm for not producing?

11.4 COMPARING A MONOPOLY TO A PERFECTLY COMPETITIVE MARKET

Let's compare the operating characteristics of perfect competition and pure monopoly. We want to see how a market is affected when it changes from

[9] Note that this is the solution that arises in the so-called multiplant monopoly, which is a monopoly that owns many plants of varying levels of efficiency and must determine how much each plant should produce to maximize profits.

being perfectly competitive to a single-price monopoly. To hold as many factors constant as possible, we first assume that the market is perfectly competitive. Then a clever entrepreneur purchases all existing firms and persuades the local government to grant him or her an exclusive license to sell the monopoly product. In this scenario, neither the cost structure of the individual firms nor the market demand curve is affected by the monopoly-producing merger. The change in operating characteristics is thus caused solely by the change in market structure.

PRICE AND OUTPUT DIFFERENCES

In the perfectly competitive market structure, the short-run market supply equals the sum of each firm's supply curve. A perfectly competitive firm's supply curve equals its marginal cost curve for all points above the minimum of its average variable cost curve. Thus, market supply is the sum of each firm's marginal cost curve—above the minimum of the average variable cost curve. When the monopoly is formed, market supply for the perfectly competitive industry becomes the monopoly's marginal cost curve, which is used to determine the optimal output position for the monopoly. This situation is illustrated in Figure 11.11.

Panel (a) in Figure 11.11 shows the market demand curve, D_{market}, and its associated marginal revenue curve, MR. The marginal cost curve, MC, represents the market supply curve for the perfectly competitive market and, too, the marginal cost curve for the monopoly once it purchases all existing firms. The perfectly competitive market produces an output rate of Q_c, the output rate above which the market supply curve intersects the market demand curve. The market clearing price is P_c for the perfectly competitive market. After the monopoly is formed, optimal output decreases to Q_m, the output rate at which MR equals MC. The market clearing price for the single-price monopoly is P_m, which *exceeds* the marginal cost of producing Q_m.

> **The market clearing price is higher and the output rate is lower after a monopoly takes over a perfectly competitive market (assuming that the cost structure does not change).**

EFFECTS ON CONSUMERS' AND PRODUCERS' SURPLUSES

On an operating level, a monopoly drives a wedge between price and marginal cost that is not present with perfect competition. Perfect competition exhausts all gains from trade by producing an output rate at which price equals marginal cost. A monopoly, however, leaves some consumers without the product even though they are willing to pay more than the marginal cost of the extra output. These lost sales cause a decrease in the total surplus generated at the market equilibrium. Panel (b) in Figure 11.11 illustrates this result. The various areas under the demand curve and above the marginal cost curve are shown in panel (b). The effects on consumers' and producers' surpluses of changing from a perfectly competitive market to a monopoly structure are described as follows:

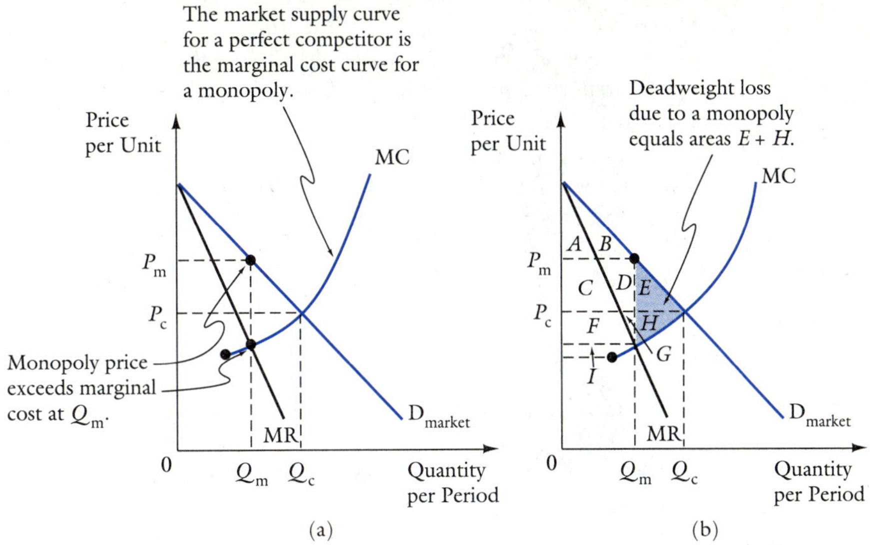

FIGURE 11.11

Comparing a Perfectly Competitive Market to a Monopoly

Panel (a) shows the output rate of a perfectly competitive industry, Q_c, and the lower output rate of a monopoly, Q_m, which is formed by combining all the competitive firms under one ownership. The monopoly price, P_m, exceeds the price charged by the perfectly competitive industry, P_c. Panel (b) shows the deadweight losses in both producers' and consumers' surpluses caused by the formation of a monopoly from a previously competitive industry. The total *deadweight loss* equals areas $E + H$, where area E represents lost consumers' surplus and area H represents lost producers' surplus. Areas $C + D$ represent a transfer of surplus from consumers to producers.

	Perfect Competition *Market Price* = P_c	**Monopoly** *Market Price* = P_m
Consumers' Surplus	$A + B + C + D + E$	$A + B$
Producers' Surplus	$F + G + H + I$	$C + D + F + G + I$
Total Market Surplus	$A + B + C + D + E + F + G + H + I$	$A + B + C + D + F + G + I$
Deadweight Loss		$E + H$

The consumers' surplus for perfect competition equals areas $A + B + C + D + E$. This is the area under the market demand curve and above the perfectly competitive price, P_c. Using the results from Chapter 10, we know that producers' surplus equals areas $F + G + H + I$ for perfect competition. The total market surplus for perfect competition is thus equal to $A + B + C + D + E + F + G + H + I$. With a monopoly, the calculation is similar. Consumers' surplus for a monopoly equals areas $A + B$, which is the area under the market demand curve and above the monopoly price, P_m. Producers' surplus equals areas $C + D + F + G + I$ for the monopoly. Thus, total market surplus under a monopoly equals areas $A + B + C + D + F + G + I$.

As the market clearing price increases from P_c to P_m, the total market surplus decreases by an amount equal to areas $E + H$, which is the difference between the total market surpluses under perfect competition and monopoly. This area—$E + H$—is the ***deadweight loss***—defined in Chapter 3—that a monopoly structure imposes on a perfectly competitive market. Deadweight loss is lost forever from the market if there is no change in demand or cost conditions over time. In the short run, the loss is composed of both lost producers' surplus, area H, and lost consumers' surplus, area E. In the long run, however, the loss falls entirely on the consumers because a perfectly competitive market offers no economic profits in the long run.

LEARNING EXERCISE 11.12

How does the deadweight loss due to a monopoly change in the long run? Draw a graph comparing the total market surplus under both monopoly and perfect competition in the long run (assume that the LATC is U-shaped).

REGULATING A NATURAL MONOPOLY

The result that a monopoly causes a loss in ***total market surplus*** relative to a perfectly competitive market assumes that a perfectly competitive market is viable. We have already mentioned, however, that one barrier to entry may be economies of scale. If economies of scale are so great that the long-run average total cost curve is downward-sloping over a significant range of output, then only one firm can survive. The firm that survives will be the one that expands output the most and, hence, enjoys the greatest decrease in average total cost. As we have shown in Figure 11.7, a ***natural monopoly*** results from this situation.

The purported presence of natural monopolies in some industries has led federal, state, and local government to develop regulatory schemes to increase the total market surplus and, particularly, the consumers' surplus portion. One approach is to regulate the market price a firm charges, which is illustrated in Figure 11.12.

The firm illustrated in Figure 11.12 is a natural monopoly because it experiences economies of scale over such a broad range of output relative to demand that two or more firms cannot operate as efficiently as one. Left on its own, the natural monopoly will produce Q_m and charge a market clearing price of P_m. Its profits at this position are equal to $[P_m - LATC(Q_m)]Q_m$, which is equivalent to areas $C + D$ in the figure. Consumers' surplus in the market at the monopoly price equals areas $A + B$. Thus, the total market surplus equals areas $A + B + C + D$. A regulatory body with control over price, however, can increase both consumers' surplus and total market surplus. Suppose the regulatory body sets a ***price ceiling*** at P_r, which is a maximum price for any unit sold. Now the monopoly receives P_r per unit for all units up to Q_r. For output rates beyond Q_r, the monopoly must lower price below P_r to sell additional units.

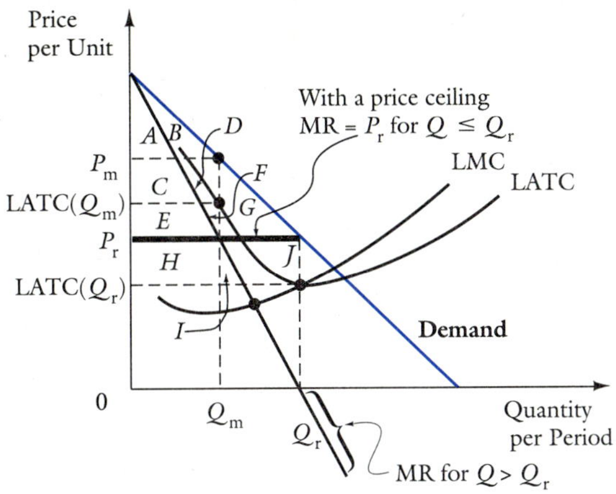

FIGURE 11.12

Regulating a Natural Monopoly with a Price Ceiling

Regulating a monopoly using a price ceiling can increase its optimal output rate and consumers' surplus. An unregulated monopoly charges P_m and produces Q_m. Imposing a price ceiling at P_R, however, alters the structure of the monopoly's marginal revenue curve. Marginal revenue equals P_R up to the output rate Q_R, after which it drops down to continue along the unregulated marginal revenue curve. Now, the optimal output rate is Q_R, at which point consumers' surplus increases by an amount equal to areas $C + D + E + F + G$. The monopoly loses profits equal to areas $C + D$, so the net gain in consumers' surplus from price regulation equals areas $E + F + G$.

The marginal revenue curve changes because of price regulation. Marginal revenue is equal to P_r for all output rates up to Q_r. At Q_r, marginal revenue drops down to the original marginal revenue curve and continues along this curve for all output rates greater than Q_r. The new marginal revenue curve causes the firm to maximize profits at the output rate of Q_r; that is, at output rates less than Q_r, marginal revenue exceeds marginal cost, and at output rates greater than Q_r, marginal revenue is less than marginal cost, so the optimal position for the firm is at Q_r.

The higher output rate increases consumers' surplus, which now equals areas $A + B + C + D + E + F + G$. The firm's long-run profits—its producers' surplus—equals areas $H + I + J$, which is less than the economic profits generated before the price ceiling. (These profits must be less; otherwise, the firm would have chosen Q_r initially.) Although the firm loses profits in this situation, the increase in consumers' surplus—areas $C + D + E + F + G$—more than offsets the firm's loss in profits—areas $C + D$. Thus, total market surplus increases as a result of price regulation.

PROBLEMS WITH PRICE REGULATION

There are several problems with price regulation of a natural monopoly. First, it requires some compromise with what we have defined as the efficient operating conditions for the market. Efficiency requires that the market price equal marginal cost ($P = \text{MC}$), but for a natural monopoly, this solution results in losses. The losses arise because marginal cost is less than average cost when average cost is falling. Setting price equal to marginal cost implies that $P < \text{AC}$, which generates operating losses.

Second, it requires the regulators to collect and interpret information on market demand and the firm's cost structure. The degree to which they are successful at this determines how effective the price ceiling is in increasing total market surplus. The monopoly, for example, may report higher than actual costs to the regulators if such reports cannot be easily verified. Reporting higher costs may move the regulated price closer to P_m, the deregulated monopoly price.

Third, changes in demand conditions may call for frequent changes in the price ceiling, which imposes an additional administrative burden on regulators. Regulators are not paid based on their performance, so they may have little incentive to adjust price frequently if this means that they perform more work.

Fourth, a natural monopoly may produce various *qualities* of the same product. In other words, it is difficult to regulate price per *constant-quality* unit. The regulators are then charged with the difficult task of setting multiple price ceilings for different qualities in order to increase the total market surplus.

Finally, if technological changes over time make the natural monopoly situation obsolete, the regulatory body may be slow to respond, making it difficult for new firms to enter the industry. In short, regulation can improve the surplus received by consumers, but it may be costly to implement and slow to respond to new technology that affects a firm's cost structure and its claim to natural monopoly status.

THE TREND TOWARD DEREGULATION

The extensive regulation of business dates back to the Interstate Commerce Act of 1887, which created the Interstate Commerce Commission (ICC) to regulate railroads and, later, all motor carrier transportation across state lines. In the 1930s, more regulations and regulatory bodies were created, such as the Securities and Exchange Commission (1933), the Federal Deposit Insurance Corporation (1933), and the Civil Aeronautics Board (1938). Much of the increased regulation in the 1930s was the result of bank and other financial crises during the Great Depression. In much of the 1980s, however, the trend was to remove government from its oversight role and to deregulate business activity. Table 11.1 summarizes some of the major acts to deregulate business that have been passed since 1978.

The argument for deregulation is that if government-imposed entry barriers are removed, the profit motive causes firms to enter markets in which market power and economic profits exist and thereby moves these markets toward a perfectly competitive equilibrium. This argument is bolstered by the theory of contestable markets.[10] A **contestable market** is one in which there are no

Contestable Market A market in which there are no sunk costs of entry and exit of firms.

[10] For a discussion of the relationship between contestable markets and deregulation, see Elizabeth Bailey and William Baumol, "Deregulation and the Theory of Contestable Markets," *Yale Journal of Regulation* 1 (1984), 111–137.

TABLE 11.1

Important Deregulation and Reregulation Legislation, 1978–1992

Title	Year	Description
Airline Deregulation Act	1978	Phased out the Civil Aeronautics Board and gave airlines control over fares charged and routes flown, subject to Federal Aviation Administration (FAA) restrictions and local airport authority rules.
Natural Gas Policy Act	1978	Set a schedule for the decontrol of interstate natural gas and wellhead prices. Natural gas prices may still be controlled *within* some states.
Motor Carrier Act	1980	Reduced the restriction on entry and exit in the long-haul trucking business and gave trucking firms more control over prices.
Depository Institutions Deregulation and Monetary Control Act	1980	Standardized the regulation of all depository institutions and allowed banks and savings and loans to expand into new services. Provided a timetable for the elimination of interest rate ceiling on deposits, known as Regulation Q.
Bus Regulatory Reform Act	1982	Allowed greater entry and exit into the interstate bus market and standardized many state laws covering bus regulation.
Garn–St. Germain Depository Institutions Act	1982	Permitted banks and savings and loans to offer money market deposit accounts (MMDAs) similar to those offered by mutual funds and securities brokers. Accelerated the timetable to eliminate interest rate ceilings.
Cable Communications Act	1984	Allowed cable companies to set rates independent of local and state regulators as long as there is effective competition in the subscriber community.
Cable Television Reregulation Act	1992	Effectively rescinded the Cable Communications Act of 1984, reregulating cable prices and service quality in many areas.

(or very small) *sunk costs* of entry or exit. In a contestable market, even firms with some market power behave like perfectly competitive firms because they know that positive economic profits cause the entry of new firms. The *potential for entry,* not necessarily actual entry, is what drives firms to operate at the zero-profit equilibrium in a contestable market.

Why are sunk costs important to the theory of contestable markets? After all, sunk costs can be ignored when a firm chooses its optimal output rate. Sunk costs are important because they are considered an avoidable cost if the firm does not enter the market. When the entry decision is contemplated, the firm expects to earn a return on the portion of its investment that is sunk after entry. This view gives existing firms some leeway in their pricing decision. Existing firms can charge an above-competitive price so long as it is not high enough to offer a competitive return on the sunk portion of a new entrant's investment. As a result, existing firms can earn positive economic profits without attracting entry. If sunk costs are zero, existing firms do not have any pricing flexibility, so they tend to act like perfect competitors.

The airline business is a frequently cited example in which there are very low or no sunk costs of entry or exit after deregulation. The major investment that an airline must make is in its airplanes. Airplanes may be leased or purchased; either way, all of the investment is not a sunk cost because airplanes can easily be sold or leased to another firm if the airline ceases operations. One consequence of deregulating the airline industry is that airlines offered better service to customers. In 1978, complaints against airlines averaged 400 per 10,000 passengers. In 1991, complaints had fallen to 180 per 10,000 passengers. In contrast, the piping that oil companies sink into the ground is (literally) sunk cost because it is very difficult to retrieve when the well goes dry. Drilling companies can move their oil derricks, but they leave behind their piping when they move to a new site.

As can be seen in Table 11.1, the removal of entry and exit restrictions has been an important characteristic of deregulation. But, as the theory of contestable markets predicts, whether this alone increases total market surplus depends on the size of sunk costs of entry and exit in these various industries. On this question, the empirical results are not fully tabulated, but the growth observed in some of these industries, such as increased passenger travel on airlines, suggests that deregulation has increased consumers' surplus in some of these markets.

Policy Application and Evaluation

Cable TV

Issue—*Should the cable television industry be regulated?*

Background

When cable television first developed in the 1950s, it came under federal, state, and local regulation. Cable operators were often required to carry public interest programming in local markets and could not generally change rates. Deregulation in the 1980s changed the landscape for cable TV operators. The Cable Communications Policy Act of 1984 provided for the complete deregulation of the prices charged by most cable companies by the end of 1986. This act prohibited state and local governments from regulating cable service rates in any area where the cable system was subject to so-called effective competition. According to the FCC, effective competition

TABLE 11.2

Changes in Basic Cable TV Rates After Deregulation

	Consumer Price Indices					
Date	Basic Cable Service	Food	Apparel	New Cars	Medical Care	Energy
Nov. 1986	$11.71	108.9	105.9	110.3	121.0	88.1
Apr. 1991	$18.84	136.7	127.2	125.2	174.4	100.5
Percentage Change	60.1	25.5	20.1	13.5	44.1	14.1

Note: The base for the CPI indices is 1982–1984 = 100.
Source: Economic Indicators, March, 1992.

exists if residents can receive three or more television stations using their own antennas. In essence, "rabbit ear" antennas that can receive three or more signals are thought to create an effective alternative to cable service. Over 88 percent of all cable systems satisfy the effective competition test and hence were deregulated by the Cable Communications Policy Act of 1984.

What Are the Effects of Deregulation?

As Table 11.2 shows, since deregulation, cable rates have increased rapidly, much faster than the prices paid for other consumer goods and services.[11] Critics of cable TV deregulation have charged that cable companies are acting as monopolies; that is, they have raised prices to monopoly levels and are earning economic profits. These critics charge that the effective competition test in the deregulation act was not sufficient to prevent existing cable companies from exercising market power. In other words, three broadcast stations are too few to represent effective competition to a cable system, because the average cable system may offer these same three stations plus 20 to 30 more as part of its basic service. Even though antenna reception is without cost, households must tolerate more atmospheric interference with antennas, so antenna reception is not really a close substitute for a cable hookup.

The cable companies counter these charges with the claim that their costs have increased rapidly since deregulation. To support their claims, cable companies point to the growth in the number of channels offered. Prior to deregulation, the average subscriber received 27 channels as part of the basic fee. In 1991, the average subscriber received 35 channels. Looking at the price per channel, then, the rates for basic cable service have increased from 43 cents in November 1986 to 54 cents in April 1991, which is an increase of only 26 percent. Adjusting for the increased service, cable rates have grown at the same rate as food prices, a rate much slower than the growth rate of medical care prices.

[11] Cable rates are found in *1991 Survey of Cable Television Rates and Services* (GAO/RCED-91-195), July 18, 1991.

A New Era in Cable TV Regulation

In spite of the cost-based arguments of the cable companies, Congress passed the Cable Television Reregulation Act of 1992. This act gave the FCC the power to determine the "reasonableness" of basic cable rates for public, educational, governmental, and local broadcast affiliates, such as ABC, NBC, CBS, Fox, and PBS. As a result, the FCC is empowered to set rates for over 56 million cable subscribers. This legislation also strengthened previous administrative rulings at the FCC. On June 13, 1991, for example, the FCC modified its definition of "effective" competition. Previously, cable systems were exempt from local and state regulatory bodies if there were three or more broadcast channels available to residents using antennas or if a competing cable system was serving 10 percent of the homes that the incumbent system could serve and was available to over one-half of the community. Under the FCC's new ruling, approximately 30 percent of the existing cable systems—mostly in rural areas—had their cable rates reregulated. Even with regulated rates, however, cable companies may be able to act like monopolies, particularly if they have access to cost data that the regulators do not have. Only the threat of entry or new technology is truly able to prevent cable companies from behaving like monopolies.

Questions for Evaluation

Does a comparison of the price growth rates shown in Table 11.2 really indicate market power? Under what circumstances will such a comparison provide evidence that firms have some market power? Will the average number of channels offered increase or decrease in the areas facing reregulated cable rates? Why?

11.5 Detecting and Preventing a Monopoly

It is one thing to say that a monopoly or some market power exists; it is quite another to measure the degree to which it exists or the likelihood that a merger of two firms will create market power. In spite of the practical difficulties with measurement, there are several methods of measurement used by policymakers. In this section, we look at the two most popular indices of market power. In addition, we will discuss the laws that govern monopoly behavior and mergers as well as the current implementation of these laws.

THE LERNER INDEX

An important difference between monopoly and perfect competition is that a monopoly does not produce an output rate at which price equals marginal cost. This result also follows from equation (11.8) on page 421, the markup pricing formula. In 1934, economist Abba Lerner used the markup pricing formula to measure the degree of monopoly power.[12] The **Lerner index** is defined as:

Lerner Index (L) A measure of supposed market power given by the ratio $(P - MC)/P$.

[12] Abba P. Lerner, "The Concept of Monopoly and the Measurement of Monopoly Power," *Review of Economic Studies* 1 (June 1934), 157–175.

$$L = \frac{P - \text{MC}}{P} \tag{11.11}$$

where MC may be either the short- or long-run marginal cost of the firm.

Obviously, the Lerner index is nothing more than the markup pricing rule for a monopolist. If the firm is perfectly competitive and it follows this rule, the result is that $L = 0$, because $P = \text{MC}$ for a perfectly competitive firm. As L increases away from zero, the greater the difference between P and MC becomes, and the larger the degree of monopoly or market power.

From the markup pricing rule shown in equation (11.8), we know that $L = -(1/\eta)$ if the monopoly is maximizing profits. Thus, the degree of market power depends on the price elasticity of the firm's demand curve. Our previous results show that a single-price monopolist never maximizes profits in the inelastic portion of its demand curve; that is, it will not select an output rate at which $-1 < \eta < 0$. This result implies that $0 < L < 1$ if the firm is a profit-maximizing monopolist. In other words, the markup for a single-price monopoly can never be more than 100 percent.

The Lerner index of monopoly power requires the ability to measure marginal cost. This is no easy task. We should remember, for instance, that long-run marginal cost is usually different from short-run marginal cost. Moreover, price must refer to a constant-quality unit. If there is asymmetric information about product quality, for example, even a perfectly competitive market may reach an equilibrium at which price exceeds marginal cost, as we saw in Chapter 10. Thus, if you use the Lerner index of monopoly power in order to compare firms, you must try to determine the quality characteristics of the goods sold and the degree to which asymmetric information is present in the market.

LEARNING EXERCISE 11.13

Suppose that $L > 1$. Is this sufficient evidence to say that a firm does not have market power? How can we use the Lerner index to solve for the price elasticity of demand? If we find that the estimated elasticity is inelastic, is this evidence against market power?

THE HERFINDAHL-HIRSCHMAN INDEX

Herfindahl-Hirschman Index (HHI)
A measure of market power equal to the sum of the squared market shares of all firms in the industry.

The **Herfindahl-Hirschman Index (HHI)** is used by the U.S. Department of Justice as a guide to whether or not a merger should be challenged. The HHI is calculated by summing the squares of the *market share* of all the firms in the market. Market share is defined as a given firm's share of some market indicator, divided by the total value of the indicator for the entire market. There are several market indicators that can be used to define market share, such as total sales, profits, unit sales, or assets. Usually, total sales are used, so a firm's market share equals its sales divided by the total sales in the market (multiplied by 100 to make a percentage). Algebraically, the HHI is defined as

$$HHI = \sum_{i=1}^{N} S_i^2 \quad (11.12)$$

where S_i is the market share of the *i*th firm and there are N firms in the marketplace.

The HHI accounts for both the distribution of the market shares of the top firms and the composition of the market outside those firms. If the relevant market consists of five firms, for example, with market shares of 40 percent, 30 percent, 20 percent, 9 percent, and 1 percent, the HHI is 2,982 = 1,600 + 900 + 400 + 81 + 1. The highest possible HHI is 10,000, when one firm has 100 percent of the market; the lowest HHI is approximately zero, in the case of a perfectly competitive market populated with firms that have small market shares. Thus, the argument is that the higher the value of the HHI, the greater the likelihood of market power.

Although the HHI may appear to be an intuitively reasonable index, it is not a clear guide to market power. An industry may be perfectly competitive, for example, but have a relatively high HHI. Suppose that four firms share the market equally. The HHI for this market is 2,500 = $(25)^2 + (25)^2 + (25)^2 + (25)^2$. The Lerner index for these firms may be zero, so there is no market power. If two of these firms merge, the HHI is 3,750 = $(50)^2 + (25)^2 + (25)^2$, but the Lerner index may remain equal to zero if the three remaining firms continue to act independently of each other. In addition, the HHI ignores potential competitors who have not yet entered the market but might do so if market power by existing firms generates economic profits. Because of these problems, the HHI is generally used as only one component for making policy decisions, not the sole component.

Learning Exercise 11.14

Assume that there are four firms in an industry. The market shares are 20 percent for firm A, 40 percent for firm B, 10 percent for firm C, and 30 percent for firm D. Suppose firm A merges with firm D. Compute the HHI for this industry both before and after the merger.

FEDERAL ANTITRUST LAW

The Sherman Act of 1890 was the first antitrust stature designed to deal with monopoly power and its undesirable consequences. The first two sections of the Sherman Act contained its main provisions:

1. Every contract, combination in the form of trust or otherwise, or conspiracy, in restraint of trade or commerce among the several States, or with foreign nations, is hereby declared illegal.
2. Every person who shall monopolize, or attempt to monopolize, or combine or conspire with any other person or persons, to monopolize any part of the trade or commerce among the several States, or with foreign nations, shall be deemed guilty of a misdemeanor.

The intention of the Sherman Act was to prevent certain types of behavior that may result in what was called *restraint of trade*. Currently, both jail terms and fines can be assessed for those found guilty of restraint of trade under the Sherman Act. At the discretion of the court, individuals may be fined up to $350,000 and sent to jail for up to three years; corporations may be fined up to $10,000,000. In addition, the court may impose other remedies in an attempt to *restore* competition. Injunctions may be used to stop certain actions, and, in extreme cases, companies may be dissolved and their assets distributed to shareholders.

The most famous application of the Sherman Act occurred in 1911 when the U.S. Supreme Court upheld a lower court decree that the Standard Oil Company was "conspiring to restrain trade in petroleum" and ordered that the company's structure be broken into separate and independent parts. Following the Standard Oil case, the government used the Sherman Act primarily to win injunctions against firms that tried to monopolize a market. These injunctions prevented firms from engaging in *monopolistic practices,* such as charging a monopoly price for an intermediate product and a competitive price for a final product, as Alcoa aluminum was found guilty of doing in 1953.

The Clayton Act of 1914 added more muscle and clarity to the Sherman Act. The many sections of the Clayton Act, for example, make it illegal to *price-discriminate*—that is, charge different prices for the same good when costs are identical—whenever such price discrimination may "substantially lessen competition or tend to create a monopoly." Price discrimination is permitted—we should say tolerated—only when it does not lessen competition, such as in the case of senior citizen discounts at movie theaters. We will discuss price discrimination in more detail in Chapter 12.

Also in 1914, the U.S. Congress passed the Federal Trade Commission Act and created the Federal Trade Commission (FTC), which was charged with the responsibility of challenging "unfair methods of competition . . . and unfair or deceptive acts or practices in affecting commerce." Because "unfair methods of competition" are difficult to define, the FTC has been somewhat limited by the courts to challenging "deceptive acts or practices." Ensuring truth in advertising and product labeling and preventing business fraud have been the primary aims of the FTC in recent years.

Today the government often is involved in less trust- or monopoly-busting and more preventive kinds of activity. The Sherman Act, Clayton Act, FTC Act, and subsequent amendments are used to prevent mergers that are likely to substantially lessen competition.[13] The implementation of the current policy is explained below in our discussion of the U.S. Justice Department merger guidelines. The merger rules are subject to interpretation—that is, there are gray areas—but they are fairly clear about when mergers are likely to be challenged. What is not clear, however, is whether these guidelines are good public policy.

[13] The Robinson-Patman Act of 1936 amended the Clayton Act to make "predatory pricing" illegal. The Celler-Kefauver Act of 1950 amended the Clayton Act to make the purchase of another company's assets illegal if such purchases will "substantially lessen competition." Previous to the Celler-Kefauver Act, the purchase of stock was illegal if it would "substantially lessen competition," but the purchase of assets was not illegal. The Wheeler-Lea Act of 1938 amended the FTC Act to make "unfair or deceptive" business practices illegal. Lastly, the Hart-Scott-Rodino Antitrust Improvement Act of 1980 amended the FTC Act so that firms must notify the FTC and the Justice Department ahead of time that they intend to merge.

$$$ Price Theory in Practice

U.S. Justice Department Merger Guidelines

As a guide to firms contemplating mergers, the Justice Department in 1984 issued its revised *Merger Guidelines.* Table 11.3 summarizes these guidelines. How the relevant market is defined is an important concern to firms contemplating a merger. Clearly, the broader the definition of the relevant market, the lower will be the concentrating effect of a merger. Judgment is involved when defining both the product and geographic market, but the guidelines specify a fairly specific procedure to follow. The U.S. Justice Department, for example, selects a particular product and the firms that make that product. Then, the Justice Department determines when ownership by a *single* firm gives that firm the power to impose a "small but significant and nontransitory" increase in price. Usually the rule is that the price may increase by 5 percent for one year. If this experiment causes consumers to find substitutes, so that it is not profitable to maintain the increased price, then the relevant market definition is broadened; that is, other products are included. The same thought experiment is repeated for the definition of the geographic market.

The judgment required to implement the guidelines involves issues that economists discuss in monopoly theory—the closeness of substitutes, for example, is understood to be one key to a firm (or two firms proposing to merge) having market power in a product or geographic market. Regardless of merger size—for example, the multibillion-dollar merger between oil giants Texaco and Getty Oil Company—if the new firm faces substantial competition in the geographic markets in which it operates and substantial competition in the products it produces, mergers generally are not likely to be challenged.

A proposed merger is studied to determine whether it is a horizontal or nonhorizontal merger, that is, whether or not the merging firms are in the same product and geographic markets. If it is a *horizontal merger,* then the post-merger HHI is calculated and a set of challenge rules are considered. For example, if there are ten firms in an industry, each with an equal market share, the pre-merger HHI is 1,000. If two of these firms propose to merge, the post-merger HHI is 1,200—an increase of 200 points—so the merger is likely to be challenged. For nonhorizontal mergers, the Justice Department considers whether the acquiring firm is a likely potential entrant in the market by means other than a merger or whether the degree of vertical integration between the two markets may substantially deter the entry of other firms.

To some extent the challenge rules are mechanical—particularly in the use of the HHI. Each merger case considers many other factors, however, such as the peculiarities of the market, the likelihood of increased or decreased competition in the market in the future, the possibility that one of the merging firms might go out of business without the merger, and the ease of entry into the relevant market. The use of such additional criteria, which are based on economic theory, is a major reason why some mergers involving relatively small firms are challenged and why other mergers involving giant firms are uncontested.

TABLE 11.3

U.S. Department of Justice—Current Merger Guidelines

U.S. Justice Department Definitions	
Market Power	The ability of one or more firms to profitably maintain prices above (or below) competitive levels for a significant period of time.
Relevant Market	A product and geographic market of sufficient size that if only a single (hypothetical) firm is present, it could profitably impose a "small but significant and nontransitory" increase in price—usually a 5 percent increase for one year.
Market Share	The dollar share, unit share, or relative capacity held in the relevant market.
Horizontal Merger	A merger between two or more firms in the same relevant market
Nonhorizontal Merger	A merger between two or more firms not in the same relevant market.
General Standards for Horizontal Mergers	
No Challenge	If the post-merger HHI is below 1,000, except in "extraordinary" circumstances
Likely Challenge	If the post-merger HHI is between 1,000 and 1,800 and the increase in the HHI is more than 100 points or if the post-merger HHI is above 1,800 and the increase in the HHI is more than 50 points, unless it is found from the presence or absence of other factors that the merger is not likely to substantially lessen competition.
Unlikely Challenge	If the post-merger HHI is above 1,800, but the merger causes the HHI to increase by less than 50 points.
Leading Firm Challenge	A challenge is likely, regardless of the post-merger HHI, if a leading firm, with a market share of at least 35 percent, merges with a firm with a market share of at least 1 percent.
Some General Standards for Nonhorizontal Mergers	
Potential Entrant Challenge	A challenge is likely if the acquiring firm is a potential entrant in the relevant market, the acquired firm has at least a 5 percent market share, entry by other firms is difficult, and the HHI is above 1,800 in the acquired firm's market.
Vertical Integration Challenge	A challenge is likely if the degree of vertical integration between two markets requires potential entrants to enter both markets simultaneously or not to enter at all; entry into the second market must make entry into the first market more difficult; and the competitive structure of the first market must be affected by the difficulty of entry.

Source: U.S. Department of Justice, *Merger Guidelines,* June 14, 1984.

LEARNING EXERCISE 11.15

Suppose the relevant market is composed of fourteen firms. Seven firms each have a 5 percent market share and seven firms each have a 10 percent market share. What mergers are possible in this industry under the "no challenge" standard for horizontal mergers?

AN ALTERNATIVE VIEW OF ANTITRUST LAWS

Judge Robert Bork, formerly on the U.S. Court of Appeals in Washington, D.C., has argued that antitrust laws should be used to promote *consumer welfare,* which for purposes of illustration we will interpret as consumers' surplus.[14] Using consumers' surplus as a guide to public policy, instead of the more strict merger guidelines, could lead to some monopoly-producing mergers if such mergers offer substantial cost reductions—often called economic efficiencies. This possibility is illustrated in Figure 11.13.

In Figure 11.13, the market demand curve, D_{market}, and its associated marginal revenue curve, MR, are assumed to be fixed. There are now two firms in the industry. The sum of the marginal cost curves for these two firms is equal to MC_{before}, which is the marginal cost curve for the industry *before* the merger. The

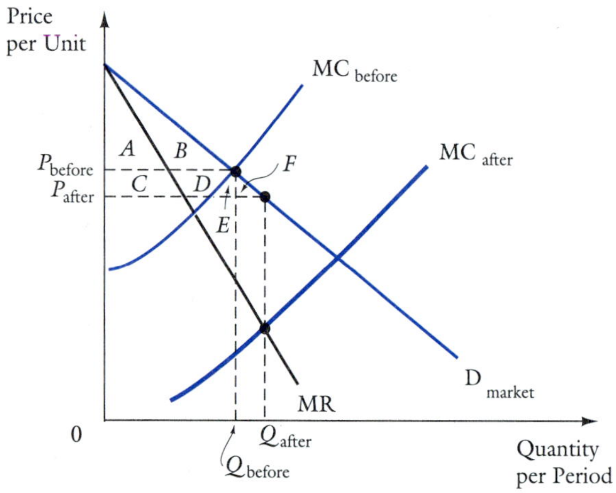

FIGURE 11.13

A Cost-Reducing Merger Can Create a Monopoly and Increase Consumers' Surplus

Cost-reducing mergers that produce a monopoly may actually increase consumers' surplus. A cost-reducing merger lowers the marginal cost curve to MC_{after} from MC_{before}, which increases the monopoly output rate to Q_{after} from Q_{before}. Consumers' surplus increases by the areas $C + D + E + F$.

[14] Robert H. Bork, *The Antitrust Paradox: A Policy at War with Itself,* New York: Basic Books, 1978.

two firms are assumed to be perfectly competitive, so they produce a total output rate of Q_{before}. The market is in equilibrium at a price of P_{before}. Consumers' surplus for the industry equals areas $A + B$. The merger of the two firms creates a monopoly, but it also greatly lowers the cost structure of both firms. The MC_{after} curve is the marginal cost curve of the merged firm. The optimal output for the monopoly is Q_{after} and the market clearing price is P_{after}. Because of the substantial cost reduction, consumers' surplus has actually increased to areas $A + B + C + D + E + F$ after the merger. Using consumers' surplus as a guide to public policy suggests that these two firms should be allowed to merge.

Current public policy, dating back to the *Brown Shoe v. United States* decision in 1962, is at odds with Judge Bork's view. Current policy questions whether a substantial cost savings is good *if it may substantially lessen competition*. In *Brown Shoe,* the Supreme Court under Chief Justice Earl Warren concluded that a substantial cost savings would adversely affect the remaining firms, making it difficult for them to remain in business after the merger. In this light, the court viewed a substantial cost savings as a negative factor because it was likely to result in monopoly power or a natural monopoly situation.

Economists disagree on the merits of a merger that creates a monopoly. Some economists argue that the cost savings are unlikely to be substantial enough to increase consumers' surplus. Others argue that even with substantial cost savings, a monopoly may try to extract some or all of the consumers' surplus by adopting nonuniform pricing practices, also called price discrimination (see Chapter 12). Nonuniform pricing transfers some consumers' surplus to the monopolist as economic profits. Because there is an incentive to extract consumers' surplus when a firm has market power, economists argue that a merger such as that described in Figure 11.13 will not be beneficial to consumers.

Chapter Summary

1. A firm has market power when its output decision can affect the *market* price of its product. Such a firm faces a negatively sloped demand curve for its product and is a price maker. By definition, a pure monopoly is the only seller, so it has market power.
2. As a profit-maximizing firm, the single-price monopolist finds the output rate at which marginal revenue equals marginal cost. Algebraically, $\text{MR} = \text{MC}$, or $P[1 + (1/\eta)] = \text{MC}$, where η is the price elasticity of demand for the firm's product.
3. At the optimal output rate, the monopolist's price markup is inversely proportional to the price elasticity of demand. The markup price rule is $[(P - \text{MC})/P] = -1/\eta$, where both marginal cost and price vary with the output rate of the firm.
4. Four barriers to entry that can create market power are the ownership of resources with no close substitutes; economies of scale; government licenses, franchises, and certificates of need; and patents. These barriers can prevent other firms from entering an industry and competing away any monopoly profits.
5. By restricting output of its members, the cartel replicates the monopoly solution. For each cartel member, however, price exceeds marginal

cost; if each member acts as a price taker, then there is an incentive to cheat—that is, to expand output to the point at which $P = \text{MC}$.

6. When a previously perfectly competitive industry is converted into a single-price monopoly, there is a deadweight loss of both consumers' and producers' surpluses in the short run. In the long run, the deadweight loss is solely from consumers' surplus because producers' surplus is zero at the long-run perfectly competitive equilibrium.
7. Federal law relies on the Sherman Act of 1890 and the Federal Trade Commission Act of 1914. When enforced, these laws can cause firms to break up into smaller, independent parts, as was the case with the Standard Oil Company, or can make firms compensate others for their anticompetitive behavior.

Trouble Spots

Concept	Reminder
Price and Output Decisions for a Monopoly	A pure monopoly is a single seller of a service or product, whereas a firm with market power may face competition from other firms but still have a negatively sloped demand curve. The analysis of the profit-maximizing decision for a pure monopoly is the same as the decision for a firm with market power as long as the demand curve is negatively sloped and it can act independently of its competitors. So, at present, there is little need to distinguish between a firm with market power and a pure monopoly.
Maximizing Profits for a Single-Price Monopolist	Sometimes students confuse the market clearing price with the level of marginal revenue or marginal cost that maximizes profits. The market clearing price is determined by finding the single price along the demand curve at which the optimal output will (all) be sold. Marginal revenue equals marginal cost below this output rate, so marginal revenue is always less than price for a firm with market power that sets a single price to all customers.
Markup Pricing for a Single-Price Monopolist	The markup pricing rule applies at the profit-maximizing output rate, *not* at all output rates. In addition, the rule uses the *marginal* cost of the optimal output rate, *not* the average cost. Even though the average cost may be more easy to compute from available data, the markup pricing rule requires marginal cost data.
A Monopolist Has No Supply Curve	Monopolies do not have supply curves. A monopoly does not take market price as given in order to determine its output rate; the monopolist sets market price by its output decision. Thus, the output rate of a monopolist is uniquely determined once market demand and its cost structure are known. There is no schedule of output rates to compute, rather, just one unique value.

Barriers to Entry	A monopoly need not be permanent for it to earn economic profits. If the barriers to entry are temporary, such as a patent that lasts for 17 years, the firm will have market power for the time the barriers are in effect. After they are removed, entry is expected to eliminate any remaining monopoly profits.

11.6 Review Questions

1. Explain why marginal revenue is less than price for a single-price monopolist.
2. Is it possible that a profit-maximizing, single-price monopolist will operate in the inelastic portion of its demand curve?
3. What is the profit-maximizing rule for a single-price monopolist? How is price related to marginal cost at the optimal output rate?
4. Explain why a monopolist does not have a supply curve. Does your explanation imply that the monopolist is never a price taker?
5. Does a monopolist always earn economic profits? Draw a diagram that shows a monopoly losing money in the short run. When will the monopolist cease operating in the short run?
6. What is the profit-maximizing rule for a monopolist that operates several plants or, equivalently, a monopolist that purchases all of the firms in a competitive industry?
7. Does a monopolist produce more or less than a comparable perfectly competitive industry? How do the prices charged under these two market structures compare to each other?
8. Of the barriers to entry discussed in the text, which ones are government created and which ones arise in the absence of government action?
9. Explain what a natural monopoly is. Why is the right of free entry insufficient here to prevent sustained economic profits?
10. Is there any difference between an effective cartel and tacit collusion agreements that effectively restrain competition?
11. Why is the incentive so great for an individual firm to cheat on a cartel agreement?
12. Explain why the Herfindahl-Hirschman and Lerner indices of market power can sometimes conflict with each other. What is the value that these indices take for a perfectly competitive market? What is the value that they take for a pure monopoly?

11.7 Price Theory Problems

1. "Because a monopolist is the only supplier of a well-defined product, there is no limit to the price it can charge." Is this statement true or false? Explain.
2. If demand increases for a monopoly, can we conclude that output and market price will increase as well?
3. How would you determine if a firm has market power? If the cross-price elasticity of demand for your product and the products produced by your competitors is zero, do you have market power? Design a test that will provide evidence for or against the proposition that a given

firm has some market power. What are the general problems you face in drawing your conclusion?

4. If a new entrant buys an existing monopoly, will the new entrant earn monopoly profits?
5. "Philosophically, I am vehemently opposed to government interference in the marketplace; however, as the owner of a liquor store, I can tell you that deregulation would be very bad for the citizenry. You wouldn't want a liquor store on every corner, would you?" Why would you predict that a liquor store owner would defend regulation of his or her industry?
6. "If a government regulatory agency ordered a public utility to price all of its output at marginal cost, the firm would lose money unless subsidy payments were made by the government." Is this statement true, false, or uncertain? Why?
7. Suppose a single-price monopolist and a comparable perfectly competitive industry experience a cost increase that causes average and marginal cost curves to shift up by 10 percent. Will the resulting *increase* in market price be greater or less for a monopoly than for the perfectly competitive industry?
8. Suppose a monopoly faces an (inverse) demand curve given by $P = 400 - Q$ and a short-run total cost curve given by $STC = Q^2 + 5{,}000$. The short-run marginal cost curve is given by $SMC = 2Q$. Find the profit-maximizing output rate and market clearing price for the monopolist. Draw a graph that illustrates your solution.
9. The Leaping Lizards Toy Company has a monopoly of Leaping Lizards toys. The (inverse) demand curve for these toys is given by $P = 10 - .01Q$. The toys are made in China and imported to the United States. The marginal cost of the toys is constant: MC = \$2.

    a. What is the profit-maximizing output rate of Leaping Lizards toys? What is the market clearing price?

    b. Assume that an antilizard tax passed by Congress places an import tariff of 50 cents per toy on each Leaping Lizard toy imported to the United States. What are the new profit-maximizing price and output rate? How much tax revenue is collected by the government?

10. Using the demand and cost structure in Price Theory Problem 9 (with no import tax), compute the producers' and consumers' surpluses at the monopoly solution. Now, assume that Leaping Lizards toys are produced by a perfectly competitive market, with each firm's marginal cost given by MC = \$2.

    a. What are the market clearing price and output rate of the perfectly competitive market?

    b. What are consumers' and producers' surpluses for the perfectly competitive market? What is the deadweight loss due to a monopoly?

11. The Pin-Strip Apparel Company operates two production facilities. The costs at these plants are as follows:

Plant 1 $TC_1(Q_1) = 500 + .1Q_1^2$

Plant 2 $TC_2(Q_2) = 100 + Q_2^2$

The firm has market power and faces an (inverse) demand curve given by

$P = 1000 - 5Q$

where $Q = Q_1 + Q_2$.

a. Draw a diagram showing the marginal cost structure of the two plants. Which plant is more efficient?
b. Calculate the profit-maximizing output rate for each plant and the market clearing price.
c. Suppose a union wage settlement raises the cost of operating plant 1 such that its total costs are given by $TC_1(Q_1) = 600 + .5Q_1^2$. How does this affect your answer to part b? Has the output rate produced by plant 2 increased relative to plant 1 because of the union wage settlement?

12. In Omaha, Nebraska, there was a question of how to maximize the tax revenue from the game keno, a popular form of gambling. Some city officials wanted to permit only one gambling house in the city, while others thought that tax revenues would increase if there were many competitors offering the game. Assume that taxes of amount T are paid for each keno player and that a linear demand curve, $P(Q) = 120 - 5Q$, and a constant marginal cost curve, $MC = 5$, describe the industry structure. If the city officials can set T to maximize their tax receipts, do they do better with a perfectly competitive market or with a monopoly?

11.8 Writing Exercise

Nearly every municipality grants or maintains some monopoly privilege. Taxi service, cable TV, and garbage collection are frequently cited examples of government-granted monopolies. Select a service or product that a local municipality provides or restricts by license or franchise in your community. In your essay, investigate the prices charged for the service, whether there is any subsidy paid or special tax charged, and whether there is any *illegal* competition. Describe any close substitutes you can identify and their prices. Investigate whether the same service is provided as a monopoly in other areas of the country. If it is not, find out how much it costs in areas where it is competitively provided. In your essay, estimate the increase in price (if any) that the government-granted monopoly is charging relative to a competitive market structure.

12 Pricing Strategies with Market Power

Preview Questions

When you finish studying this chapter, you should be able to answer the following questions:

- What is price discrimination?
- How do first-, second-, and third-degree price discrimination differ from each other?
- What is bundling?
- How do pure bundling and mixed bundling strategies differ from each other?
- How do two-part tariffs extract consumers' surplus?
- What are exclusive dealing and requirements contracts?
- How does an English auction differ from a Dutch auction?
- What does the winner's curse mean to auction participants?

How would you price a laboratory mouse? Not just any lab mouse, but a genetically engineered lab mouse. In April 1988, Harvard University was issued a patent on a genetically engineered mouse. These mice are altered so that they are predisposed to getting cancer. Medical and university-based researchers use such mice in experiments, most of which are trying to find a cure for cancer. With the patent, Harvard has market power, or should we say mouse power, in the laboratory mouse market. Should Harvard charge one price for all its mice? Should it offer quantity discounts? Should it bundle small mice with larger mice? Or should it charge a membership fee to researchers, who would then pay an extra charge for each mouse they use? A firm with market power must choose among these and many other possible pricing strategies, because acting as a single-price monopolist may not be the strategy that maximizes profits.

A pure monopoly is fairly rare, but firms with market power—even if it is temporary—are more common. Often it is government policy that creates the market power some firms have. For example, some firms have market power in industries that have only a few producers because government-created trade barriers protect these firms from international competition. Although the market power these firms enjoy may not be sustainable in the long run—as trade barriers may be changed or removed—when firms have market power, they will use it to try to increase profits.

As they try to increase profits, managers of firms with market power must cope with a more complex environment than managers of perfectly competitive firms. Managers in perfectly competitive firms take market price as given, so they focus on cost-reducing strategies. But firms with market power can affect the market price, so managers must address both cost-reducing *and* pricing strategies in order to increase profits. This chapter focuses on various pricing strategies that managers of firms with market power use to increase profits. All of these strategies have one common denominator: They try to increase profits at the expense of consumers by extracting more consumers' surplus than the simple single-price monopoly solution.

In this chapter, we investigate how firms with market power use price discrimination to increase profits. Price discrimination occurs in any pricing strategy that involves charging different customers different prices for the same product, holding cost and product constant. We describe three common types of price discrimination—first-, second-, and third-degree—and discuss several purported examples of each type. We also investigate bundling, which is the practice of selling a package containing more than one product, as well as the two-part tariff, which is the practice of charging a unit price and an access fee for the right to buy a product. We will discuss the auction as the third method of increasing profits by extracting consumers' surplus. Finally, we examine public policy toward price discrimination and offer a critical appraisal of the purported examples of discriminatory pricing. As you might expect, price discrimination is often *de jure* illegal if it substantially lessens competition. Many such practices are ignored by government officials when they have little or no effect on competition in a given market.

12.1 Pricing to Extract Consumers' Surplus

Our discussion of market power in Chapter 11 focused exclusively on setting a *single price* for all consumers. The single price was found by choosing an output rate that equates marginal revenue to marginal cost in order to maximize profits. But firms do not generally charge a single price to all customers. Movie theaters offer discounts to children and senior citizens; restaurants offer "early bird" prices to patrons; retail stores offer discounts to shoppers who clip discount coupons from newspapers; and airlines offer a host of discount fares to travelers who meet certain restrictions, such as staying over on a Saturday night before returning home. In this section, we discuss why firms with market power try to adopt a multiprice strategy. As in our previous discussions, our focus is on how such strategies increase a firm's profits.

Consumers' Surplus as Potential Profits

When the operating behavior of a monopoly was compared to the behavior of a perfectly competitive firm, we found that *total market surplus* was reduced under a monopoly. The fall in total market surplus, however, is not the only effect that a monopoly or a firm with market power has on a (previously) competitive market. There is a redistribution of surplus, from consumers to the firm(s) with market power as it institutes a monopoly price. In Figure 12.1, we show the transfer of consumers' surplus in the standard single-price monopoly case.

The long-run marginal cost curve (LMC) for the firm is assumed to be constant, which implies that LMC = LATC. (This assumption is made for expositional convenience only; our conclusions do not change if we use U-shaped cost curves.) The market demand curve and its associated marginal revenue curve have the usual shape. If a competitive market exists, then the total industry output equals Q_c and market price equals P_c. Consumers' surplus equals areas $A + B + C + D + E$ under the perfectly competitive market structure. Alternatively, if a monopoly, or a firm with market power, takes over, total industry output decreases to Q_m, the point at which marginal revenue equals marginal cost. The monopoly charges P_m per unit for its output and earns $(P_m - \text{LATC})Q_m$ in economic profits.

Consumers' surplus under the monopoly equals areas $A + B$, which is a *decrease* from the consumers' surplus generated under the perfectly competitive market structure. The decrease in consumers' surplus—areas $C + D + E$—is composed of monopoly profits, equal to areas $C + D$, plus a deadweight loss, equal to area E. Thus, the change in industry structure transfers some previously accruing consumers' surplus to the monopoly in the form of additional

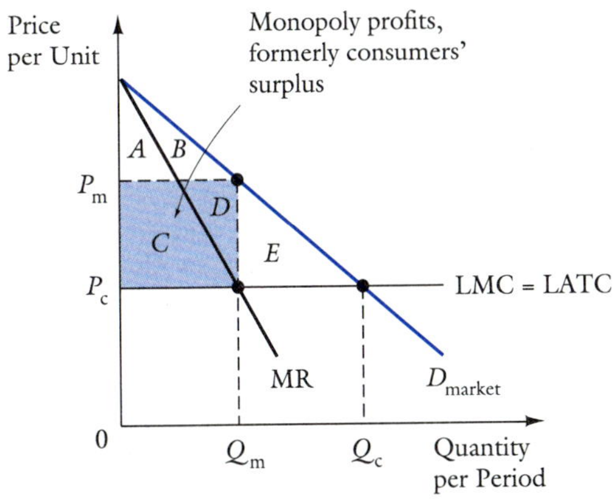

FIGURE 12.1

The Transfer of Consumers' Surplus to a Monopoly

When ownership in a perfectly competitive industry is transferred to a single entity, a monopoly is created. The pricing and output decisions of the monopoly transfer some consumers' surplus to the monopoly in the form of monopoly profits. If the perfectly competitive industry produced Q_c and charged P_c in equilibrium, then the monopoly produces Q_m and charges P_m in equilibrium. Consumers' surplus in the perfectly competitive industry equals areas $A + B + C + D + E$. Under the monopoly structure, areas $C + D$ are transferred to the monopoly as economic profits.

monopoly profits. To a firm contemplating a merger or another action that creates market power, consumers' surplus represents a new source of potential profits.

DROPPING THE SINGLE-PRICE ASSUMPTION

Once a monopoly or a firm with market power begins to view consumers' surplus as potential profits, there is an incentive to find a way to extract more consumers' surplus than that offered by the single-price solution. In Figure 12.2, we show how the firm may increase its profits if it can separate consumers into two distinct groups.

The demand and cost structure shown in Figure 12.2 is the same as that presented in Figure 12.1. The only difference is that the firm has (somehow) placed consumers into two groups: a high-value group, composed of consumers who are willing to pay *at least* P_{high} (equal to P_m in Figure 12.1) for the product, and a low-value group, composed of consumers who will pay *at most* P_{high} for the product.[1] The location of these two groups is marked on the market demand curve and is also shown on the two smaller graphs in the figure.

The firm can now increase its profits if it successfully charges two different prices to these two groups. The marginal revenue curve for the high-value group equals MR_{high}, which is the same as the marginal revenue curve in Figure 12.1 except that it stops at output rate Q_{high} (equal to Q_m in Figure 12.1). Note that MR_{high} = LMC at Q_{high}. Thus, the firm maximizes profits generated from the high-value group by selling Q_{high} units and charging P_{high} to each member of the high-value group. These profits are equal to those generated in Figure 12.1, so up to this point in our analysis nothing has changed.

Now, for output rates beyond Q_{high}, the firm is selling to the low-value group. If we chop the demand curve into two pieces at the point above Q_{high}, then the lower segment is the demand curve for the low-value group. By focusing solely on this segment, we can compute the marginal revenue curve for the low-value group. This curve, labeled MR_{low}, begins at the point where the demand curve is split. The firm must now decide how much extra output to produce to maximize profits from selling to the low-value group. In Figure 12.2, we see that MR_{low} = LMC at the output rate Q_{total}.[2] Thus, to maximize profits from the low-value group, the firm sells Q_{low} (equal to $Q_{total} - Q_{high}$) additional units and charges P_{low} to each member of the low-value group. The *additional* profits generated from these sales equal the shaded area in Figure 12.2. Note that these additional profits include a portion of the deadweight loss caused by a monopoly in Figure 12.1, and previously they were part of consumers' surplus under a perfectly competitive market structure. Thus, by separating consumers into two groups and adopting a two-price strategy, the firm can capture more consumers' surplus and thus more profits.

Because there are additional profits created from the low-value group, the firm is better off when it charges two different prices rather than a single price to all consumers. This situation is referred to as price discrimination. With

---

[1]For simplicity, assume that consumers purchase only 1 unit of the product.

[2]For the purposes of computing MR_{low}, the vertical axis may be thought of as extending up from Q_{high}.

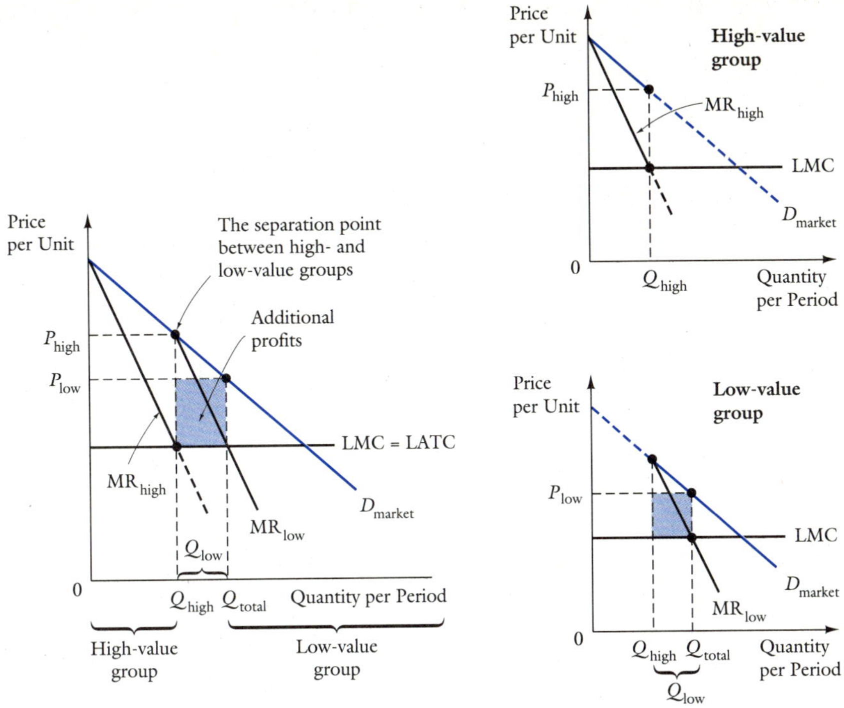

FIGURE 12.2

Separating Consumers Into Two Groups and Charging Different Prices Increases Profits

If a single-price monopolist can divide its customers into high-value and low-value groups, it can increase profits by charging each group a different price. The high-value group includes all customers who will pay P_{high} or more for the product. The low-value group includes those customers who will pay *less than* P_{high} for the product (e.g., they will buy no units if $P \geq P_{high}$). The marginal revenue curve for the low-value group begins at the "splitpoint" along the demand curve that divides the two types of customers. The monopolist charges P_{high} to the high-value group and P_{low} to the low-value group. The optimal quantity sold to the high-value group is Q_{high}. At price P_{low}, the low-value group buys Q_{low} units, so the total produced equals $Q_{high} + Q_{low} = Q_{total}$. By segmenting the demand curve, a monopoly can increase profit. The amount of the profit increase is shown by the shaded area.

Price Discrimination Charging different buyers a different price for different units of a similar product when cost differences do not justify the observed price differences.

price discrimination, a firm charges consumers two (or more) different prices for a similar product where the differences in price do not reflect differences in cost. In this example, there are two different prices, the product is identical, and its cost of production is the same for all consumers. As this example shows, a firm that can effectively price-discriminate earns more profits than a firm that charges a single price to all consumers.

A word of caution before we continue: You should realize that charging different prices to different people for different units because of differences in the cost of service is not generally price discrimination. This is normally **price differentiation:** differences in prices that reflect differences in marginal cost. The larger-size box of detergent, for example, is cheaper per ounce because it costs less to produce and transport on a per-ounce basis. Cost differences nearly always result in different prices. But it is also true that a single price does not necessarily indicate an absence of price discrimination. If production costs vary by customer and all consumers are charged the same price, this is a case of price discrimination.

Price Differentiation
Price differences that reflect differences in marginal costs.

LEARNING EXERCISE 12.1

How has consumers' surplus changed when the firm price-discriminates in Figure 12.2? Has consumers' surplus increased relative to the monopoly solution shown in Figure 12.1? How has the deadweight loss changed?

IDENTIFICATION AND ARBITRAGE ARE CRUCIAL

The firm is better off if it can price-discriminate, but can it successfully accomplish this goal? There are two key elements to successful price discrimination: identification and arbitrage. The firm must have a way to successfully divide consumers into groups according to their reservation prices, or willingness to pay, for its product. The **reservation price** equals the maximum a consumer is willing to pay for a given unit of a good. Reservation prices for a single consumer are found from that consumer's demand curve; that is, the demand curve represents the schedule of *maximum* prices a consumer is willing to pay for each quantity purchased.

Reservation Price
The maximum a consumer is willing to pay for a given unit of a good.

Some professions offer more opportunities to discover a consumer's reservation prices than others. Tax accountants, for example, learn exactly how much an individual earns over the course of a year and may use this information to charge their clients higher fees. For other products, such as retail merchandise, consumers are more anonymous, so firms may not know their customers to a high degree. Firms with market power that sell to relatively anonymous consumers must devise schemes that reveal who among a large group of customers is willing to pay more than others. Discount coupons and bundling of products—discussed below—are often used by firms to price-discriminate under these circumstances. The key, though, is that the firm must *identify* how much its customers are willing to pay before it can effectively price-discriminate.

Successful price discrimination is short-lived if a firm cannot prevent arbitrage. **Arbitrage** is a situation in which price differences offer profit-making opportunities to market participants. Arbitrage occurs, for example, when consumers who pay the low price sell the product to consumers who are charged the high price. To complete the sale, the low-price consumers undercut the high price charged by the firm with market power. This action closes the gap between the prices charged to each group and eventually causes a single price to exist for all consumers. The price paid for U.S. government securities in New York and Tokyo, for example, can never differ by more than a fraction of a cent because of arbitrage. If Treasury securities were significantly more

Arbitrage
The purchase and resale of an asset in order to gain from observed price differences.

expensive in Tokyo, traders would buy Treasury securities in New York and simultaneously sell them in Tokyo for an instant profit. In contrast, price discrimination for medical services is much less difficult to implement because arbitrage is very costly or impossible. Resale of a coronary bypass operation is impossible, for example.

Basically, for the firm to successfully price-discriminate, it is necessary that buyers can be separated at a reasonable cost and that arbitrage is not practical. For example, charging senior citizens and children a lower price than other moviegoers can be done relatively easily and at low cost. Usually, these groups of buyers are visually identified. Alternatively, some movie theaters issue senior citizen discount cards that are presented at the ticket window. Also, it is fairly easy to prevent arbitrage because the market for ticket sales is in the front of the theater, and monitoring any resale activity is fairly simple and inexpensive. Many movie theaters do not sell tickets in advance, so they can prevent arbitrage. Movie tickets for that day's shows go on sale when the box office opens. Tickets for the next day's shows go on sale the next day. The only exception seems to be when someone chooses to buy out an entire performance, in which case everyone attending that performance pays effectively the same price, so arbitrage is not important. In short, if a firm cannot prevent arbitrage, it cannot successfully price-discriminate.

PRICE DISCRIMINATION BREAKS DOWN WHEN IDENTIFICATION IS COSTLY

Bargaining is the usual and maybe the most effective method of determining someone's reservation price. But bargaining for some products can be very costly relative to the profits gained from price discrimination. In the United States, charging more for aspirin to someone who has a headache is simply too costly. You must hold up other customers who want to pay for their purchases to bargain with someone who feels bad. Even though the individual may have a reservation price higher than the posted price, you will gain very little in profits on the transaction and will probably lose one or more customers in the process. In poorer countries, however, bargaining for simple necessities—such as aspirin—is more likely. Because incomes are relatively low in poorer countries, the time cost of bargaining is lower, and bargaining is more common. In addition, when the potential gains from bargaining are high to both parties, as when bargaining for a new car, more bargaining occurs.

$$$ Price Theory in Practice

THE CASE OF ROBERT SUTTON: ARBITRAGER OF NEW AND OLD OIL PRICES

Beginning after the oil embargo by the Organization of Petroleum Exporting Countries (OPEC) in 1973, the United States adopted a system of price controls on domestically produced crude oil. By discouraging domestic oil production, these controls contributed to the long lines motorists found at gas stations during various periods in the 1970s. Growing resentment by consumers led to the near-total decontrol of oil prices in January 1981. Since then, there have been no long lines at gas stations.

The oil pricing policy adopted by the U.S. government evolved over time, but it was basically a case of government-sanctioned price discrimination. The government defined two types of oil: old and new. Old oil came from wells that were drilled prior to 1976, and new oil came from wells drilled after this date. The nominal price set by the government for new oil averaged about $13 per barrel during the 1976–1981 period. The nominal price of old oil averaged about $5 per barrel over the same period. New and old oil were identical to each other for all practical purposes, but the government mandated two different prices based on when the oil was discovered. There was also a third type of oil, known as stripper oil, which came from wells that produced less than 10 barrels a day. The nominal price of stripper oil was not controlled and varied with the world price of oil, which ranged from $13 to $38 over this period.

The real reason the government set up this scheme is unclear. Purportedly, it did not want companies that had discovered oil many years earlier—which is oil that was less costly to extract—to benefit from the rapidly increasing price of oil. Firms that discover new oil fields face higher exploration and extraction costs. The higher price set for new oil helped them to cover these higher costs.

Whatever the government's reason, it set up a discriminatory price structure for oil. As noted above, a discriminatory pricing strategy will be successful only if arbitrage can be prevented. Although the government made it illegal to violate the price controls, the potential profits lured many arbitragers to try, and some were quite successful for a short time. Obviously, at the average price, if you *convert* a barrel of old oil into new oil, you can more than double your money invested. And if you convert old oil into stripper oil, you might earn an even greater return. By the end of the price control period, the government had filed suit against more than eighty companies, charging them with violating the price controls by converting old oil into new or stripper oil.

The case of Oklahoma oilman Robert B. Sutton is perhaps the best known. Sutton sold postage meters before he became a multimillionaire in the business of *reselling* oil. In his heyday, he controlled an oil refinery, a Bahamas resort hotel once owned by Howard Hughes, and two private jets. His companies, BPM Ltd. and the Scurry Oil Co., went into bankruptcy after oil prices were decontrolled. Sutton was subsequently charged in a 17-count criminal indictment with falsely certifying over 240 million barrels of old oil as either new or stripper oil. The government alleged that consumers were overcharged $1 billion by Sutton's companies. Sutton was found guilty in 1984, sentenced to five years in prison, and ordered to repay approximately $211 million plus interest to the government.

The reselling activities of Robert Sutton, his companies, and other companies were an attempt to move the oil market to a single-price equilibrium. The amount of economic profits to be earned from arbitrage was simply too great to make government-mandated price discrimination sustainable. Without government intervention in the form of lawsuits, these arbitragers would likely have eliminated the government-imposed discriminatory pricing in the oil market long before prices were decontrolled.

LEARNING EXERCISE 12.2

How would a more vigorous legal attack on arbitragers affect the longevity of the two-price equilibrium in the oil market? What do you predict happened to production levels from old-oil wells after prices were decontrolled?

12.2 Three Degrees of Price Discrimination

Traditionally, economists define three types of price discrimination, labeled first-degree, second-degree, and third-degree price discrimination. Keep in mind, however, that there are more than just three methods of increasing profits by extracting consumers' surplus, as we will show when we discuss bundling, tying, and other pricing schemes below. Before we describe these more elaborate schemes, let's consider the traditional approaches to price discrimination.

First-Degree Price Discrimination

First-Degree Price Discrimination
Price discrimination in which all consumers' surplus is extracted by charging each consumer the highest price he or she will pay for each unit of the good purchased.

In **first-degree price discrimination,** the monopolist or the firm with market power charges *each* buyer his or her *reservation price* for each unit purchased. When price is below the buyer's reservation price, the product or service is purchased. When price is above the buyer's reservation price, no purchase is made. First-degree price discrimination is also called *perfect price discrimination* because all of the consumers' surplus is transferred to the producer. Consider, for example, the purchase of a new car. Suppose you have selected the type of car that you want and now the only question is the price you will pay. You will probably enter into some sort of bargaining with the car dealer. You want the lowest price you can get and the dealer wants the highest price you will pay, subject to some minimum amount. The minimum for the dealer is the present value of the amount that the dealer believes another buyer will pay for the same car. At some point in the bargaining process, you may reveal your reservation price to the dealer. You may do this inadvertently by discussing your income for possible financing purposes or by discussing what you think you would pay another dealer for a similar car. At this point you are likely to be given a final offer, which is a "take it or leave it" offer. The dealer says you can have the car for your reservation price; otherwise, you can go elsewhere and bargain with another dealer. If you accept the offer, the transaction will be an example of perfect price discrimination.

Figure 12.3, on page 474, illustrates first-degree, or perfect, price discrimination. For comparison, the profit-maximizing price and output are P_m and Q_m, respectively, for a single-price monopoly. In this case, profits equal areas $C + D$. Now, by charging each consumer his or her reservation price, the firm slides down its demand curve as it sells additional units.[3] In other words, each point on the market demand curve represents a price at which the firm sells 1

[3]Again, we are assuming that each consumer purchases a single unit of the product or service.

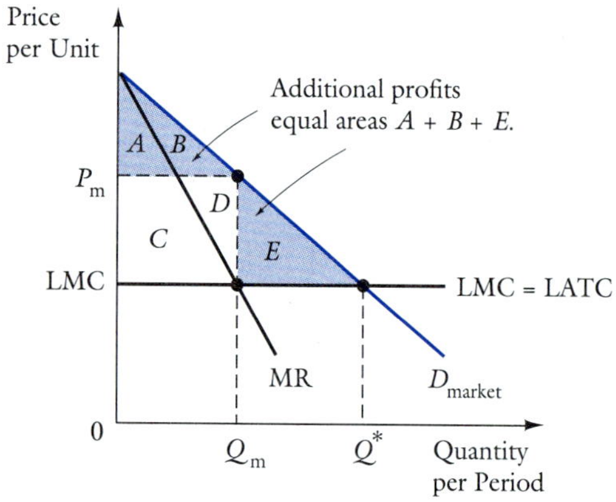

FIGURE 12.3

Charging Each Consumer His or Her Reservation Price: A Case of First-Degree Price Discrimination

With first-degree price discrimination, each customer is charged the maximum he or she is willing to pay. A perfect price-discriminating monopolist produces Q^* units compared to a single-price monopolist that produces Q_m units. The single-price monopolist earns profits equal to areas $C + D$, whereas the perfect price discriminator earns profit equal to areas $A + B + C + D + E$. The additional profits earned from perfect price discrimination equal areas $A + B + E$.

unit to a customer whose reservation price equals that price on the demand curve. Under this approach to pricing, the firm then sells a total of Q^* units. The firm stops at Q^*, because the next customer is not willing to pay (at a minimum) the marginal cost, LMC, of the $Q^* + 1$ unit. At Q^*, the firm earns profits equal to areas $A + B + C + D + E$, which is the entire area under the demand curve *above* the LMC curve. The increase in profits relative to the single-price, or nondiscriminatory, monopoly equals the shaded region in Figure 12.3. Clearly, the firm is significantly better off if it can be a perfect price discriminator even though the consumer is not. All of the consumers' surplus is transferred to the firm as economic profits when perfect price discrimination is successful; there is, however, no deadweight loss of *total market surplus* (ignoring any transaction costs).

How does a firm discover what someone is willing to pay? Signals are often used. If your time is valuable and you are in a hurry, you may not be willing to spend much time bargaining for a car. A successful car dealer notices this, offering you a smaller discount than to another customer who has indicated a willingness to spend time bargaining or shopping at other dealers. In some other situations, financial data are used to estimate your reservation price. Colleges require students and parents to disclose income tax returns or equivalent information about income and assets before awarding scholarships. These awards are nothing more than a tuition discount. Alternatively, restrictions may be imposed on how and when you can use a product to identify those with relatively low reservation prices. Commercial airlines place travel restrictions on their discount tickets in an attempt to identify those travelers with relatively low reservation prices. Such air travelers may find that they must connect with another plane, travel late at night, and stay over a Saturday night to receive the lowest ticket price. Lastly, some firms can identify the reservation prices of customers by their purchase habits. Hotels normally charge walk-in customers more than they charge customers who make phone reservations. Your choices are limited at 10 P.M., for example, and it is costly for you to search for other hotels at this hour, particularly if you are not familiar with the city. In contrast, in advance you can cheaply call another hotel if you think the rate quoted over the phone is too high.

SECOND-DEGREE PRICE DISCRIMINATION

Second-Degree Price Discrimination A pricing scheme that sorts buyers imperfectly based on their reservation prices.

Second-degree price discrimination occurs when there are many buyers within each market and sellers cannot perfectly determine each buyer's reservation prices. A declining rate schedule embodying *quantity discounts* is an example of second-degree price discrimination. Many retailers, for example, sell socks and undergarments in packages or separately. The packaged goods invariably have a lower unit price compared to the price charged separately. Some electric utilities charge lower prices for each additional *block* of electricity used. Those customers who use a specified large amount of electricity can buy the next block at a lower price. Second-degree price discrimination induces greater consumption by offering quantity discounts that are made in a stepladder fashion. Figure 12.4 illustrates an application of second-degree price discrimination.

Figure 12.4, on page 476, shows three pricing blocks offered by an electric utility company. In the first block, a *single* consumer who uses up to Q_1 kilowatt hours (kwh) per month pays a price of P_1 per kwh. For this block, the consumer's surplus, equal to areas $A + B$, is paid to the firm. A price of P_2 is charged for electricity consumed between Q_1 and Q_2, the second block. At price P_2, some additional consumers' surplus, equal to area C, is transferred to the firm. Finally, for consumption between Q_2 and Q_3, the consumer pays P_3, which equals the marginal cost of producing electricity. There is no transfer of consumers' surplus for the third block because price equals marginal cost for all electricity consumed in this block. The firm receives profits equal to areas $A + B + C$ from this particular consumer. Notice that the consumer retains some of his or her consumers' surplus with a block pricing structure. The shaded *triangular* areas in Figure 12.4 represent consumers' surplus that stays with the individual in this situation.

It is useful to remember that block pricing is discriminatory in this example because it does not reflect any cost differences arising from servicing different blocks. If the marginal cost curve (LMC) fell as we moved between blocks, then cost differences would help justify some of the price differences we find with block pricing.

Multipart Pricing Another name for second-degree price discrimination.

Another name for second-degree price discrimination is multipart pricing. **Multipart pricing** is the case in which firms charge successively lower prices for additional units as more units are purchased. Multipart pricing occurs, for

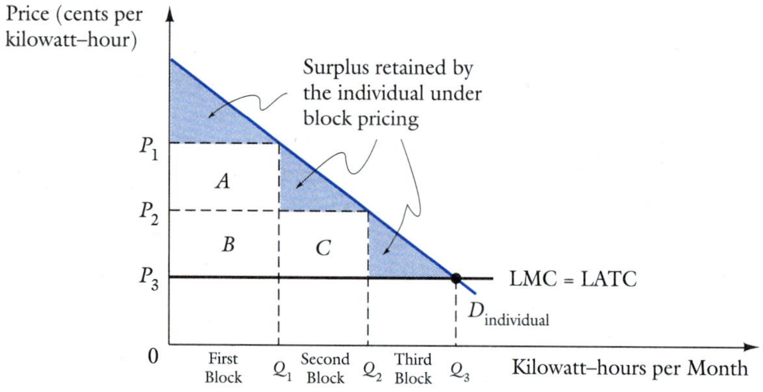

FIGURE 12.4

The Effects of Second-Degree Price Discrimination on Electricity Demand for an Individual

Using second-degree price discrimination, units sold are priced in blocks: The first block sells for a high price, P_1; the second block sells for a lower price, P_2; and the third block sells for an even lower price, P_3. An electric company that uses a block pricing strategy earns profits equal to areas $A + B + C$. Because this form of price discrimination is imperfect, individuals retain some consumers' surplus, which equals the total of the shaded areas.

example, in supermarkets when you can buy one can of soup for 89 cents and two cans for $1.59. In other words, the price of the first can is 89 cents—equivalent to P_1 in Figure 12.4—and the marginal price of the second can is 70 cents—equivalent to P_2 in the figure. Multipart pricing often arises when firms have imperfect information about demand. Firms do not know what different consumers are willing to pay, so they give consumers the option of choosing between price structures. Roadside fruit stands, for example, often practice price discrimination. Oranges may be placed into different display bins labeled "Delicious," "Extra Sunshine Delicious," and "Highest-Grade Super Delicious," for example.[4] The oranges are ***not*** sorted by size or grade; they come mixed together in the back of a large trailer truck. But each bin has a different price, with the "Highest-Grade Super Delicious" having the highest price. Consumers reveal their willingness to pay by the bin they choose.

There is a difference between multipart pricing, which is second-degree price discrimination, and first-degree, or perfect, price discrimination. Multipart pricing is an ***imperfect*** way to extract surplus from each consumer. It is a way of dealing with multiple purchases when one-on-one bargaining or other methods of discrimination are costly to implement. In other words, it can be costly to systematically discover a consumer's reservation price for each

[4]This example relates the experiences of one of the authors' college roommate, who managed an orange grove in Florida.

successive unit of a product or service. Block pricing is a compromise that recognizes these costs. Alternatively, when only one or two units are purchased, as in the car example, firms may try to implement first-degree price discrimination, which extracts all of the consumers' surplus in the market.

LEARNING EXERCISE 12.3

How much electricity does the consumer described in Figure 12.4 purchase under the block pricing structure?

THIRD-DEGREE PRICE DISCRIMINATION

Third-Degree Price Discrimination
Charging different prices in different markets for the same product; those consumers with relatively inelastic demands pay higher prices.

Third-degree price discrimination occurs when a firm charges different prices in different markets for the same product and transportation and distribution costs cannot explain the different prices. Consider the example of the RealPure Pharmaceutical Company, which makes two types of medicine for high blood pressure. The first type is marketed under the brand name Purelo and is advertised nationally to physicians and hospitals in trade magazines and direct mail brochures. The second type is called LoPress and is also advertised, but as a generic drug. The second drug is chemically equivalent to the first drug; in fact, the two drugs are made in the same plant using the same workers and equipment. The only difference between the two drugs is the label; the firm spends the same amount of money advertising and marketing both drugs.[5]

The RealPure Pharmaceutical Company believes that there are two distinct markets for its high-blood-pressure drug. The first market is composed of consumers who believe that a brand name product is better for them than a generic product. These consumers are willing to pay more for the brand name drug; that is, they have, on average, a higher reservation price for the brand name drug. The second group is the generic group of consumers, who believe that a generic drug is equivalent to a brand name drug, so they always buy the generic because it is cheaper. The net effect is that the brand name group is less responsive to price changes than the generic group. In terms of market demand curves, the brand name group has a less elastic demand than the generic group. This difference in elasticities will be important in determining the optimal price to charge each group, as we will show below. Figure 12.5, on page 478, illustrates this case.

Figure 12.5 shows three panels that highlight the demand and cost structure for the RealPure Pharmaceutical Company. Panel (a) shows the demand for Purelo, the brand name drug. The marginal revenue curve for this drug is shown as MR_b. Panel (b) shows the demand for LoPress, the generic drug. The marginal revenue curve is shown as MR_g. In panel (c), the total demand (D_{total}) for both drugs is computed by summing the two demand curves shown in panels (a) and (b). The marginal revenue curve for D_{total} equals the

[5]Advertising expenditures are often higher for brand name drugs. We have assumed that they are equal here to simplify the example.

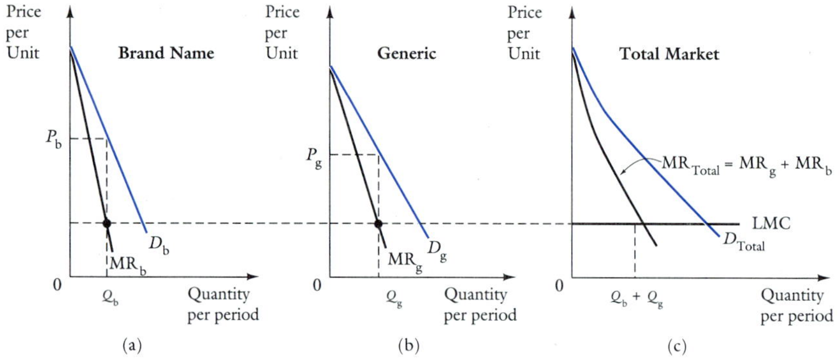

FIGURE 12.5

Third-Degree Price Discrimination in Brand Name and Generic Drug Markets

Using third-degree price discrimination, markets are separated according to their price elasticity of demand. The demand for brand name drugs shown in panel (a) is relatively inelastic compared to the demand for generic drugs shown in panel (b). By equating the long-run marginal cost (LMC) to the marginal revenue curve, the monopolist sets an optimal price and quantity in each market. The price for brand name drugs, P_b, is higher than the price for generic drugs, P_g, because demand is more inelastic for brand name drugs. The total market demand is shown in panel (c).

sum of the individual marginal revenue curves; that is, $MR_{total} = MR_g + MR_b$. The firm's long-run marginal and average total costs are also shown in panel (c).

In order for RealPure Pharmaceutical Company to maximize profits, it must equate marginal revenue and marginal cost in *both* markets. This result implies that $MR_g = LMC$ *and* $MR_b = LMC$. Because the marginal cost of producing the two drugs is the same in both markets, the rule for profit maximization implies that

$$MR_b = MR_g = LMC \tag{12.1}$$

at the optimal output rate.

To solve for the optimal output rate in each market, the firm finds the output rate at which $MR_{total} = LMC$. This point gives the total amount produced of both drugs. To find the amount produced of each drug, the firm traces back from the $MR_{total} = LMC$ intersection point to the marginal revenue curve in each market. For the generic brand, $MR_g = LMC$ at the output rate of Q_g, which implies that the market clearing price in the generic market is P_g. Similarly, for the brand name product, $MR_b = LMC$ at the output rate of Q_b, so the market clearing price in the brand name market is P_b.

Figure 12.5 shows that $P_b > P_g$; the brand name drug is sold for a higher price than the generic drug. This inequality arises because we have assumed that the demand for the generic drug is more elastic than the demand for the brand name drug. To see this result, recall from Chapter 11 (equation 11.4) that $MR = P(1 + \frac{1}{\eta})$ is the general equation for marginal revenue when the firm charges P per unit for its product. In the drug case, the firm is charging two prices in two distinct markets, so $MR_b = P_b(1 + \frac{1}{\eta_b})$ and $MR_g = P_g(1 + \frac{1}{\eta_g})$. The prices charged are found by solving for the output rate at which $MR_b = MR_g = LMC$. At this solution, $MR_b = MR_g$ must hold. Substituting the two general marginal revenue equations into the latter equality gives

$$P_b(1 + \frac{1}{\eta_b}) = P_g(1 + \frac{1}{\eta_g}) \tag{12.2}$$

We can rearrange equation (12.2) to show that if $\eta_b > \eta_g$, then $P_b > P_g$.[6] Because both η_b and η_g are price elasticities of demand, they are always negative numbers. Thus, the condition that $\eta_b > \eta_g$ implies that the demand for the generic drug is more elastic (larger in absolute value) than the demand for the brand name drug at the optimal solution. This is a maintained assumption in our analysis, so our result that $P_b > P_g$ follows from this assumption.

There are other examples indicating that third-degree price discrimination may be fairly common. Charging students a lower price for movies, magazines, and professional journals is a common example of third-degree price discrimination. Charging senior citizens a lower price than other buyers for movies and spectator events is another common example. Note that both senior citizens and students normally have more elastic demands because they tend to have lower incomes. Lastly, so-called foreign dumping—selling domestically produced products abroad at lower prices than are charged domestically—is another purported example of third-degree price discrimination.

LEARNING EXERCISE 12.4

Suppose the marginal cost of producing a brand name drug exceeds the marginal cost of producing a generic drug. What rule would the RealPure Pharmaceutical Company use to maximize profits? Does your answer imply that the firm is practicing price discrimination?

[6]Dividing the left-hand side of equation (12.2) by the right-hand side and assuming that $P_b > P_g$ gives

$$\frac{P_b}{P_g} = \left(\frac{1 + \eta_g}{1 + \eta_b}\right)\frac{\eta_b}{\eta_g} > 1$$

Multiplying by $(1 + \eta_b)\eta_g$ and reducing terms gives $(P_b/P_g) > 1$ if $\eta_b > \eta_g$.

INTERTEMPORAL PRICE DISCRIMINATION

Intertemporal price discrimination is a variation on third-degree price discrimination. With **intertemporal price discrimination,** the *different* markets are defined at two different points in time. Some consumers, for example, choose not to wait for a movie to appear in a video rental store, so they pay more to watch it at a movie theater. Similarly, both fiction and nonfiction books are usually published in more expensive hardcover versions because some consumers will pay more for these versions rather than wait for the paperback editions. In effect, consumers who buy hardback books have less elastic demand curves than consumers who buy paperback books. Although there are cost differences that help explain the lower prices in both of these examples, they are probably not so great as to justify the observed price differences.

Intertemporal Price Discrimination Charging different prices for the same product at different points in time, which are not justified by cost differences.

Peak-load pricing is sometimes considered a special case of intertemporal price discrimination. Firms that use peak-load pricing charge higher prices during periods of increased demand. In some parts of the country, for example, electric utilities charge customers higher prices for electricity consumed during the day versus the night and charge higher prices during the winter months. Phone companies charge higher prices for long-distance calls made during the day versus the night. These are periods of peak, or greatest, demand. Peak-load pricing is not a simple example of price discrimination. More often than not, companies face higher costs during peak periods, which can explain the higher prices charged. Electric utilities, for example, service peak periods from spinning reserves and "peaking" units that cost more to operate than their other power plants.

Peak-Load Pricing Charging peak users more than off-peak users.

Hotels in vacation areas also use peak-load pricing. Hotel rates in Maine increase in the summer and decrease in the winter. Analogously, hotel rates and lift tickets at ski areas increase in the peak winter months in Colorado. Again, costs also increase in these periods, so it is not clear whether these prices truly reflect intertemporal price discrimination.

There is really no difference between intertemporal price discrimination and third-degree price discrimination *if the marginal cost of production is the same during peak and off-peak periods.* Equation (12.2) can be applied to determine the optimal prices for the two (temporal) markets. If costs are different, however, the optimal solution is to try to practice either first- or second-degree price discrimination in the two periods, separately. If this is not possible, then the single-price monopoly approach can be applied to each period to maximize profits.

12.3 BUNDLING

If you open nearly any mail-order catalog for computer software and peripherals, you will find some software products sold in packages of two or more products. Microsoft Corporation, for example, markets four products, Word, Excel, PowerPoint, and Mail, in one package called Microsoft Office. The price of such packages is substantially less than the price you pay if the individual items are bought separately. We call such packages **bundles** because they include more than one product or service.[7]

Bundle
A package of two or more products or services.

There are many other examples of bundling of products. Restaurants offer à la carte and full-course meals. The items served in the full-course meal are often available from the à la carte menu, but for a higher cost. Season tickets to sports events are a bundle of tickets to each individual game. Music and other entertainment organizations also sell season tickets. Colleges often sell a bundle of 15 to 18 credit hours of course work for one price, which is less than the price you would pay if you bought courses at the per-credit-hour price for the same total amount of credits. Automobile service stations sell tune-ups, which involve replacing spark plugs, setting the timing or checking the electronic ignition, and checking the filters. Of course, each of these services can be purchased separately at a higher total price than the bundle itself.

Why do firms bundle their products? There may be several reasons, not the least of which is that bundling may be less costly. In other words, bundling may economize on the transaction costs consumers and producers face. Although economizing on transaction costs may be the most common reason for bundling, it is also possible for firms that have market power to use bundling as a method of price discrimination. If bundling helps the firm price-discriminate, then bundling increases profits.

PURE BUNDLING

Pure Bundling
When two or more products are sold only as a package.

Sometimes a firm chooses not to sell its products individually but only as a bundle. This is known as **pure bundling.** The classic case of pure bundling occurred in 1939 with the rental of the film *Gone with the Wind* as a package with the film *Getting Gertie's Garter. Gone with the Wind* was a smash hit in 1939 but *Getting Gertie's Garter* was a flop. Even as a flop, *Getting Gertie's Garter* appealed to some audiences more than others. Movie theaters were willing to pay more for *Getting Gertie's Garter* in some areas of the country than in other areas. Similarly, there were some places where *Gone with the Wind* was not as big a hit as in other areas—movie patrons went back to see it only twice, not three times, in these areas. The key to the successful pure bundling of these two films was that *Gone with the Wind* did relatively better in areas where *Getting Gertie's Garter* did relatively worse. In other words, across all theater owners, the willingness to pay for *Getting Gertie's Garter* was *negatively* related to the willingness to pay for *Gone with the Wind.* The use of pure bundling allowed the producers of *Gone with the Wind* to take advantage of the negative correlation between the different willingness to pay for these films, and thus to make greater profits.

A more modern example of pure bundling occurs frequently with the marketing of professional athletes as sponsors and promoters of products. To show

[7]For a more detailed discussion of bundling, see William James Adams and Janet L. Yellen, "Commodity Bundling and the Burden of Monopoly," *Quarterly Journal of Economics* 90 (August 1976), 475–498, and William M. Cready, "Premium Bundling," *Economic Inquiry* 29 (January 1991), 173–179.

exactly how a pure bundling strategy can increase profits, let's consider the case of bundling former basketball star Michael Jordan with football star Boomer Esiason. These athletes offer their services as promoters or sponsors to large sporting goods companies and other firms. These services are marketed by agents who generally earn a percentage of the promotional fees received by the athletes. The athletes sometimes work together to promote the same product, but at other times they are sole promoters. When athletes are marketed together by agents, the package is a case of pure bundling. When they are marketed separately, the package is considered a case of mixed bundling, which we will discuss below.

Michael Jordan was one of the all-time great basketball players, and he is still sought after as a sponsor for products. Before retiring, Jordan's salary from basketball in 1992 was estimated to equal $3.9 million, which is only about 12 percent of the estimated $32 million he received from endorsing and promoting products. Boomer Esiason did not do as well. As a professional quarterback his salary in 1992 was estimated to exceed $1 million, but his endorsements were estimated to generate only $200,000. Clearly, Michael Jordan is a more popular individual from the point of view of firms hiring sponsors and promoters of their products.

The key to successfully bundling these two athletes, however, is that they use the same sports agent to market their services *and* some firms have a preference for a football star over a basketball star. In other words, all firms will pay Michael Jordan more than they will pay Boomer Esiason to sponsor their products, but some firms will pay Boomer Esiason more than other firms because they want a football star marketing their product. Pure bundling of these two athletes will be successful if the firms who will pay relatively more for Boomer Esiason are the same ones that will pay relatively less for Michael Jordan. Across all firms, the willingness to pay for Boomer Esiason is negatively related to the willingness to pay for Michael Jordan.

Reservation Prices Are Negatively Related

To see how such a negative relationship can be used to increase the profits of the sports agent marketing these athletes, suppose there are just two types of firms desiring their promotional services: a football-product type and a basketball-product type. In addition, suppose that the two types of firms are equally distributed, so an imbalance in the number of football-product-type or basket-product-type firms is not a factor in the pricing decision. The reservation prices per year for these two types of firms is summarized as follows:

Negatively Correlated Prices

	Michael Jordan	Boomer Esiason	Total
Football-product firm	$470,000	$90,000	$560,000
Basketball-product firm	$500,000	$50,000	$550,000

The owner of a football-product-type firm is willing to pay at most $470,000 per year to hire Michael Jordan and at most $90,000 per year to hire Boomer Esiason. Similarly, the owner of a basketball-product firm is willing to pay at most $500,000 per year to hire Michael Jordan and at most $50,000 per year to hire Boomer Esiason. A negative correlation exists between these reservation prices because the football-product firm is willing to pay more for Boomer Esiason and less for Michael Jordan than the basketball-product firm.

If the sports agent markets these athletes separately, the most that can be charged is $470,000 for Michael Jordan and $50,000 for Boomer Esiason (assuming that perfect price discrimination is not possible). With a separate pricing strategy, total revenues across firm types equals $520,000 times 2 firms, or $1,040,000. In contrast, if the sports agent adopts a pure bundling strategy—marketing Michael Jordan and Boomer Esiason as a package—he or she can charge $550,000 to both types of firms. This is the maximum amount that the basketball-product firm will pay for both athletes. The football-product firm will pay $560,000, but the company cannot charge more than $550,000 if it wants to sell these athletes to basketball-product firms. With a pure bundling strategy, the sports agent's revenues are $1,100,000 from the two types of firms. By producing more total revenues without any additional cost, the pure bundling strategy proves to be more profitable for the sports agent. The pure bundling strategy is illustrated in Figure 12.6 on page 484.

In Figure 12.6, we plot the reservation prices of the two types of firms. The vertical axis measures the yearly reservation price (r_2) that firm owners will pay for hiring Michael Jordan. The horizontal axis measures the yearly reservation price (r_1) that firms will pay for hiring Boomer Esiason. The reservation price points for the two types of firms are plotted and labeled in the figure. The negatively sloped line that passes through the basketball-product firm's reservation price point is called the **bundle price line.** The reservation prices defining any point on the bundle price line sum to equal the bundle price (P_B); that is, the bundle price line holds the bundle price constant and solves for the reservation prices that sum to equal this constant. The bundle price line passes through the basketball-product firm's reservation price point because the reservation prices of the basketball-product firm sum to equal the bundle price—that is, P_B = $500,000 + $50,000 = $550,000.

Bundle Price Line
The set of reservation prices that sum to the bundle price. For two products, the bundle price line is formed from the equation $r_2 = P_B - r_1$.

In general, the bundle price equals the sum of the two reservation prices because the most firms will pay for the bundle cannot exceed the sum of what firms will pay for its separate components. Algebraically, $P_B = r_1 + r_2$, or rearranging terms, $r_2 = P_B - r_1$. Using the basketball-product firm's reservation prices implies that P_B = $550,000, so r_2 = $550,000 – r_1 is the equation of the bundle price line shown in Figure 12.6. Notice that with P_B = $550,000, firms whose reservation price points lie below the bundle price line will not hire the two athletes as a package. Analogously, any firms whose reservation price points lie on or above the bundle price line will hire both athletes.

Pure bundling is superior to a separate pricing strategy, but neither strategy extracts all of the willingness to pay, or surplus, in the market. The total benefits for these two types of firms equals the sum of the four reservation prices. Total benefits equal $1,110,000 ($470,000 + $500,000 + $90,000 + $50,000) per year for the two types of firms. With revenues equal to $1,100,000, the sports agent leaves $10,000 in surplus in the market ($1,110,000 – $1,100,000). If the sports agent knows the reservation prices of

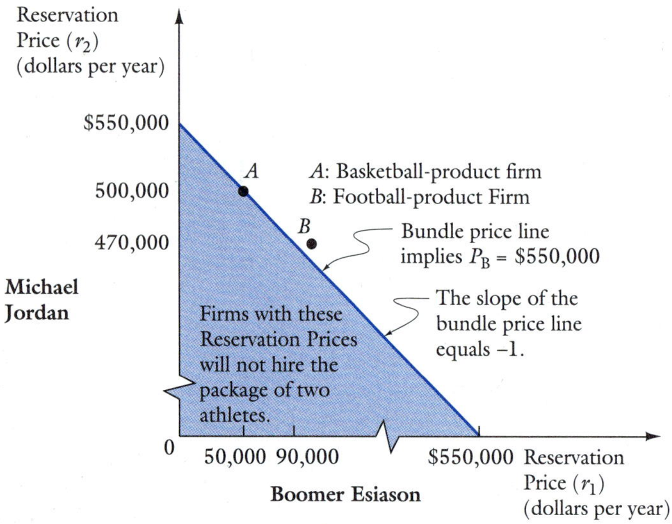

FIGURE 12.6

A Pure Bundling Strategy Can Increase Profits

The optimal price, P_B, for the pure bundling strategy equals \$550,000. Because there are two athletes in the bundle, there are many combinations of reservation prices that equal the optimal bundle price. The bundle price line is a straight line that represents all of these combinations. Algebraically, the bundle price line is defined by $P_B = r_1 + r_2$, or, in the figure, as $r_2 = \$550{,}000 - r_1$. The two reservation prices of the basketball-product firm place it on the bundle price line at point *A*. The two reservation prices of the football-product firm places it *above* the bundle price line at point *B*. Firms whose reservation prices place them on or above the bundle price line will purchase the bundle. Firms whose reservation prices place them *below* the bundle price line will not purchase the bundle.

both types of firms, he or she can offer perfectly discriminatory prices and extract all of the firms' willingness to pay. The best that the agent can do without such information, however, is to offer the pure bundle at a price of P_B = \$550,000 to each type of firm. Note that if the reservation price points for both firms lie on the bundle price line, then the bundle pricing strategy extracts all of the firms' surplus.

Learning Exercise 12.5

Suppose the reservation prices of the two firms are as follows:

	Michael Jordan	Boomer Esiason
Football-product firm	$490,000	$100,000
Basketball-product firm	$525,000	$65,000

Does a pure bundling strategy extract all of the firms' surplus?

Positively Related Reservation Prices Do Not Increase Profits

By plotting the reservation prices of the two types of firms in Figure 12.6, we can see that there is a negative correlation between them. If you draw a straight line between the two points shown, for example, it has a negative slope. If we were to reverse this relationship, so that reservation prices were positively correlated, then we would not increase profits using a pure bundling strategy.[8] To see this, suppose that we switch the amounts that the two firms are willing to pay for Michael Jordan. The reservation prices of the two types of firms are shown in the following table.

Positively Correlated Prices

	Michael Jordan	Boomer Esiason	Total
Football-product firm	\$500,000	\$90,000	\$590,000
Basketball-product firm	\$470,000	\$50,000	\$520,000

These reservation prices are positively correlated. The football-product firm is willing to pay more for both Michael Jordan and Boomer Esiason. In this situation, if the sports agent bundles the two athletes, the most that he or she can charge for the bundle is \$520,000, because this is the maximum that a basketball-product firm will pay for both athletes. This strategy offers only \$1,040,000 in yearly promotional income from the two firms. Thus, pure bundling does not increase revenues relative to the separate pricing strategy when reservation prices are positively correlated. This result is illustrated in Figure 12.7 on page 486.

Panel (a) in Figure 12.7 shows how a separate pricing strategy affects who hires these two athletes. Suppose that Boomer Esiason's promotional services sell for P_1 per year and Michael Jordan's promotional services sell for P_2 per year. Firms whose reservation prices lie in quadrant I hire both athletes; that is, $r_1 \geq P_1$ and $r_2 \geq P_2$ for these firms. Firms whose reservation prices lie in quadrant II hire only Michael Jordan; that is, $r_1 < P_1$ and $r_2 \geq P_2$ for these firms. Using the set of positively correlated reservation prices, for example, if P_1 = \$100,000 and P_2 = \$500,000, then the football-product firms hire Michael Jordan, but not Boomer Esiason. At these prices, the basketball-product firm owners do not hire either athlete. Firms whose reservation prices place them in quadrant III do not hire either athlete; that is, $r_1 < P_1$ and $r_2 < P_2$ for these firms. Finally, firms whose reservation prices lie in quadrant IV hire only Boomer Esiason; that is, $r_1 \geq P_1$ and $r_2 < P_2$ for these firms. Thus, a separate pricing strategy divides the reservation price graph into four quadrants that define the willingness of firms to hire one athlete, both athletes, or no athletes at all.

Panel (b) in Figure 12.7 is divided into four quadrants using the prices P_1 = \$50,000 and P_2 = \$470,000, which are the optimal prices to charge if the sports agent uses a separate pricing strategy when reservation prices are positively correlated. We have also plotted and labeled the reservation price points

[8]For a complete discussion of how correlation between reservation prices affects profits, see Richard Schmalensee, "Gaussian Demand and Commodity Bundling," *Journal of Business* 57 (January 1984), S211–S230.

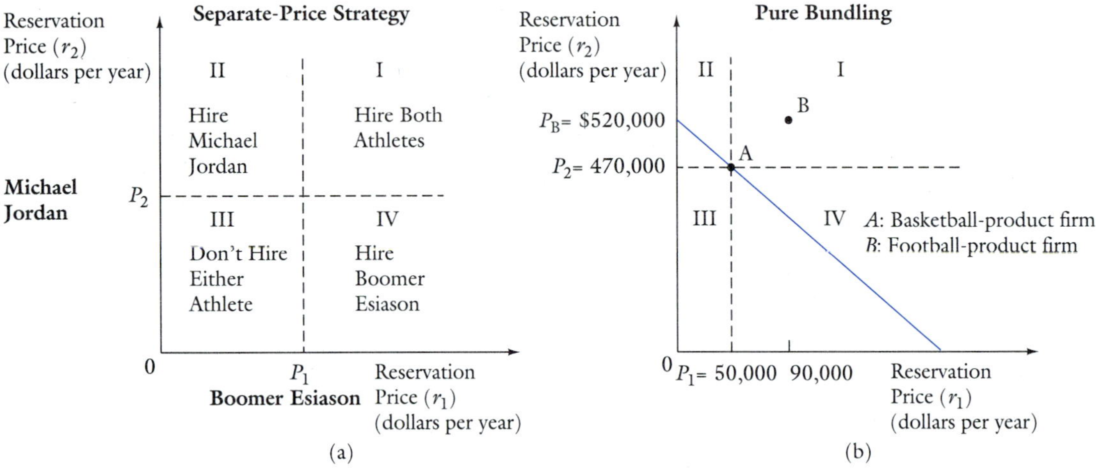

FIGURE 12.7

Comparing Pure Bundling to a Separate-Price Strategy with Positively Correlated Reservation Prices

In panel (a), the sports agent adopts a separate pricing strategy by charging P_1 for Boomer Esiason and P_2 for Michael Jordan. The four quadrants—I, II, III, and IV—define the firm's decisions based on its reservation prices. For example, if a firm's reservation price for Boomer Esiason exceeds P_1 and its reservation price for Michael Jordan exceeds P_2, then its reservation price point lies in quadrant I and it will hire both athletes. Panel (b) shows the bundle price line and the optimal single-price strategy for the case in which the firm's reservation prices are positively correlated. Because the reservation price points, *A* and *B*, of the two types of firms lie in quadrant I of the optimal single-price strategy, there is no additional profit from bundling the two athletes.

for both the football-product and basketball-product firms for this situation. Note that if you draw a straight line between these two points it has a positive slope, indicating that there is a positive correlation between the reservation prices of the different firms.

The bundle price line for the positively correlated case is also shown in panel (b). Because the bundle price (P_B) is \$520,000, the equation for the bundle price line is $r_2 = \$520,000 - r_1$. As was the case in Figure 12.6, firms whose reservation price points lie on or above this line will hire the package of both athletes; those whose points lie below the bundle price line will not hire the package. Note that the bundle price line passes through the reservation price point of the basketball-product firms. Because this point is also the intersection point of the four quadrants, the bundle price does not generate any more revenue than the separate pricing strategy.

MIXED BUNDLING

Up to now, the analysis assumed that the sports agent selects *either* a separate pricing strategy or a pure bundling strategy. But it is very possible, and likely, for a sports agent to mix the two strategies, offering, for example, to sell the

Mixed Bundling
When two or more products are sold separately and in bundles.

services of either athlete separately *and* as a bundle. This approach, which is called **mixed bundling,** is used for many products. Many restaurants, for example, arrange their menus with prix fixe and à la carte selections. Generally, a restaurant patron can buy the items in the prix fixe offering separately in the à la carte section, although the total bill will be greater. Many software and video products are also sold using a mixed bundling strategy. CBS/Fox video bundles the *Star Wars* trilogy as a package and also sells each video in the series separately. Other videos are sold similarly, such as the *Indiana Jones* trilogy, the *Ghostbusters* films, the *Rocky* series, and many of the older television shows. The bundle is attractive to some customers because it sells at a discount relative to the price paid when each movie is purchased separately.

We can see why mixed bundling is attractive to some customers, but why is it attractive to the firm with market power? Mixed bundling can often increase a firm's profits over either a pure bundling strategy or a separate pricing strategy when reservation prices are *imperfectly* correlated or when there are differential marginal costs. (Note that in our discussion of pure bundling we implicitly assumed that marginal costs were zero to keep the example simple.) To see how mixed bundling can increase profits, let's consider how RCA/Columbia Home Video can price the two *Ghostbusters* films, *Ghostbusters* and *Ghostbusters II.* Let's first consider the case in which reservation prices are imperfectly correlated, then the case in which there are differential marginal costs.

Reservation Prices for the *Ghostbusters* Videos

The first *Ghostbusters* film generated the second-highest nominal box office revenues of any comedy film in history (*Home Alone* is number one), exceeding $200 million worldwide. *Ghostbusters II* was not as successful, but it still earned over $100 million. Among moviegoers, there is a range of preferences as to which is the better film. Some moviegoers with small children prefer the original film, *Ghostbusters,* because the second film, *Ghostbusters II,* includes many scary scenes with Oscar, a character who is just a baby. Other moviegoers like both films, and some really like the scary scenes in the second movie, preferring *Ghostbusters II* to *Ghostbusters.* With such a wide variance of opinion, there is expected to be a significant variance in reservation prices for these two home videos. Figure 12.8, on page 488, illustrates this situation.

The reservation prices of four home video buyers are plotted in Figure 12.8. The vertical axis measures the reservation price (r_2) for *Ghostbusters II* and the horizontal axis measures the reservation price (r_1) of the original *Ghostbusters* film. Customer A likes scary movies and really likes the *Ghostbusters II* film. This customer is willing to pay up to $90 for the *Ghostbusters II* video but will pay at most $5 for the *Ghostbusters* video. Customer B is more to the middle of the moviegoer spectrum. This customer has a reservation price of $60 for the *Ghostbusters* video and $50 for the *Ghostbusters II* video. Customers C and D both have small children at home. Customer C has a reservation price of $70 for the *Ghostbusters* video and $10 for the *Ghostbusters II* video. Customer D has a reservation price of $75 for the *Ghostbusters* video and $5 for the *Ghostbusters II* video.

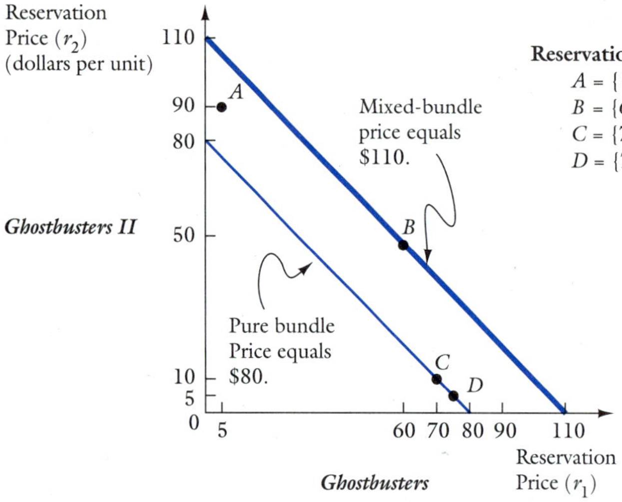

Strategy	P_1	P_2	P_3	Profits
Separate prices	60	50	—	$280
Pure bundle	—	—	80	$320
Mixed bundle	70	90	110	$340

FIGURE 12.8

An Optimal Mixed-Bundling Strategy

The reservation price points for *Ghostbusters* and *Ghostbusters II* are shown for four home video customers. The table shows the optimal pricing policy for separate pricing, pure bundling, and mixed bundling strategies. Profits are greatest under a mixed bundling strategy in which the seller offers the videos for sale separately *and* in a bundle, with the price of the bundle less than the sum of the two separate prices. The mixed bundling strategy is more profitable here because some customers have a strong preference for one or the other film, which is reflected in their reservation prices.

Imperfectly Correlated Reservation Prices

As may be seen from Figure 12.8, we cannot draw a *straight* line that passes through all four reservation price points, so they cannot be perfectly negatively correlated. But the reservation price points, as plotted, show a downward, or negative, *trend* in the figure. As a result, the reservation prices of these four customers are *imperfectly* negatively correlated.

In this situation, RCA/Columbia home video finds it optimal to adopt a mixed pricing strategy. To see this, consider the optimal prices the company charges for the three possible strategies: separate pricing, pure bundling, and mixed bundling. The table at the bottom of Figure 12.8 shows the optimal prices for each strategy. For the separate pricing strategy, the *Ghostbusters* video sells for \$60 (P_1) and the *Ghostbusters II* video sells for \$50 (P_2).[9] At these prices, customers B, C, and D purchase the *Ghostbusters* video and customers A and B purchase the *Ghostbusters II* video. With marginal costs set at zero, the firm's profits equal its total revenue. Thus, profits for the separate pricing strategy equal \$60 × 3 plus \$50 × 2, or \$280.

If a pure bundling strategy is used, the optimal bundle price (P_B) is \$80. At this price, the bundle price line passes through customer C's reservation price point. All customers purchase the bundle at this price because all reservation price points lie on or above the bundle price line. The profit generated from a pure bundling strategy equals \$320.

Now, let's consider a mixed bundling strategy. With this strategy, the firm is trying to capture some consumers' surplus not extracted by the separate pricing and pure bundling strategies. Because customer A places a high value on the *Ghostbusters II* video and customers C and D place a low value on this video, it makes sense to try to separate these three customers with the optimal pricing strategy. If the firm charges P_1 = \$70 for the *Ghostbusters* video and P_2 = \$90 for the *Ghostbusters II* video, then these three consumers are effectively separated by their purchase decisions. Customer A buys only the *Ghostbusters II* video, and customers C and D buy only the *Ghostbusters* video. Customer B will not buy either video at these prices, but because the sum of customer B's reservation prices exceeds the sum of any other customer's reservation prices, customer B can be attracted to purchase a bundle of both videos. If P_B = \$110, then the bundle price line passes through customer B's reservation price point and this customer purchases the bundle. The total profits of the mixed bundling strategy equals \$340, which exceeds the profits generated by either the separate pricing or pure bundling strategies.

Because reservation prices are imperfectly correlated, the firm increases profits with the mixed bundling strategy. Mixed bundling, however, does not extract all of the consumers' surplus. The total consumers' surplus equals the sum of the reservation prices (\$365) minus total expenditure (\$340). Thus, the mixed bundling strategy leaves \$25 in consumers' surplus. Obviously, if perfect price discrimination is possible, then all of the consumers' surplus can be extracted by the firm.

LEARNING EXERCISE 12.6

Suppose the reservation prices of four consumers are as follows:

	Ghostbusters	*Ghostbusters II*
Consumer E	\$30	\$55
Consumer F	25	60
Consumer G	75	50
Consumer H	90	30

Find the optimal prices for separate pricing, pure bundle, and mixed bundle strategies. Which strategy offers the greatest profits?

[9] Try any other combination of prices to convince yourself that these are the optimal prices for the separate-pricing strategy. No other combination results in more total revenue.

12.4 Two-Part Tariffs

Two-Part Tariff
A pricing strategy in which consumers are charged both access and usage fees.

A **two-part tariff** is another method used by firms to extract consumers' surplus.[10] Firms that use a two-part tariff charge customers an access fee, commonly an entrance fee to a nightclub or an amusement park, and a price per unit for whatever units are bought. In effect, the access fee grants customers the right to buy the product or service at the unit price charged. For example, years ago the Walt Disney Company charged customers an entrance fee and a ride fee at its amusement parks.[11] Disney issued a ticket coupon book, with ride coupons labeled A through E. The E coupons were the most valuable because they were tickets to the "best" rides. If you ran out of coupons, you could buy more. The Disney scheme was a little more elaborate than a standard two-part tariff because Disney charged an entrance fee and *five different prices,* not just one price, for its products. But the principle behind Disney's actions was the same as that of a firm that charges an access fee and only one price—that is, to extract consumers' surplus in order to increase profits.

If we focus our attention on the standard two-part tariff, we see that the problem a firm with market power faces is how to choose both an access fee and a unit price to maximize profits. What should the firm do? If it sets a high access fee and a low unit price, it will sell more units but to fewer people, because the high fee reduces the number of customers willing to pay the access charge. Alternatively, the firm can set a low access fee and a high unit price. In this situation, the firm will have relatively more customers but fewer unit sales. Clearly, the firm faces a trade-off between a high access fee with a low unit price and a low access fee with a high unit price.

Identical Customers

To understand more of the details of this price trade-off, let's look at the problem in a very simple setting. Suppose the firm's customers are all identical in that they all have an identical demand curve for the firm's product. In this case, the optimal access fee and unit price for a typical consumer are also optimal for all consumers. Figure 12.9 illustrates this situation.

In Figure 12.9, the demand curve of a typical consumer is shown as D_{typical} and the cost structure is such that long-run marginal costs (LMC) are constant and equal to long-run average total costs (LATC). The optimal unit price for the firm is to charge P^* = LMC. At this price the typical consumer buys Q^* units of the firm's product. The shaded area under the demand curve and above P^* is consumer surplus for the typical customer. The optimal access fee (T^*) equals this area; that is, the firm charges an access fee that extracts all consumers' surplus. Because LMC = LATC at all output rates, the firm earns zero profits from its unit sales. Algebraically, $\pi(Q^*) = [P^* - \text{LATC}(Q^*)] \times Q^* = 0$.

[10]The word *tariff* usually applies to a tax on imported goods. By convention, however, the word *tariff* is another word for *price* in the phrase *two-part tariff.*

[11]For an analysis of the old Disney pricing scheme, see Walter Oi, "A Disneyland Dilemma: Two-Part Tariffs for a Mickey Mouse Monopoly," *Quarterly Journal of Economics* (February 1971), 77–96.

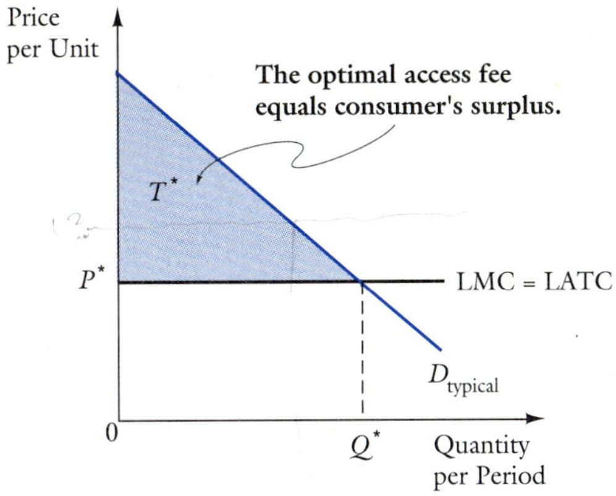

FIGURE 12.9

A Two-Part Tariff with Identical Consumers

A two-part tariff can extract all consumers' surplus if consumers have identical demand curves. The optimal tariff, T^*, equals the shaded area, which is the area under the typical demand curve, $D_{typical}$, above the long-run marginal cost curve, LMC. The optimal per unit price, P^*, equals the LMC, so the typical consumer buys Q^* units.

The firm's profits, then, are equal to the total access fees collected. If there are 50 customers ($N^* = 50$) then the firm's profit equals $N^* \times T^*$.

In this example, the trade-off between the high access fee with a low unit price and a low access fee with a high unit price is very "lumpy." Because all customers are identical, if one customer drops out because of a higher access fee, they all do, and if one customer is willing to pay the access fee, they all are. Similarly, if one customer is willing to purchase Q^* at the unit price of P^*, all other customers are, too. The trade-off, then, is one in which all customers are either in or out of the market. At the unit price of P^*, for example, if the firm charges an access fee *higher than* T^*, it loses all of its customers. Alternatively, if it raises its unit price above P^* while holding the access fee at T^*, it will not sell any units; in fact, with this arrangement customers will not pay the access fee because they don't plan to buy any units, so the firm loses all of its customers here, too.[12]

LEARNING EXERCISE 12.7

Show that if the firm raises or lowers the unit price in Figure 12.9 above or below P^*, its profits decrease. (Remember to adjust the optimal access fee, T^*, at the same time.)

[12]When the firm charges an access fee of T^*, it cannot also charge a unit price higher than P^* because it cannot extract the consumers' surplus twice.

TWO CUSTOMER GROUPS

Now, let's suppose that not all customers are identical. Assume that there are two groups of customers, the *high* and *low* demand groups, with an equal number of consumers in each group. To add more realism, assume that these two groups are users of cellular phones. The high-demand group is composed of businesspeople who are willing to pay relatively more for the use of a cellular phone. The low-demand group is composed of households who use cellular phones only occasionally, such as to find directions when a member of the household is lost. Figure 12.10 illustrates this situation.

There are two possible solutions to the case of two groups of customers. The first solution is that the firm's profits are maximized by serving *both* groups of customers. This is the solution shown in Figure 12.10, where the optimal access fee (T^*) equals area A under the demand curve, D_{low}, and the optimal unit price equals P^*. By raising price above marginal cost, the increase in profits more than offsets the losses from a lower access fee. If the firm charged price = LMC = LATC, for example, its profits would equal 2 times the optimal access fee. (Note that there are two groups paying the access fee.) In terms of Figure 12.10, profits equal areas $(A + B + C) \times 2$. By raising price above marginal cost, however, profits equal areas $(2 \times A) + B + (B + C + D)$. The difference between these two profit calculations reduces to a comparison between area C and area D. Because area D nearly always exceeds area C, it is

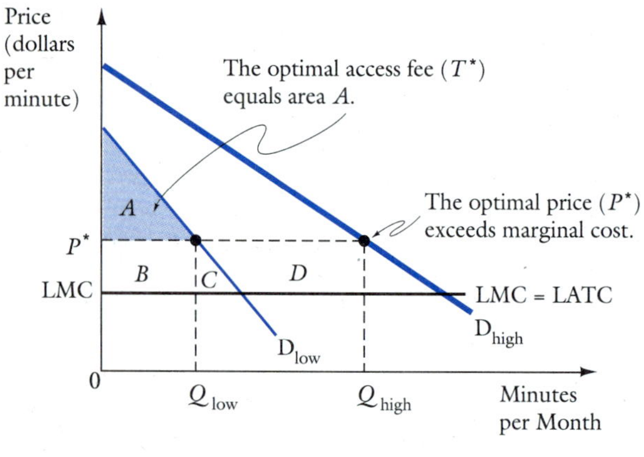

FIGURE 12.10

A Two-Part Tariff for Cellular Phones with Two Groups of Customers

If there are two types of consumers, one type with high demand, D_{high}, and another type with low demand, D_{low}, the optimal tariff is not expected to extract all consumers' surplus. In the cellular phone case, the optimal access fee, T^*, equals area A, the shaded area under D_{low}. The optimal unit price, P^*, exceeds the long-run marginal cost (LMC) of phone service. With heterogeneous demands, the optimal access fee exceeds marginal cost whenever area D exceeds area C.

optimal for the firm to raise price above marginal cost. Thus, the optimal access fee does not extract all of the consumers' surplus, not even for the low-demand group.

How do we find the optimal P^* and T^*? To determine the exact values for these choice variables, we must know the algebraic form of D_{low} and D_{high}. With this information, we can specify the firm's profit function. The general profit function for this problem is given by $2T^* + (P^* - \text{LATC}) \times (Q_{low} + Q_{high})$, where Q_{low} and Q_{high} are derived from the demand equations D_{low} and D_{high}. Maximizing the general profit function with respect to P^* gives the optimal solution for both P^* and T^*.[13]

The second solution arises when the number of persons in each group is significantly different. If the high-demand group is sufficiently large relative to the low-demand group, the firm may maximize profits by setting price to exclude the low-demand group. In this situation, the firm chooses the solution described in Figure 12.9 as it applies to the high-demand group. In other words, the firm charges a unit price equal to marginal cost and an access fee that extracts all the consumers' surplus for the high-demand group.

LEARNING EXERCISE 12.8

Using the two demand curves for cellular phone service in Figure 12.10, determine the conditions under which the firm will exclude the low-demand group. What are the areas that must be compared?

$$$ Price Theory in Practice

THE MICKEY MOUSE MONOPOLY—REVISITED

The use of two-part tariffs was pioneered by the Disney Company in the late 1960s. Disney's basic pricing strategy was to charge an admission price plus a ride charge. As the years passed, Disney modified this scheme to charge different prices for various groups of rides, and, finally, to charge only one admission price with the rides included. The evolution of Disney's prices is informative because it illustrates how changing a pricing strategy affects costs as well as revenues.

The opening of Disney World in Orlando, Florida, represented an advance in theme park and ride technology that created higher marginal operating costs for some rides. The A-to-E coupon booklet was an attempt to differentially price rides based largely on their relative marginal operating costs. But multipart pricing created additional implementation and monitoring costs. Ticket lines grew longer for patrons who wanted additional coupons, because it took more time to handle a transaction. The costs of servicing rides also increased as ticket collectors had to check patrons for the correct coupons. Cases of angry patrons were more frequent as confusion arose over what coupon was required

---

[13]The access fee, T^*, equals the area under the demand curve D_{low} and above the optimal price. This area is computed using a given P^*. Thus, the optimal T^* is a by-product of the optimal P^*.

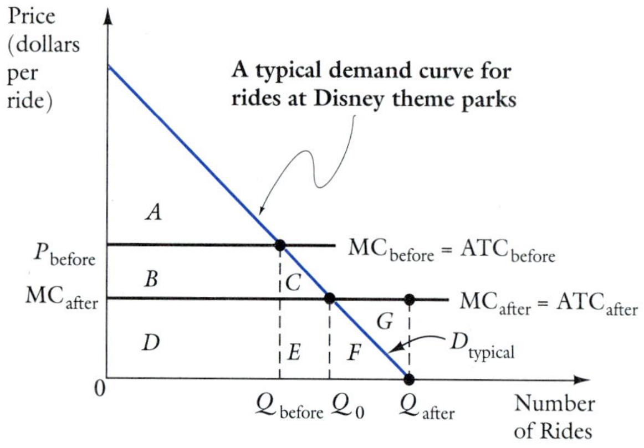

FIGURE 12.11

The Effects of Disney's GuestPass on Costs and Profits

The Disney company dropped the two-part tariff in favor of a GuestPass pricing strategy that extracts more consumers' surplus. With the two-part tariff, Disney charged area A as a park entrance fee and $P_{before} = MC_{before}$ as the price per ride. By dropping the per ride price to zero, Disney lowered marginal costs to MC_{after} because the company no longer needed as many people to collect ride coupons. The optimal park fee equals the entire area under $D_{typical}$, the typical demand curve, which equals areas $A + B + C + D + E + F$. By charging a zero price, Disney is losing money on rides produced in the range between Q_0 and Q_{after} because part of these costs lie above $D_{typical}$, that is, area G. But its new strategy increases profits as long as the costs savings, $B + C$, exceed area G.

on a particular ride. Patrons who had waited in particularly long lines were very perturbed to find that they had the wrong coupon for the ride.

In the late 1970s, Disney dropped the A-to-E coupon strategy for the "around the neck" ticket that later became the GuestPass, which you could keep in your pocket or purse. The GuestPass is all-inclusive, one price for admittance to the theme park and a *zero* price for rides. Figure 12.11 illustrates the effect of the GuestPass on costs and profits for the Disney Corporation.

Figure 12.11 shows the typical demand curve ($D_{typical}$) for rides on a Disney attraction. Using the A-to-E coupon strategy, Disney faces a marginal cost of servicing the *typical* ride equal to MC_{before}. In this situation, the optimal strategy is to charge an admission fee equal to area A with the coupon price (P_{before}) set equal to the marginal cost of the ride. The average patron consumes Q_{before} rides under the coupon-pricing strategy. The average profits generated are thus equal to area A. Using the GuestPass, or single-fee strategy, Disney charges a fee equal to areas $A + B + C + D + E + F$. The marginal cost of servicing rides *decreases,* because it is no longer necessary to collect and process coupons; that is, if you have been admitted to the park, you can ride the rides. The marginal cost curve falls to MC_{after} when Disney begins to use the GuestPass. The revenue generated for the typical demand curve equals the price paid for the GuestPass, or areas $A + B + C + D + E + F$. Because the price of a ride is zero, the typical patron consumes

Q_{after} rides. The total cost of producing Q_{after} rides equals areas $D + E + F + G$. Thus, profit generated from the typical patron equals areas $A + B + C - G$. The GuestPass strategy increases profits if areas $B + C$ exceed area G.

By servicing Q_{after} rides, Disney incurs a marginal cost that exceeds the typical consumer's willingness to pay for some rides. In other words, all rides *beyond* Q_0 are valued on the demand curve at a price below their marginal cost. Thus, Disney loses area G in its profit calculation. Because marginal costs fall with the coupon-pricing strategy, however, Disney can recoup these loses if areas $B + C$ are larger than area G. Because the Disney Corporation has enjoyed increased profits throughout the nonrecession periods of the 1980s and 1990s, it is very likely that the GuestPass strategy has proved superior to the coupon-pricing strategy.

Learning Exercise 12.9

Patrons at Disney's theme parks pay a different price for each ride by waiting in line—sometimes a very long line. How does this problem affect the above analysis of *the GuestPass strategy?*

12.5 Tying, Requirements Contracts, and Exclusive Dealing

Tying
A requirement that links the purchase of one product or service to the purchase of another product or service.

Tying refers to a situation in which one firm links the purchase of its product or service to the purchase (or nonpurchase) of some other product or service. Bundling is a type of tying arrangement, but tying can take other forms. A diet center, such as Jenny Craig, may require its customers to purchase specially prepared food as part of its contract with patients. Such contracts generally state that clients must buy a minimum amount of food each week from the diet center, say at least 15 meals per week. The evaluation and counseling therapy offered by the diet center is thus *tied* to the purchase of a certain amount of its specially prepared food. This form of tying arrangement is called a **requirements contract** because customers are *required* to purchase a minimum quantity of a second product from the firm.

Requirements Contract
An agreement to purchase a certain quantity of products from a particular firm over a given time period.

Exclusive Dealing
An agreement not to purchase a product or service from any other firm.

Exclusive dealing contracts are another form of tying arrangement. With an exclusive dealing contract, customers agree to purchase certain products only from a particular firm. Exclusive dealing is a special type of a requirements contract in which customers are required to buy *all* of a product or service from the firm. In other words, with a requirements contract, customers may look to other firms for the *required* good once the minimum purchase level is reached. At the diet center, for example, if customers eat more than 15 meals in a given week, they can buy these meals from any firm of their choosing. With an exclusive dealing contract, however, customers agree to buy all meals from the diet center. Exclusive dealing is not always a case of tying. Exclusive dealing arrangements may try to bind a customer to the purchase of one particular good or service independent of any other purchase the customer may make.

Why do companies use such practices? We have seen that bundling of goods can increase profits by extracting more consumers' surplus.

Alternatively, it may be a way to economize on transaction costs. For bundling to extract consumers' surplus, however, the firm must have some market power over both of the products in the bundle. If the firm has market power over only one product, its ability to extract any profits from the good that it does not control is limited.

Former Federal Judge Robert Bork argued that it is a fallacy to think that a monopoly over one product or service grants a firm the ability to monopolize another product or service via exclusive dealing or requirement contracts.[14] Bork analyzed two famous court cases that challenged exclusive dealing: *Standard Fashion* (1922) and *Griffith Theaters* (1948). In *Standard Fashion,* the firm used an exclusive dealing contract to keep competitors' dress patterns out of certain retail outlets. In *Griffith Theaters,* Griffith allegedly used its monopoly over theaters in small towns where there were no competing theaters to extract favorable terms from film distributors in towns where there was competition. In Bork's words, the claim is that

> the uniqueness of Standard's line of patterns . . . gives it market power which it can use to demand exclusivity and injure rivals or new entrants.

But, in Bork's view (and the view of many other economists),

> that argument repeats the fallacy of the *Griffith* case . . . in a new context. Standard can extract in the prices it charges retailers all that the uniqueness of its line is worth. It cannot charge the retailer that full worth in money and then charge it again in exclusivity the retailer does not wish to grant. To suppose that it can is to commit the error of double counting.[15]

By "double counting," Bork meant that the firm cannot extract the same consumers' surplus twice. His argument is certainly correct about consumers' surplus, but it ignores the possibility that the monopolized good and a competitively produced good tied to it may interact in some manner. If you follow the advice of the diet center counselors, "Exercise and eat the right foods," you may lose weight, but if you follow this advice and eat the diet center's food, you may lose weight *faster*. For example, the diet center's food may be specially prepared to cause more rapid weight loss than the food that you might prepare.

Similarly, a firm that buys a monopolized product as an input to produce a third product may find that its costs decrease because of the nature of its production process. The monopolized product may interact with another, competitively produced input to lower the firm's costs. In this instance, the monopoly may *tie* the purchase of the competitive input to the monopolized input with an exclusive dealing contract in order to extract some or all of the reduced costs.[16] In effect, the exclusive dealing contract can be used to capture the cost savings, not any monopoly profits, in the second good.

---

[14]See Robert H. Bork, *The Antitrust Paradox: A Policy at War with Itself,* New York: Basic Books, 1978.

[15]Ibid., p. 306.

[16]For a detailed analysis of this case and how a tying contract can increase profits, see John S. McGee, "Compound Pricing," *Economic Inquiry* 25 (April 1987), 315–339.

Although exclusive dealing and requirements contracts are fundamentally illegal under the Clayton Act of 1914, their purpose may not always be anti-competitive. Firms may use such agreements to protect their goodwill and brand name. The diet center's advertisements may claim, for example, that it guarantees the loss of 10 pounds in a month or the customer's money will be refunded. Without the use of its specially prepared food, however, there may be little chance that a customer will lose 10 pounds in a month, so the center uses a requirements contract to help make its advertising truthful. A manufacturing firm may also invest in training its (independent) dealers' sales staff. An exclusive dealing contract protects the manufacturer's investment.

Many franchise agreements for fast-food outlets such as McDonald's, Burger King, and Kentucky Fried Chicken formerly required franchisees to purchase inputs—food, materials, and supplies—from the parent company. These firms argued that such arrangements help to control the quality of the products produced by the franchisees, thereby guaranteeing to customers that their products are the same everywhere. Recently, such practices have stopped, as the courts have ruled that other mechanisms—random inspection and monitoring—can be used to ensure quality.

12.6 Auctions

Auctions have a long and rich history as a method of allocating goods. Perhaps the earliest reference to a regularly organized auction is the Babylonian marriage market, in which brides were auctioned to Babylonian men. But to appreciate the real flavor of an auction, there may be no place in the world like the Dorotheum in Vienna, Austria. The Dorotheum began in 1707 under Emperor Josef I. It currently conducts two to three auctions per day, placing between 800 and 1,000 items for sale at each auction. Thousands of visitors from all over the world, not to mention Austrians, descend upon the Dorotheum on any given day in search of a "good buy."

What makes an auction an appealing method of allocating goods? To answer this question, let's consider how an auction works to the benefit of both buyers and sellers.

The Auction Mechanism

Whether in Babylon, in Vienna, or at a school fund-raiser, auctions are used to sell a variety of goods and services. It is noteworthy that some auctions have been used for several hundred years. For a market mechanism to remain in existence so long, it must provide an efficient method of allocating goods between buyers and sellers. Thus, those with some market power—the current owners of the good to be auctioned—must gain from using an auction to sell their product or service. The auction must provide the *least-cost* method of identifying who will pay the greatest amount for the item, even if the winner does not actually reach his or her *maximum* willingness to pay. Viewed in this light, then, auctions may be a vehicle for increasing profits if a firm has market power in some products or services.

Whether an auction can successfully extract all or just part of the consumers' surplus depends on the type of auction used, the good that is auctioned, and how bidders react to the rules of the auction. There are many types of auctions, and each has slightly different rules about bidding and the selection of a winner.[17] Let's review the four basic types of auctions.

English Auction

The **English auction** is the most commonly used auction mechanism in the world. The rules are very simple. Bidders announce or otherwise indicate their bids in an open forum. The auctioneer continues the bidding until only one bidder remains. There are two distinguishing features of an English auction. First, to bid you must announce a price higher that the last bid, so this is an increasing-price auction.[18] Second, your bid and the bids of others are known to everyone participating in the auction. In fact, auctioneers make a point of repeating the last bid so that everyone is aware of the price they must beat. Sotheby's and Christie's auction houses primarily use English auctions when they sell merchandise.

English Auction
An auction in which prices are announced to all participants and the highest bidder wins.

Dutch Auction

A **Dutch auction** operates as nearly the reverse of an English auction. In a Dutch auction, the auctioneer starts with a high price and systematically lowers the price until one bidder accepts the offer, usually by pressing a buzzer. With a Dutch auction, you do not know what the other bidders might bid; you find out only what the winning bidder bids. In this sense, the Dutch auction provides less information about the other bidders than the English auction. Most Dutch auctions are run automatically; that is, they use a clock-like device that ticks down every few seconds to a new lower bid. In this respect, one may reason that the Dutch auction takes less time to conduct than an English auction. Thus, the Dutch auction is likely to be preferred over the English auction method for the sale of perishable products. The Dutch auction mechanism, for example, is used to sell fresh-cut flowers in the Netherlands and fresh fish in Marseilles, France, and Tel Aviv, Israel.

Dutch Auction
An auction that starts with a high price—selected by the auctioneer—which is successively lowered until someone accepts the price.

First-Price Sealed-Bid Auction

Many goods are sold using sealed bids; that is, goods are sold at an auction in which the bids are not subject to change when information about the bids of others is known. Bids are sealed and time stamped when submitted. These auctions are called **first-price sealed-bid auctions** because the good is sold to the earliest high bidder. If there is a tie between the highest bidders, the winner is determined by the time stamp: the one with the earliest time stamp wins. The U.S. government uses first-price sealed-bid auctions to sell oil and gas

First-Price Sealed-Bid Auction
An auction in which sealed bids are all opened at once on a given date. The highest bidder wins and pays the amount bid.

[17]For an extensive survey of the auction literature, see R. Preston McAfee and John McMillan, "Auctions and Bidding," *Journal of Economic Literature* 25 (June 1987), 699–738, and Paul Milgrom, "The Economics of Competitive Bidding: A Selective Survey," in *Social Goals and Social Organization*, Leonid Hurwitz, David Schmeidler, and Hugo Sonnenschein (eds.), Cambridge: Cambridge University Press, 1986.

[18]The word *auction* evolved from the Latin word *augere*, which means "to increase."

leases on government-owned lands and parcels in the Gulf of Mexico. This auction mechanism is also used by the government to sell surplus equipment and materials, such as silver from the U.S. strategic metals stockpile, and a variation of it is often used to sell U.S. Treasury Bills.

Second-Price Sealed-Bid Auction

Second-Price Sealed-Bid Auction
An auction in which sealed bids are all opened at once on a given date. The highest bidder wins but pays the amount bid by the second-highest bidder.

The **second-price sealed-bid auction** is equivalent to the first-price sealed-bid auction in all respects except that the winning bidder pays the price bid by the second-highest bidder. Although this auction mechanism is rarely used, it is useful to our present discussion because it helps us understand the theoretical properties of the other three auctions.

$$$ Price Theory in Practice

AUCTIONS FOR NEW BOOKS

When Mikal Gilmore decided to write a book about his brother, executed murderer Gary Gilmore, he spurned the traditional route of approaching a single publisher with the idea. Instead, he held an auction. A number of publishers were notified that an auction would take place on Tuesday, April 23, 1991. Bids were to be submitted to Gilmore's agent, Richard Pine. Bidding started at $75,000. Doubleday Publishing won with a bid of $700,000.[19]

Welcome to the new world of deal making between authors and publishers. In the past, authors commonly had relationships with a single publishing house that lasted their lifetime. An agent—if the author even had one—would go to the publishing house to negotiate the advance the author would receive for a book. Now, auctions bring the publishers to the author. Usually, it works this way: Agents send out book proposals to many publishers and set an auction date. The bidding process can be formal. Publishers may be asked to formally submit bids by a certain deadline, with no bids opened until after the deadline. Or the bidding process can be more informal. Agents may receive and open initial bids and then negotiate a final bid among several publishers. The bid for the Gilmore book was informal. Over two days, 11 publishers made a flurry of phone calls to Mr. Pine before a final bid was agreed to.

The auctions have allowed authors to receive up-front payments that had been unheard-of previously. For example, in 1990 Dell Publishing paid $12.3 million for two books by Ken Follett, and HarperCollins Publishers paid $20 million for three books by Jeffrey Archer. Authors and agents say they would never have received such advances if they had gone directly to a single publisher as they had before. They credit the competitive forces of auctions for the increase in advances.

Of course, auctions will do little to increase the price of a product for which there is little or no demand. In 1990, the agent for Daniel Ortega, former president of Nicaragua, set up a well-planned auction to sell Ortega's proposed autobiography. The agent suggested the advance might hit $1 million. Low six-figure offers were all they received. As a result, Ortega decided not to write the book.

---

[19]Roger Cohen, "Auctions Change the Way Writers and Agents Think," *The New York Times*, April 29, 1991, p. C1.

The publishing business also has shown that auctions are not immune to efforts to manipulate prices. In 1991, Derek V. Goodwin sold the proposed book *Just Killing Time* at auction for $920,000. The bidding had been swayed by endorsements from authors John le Carré and Joseph Wambaugh that had been sent to publishers. The endorsements, however, turned out to be faked, and publisher Simon & Schuster withdrew its top bid.

Learning Exercise 12.10

A book is sold to the highest bidder at auction, but is the amount bid likely to be the maximum the winner is willing to pay?

REVENUE EQUIVALENCE THEOREM

To analyze how bidders react to each of the four types of auctions, we must make some assumptions about the information available to bidders and their reservation prices. Suppose that all bidders are risk-neutral; that is, every bidder will accept a fair gamble. In a fair gamble, an individual expects to win an amount exactly equal to the cost of playing.[20] Also assume that the reservation price of each bidder is known only to that bidder and is not related to the reservation price of another bidder.[21] The assertion that there is no relationship between bids is another way of saying that beauty is in the eyes of the beholder. In other words, what one bidder is willing to pay is dependent on his or her own view of the product or service. Taken together, these assumptions define the so-called **independent private values model** of bidding behavior.

Independent Private Values Model
A model of bidding behavior in which each bidder's reservation price is independently determined and is known only to each bidder.

A remarkable result arises when the independent private values model is used to compare the English, Dutch, first-price, and second-price auctions. The result is known as the **revenue equivalence theorem,** which says that these four auctions are each expected to generate the *same* amount of revenue to the seller of the auctioned good. To understand this result, suppose that you are planning to auction an important piece of art—say, a painting of a Campbell's soup can by Andy Warhol. The revenue you can expect to receive under *any* of these four auctions is equal to the reservation price of the second-highest bidder at the auction. This theorem is easy to understand for the English auction. With the English auction, the bidder with the highest reservation price knows the bids of his or her competitors. As the price increases, bidders drop out until only two are left. The bidder with the highest reservation price must then only bid a fraction more than the bidder with the next-highest reservation price to win. Thus, the seller can expect to receive only the next-highest reservation price (plus an infinitesimal fraction) from the auction.

Revenue Equivalence Theorem
The result that the expected revenues from either English, Dutch, first-price, or second-price auctions are equal.

The revenue equivalence theorem clearly applies to the second-price sealed-bid auction, but it is less obvious for the Dutch and first-price sealed-

[20]Risk neutrality and fair gambles are explained further in Chapter 15.

[21]We must also use the technical assumption that bidders follow a symmetric bidding strategy, which is the same as saying that each bidder's strategy mirrors that of the other bidders.

bid auctions. With both of these auctions, the bidder with the highest reservation price plays a guessing game to determine the second-highest reservation price. In the Dutch auction, once the bid clock ticks past the reservation price of the bidder with the highest reservation price, the bidder is taking a chance that someone else may win by pressing the buzzer first. The longer the bidder waits, the more chance he or she takes. In effect, the highest bidder must estimate what the second-highest reservation price is. Given that all bidders use a similar bidding strategy, then on average the highest bidder can correctly estimate the second-highest reservation price. On average, the highest bidder waits until just before the next bidder is ready to bid to accept the price shown on the bid clock. Thus, the revenue generated is equal to the next-highest reservation price (plus an infinitesimal fraction).

With the first-price sealed-bid auction, the bidder faces a problem similar to that faced in the Dutch auction. The second-highest reservation price is not known, and the bidding process does not reveal it. Again, the bidder with the highest reservation price must estimate the second-highest reservation price. Under the assumptions of the independent private values model, the estimate will be correct on average. Thus, the revenue generated from this auction is also equal to the next-highest reservation price (plus an infinitesimal fraction), as the theorem suggests.

The problem with the revenue equivalence theorem is that it does not give the seller much advice about which auction to use. You want to maximize the revenue from selling your painting, for example, but the revenue equivalence theorem implies that you are likely to be indifferent between these different types of auctions.

The revenue equivalence theorem really begs the question of why the English auction is the most popular type of auction. There are different possible answers to this question. One answer is that the English auction may be the least costly to operate. (Given that the four auctions are expected to produce the same revenue, the seller would want to use the auction that is the least costly to operate.) Another answer may be that the English auction offers a lower variance of revenues than either the Dutch or first-price auctions. In other words, if you repeatedly auction similar goods, such as watches or automobiles, the revenues generated by the English auction vary less than those of either the Dutch or first-price auctions. This would be valuable to a seller who is averse to risk, which would imply a preference to using the English auction. Lastly, the English auction may be preferred because it offers more flexibility to bidders. Bidders may change their bids in response to other bids, which cannot be done in the other auctions. This flexibility may attract more bidders, thus offering sellers the possibility that bidders with higher reservation prices may participate in the auction.

COMMON VALUE AUCTIONS

There are many auctions in which the independent private values model does not apply because the commodity sold has a *standardized* or *common* value.

What is often unknown is not the price of the commodity being auctioned, but how much you are buying; that is, you know price, P, but you must bid total revenue (P times Q), and Q is not known. These auctions are called **common value auctions.** When the government auctions an oil lease in the Gulf of Mexico, it is conducting a common value auction. Companies participating in these auctions carefully estimate the *quantity* of oil they expect to extract in order to determine their bids. These calculations are subject to error, because Mobil, Texaco, Exxon, and the many other oil companies that bid on oil leases do not really know what they will find under the ocean until they actually drill a well. Because of errors in the estimates of recoverable oil, the bids submitted can disagree with each other, sometimes by a large amount.

Common Value Auction
An auction in which product price is the same for all bidders and is generally known but quantity is unknown.

As a result, the high bidder often experiences mixed emotions upon learning the results of the auction. There may be elation because the high bidder is the winner—and also regret if the other bids are significantly less than the winning bid. In other words, by winning, the high bidder learns that its estimate of the recoverable oil in a government field exceeds that of everyone else, which probably means that it has erred and is overly optimistic about quantity. This dilemma is known as the **winner's curse.**

Winner's Curse
The problem faced by the high bidder at a common value auction if the winning bid is significantly greater than the other bids.

The winner's curse is not present in the independent private values model because the values are unique to each bidder. But the winner's curse is present in any auction in which there is a known market price for the auctioned good or in auctions in which market price is unknown but all participants agree that the good has a common value.

WHY ARE AUCTIONS USED?

Auctions are really very popular. During the economic slump in 1990–1991, for example, an estimated $12 billion worth of real estate was sold at auction. It is reasonable to ask, then, why auctions are used. After all, there are many other ways to find buyers for goods. One reason may be that auctions firmly establish the rules under which a seller will part with a good. Sellers make firm commitments to auction companies that market their goods. Often a minimum price is established, but if the bidding exceeds this price, the good is sold; the seller cannot back down from the commitment. In contrast, when auctions are not used, buyers may enter into negotiations with a seller, but they may be wasting their time if the seller has not made a definitive commitment to sell. Many real estate deals fall apart because the seller backs out after a period of negotiating. With an auction, buyers are assured that they are not wasting their time negotiating with a seller.

In addition, there are many goods that do not have a known market price. An auction is a method of creating a market, even though it is a temporary one, so that these goods can be valued. The art world was generally surprised, for example, when Van Gogh's *Irises* sold for over $53 million in 1987. A painting of this quality and history is sold very infrequently, so there was no recently quoted price for the seller to use as a reference. An auction is a relatively low-cost method of providing a market price.

$$$ Price Theory in Practice

The Solomon Brothers Treasury Auction Scandal

Although the revenue equivalence theorem shows that the English, Dutch, first-price, and second-price auctions offer equivalent revenues, a 1991 auction scandal in the U.S. Treasury note market suggests that other factors are important when selecting an auction method.

The scandal involved Solomon Brothers, a prominent Wall Street securities firm. Solomon Brothers admitted to submitting bids for more than the allowed share of Treasury notes in two different auctions. The auction rules restrict bidders to owning less than 35 percent of the total notes sold. By violating the rules, Solomon Brothers acquired 57 percent of the five-year notes sold in February 1991 and bid for 46 percent of the four-year notes sold in December 1990. The 35 percent rule is arbitrary, but its purpose is to prevent any one dealer from achieving a monopoly or market power over a given issue of notes.

What Solomon Brothers did is actually not that important, because the firm admitted its mistake and quickly reorganized to prevent any further violations of the rules. Further, it is doubtful that Solomon Brothers achieved any market power by its actions. The important lesson of this scandal is that the auction mechanism used by the U.S. Treasury is flawed because it tends to encourage abuse.

U.S. Treasury notes are auctioned using a first-price sealed-bid auction. In contrast to the sale of a single object, such as a painting, the Treasury sells billions of dollars (face value) of notes. Bidders are asked to specify a price *and* quantity when they submit bids. The Treasury ranks these bids from highest to lowest and goes down the list until it has sold the quantity of bills placed in auction. The winning bidders must then buy the quantity requested *and pay the price that they bid*. In other words, the bidder who submitted the lowest bid accepted by the Treasury pays less than other accepted bids for the *same* product. There is a variation of the winner's curse working here. Those who submitted high bids paid more than those who submitted low bids, but both *winners* are buying the same product. In effect, this is discriminatory pricing.

With firms risking billions of dollars, discriminatory pricing encourages them to collude on their bids or use other means to avoid the winner's curse; that is, no firm wants to be the high bidder and suffer from the winner's curse. Collusion among firms leads to very similar bids, so the high bidder loses less from the winner's curse. Alternatively, if a firm can capture nearly all of the supply at a given auction, as Solomon Brothers tried to do, then there is no winner's curse because the resulting market power allows the firm to resell the notes at a profit.

The Treasury Department has known about this problem for many years, ever since economist and Nobel Laureate Milton Friedman testified to Congress in 1959 about the potential for collusion in Treasury auctions. Friedman's suggestion then was that the Treasury use a variation of the second-price sealed-bid auction. In Friedman's auction, the Treasury charges all winning bidders the price paid by the lowest acceptable bid, so everyone pays the *same* price. The *revenue equivalence theorem* suggests that the Treasury will raise the same amount of money using this auction as the first-price sealed-bid auction. In addition, if there is no price discrimination, then there is much less incentive to collude, and it is likely that there will be fewer auction scandals like the one that Solomon Brothers helped create.

In response to the Solomon Brothers scandal, the Treasury decided to experiment with its auction procedure. Between September 1992 and August 1993, the U.S. Treasury auctioned its two- and five-year notes using Friedman's suggestion. The results of these experiments have not yet been fully analyzed.

LEARNING EXERCISE 12.11

Holding everything else equal, do you expect the bids to be higher or lower in Friedman's second-price sealed-bid auction when compared to the Treasury's current auction mechanism?

12.7 PUBLIC POLICY TOWARD PRICE DISCRIMINATION

The Robinson-Patman Act of 1936 amended the Clayton Act of 1914 to effectively prohibit price discrimination. The Robinson-Patman Act made it illegal to charge different prices for goods of "like grade and quality" if these differences could not be justified by differences in production costs. Of course, trying to determine whether two products are of "like grade and quality" is difficult, as the government found in its case *Federal Trade Commission v. Borden Company* (1966), which we discuss below.

The Robinson-Patman Act also prohibited another form of price discrimination called **predatory pricing.** There is much controversy surrounding the court's interpretation of predatory pricing. To an economist, pricing would perhaps seem *predatory* if a firm's strategy was to charge a price *below* marginal cost, but the courts have ruled that pricing substantially below competitors' prices can be predatory. The *Utah Pie Co. v. Continental Baking Co.* (1967) case—discussed below—best illustrates the court's interpretation of predatory pricing. It would seem, then, that the act was designed to protect other firms, not consumers or competition in the broader sense, and, in fact, the court has tended to interpret the act in this manner.

Predatory Pricing
A pricing policy intended to extract market share and profits from competitors by temporarily pricing below marginal cost.

FEDERAL TRADE COMMISSION v. BORDEN COMPANY

The Borden Company sold evaporated milk under its nationally advertised brand name and also sold evaporated milk to large regional firms, which placed their own brand names on the cans. The milk sold under the regional brand names was physically and chemically identical to the milk sold under the Borden brand name, but the regional, or private, brand names sold for prices *below* the Borden brand name milk. The FTC ruled that this was price discrimination and issued a cease and desist order to Borden. The U.S. Court of Appeals reversed the FTC decision, finding that the Borden brand name was an important characteristic of its evaporated milk. The U.S. Court of Appeals said, "Consideration should be given to all commercially significant distinctions which affect market value, whether they be physical or promotional."

The Borden Company argued that the higher price charged for its brand name milk was justified on the basis of cost differences. Borden claimed that it spent large sums of money to ensure the quality of its milk and used advertising to develop its brand name so that consumers understood that its milk was of high quality. Borden's defense illustrates our discussion of a competitive market under asymmetric information in Chapter 10. Because the evaporated milk is in a can, consumers do not know its actual quality until after it is bought. Recognizing this problem, Borden spent money on a specific asset—its brand name—to *signal* consumers that it sold high-quality milk. In this case, the market equilibrium requires Borden to charge a *quality-assuring price* for its product, which we may expect to be higher than that charged by the regional firms who do less advertising.

The U.S. Supreme Court, however, overturned the appeals court ruling. To the U.S. Supreme Court, the Robinson-Patman Act specified "like grade and quality," not "like grade, quality, *and brand*." The Supreme Court reasoned that if it allowed brand name to affect its interpretation of the Robinson-Patman Act, companies would have a back door by which they could practice discriminatory pricing. The Supreme Court suggested that Borden (or any company) might choose to sell the brand name product to some retail outlets and withhold the nonbranded, or privately branded, product from these stores. Alternatively, it might sell the privately branded product and not the brand name product. The court saw this possibility as a way to circumvent the laws against price discrimination even though, as we have noted, there may be sensible economic reasons for charging a higher price for the brand name product.

UTAH PIE CO. v. CONTINENTAL BAKING CO.

Utah Pie was a family-owned company that had sold pies in Utah and surrounding states for over thirty years. In 1957, Utah pie entered the frozen pie business. The company's pies were quite successful, capturing 66.5 percent of the market in 1958, 34.3 percent in 1959, 45.5 percent in 1960, and 45.3 percent in 1961. Even with such success, Utah Pie was a small company employing only 18 people at the time of the lawsuit, 9 of whom were members of the founding family. The defendants in this case, Continental Baking Company, Pet Milk Company, and the Carnation Company, were all much larger than the Utah Pie Company.

Utah Pie charged that the defendants had engaged in predatory pricing by selling pies below cost. What the defendants actually did was to lower their prices to meet or beat the prices charged by Utah Pie. Utah Pie had built its frozen pie plant in Salt Lake City, so it enjoyed a somewhat lower cost than the national firms in servicing the area when transportation charges are included. To enter the frozen pie market, Utah Pie offered its pies at a price below that charged by defendants. That the defendants responded to this by lowering their prices is not a surprise. What is difficult to determine, however, is whether this action is really predatory pricing. The Supreme Court thought so and found the defendants guilty of predatory pricing. Whether the court was right cannot be truly known, but it is clear that the issues were largely empirical. Specifically, consumers in the Utah Pie region benefited from the lower prices the new competitors created, but if Utah Pie had been driven out of business, consumers might have lost in the future because of higher prices. Whether the low prices would have driven Utah Pie out of business was an empirical question. Focusing on price and cost comparisons, the court concluded in the affirmative. Unfortunately, the effect was that the court granted Utah Pie a local monopoly.

Although court decisions have not reversed the Utah Pie decision, the FTC and the U.S. Justice Department have moved away from imposing the price and cost comparisons in the Utah Pie ruling on other companies. That is, the government has placed more emphasis on the competitive effects of discriminatory pricing and consumer benefits than on the damages a single firm may suffer. This view has led to relatively few Robinson-Patman cases coming to trial in the past twenty years. Companies are forewarned, however, that the government may change its mind in the future and revert to the standards adopted in the Utah Pie decision. Thus, aggressive pricing strategies may bring forth a charge of price discrimination, particularly if such strategies are successful.

12.8 A Critique of Price Discrimination

Before we leave the subject of price discrimination, it is useful to reflect upon our purported examples of discriminatory pricing and ask whether there may be another explanation.[22] Charging a lower price for the salad bar to customers who order an entrée, for example, may reflect cost differences, not price discrimination. Patrons who order an entrée may consume less food at the salad bar, thus lowering a restaurant's costs. Similarly, the higher cost of dinner as compared to lunch may partly reflect the time that patrons stay in the restaurant to eat these meals. Dinner patrons typically stay longer, increasing the restaurant's opportunity costs because it is not serving new customers. The so-called lingering theory may also explain why items such as coffee, tea, and wine are priced far above their marginal costs of production. Patrons who order these items tend to linger longer than, say, patrons who order soft drinks, which are priced closer to their marginal costs.

The lingering theory is credible because it is hard to imagine that the restaurant business in most cities and towns is anything but competitive. There are no barriers to entry. The only exclusivity that a restaurant can claim is its recipes, which may or may not be known to competitors. These recipes can grant some restaurants market power—say, the exotic French restaurant—but it is unlikely that recipes offer market power to the hamburger shop, the sandwich deli, or other restaurants that serve fairly standard meals. Yet, these restaurants charge higher prices for their dinner meals, too. So, the lingering

[22]For a discussion of alternative explanations of seemingly discriminatory pricing, see John R. Lott, Jr. and Russell D. Roberts, "A Guide to the Pitfalls of Identifying Price Discrimination," *Economic Inquiry* 29 (January 1991), 14–23.

theory or some other cost-based explanation is probably the reason for the pricing strategy found in restaurants.

We suspect that nearly every example we have offered of price discrimination by firms purported to have market power can also be rationalized with a cost-based explanation. Discount coupons may be the most difficult to explain, but they have a cost-based explanation, too.[23] Shoppers who clip discount coupons may tend to shop during off-peak hours when stores are less congested. Servicing these customers is less costly than trying to service customers who shop during peak hours when there are longer checkout lines and more part-time employees are needed to handle the congestion.

Another perplexing pricing strategy is that used by commercial airlines. Although some airlines may have market power on some routes, the restrictions they impose on air travelers tend to be found on almost every route they fly. The requirement that you purchase your ticket one week in advance for a discount is quite common. The discount is greater if you can stay over a Saturday night, and greater still if you buy a nonrefundable ticket. Although we are not inclined to rule out price discrimination totally, these rules do affect the airline's costs. If you purchase a nonrefundable ticket, the airline is *less likely* to fly with an empty seat because you have canceled your trip at the last minute. The opportunity cost of selling such a ticket is therefore lower. If you buy your ticket one week ahead of your trip, you are likely to receive your seat assignment at that time, which reduces the airline's cost of serving you when you actually check in for departure. Analogously, travelers who wait until the last minute to make their plans known require more service—buying a ticket, seat assignment, last-minute luggage check-in—and thus increase an airline's costs.

One restriction that is difficult to explain is the Saturday night stay. It is tempting to accept that this may be a method of discriminating against business travelers, whose plans are not usually flexible enough to allow a Saturday night stay over. It is possible, however, that this requirement is an example of lowering price for off-peak customers. The traveler who stays over on a Saturday night is likely to return on Sunday, which is one of the slowest days of the week for air travel. Because there is less congestion, airlines may face a lower cost of serving customers who travel on Sundays.

Economists tend to find themselves in two camps on the subject of price discrimination. On the one hand, some economists believe that in industries with no barriers to entry, purported examples of discriminatory pricing are just that: purported examples, not real examples. This camp of economists relies on cost differences to explain price differences between customers. On the other hand, some economists believe that entry to an industry is never free and that information about economic profits may be costly to obtain, so that there are barriers to entry in most industries, even if they are only temporary. If such barriers allow existing firms to exercise market power, then these firms will try any of the discriminatory pricing strategies mentioned above in an attempt to extract consumers' surplus. To these economists, both cost and discriminatory

[23]Tuition discounts in the form of scholarship may also be very difficult to explain using a cost-based approach.

pricing can be used to explain price differences between customers. We will leave it for you to decide which camp is more correct for a given situation.

Chapter Summary

1. Price discrimination arises when consumers are charged different prices for identical products and the difference in price cannot be justified by the differences in costs of servicing consumers. The primary purpose of price discrimination is to increase profits by extracting more consumers' surplus.
2. In first-degree price discrimination, consumers pay their reservation price for each good purchased. With first-degree price discrimination, the firm extracts all consumers' surplus. With second-degree price discrimination, consumers pay different prices depending on the quantity purchased. The price charged falls in discrete lumps as quantity increases. With third-degree price discrimination, consumers can be separated into distinct markets in which different prices are charged for an identical product.
3. Bundling is a method of packaging goods in which more than one product is sold as part of the total bundle. A firm with market power may use bundling as a method of price discrimination.
4. In a pure bundling strategy, the firm sells only the bundle; none of the products are sold separately. In a mixed strategy, the firm sells both the bundle and the individual products, except that the bundle is less costly than the sum of the prices of the individual products.
5. A two-part tariff consists of an access fee and a usage, or per-unit, charge. An optimal two-part tariff extracts consumers' surplus using the access fee. For the case in which consumer demands are identical, the optimal two-part tariff can extract all consumers' surplus.
6. An exclusive dealing agreement obligates one firm to purchase goods or services from another firm. A requirements contract is a slight variation on exclusive dealing in that the firm is required to purchase a certain quantity of goods and services from another firm over a given time period. The general marketplace can be used for purchases after the agreed-to requirements are satisfied.
7. In an English auction, bids are made in an open forum with an auctioneer announcing the current bid to all participants. To bid, you must offer to pay an amount that exceeds the current bid. In a Dutch auction, the auctioneer announces successively lower prices to all participants. The first participant to respond wins the bidding.
8. In a common value auction, the item sold has a uniform market price, but bidders are uncertain of the quantity to be purchased. The winning bidder suffers from the winner's curse if the winning bid is significantly above the other bids. The curse is that the other bids provide information about quantity that the winner does not have until the auction is finished.

Trouble Spots

Concept	Reminder
Pricing to Extract Consumers' Surplus	Firms with market power are forgoing potential profits if they do not try to capture consumers' surplus. But price discrimination may be very expensive to implement, leaving the single-price monopoly solution as optimal. Because the cost of implementing price discrimination varies across countries, we may observe less discriminatory pricing in the United States compared to poorer countries.
Identification and Arbitrage Are Crucial	Arbitrage is not to be considered a single event. If arbitrage is to successfully prevent a firm from practicing price discrimination, it must become systematic, so that nondiscriminatory prices are continuously available to consumers.
Second-Degree Price Discrimination	We can think of second-degree price discrimination as a "lumpy" version of first-degree price discrimination. Instead of extracting all consumers' surplus for every unit sold, second-degree price discrimination extracts lumps of consumers' surplus with "blocks" of units sold. Not all of the consumers' surplus in each block is extracted because a single price is charged over the whole block.
Bundling	Bundling is usually the packaging of two or more physically distinct products, but the concept is more general than this definition. You can think of different-sized laundry detergent boxes as a bundled product. One box may contain 12 ounces of detergent and the other box may contain a bundle of 12 ounces and 8 ounces of detergent. This is particularly true when both 12-ounce and 8-ounce boxes are available, too.
Auctions	Try not to confuse reservation prices with bids at an auction. The reservation price is the *most* that an individual will bid. The actual bids made are a function of reservation prices but are not generally equal to them.

12.9 Review Questions

1. Explain the difference between a single-price monopolist and a monopolist that practices first-degree price discrimination. Which type of firm earns the highest profits?
2. If a firm with market power has a choice between first- and second-degree price discrimination, which approach is it likely to prefer if both cost the same amount to implement?
3. What type (degree) of price discrimination might a physician practice with respect to an emergency case of appendicitis that cannot be prac-

ticed for an annual physical exam? What might limit his or her power to do so?

4. In what way is first-degree price discrimination merely a special case of second-degree (multipart) price discrimination?
5. "The reason movie theaters charge young adults and senior citizens less than the rest of us is because theater owners want to help these two low-income groups." Comment.
6. The airlines have a long history of seemingly discriminatory fares, whether or not the airlines were regulated. Airlines charge the least for tickets purchased substantially in advance of travel and charge less for travel on certain days of the week. Under what circumstances do such arrangements imply that full-fare passengers are subsidizing the discount-fare passengers?
7. Explain the difference between peak-load pricing and third-degree price discrimination. Under what condition is peak-load pricing not an example of price discrimination?
8. Explain how pure bundling can increase a firm's profits. Under what circumstances would the firm prefer pure bundling to mixed bundling? Cite an example of a product(s) sold using these two strategies.
9. Define a two-part tariff. Show how a two-part tariff can generate the same profits as first-degree price discrimination.
10. Explain why a firm and its customers might agree to an exclusive dealing arrangement or a requirements contract.
11. What is the revenue equivalence theorem? What does it imply about the revenues generated from the English, Dutch, first-price, and second-price auctions?
12. Explain the winner's curse. Why does the winner's curse affect a common value auction and not an auction that follows the independent private values model?
13. Explain how the government's past efforts to prevent price discrimination may have promoted local monopolies in some businesses.

12.10 Price Theory Problems

1. To successfully price-discriminate, a firm must separate customers with more elastic demands, who are charged less, from customers with inelastic demands, who are charged more. Explain how the following practices can be used to separate customers in this manner. In addition, develop a cost-based explanation for these practices.
    a. Charging lower prices at the copy center for larger numbers of copies.
    b. Offering free coffee with lunch to workers housed in the same office building as the sandwich shop.
    c. Offering Florida residents a 50 percent lower price to Disney World in Orlando, Florida, than nonresidents pay.
    d. Selling Nintendo's Game Boy cartridges with a coupon offering a $5 rebate from the manufacturer.

e. Distributing discount tickets to next week's football game during halftime at this week's game.

2. Explain why automobile companies offer some options as part of the car's base price, such as air conditioning, and price some options separately, which customers may choose not to buy. Why do "luxury options," such as leather seats and airbags, have higher markups than more "standard" options, such as window tinting and undercoating?
3. Explain why Kellogg sells toys on the back of Kellogg's Corn Flakes and Rice Krispies boxes. To buy these toys, customers must send a "proof of purchase" along with a check or money order. How would your answer change if the toys were available at the local toy store for a higher price? What if they were not available at all?
4. Suppose your firm faces a linear (inverse) demand curve given by $P = 1{,}000 - Q$, with the corresponding marginal revenue curve given by $MR = 1{,}000 - 2Q$, and that your marginal cost of production is constant at \$200 per unit.
   a. What is the profit-maximizing output rate if you charge a single price? What is the market clearing price? What are your profits?
   b. Suppose you can implement first-degree price discrimination; what are your profits?
   c. If your marginal costs increase to \$300 because it is costly to price-discriminate, will you price-discriminate or use a single price?
5. Your company sells a product called EthnicSpices in both California and New York. These two markets are geographically separated, so arbitrage is not possible. The demand and marginal revenue curves for EthnicSpices in these two markets are given by

$$P_{NY} = 20 - Q_{NY} \qquad MR_{NY} = 20 - 2Q_{NY}$$

$$P_{CA} = 10 - Q_{CA} \qquad MR_{CA} = 10 - 2Q_{CA}$$

   where the subscripts refer to New York (NY) and California (CA). Suppose the marginal cost of producing and distributing EthnicSpices is constant and equal to \$2 per unit.
   a. What is the optimal price you will charge if you engage in third-degree price discrimination? How much will you sell in each market, and what are your total profits?
   b. What is the deadweight loss due to monopoly pricing in each of these markets?

6. You operate a movie theater and have noticed that demand for movies varies during the day. The early moviegoers are more sensitive to price than the evening moviegoers. Suppose the demand and marginal revenue curves for the *typical* consumer in these two time periods are given by

$$P_{early} = 6 - Q_{early} \qquad MR_{early} = 6 - 2Q_{early}$$

$$P_{late} = 8 - Q_{late} \qquad MR_{late} = 8 - 2Q_{late}$$

In addition, suppose that the marginal cost of showing a movie is constant and is equal to $2 per customer.

a. What is the optimal price you will charge if you engage in third-degree price discrimination? What are your profits from a typical moviegoer in both time periods?
b. Now, suppose that you can implement a two-part tariff in both time periods. What is the optimal admission charge in the two periods, and what are your profits from a typical moviegoer in each period?

7. Suppose there are three customers in the market who typify all other customers. Your firm sells two goods—A and B—and has some market power. The reservation prices of these customers are as follows:

Customer	Good A	Good B
Sam	$25	$75
Betty	$50	$50
Yoling	$80	$20

a. Suppose the marginal cost of each product is zero. What is the optimal bundling strategy for the sale of these two goods? Does pure bundling extract more consumers' surplus than mixed bundling?
b. Now, suppose that the marginal cost of producing the good A is $30 and the marginal cost of producing good B is $25. What is the optimal bundling strategy for the sale of these two goods? Does pure bundling extract more consumers' surplus than mixed bundling in this case?

8. Suppose there are four customers in the market who typify all other customers. As in question 7, your firm sells two goods—A and B—and has some market power. The reservation prices of these customers are as follows:

Customer	Good A	Good B
Alice	$20	$5
Ben	$15	$20
Bob	$15	$15
Joyce	$5	$20

a. Suppose the marginal cost of each product is zero. Find the optimal prices to charge for a single price strategy, pure bundling, and mixed bundling. Which of these three is the optimal bundling strategy for the sale of these two goods?
b. How much consumers' surplus remains with consumers when your firm uses the optimal strategy?

9. Suppose you are the owner of a large marina that has market power due to environmental laws that have effectively restricted other firms

from entering your business. You face a typical (inverse) demand for the monthly rental of dock space given by $P = 200 - Q$, where Q is the length in feet of the dock and P is the price per foot per month. The corresponding marginal revenue curve is given by $MR = 200 - 2Q$. Your marginal cost of servicing boats is increasing with the length of the dock space rented: $MC = 50 + Q$, with $TC = 1{,}000 + 50Q + .5Q^2$.

a. What is the profit-maximizing dock rental length (Q) if you charge a single price? What is the market clearing price? What are your profits?
b. Suppose you can implement a two-part tariff. What are the optimal usage fee and access fee? What are your profits?

10. Some firms offer free airtime to customers to get them to sign up for cellular phone service. This is usually done by offering two payment options. For example, the first option charges customers \$50 per month for up to 100 minutes of airtime, after which they pay 75 cents per minute. The second option charges customers \$50 per month and 25 cents per minute for all airtime used. Explain why firms might offer these two options. What types of customers are likely to choose the first option? What types of customers are likely to choose the second option?
11. Using a graph, compare peak-load pricing to a two-part tariff with two different demand curves. First assume that the marginal cost is the same for serving both demands, then assume that the higher demand causes a higher marginal cost. What is the profit-maximizing pricing method in the two instances?
12. Draw a graph comparing the bids received for Treasury securities using the pay-what-you-bid auction versus the one proposed by Milton Friedman. Recall that in Friedman's auction all bidders pay the lowest acceptable bid. After the bids are ranked from highest to lowest, the lowest acceptable bid is the one that just exhausts the quantity of Treasury securities to be sold. You should let the revenue equivalence theorem guide you in drawing your graph.

12.11 Writing Exercise

Develop an essay that takes only one side of the price discrimination issue. Do you think that there is rampant price discrimination—grocery stores, restaurants, airlines—or do you think that the price differences we observe in these markets are justified by cost differences? Select a specific case, either one reported here or elsewhere, that is also observed in your area. Investigate this case in depth by interviewing the firm's managers to determine their explanation for the observed pricing strategy. Act independently as well by observing the behavior of the firm's customers. Be sure to base your conclusions on the evidence you discover.

13 Monopolistic Competition, Oligopoly, and Game Theory

Preview Questions

When you finish studying this chapter, you should be able to answer the following questions:

- How does monopolistic competition differ from perfect competition?
- Do oligopolists collude, act strategically, or both in order to maximize profits?
- What do Cournot duopolists assume about each other's output rate?
- Why are prices fairly stable in the kinked demand curve model?
- How does a dominant firm set the market price in its industry?
- What is the payoff matrix in a game?
- How do game participants use the Nash equilibrium concept?

In August 1993, newspapers revealed that IBM Corporation planned to engineer and produce a clone of the microprocessor chips developed by Intel Corporation. The Intel chips—386, 486, and Pentium—are the "brains" inside the majority of desktop and notebook computers. IBM and Intel do not operate in a vacuum. If IBM's plans become a reality, Intel and other chip manufacturers will react. Some companies, such as Advanced Micro Devices and Cyrix, may simply cut the prices on their computer chips to compete. Intel, however, may choose a different path. The proposed clones mimic Intel's patented chip designs, so Intel may sue to challenge IBM's design in court. If Intel sues and wins, IBM may face large damage payments and possibly be forced out of the clone business. Because other firms will respond to IBM's plans, the chip-making market place is different from a perfectly competitive market. The chip-making marketplace is composed of strategic firms, who pay careful attention to and react to the actions of other competitors.

The common playground assertion "I'll do what you do if you do what I do" poses a dilemma for anyone who considers its implications. How can you make a deal that involves circular reasoning? Who takes the first step in such a deal? When is a second step appropriate? Agreements that involve circular reasoning are difficult to follow because they do not specify an end, and it is hard to see how one begins. These concerns aside, firms have been known to act as the quote suggests; that is, they follow each other's price and quantity actions if other firms follow their actions. The models of perfect competition and pure monopoly do not involve interactions of this nature. In perfectly competitive markets, firms act independently, and in a monopoly or cartel, firms cooperate either explicitly or implicitly to set market price. But the behavior of firms in most markets falls between these two extremes. As the quote suggests, firms can generally expect that other firms will respond to their actions and that they will respond to the actions of others.

In this chapter, we study market structures that lie between perfect competition and pure monopoly. We will consider the case of monopolistic competition, in which firms have some market power but are limited in their exercise of this power by free entry and the availability of close substitutes. We will also develop models in which firms take account of and react to other firms' pricing and output decisions. We consider the kinked demand curve model, oligopoly models, price leadership models, models with consistent conjectures, and dominant strategy and Nash equilibrium models from game theory. In these reaction-type models, each seller is aware that the other sellers may take retaliatory actions to offset or hinder aggressive pricing and output decisions. In contrast to perfect competition, both rivalry and strategic competition among a few firms affect the output produced in these models.

13.1 Monopolistic Competition

The search for a model that has the characteristics of both perfect competition and pure monopoly led to the theory of **monopolistic competition,** developed by Harvard's Edward Chamberlin and Cambridge's Joan Robinson. Chamberlin's book was titled *The Theory of Monopolistic Competition* and Robinson's book *The Economics of Imperfect Competition*. Both books were first published in 1933. The market structure we develop in this section is based on Chamberlin's work.

Monopolistic Competition
An industry in which there is free entry and each firm faces a negatively sloped demand curve. Economic profits are zero in the long run.

What Is Monopolistic Competition?

A monopolistically competitive market is characterized by differentiated products and the free entry and exit of firms. In effect, all the assumptions of the perfectly competitive model apply except that the products are not homogeneous. Let's discuss how the lack of a homogeneous product affects the behavior of monopolistically competitive firms.

Product Differentiation

Many products are thought of as close but imperfect substitutes. If you shop for potato chips, for example, you can choose from chips loosely packed in bags or chips neatly stacked in cylindrical containers. You can also buy regular chips, thick chips, lightly salted chips, chips with ridges, "old-fashioned" chips, barbeque chips, cheese-flavored chips, and so on. There are certainly differences between these chips, and, as a result, many consumers prefer one type of potato chip to another. But there are also several firms that produce these different types of potato chips. The important question is whether these same consumers prefer the potato chips produced by one company over those produced by another company. If they do, then such preferences imply that some consumers are willing to pay more for the chips that they prefer.

Firms that can successfully differentiate their products gain some market power over price. If there is free entry of firms producing close substitutes, then these firms are described as monopolistic competitors. Frito-Lay, for example, produces Ruffles, which is the most popular ridged potato chip sold in the United States. Consumers who like ridged potato chips are willing to pay a little more for Ruffles than the ridged chips of Frito-Lay's competitors. Perhaps it is the fancy package Frito-Lay uses, the "Ruffles have ridges" slogan, or simply the consistent quality and taste of Ruffles chips that makes consumers willing to pay more. Whether the preferences shown are based on fact or fantasy does not matter. What matters is that such preferences give Frito-Lay *some* power over the market price of Ruffles potato chips.

Frito-Lay's competitors—General Foods, Keebler, and Anheuser-Busch—compete by offering close substitutes at an attractive price. Thus, Frito-Lay's pricing power is *limited* because consumers' choices are affected by the *relative* price of competing products. If Frito-Lay increases the price of Ruffles chips sufficiently, the increase in relative price causes some *less committed* consumers to choose other chips. In effect, Frito-Lay faces a negatively sloped demand for Ruffles chips that is more price-elastic than the demand curve Frito-Lay would face if it did not have any competitors in the ridged-chip market. The presence of competition from existing firms and potential entrants limits Frito-Lay's market power. Frito-Lay charges a price that exceeds marginal cost, but because of competition from close substitutes, its price is less than that charged by a pure monopoly with no close substitutes.

Product differentiation takes many forms. The products may be physically and chemically different—which is the case with beer and wine—so that consumers' preferences are affected by tangible product characteristics. Products may also be different for less tangible reasons, such as perceived quality enhanced by brand names or advertising slogans. In addition, other factors such as sales location can be used to differentiate products. The closer a sales outlet is to a major highway, the more convenience it usually offers customers. In addition, many apparel and auto manufacturers want consumers to buy "American-made" products, and some small firms advertise that they are local suppliers, not big, out-of-state firms that are not concerned about local customers. These patriotic appeals may affect the preferences of some individuals, giving domestic or local manufacturers some market power relative to foreign or out-of-state firms.

Free Entry and Exit of Firms

There are no barriers to entry or exit in a monopolistically competitive market. A firm that successfully differentiates its product expects other firms to try to replicate its product or marketing strategy if it is earning economic profits.

Economic profits attract entry. New entrants tend to decrease demand for a successful firm's product. With more close substitutes from which to choose, the cross-price elasticity of demand may increase, causing successively larger decreases in the firm's demand curve as relative prices change. Alternatively, more competition may further narrow the market niche that a firm has carved for itself, which decreases demand for the firm's product. The market for travel and entertainment magazines offers evidence of this increasing differentiation. The general interest magazines—*Holiday* and *Travel*—have lost market share to the more specialized magazines, such as *Caribbean Travel* and *New England Inns*. The net effect is that free entry decreases demand for a firm's product and eventually squeezes out all economic profits.

SHORT-RUN EQUILIBRIUM FOR THE MONOPOLISTIC MARKET

With limited market power, the monopolistically competitive firm faces a negatively sloped demand curve. Figure 13.1 shows the monopolistically competitive firm's demand curve, which is labeled D_{SR}. The elasticity of D_{SR} depends partly on the costs of substituting among firms. If switching to another firm's product is relatively costless, then D_{SR} is more elastic. If this were a perfectly competitive model, for example, D_{SR} would be ***horizontal*** at price P^*. If substitution is relatively expensive, then D_{SR} becomes more inelastic. In other words, if it is relatively expensive to substitute among firms, consumers cannot take advantage of relative price changes, so the monopolistic firm's demand curve adjusts to reflect the lack of substitutes.

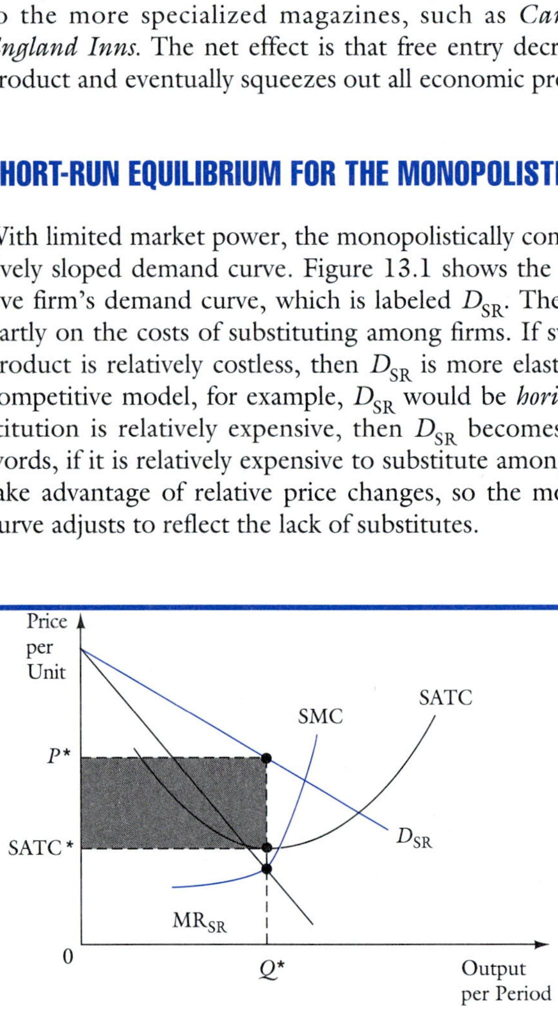

FIGURE 13.1

A Monopolistically Competitive Firm in Short-Run Equilibrium

Short-run equilibrium for a monopolistically competitive firm implies that marginal revenue equals marginal cost at an output rate Q^*. At this equilibrium, the firm earns economic profits equal to $(P^* - \text{SATC}^*) \times Q^*$, which equals the shaded area in the figure.

Short-run equilibrium for the monopolistic market is achieved when no firm has an incentive to change its own price or output. This occurs only if marginal revenue equals marginal cost at each firm's output rate. In Figure 13.1, the profit-maximizing output rate is Q^*, the output at which the perceived marginal revenue curve, MR_{SR}, intersects the short-run marginal cost curve, SMC. The market clearing price is P^*, which corresponds to output rate Q^*. There is no incentive for the firm to change its short-run behavior at this point. Moreover, there is no incentive for any firm to change its behavior if it is operating at the output rate that equates marginal revenue to marginal cost. Thus, the market is in short-run equilibrium at a price of P^*.

LEARNING EXERCISE 13.1

If the monopolistic firm in Figure 13.1 was given a patent that effectively eliminated its close competitors, how would its demand curve change?

LONG-RUN EQUILIBRIUM FOR THE MONOPOLISTIC MARKET

In our example of the short-run equilibrium, positive economic profits are made by each individual firm. The shaded area in Figure 13.1 represents the economic profits earned by a typical monopolistically competitive firm. Positive economic profits attract entry in the long run, which has two effects:

1. Market supply increases, causing price to fall.
2. New firms cause the demand curve to shift to the left as each firm receives a lower market share. (Note that this result also occurs in perfect competition as firms move down their marginal cost curve.)

These two effects stop when there is no reason for new entry, that is, when there are no economic profits to attract new firms. Figure 13.2, on page 520, illustrates the long-run equilibrium position of a monopolistically competitive firm.

In Figure 13.2, the decrease in the firm's demand curve changes its profit-maximizing output rate. Now the firm produces Q_{LR} and charges P_{LR} to maximize profits. This output rate is given by the point of tangency between the firm's demand curve and its long-run average cost curve, LATC. Thus, P_{LR} equals $LATC_{LR}$, so the firm earns *no* economic profits in the long run. In the potato chip market, for example, the product differentiation developed for Ruffles causes Charles Chips Company to promote Waffles potato chips and Anheuser-Busch, Keebler, and General Foods to offer ridged potato chips. For these companies, the market equilibrium recognizes their product differentiation but offers no economic profits for the effort.

Note that both the firm *and* the market are in equilibrium at a price of P_{LR}. The firm's output rate maximizes profits and lies at the intersection point between its demand curve and its long-run average cost curve. The market is in equilibrium because all individual firms are in equilibrium and because there is no incentive for new firms to enter.

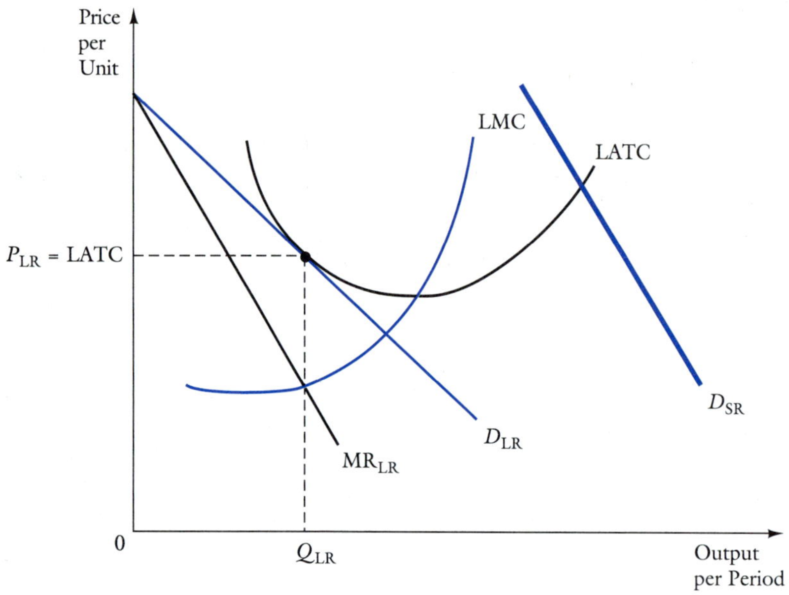

FIGURE 13.2

Long-Run Equilibrium in a Monopolistically Competitive Market

In the long run, positive economic profits attract new entrants, which has the effect of reducing the demand for the firm's products. The long-run equilibrium is reached when marginal revenue equals marginal cost at an output rate, Q_{LR}, at which the firm's demand curve, D_{LR}, is tangent to the long-run average total cost curve, LATC. At this point, the optimal price, P_{LR}, equals long-run average cost. At this equilibrium, the firm earns zero economic profits.

EXCESS CAPACITY IN MONOPOLISTIC MARKETS

In Chapter 10, we showed that the long-run equilibrium for a perfectly competitive market occurs when all firms operate at the minimum point on their long-run average cost curve. At this point, there is no *excess capacity* in the industry. This result arises because the *horizontal* demand curve facing each individual firm shifts down with new entry until price equals the lowest point of the long-run average cost curve. Then entry or exit stops in the perfectly competitive industry. If a firm operates at an output rate below this minimum point, there is excess capacity.

We can compare the optimal long-run operating position of a monopolistic firm to that of a perfectly competitive firm. Looking at Figure 13.2, we see that the monopolistically competitive firm produces an output rate that is less than the one at which the long-run average cost curve reaches a minimum. This result implies that there is *excess* capacity in the monopolistically competitive industry; that is, if the industry produced more, average cost would decrease for each firm.

Paying for Product Differentiation

As long as there is any negative slope whatsoever to the perceived demand curve, there is no way that an individual firm can operate at the minimum point on its long-run average cost curve. Chamberlin suggested that the difference between the actual long-run average cost of production for a monopolistically competitive firm and its *minimum* long-run average cost represented the "cost" of producing "differentness." In other words, Chamberlin did not label this difference in average unit cost a measure of excess capacity, but rather a charge for product differentiation.

Indeed, Chamberlin argued that it is rational for consumers to have a taste for differentiation; that is, consumers willingly accept the increased average cost in return for choice and variety of output. We know that the so-called excess capacity problem is a result of heterogeneity across products; if there were no heterogeneity and all other assumptions in the model were retained, the firm would become a perfect competitor, operating at the minimum point on its long-run average cost curve.

Monopolistic Competition is Inefficient

The long-run equilibrium solution for a monopolistic industry results in a price that exceeds marginal cost. From Chapter 10, we know that price equals marginal cost under perfect competition and that perfect competition is efficient in that all gains from trade are exhausted at the equilibrium solution. This is not the case with monopolistic competition. At the monopolistic equilibrium, consumers value additional units of the monopolistically produced product at more than the firm's marginal cost. Because the firm refuses to produce more, however, the gains from trade are not fully exhausted. It refuses to produce more because its present zero profit is the best that it can do in the long run. So the monopolistic equilibrium is not efficient.

COMPARING MONOPOLISTIC COMPETITION, PERFECT COMPETITION, AND MONOPOLY

Monopolistic markets are different from perfectly competitive and monopolized markets, but the differences may be fairly subtle, particularly in the short run. Figure 13.3, on page 522, shows the operating differences between firms in each of these market structures. Positive economic profits may exist in any of these market structures in the short run. In the long run, however, positive profits can arise only in a monopoly. The firm in a monopolistic industry operates at an output rate at which price equals its long-run average total cost. The perfectly competitive firm also operates at such a position, except that price equals the *minimum* of the long-run average total cost curve. This difference is the reason there is excess capacity in monopolistic firms. For the monopoly, however, neither condition generally holds in the long run because the monopolist can make positive economic profits, so price generally exceeds long-run average cost.

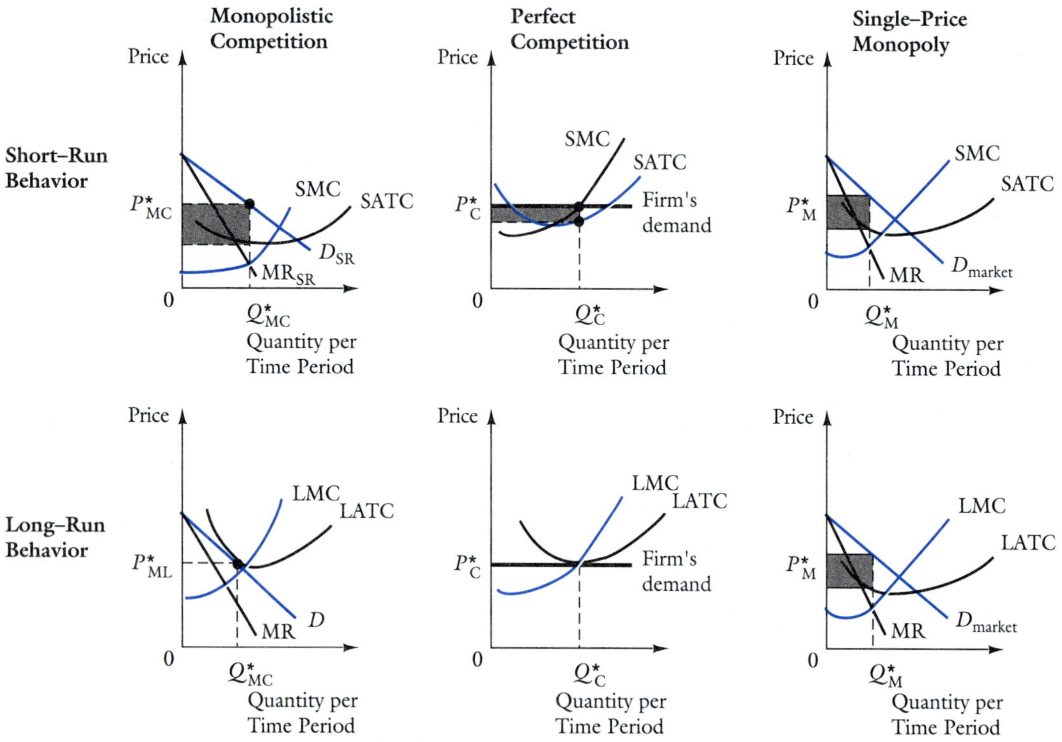

Comparing Monopolistic Competition, Perfect Competition, and Single-Price Monopoly

The short- and long-run relationships between monopolistic competition, perfect competition, and monopoly are shown. The shaded areas represent profits under each industry structure.

CRITICISMS OF THE MONOPOLISTIC COMPETITION MODEL

The basic idea of monopolistic competition has been criticized by many economists. The notion that products are close substitutes and thus firms that produce them are monopolistic competitors is often difficult to formalize. For example, pretzels may be a close substitute for potato chips. But pretzels may be a substitute for crackers, which may be a substitute for toast, which may be a substitute for muffins, which may be a substitute for danishes, which may be a substitute for waffles, which may be a substitute for eggs. But one does not *normally* think of eggs as a substitute for pretzels. Thus, the whole notion of differentiation by product groups composed of close substitutes is difficult to operationalize.

In an attempt to overcome some of this difficulty, economists have modified the monopolistically competitive model. In the section that follows, we develop a model of monopolistic competition in which firms differentiate themselves by location, not by product characteristics. This model is consistent with the idea that firms may price their products to take into account the waiting or travel time of customers.

LEARNING EXERCISE 13.2

From the viewpoint of efficiently allocating resources, which is more important, price equal to marginal cost or price equal to the minimum of the long-run average total cost curve?

13.2 SPATIAL COMPETITION

Firms may try to differentiate themselves along dimensions other than the physical characteristics of the goods or services they produce. In fact, *ceteris paribus,* the goods or services they produce may be perfect substitutes; consumers may prefer one firm over another because it is located closer to the consumer's residence or job site. In other words, when we include transportation cost as part of the price of a product, consumers who are otherwise indifferent between firms show a preference for the nearby firm. Obviously, the full price charged by the nearby firm is less than that of its more distant competitor. Competition along the transportation cost dimension is called **spatial competition.** Let's develop a simple model of spatial competition to show how consumers are sorted among firms and how the optimal number of firms can be determined in an industry.

Spatial Competition
Competition between firms for location and distribution of products or services.

A SIMPLE CITY MAP

Figure 13.4, on page 524, shows a city that was built around a circular roadway. There are four commercial zones inside the roadway—A, B, C, and D—and four housing developments outside the roadway. The commercial zones span the entire strip between any two housing developments. Businesses can locate at any point within a commercial zone. Each housing development contains 250 households, so there are 1,000 households in the city. Currently there are two fast-food restaurants, located at points A and B on the map. Each restaurant serves hamburgers, French fries, and soft drinks, and each restaurant charges $4.20 per meal.

The circumference of the roadway is exactly 1 mile, and the housing developments are ¼ mile in length, with houses spread evenly within each development. Currently, residents in Country Greens and Lake Villas patronize the fast-food restaurant in location A, while residents in Coral Estates and Calloway Hills patronize restaurant B. Thus, each restaurant serves 500 meals per day, that is, one to each household. Households group themselves in this manner because the food sold at each restaurant is identical (i.e., the meals are perfect substitutes), so the transportation cost alone affects the choice of restaurants.

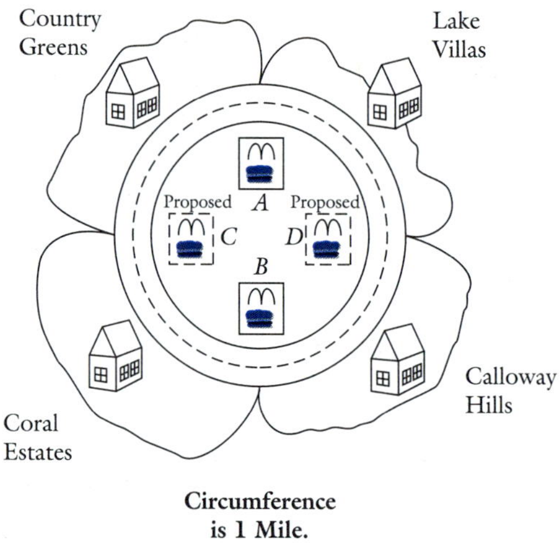

FIGURE 13.4

A Simple City Map

Commercial and residential areas are distributed uniformly around a circular roadway. The circumference of the roadway is one mile. There are two existing fast-food restaurants located at points *A* and *B*, and two new fast-food restaurants are proposed to be built at points *C* and *D*.

THE FULL PRICE OF A MEAL

Let's assume that the transportation cost for any household is t dollars per mile and that the distance to a restaurant is d for a given household. Then, the full price of a fast-food meal equals the \$4.20 charge plus the transportation cost. The cost of a round trip to the restaurant equals $2td$, so the full price of a meal equals \$4.20 + $2td$. With households evenly distributed around the circular roadway, the average one-way distance traveled equals ⅛ mile, that is, one-half the length of a housing development. A round trip covers ¼ mile. For example, suppose that t = \$4 and d = ⅛ mile; then the transportation cost equals 2(\$4)(⅛), or \$1, so the full price of a meal is \$4.20 + \$1 = \$5.20.

The meal price at restaurants is a function of each restaurant's cost. The average and total costs will vary with output. Assuming that the *daily* total costs (TC) of each restaurant are linear in output, then

$$\text{TC} = \text{FC} + mQ \qquad (13.1)$$

where FC is the fixed cost, Q is output, and m is the variable cost of a meal.

Using this formulation, average cost (AC) equals FC/Q + m, which implies that average cost declines as output increases. In other words, the more patrons a restaurant serves, the lower its average costs. If these restaurants face a total cost function, measured in dollars per day, given by TC = 100 + 4Q, then the average cost of serving 500 customers per day equals \$4.20. If two new restaurants open up at locations C and D in Figure 13.4, then the 1,000 households will be split among four restaurants, with each restaurant serving 250 households per day. In this case, the average cost of a meal increases to \$4.40 (i.e., \$100/250 + \$4).

Although the average cost of a meal increases, the *average* transportation cost decreases because the new restaurants are better situated for some households in each development. With two new restaurants at locations C and D, the average length of a one-way trip is cut in half. Thus, households travel an average of $1/16$ mile each way. With $t = \$4$ and $d = 1/16$ mile, the transportation cost equals $2(\$4)(1/16)$, or 50 cents. The full price of a meal is now \$4.40 + \$.50 = \$4.90, which is 30 cents *less* than before. An increase in the number of restaurants lowers the full price of a meal if the reduction in transportation cost more than offsets the increase in average cost at each restaurant.

Note that the price a restaurant charges (assuming that it breaks even) has increased from \$4.20 to \$4.40 per meal with the addition of two new restaurants. But the *full* price paid by customers falls from \$5.20 to \$4.90 per meal. Customers are better off with the two new restaurants even though the *market* price of meals has increased.

THE OPTIMAL NUMBER OF RESTAURANTS

How many restaurants can we expect to find in the long run in Figure 13.4? To answer this question, let's assume that competition between restaurants forces them to a zero-profit equilibrium in the long run. In this case, the quoted price, or market price, of a meal equals the average cost of producing a meal. If there are *no* transportation costs to consider, then it is optimal to have only one firm because this firm can achieve the greatest scale economies given a linear total cost function. For example, with zero transportation cost and one restaurant, the full price of a meal equals its average cost of \$4.10 (i.e., \$100/1,000 + \$4).[1] With *positive* transportation costs, more than one restaurant is optimal in the long run.

When do we stop adding more restaurants? If we treat the number of restaurants as a continuous variable, then we can use calculus to solve for the optimal number. Let L represent the total population. The average cost of a meal is given by $\text{AC} = (N/L)\text{FC} + m$, where (N/L) is the proportion of customers served by each restaurant. Distributing restaurants evenly around the 1-mile circular roadway implies that the distance between restaurants equals $(1/N)$ miles. The farthest a customer will travel is $(1/2N)$ miles. The average distance is one-half this amount, or $(1/4N)$ miles. Thus, the average round-trip transportation cost equals $2t(1/4N)$. The full price of a meal equals the sum of the average meal cost and the average transportation cost, or $(N/L)\text{FC} + m + 2t(1/4N)$. Minimizing the full price with respect to N gives the solution for the optimal number of restaurants:

[1]We are assuming that the restaurant does not act like a monopoly.

$$N = \sqrt{\frac{tL}{2FC}} \tag{13.2}$$

What equation (13.2) reflects is that if an additional restaurant *increases* the full price of a meal, it will not be built and operated in the long run. Thus, the optimal number of restaurants is the number that minimizes the full price of a meal. The theoretical solution is compelling, but there may be differences between theory and reality. The actual number of restaurants is affected by factors such as local zoning codes and the availability of licenses for liquor and other beverages. Restrictions such as these may limit the number of restaurants so that the optimal number is never achieved.

Models of spatial competition show that firms compete in dimensions other than the posted price of their products. When location is introduced directly, we can solve for the optimal number of firms in a given market area. The benefit of these models is that they show that firms are acting to lower the full price paid by consumers, even though they may incur higher costs at this solution.

Learning Exercise 13.3

Using the parameters given above, determine the full price of a meal if there are five restaurants proportionately spaced around the circular roadway. Does the full price increase or decrease relative to the price when there are only four restaurants?

13.3 Oligopoly

Firms that react to the actions of other firms in the same market are considered strategic competitors. For example, a monopolistically competitive firm affects its own demand when it changes the relative price of its product. By raising the relative price, the firm loses customers to other firms who offer a close substitute or to new entrants who see a profit opportunity. Similarly, if a firm lowers the relative price of its product, it may gain customers from other firms.

It is difficult to model strategic behavior because there are many different ways to approach the problem. As long as firms do not cooperate to reach the monopoly solution discussed in Chapter 11, there may be many different market equilibrium solutions. In this section we consider several approaches. All are potentially useful in explaining the behavior of firms in an oligopoly. An **oligopoly** is a market composed of only a *few* firms that account for most of the market sales. Firms in oligopolistic industries are in a position to affect market price and the demand for other firms' products by their actions; thus, they are generally regarded as strategic competitors.

Oligopoly
A market structure in which there are relatively few firms and each firm takes account of the others' reactions.

Strategic competition implies that oligopolists may spend much of their time trying to second-guess each other because there are a large number of possible ways in which firms can act and react. We start with a very simple model of oligopoly, known as **duopoly** because there are only two firms in the market. We then present a discussion of the kinked demand curve,

Duopoly
A market structure in which there are only two firms.

implicit collusion, and price leadership models, which illustrate other forms of strategic competition.

THE COURNOT DUOPOLY MODEL

In 1838, French mathematician Antoine Augustin Cournot published a theory of duopoly.[2] Unfortunately for Cournot, this theory did not become widely known or discussed until the 1930s. Although the Cournot model is an intrinsically interesting model and is used as a basis of departure for further analysis, it embodies some rather restrictive assumptions. Let's investigate the Cournot model in detail.

Assumptions of the Cournot Model

In the Cournot duopoly model, the two firms sell identical products at identical costs. Marginal costs are assumed to be constant, and each firm knows exactly the shape of the market demand curve. It is further assumed that buyers and sellers have perfect information, so both firms behave in exactly the same way. Therefore, each duopolist sells the product at exactly the same price and produces the same output rate.

The question each firm faces is how to choose output to maximize profits. Cournot used the Nash equilibrium concept to solve this problem. The **Nash equilibrium** concept requires that each firm select a course of action that is best for it given the actions of other firms. (The Nash equilibrium concept is developed more fully below.) Specifically, Cournot assumed the following behavioral rule:

Nash Equilibrium A strategy (or action) that is optimal for each firm given the decisions of all other firms.

> **Each duopolist, in selecting its own rate of output, assumes that the other duopolist's output will remain constant.**

Of course, this assumption involves self-delusion because each duopolist assumes that it can act without provoking an output reaction from the other firm. This is, in essence, a no-learning-by-doing model. Nonetheless, Cournot was able to show that, given his assumptions, the two duopolists will approach a Nash equilibrium solution for their rate of output.

THE COURNOT-NASH EQUILIBRIUM

In order to understand how the Cournot duopoly model works, we will start with a market demand function for a specific commodity. To retain the flavor of Cournot's original application, we will use mineral water as the commodity.

[2]Antoine Augustin Cournot, *Recherches sur les Principes Mathématiques de la Théorie des Richesses* (Paris, 1897). English translation by N. Bacon, New York: Macmillan, 1938.

Figure 13.5 shows the industry demand curve, D_{market}, and its corresponding marginal revenue curve, MR_{market}. Firm 1 moves first, and firm 2 is temporarily inactive; that is, firm 2 does not produce any mineral water in the initial step. Hence, D_{market} is the demand curve facing firm 1. To maximize profits, firm 1 sets a rate of output at which marginal revenue equals marginal cost. As shown in Figure 13.5, firm 1 produces an output rate of 1,000 bottles per day in the first round. Remember that this is the initial round, so firm 2 has not yet begun production.

Now, firm 2 enters the market with the second round. It takes the output rate of firm 1 as fixed at 1,000 bottles per day. Firm 2 believes that its demand curve is D_{market} *minus* the rate of output of firm 1; that is, firm 2's demand curve is $D_{1,000}$, which equals D_{market} minus 1,000 bottles per day. The marginal revenue curve for firm 2 is $MR_{1,000}$. Firm 2 maximizes profits by finding the

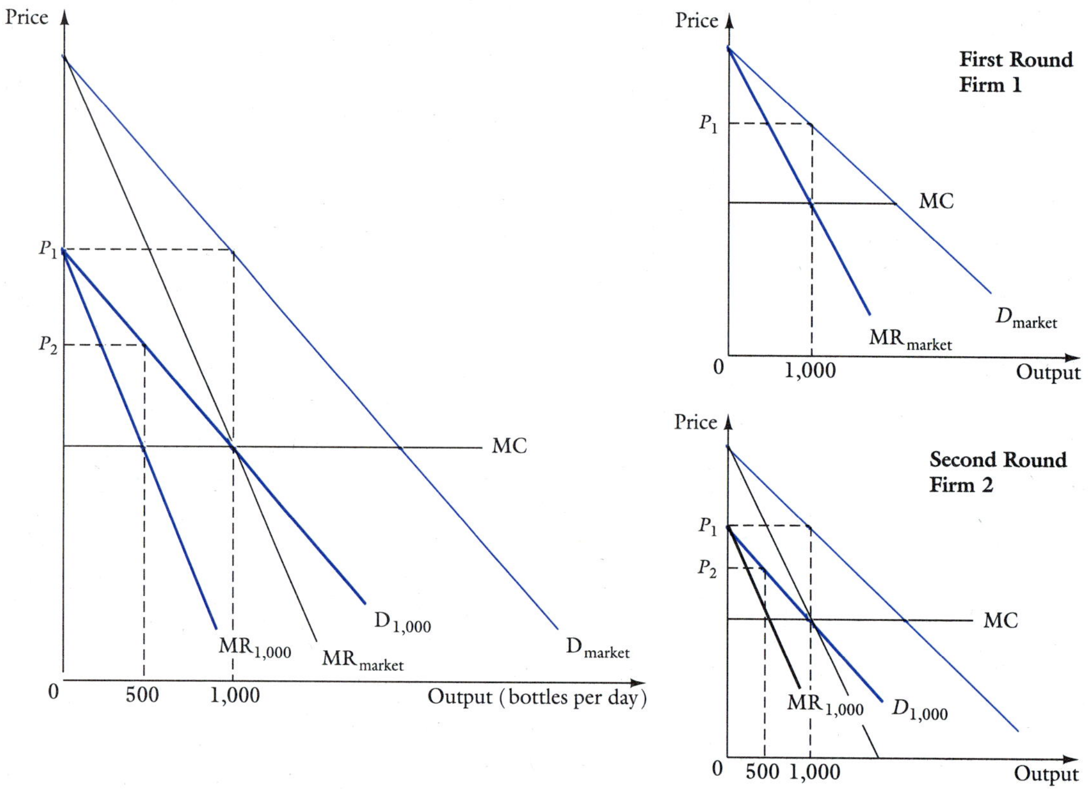

FIGURE 13.5

The Cournot Duopoly Model: Iterating Towards an Equilibrium

In the first round of the Cournot duopoly model, firm 1 maximizes profit assuming that firm 2's output is zero. Firm 1 produces 1,000 bottles per day and sets price at P_1. In the second round, firm 2 acts as if firm 1's output is fixed at 1,000 bottles per day and maximizes profits using the residual demand curve, D_{1000}. Firm 2's optimal output rate is 500 bottles per day, which clears the market at price P_2 when combined with the 1,000 bottles produced by firm 1. These firms continue to iterate in this manner until they reach a Cournot-Nash equilibrium.

output rate at which $MR_{1,000}$ equals MC. As shown in Figure 13.5, firm 2 produces 500 bottles per day in the second round of this equilibrium game.

Firm 1 has the third move. Because firm 2 is producing 500 bottles per day, it is no longer optimal for firm 1 to produce 1,000 bottles per day. In other words, the assumption that firm 2 produces nothing is no longer correct. The demand curve for firm 1 equals the market demand curve minus 500 bottles per day. Although we have not drawn this demand curve in Figure 13.5, you should realize that it lies *between* $D_{1,000}$ and D_{market}; it does not lie below $D_{1,000}$. Similarly, the marginal revenue curve on the third move lies *between* $MR_{1,000}$ and MR_{market}. In the third move, then, firm 1 selects a rate of output *between* 500 and 1,000 bottles per day.

The sequence of moves continues just as described above, with each firm taking the other firm's output as fixed in order to make its output decision. Although this process may seem endless, it will not go on indefinitely. The two firms will eventually reach an output rate that is self-validating. That is, the output rate that firm 1 assumes for firm 2 is equal to firm 2's optimal output rate *and* the output rate that firm 2 assumes for firm 1 is equal to firm 1's optimal output rate. On this move, these firms are at a Nash equilibrium. In Figure 13.5, the Nash equilibrium lies between 500 and 1,000 bottles per day, with each firm producing the same output rate.

Cournot Reaction Functions

Reaction Function
An equation that defines the response of one firm to the actions taken by other firms.

One approach we can take to solve for the Cournot-Nash equilibrium is to describe how each firm reacts to the other firm's output rate. A **reaction function** is an equation that specifies the optimal output rate for one firm given the other firm's output rate. There are two reaction functions in the duopoly model:

$$Q_1^* = f_1(Q_2) \quad (13.3)$$

$$Q_2^* = f_2(Q_1) \quad (13.4)$$

Equation (13.3) specifies the optimal output rate for firm 1, and equation (13.4) specifies the optimal output for firm 2. For example, in the first move by firm 1 above, the output rate of firm 2 was set at zero, so $Q_1^* = 1{,}000 = f_1(0)$. In the second move, made by firm 2, firm 1's output rate was set at 1,000, so $Q_2^* = 500 = f_2(1{,}000)$. These moves continue until an equilibrium is reached. The Cournot-Nash equilibrium occurs when

$$Q_1^* = f_1(Q_2^*) \textit{ and } Q_2^* = f_2(Q_1^*)$$

In other words, the optimal output rate of each firm equals what the other firm had assumed. The key to using this equilibrium approach is to learn how to set up the duopoly problem so that you can solve for each firm's reaction function.

The Cournot Model with a Linear Demand Curve

Here we develop a numerical example of the Cournot model so that you can see how to solve for the reaction functions directly. Suppose that the (inverse) market demand curve is given by:

$$P = 4{,}000 - 2(Q_1 + Q_2) \tag{13.5}$$

where Q_1 is the output rate of firm 1 and Q_2 is the output rate of firm 2. In addition, the marginal cost of each firm is assumed to be constant:

$$MC_1 = MC_2 = 400 \tag{13.6}$$

This assumption implies that average costs are constant and equal to marginal costs. Thus, the total costs of firm 1 can be written as $400Q_1$ and the total costs of firm 2 can be written as $400Q_2$.

To solve for the reaction functions, let's start with firm 1's optimization problem. The total revenue for firm 1 is TR_1:

$$\begin{aligned} TR_1 = P \times Q_1 &= 4{,}000Q_1 + 2(Q_1 + Q_2) \times Q_1 \\ &= 4{,}000Q_1 + 2Q_1^2 + 2Q_2 \times Q_1 \end{aligned} \tag{13.7}$$

The marginal revenue curve for firm 1, MR_1, is equal to the incremental change in total revenue, ΔTR_1, resulting from an incremental change in output, ΔQ_1:

$$MR_1 = \frac{\Delta TR_1}{\Delta Q_1} = 4{,}000 - 4Q_1 - 2Q_2 \tag{13.8}$$

To solve for the firm's optimal output rate, we set marginal revenue equal to marginal cost. Marginal cost is assumed to be constant and equal to \$400, the same for both firms. For firm 1 we set MR_1 equal to \$400 using equation (13.8). This gives an expression of Q_1 as a function of Q_2. Simplifying for equation (13.8) gives *firm 1's reaction function:*

$$Q_1^* = f_1(Q_2) = 900 - \frac{1}{2}Q_2 \tag{13.9}$$

Following the same steps, we can find *firm 2's reaction function:*

$$Q_2^* = f_2(Q_1) = 900 - \frac{1}{2}Q_1 \tag{13.10}$$

The equilibrium for this problem is solved by substituting Q_2^* from equation (13.10) into equation (13.9), which gives the optimal output rate for firm 1. This substitution implies that $Q_1^* = 600$. Substituting this value into equation (13.10) gives $Q_2^* = 600$, too.

Another way to see this solution is to graph the reaction functions of the two firms. Figure 13.6 plots these reaction functions using Q_1 for the vertical axis and Q_2 for the horizontal axis. The reaction function, or curve, for firm 1 intersects the vertical axis at 900 units ($Q_2 = 0$) and intersects the horizontal axis at 1,800 units ($Q_1 = 0$). From equation (13.9), we see that the reaction function is linear, so the reaction curve is a straight line connecting these two points. Analogously, the reaction curve for firm 2 is also a straight line. The Cournot-Nash equilibrium occurs at the intersection of these two curves, which, from the discussion above, we know is at the output rate of 600 units for each firm.

We can contrast this result with that of a pure monopoly and that of a perfectly competitive market. If these two firms merged to form a pure monopoly, then the optimal output rate would be 450 units for each firm, or 900 units for the whole market. Alternatively, in a perfectly competitive industry, the two firms would set price equal to marginal cost to solve for

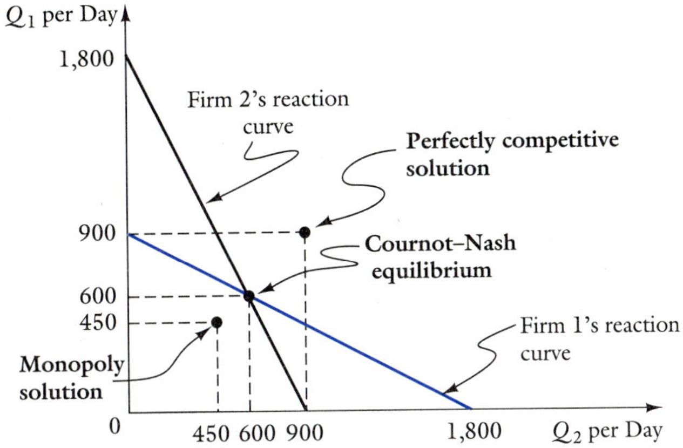

FIGURE 13.6

The Reaction Curves of the Cournot Duopolists

The intersection of the two firms' reaction curves determines the Cournot-Nash equilibrium output rate in the duopoly model. In this example, each firm produces 600 units per day. In contrast, at the perfectly competitive solution, each firm produces 900 units per day, and at the monopoly or cartel solution, each firm produces 450 units per day.

their output rates. The perfectly competitive solution implies that each firm produces 1,800 units for a total of 3,600 in the market. As you can see from Figure 13.6, the Cournot-Nash equilibrium solution lies between the equilibrium solutions for the pure monopoly and the perfectly competitive industry. This is one reason why economists call the Cournot model an example of *imperfect* competition.

LEARNING EXERCISE 13.4

Solve for the profits of each firm at the monopoly, Cournot-Nash, and perfectly competitive solutions. Is the relationship between the profits for these three models what you expected?

THE KINKED DEMAND CURVE MODEL

Kinked Demand Curve A demand curve that has a kink, or abrupt change in slope, at some price, which causes a gap in the marginal revenue curve.

Another example of how firms use price and output strategies to compete is the kinked demand curve model. In the **kinked demand curve** model, the other firms react asymmetrically to a price change. A firm that raises price must go it alone because other firms will not match an increase in price, but if a firm lowers price, all firms match the lower price. This behavioral assumption implies that each firm faces a demand curve with a kink at the current market price. Let's examine how each firm operates in the presence of a kinked demand curve.

Figure 13.7 shows two demand curves that intersect at the current market price, $P_{current}$. Demand curve D_{match} is drawn under the assumption that any change in the firm's price is ***matched*** by all other firms. Thus, relative prices are not changed along D_{match}. Demand curve $D_{no\ match}$ is drawn under the assumption that no other firm matches the given firm's price change. Obviously, $D_{no\ match}$ is more elastic than D_{match} at price $P_{current}$.

Using the behavioral assumption of the kinked demand curve model, the firm faces demand curve $D_{no\ match}$ if it raises price above $P_{current}$ and faces demand curve D_{match} if it lowers price below $P_{current}$. The firm's demand curve is thus the heavily shaded kinked demand curve, which has a kink at the current market price.

Price Stability in the Kinked Demand Curve Model

Given the kinked nature of the firm's demand curve, the marginal revenue curve the firm faces is similarly distorted. Figure 13.8 shows the marginal revenue curve associated with the firm's kinked demand curve. At output rates less than $Q_{current}$, the firm operates on the $D_{no\ match}$ demand curve, so its marginal revenue curve is the one that corresponds to this demand curve. At output rates greater than $Q_{current}$, the firm operates on the D_{match} demand curve, so its marginal revenue curve is the one that corresponds to this demand curve. Because $D_{no\ match}$ and D_{match} have different slopes, these two marginal revenue curves ***do not*** intersect at $Q_{current}$, which is where the kink is found. The marginal revenue curve is therefore ***discontinuous*** at the kink.

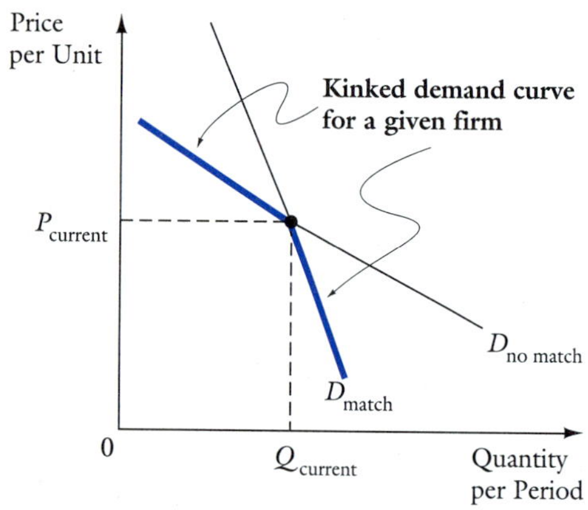

FIGURE 13.7

The Shape of the Kinked Demand Curve

For any firm we can define a demand curve, D_{match}, for which all competitors match its price changes and a demand curve, $D_{no\ match}$, for which no competitors match its price changes. These two demand curves intersect at the current price, $P_{current}$, and output rate, $Q_{current}$, of the firm. If competitors match all price decreases but do not match price increases, the firm faces a kinked demand curve. The kinked demand curve equals $D_{no\ match}$ when prices increase above $P_{current}$ and equals D_{match} when prices fall below $P_{current}$.

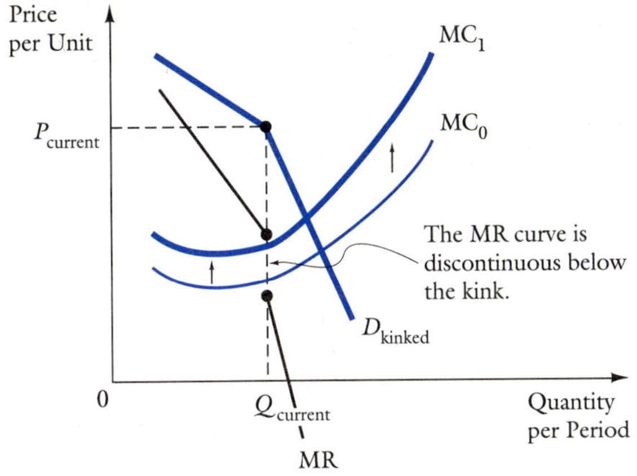

FIGURE 13.8

Price Stability in the Kinked Demand Curve Model

Price stability arises in the kinked demand curve model because the marginal revenue curve is discontinuous at the kink point. If marginal cost increases from MC_0 to MC_1, it is optimal for the firm to produce $Q_{current}$ and charge $P_{current}$ even though profits are reduced.

The gap in the marginal revenue curve has a stabilizing effect on the firm's ability to adjust to changes in its marginal cost structure. When marginal cost increases within the gap—say, from MC_0 to MC_1 in Figure 13.8—the firm does not change its optimal output rate. In other words, even though costs have increased, the rule that marginal revenue equals marginal cost implies that $Q_{current}$ is still the optimal output rate. Because the output rate does not change, market price does not change. As a result, this model has been suggested as a possible explanation for cases when market prices remain relatively constant in the face of increasing input costs.

LEARNING EXERCISE 13.5

Show that the size of the gap in the firm's marginal revenue curve increases as the kink becomes more pronounced.

What's Wrong with the Kinked Demand Curve Model?

When the kinked demand curve model first appeared, it was regarded as innovative and useful. After extensive examination, however, economists have seriously challenged its basic assumptions and predictive powers.

The basic theoretical problems concern how the initial price $P_{current}$ is determined. If we start off the model with $P_{current}$ as given, the analysis is consistent, but if we do not know how $P_{current}$ is reached, we do not have a general theory of the initial market equilibrium. Without a method of determining the market equilibrium, the model has limited usefulness.

Nor does the empirical evidence support the existence of a kinked demand curve in many industries. Economist and Nobel laureate (late) George Stigler showed that in seven industries containing only a few firms, price increases by one firm were met with price increases by other firms. Thus, there was no asymmetry in the reaction of rivals to changes in a single firm's price, although that is the claim inherent to the kinked demand curve model.[3] One empirical study does not disprove a theory, but it does cast doubt on the robustness of the kinked demand curve model.

THE STACKELBERG MODEL: MOVING FIRST HAS ITS ADVANTAGES

The Cournot-Nash model assumes that each firm continues to adjust its own output, given the other firm's output, until it reaches an equilibrium that is self-fulfilling. Firms play each round with the final equilibrium as their goal. They can avoid the round-by-round play and move directly to the final equilibrium solution if they solve the two reaction functions shown in equations (13.9) and (13.10) in the first round. This is often a shortcut to the final result. One virtue of reaching the result in the first round is that both firms can avoid the first-mover advantage. The **first-mover advantage** arises when the firm that goes first is given a profit advantage over the other firm.

First-Mover Advantage
The firm that sells output first has a profit advantage over firms that enter the market later.

We can see how the first-mover advantage affects the profits of the two firms from Figure 13.5 on page 528. Firm 1, which sets output first, chooses to produce 1,000 bottles per day, whereas firm 2 optimally chooses to produce 500 bottles per day. Firm 1 receives a price of P_1 for its output. Because marginal cost is constant, it is also equal to average cost. Thus, firm 1 receives $(P_1 - \text{MC}) \times 1{,}000$ in profits. Firm 2 receives P_2 for its output and faces a constant marginal cost of production. Thus, firm 2's profits are $(P_2 - \text{MC}) \times 500$. Because P_1 is greater than P_2, firm 1 has a profit advantage over firm 2, which arises because firm 1 goes first. If firm 2 had gone first, it would have the profit advantage.

The firm that moves first does not have a profit incentive to continue toward the Cournot-Nash equilibrium. By continuing to produce 1,000 bottles per day, firm 1 can maintain its profit advantage over firm 2. This variation of the Cournot setup is known as the *Stackelberg model*. The Stackelberg model provides insight into many real-world practices. Software companies that compete in markets in which there are only a few strong competitors often try to capture the first-mover advantage. Aldus Corporation, which makes PageMaker, is one example. The PageMaker software is a high-end page layout program. Its major competitor is QuarkXPress, produced by Quark Corporation. Aldus announced a significant revision in PageMaker, called PageMaker 5.0, in the late summer of 1992, with shipment expected in early 1993. Unfortunately for users, the product did not ship until the summer of 1993. In the meanwhile, Aldus

[3]George Stigler, "The Kinked Oligopoly Demand Curve and Rigid Prices," *Journal of Political Economy* 55 (October 1947), 432–449.

accepted thousands of orders from customers. Many of these customers might have bought QuarkXPress if they had known how long they would have to wait for PageMaker 5.0.

THE BERTRAND-EDGEWORTH DUOPOLY MODEL

There are many ways to change the basic Cournot model. One change is to drop the assumption that the other firm's output is held constant. A firm's output is the variable that is probably least likely to remain constant. French mathematician Joseph Bertrand suggested that a solution to the duopoly problem should be based on the assumption that the *price* charged by the other firm is constant. This approach is more in line with the price-taker assumption of perfect competition. English economist Francis Y. Edgeworth took up this suggestion and developed a new duopoly solution.

Assumptions of the Bertrand-Edgeworth Model

The Bertrand-Edgeworth model makes two changes in Cournot's original assumptions. The first assumption is that for very short time periods, two different prices for output may be quoted in the market.

The second assumption is that each duopolist selects the price that maximizes profit, and this price is selected on the assumption that the other duopolist continues to charge the same price even after the first firm sets a different price. In other words, Bertrand-Edgeworth assumes that firms use a Nash equilibrium strategy in *prices* instead of quantities.

Equilibrium in the Bertrand-Edgeworth Model

The Bertrand-Edgeworth assumptions imply that if the duopolists charge the *same* price for the product, they will divide the market equally. Alternatively, if one duopoly charges a price of P_{fixed} and the other duopolist charges a price *greater than* P_{fixed}, the higher-priced duopolist will not sell any output. Similarly, if the duopolist charges a price *less than* P_{fixed}, it will capture the entire market. Obviously, the optimal strategy is to undercut your competitor and capture the market as long as the price charged is greater than or equal to marginal cost. Profits are higher here than when the firm shares output equally or the firm sells nothing. Because both firms follow this strategy, the Bertrand-Edgeworth assumptions drive firms to set price equal to marginal cost and to share the market demand equally. In effect, the firms iterate to a perfectly competitive solution.

The Bertrand-Edgeworth model demonstrates that a seemingly simple change in the Cournot model—that is, that firms compete on the basis of price, not quantity—causes a significant change in market equilibrium. While the Cournot model led to a solution between monopoly and perfect competition, the Bertrand-Edgeworth model converges (probably quickly) to the competitive equilibrium at which price equals marginal cost.

$$$ Price Theory in Practice

FTC versus Ethyl, Du Pont, Nalco, and PPG

In the late 1970s, the Federal Trade Commission (FTC) brought suit against four makers of a chemical additive to leaded gasoline. The FTC charged these firms with conspiring to fix the price of the chemical additive, an activity it saw as an unreasonable restraint of trade. At issue were certain business practices prevalent among these firms. The firms consistently provided advance notice of price increases but not decreases, used most-favored-customer clauses, and stopped making public announcements of all their price changes.

The FTC charged that advance notice of only price increases helped firms collude. For example, if one firm did not choose to follow the lead of the firm announcing the higher price, there was time to communicate—by whatever means—this information to the other firms. The FTC also considered most-favored-customer clauses anticompetitive in this case. These clauses required firms to lower price for *all* customers if they made a *lower* offer to any one customer. Certainly, this activity would raise the cost of any selective price-cutting steps these firms might undertake.

In addition, the FTC was concerned about the cessation of public press announcements. Public announcements of price changes had been common practice in this industry. When they ceased, the FTC was troubled by the fact that the speed at which firms matched each other's price changes did not change. Thus, the FTC felt that there might be some implicit collusion among firms.

A further concern in this case was the lack of potential entrants to the industry. The concern was not that there were any traditional entry barriers but rather that the chemical additive faced a decreased demand in the future. In order to meet tougher pollution standards, leaded gasoline was being phased out of production and was not used in new automobiles. A new firm wanting to enter the industry would require a significant capital investment in equipment that would last for twenty or more years even though the lead additive business might disappear in less than ten years. Thus, existing firms had little concern that economic profits would attract entry.

The administrative judge at the FTC ruled against these firms, but the decision was overturned by the U.S. Second Court of Appeals.[4] The court found that many of these practices, such as most-favored-customer clauses, existed in other industries that are regarded as competitive, so there was no clear evidence that these firms behaved in an anticompetitive manner. Today, however, just as the FTC predicted, the lead-additive business is almost nonexistent.

Learning Exercise 13.6

Most-favored-customer clauses raise the cost of selective price-cutting activity, but is there a competitive (i.e., noncollusive) explanation for such clauses?

[4] *E. I. Du Pont de Nemours & Co. v. FTC*, 729 F. 2d 128 (2nd Cir., 1984).

THE MODEL OF PRICE LEADERSHIP

Among the various models of implicit collusion that have been presented to explain oligopolistic industries, one has had a relatively long life. This is the model of *price leadership*. In this model, and others that have been proposed, there is no formal or explicit cartel arrangement.

Behavior of the Dominant Firm

It is sometimes alleged that pricing in oligopolistic industries is controlled by a dominant firm, in other words, the largest or lowest-cost firm in the industry. The basic assumption is that the dominant firm sets the price and allows other firms to sell all they can at that price. The dominant firm then sells the rest. Given this assumption, a solution for market price and quantity can be derived.

The first thing we must do is derive the demand schedule for the dominant firm. This is done in Figure 13.9 on page 538. First, we draw the market demand schedule D_{market}. Then, we draw the supply schedule of all the smaller firms taken together. This is shown as S_{small}, which is the horizontal summation of the marginal cost curves of all of the smaller firms above their respective minimum average variable cost curves. To find the demand curve of the dominant firm, we need to find (1) a point at which all the smaller firms supply the entire market demand and the dominant firm supplies zero demand and (2) a point where the dominant firm supplies the entire market and the small firms supply zero. In what follows, we add a third point in between.

Look at price P_1. At price P_1, the small firms want to supply the total quantity that the market will purchase, or the quantity from the vertical axis to point E on the demand curve D_{market}. Remember that we assume the dominant firm sets the price and allows other firms to sell all they can at that price. If the dominant firm set the price at P_1 and followed this assumption, it would allow the small firms to supply everything, Q_1; the dominant firm would supply nothing at price P_1. *The price* P_1 *is therefore the* vertical *intercept of the dominant firm's demand curve.*

Now pick a price P_2 less than P_1. The smaller firms will provide output Q_{small}, the horizontal distance from the vertical axis to point A on the summed marginal cost curve. At price P_2, total quantity demanded is equal to Q_{total}, or the horizontal distance from the vertical axis to point C on the demand curve. We measure back from point C an amount equal to Q_{small} to find out how much is left over for the dominant firm. This gets us to point B. Thus, the dominant firm will supply output equal to $Q_{dominant}$, the horizontal distance from P_2 to point B.

Now we go to price P_3. At this price, the small firms will provide no output because their costs are too high. The dominant firm will provide the entire market, or the horizontal distance from the vertical axis to point F on the market demand curve. Thus, the dominant firm's demand curve is the thick, *kinked* demand curve that runs from the vertical axis at price P_1 through point B to point F and then along the market demand curve.

The dominant firm has the first move in the price leadership model. Given the first move, the dominant firm acts as a firm with market power. We can

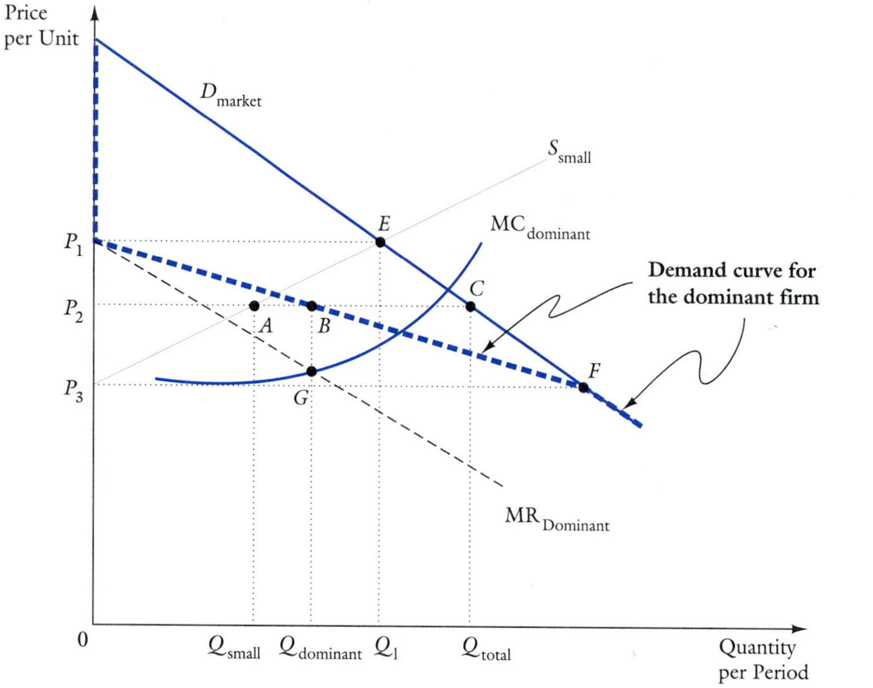

FIGURE 13.9

Price Leadership by a Dominant Firm

The market demand curve is D_{market} and the supply curve of all small firms is S_{small}. At a price of P_1, the small firms supply Q_1, which is exactly the quantity demanded by the market (point E). At prices below P_3, the small firms supply nothing, so the dominant firm provides any output supplied. Thus, the demand curve for the dominant firm equals zero for prices above P_1, equals the difference between D_{market} and S_{small} for prices between P_3 and P_1, and equals D_{market} for prices less than P_3. The dominant firm's optimal output rate, $Q_{dominant}$, is found from the intersection of its marginal cost, $MC_{dominant}$, and marginal revenue, $MR_{dominant}$, curves (point G). The dominant firm charges P_2 per unit. At this price, the small firms produce Q_{small} (point A) and the total quantity supplied is Q_{total} (point C).

now draw a marginal revenue curve for the dominant firm, $MR_{dominant}$. The marginal cost curve for the dominant firm is labeled $MC_{dominant}$. It intersects the dominant firm's marginal revenue curve, $MR_{dominant}$, at point G. The dominant firm's profit-maximizing rate of output is therefore given as $Q_{dominant}$. The profit-maximizing price set by the dominant firm will be P_2. The smaller firms, in the aggregate, will produce Q_{small}. At price P_2, total market demand is satisfied by the combined outputs $Q_{dominant}$ and Q_{small}. A price-quantity solution is obtained. It is stable because of our assumption that the small firms behave passively as price takers. In other words, small firms are eliminated from consideration as rivals in the usual sense of the term.

LEARNING EXERCISE 13.7

Suppose the market demand curve is given by $P = 100 - Q$, total supply of the "small" firms is $P = 25 + Q$, and the marginal cost of the price leader is constant and equal to \$25. Solve for the price leader's demand curve and equilibrium output rate.

Price Leadership and the Cost of Information

The main problem with the price leadership model is the information requirement it imposes on the leading firm.

Information about future demands for a commodity, future alternative sources of supply, future production costs, and future changes in technology is not free. Information is a scarce resource, and other resources must be expended to obtain it. The firm needs to know where to set output and price in order to maximize profits, and it is costly to obtain the information on which to base its decisions. Thus, we might predict that in some instances some firms would prefer to allow other firms to generate that information. Firms would like, if they could, to be free riders on the information obtained by other firms that would help them set their profit-maximizing prices.

What better way to be a free rider than to allow the dominant firm in the industry to do all the market research to determine the profit-maximizing price? It is possible that price leadership by a dominant firm has nothing to do with collusion or shared markets but rather reflects the fact that smaller firms allow the larger firm to spend all the resources necessary to obtain the information for setting a profit-maximizing price. Price leadership by a dominant firm can be couched within the theory of information and the problem of the free rider.

13.4 Game Theory

Game
A situation in which the interaction of firms or consumers affects decision making.

In the model of monopolistic competition and oligopoly, the reactions of other firms play an increasingly important role. When the reactions of other firms affect a given firm's decision, we say that the firms involved are playing a *game*. A **game** is a situation in which firms recognize the mutual interdependence of their actions. We can thus use models of game theory to describe the behavior of strategic firms. Game theory attempts to describe situations in which firms or individuals *rationally* interact while attempting to achieve their individual goals.[5] In fact, game theory is a formal approach to the problem a firm faces when it must consider how other profit-maximizing firms will react to its actions. Let's explore the basics of game theory.

[5]Game theory evolved from the classic book by John von Neumann and Oskar Morganstern, *The Theory of Games and Economic Behavior,* which was published in 1944 by Princeton University Press. For a more contemporary discussion of game theory, see Ken Binmore, *Fun and Games—A Text on Game Theory* (Boston: D. C. Heath & Company, 1992), or for a more advanced treatment see Roger Myerson, *Game Theory: Analysis of Conflict* (Cambridge: Harvard University Press, 1991).

COOPERATIVE AND NONCOOPERATIVE GAMES

The games that individuals or firms play are of two general types: noncooperative and cooperative. The standard cartel arrangement, for example, is cooperative. In a cartel, firms act in a coordinated manner to achieve a common goal—reduced industry output, a higher price for the product they produce, and higher profits. A **cooperative game** allows agreements between firms, which often is to act in a predetermined manner. In contrast, a **noncooperative game** arises when it is too costly to negotiate and enforce cooperative agreements. The ordinary interaction between retail dress outlets, for example, is noncooperative. There is no formal agreement between outlets to cooperate, so each outlet attempts to attract customers away from other outlets to maximize its profits. Most real-world games have both noncooperative and cooperative aspects, but we will focus on noncooperative games.

Cooperative Game
A situation in which firms collude or otherwise coordinate their actions.

Noncooperative Game
A situation in which firms do not collude or coordinate their actions; they act independently, but they know that their payoffs depend on the actions of other firms.

Negative-Sum, Zero-Sum, and Positive-Sum Games

Games may be classified by whether their total payoffs are negative, zero, or positive. A **negative-sum game** is one in which the players all lose or are worse off after the game is played than they were before it started. Firms or individuals that seek "revenge" often play negative-sum games. In the movie *Days of Thunder,* actor Tom Cruise played a stock car driver on the NASCAR racing circuit. In one scene, Cruise loses a race because another driver purposely bumps his car, which makes him lose control and spin out on the track. Seeking revenge, Cruise rams his car into the offending driver's car during the winner's victory lap, destroying both cars. Both drivers were made worse off in this negative-sum game. Mergers in which the firm to be acquired has a "poison pill" antitakeover provision in its bylaws may be a form of negative-sum game, too. When the firm is acquired, the poison pill provision is implemented, which generally causes a decrease in the value of the acquired firm's assets and hence causes the acquiring firm to lose part of its investment. Both firms lose in this game.

Negative-Sum Game
A game in which the players are worse off after the game is played.

One may ask why anyone would play a negative-sum game. The answer is often that another party to the game, one who may not play directly, can gain from the game. A poison pill contract may look like it supports existing management, but shareholders can change these provisions if they wish. The poison pill provision may act as a signal to takeover firms that the offer must be really good for it to be worth considering. In this respect, shareholders may hold out for higher offers because offers that are marginally above the current market price are not that beneficial when the costs of evaluating the offer are taken into consideration.

A **zero-sum game** is one in which one player's losses—if any—are exactly offset by other players' gains. The total gains in a zero-sum game are therefore zero. An ordinary bet or wager between friends is such a game, if we measure gains and losses solely in terms of money. Participants in futures markets play a zero-sum game. Once a futures contract has been purchased, the future price for delivery on a specific date is fixed. During the next hour, on the next day, or anytime before the delivery date, the *market* price of the contract may change. If the price increases, the buyer is made better off at the expense of

Zero-Sum Game
A game in which the gains and losses of players exactly offset each other.

the seller. In other words, what the buyer gains is offset by what the seller loses as the price rises. Equivalently, if the price falls, what the seller gains is offset by what the buyer loses.

Positive-Sum Game
A game in which participants gain from playing.

A **positive-sum game** is one in which both players are better off after the game than they were before the game. A voluntary exchange between individuals and firms is such a game if we measure gains in terms of consumers' and producers' surpluses. In fact, positive-sum games are the basis for all voluntary transactions in competitive markets, except those that are at the margin. When consumers actually purchase goods at a fixed price per unit, consumers' surplus is realized and firms gain profits, which may be positive in the short run. Without such transactions, neither firms nor consumers realize any gains.

Although it might seem that positive-sum games are cooperative and zero-sum games are noncooperative, that is not strictly true. Even with positive-sum games, there can still be competition over the division of the gains as long as each player ends up better off than he or she was before the game began. When you go to purchase a new car, you will probably bargain on price. The bargaining itself is noncooperative because a lower price gives you more consumers' surplus but reduces the dealer's profits. Without some actual agreement, however, neither you nor the dealer realize any surplus, so you have an incentive to cooperate at some point in the bargaining process.

It is also important to note that few real-world situations correspond exactly to one of the above types of games. Often a real-world situation involves several different games running simultaneously, or it has the potential to change from one type of game to another.

The Payoff Matrix for a Game with Two Choices

Payoff Matrix
A chart that summarizes the gains and losses for all participants' actions.

It is conventional to represent the alternative outcomes in a simple game situation in a diagram called a **payoff matrix.** A payoff matrix shows the gain or loss to each player for each choice made by that player and by other players. Suppose we consider the problem faced by General George B. McClellan, commander of the Union forces, and General Robert E. Lee, commander of the Army of Northern Virginia, during the battle at Antietam, Maryland. This was an important battle during the Civil War; many historians believe that aggressive action on the part of McClellan could have lead to a swift end to the war. To keep things simple, let's assume that both commanders are considering the probable loss in lives from the actions that they take. Neither commander wants to be responsible for a massive loss of lives within his own army. To set the stage, assume that the battle has raged for two and one-half days and that the losses on both sides are heavy.[6] McClellan is considering two options: either continue the advance on Lee's position or hold the ground and await reinforcements. Lee is also considering two options: retreat across the Potomac River back into Virginia and carry on the fight there or hold

[6]In this battle, there were 12,410 Union casualties and 13,724 Confederate casualities.

General Robert E. Lee \ General George B. McClellan	Advance the Battle	Hold Ground and Await Reinforcements
Retreat Across the Potomac River	21,000 / 16,000 (Cell 1)	14,500 / 12,500 (Cell 2)
Hold Ground and Await Reinforcements	28,000 / 18,000 (Cell 3)	19,000 / 15,000 (Cell 4)

Confederate Casualties / Union Casualties

The amounts shown are the *expected* number of casualties given the strategies chosen.

FIGURE 13.10

The Payoff Matrix at the Battle of Antietam, Maryland, September 1862

The payoff matrix shows the interdependence of each general's decision. If General Lee decides to retreat across the Potomac, for example, the expected number of casualties to Lee's troops will be 21,000 or 14,500 depending on what action General McClellan takes. Similarly, General McClellan's casualties are affected by the action General Lee takes.

the ground until reinforcements arrive and then try to win a battle in a northern state.[7] The payoff matrix for this game is shown in Figure 13.10.

In Figure 13.10, the choices considered by General Lee are listed on the left-hand side of the payoff matrix and the choices considered by General McClellan are listed across the top of the payoff matrix. The four cells of the matrix represent the payoffs from the choices made by *both* commanders. Each cell shows two numbers. The number at the top of each cell is the expected number of casualties in the Confederate army, and the number at the bottom of each cell is the expected number of casualties in the Union army. In cell 1, for example, McClellan chooses to advance the battle and Lee chooses to retreat across the Potomac River. The outcome, or payoff, is that Lee has 21,000 casualties and McClellan has 16,000 casualties. Alternatively, if McClellan chooses to hold ground

[7]It was important that the Confederate army win a major battle in a northern state because European banks, which were lending money to the Confederate government, needed reassurance that their investments might bring a positive return. If the Confederacy could not win in the northern states, it stood little chance of winning a negotiated peace with the North.

and await reinforcements *and* Lee chooses the same strategy, then the payoff, shown in cell 4, is 19,000 casualties for the Confederate army and 15,000 casualties for the Union army.

The point of this example is to show you that the payoffs depend on the actions chosen by *all* parties. The payoff matrix is a simple way of showing such interaction.[8] The payoff matrix, however, does not tell us what the commanders should do; it only shows the consequences of their decisions. We do not know what the *best* choice is for either the offense or the defense without knowing the decision strategy of each commander, so let's consider some strategies that game participants can adopt.

LEARNING EXERCISE 13.8

Draw a payoff matrix in which General McClellan has a choice of three options but General Lee continues with only two options.

DOMINANT STRATEGIES IN NONCOOPERATIVE GAMES

A *strategy* is a rule that game participants can use to make a choice. In a football game, for example, one strategy an offensive coach can follow is to try for a touchdown on every play. If this occurs, the defensive coach can choose to defend against the deep pass on every play. If the strategy of the defensive coach is to prevent a touchdown on every play, then the offensive coach has a problem because his strategy is too simple. The defensive coach can always prevent a touchdown by using a deep-coverage formation on every play. Alternatively, the offensive coach may adopt a strategy of choosing plays randomly—say, 50 percent are pass plays and 50 percent are running plays—in an attempt to fool the defensive coach and actually score some touchdowns.

Obviously, there are many possible strategies that can be adopted by football coaches, and this is also true for firms and individuals involved in game situations. Some strategies may be better than others in that they offer higher payoffs to players who adopt them. Some strategies may be successful for certain actions that competitors take but not for others. It is possible, however, that some strategies may be successful *no matter what actions competitors take.* A strategy that is better no matter what decision another player makes is called a **dominant strategy.** A payoff matrix in which a dominant strategy is optimal is shown in Figure 13.11 on page 544.

Dominant Strategy
A choice that is optimal in a noncooperative game, no matter what other firms do.

Figure 13.11 shows the payoff matrix for a choice between cover pictures by *Time* and *Newsweek* magazines. Late in 1992, both Russian President Boris Yeltsin and the AIDS epidemic were in the news. These magazines had to decide which story to feature on their cover pages. The payoff for each choice is in terms of weekly magazine sales. If both *Time* and *Newsweek* feature Boris

[8]Games are represented in their *normal form* (also called the *strategic form*) by payoff matrices. An alternative and equivalent approach is to draw a decision tree that shows all the possible actions each participant can take. Games are represented in *extensive form* by decision trees. For an introduction to decision trees, see Scott Bierman and Luis Fernandez, *Game Theory with Economic Applications,* New York: Addison-Wesley, 1993.

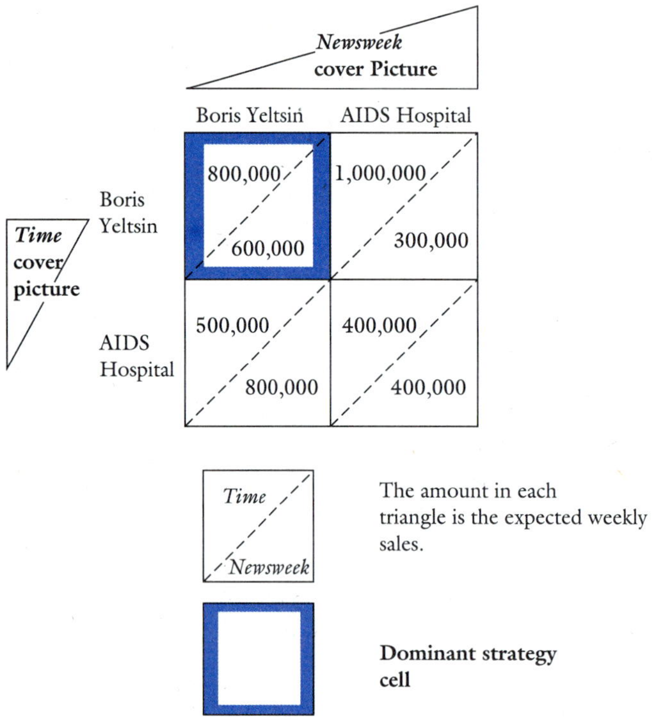

FIGURE 13.11

The Case of a Dominant Strategy

The decision to run Boris Yeltsin or an AIDS hospital as the cover story for either *Time* or *Newsweek* affects each other's magazine sales. A dominant strategy arises with one choice—in this case Boris Yeltsin—and dominates all other choices *Time* and *Newsweek* could make.

Yeltsin on their covers, then *Time*'s sales amount to 800,000 magazines and *Newsweek*'s to 600,000 magazines. Alternatively, if *Newsweek* features an AIDS hospital on its cover, then *Time*'s sales jump to 1 million magazines and *Newsweek*'s sales drop to 300,000 magazines. The remaining payoff cells are interpreted similarly.

A particular choice *dominates* the other choice for both magazine companies in this problem. *Time* should put Boris Yeltsin on its cover no matter what *Newsweek* does. *Time*'s sales are either 1 million (if *Newsweek* runs the AIDS hospital) or 800,000 (if *Newsweek* runs Yeltsin), which exceed its sales if it runs the AIDS hospital on the cover, regardless of *Newsweek*'s cover picture. *Newsweek* should run Yeltsin on its cover, too. *Newsweek*'s sales with Yeltsin on the cover are 600,000 (if *Time* also runs Yeltsin) or 800,000 (if *Time* runs the AIDS hospital). In both cases, *Newsweek*'s sales exceed its sales from placing the AIDS hospital on the cover, regardless of what *Time* puts on its cover.

Thus, each magazine will run a cover photo of Boris Yeltsin, which is the dominant strategy for this game.

LEARNING EXERCISE 13.9

Suppose the payoff to *Newsweek* is 350,000 magazine sales if it runs the Boris Yeltsin story and *Time* runs the AIDS story. Is there a dominant strategy for this new payoff matrix?

THE NASH EQUILIBRIUM CONCEPT

Because sales were higher with Boris Yeltsin on the cover of *both* magazines, the game in Figure 13.11 had a solution, or equilibrium, in which the choices of both participants were not subject to change *even if they knew their competitor's cover choice before they chose their cover.* In other words, neither *Time* nor *Newsweek* would change its mind if it knew what was on the other's cover before it made its decision. But not every game has a dominant-strategy solution. In some cases, participants would rather change their minds if they knew their opponent's choice. In such situations, the approach suggested by John Nash in 1950 is often used to find a solution.[9]

The *Nash equilibrium* concept requires that each participant choose an action that is best *given the opponents' actions.* This approach is different from a dominant strategy because a dominant strategy arises when a player can select the best action *regardless of the opponents' actions.* In Figure 13.12, on page 546, we have changed the payoff matrix for *Time* and *Newsweek* to illustrate the Nash equilibrium concept.

The new payoffs in Figure 13.12 complicate the choice problem for *Time* and *Newsweek.* Now, the optimal cover choice for *Time* depends on the choice made by *Newsweek.* If *Newsweek* chooses to run Boris Yeltsin on the cover, then *Time* should run the AIDS hospital story on the cover (1 million sales versus 500,000 sales). But if *Newsweek* runs the AIDS hospital, then *Time* should run the Boris Yeltsin story (800,000 sales versus 600,000 sales). The same problem arises for *Newsweek.* If *Time* runs the Yeltsin story on the cover, then *Newsweek* should run the AIDS hospital story (600,000 versus 500,000). Alternatively, if *Time* runs the AIDS hospital story on the cover, then *Newsweek* should run the Yeltsin story (650,000 sales versus 400,000 sales).

The Nash equilibrium concept offers a solution to the problem faced by *Time* and *Newsweek,* but it is not a *unique* solution. *Time* can run the AIDS hospital story and *Newsweek* can run the Boris Yeltsin story, *or Time* can run the Yeltsin story and *Newsweek* can run the AIDS hospital story. Each of these solutions is self-confirming; that is, *Time* makes the optimal choice given *Newsweek*'s choice and *Newsweek* makes the optimal choice given *Time*'s choice, and *Newsweek*'s optimal choice is what *Time* assumed it would be and *Time*'s choice is what *Newsweek* assumed it would be. The problem is that we do not know exactly what these magazines will do. The Nash equilibrium con-

[9] John Nash, "The Bargaining Problem," *Econometrica* 18 (1950), 155–162.

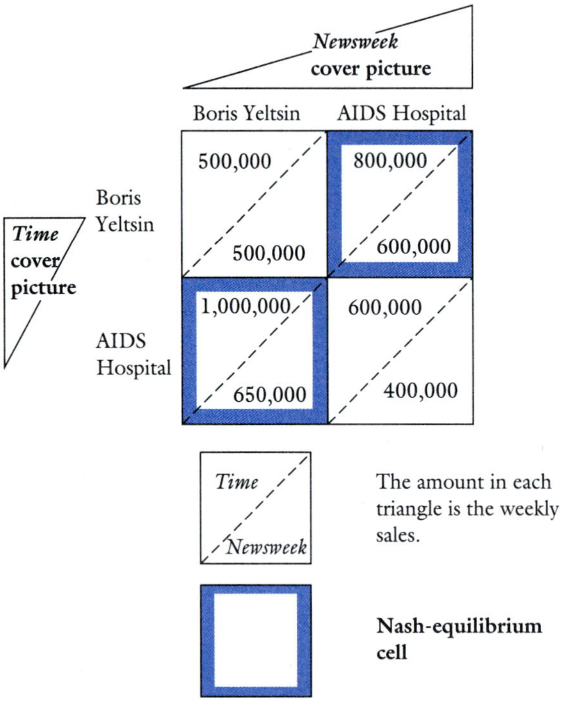

FIGURE 13.12

A Pair of Nash Equilibrium Strategies

A Nash equilibrium strategy implies that *Time* and *Newsweek* can eliminate some choices that both firms might make, but because there are two Nash equilibrium cells, the actual choice or action is difficult to predict.

cept has identified two cells in Figure 13.12 as possible solutions and has eliminated two other cells, but it has not identified which of the two optimal cells is chosen.

A First-Move Solution

One way to resolve the problem of multiple Nash equilibria is to allow one party the first move. Given this move, the other party is expected to choose an optimal response. Suppose *Time* makes the first move. *Time* will want to run the AIDS hospital story on its cover because this action maximizes its sales given that *Newsweek* is using a Nash equilibrium strategy. To tell *Newsweek, Time* may "accidentally" send a fax of its cover page to *Newsweek* while it is still in layout form. If *Newsweek* believes that *Time* is really planning to run the AIDS hospital story, then it is optimal for it to run Boris Yeltsin on its cover.

For the payoff matrix in Figure 13.12, it actually does not matter who goes first because the solution will be the same. In some games, however, the solution changes depending on who has the first move. Because of

this, the firm that moves first has an advantage, so it is difficult to agree ahead of time on which firm will have the first move.

The first-move advantage may be particularly important when firms introduce new products to a market. The firm that is the first to advertise and to supply customers may be likely to retain these customers over time and gain some market power. As a result, coordinating who goes first may be nearly impossible. Computer software and hardware companies, for example, have become notorious for trying to use first-move strategies to their advantage. All the major computer companies, such as IBM, Apple, Compaq, Dell, and DEC, have participated in the game of preannouncing "vaporware"—products that will not be ready for delivery for several months. The idea is to preempt the sales of rival products with such announcements. These announcements did harm to some companies—for example, IBM and its OS/2 software product—because they could not deliver the product on time. Customers lost interest and companies lost significant credibility.

LEARNING EXERCISE 13.10

Suppose *Newsweek*'s sales are 600,000 if it runs Boris Yeltsin and *Time* runs the AIDS story. Find the first-move solution for each firm.

A "Cheap Talk" Solution

The problem faced by *Time* and *Newsweek* arises because we have assumed that they are playing a *noncooperative* game with multiple solutions. If there is a way for them to communicate with each other—that is, cooperate—then they may find a way to select between the multiple Nash equilibrium solutions shown in Figure 13.12. When such communication takes place in noncooperative games, it is called **cheap talk.** Cheap talk is presumed to be costless because it does not commit either side to a given action; its purpose is to inform both parties of each other's reasoning. *Time* or *Newsweek* may communicate that it is considering only two possible cells (outcomes), that is, the Nash equilibrium cells. This information reveals that a Nash equilibrium strategy is being used, but it is not yet enough to solve the problem of choice each side faces.

Cheap Talk
Costless communication of information to firms in a noncooperative game.

With the knowledge that each side is considering Nash equilibrium strategies, the magazines can use cheap talk to identify a possible solution. In Figure 13.12, *Time* sells 1 million magazines when it runs the AIDS hospital and Newsweek runs Yeltsin. This is the *absolute* best that *Time* can do in this game. *Newsweek* sells 650,000 magazines when it runs Yeltsin on the cover and *Time* runs the AIDS hospital story. This is the *absolute* best that *Newsweek* can do in this game. Additional cheap talk between *Time* and *Newsweek* can be helpful to inform each other of the absolute best outcome for each magazine. With this information, it is likely that both parties will agree that *Time* should run the AIDS hospital story and that *Newsweek* should run the Yeltsin story.

Mixed Strategies

The Nash equilibria for the *Time* and *Newsweek* game both are called **pure strategies.** In pure strategies, once a choice has been made, each company sticks to its decision. But not every game lends itself to a pure strategy solution. Consider the game of rock, paper, and scissors, which is often played by children as a game of elimination. In this game, a closed fist is a rock, an open hand is paper, and two fingers extended are scissors. The rules are that paper covers rock, scissors cut paper, and a rock smashes scissors. If two people are playing the game and one shows scissors while the other shows paper, the one who shows paper is eliminated. Similarly, if one shows scissors and the other shows rock, the one who shows scissors is eliminated.

Pure Strategy
The choice of a single, unchanging action in a noncooperative game.

A *pure strategy* in the game of rock, paper, and scissors would be to always show the same item, such as always show a rock. This would be a very bad strategy because the other player can always show paper, which eliminates the one who shows the rock. In fact, there is no pure-strategy Nash equilibrium for this game because any one item can be dominated by another item. The

Mixed Strategy Choosing to alternate between actions according to some probability measure.

only Nash equilibrium to this game is a **mixed strategy.** A mixed strategy implies that players randomize their actions; that is, they choose an optimal probability for each action and randomly switch between actions based on these probabilities. In the rock, paper, and scissors game, the optimal probability is for players to choose paper one-third of the time, scissors one-third of the time, and rock one-third of the time. At any given point, then, opponents will not know what a given player is planning to show.

Mixed strategies are particularly useful for firms that desire to keep their competitors guessing about their *true* strategy. Some brokerage firms, for example, use mixed strategies when they trade commodities. In commodities trading, firms are identified by the jackets and badges its employees wear on the trading floor. Members of particularly successful firms are watched carefully by other traders, who want to "free ride" on their success. To disguise whether they are net buyers or net sellers, firms may execute several random trades. If the firm desires to be a net buyer, for example, it might sell a fixed amount of a commodity 40 percent of the time and buy the same amount 60 percent of the time. These firms execute such strategies through several brokers, so other traders have a very difficult time figuring out what they are doing.

A Tit-for-Tat Strategy

Tit-for-Tat Strategy Choosing a cooperative solution as long as other firms cooperate.

Mixed strategies are feasible if a game is *repeated* over time. Repetition is required so that participants can fully randomize their actions. With repeated games, however, there is the distinct possibility that participants will adopt a **tit-for-tat strategy.** In a tit-for-tat strategy, each participant cooperates with the other players so long as the other players choose actions that are not harmful to them. Two airline companies that compete for customers on the Atlanta-to-Denver route might adopt a tit-for-tat pricing strategy. One airline—it does not matter which one—might announce a high price for tickets on this route. If the other airline adopts a tit-for-tat strategy, it will cooperate and announce a high price, too. The ticket price on the Atlanta-to-Denver route will remain high for as long as both airlines leave well enough alone. As soon as one airline lowers price in an attempt to increase air travel on its planes, the other airline will match the lower price. Thus, any potentially harmful actions of one firm will be matched by the other firm under a tit-for-tat strategy.

The tit-for-tat strategy is not a Nash equilibrium strategy, but it does appear to dominate the Nash equilibrium and many other strategies for repeated games. In a cleverly designed and cleverly executed experiment, Robert Axelrod of the University of Michigan found that a tit-for-tat strategy dominates all other strategies.[10] Axelrod asked participants to submit strategies to solve a repeated version of the Prisoner's Dilemma game (discussed below). After 200 iterations of the game, the tit-for-tat strategy emerged above all other strategies by a significant margin. Other experiments by Axelrod have confirmed his initial findings.

What is interesting about Axelrod's results is that they imply that the *backward reasoning* of repeated games may not be as helpful as one might first

[10]Robert Axelrod, *The Evolution of Cooperation,* New York: Basic Books, 1984.

think. With backward reasoning, a participant looks ahead to the next or any future period and asks, "What is an optimal strategy in this period?" Once this strategy has been selected, the participant goes back one period and answers the same question. Once the strategy is selected for this period, the participant goes back another period and repeats the exercise. Eventually, the participant gets back to the present period and selects a strategy for this period, which is optimal given that the strategies for all future periods have been selected optimally.

One implication of backward reasoning is that players may not make reputation investments if they are worthless in the last period of the game. A player's reputation—say, for sticking consistently to one action, such as charging a high airfare on the Atlanta-to-Denver route—is worthless in the last period if cheating on the agreement is costless. By lowering price in the last period of the game, for example, one airline can gain customers and profits at the expense of the other airline. Now, if reputation investments are worthless in the last period, backward reasoning implies that they are worthless in the next-to-last period, and so on, all the way back to the present period. A tit-for-tat strategy implies a reputation for consistent behavior. But if the game will end sometime in the future, then backward reasoning implies that a tit-for-tat strategy is not optimal. Players will cheat in the last period; that is, they will do something to make themselves better off at the expense of the other players. So, backward reasoning would suggest a tit-for-tat strategy cannot be maintained. Nonetheless, the tit-for-tat strategy was a preferred strategy in the repeated-game experiments conducted by Axelrod, which suggests that cooperation in seemingly noncooperative situations may occur more often than one might think.

$$$ Price Theory in Practice

Do Airlines Play a Tit-for-Tat Game?

What airfares would you try to charge if you ran a domestic airline? How would you react when a competitor announced a fare increase? How would you react to a fare decrease? Would you react at all? If you don't react, you are not playing the game the way that U.S. airlines play it. Domestic airlines typically match *both* fare decreases *and* fare increases announced by other airlines, or at least they announce that they plan to match these changes (often they fail to implement fare increases). This behavior is similar to a tit-for-tat strategy. Let's look at the behavior of the domestic airline industry during the six months between December 1991 and May 1992.

Table 13.1 shows that both cooperation and competition exist among the major airlines. On December 10, 1991, Continental Airlines announced a $20 increase in round-trip airfares, which was matched by United Airlines two days later. All the major carriers went along with this fare increase. Then United Airlines announced an across-the-board 2 percent increase, which the other major carriers adopted on January 3, 1992. A subsequent increase of 2 percent failed to gain support and was adopted only for excursion fares. On March 9, 1992, American lowered fares for international travel, which set off a chain reaction of fare reductions. The price cutting reached a peak on May 28, 1992, when American effectively cut its prices in half for summer travel. Consumers responded quickly. Nearly every major carrier sold out its allocation of discount seats in seven days.

Do the airlines follow a tit-for-tat strategy? Certainly there is a strong element of a tit-for-tat strategy in their behavior, but it is not fully symmetric between price increases and price decreases. As a group, the major carriers will match fare decreases more often than they will match fare increases. Matching fare decreases is probably noncooperative behavior in this industry. But because they will match *some* fare increases, the airlines are not totally noncooperative. The mixture of cooperative and noncooperative behavior suggests that a tit-for-tat strategy does not completely explain the behavior of the airline industry.

TABLE 13.1

News Announcements by Domestic Airlines, December 1991 to June 1992

Date	Airline	Action	Announcement/Competitors' Response
Dec. 10, 1991	Continental	Increase	*Effective December 19:* Increases restricted round-trip fares by $20; eliminates 15 percent discounts on one-way advance purchase tickets. No immediate response by competitors.
Dec. 13, 1991	United	Match	*Effective December 19:* United matches Continental's $20 fare increase but does not eliminate advance purchase discounts.
Dec. 19, 1991	General		All major airlines increase fares on restricted tickets by $20.
Dec. 25, 1991	United	Increase	*Effective January 3:* Increases domestic airfares by 2 percent. Northwest, American, and Alaska Airlines match United's fare increases.
Jan. 3, 1992	General		All major airlines increase fares 2 percent.
Feb. 20, 1992	United	Increase	*Effective March 3:* Increases domestic airfares by 2 percent. USAir and Alaska Airlines match United's fare increases.
Feb. 26, 1992	Northwest	Match	Northwest matches United's 2 percent fare increase only on full-price tickets.
Feb. 29, 1992	Delta	Match	Delta adopts a 2 percent fare increase only on excursion tickets, not on business tickets.
Mar. 3, 1992	United	Revision	*Effective March 6:* United raises excursion fares by 2 percent; United drops plans to raise fares by 2 percent across the board. Delta and American airlines match United's limited fare increases.
Mar. 9, 1992	American	Decrease	American offers two-for-one tickets to buyers who pay full fare on many of its international flights. Northwest and Delta match American's offer immediately.
Mar. 11, 1992	Northwest	Decrease	Northwest revives 30-day advance purchase fares, which offer discounts of about 10 percent on most routes. American, Delta, United, and USAir match the offer immediately.

TABLE 13.1

News Announcements by Domestic Airlines, December 1991 to June 1992 (continued)

Date	Airline	Action	Announcement/Competitors' Response
Mar. 13, 1992	General	Revision	The plan by major airlines to raise excursion fares by 2 percent is rescinded.
Apr. 10, 1992	American	Decrease	American announces a broad overhaul of airfares. Current coach fares will fall an average of 38 percent and first-class fares will fall between 20 to 50 percent, but some discount fares will rise. All major carriers match the new fare structure.
Apr. 13, 1992	TWA	Decrease	TWA lowers fares to remain 35 to 40 percent cheaper than its rivals after American's new fares are implemented.
Apr. 14, 1992	Continental	Decrease	Continental announces excursion fares between Florida and the Northeast and parts of the Midwest that are 20 percent less than American's new fares. USAir announces similar fare reductions.
Apr. 21, 1992	American	Decrease	American reduces coach and discount fares on many routes and changes its advance purchase requirement from 21 to 14 days. United matches these changes immediately.
May 27, 1992	Northwest	Decrease	Northwest introduces a two-for-one leisure fare on all domestic flights except those between Alaska and Hawaii. The new fare allows an adult and a child to fly for the price of an adult ticket. Northwest also shortens the advance purchase requirement from 14 to 7 days for family travel.
May 28, 1992	American	Match	*Effective May 29:* American matches Northwest's two-for-one discount and extends it to all ticket purchases, not just adult-and-child tickets. The offer expires on June 5. All major carriers match American's discount plan.

Source: The New York Times, selected issues, December 1991 to May 1992.

LEARNING EXERCISE 13.11

Explain how the behavior of the airline industry is similar, but not identical, to the behavior predicted by the kinked demand curve model.

FOUR STEPS TO REMEMBER IN A GAME

Game theorists have identified four steps that participants should generally follow when confronted with a game, that is, when they find that their payoffs depend on the actions of others. We will discuss these steps in the order in which a participant should consider them.[11]

[11]A modified version of these four steps has been suggested by Avinash Dixit and Barry Nalebuff, *Thinking Strategically: The Competitive Edge in Business, Politics, and Everyday Life,* New York: Norton, 1991.

1. Look Ahead, Then Reason Back, But Don't Rule Out a Tit-for-Tat Strategy

For repeated games or games that involve a sequence of moves, or choices, players should look to the *end* of the game and ask what action is optimal in the last period, then use backward reasoning to find the action that is optimal now. After having analyzed the game in this manner, players should ask what the payoff would be if all players followed a tit-for-tat strategy. If a tit-for-tat strategy offers higher payoffs, players should use a little "cheap talk" to inform the other players of this result. The reactions of the other players—enthusiastic or skeptical—may indicate how to proceed.

2. If You Have a Dominant Strategy, Use It If You Don't Cooperate

Dominant strategies, for lack of a better word, dominate other strategies. If you can find a dominant strategy, such as we found in Figure 13.11, then use it if you cannot cooperate with the other participants.

3. Try to Eliminate Some Possible Choices

In the *Time* and *Newsweek* game, there were only two possible choices for the cover picture: Boris Yeltsin or an AIDS hospital. But there may be many more choices in an actual game. *Time* and *Newsweek,* for example, may confront three or four big stories in a given week. Choosing between these stories is a more complicated game, but one way to proceed is to try to *eliminate* some particular actions. Suppose that a story on the elections to Congress is also newsworthy, and the magazines could run a picture of Capitol Hill on their covers. If either *Time* or *Newsweek* finds that such a story offers *lower* sales, regardless of what picture the other magazine runs, then the Capitol Hill story can be eliminated from consideration—it is dominated by either Boris Yeltsin or the AIDS hospital stories. Thus, to simplify a game, players should eliminate any actions that are dominated by the other remaining choices.

4. If You Don't Find a Dominant Strategy, Consider a Nash Equilibrium

As you can see from Figure 13.12, on page 516, not every game has a dominant strategy, so players must consider other ways to make a choice. The Nash equilibrium concept is one method of narrowing down the possible choices. In Figure 13.12, the Nash equilibrium concept eliminates two of the four cells. Obviously, you are still stuck with the problem of which of the two remaining cells to choose, but "cheap talk" or a first-move agreement may help resolve this problem. Thus, players can use the Nash equilibrium concept to simplify a game that does not have any dominant strategies.

A FINAL THOUGHT ABOUT GAME THEORY

To many economists, game theory is like a solar-powered car: they think that it may be the vehicle of the future in economics. These economists believe that advances in the understanding of markets are likely to evolve from models of game theory. Certainly, much of our understanding of bargaining behavior and auctions owes its roots to game theory. To other economists, however, game theory is a frustrating method of analysis because it does not provide *unique* solutions to many games. We hope this result is clear from the above discussion. The equilibrium analysis offered by the intersection of supply and demand curves is more appealing because it leaves little doubt about where both market price and quantity are heading. In spite of the frustrating nature of game theory, its continued development will surely add to the four steps outlined above and improve our understanding of the behavior of individuals and firms.

$$$ Price Theory in Practice

The Prisoner's Dilemma

The classic example of a game is the so-called prisoner's dilemma. The prisoner's dilemma exists whenever there are gains to be realized by cooperation between participants yet a given participant can realize even greater gains by cheating on the cooperative arrangement while *all* other participants continue to abide by it. The name *prisoner's dilemma* is used because prisoners are often confronted by such a game.

Suppose that Sam and Carlos have been arrested for allegedly importing illegal drugs into the United States. After the arrest, the local district attorney meets with each suspect separately. The district attorney explains the case against them and outlines their likely punishment. The details of these two conversations are summarized in Figure 13.13.

As Figure 13.13 shows, Sam and Carlos are going to jail no matter what either of them does. The lengths of their jail terms, however, depend on each other's actions. If they both confess, they each receive six years. If they do not confess, they each receive three years. If only one of them confesses, that person receives two years and the other person receives fifteen years. Obviously, with these jail sentences, there is an incentive to cheat if they had agreed beforehand not to confess. But because they are both better off if they do not confess, they face the prisoner's dilemma: do they confess for a lower sentence at the other person's expense? Both players realize this dilemma, so they both confess and spend six years in jail. In fact, the *dominant* strategy in this game is for both Sam and Carlos to confess.

The prisoner's dilemma illustrates that cooperation is better than a noncooperative dominant strategy. The problem that Sam and Carlos face is one of monitoring and enforcing a cooperative solution, which is no different from the problem a cartel faces when its members agree to reduce output. Cartel members know that individually they can gain by cheating, that is, by increasing output above their individual quota. The problem that the cartel and prisoners face is how to convincingly precommit to a particular behavior. With prisoners, it is difficult to be convincing, but firms may make investments in specific assets, which were discussed in Chapter 7, to convince others of their intentions.

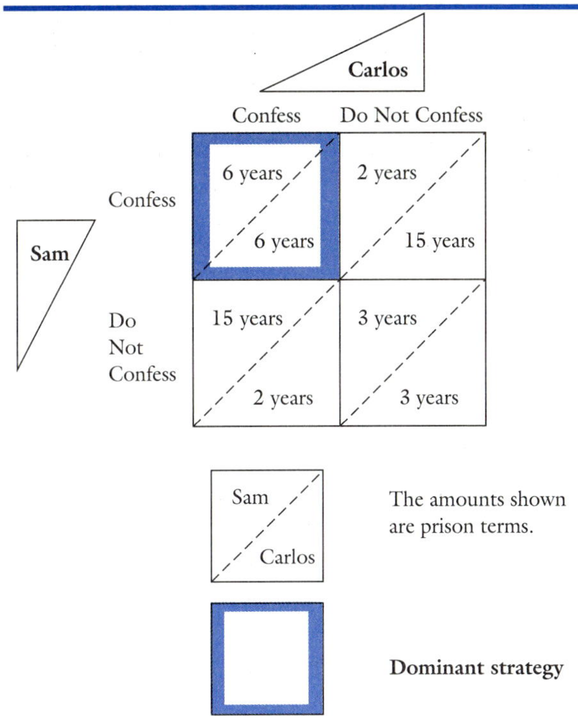

FIGURE 13.13

The Prisoner's Dilemma

The prisoner's dilemma game shows that prisoners can be placed in an environment in which they have incentive to confess. Given the prison sentences if one confesses and the other does not, a dominant strategy is for both Sam and Carlos to confess to their crimes.

LEARNING EXERCISE 13.12

How do a prisoner's age and life expectancy affect his or her incentive to cheat? Suppose that Sam is expected to live for only two more years and Carlos knows this. What is the likely outcome of the game?

13.5 ENTRY DETERRENCE

Existing firms have an incentive to try to prevent entry by new firms, which eliminates economic profits. To the extent that they cooperate with each other in this activity, the market structure is expected to be less than competitive. Obviously, enlisting the aid of local, state, and federal government entities is one possible approach, but it is not usually successful. Instead, existing firms can adopt pricing and investment strategies that *may* deter entry. Let's consider how such strategies are supposed to work.

LIMIT PRICING STRATEGIES

Limit pricing strategies were first formulated in the 1950s. With limit pricing, existing firms signal to a potential entrant that they will not change their output rate after entry. The entering firm, then, must realize that entry will *lower* the market price. The strategy of the existing firms is to charge an above-competitive price, but one that is not so high as to make entry profitable. That is, the limit price is below the point at which the new firm can enter the market, sell its output at the new lower price, and make a profit.

Limit Pricing
The practice of setting a price above marginal cost to deter new entry.

Suppose, for example, that the price elasticity of demand equals –2 at the existing market price of $10. If a new firm enters, causing supply to increase by 5 percent, then the new market price will fall by 10 percent (–2 × 5 percent) to $9. If the average total cost of production for all firms (including the new entrant) is $9.50, then *everyone* is losing money at the new price. But the potential entrant can reason through this scenario prior to entering and will not enter the market. The price will remain at $10 and all firms will earn economic profits of $.50 per unit ($10 – $9.50).

There is one basic problem with a limit pricing strategy. Limit pricing presumes that the new entrant believes the existing firms will *not* change their output rates. But why should a new entrant believe this? If the existing firms begin to lose money at the new price of $9, they may lower their output rates in order to lower total costs. Thus, they may be expected to *make room* for the new entrant. If this is the case, limit pricing will not act as an entry deterrent.

STRATEGY OF RAISING ENTRY COSTS

Another strategy existing firms may adopt to deter entry is to try to raise the costs faced by a new firm. There may be many ways that such a strategy can be implemented. For instance, if new entrants use a different production technology than existing firms, it may pay for existing firms to try to increase certain factor costs. Many foreign competitors, for example, use more labor in the production of goods. Domestic firms may lobby for "fair" import duties on these goods. These import duties (taxes) may be set so as to compensate for the difference in wage rates between foreign and domestic firms. Foreign firms that use less costly labor are adversely affected, which reduces their incentive to enter the domestic market.

Existing firms sometimes raise the costs of entry by threatening to start a price war if entry occurs. Lower prices reduce profits and thereby discourage entry, but such a threat must be credible. For credibility, existing firms may invest immediately in the extra capacity needed to expand output during a price war. Capacity investments often have a large *sunk cost* component, so by making such investments existing firms are sending a signal that they *will* launch a price war. Obviously, capacity investments are costly, but if they deter entry, existing firms may earn a return in the form of economic profits.

STRATEGY OF RAISING CUSTOMERS' SWITCHING COSTS

Existing firms can try to make it costly for customers to switch to a new entrant. After the separation of the Baby Bells from AT&T, for example, AT&T fought against allowing any competitors simple access to long-distance lines by dialing 1 before the area code and phone number. MCI, Sprint, and other companies had to tell customers to dial a local seven-digit number to gain access to their long-distance lines. Imagine how costly this is for customers of these other companies. AT&T lost this battle, but you can clearly see that its purpose was to raise the cost of switching to a competing company.

Some computer companies use the strategy of raising switching costs. Xerox Corporation and Sun Microsystems produce proprietary computers and accompanying software that generally will not run on competitors' computers. Customers who consider switching face a large investment in retraining as a result.

Colleges and universities sometimes use a high-switching-cost strategy. First-year students find that some of the courses they take are transferrable to other schools, but many are not. Nontransferrable courses must be repeated if the student switches to another school. As the costs of switching schools increases, the likelihood that a student will not switch increases. The strategy of increased costs of switching can be effective only when it is not anticipated ahead of the purchase commitment. Students who are caught off guard are affected by this strategy, but those who anticipate this action can rearrange their schedules or negotiate for scholarships to help lower the switching costs. Generally, then, it is a lack of information that makes this strategy successful.

WHERE ARE WE IN THE THEORY OF OLIGOPOLY?

If you found this chapter to be analytically somewhat less conclusive than the chapters on competition and monopoly, you are not alone. Generally, we find that most oligopolisitic models predict that the market equilibrium will be allocatively inefficient relative to the perfectly competitive market. The exception is the Bertrand-Edgeworth model. Beyond this, however, it is less clear which model is likely to arise in a given market. As noted above, there are many possibilities.

The theory of oligopoly and monopolistic competition is the most perplexing of the models of industrial structure. It is particularly perplexing because if we think of an oligopoly as an industry with only a few sellers, then oligopoly is widespread in many basic industries, and especially common in manufacturing industries, as we have noted above. But we do not really know the extent to which these firms recognize their interdependence. Progress in the field of game theory has helped us understand the strategies firms may consider. But, depending on the specific assumptions we make, we may come up with different models and different solutions for price and output. Unfortunately, economic theory does not suggest which assumptions to use to narrow our selection of models.

Chapter Summary

1. Monopolistic competition differs from perfect competition: a firm in a monopolistic industry sells a differentiated product, so it faces a negatively sloped demand curve and acts as if it has limited market power. Firms in a perfectly competitive industry sell homogeneous products and are price takers.
2. By definition, an oligopolized market contains only a few firms. These firms recognize the effects of each others' output decisions on market price, so each firm is playing a game when it chooses its output or price. Whether these firms explicitly or implicitly collude to set a monopoly price and output rate, however, depends on the costs of enforcing such a collusion and the chance of being discovered.
3. Cournot duopolists assume that the other firm will not change its output rate if they increase or decrease their output rate. This assumption leads to an equilibrium output rate between the rates produced by perfectly competitive duopolists and a monopolized industry.
4. In the kinked demand curve model, there is a gap in the firm's marginal revenue curve at the current market price. Thus, marginal cost may increase somewhat, but the optimal price and output rate of the firm are unchanged.
5. A dominant firm determines its demand and marginal revenue curve by subtracting the supply of its perfectly competitive "fringe" firms from the market demand curve. Given this demand curve, the firm sets output and price to maximize profits.
6. Games played by either cooperative or noncooperative firms offer conditional payoffs. A payoff matrix summarizes the gain or loss for each firm as a function of the actions taken by other firms.
7. The Nash equilibrium is one possible solution to a noncooperative game. In a Nash equilibrium, each firm selects an action that is "best," given the opponents' actions. One problem with the Nash equilibrium concept is that there may be multiple equilibria from which to choose.

Trouble Spots

Concept	Reminder
Product Differentiation	Although we can distinguish products by physical characteristics and other attributes, these differences are not the sole basis for product differentiation. It is the behavior and choices of consumers that establishes whether products are close substitutes. If the cross-price elasticity of demand is relatively large between two products with very different characteristics, then the two products are close substitutes. Alternatively, if two products are physically very similar and the cross-price elasticity of demand is close to zero, then they are not close substitutes.

Long-Run Equilibrium for the Monopolistic Market	In long-run equilibrium, monopolistic competitors earn zero economic profits. We have shown the zero-profit output rate as the one that lies directly below the point of tangency between the firm's long-run average cost curve and its perceived demand curve. It is not possible for these curves to intersect at this solution. If they did, the firm could produce less and increase profits, which contradicts the notion that the firm is in long-run equilibrium.
The Nash Equilibrium Concept	Often it is difficult to understand the difference between the Nash equilibrium concept and dominant strategies. Recall that a dominant strategy is optimal no matter what your opponents do and a Nash equilibrium is an action that is optimal given your opponents' choices. Although these are different ideas, one encompasses the other. Dominant strategies are a special type of Nash equilibrium because if your actions are optimal no matter what your opponents do, they are also optimal for *any* given choice your opponents make.

13.6 Review Questions

1. Explain how advertising can be used to differentiate products in a monopolistically competitive industry.
2. How do you determine if a firm has successfully differentiated its products from those of other firms?
3. How do you distinguish between perfectly competitive and monopolistically competitive industries in both the short and long run?
4. What is meant by the term *excess capacity*? Does the monopolistically competitive market have excess capacity relative to a perfectly competitive market? Does it have excess capacity relative to a pure monopoly?
5. In the Cournot duopoly model, what does each firm assume about the reaction of the other firm to a change in output?
6. What is the basic behavioral assumption of the kinked demand curve model? Explain why this assumption causes a kink in the firm's marginal revenue curve. What are some of the criticisms of the kinked demand curve model?
7. What is the adjustment variable in the Bertrand-Edgeworth model, price or output? Explain why the Bertrand-Edgeworth model approaches the equilibrium output rate and price found in a perfectly competitive situation.
8. How does a dominant firm determine its demand curve in the price leadership model? What does this model assume about the behavior of the remaining (nondominant) firms?
9. What is the difference between cooperative and noncooperative games? Are there any negative- or zero-sum *cooperative* games?
10. Explain how to determine if a strategy is a dominant strategy. Are dominant strategies *stable* if the game is played repeatedly?
11. What is a tit-for-tat strategy? Is such a strategy cooperative or noncooperative? Is this a good strategy for the prisoner's dilemma?

12. What is the first-move solution to a game? How does the first-move solution affect the payoff matrix for the firms that do not move first? Does the first-move solution affect the equilibrium of a noncooperative game that has a dominant-strategy solution?
13. What is the difference between mixed and pure strategies in a game?
14. Explain how investments in assets that have little or no salvage value (i.e., sunk costs) can be used to deter entry.

13.7 Price Theory Problems

1. Compare the assumptions underlying the perfectly competitive market with those of the monopolistically competitive market. How are they similar, and how do they differ?
2. Assuming that all firms are faced with identical cost curves, compare the long-run equilibrium result (the relationship between the various per unit cost and revenue variables) of a perfectly competitive industry with that of a monopolistically competitive industry.
3. Gasoline may appear to be a fairly homogeneous product, but oil companies spend significant sums on advertising that attempts to differentiate their products. What are some of the ways in which oil companies can differentiate their products?
4. Suppose your monopolistically competitive firm, Fine-Tune, is presently selling 100 tune-ups per week at a price of $75 each. As the owner-operator, you initiate an ad campaign on a local FM radio station, promising "a tune-up you *won't* remember." As a result, you find yourself fine-tuning 140 cars per week instead of 100. What is the "marginal revenue" of the ad campaign? What additional information do you need in order to determine whether your profits have risen? If your profits did increase, would you increase your advertising expenditures? If your profits do increase, how will your competitors react?
5. If people do not prefer differentiated products to standardized products, why would a business expend resources seeking to destandardize its particular product? Is a Chiquita banana really just a banana? If so, according to whom? Why do you think that advertising and minor changes in product design are so prevalent in many oligopolistic industries?
6. Under the kinked demand curve model, why do shifts in the marginal cost curve quite often cause no change whatsoever in price or output? Is this result consistent with long-run efficiency in an industry?
7. Suppose that two cookie companies, Mrs. Sweet and Tasty Bakery, can produce either a "soft 'n chewy" or a "crunchy" cookie. The payoff matrix for these two firms is shown on the next page.

Tasty Bakery

		Soft 'n chewy	*crunchy*
Mrs. Sweet	Soft 'n Chewy	π_S = \$800 π_T = \$800	π_S = \$1,000 π_T = \$1,400
	Crunchy	π_S = \$1,200 π_T = \$1,400	π_S = \$900 π_T = \$900

where π_S is Mrs. Sweet's profit and π_T is profit for the Tasty Bakery.

a. Does either firm have a dominant strategy in this game?
b. Identify the Nash equilibria for this game.
c. If the Tasty Bakery has the first move, what action will it take, and what will Mrs. Sweet do?

8. Suppose that two publishing firms, Fastread, Inc., and Paperbook, Inc., are considering the choice between publishing a series of mystery novels or romance novels. The decisions each firm makes affect the profits of the other firm. The weekly payoff matrix for these two firms is as follows:

Fastread, Inc.

		Mystery Series	*Romance Series*
Paperbook, Inc.	Mystery Series	π_F = \$200 π_P = \$300	π_F = \$5,000 π_P = \$3,000
	Romance Series	π_F = \$1,000 π_P = \$4,000	π_F = \$500 π_P = \$500

where π_F is Fastread's profit and π_P is profit for the Paperbook.

a. Does either firm have a dominant strategy in this game?
b. Identify the Nash equilibria for this game.
c. What is the cooperative outcome in this game?
d. Which firm gains the most from cooperation? How much of a bribe would that firm need to offer the other firm to ensure collusion?

9. The two vendors of hot dogs at a seasonal arts festival know that the festival will last for only four days. Explain why a tit-for-tat

strategy is not likely to be a successful approach to pricing for these vendors.

10. Suppose that the United States and Japan are considering a new import and export policy. Both countries can either impose a high tax or a low tax on imports from each other. The payoffs from these policies are measured in terms of each country's gross domestic product (GDP). The annual payoff matrix for these two countries is as follows (the amounts shown are in trillions of dollars):

		United States	
		Low Tax	*High Tax*
Japan	Low Tax	$GDP_{US} = \$5$ $GDP_J = \$3$	$GDP_{US} = \$4$ $GDP_J = \$1$
	High Tax	$GDP_{US} = \$6$ $GDP_J = \$3$	$GDP_{US} = \$4$ $GDP_J = \$2$

a. Does either country have a dominant strategy in this game?
b. Identify the Nash equilibria for this game.
c. If Japan has the first move, what will it do? What will the United States do in return?

11. Suppose that the (inverse) market demand curve for baby diapers is $P = 12 - Q$. There are two firms that produce baby diapers, each with a constant marginal cost of $2 per unit. Complete the table below for each of the three industry structures indicated.

Industry Structure	Market Price	Q_1	Q_2	π_1	π_2	$\pi_1 + \pi_2$
Monopoly						
Cournot-Nash						
Perfect Competition						

12. If the dominant firm sets the price, what sort of behavior is assumed on the part of the rest of the oligopolists? If the low-cost firm is the price leader, how can it run the other firms out of business? Why might it prefer not to do so?

13.8 Writing Exercise

We have described only some of the many ways in which firms can act strategically. Strategic competition is not limited to firms; it may arise in personal relationships, too. Write an essay describing at least three cases of strategic competition, either between firms or individuals, and explain the final outcome in each case. Be sure to identify whether the participants acted cooperatively, noncooperatively, or both cooperatively and noncooperatively. Could you predict the behavior of the participants using any of the models described in this chapter?

14

Labor and Other Factors of Production

Preview Questions

When you finish studying this chapter, you should be able to answer the following questions:

- Why is a factor demand curve called a derived demand curve?
- What is the optimal employment rule for a factor of production?
- How do quasi-fixed costs affect the employment of labor?
- Under what conditions does the labor supply curve bend backward?
- What is the meaning of economic rent?
- How does a monopsonist determine the optimal employment of an input?
- What factors affect the reservation wage during job search?

The news in 1993 and 1994 was not good for workers at large industrial companies. Kodak and IBM announced massive restructuring programs, reducing their combined workforce by over 100,000 employees. General Motors, USX, Apple Computer, and many others also announced plans to scale back their workforces. In contrast, some smaller companies grew. Office Depot, a retailer of office equipment and supplies, expanded its workforce. Many banks and savings and loan companies expanded as well. For the labor force and many office building owners, these changes are quite significant. Unemployed workers must search for new jobs in businesses that are growing, and office building owners must woo new tenants. A realignment of resources occurs that often involves large costs, which profit-maximizing firms will generally try to avoid.

When should firms expand or contract? How do these decisions affect profits? How does the structure of these industries affect employment decisions? In this chapter, we will analyze these basic questions. Up to now, we have found that the type of output market—competitive, monopoly, or monopolistic—affects the output and price decision of firms. We will show that the type of factor market also affects the behavior of firms, particularly the hiring and wage decisions of firms. We begin our analysis by looking at competitive factor markets and then examine how profit-maximizing firms behave when factor markets are monopolized. Then, we examine the special case of a bilateral monopoly, in which both the sellers and buyers have some monopoly power, and discuss both the standard and theoretically correct solutions to this problem. Our emphasis in this chapter is on the demand and supply of labor, but we analyze other factors of production throughout the discussion. We also develop a model of reservation wage job search to show how job search affects labor supply decisions. This model helps us better understand the problem confronted by the thousands of workers laid off in 1993 and 1994.

14.1 The Demand for Factors of Production

Before we begin our discussion of the demand for factors of production, there is one point about factor markets that needs clarification. There is a reversal of the roles firms and households play in factor markets as compared to roles played by these same firms and households in commodity markets. Business firms produce or supply goods and services to commodity markets, and households or consumers purchase or demand these goods and services. In factor markets, however, businesses *demand* factors of production, for which they give up money income in the form of wages, rents, and profits, and households sell or *supply* factors of production in exchange for money income.

A business's demand for factors of production is actually *derived from* the commodities it sells. Similarly, a household's supply of labor services is *derived from* its desire for income, which it uses to purchase commodities or services. In this section, we explain how the demand for factors is derived from the sale of the firm's output. In the next section, we discuss factor supply, with special emphasis on the supply of labor.

Factor Demand with Only One Variable Input

We first examined the firm's optimal input combination when we discussed production costs in Chapter 9. We studied the relationship of two variable inputs, capital and labor, and derived both the cost-minimizing and profit-maximizing combination of each input under the assumption that output and input prices were fixed. Let's review the profit-maximizing results from Chapter 9 as they apply to the choice of only one variable input—say, the labor input.

The basic rule the firm follows is that it tries to hire an extra unit of an input as long as the extra cost generated is less than (or equal to) the extra revenue produced by the new input. Clearly, this rule increases the firm's profits because an extra unit of an input is not hired if its cost exceeds the resulting revenue it generates. Recall that the extra revenue generated by an input is the *value of the marginal product (VMP)*, or, in the more general case in which output price is not constant, the *marginal revenue product (MRP)* of an input. The VMP equals the marginal product (MP) of an input times the output price (P) and applies to competitive firms. The MRP applies to firms that have some market power. For these firms, the extra revenue generated equals marginal product times marginal revenue (MR). For the case in which labor is the variable input, we can write

$$\text{VMP}_L \text{ is defined as } P \times \text{MP}_L \tag{14.1}$$

$$\text{MRP}_L \text{ is defined as MR} \times \text{MP}_L \tag{14.2}$$

The extra cost of an input equals the input's rate of pay, either per hour, per week, per month, or per year, depending on the terms of employment. If we can employ labor at an hourly wage of w, for example, then w is the extra, or marginal, cost of another hour of labor. Following the rule above, a *perfectly competitive firm* expands the hours of labor employed until the value of labor's marginal product equals w. Analogously, a firm with *market power* expands labor hours until the marginal revenue product equals w:

$$\text{For a perfectly competitive firm,} \quad \text{VMP}_L = w \tag{14.3}$$

$$\text{For a firm with market power,} \quad \text{MRP}_L = w \tag{14.4}$$

Equations (14.3) and (14.4) hold for the important case in which the *labor market* is competitive; that is, a single firm cannot affect the market wage rate of workers. If the labor market is not competitive, then we must adjust these equations (see section 14.3) for changes in the wage rate caused by the firm's hiring decision. In other words, we must account for the special case in which the *firm* (as opposed to the market) faces an upward-sloping supply curve of labor.

The Derived Demand Curve for Labor

We can use equations (14.1) to (14.4) to describe the derived demand for labor by both a perfectly competitive firm and a firm with market power. Equation (14.3), for example, shows the functional relationship between the market wage rate and the amount of labor hours employed by a competitive firm. A certain amount of labor hours gives rise to a certain value of the marginal product, which equals the wage rate if the firm is at the optimum position. The value of the marginal product can thus be interpreted as a curve showing the *maximum* a firm is willing to pay for any given quantity of labor. As such, the value of the marginal product is the competitive firm's demand curve for labor. Similarly, the marginal revenue product is the labor demand curve for a firm with market power. (Technically, these are short-run demand curves because capital is fixed.) Factor demand is a **derived demand** because it is partly determined by the market for the firm's output. In other words, demand for the firm's output has created a demand for inputs to produce the output. The two derived demand curves for labor are shown in Figure 14.1.

Derived Demand
Demand for an input that is derived from the demand for final output produced by a firm. The demand for all inputs is a derived demand.

As Figure 14.1 shows, both demand curves have a negative slope. Because these firms are assumed to maximize profits, we know from Chapter 8 that each firm operates only in the region of diminishing marginal returns. Thus, the marginal product of labor decreases as more labor is hired. For the competitive firm, this result implies that $P \times \text{MP}_L$ decreases as labor hours increase because the market price of output, P, is fixed. For the firm with market

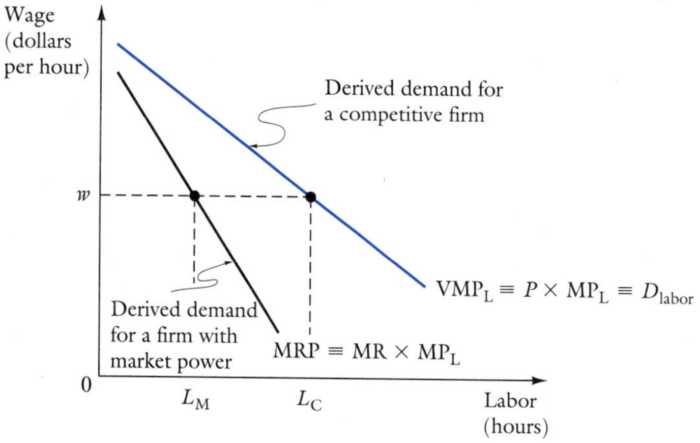

FIGURE 14.1

The Derived Demand Curve for Labor

The derived demand curve for labor when labor is the only variable input equals the value of the marginal product curve (VMP_L) if the output market is perfectly competitive; otherwise, it equals the marginal revenue product curve (MRP_L) if the firm has some market power in its output market. This curve is the firm's demand for labor (D_{labor}). At a given wage rate, w, the perfectly competitive firm employs more labor, L_C, than the firm with market power, L_M.

power, $MR \times MP_L$ decreases, too, because marginal revenue decreases as more output is sold. (Recall that $MR < P$ for a negatively sloped demand curve.) Thus, for the firm with market power, both MR and MP_L decrease as labor hours increase, which implies that the marginal revenue product curve lies below the value of the marginal product curve.[1] In other words, the marginal willingness to pay for an extra hour of labor is greater for the perfectly competitive firm than for the firm with market power.

The Optimal Employment of Labor

The optimal amount of labor hired is determined by solving either equation (14.3) for the perfectly competitive firm or equation (14.4) for the firm with market power. Because both firms are hiring labor in a competitive market, wages are taken as given. At a wage rate of w in Figure 14.1, we see that the perfectly competitive firm employs L_C hours of labor and the firm with market power employs L_M hours of labor to maximize profits. Obviously, $L_C > L_M$ because the perfectly competitive firm produces a larger output, *ceteris paribus*, than the firm with market power.

[1]The firm with market power is assumed to set a single price for its output in this discussion. Discriminatory pricing and bundling are not explored in this analysis.

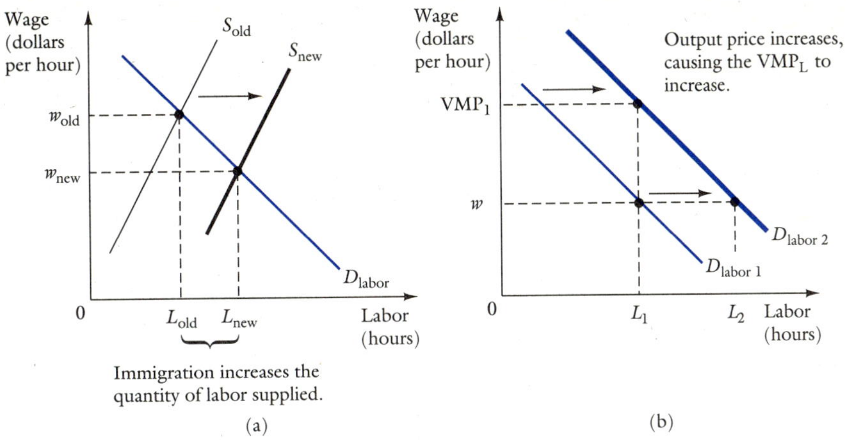

FIGURE 14.2

The Optimal Employment of Labor Is Affected by a Change in the Wage Rate and the Output Price

Changing conditions in either the input or output market affect the employment of labor. In panel (a), an influx of new immigrants shifts the supply of labor from S_{old} to S_{new}, which decreases wages and increases the quantity of labor employed from L_{old} to L_{new}. In panel (b), an increase in the output price causes the demand for labor to increase from $D_{labor\ 1}$ to $D_{labor\ 2}$. At employment level L_1, the value of the marginal product (VMP_1) exceeds the wage rate, w, so the firm has an incentive to increase employment of labor. If wages remain unchanged, employment increases to L_2.

When conditions change in either input or output markets, the optimal use of an input changes. In panel (a) in Figure 14.2, for example, a sudden liberalization in immigration laws leads to an influx of foreign labor into the domestic labor market. The wage rate falls from w_{old} to w_{new} as a result of the increase in the supply of labor. The demand curve, D_{labor}, is not affected, but the optimal quantity of labor demanded increases from L_{old} to L_{new}. (Note that it does not matter whether the derived demand curve is for a perfectly competitive firm or a firm with market power. The effect is the same: an increase in the optimal quantity of labor employed.)

Now, in panel (b) in Figure 14.2, suppose that the output price increases. The value of the marginal product (or the marginal revenue product) increases as a consequence, which causes the factor demand curve to increase from $D_{labor\ 1}$ to $D_{labor\ 2}$.[2] The firm is initially employing L_1 units of labor at a wage rate of w. On the new demand curve, $D_{labor\ 2}$, L_1 units of labor generate a value of the marginal product equal to $VMP_1 > w$. It is now profitable for the firm to expand

[2]This discussion assumes that there is only one variable input. With two or more variable inputs, the effects of changing the output prices are ambiguous. We discuss this further in the section "Factor Demand with Several Variable Inputs."

output, because the extra revenue generated exceeds the extra cost. With wages unchanged, the firm's new profit-maximizing level of labor employment equals L_2. Thus, a higher output price causes increased employment of labor, the only variable input.

A Example of the Derived Demand for Labor

Let's consider how a competitive firm actually determines the optimal quantity of labor. Consider the case of the AirTight Balloon Company, which has invested in two balloon-making machines, one of which has more hourly production capacity than the other. The firm does not plan to make any additional capital investment, so capital is fixed. The company sells balloons for 25 cents each in a perfectly competitive market. Labor is competitively supplied to this industry at the market wage (w) of \$5 per hour. The output produced and the marginal product of labor are shown in the table in Figure 14.3.

As can be seen from the table in Figure 14.3, the first employee produces 580 balloons per hour, the second employee increases the output rate to 650

w = \$5.00 per hour
P = \$0.25 per unit

Labor	Capital	Q	MP_L	$P \times MP_L$
1	2	580	–	–
2	2	650	70	\$17.50
3	2	700	50	12.50
4	2	730	30	7.50
5	2	750	20	5.00
6	2	760	10	2.50
7	2	765	5	1.25

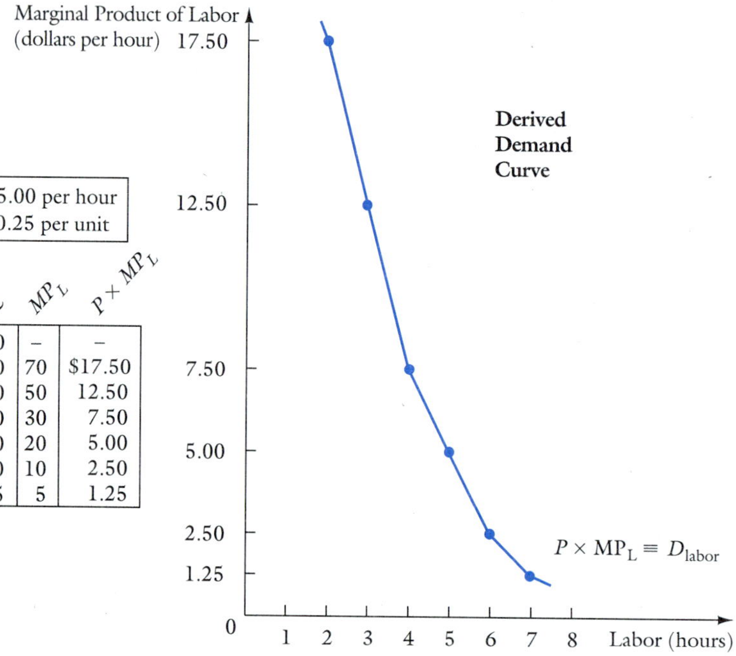

FIGURE 14.3

The Derived Demand for Labor in the AirTight Balloon Company

The table shows how to compute the value of the marginal product of labor, $P \times MP_L$, when labor is the only variable input. This is the firm's demand curve for labor, D_{labor}. The figure plots these values to show the derived demand curve for labor.

balloons per hour, the third employee increases the output rate to 700 balloons per hour, and so on. Recall that from Chapter 8, the extra output produced by hiring another employee is the marginal product of labor for that worker. The second employee's marginal product, for example, equals 70 balloons per hour. Multiplying this employee's marginal product by the price of balloons yields the value of the marginal product for the second employee, which equals $14.50. Performing this calculation for each employee yields the value of the marginal product schedule shown in the table.

The graph in Figure 14.3 plots the value of the marginal product for each of the first seven employees, which is the derived demand curve for labor. With the wage rate equal to $5 per hour, it is optimal for the firm to hire five employees. In other words, the first five employees contribute more to revenue than to costs (or an equal amount in the case of the fifth employee). The sixth employee, however, contributes only $2.50 to hourly revenue while creating $5 in extra hourly costs, so the firm will not hire the sixth employee. The firm hires five employees to maximize profits in the short run, which can be found from equating the market wage rate to the derived demand curve for labor.

$$$ Price Theory in Practice

DAVID LETTERMAN'S MARGINAL REVENUE PRODUCT

Computing the marginal revenue product for an individual may be a difficult task because many factors can change *after* a new worker is hired that affect both the quantity and price. Even so, the example provided by the 1993 TV deal signed by David Letterman, star of *Late Show with David Letterman,* is instructive.[3]

Letterman was star of the NBC show, *Late Night,* until CBS approached him with a contract offer worth $14 million per year for three years. The deal called for Letterman to move his after-midnight talk show to an 11:30 P.M. time slot on CBS, going head-to-head with *The Tonight Show* starring Jay Leno. Letterman's *Late Night* show was very popular. It generated $51 million in revenues and earned an estimated $20 million per year in profits for NBC. NBC tried to keep Letterman, but he wanted to host *The Tonight Show,* which meant that NBC would have to buy out Leno's contract. In the end, keeping Letterman was too expensive for NBC.

But did CBS make a good deal? Letterman was a risky proposition because his after-midnight audience was younger than the 11:30 P.M. audience. In addition, the ratings of *The Tonight Show* had held up after Leno replaced Johnny Carson, so Letterman might not attract the advertising revenue needed to make the show a hit.

The risky bet paid off, however, as Letterman's show surged ahead of *The Tonight Show* and ABC's investigative news show *Nightline,* starring Ted

[3]The information used in this discussion is from "Exit Laughing," *Newsweek,* December 21, 1992, "Good Night, Dave," *Newsweek,* January 25, 1993, "Dave Tops 10 List," *Advertising Age,* December 20—27, 1993, "Late Night Isn't Just Joking Around," *Advertising Age,* August 30, 1993, "At the End of Week One, Letterman Looms Large," *MediaWeek,* September 6, 1993, "Late-Night Gamble," *The New Yorker,* February 1, 1993, and "Leno Letterman War," *The New York Times Magazine,* January 30, 1994.

Koppel, in the television ratings. Before Letterman's show went on the air, advertisers were betting that Letterman would tie *The Tonight Show* in the ratings; they were paying about $35,000 for a 30-second spot on either *The Tonight Show* or the *Late Show with David Letterman*. By May 1994, however, a 30-second spot on Letterman's show was selling for $55,000.

What is Dave Letterman's marginal revenue product? Because CBS moved from third to first place in the ratings for the 11:30 P.M. time slot, it is reasonable to say that its revenues for a 30-second slot increased by *at least* $20,000 (from $35,000 to $55,000). CBS sells sixteen 30-second spots on the *Late Show with David Letterman* each night. Thus, CBS gained $320,000 per night by signing Dave Letterman, which is about $54 million in extra revenue for a 200 show season, after subtracting commissions paid to advertising agencies. Dave Letterman's marginal revenue product ($54 million) greatly exceeded his marginal cost ($14 million).

LEARNING EXERCISE 14.1

If there were two Dave Lettermans would you expect them to work for the same network? Under what conditions would they be likely to work for the same or different networks?

FACTOR DEMAND WITH SEVERAL VARIABLE INPUTS

Our analysis becomes more complicated when more than one factor of production varies. To keep the analysis manageable, we will focus on the case in which there are only two variable factors of production: labor and capital. In effect, this is a long-run analysis because both inputs can change. We will also focus on demand for an input by competitive firms, because factor demand by firms that have market power is nearly equivalent; all we must do is replace the VMP curve with the MRP curve in our discussion. Now, with more than one variable factor of production, the VMP curve no longer represents the derived demand curve for a given input, but it can be used to determine the derived demand curve.

An Intuitive Explanation of Factor Demand

When the price of labor falls, the quantity of labor demanded increases, as represented by a lower wage line, which intersects the VMP curve at a larger quantity of labor. A lower price of labor reduces the firm's marginal cost of production, thereby increasing its output. As a result, the firm is likely to invest in additional capital to expand capacity. As the quantity of capital used increases, the marginal product of labor, MP_L, increases because each unit of labor is now being used with more capital. If another balloon-making machine is purchased, for example, it causes the productivity of existing workers to increase; that is, workers who previously shared duties on the other machines can work on a new machine without the same amount of sharing. In other words, when the firm purchases more capital, each unit of labor has more

the profession or some other form of certification. Practicing in the profession without a license is generally prohibited by law, and in many cases an applicant must have graduated from an approved educational program as a step to obtaining a license. There are good arguments for and against this type of system.

Proponents of the system point to the need to protect consumers of the services provided from unscrupulous or incompetent practitioners. Arguments against professional regulation point out that such groups tend to restrict the supply of new entrants into the profession for reasons irrelevant to competence or integrity, thus elevating the wages of those currently practicing.

An interesting development in most major professions in recent years is the dramatic increase in the number of paraprofessionals. A *paraprofessional* is a practitioner with some training but less comprehensive or extensive training than a full-fledged member of the profession. Medical technicians and legal assistants, for example, are paraprofessionals. The paraprofessional is licensed to carry out limited, but frequently encountered, tasks. Paraprofessionals are usually required to practice under the direction and supervision of a fully licensed professional rather than dealing directly with the public as solo practitioners.

If a paraprofessional is a *substitute* for the professional in certain frequently provided types of services, then the prohibition against paraprofessionals engaging in solo practice is one way in which professionals can restrict the extent to which paraprofessionals undercut their market share. If paraprofessionals have skills that *complement* the work of a licensed professional, however, then such restrictions allow professionals to control the quality of their work and protect the public from the problem of asymmetric information. In other words, the training of a medical paraprofessional, such as a paramedic, for example, may not provide him or her with the skills necessary for many medical tasks. Thus, if paramedics begin to offer these services, the general public may be adversely affected because of a lack of advance knowledge about each paramedic's medical skills.

The legal profession offers some insight into the answer to whether paraprofessionals are substitutes or complements for professionals. A study by Robert Feinberg examined the growth in the number of paralegals compared to attorneys and other employees in law firms.[7] Feinberg computed the elasticity of substitution between paralegals, licensed junior attorneys, and legal secretaries (and other existing skilled law firm workers). The **elasticity of substitution** measures how the relative use of an input changes when its relative price changes. A negative elasticity of substitution between two inputs implies that they are substitutes in production; that is, as the relative price of the input increases, its use decreases compared to the other input. A positive elasticity of substitution implies that the inputs are complements in production. Feinberg found a very low elasticity of substitution between paralegals and lawyers (– .15) but a high elasticity of substitution between paralegals and legal secretaries (– .92). Similarly, the study found the price elasticity of demand for junior lawyers to be low (– .14) and that of paraprofessionals to be more elastic (– .58).

Elasticity of Substitution
A measure of the relative responsiveness of the capital-labor ratio to a change in the ratio of factor prices.

[7]Robert M. Feinberg, "Paralegals and Substitution Among Labor Inputs in the Law Firm," *Journal of Industrial Economics* 33 (September 1984), 99–104.

In short, paralegals appear to be substitutes for professionals, but the low elasticity of substitution suggests that many of their tasks may be complementary to those performed by professionals. Whether such results will arise for other occupations is an empirical matter. As the issue stands now, both proponents and opponents of an expanded role for paraprofessionals can claim some empirical support for their positions.

LEARNING EXERCISE 14.3

Can you explain the growth of paraprofessionals using just the growth in demand for the general profession? If demand for legal services decreased, do you expect that many professional attorneys would perform the tasks now performed by paralegals?

14.2 FACTOR SUPPLY

Up to this point, we have studied the demand for inputs by firms. We will now turn to an analysis of the supply of factors that firms use in production. We divide this discussion into two parts, one that discusses the supply of all nonlabor factors and another that discusses the supply of labor.

THE SUPPLY OF NONLABOR FACTORS

Nonlabor factors of production include capital (such as buildings and machines), materials, land, and energy. The supply of these factors is determined by the market structure in which they are produced. If these factors are produced in a competitive market, then the supply curve is the horizontal sum of the marginal cost curves (above the minimum of the average variable cost curve) of each factor-producing firm. If the factor is produced in a constant-cost industry, then its long-run supply is horizontal at the level of the minimum of the long-run average cost curve. If the factor is produced in an increasing cost industry, then its long-run supply curve is positively sloped. Similarly, if the factor is produced in a decreasing-cost industry, then its long-run supply curve is negatively sloped.

In contrast, if the factor is produced by a nondiscriminating monopoly, then there is no supply curve for the monopoly. The monopolist produces a specific quantity of the factor to maximize profits. If demand changes, then another optimal quantity may be chosen, but, as we saw in Chapter 11, there is no unique relationship between price and quantity for a monopoly. For other industry structures, the particular assumptions of the industry determine the shape of the market supply curve. There are really no general statements we can make about these noncompetitive industry structures in order to determine the nature of factor supply; each structure must be dealt with separately.

The supply curve for a nonlabor factor of production, then, is determined by the nature of the industry in which it is produced.

LABOR SUPPLY OF INDIVIDUALS

Labor deserves special attention because individuals make choices to increase their satisfaction, whereas firms that produce nonlabor factors make choices to maximize profits. Thus, the labor supply decisions of individuals may differ from what we might expect a profit-maximizing firm to do. For example, as the price of its output increases, a profit-maximizing firm increases the quantity produced. But, as wages increase, individuals face a trade-off between income and leisure when considering whether or not to increase the time spent in the labor force. As explained in Chapter 6, we know that as wages increase, the *substitution effect* encourages more work because leisure becomes relatively more expensive. If leisure is a normal good, however, the *income effect* encourages the consumption of more leisure—because the individual can afford more of all products and services, including leisure—as wages increase. For low wage rates the substitution effect tends to dominate, but for high wage rates the income effect may dominate, leading to a backward-bending labor supply curve. Figure 14.6 on page 582 illustrates the substitution and income effects caused by an increase in wages.

Figure 14.6 shows the trade-off between daily income and leisure for an hourly worker. This graph is similar to the trade-off we derived in Chapter 6 between expenditures and leisure. The principal differences here is that we are focusing on income, which equals expenditures on goods, and daily choices of leisure, not weekly choices. Recall from our earlier discussion that the horizontal axis measures more leisure consumption—less work time—as you move toward the right and less leisure consumption—more work hours—as you move toward the origin. The individual's wage rate equals \$5 per hour initially, so if it were possible to work all 24 hours in a day, daily income would equal \$120. This is shown as point *A* in Figure 14.6. If the individual does not work, then daily income equals zero and 24 hours of leisure are consumed, which corresponds to point *B* in the figure. The straight line that connects these two points represents the individual's *full income constraint*, which was defined in Chapter 4. The full income constraint shows the various combinations of income and leisure consumption that are obtainable at a given wage rate.

The maximum satisfaction the individual can achieve is given by indifference curve U_1 in Figure 14.6. The optimal bundle is defined as the point of tangency between indifference curve U_1 and the initial full income constraint. Point *C* represents the optimal bundle, which contains 16 hours of leisure, or equivalently 8 hours of work, and \$40 in daily income.

Increasing the Wage Rate

When the wage rate increases to \$10 per hour, the full income constraint pivots at point *B* until it intersects the vertical axis at \$240, which is point *D*. The new optimal bundle is given by point *F*, which is the point of tangency between indifference curve U_2 and the new full income constraint.

The movement from the old to the new bundle illustrates the opposing nature of income and substitution effects for labor supply. The substitution effect is given by the change from point *C* to point *E*, or the change from 16

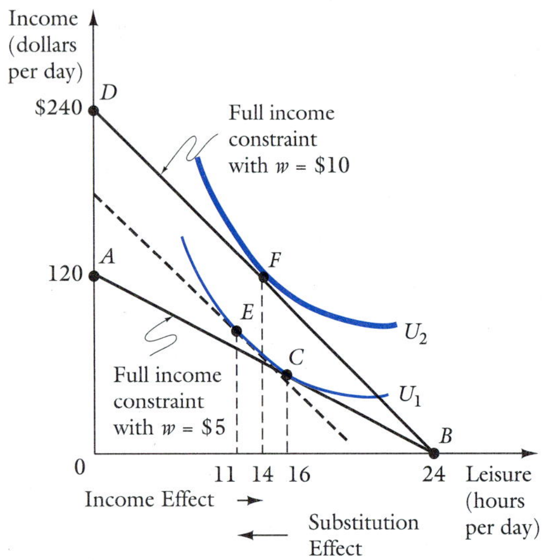

FIGURE 14.6

Comparing Income and Substitution Effects of a Wage Increase

The straight line between points *A* and *B* represents the full income constraint when the wage rate is $5 per hour. The individual initially chooses point *C* as the optimal bundle, which is composed of 8 hours per day of work and 16 hours per day of leisure. When wages increase to $10 per hour, the straight line between points *D* and *B* represents the new full income constraint. The new optimal bundle is given by point *F*, which is composed of 10 hours of work and 14 hours of leisure. The transition from point *C* to point *F* can be divided into substitution and income effects. The substitution effect equals the change from point *C* to point *E* in which work effort is *increased* by 5 hours. The income effect equals the change from point *E* to point *F* in which work effort *decreases* by 3 hours. The *net* effect is to increase work effort by 2 hours.

hours to 11 hours of leisure. This change is due solely to the effect of a higher relative cost of leisure, holding satisfaction constant—that is, keeping the individual on indifference curve U_1. For the substitution effect alone, we see that the individual increases work effort from 8 hours to 13 hours per day.

The income effect works in the opposite direction. From point *E*, the individual moves to point *F*—the optimal bundle—at which 14 hours of leisure are consumed. The move from point *E* to point *F* is caused by a parallel shift in the full income constraint—the dashed line to the new full income constraint—which is equivalent to an increase in income. With leisure a normal good, more income implies that more leisure is consumed. The *net* effect—accounting for both income and substitution effects—is that the individual increases work effort from 8 to 10 hours per day, earning $100 in daily income at point *F*.

Backward-Bending Labor Supply Curve

In Figure 14.6, the individual increases the time spent in work when the wage rate increases. Thus, over this range of wages, the labor supply curve has a *positive* slope. But labor market experience suggests that the labor supply of an individual is not always positively sloped. For many individuals, the income effect dominates the substitution effect at higher wage rates, which causes the individual's labor supply curve to become negatively sloped. We can represent the case in which the income effect dominates the substitution effect by drawing a backward-bending labor supply curve. Figure 14.7 illustrates one such curve for the individual in Figure 14.6.

At the initial wage of $5 per hour, the individual supplies 8 hours of work effort per day, which is shown as point *A* in Figure 14.7. For an increase in wages to $10 per hour, the substitution effect dominates the income effect and work effort increases to 10 hour per day, which is given by point *B*. As shown in the figure, the substitution effect continues to dominate until the wage rate equals $25 per hour, at which point the individual supplies 15 hours of work effort per day—point *C*. For wages greater than $25 per hour, the income effect dominates and the individual reduces work effort in exchange for more leisure hours. The labor supply curve, $S_{\text{individual}}$, has a backward bend to it beginning at $25 per hour. In short, employers may increase wages thinking that that will increase work effort, but such action is successful only at lower

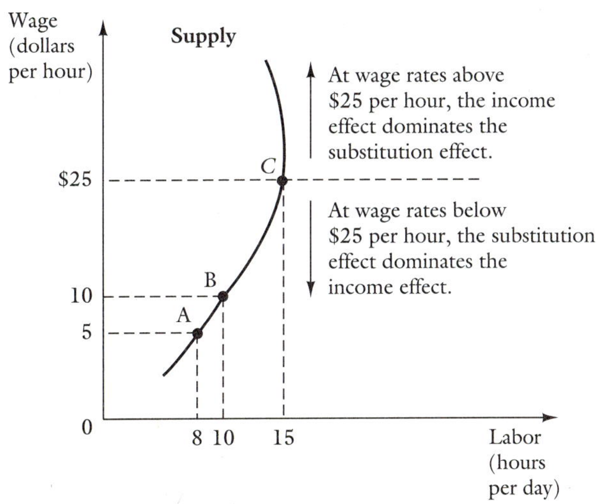

FIGURE 14.7

A Backward-Bending Individual Labor Supply Curve

The individual labor supply curve has a positive slope when the substitution effect dominates the income effect. At point *C*, the supply curve begins to slope backward. At wage rates above $25 per hour, the income effect dominates the substitution effect.

wage rates. The backward-bending characteristic makes labor supply different from the supply of nonlabor factors of production.

LEARNING EXERCISE 14.4

Redraw Figure 14.6 to show the case in which the income effect dominates the substitution effect in labor supply.

EQUILIBRIUM IN THE LABOR MARKET

The labor market reaches an equilibrium when the wage rate equates quantity demanded to quantity supplied. To find quantity demanded in the market, we follow the steps outlined in Figure 14.5 on page 575. To find the market supply curve, we sum (along the horizontal axis) all the individual supply curves for workers of similar skills and abilities. The intersection of market supply and demand curves gives the equilibrium wage and amount of labor services employed. Figure 14.8 illustrates such a labor market equilibrium for the case of manufacturing workers.

Figure 14.8 shows that wages in manufacturing average $12 per hour (higher with benefits added) in 1992. At this wage rate, approximately 775 million worker-hours are employed each week. (Note that worker-hours are computed by multiplying the average weekly hours worked times the number of employed manufacturing workers.) This exercise can be repeated for other industries to find the labor market equilibrium, and it can be done for local

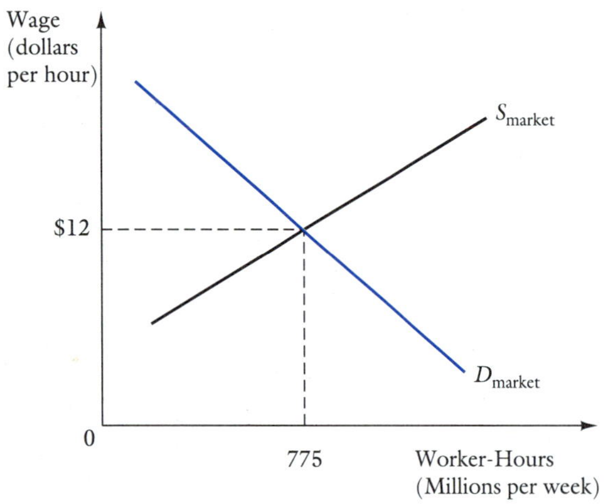

FIGURE 14.8

Labor Market Equilibrium in U.S. Manufacturing, 1992

The labor market reaches an equilibrium when quantity supplied equals quantity demanded at the prevailing wage rate. In 1992, U.S. manufacturing workers earned $12 per hour and supplied 775 million hours of work.

and regional labor markets when there is a cost to labor mobility. An important point to remember, however, is that the supply and demand curves are defined for individuals with similar skills and abilities. Because of the difficulty of creating a homogeneous group of skills, we have described the equilibrium wage as the average wage rate. In any practical setting, individuals with differing skills will be mixed together, and there will be multiple wage rates that reflect these skill differences.

$$$ Price Theory in Practice

Does the Economy-wide Supply Curve of Labor Have a Backward Bend?

The supply curve in Figure 14.8 shows a positive slope throughout the full range of wages. This may seem odd at first because we have drawn the individual supply curve in Figure 14.7 with a backward-bending segment. So, the simple math of adding up such backward-bending curves suggests that the total, or market,

TABLE 14.1

Historical Labor Force Statistics

Year	Average Weekly Hours	Index of Real Weekly Earnings	Employed Civilian Labor Force (1,000s)	Estimated Total Weekly Hours (1,000s)
1914	49.4	100	36,281	1,792,281
1920	47.4	120	39,208	1,858,459
1925	44.5	127	43,716	1,945,362
1930	42.1	127	44,183	1,860,104
1935	36.6	133	41,673	1,525,231
1940	38.1	163	47,520	1,810,512
1945	43.5	226	52,820	2,297,670
1950	40.5	223	58,920	2,386,260
1955	40.7	261	62,171	2,530,359
1960	39.7	278	65,778	2,611,386
1965	41.2	314	71,088	2,928,825
1970	39.8	317	78,678	3,131,384
1975	39.4	324	85,846	3,382,332
1980	39.7	322	99,303	3,942,329
1992	41.0	373	126,982	5,206,262

Sources: Ehrenberg and Smith, *Modern Labor Economics* (5th edition), New York: HarperCollins Publishers, 1994; U.S. Department of Commerce, *Historical Statistics of the United States—Colonial Times to 1970,* New York: Kraus International Publications, 1989.

supply curve will have a backward-bending segment, too. But the simple math may not be correct if the backward bend begins at different wage rates for different individuals. In other words, the income effect may begin to dominate the substitution effect at different points along the labor supply curve for different individuals. In this case, as we add together the various individual labor supply curves, the backward-bending segments for some individuals may be offset by positively sloped segments for other individuals. This causes the market supply curve to have a positive slope over all but the very highest wage rates.

The heterogeneity across individual supply curves may be particularly important when the *net inflows* of new workers are considered. An increase in wages, for example, may tend to reduce work effort for some individuals on the backward-bending portion of their labor supply curves, but higher wages may also attract new workers and thereby increase the total quantity of work effort. We can see this effect if we look at the behavior of the aggregate labor force over long time periods, as shown in Table 14.1 on page 585.

In Table 14.1, we see that there is a general tendency for the average weekly hours worked to decrease as real wages increase over time. If the labor force is static—that is, there are no new entrants—then the average tendency is for less work effort over time. Figure 14.9 shows the shape of the (intertemporal) labor supply curve, holding the number of workers at 1914 levels but varying real wages and the average weekly hours worked. There is a slight negative slope to this curve, perhaps indicating that the *average* income effect is slightly greater than the *average* substitution effect.

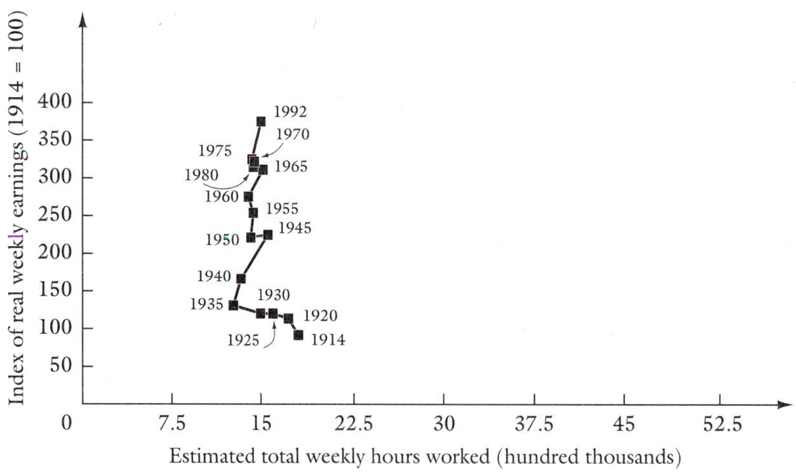

FIGURE 14.9

Weekly Labor Supply in the United States, Holding the Size of the Labor Force Fixed at 1914 Levels

The intertemporal behavior of labor supply shows a slight bias toward less work as real wages increase and the labor force is held constant at 1914 levels.

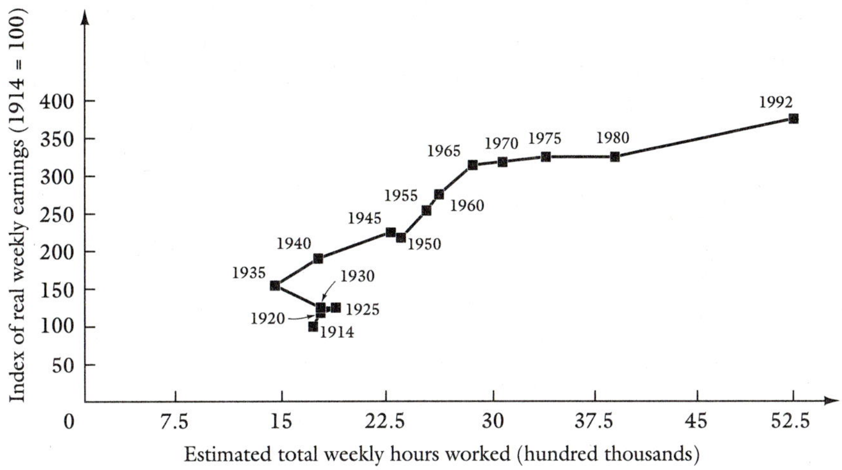

FIGURE 14.10

Weekly Labor Supply in the United States Allowing for New Entrants, 1914–1992

When new entrants are included the intertemporal behavior of labor supply exhibits a positive slope between most time periods. The exception is the 1975 to 1992 period in which real wages were nearly constant, but hours worked increased significantly.

In contrast, Figure 14.10 shows the behavior of the dynamic labor supply curve using the actual employed civilian labor force to estimate the total weekly hours worked. These totals are shown in Table 14.1, too. As you can see, entry makes a significant difference in the shape of the (intertemporal) labor supply curve. The labor supply curve has a positive slope across nearly all periods. The only exceptions are the 1930–1935 and 1975–1989 periods. The former period includes the Great Depression, in which over 20 percent of the labor force was unemployed in some years. The latter period has roughly a zero slope. Over this period, workers who were part of the postwar baby boom and a significant number of women entered the workforce for the first time; this held real wages constant as total hours worked increased.

In summary, if we look at the labor force as a static entity, there appears to be a slight tendency for the income effect to dominate the substitution effect, but new entrants over time have overwhelmed the influence of this effect.

Learning Exercise 14.5

Using the data in Table 14.1, compute the elasticity of supply between 1940 and 1945 and between 1945 and 1950. What factors might explain the change in the elasticity of supply?

RESERVATION WAGES AND ECONOMIC RENTS

Another way to interpret an individual's labor supply curve is to view it as descriptive of the minimum wage rate necessary to elicit the resulting labor effort. That is, the labor supply curve shows the *least* amount that a firm can pay for each level of labor effort. We call the least amount an individual will accept for a given amount of labor effort the **reservation wage**.

Reservation Wage
The lowest wage that will elicit a given level of labor effort.

The concept of a reservation wage is important because it represents a switching point in the individual's behavior. To induce the individual to *switch* from consumption of leisure to providing (more) work effort, a firm must offer to pay an amount *at least* as large as the individual's reservation wage. Obviously, if a firm pays more than the necessary reservation wage to some individuals, these individuals gain because they were actually willing to provide their labor services for less. When the actual wage rate exceeds the individual's reservation wage for the labor services provided, we say that firms are paying an economic rent. An **economic rent** for labor services is defined as the difference between the total payment received by an individual and the individual's reservation wage for the services provided.

Economic Rent
A payment to a factor of production above what is necessary to keep a given quantity of the factor in its current employment and quality.

We can illustrate the concept of an economic rent using an example from the entertainment market. Madonna has become a successful singer and movie actress. Many movie studios and recording companies are willing to pay her millions of dollars for her services, but Madonna's time is limited. Figure 14.11 offers a view of Madonna's labor supply curve, $S_{Madonna}$, and the corresponding demand curve, $D_{Madonna}$, for her services as a movie actress.

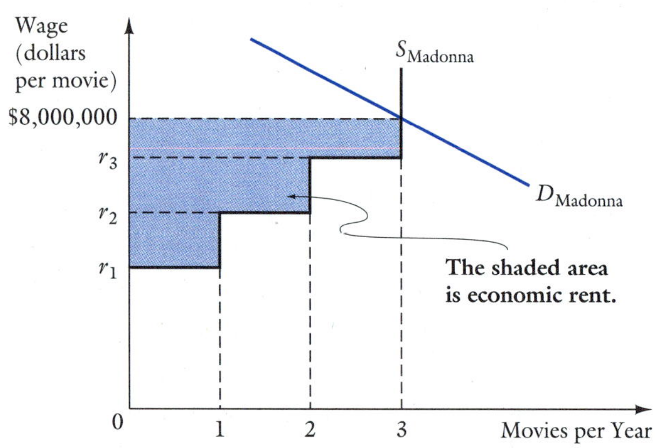

FIGURE 14.11

The Market Value of Madonna's Time as a Movie Actress

Reservation wages r_1, r_2, and r_3 represent the prices at which Madonna will supply her movie actress services during one year. She cannot participate in more than three movies each year, so $S_{Madonna}$ represents her labor supply curve. The demand for her movie services is given by $D_{Madonna}$. The market reaches an equilibrium at $8 million per movie. At this wage Madonna earns economic rents equal to the shaded area.

As can be seen in Figure 14.11, the lowest wage that Madonna is willing to accept to appear in *one* movie is r_1. This is her reservation wage for the first movie during the year. Similarly, she will appear in a second movie if offered at least r_2 dollars and in a third movie if offered at least r_3 dollars. Her supply curve is vertical after three movies because she does not have the time available to appear in more than three movies a year.

Now, you may ask why Madonna places a different reservation wage on the first, second, and third movies. The basic answer is that she is giving up more and more leisure time as she accepts additional movie contracts, so to overcome her preference for increasingly scarce leisure time, she requires more income with which to purchase goods that provide satisfaction. The satisfaction generated by the consumption of extra goods compensate her for the leisure time she must give up to appear in another movie.

As drawn in Figure 14.11, the demand for Madonna's movie actress services exceeds three movies per year at the wage of r_3 per movie. Thus, she rations her time by charging a price of $8,000,000 per movie, which exceeds her reservation wage, r_3, for three movies. At a price of $8,000,000 per movie, quantity demanded equals quantity supplied, so Madonna and the various movie studios that seek her services are in equilibrium.

At the equilibrium wage, Madonna earns economic rents for her movie services equal to the area above the supply curve and below the $8 million price line, which is the shaded area in Figure 14.11. This area represents compensation received by Madonna that exceeds the reservation wage(s) necessary to elicit her work in movies. Note that economic rents are computed as if each movie is priced separately, that is, as if wage discrimination was possible when pricing each movie. This approach is analogous to the computation of consumer's surplus over different quantities. Consumer's surplus equals the difference between the maximum a consumer is willing to pay and the actual price paid for ***each unit,*** summed over all units bought. The maximum for each unit is used because this is a measure of the consumer's valuation of that particular unit. Similarly, the reservation wage necessary to elicit Madonna's services for ***each movie*** is used because this is a measure of her minimum valuation of the time required for each movie.

Economic rents are to individuals what economic profits are to firms. Economic rents represent payments over and above what is necessary to compensate individuals for their (perceived) opportunity costs. Similarly, economic profits to firms are payments that remain after the opportunity cost of all resources used in production is subtracted from revenues. Just as positive economic profits attract new firms to a particular market, positive economic rents tend to attract individuals to a particular labor market. Many young actresses and singers, for example, are likely to try to imitate Madonna in an attempt to capture some of her economic rents.

LEARNING EXERCISE 14.6

Compute Madonna's economic rent if the demand curve intersects her supply curve at the reservation wage rate r_2.

HUMAN CAPITAL AND WAGE DIFFERENCES

Our analysis of the labor market equilibrium suggests that a single wage rate arises for all individuals with the same marginal revenue product. But actual experience suggests that the marginal revenue product must vary because wages vary significantly in many occupations and within most firms, even for individuals with the same title and responsibilities. Much of the explanation for these differences can be attributed to the individual worker's investment in **human capital.** Human capital investments are broadly defined as those that increase a worker's present or future productivity. Human capital investments include on-the-job training, formal education, and health maintenance activities. Not only is it likely that these investments increase productivity, but it is also likely that these increases will persist over time, so we can regard such investments as durable and highly related. Thus, workers entering an on-the-job training program may show one level of productivity increase and workers who enter a follow-up training program may show another level of productivity increase. The second level of increase, however, may not be possible without completing the initial on-the-job training program. Because human capital investments vary greatly across workers, we expect marginal product and wages to vary significantly, too.

Human Capital
Any activity that increases a worker's present or future marginal productivity.

In a perfectly competitive world, we would expect to find wages equalized for workers who make the same human capital investments. Although the results are not definitive, empirical research suggests that wages are not equalized even after adjusting for human capital differences. Of course, the basic question is, why? Some might argue that there is discrimination, particularly against women and minorities, who typically earn less in the labor market. But such arguments often fail to recognize the obvious gains to be had by firms that don't discriminate. Firms, perhaps run by women or minorities, could attract the most productive underpaid workers from firms that do discriminate by offering these underpaid workers a higher, but competitive, wage. Such behavior makes the discriminating firm worse off because it loses low-paid but productive workers and makes the less discriminating firm better off because its profits increase. This argument suggests that systematic discrimination is not expected to persist for long periods of time; there is too much to gain in profits from not discriminating. The argument is clear, but it does not explain the data.

Another explanation for wage differentials is that there are factors external to the labor market that generate wage differences. Wages in some regions of the country may be lower because these areas are desirable places to live or because the cost of living is lower. The relative desirability of an area and differences in the cost of living create compensating wage differentials (discussed below) that can account for wage differences.

Finally, government policy may affect wages and cause wage differences for workers with similar skills. Labor is not very mobile between two countries, for example. Work permits in most countries are temporary and are difficult to acquire if you are a nonresident. Such restrictions can create shortages of labor that change relative wages. Firms may try to respond by moving production facilities to the country with the low-cost labor supply. But such actions may carry a cost, too. Import restrictions on goods may limit the gains firms might realize from relocating plants. The textile industry in the United States would be significantly smaller, for example, if textile import quotas and taxes were eliminated. This result may arise in the future since the North American Free Trade Agreement has become law. NAFTA will phase out tariff and quota restrictions over ten years. Foreign governments may change their policies, too, so that firms face higher costs. In the worse case, investments can be confiscated, and all of the advantage to low-cost foreign labor is lost in the process.

COMPENSATING WAGE DIFFERENTIALS

We have noted that wages may differ across employees because of varying levels of human capital investment, but wages may also differ across firms for individuals with the same level of human capital investment. Consider the case of two shoe manufacturing plants, one located in the city close to residential areas where workers live and the other located a 30-minute drive from the city. If both firms provide identical working conditions and wages, the plant located outside the city will have a difficult time recruiting workers. Why? Simply, workers who accept employment at the more distant plant must commute farther than those who work at the in-city plant. Time spent commuting is time not spent in leisure, and this reduces a worker's satisfaction (or utility) relative to working at the nearby plant.

To compete for workers, the more distant plant must offer higher wages than the in-city plant. The higher wages provide workers with extra income compared to the in-city workers. The extra income may be used to purchase goods that provide enough satisfaction to offset the effects of the workers' lost leisure time. Assuming a pool of homogeneous workers, the extra income is enough to make workers *indifferent* between working at the out-of-town firm or the in-city firm.

The *extra* wage offered by the out-of-town firm is called a compensating wage differential. The **compensating wage differential** represents an amount of income that workers receive for accepting certain working conditions that are less desirable than what other firms offer.

Compensating Wage Differential
Extra wages paid to otherwise equally productive workers in order to compensate for a less desirable working environment.

The compensating wage differential may pay for more than just differences in the time spent commuting. Some firms offer unclean, unsafe, or unpleasant working conditions compared to other firms. These less desirable firms pay a higher wage than firms that are cleaner or safer or that provide more pleasant working conditions. Other firms operate in areas that pose a health risk. Holding other factors constant, firms in Los Angeles, for example, pay higher wages because air pollution affects workers' health and the desirability of living and working in the area. In addition, firms that operate coal mines typically pay higher wages than firms that operate copper and zinc mines because of the health risk that black lung disease poses for workers.

When workers have identical skills and preferences, the compensating wage differential represents an *exact* payment for the extra "costs" workers incur at the less desirable firm. In such cases, no worker receives more than any other worker to compensate for the firm's working conditions. When workers' preferences differ, however, there is a sorting of workers to firms based on each worker's valuation of the extra costs imposed by less desirable firms. In this situation, there is no single compensating wage differential for all workers; it varies because preferences vary across workers. In the commuting example, workers who place a relatively high value on leisure time will prefer to work at the in-city firm, whereas workers who place a relatively low value on leisure time will prefer the higher wages offered by the firm located out of town. Thus, workers will sort themselves between the in-city and out-of-town firms partly on the basis of their relative valuation of leisure time. The exact size of the resulting compensating wage differential is less clear in this situation because it depends on the cost imposed—the 30-minute commute that takes away from leisure time—and the distribution of the weights each individual places on this cost. If relatively more workers place a higher weight on lost leisure time, then the compensating wage differential increases. Alternatively, if relatively more workers place a low weight on lost leisure time, then the compensating wage differential decreases.

Compensating wage differentials allow the labor market to reach an equilibrium employment level and wage rate at which working conditions at firms and preferences of workers can vary.

EFFICIENCY WAGES AND LONG-TERM EMPLOYMENT

Some firms find that they benefit from long-term employment arrangements with workers. Many corporations and professional associations have historically retained employees for long periods of time, in many cases until they retire. In such situations, long-term continuity of the workforce is valued because it increases profits. The personal service provided by an attorney or an accountant, for example, builds a trust relationship that may be amortized over many years for the initial time investments by both employer and employee to pay off. But long-term employment arrangements can also create opportunities for shirking (see Chapter 7). For example, employees may claim that they are spending time cultivating business relationships for a future payoff when, in fact, there is little likelihood of a future payoff. An employee who shirks lowers profits and, because he or she is likely to be dismissed, disrupts the continuity of long-term employment arrangements. In such circumstances, managers of firms may adopt incentive pay schemes to help prevent shirking and other forms of opportunistic behavior.

One incentive plan that economists have debated is called efficiency wages. With **efficiency wages,** employees are paid more than they are worth to other firms; in effect, they receive an above-market wage rate. The idea behind efficiency wages is that employees are less likely to shirk—reducing absenteeism—and turnover will be lower if employees would earn a lower wage at another firm. Shirking carries not just the loss of a job but a lower future wage. Firms that pay efficiency wages may save on monitoring costs and lost output; thus, they expect to increase profits. The concept of efficiency wages has been used by the boards of directors at some firms to justify the high salaries paid to executives.

Efficiency Wages Paying wages that exceed the value of an employee's marginal product in order to discourage shirking or opportunistic behavior.

Obviously, the need for a long-term employment relationship is important to the use of efficiency wages. If the firm's product and marketing methods are such that profits are unaffected by high turnover rates in the labor force—which is unlikely because of quasi-fixed hiring costs—then efficiency wages have less value. The firm could hire at the going market wage and replace any fired employees at the same wage rate. Construction firms in many areas operate in this manner. Efficiency wages would not increase output relative to the marginal product of a new worker, so the firm would not gain by paying an above-market wage rate.

Although efficiency wages appear to be one solution to the problems of shirking and high turnover rates, it is not entirely clear that firms actually adopt efficiency wages in the simple manner that we have described. The reason is that the VMP of each worker can be difficult to measure. When we can directly measure the VMP, we tend to find that firms use other forms of incentive pay, such as piece rates or commissions, to reward employees for their productivity. In this respect, efficiency wages may arise as a last resort when other incentive schemes cannot be implemented (for example, in firms where workers operate in teams in which there is a significant investment in team-specific training). There is some evidence, for example, that efficiency wages may be paid to employees with more seniority at some service-oriented firms; that is, workers with more seniority may earn wages above the value of their marginal products. The reason for this result may be due to the reputation that many senior employees have built up over their years of service. This reputation draws business to the firm that may not have been directly solicited by these employees. If such employees leave the firm, they impose a cost in terms of lost profits on the firm because their network of contacts and clients may value the services of the firm less. As a result, firms may pay efficiency wages to keep senior employees around.

Another explanation has been offered for the relatively high wages paid to more senior workers at some firms. These employees may have accepted employment based on a long-term wage profile: low wages relative to productivity in the beginning, with high wages relative to productivity in the later years. When we look at the later years, it appears that efficiency wages are paid, but if we look over the *entire* period of their employment, these workers may actually earn the value of the marginal product; they are just not paid the full VMP contemporaneously with their effort.

Efficiency wages are a means that firms can use to reduce shirking and turnover rates, but it is likely that such wages are to be found only when other incentive pay plans cannot be implemented at low cost.

$$$ Price Theory in Practice

Did Ford Motor Company Pay Efficiency Wages in 1914?

The actions taken by the Ford Motor Company in 1914 are often cited as an example of efficiency wages. On January 6, 1914, Henry Ford, president of the Ford Motor Company, announced a new wage and profit-sharing plan that would institute an above-market wage for most workers. Under the terms of the plan, the company

- Reduced work from 9 to 8 hours per shift and increased the number of shifts from two to three, so that the plant operated 24 hours per day.
- Increased the minimum wage paid to any male employee 22 years old or older from \$2.34 to \$5.00 per day.

- Distributed among employees 50 percent of all yearly profits, a sum estimated at $10 million in 1914.
- Increased the workforce from 22,500 to 26,500 workers.

Ford's motivation for introducing a profit-sharing plan and $5 daily wage has been debated by economists. The standard explanation is that Ford was unsuccessful in attracting a certain quality and quantity of workers. The facts, however, lend little support to this theory. Throughout 1913, the Ford Motor Company faced an excess labor supply. Unemployed workers from the Midwest and the eastern United States came to the Ford Motor Company's employment office daily seeking new jobs. Thus, Ford had little incentive to increase wages to $5 per day to attract more workers. In addition, it was unlikely that Ford was looking for more skilled workers. Under Ford's automated assembly line, jobs were menial routines and could have been performed by the least skilled workers. Ford's engineers were actually "de-skilling" the jobs as they perfected the assembly process. The Ford Motor Company boasted that *any* man could be a Ford employee after a 15-minute production lesson from any of its supervisors. The company did not demand many highly skilled workers, so it is unlikely that Ford offered higher wages and a share of profits to attract additional skilled labor.

A better explanation for Ford's plan and the $5 per day wage involves turnover costs. In 1913, worker dissatisfaction at Ford took visible form when the annual employee turnover at the plant reached 370 percent. In March 1913, 7,300 employees left the company. Of these numbers, 18 percent were discharged, 11 percent quit, and 71 percent were "5-Day Men" who had missed 5 work days in a row without an excuse and had therefore forfeited their jobs.[8] In addition, in 1913 the Ford Motor Company had a 10 percent daily absentee rate. This meant that on any given day 1,300 or 1,400 less experienced replacement workers took the helm at new tasks and machines. High absenteeism lowered plant efficiency and lowered productivity. Workers claimed that the high absentee rate was caused by the routinized work on the assembly lines. Workers lacked incentive and drive to perform the endlessly repetitive tasks. One Ford employee summed up the workers' feelings when he poignantly said, "If I keep putting on Nut No. 86 for about 86 more days, I will be nut No. 86 in the Pontiac bughouse."[9] Workers were clearly unhappy. They listed among their gripes:

- Long hours. The day was too long and the work exhausting.
- Low wages. Workers felt they were being underpaid and were always looking for a change in occupation, which contributed to the high turnover rate.

It is clear that Ford knew of the worker's complaints and that he thought carefully about how to address them. On January 15, 1914, Henry Ford announced the goals of his new plan:

[8]Daniel M.G. Raff and Lawrence H. Summers, "Did Henry Ford Pay Efficiency Wages?" *Journal of Labor Economics,* vol. 5, 1987, pp. 557–586.

[9]Stephen Meyer, *The Five-Dollar Day: Labor Management and Social Control in the Ford Motor Company, 1908–1921,* Albany: State University of New York Press, 1981.

> We shall get increased efficiency. The men will get half the profits. Is it not to their interest to increase their output and thus increase their share of the profits? If there are no profits, then, of course, there will be no sharing. . . . We shall continue to make our cars better and cheaper, and we shall cut the price regularly every fall. With increased economy in manufacture we shall be able to lower the price next fall by fully $30—perhaps by more.[10]

Did Henry Ford pay efficiency wages? Henry Ford never viewed the situation this way. He stressed this point emphatically when he said, "It [the profit-sharing plan] is not, I may emphasize, an increase in wages. It is a system of profit-sharing, which, we believe will be successful in operation. . . . It is a sort of dividend."[11] Ford's goal was to maximize profits by reducing turnover and hiring costs, not necessarily to attract more productive workers. Yet, the goals of an efficiency wage are not only to attract more productive workers but also to decrease turnover, reduce labor costs, and improve worker morale and loyalty, which were also Ford's goals. Under the plan, workers were given shorter shifts, higher wages based on the preceding year's profits, and a chance to earn an even higher income if profits continued. Ford's plan was not intended to attract more productive workers, but it did meet the other goals. By reducing turnover and labor costs and improving morale and loyalty, it resembled an efficiency wage program. Thus, Henry Ford coupled wages with an increased concern for workers' financial well-being to produce a more efficient and profitable company. Workers were given an incentive not only to work for themselves but also to work for the company.

Learning Exercise 14.7

What were the effects of Ford's supracompetitive wage on other motorcar companies, such as Pontiac or Dodge?

14.3 Monopsony and Union Bargaining

Up to this point we have assumed that the labor market is characterized by many firms acting as buyers, each of them unable to affect the equilibrium wage rate. We now assume that the firm buying labor is, relative to the market, large enough so that a change in its demand for labor affects the market demand and the wage rate for labor. Such a firm has market power over the price paid for an input. The most extreme case of this type of market power occurs when there is only one firm buying a particular input, such as was nearly the case with AT&T's hiring of telephone operators before the firm was broken up by the courts. Another example is a coal-mining town, in which the coal mine is the only buyer of miner services. A market with only one buyer is called a **monopsony.** In this section, we examine how a monopsony chooses its optimal quantity of labor services.

Monopsony
A market structure in which there is a single buyer of an input.

[10] *The Commercial and Financial Chronicle,* January 17, 1914, p. 233.

[11] *The Commercial and Financial Chronicle,* January 17, 1914, p. 233.

AVERAGE AND MARGINAL FACTOR COST CURVES

A labor monopsonist faces an upward-sloping supply curve of labor because, as the only buyer of a particular type of labor, it faces the entire market supply curve. Thus, if the monopsonist desires to increase its use of labor, it must raise the wage rate to attract more workers into the market. The monopsonist must pay a higher price for the last unit of the input, but if no price discrimination in *purchasing* is possible, the monopsonist must also pay a higher price on all previous units purchased.

The supply curve of an input is often called the **average factor cost (AFC) curve,** just as the demand curve for an output is often called the average revenue curve. In Chapter 11, we derived a curve marginal to the average revenue, or demand, curve to represent the marginal revenue obtained by a monopolist from an extra unit of sales. We can define an analogous curve for the supply, or average factor cost, curve. The curve that represents the additional cost incurred from hiring another worker is called the *marginal expenditure curve,* or more commonly the **marginal factor cost (MFC) curve.** An example of how marginal factor costs are computed for a monopsonist is presented in Table 14.2.

Average Factor Cost (AFC) Curve
Another name for the factor supply curve; at any point on the supply curve, the price given is equal to the average (per unit) factor cost.

Marginal Factor Cost (MFC) Curve
A curve showing the change in total factor cost due to a one-unit change in the use of that factor.

In Table 14.2, the wage rate increases as the monopsonist increases its employment of labor. Starting from a base of 10 workers each earning $5.00 per hour, the monopsonist can attract an additional employee if wages are increased to $5.20. Because there is no wage discrimination, all workers earn $5.20 per hour. The total labor cost increases from $50 to $57.20 per hour. The change in total labor costs equals the marginal factor cost of the eleventh worker, which is $7.20. In other words, to attract the eleventh worker the monopsonist must offer a wage of $5.20. This decision implies that the existing 10 workers will now earn an extra 20 cents per hour. The marginal factor cost of the eleventh worker is thus $5.20 plus $0.20 × 10 workers, which equals $7.20. The marginal factor cost for each of the other workers is com-

TABLE 14.2

Computing the Marginal Factor Cost of Labor

Quantity of Hourly Workers	Wage Rate ($/hour)	Total Labor Cost ($/hour)	Marginal Factor Cost ($/hour)
10	$5.00	$50.00	—
11	5.20	57.20	$ 7.20
12	5.50	66.00	8.80
13	6.00	78.00	12.00
14	6.75	94.50	14.50
15	7.50	112.50	18.00

puted in the same manner. Note that the marginal factor cost exceeds the wage rate at each level of employment. This must be true because the extra pay of the existing workers is added to the wage rate of the last worker to compute the marginal factor cost. This result implies that the marginal factor cost curve lies above the average factor cost curve. We show this relationship in Figure 14.12 below.

The MFC and AFC curves in Figure 14.12 are drawn using the data provided in Table 14.2. We have drawn a smooth curve between these data points to illustrate the general appearance of these curves. As the diagram shows, a monopsony faces a marginal factor cost that exceeds what a competitive buyer would face; that is, a competitive buyer cannot affect wages by its employment decision, so its marginal wage cost moves along the labor supply curve (AFC).

MONOPSONIST'S CHOICE OF LABOR: ONE VARIABLE INPUT

We assume that the pure monopsonist, like anyone else, maximizes profit. For a monopsonist, however, the marginal factor cost curve replaces the wage rate as the marginal cost of hiring additional workers. If labor is the only variable input, then either the VMP_L or MRP_L curves may be used to describe the revenue contribution of additional labor units. Thus, to maximize profits, the wage terms in equations (14.3) and (14.4) on page 567 are replaced by the marginal factor cost (MFC_L) of each worker:

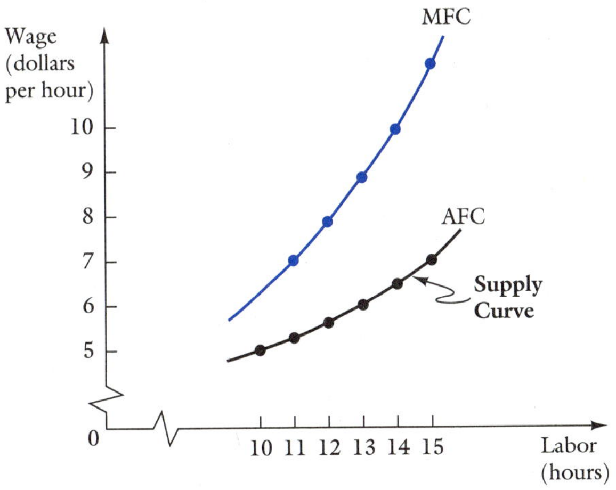

FIGURE 14.12

Comparing MFC and AFC Curves

The average and marginal factor cost curves shown are derived from the data in Table 14.2. The AFC curve is the supply curve of labor. The MFC measures the additional cost the firm incurs because its employment decisions affect the wages paid to all workers.

In a perfectly competitive output market, $VMP_L = MFC_L$ (14.5)

When there is market power in the output market, $MRP_L = MFC_L$ (14.6)

If the monopsonist sells its output in a perfectly competitive output market, then equation (14.5) is used to determine the optimal quantity of labor to employ. Alternatively, if the monopsonist has some market power over price in the output market, then equation (14.6) is used to determine the optimal quantity of labor to employ. Figure 14.13 illustrates how a monopsonist chooses the optimal quantity of labor for the case in which its output sells in a perfectly competitive market.

In Figure 14.13, the profit-maximizing monopsonist hires labor up to the point at which $VMP_L = MFC_L$. This occurs at the intersection of the VMP_L curve with the MFC_L curve, or at point *A*, which gives the profit-maximizing rate of employment of labor, L^*. Now, how much does the monopsonist have to pay per unit for that amount of labor? The answer is found from the supply curve, S_{labor}. Point *B* on the labor supply curve corresponds to the desired quantity of labor, L^*. The wage rate that must be paid is w^* to attract this number of workers. We have, then, the wage and employment optimum for a monopsonist selling its output in a purely competitive market when there is only one variable factor of production.

The first time you see Figure 14.13, you may think that the wage rate should equal the marginal factor cost of L^* units of labor, MFC_L^*. After all, that is where we observe the intersection of the marginal factor cost curve with

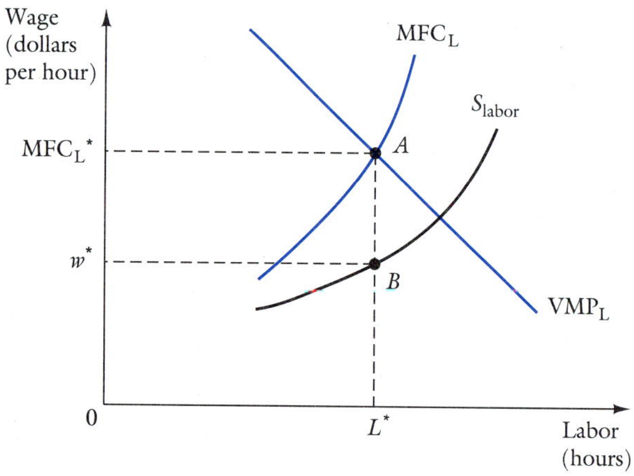

FIGURE 14.13

Optimal Employment of Labor by a Monopsonist Who Sells Output to a Competitive Market

If labor is the only variable input, the value of the marginal product, VMP_L, is the monopsonist's derived demand for labor. Equating the marginal factor cost curve, MFC_L, to the VMP_L curve at point *A* gives the optimal quantity of labor hours, L^*. The wage paid to workers, w^*, is determined from the supply curve of labor, S_{labor}, at point *B*.

the VMP_L curve (which is the demand curve for labor). The intersection at point *A*, however, gives us information only about the optimal quantity of labor hired by a monopsonist. Once the optimal quantity is determined, the monopsonist does not have to pay the marginal factor cost to attract the quantity L^* of labor per hour. The monopsonist has to pay only the wage rate w^*, which lies on the supply curve for labor. Remember, it is the supply curve of labor that indicates the quantity of labor forthcoming at each and every wage rate, not the marginal factor cost curve.

LEARNING EXERCISE 14.8

Redraw Figure 14.13 for the case in which the monopsonist has market power in its output market. Does the monopsonist with market power employ more or less labor than the monopsonist that sells in a competitive output market?

THE CASE OF A BILATERAL MONOPOLY

Bilateral Monopoly A situation in which a monopolist sells to a monopsonist.

A monopsony gives a firm market power in its input market. The input market affected may respond by organizing itself into a monopoly to sell to the monopsonist. A labor union may coalesce to "sell" labor services to a monopsonist. Baseball and many other professional sports are examples of this situation, which is called a **bilateral monopoly** because *both* the buyer and seller have some market power. Let's explore how a bilateral monopoly might operate, using baseball as an example. First, we consider how the players' union is expected to behave when the owners are competitive; then, we examine how the solution may change when the owners act as a monopsonist. This is the standard approach to the bilateral monopoly problem. We also discuss how heterogeneous players affect the bilateral monopoly problem and examine the solution that arises if the owners and the players' union recognize that they are both better off by maximizing joint profits, which is the theoretically correct solution. Last, we discuss the efficiency of a bilateral monopoly compared to a competitive market.

Wage and Employment Decisions for the Players' Union

To simplify our analysis, let's begin by assuming that all baseball players contribute equally to a team's success and that a players' union represents *all* players. Neither of these assumptions is completely true, of course, but for now let's use them to look at the basic problem a players' union faces.[12] Figure 14.14 on page 600 shows the market situation confronted by the players' union when the owners act as perfect competitors.

Figure 14.14 shows the supply curve for baseball players represented by the players' union, $S_{players}$, and the demand curve for baseball players, $D_{players}$,

[12]Players have different abilities, and free agency in baseball and other professional sports causes many players to hire their own agents or negotiate directly with team owners for contract conditions. These contracts are over and above what the players' union may negotiate.

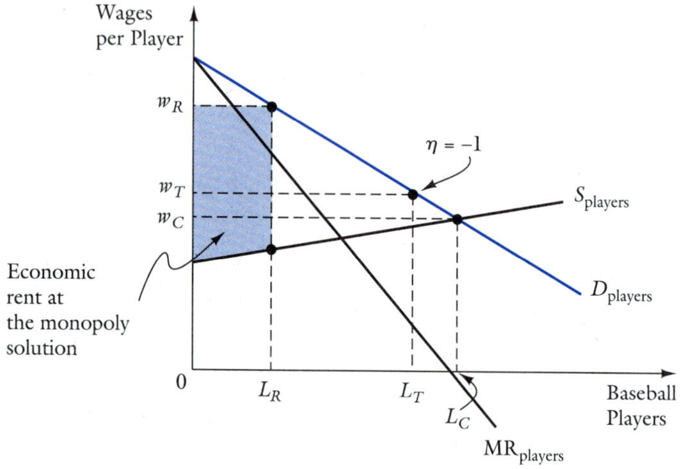

FIGURE 14.14

Monopoly Power for the Players' Union

Given supply ($S_{players}$), demand ($D_{players}$), and marginal revenue ($MR_{players}$) curves for baseball players, a players' union that acts as a monopoly requests a wage of w_R per player. Team owners will hire only L_R players at this wage, generating economic rents equal to the shaded area. If the players' union seeks to maximize total wage paid to players, it may request a wage of w_T per player, which generates employment of L_T players. If the union is dissolved and the players compete, then the market equilibrium wage rate equals w_C and L_C players are employed.

when the team owners act competitively. If the union seeks a competitive wage, then L_C players will be employed at a wage of w_C per player. This wage and employment level maximizes the *sum* of the consumers' surplus for the team owners and the economic rents of the players.[13] The problem with this solution is that the players do not need a union if this is their desired goal. Competition by owners and players, acting on their own, reaches the competitive solution. If the competitive solution is the final outcome, players are better off without the union so that they do have to pay any union dues. Thus, in order to survive, the players' union must offer an alternative to the competitive solution.

Two alternative solutions are shown in Figure 14.14. One solution is for the players' union to act as a monopolist. In this solution, the team owners' marginal revenue curve, $MR_{players}$, is equated to the players' supply curve to find the employment level and wage rate that maximize economic rents. (Note that the supply curve reflects the marginal opportunity costs—that is, reservation wage—of each additional professional baseball player.) There are L_R players hired, and each player receives wages of w_R at the monopoly solution. Total

[13]Recall that consumers' surplus equals the area under the market demand curve above price. Consumers' surplus accrues to the team owners here because it is they who have a demand for the services of baseball players.

economic rents earned by players are equal to the shaded area in Figure 14.14. Obviously, the players who are employed at this solution are better off than at the competitive solution, but there are $L_C - L_R$ players who are not employed, and they are worse off.

The other solution shown in Figure 14.14 is for the players' union to maximize the total wages paid to its members. This occurs at the point at which the price elasticity of demand equals minus 1 ($\eta = -1$). At this point, L_T players are employed and wages are equal to w_T. Total employment is higher at this solution compared to the monopoly solution, but not as high as the competitive solution.

The question is, how will the players' union act? Will it act like a monopolist? Will it act to maximize total wages paid? What will it do? The answer depends on how the union is organized. If it is run democratically with its leaders elected by a *majority* vote of its members, then it is likely to act as a monopolist *if a majority of its members are employed at the monopoly solution.* The monopoly solution provides the greatest economic rents and, hence, potentially the largest amount of dues paid by union members. If a majority of a union's members are not employed at the monopoly solution, however, then it is more likely that the union will move toward the maximum total wages solution in an attempt to find employment for a majority of the "voting" members. Obviously, the union's leaders must satisfy the majority if they are to remain in office, and this fact will predict the behavior of the union. For convenience, we will assume that the union has a mandate to act as a monopolist.

LEARNING EXERCISE 14.9

In Figure 14.14, assume that L_C is the size of the union membership and that each member pays dues equal to H per contract-year. Under what conditions will a *majority* of union members vote to disband the union in favor of a competitive solution? (Hint: Find the largest number of players who would be willing to pay, say, H in dues from their wages and compare this number to L_C.)

Bilateral Monopoly: The Standard Approach

If the baseball team owners organize themselves to bargain with the players' union, then we have a case of bilateral monopoly. In other words, the union acts as a monopoly by being the sole seller of players' services and the owners act as a monopsony by being the sole buyers of players' services. As assumed above, players have similar skills and the players' union seeks an agreement that maximizes economic rents for its members. In contrast, the owners seek the monopsonist solution at which optimal employment is determined by the marginal factor cost curve. These two goals are illustrated in Figure 14.15 (page 602).

The demand and supply curves for baseball players are shown as D_{players} and S_{players}, respectively, in Figure 14.15. The marginal revenue curve, MR, is shown under the assumption that a single wage is paid to all players. The marginal factor cost curve, MFC, is shown under the same assumption. The optimal bar-

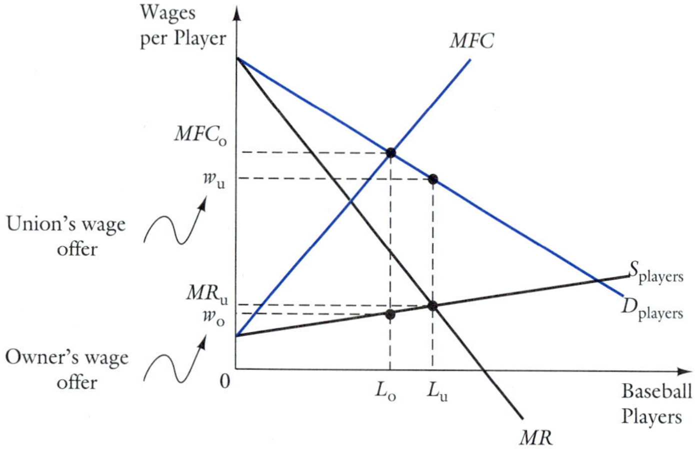

FIGURE 14.15

The Case of a Bilateral Monopoly

In a bilateral monopoly, the players' union determines its asking wage from the point on the demand curve, $D_{players}$, above the intersection of the curves for marginal revenue, MR, and supply, $S_{players}$. Thus, the players' union asks for w_u per player. The owners, acting as a monopsonist, counter with an offer of w_o per player, which is the point from $S_{players}$ below the intersection between the marginal factor cost curve, MFC, and $D_{players}$. The gap between w_u and w_o is the bargaining area between the two sides. The relative bargaining strength of the two sides determines the final wage of the players.

gaining position for the players' union is found at the intersection of the MR and $S_{players}$ curves.[14] Thus, the players' union will ask the owners to employ L_u baseball players and pay each of them w_u. In contrast, the optimal position for the owners is found at the intersection of the MFC and $D_{players}$ curves. The owners will thus offer to employ L_o players and pay each player w_o. Obviously, there is a significant difference of opinion between the union and the owners on wages and a smaller difference of opinion on employment levels.

The relevant question is, how does the difference of opinion resolve itself? Generally, the answer is that both sides will compromise somewhat, so that the game of baseball can continue to be played. Now, how much each side is willing to compromise depends on the relative bargaining strength and financial durability of each side. If the union can make a credible threat that it will go on strike against the owners, then it can increase its bargaining position. To make a credible threat, however, it must have the financial resources to help defer part of the opportunity costs incurred by players during a strike; that is, it must offer strike pay to players and it must offer the probability of a signifi-

[14]Note that the supply curve, $S_{players}$, represents the marginal cost curve when the owners are not acting as a monopsonist.

cant wage increase at the end of the strike. During 1994, for example, the players' union went on strike in the middle of the playing season, which was costly to both owners and players. The owners can improve their bargaining position if they show a willingness to wait out a strike, that is, to exhaust the financial staying power of the players' union. The final result is going to be a wage rate between w_o and w_u. It will be closer to w_o if the owners have a better bargaining position; otherwise, it will be closer to w_u.

The Effects of Heterogeneous Players: Superstars

How will the bilateral monopoly problem change when players have varying abilities or, more important, when the VMP of players varies? In baseball, in other sports, and in most professions the VMP varies across employees. This situation is particularly apparent for the superstars in a firm. These individuals are the star performers. In baseball, players such as Dwight Gooden, Roger Clemens, and Barry Bonds excel above most other team members and attract fans to the baseball stadium. The added value of a baseball players' union to the superstars on a team is less clearly defined. For example, superstars demand wages significantly higher than the average wage of the team, so these players are likely to hire their own agents to negotiate salaries and benefits, which reduces the value of the players' union.

Placing the superstars aside, if the VMP of players varies significantly, even at the lower levels, the negotiating process will tend to become player-specific. The advantage of having a union bargain for all players is thus reduced. After the development of free agency in baseball in 1975, for example, the role of the players' union changed from one of negotiating salaries and benefits that affect many players—that is, salary schedules for players in their first year, second year, and third year—to negotiating *minimum* salary scales, which affect only a few players, and general working conditions, such as time off between games, the number of games played, and the size of the roster. In general, the more the VMP varies across employees, the fewer the issues for which a union will be used as a negotiating agent. This decreases the general bargaining strength of a union relative to the team owners (or the managers of a given firm).

Bilateral Monopoly: The Joint-Profit Solution

A basic weakness with the standard approach is that the two sides alternate in their view of each other. When the union is presenting an offer, it is a monopoly and the owners are viewed as perfect competitors. This allows the union to compute a marginal revenue curve from the owners' derived demand for players. Similarly, when the owners are presenting an offer, they view the players as competitive and themselves as a monopsonist. This allows the owners to compute a marginal factor cost curve from the players' supply curve.

The problem with the standard approach is that when the two sides view each other correctly, then one is a monopoly and the other is a monopsonist.

These are the facts. We know from our discussion of monopoly in Chapter 13 that a monopoly does not have a supply curve. Thus, the owners are really not able to compute a marginal factor cost curve from $S_{players}$. Following the reasoning presented in Chapter 13, we can also show that a monopsonist *does not have a derived demand curve.* Thus, the players' union really cannot use the competitively determined derived demand curve to compute a marginal revenue curve. These results suggest that the standard approach does not adequately describe the bilateral monopoly problem.

Economists Roger Blair, David Kaserman, and Richard Romano have revisited a solution to the bilateral monopoly problem that was first suggested by A. L. Bowley in 1928.[15] This solution allows for bargaining behavior. The two sides recognize that they each have market power, so it is reasonable for them to entertain a solution in which their *joint* profits are maximized. In other words, what would the solution be if the owners and players' union acted together, or jointly? By acting together they generate the greatest profits from the market.

The usefulness of the joint profit maximization solution is that it determines a *unique* employment level of players. There is no range of employment, such as between L_o and L_u shown on Figure 14.15, that must be bargained over. The employment level is unique because the amount of output to be produced—baseball games and innings played—is uniquely determined in the joint profit-maximizing solution.

Although the employment level is determined, the wage paid to players is not given by the joint-profit solution. A range of possible wages may arise. Bargaining is the only way to resolve what wage is paid. In effect, if the players' union is a better bargainer, then it negotiates a high wage and receives all or nearly all of the joint profits. Alternatively, if the owners are better bargainers, then they negotiate a low wage and receive all or nearly all of the joint profits. What is important is that even if one party has a dominant bargaining position, so that it can set a wage that gives the other party zero profits, the dominant party will still select the joint profit-maximizing employment level.

Bilateral Monopoly: The Question of Efficiency

In terms of efficiency, it does not matter whether the result is the Bowley solution (from 1928) or the range of solutions implied by the standard approach. A bilateral monopoly does not produce a competitive output rate or employ a competitive quantity of labor. As such, there is a loss of efficiency when the bilateral monopoly is compared to a competitive market. The exact size of the loss depends on the shape of market supply and demand curves in a competitive environment and on the size of the output reduction. Clearly, the larger the output reduction, the larger the loss of efficiency relative to the competitive solution.

[15]Roger D. Blair, David L. Kaserman, and Richard E. Romano, "A Pedagogical Treatment of Bilateral Monopoly," *Southern Economic Journal* 55 (April 1989), 831–841.

MATH NOTEPAD

The Bowley Solution to Bilateral Monopoly

The Bowley solution arises when both firms recognize that they are better off if they follow a plan to maximize joint profits. This result arises regardless of which firm has more bargaining power. To understand why, let's formulate the joint profit problem for our baseball union problem.

Owners face a production function, $Q = f(K, L)$, where Q is output, K is the capital input, and L is the employment level of players. The per unit cost of capital is r and the wage paid to players is w. Owners face an (inverse) demand for their output, defined by $P = g(Q)$; that is, price per unit, P, is some function of output, Q. The players' union faces an opportunity cost of attracting additional players to the game, defined by $C(L)$, where $C(L)$ is increasing in L. The slope of this function defines the supply curve of players, S_{players}, in Figure 14.15.

The profit function of the owners is written as follows:

$$\pi^{o} = P(Q)Q - wL - rK$$

The profit function of the players' union is written as follows:

$$\pi^{u} = wL - C(L)$$

By adding together these two profit functions, $\pi^{o} + \pi^{u}$, we can derive the joint profit function, which is written as follows:

$$\pi^{j} = P(Q)Q - C(L) - rK$$

Maximization of π^{j} yields the largest profits available for the owners and players' union to share. Note that the maximization of π^{j} produces a unique solution for L, the employment level of players. The same solution for L arises independent of who has the greater bargaining power. To see this, consider the case in which the owners have absolute bargaining power. In this case, the owners will maximize profits subject to the restriction that the players' union's profits are zero; that is, the players' union does not share in any of the profits:

$$\text{Max. } \pi^{o} \text{ subject to } \pi^{u} = 0.$$

The constraint that $\pi^{u} = 0$ implies that $wL - C(L) = 0$. Rearranging this expression to solve for w gives

$$w = C(L)/L$$

Using this result to substitute for w in the owners' profit function gives

$$\begin{aligned}\pi^{o} &= P(Q)Q - [C(L)/L]L - rK \\ &= P(Q)Q - C(L) - rK \\ &= \pi^{j}\end{aligned}$$

Thus, the owners' profit function is identical to the joint profit function when the owners have absolute bargaining power. In this case, the solution for L is the same as the joint profit solution. If we reverse the bargaining power, so that the players' union has absolute bargaining power over the owners, then we will find the same result; that is, the profit function for the players' union reduces down to the joint profit function. Clearly, both the players' union and the owners will desire the same employment level for baseball players if they recognize that they are better off when joint profits are maximized.

RANK-ORDER TOURNAMENTS

Many superstars reach their lofty positions through participating in some form of rank-order tournament. In a **rank-order tournament,** individuals who finish in the top ranks receive many times more income than lower-ranked participants. In golf tournaments, for example, the annual winnings by the top ten players are nearly six times higher than the winnings of the second ten players, even though the average game scores of these same players are generally within 5 percentage points of each other. In golf and many other sports, participants compete for large sums of money to be distributed according to the players' final ranking in the tournament, not by any scheme that uses the relative size of each player's effort (say, as measured by their golf scores).

Rank-Order Tournament
A reward system in which pay is based on a participant's ranking relative to other participants.

The pay scheme embodied in a rank-order tournament arises partly because of the way such tournaments are produced. Television and cable TV technology have created a potentially enormous audience for many services, such as concerts, tennis, golf, and the nightly news. With television and video technology, a service (or tournament) is produced only once for potentially many millions of customers. In contrast, most goods must be created many times to meet consumers' demand. One restaurant meal, for example, is produced for each customer, whereas a music concert is produced just once and consumed by many individuals.

Because television production costs do not vary with the size of the audience, producers of shows desire to offer a product that attracts the largest number of viewers. More viewers generate more advertising revenues, so more viewers increase profits. In sports programs and the nightly news, the size of the viewing audience is related to the *quality* of the program. Two tennis players that are not ranked in the top 20 in the world may play well, but their match is not expected to be as good as the match played by two players ranked in the top 20. These "lower-quality" players are expected to attract a dismally small audience to the tennis stadium and a correspondingly small number of television viewers. Only the most successful (past and present) tennis players attract stadium fans and large numbers of television viewers. Thus, producers of such events use a rank-order tournament with disproportionately large rewards for the top performers, because it is these individuals who generate the largest portion of their revenues.

There is a partial winner-take-all characteristic inherent in rank-order tournaments; that is, the winner gets a disportionate share of the prize money. We can also find evidence that this characteristic affects wages in situations not related to sporting events. For example, nearly every local station competes for viewers during the evening hours. Because most viewers demand to know the day's news events at this time, most local stations offer a nightly news program. To win the largest viewing audience, the stations that are not at the top of the ratings will change formats and personnel. Often the lower-ranked stations try to hire the news anchors from the top-ranked station or from a top-ranked station out of the area. Because the top-ranked station receives a disproportionate share of the advertising dollars spent on news programs, a news anchor who can vault a lower-ranked show into the top spot is in a position to command a relatively high salary. But how much will such a news anchor be paid?

Suppose that Connie Hennings is a news anchor who has demonstrated that she can attract the largest number of television viewers. She is currently anchor for the highest-ranked television station in the Dallas–Ft. Worth market. Managers of the second-highest-ranked television station desire to hire her. If they do, then they will earn the advertising revenues currently earned by the highest-ranked station. It is not clear how far down in the rankings the current top-ranked station will fall, but the best it can do is to swap places with the number two station if it loses Connie Hennings. The earnings data for the two stations reveal that the highest-ranked news program earns $2 million more in advertising revenue than the second-highest-ranked station. What is the most that the second-highest-ranked station will offer Connie Hennings? They should be willing to pay her $1,999,999.[16] Thus, if Connie Hennings is as good at bargaining as she is at reading the news on T.V., you can expect her to receive superstar wages. (Note the winner-take-all nature of this situation: without Connie Hennings, the second-ranked station cannot become number one.)

Learning Exercise 14.10

How do you determine how much the highest-ranked station will counteroffer to keep Connie Hennings? Does it matter to your answer if they fall to number three in the rankings without her?

14.4 Searching for the Best Job Offer

We have discussed labor market equilibrium without addressing the question of how employers and employees find each other. Job search and selection decisions are important factors in all labor markets. In cyclical businesses, for example, employees are likely to be temporarily unemployed during periods of recession. In these periods, they may actively search for supplemental or new employment. What are the conditions under which an individual will accept a

[16]You may also add in the wages the station pays any anchor that Connie Hennings is expected to replace because these wages are a cost savings to the station.

job offer? How long is someone likely to search? These are the questions we consider in this section.

RESERVATION WAGE SEARCH

In our discussion of economic rents, we introduced the concept of a reservation wage, which is the lowest wage that someone is willing to accept in order to produce a given amount of effort. The reservation wage is determined from the individual's labor supply curve. In effect, the reservation wage represents the trade-off between work and leisure when wages are known. When jobs are not immediately available and job search is required to determine wage offers, however, the calculation of a reservation wage is changed. The reservation wage is still affected by the satisfaction received from leisure time relative to goods consumed, but it is also affected by the distribution of wage offers in the labor market.

Suppose that you are an accountant and that *all* firms pay \$20 per hour for accounting services. If you are willing to work 40 hours per week for \$20 per hour, you will accept the first job offered at \$20 per hour, *ceteris paribus*; that is, it makes no sense for you to continue searching if all other offers are the same. Now, suppose that there is a range of wages offered to accountants and that \$20 per hour is the *average* wage offer, \$30 per hour is the *maximum*, and \$10 per hour is the *minimum*. If your first job offer is \$20 per hour, will you accept it? The answer depends on how the new information about the wage offer distribution changes your reservation wage. Does the fact that there are jobs paying more than \$20 per hour cause you to raise your reservation wage? If so, then you may not accept the first job offer if it is for \$20 per hour. What this example illustrates is that the variability of wages may affect your decision to accept a particular wage offer.

DETERMINING THE RESERVATION WAGE

We can formalize the choice of a job offer by showing how an individual might set the reservation wage in response to information about the wage offer distribution. Let's continue with the example above and assume that wage offers for accountants are uniformly distributed between \$10 and \$30, with the average wage equal to \$20. The uniform distribution is shown in the two panels in Figure 14.16.

Panel (a) in Figure 14.16 represents the distribution of wage offers for a large number of accounting firms. Hourly wage offers vary across firms, but every wage offer is between \$10 and \$30 per hour and has the same likelihood of arising during job search. Because Figure 14.16 is a probability distribution, the total area of the rectangular box in the figure equals 1. The distribution is symmetric at \$20, so one-half of the area lies below \$20 and one-half of the area lies above \$20, which implies that the average wage offer is \$20 per hour. Another way to see that \$20 is the average wage offer is to realize that with every wage equally likely, the average of the highest and lowest wages equals the average wage, that is, $\$20 = (10 + 30)/2$.

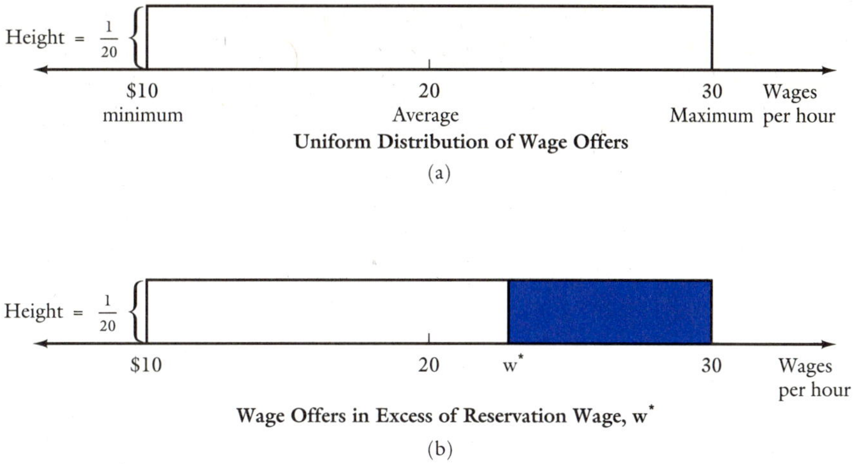

FIGURE 14.16

Wage Offers

If wage offers for accountants are distributed uniformly between $10 and $30 per hour, they have a rectangular distribution shown in panel (a). The height of the rectangle equals 1/20, which is 1 divided by the difference between the maximum and mimimum wage offers. The average wage offer is $20 per hour, which is the average of the maximum and minimum wage offers because all wage offers are equally likely. In panel (b), if the reservation wage is w^*, then any wage offer above w^* is accepted and any wage offer below w^* is rejected. The shaded area of the distribution is thus the region from which acceptable wage offers are drawn. This job search rule implies that the average accepted wage exceeds the individual's reservation wage.

At this point one may ask, why is there a distribution of wage offers? Why don't firms offer one wage? There are many possible answers to this question. Firms seeking individuals with more experience, better personalities, or certain skills may offer higher wages. Firms may also advertise a range of wages and may make offers after evaluating a candidate's credentials. These offers may vary across firms because the screening and evaluating procedures firms use are not identical. For these reasons alone, there will be a distribution of wage offers for any given individual.

We assume that when an individual searches for an accounting job, wage offers are drawn from the distribution randomly. In other words, there is no special information that allows the individual to preselect certain firms. This may be unrealistic in some cases because job searchers may carefully investigate firms before applying for some jobs. Although possibly unrealistic, it may not change the likelihood that wage offers are drawn from the uniform distribution in Figure 14.16 if the prescreening of firms generates a variety of offers that are representative of a uniform distribution.

Assume that the individual sets a reservation wage of w^* (determined below). Then, the search rule is that if a wage offer exceeds w^*, the job is accepted; if not, it is turned down and job search continues. This search rule implies that the *actual* wage accepted is expected to exceed the reservation wage. Panel (b) in Figure 14.16 illustrates this situation.

The reservation wage, w^*, is shown to be slightly higher than \$20 per hour in panel (a) in Figure 14.16. (This is an arbitrary position, so we can't infer any general results from its placement.) The shaded area to the right of w^* represents the probability that a given wage offer exceeds the reservation wage. Obviously, the higher the reservation wage (closer to \$30), the lower the probability that a job offer exceeds it. If the individual follows the search rule defined above, then only wage offers drawn from the shaded area in panel (b) are accepted. Under these circumstances, the average *accepted wage* equals the average of the wages in the shaded area of the figure. Thus, the average accepted wage equals $(30 + w^*)/2$, which exceeds the reservation wage.

How do we determine the reservation wage? The answer is that we must compare the expected gain from continued search to the extra cost of search to determine the reservation wage. Let's assume that the average cost of visiting another firm and waiting to hear its offer equals \$2 per hour. The expected gain from continued search equals the increase in wages the individual may receive times the probability of receiving the higher wage. The probability of receiving a wage higher than w^*, the reservation wage, equals the area in the uniform distribution above w^*. We can write this probability algebraically as

$$\text{Probability of a wage offer} > w^* = \frac{30 - w^*}{20} \tag{14.7}$$

The gain from continued search equals how much the individual can expect wages to increase (above w^*) if he or she continues to search *and* finds an acceptable offer. Because individuals will accept an offer only if it is greater than w^*, the average accepted wage is $(30 + w^*)/2$, as discussed above. Thus, if the current offer equals w^*, the net gain from another round of search equals $(30 + w^*)/2 - w^*$, or $(30 - w^*)/2$. Multiplying the net gain by the probability that the job seeker finds an offer that exceeds the reservation wage, equation (14.7), gives the expected gain from continued search:

$$\begin{aligned} \text{Expected gain from continued search} &= \frac{(30 - w^*)}{2} \times \frac{(30 - w^*)}{20} \\ &= \frac{(30 - w^*)^2}{40} \end{aligned} \tag{14.8}$$

The individual must equate the expected gain from continued search as shown in equation (14.8) to \$2 per hour cost of additional search in order to determine the *optimal* reservation wage. The optimal reservation wage offers the greatest increase in wages relative to the costs of searching for job offers. Equating equation (14.8) to the \$2 per hour cost of search and rearranging terms gives

$$w^* = 30 - \sqrt{80} = \$21.06 \tag{14.9}$$

Thus, the optimal reservation wage exceeds the average wage offered to accountants in this particular case. The job seeker will accept any job offer that exceeds \$21.06 per hour; otherwise, it is better to keep searching for a job from another firm.

LEARNING EXERCISE 14.11

If the cost of continued search increases to \$4 per hour, what is the optimal reservation wage? Is there likely to be more or less search as a result?

SOME RESULTS ON RESERVATION WAGE SEARCH

The optimal reservation wage selection rule has several implications for the structure of the labor market. First, the amount of job search is affected by the relative level of the reservation wage. If the distribution of offers is fixed, a higher reservation wage implies a longer expected duration of job search, which implies that measured unemployment rates are expected to be higher as reservation wages increase.

Second, reservation wages are affected by the cost of continued search. If the cost of continued search decreases, then we can expect an individual's reservation wage to increase and, accordingly, we expect the duration of unemployment to increase. Each state administers an unemployment insurance program for private sector employees. Employees who lose their jobs because of a layoff (not because of wrongful behavior) are eligible for unemployment insurance payments, which usually last about 26 weeks. In effect, these payments lower the cost of continued search by lowering the opportunity cost of refusing a job offer. Empirical research has found that an extra \$1 of unemployment benefits increases reservation wages by 44 cents and that when benefits are exhausted reservation wages fall by 14.5 percent of the pre-unemployment wage rate.[17]

Third, reservation wages are generally not fixed over time. As individuals search, they deplete their "rainy day" savings accounts. This factor causes reservation wages to fall over the period of unemployment because individuals realize that the resources needed for continued search face exhaustion at some point. In addition, search provides more information about the actual distribution of wage offers, so individuals revise their expectations downward if they were overly optimistic to begin with. These new expectations produce a new reservation wage and increase the likelihood of finding an acceptable wage offer.

Finally, reservation wage search implies that individuals with similar skills may accept jobs with different wages because wage offers depend partly on the search process. Some individuals may select a firm that offers an acceptable wage closer to their reservation wage, while other individuals may get lucky and find a job at a relatively higher wage. Thus, there is an element of luck

[17]See Raymond P. H. Fishe, "Unemployment Insurance and the Reservation Wage of the Unemployed," *Review of Economics and Statistics* 64 (February 1982), 12–17.

inherent in the actual distribution of wages in the labor market; it is not all determined by the value of an individual's marginal product.

Chapter Summary

1. Factor demand is called a derived demand because it is derived from the demand for the final output of the firm. Without a market for the firm's output, the firm has no need for the factors used to produce the output.
2. The optimal employment rule depends on the structure of the output market. Perfectly competitive firms hire an input up to the point at which the value of the marginal product equals the input's marginal cost ($VMP_L = w$ for labor inputs). A firm with market power hires an input up to the point at which the marginal revenue product equals the input's marginal cost ($MRP_L = w$ for labor inputs).
3. Quasi-fixed costs do not vary directly with output; instead, they tend to vary with the amount of inputs. Hiring and training costs for new workers are examples. Quasi-fixed costs imply that firms compare the present value of the extra revenue from hiring a new employee to the present value of extra costs, including quasi-fixed costs. If the present value of extra revenues exceeds the present value of extra costs, then a new employee is hired.
4. Wage changes cause both income and substitution effects. The labor supply curve is positively sloped when the substitution effect (more work) exceeds the income effect (more leisure). A backward bend develops when the income effect overcomes the substitution effect.
5. The labor supply curve shows the least amount that an individual will accept to provide a given level of labor effort. If the wage received exceeds the least amount for the effort supplied, the individual receives an economic rent, which is the difference between the total wages paid and the least amount needed to elicit the labor effort provided.
6. A monopsonist is the only buyer of one input, which gives it market power over the input's price. If quantity demanded of the monopsonized input increases, the monopsonist pays a higher wage. Thus, the monopsonist faces an increasing marginal factor cost curve. Optimal employment is determined by equating the value of the input's marginal product to the input's marginal factor cost.
7. The reservation wage is affected by the trade-off between leisure and work and many factors specific to the labor market. A reduction in job search costs, for example, causes reservation wages to increase. Limited assets of the unemployed and new information about the distribution of wages offers also affect reservation wages.

Trouble Spots

Concept	Reminder
Factor Demand with Only One Variable Input	Factor demand with labor as the only one variable input is determined by equating the VMP to the wage rate for perfectly competitive firms or by equating the MRP to

	the wage rate for firms with market power. These results define an unambiguous functional relationship between wages and employment levels. Higher employment levels will maximize profits only if wages are lower for all workers. Thus, the derived demand curve for labor has a negative slope.
Factor Demand with Several Variable Inputs	With more than one variable input, the interaction between inputs affects the factor demand curve for a single input. If the wage rate falls, for example, the firm's marginal costs decrease, which causes profit-maximizing output rate to increase. To produce the higher output, the firm generally increases the use of all variable inputs. With complementarity between inputs, productivity of any given input increases. Thus, the firm hires a larger amount of any given input compared to the case in which there is only one variable input.
Labor Supply of Individuals	We treat the labor supply of individuals separately from the supply of other factors because individuals optimize by maximizing the satisfaction received from their actions, whereas other factors are supplied by firms that are assumed to maximize profits. These different objective functions can lead to different results, such as the backward-bending labor supply curve.
Average and Marginal Factor Cost Curves	The power of a monopsonist is comparable to the power of a monopolist: a monopolist can affect the market price of its output and the monopsonist can affect the market price of an input. By its hiring decision, the monopsonist determines the market price of the monopsonized input. Thus, the marginal cost of the input varies as more units are employed, which gives rise to the marginal factor cost curve.
The Case of a Bilateral Monopoly	There is no obvious equilibrium solution in the case of a bilateral monopoly. The outcome will depend on factors, such as bargaining ability and financial strength, that are not directly incorporated into the analysis.

14.5 Review Questions

1. Most of the analysis in this chapter uses labor as the variable input in the short run. Can you identify a firm whose short-run fixed costs are labor and whose variable costs are capital?
2. "Capital and labor compete with one another. This point was not lost on the workers of Flanders, who sabotaged the machines of the early industrial era with their wooden shoes [*sabots,* thus the origin of the word *sabotage*]; they knew well what the situation was." Comment critically.

3. What factors determine the amount of labor a perfectly competitive firm hires in the short run if labor is the only variable input?
4. When there is only one variable input, how does a monopoly seller's demand for that input differ from the demand of a perfectly competitive seller?
5. Does a perfectly competitive firm have to worry about the impact its own demand for labor has on the going wage rate?
6. If the capital input of a firm is not fixed, why is it wrong for a firm to simply "ride" its VMP_L curve up and down to determine the quantity of labor demanded as the relative price of labor changes?
7. A chicken sexer is someone who is skilled at distinguishing male and female chicks. Chicken sexers often earn over $200 per day, and a good chicken sexer can classify several thousand chicks in a single shift with a high degree of accuracy. Which determinant of factor demand elasticity do you think would bear most heavily on the demand for sexers' services? Why?
8. Why is it inaccurate to sum the labor demand curves of individual firms horizontally to arrive at the total industry demand for labor?
9. Why do you think many bank clerks earn less than many blue-collar workers having the same set of abilities? Is this an example of paying efficiency wages to blue-collar workers?
10. Assuming that the work of a certified public accountant is no more or less pleasant than that of a supermarket checker and that neither group is unionized, why would we expect to see the CPA's real wages higher in the long run?
11. "I can see why the market supply curve of labor would be upward-sloping when the substitution effect overcomes the income effect. The supply of land, however, must be straight up and down (perfectly inelastic with respect to its price). After all, there's only so much land." Comment critically.
12. "Because not all workers are completely mobile, we should not expect wage differentials among firms or different regions of the country to be completely eliminated." Do you agree or disagree, and why?
13. "Do sellers that are monopolists in the output market have monopsony power over nonunionized labor in a competitive labor market?" Evaluate this question.
14. "Mining towns often depend on a single employer. If a mine worker doesn't like the wages offered, what can he or she do? In fact, the worker will surely be fired if there are complaints or attempts to organize a union." Comment on this situation critically.
15. "People with highly specialized skills—such as harbor pilots and movie directors—often earn economic rents." Comment on the validity of this claim.
16. Explain why people receiving unemployment insurance payments are likely to remain unemployed longer than someone without such payments. How do unemployment insurance payments affect reservation wages?

14.6 Price Theory Problems

1. Is the Disney Company's demand for character actors to dress up as Mickey Mouse in its theme parks a good example of a monopoly seller hiring in a perfectly competitive labor market? How would you decide?
2. The following table lists labor employed and daily output for the FancyTie Company.

Quantity of Hourly Workers	Daily Output Rate	Marginal Product of Labor
1	100	–
2	?	80
3	220	?
4	?	20
5	244	?
6	?	2

Fill in the missing values for the FancyTie Company.

   a. If FancyTie sells its output in a competitive industry at $8 per tie and can hire labor at $16 per hour, what will be the profit-maximizing quantity of labor employed?
   b. Suppose the workforce at the FancyTie Company organizes a union, which demands a wage rate of $32 per hour. If FancyTie accepts the union offer, how will employment change? Given this result, do you think a majority of the workers will support the union's demands?

3. An economist has estimated that the average 1990 salary of Fortune 500 CEOs was $2.4 million and that they worked an average of 2,560 hours during the year. In 1991, the average salary increased to $2.7 million and the CEOs worked an average of 2,504 hours during the year. Is this evidence of a backward-bending labor supply curve? What other factors may explain these data?
4. "Teaching methods in colleges and universities have changed little in the past twenty years, yet salaries of professors have increased more than twofold. This is evidence that paying workers according to the value of their marginal product is a questionable theory in practice." Comment on this claim. How do average class size and innovations in display technology—laser disks and overhead projectors—affect your analysis? How do research and grant writing enter into the discussion? Is there a winner-take-all characteristic in the reward structure for college and university professors?
5. Individuals are usually very reluctant to discuss their salary or wages with co-workers. What economic motive do they have to keep such information secret? Why do managers of firms encourage secrecy? When workers are unionized, wage information is often revealed in the form of salary schedules. Why do unions prefer to reveal wage information?

6. Explain why discrimination in hiring and wage decisions for a perfectly competitive firm is inconsistent with profit maximization. Can you make the same claim for a pure monopoly?
7. Suppose a monopsonist's (inverse) demand curve for labor is given by $w = 80 - 4L$, where w is the hourly wage and L is the quantity of labor hours employed.
    a. If the supply curve of labor is $w = 4L$ and the marginal factor cost curve (MFC) is $w = 8L$, what is the optimal employment of labor and what is the wage paid?
    b. How would your response to part (a) change if the output industry was perfectly competitive?
    c. Suppose the workers organize a labor union. What is the rent-maximizing wage demand by the union? [Note: marginal revenue (MR) is given by $w = 80 - 8L$.]
8. In the mid-1970s, the U. S. Congress eliminated the military draft in favor of an all-volunteer army. What effect did this have on the wages paid in the military? Did this action increase or decrease the overall quality of military personnel? How did this action affect the training programs offered to new recruits?
9. Suppose that hourly wage offers for plumbers are distributed uniformly between \$15 and \$30. If the opportunity cost of each job search is \$3 per hour, what is the optimal reservation wage for plumbers? What is the probability that an acceptable job offer is found on the first search?
10. Assume that two people have equal preferences and abilities except that the one who goes to college becomes more productive. Would you expect both people to attend college if one chooses to go? How do tuition levels affect this decision if both people have the same wealth and family income?

14.7 Writing Exercise

Write an essay that analyzes the decision of a household to have children. Assume three possible scenarios: (1) both the husband and the wife are college graduates with good jobs; (2) the husband is a college graduate and the wife is not, but the husband is ten years older than the wife; and (3) neither the husband nor the wife are college graduates. Discuss the relative number of children you expect to find born in each scenario. Explain the effect the couple's residence in a city or in the country has on your analysis. Be careful to specify the economic rationale for your observations.

15 Intertemporal Markets and Decision Making Under Uncertainty

Preview Questions

When you finish studying this chapter, you should be able to answer the following questions:

- What is the price of intertemporal consumption?
- How do you compute the present value of future income?
- What is the intertemporal budget constraint?
- How do you determine the optimal path of consumption over time?
- What markets have developed to transfer risk?
- What is the difference between the descriptions risk neutral, risk averse, and risk lover?

Let's consider the subject of death with a serious tone. It is 1986 and Sean Reilly has a terminal illness. His doctor says that he has six months to live; the experimental treatment he is taking is not effective. He has exhausted all of his assets, except for a life insurance policy that will pay $100,000 to his wife (they have no children). He and his wife have dreamed of traveling to Ireland to visit his ancestral home, but they don't have the financial means to arrange the trip. Sean Reilly dies without seeing Ireland.

The plight of Sean Reilly illustrates the need for a new market, one in which life insurance can be redeemed (at a discount) before death. In 1988, American Life Resources Corporation and several other companies responded to this need by offering to buy the life insurance policies of terminally ill patients. These companies, known as viatical settlement organizations, purchase life insurance policies at a discount to their face value. The policyholder receives money to which he or she would otherwise never have access. Today, there are over fifty companies offering viatical settlement plans.

For the terminally ill and perhaps all of us, time is our most scarce economic resource. The scarcity of time gives it value; that is, it can be used for leisure or it can be used to obtain income through work. Time also presents trade-offs for consumption decisions: Do we choose to save income today for more consumption in the future, or do we choose to borrow against our future income to have more consumption today? While this question is important to everyone, it is clearly important to those who are terminally ill. So far, we have not addressed the question of saving and borrowing. How much do you save? How much do you borrow? What affects your decision to save or borrow?

Nor have we considered how uncertainty affects our consumption decisions. We have assumed that consumers choose between alternatives that are "certain" or "riskless." If you plan a picnic in a local park, bad weather or a dead battery in your car may affect your level of satisfaction. Fire, flood, illness, or other unexpected disasters may substantially lower your income, just as winning a state lottery may unexpectedly make you rich.

Insurance markets arise because uncertainty affects your consumption decisions. Life insurance, flood insurance, and health insurance offer you a way to transfer some risk to others. Your decision on how much risk to bear is thus affected by the price of insurance and its availability.

This chapter extends our basic model of choice to consumption over time and choices under uncertainty. We discuss the preference for consumption today versus consumption in the future and the saving and borrowing decisions that individuals make, and we describe the market for intertemporal consumption. In addition, we explain how risk affects various consumption decisions, such as whether to purchase insurance. We also discuss the many financial markets that have arisen to transfer risk using the price system.

15.1 Consumption Over Time

When we started our formal analysis of choice in Chapter 5, the choice you confronted was between where to eat lunch, McDonald's or Le Bistro—or, more abstractly, between good X_1 and good X_2. The two goods were to be consumed "today," or, in the case of lunch, during the upcoming week. You were faced with an **atemporal** consumption decision: how much to consume of each good during a given period of time. We found the solution using indifference curves and the budget line.

Atemporal
A single period of time.

Similarly, we can consider your consumption choices between different time periods, that is, between consuming goods in the "present" and consuming them in the "future." Such choices are called **intertemporal** choices because they involve different time periods and are linked by borrowing and savings. You can save present income to spend in the future or you can borrow against future income to consume more in the present. Generally speaking, your choice requires you to compare consumption expenditure in the present to consumption expenditure in the future. How much do you prefer one over the other at the margin? Do you save or borrow in the present? If you manage a business, you frequently are confronted with intertemporal choices. Do you borrow funds to buy the current computer technology or save to buy a more advanced technology in the future? Do you pay higher dividends to shareholders, or do you retain the company's earnings, thus investing for higher earnings in the future? The price of saving for future consumption expenditure is the current consumption expenditure you give up. The price for borrowing to increase current consumption expenditure is the future income (or consumption) you forgo as a result of repaying your loan.

Intertemporal
More than one period of time.

THE PRICE OF SAVING AND BORROWING

Interest Rate
The rate of exchange between goods today and goods in the future.

In order to determine your optimal choice between present goods and future goods, we must define your intertemporal budget constraint and preferences. The budget constraint depends on the price of present consumption versus future consumption. This price is called the **interest rate**, *r*; it measures the rate of exchange between present and future goods over a given time period. Specifically, an *annual* interest rate measures the price of consuming a good today compared to one year from now. The level of the interest rate in our open economy is determined by the market for loanable funds, also called the credit market.

The credit market brings together two types of people: those who want to save and those who want to borrow. Those people who want to save some of their present income are the *suppliers* of credit, and those who want to borrow—repaying in the future—are the *demanders* of credit. In other words, the credit market brings together people who are willing to exchange present and future consumption.

THE EQUILIBRIUM INTEREST RATE

Figure 15.1 shows supply and demand curves for the international credit market. The intersection of these curves determines the equilibrium market rate of interest. The equilibrium interest rate balances the borrowing desires of individuals, corporations, and governments with the saving desires of the same three groups.

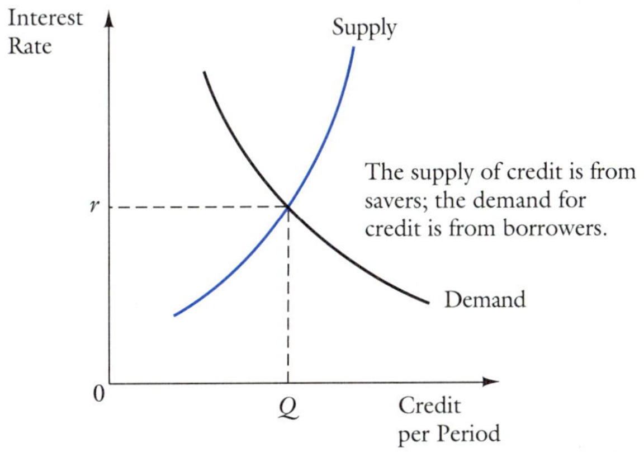

FIGURE 15.1

The Equilibrium Interest Rate for the Credit Market

The credit market determines the equilibrium interest rate. The credit market brings together borrowers, who wish to spend more than their present income allows, with savers, who do not wish to spend all of their current income. The demand for credit is determined by borrowers and the supply of credit is determined by savers.

Although we will use the same interest rate for borrowing and lending, it is important to note that different borrowers can face different interest rates. The difference is explained by the riskiness of the borrowers' projects, the collateral offered, and the past record of repayment.

For simplicity, we assume that any one saver or borrower is a very small part of the entire credit market, and therefore a single consumer can borrow or lend as much as he or she wishes without affecting the equilibrium market rate of interest. Let's denote the equilibrium rate of interest by r. Then 1 plus the rate of interest, or $(1 + r)$, is the rate at which future dollars and current dollars are exchanged. For our purposes, the future is the next year. That is, by spending \$1 on consumption today, you forgo $\$(1 + r)$ of income that could be spent on consumption in the next year. We say that $\$(1 + r)$ is the **future value (FV)** of \$1 of present income. Looked at another way, you must repay $\$(1 + r)$ in the future in order to borrow and buy \$1 worth of goods at current prices now. In this light, \$1 is the **present value (PV)** of $\$(1 + r)$ of future income.

Future Value (FV) The value of income or consumption in a future period.

Present Value (PV) The current value of any sum to be received or paid in the future.

The concepts of future value and present value are very important. Let's develop another example to help illustrate these two concepts. Suppose the equilibrium annual interest rate is 10 percent ($r = 10\%$). If you deposit \$100 in a bank today, you will find that your deposit has grown to \$110 one year from now. By saving \$100 of present income, you can purchase \$110 worth of consumption a year from now. The *future value* of your \$100 is $\$100(1 + r)$, or \$110, when $r = 10\%$.

Now, let's reverse the situation.[1] Assume that you do not have \$100 today to deposit in a bank but that you desire to buy \$100 worth of goods today. What can you do? If you expect to earn \$110 one year from now and you can substantiate this fact to your bank, then you can borrow \$100 today if you commit to repay the bank \$110 at the end of one year. In this case, the \$100 is the *present value* of the \$110 you have promised to repay one year from now. Algebraically, we say that $\$100 = \$110/(1 + r)$, where $r = 10\%$.

The relationship between present value (PV) and future value one year from now (FV_1) is given by the following equation:

$$PV = \frac{FV_1}{(1 + r)} \tag{15.1}$$

where the interest rate, r, is defined for a given time period—say, one year—and PV and FV_1 are monies received at the beginning and end of the time period, respectively.

The basic relationship between present and future periods can be extended to periods extending beyond one year. For example, if you deposited \$100 in a bank for two years at an *annual* interest rate of 10 percent, your deposit would grow to \$110 at the end of the first year and then grow to $\$121 = \$110(1 + r)$ at the end of the second year. Now, the future value is \$121 and the present value is \$100. The relationship between the

[1] Our example assumes that you can save and borrow at the same rate of interest. Although this is generally not correct, we will use this assumption to simplify the exposition of the intertemporal budget constraint.

present value (PV) and the future value *two years from now* (FV_2) is given by the following equation:

$$PV = \frac{FV_2}{(1 + r)^2} \tag{15.2}$$

Equation (15.2) is a slight generalization of equation (15.1). The two main differences are that the future value, FV_2, is paid two years from now and the denominator, $(1 + r)$, is squared. The denominator is squared because we must bring the future dollars back *two* years, instead of one, to reach the present. We can generalize the relationship between present and future dollars to any number of years. Specifically, if FV_n represents the future value n years ahead, then the present value of these dollars is given by the following equation:

$$PV = \frac{FV_n}{(1 + r)^n} \tag{15.3}$$

LEARNING EXERCISE 15.1

Your college gives you a choice: Pay \$5,000 in tuition now or pay \$6,000 at the end of the year. Assuming that you can borrow or lend at an annual interest rate of 15 percent, what is the "best" decision?

Price Theory in Practice

BORROWING TO BUY A HOME

When you buy a home you will probably borrow money from a bank that will be repaid over the next 30 years. Your ability to repay the loan depends on your income over many years in the future. To compute how much debt you can repay, we must determine how much money you can set aside for loan payments each year for the next 30 years. Let's say that you can reasonably expect to be able to pay \$10,000 per year on a home mortgage loan. If the loan is for 30 years, then the present value of the \$10,000 payment is given by the following equation:

$$PV = \frac{L_1}{(1 + r)} + \frac{L_2}{(1 + r)^2} + \cdots + \frac{L_{30}}{(1 + r)^{30}}$$
$$= \frac{10{,}000}{(1 + r)} + \frac{10{,}000}{(1 + r)^2} + \cdots + \frac{10{,}000}{(1 + r)^{30}}$$

This may be simplified using the summation operator:

$$PV = \sum_{t=1}^{30} \frac{L_t}{(1 + r)^t} = \sum_{t=1}^{30} \frac{\$10{,}000}{(1 + r)^t} \tag{15.4}$$

where t is an index for the years, L_t represents the total loan payments in year t, and the summation symbol, $\sum_{t=1}^{30}$, means that the term it precedes is to be added successively until the time index equals its terminal value. Here the terminal value is 30. In effect, the summation symbol implies that you are to compute the ratio $\$10{,}000/(1 + r)^t$ for each value of the time index between 1 and 30 and then add these terms together to compute the present value (PV). Note that equation (15.4) is a generalization of equation (15.3). Equation (15.3) gave the present and future value relationship for a *given* period in the future, whereas equation (15.4) gives this relationship for a sequence of future periods in which dollars are paid.

If the current market interest rate on home mortgages is 10 percent, then equation (15.4) implies that the present value of your $10,000 annual payment is $94,269. Assuming that you meet the other qualifications for a loan that the bank may require, you can expect to borrow up to $94,269 for the purchase of a home. If the home costs more than this amount, you will be expected to provide the difference yourself.

This example illustrates how the concept of present value may be generalized to more than one time period. In many cases, you will be faced with choices, such as the home loan decision, in which the present value formula shown in equation (15.4) will be helpful.

Learning Exercise 15.2

Assume that you will earn $25,000 (after taxes) during each year for the next four years. If the interest rate is 12 percent, what is the present value of this income stream?

REAL AND NOMINAL INTEREST RATES

So far we have been discussing the *nominal* rate of interest, which is the interest rate reported in newspapers and quoted by banks for loans and deposits. The nominal interest rate includes an allowance for changes in the cost of living between time periods. When you deposit $100 in a bank offering 10 percent annual interest, for example, you are paid $110 at the end of the year. In money, or nominal, terms you earn $10 in interest. But the purchasing power of the $100 deposit is affected by economy-wide inflation. If the prices of the goods and services you buy increase by 4 percent during the year, then what you could purchase for $100 at the beginning of the year will now cost $104. Thus, $4 of the $10 in interest earned over the year compensates you for your lost purchasing power. The remaining $6 in interest increases your purchasing power in the next year and thus represents a *real return* on your $100 deposit. In this example, the **real rate of interest** on your deposit is 6 percent.

Real Rate of Interest
Rate of return measured in terms of the goods or services you can purchase in future periods after adjusting for inflation.

The *real rate of interest* measures your return in terms of the goods or services you can purchase in the next period after adjusting for inflation. In contrast, the *nominal rate of interest* measures your return in terms of the money you receive for your deposit, not adjusted for inflation. When there is inflation, there is always a difference between real and nominal rates of interest, so it is reasonable to ask which interest rate affects behavior. Because goods and services provide you with satisfaction, it is the real rate of interest earned on your deposit, not the nominal rate of interest quoted by the bank, that affects your level of satisfaction and your intertemporal consumption choices. Continuing with the example above, if you expect inflation to increase to 8 percent next year, you will be much less willing to deposit \$100 in a bank offering a nominal rate of 10 percent because your real rate has fallen to 2 percent. To earn the same real rate of interest as before, the bank must offer a nominal rate of 14 percent on your deposit—8 percent to cover inflation and 6 percent to increase your purchasing power. To simplify the discussion that follows, we will hold the inflation rate at zero, so that real and nominal rates of interest are equal.

MATH NOTEPAD

Computing the Real Rate of Interest

We can compute the real rate of interest from the relationship

$$(1 + r_{nominal}) = (1 + p^e) \times (1 + r_{real})$$

where p^e measures the expected inflation rate. Rearranging this expression gives

$$r_{nominal} = r_{real} + p^e + p^e \times r_{real}$$

which is commonly called the *Fisher equation.* If interest is compounded continuously, the $p^e \times r_{real}$ term drops out of the expression, giving the more common form of the Fisher equation:

$$r_{nominal} = r_{real} + p^e$$

THE INTERTEMPORAL BUDGET CONSTRAINT

Intertemporal Budget Constraint A budget constraint that shows the trade-off between present consumption and future consumption when present and future income are known with certainty.

We can use the relationship between present and future values to define the **intertemporal budget constraint.** Let's denote present consumption expenditure by C_1 and future consumption expenditure by C_2 (the next year). In the present year, you expect to earn income equal to M_1, and in the future, you expect to earn income equal to M_2. If you cannot borrow *or* save—that is, you do not have access to the credit market—all you can do is spend your present income on present consumption and spend your future income on future consumption, in which case $C_1 = M_1$ and $C_2 = M_2$. If you can borrow or save, then present and future consumption may not equal present and future income. If you are a prodigal person or receive most of your income in the second period, you may desire to borrow to increase present consumption. If you borrow against *all* of your future income, your *maximum* present consumption, C_1^{max}, will be given by the following equation:

$$C_1^{max} = M_1 + \frac{M_2}{(1 + r)} \qquad (15.5)$$

where r is the interest rate and the loan amount equals $M_2/(1 + r)$ dollars.

Suppose, for example, that the interest rate is 10 percent for money borrowed against next year's income, M_1 = \$10,000, and M_2 = \$10,000. Substituting these values into equation (15.5) will result in C_1^{max} = \$10,000 + \$10,000/1.10 = \$19,091. So, the most that you could consume this year, assuming that you borrowed against all of your future income, is \$19,091.

In contrast, if you are a frugal person or you receive most of your income in the first period, you may desire to save part of your present income to increase your future consumption. If you save all of your present income, your maximum future consumption, C_2^{max}, will be determined by the following:

$$C_2^{max} = (1 + r)M_1 + M_2 \tag{15.6}$$

To illustrate, let's use the values we used for r, M_1, and M_2 to compute equation (15.5). Substituting these values into equation (15.6) gives $C_2^{max} = (1.10)\$10{,}000 + \$10{,}000 = \$21{,}000$. So, the most you could consume next year, assuming that you saved all of your present income, is \$21,000.

These two extreme points can be used to construct the intertemporal budget constraint. This is done in Figure 15.2. The intertemporal budget constraint is a straight line connecting C_1^{max} and C_2^{max} in Figure 15.2. The intertemporal budget constraint passes through the point at which $C_1 = M_1$ and $C_2 = M_2$. Recall from Chapter 4 that the slope of the budget line for two commodities purchased today is equal to the relative price ratio with a minus sign in front. By analogy, the slope of the intertemporal budget constraint equals the relative price of consumption in the present to consumption in the future, which is equal to $-(1 + r)$. In effect, the slope of the

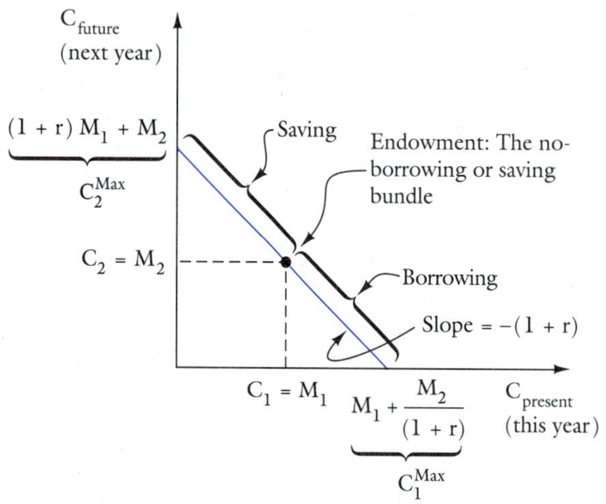

FIGURE 15.2

The Intertemporal Budget Constraint

The intertemporal budget constraint shows the trade-off between present and future consumption. An individual has an endowment of present (M_1) and future (M_2) income. Saving or borrowing at the market interest rate, r, makes available additional intertemporal consumption bundles. The trade-off between present and future consumption is equal to $(1 + r)$; that is, an extra \$1 of present consumption will cost $\$(1 + r)$ of future consumption.

intertemporal budget constraint measures the market-determined rate of trade-off between present and future consumption. An extra dollar of present consumption implies that you forgo \$(1 + r) of future consumption. Alternatively, reducing present consumption by \$1 increases future consumption by \$(1 + r).

A closer inspection of Figure 15.2 will reveal the exact form of the trade-off you face between present and future consumption. Between the present and the future you will spend all of your income. The most you can spend on future consumption is defined by equation (15.6). Whenever you increase present consumption by \$1, you decrease future consumption by \$(1 + r). So, if you consume C_1 dollars of present consumption, you reduce the amount available for future consumption by $(1 + r)C_1$ dollars. This implies that the relationship between future consumption, C_2, and present consumption, C_1, is given by the following equation:

$$C_2 = (1 + r)M_1 + M_2 - (1 + r)C_1 \tag{15.7}$$

where the *first* two terms on the right-hand side represent the maximum possible spending on future consumption and the *third* term shows how present consumption reduces future consumption.

Equation (15.7) is the algebraic representation of the intertemporal budget constraint. It shows that the trade-off between present and future consumption equals $-(1 + r)$; that is, an extra dollar of present consumption costs $(1 + r)$ dollars of future consumption. This is the equation used to draw the intertemporal budget line shown in Figure 15.2.

Continuing with the simple numerical example we used for equations (15.5) and (15.6), we see that the intertemporal budget line is given by $C_2 =$ (1.10)\$10,000 + \$10,000 – (1.10)C_1, which reduces to C_2 = \$21,000 – (1.10)C_1. This example confirms the results of our previous discussion. The most you can consume in the second year is \$21,000 if $C_1 = 0$, and for every \$1 of consumption in the present year you reduce the next year's consumption by \$1.10.

LEARNING EXERCISE 15.3

Redraw Figure 15.2 under the assumption that your savings earns 8 percent interest, but if you borrow, you pay 12 percent interest.

HOW INTEREST RATES AFFECT THE INTERTEMPORAL BUDGET CONSTRAINT

If the interest rate changes, so, too, must the slope of the intertemporal budget constraint, –(1 + r). The two panels in Figure 15.3, on page 626, show the effects of increasing and decreasing the interest rate on the intertemporal budget constraint. These panels are constructed for a specific example to help you understand how to apply the equations shown above. We have assumed that the variables defining the intertemporal budget constraint have the following initial values:

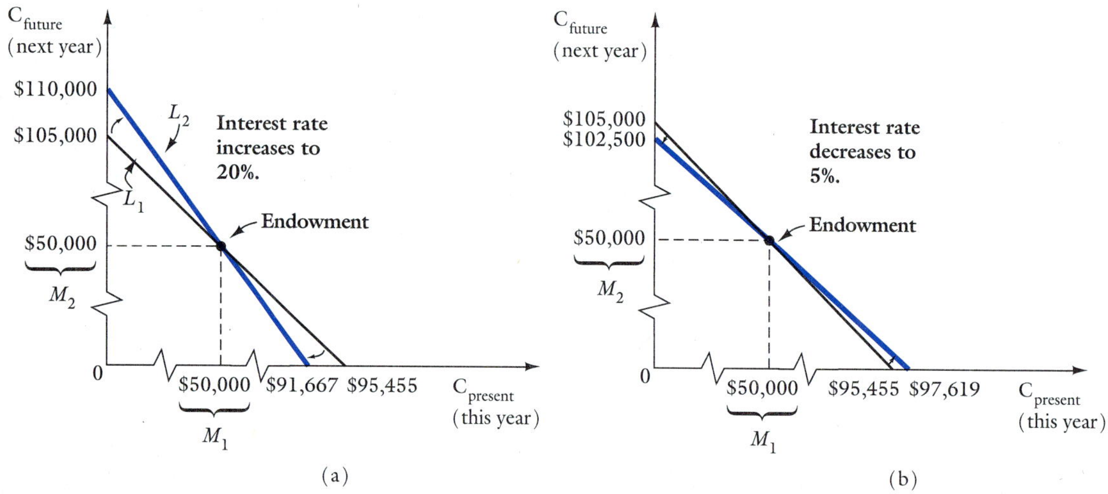

FIGURE 15.3

The Effects of Changing the Interest Rate on the Intertemporal Budget Constraint

Panel (a) shows the effect of an increase in the market interest rate from 10 to 20 percent. The intertemporal budget line pivots at the endowment point, which is not affected by a change in interest rates. More future consumption is available for savers, but less present consumption is available for borrowers. Panel (b) repeats the exercise with the market interest rate decreasing from 10 to 5 percent. Now, more present consumption is available to borrowers and less future consumption is available to savers.

$$M_1 = \$50{,}000$$
$$M_2 = \$50{,}000$$
$$r = 10\%$$

where income in each period is stated in after-tax dollars.

Using these values, the maximum you can consume in the present year is defined by equation (15.5), which implies that $C_1^{max} = \$95{,}455$ (equal to $\$50{,}000 + \$50{,}000/1.10$). The maximum you can consume in the next year is defined by equation (15.6), which implies that $C_2^{max} = \$105{,}000$ [equal to $\$50{,}000 + \$50{,}000(1.10)$]. These values define the initial position of the intertemporal budget constraint, which is shown as budget line L_1 in both panels in Figure 15.3. Now, a change in the interest rate causes the intertemporal budget constraint to pivot at the point for which $C_1 = \$50{,}000$ and $C_2 = \$50{,}000$. The new budget line is shown as L_2. The reason the pivot occurs at this point is that this point represents your income, M_1 and M_2, in the two time periods. Because M_1 and M_2 do not change when the interest rate changes, your intertemporal budget line pivots on this point. Thus, the endowment point, $C_1 = M_1$ and $C_2 = M_2$, represents the pivot point for the intertemporal budget constraint when the interest rate changes.

In panel (a), the interest rate increases to 20 percent. The effect is that the intersection point on the future consumption axis *increases* to $110,000 [equal to $\$50{,}000 + \$50{,}000(1.20)$] while the intersection point on the present consumption axis *decreases* to \$91,667 (equal to \$50,000 + \$50,000/1.20).

The interest rate increase has a mixed effect on the bundles of present and future consumption you can purchase—those bundles to the right and left of the endowment point. If you are saving some of your present income—you are to the left of the endowment bundle—then the increase in interest rates has increased your *future* consumption opportunities. In contrast, if you are borrowing for more present consumption—you are to the right of the endowment bundle—then the increase in interest rates reduces your *present* consumption opportunities. Intuitively, we see that if you are saving and interest rates go up, you earn more on your savings, so your future consumption possibilities must increase. If you are borrowing, then an increase in interest rates raises the cost of borrowing, so you have less income to spend on present consumption.

Panel (b) of Figure 15.3 shows the effects of an interest rate decrease from 10 to 5 percent. A falling interest rate causes the intertemporal budget line to pivot in the opposite direction from that shown on panel (a) of Figure 15.3. The effect is that the intersection point on the future consumption axis *decreases* to \$102,500 [equal to \$50,000 + \$50,000(1.05)] while the intersection point on the present consumption axis *increases* to \$97,619 (equal to \$50,000 + \$50,000/1.05).

When the interest rate decreases, borrowers find that they have more intertemporal consumption bundles available while savers find that they have fewer such bundles available. The reason is that a decline in interest rates lowers the cost of borrowing money and decreases the return to saving money. In effect, the relative price of present consumption has decreased; it no longer costs \$1.10 of future consumption for every \$1 of present consumption; the cost is now \$1.05 of future consumption for every \$1 of present consumption.

LEARNING EXERCISE 15.4

Draw the intertemporal budget constraint when your income in the present and future periods is unequal; that is, assume that $M_1 = \$40,000$ and $M_2 = \$60,000$.

INTERTEMPORAL PREFERENCES

Now that we have defined the intertemporal budget constraint, let's describe your preferences for present and future consumption.

First, present and future consumption expenditure may be considered substitutes; after all, they just represent consumption expenditure in two different time periods. We assume that present consumption is generally preferred to future consumption, *ceteris paribus.* If you are offered a commodity, say a one-year membership in a health club, with a choice of either having it today or having it next year, you will generally prefer to have the membership today. To defer the membership implies that you give up the option to use the health club during the coming year. The option of using the health club now is generally valuable. Thus, you will normally offer a higher price for a health club membership that you receive today than for one that you will receive one year from now. This is, of course, the analogue of why individuals usually must be rewarded by a higher market interest rate in order to encourage them to save more. Saving is the decision *not* to consume in the present period. If someone wishes to increase her present consumption but does not have enough current income, she must borrow to accomplish her goals. To borrow, she must offer someone else an incentive to save the money she needs to borrow. Generally, your saving behavior will not change unless there is an additional reward for saving. In equilibrium, your reward is the market rate of interest you receive on your savings.

But how do we know whether you will be a saver or a borrower at the equilibrium interest rate? The answer depends on your preferences for present and future consumption and your endowment. Just as we can define your preferences for two commodities by using a set of indifference curves, we can define your preferences for present and future consumption by using indifference curves. Figure 15.4 shows a set of three typical indifference curves that define your preferences for different intertemporal consumption bundles. Note that the farther away from the origin you are on an indifference curve, the higher your satisfaction, because indifference curves that are farther away from the origin allow for greater consumption in *both* present and future periods.

The intertemporal indifference curves in Figure 15.4 have a negative slope, which implies that you must give up some future consumption to gain an extra $1 of present consumption, holding satisfaction constant. The *absolute* value of the slope of an intertemporal indifference curve at a given bundle is called the

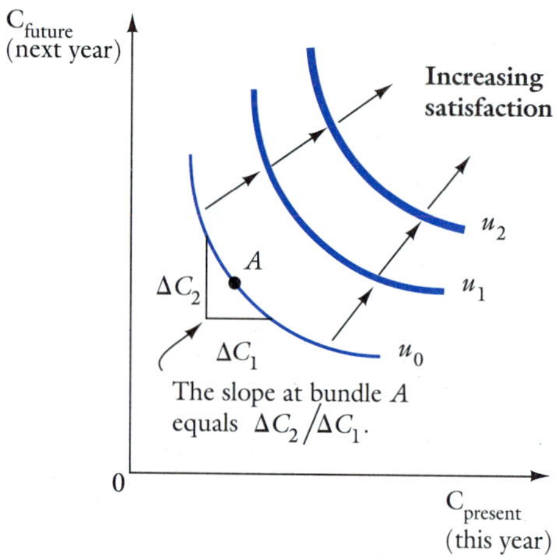

FIGURE 15.4

Three Intertemporal Indifference Curves

Three indifference curves expressing your preferences for intertemporal consumption bundles are shown. Indifference curves that are farther away from the origin represent more satisfaction. The slope of an indifference curve at bundle *A*, for example, is equal to the change in next year's consumption (ΔC_2) divided by the change in this year's consumption (ΔC_1).

Marginal Rate of Time Preference
The rate at which you can trade-off future consumption for present consumption; an extra \$1 of present consumption will cost \$(1 + *r*) of future consumption.

Positive Time Preference
The property that the marginal rate of time preference is greater than unity.

Negative Time Preference
The property that the marginal rate of time preference is less than unity.

Neutral Time Preference
The property that the marginal rate of time preference is equal to unity.

marginal rate of time preference (MRTP). For example, at bundle *A* in Figure 15.4, the MRTP is equal to $|\Delta C_2/\Delta C_1|$. The MRTP is analogous to the marginal rate of substitution discussed in Chapter 5. Recall that the marginal rate of substitution defined your subjective rate of trade-off between the two commodities shown on each axis. Similarly, the MRTP defines your subjective rate of trade-off between present and future consumption.

If the MRTP > 1, then you must receive *more than* \$1 of future consumption in order to give up \$1 of present consumption. For bundles in which this occurs—and it is expected to be the typical situation at the optimal bundle—you have a **positive time preference.** In contrast, if MRTP < 1, then you are willing to give up \$1 of present consumption for *less than* \$1 of future consumption. For these bundles, you have a **negative time preference.** The latter situation is unlikely to be very common, as the reasoning behind the health club membership example suggests. In other words, consumption of a good now is generally preferred over consumption of the same good at a future date. Finally, if MRTP = 1, you have a **neutral time preference** at your current intertemporal consumption bundle, which means that you are willing to give up \$1 of present consumption for exactly \$1 of future consumption.

While the optimal bundle is likely to exhibit MRTP > 1, other bundles along an intertemporal indifference curve may not have this property. In fact, just as the marginal rate of substitution declines as you move down an indifference curve for two commodities, the MRTP is expected to decline as you move down an intertemporal indifference curve. So, if you are at a bundle that contains significantly more future consumption than present consumption, you are likely to find that MRTP > 1. In contrast, if you are at a bundle that offers significantly more present consumption than future consumption, then MRTP < 1 may hold. Figure 15.5 on page 630 illustrates the declining MRTP property for intertemporal indifference curves.

In Figure 15.5, bundle *A* contains more future consumption than present consumption. The reverse is true at bundle *B*. We find that MRTP > 1 at bundle *A* and that MRTP < 1 at bundle *B*. Bundle *A* might represent the situation in which you are to inherit \$5 million three years from now, but for now you must live on your income from odd jobs and part-time work. With the MRTP > 1, you are willing to give up more than \$1 of your future inheritance to increase your present consumption by \$1. Bundle *B* might represent the situation of a refugee who is fleeing his country before he is arrested. The refugee may have assets that cannot be transported, such as a house and appliances, and these will be confiscated if he is caught by the authorities. In such cases, the trade-off between present and future consumption may be such that MTRP < 1. The refugee is willing to give up \$1 of present assets for less than \$1 of future assets. In effect, the refugee is willing to sell his assets at a steep discount to escape arrest and the subsequent loss of all assets.

THE OPTIMAL TIME PATH FOR CONSUMPTION

We can combine the intertemporal indifference curve in Figure 15.5 with the intertemporal budget constraint in Figure 15.2 to find the optimal intertem-

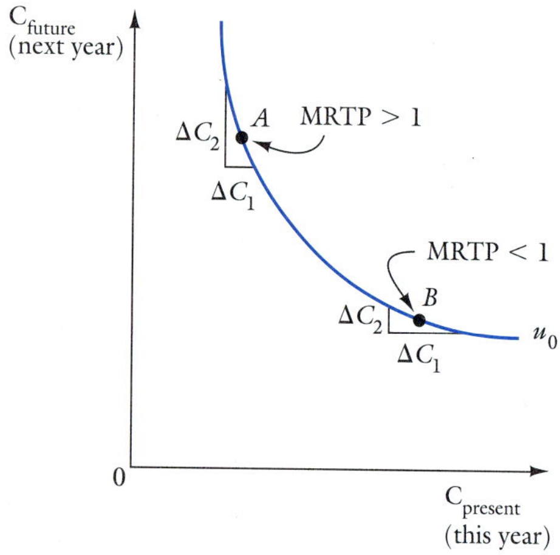

FIGURE 15.5

The Marginal Rate of Time Preference (MRTP) Decreases as You Move Down the Indifference Curve

The absolute value of the slope of an intertemporal indifference curve is equal to an individual's marginal rate of time preference (MRTP). As you move down an intertemporal indifference curve, the MRTP falls.

poral consumption bundle. This bundle is shown in Figure 15.6. The intertemporal budget constraint is tangent to the highest indifference curve, U_1, at bundle $E_{optimal}$. At the optimal bundle, equilibrium consumption is C_1^* and C_2^* in the present year and next year, respectively. Note that at the optimal bundle you are saving some of your present income. The amount of saving is equal to $M_1 - C_1^*$. At the current interest rate, r, this amount of saving allows you to increase future consumption to an amount that exceeds future income. The increased amount of future consumption is equal to $C_2^* - M_2$. This increase is equal to your savings plus the interest you earn, that is, $C_2^* - M_2 = (1 + r)(M_1 - C_1^*)$.

At the equilibrium bundle, your rate of trade-off between present and future consumption equals the rate of trade-off determined by the international market for credit. In other words, the MRTP equals the absolute value of the slope of the intertemporal budget constraint:

$$\text{MRTP} = (1 + r) \qquad (15.8)$$

Thus, as long as the international credit markets reach an equilibrium at which $r > 0$, we can say that you will reach an equilibrium at which MRTP > 1. That is, the equilibrium bundle will exhibit a positive rate of time preference. We should note that, psychologically, nothing precludes a negative rate of time preference in the equilibrium bundle except that this requires a negative equilibrium interest rate, $r < 0$. Such a possibility is counterintuitive: The market would be saying that savers are paying borrowers for the privilege of saving. This situation does not occur—at least, it does not occur at the time the saving decision is made. It may occur after the fact—for example, when a high rate of

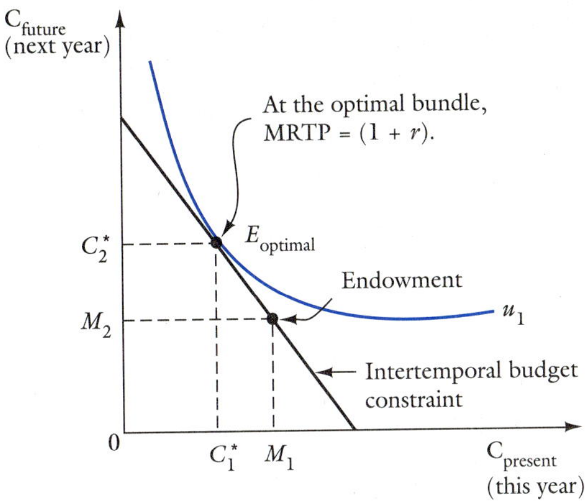

FIGURE 15.6

The Optimal Intertemporal Consumption Bundle

The equilibrium intertemporal consumption bundle is the one for which MRTP = $(1 + r)$, where r is the market rate of interest. The individual shown is in equilibrium at bundle E_{optimal}, which implies that he or she is a saver. At this point, saving for this year equals $M_1 - C_1^*$.

inflation has decreased the real value of the money saved, so that the interest paid does not offset the decline in value caused by inflation.

$$$ Price Theory in Practice

PERMANENT INCOME AND LIFE CYCLE HYPOTHESES

At one time, economists believed that present consumption was almost entirely determined by present income. If your present income rose 20 percent, so the theory went, then your present consumption would be expected to rise by about 20 percent.

Careful examination of household consumption data during the 1950s by Milton Friedman, Franco Modigliani, and Richard Brumberg found this theory was inconsistent with actual behavior.[2] Friedman and Modigliani and Brumberg found that a change in present income does not cause a nearly identical change in present consumption. Instead, present consumption changes by a significantly smaller fraction. Modigliani and Brumberg formulated the *life cycle hypothesis* to explain this result. They suggested that consumption decisions are planned for many years into the future—that is, over an individual's life cycle. So, the effects of a change in present income are spread over both present and future consumption

[2] See Milton Friedman, *A Theory of the Consumption Function,* Princeton, NJ: Princeton University Press, 1957; and Franco Modigliani and Richard Brumberg, "Utility Analysis and the Consumption Function: An Interpretation of Cross-Section Data," in *Post Keynesian Economics,* K. Kurihari, ed., London: Allen & Unwin, 1955.

decisions. This theory predicts that not all of the rise in present income is spent in the present, and this is what the actual consumption data show.

Friedman's theory of consumption, called the permanent income hypothesis, produced a similar prediction. Friedman said that present consumption is primarily determined by your **permanent income.** By permanent income, Friedman meant the present value of the stream of future income. Equation (15.4), for example, can be used to compute your permanent income, assuming that you can estimate your income into the future. Because consumption is a normal good, an increase in permanent income will increase consumption in all future periods. If permanent income increases because present income increases, the rise in income will be spread over the present and many future periods. As with the life cycle hypothesis, consumption in the earliest period does not increase by an amount that is directly proportionate to the change in present income.

Permanent Income The present value of the expected future stream of labor income.

The life cycle and permanent income hypotheses represent one of the first applications of the intertemporal choice model. The model was put to good use: It helped explain consumption patterns at a time when they were not clearly understood.

LEARNING EXERCISE 15.5

A natural disaster, such as a hurricane or earthquake, can cause permanent losses in wealth. What effect do you expect a natural disaster to have on present and future consumption?

15.2 DETERMINANTS OF INTEREST RATES

Your decision to save or borrow depends on the interest rate and other variables. Nominal interest rates can vary significantly, and this can cause important changes in saving and borrowing decisions. Historically, interest rates of all types have followed a roller coaster path through time, changing dramatically in some periods and remaining relatively stable during other periods. During the Great Depression in the 1930s, for example, interest rates on long-term government bonds averaged less than 3 percent. And for most of the 1940s, long-term government bonds averaged less than 2.5 percent. In contrast, in the late 1970s and early 1980s, interest rates on long-term government bonds exceeded 10 percent. One particularly dramatic example of how interest rates can change occurred in October 1907, when the interest rate charged on loans secured by common stocks increased from 5 percent to 125 percent in one week! Why do interest rates change, sometimes slowly and at other times quite dramatically? Why do they vary across different investment options, such as mortgage loans and new car loans? Let's discuss the basic reasons.

RISKY INVESTMENTS

There are many different investment options. You can buy common stocks, corporate bonds, foreign government bonds, limited partnership shares in oil drilling ventures, real estate, "old master" paintings, gold coins—the list seems endless. These options are all risky in the sense that investors do not know their future value or their future income stream today. The relative riskiness of these investments affects their relative return in four ways:

1. The *default risk* varies across investments. A credit card loan is likely to have a greater probability of default than a new car loan, which is likely to have a greater probability of default than a home mortgage loan. *Ceteris paribus*, the market interest rate on credit card loans exceeds the interest rate on car loans, which exceeds the interest rate on mortgage loans.
2. *Collateral* affects the riskiness and return on an investment. A deposit in a bank is insured by the Federal Deposit Insurance Corporation (FDIC) up to $100,000. In effect, your deposit is a loan to the bank that is fully collateralized by the FDIC, so there is no loss if the bank should fail. In contrast, if you buy commercial paper issued by some large corporations, you are making an unsecured loan. If these companies enter into bankruptcy before you are repaid, you must wait in line with other creditors for payment. Generally, the higher the expected value of the collateral, the lower the interest rate on the investment.
3. *Collection costs* affect the interest rate on risky investments. If your investment is in default, the expected cost of recovering all or part of what is owed affects the interest rate. Some bankruptcy cases last for many years while others are resolved in much less time. The shorter the expected length of time in default or the lower the collection costs, the lower the interest rate.
4. A *varying payment stream* affects the interest rate on risky investments. Some investments, such as bonds, offer a payment schedule that indicates the amount and date of certain payments. In contrast, common stocks and many real estate investments make payments only if the investment produces profits, which can vary from period to period. When comparing two otherwise equivalent investments, most investors place a higher value on the one with the less variable payment stream, so it offers a lower return.

In addition to the above, most investments can be regarded as *physically different assets*. Gold coins, for example, do not look or feel the same as a painting by the great French impressionist Claude Monet. Thus, the satisfaction generated—not necessarily the monetary return—may differ across various investment options, which may lead to a different interest rate for certain investments.

INFLATION PREMIUM

Although death and taxes may be certain, inflation is not, but its past history makes it an ongoing problem for credit markets. Economy-wide inflation affects the purchasing power of the future income stream of an investment, which affects nominal interest rates as noted in our discussion of real and nominal interest rates. The inflation premium increases the interest rate, or return, on an investment. It may be a constant effect for investments maturing at various points in time, or it may affect maturities differently. For example, if investors expect inflation to remain at 4 percent each year over the next 10 years, then all investments maturing within the next 10 years will carry a constant 4 percent per annum inflation premium. In contrast, if investors expect that inflation will increase in the future from its present rate of 4 percent, then investments with more distant maturities will carry a higher inflation premium than investments maturing in the near future. Thus, interest rates will be higher on investments with more distant maturity dates.

TERM STRUCTURE

The **term structure** is a profile of the market interest rate on a particular investment over different maturity dates in the future. Generally, the more distant the date of maturity, the higher the market interest rate on the investment. The term structure is often helpful to investors because it defines the interest rate profile for a *specific* investment. Thus, the relative riskiness associated with *different* investments that have *different* maturities is controlled for in a graph of a specific investment's term structure. For instance, a car loan may mature in 4 years and a mortgage loan may mature in 30 years. These investments are different along two dimensions: car versus mortgage and 4 years versus 30 years to maturity. On a term-structure profile, we look at only one investment, say, a mortgage, and plot the interest rate at different maturity dates, so we can avoid the issue of whether a mortgage per se is more or less risky than a car loan. In this light, the term structure shows the market-determined profile of the relative *time* riskiness of an investment.

Term Structure
A profile of the interest yield of an asset for various maturities.

Figure 15.7 shows an example of the term structure of interest rates for U.S. government bonds on September 17, 1992. The interest rate for bonds that mature in less than 1 year is less than 3.5 percent, but as maturity increases, the interest rate increases until we reach 7.31 percent for 30-year government bonds. Historically, this is a very steep term-structure curve. Since 1926, for example, the average differential between long-term government bonds and 90-day Treasury bills has been about 1 percentage point. In the 1970s and 1980s, the differential increased to a little more than 2 percentage points. On Figure 15.7, the differential is 3.81 points! Thus, this term structure curve is unusual.

What causes the term structure to change its shape? Why is it steeper in some periods and flatter in others? There are several theories for why the term structure changes its shape over time. One view, known as the **expectations hypothesis,** is that the term structure is rising because investors expect shorter-term interest rates to rise in the future. Thus, relatively longer-term rates are a reflection of this belief. The steeper the yield curve, the more rapidly investors expect shorter-term rates to rise. The flatter the yield curve, the slower rates are expected to rise. According to the expectations hypothesis, periods of rapidly increasing inflation should represent periods in which the term structure is relatively steep. Professor Eugene F. Fama of the University of Chicago has found evidence to support the expectations hypothesis, but he has also

Expectations Hypothesis
The shape of the term structure is determined by expectations of future changes in shorter-term yields.

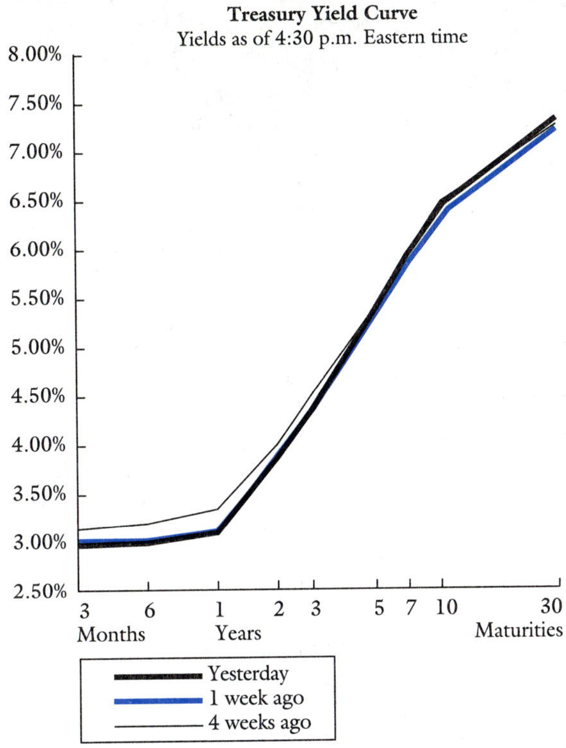

FIGURE 15.7

The Term Structure for U.S. Treasury Securities, September 17, 1992.

The term structure of U.S. Treasury securities on September 17, 1992, is shown. The yield curve is fairly flat for securities maturing in one year or less and then is relatively steep, climbing to a yield of 7.25 percent for 30-year bonds.

Source: Technical Data's Bond Data, *The Wall Street Journal*, September 17, 1992.

found that the theory is lacking because shorter-term rates do not rise by the full amount predicted by longer-term rates.[3] Thus, the relatively steep curve in Figure 15.7 does not necessarily imply that shorter-term rates will increase after September 1992.

Liquidity Preference Theory
The shape of the term structure is determined by the relative mix of long- and short-term investors.

An alternative view of the behavior and shape of the term structure curve, called the **liquidity preference theory,** suggests that there are not enough investors willing to accept the risk of longer-term investments. Some investors want to invest funds for longer-term maturities and some for shorter-term maturities. Similarly, some companies, households, and financial institutions

[3] See Eugene F. Fama, "The Information in the Term Structure," *Journal of Financial Economics* 13 (December 1984), 509–528.

want to borrow funds to repay in the near future and some want to repay in the more distant future. The liquidity preference theory suggests that there are fewer individuals or institutions (or the amount of funds) willing to lend for longer-terms than the number of individuals or institutions (or the amount of funds) desiring to borrow for repayment in the distant future. This shortage of long-term investors or imbalance of funds creates a relative risk premium for long-term assets. Long-term assets must yield more to induce investors to accept longer-term risks.

Both the liquidity preference theory and the expectations hypothesis predict that the term structure curve will have a positive slope when investors expect short-term rates to increase in the future; each theory suggests that there is a risk premium on longer-term assets, but for different reasons. The expectations theory explains the positively sloped yield curve on the basis of inflation, whereas the liquidity preference theory explains it in terms of the relative supply of short- and long-term investors. There is a difference between the two theories: The expectations hypothesis claims that short-term rates will rise in the future to confirm the relatively higher long-term rates, whereas the liquidity preference theory does not make such a claim. Thus, which theory is actually correct affects the future behavior of interest rates, which affects decisions made by both households and firms.

Learning Exercise 15.6

Collect monthly data on 90-day Treasury bill rates and 20-year government bond rates since September 1992. Do these data show that the shorter-term rates have increased as predicted by the expectations hypothesis?

$$$ Price Theory in Practice

Nominal Versus Real Returns, 1926–1991

The relative riskiness of investments differs over time. In some periods, fixed-payment assets, such as government and corporate bonds, outperform common stocks and other assets whose payment stream is relatively uncertain. In other periods, common stocks outperform bonds. Over very long periods of time, however, common stocks and other assets that have uncertain payment streams outperform assets with contractually fixed payment streams.

Table 15.1 shows the 66-year performance of five different investment options: common stocks, small company stocks, long-term corporate bonds, long-term government bonds, and U.S. Treasury bills. Stocks offer an uncertain and varying payment stream, whereas bonds and bills offer a commitment to a predetermined payment stream. As Table 15.1 shows, investors place a risk premium on stocks compared to these other assets. Further, when adjusted for inflation, bonds and bills offer very low returns compared to stocks. These results suggest that stocks may be the only asset that offers longer-term protection against the risk of inflation. Thus, the so-called buy-and-hold strategy of investing in the stock market is not without empirical support.

TABLE 15.1

Summary of Annual Returns, 1926–1991

Asset	Annual Returns	Inflation-Adjusted Annual Returns
Common Stocks	10.4%	7.0%
Small Company Stocks	12.1	8.7
Long-Term Corporate Bonds	5.4	2.2
Long-Term Government Bonds	4.8	1.6
U.S. Treasury Bills	3.7	0.5

Source: Stocks, Bonds, Bills, and Inflation, 1992 Yearbook, Ibbotson & Associates, Chicago, IL; pp. 26–27.

LEARNING EXERCISE 15.7

What explains the difference in return between long-term corporate bonds and government bonds?

15.3 MARKETS FOR RISK TRANSFER

It is important to realize that risk does not "go away" in the world. You can transfer your risk to others, as we discuss below, or you can live with it yourself. If you keep the risk you face, then you bear any consequent costs. That is, if you become unemployed, it is your income that is affected, not someone else's. If you are sick and cannot work, you bear the lost income. Alternatively, if your employer will pay you while you are sick, then your employer bears the risk, not you. The risk is still there; the question is, who bears the cost associated with it?

Generally speaking, certainty is a scarce good, and for most people it has positive value. In other words, individuals are willing to pay to limit the risk they are exposed to, particularly risk that can cause a substantial change in income or wealth. Markets have arisen to help *transfer* risk between those who want less risk and those who are willing, at some price, to accept more risk.

INSURANCE MARKETS

One of the markets that has developed to transfer risk is the insurance market, in which each individual pays an insurance premium to transfer part or all of a given risk to an insurance company. Automobile, health, life, and fire insurance are probably the most common types of insurance. With automobile insurance, for example, an insurance company accepts part of the risk that you will be involved in a car accident. The insurance policy you buy will pay for some or all of the costs you incur as a result of such an accident.

By insuring many people against similar risks, an insurance company collects a pool of funds to pay policyholders who are affected by accidents. Consider a simple numerical example. Suppose there are 1,000 houses in your hometown. On the average, we can assume that ten houses catch fire each year. The average loss from smoke and flames is about $50,000 per home. The total annual loss from house fires in your hometown is expected to be $500,000. The chance of any one home catching fire is 10/1,000, or 1 in 100 or 1 percent. As a homeowner, your expected losses are equal to the probability of a loss times the amount of the average loss, that is, 1 percent times $50,000, which is equal to $500.

Although your expected losses are relatively small, your actual losses are 100 times greater if you actually have a fire in your home. You, and the other homeowners, may find it beneficial to pool your risks because of the relative size of the actual losses you face. If all homeowners buy insurance, paying a premium of $550 per year into a common reserve fund, then there will be a pool of $550,000 to cover annual losses. It is expected that $500,000 will be paid to the ten homeowners whose homes catch fire during the year, with the $50,000 extra used to pay overhead, operating expenses, and profits of the insurance company.

Note that in this example, the insurance premium of $550 exceeds the expected annual loss per homeowner of $500. If there are no other costs to consider, then homeowners must place a higher value on full reimbursement for a potential loss than on their expected loss, or they would not purchase such an insurance policy. The presence of persons who place a relatively high value on avoiding risk is one explanation for the success of insurance markets. These people are willing to pay more than the expected loss to escape a risky situation. By pooling risks, owners of insurance companies are exposed to the average risk, so the amount a given policyholder is willing to pay is more than enough to cover the expected losses.

SWAP MARKETS

The market for swaps developed almost overnight during the 1980s. Today, the market is estimated to exceed $3 trillion, measured by the face value of assets outstanding that have been swapped. A **swap** is a transaction that transfers risk between two parties. There are many assets that can be swapped, such as currencies, commodities, and equities, but frequently companies swap assets that offer a fixed payment for assets that offer a variable payment. A commercial bank, for example, may swap a loan made at a fixed rate for a loan made at a variable rate by an insurance company. The bank removes the asset whose payment does not change and replaces it with an asset whose payment *does* change with general economic conditions. A bank gains from such a swap because its depositors are usually paid a rate of interest on their deposits that fluctuates with general economic activity. By swapping for a variable-rate loan, whose repayment rate fluctuates, the bank is more closely matching its cost of deposits with its revenue stream. On the other side of the swap, an insurance company has costs that are tied to average risks, which don't fluctuate with

Swap
An exchange of assets that have different payment characteristics. For example, the exchange of a fixed-rate loan for a variable-rate loan is a swap.

general economic conditions, so the fluctuating loan causes its revenue stream to change when its costs do not change. The fixed-rate loan smoothes the fluctuations in the insurance company's revenue stream so that they are more like the (smooth) change in the cost stream. This form of interest rate swap is known as a "plain vanilla" swap. Plain vanilla swaps represent about 55 percent of all swap transactions.

The risk of changing economic conditions is transferred in the swap between the bank and the insurance company. The bank accepts the risk that interest rates may fall, thereby reducing its revenue stream, but this risk is offset by the decline in deposit costs that accompanies a fall in interest rates. The insurance company "locks in" a payment stream that will not fall if interest rates decline. The insurance company's cost stream does not change much when interest rates increase, so it benefits from a fixed-interest-rate loan. The transfer of risk with a loan swap has benefited both the insurance company and the bank.

Although interest rate swaps dominate the swap market, the first major swap transaction was a currency swap. In August 1981, the World Bank and IBM Corporation entered into a currency swap. The details of this swap help explain why currency and other asset swaps have become increasingly popular. In 1980, the IBM Corporation in the United States issued Swiss franc- and German mark-denominated debt. This debt required IBM to repay its lenders in Swiss francs and German marks. The proceeds were used to help IBM expand its European operations. IBM sells its products in Germany and Switzerland, and it is paid in German marks and Swiss francs. Between 1980 and 1981, the U.S. dollar appreciated against both of these currencies, so IBM had significant paper profits on its debt issue. The World Bank issued $290 million in Eurobonds, which is debt that is sold in Europe and repaid in U.S. dollars. The World Bank had initially desired to borrow in both Swiss francs and German marks, but it had a large amount of debt outstanding in these currencies, so it faced a higher interest rate if it issued Swiss franc- or German mark-denominated bonds instead of Eurobonds. The currency swap with IBM Corporation let the World Bank borrow in Swiss francs and German marks at IBM's borrowing cost and also let IBM realize the profits on its appreciated debt. Thus, both parties gained from the swap.

Basically, currency swaps allow firms and other institutions access to loans in other currencies, which they may not have access to otherwise. For instance, many countries have exchange controls that limit the access of foreign firms to credit in their markets; they also have restrictions on the lending activity of banks to foreign firms. By arranging a currency swap, firms and other institutions can circumvent some of the local rules and regulations affecting foreign credit markets.

FUTURES MARKETS

We have discussed markets dealing in time—the credit market—and we have discussed two markets dealing with risk transfer—the insurance and swap markets. There is a market in which both elements, time and uncertainty, are found. It is the **futures market,** in which people agree in the present to buy or sell a good for delivery at a particular date in the future at a specific price. Some of the participants in the trading of **futures contracts** are called speculators. Before we analyze speculation and its effect on the allocation of resources over time and on the degree of risk taking by separate groups of individuals, we will briefly explain the market for futures.

Futures Market
The market in which futures contracts are traded.

Futures Contract
A contract for delivery of a given amount of a commodity, or the cash equivalent, at a known future date, with the price to be determined at the time of purchase.

Many of us contract for a product that is to be delivered at a future date. Most mail-order companies accept orders over the phone and deliver the merchandise two or three days later. You may order a new car with special options not available on the cars shown at the local dealership. You will probably wait a few months for the car to be produced and shipped. Some people have waited up to five years for custom-made watches. More commonly, a farmer may agree to deliver 1 million bushels of grain to a grain elevator operator at a specific month in the future at a price that is agreed upon by both parties today. Such a contract is called a **forward contracts.**

Forward Contract
The same as a futures contract except that its terms may be more flexible. Forward contracts are not traded on organized futures exchanges.

Contracting Through Time

A forward contract is not, strictly speaking, the same as a futures contract; the latter applies only to those contracts executed in "formal" exchange markets. There are a number of such markets: the Chicago Board of Trade, the Chicago Mercantile Exchange, the London International Financial Futures Exchange, the Tokyo Commodity Exchange, and others throughout the world. A recent count indicated that over thirty exchanges around the world were trading futures contracts. In the United States there are futures markets for frozen orange juice concentrate, oats, soybeans, wheat, corn, cotton, sugar, barley, lard, livestock, soybean oil, lumber and plywood, frozen chickens, potatoes, silver, rubber, cocoa, copper, wool, pork bellies, platinum, foreign exchange, government-insured mortgages, Eurodollar deposits, T-bills, T-bonds, stock market indices, pollution rights, and foreign currencies. The financial contracts—T-bonds, Eurodollar deposits, T-bills, stock indices, and foreign currencies—are far and away the most important; they represent over one-half of the trading volume in all futures contracts.

Futures contracts are made for standard qualities and quantities of a commodity. For example, in the futures market for frozen orange juice concentrate, a standard contract is for 15,000 pounds of concentrate. Futures contracts call for delivery at a standard time during the year. Futures contracts can be purchased and sold only through brokers who are members, or affiliates of members, of an exchange that trades futures contracts.

The difference between forward and futures contracts is more profound than the simple explanation above indicates. In a futures market, transactions are strictly impersonal; buyers and sellers know nothing but the price, the time, a few attributes of the product, and the place of delivery. In other words, in a futures contract it might be stated that 40,000 bushels of Minnesota no. 2 red wheat will be delivered in Winnipeg between November 3 and November 10, 1996. Clearly, there are many economies of transaction here. In other words, the transaction costs are relatively low in a futures market, which is why futures markets have gained importance over time. In contrast to futures contracts, forward contracts permit more "custom-made" contracting. The buyer and seller engage in personal rather than impersonal dealing and can specify many more aspects of the transaction than is possible in an organized futures market.

Going Long and Short

If you *buy* a futures contract today, you agree to accept delivery of a specified amount of, say, wheat at a specified date in the future at a specified place. You also agree to pay the price specified in the futures contract. When you buy a futures contract, you take a **long position** in the underlying commodity. The price that is specified in the futures contract is called the *futures price.* You might look in the newspaper today and find out that the futures price of wheat to be delivered three months from now is so many dollars per bushel. You can compare the futures price with today's **spot price,** which is the price of wheat bought *on the spot,* or currently. It is also called today's *cash price.* By holding the long side of a futures contract, you will gain if the price *increases* over the life of the contract.

Long Position
The holdings of someone who has bought a futures contract for delivery or has bought the underlying commodity.

Spot Price
The current, or cash, price of a commodity; the price for on-the-spot delivery.

On the other side of the transaction is the seller of a futures contract. The seller agrees to deliver a specified amount of a commodity on a specified date at a specified price. Those who have agreed to deliver commodities in the future at a stated price are said to have a **short position,** or to be *short,* or to have *gone short.* They have sold futures contracts. If you take a short position in a futures contract, you will profit if the price *falls* over the life of the contract.

Short Position
The holdings of someone who has agreed to deliver a commodity at a specified time in the future at a currently agreed-upon price.

Note that futures contracts generally are not settled at maturity by actual physical delivery of the commodity to a warehouse. Rather, most futures contracts are either closed out before their maturity date or settled by payment of the difference between the price stipulated in the contract and the spot price of the commodity at the date of maturity. Hence, if the futures price of wheat was \$5 when the contract was written and the spot price was \$5.10 at the date of maturity, the seller of the futures contract would pay the purchaser of the futures contract 10 cents times the number of bushels specified in the contract to settle the contract obligation.

Hedging

A crucial function of the futures market is that it allows individuals to shift risk from those less willing to bear it to those more willing to bear it, for a given fee. The process of using the futures market to eliminate risk is called **hedging.** Those who engage in this activity are called *hedgers.* Consider the operator of a grain elevator (a place to store grain) who buys corn from farmers at harvest time. The grain elevator operator stores the corn and sells it to processors (millers) over the period between corn harvests. The grain elevator operator wants to specialize in storing corn. He or she does not want to specialize in predicting the future spot prices of corn. Knowing that there are fluctuations in the spot price of corn, the grain elevator operator may wish to reduce the possibility of loss due to a reduction in the spot price of corn later on. A loss can occur, for example, if the elevator operator buys

Hedging
Holding a given position in the spot market and the opposite position in the futures market.

corn today at $5 per bushel and two months from now sells corn for $3 per bushel. In reducing the possibility of loss, however, the operator also reduces the possibility of profit.

Using the futures market, it is possible for the grain elevator operator to transfer to someone else some of the risk that the spot price of corn will fall, in exchange for transferring the potential gains that may arise if the spot price of corn rises. What the elevator operator does is sell futures contracts in corn at the same time as he or she buys the corn from farmers. This strategy "locks in" a price for the corn stored in the grain elevator.

Speculation

Those who do not simultaneously hold both long spot and short futures positions in a particular commodity are called *speculators*. Speculators are betting that the *future* spot price of a commodity will be different from the spot price quoted today. For example, the purchaser of a futures contract from the grain operator at $2.05 per bushel of corn is betting that in six months the spot price of corn will be greater than $2.05. If corn is selling for $2.15 per bushel in six months, the speculator who has bought corn futures contracts makes a profit of 10 cents per bushel. Speculators also sell futures contracts. When they sell a futures contract, they are betting that the spot price of the commodity on the date of maturity of the contract will be lower than the current futures price. The difference is their profit on each unit of the commodity sold. They are betting that there will be a difference between the actual futures price and the current futures price.

Speculation and Risk Taking

To be sure, it is possible for hedgers to shift risk onto speculators; however, speculation is not limited to futures markets. Anyone who has any "nonindexed" assets or liabilities is by definition a speculator. A nonindexed asset is one whose price does not move positively with inflation. These include an automobile, a house, or major appliances as well as stocks, bonds, or futures contracts. The value of assets can go up or down, depending on shifts in the supply and demand curves of the assets in question. Owners usually have nothing to do with the shifts in supply and demand; unanticipated changes in the rate of inflation, for example, can alter the burden of liabilities. Hence, owners of assets or liabilities are affected constantly by "the market." To the extent that you have a short or long position in an asset, you are by definition a speculator. You can reduce speculation by renting and leasing assets rather than by owning them because by leasing you don't go short or long. But even then you cannot eliminate speculation completely. A long-term lease involves speculation because you could be "locked into" a high monthly lease fee during a period in which the value of the asset you are leasing falls in the open market. When this happens, new leases will be written at a lower rate. You will suffer a reduction in your wealth compared to what your wealth would have been had you not signed the long-term lease but rather had signed a series of consecutive short-term leases.

$$$ Price Theory in Practice

The Future Value of Television Time

While active futures markets trade agricultural, metallurgical, and financial commodities, many other commodities are bought and sold for delivery in the future that are not traded on organized exchanges. One such forward market peddles the advertising time available during the television networks' new lineup of shows.

The market for the ad time works the same way as a futures market for wheat. But instead of farmers, who are unsure what price wheat will bring at harvest time, there are network executives who are unsure whether a crop of new shows will earn high ratings and top dollar for advertising time or low ratings and bargain basement advertising revenue.

Suppose you are an executive for the Fox Television Network and the network is scheduling, for the first time, the animated cartoon show *The Simpsons.* You are uncertain whether prime-time audiences will watch a show that is centered on a school-age underachiever named Bart whose favorite saying is "Don't have a cow, man." So, prior to the fall season, you decide to hedge your bet. You sell a block of advertising time during several episodes of the show to a firm that specializes in buying television time. Such firms are usually found as divisions within large advertising agencies. This decision limits your losses if the show is a total flop, but it also limits your return if the show is a big success. In effect, you have sold a forward contract on *The Simpsons* that obligates Fox Television Network to sell advertising time on the show for a price that you agree to today.

The buyer of the advertising time is speculating that *The Simpsons* is going to be a success, at least more of a success than you think. The agreement fixes price, so it assures that the buyer will not have to pay premium prices if the show tops the ratings. The buyer can then break up the block of time into pieces and sell 30-second or 1-minute segments to companies seeking to advertise their products, such as Burger King or McDonald's. Because *The Simpsons* was successful, the buyer profited handsomely on this transaction.

This market works just like an organized futures exchange. The speculator is the buyer here. If the buyer is wrong in his or her beliefs about the success of a new television show, then the actual price of advertising time falls and the buyer suffers a loss.

Learning Exercise 15.8

Name two other commodities that are offered for sale in the future at fixed prices today. How can speculators profit from buying or selling these commodities (football tickets, hotel rooms at the Olympics, airline tickets, cruise tickets, concert tickets, etc)?

15.4 Uncertainty

We have described how you choose an optimal consumption path through time and how markets arise to facilitate this decision, but we have not allowed risk or uncertainty to affect your choices. Unfortunately, the world we live in is rarely so specific when it comes to defining the future, particularly your future income. We assumed that you know your income in the future, M_{future}, in Figure 15.6 because this information is necessary to define how your future consumption changes when you increase your present saving. What if future income is not known? How does such uncertainty affect your optimal decisions? There are different ways to approach this question, but in all approaches your attitude toward risk bearing affects the choice you make.

Different Attitudes Toward Risk

Let's examine the different views you may have toward risk. Imagine, for instance, that someone offers to bet you $10 that the toss of a coin will come up "heads." If the coin shows "tails" when it lands, you will win $10; if the coin shows "heads" when it lands, you will lose $10. If a "fair" coin is used, your chances of winning or losing this bet are 50/50. To determine the average, or *expected,* net gain from playing this game, you must make the following calculation:

$$\begin{aligned}\text{Expected Net Gain} &= (\text{Probability of Losing})(\text{Payout if You Lose}) + \\ &\quad (\text{Probability of Winning})(\text{Payout if You Win}) - \\ &\quad (\text{Amount You Pay to Play the Game}) \\ &= \$.50 \times \$0 + \$.50 \times \$20 - \$10 \\ &= \$0 \qquad (15.9)\end{aligned}$$

The first two terms in equation (15.9) are the probability-weighted values of losing and winning the bet; they sum to equal the **expected value** of the bet. (Note that the probabilities of the different events must sum to 1.) The last term is the amount you pay to play the game, or rather your bet. The difference between the expected value of the bet and the amount you *pay* to play the game is the **expected net gain.** This is a **fair bet** because what you pay to play is equal to the expected value of the bet; that is, the expected net gain is equal to zero. Assuming that there are no religious or legal reasons for you to refuse such a bet, your attitude toward risk can be explained by your attitude toward this type of bet. If you are *indifferent* between keeping $10 that you pay to play the game, which is yours with certainty, and accepting this risky bet, then you are said to be **risk neutral.** As a risk-neutral person, you are indifferent between a fair bet and holding onto the money you would have at risk in the bet. Stated another way, you are risk neutral if you receive the same satisfaction from how you would spend the $10 that you have with certainty and how you would spend your expected winnings.

In contrast, if you refuse to accept this bet in its current form but will accept it at some *positive* expected net gain, then you are said to be **risk averse.** A risk-averse person must expect to win more than the bet that he or

Expected Value
The probability-weighted value of each outcome to a particular game or risky situation.

Expected Net Gain
Equal to the expected value of a risky game minus its cost.

Fair Bet
Also called a fair game; a situation in which the expected value of a risky game is equal to the cost of playing the game.

Risk Neutral
An individual who is indifferent between holding on to the money required to accept a fair bet and accepting a fair bet.

Risk Averse
An individual who plays a risky game only if it has a positive expected net gain.

she places; that is, the person must be compensated for placing $10, which he or she owns with certainty, at risk in a bet. In other words, although the game described above is a fair bet, this is not enough to induce a risk-averse person to play. Suppose, for example, that you refuse to play the game as we have described it, but you will play if the amount you win—should you win—is increased to $25. The amount you pay is still $10. With this change, the *expected net gain* is $2.50.[4] By revealing that you will play the game at a *positive* expected net gain but not at a zero expected net gain, you have shown that you are risk averse.

Risk Lover
An individual who will play a risky game when it has a negative expected net gain.

Analogously, you are said to be a **risk lover** if there are some bets with *negative* expected gain that you are willing to accept. A risk lover prefers to place $10 at risk in the bet and is willing to pay (some amount) to play such games. Hence, the risk lover will accept some bets that have a negative expected net gain; that is, on average, the risk lover loses money on the bet.

LEARNING EXERCISE 15.9

Pedro, Henry, and Judy are each offered the following gamble: Pay $25 and win $100 if two flips of a balanced coin show "heads" on both flips. Pedro refuses to play, but Henry and Judy accept. They are also offered another gamble: Pay $10 and win $25 if the roll of two dice shows a number greater than 9. Pedro and Judy refuse to play this game, but Henry plays. What can you say about Pedro's, Henry's, and Judy's attitudes toward risk?

DECISION MAKING UNDER UNCERTAINTY

Your attitude toward risk affects your choices when outcomes are uncertain. To illustrate, let's suppose that your future income is uncertain because there is a chance that you may be injured on the job and thus unable to work. Although most employers offer disability insurance to their employees, it can also be purchased separately from the insurance market. If you become disabled and you have a disability insurance policy, part or all of your regular salary is paid, normally until you reach age 65. To understand how your attitude toward risk affects whether you buy disability insurance, let's assume the following values for your future income and the probability of becoming disabled:

$$M_{\text{disabled}} = \$0$$
$$M_{\text{not disabled}} = \$50{,}000$$
$$p_{\text{disabled}} = 2\%$$
$$p_{\text{not disabled}} = 98\%$$

where $p_{\text{disabled}} + p_{\text{not disabled}} = 100$ percent, which is always true for the probability of two mutually exclusive and exhaustive events.

[4] Your expected net gain is equal to (.5)($0) + (.5)($25) – ($10), which is equal to $2.50.

Let's also assume that you have five years until retirement. Your income for the next five years depends on whether you are disabled. If you are *not* disabled, you earn $50,000 each year until retirement. If you are disabled and not insured, you earn nothing until retirement. Thus, your expected annual income equals

$$\begin{aligned}\text{Expected Annual Income} &= (\$50{,}000 \times p_{\text{not disabled}}) + (\$0 \times p_{\text{disabled}}) \\ &= (\$50{,}000 \times .98) + (\$0 \times .02) \\ &= \$49{,}000 \qquad (15.10)\end{aligned}$$

In effect, you *expect* to earn $49,000 in each of the next five years, which we can call your average income. Now, suppose an insurance company that has a large pool of policyholders offers to insure you completely against the possibly that you become disabled for a premium of $1,000 per year; that is, if you become disabled, the insurance company will pay your annual salary of $50,000 until you retire. The insurance company's offer is a fair bet because your expected annual loss of $1,000 ($50,000 – $49,000) is exactly equal to the annual premium. If you are risk neutral, you are indifferent between buying and not buying the insurance. If you are risk averse, however, you will buy the insurance because you are actually willing to pay more than the *fair bet* premium for disability insurance. If you are a risk lover, you will not accept the offer because you receive more satisfaction from the risky situation than from the certainty of receiving $49,000 per year ($50,000 – $1,000) for five years.

This situation is slightly different from the coin toss game in which you bet $10. The difference is that you have the $10 with certainty in your pocket in the coin toss and you are considering giving it up in exchange for a risky bet whose outcome is not known. Here you face an uncertain future income because of the chance of disability, so you begin in an uncertain situation in this example. The insurance company is offering to move you into a situation of complete certainty by insuring your future income stream against disability. Because you are *stuck* with the uncertainty, we must transpose our comments about what you will do when you are risk averse. Instead of offering you a bribe to give up your "certain" income, if you are risk averse you will be willing to *pay* to escape the "uncertain" situation that you are in. This is why you are willing to buy disability insurance when it is a fair bet at $1,000 per year. In effect, as a risk-averse person, you are giving up some "uncertain" income to purchase a "certain" income stream.

Now suppose that the insurance company offers disability insurance for $1,200 per year. Will you accept this offer? If you are risk neutral or a risk lover, you will not. If you are risk averse, you might or you might not; it depends on the *degree* to which you are averse to risk. If you accept the offer, then we know that you are willing to pay a premium of at least $200 to avoid the risk. If you don't accept the offer, you may still be risk averse, but the premium you place on avoiding the risk of disability is less than $200.

It should be clear that if the insurance company sells disability policies for $1,200 per year to a large number of individuals, it expects to gain $200 per year. If you accept such an offer, however, you gain too because the premium that you place on avoiding risk is at least $200 per year. Thus, by transferring the disability risk to an insurance company, both you and the insurance company can be made better off. What is important is that your attitude toward risk determines whether you will buy insurance. A risk lover or risk-neutral individual, *ceteris paribus*, will not buy insurance that is priced higher than its fair value, but a risk-averse individual may buy such insurance if his or her risk premium is sufficiently large.

USING UTILITY TO DESCRIBE ATTITUDES TOWARD RISK

There is a long tradition in economics of using utility functions to describe an individual's attitude toward risk and the choices made in uncertain situations. Mathematician John von Neumann and economist Oskar Morgenstern pioneered this approach, and it often bears their names. Specifically, the **von Neumann-Morgenstern utility function** equals the mathematical expectation of an ordinary utility function.[5]

von Neumann-Morgenstern Utility Function
The expected utility an individual receives when facing uncertain states of consumption.

To illustrate, let's say that your utility is a function of consumption in two possible states of the world. Following the example above, consumption equals \$50,000 if you are not disabled ($C_{\text{not disabled}} = \$50{,}000$); consumption equals \$0 if you are disabled ($C_{\text{disabled}} = \$0$). (To simplify the discussion, we are assuming that your consumption equals your income, which implies that there are no taxes to pay.) Your utility is specified as U(C), where C is consumption. Now, you will consume either \$50,000 or \$0, so your actual utility will be U(\$50,000) or U(\$0). What von Neumann and Morgenstern suggested was that you evaluate this situation by computing your expected utility (EU). Specifically, your expected utility can be written as

$$\begin{aligned} \text{EU}(C) &= p_{\text{disabled}} \times \text{U}(C_{\text{disabled}}) + p_{\text{not disabled}} \times \text{U}(C_{\text{not disabled}}) \\ &= .02 \times \text{U}(\$0) + .98 \times \text{U}(\$50{,}000) \end{aligned} \tag{15.11}$$

where we have used the probabilities specified above to substitute for the probabilities of becoming disabled and not disabled.

The question that you face is whether you should buy insurance to protect your future consumption stream against the possibility of becoming disabled. How do you decide? According to von Neumann and Morgenstern, you must compare your expected utility, equation (15.11), to the utility (or satisfaction) that you will receive if you buy the insurance. The utility that you receive if you buy insurance equals U(C – premium), or U(\$50,000 – \$1,000) = U(\$49,000). In other words, if you buy the insurance, you consume \$50,000 (guaranteed) minus the premium cost of the insurance. If the insurance is a fair bet, then its premium is \$1,000 and you consume \$49,000 each year for the next five years.

Now the question is easy to answer: Which is greater, your expected utility of consumption *without* insurance or your utility of consumption *with* insurance? That is, compare EU(C) in equation (15.11) to U(\$49,000). If U(\$49,000) > EU(C), then buy the insurance; if it is not greater, then don't buy the insurance.

[5] If U(C) is utility of consumption, then *expected utility* is written as EU(C) = p_1U(C_1) + p_2U(C_2), where p_1 and p_2 are the probabilities of consumption being C_1 and C_2, respectively.

With insurance priced fairly, your attitude toward risk is revealed by your decision to buy or not buy insurance. If you buy the insurance, then U($49,000) > EU(*C*) and you have revealed yourself to be risk averse. If you do not buy insurance, then U($49,000) ≤ EU(*C*), and you are either risk neutral or a risk lover. If insurance is not priced as a fair bet, your attitude toward risk may still be revealed, but the information may be ambiguous. That is, if the insurance premium equals $1,200 (see above), which is not a fair bet, and you buy it, you must be risk averse, but if you don't buy you can still be risk averse; it's just that the $200 premium exceeds your degree of risk aversion.

VISUALIZING ATTITUDES TOWARD RISK

The utility function approach lends itself to a visual description of risk aversion, risk neutrality, and risk-loving behavior. Figure 15.8 shows these three attitudes toward risk and compares them to the von Neumann–Morgenstern utility function, which is always a linear function.

Panel (a) shows the relationship between expected utility, EU(*C*), and the ordinary utility function, U(*C*), for an individual who is risk averse. Risk aversion is revealed by the concave shape of the utility function. The expected utility function is a straight line connecting U($0) and U($50,000). We can see that U($49,000) > EU(*C*) for this individual, so he or she will buy disability insurance if it is fairly priced.

Panels (b) and (c) show the relationship between utility and expected utility for risk-neutral and risk-loving individuals, respectively. For risk-neutral individuals, ordinary utility, U(*C*), and expected utility, EU(*C*), overlap and are thus equal to each other between $0 and $50,000. In this case, U($49,000) = EU(*C*). For risk lovers, the ordinary utility function is convex in shape. For these individuals, U($49,000) < EU(*C*).

RISK AND INCOME

Although difficult to prove, it is probably the case that most people act like risk lovers when the amounts they stand to lose are small in relation to their income. That is, when people gamble in Las Vegas, in Atlantic City, in Europe, or on cruise ships, they typically do not risk a large fraction of their income or wealth. Such gambling is produced with the odds of winning stacked against the players, so players must be risk lovers to some degree to play. It is also likely that for most people, risk becomes a "bad" when the possible losses become a large share of their income or wealth position. In the disability case, a substantial portion of your future income is at risk due to the chance of becoming disabled. In such situations, most people will probably act in a risk-averse manner. Each individual decides on the turning point between risk-taking bets and risk-averse bets. Virtually all of us will risk some small proportion of our wealth or income in situations with uncertain outcomes, and most people will become more risk averse in situations involving proportionately greater losses.

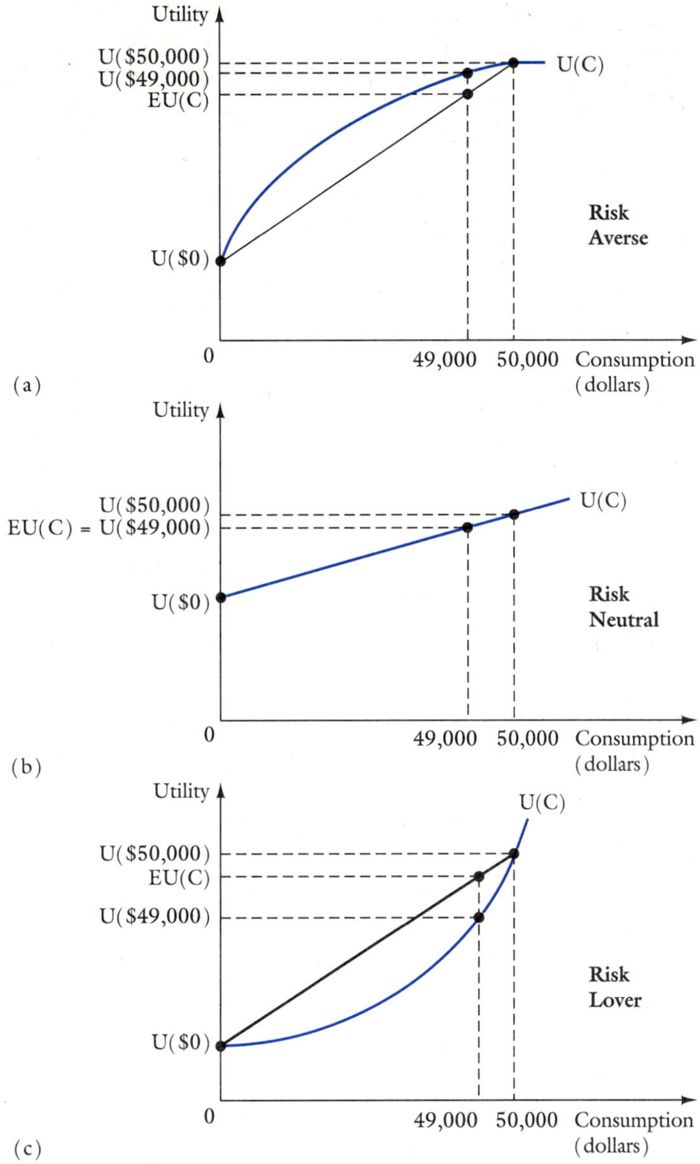

FIGURE 15.8

Visualizing Attitudes Toward Risk

An individual's attitude toward risk is revealed by the shape of his or her utility function. In panel (a), the individual is risk averse because the utility received from $49,000 with certainty, U($49,000), is greater than the expected utility received when the individual is at risk of a disability, EU(C). The utility function has a concave shape here. Analogously, in panel (b) the individual is risk neutral because U($49,000) = EU(C), and the utility function is linear. Finally, in panel (c), the individual is a risk lover because U($49,000) < EU(C), and the utility function is convex.

A RISKY CONCLUSION

The lesson of this chapter is that the world and all our dealings in it are risky, particularly when we consider intertemporal decisions. It is costly to reduce risk by shifting it to others or by taking precautions in the way in which we order our affairs. Just how much risk we are willing to bear rather than pay the price for increased security is largely a function of how much risk we are already bearing and what percentage of our total income or wealth position is at risk. If you reflect on the basic propositions of consumer choice and demand theory that you learned in previous chapters, you will realize that certainty, or risk reduction, is a scarce good governed by the same general principles of choice that apply to all other goods.

Chapter Summary

1. Consuming more in one period reduces the amount that you can consume in all other periods. The value 1 plus the interest rate measures the market-determined rate of trade-off between consumption in two adjacent periods. For example, \$1 of consumption in the present will cost $\$(1 + r)$ of consumption in the next, future period.
2. To reduce future income to present value, the income in the future is divided by 1 plus the interest rate, where the interest rate is defined for the period of discounting. If the future income occurs one year hence, for example, a one-year interest rate is used in equation (15.1) to compute the present value.
3. The intertemporal budget constraint shows the bundles of present and future consumption that may be consumed given present and future incomes and the interest rates for saving and borrowing.
4. The optimal intertemporal consumption bundle is found by equating the marginal rate of time preference to the market-determined price of intertemporal consumption, which is 1 plus the interest rate. If the interest rate is positive, then the equilibrium bundle will exhibit a positive rate of time preference; that is, you will require more than \$1 of future consumption in order to give up \$1 of present consumption.
5. Insurance and futures markets have evolved over time to transfer risk, at a price. An insurance company can pool the risk of a hazard and find that its losses are determined by statistical averages. A futures market combines uncertainty and time preference to transfer risk. Futures contracts commit buyers to a price today in exchange for delivery of the commodities at some future date.
6. A risk-averse person will not accept a gamble that has zero expected net gain. The expected net gain must be some positive value before the risk-averse person will play. A risk-neutral person is indifferent between accepting a gamble with zero expected net gain and keeping the money required to play. A risk lover will accept a gamble at some negative expect net gain; that is, the risk lover will lose money, on average, in the gamble.

Trouble Spots

Concept	Reminder
The Price of Saving and Borrowing	The interest rate in an open economy, such as the United States, is determined by the international market for credit. The rate equilibrates the money allocated to saving with the money demanded by borrowers; it does not *balance* the number of borrowers and savers.
The Equilibrium Interest Rate	Present values represent the purchasing power of your income in terms of goods you can buy today. Future values show the purchasing power of your income in terms of the goods you can buy in the future. These values are related to each other through the interest rate, as shown by equation (15.1).

15.5 Review Questions

1. Briefly explain how the equilibrium interest rate is determined.
2. What is the intertemporal budget constraint? Does it imply a trade-off between present and future consumption? What is exact form of the trade-off?
3. Suppose that Bob's time preferences are such that he is indifferent between 11 fresh peaches now and 10 a year from now. Does this prove that the interest rate must be negative? Explain.
4. "I can't understand people who will fork over $5 or $10 to see a first-run movie when they could see it for about half that price a few months later, or even watch it on TV for free a few years later." What does time-preference theory say about this?
5. If the interest rate increases and you are presently borrowing, how are your intertemporal consumption opportunities affected? If the interest rate decreases and you are borrowing, how are they affected?
6. Explain why an absolutely certain contractual right to receive $1 in the future is less valuable than having $1 right now. Assume that no inflation or deflation is expected.
7. How is it possible that an absolutely reliable annuity of $1 per year, to be paid or received for 20 years, has a present value of less than $20?
8. Explain the permanent income hypothesis and the life cycle hypothesis. How are they related to the intertemporal consumption model?
9. Is it possible for someone to eliminate *all* financial risk by investing properly? Discuss.
10. Explain how futures markets transfer risk between buyers and sellers of futures contracts.
11. What can you say about the risk preferences of visitors to Las Vegas casinos? How do you know that your answer is true? What about the risk preferences of those individuals who always buy used cars?
12. Is there any relationship between your attitude toward risk and your decision to borrow or save in the present period? That is, if you are risk averse, are you more or less likely to save money?

15.6 Price Theory Problems

1. International fashion designer Alfredo Lorenz has had a bad year: his coarse leather fashions did not sell well. He managed to earn only \$10,000 after taxes. Next year, a long-awaited change in the world climate will make it colder in many cites where Alfredo sells his clothes. The cooling trend is expected to increase sales significantly, and he is expected to earn \$100,000 after taxes.
    a. Draw Alfredo's intertemporal budget constraint, assuming that he can borrow or save at a 10 percent interest rate.
    b. Assume that it is optimal for Alfredo to borrow \$35,000 in the present period. Locate his optimal consumption bundle on the intertemporal budget line. What is the marginal rate of time preference for this bundle?
    c. Given Alfredo's optimal bundle, is he better or worse off when interest rates increase?

2. As luck would have it, you have won \$50,000 in Florida's instant winner lottery. Draw a graph indicating how winning the lottery affects your intertemporal budget constraint. Show the conditions under which you will spend all of your winnings in the present period.
3. Suppose you buy a United States government two-year note. The note entitles you to the following: You will receive \$100 per year in interest, and when the note matures, you will also receive the bond's face value of \$1,000. If you earn 10 percent per year on your investment, what is the maximum price you will be willing to pay for the bond? What is the most you would be willing to pay if the interest rate was 8 percent per year?
4. Suzanne has had credit problems in the past, so she is not able to borrow money. She earns \$25,000 per year, which is not expected to change next year.
    a. Draw Suzanne's intertemporal budget constraint if the interest rate on savings is 10 percent.
    b. A newly insured savings and loan has just opened for business in Suzanne's hometown. The bank has agreed to let her borrow at 15 percent interest. Draw Suzanne's new intertemporal budget constraint.

5. Suppose your marginal rate of time preference is constant along your intertemporal indifference curve. Describe the possible solution bundles that might arise. If you find that it is optimal to consume in the present period, what is the relationship between the MRTP and the interest rate?
6. Suppose you own a bar near the University of Nevada at Las Vegas. Every time the basketball team wins a home game, business is brisk and you clear \$200 for the day. When it loses, business is slow, and on those days you clear only \$50. The problem is, you don't like risk; you would prefer a certain income to an uncertain one. Fortunately for you, gambling is legal in Nevada, and there are hordes of people who

like to shoulder risk, among other ways, by wagering on athletic events. Assuming you can get even odds, how much should you bet per game and on which team, in order that you will be "hedged" against the team's having a bad (or good) season?

7. Suppose a group of 1,000 women, all age 25, decide to "cut out the middle persons" by forming a mutual pregnancy-insurance league. From statistics, they ascertain that for every 1,000 women age 25 an average of 15 conceptions occurs per year. Medical expenses in their area average $8,000 per pregnancy. Based upon these figures, what annual insurance premium would they assess one another to take care of the costs of expected pregnancies? Can you anticipate any potential problems with their scheme to beat the insurance companies out of some business?
8. In present value terms, what two financial rights do you buy when you purchase a share of common stock? Does the past performance (earnings, etc.) of the firm have any bearing on either of these two rights?
9. Why might a speculator in commodities futures want to have instantaneous reports on changes in weather throughout the world? How much should a speculator spend generating weather information? Should he or she go as far as to have an in-house weather service generating its own weather forecasts?
10. Suppose you run a printing business specializing in rush jobs. Would you want any special clauses in the contracts you make with your suppliers of ink, paper stock, and other essential inventory?
11. Does the law of demand imply that there are fewer individuals with a high degree of risk aversion than a low degree of risk aversion? After all, as the price of insurance increases, the face value of policies sold decreases.
12. Derive the income and substitution effects of an increase in interest rates for the following cases:
    a. You are a saver before and after the increase in rates.
    b. You are a borrower before and after the increase in rates.
    c. You are a borrower before and a saver after the increase in rates.

15.7 Writing Exercise

Carefully study the financial pages of your local newspaper. Select a commodity traded on a futures exchange and for two weeks keep track of its daily closing price, daily high price, daily low price, volume, and open interest. Also, keep a careful record of changes in the one-year Treasury bill rate. Develop and analyze a graph of these data. Do you see any trends in the data when they are plotted? Construct the first differences of the price series; that is, subtract yesterday's price from today's price. Analyze the first-difference series. Do you see any trends in this series? If option contracts are traded for the commodity you choose, repeat the analysis using the data for the option contracts. What conclusions can you draw from your study about the behavior of prices and interest rates?

16

General Equilibrium and Voluntary Exchange

Preview Questions

When you finish studying this chapter, you should be able to answer the following questions:

- How do general and partial equilibrium analysis differ?
- What is an Edgeworth box diagram?
- What conditions are necessary for efficient exchange between individuals?
- What are the conditions for an efficient use of inputs in production?
- How do we derive a production possibilities frontier?
- What conditions are necessary for output (or product mix) efficiency?

In the early morning hours of August 24, 1992, Hurricane Andrew slammed into South Florida, causing at least $12 billion in damage to homes and property. In the days following the hurricane, prices of orange juice futures edged upward; entrepreneurs in Atlanta, who had benefited when Hurricane Hugo struck South Carolina, secured rental contracts for trucks (used to haul generators and soft drinks); and the stock price of several insurance carriers started to drift downward. These changes are linked to a single event—the hurricane—but they illustrate a more general principle. Markets are linked together, either by an external event or by relative prices: they are related.

Except on a few occasions, we have discussed markets as though they were completely isolated; that is, we have analyzed only what happens in one particular market when, for example, a relative price changes, a tax is levied, or a new law is passed. This approach provides only a limited view of what happens in markets.

It is no surprise that there are interrelations among the many markets in our economy. When there is a freeze in Florida, the price of Florida oranges increases, but so does the price of California grapefruit. An increase in the tax on jet fuel affects the price of airline tickets and has an impact on hotel room prices in resort communities served mainly by air travel, such as Tahiti. A new law that reduces trade restrictions between two countries—the United States and Canada, for example—has an effect on employment and production in both countries. The goal of this chapter is to connect these various effects so that you see how economic analysis describes the general behavior of many interrelated markets, not only the behavior of a single isolated market.

We begin by comparing the general equilibrium of many markets to the partial equilibrium of a single market. Then we develop the efficiency conditions for general equilibrium. These efficiency conditions apply to exchange between individuals, the use of inputs by firms, and the product mix in the economy. We show that a perfectly competitive economy satisfies these efficiency conditions.

16.1 General Equilibrium Analysis

The equilibrium analysis of a single market is called **partial equilibrium analysis.** Partial equilibrium analysis always involves the *ceteris paribus* qualification. In such analysis, it is assumed that all other factors are held constant. Not all factors are constant, however, or no change would be possible. In essence, partial equilibrium analysis allows us to focus on a single market and view it in isolation from all other markets. For analytical purposes, we view the market as independent and self-contained. But we know that markets interact. When we attempt to take account of the interactions between markets, we enter the realm of general equilibrium analysis.

Partial Equilibrium Analysis
Analyzing market responses in isolation without taking account of the interrelations between markets.

General equilibrium analysis describes the equilibria of markets that are interrelated; that is, it accounts for the interrelations among prices and quantities of various goods and services. Just as partial equilibrium analysis does not allow other things to vary, general equilibrium analysis does not require that other things be constant. Something must be **exogenous** (determined outside the system), or "given," for us to start the analysis. But once the exogenous variable changes, a complete general equilibrium analysis allows *all* affected markets to adjust to reach a new equilibrium. We can show the rudiments of general equilibrium analysis in a graphical example. For simplicity, let's limit the analysis to two markets: apples and grapes.

General Equilibrium Analysis
Economic analysis that takes into account the interrelations between markets.

Exogenous
Originating from outside the model.

An Analysis of Two Interdependent Markets

Let's assume that customers consider apples and grapes to be substitutes. Thus, any change in the relative price of the two products has an impact on the quantity demanded in *both* markets. Figure 16.1 shows the initial equilibrium for these two markets.

The apple market is shown in panel (a) and the grape market is shown in panel (b). Initially, the demand for apples is given by D^0_{apples} and the supply curve is given by S_{apples}. The apple market is in equilibrium at a price of 20 cents per pound, at which Q^0_a pounds of apples are sold. The initial demand for grapes is given by D^0_{grapes} and the initial supply is given by S^0_{grapes}. The grape market is in equilibrium at a price of 80 cents per bunch, at which Q^0_g bunches of grapes are sold. Suppose that the initial equilibrium is disturbed by

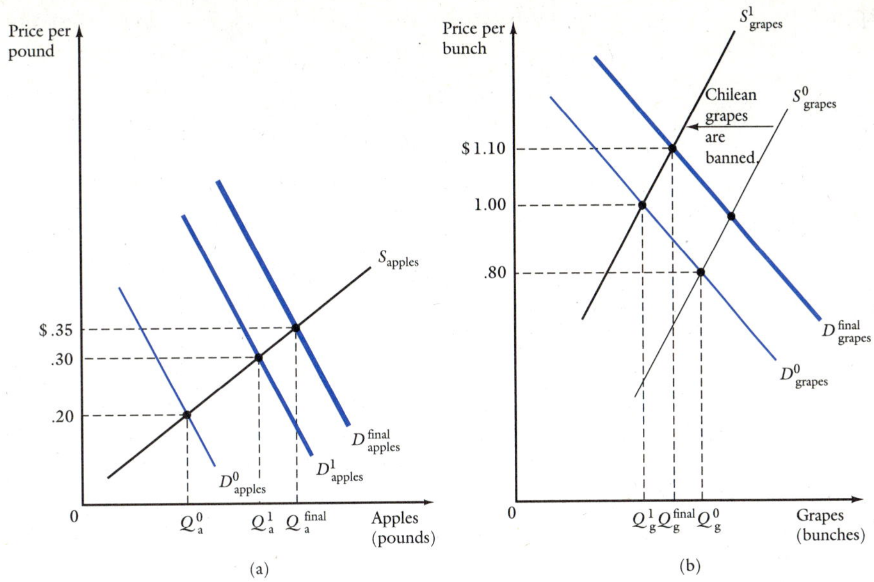

FIGURE 16.1

The Effect of a Ban on Chilean Grapes on the Grape and Apple Markets

Panels (a) and (b) show the demand and supply curves for the apple and grape markets in the United States. Initially, the apple market is in equilibrium at a price of 20 cents per pound with sales of Q^0_a pounds and the grape market is in equilibrium at a price of 80 cents per bunch with sales of Q^0_g bunches. The ban on Chilean grapes causes the supply of grapes to shift to the left—from S^0_{grapes} to S^1_{grapes}—in panel (b). The grape market adjusts to a *partial equilibrium* at a price of $1 per bunch with sales of Q^1_g bunches. The apple market then adjusts to new relative price of apples to grapes with a rightward shift in the demand for apples—from D^0_{apples} to D^1_{apples}—reaching a partial equilibrium at 30 cents per pound with sales of Q^1_a pounds in panel (a). The grape market then reacts to the new relative price, and the feedback process continues until a final equilibrium is reached in both markets; this is the general equilibrium solution.

the discovery that someone has tampered with grapes imported from Chile. Customs inspectors have found traces of a deadly poison on some Chilean grapes. In response, the U.S. government bans all grape imports from Chile until a thorough investigation can be completed.

Now, the market supply of grapes decreases to S^1_{grapes} and, *if the price of apples remains at 20 cents per pound,* the equilibrium price of grapes increases to $1 per bunch, at which Q^1_g grapes are sold. Obviously, the higher price reduces the quantity of grapes demanded, but it also affects the apple market. Measured from the initial equilibrium, the relative price of apples decreases from $.20/$.80 to $.20/$1, or from ¼ to ⅕. Apples are now relatively cheaper to consume than grapes. This change in relative prices causes the demand for apples to increase, shifting rightward to D^1_{apples} in panel (a). *Given that the price of grapes is $1 per bunch,* the apple market reaches an equilibrium at a price of 30 cents per pound, at which Q^1_a pounds of apples are sold.

These two markets are not yet at their final equilibrium. The changing demand for apples and, consequently, the higher price of apples alters the relative price of apples and grapes again. The relative price of grapes falls from $1/$.20 to $1/$.30, or from $^5/_1$ to $^{3.33}/_1$. Grapes are now relatively cheaper, so the demand curve for grapes increases by shifting to the right in panel (b). But such a move affects the relative price again, this time lowering the relative price of apples, and the demand curve for apples increases in response. The repeated changes in the relative price of apples and grapes cause these markets to reach a *final* equilibrium when the demand for apples is given by $D^{\text{final}}_{\text{apples}}$ and the demand for grapes is given by $D^{\text{final}}_{\text{grapes}}$. (Intermediate shifts in D_g are not shown.) The final equilibrium price in the apple market is 35 cents, at which Q^{final}_a pounds are sold. The final equilibrium price in the grape market is $1.10, at which Q^{final}_g bunches of grapes are sold.

Note that the final equilibrium prices given by our graphical approach are hypothetical, based on presumed changes in the apple and grape markets. If we want to compute the equilibria for actual markets, we need to estimate the demand and supply functions for these markets. Given these functions, we can compute the final equilibria analytically by solving for the intersection between quantity supplied and quantity demanded in the two markets after the grape embargo is imposed.

LEARNING EXERCISE 16.1

Using a graphical analysis similar to Figure 16.1, describe the likely effects that the *removal* of the ban on Chilean grapes will have on both the apple and grape markets.

COMPARING GENERAL AND PARTIAL EQUILIBRIUM ANALYSES

The analysis of the apple and grape market shows the difference between general and partial equilibrium analyses. The discussion above is a general equilibrium analysis: An exogenous event occurred—banning grape imports from Chile—and then we followed *all* of the relative price changes until they led to a final equilibrium in the two markets. All the feedback effects between the apple and grapes markets are accounted for in this analysis. In contrast, a *partial* equilibrium analysis of the grape embargo against Chile focuses on just the initial shift in supply and its effects on the price and quantity of grapes transacted. A partial equilibrium analysis of the grape embargo is shown in Figure 16.2.

Figure 16.2 recreates the grape market described in panel (b) of Figure 16.2, except that there are no feedback effects from the changing relative price of apples, which would cause the demand for grapes to increase. In other words, the *ceteris paribus* assumption holds. A partial equilibrium analysis states that the effect of the grape embargo is to increase the price of grapes

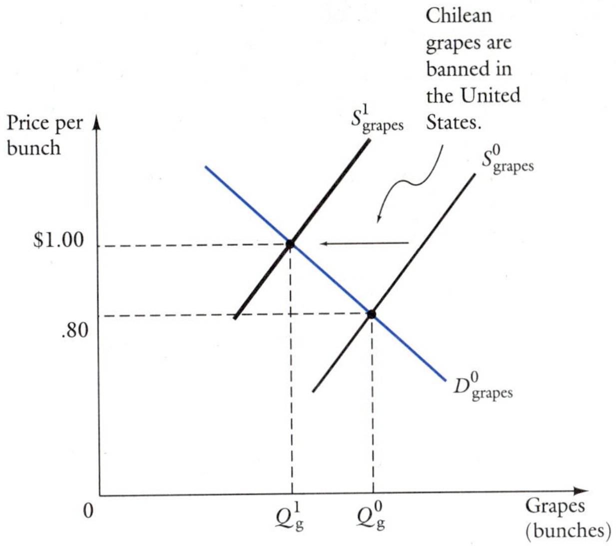

FIGURE 16.2

A Partial Equilibrium Analysis of a Ban on Chilean Grapes

A partial equilibrium analysis of the Chilean grape ban focuses on the equilibrium reached in the grape market, holding the price of apples constant. The grape ban shifts the supply of grapes to S^1_{grapes} from S^0_{grapes}. The partial equilibrium is reached at a price of $1 per bunch with sales of Q^1_{grapes} bunches.

from 80 cents to $1 per bunch and to decrease the quantity of grapes sold from Q^0_g to Q^1_g. Clearly, the partial equilibrium analysis is incomplete. At the final equilibrium, the price of grapes is higher than $1 and the quantity of bunches of grapes sold will not be more than Q^0_g. Thus, the *partial* equilibrium shows just *part* of the final result.

You may be tempted to conclude that all of our previous analysis is wrong because it was not a general equilibrium approach. Such a conclusion, however, is only partially correct. Partial equilibrium analysis describes the *initial* effect of an exogenous change. In nearly every market, for example, the initial effect is bigger than the subsequent feedback effects, so the initial tendency of prices and quantities as described by partial equilibrium analysis is correct. Because the initial effect dominates the feedback effects in nearly all cases, partial equilibrium analysis shows the correct *direction* for both prices and quantities. The final equilibrium price of grapes, for example, will not be less than 80 cents, because the feedback effects of a higher relative price of apples will not shift the demand for grapes sufficiently far to cause a different result. As a consequence, we may think of partial equilibrium analysis as a description of the initial effect; this becomes very useful when we need to know the direction of price and quantity changes. When *absolute* magnitudes are important and feedback effects are relatively large, however, a general equilibrium analysis is the better approach.

The example of gasoline consumption following the Arab oil embargo of 1973 illustrates the difference between partial and general equilibrium analysis. The oil embargo increased the price of crude oil by over 200 percent in less than a year. Initially, consumption of crude oil and gasoline (which is derived from crude) decreased, but not substantially. Other products, such as plastics and chemicals, were affected by the higher crude oil price, but the initial response was also small. Over time, however, the higher relative price of gasoline affected the demand and supply of many products. For example, automobile manufacturers began to make lighter cars to increase their fuel economy, consumers installed insulation in their homes to lower electricity consumption, firms invested in solar energy technology, and refining facilities were built to extract oil from tar sands. A partial equilibrium analysis shows an inelastic demand in most markets affected by crude oil prices, but a general equilibrium analysis, which also encompasses changes over time, traces substantial changes in demand and supply to the initial change in crude oil prices.

LIMITS TO GENERAL EQUILIBRIUM ANALYSIS

A note of warning: The distinction between general and partial equilibrium analysis is, in practice, one of degree. After all, there is a limit to how many markets we can include in any analysis. That limit is set either by the cerebral limits of the economist doing the analysis or by the capabilities of the computer that he or she is utilizing. A complete general equilibrium analysis requires the setting up of an almost infinite set of simultaneous equations, and this is a task no one has yet undertaken.

When economists talk of general equilibrium analysis in dealing with practical problems, they are referring to an analysis that takes into account several markets and the interrelations among them. In these markets, the feedback effects cause a measurable change in either demand or supply, or both. If the goal is to predict what will happen when the economic environment changes, then the choice of partial or general equilibrium analysis depends on (1) the question being asked and (2) the degree to which the answer changes if more than one market is considered. Basically, it is a matter of determining what things can be held constant to simplify a problem without invalidating the analysis.

LEARNING EXERCISE 16.2

Explain how the cross-price elasticity between two markets helps determine whether the feedback effects from one market are likely to affect another market.

WELFARE ECONOMICS

Welfare economics is the study of the social desirability of different economic outcomes. *Social desirability* is a term that refers to how the whole group of participants in a market are benefiting, not just one participant. General equi-

Welfare Economics The study of the social desirability of different economic outcomes.

librium analysis also is used in welfare economics. It is used to examine how well-off individuals are, given their choices and the market setting. If the market setting changes, choices may change and the benefits derived for each individual may change, too. Thus, the social desirability of the outcome may change. We will discuss two results from welfare economics below.

16.2 Voluntary Exchange Between Individuals

At the root of general equilibrium analysis is the interaction between different markets. Markets are interrelated because purchase decisions are affected by individual budget constraints. Budget constraints force individuals to make trade-offs between different goods, a process that links markets for goods together. In this section, we develop the interaction between markets at the level of the individual. We show how exchange between individuals is beneficial and how such decisions are made in a general equilibrium environment. To simplify the theory of exchange, we use just two consumers, who are endowed with goods, rather than income, as their budget constraint. Given these endowments, we derive a general equilibrium condition for efficient exchange between these individuals. Note that the analysis is dependent on the initial endowments.

If we change the initial endowments, we will change the equilibrium solution.

The Edgeworth Box

Edgeworth Box
A rectangular graph portraying two individual commodity spaces superimposed on each other, with each individual's origin at a diagonally opposite corner of the box. We use the box to analyze exchange between two individuals.

The **Edgeworth box,** named after the English mathematical economist Francis Y. Edgeworth (1845–1926), is a graphical technique for illustrating how two individuals (or countries) can gain from voluntary exchange. To illustrate, let's consider a situation in which there are two commodities—food and clothing—whose total supply is fixed. Let Mary and Tom be our two individuals. Their respective commodity spaces are presented in panel (a) and panel (b) of Figure 16.3 on page 662. The origin for the commodity space that pertains to Mary is labeled as O_M. The origin for the commodity space that pertains to Tom is labeled as O_T.

Both Mary and Tom are endowed with an initial quantity of clothing and food. Mary's *endowment* of 25 units of clothing and 5 units of food is shown as point *A* in panel (a). Tom's endowment of 15 units of clothing and 35 units of food is shown as point *B* in panel (b). As we will show below, Mary and Tom may find it in their interest to change their initial endowments by voluntarily trading with each other.

Now, we wish to combine these two commodity spaces together. We do this by rotating Tom's commodity axes 180° so that Tom's origin, O_T, is in the upper right-hand corner. We can see this new arrangement in the two panels of Figure 16.4 (page 662). Panel (a) is the same, but panel (b) appears to be upside down; actually, it has been rotated in a counterclockwise direction.

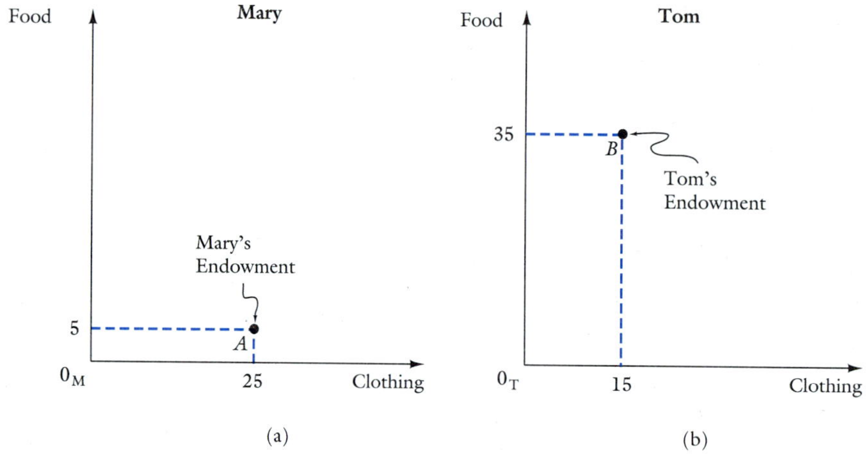

FIGURE 16.3

Endowments of Food and Clothing for Mary and Tom

The endowments of food and clothing for Mary and Tom are shown in panels (a) and (b), respectively. Mary is endowed with 5 units of food and 25 units of clothing, and Tom is endowed with 35 units of food and 15 units of clothing.

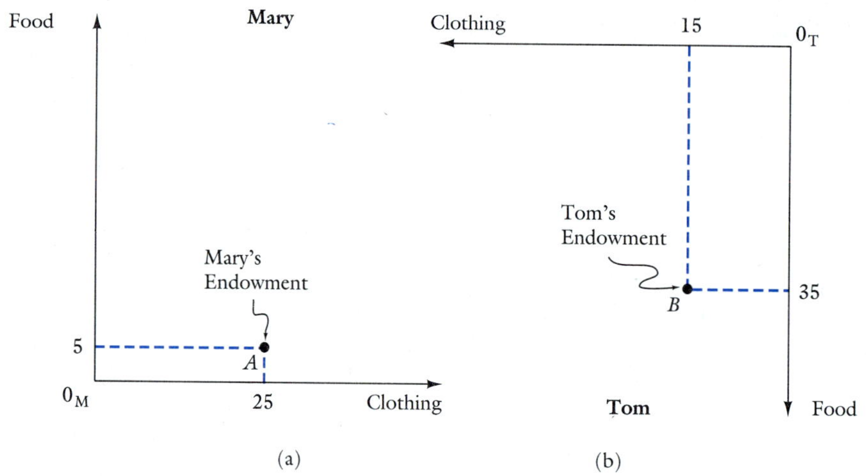

FIGURE 16.4

Rotating Tom's Commodity Space

Mary's endowment and Tom's endowment are duplicated from Figure 16.3, except that Tom's commodity space has been rotated 180°.

We now wish to fit the two commodity spaces together. At first glance, it might appear that there is a problem with the length of the horizontal and vertical axes. There is no problem, however, when we assume that fixed supplies of clothing and food must be shared by Mary and Tom. In other words, the amount of clothing consumed by Mary plus the amount of clothing consumed by Tom equals the total available supply of clothing, which is the sum of Mary's and Tom's endowment of clothing, or 40 units. The same is true for the total supply of food.

Thus, what we want to do is combine the commodity spaces in panels (a) and (b) in Figure 16.4 in such a way that

1. The length of *any* line measuring clothing equals the total supply of clothing, which is 40 units, and
2. The length of *any* line measuring food equals the total supply of food, which is 40 units.

We do this by sliding panels (a) and (b) in Figure 16.4 toward each other until we have the proper overlap on each axis. This adjustment gives us the result we see in Figure 16.5 on page 664. This configuration is called the *Edgeworth box.* Note that if we change either Tom's or Mary's endowment of either good, we will change the Edgeworth box. The initial endowments determine the length of each side, so by changing initial endowments, we change the shape of the box.

The endowments of Mary and Tom are completely described by a specific point within the Edgeworth box. In this case, point E represents how much of the available supply of clothing and food is given to Mary and Tom in their endowments. Mary's endowment of clothing, for example, is found to equal 25 units, which is the amount on the clothing axis at the *bottom* of the box. In contrast, Tom's endowment of clothing equals 15 units, which is the amount on the clothing axis at the *top* of the box. Similarly, point E also defines the endowment of food for Mary and Tom, which can be seen from the right and left axes of the Edgeworth box, respectively.

Placing Indifference Curves in the Edgeworth Box

We can describe Mary's and Tom's preferences for food and clothing using indifference curves. Recall from Chapter 5 that indifference curves are typically convex to the origin. Because Mary's axes have not been rotated, her indifference curves will appear normally shaped. In Figure 16.6 on page 665, indifference curve U_{M}^{0} represents Mary's level of satisfaction from her initial endowment. Analogously, indifference curve U_{M}^{1} represents a higher level of satisfaction because it is farther away from Mary's origin, O_{M}, than indifference curve U_{M}^{0}.

In contrast to Mary's normal-appearing indifference curves, Tom's indifference curves must be rotated to conform to the rotation of his axes. Thus, Tom's indifference curves have the appearance and shape of a curve traced by the minute hand of a watch moving over the first 15 minutes of an hour. In Figure 16.6, indifference curve U_{T}^{0} represents Tom's level of satisfaction from

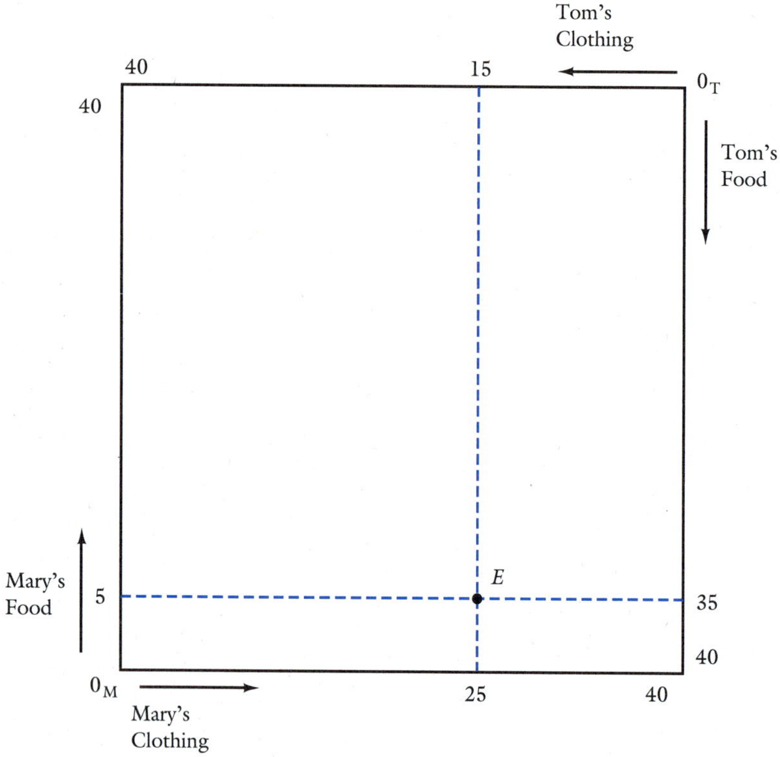

FIGURE 16.5

The Edgeworth Box

The Edgeworth box is constructed by sliding the commodity space diagrams of Mary and Tom shown in Figure 16.4 together until their endowment points overlap. The lengths of the sides of the Edgeworth box measure the total quantity available of the commodities.

his initial endowment. Similarly, indifference curve U_T^1 represents a higher level of satisfaction because it is farther away from Tom's origin, O_T, which is in the upper right-hand corner of the Edgeworth box.[1]

Obviously, if Mary could move to indifference curve U_M^1 and Tom could move to indifference curve U_T^1, they both could be made better off than they are at the initial endowment point. The problem they face, however, is that such a move by *either* of them must make the other one worse off when there is a fixed supply of both food and clothing. At point *F*, for example, Mary is better off because she has increased her holdings of food by 10 units, but Tom

[1] Note that Tom's indifference curves are convex to Tom's origin and Mary's are convex to her origin.

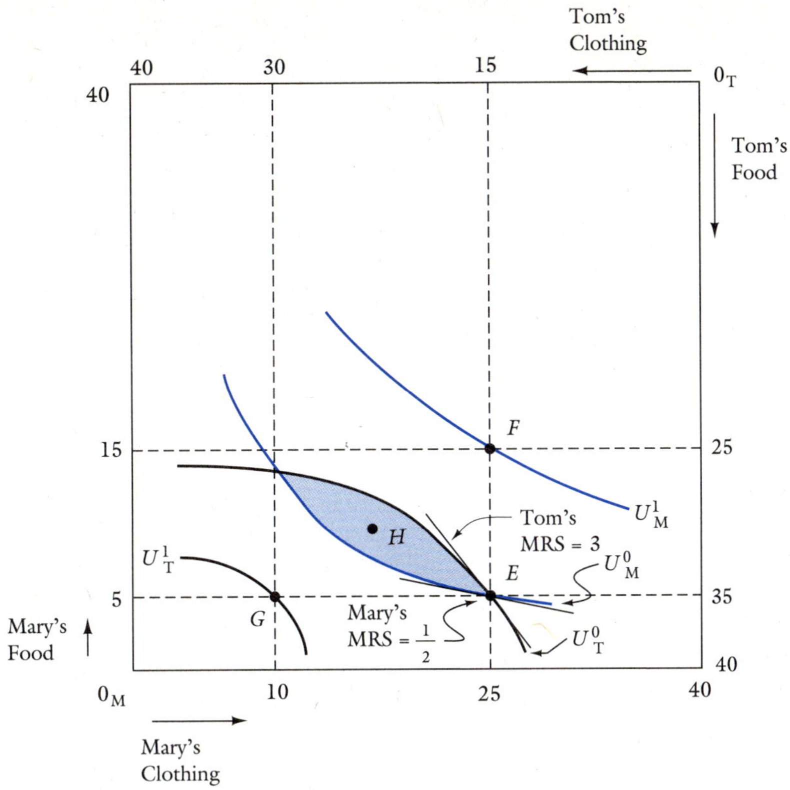

FIGURE 16.6

The Edgeworth Box with Indifference Curves and the Region of Mutual Advantage

The Edgeworth box is shown with Mary's and Tom's indifference curves added. Mary's indifference curve, U_M^0, represents the satisfaction she receives from endowment point *E*. Tom's indifference curve, U_T^0, represents the satisfaction he receives from endowment point *E*. The shaded area between these two curves represents the region of mutual advantage, where both Mary and Tom can gain from additional trade. Note that Mary's MRS is not equal to Tom's MRS at the endowment point, which also indicates that there are gains from moving to another allocation point, such as point *H*, in the region of mutual advantage.

is worse off because the 10 units came out of his endowment of food. Alternatively, Tom is better off at point *G* because his holdings of clothing have increased by 15 units, but Mary is worse off because her holdings of clothing decreased by the same 15 units. Thus, Mary will not voluntarily trade with Tom if it places them at point *G* in the Edgeworth box, and Tom will not voluntarily trade with Mary if it places them at point *F* in the box.

No voluntary trade takes place if it makes *one* party worse off.

Gains from Voluntary Exchange

Given the initial endowment and the shapes of Mary's and Tom's indifference curves, there is an area in which they both could gain from trade with each other. The shaded area in Figure 16.6 represents the points at which both Mary and Tom can be made better off through exchanging food and clothing. At point *H,* for example, Mary decreases her holdings of clothing and increases her holdings of food to reach a point that lies above her initial indifference curve, a point that is preferred to her initial endowment. The same may be said for Tom at point *H,* except that he gives up some food to gain some clothing. This shaded area is called the *region of mutual advantage* (or the core) because *both* persons are better off if they can move to a point in this region. Note that the region of mutual advantage is the only region in the Edgeworth box in which *voluntary* exchange takes place. Thus, any movement from the initial endowment to a point outside the region of mutual advantage must be done without the voluntary participation of at least one of the participants.

LEARNING EXERCISE 16.3

How does the size of the region of mutual advantage change as the degree of substitution between the two goods increases?

EFFICIENT EXCHANGE: EQUATING THE MARGINAL RATES OF SUBSTITUTION

Whenever there is a region of mutual advantage, there are gains from trade. As long as the transaction costs of trading are small (we assume that they are zero here), Mary and Tom will trade with each other. They will continue to trade until they reach a point of **exchange efficiency,** a point at which the region of mutual advantage vanishes. In other words, Mary tries to find a bundle of clothing and food that offers her more satisfaction than her existing bundle, and Tom does the same. As long as there is a region of mutual advantage, they have not exhausted all of the gains from trade and they have not reached a point of efficient exchange. Only after they reach a trade in which the region vanishes will they stop trading; then they will have achieved exchange efficiency. Figure 16.7 illustrates this situation.

Exchange Efficiency An allocation of goods at which the MRS is equated across all individuals.

In Figure 16.7, the last trade Mary and Tom make leaves Mary with 20 units of clothing and 10 units of food and Tom with 20 units of clothing and 30 units of food; this situation is represented by point *H* in the Edgeworth box. Mary receives satisfaction given by indifference curve U^*_M and Tom receives satisfaction given by indifference curve U^*_T. These two indifference curves are tangent at point *H,* which is why the region of mutual advantage vanishes with this trade. The tangency result implies that the slopes of these two indifference curves are equal to each other at point *H.* In Chapter 5, we showed that the marginal rate of substitution (MRS) equals the absolute value of the slope of an indifference curve, so we know that Mary's MRS equals Tom's MRS at point *H.* An analysis of this result offers us another way to interpret the gains from trade for Mary and Tom.

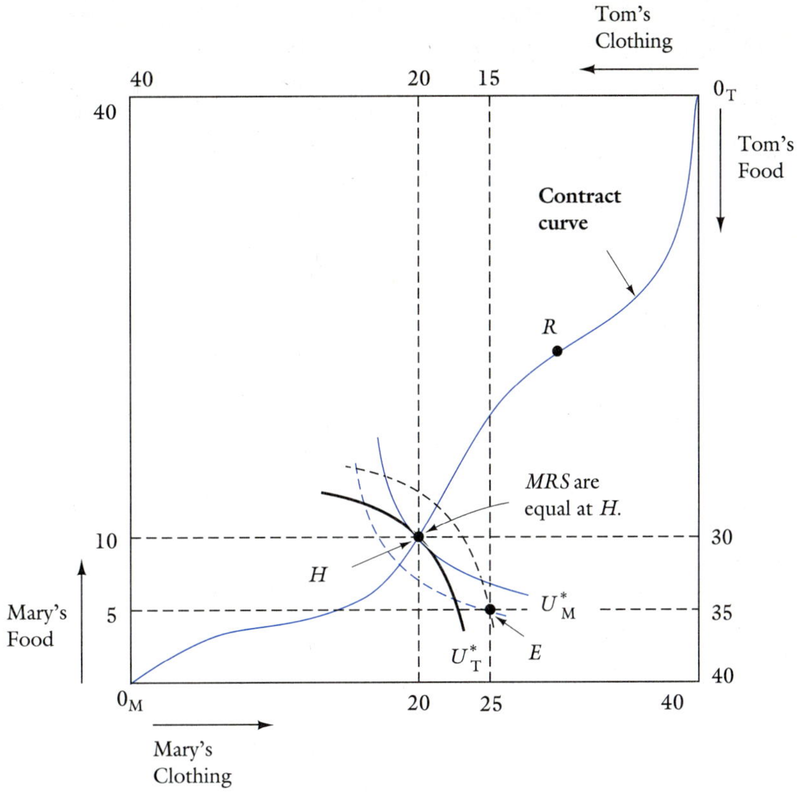

FIGURE 16.7

The Gains from Trade are Exhausted Along the Contract Curve

Efficient exchange is reached at an allocation, such as given by point *H*, at which Mary's MRS equals Tom's MRS. At an efficient allocation point Mary's and Tom's indifference curves are tangent. The collection of these points of tangency forms the contract curve.

Suppose at the initial endowment—point *E* in Figure 16.7—Mary's MRS equals ½ and Tom's MRS equals 3. Mary's MRS implies that she is willing to exchange ½ unit of food for 1 unit of clothing *without it affecting her level of satisfaction*. Equivalently, Mary is willing to exchange 1 unit of food for 2 units of clothing. Tom's MRS implies that he is willing to exchange 3 units of food for 1 unit of clothing *without it affecting his level of satisfaction*. Equivalently, Tom is willing to exchange 6 units of food for 2 units of clothing. Clearly, with these rates of exchange there is room for trade between Mary and Tom that will make them both better off. If Tom offers Mary 2 units of food for 2 units of clothing, then *both* Tom and Mary gain. Mary gains because she is willing to give up 2 units of clothing for just 1 unit of food and Tom gains because he is willing to offer (at most) 6 units of food for 2 units of clothing.

Whenever Mary's MRS differs from Tom's MRS, there is room for mutually advantageous trade. In other words, Mary can make Tom an offer that benefits both Mary and Tom if it is accepted. Equivalently, Tom could make Mary an offer that benefits them both if it is accepted. The fact that beneficial trade is possible whenever Mary's MRS differs from Tom's MRS causes the marginal rates of substitution to converge with trade. Thus, Mary and Tom stop trading—reach a point of *efficient exchange*—when their marginal rates of substitution are equal. Now we can draw the following general conclusion:

The gains from trading two goods are exhausted if the marginal rates of substitution are equated at the current allocation:

$$MRS^{Mary}_{clothing,\ food} = MRS^{Tom}_{clothing,\ food}$$

PARETO OPTIMALITY

The point at which the marginal rates of substitution are equal is called a Pareto-optimal allocation. Point *H* in Figure 16.7 represents such an allocation. At a **Pareto-optimal allocation,** there is no way that additional (voluntary) trade can make both participants better off.

Pareto-Optimal Allocation
Another term for *exchange efficiency.*

Any trades that take place from a Pareto-optimal point must make at least one person worse off.

The Pareto-optimal concept was named after Vilfredo Pareto (1848–1923), a nineteenth-century Italian economist who developed the implications of mutually beneficial trade.

THE CONTRACT CURVE

The concept of Pareto optimality can help us define the set of points at which the region of mutual advantage disappears. We reached Pareto-optimal allocation for Mary and Tom—point *H*—by starting from a given initial endowment—point *E*. It is generally true that if we start at another endowment point, we will end up with an allocation that is different from that described by point *H*. The new solution will also be Pareto-optimal, so that the marginal rates of substitution for Mary and Tom will be equal. If we repeat this exercise over and over by changing Mary's and Tom's initial endowments (keeping the total size of the Edgeworth box constant), we will find many Pareto-optimal allocations. When we find all of the Pareto-optimal solutions, we will have defined a curve called the contract curve. The **contract curve** represents *all* of the possible equilibrium combinations that might arise between Mary and Tom when trade is possible.

Contract Curve
The locus of allocation points in an Edgeworth box that are exchange-efficient (i.e., Pareto-optimal).

Note that the given endowment of Mary and Tom may result in an allocation other than point *H*, as long as it is on the contract curve. The relative bargaining power of Mary or Tom may move the final solution to the right or left of point *H*.

An example of the contract curve is shown in Figure 16.7, on page 667. All points along the contract curve are Pareto-optimal, so one individual cannot be made better off without reducing the welfare of the other once an allocation on the contract curve is reached. Another way to say this is that we cannot move from point H on the contract curve in Figure 16.7 to point R, which is also on the contract curve, without making either Mary or Tom worse off. In this case, we would make Tom worse off because his consumption at point R contains less of both clothing and food than he is consuming at point H. Once we have reached a Pareto-optimal allocation, there is no room for voluntary trade, even if it is to another Pareto-optimal allocation.

The contract curve illustrates an important characteristic of exchange between two individuals: namely, that there are generally many possible final allocations that can arise from an initial endowment. This occurs because the region of mutual advantage contains many points that lie on the contract curve. Although the final allocation is a point on the contract curve, it is not clear which point will arise from a given endowment of goods. The relative bargaining skills of Mary and Tom will most likely determine the final result. If Mary is a better bargainer than Tom, then the final allocation is likely to lie close to Tom's initial indifference curve, U_T^0, which gives Mary a large gain. Alternatively, if Tom is the better bargainer, then the final allocation is likely to lie closer to Mary's initial indifference curve, U_M^0, which gives Tom a large gain. We cannot determine which of the points on the contract curve will arise as the final allocation because we do not know how bargaining between the two parties will evolve. In short, the Edgeworth box does not predict the exact outcome.

EXCHANGE EFFICIENCY IN PERFECT COMPETITION

One drawback to the two-person model of exchange is that the final allocation depends on the relative bargaining power of the participants. Although exchange efficiency is achieved, the actual allocation on the contract curve cannot be predicted without knowing the bargaining power of the two individuals. One way to deal with this problem is to introduce a competitively determined price system. In a competitive system, we can determine the final allocation point using the equilibrium relative price ratio. Because prices are determined competitively—that is, market participants are price takers—we can show that a perfectly competitive economy achieves exchange efficiency.

Let's assume that there are many Marys and Toms in the economy, so that each Mary and Tom is a price taker; they cannot affect the price of clothing, P_c, or food, P_f, by their trading behavior. Each Mary and Tom is endowed with a certain quantity of food and clothing. If there is no collusion, then we have a perfectly competitive economy in which prices are used to set the terms of trade. The equilibrium relative price ratio, P_c/P_f, in this economy is the one in which quantity demanded equals quantity supplied in *both* the food and clothing markets. All exchanges between any members of the economy take place at the equilibrium relative price ratio. Any other ratio of exchange would make one party worse off.

For example, suppose that the equilibrium relative price ratio is 1; that is, the price of clothing equals the price of food ($P_c = P_f$). Further, suppose that a typical Tom and a typical Mary are endowed with food and clothing as described by point E in Figure 16.8 (this is the same endowment that we used above). At this endowment, the typical Mary's MRS equals ½ and the typical Tom's MRS equals 3. The equilibrium price line is shown as the straight line that passes through the endowment point of the typical Tom and the typical Mary. The slope of this line equals –1 times the equilibrium price ratio, $(-P_c/P_f)$.

If a typical Tom offered to trade a typical Mary at a rate different from the equilibrium price ratio, it would be a bad deal for a typical Mary. Suppose that

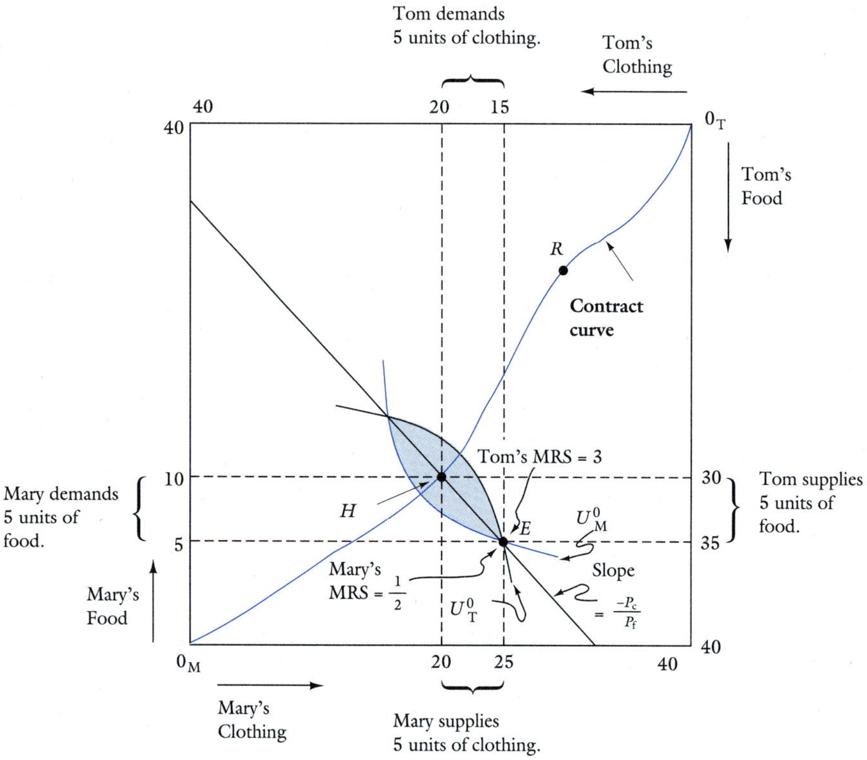

FIGURE 16.8

A Competitive Equilibrium Solution

In a competitive market, Mary and Tom can trade at the equilibrium relative price ratio of clothing and food. In fact, any other rate of exchange is disadvantageous to one of them. Thus, they are expected to move from their endowment at point E to point H on the contract curve by trading clothing for food at the rate P_c/P_f. In this trade, Mary supplies 5 units of clothing to Tom and Tom supplies 5 units of food to Mary. Because the MRS of Tom and Mary equals P_c/P_f at point H, the competitive market is efficient in exchange.

a typical Tom and a typical Mary offered 1 unit of food for 2 units of clothing. When we just look at the marginal rates of substitution for a typical Tom and a typical Mary, it might seem that this is a beneficial trade. The typical Mary receives *exactly* what her MRS requires and the typical Tom pays *less* than his MRS requires. In other words, Mary is no worse off and Tom is better off. But given that the equilibrium price ratio is 1, it is actually a bad deal for the typical Mary and a good deal for the typical Tom. The equilibrium price ratio implies that the typical Mary can trade 1 unit of clothing for 1 unit of food *with someone else in the market.* She does not have to give up the extra unit of clothing if she trades at the market price ratio. By analogy, if the typical Tom trades with the market, he will receive only 1 unit of clothing for the 1 unit of food. Obviously, if he can convince the typical Mary to give up 2 units of clothing, he is in a much better position. The typical Mary, though, will not accept the typical Tom's offer.

Given the opportunity to trade at the equilibrium price ratio, if the typical Mary trades with the typical Tom at Tom's terms, she is overpaying for the food she is receiving. Thus, as long as the typical Mary knows the equilibrium price ratio, she will not make a trade at any ratio less advantageous than the equilibrium price ratio. This observation also holds for the typical Tom. He is not willing to offer a better deal than he can get from "selling" (or "buying") at the equilibrium price ratio. Thus, both the typical "buyer" and the typical "seller" are expected to accept trades only at the equilibrium price ratio.[2]

Looking at the situation in Figure 16.8, we see that there is room for mutually advantageous trade between the typical Tom and the typical Mary at the equilibrium price ratio. The competitive price line intersects the contract curve at point *H,* a Pareto-optimal allocation. Thus, the typical Tom and the typical Mary can agree on a single trade that will place them at point *H;* that is, the typical Tom will offer the typical Mary 5 units of food for 5 units of clothing. After making this trade, the typical Mary and the typical Tom will not trade again—they have reached an equilibrium in which quantity supplied equals quantity demanded. If they try to move away from this point, they will find that one of them is made worse off.

The reasoning above suggests that when the typical Tom and the typical Mary are price takers, the perfectly competitive equilibrium will be on the contract curve, which means it will be a Pareto-optimal allocation. Thus, the perfectly competitive equilibrium achieves exchange efficiency. We can characterize the perfectly competitive equilibrium by the following observation:

A perfectly competitive equilibrium is reached when the marginal rate of substitution of each individual equals the price ratio:

[2] Some economists may argue that the price ratio can be out of equilibrium and so some trades may take place at a disequilibrium price ratio. Although this is possible, if participants are aware of the disequilibrium, one side of the transaction—either the buyer or seller—has an incentive to wait for a deal at the equilibrium price ratio, which causes the existing disequilibrium price ratio to converge to equilibrium. We ignore the problems presented by a disequilibrium price ratio because there is a strong incentive to converge to an equilibrium price ratio.

$$MRS_{\text{clothing, food}}^{\text{typical Mary}} = \frac{P_{\text{clothing}}}{P_{\text{food}}} = MRS_{\text{clothing, food}}^{\text{typical Tom}}$$

This statement is true for two reasons: (1) The marginal rates of substitution are equal at all points on the contract curve, and (2) each individual has an incentive to trade whenever the MRS is not equal to the equilibrium price ratio. Thus, individuals will stop trading when they have exhausted all gains from trade—that is, at some point on the contract curve in the region of mutual advantage—and when their MRS equals the equilibrium price ratio. Because the equilibrium price ratio is constant across all individuals, it equals the MRS for every individual at the perfectly competitive equilibrium.

TWO THEOREMS OF WELFARE ECONOMICS

The result that the perfectly competitive equilibrium exhausts all gains from trade—that is, satisfies the conditions for efficient exchange—was discussed in Chapter 10. This result is called the *invisible hand theorem,* named so because of Adam Smith's intellectual contribution to the understanding of competitive markets. It is also called the *first theorem of welfare economics* and is often restated to say

The perfectly competitive equilibrium is a Pareto-optimal allocation.

In effect, if market participants act as price takers and the other assumptions of perfect competition are satisfied, then we are assured that all gains from trade are exhausted and that the competitive equilibrium allocation lies on the contract curve. One question that this theorem does not address, however, is whether all of the possible allocation points along the contract curve correspond to a competitive equilibrium. In other words, suppose that you do not think that Mary is dealt a fair allocation with her initial endowment. Mary has more clothing than Tom, but she has quite a bit less food. You may think that this is unfair and you would like to change this endowment. A new endowment will lead to a final allocation at some other point on the contract curve, say, point *R* in Figure 16.8. The question remains, is there a competitive equilibrium that corresponds to the new allocation?

Under fairly general assumptions, the answer is yes. This result is called the *second theorem of welfare economics* and is stated

Any allocation on the contract curve can be achieved by a competitive equilibrium.

The conditions that produce this result are mainly technical, but an important one is that the indifference curves of Tom and Mary must be convex to their respective origins. Convexity creates the region of mutual advantage, which yields beneficial trades. As long as we can define a price ratio that generates a price line, as in Figure 16.8, which passes through the region of mutual advantage, then it will intersect the contract curve. By varying the price ratio, we can intersect the contract curve at other points in the region of mutual advantage, too, so any point along the contract curve within the region of mutual advantage can be a competitive equilibrium.

The second theorem of welfare economics illustrates an important result about the relationship between efficiency and equity, or fairness. The initial allocation for Mary may be unfair or inequitable, so you might desire to change it. Economists cannot tell you whether it is a good or bad idea to change the initial endowments of Mary and Tom. But we can say that if you do change it, then the economy is likely to reach another competitive equilibrium by starting from the new endowment point. Thus, the issues of efficiency and equity (or fairness) are logically separate from each other. We can examine efficiency issues with authority, but equity or fairness issues are not generally part of this discussion.

$$$ Price Theory in Practice

The Divide and Choose Problem

There is an old story that an elderly gentleman was worried about how to divide his estate between two greedy children. This gentleman worried that no matter how it was done, there would be endless bickering and bad feeling. A wise counselor said there was a way to avoid the problem and to deter greed by each child. The counselor said: "In your will, leave instructions that one of your children is to take your possessions and divide them into two groups. The *other* child then gets to pick whichever of the two groups of goods he or she wants. This way, if the first child, the divider of the goods, tries to be greedy, it will backfire as the second child, the chooser, gets to pick the more valuable pile of goods. This will ensure a fair division. Neither child can say he or she did not have a choice."

Would you rather be the Divider or the Chooser in such a situation? What does the theory of efficient exchange suggest? The correct answer is that you would rather be the divider. To see this result, let's examine one possible case.

We assume that the two children, Divide and Choose, know each other very well, so each knows the value the other places on the goods to be inherited. They do not have identical preferences; they just know each others' preferences. To simplify the analysis, assume there are only two types of goods to be divided so that we can use the Edgeworth box to illustrate this problem. Figure 16.9, on page 674, shows the basic setup of the divide and choose problem.

The gentleman left two goods to be divided, which we will call *A* and *B*. The total quantity of these goods defines the borders of the Edgeworth box in Figure 16.9. There are 300 units of good *A* and 80 units of good *B* in the estate. The Divider is responsible for dividing goods *A* and *B* into the two piles, such as at point *X* or point *Y*. Point *X* contains 200 units of good *A* and 25 units of good *B* for the Divider and 100 units of good *A* and 55 units of good *B* for the Chooser. Point *Y* is the mirror image of point *X*; that is, the Divider's bundle is switched with the Chooser's bundle. Points *X* and *Y* allow us to see the alternative quantities the Divider and Chooser receive, depending on which of the two piles the Chooser selects.

Figure 16.9 shows two indifference curves, C_1 and C_2, for the Chooser. These curves represent the satisfaction provided by points *Y* and *X*, respectively.

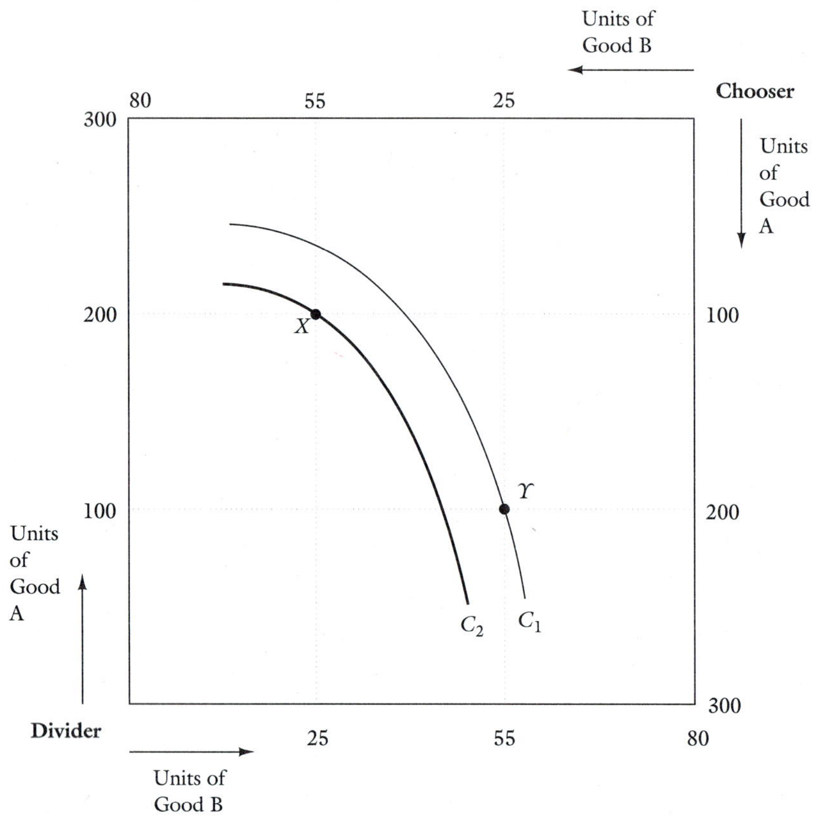

FIGURE 16.9

Choosing Between Bundles Offered by the Divider

The Divider splits the two goods in the estate with knowledge of the Chooser's preferences. The two allocation points, X and Υ, are mirror images of each other and represent two outcomes available to the Chooser. Because the allocation at point X offers more satisfaction to the Chooser—indifference curve C_2 compared to indifference curve C_1—the Chooser selects this allocation.

Because indifference curve C_2 represents a higher level of satisfaction than indifference curve C_1, the Chooser will select the division given by point X. Of course, because the Divider knows the Chooser's preferences, the Divider knows that point X is preferred to point Υ and deliberately combined the bundles of goods that way—so as to maximize what the Divider gets out of the arrangement.

Figure 16.10 shows how the Divider has benefited from being the divider. By carefully selecting the piles of goods to account for the Chooser's preferences, the Divider can offer a bundle that the Chooser will select that puts the Divider on a higher level of utility. The Divider receives satisfaction at point X given by indifference curve D_2, which exceeds the satisfaction at point Υ given by indifference curve D_1.

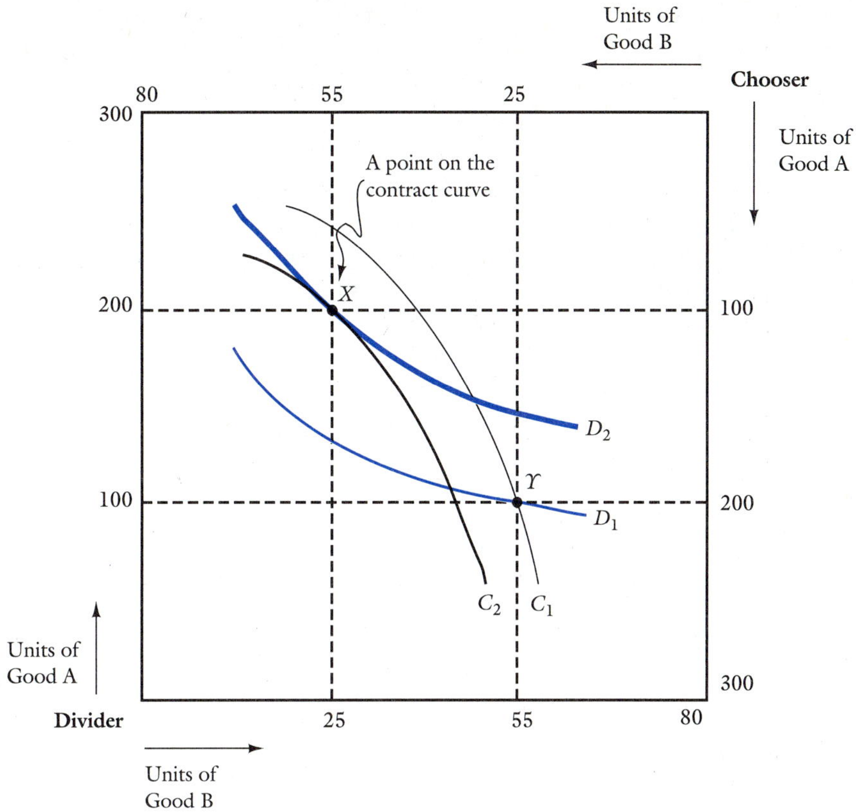

FIGURE 16.10

The Divider Arranges for a Solution on the Contract Curve

The Divider knows that the Chooser will select the allocation at point *X*, so the goods are split in such a way that the Divider's satisfaction is maximized (subject to the Chooser's preferences) by the allocation at point *X*. As shown, the Divider receives satisfaction given by indifference curve D_2, which exceeds the satisfaction given by indifference curve D_1 that includes allocation point *Y*.

Point *X* in Figure 16.10 is actually the solution to a maximization problem for the Divider. If the Divider knows the Chooser's preferences completely, the Divider can find the split that maximizes his or her satisfaction subject to the Chooser's decision. In other words, the Divider's advantage comes from being in a position to maximize for himself or herself, subject only to the Chooser's selection, which the Divider can determine if the Chooser's indifference curves are known.

The combination that results from the Divider's maximization problem is on the contract curve because it makes no sense for the Divider to trade after the choice if he or she can select the composition of the bundle beforehand. In other words, there will be no additional gains from trade after the piles are distributed. Because the Divider maximizes his or her satisfaction over the *entire set of bundles* in the Edgeworth box (constrained by the Chooser's preferences) and the Chooser maximizes only over two particular bundles, it is better to be the Divider than the Chooser.[3] Although it may sound funny, it is correct to say that the Divider has more to choose from than the Chooser.

LEARNING EXERCISE 16.4

Suppose that instead of trying to be clever, the elderly parent had simply divided things 50/50, so that the goods are allocated in equal bundles: 150 units of good A and 40 units of good B to each child. How will this solution differ from the divide and choose solution?

16.3 Efficient Production

In this section, we extend the analysis of exchange between individuals to firms and their choice of inputs. This is necessary because the previous discussion treated production as given—that is, each individual was *endowed* with a fixed supply of goods. But goods do not drop out of the sky; they are produced by firms. In this section, we explain the general equilibrium conditions under which goods are efficiently produced and show that a perfectly competitive economy satisfies these conditions.

INITIAL EMPLOYMENT

Let's continue to assume that there are two goods, food and clothing, but now let's state that they are produced by two inputs: capital (K) and labor (L). For simplicity, the total quantities of capital (K_{total}) and labor (L_{total}) available per time period are fixed; we also assume that they are always fully employed. Any increase in production in the food industry, then, must take some inputs away from the clothing industry, and vice versa. In Figure 16.11, we show the initial employment levels of capital and labor in the production of food and clothing.

The capital and labor used in the production of clothing are measured from the origin labeled O_C (lower left-hand corner of the diagram). The capital and labor used in the production of food are measured from origin O_F (upper right-hand corner). By assumption, the use of capital in the clothing and food industries equals the total amount of capital available; the same is true for labor. Thus, given the initial use of capital and labor represented by point A in Figure 16.11, we know that the clothing industry uses K_c in capital and the food industry uses K_f in capital, so $K_c + K_f = K_{\text{total}}$. With respect to labor, at point A, the clothing industry uses L_c, the food industry uses L_f, so $L_c + L_f = L_{\text{total}}$.

[3] It is possible that the Divider and Chooser may be indifferent between who is the divider and who is the chooser. In this case, the Divider's and Chooser's preferences are such that they would create the same bundles to choose from.

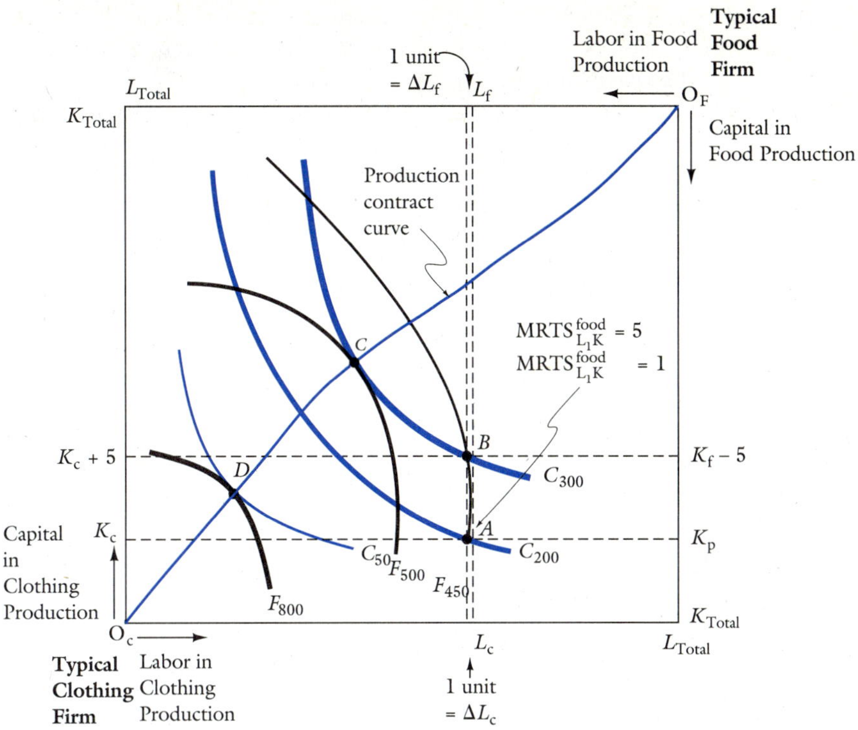

FIGURE 16.11

The Edgeworth Box for Production

The Edgeworth box for production shows the initial input mix at point *A* for the typical food firm and the typical clothing firm. The total quantity of inputs is fixed in this analysis, so increases in production in one industry require that inputs be transferred from the other industry. Production isoquants for the two typical firms are shown. The initial input mix in the two industries is not technically efficient because the firm's MRTS values are not equal. Rearranging the input mix increases output in both firms. Efficient product occurs along the production contract curve, which shows the input combinations for which the MRTS values of the two firms are equated.

Figure 16.11 is an Edgeworth box diagram, but in this case we are using it to depict a production relationship, so we call it an *Edgeworth production box* or an *Edgeworth box for production*.

THE PRODUCTION FUNCTION

In Figure 16.11, we also show the production isoquants (see Chapter 8) for a typical food producer and a typical clothing producer. The initial allocation of inputs between the production of food and clothing allows the typical clothing firm to produce 200 units of clothes, which is described by the isoquant C_{200}.

Similarly, the typical food firm can produce 450 units of food, as described by the isoquant F_{450}. (Note that the food isoquant has been rotated 180° in the Edgeworth production box.) These isoquants represent the highest production possible, given the initial allocation of inputs.

Recall from Chapter 8 that the marginal rate of technical substitution (MRTS) equals the ratio of the marginal product of labor (MP_L) to the marginal product of capital (MP_K); that is, $MRTS_{L,K} = MP_L/MP_K$. The $MRTS_{L,K}$ is the ratio at which labor can be substituted for capital *without changing the output rate*. Geometrically, the $MRTS_{L,K}$ equals the absolute value of the slope of an isoquant at a given point. At point *A*, we can see that the slope of the clothing isoquant *does not* equal the slope of the food isoquant because these isoquants are not tangent to each other. Thus, $MRTS^{clothing}_{L,K} \neq MRTS^{food}_{L,K}$ at the initial allocation of inputs. When comparing the production functions for food and clothing, the clothing isoquant is "flatter" at point *A* than the food isoquant, so we can state that $MRTS^{food}_{L,K} > MRTS^{clothing}_{L,K}$ at the initial allocation of inputs.[4] As shown in the figure, $MRTS^{food}_{L,K} = 5$ and $MRTS^{clothing}_{L,K} = 1$. Thus, the marginal product of labor is low relative to the marginal product of capital in the clothing industry when compared to the food industry. This result implies that one or both of the typical producers in these two industries can increase their output if they can rearrange their initial allocation of capital and labor.

TECHNICAL EFFICIENCY

Technical efficiency in production implies that firms have an incentive to rearrange their input mix whenever a new mix results in higher output rates. Consider what is gained if the typical food firm substitutes 5 units of capital for 1 unit of labor. The capital given up is sent to the typical clothing firm in exchange for labor. Total food output remains unchanged, but now the clothing industry has 5 additional units of capital and 1 less unit of labor. Because $MRTS^{clothing}_{L,K} = 1$, total clothing output remains unchanged if 1 unit of capital is exchanged for 1 unit of labor. The action of the typical food producer, however, provides the clothing firm with 5 units—not 1 unit—of capital for 1 unit of labor. Thus, the output in the typical clothing firm must increase.

Figure 16.11 shows this result as a move from point *A* to point *B*. The food firm continues to produce 450 units of food because point *B* lies on isoquant F_{450}. The clothing firm, however, has moved to isoquant C_{300}, at which 300 units of clothing are produced, compared to 200 units previously.

This example illustrates that output can increase whenever the $MRTS_{L,K}$ is not equated across firms. Thus, firms have an incentive to change their input mix if the values for $MRTS_{L,K}$ are not equal. Once the $MRTS_{L,K}$ values are equated across firms, any change in the input mix must cause at least one firm's output rate to decrease. But then there is no incentive for the firm

[4] The MRTS equals the absolute value of the slope of an isoquant at a given point. Because the clothing isoquant is "flatter" than the food isoquant at point *A*, the absolute value of its slope is less than the absolute value of the slope of the food isoquant. The fact that the food isoquant is rotated 180° does not change this result.

whose output decreases to change its input mix, so there are no further changes in the input mix whenever the $MRTS_{L,K}$ values are equal across firms. This result gives rise to the definition of **technical efficiency.**

Technical Efficiency
The condition that the MRTS values are equated across firms, so that there are no mutual gains in output across industries when the input mix is reallocated.

Production by firms is *technically efficient* when

$$\mathbf{MRTS}_{L,K}^{\text{clothing}} = \mathbf{MRTS}_{L,K}^{\text{food}}$$

for all firms. When this condition holds, there are no further output gains for *all* firms from changing the input mix.

Technical efficiency for firms is analogous to exchange efficiency for individuals. When exchange efficiency is achieved, additional trades will not make *both* individuals better off. Similarly, when technical efficiency is reached, any further changes in the input mix will not increase the output of *both* firms.

In Figure 16.11 on page 677, neither point *A* nor *B* is technically efficient. In both cases, output can increase if these typical firms change their input mix. The condition for technical efficiency implies that the isoquants of the two firms are tangent; that is, technical efficiency occurs at a point at which the isoquants have the same slope. At points *C* and *D*, for example, the isoquants of the two firms are tangent. Thus, points *C* and *D* are both technically efficient, although it is unlikely that point *D* can be reached from the initial allocation—point *A*—because point *D* implies a lower output rate for the typical clothing firm.

Production Contract Curve
The set of input mixes in an Edgeworth production box that are technically efficient.

There are actually many points in the Edgeworth box for production that are technically efficient. The **production contract curve** shown in Figure 16.11 defines all of the points that are technically efficient. At any of these points, the output gains for both firms from changing the input mix are exhausted.

TECHNICAL EFFICIENCY IN PERFECT COMPETITION

Perfectly competitive firms maximize profits. As we learned from Chapter 10, a profit-maximizing firm is also a cost-minimizing firm. That is, the input mix selected by a profit-maximizing firm produces its chosen output at least cost. If the price of labor is *w*, the price of capital is *r*, and both the labor and capital markets are competitive, then the cost-minimizing firm equates the ratio of marginal products (MP_L/MP_L) to the ratio of relative input prices to determine the least-cost input mix (see Chapter 9). Because the marginal rate of technical substitution is defined as the ratio of marginal products, the cost-minimizing firm solves

$$MRTS_{L,K} = \frac{w}{r} \qquad (16.1)$$

at the optimal input mix.

Now in a competitive economy, *all* profit-maximizing firms solve equation (16.1) when they select an input mix. Because the ratio of input prices, w/r, is constant across firms, the $MRTS_{L,K}$ is equated across *all* firms. Thus, all perfectly competitive firms choose an input mix somewhere along the production contract curve, so all perfectly competitive firms are technically efficient.

$$$ Price Theory in Practice

Gains from Trade with Mexico

Mexico's biggest producer of women's clothing wasted no time when the United States and Mexico began talks in 1991 to establish a free trade agreement between the two countries. The clothing maker, called Vanity, started to plan how to expand into the heavily protected clothing and textile industry in the United States. The firm invested in a computerized design machine. It also improved the quality of its cloth, importing 85 percent instead of 15 percent of its cloth. At the same time, the Mexican ceramic tile maker Interceramic invested $50 million in a new plant and research laboratory. The firm also signed on Armstrong World Industries of Lancaster, Pennsylvania, to market Interceramic's products in the United States. The firm expected an increase in sales when the 21 percent tariff (tax) on ceramic tiles imported to the United States would be eliminated. The North American Free Trade Agreement (NAFTA) passed in 1993 and provided a phaseout of tariffs over 15 years, but many tariffs were eliminated immediately.

The actions of these firms show how free trade affects Mexico and the United States. The Edgeworth box shows us that both countries can gain from voluntary exchange when the endowments of each country are fixed.[5] In this case, Mexico has a *comparative advantage* in labor-intensive industries because of its lower relative cost of labor. (Recall that comparative advantage was defined in Chapter 1.) A country has a comparative advantage in a particular production activity if it faces the lowest opportunity cost in that activity. Mexican clothing manufacturers and tile makers, for examples, have a comparative advantage over most U.S. counterparts. These firms plan to expand production to meet demand in the United States. Mexican workers earned an estimated 57 cents per hour compared with $10.86 per hour in the United States in 1993. Productivity differences can explain much of the wage difference. Even so, labor-intensive industries will export more products because they can be produced at a lower cost in Mexico than in the United States.

U.S. firms will also benefit from free trade. Generally, the United States has a comparative advantage in goods that are capital-intensive, technology-intensive, or intensive in skilled labor. For example, much of the physical capital—such as computers and machine tools and dies—that Mexican industries need in order to expand production is imported from the United States. The United States also benefits from the greater export of services to Mexico, such as the marketing services purchased by Interceramic and financial services provided by large banking firms. Thus, as Mexican firms expand production, the demand for capital equipment made in the United States and for loans increases, which expands output and labor demand in capital-producing and financial service industries.

Although free trade makes the economies of Mexico and the United States more efficient, there are those who will be hurt (at least initially) by free trade.

[5] Free trade between Mexico and the United States may actually increase the resource endowment of both countries (assuming that both labor and capital are mobile), so there may be an additional gain beyond the gain from voluntary trade arising from the free trade agreement.

In other words, as firms adjust to equate MRTS to w/r in both Mexico and the United States, there will be a sorting of jobs between the two countries. Employment opportunities will increase in Mexico, which will increase wages of Mexican workers, while employment opportunities in some labor-intensive industries in the United States will decrease. Thus, U.S. wages in certain industries will fall. This process will make both economies more technically efficient.

Obviously, the technical efficiency generated by free trade with Mexico is not achieved without political and economic pain. In the United States, workers in industries that produce clothing, autos, glass products, and footwear are among those expected to be hurt as lower-cost substitutes become available from Mexico. Unions representing those workers, led by the AFL-CIO, are opposed to free trade. Opponents point to the *maquiladora* program as an example of how U.S. jobs are lost to low-paid workers in Mexico. The program, started in 1965, allows the northern border area of Mexico to attract assembly operations from the United States. The *maquiladoras,* or participating firms, are permitted to import duty-free raw materials, components, and machinery from the United States with the stipulation that the plants export their output. The number of operations has grown steadily from 12 in 1965 employing 3,000 workers to more than 1,800 in 1990 employing more than 400,000 workers. Many of these operations were drawn away from the United States; for example, a number of wood furniture firms relocated from the Los Angeles area to just south of the Mexican border.

But the attraction of opening markets to free trade is that there are *net* gains from trade; the gains of the export industries outweigh the losses of industries hurt by imports. At the same time, consumers gain from lower prices. They can buy clothes, ceramic tiles, and car parts made in Mexico at a lower price than if they had been made in the United States. The lower prices allow U.S. consumers to increase their consumption basket of goods—that is, to buy more of all goods—which increases the demand for labor in the United States.

LEARNING EXERCISE 16.5

If a free trade partner with the United States, such as Mexico, signs a free trade agreement with a country that does not have such an agreement with the United States, does this imply that the United States has effectively "signed" a free trade pact with this third country? How can the United States enforce its trade restrictions against this third country? How can the third country avoid such restrictions?

16.4 The Production Possibilities Frontier

Technical efficiency defines a set of equilibrium points for inputs to the production process, but in order to select a unique point on the production contract curve we must consider the economic conditions in the output market. For example, how much will consumers pay for the outputs produced? For output markets to reach a general equilibrium, firms must produce a combination of goods that *matches* consumers' willingness to pay for the combination.

General equilibrium requires that quantity supplied equals quantity demanded at the prevailing price in each market. To integrate the production analysis with the analysis of consumer exchange, we must translate the efficient production combinations, represented by the production contract curve, to a set of output combinations, which shows us the production possibilities frontier. The **production possibilities frontier** represents the maximum attainable output combinations of two goods when the initial inputs are fixed. Once we have derived a production possibilities frontier, we can show how consumers' preferences affect the equilibrium in each market.

Production Possibilities Frontier The mapping of the production contract curve into output space. The frontier shows the maximum technologically efficient rates of output for a given endowment of inputs.

DERIVING THE PRODUCTION POSSIBILITIES FRONTIER

The way we derive a production possibilities frontier is to transfer the contract curve from the Edgeworth production box to an output graph. Every point on the production contract curve corresponds to a given amount of food and clothing output. At point *C* in Figure 16.11 on page 677, for example, labor and capital are allocated among firms such that the typical food firm produces 500 units of food and the typical clothing firm produces 300 units of clothes. Other points on the production contract curve represent different combinations of output. Graphing the output relationship across *all* points on the contract curve gives the production possibilities frontier.[6] An example of the production possibilities frontier is shown in Figure 16.12.

In Figure 16.12, points *A, B, C,* and *D* are extracted from the Edgeworth production box shown in Figure 16.11. Points *A* and *B* are not on the production contract curve, so they do not lie on the production possibilities frontier. In contrast, points *C* and *D* are on the production contract curve, so these points lie on the production possibilities frontier. Thus, we can say that points below the production possibilities frontier are technically inefficient, while all points on the frontier are technically efficient (by definition).

MARGINAL RATE OF TRANSFORMATION

Note that the shape of the production possibilities frontier in Figure 16.12 is concave to the origin. The production possibilities frontier is concave because the *opportunity cost* of shifting production from one good to another is increasing as we move down the curve. We measure the opportunity cost of one output in terms of the other as the absolute value of the slope of the production possibilities frontier, which is called the **marginal rate of transformation (MRT).** In Figure 16.12, we can see that the MRT at point *D* equals ½. This implies that ½ unit of food must be given up—not produced—in order to produce 1 additional unit of clothing. In other words, at point *D,* the opportunity cost of an additional unit of clothing equals ½ unit of food. As we move farther along the production possibilities curve to point *C,* the MRT increases to

Marginal Rate of Transformation (MRT) The slope of the production possibilities frontier at a given point. The MRT equals the ratio of the marginal cost of the output shown along the horizontal axis to the marginal cost of the output shown along the vertical axis.

[6] The production possibilities frontier applies to the entire economy, so we are treating the Edgeworth production box and the resulting production contract curve for the two typical firms as representative of all firms in the food and clothing industries.

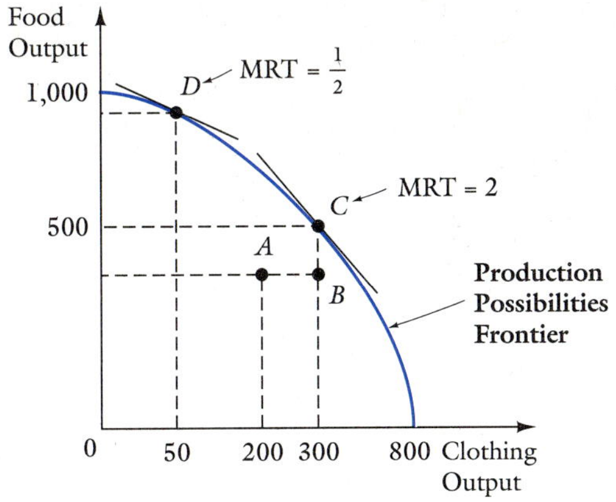

FIGURE 16.12

The Production Possibilities Frontier

The production possibilities frontier plots the output created along the production contract curve. The output of the food industry is shown along the vertical axis and the output of the clothing industry is shown along the horizontal axis. Output rates below the frontier, such as shown at points *A* and *B*, are not technically efficient. As firms move along the production possibilities frontier, the relative opportunity cost of producing one output or the other changes. The marginal rate of transformation (MRT), which equals the absolute value of the slope of the production possibilities frontier, measures the relative opportunity cost of a given output mix. The MRT increases as we move from point *D* to point *C*, indicating that the relative opportunity cost of producing more clothes and less food is increasing.

2, so the opportunity cost has increased. Now, 2 units of food must be given up in order to produce 1 additional unit of clothing.

We can relate the marginal rate of transformation to the marginal cost of clothing and food production. At point *D* in Figure 16.12, for example, we give up producing ½ units of food by transferring some inputs to the production of 1 unit of clothing. This implies that the marginal cost of the clothing units is twice the marginal cost of the food units at this point. That is, the capital and labor given up for 1 unit of food production generates one-half of the marginal cost of the capital and labor used to produce 1 extra unit of clothing. Therefore, 1 extra unit of clothing production requires the amount of capital and labor used to produce 2 units of food. This result implies that the marginal rate of transformation equals the ratio of marginal costs at any point on the production possibilities curve. Analytically, we write

$$\text{MRT} = \frac{\text{MC}_c}{\text{MC}_f} \tag{16.2}$$

To better understand equation (16.2), suppose that the marginal cost of clothing production (MC_c) is \$8 per unit at point *D*. Because the MRT = 2, we know that the marginal cost of food production (MC_f) must be \$4 per unit. Thus, we can rearrange equation (16.2), which is the opportunity cost of producing 1 extra unit of clothing at a given point, to state that $MC_f = MC_c/MRT$, which allows us to solve for MC_f. Another way to look at this relationship is to say that the ratio MC_c/MRT measures the dollar value of the additional capital and labor needed to produce another unit of food. Thus, at point *D*, we need \$4 of additional labor and capital to produce 1 extra unit of food.

LEARNING EXERCISE 16.6

Suppose that improved technology allows food producers to supply 1.5 times more food using the same inputs. How does this change affect the shape of the production possibilities frontier?

GENERAL EQUILIBRIUM FOR BOTH FIRMS AND CONSUMERS

The production decisions of firms are consistent with the exchange demands of consumers only when the terms of trade between consumers and firms are equated. A consumer is willing to trade food for clothing based on his or her MRS, and if exchange is efficient, then the MRS values are equal across all consumers. The terms of trade for firms are determined by the opportunity cost of producing additional units of clothing compared to food, which equals the MRT, which is equal across all firms if firms are technically efficient. *Thus, a general equilibrium is reached between firms and consumers when*

$$MRS = MRT \tag{16.3}$$

for all consumers and firms in the economy. This equation is known as the **output efficiency** condition because it specifies an equilibrium for the output markets. This equation ensures that the product mix in the economy is the one that consumers demand, given the opportunity costs of production.

Output Efficiency The condition that the MRT equals the MRS for all consumers and firms in the economy. This condition ensures that the output mix reflects consumers' relative willingness to pay.

It is important to note that the economy may be efficient in exchange between consumers and technically efficient in production, but not efficient in output because firms are not producing a product mix that reflects consumers' relative willingness to pay. For example, firms may produce a minuscule amount of clothing and a large amount of food very efficiently, and consumers may exchange these goods between themselves efficiently, but the lopsided product mix may be an *inefficient* choice for the economy because $MRS \neq MRT$. Consumers are likely to be made better off if firms allocate more resources to producing clothing and less to producing food ($MRS_{clothing,food} > MRT$). The output efficiency condition ensures that there is no dissimilarity between the relative valuation consumers place on goods and the relative opportunity costs firms incur when the goods are produced.

To understand why the output efficiency condition, equation (16.3), must hold in a general equilibrium, suppose that the $MRS_{clothing,food} = 3$ and the $MRT = 2$ at the current allocation. Consumers are willing to trade 3 units of food for 1 unit of clothing at this allocation. But with the $MRT = 2$, the opportunity cost of producing 1 additional unit of clothing is only 2 units of food. Clearly, there is room for trade between consumers and firms. Consumers are willing to pay more (in terms of food units) for an extra unit of clothing than it will cost firms to produce an extra unit of clothing. Thus, a general equilibrium has not been reached: Both the food and clothing markets will be affected by continued trade between firms and consumers. When consumers demand more clothing and less food, the economy moves farther down the production possibilities frontier, which causes the MRT to increase, so the value of the MRT approaches the value of the MRS. Trade continues in this direction until equation (16.3) is satisfied.

$$$ Price Theory in Practice

EXPENDITURES ON CHILDREN

Employing some simplifying assumptions, we can treat the family unit as a closed economy and analyze it within a general equilibrium framework. Such an approach was taken in modeling the expenditures made by parents on their children's education.[7] The basic question studied was how the family's resources are allocated among siblings when the children have different innate abilities and the parents have an aversion to inequality in the distribution of the lifetime earnings of their offspring. Parents observe the ability of their children as they grow. Parents can use this information to estimate how well each child will do in the labor market. If parents estimate that a child will not do well in the labor market, do they give the less gifted child more resources in an attempt to help him or her catch up with the more gifted children? Empirical estimates of the model's parameters using data on twins suggest that parents do indeed act this way and consequently spend more on the education of less able children.

To introduce the model, assume that earnings are the sole determinant of an adult's economic well-being and that expected lifetime earnings depend only on the individual's genetic makeup and the amount of education received as a child. Parents affect their children's subsequent economic status through the amount of resources they devote to education, and it is further assumed that parents provide all resources for their childrens' education. Parental expenditures on education, therefore, increase a child's expected lifetime earnings, but at a decreasing rate. In addition, assume that the family's total educational budget is determined independently of the parents' own consumption, parents do not give bequests or any other gifts to their children, and the price per year of schooling is the same for all children and independent of the level of education attained.

A given total of parental spending on education, along with the scholastic ability of the offspring, determines the expected lifetime earnings for the children. As total spending on education is reallocated between children, lifetime earnings change. The *expected earnings frontier* shows how changing the mix of education expenditure among children affects lifetime earnings. The expected earnings frontier is illustrated in Figure 16.13 (page 686) for a family with two children. As can be seen from the skewed nature of the earnings frontier, the potential earnings of child 2 are higher than those of child 1 because of different

[7] Jere R. Behrman, Robert A. Pollack, and Paul Taubman, "Parental Preferences and Provision for Progeny," *Journal of Political Economy* 90 (February 1982), 52–73.

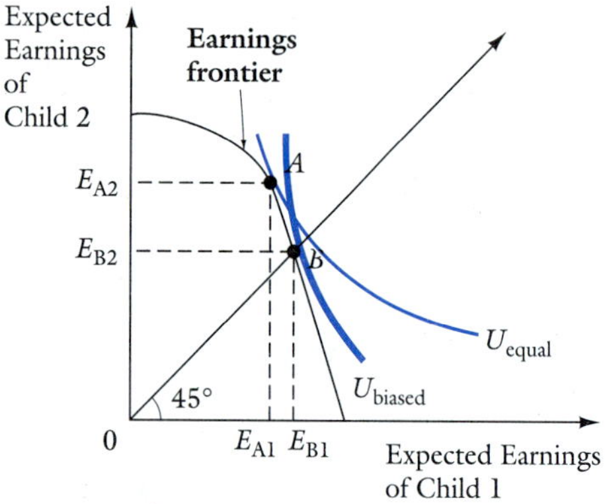

FIGURE 16.13

Allocation of Resources by Parents to Children with Different Scholastic Ability

The earnings frontier shows the lifetime expected earnings potential of two children based on the resources allocated to schooling by their parents and the scholastic ability of the children. If parents' preferences are symmetric (U_{equal})—that is, there is no bias toward one child or the other—parents choose to allocate schooling resources such that child 1 earns E_{A1} and child 2 earns E_{A2}. Because child 2 has more scholastic aptitude than child 1, parents may bias their preferences toward the less endowed child (U_{biased}). School resources may thus be allocated so that each child has the same expected lifetime income ($E_{B1} = E_{B2}$).

ability. Also shown in Figure 16.13 are two possible preference maps for the parents. The indifference curve U_{equal} is drawn symmetrically around the 45° line to indicate equal concern for the children's economic well-being. In other words, with a symmetric indifference curve, the expected earnings of each child are given equal weight in the parent's preferences. The indifference curve U_{bias} is not symmetric but rather tilted toward child 1, who has a lower earnings potential.

Note that equal concern as represented by U_{equal} rules out unequal treatment based on parental preferences, but it does not guarantee equal expected earnings. Differences in ability may result in systematic differences in earnings between the children in a family, as the skewed shape of the earnings frontier indicates. Point *A* on the earnings frontier in Figure 16.13 shows this possibility. Even though the parents weight each child equally in their preferences, different abilities skew the earnings frontier toward child 2, who earns E_{A2} compared to E_{A1} for child 1.

Because children's abilities differ, parents may adopt compensating strategies to help equalize earnings among the children. Point *B* on the earnings frontier shows the optimum solution when parent's preferences have adjusted to show a bias toward the less able child. In this situation, child 1 earns E_{B1} and child 2 earns E_{B2} from the parent's distribution of education resources. Note that E_{B1} exceeds E_{A1}, so that child 1 is favored over child 2.

To test whether parents adopt compensating strategies, the researchers analyzed a sample of 914 white male fraternal twins born in the United States between 1917 and 1927. The results suggested that both earnings inequality and basic investment considerations, such as the future returns to a college education, are important determinants of the allocation of resources within families. In general, the results implied that parents do favor their less gifted children; that is, they spend more on the education of their less able children. These findings indicate a fairly strong parental aversion to earnings inequality.

LEARNING EXERCISE 16.7

If parents adopt compensating strategies, can children change the outcome by trade among themselves? What do parents do to prevent arbitrage by children?

GENERAL EQUILIBRIUM AND THE EFFICIENCY OF PERFECT COMPETITION

The condition for output efficiency, equation (16.3), is satisfied in perfect competition. We know from the discussion of exchange efficiency and perfect competition that $MRS_{clothing,food} = P_c/P_f$ when consumers are in equilibrium. We also know that $MRT = MC_c/MC_f$ as a by-product of the definition of the opportunity cost of producing additional units of clothing. Now, in perfect competition all firms are price takers, so they choose an output rate such that $P_c = MC_c$ and $P_f = MC_f$ to maximize profits. This result implies that

$$\frac{P_c}{P_f} = \frac{MC_c}{MC_f} \tag{16.4}$$

for perfectly competitive markets.

Combining equation (16.4) with equation (16.2) and our result that $MRS_{clothing,food} = P_c/P_f$ in perfect competition produces the following conclusion:

Perfectly competitive markets reach an equilibrium that exhausts all gains from trade between consumers and firms:

$$MRS_{clothing,food} = \frac{P_c}{P_f} = \frac{MC_c}{MC_f} = MRT$$

In effect, the assumptions of perfect competition lead both firms and consumers to interact in such a manner as to undertake all mutually advantageous trades. Firms do so to maximize their profits and consumers do so to increase their satisfaction. This interaction determines a unique product mix for the economy to produce given the initial endowment of resources. It is truly amazing, as Adam Smith first noted, that by pursuing their own self-interest, consumers and firms are "led by an invisible hand" to promote an outcome that they did not necessarily intend, that is, the exhaustion of *all* gains from trade for *all* participants in the economy.

TABLE 16.1

Efficiency Conditions for a Two-Good, Two-Input Economy

Exchange Efficiency
$MRS^{Mary}_{clothing,food} = MRS^{Tom}_{clothing,food}$
Technical Efficiency
$MRTS^{clothing}_{L,K} = MRTS^{food}_{L,K}$
Output Efficiency (Product Mix)
$MRT = \frac{MC_{clothes}}{MC_{food}} = MRS^{typical\ consumer}_{clothes,food}$

LEARNING EXERCISE 16.8

Suppose that $P_c/P_f > MC_c/MC_f$. How should production of food and clothing change to reach an efficient output mix?

A SUMMARY OF ECONOMIC EFFICIENCY

The exchange efficiency, technical efficiency, and output efficiency conditions are summarized in Table 16.1.

When the three efficiency conditions in Table 16.1 are satisfied, the economy reaches a general equilibrium solution. The general equilibrium solution, however, is not independent of the initial endowment of resources. Exchange between consumers is efficient anywhere along the contract curve and firms are technically efficient anywhere along the production contract curve. But the relative position of consumers and firms along these curves is affected by their initial endowments. Consumers who are endowed with more income (or goods) are expected to consume more goods than consumers endowed with less income. The economy may produce such goods efficiently and reach a general equilibrium solution, but the relatively poorer consumers (those endowed with less) still will be less than satisfied because they receive less. Thus, the efficiency conditions predict the general tendency of markets to exhaust all gains from trade; they do not predict anything about the attitude of consumers toward their initial positions in the economy.

Chapter Summary

1. General equilibrium analysis examines interrelationship between markets when describing equilibrium adjustments. Thus, both direct and feedback effects between markets are used to describe the final equi-

librium point. Partial equilibrium analysis holds the response of other markets constant, so feedback effects are not included in this analysis.

2. An Edgeworth box diagram is a graphical technique that is used to represent the exchange possibilities between two individuals (or two firms). The L-shaped part of the box (left-hand side) represents the axes for a standard indifference curve graph, while the opposite corner represents axes for a "rotated" map of indifference curves.
3. Efficient exchange occurs if there are no remaining gains to both parties from trading to another allocation point. The MRS values of all individuals are equated at the efficient allocation point, which lies on the contract curve.
4. Production is organized efficiently when output cannot be increased by a reallocation of inputs across firms in the same of different industries. We say that firms are technically efficient in their input choices when the MRTS values are equated for *all* firms.
5. The production possibilities frontier is a curve showing the various rates of output that can be produced by technically efficient firms from a given endowment of inputs. In effect, the production possibilities frontier is a mapping of the production contract curve into output space.
6. Even if consumers are efficient in exchange and firms are efficient in production, the economy can be inefficient in its choice of an output mix. A general equilibrium is reached when the marginal rate of substitution (MRS) for every consumer equals the marginal rate of transformation (MRT) for all firms, that is, MRS = MRT.

Trouble Spots

Concept	Reminder
Comparing General and Partial Equilibrium Analyses	Although we distinguish between general and partial equilibrium analyses by the extent to which feedback effects are included, both approaches describe a market equilibrium. The difference is that for general equilibrium more variables are allowed to adjust in order to reach the final equilibrium. Partial equilibrium analysis describes an equilibrium in which some variables are held constant, even though they may change in a general equilibrium analysis.
The Edgeworth Box	When we construct an Edgeworth box diagram, we slide the two panels toward each other until the endow ment points overlap. In this position, the length of each side of the Edgeworth box exactly equals the *total* endowment for both individuals (or firms).
Exchange Efficiency in Perfect Competition	Exchange efficiency requires that the final allocation lie on the contract curve, that is, at a point at which the MRS values are equal for the two individuals. Perfect

competition creates this result because all individuals act as price takers and choose a bundle for which the MRS equals the price ratio. Any market structure with these two characteristics will also be efficient in exchange.

16.5 Review Questions

1. Explain why markets are interrelated. Focus on the role of the budget constraint in your answer. Is partial equilibrium analysis consistent with a binding budget constraint?
2. When would general equilibrium analysis be more appropriate than partial equilibrium analysis? Does voluntary exchange always make both parties better off?
3. In a two-person, two-good world, what condition must exist for there to be a general equilibrium in exchange?
4. What is the contract curve, and how is it related to general equilibrium in exchange?
5. "Given an initial endowment of two goods between two people, we can say that exchanges will place the two individuals on the contract curve, but we cannot say exactly where the final allocation will be." Is this statement true or false, and why?
6. Assume that the distribution of goods has reached a point on the contract curve. Now one or both of the persons' preferences change, for whatever reason. What must then occur?
7. What do points within an Edgeworth box for production represent? Are the initial endowments of productive resources stocks or flows?
8. What is the condition for technical efficiency in firms? Are perfectly competitive firms technically efficient? Explain why or why not.
9. Explain why it is inefficient to produce at some point that lies below the production possibilities frontier.
10. Why must MRS and MRT be equal in order for all consumers and firms to achieve a general equilibrium in both consumption and production?

16.6 Price Theory Problems

1. Repeat the analysis of the ban on Chilean grapes under the assumption that grapes and apples are complements (i.e., they tend to be consumed together in a fruit bowl, not separately). Discuss how the final equilibria in the two markets differ from the previous analysis.
2. Suppose that a unit tax is levied on Chilean grapes instead of a ban. The unit tax is set such that it causes the supply of grapes to shift as if a ban was imposed (i.e., S^0_{grapes} shifts to S^1_{grapes} in Figure 16.1 as a result of the tax). Is your analysis of the effects of the tax the same as the effects of a ban? Does your answer depend on where the tax receipts are spent? How does the analysis change if the tax receipts are used to pay apple consumers a *subsidy* for each pound of apples purchased?

3. *True or False*. If two goods are perfect substitutes, then a partial equilibrium analysis leads to the same conclusion as a general equilibrium analysis when a unit tax is imposed on one good.
4. Suppose that rubies (R) and emeralds (E) are substitutes for each other in the minds of consumers. The (inverse) market demand for these commodities in the United States is given by the following equations:

$$P_R = 10{,}000 - 10Q_R + 0.2P_E$$

$$P_E = 12{,}000 - 20Q_E + 0.1P_R$$

The supply of rubies and emeralds is fixed in the short run with Q_R = 200 and Q_E = 400.

   a. What are the current equilibrium prices of rubies and emeralds?
   b. Suppose that rubies imported from Sri Lanka are banned for political reasons. Sri Lanka produces one-half of the rubies sold in the United States. Holding the price of emeralds constant at the level in part (a), what will be the new (partial) equilibrium price of rubies? What is the *general* equilibrium price of rubies and emeralds?

5. In the analysis of exchange between two individuals, explain how efficient exchange is achieved if
   a. The two goods are perfect substitutes for both individuals.
   b. The two goods are perfect complements for both individuals.
   c. The two goods are perfect substitutes for one individual and perfect complements for the other individual.

6. Harry is endowed with 10 coupons that can be redeemed for video rentals during the next week and 2 bags of microwave popcorn. Susan is endowed with 1 coupon that can be redeemed for video rentals during the next week and 7 bags of microwave popcorn. At these endowments, Susan's marginal rate of substitution ($MRS_{c,p}$) of coupons for popcorn equals ⅓ and Harry's $MRS_{c,p}$ equals 4.
   a. Construct an Edgeworth box diagram of the initial endowments of Harry and Susan.
   b. Is the initial endowment efficient? Explain how their allocations will change as Harry and Susan move to a point on the contract curve.

7. Suppose that the economy produces two goods, food and clothing, using two inputs, capital and labor. The current input mix in the food industry yields a marginal rate of substitution ($MRTS_{L,K}$) of labor for capital equal to 3, and the current input mix in the clothing industry yields a $MRTS_{L,K}$ equal to 1. Is this input mix technically efficient? How can the input mix be changed to achieve technical efficiency in production?

8. Suppose that the food and clothing industries have a constant marginal cost for all output rates. What is the shape of the production possibilities frontier? If food and clothing are *not* perfect substitutes, will any output mix be efficient?

16.7 Writing Exercise

General equilibrium theory suggests that consumers and producers are better off when they can trade freely among themselves. But many governments impose restrictions on free trade. The United States and Japan voluntarily restrict the number of Japanese-made automobiles sold in the United States. There are also restrictions on sugar imports in the United States and exports of many agricultural products to other countries. Select a commodity that is subject to either import or export restrictions (or both) and analyze the effects that these restrictions have on domestic and foreign units sold and prices. In addition, discuss how the restrictions affect employment in the industries affected and whether domestic and foreign consumers benefit on net from the restrictions.

17

Market Failure and Externalities

Preview Questions

When you finish studying this chapter, you should be able to answer the following questions:

- What factors can cause inefficiencies in a competitive market?
- What is the difference between rival and nonrival goods?
- How does exclusivity of a good affect the free rider problem?
- How can the tragedy of the commons be prevented?
- How do transaction costs affect market efficiency in the presence of externalities?
- Does a Pigouvian tax resolve the problem created by an externality?

Las Vegas receives four inches of rain per year but has one of the nation's highest per capita uses of water. For years, the area had been surviving on the surplus that accumulates in its aquifer from annual rain and mountain runoff, but desert development has made this source inadequate. Las Vegas proposes to harvest water underneath vast, sparsely populated areas of Nevada. State laws allow municipalities to claim any water not currently being used by agricultural interests or ranches. The U.S. Fish and Wildlife Service and neighboring Nevada counties, who stand to lose part of their water reserves if the aquifer is tapped, argue that the pumping will lower the water table needed by ranchers and farmers in the area. While not currently used, the water is a reserve for future needs. In addition, close to one-third of North America's native fishes live in the dry West, and while Las Vegas consumes water to create lakes, amusements, and green lawns, entire desert fish species may become extinct as their small desert springs dry up. The bottom line is that if Las Vegas uses the water, others are affected.

Competitive markets work well; they are efficient and achieve a Pareto-optimal allocation of resources. But the proof that competitive markets are efficient does require a particular type of market setting with specific assumptions. If the setting changes, efficiency and Pareto optimality may be lost. The assumptions of competitive markets are not satisfied for water use by Las Vegas, for example. If Las Vegas consumes water from other areas of Nevada, ranchers and agricultural interests are affected. Action taken by Las Vegas imposes a cost on these groups that is not taken into account by the market for water as presently structured in the West.

In this chapter we explore the reasons why markets may not operate efficiently and examine the effects of these inefficiencies. In other words, we examine what can go wrong and how it affects market output rates and the welfare of market participants. Our emphasis is on the type of goods produced—public goods or private goods—and whether externalities are created in the production process. Externalities create either costs or benefits that are not taken into account by competitive markets. For example, the cost that Las Vegas imposes on ranchers and agricultural interests can be considered a negative externality. We also discuss the effects of market or monopoly power and asymmetric information on market efficiency and the so-called tragedy of the commons.

17.1 What Causes Market Inefficiency?

Our discussion of general equilibrium in Chapter 16 has shown that perfectly competitive markets are allocatively efficient. Thus, ignoring questions about whether individuals are happy with their initial endowment, as long as the assumptions of perfect competition are satisfied, we can expect the economy to operate efficiently. If the assumptions underlying the perfectly competitive model are not satisfied, however, the allocation of goods may not be efficient. In this section, we consider how violating some of the assumptions of perfect competition affects the efficiency of the economy.

There are five cases to consider: market or monopoly power, taxes and subsidies, asymmetric information and moral hazard, pure public goods, and externalities. We discuss the first three cases in section 17.1 and leave pure public goods and the case of externalities for a more detailed explanation in sections 17.2 and 17.3.

Market or Monopoly Power

We saw in Chapter 11 that firms with market power do not equate price to marginal cost. Typically, $P > MC$ for firms with market power. Such firms produce less output than perfectly competitive firms. Thus, given that perfectly competitive firms produce an efficient output mix, firms with market power cannot produce an allocatively efficient output mix as long as they produce where $P > MC$. Consider the case of the food and clothing industries. If the clothing industry is monopolized and the food industry is competitive, then the economy will produce too little clothing and too much food. (Note that the resources that are freed from clothing production are used to produce food, so we remain on the production possibilities frontier.)

Figure 17.1 illustrates the inefficiency caused by a monopoly in the clothing industry. Point *A* represents the perfectly competitive solution. At this point, the clothing industry produces 300 units per period and the food industry produces 500 units per period. When a monopoly is introduced, the economy moves to point *B*. The output rate of the monopolized clothing industry falls to 100 as input resources are redirected to the food industry, which now produces 800 units per period.

The monopoly equates marginal revenue to marginal cost. Because price exceeds marginal revenue for a single-price monopolist, the price of clothing exceeds the marginal cost of clothing at point *B* in Figure 17.1. This result implies that the marginal rate of transformation is not equal to the marginal rate of substitution at the monopoly solution. Thus, the monopoly solution is not efficient.

To understand this result, note that both exchange and technical efficiency conditions still hold. That is, consumers still equate their marginal rates of substitution, because they all face the same relative price ratio. Producers still equate their marginal rates of technical substitution, because they all face the same input cost ratios. The difference is that now the price and marginal cost ratios are not equal to each other. The monopoly solution has driven a wedge between the price of clothing and its marginal cost ($P_c > MC_c$). We find that $P_c/P_f > MC_c/MC_f$ at point *B*, even though $P_f = MC_f$. Thus, the marginal rate of substitution is not equal to the marginal rate of transformation. In other words, the economy does not achieve output efficiency with a monopoly in the clothing industry.

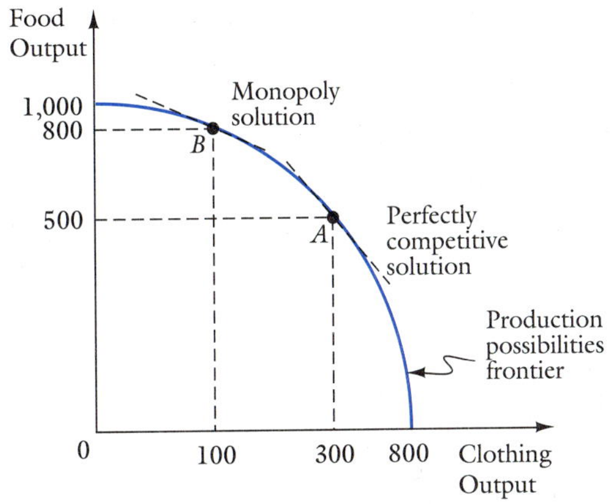

FIGURE 17.1

An Inefficient Solution Caused by Monopoly Power

The production possibilities frontier shows the output possibilities for the food and clothing industries. If both industries are perfectly competitive, the optimal output mix is given by point *A*. When the clothing industry is monopolized, the output mix changes to point *B*, at which clothing output decreases and food output increases to the perfectly competitive solution. The monopoly solution is inefficient.

Market power in an input market causes inefficiency, too. A monopsony in the market for labor, for example, reduces the employment of labor in the clothing industry. The monopsonist equates the marginal rate of technical substitution to the ratio of marginal factor costs. The problem is that the marginal factor cost of labor (MFC_L) exceeds its wage rate. Thus, the monopsonist equates $MRTS_{L,K} = MFC_L/r$ and the competitive firm equates $MRTS_{L,K} = w/r$. The result is that the economy does not achieve technical efficiency, because the marginal rates of technical substitution between the food and clothing sectors are not equated.

A labor union causes a similar result. If the clothing sector is unionized, then wages paid in the clothing industry rise above competitive levels and fewer workers are employed producing clothes. The excess workers enter the food industry, reducing the wages of these workers. Thus, the relative cost of inputs is different in the food and clothing industries. In this case, the MRTS values are not equal in these two industries, so firms are not operating at a point on the production contract curve in the Edgeworth production box. If they are not on the production contract curve, then they cannot be on the production possibilities frontier; they must be operating somewhere below the frontier, which is inefficient.

LEARNING EXERCISE 17.1

Show how the equilibrium product mix changes in Figure 17.1 if the food industry is monopolized and the clothing industry is competitive.

TAXES AND SUBSIDIES

Taxes and subsidies create output inefficiency in the same manner that a monopoly in the output market does. A unit tax of τ_c, for example, drives a wedge between the price consumers pay for clothing and the price received by producers. If consumers pay P_c, then producers receive $(1 - \tau_c)P_c$. Consumers achieve exchange efficiency because they all face the price ratio P_c/P_f. Producers, too, are efficient because they still face a common relative input price ratio. The difference now is that producers face a different relative (output) price ratio than consumers. Producers set $(1 - \tau_c)P_c$ equal to their marginal cost of clothing to determine their output rate. But this implies that the price consumers pay, P_c, exceeds the marginal cost of clothing in equilibrium. Thus, the marginal rate of transformation cannot equal the ratio of output prices in equilibrium. The economy is not output efficient. In effect, clothing firms produce too little output relative to the perfectly competitive solution.

Subsidies cause a similar result, except that they encourage more, not less, production than the efficient solution. The analysis is the same as that given for taxes, except that we multiply by $(1 + s_c)$, where s_c is the per unit subsidy, instead of $(1 - \tau_c)$ to determine the net price received by the clothing firm. The result is that clothing firms produce too much output relative to the perfectly competitive solution.

These results have been used to argue that taxes and subsidies cause distortions in the economy. Supply-side economists have carried this idea further to argue that if taxes and subsidies are reduced, then the distortions will decrease and the economy will operate more efficiently. Although this may be true in some instances, the analysis is not a complete proof of that claim. The reason is that the tax receipts and other monies are used for some purpose by the government. The taxes collected may be used to produce goods that the private sector will not produce (see the discussion of public goods in section 17.2). Compulsory taxes may be the only way to fund the provision of certain goods and services that improve the welfare of consumers and producers (roads and national defense). Thus, we cannot determine whether eliminating taxes (or subsidies) makes the economy more efficient unless we analyze how the revenue is used.

ASYMMETRIC INFORMATION AND MORAL HAZARD

In the strictest sense, asymmetric information creates inefficiency in the economy. If consumers do not know market prices for some commodities, they cannot satisfy the *condition for efficient exchange*, $MRS_{clothing,food} = P_c/P_f$. They may purchase food and clothing, for example, at prices different from the market price. Thus, their consumption of either food or clothing will be too little or too much, depending on whether they pay more or less than the actual market price. Similarly, firms may over- or under-invest in inputs if they are not aware of market clearing input prices, which causes inefficiency in production among firms.

Sometimes the information asymmetry affects the full price paid for a good or service. Today, almost no one lacks information on the adverse health effects of smoking. But before there were warning labels on each pack of cigarettes, some people doubted or did not know about the likely effects. Without such information, consumers who smoke may overinvest in consumption of cigarettes. With such information, the full price of their actions is known (and higher), so consumers who were previously uninformed may be expected to purchase fewer cigarettes.

The health profession is one example in which asymmetric information affects both production and consumption choices. For many illnesses, a doctor does not know what is wrong with a patient and the patient does not know what services to purchase. The symptoms are very similar for many diseases, so it is hard to distinguish between diseases even with extensive testing. The first few tests may be inconclusive, suggesting that a patient has a fever-induced rash caused by a cold virus. Further testing, such as a spinal tap for viral encephalitis, which is a life-threatening disease, may be negative. Doctors perform these tests to diagnose the illness, even though most illnesses, particularly viruses, are cured without medical treatment.

The patient is seeking help from the doctor but does not know how much help to buy. On the one hand, if the patient has viral encephalitis, he or she should purchase a large quantity of medical services. On the other hand, if the patient is reacting to a particularly troublesome flu virus, a small amount of medical services along with bed rest and fluids may be the optimal choice. These choices, however, are often made by the doctor, who may face constraints that the patient does not. The threat of a malpractice suit, for example, may cause the doctor to order unnecessary tests in order to minimize the likelihood of a lawsuit. Thus, the doctor may overinvest in producing medical services when there is asymmetric information. If the patient could indemnify the doctor against a suit, he or she might order fewer tests in order to pursue the most likely cause of the patient's illness.

Asymmetric information may also cause monopoly-like problems in some markets. If consumers are not aware of who a firm's competitors are or their prices, the firm may face a negatively sloped demand curve. As such, $P > MC$ may exist (at least for some period of time). This situation creates an inefficiency equivalent to that caused by firms with market power over the output price.

In other circumstances, such as whether consumers know the quality of a product before its purchase, asymmetric information may not vitiate our conditions for market efficiency. The model of competition under asymmetric information developed in Chapter 10 showed that markets for both high- and low-quality products reach an equilibrium at which $P = MC$. In this model, specific assets were important because they were the means by which firms "collateralized" their claims of producing a high-quality product. Without specific assets, the market for the high-quality product would not exist, which would be inefficient. Thus, asymmetric information may not produce inefficiencies if the market can develop a mechanism—such as investment in specific assets—that overcomes the problem posed by asymmetric information.

Moral hazard also poses a problem for market efficiency. Recall from Chapter 7 that a moral hazard situation may arise because of incentives created after an agreement is concluded. Homeowner insurance policies, for example, reimburse homeowners for losses due to theft or natural disasters. The basic problem insurance poses is that once the contract is signed, it gives the homeowner incentive to be less careful. Thus, more risk is imposed on the insurance company. Insurance companies that paid claims to the victims of Hurricane Andrew in 1992 understand the perverse incentives insurance can create. Some of the homes that were damaged were not protected by the homeowners in any manner, such as with plywood to cover doors and windows. Homeowners fled the storm leaving their homes unprotected, with the knowledge that insurance would pay for the damages. The moral hazard problem changes the market price faced by the homeowner and the insurance company after the contract is agreed to. Thus, it creates an output inefficiency in the economy.

17.2 Pure Public Goods

Pure public goods create inefficiencies because the private market does not supply a quantity that reflects the consumer demand for such goods. Instead, the private market typically undersupplies or simply does not supply pure public goods. The inefficiency this creates depends on the extent to which there are public goods in the economy. To examine the question of inefficiency, we must first define a pure public good.

WHAT IS A PURE PUBLIC GOOD?

Nonrival Good
A good for which additional units can be provided at zero marginal cost.

To distinguish pure public goods from other goods, we use two concepts: *nonrivalry* and *nonexclusivity*. A **nonrival good** is one in which additional units can be provided to another consumer at zero marginal cost. An empty seat on a jet just before takeoff is a nonrival good because the marginal cost to the airline of filling that seat is zero. This is one reason employees at some airlines can fly for free if they fly standby. They wait until all the other passengers have boarded; at this point, servicing these employees poses a (nearly) zero marginal cost to the airline. A lighthouse on the coast is also a nonrival good. Many ships may take advantage of the light without affecting its marginal cost.

Nonexclusive Good
A good for which it is costly to exclude consumption by another person.

Pure Public Good
A good that has a marginal cost of zero (nonrival) and that is nonexclusive across consumers.

There is a subtle difference between an airline seat and a lighthouse. The airline can *exclude* an additional passenger from flying in an empty seat, but once the lighthouse is turned on, passing ships cannot be excluded from its light. The lighthouse is said to be *nonexclusive*. A **nonexclusive good** is one in which it is very costly to exclude consumption by another person. *Because the lighthouse is* both *nonrival* and *nonexclusive, it is a pure public good,* whereas the airline seat is exclusive (although nonrival) and is not a pure public good. A **pure public good** is thus defined by whether it has the characteristics of nonrivalry *and* nonexclusivity. (Some economists drop the nonrivalry characteristic and call any good that is nonexclusive a public good, dropping the "pure" modifier.) Although much of the following analysis can be applied to nonexclusive goods (rival or nonrival), we will mainly focus on the *pure* case of a public good, which requires that the good be both nonrival *and* nonexclusive.

Figure 17.2, on page 700, provides a summary of the characteristics—rivalry, nonrivalry, exclusivity, and nonexclusivity—of goods and lists some goods that exhibit these various characteristics.

As Figure 17.2 shows, most of the goods we consume are both rival and exclusive. Our purchase of clothes at a department store, for example, prevents anyone else from buying that particular garment (exclusive) and affects costs because an additional garment cannot be consumed unless additional costs are borne by the manufacturer. Marginal costs of additional output are not zero, so clothes are *rival* goods.

Fishing and on-line computer services are rival goods, but they are also nonexclusive. You cannot prevent others from fishing (if they have a license) in a lake near where you are fishing, but their fishing helps reduce the likelihood that you will catch many fish.[1] That is, with a fixed quantity of fish in the lake, additional fishing reduces the quantity of fish available to others and thereby increases the marginal cost of fishing. Similarly, additional subscribers to an on-line computer network slow down the access time of existing subscribers, thereby raising their costs. In effect, if there is low demand for fishing or only a few people signed onto a computer network, these goods are nonexclusive and show very little rivalry. As demand increases, the lake and the computer network become congested, which increases the rivalry among users.

---

[1] Conceptually speaking, an activity that is truly nonrival cannot be licensed at low cost.

	Exclusive	Nonexclusive
Rival	**Most goods** Clothes Shoes Furniture Food	On-line computer services Fishing Congested Highways
Nonrival	When not at capacity: Airline seats Concert seats Horse racing	**Pure public goods** National defense Streetlights Air raid sirens

FIGURE 17.2

General Characteristics of Goods

Goods can be grouped by whether they have rivalry and exclusivity features. Several examples of rival or nonrival and exclusive or nonexclusive goods are shown.

With pure public goods, such as national defense, consumption by one individual *does not* affect the consumption of others and does not affect the marginal cost of providing another individual with the public good. In effect, once a pure public good is produced, it is available for all to consume. One reason these goods are government provided is that it may be difficult for private markets to develop for such goods. If consumers know that such a good is available to them once it is produced for someone else, they have an incentive to wait until someone else acquires the good. But everyone has this incentive, so it is difficult to find an individual who is willing to pay for the initial production of a pure public good. Without some sort of exclusion mechanism, the private sector is not likely to supply a pure public good, because it cannot use the price system to ration production. This is one argument for government providing some services, such as national defense.

A NOTE ON PRIVATE SECTOR SUPPLY OF NONEXCLUSIVE GOODS

We have presented the characteristics of goods in a either/or manner. A good is *either* exclusive *or* it is nonexclusive; a good is *either* rival *or* it is nonrival. Although this approach sharpens our focus on what we call pure public goods—which are nonrival and nonexclusive—it ignores the possibility that exclusivity can be created at some cost. Private firms look at the *degree* to which a good is nonexclusive when deciding whether private production is feasible. In other words, private firms may produce some nonexclusive goods when it is possible for them to implement an excludability plan at a profitable price. Private firms organize concerts in public parks, for example, where exclusivity is generally thought to be absent. These firms select parks that offer them an area in which "gate crashing" can be prevented at relatively low cost. Often open-air arenas or grandstands located in public parks can be isolated from the less exclusive parts of a park. In these areas private firms can organize a concert and exclude free riders at a profitable price. A **free rider** is an individual or firm who can share in the consumption of a good without sharing in the payment for its cost of production. In such circumstances, there is less reason for the government to provide certain services, such as concerts.

Free Rider
An individual (or firm) who can share in the consumption of a good without sharing in its cost.

MARKET DEMAND FOR NONEXCLUSIVE GOODS

Competitive markets in long-run equilibrium offer a quantity of goods at which $P = \text{MC}$ for all firms. This is another way of saying that marginal benefit (P) equals marginal cost in competitive markets. As we have seen above and in Chapter 10, output efficiency arises when marginal benefit equals marginal cost, because no one who values an additional unit of production above its marginal cost is excluded from buying the good. The only people excluded are those who value additional production below its marginal cost. This is efficient because such exclusion prevents resources from being wasted.

The marginal benefit of each output rate is determined from the market demand curve, which equals the sum of all individual demand curves. This sum is over quantity demanded *at a given price* and is appropriate only when the good being demanded is exclusive. That is, each consumer's consumption is exclusive to that consumer; output is not shared with any other consumer. If you purchase a pair of shoes, for example, your purchase does not provide other consumers with a pair of shoes.

With nonexclusive goods, however, your consumption of a good does not preclude others from consuming it. Now, the marginal benefit schedule *is not* the sum over quantity demanded at a given price, because once *one* good is produced, it provides benefits for everyone. When the second good is produced, it provides benefits for everyone, too, and so on. Instead of summing horizontally along the quantity axis, we must sum *vertically* along the price axis to determine the market demand curve for nonexclusive goods. This result is shown in Figure 17.3 on page 702.

There are two individual demand curves in Figure 17.3, D_1 and D_2 for individuals 1 and 2, respectively. First, suppose that these demand curves are for an exclusive or "private" good; then the market demand curve, $D_{\text{exclusive}}$, equals the *horizontal* sum of these two curves. At a market price of \$5 per unit, for example, zero units are purchased by individual 1 and 3 units are purchased by individual 2. Thus, market demand equals 3 units when price is \$5. Similarly, at a market price of \$4 per unit, 3 units are purchased by individual 1 and 5 units are purchased by individual 2 for a total market demand of 8 units when price is \$4.

Now, suppose that the demand curves in Figure 17.3 are for a nonexclusive or pure public good. Then the market value of each unit equals the sum of the *values* placed on this unit by individuals 1 and 2. If individual 1 places a value of \$4.75 on the first unit and individual 2 places a value of \$6.75 on the

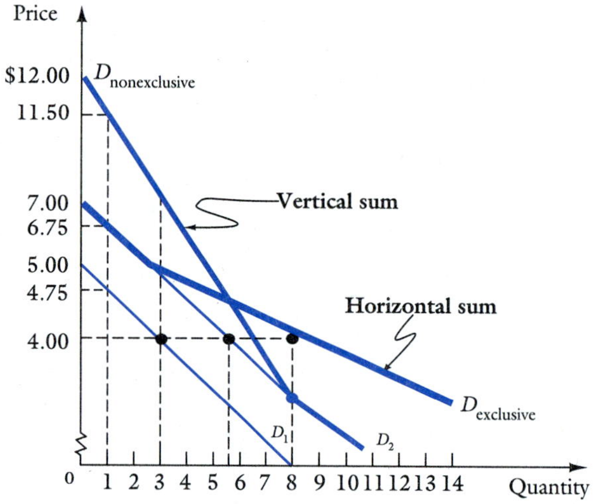

FIGURE 17.3

Comparing Market Demand for Exclusive and Nonexclusive Goods

The market is composed of two individual demand curves, D_1 and D_2. The type of good determines how these two demand curves are combined to compute the market demand curve. If the good is exclusive, the demand curves are added along the quantity, or horizontal, axis, holding price constant, which gives the market demand curve $D_{exclusive}$. If the good is nonexclusive, the demand curves are added along the price, or vertical, axis, holding quantity constant, which gives the market demand curve $D_{nonexclusive}$.

first unit, then market value of the first unit equals \$11.50 (\$4.75 + \$6.75). Similarly, if three units of the nonexclusive good are produced, the value placed on the *third* unit equals \$9 (\$4 + \$5). Therefore, the market demand curve for a nonexclusive good is the *vertical* sum of the two demand curves, D_1 and D_2, which is shown as $D_{nonexclusive}$.

EFFICIENT SUPPLY OF PURE PUBLIC GOODS

The efficient output of a pure public good occurs at an output rate at which marginal benefit equals marginal cost. Although the marginal cost of supplying another consumer with the good is zero, the actual cost of production is not zero. Marginal production costs may be positive and increasing for most public goods, such as national defense. Thus, the efficient output of a pure public good equates marginal benefits to marginal production costs. Figure 17.4 shows the efficient supply of a pure public good.

Figure 17.4 uses the demand for a nonexclusive good, $D_{nonexclusive}$, described in Figure 17.3 as the market demand curve. The marginal cost (MC) of producing the good shown is positive and increasing. It is optimal to produce Q^* units of this pure public good. This is the output rate at which

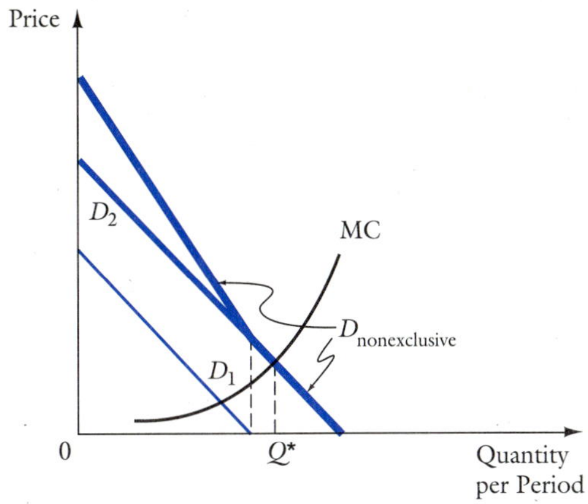

FIGURE 17.4

Efficient Supply of a Pure Public Good

The marginal cost of producing a pure public good is shown as MC. Using the market demand curve, $D_{nonexclusive}$, the optimal quantity supplied is Q^*, which is the output rate at which marginal benefit equals marginal cost.

P = MC. There is only one caveat to this statement. The output rate Q^* is optimal as long as the *total* costs of production are covered at this solution (most likely paid by the consumers of the pure public good). In other words, total payments by consumers of the pure public good must exceed total production costs for there to be an efficient supply of *any* units of the pure public good.

LEARNING EXERCISE 17.2

If a good is nonexclusive and MC = 0, what is its optimal output rate?

THE FREE RIDER PROBLEM

The question of how to pay the costs of a pure public good or any nonexclusive good gives rise to the problem of free riders. Immigrants to the United States, for example, are free riders in the consumption of national defense. Once an immigrant arrives, he or she enjoys the same national defense protection as existing residents, but he or she did not pay any of the production costs in taxes. Programs on public television are produced with a large free rider component. Public television has many more viewers than contributors.

The free rider problem creates a perverse incentive. If individuals are asked to *voluntarily* pay for national defense services, they have an incentive not to contribute if they think that the contributions of others will cover total production costs. Thus, the individual can free ride on everyone else. But if everyone thinks this way, then contributions will be small or nonexistent and the good will be undersupplied or not supplied at all. Thus, payment for national defense and other pure public goods cannot generally be based on voluntary transactions if such goods are to be efficiently produced.

The government, with its power to levy taxes that are nonvoluntary, is the logical choice to provide national defense and other pure public goods. The private sector does not have the power to tax or impose other involuntary payments on customers, so private firms are unlikely to produce pure public goods unless they can solve the free rider problem. This result explains why we claim that pure public goods cause inefficiencies for an economy; that is, it is typically inefficient for the private sector to produce pure public goods.

We can make two additional points about public sector production of goods. First, it is the nonexclusive component that generates the free rider problem, so the rivalous or nonrivalous nature of a good does not affect whether the private sector will produce the good. Second, exclusivity may not be an entirely objective criterion on which to base public sector production. As noted above, the private sector can expend resources to generate exclusivity, so exclusivity becomes a choice variable for many goods. Similarly, the government may choose not to enforce property rights for some goods, which makes these goods nonexclusive.

HYBRID PRODUCTION: THE CASE OF PRIVATIZATION

Although the private sector is not expected to supply an efficient quantity of a pure public good, it is possible that the public sector—that is, government—may not be efficient either. Shirking by workers is obviously a common problem with government-sponsored production. The lack of ownership of profits combined with the civil service system in government, which often guarantees jobs, causes convoluted incentives for workers. For example, government workers may be absent from their jobs more often than their private sector counterparts. Political patronage may pad the payroll of government enterprises. Thus, government may not use an efficient quantity of workers compared to the private sector. These problems create social losses compared to private sector production.

One solution to this problem that has gained attention is privatization. With **privatization,** the government contracts with private firms to produce the public good. The government negotiates either a fixed unit price or a fixed contract price. In this environment, firms can behave as price takers and minimize the cost of producing output as a by-product of profit maximization. The government must monitor output, however, because private firms may cut costs by producing *less than* the optimal quantity of the public good instead of producing the optimal quantity at a lower total cost. With monitoring, privatization solves the free rider problem because the government continues to collect (mandatory) taxes from consumers of public goods. Thus, the revenue stream of a private firm is not at risk when a nonexcludable good is produced via privatization.

Privatization
Government contracting with private firms to produce publicly financed goods and services.

$$$ Price Theory in Practice

PRIVATIZATION OF PRISONS

Many local and state governments are turning to the private sector for the provision of selected public goods. The trend toward privatization has been a rocky

TABLE 17.1

State Private Prisons

State	Number of Facilities	Private Capacity	Total Capacity	Percent Private
Kentucky	3	1,000	8,289	12.1
Louisiana	2	1,220	17,257	7.1
New Mexico	1	200	3,034	6.6
Texas	4	2,000	40,789	4.9
Florida	1	1,000	39,999	2.5

road, but as more demands for public sector services compete with limited tax revenues, governments have turned increasingly to the private sector for relief. Prisons offer one example of the potential benefits of privatization.

The war on drugs and harsher prison sentences in the United States during the 1980s resulted in overflowing federal prisons and significant incarceration costs. Building a prison now costs $50,000 per bed and operating it costs $25,000 per inmate per year. As a result, federal officials want to know if private firms can do the same job at a lower cost.

Since 1980, Florida, Kentucky, Louisiana, New Mexico, and Texas have either opened privately operated prisons or contracted with private firms to operate prisons. Table 17.1 summarizes the extent of privatization in these 5 states. In addition to these efforts by state governments, 16 local governments have private jails. The city of Detroit has the largest, a 400-bed private facility. At the federal level, however, private firms have been contracted only to run centers for noncitizens and unsentenced offenders.

Audited results from several of the 5 states show that the private firms provide prison space at a lower cost than public prisons.[2] Table 17.2, on page 706, shows these results for 8 different facilities in 4 states. Cost savings for private firms exceed 10 percent in every facility except St. Mary's in Kentucky. The states generally anticipate savings of this magnitude. In Texas, Louisiana, and Florida, for example, cost savings of 10 percent are written into contracts with private firms. In Louisiana it is estimated that privatized prisons saved the state $5.9 million over a 5-year period. In addition to operating savings, some state officials believe private firms lower the time costs of constructing prisons, particularly when new prisons are required by court order. In New Mexico, for example, it took only 9 months to build a private women's prison when it was expected to have taken the state 3 years.

The exact cause of these savings is not known. We can speculate that the private sector can manage employee absenteeism, turnover, and general shirking in a more effective manner than the public sector. Whatever the reason for these gains, they indicate that the private sector can reduce the social losses caused by inefficient public sector production.

[2] "Private Prisons: Cost Savings and BOP's (Bureau of Prisons') Statutory Authority Need to Be Resolved," U.S. General Accounting Office, Report to House of Representatives, February 1991.

TABLE 17.2

Government Versus Privately Operated Per Diem Prison Costs

Private Facility	Government Per Diem	Private Per Diem	Private Savings (%)
St. Mary's, KY	$28.00	$26.89	4.0
Beattyville, KY	32.00	26.89	16.0
Grants, NM	80.00	69.75	12.8
Winnfield, LA	29.50	26.00	11.8
Cleveland, TX	42.53	35.25	17.1
Venus, TX	42.53	35.25	17.1
Kyle, TX	42.53	34.79	17.2
Bridgeport, TX	42.53	34.79	17.2

Although the experience of these states shows that private firms can operate prisons at a lower cost than the government, other states have been reluctant to privatize their prisons. Some states believe that the private prisons offer a lower level of safety and service compared with government-run prisons, although there is no clear evidence that this is actually the case. Other states are waiting for better information on cost savings. Obviously, cost savings at any level suggest that privatization—at least in prisons—is a way to improve the efficiency of the economy.

LEARNING EXERCISE 17.3

List some of the reasons why you think government officials might oppose privatization efforts. Is there an economic basis for their opposition?

THE TRAGEDY OF THE COMMONS

Tragedy of the Commons Inefficient use of a resource because exclusion of others is too costly.

The **tragedy of the commons** results when exclusion of others from the use of a resource is relatively costly compared to its benefit, so the resource tends to be overused. In other words, property rights are not completely specified and there is a relatively high cost of excluding others. For example, in colonial times and when the western areas of America were developed, vast tracts of land were regarded as common areas for all residents to use. These tracts were generally used for grazing of cattle or sheep or for herding purposes between winter and spring seasons. Today, the tract of land called Boston Common in Boston, Massachusetts, traces its origin to the practice of creating common areas for citizens to use. The benefits of trying to prevent individuals from using these tracts of land were too low relative to the cost of monitoring. Thus, private ownership of many parcels of land was not meaningful. The problem with common ownership, or common areas, however, is that they are overutilized relative to how a single owner would use the resource.

To see how the tragedy of the commons arises, let's consider the case of Kuwait and Iraq, who share an oil field on their border. The oil field is a geological formation that was present long before the border between Kuwait and Iraq was defined. The oil field runs for many miles underground, and both countries use drilling rigs to extract oil from the field. The problem is that drilling too many oil wells lowers the overall yield from the oil field. This situation is illustrated in Figure 17.5.

Figure 17.5 shows the value of the marginal product ($P_{barrel} \times$ MP) and average product ($P_{barrel} \times$ AP) curves for drilling rigs in the Iraq/Kuwait oil field. The value is determined here by multiplying the marginal and average product of an oil well (measured in barrels of oil) by the price of a barrel of crude oil (P_{barrel}). As the number of new wells increases—that is, more drilling rigs are built—the value of the average and marginal product of an oil well first increases and then decreases. This results follows from the classical shape of the average and marginal product curves as described in Chapter 8, holding the price of a barrel of crude oil constant.

Because Iraq and Kuwait share the same field, they each receive the value of the average product of a new well when they install another drilling rig. In effect, Iraq and Kuwait are drinking oil from two straws in the same cup. The output they receive must be an average because they are sucking on the straws at the same time. To maximize their individual gain, they will equate the marginal cost of another well to the value of the average product of that well. In total, they drill $T_{Iraq} + T_{Kuwait}$ wells in the commonly owned oil field. This solution is not optimal, however, from the point of view of a single owner of the oil field. A single owner receives the value of the marginal product—not the

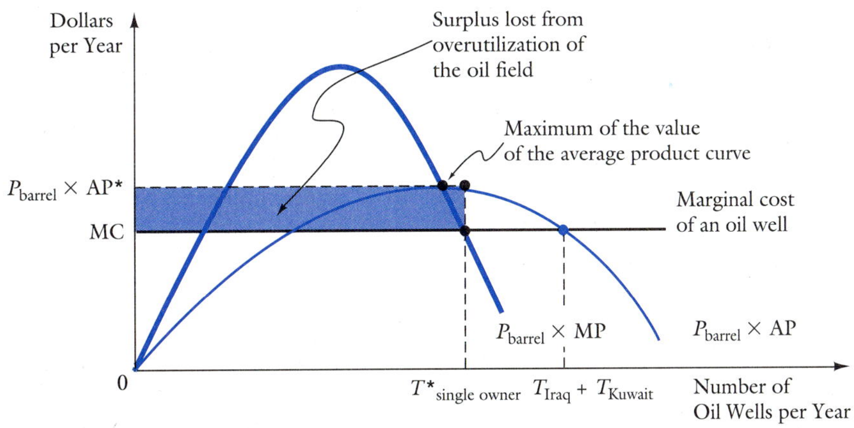

FIGURE 17.5

The Tragedy of the Commons

The tragedy of the commons causes overutilization of the oil field shared by Iraq and Kuwait. With each country acting independently, the number of oil wells drilled equals $T_{Iraq} + T_{Kuwait}$, the quantity at which the value of the average product equals the marginal cost of drilling an oil well. If the field were operated under a single ownership, the optimal number of wells would be $T^*_{single\ owner}$. Thus, the excess production without a single owner causes a loss of surplus equal to the shaded area.

average product—when new wells are drilled; that is, there is no sharing with anyone else. Thus, to maximize a single owner's gain, T^* wells are drilled with $AP = AP^*$. The gain received by the single owner equals the shaded rectangle in Figure 17.5. This gain is also the lost surplus forgone by Iraq and Kuwait because they do not drill the optimal number of wells.

The tragedy of the commons causes Iraq and Kuwait to overuse their commonly held resource. But how can inefficient utilization be prevented? In general, it is prevented by contracting with all parties to create a single management of the resource. The single manager will thus act to maximize the surplus of all of the contracting parties. The only problem with this solution is that it is like a cartel arrangement, and the problem with cartel arrangements is cheating. The manager must therefore have an effective method of preventing cheating for the arrangement to work. In the case of Iraq and Kuwait, cheating on their extraction agreement was commonplace. This was cited by many observers as one of the reasons Iraq invaded Kuwait in August, 1990. The invasion created a single owner—for four months—of the oil field on Kuwait's northern border. Fortunately for Kuwait, the United Nations and its member countries took a dim view of Iraq's invasion.

$$$ Price Theory in Practice

Common Property and Cape Cod Fishing

In the Atlantic Ocean just off Cape Cod, Massachusetts, New England's renowned fishing fleet used to haul in large catches of prized haddock. Today, the haddock cannot be found; codfish and flounder are also relatively scarce.

The New England coastal waters, once among the country's most fertile fishing grounds, have become an example of the tragedy of the commons. The barren waters have paid the price for the stream of boats that have returned to shore again and again with as much fish as they could haul. Each boat operator had little incentive to limit the catch because it would only mean a larger catch for the next boat. Now the catches are smaller for everyone, about half what they were 10 years ago.

Ironically, the current problem of overfishing sprang from a government effort 14 years ago to help the New England fishing industry. To prevent foreign fleets from fishing along the New England coast, the United States declared a 200-mile boundary around its shores. The problem was that in the wake of the departing foreign ships, New Englanders moved in with their nets to harvest the fish. They filled the void vacated by the foreign ships, aided by a government loan program that helped the New England owners to expand their fleets. The New England ground fishing fleet—the trawlers that fish for species that live on the ocean floor—grew from 590 vessels in 1976 to more than 1,000 in the early 1980s. The expanded fleet meant that the 200-mile limit probably did not change the number of boats fishing the waters off Cape Cod; only the nationality of the people on them changed.

With overharvesting of common property, the government can act as property owner and limit catches to maximize the benefit to society. But the government abdicated that role in 1982 when fishery managers from the New England Fishery

Management Council caved in to pressure and lifted catch quotas and trip limits. Meanwhile, the tendency to overfish was fueled by an increase in demand for fish as Americans' dietary preferences turned away from beef and toward fish.

The state-of-the-art electronic equipment many boats now carry added a new dimension to the fishing tragedy. The new equipment allows boat operators to track down schools of fish with amazing accuracy. Fish have always bounced back from cycles of overfishing, but some scientists say this time may be different.[3] The big fleets and technology now have the capacity to nearly eliminate the marketable fish population, scientists say.

Scientists can see the results. Off the New England coast, stocks of flounder and haddock are near record lows, the cod population is down, and bluefin tuna and swordfish have been nearly depleted. Boat owners, too, are living with the results. A typical 76-foot trawler used to catch as much as 30,000 pounds of fish on a two- or three-day fishing trip. Now the same trip brings in 15,000 pounds.

Still, the New Englanders are not setting limits. Their self-interest is evident as they crowd public meetings lobbying against conservation measures. Many are struggling to pay off the expensive boats they bought during the boom years. They cannot afford to catch fewer fish.

The lessons are not easily learned. In New Bedford, Massachusetts, the area's scalloping fleet is doing well because scallops are still in ample supply. But they may not be for long. The price of scallops has encouraged some operators to work almost around the clock. They return to port after a 10- or 12-day trip, unload, resupply, and head out to sea with a fresh crew in as little as 6 hours. They rush out to dredge up the scallops before someone else does.

LEARNING EXERCISE 17.4

If the U.S. government decided to auction the rights to catch a particular type of fish—haddock, cod, flounder, and so on—to the highest bidder, would this solve the tragedy of the commons in fishing? What makes this potential solution impractical and costly?

17.3 EXTERNALITIES

Externalities generally pose a problem for an economy trying to reach an efficient output (or input) mix. In Chapter 3, we defined an externality as an action by one individual or firm that produces benefits *or* costs that affect another individual or firm. An externality can be positive or negative, depending on whether it imposes benefits or costs on others. Air pollution by automobiles and factories, for example, is considered a *negative externality* because it imposes health-related costs on others not involved in the decisions that generate the pollution. If the decision was theirs alone, those affected by a

[3] Lawrence Ingrassia, "Overfishing Threatens to Wipe Out Species and Crush Industry," *The Wall Street Journal,* July 16, 1991.

negative externality would like to see it reduced, but those causing the negative externality don't weigh its cost in the same manner, so they do not want to change their externality-producing actions to accommodate others. A paper mill, for example, pollutes the air with foul-smelling emissions. The emissions are a by-product of the paper production process, so the mill gains nothing by investing in emissions-reducing equipment. Those living near the mill, however, would gain if the mill reduced its output or otherwise reduced its emissions.

In contrast, when your neighbor plants flowers in the spring, you probably enjoy their beauty, so we can think of your neighbor's flowers as a *positive externality.* You would probably like your neighbor to plant more flowers because of the benefits you receive. But your neighbor doesn't view the problem the same way you do. She must spend time planting and maintaining these flowers, so the cost of planting and maintaining additional flowers may outweigh the benefits she receives. In other words, you want more production of a good that generates a positive externality, but the producer is probably satisfied with the current output. Because producers and consumers differ in terms of the desired output of the externality-producing product, there is the *potential* for an inefficient outcome.

In this section, we first show how externalities affect the efficient level of production. Then we show that the efficient outcome always arises if the transaction costs of negotiating and contracting are low. This result, known as the *Coase theorem,* was first mentioned in Chapter 3.

EXTERNALITIES AND OUTPUT EFFICIENCY

To understand the effects of an externality, let's consider the example of fishing and citrus farming. Citrus farming produces a negative externality for fishing because fruit trees must be sprayed with fertilizer and disease-killing chemicals to ensure a high crop yield. Without regular spraying, the citrus crop is expected to be smaller, as more fruit is diseased and less fruit matures because of insufficient fertilizer. Rain washes these chemicals into nearby lakes, which kills fish and reduces the size of the catch. Figure 17.6 describes the market for citrus output and the external costs that citrus production imposes on the fishing fleet.

The market demand for the citrus output is given by D_{citrus}, and the market supply provided by all citrus farmers is shown as S_{citrus}. Because citrus output is competitively produced, market supply equals the sum of the marginal cost curves for each citrus farmer (above the minimum of the average variable cost curve), that is, $S_{\text{citrus}} = \Sigma$ MC. Thus, the competitive equilibrium output rate equals Q_c pounds per year, which sells for P_c per pound.

Because citrus production reduces the fish catch, there is an additional cost created by citrus output. At zero citrus output the external cost is zero, but as citrus output increases the external cost increases, too. On a per unit basis, we assume that the external cost (E_c) imposed on the fishing industry is increasing as more citrus is produced. The **marginal social cost (MSC)** represents the *sum* of the marginal cost of producing citrus and the per unit external cost imposed on the fishing industry, that is, MSC = Σ MC + E_c. This implies that

Marginal Social Cost (MSC)
The sum of marginal production cost and the marginal external cost: MSC = ΣMC + E_c.

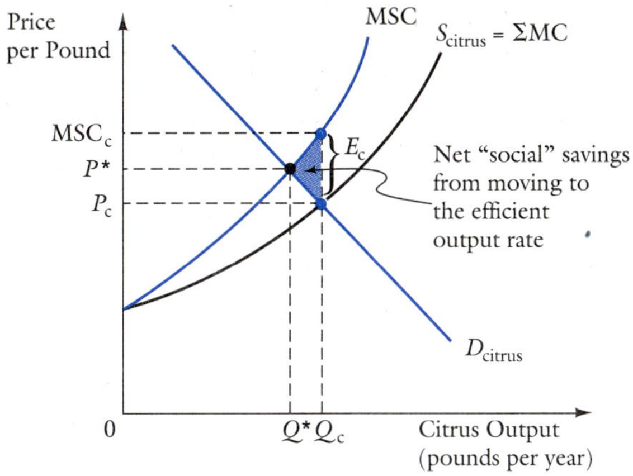

FIGURE 17.6

External Costs: Citrus Farmers Have the "Rights" to Pollute

A negative externality created by citrus farmers causes losses to the fishing fleet that are proportional to citrus output. The marginal cost curve for citrus production, $S_{citrus} = \Sigma MC$, does not include these external costs. Adding these external costs to the marginal cost curve gives the marginal "social" cost curve, MSC. When citrus farmers produce the competitive output rate, Q_c, and charge a price of P_c, they impose an external cost of E_c per unit on fishing. By reducing their output rate to the "socially" optimal rate of Q^* and charging price P^*, citrus farmers generate a net "social" savings equal to the shaded triangular area.

the per unit cost of the externality equals the difference between MSC and Σ MC at any given output rate (i.e., $E_c = \text{MSC} - \Sigma\ \text{MC}$). Thus, the area *between* the MSC and Σ MC curves up to a given level of citrus output equals the *total cost* of the externality for that level of output.[4]

From an efficiency viewpoint, citrus farmers are producing too much citrus output at the competitive equilibrium. Although consumers value the last unit of citrus output at P_c, the competitive equilibrium price, this unit actually creates a marginal cost of MSC_c when *both* the marginal cost of citrus production *and* the unit cost of the negative externality are considered. Because $MSC_c > P_c$, the competitive equilibrium output rate is inefficient; it is too large. In other words, the presence of an external cost, $E_c = MSC_c - P_c$, drives a wedge between the competitive equilibrium price and the marginal social cost of production.

The efficient output rate is the one at which marginal benefit (as measured by the market demand curve) equals marginal social cost. This occurs at Q^*, where the MSC curve intersects D_{citrus}. At this output rate, the market clearing price is P^*, which equals MSC*, the marginal social cost of producing Q^* pounds of citrus. The net social savings created by moving from Q_c to Q^*

[4] We are assuming that there is no fixed-cost component to the citrus externality.

equals the shaded area in Figure 17.6. This area is the difference between the total social costs of producing the extra ($Q_c - Q^*$) pounds of citrus minus the total benefit of this extra output, where total benefit equals the area under the demand curve between Q^* and Q_c. Whenever there are positive net social savings from reducing output, it is efficient to reduce output. Similarly, if there are positive net social gains from increasing output, it is efficient to increase output. Because competitive firms typically ignore the social cost of externalities, they do not produce the efficient output rate.

Learning Exercise 17.5

Using a graph similar to Figure 17.6, show that the competitive output rate is too small in the presence of a *positive* externality. Show the net social *gain* in benefits when the socially efficient output rate is produced.

$$$ Price Theory in Practice

Economic Costs Arising from Using Fossil Fuels

As concern rises worldwide about global warming and other threats to the planet, environmentalists and many political leaders have called for reduced dependence on fossil fuels, one of the primary causes of pollution and (possibly) global warming. One way to reduce consumption is for the government to raise the price of fossil fuels, such as oil and coal. The claim is that current prices do not reflect the *full cost* to society of consuming fossil fuels. Thus, it is argued, fuel producers should be taxed to reduce the negative externality—the carbon dioxide that warms the atmosphere—caused by their output. That means firms would face a higher marginal cost curve and, at any given price, produce less fuel than they would otherwise.

Difficulties arise in implementing the idea: For example, how do we measure the true cost of these fuels to determine the optimal tax? In some cases, there are estimates of the costs of pollution. The Environmental Protection Agency (EPA), for example, estimates that pollution from burning fuels reduces crop yields in the United States by 12 percent each year, which cost an estimated $2.5 billion in lost crops in 1990. Other estimates, however, put the crop losses as high as 30 percent. Estimating environmental costs is more difficult when we consider the effects of pollution on human life. Respiratory disease and other pollution-related ailments are estimated to cost anywhere from $12 billion to $82 billion annually. Because of the wide range of estimates, implementing an effective tax policy is likely to be prone to error.

In specific cases, however, a tax or regulatory policy may have limited success. In Wisconsin, for example, regulators have approved non–fossil fuel plants even though their operating costs are as much as 15 percent more than oil- or coal-burning plants. Lengthy hearings were held to justify the added cost of these plants based on evidence showing the savings in health costs for the residents of Wisconsin. Some states, such as New York, California, and Oregon, add surcharges to the cost of various fuels based on the pollution the fuel is expected to produce. Only then is the lowest-social-cost fuel for the plant chosen. The surcharges imposed on fossil fuels are not arbitrary; they are based on evidence showing the increasing health risk posed by fuels with a higher sulfur content.

Although reducing the negative externality created by fossil fuels is an efficient goal, there may be no simple, universal approach to the problem because the actual social costs vary widely from region to region and across different fuels. Thus, consumers affected by these externalities may have to wait until scientists and economists provide more accurate estimates of the incidence and costs of such pollutants before effective solutions are implemented.

LEARNING EXERCISE 17.6

How would you measure the economic damage caused by air pollution that affects you?

THE COASE THEOREM AND PROPERTY RIGHTS

Property Rights
The ownership assignment of resources.

You may have the impression that lake polluting citrus farmers are going to produce the competitive output rate, Q_c, because the fishing fleet has no control over their decisions. This is not necessarily correct. What the citrus farmers will actually do depends on how costly it is to negotiate with the fishing industry and who has the **property rights** to pollute the lakes. Suppose that there is no law against polluting lakes with chemical runoff, so the citrus farmers have the property rights to pollute the lakes. In addition, assume that the fishing industry and citrus farmers can negotiate with each other at a very low cost, say zero. Then it would benefit the fishing industry to offer a *bribe* to the citrus farmers to reduce their output rate. The appropriate bribe is described in Figure 17.7 (page 714).

If the citrus farmers produce Q_c instead of Q^*, the additional cost imposed on the fishing industry equals areas $A + B + C$ in Figure 17.7. Thus, the maximum the fishing fleet will be willing to pay to citrus farmers equals areas $A + B + C$. Fortunately for the fishing fleet, the citrus farmers are probably willing to accept less. Area A represents the producers' surplus generated when output increases from Q^* to Q_c. Thus, citrus farmers are willing to reduce output to Q^* for any bribe amount that exceeds area A.

A bribe equal to area A is likely to work for the fishing industry if consumers of citrus output are a fairly disorganized group. If consumers are organized, they may make a counteroffer to citrus farmers to have them increase their output back to Q_c. Consumers are unhappy at the reduction to Q^* because they lose consumers' surplus equal to area B. Thus, if area B exceeds area A, they could counter the fishing industry's offer with an amount equal to area B. To combat this problem, the fishing industry must make another offer that exceeds area B in size.[5] This is easy for the fishing industry to do because

[5] The fishing industry might end up paying off citrus consumers, too, which would be efficient because they lose consumers' surplus when output is reduced. Although this is efficient, consumers may not have any rights that cause the fishing industry to bribe them, so this bribe may not be paid.

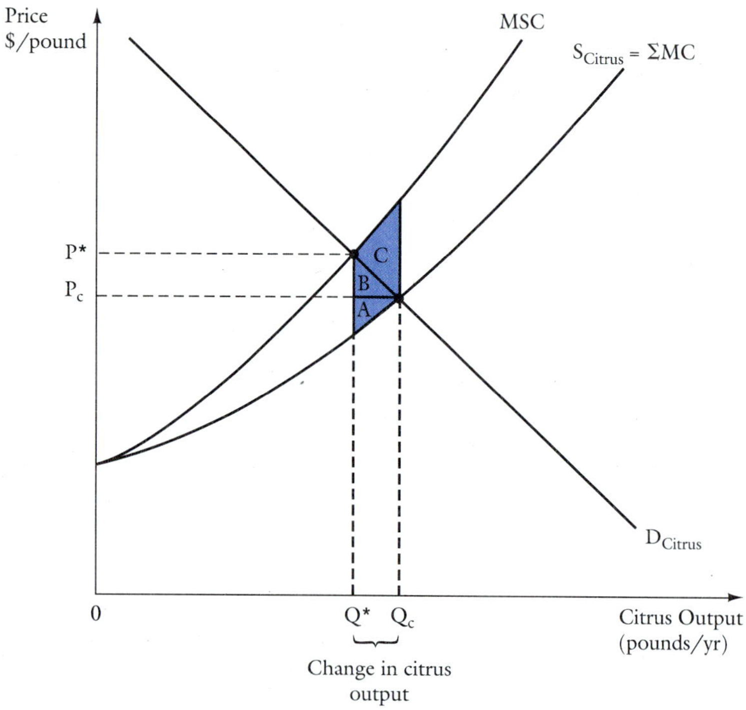

FIGURE 17.7

Fishing Fleet Can Bribe Citrus Farmers to Reduce Their Output

When the transaction costs of bargaining between citrus farmers and fishing fleet are low and citrus farmers have the "rights" to pollute, fishing fleet can bribe citrus farmers to reduce their output to the "socially" optimal rate. The net losses to fishing fleet equals areas $A + B + C$. The lost profits to citrus farmers equals area A, so it is mutually advantageous to fishing fleet to bribe citrus farmers to reduce their output rate.

their total losses equal areas $A + B + C$. The final result will be that citrus farmers reduce their output rate to Q^* if it is costless to negotiate such bribes.

The Fishing Industry Has the Property Rights to Prevent Pollution

The Coase theorem tells us that the final result—citrus output of Q^*—arises regardless of who has the property rights to create (or prevent) an externality when transaction costs are low. As we have seen, when citrus farmers have the property rights to use fertilizer and other chemicals in their production process, the fishing industry will offer them bribes to reduce output to the socially efficient level. The Coase theorem states, however, that we could pass a law that gives the fishing industry the right to "control" the chemical runoff into lakes, and we would still find that citrus farmers produce Q^*. Figure 17.8 describes this case.

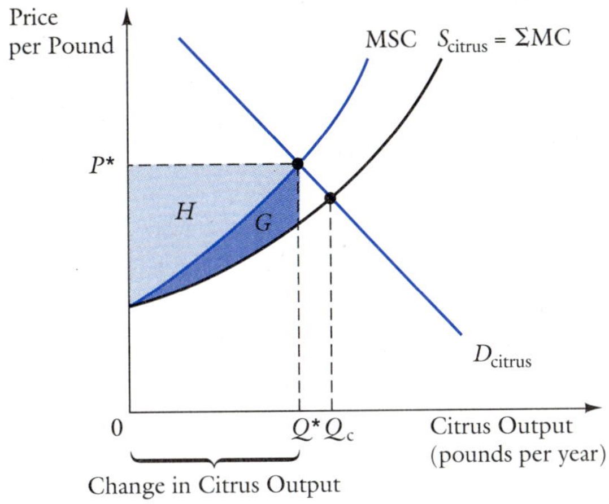

FIGURE 17.8

Fishing Industry Have the "Rights" to Control Pollution in the Lakes

When the transaction costs of bargaining between citrus farmers and fishing interests are low and fishing interests have the "rights" to prevent pollution, citrus farmers will pay for the right to produce the "socially" optimal rate. The net losses to fishing when Q^* is produced equal area G (the pollution costs). The lost profits to citrus farmers equal areas $G + H$, so it is mutually advantageous to citrus farmers to pay fishing interests for the "rights" to pollute the lakes to the extent determined by the "socially" optimal output rate.

With the fishing industry in control of the "rights" to allow chemical runoff into lakes, citrus farmers must pay the fishing industry for the "rights" to use fertilizer and other chemicals. The producers' surplus generated from producing Q^* units of output using fertilizer and other chemicals equals areas $G + H$ in Figure 17.8.[6] The negative externality from chemical runoff imposes a total cost of area G on the fishing fleet. Because areas $G + H$ exceed area G, citrus farmers can afford to pay area G for the rights to produce Q^* pounds of citrus each year.[7] Thus, the final result is that citrus farmers produce Q^* regardless of who has the property rights to cause (or prevent) the externality.

LEARNING EXERCISE 17.7

How does the payment by citrus farmers to the fishing industry change if they can produce citrus without fertilizer and other chemicals at a higher marginal cost?

[6] For simplicity, we are assuming that citrus cannot be produced without fertilizer and other chemicals, so if the fishing industry is unwilling to sell pollution rights, there will be no citrus output.

[7] Although the producers' surplus exceeds the total cost of the externality in this example, this may not always be the case. In such situations, both consumers and producers of citrus will have to pay the fishing industry for the rights to pollute lakes with fertilizer and other chemicals.

Efficiency Restored?

When transaction and other negotiating costs are low (or zero), the Coase theorem restores the efficiency of the economy. In other words, the output rate produced is the one at which marginal benefit (P) equals MSC. If there are significant transaction or negotiating costs, however, then bribes or other payments may not arise, which means that the efficient outcome may not arise. Thus, the efficiency of an economy in the presence of externalities depends on the size of transaction costs between the parties generating and affected by the externality.

Changing Property Rights Affects the Distribution of Wealth

Although the socially efficient output rate is reached when transaction costs are low regardless of who has the property rights to pollute the lakes, there is an effect on the distribution of wealth when property rights change. When citrus farmers have the property rights to pollute, they receive a bribe from the fishing industry to reduce their output rate. Thus, citrus farmers are paid when they have the rights to pollute, so their wealth increases. Alternatively, when the fishing industry owns the property rights, citrus farmers and possibly consumers must pay to allow any chemical runoff into the lakes. Thus, the wealth of the fishing fleet increases when the industry has the rights to pollute. In a low-transaction-costs economy, then, the only effect of changing property rights is to change the distribution of wealth.

$$$ Price Theory in Practice

DURABLE GOODS AS RENEWABLE RESOURCES

Durable goods pose an externality problem different than the problem between citrus farmers and the fishing industry. Durable goods wear out, but they don't disappear in the process. They end up in landfills or empty lots in some neighborhoods. A rusty refrigerator, automobile, or washing machine is unsightly and hazardous. Recycling is a way to help reduce this externality. After a period of decline in automobile recycling, because plastic made recycling and sorting more costly, the automobile industry is once again leading many other industries in developing durable goods that can be recycled at low cost.

A two-seat roadster called the Z1, introduced in Europe by BMW in 1988, has plastic body panels that come off with the removal of a few fasteners. The plastic panels can then be recycled easily. In 1991, BMW also began stamping the plastic parts in its smaller cars so they can be grouped by type of plastic for recycling. Other automakers are not far behind BMW. In Germany, a subsidiary of General Motors has made some parts on its Calabria models from recycled battery cases and designed these parts for easy removal.

The BMW roadster is an early glimpse of what may lie ahead. Manufacturers are starting to change their products, because of increased concern for the environment and the apparent willingness of consumers to pay more for products that do less harm to the environment than other products. Manufacturers have also found it more profitable to recycle as the relative price of recycled products has increased due to increased demand. As a result, more firms are designing their products with recycling in mind. That means making products that are easy to take apart. It also means making a part of only one kind of plastic and stamping parts by type, as BMW has done.

Plastics present a particular obstacle to recycling because the firms that recycle plastics want only pure plastic resins. Although composite plastics made from several different compounds have some uses, they are inferior materials and are more expensive to recycle. Some composite plastics, for example, cannot be melted at low temperatures, which raises costs. As a result, plastics are more likely to be recycled and draw a higher price if they are marked and sorted.

Cars are a good example of the challenge. The typical American car weighs 2,400 pounds and uses as many as 60 different types of plastic, for a total of about 180 pounds of plastic. Use of plastic has allowed the average car weight to drop from nearly 4,000 pounds 20 years ago. Making automobiles lighter has been one method used by automakers to meet U.S. fuel efficiency standards mandated after the oil shock of 1974. The Corporate Average Fuel Economy (CAFE) standards required that new passenger cars in the United States—which in 1974 averaged 14 miles per gallon—average 18 miles per gallon by 1978 and 27.5 miles per gallon by 1985. The standards spurred, for example, the fuel efficiency of new cars sold by General Motors to rise from 12 miles per gallon in 1974 to 27.1 miles per gallon in 1990, down slightly from 27.6 miles per gallon in 1988.

Changes can be found outside the car industry as well. In 1991, Minnesota Mining and Manufacturing Co. (3M) introduced a plastic desk organizer with pieces that snap apart. Each part is marked with its type of plastic. Whirlpool says it is developing new fasteners to get away from screws because they make disassembly difficult.

Now, more firms are studying ways to approach recycling. Many fear that if they do not develop their own plans, the government is likely to mandate what firms must do in order to reduce the negative externality. Laws regarding durable goods and recycling already are being written in the United States and in other countries. At least eight states ban appliances from landfills, requiring that appliances first be taken apart to recover useful materials. The German government has proposed making car companies responsible for disposal of worn-out vehicles. Germany also is considering taxes on products based on the cost of disposing the product and its packaging. Several bills have also been proposed in the U.S. Congress that are similar in effect to the German proposals.

Learning Exercise 17.8

The incentive to recycle is a matter of relative benefits and costs. If the burden of recycling cars is imposed on car manufacturers, will the price of new cars increase?

DO TAXES (OR SUBSIDIES) OFFER A BETTER SOLUTION?

When we first considered the problem of externalities, we suggested that the government could impose a tax on firms that produce negative externalities and offer a subsidy to firms that produce positive externalities. The idea was that an optimal tax would reduce output to the socially efficient rate and an optimal subsidy would increase output to the socially optimal rate. With a negative externality, for example, setting the tax (τ) equal to the externality cost per unit—that is, $\tau = (MSC - \Sigma\ MC)$—reduces output to Q^* because this tax has the effect of making MSC the supply curve for the market. (A tax defined in this manner is called a Pigouvian tax; it was first suggested by British economist A. C. Pigou.) At the socially optimal output rate, the **Pigouvian tax** equals the marginal damage caused by the externality. Figure 17.9 shows how the Pigouvian tax is determined.

Pigouvian tax A tax on each unit of pollution-causing output in an amount equal to the marginal damage caused by the externality.

Prior to the Pigouvian tax, the citrus market supplies Q_c pounds of citrus per year. The Pigouvian tax (τ) causes the supply curve for citrus, S_{citrus}, to shift vertically by an amount equal to the tax. Now the market supply curve for citrus is given by $S_{citrus} + \tau$. Because the Pigouvian tax is set equal to the marginal effluent, or damage, cost at the socially optimal output rate (Q^*), the citrus market reaches a new equilibrium at Q^*. Thus, the Pigouvian tax resolves the inefficiency caused by the externality.

We may ask what happens to the tax revenues collected from the citrus market. This is a tricky question to answer. The spending of these funds may affect the optimal solution in the citrus market if they are dispersed in a manner that affects either the market supply or demand for citrus, or the marginal

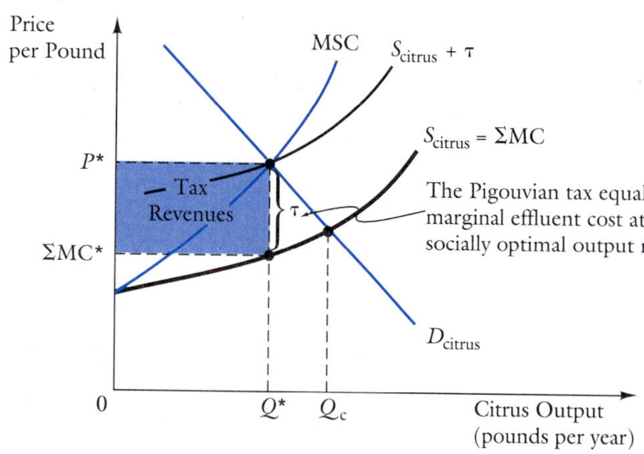

FIGURE 17.9

Using a Pigouvian Tax to Elicit the Socially Optimal Output Rate

A Pigouvian tax causes the supply curve of citrus to shift upward from S_{citrus} to $S_{citrus} + \tau$. Because the tax is set equal to the marginal cost of the externality at the socially optimal output rate (Q^*), the market reaches a new equilibrium at the socially optimal output rate. The tax also generates revenues equal to the shaded area, which may affect the size of the tax rate (τ) if these revenues are distributed in a manner that affects either the demand or supply of citrus.

externality cost. If the tax funds are somehow directed to the fishing industry—for example, to help lower the burden the industry bears from the socially optimal quantity of effluent discharge—then they may reduce the marginal effluent cost. In other words, an extra pound of citrus output increases the chemical discharge in lakes but also generates extra tax revenue to help offset the lost income from the additional effluent. Thus, the socially optimal output rate changes because the use of the tax funds affect the citrus market equilibrium. In this situation, a general equilibrium model is needed to determine the correct Pigouvian tax.

A Pigouvian tax (or subsidy) can create an allocatively efficient solution (assuming that we have the information necessary to implement it), but it may be unnecessary if private trades produce the efficient outcome. The Coase theorem shows us that if transaction costs are low, the optimal solution can be reached without government assistance. Of course, this assumes that the parties involved negotiate in good faith. Coase's point was that in a low-transaction-cost economy, the main effect of government is to change the distribution of wealth by the assignment of property rights; government does not need to interfere with the output rate of firms.

When transaction costs are high, which they generally are, so that negotiating payments or bribes is expensive, it may be efficient for government to use taxes or subsidies to influence the output rate of externality-producing firms. But such actions must be carefully considered because of the dynamic nature of the economy; the present tax (or subsidy) may be correct, but it can become suboptimal as the structure of markets changes over time. Thus, for any tax (or subsidy) policy to work effectively, it must be reevaluated and changed on a regular basis to keep pace with the dynamic economy.

LEARNING EXERCISE 17.9

Explain how the government can use output restrictions instead of taxes to cause the market to produce the socially optimal output rate in the presence of a negative externality.

$$$ Price Theory in Practice

INTELLECTUAL PROPERTY RIGHTS

To what extent does a person own the property rights to unpublished material he or she may have written, for example, in letters and diaries? For years, copyright law allowed book authors to quote "bits and pieces" of unpublished material without infringing on the writer's property rights. That "fair use" practice, however, has been dramatically curtailed in recent court cases that have set off a battle between book authors and, in a new twist, computer software writers.

In 1987 and again in 1989, the U.S. Court of Appeals in New York sought to protect property rights to unpublished material by ruling that book authors had overstepped the "fair use" of material allowed by copyright law. In the first case, the court ruled that author Ian Hamilton had no right to quote or paraphrase from 59 letters written by author J. D. Salinger. In the second case, the court found that author Russell Miller had drawn too heavily from the unpublished writings of L. Ron Hubbard, founder of the Church of Scientology. Hamilton and Miller had written biographies of Salinger and Hubbard, respectively.

Although the rulings drew criticism from book authors, they were applauded by computer software writers, who share concerns about property rights with the writers of unpublished letters and diaries. The consequences for software writers, however, may be more far-reaching. The old practice allowed someone to use small sections of unpublished computer code. In the software-writing business, a small piece of program code may be the essential innovation of the program. Under the "fair use" doctrine, the writer of the software is denied the property rights to the new versions of his or her program.

A major effect of the court rulings, then, is to protect the property rights of American software producers, who control as much as 70 percent of the world market. The new ruling makes it easier for software producers to take legal action against rivals who create software packages that "mimic" the producers' popular computer programs.

In response, authors are asking Congress to rewrite the copyright laws to again allow them to make "fair use" of small amounts of unpublished works. Under the new court rulings, authors often cannot even paraphrase unpublished work. Newspapers and televisions fear that the restrictions may ultimately be applied to their investigative reports. These days the only safe route for authors who want to use unpublished material is to receive written permission from the writers of the material or the heirs of that person. Such written permission may be costly, however. So far there appear to be no notable examples of persons or heirs who have sold the rights to unpublished documents to biographers. In 1989, Arun Gandhi considered auctioning 60 letters written by his famous grandfather, Mahatma Gandhi, through Christie's in London.[8] That possibility, however, was apparently quashed by family opposition. Historically, public figures or their heirs have either allowed biographers unrestricted access to documents or burned them to avoid unwanted publicity. The explorer and writer Richard Burton (1821–1890), for example, left papers that were burned by his wife after his death.

The U. S. Congress has tried to write a law that is acceptable to both book authors and software writers, but with little success. As it stands now, the production of computer software is expected to increase, but the number of books published is expected to decrease. The problem with that, authors and publishers say, is that important biographies—perhaps some of critical or historical significance—will not be written because authors cannot use important unpublished information.

[8] "To Auction the Mahatma's Letters Is Not the Gandhian Way," *The New York Times,* Dec. 1, 1989, p. A34.

LEARNING EXERCISE 17.10

How will the *relative* price of biographies and computer software change as a result of the court's ruling?

Policy Application and Evaluation

NORTHERN SPOTTED OWL

Issue—*Should we save the northern spotted owl?*

Background

Often government regulation affects the production and employment practices of firms. The case of the northern spotted owl is one such example. The northern spotted owl was listed as a threatened species under the Endangered Species Act of 1973 on June 26, 1990. Unlike most other species protected by the Endangered Species Act, the owl lives in a very large geographic range, which stretches from southern British Columbia, Canada, to Marin County, California. Thus, the designation of the owl as an endangered species affected a large populated area in the western states. In April 1993, the effect of the owl's protection on the timber industry was debated at a timber summit led by President Bill Clinton in Portland, Oregon. Environmentalists and timber industry supporters disagreed on how far protection for the owl should go. Environmentalists argued that timber harvest practices have led to habitat loss and fragmentation for the owl, a negative externality. Advocates for the timber industry contended that the owl conservation laws would put too many people out of work and raise the cost of timber, which is primarily used to build homes.

Save the Owl

The major concern of environmentalists is that planned timber harvest levels are too high given the social value of the spotted owl. Clear-cutting as a forest management practice, combined with increasingly shorter rotation lengths, have decreased the overall forest age in the Northwest and decreased habitat suitable for the owl. Owl habitat requirements include extensive forested areas characterized by large trees (over 30 inches in diameter at breast height, 150 to 200 years old) and smaller trees. Timber harvest plans target the old trees, so they are becoming relatively scarce. Cutting plans for the next 50 years are expected to reduce the average age of harvested trees to 80 to 90 years old on Forest Service lands, to 50 years old on U.S. Department of Interior lands, and to 45 to 65 years old on private land. A study by the U.S. Fish and Wildlife Service shows that National Forests in the Pacific Northwest are expected to contain only 25 million cubic feet of timber by the year 2040. In 1952, the total figure was close to 50 million cubic feet.

In addition to rapid harvesting, the protection of biological diversity appears to be of increasing concern to Congress and the American public. The designation of a critical habitat area for the spotted owl contributes to maintaining regional biodiversity in the Pacific Northwest. The habitat of the northern spotted owl represents a unique forest ecosystem of diverse plants and animal species.

Saving the Owl Will Cost Jobs

The view of the timber industry is markedly different from that of environmentalists. The timber industry claims that it is replanting six trees for every one harvested and that there are more trees in the Pacific Northwest now than there were 40 years ago.[9] Timber industry officials argue that saving the old growth forests in which the northern spotted owl lives would put too many people out of work. Furthermore, timber industry officials question the "value" of the owl in terms of maintaining biodiversity in the Northwest region. In the long run, they say, the benefits, if any, that the spotted owl offers to society are minuscule when compared to the losses of thousands of jobs and the income to workers if timber companies lose the right to harvest trees.

What Is Expected to Happen?

The annual timber harvest in Washington and Oregon has been slashed by more than half since the first court-ordered injunction to protect the owl was issued in 1989.[10] The question that arises is whether or not this reduction in the stock of cutting trees has permanently increased the average cost of timber. There seems to be two views about the answer to this question.

Environmental economists argue that stumpage price (the price of logs before transportation and milling costs are added) in the region is expected to increase only temporarily as a result of reduced Federal timber supplies. Higher prices induce private timber owners to increase their harvest, at least in the short term, by harvesting timber sooner than originally planned. This has a mitigating effect on the increasing stumpage price. The Forest Service estimated that implementing an owl conservation plan would result in 30 percent higher stumpage prices in the Northwest in the short term and that private timber owners would respond by increasing their annual harvest in the region by at least 4.2 percent. In the long run, more timber will be planted, which will place downward pressure on stumpage prices.

Other economists disagree with this analysis. They argue that the average cost of timber will increase permanently as a result of owl conservation measures that lead to a reduction in the stock of cutting trees. The elimination of a stock of accessible cutting trees is a permanent change in the supply of harvestable timber. Timber firms will have to search in more remote areas for new supplies. More remote or deeper forests yield more expensive timber because of the higher costs of transporting workers and raw logs to and from these areas. Characteristically, these deep-forest areas are far from any existing logging roads or, at times, any roads at all. The increasing cost the timber industry incurs in reaching the trees and transporting the logs will offset any short-run incentive to increase output.

---

[9] *The New York Times,* Friday, April 2, 1993, p. A9.

[10] *The New York Times,* Friday, April 2, 1993, p. A9.

As the price of timber rises in the short run or long run, less will be purchased. Thus, employment in the timber industry will be reduced to reflect the decreased demand. Government-projected employment losses due to the owl protection plan is estimated at 32,436 jobs, which breaks down to 6,528 unemployed workers in Washington, 21,589 in Oregon, and 4,319 in California. The timber industry contends that 100,000 people will ultimately lose their jobs.

The Policy Proposal

After considering both sides in the debate, President Clinton proposed a plan to resolve the fate of the Pacific Northwest's ancient forests. The plan was intended to strike a middle ground. Some of the highlights of the Clinton timber plan include

- Logging of about 12 billion board feet of timber over 10 years, or about 1.2 billion board feet annually on federal lands in the Pacific Northwest that produced over 5 billion board feet annually throughout the 1980s
- Establishing reserves for the spotted owl
- Establishing logging buffer zones around sensitive streams and watersheds. (Streams and watersheds help to maintain the area's biodiversity.)
- Asking Congress to spend $1.2 billion over five years to aid the region's displaced workers through grants, small business loans, and job training.

Neither environmentalists nor timber logging advocates completely supported the plan. Each side felt their needs were not fully accounted for or met. The Clinton timber plan caused heated debates in Congress between the pro-environment advocates and the pro–timber economy supporters.

Questions for Evaluation

Why would environmentalists disagree with the Clinton timber plan? How can we value biodiversity? Is biodiversity a positive externality? If the northern spotted owl is genetically similar to the Chinese spotted owl, do we need to save both owls? What will happen to the value of homes in logging and timber towns as a result of the Clinton plan?

Chapter Summary

1. There are four main causes of market inefficiency: market or monopoly power over price, asymmetric information about conditions in a market or about product quality, the presence of pure public goods for which the private sector will not produce or will produce too little, and positive and negative externalities.
2. A rival good can be produced only by using additional resources that have positive value. Extra units of a nonrival good can be produced at zero marginal cost. An owner of a radio, for example, can select another radio station by pressing a tuner button. The radio station has produced music for another listener at zero marginal cost.

3. With an exclusive good, consumption by one individual effectively precludes consumption by another individual. The free rider problem exists because some goods are nonexclusive. Thus, if the good is exclusive, the free rider problem is solved.
4. The tragedy of the commons exists because property rights to particular resources are too costly to enforce relative to the benefits of such enforcement. If the relative costs and benefits of enforcing property rights are changed sufficiently, say by single ownership of a resource, the overuse of a common resource will stop.
5. Externalities generally reduce the efficiency of an economy because the optimal output is not produced. But this statement depends on the size of transaction costs, as the Coase theorem shows. If transaction costs of bargaining and negotiating are low, then the parties affected by an externality can negotiate a side payment to arrange for production of the efficient output rate. High transaction costs, however, make such payments too costly to arrange.
6. A Pigouvian tax induces the socially optimal solution on an (otherwise) free market in which the polluter has the right to pollute without fear of legal or governmental challenge. The Pigouvian tax equals the marginal damage cost at the socially optimal output rate. The tax does not eliminate the externality or change property rights, but it does decrease the damage caused by the externality.

Trouble Spots

Concept	Reminder
The Free Rider Problem	Free riders are a problem because they may consume a pure public good, but they don't have to pay a share of its cost. Free riders are likely to pose less of a problem for nonexclusive goods with positive marginal costs of production. Because additional production requires additional cost, firms can (partially) exclude free riders by not incurring these additional costs. For example, free riders sitting just *outside* a concert area in a public park can hear the concert, but not very well. If speakers are located near the back of the concert area, hearing improves, but this requires additional cost that the concert promoter can avoid.
The Tragedy of the Commons	The tragedy of the commons arises when private ownership rights are not enforceable. Landowners in the western United States in the 1800s, for example, were not able to prevent cattle from other ranches from using their land until the development of the barbwire fence. The barbwire fence effectively defined the property rights of ranch owners. We can say that private ownership, per se, is not sufficient to

prevent the tragedy of the commons; the ownership rights must be enforceable at relatively low cost for the tragedy to be prevented.

17.4 Review Questions

1. Explain how market or monopoly power affects the efficiency of a competitive market.
2. Why does asymmetric information pose a problem for market efficiency? If information is available, but costly to obtain, does the lack of information continue to cause market inefficiency?
3. Explain the difference between rival and nonrival goods and between exclusive and nonexclusive goods. What are the characteristics of a pure public good?
4. What types of goods give rise to the free rider problem?
5. Why will private sector firms fail to provide goods that are nonexcludable?
6. What makes the tragedy of the commons a tragedy? How can the tragedy be eliminated?
7. List two examples of a negative externality and two examples of a positive externality. Can an externality be an exclusive good, that is, a good for which others are excluded from consuming?
8. Explain the significance of the Coase theorem. How does the Coase theorem help restore efficiency to an economy in which some goods are producing negative externalities?
9. If transaction costs are low or zero, does the assignment of property rights affect the output rate of the externality-producing good?
10. Explain how a Pigouvian tax can be used to cause the market to produce the socially optimal output rate. How does the distribution of the tax receipts affect the socially optimal solution?

17.5 Price Theory Problems

1. Public goods are likely to be provided by the public sector, but can they be produced privately for distribution by public authorities? What is the single act that public authorities must be able to do in order to provide public goods? Can this act be performed by the private sector under contract with the public sector?
2. Classify the following goods as rival or nonrival and exclusive or nonexclusive:
    a. Crime Watch services in a local neighborhood
    b. A police speed trap
    c. A haircut
    d. A thunderstorm
    e. Public television
    f. A telephone call on a normal day
    g. A telephone call on Mother's Day
    h. A magazine at a newsstand

  i. A charm bracelet
  j. A fax machine in a busy office
  k. A lifeboat on the Titanic
  l. Paper money

3. Many scientists are worried about the extinction of certain animals and plants as vast tracts of jungle in South America are converted into agricultural land. The concern is that the DNA, or genetic code, of a species is lost forever. The genetic code could provide important services in the future, such as the development of new drugs. What scheme could you develop to encourage farmers to preserve rare plants and animals? How can patents and established property rights to the preserved DNA fit into your scheme? How is your scheme affected if the rare plants and animals are found in some other location on the globe?
4. Explain the economic difference between flowers planted in your front yard, in full view of your neighbors, and flowers planted in the backyard that only you can see. Are there too few flowers planted in your front yard? Why or why not? If you don't like your neighbors—that is, you can't stand to talk to them—how will your answer change?
5. One way to move to the socially optimal output rate in the presence of a negative externality is to impose an output restriction on the offending industry. An alternative is to impose an appropriately determined Pigouvian tax. Explain the economic difference between these two approaches using a general equilibrium analysis. (Note that the tax revenue must go somewhere.) Is there an economic reason to prefer one approach over the other if demand is highly variable over time?
6. Output restrictions can reduce the amount of the externality-producing good to replicate the Pigouvian tax solution. Can output restrictions or controls cause the market to produce the socially optimal output rate when there is a positive externality? Can appropriately defined price controls recreate the socially optimal solution?
7. It is currently illegal to buy and sell human organs and tissues. One reason this law is effective is that it is costly to determine who is a suitable match for a given organ. Many factors, including blood type, age, genetic disorders, and medical history, affect the likelihood that an organ will be rejected by a recipient. Suppose, however, that a new antirejection drug eliminated all matching factors except blood type. Now, how would the number of transplants change? Is it likely that organs will be bought and sold like other commodities? Does the Coase theorem offer an explanation of the new equilibrium?
8. Many restaurants set aside nonsmoking areas for their patrons. Oftentimes patrons wait for seats in these areas while the seats in smoking areas are vacant. What does this situation tell you about the transaction costs of bargaining with restaurant patrons? Does the addictive nature of smoking affect the incentive to bargain with smokers?

17.6 Writing Exercise

Create a list of five positive and five negative externalities. Explain how the property rights to produce these externalities are currently allocated. Find a specific case in which a local, state, or federal government has sought to change or has changed the allocation of these rights. Explain who gains and who loses with the change. Document whether these two (or more) groups "fought" each other over the proposed change in the assignment of property rights. How much money and time did each group spend in their effort? Explain whether the cost of organizing one side or the other affected the final outcome.

Appendix A
Glossary

Absolute Advantage The ability to produce an output with fewer inputs than someone else. (1)

Absolute Prices Pure numbers measured in current dollar values. (2)

Adverse Selection A problem arising when agents possess information that is valuable to the principal before the principal has contracted for their services. (7)

Agent A term describing the individual or party responsible for performing the action requested by the principal. (7)

Allocative Efficiency A situation in which all gains from voluntary trade are realized. (10)

Arbitrage The purchase and resale of an asset in order to gain from observed price differences. (12)

Arc-Price Elasticity of Demand Price elasticity of demand measured between any two points on a demand curve rather than at a single point. (2)

Asymmetric Information Information that is known to one party to a contract or transaction that is not known to the other party. (7)

Atemporal A single period of time. (15)

Average Factor Cost Curve (AFC) Another name for the factor supply curve; at any point on the supply curve, the price given is equal to the average (per unit) factor cost. (14)

Average Fixed Cost (AFC) Total fixed cost divided by output. (9)

Average Product Total output divided by the number of units of the variable input used. (8)

Average Total Cost (ATC) Total of all fixed and variable costs divided by output. (9)

Average Variable Cost (AVC) Total variable cost divided by output. (9)

Bargaining The process of negotiating the price of a product. (2)

Barriers to Entry Any impediments to entry into an industry that give existing firms market power. (11)

Bilateral Monopoly A situation in which a monopolist sells to a monopsonist. (14)

Board of Directors A group elected by the shareholders to represent their interests with the firm's managers. The board of directors has the fiduciary responsibility to monitor the firm's managers. (7)

Budget Constraint An equation showing the maximum combination of different goods a consumer can purchase with a given income. (4)
Budget Line Algebraic rearrangement of the budget constraint to show the trade-off between two goods when income and prices are fixed. (4)
Bundle A specific collection of goods. (4)
A package of two or more products or services. (12)
Bundle Price Line The set of reservation prices that sum to the bundle price. For two products, the bundle price line is formed from the equation $r_2 = P_B - r_1$. (12)
Cardinal Utility A summary measure of satisfaction that places a numerical value on the satisfaction received from a bundle of goods. (5)
Cartel A group of firms that have agreed to coordinate price and output decisions in an attempt to gain market power. (11)
Ceteris Paribus Other things being the same. (2)
Cheap Talk Costless communication of information to firms in a noncooperative game. (13)
Common Value Auction An auction in which product price is the same for all bidders and is generally known but quantity is unknown. (12)
Comparative Advantage The ability to perform a given task at a lower opportunity cost than someone else. (1)
Compensated Demand Curve A demand curve generated by changing the price of one good and compensating (or taxing) the individual to keep him or her on the original indifference curve. (6)
Compensating Wage Differential Extra wages paid to otherwise equally productive workers in order to compensate for a less desirable working environment. (14)
Complement Good A is a complement to good B if the demand for good A varies directly with the price of good B. (2)
Complementarity Two factors of production are complementary if increased use of one raises the marginal product of the other. (14)
Complements in Production Input A is a complement to input B if the use of input A varies directly with the price of input B. (2)
Completeness A property of preferences that implies bundles of goods can be ranked as preferred, indifferent, or less preferred to one another. (5)
Composite Good Combines the purchases of all but one good. The combined goods are called "all other goods." (4)
Constant-Cost Industry An industry in which average and marginal cost curves remain unchanged as the output of all firms changes. (10)
Constant Economies of Scale Output increases proportionate to the change in inputs causing average total costs to remain constant; may result from constant returns to scale or such external-to-the-firm changes as fixed factor prices. (9)
Constant Returns to Scale The long-run characteristic that a change in all inputs by a fixed percentage causes output to change by the same fixed percentage. (8)
Consumers' Surplus The benefit to consumers from purchasing a given quantity of a good; it equals the difference between the value placed on each unit and its price summed over all purchases. (3)
Contestable Market A market in which there are no sunk costs of entry and exit of firms. (11)

Contract Curve The locus of allocation points in an Edgeworth box that are exchange-efficient (i.e., Pareto-optimal). (16)

Cooperative Game A situation in which firms collude or otherwise coordinate their actions. (13)

Corner Solution A bundle, lying at either end of the budget line, that provides more satisfaction than any other bundle on the budget line. (5)

Credible Signal An action taken or message sent by an individual or firm that is believed by the marketplace. (7)

Cross-Price Elasticity of Demand The percentage change in the quantity demanded of good *X* divided by the percentage change in the price of good *Y*; to be contrasted with price elasticity of demand. (6)

Deadweight Loss The permanent loss in consumers' and producers' surpluses because of a change in the market environment, for example, a new government program. (3)

Decreasing-Cost Industry An industry in which average and marginal cost curves shift down as the output of all firms changes. (10)

Decreasing Returns to Scale The long-run characteristic that a change in all inputs by a fixed percentage causes output to change by less than the fixed percentage. (8)

Demand Curve The relationship between quantity purchased and price. (2)

Derived Demand Demand for an input that is derived from the demand for final output produced by a firm. The demand for all inputs is a derived demand. (14)

Diminishing MRS The property that the MRS_{xy} decreases as the amount of good *X* increases and the amount of good *Y* decreases on a given indifference curve. (5)

Diseconomies of Scale Output rises less than in proportion to a change in inputs, causing average total cost to increase, may result from either decreasing returns to scale or such external changes as an increase in the price of inputs. (9)

Diseconomies of Scope Production of multiple outputs in one firm is more expensive than the costs of producing the same outputs in separate firms (or plants). (9)

Disequilibrium A situation in which, at prevailing prices, quantity demanded does not equal quantity supplied. (2)

Dominant Strategy A choice that is optimal in a noncooperative game, no matter what other firms do. (13)

Duopoly A market structure in which there are only two firms. (13)

Durable Resource An input, such as capital, that provides a flow of services over time to the firm. (9)

Dutch Auction An auction that starts with a high price—selected by the auctioneer—which is successively lowered until someone accepts the price. (12)

Economic Depreciation The change in market value (adjusted for inflation) of an asset between two points in time. (9)

Economic Efficiency Selecting an input along the least-cost expansion path. (9)

Economic Rent A payment to a factor of production above what is necessary to keep a given quantity of the factor in its current employment and quality. (14)

Economies of Scale Output increases more than in proportion to the change in inputs, causing average total costs to decrease; may result from increasing returns to scale or such external-to-the-firm changes as falling factor prices. (9)
Economies of Scope Production of multiple outputs in one firm is less expensive than the costs of producing the same outputs in separate firms (or plants). (9)
Edgeworth Box A rectangular graph portraying two individual commodity spaces superimposed on each other, with each individual's origin at a diagonally opposite corner of the box. We use the box to analyze exchange between two individuals. (16)
Efficiency Wages Paying wages that exceed the value of an employee's marginal product in order to discourage shirking or opportunistic behavior. (14)
Elastic Price elasticity of demand greater than 1 in absolute value. (2)
Elasticity of Substitution A measure of the relative responsiveness of the capital-labor ratio to a change in the ratio of factor prices. (14)
Engel Curve The set of points showing the various quantities of a commodity purchased at different levels of income. (6)
English Auction An auction in which prices are announced to all participants and the highest bidder wins. (12)
Equimarginal Principle The optimum for any problem comparing benefits and costs occurs at the point where marginal benefit (MB) equals marginal cost (MC). (1)
Exchange Efficiency An allocation of goods at which the MRS is equated across all individuals. (16)
Excise (or Unit) Tax A tax per unit of the good sold. (3)
Exclusive Dealing An agreement not to purchase a product or service from any other firm. (12)
Exogenous Originating from outside the model. (16)
Expectations A belief about the future. (2)
Expectations Hypothesis The shape of the term structure is determined by expectations of future changes in shorter-term yields. (15)
Expected Net Gain Equal to the expected value of a risky game minus its cost. (15)
Expected Value The probability-weighted value of each outcome to a particular game or risky situation. (15)
Expenditure Index The ratio of expenditures in one time period to expenditures in another—usually previous—time period, computed using the prices and quantities observed in these periods. (6)
Externality A cost or benefit imposed on others who are not party to creating the cost or benefit. (3)
Factor Price Effect The effect the change in output for the whole industry has on factor prices, causing average and marginal cost curves to shift. (10)
Fair Bet Also called a fair game; a situation in which the expected value of a risky game is equal to the cost of playing the game. (15)
Feasible Set The various combinations of bundles that you can buy with your budget, or income. (4)

Firm An organization in which there is more than one employee working as part of a team to produce a good or service. The team is linked together by explicit and implicit contracts. (7)
First-Degree Price Discrimination Price discrimination in which all consumers' surplus is extracted by charging each consumer the highest price he or she is willing to pay for each unit of the good purchased. (12)
First-Move Advantage The firm that sells output first has a profit advantage over firms that enter the market later. (13)
First-Price Sealed-Bid Auction An auction in which sealed bids are all opened at once on a given date. The highest bidder wins and pays the amount bid. (12)
Fixed Costs (FC) Costs that are not avoidable in the present planning horizon, usually due to a fixed input. (9)
Fixed Input An input that does not change under the present planning horizon. (8)
Fixed Proportions A production technology that holds the ratio of inputs constant as output increases. (8)
Flow The change in the stock of a resource between two points in time. (2)
Forward Contract The same as a futures contract except that its terms may be more flexible. Forward contracts are not traded on organized futures exchanges. (15)
Free Rider An individual (or firm) who can share in the consumption of a good without sharing in its cost. (17)
Full Income The amount of income a consumer can earn if all available time is spent working. (4)
Full Income Constraint An equation showing how a consumer's full income is allocated to the "purchase" of both goods and leisure. (4)
Future Value (FV) The value of income or consumption in a future period. (15)
Futures Contract A contract for delivery of a given amount of a commodity, or the cash equivalent, at a known future date, with the price to be determined at the time of purchase. (15)
Futures Market The market in which futures contracts are traded. (15)
Game A situation in which the interaction of firms or consumers affects decision making. (13)
General Equilibrium Analysis Economic analysis that takes into account the interrelations between markets. (16)
Giffen Good A good that is so inferior that a fall in price causes quantity demanded to decrease; that is, the demand curve slopes upward. (6)
Hedging Holding a given position in the spot market and the opposite position in the futures market. (15)
Herfindahl-Hirschman Index (HHI) A measure of market power equal to the sum of the squared market shares of all firms in the industry. (11)
Holdup Problem When one party takes an action that prevents another party from fully earning a normal return on its investment in a specific asset. (7)
Homogeneous Products The collection of all products that consumers view as perfect substitutes for each other. (10)
Horizontal Integration A merger that involves firms selling commodities that are close substitutes. (11)

Human Capital Any activity that increases a worker's present or future marginal productivity. (14)
Income-Consumption Curve The set of equilibrium bundles generated from successive increases in income, holding nominal and relative prices constant. (6)
Income Effect When the price of one good changes, the part of the change in quantity demanded that is due to a change in purchasing power, or real income. (6)
Income Elasticity of Demand The responsiveness of quantity demanded to changes in income; the percentage change in the quantity demanded of a good divided by the percentage change in income. (6)
Increasing-Cost Industry An industry in which average and marginal cost curves shift up as the output of all firms changes. (10)
Increasing Returns to Scale The long-run characteristic that a change in all inputs by a fixed percentage causes output to change by more than the fixed percentage. (8)
Independent Private Values Model A model of bidding behavior in which each bidder's reservation prices is independently determined and is known only to each bidder. (12)
Indifference Curve A collection of bundles that offer the same level of satisfaction. (5)
Industry A group of firms that sell the same or related goods and services. (1)
Inelastic Price elasticity of demand less than 1 in absolute value. (2)
Inferior Good A good for which purchases decrease as income increases and increase as income decreases. (6)
Inflection Point The point where the total product curve changes from increasing at an increasing rate to increasing at a decreasing rate. (8)
Informal Collusion Informal agreements between two or more firms, designed to affect market price and output. (11)
Interest Rate The rate of exchange between goods today and goods in the future. (15)
Interior Solution A bundle on the budget line at which the MRS equals the price ratio. (5)
Intertemporal More than one period of time. (15)
Intertemporal Budget Constraint A budget constraint that shows the trade-off between present consumption and future consumption when present and future income are known with certainty. (15)
Intertemporal Price Discrimination Charging different prices for the same product at different points in time, which are not justified by cost differences. (12)
Inventory The stock of output or resource inputs that is available to the firm at a given point in time. (9)
Isocost Line The line along which total costs are constant in a graph with inputs on both axes. The isocost line shows the combinations of labor and capital that produce the same total cost. (9)
Isoquant The locus of points showing all the combinations of capital and labor that will yield the same output level. (8)
Kinked Demand Curve A demand curve that has a kink, or abrupt change in slope, at some price, which causes a gap in the marginal revenue curve. (13)

Laspeyres Index The ratio of expenditures in one time period to expenditures in another—usually previous—time period, computed using the prices observed in these periods, while holding quantities at their initial levels. (6)
Law of Demand An inverse relationship exists between quantity demanded and price. (2)
Law of Diminishing Marginal Utility An assumption that marginal utility decreases as you consume more of a good. (5)
Law of Diminishing Returns With a given technology and at least one fixed input, the marginal product of a variable input will eventually decrease. (8)
Law of Supply A positive relationship exists between quantity supplied and price. (2)
Least-Cost Expansion Path The set of input combinations that produce each level of output at least cost. (9)
Lemons Problem A phenomenon in which consumers will pay at most the low-quality price for products because they cannot determine quality before a purchase. (10)
Lerner Index (*L*) A measure of supposed market power given by the ratio $(P - \text{MC})/P$. (11)
Limit Pricing The practice of setting a price above marginal cost to deter new entry. (13)
Liquidity Preference Theory The shape of the term structure is determined by the relative mix of long- and short-term investors. (15)
Long Position The holdings of someone who has bought a futures contract for delivery or has bought the underlying commodity. (15)
Long Run The planning horizon for which all inputs are variable. (8)
Long-Run Supply Curve The curve that shows the output rate of a firm in the long run at various market prices. (10)
Luxury Good A good whose income elasticity is greater than 1. (6)
Managerial Costs The costs of organizing, monitoring, and coordinating production within the firm. (7)
Marginal Analysis Using incremental changes to make optimal decisions. (1)
Marginal Cost (MC) The amount that total cost changes when output changes by a small amount—usually by one unit. (7) The change in total cost (or in variable cost) due to a one-unit change in the rate of output. (9)
Marginal Factor Cost Curve (MFC) A curve showing the change in total factor cost due to a one-unit change in the use of that factor. (14)
Marginal Product The change in output due to a small change (i.e., one-unit change) in a variable input, all other inputs held constant. (8)
Marginal Rate of Substitution (MRS) Measures the trade-off between an additional unit of good X (horizontal axis) and good Y (vertical axis), holding satisfaction constant. (5)
Marginal Rate of Technical Substitution The rate at which labor can be substituted for capital, holding output constant, or the ratio of the marginal product of labor to the marginal product of capital (i.e., $\text{MRTS} = \text{MP}_L/\text{MP}_K$). (8)
Marginal Rate of Time Preference The rate at which you can trade-off future consumption for present consumption; an extra \$1 of present consumption will cost $\$(1 + r)$ of future consumption. (15)

Marginal Rate of Transformation (MRT) The slope of the production possibilities frontier at a given point. The MRT equals the ratio of the marginal cost of the output shown along the horizontal axis to the marginal cost of the output shown along the vertical axis. (16)
Marginal Revenue (MR) Change in total revenue associated with a small (or one-unit) change in the quantity sold. (2) Equivalently the amount that total revenue changes when output changes by a small amount—usually by one unit. (7)
Marginal Social Cost (MSC) The sum of marginal production cost and the marginal external cost: MSC = ΣMC + E_c. (17)
Marginal Utility Measures the change in total utility generated from consuming an extra unit of one good. (5)
Market The total collection of buyers and sellers participating in exchange of a given good or service. (1)
Market Demand The (horizontal) sum of the demand curves of all participants in the market. (2)
Market Equilibrium A situation in which, at the prevailing price, quantity supplied equals quantity demanded. (2)
Market Power The ability to affect the market price by changing the firm's output rate. (11)
Market Supply The (horizontal) sum of the supply curves of each firm in the market. (2)
Merger The joining of two or more firms together under a single ownership. (11)
Mixed Bundling When two or more products are sold separately and in bundles. (12)
Mixed Strategy Choosing to alternate between actions according to some probability measure. (13)
Money Illusion A situation in which consumers think the feasible set has changed just because income and all prices change proportionately. (4)
Monopolistic Competition An industry in which there is free entry and each firm faces a negatively sloped demand curve. Economic profits are zero in the long run. (13)
Monopoly Power The same as *market power.* (11)
Monopsony A market structure in which there is a single buyer of an input. (14)
Moral Hazard A problem arising when agents discover information that is valuable to the principal after the principal has contracted for their services. (7)
Multipart Pricing Another name for second-degree price discrimination. (12)
Nash Equilibrium A strategy (or action) that is optimal for each firm given the decisions of all other firms. (13)
Natural Monopoly A case in which only one firm can successfully compete in the market because economies of scale are so large relative to demand that this firm has an absolute cost advantage over other firms. (11)
Necessity Good A good whose income elasticity is positive but less than 1. (6)
Negative-Sum Game A game in which the players are worse off after the game is played. (13)
Negative Time Preference The property that the marginal rate of time preference is less than unity. (15)

Neutral Time Preference The property that the marginal rate of time preference is equal to unity. (15)
Nominal Income The flow of money received in a given period. (2)
Noncooperative Game A situation in which firms do not collude or coordinate their actions; they act independently, but they know that their payoffs depend on the actions of other firms. (13)
Nondurable Resource An input to production that is transformed or otherwise used up during the production process. (9)
Nonexclusive Good A good for which it is costly to exclude consumption by another person. (17)
Nonprofit Firm An organization that has no shareholders, restricts the distribution of its assets, and tends to equate annual revenues to annual costs. (7)
Nonrival Good A good for which additional units can be provided at zero marginal cost. (17)
Nonsatiation The "more is better" property of preferences. A bundle with more of one good and no less of any other is preferred or indifferent to an otherwise equivalent bundle. (5)
Normal Good A good for which purchases increase as income increases and decrease as income decreases. (6)
Oligopoly A market structure in which there are relatively few firms and each firm takes account of the others' reactions. (13)
Open Interest The number of futures contracts outstanding. (3)
Opportunity Cost The cost of the next-highest-ranked alternative action. (1)
Ordinal Utility A summary measure of satisfaction that ranks bundles of goods but does not assign a numerical value to utility. (5)
Ordinary Demand Curve A demand curve generated by changing the price of one good, holding nominal income and all other prices constant. (6)
Output Efficiency The condition that the MRT equals the MRS for all consumers and firms in the economy. This condition ensures that the output mix reflects consumers' relative willingness to pay. (16)
Pareto-Optimal Allocation Another term for *exchange efficiency.* (16)
Partial Equilibrium Analysis Analyzing market responses in isolation without taking account of the interrelations between markets. (16)
Patent A government-granted right to the exclusive use of an invention, which expires after 17 years. (11)
Payoff Matrix A chart that summarizes the gains and losses for all participants' actions. (13)
Peak-Load Pricing Charging peak users more than off-peak users. (12)
Perfect Competition A market structure in which firms are price takers, entry and exit are unrestricted in the long run, information is known by both buyers and sellers, and a homogeneous product is sold. (10)
Perfect Complements Goods that generate right-angled indifference curves. (5)
Perfect Substitutes Goods that generate straight-line indifferent curves. (5)
Perfectly Elastic A demand curve that has a price elasticity equal to $-\infty$. (2)
Perfectly Inelastic A demand curve that has a price elasticity equal to 0. Quantity demanded is not affected by price changes. (2)
Permanent Income The present value of the expected future steam of labor income. (15)

Pigouvian Tax A tax on each unit of pollution-causing output in an amount equal to the marginal damage caused by the externality. (17)

Planning Horizon The length of time associated with the profit-maximizing decision to change one or more inputs. (8)

Point Elasticity of Demand Price elasticity of demand measured at a single point on a demand curve. (2)

Poison Pill Special provisions adopted by a firm, often without the vote of shareholders, that make a corporate takeover more costly for the acquiring company. (7)

Positive-Sum Game A game in which participants gain from playing. (13)

Positive Time Preference The property that the marginal rate of time preference is greater than unity. (15)

Posted-Offer Pricing The price of labeling goods with prices before demand is known. (2)

Predatory Pricing A pricing policy intended to extract market share and profits from competitors by temporarily pricing below marginal costs. (12)

Present Value (PV) The current value of any sum to be received or paid in the future. (15)

Price Ceilings A maximum price for market transactions, for example, rent controls in some cities. (3)

Price-Consumption Curve The set of equilibrium bundles generated from successive changes in the price of one good, holding income and other prices constant. (6)

Price Differentiation Price differences that reflect differences in marginal costs. (12)

Price Discrimination Charging different buyers a different price for different units of an identical product when cost differences do not justify the observed price differences. (12)

Price Elasticity of Demand The ratio of the percentage change in quantity demanded to the percentage change in price. (2)

Price Floors A minimum price for market transactions, for example, the minimum wage. (3)

Price Maker A firm that can affect the market price by its output decision. (10) A firm with market power. (11)

Price Markup The fractional difference between price and marginal cost. (11)

Price Taker A firm that cannot affect market price by its output decision. (10) A situation in which market prices are not affected by your consumption decisions. (4)

Principal A term describing the individual or party who initiates some action. (7)

Private Costs All costs explicitly or implicitly incurred by individuals or firms. (9)

Privatization Government contracting with private firms to produce publicly financed goods and services. (17)

Producers' Surplus The benefit to firms from producing a given output rate; it equals the difference between the price and marginal cost summed over all units sold. (3)

Production Any use of resources that converts one commodity into a different commodity; production, therefore, includes storing, wholesaling, transporting, and repackaging services as well as manufacturing. (8)

Production Contract Curve The set of input mixes in an Edgeworth production box that are technically efficient. (16)
Production Function The mathematical expression of the technical relation between output and one or more inputs. (8)
Production Possibilities Frontier The mapping of the production contract curve into output space. The frontier shows the maximum technologically efficient rates of output for a given endowment of inputs. (16)
Production Schedule A table or chart showing the relationship between input and output quantities. (8)
Profit The difference between total revenue and total cost. (3)
Property Rights The ownership assignment of resources. (17)
Pure Bundling When two or more products are sold only as a package. (12)
Pure Monopoly A single seller or supplier of a well-defined commodity for which there are no close substitutes. (11)
Pure Public Good A good that has a marginal cost of zero (nonrival) and that is nonexclusive across consumers. (17)
Pure Strategy The choice of a single, unchanging action in a noncooperative game. (13)
Quality-Assuring Price A price that will induce firms to produce a high-quality product and not to cheat consumers by switching to the low-quality product in some period in the future. (10)
Quantity Demanded The number of units purchased at a given price. (2)
Quantity Discounts A price discount received when a consumer buys more than one unit of a good. (4)
Quantity Supplied The amount offered for sale at a given price. (2)
Quasi-Fixed Costs Costs that are "lumpy" and do not vary continuously with the firm's output rate. (14)
Rank-Order Tournament A reward system in which pay is based on a participant's ranking relative to other participants. (14)
Rationality Assumption Individuals maximize according to their own self-interest. (1)
Reaction Function An equation that defines the response of one firm to the actions taken by other firms. (13)
Real Income Nominal income divided by an index of absolute prices. (2)
Real Rate of Interest Rate of return measured in terms of the goods or services you can purchase in future periods after adjusting for inflation. (15)
Relative Prices Price of one good compared to another. (2)
Rent-Seeking Behavior An attempt to secure monopoly profits by investing resources to influence public policy. (11)
Representative Consumer A consumer whose demand is like the demand of many other consumers. (2)
Requirements Contract An agreement to purchase a certain quantity of products from a particular firm over a given time period. (12)
Reservation Price The maximum a consumer is willing to pay for a given unit of a good. (12)
Reservation Wage The lowest wage that will elicit a given level of labor effort. (14)
Residual The residual of a firm is its profits, that is, the difference between total revenues and total costs, including the opportunity cost of all resources used. (7)

Residual Claimants The owners of a firm's profits. If the firm is a corporation, then the owners are the shareholders. (7)
Revenue Equivalence Theorem The result that the expected revenues from either English, Dutch, first-price, or second-price auctions are equal. (12)
Risk Averse An individual who plays a risky game only if it has a positive expected net gain. (15)
Risk Lover An individual who will play a risky game when it has a negative expected net gain. (15)
Risk Neutral An individual who is indifferent between holding on to the money required to accept a fair bet and accepting a fair bet. (15)
Sales Tax A percentage tax placed on the total receipts of a transaction. (3)
Scarcity The concept that resources are limited compared to wants. (1)
Second-Degree Price Discrimination A pricing scheme that sorts buyers imperfectly based on their reservation prices. (12)
Second-Price Sealed-Bid Auction An auction in which sealed bids are all opened at once on a given date. The highest bidder wins but pays the amount bid by the second-highest bidder. (12)
Shareholders Owners of shares in a corporation; shareholders own the rights to the firm's residual payments. (7)
Shirking Changing work effort in a manner that imposes a cost on other team members. (7)
Short Position The holdings of someone who has agreed to deliver a commodity at a specified time in the future at a currently agreed-upon price. (15)
Short Run The planning horizon for which at least one, but not all, inputs are fixed. (8)
Short-Run Supply Curve The curve that shows the output rate of a firm in the short run at various market prices. (10)
Shortage Quantity demanded exceeds quantity supplied at a given price. (2)
Shutdown Rule A firm ceases operating if its average revenue is less than its average variable costs. (10)
Single-Price Monopoly A monopolist that charges the same price for all units sold. (11)
Social Costs Private costs plus costs imposed on other members of society who are not parties to the transaction, that is, third parties. (9)
Spatial Competition Competition between firms for location and distribution of products or services. (13)
Specialization Developing skills for a limited number of tasks. (1)
Specific Asset A good, service, or intangible that is more valuable in its present use than in any other alternative use. Some specific assets have no alternative use, making them a sunk cost. (7)
Spot Price The current or cash price of a commodity; the price for on-the-spot delivery. (15)
Stock Quantity of a resource available at a given point in time. (2)
Subsidy A payment made to either buyers or sellers for each transaction. (3)
Substitute Good Good A is a substitute for good B if the demand for good A varies inversely with the price of good B. (2)
Substitutes in Production Input A is a substitute for input B if the use of input A varies inversely with the price of input B. (2)

Substitution Effect When the price of one good changes, the part of the change in quantity demanded that is due to a change in relative prices. (6)
Sunk Cost An investment that has a zero opportunity cost. (7)
Surplus Quantity supplied exceeds quantity demanded at a given price. (2)
Swap An exchange of assets that have different payment characteristics. For example, the exchange of a fixed-rate loan for a variable-rate loan is a swap. (15)
Tastes A description of the goods and services that you like and dislike. (2)
Team A collection of individuals working jointly to produce a product or service or a specific part of a product or service. (7)
Technical Efficiency The technical relation between output and inputs as defined by the production function. (9)
The condition that the MRTS values are equated across firms, so that there are not mutual gains in output across industries when the input mix is reallocated. (16)
Term Structure A profile of the interest yield of an asset for various maturities. (15)
Third-Degree Price Discrimination Charging different prices in different markets for the same product; those consumers with relatively inelastic demands pay higher prices. (12)
Tit-for-Tat Strategy Choosing a cooperative solution as long as other firms cooperate. (13)
Total Cost (TC) The sum of total variable and fixed costs. (9)
Total Market Surplus The sum of consumers' and producers' surpluses. (10)
Total Product Curve A curve showing the physical output that results from the production process. (8)
Total Revenue Price per unit times quantity sold for a given time period. (2)
Total Variable Cost (TVC) The total cost of the variable inputs to the production process; this cost varies as the output rate changes. (9)
Tragedy of the Commons Inefficient use of a resource because exclusion of others is too costly. (17)
Transaction Costs Costs that arise from negotiating and completing a transaction with another firm or independent party. (7)
Transitivity The logical consistency property of preferences. If bundle *A* is preferred to bundle *B* and bundle *B* is preferred to bundle *C*, then transitivity implies that bundle *A* is preferred to bundle *C*. (5)
Two-Part Tariff A pricing strategy in which consumers are charged both access and usage fees. (12)
Tying A requirement that links the purchase of one product or service to the purchase of another product or service. (12)
Unitary Elastic Price elasticity of demand equal to 1 in absolute value. (2)
Variable Input An input that may change under the present planning horizon in order to change output. (8)
Variable Proportions A production technology that permits the ratio of inputs to vary along an isoquant. (8)
Vertical Integration A merger that involves one firm buying either a seller of one of its inputs or a purchaser of its outputs. (11)
von Neumann–Morgenstern Utility Function The expected utility an individual receives when facing uncertain states of consumption. (15)

Wants Individual consumption when income is not a constraint. (1)
Wealth A stock of assets at a given point in time. (2)
Welfare Economics The study of the social desirability of different economic outcomes. (16)
Winner's Curse The problem faced by the high bidder at a common value auction if the winning bid is significantly greater than the other bids. (12)
Zero-Sum Game A game in which the gains and losses of players exactly offset each other. (13)

Appendix B

Answers to Learning Exercises and Price Theory Problems

Chapter 1

LEARNING EXERCISES

1.1 Scarcity in the production of a periodical might cause the editors to list the obituaries of only important people or to shorten a story. If scarcity were not a problem, the classified ads in the back of the newspaper would be printed in larger, more readable type.

1.2 You might take medicine, sentimental pictures, or current work in progress. In other words, if given the choice you would take an item with greatest personal or monetary value relative to the other items in your house (the item with the highest opportunity cost to replace).

1.3 Married couples can split the household chores according to their respective comparative advantage. Chores such as paying bills, repairing household items, and cleaning can be allocated according to comparative advantage to save time for both individuals.

PRICE THEORY PROBLEMS

1. *TV Guide* readers are less interested in the commercials; they want to know what programs are playing. Using scarce space and resources to list commercials is not justified by the value readers place on this information.

2. Actual data are used to determine if a theory is accurate because these are the data the theory is supposed to explain. Without a way to empirically validate a theory, it will remain open to criticism.
3. The rental expense of a video and the expense of a restaurant meal before the movie are not included in the opportunity cost.
4. You study for each exam until the marginal return from an extra hour of study is equal for the two courses.
5. You would spend twenty to thirty minutes commuting. At this point the marginal value ($70 – $50 = $20) of commuting is equal to the marginal cost ($20 per hour) of what you would give up at your job.
6. Answers (a) and (d) are "what should be" questions that require an opinion. Answers (b) and (c) require positive economic analyses.

Chapter 2

LEARNING EXERCISES

2.1 Absolute change is 63 percent. Relative change is 11.8 percent.

2.2 Because they are substitutes, the demand for new Steinways moves directly with the price of used Steinways.

2.3 4,500; 3,205

2.4 –7; –3; –1.4; –.7; –.6

2.5 4 vans.

2.6 Approximately 196 percent increase in ticket sales.

2.7 2; 18 percent.

2.8

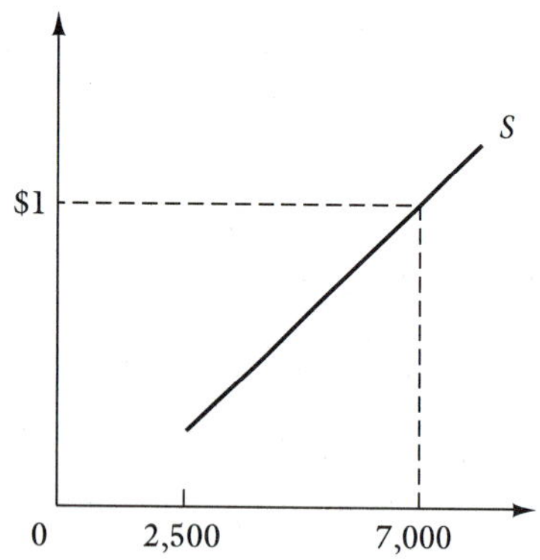

2.9 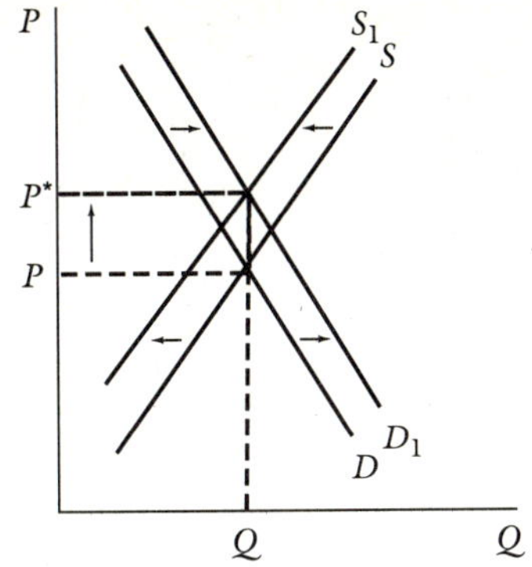

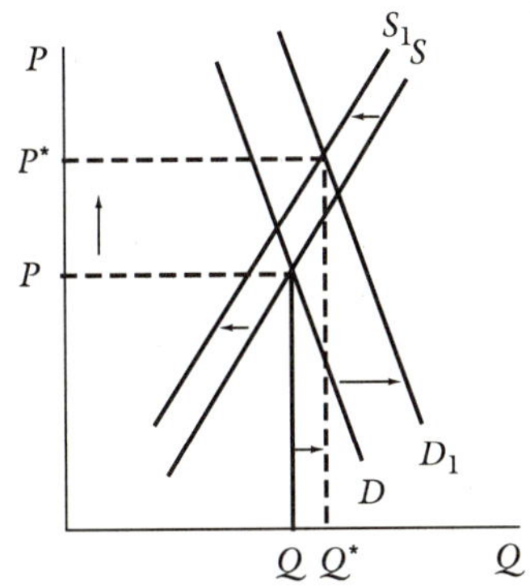

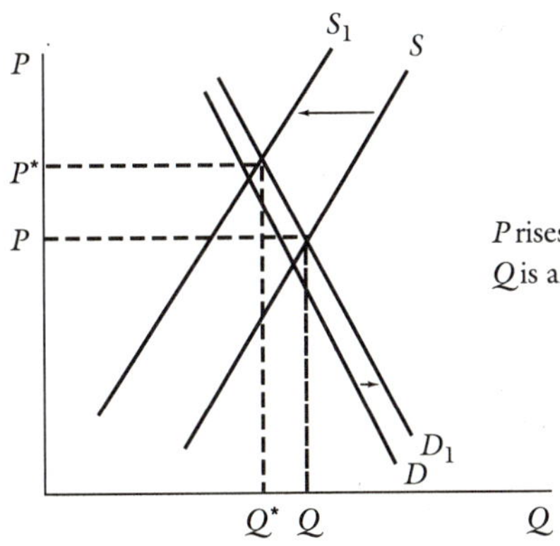

P rises to P^*
Q is ambiguous

PRICE THEORY PROBLEMS

1. The price of gas will rise. You could purchase more fuel for your car in anticipation of the price increase. The producers may have an incentive to reduce the supply of gas now so that they can sell it at a higher price later.
2. Students will see 20 percent fewer movies and senior citizens will see 10 percent fewer movies. We cannot say who has the greatest absolute change in quantity demanded.

3. −9; −2.02; −2.04; −.9; increases and then decreases.
4. $Q = a/P$, where a is a constant.
5. A stepwise demand curve looks like a staircase. The vertical segments are part of the demand curve; the horizontal segments represent gaps in the demand curve. Individuals buy additional units only after the price has risen the height of the next step. Aggregation across individuals smooths the steps because individuals are likely to have steps of different heights.

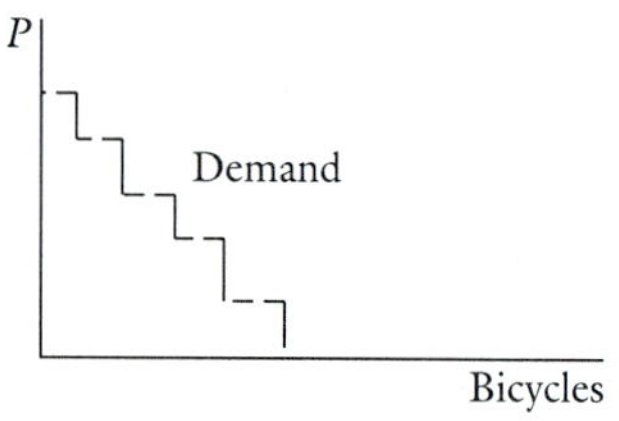

6. a. The supply curve for gold will shift to the right. The demand for lead should also rise as more people want lead to turn into gold.
   b. The new equilibrium price of gold should converge to the old equilibrium price of lead.
7. a. Lowering the cost to the airline should lower the cost of air travel, increasing supply at each price.
   b. Terrorist attacks increase the risk (cost) of air travel and should reduce demand.
   c. With more disposable income, people might travel more, causing demand for air travel to increase.
   d. Spring break represents a seasonal increase in demand.
   e. Buses are substitutes for air travel, so the demand for air travel will decrease.
8. a. $Q = 14{,}000 - 1{,}000P$ for the demand curve.
   b. $P = \$2$; $Q = 12{,}000$
   c. $42{,}000 - 3{,}000P = 20{,}000 + 2{,}000P$
   d. $(42{,}000 - 20{,}000)/5{,}000 = \$4.40$; $Q = 28{,}800$
9. a.

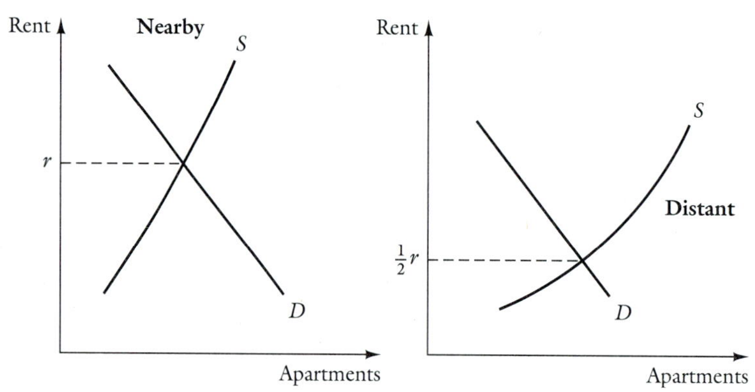

b. 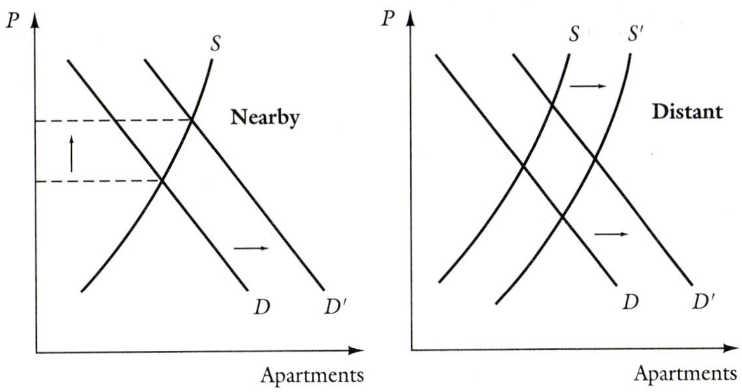

The price changes depend on the relative elasticity of demand and supply.

10. a. $1,000
    b. –6.25; decrease
    c. $580
11. a. Demand shifted to the right initially; then supply increased each day after the hurricane.
    b. –.69; –.45
    c. It increases initially and then remains at the higher level for a few days.
12. a. Items in (a), (d), and (e) are purchased through bargaining because they either are very expensive or are not purchased in discrete packages. The other items would probably not be bargained for in the United States. College tuition is usually divided into a set of per credit fees, and the other items are relatively less expensive than the cost of the time required to bargain.

CHAPTER 3

LEARNING EXERCISES

3.1 $P = 1 + (4{,}000/7{,}596) \times .20 = \$1.11$; $Q = 8{,}096 - 3{,}596(1.11) = 4{,}104$

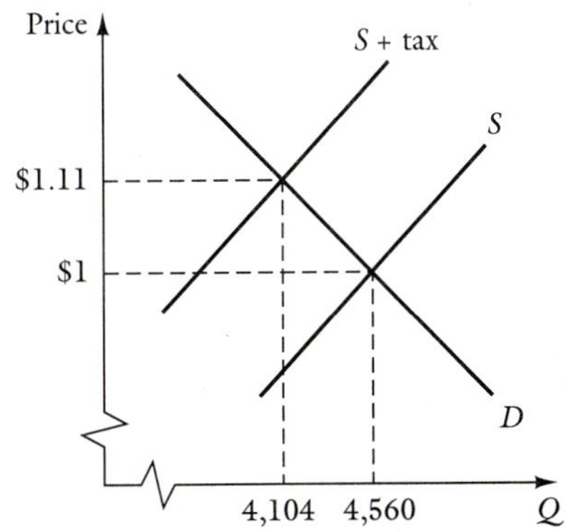

3.2 When the demand curve is horizontal, the per-unit burden shifts to the producer. When the supply curve is vertical, the per-unit burden shifts to the consumers.

3.3 The equilibrium will be the same, only demand will shift rather than supply.

3.4 (50 units × \$2)/2 = \$50

3.5 Subtract the area of the consumers' surplus under the world demand curve at the quota price from the area of the consumers' surplus under the world demand curve at the new free market price.

3.6

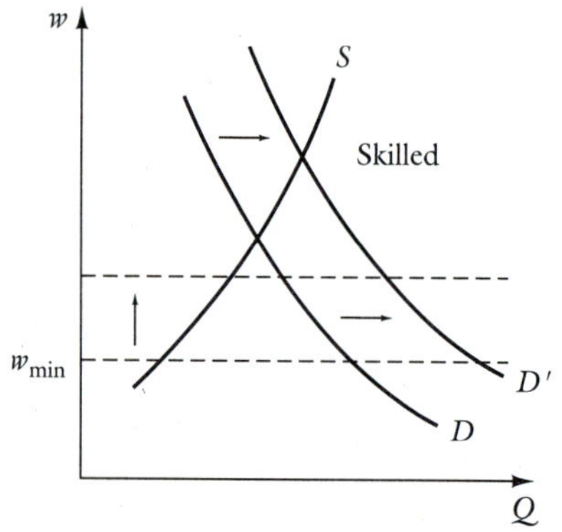

Demand will shift to the right because skilled workers have become relatively less expensive when the minimum wage increases.

3.7 Subtract the number of defaults with no limit from the number of defaults if there had been a limit on a particular day. If this number is statistically significant, the number of defaults has decreased.

3.8 You would not call if having your neighbor stop mowing is worth less than \$50. With a \$75 fine, your neighbor would stop mowing if it is worth only \$20 to him. If it was worth \$80 to your neighbor, he would not stop.

3.9 New P = \$300, Q_d = 1.2. \$1,500 million versus \$720 million.

PRICE THEORY PROBLEMS

1. The market equilibrium price of taxi rides will rise due to the tax. Depending on the elasticity of the demand and supply curves for taxi rides, the tax will be divided between the producers (taxi drivers) and consumers (passengers).

2.

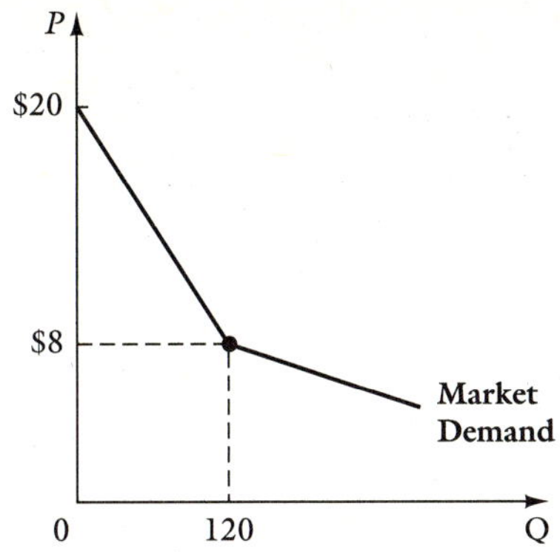

a. $D_t = 400 - 35P$ if $P \leq \$8$
b. $400 - 35P = 45P$; $P = 5$; $Q = 225$
c. $P_d = 1{+}(45/80)\text{tax} = 8.38$; $Q = 106.7$
d. $\frac{2}{3}$

3.

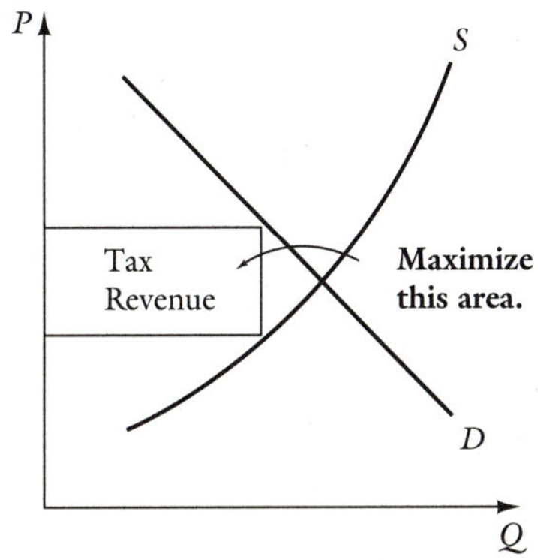

4. a. $P = \$400$; $Q = 25{,}000$
   b. $Q_d = 30{,}000$; $Q_s = 20{,}000$; producers lose $2,250,000; consumers gain $1,750,000, so deadweight loss = $500,000.
5. Dialysis companies and organ procurement organizations benefit; consumers who need an organ transplant probably lose.
6. Unskilled workers include teenagers, first-time job entrants, and people with little education or training; they are affected by a minimum wage. Employers can move their companies to a country where there is no minimum wage.
7. Yes. A quota that limits the supply of workers below equilibrium will cause the wages of workers to rise.
8. Consumers' quantity demanded for gasoline exceeded quantity supplied. If producers limited your purchases to less than your demand, you would wait in a second line if the value of your time justified the wait.
9. If your roommate is well educated in physics, you may benefit on your physics test from your roommate's knowledge. While having good

health in itself is important, the real external benefit from good health is your ability to do other activities or work better.

10. If the costs of negotiating are zero, everyone will bargain and all will arrive at a point at which each party maximizes. When property rights are not well defined, the value of undocumented property is less than that of legally owned property. This creates a negative externality for the whole society through higher transaction costs attached to transferring ownership.

Chapter 4

LEARNING EXERCISES

4.1

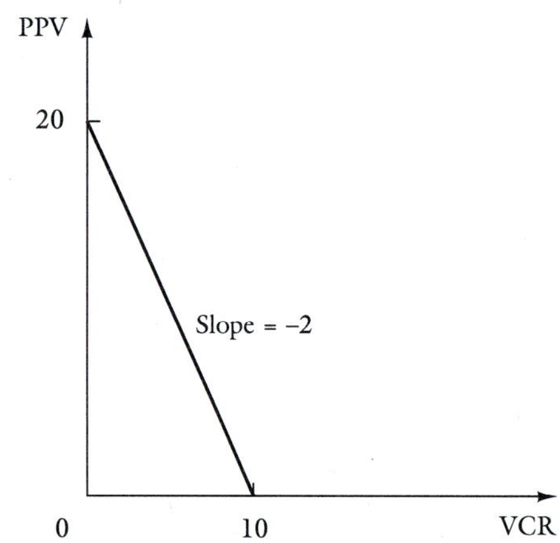

4.2

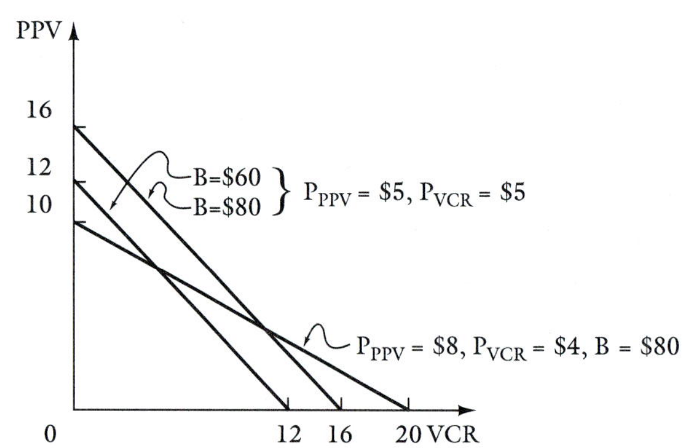

4.3

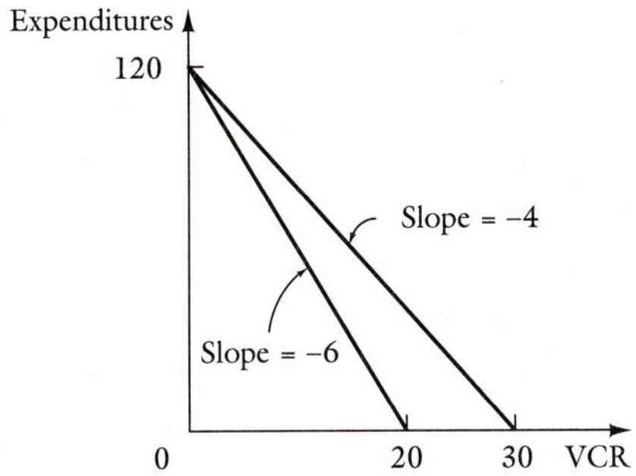
Expenditures
120
Slope = −4
Slope = −6
0
20
30
VCR

4.4

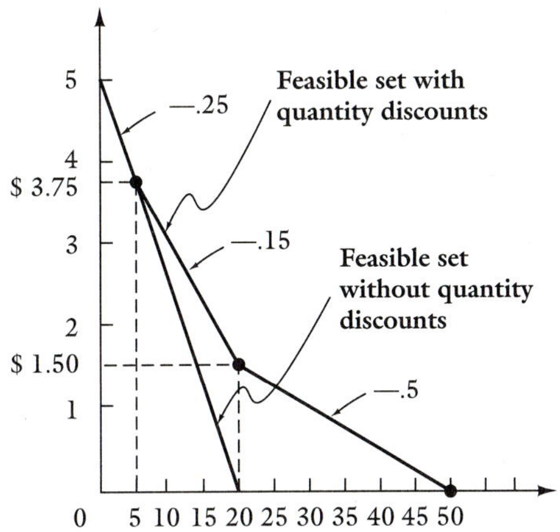
5
4
$ 3.75
3
2
$ 1.50
1
0
—.25
—.15
—.5
Feasible set with quantity discounts
Feasible set without quantity discounts
5 10 15 20 25 30 35 40 45 50

4.5

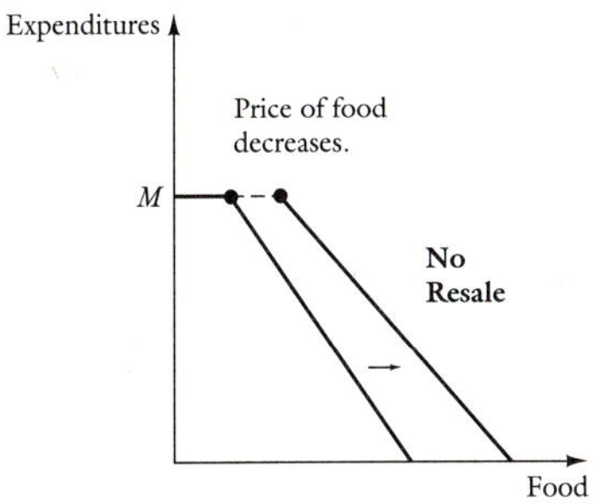
Expenditures
Price of food decreases.
M
No Resale
Food

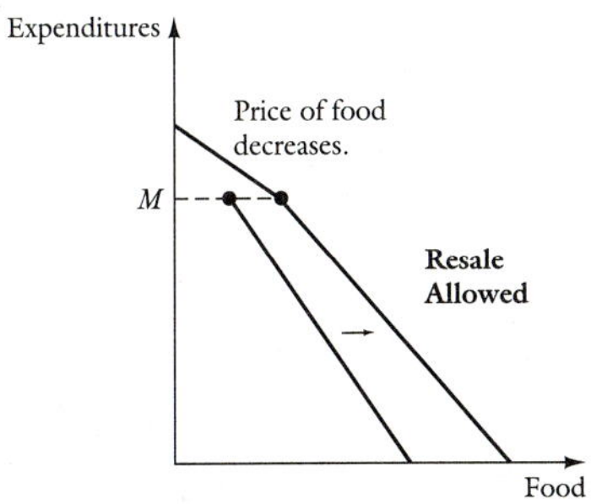
Expenditures
Price of food decreases.
M
Resale Allowed
Food

4.6 No change.

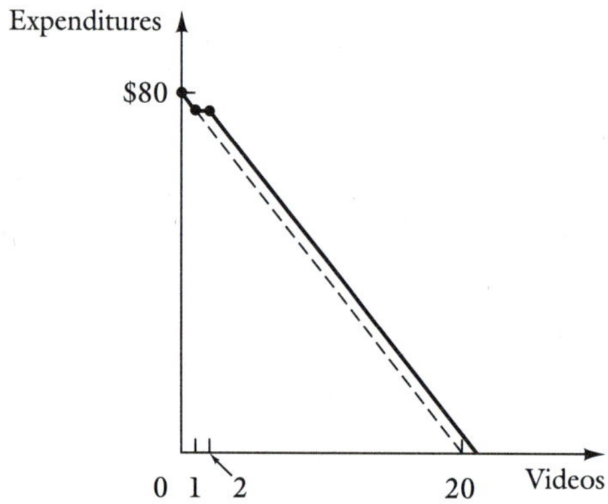

4.7

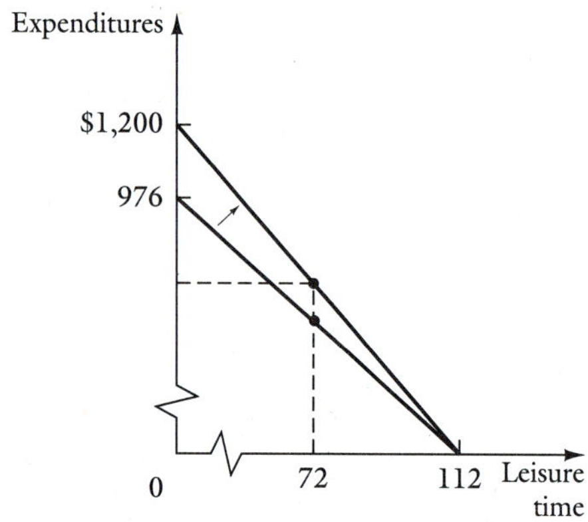

4.8 \$1,538 + 40×10 = \$1,938; \$1,538/40 = \$38.45 per hour.

4.9 The wage rate paid to women relative to men for the same task has risen throughout the last 20 years. As women's wages have increased, the cost of one additional hour of leisure has also increased. This creates an incentive for women to enter the job market.

PRICE THEORY PROBLEMS

1.

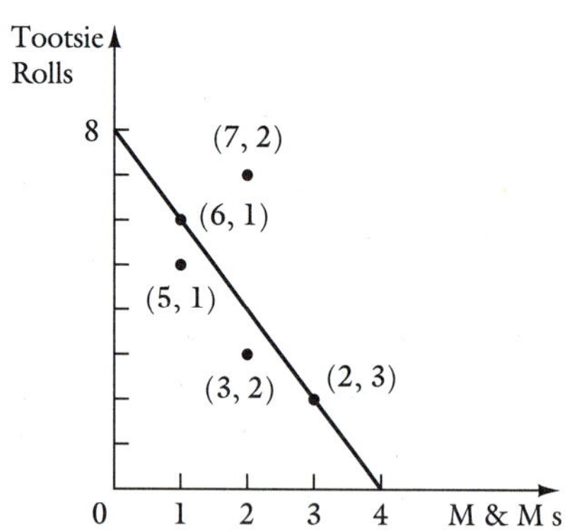

2. a. $P = 10 - \frac{1}{2}T$ (using $80 = 8P + 4T$)

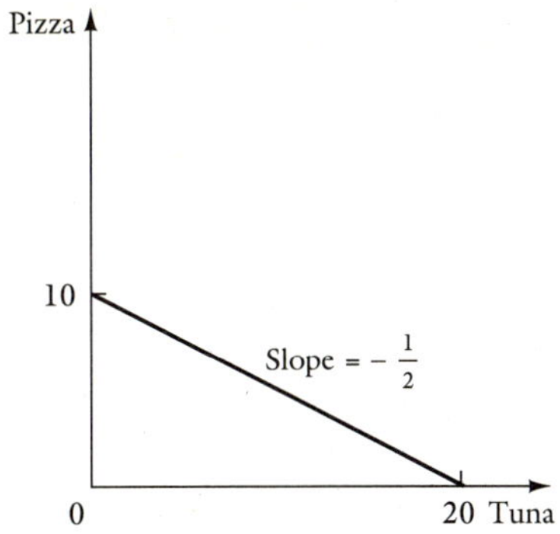

b. 1 pizza is equal to 2 tuna salad sandwiches. The slope of the budget line equals $-\frac{1}{2}$.

c. You could buy 10 pizzas or 20 tuna salad sandwiches.

3. a. False.

b. True.

c. True.

4. (a) and (b)

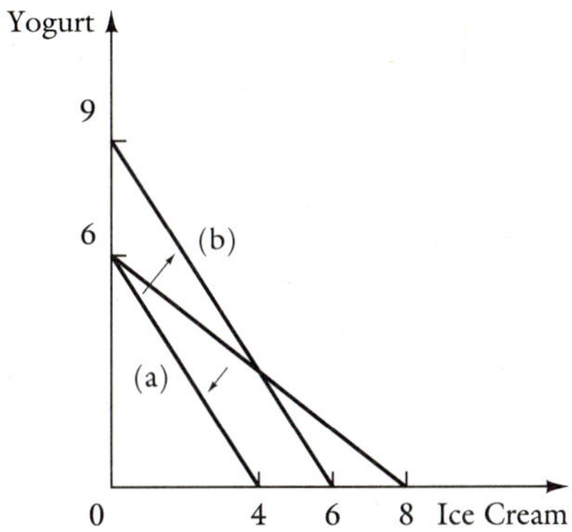

c. No, some bundles in your original set are below the new budget line.

5.

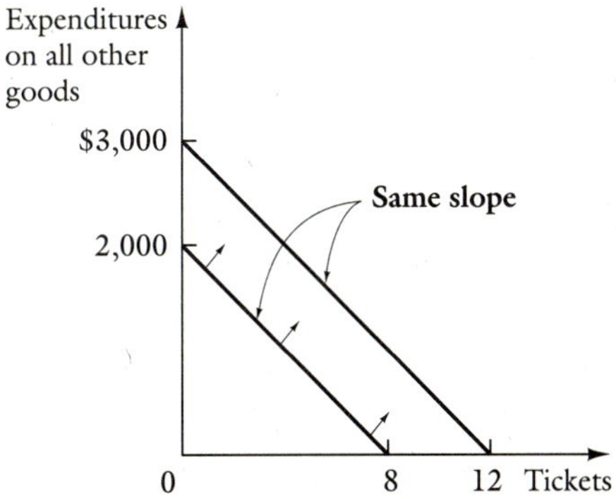

Slope equals −250.

6.

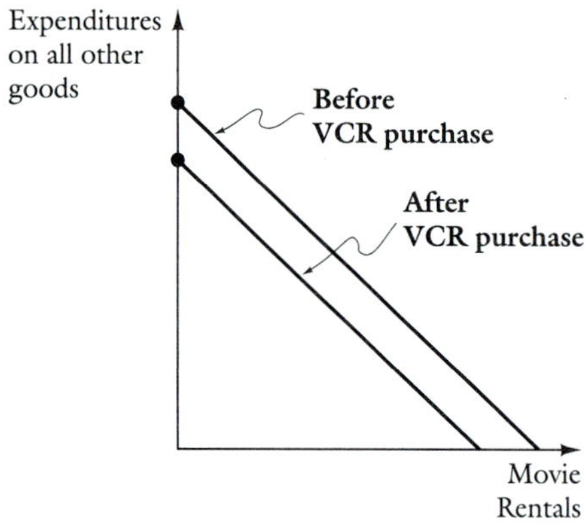

7.

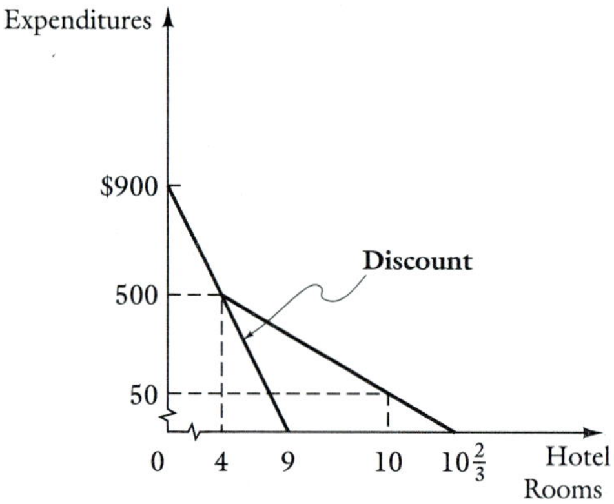

8.

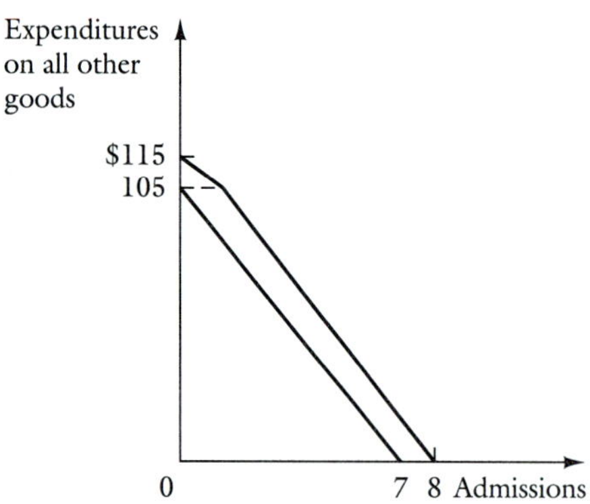

9. a. $60,000
   b. 27,000/15 = 1,800 hours
   c. 20 × 1,800 = $36,000

d.

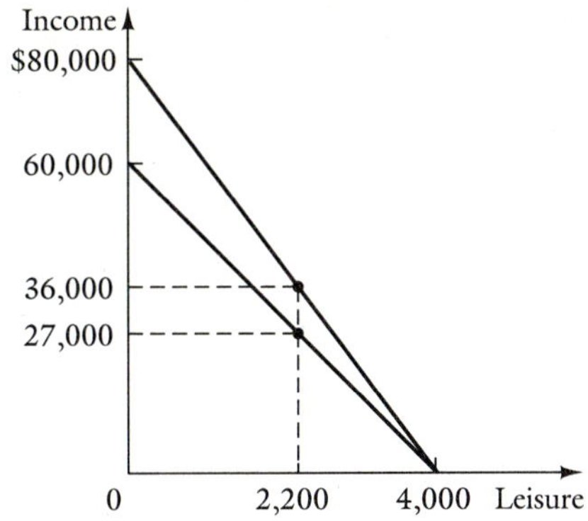

10.

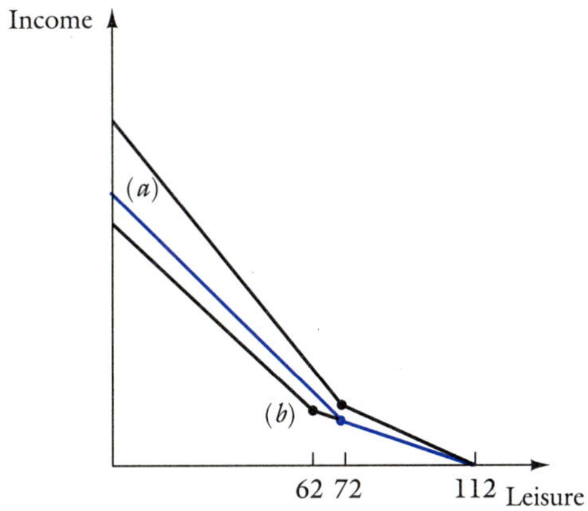

11. $T_{total} = T_{work} + T_{leisure} + T_{household}$

12. a.

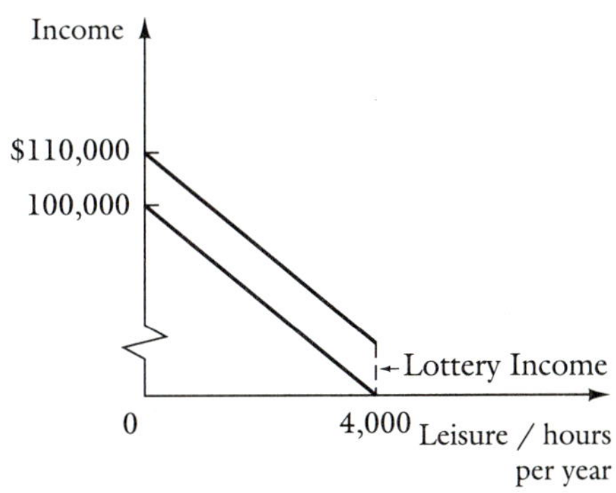

b. You have less income.

Chapter 5

LEARNING EXERCISES

5.1 Bundle *E* is preferred to bundle *A;* bundle *C* is preferred to bundle *B;* we don't know the relationship between bundle *D* and bundle *C.*

5.2

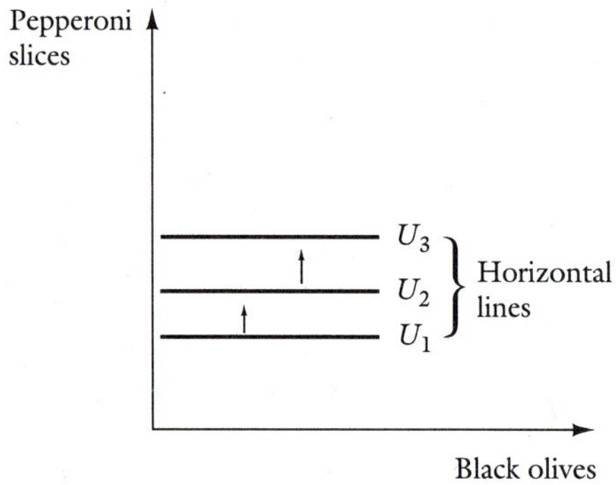

5.3 No, an intersection point will violate the assumptions of nonsatiation and transitivity.

5.4 No, completeness, nonsatiation, and transitivity apply to famous people, too. These assumptions don't make famous people different.

5.5

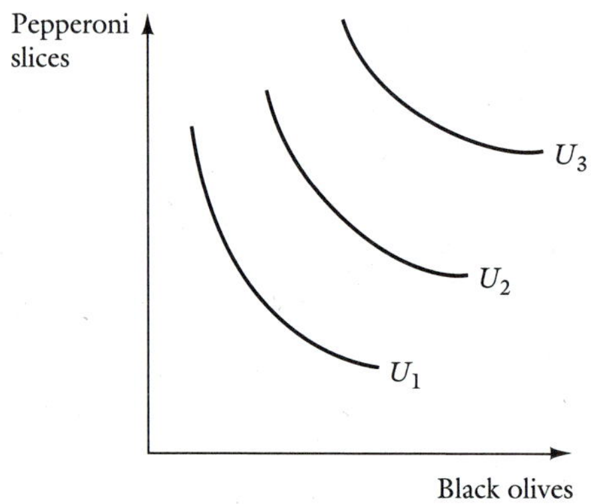

5.6

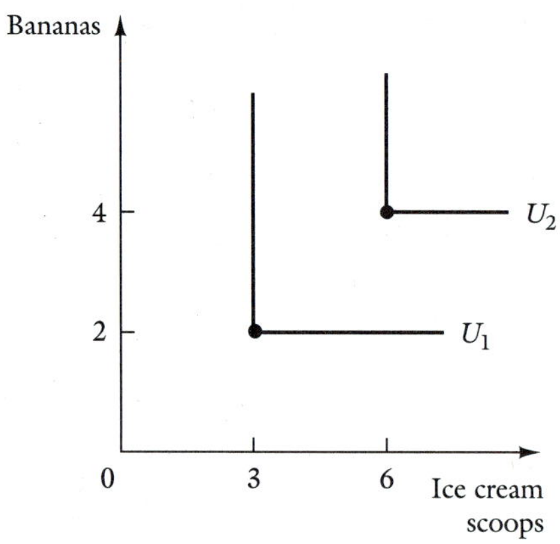

5.7 No, as long as the budget line is straight.

5.8 You have not maximized by selecting this bundle because bundle *B* offers more satisfaction.

5.9 The optimal bundle may lie anywhere on the budget line.

5.10 This is another kink in the full income constraint after 8 hours of overtime. The slope of the full income constraint increases after this point.

5.11

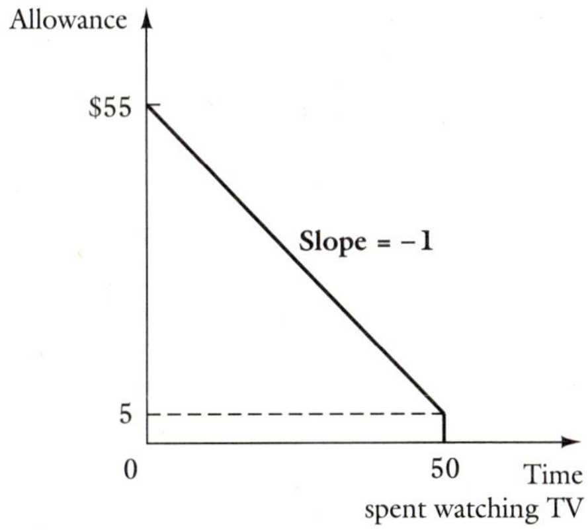

PRICE THEORY PROBLEMS

1. a. Consistent if the consumer is indifferent; otherwise, inconsistent.
   b. Generally inconsistent. It implies that there are no substitutes.
   c. Consistent, but physically impossible.
   d. Consistent. The American Express card is a perfect complement to travel away from home.
2. Additional units of this good do not increase satisfaction. Yes.
3. a. Usually perfect complements.
   b. Substitutes.
   c. Perfect substitutes in exchange at a ratio of 5 nickels to 1 quarter.
   d. Complements.
   e. Substitutes.
   f. Complements.

4.

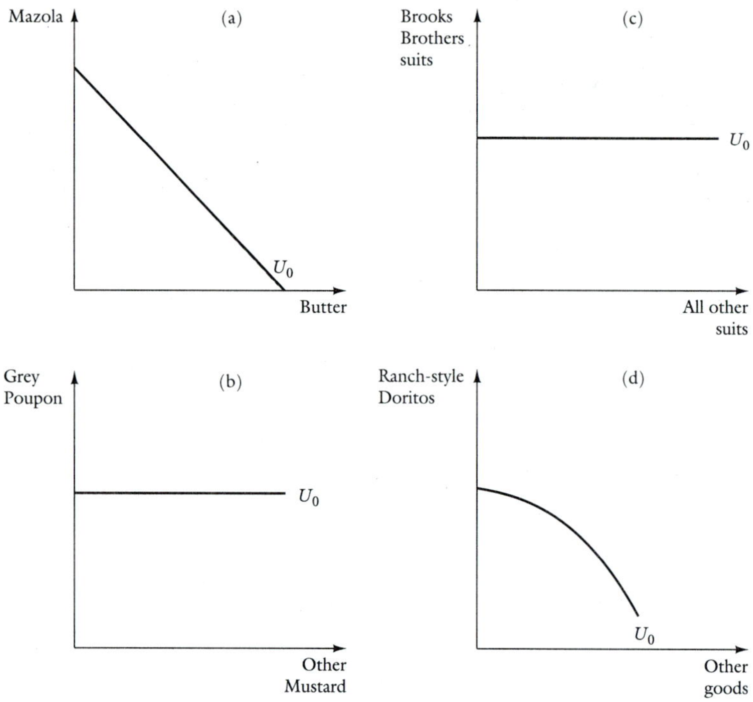
Mazola
(a)
U_0
Butter
Brooks Brothers suits
(c)
U_0
All other suits
Grey Poupon
(b)
U_0
Other Mustard
Ranch-style Doritos
(d)
U_0
Other goods

5.

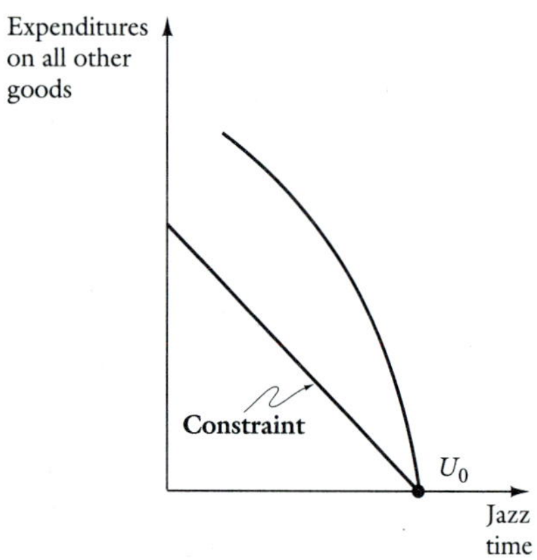
Expenditures on all other goods
Constraint
U_0
Jazz time

6. a.

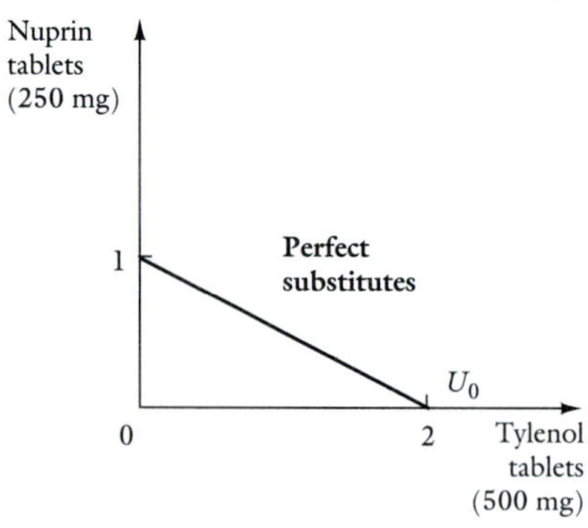
Nuprin tablets (250 mg)
1
Perfect substitutes
U_0
0
2
Tylenol tablets (500 mg)

b. The MRS is 1 to ½ in terms of tablets.

7. 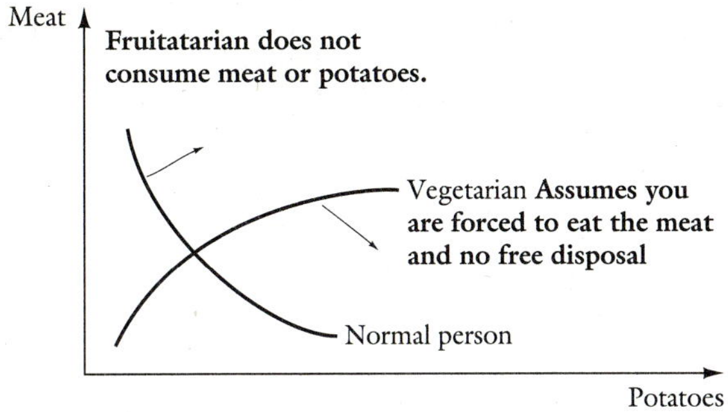

8. a. She likes milk better than root beer.
   b. We can't determine the relationship here.
9. (Leisure, work, expenditures); (50, 50, \$480); (30, 40, \$1,000); (20, 60, \$1,000).
10. a. True, as long as they face the same relative prices.
    b. True.
11. For you, $MRS_{corn,dinners} = P_{corn}/P_{dinners}$. For your sister, $MRS_{corn,dinners} > P_{corn}/P_{dinners}$ at your current bundle.
12. $MRS_{cotton,cotton\text{-}polyester} > P_{cotton}/P_{cotton\text{-}polyester}$.
13. a. 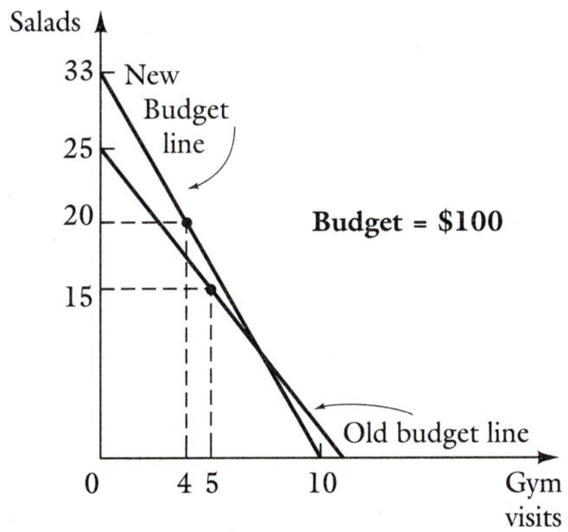

    b. We cannot say if you are better off.
14. a. Yes.

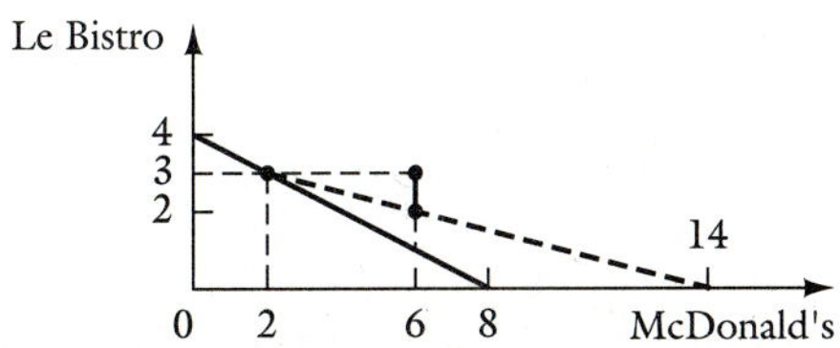

b. You must change your consumption unless these goods are perfect complements.

15.

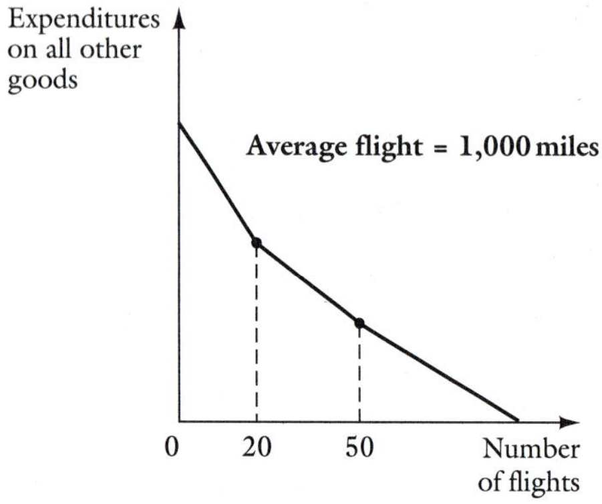

16.

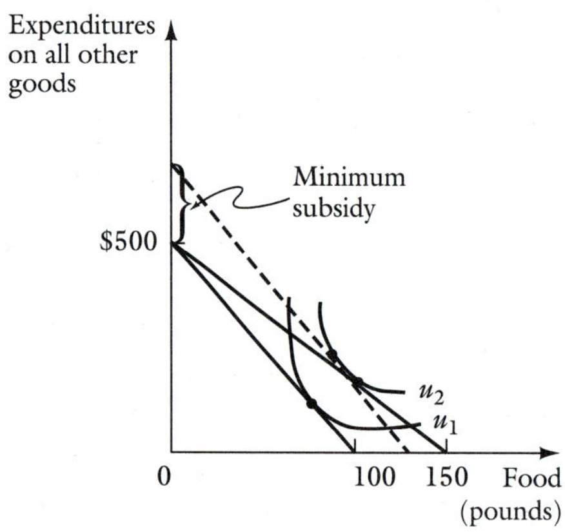

17. American workers are choosing more leisure at the optimal solution. The income effect overcomes the substitution effect.

18. a.

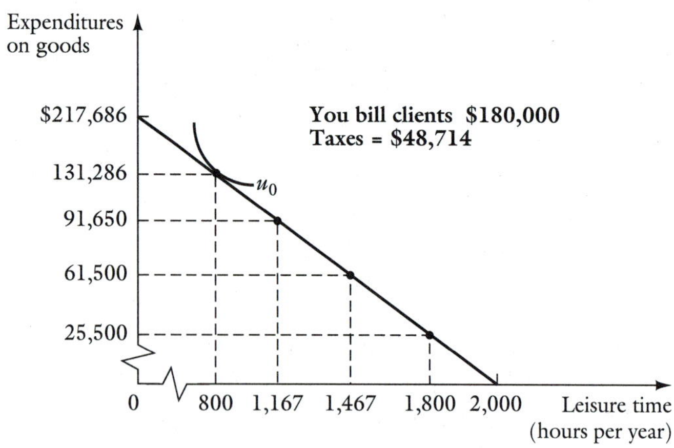

b. Taxes = $48,714; Expenditures = $131,286.

CHAPTER 6

LEARNING EXERCISES

6.1

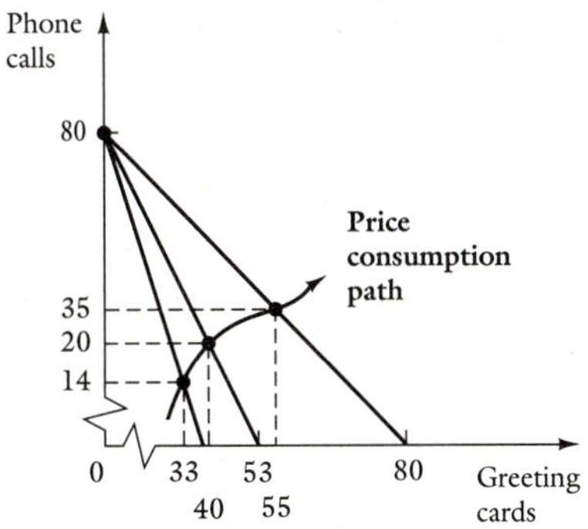

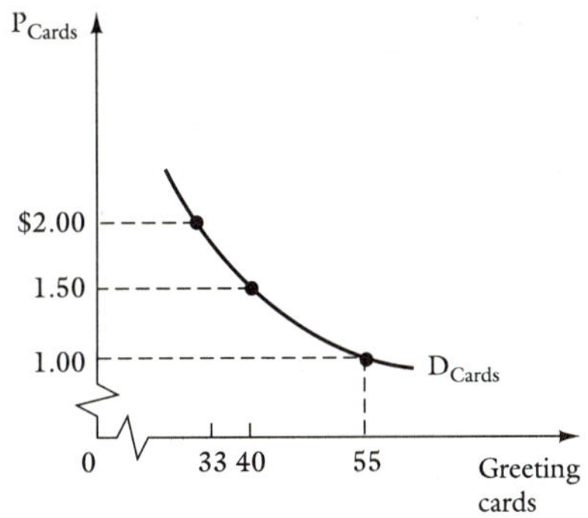

6.2 This violates the nonsatiation assumption.

6.3 12 percent.

6.4 1.3

6.5 Overseas, because of the high fixed cost of relocating managers.

6.6

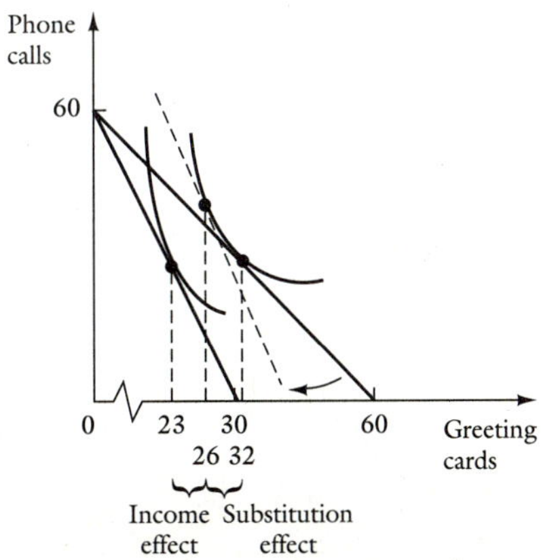

6.7 Demand for crackers increases by 30 percent; demand for butter decreases by 6 percent.

6.8 Companies located overseas—the Bahamas, Mexico, Hong Kong—because they could sell boats without paying the tax.

6.9

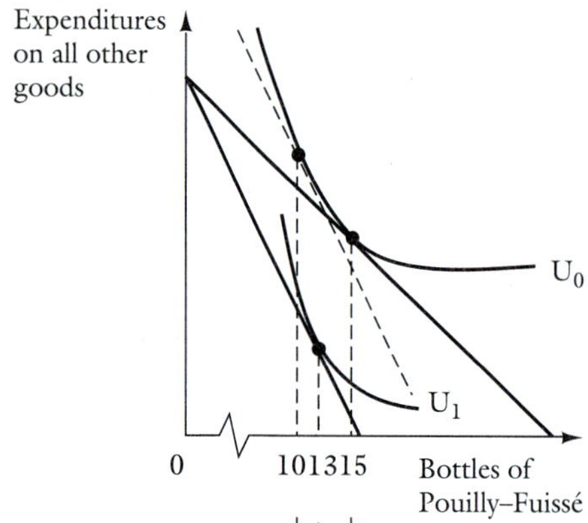

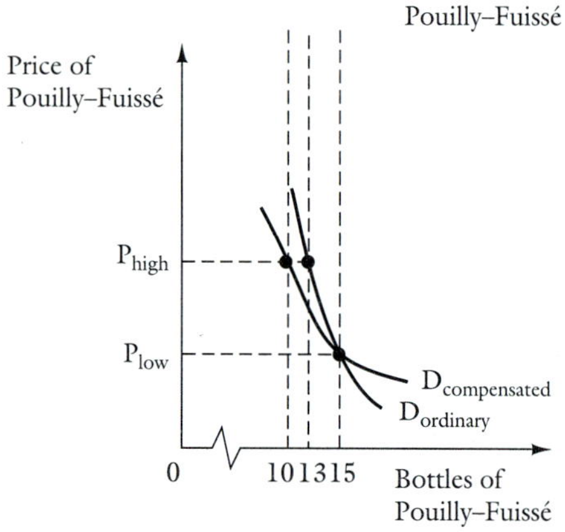

6.10 Positively sloped.

6.11 $E = 1.22$; $L = 1.10$. You are better off because $L < E$.

PRICE THEORY PROBLEMS

1. (a) and (b)

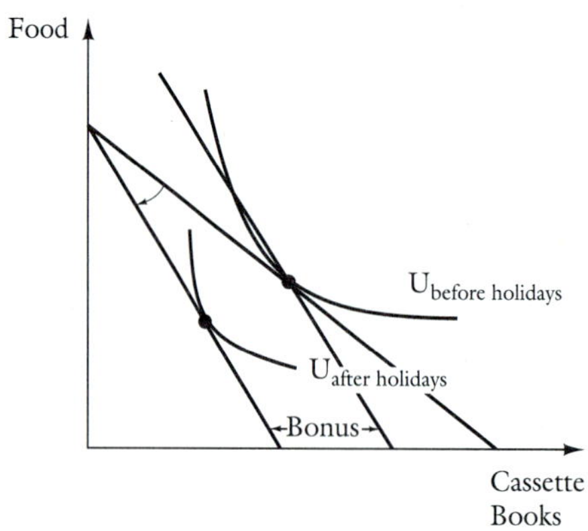

2. a. True.
   b. True.
   c. It is straight until the individual substitutes the other good in consumption.
3. This is neither true nor false but depends on how inferior the good is.
4. a. The shipping cost lowers the relative price of high-quality French wine to U.S. consumers.
   b. The fixed cost of registering high-quality diamonds is relatively lower for expensive diamonds.
5. Changes in real income can be measured using the current bundle or the past bundle. Using the past bundle, the 10-percent increase in income just compensates you for the change in food prices, so you are no better off. Because we don't know the current bundle, we can't say whether you are now better off or worse off.
6. Food stamps create an increase in demand for food via the income effect. Households that do not receive food stamps face higher food prices and thus reduce their consumption of food.
7. Share equals 80 percent; income elasticity equals 1.05.
8.

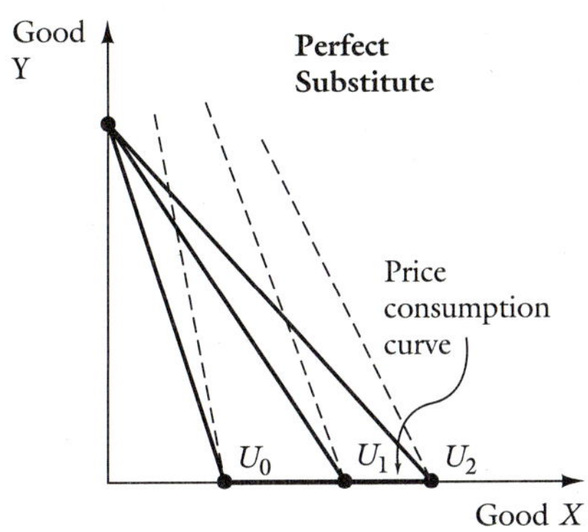

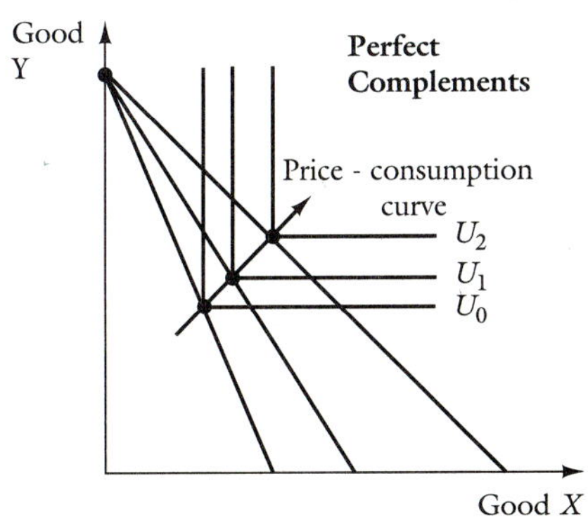

9. a. Negative.
   b. Positive.
   c. Positive.

d. Negative.
e. Negative.
f. Positive.

10. Families would not receive welfare payments after earning \$300 under System 2 and \$100 under System 3. The greatest incentive for work is provided under System 1.

11. If there are no administrative costs, you have the same income as before the tax. Administrative costs impose a net tax burden on consumers, so they cannot all have the same income as before.

12. a. $L = 1.24$; $E = 1.25$.
b. Better off.

13. a. $160X_1 + 50X_2 = 2{,}400$.
b. $L = 1.24$; $E = 1.20$.
c. Cannot say if you are worse off.

Chapter 7

LEARNING EXERCISES

7.1 Find Q such that $MR(Q) = MC(Q)$. $Q = 150$.

7.2 The value of a spouse's time has risen in the market relative to the price of child-care services.

7.3 If the individual chooses to work harder than the other team members, she is subsidizing the other members.

7.4 An increase in fines would reduce cheating if monitoring efforts remained the same. A decrease in tax rates lowers the return to cheating and thus is expected to reduce cheating.

7.5 Decrease.

7.6 The investment behavior would be different because Mr. Paul would absorb all of the losses. No deposit insurance would encourage more monitoring by depositors.

7.7 The builder will not reveal the problem.

7.8 Moral hazard: Bank insurance, wills, and fire insurance.

Adverse selection: Employee hiring, contracts, and loans.

7.9 Your investment in materials is a sunk cost, but your friend's offer lowers your *ex ante* computed return.

7.10 Better Business Bureaus will invest more time in monitoring their members, which will cost more.

PRICE THEORY PROBLEMS

1. It is costly to determine the piecework in joint production.
2. False. Proxy fights are a mechanism of transferring ownership that lets shareholders, not managers, decide the fate of the company.
3. The cost of search and negotiating.
4. Row 2: \$200, \$270; row 3: \$100, \$100; row 4: \$100, \$30; row 5: \$100; row 6: \$80; row 7: \$700, \$100; row 8: \$700; row 9: \$900, \$200.
5. $MR(Q) = \$1{,}000$, so $MR(Q) = MC(Q)$ at $Q = 475$.
6. 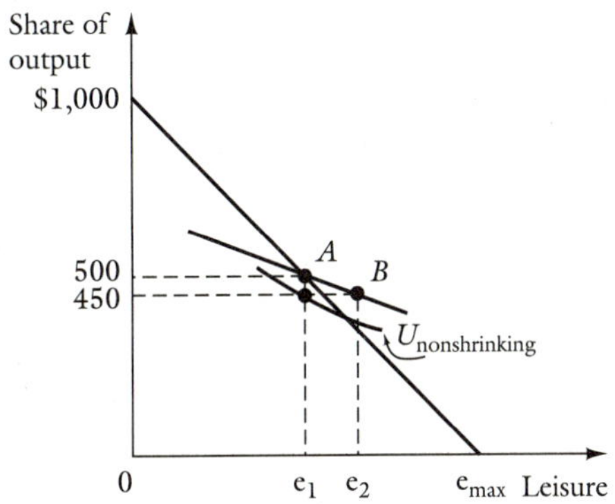

   They receive less satisfaction.

7. Shirking is always detected, but the penalty determines whether it is reduced.
8. If corporations tried to audit their own books, shareholders would be concerned about opportunistic behavior. Large corporations choose large accounting firms in part because these firms will receive only a small amount of total revenue from the large corporation, which makes bribery more difficult.
9. Managers who make specific investments in a corporation may see the value of these investments fall to zero if they are fired after a takeover. To convince managers to make such investments, companies must offer compensation to managers who are fired.
10. Managers will have a more difficult time hiring and firing employees. If there are a large number of employees, the profit-maximizing goal is likely to be the consensus choice. If the shares can be sold to outsiders, managers have more freedom to reallocate resources because those who don't like the choices can sell out to others who do.

11. a. Moral hazard.
    b. Moral hazard.
    c. Adverse selection.
    d. Adverse selection and moral hazard.
    e. Adverse selection.
    f. Moral hazard.
    g. Adverse selection.
12. a. Specific.
    b. Nonspecific.
    c. Partly specific.
    d. Nonspecific.
    e. Specific.
    f. Specific.
    g. Nonspecific.
13. Deductibles help to reduce the costs imposed by moral hazard. If a law eliminated deductibles, then insurance premiums would increase, but the effect on claims would depend on whether any other mechanism developed to deter moral hazard problems.
14. Adverse selection; moral hazard. The market price of used cars will increase and the price of returned cars will decrease.

CHAPTER 8

LEARNING EXERCISES

8.1 We can explain why the cassette tape player replaced the eight-track tape player in automobiles in terms of the opportunity costs. It is more costly (in terms of car space and the monetary cost of the tape) to have an eight-track tape player in automobiles. The same explanation applies to the new CDs. Although the CD player generally has better quality than the cassette tape player, it is more expensive and takes up more room.

8.2 a. Wine glasses are fixed and the number of guests invited is variable.

b. Fixed input is the capacity of the hard disk; variable inputs are the programs installed.

c. Number of phone calls is variable and phone lines are fixed.

8.3

$Q = 2K + 3L$

For $Q = 90$

$2K + 3L = 90$

$2K = 90 - 3L$

$K = 45 - 1.5L$

$$\text{MRTS} = \frac{dK}{dL}$$

$$= -1.5 = \frac{\text{MP}_L}{\text{MP}_K}$$

L	K	Q
10	30	90
20	15	90
30	0	90

For $Q = 120$

$2K + 3L = 120$

$2K = 120 - 3L$

$K = 60 - 1.5L$

$$\text{MRTS} = \frac{dK}{dL}$$

$$= -1.5 = \frac{\text{MP}_L}{\text{MP}_K}$$

L	K	Q
10	45	120
20	30	120
30	15	120

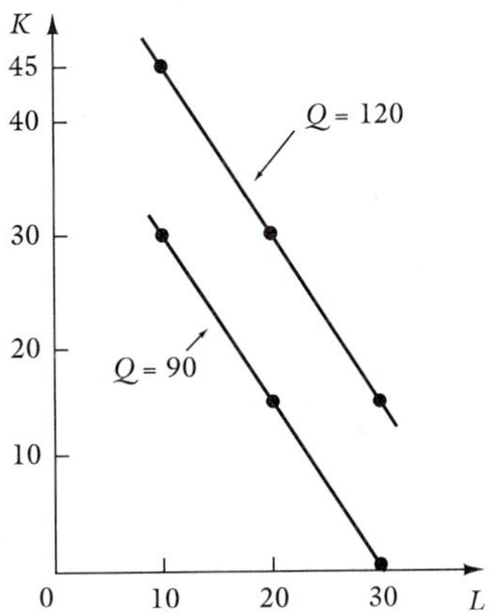

The MRTS values of these two isoquants are exactly the same at all points. In other words, K and L are perfect substitutes. It says that a firm is able to substitute 1 unit of K for 1.5 units of L at any level of output.

8.4 For $L = 4$, $\text{MP}_L = 3/4$ and $\text{AP}_L = 3/2$. For $L = 16$, $\text{MP}_L = 3/8$ and $\text{AP}_L = 3/4$.

8.5

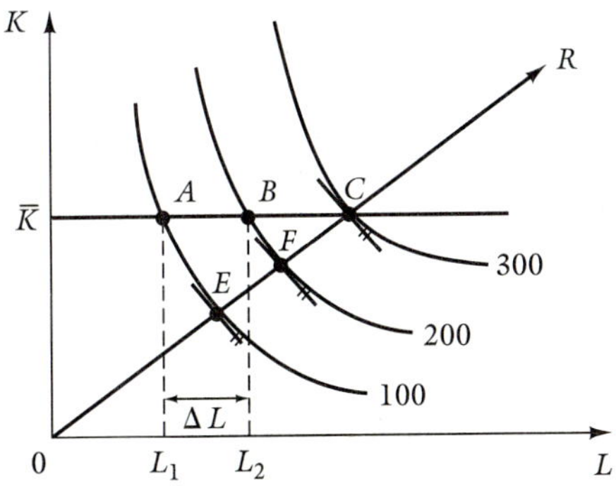

Assuming a constant-returns-to-scale technology, the slopes at points *E, F* and *C* are the same. In contrast, the slopes at points *A, B* and *C* are different. Moving from *A* to *B*, *K* is held constant while *L* rises. The slope is steeper at point *A* than at point *B*. It means that MRTS falls as more and more of *L* is employed for a fixed capital stock. Note that with constant returns to scale, $MP_L = F(KL)$, so, holding *K* constant, MP_L falls as *L* rises. Or equivalently, MP_K rises as *L* rises. By the same token, we can show that holding *L* constant, MP_K falls as *K* rises.

8.6 For $K = 8$ and $L = 8$, $MP_K = ½$ and $MP_L = ½$, so MRTS = 1. For $K = 1$ and $L = 8$, $MP_K = \sqrt{2}$ and $MP_L = 1/(4\sqrt{2})$, so MRTS = ⅛. These points do not lie on the same isoquant because they generate different output rates.

8.7 Although the technologies used by the French and British engineers are different—the French is more capital-intensive while British is more labor-intensive—one can expect the marginal product of labor to be equal in these two countries. Assuming a constant-returns-to-scale technology for both sides, factor returns will be equalized if there is free trade between both countries.

8.8 Examples are as follows: Searching for books using an on-line computer network that links all university libraries in the United States and use of E-mail network for office-to-office information exchanges.

PRICE THEORY PROBLEMS

1. Row 2: $L = 7$, $MP_L = 27$; row 3: TP = 170, $AP_L = 21.1$; row 4: TP = 180, $MP_L = 10$.
2. Total product reaches its highest point at MP = 0, but this also implies that MP must start to fall before TP. By the same token, MP must fall before AP because MP intersects AP at its maximum. In effect, MP changes at a much faster rate than AP. Intuitively, we see that even small changes in labor affect MP, whereas it requires a large change to influence AP.

3. a.

Assume $K = 5$

$Q = 5\overline{K} + 4L$

L	TP	MP_L	AP_L
1	29	–	29
2	33	4	16.5
3	37	4	12.3
4	41	4	10.2

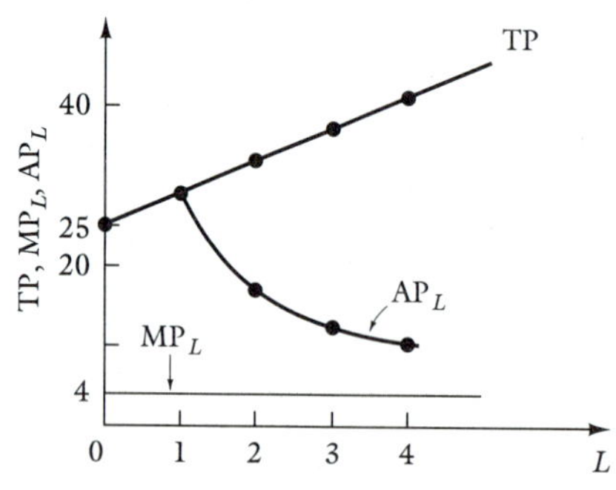

b. $Q = KL^2 \quad \overline{K} = 5$

L	TP	MP_L	AP_L
1	5	–	5
2	20	15	10
3	45	25	15
4	80	35	20
5	125	45	25

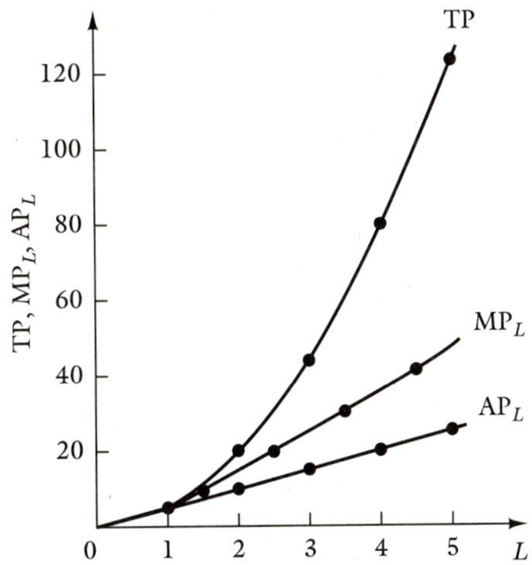

c. $Q = \min\{K,L\} \quad \overline{K} = 5$

L	TP	MP_L	AP_L
1	5	–	5
2	5	0	2.5
3	5	0	1.6
4	5	0	1.2
5	5	0	1
6	6	1	1
7	7	1	1

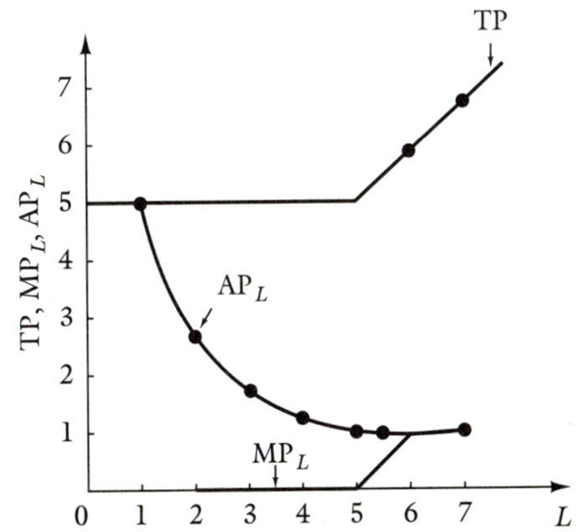

4. In the short run, at least one input is fixed, while in the long run all inputs can be varied. A firm's fixed inputs are fixed in the short run. This is because at least one input, such as capital (e.g., an assembly

line), is too costly to change in the short run. Technically, it is difficult to define the length of time that corresponds to the short run or long run because the length of time required to change the production process varies from firm to firm and from industry to industry. For example, the length of time required to install a new generator for a utility company is much longer than the time required to install a new gas stove in a restaurant.

5. a. The production is a service. The car dealer takes requests for potential buyers and matches them with potential sellers.
   b. The processed pitted apricots are a new commodity, produced using f(pitted apricots, sunshine, labor, capital).
6. a. Decreasing.
   b. Constant.
   c. Constant.
   d. Increasing.
7. Along an isoquant, one can obtain information about all technically possible input combinations of (K, L) which are used to produce a given output rate. In addition, the slope of an isoquant measures the technological substitution possibilities between capital and labor, MRTS. As a firm moves upward and to the left it substitutes capital for labor; this can be caused by an increase in the relative price of labor.
8. For constant or decreasing returns, the marginal products of capital and labor vary inversely with K and L, respectively. For increasing returns, a general answer cannot be determined.

Chapter 9

LEARNING EXERCISES

9.1 (a) Cash: no difference.

(b) Accounts payable: Accounts payable allows firms to delay their current payments to the future. In an economist's view, the present value of a 1-month account payable is \$10,000/1+r, where r is the monthly interest rate, while for an accountant, the value of the account payable is \$10,000.

(c) Marketable securities or long-term debt: In an accountant's statement, the values of marketable securities and long-term debt are based upon the values when these items first enter the balance sheet. Thus, they do not necessarily reflect the current opportunity costs of an asset or a debt.

9.2 Sunk costs: An investment in a dry oil well is a sunk cost because the investment cannot be recovered by subsequent resale. It is not a fixed cost because fixed costs are those a firm pays for regardless of its output level. For a dry well, there is not any output at all. New-car insurance is also a sunk cost. Unless the insurance can be transferred or resold, it is a sunk cost to the insured for a given period of time.

Fixed costs: A concert piano for a symphony orchestra is a fixed cost for the producer because it is an investment that can be recovered from future performances. For example, the piano can be used for other shows besides the concert. In contrast, the set-up cost for a given concert is a sunk cost.

Sunk costs and fixed costs: Monthly bank fees for a checking account are a sunk cost to a customer because the fee can not be recovered by subsequent resale. Fees are also a fixed cost because the customer can withdraw as many checks as he or she wishes in a month as long as he or she pays a certain fixed amount of fees.

9.3 By definition, sunk costs cannot be recovered by subsequent resale and have zero opportunity cost for all decisions that firms may make. If a government purchases a weapons system that has no future resale value, it is a sunk cost with no opportunity costs.

9.4 $\text{ATC} = Q + 10 + 16/Q$

$\text{TC} = \text{ATC} \times Q = Q^2 + 10Q + 16$

$\text{TC} = \text{FC} + \text{TVC}$, so $\text{FC} = 16$ and $\text{TVC} = Q^2 + 10Q$

$\text{AVC} = \text{TVC}/Q = Q + 10$

To find the MC of the sixth unit of output, we calculate TC and MC at each output level in the following table. As it shows, the MC of the sixth unit is $21.

Q	TC	MC
1	27	9
2	40	13
3	55	15
4	72	17
5	91	19
6	112	21

9.5 Given AVC = 20 and $AP_L = 2$, $\text{AVC} = w/AP_L = \$40$.

9.6

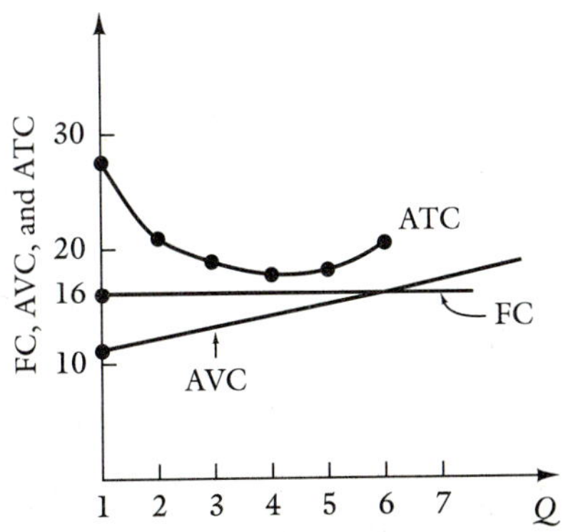

To draw the graph of ATC, AVC, and FC, the following table is used:

Q	ATC	AVC	FC
0	16	0	16
1	27	11	16
2	20	12	16
3	18.3	13	16
4	18	14	16
5	18.2	15	16
6	18.7	16	16

9.7

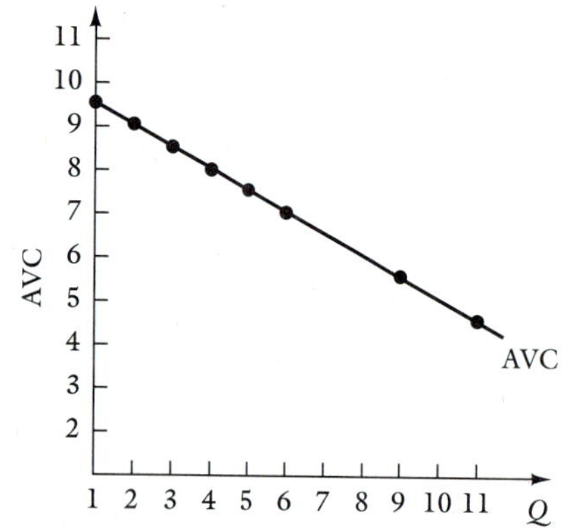

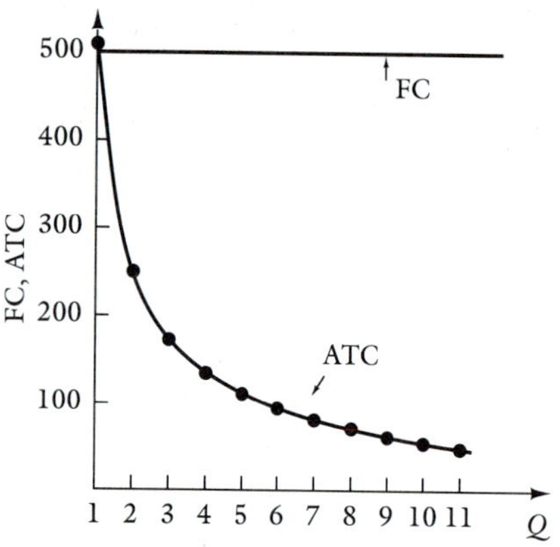

Given $TC = 500 + 10Q - 0.5Q^2$, then $ATC = TC/Q = 500/Q + 10 - 0.5Q$ (nonlinear function), $FC = 500$, $TVC = 10Q - .05Q^2$, and $AVC = TVC/Q = 10 - .05Q$ (a linear function).

Q	AVC	ATC
1	9.5	510
2	9	259
3	8.5	175
4	8	133
5	7.5	105
6	7	90
7	6.5	78
8	6	69
9	5.5	61
10	5	55
11	4.5	50

9.8 Product liability costs are expected to increase because the larger number of units implies that the expected number of defects is greater.

9.9 Given $Q = K^{1/2}L^{1/2}$, the least-cost combination of K and L for a given output level, 100, solves the first-order conditions: MRTS = w/r, where w = \$10 and r = \$20. Solving for the marginal product gives L = 100 and K = 25. If $w = r$ = \$20, then the least-cost combination is L = K = 100.

9.10 If K is fixed, we are along an SR expansion path.

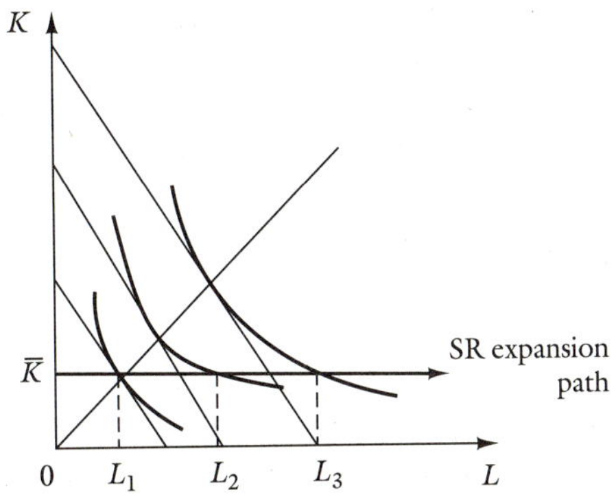

9.11 As the two products become better substitutes in production, the isoquant becomes more linear. In the limiting case of perfect substitutes, an increase in the price of silver causes firms to substitute completely to photopolymers.

9.12 This is possible only if the LATC is a constant; otherwise the SRTC curves do not necessarily touch the LATC at its lowest point. By definition, the LRTC is a collection of SRTCs. Each point (each output level) along the LRTC represents the minimum cost of producing that output and does not necessarily correspond to the minimum point of every SRTC. For example, LATC can be decreasing or increasing while SRTC can be increasing or decreasing.

9.13

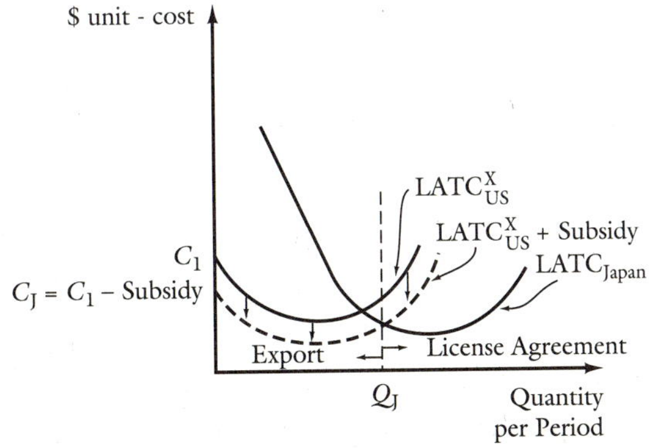

A per unit subsidy to U.S. beer exports will shift down the $LATC_{US}$ by that amount. This will increase exports. Similarly, a per unit increase in Japanese tariffs will shift up the $LATC_{US}$ and it can offset the effects of a U.S. subsidy when the unit tariff rate equals the subsidy.

9.14 The cost-minimizing allocation of output can be solved by equalizing the MCs in two plants: $MC_N = MC_O$, where $MC_N = 15 = 2Q_N$, $MC_O = 5 + 8Q_O$, and $Q_O + Q_N = 100$, so $Q_O = 35$ and $Q_N = 65$.

PRICE THEORY PROBLEMS

1. By keeping an old machine idle, the firm loses the opportunity cost from selling the machine. These costs include the money income from resale and its potential interest receipts during the time the machine is idle. In addition, the machine takes up space that can be used by the firm.
2. The opportunity costs of that waiting time are most likely zero in this case. This is because during the assembly process, each person assembles part of the product, and this person cannot be assigned to any other work. Because there is no alternative use of this labor when the worker is waiting on the assembly line, his or her opportunity costs are zero. This conclusion does not depend on whether the employee's wage is paid by hours or paid by pieces; it depends on the structure of the production process.
3.

Units	Total cost	Fixed cost	Variable cost	ATC	AVC	AFC	MC
0	\$400						
1	A	B	C	D	E	F	\$40
2	G	H	\$100	I	J	K	L
3	M	N	\$200	O	P	Q	R
4	\$750	S	T	U	V	W	X

A = 440	G = 500	M = 600	S = 400
B = 400	H = 400	N = 400	T = 350
C = 40	I = 250	O = 200	U = 187.5
D = 440	J = 50	P = 66.7	V = 87.5
E = 40	K = 200	Q = 133	W = 100
F = 400	L = 60	R = 100	X = 150

4. a.

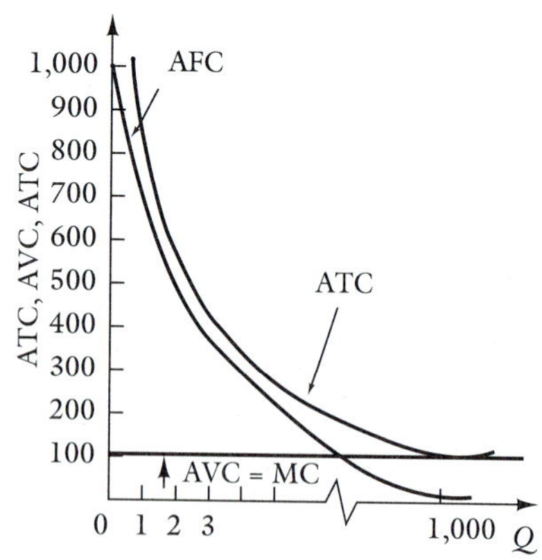

Q/m	MC	FC	AVC	AFC	ATC
0	0	1,000	O	1,000	1,000
1	100	1,000	100	1,000	1,100
2	100	1,000	100	500	600
3	100	1,000	100	333	433
4	100	1,000	100	250	350
5	100	1,000	100	166	266
6	100	1,000	100	142	242
...	...	...	...	...	...
10	100	1,000	100	10	110
...	...	...	...	...	...
100	100	1,000	100	10	110
...	...	...	...	...	...
1,000	100	1,000	100	1	101
...	...	...	...	...	...

b. No, there is no output level that minimizes the average total cost of production. The output rate at which the ATC reaches its minimum point is when MC = ATC, but, in this example, ATC will never intersect MC.

5. Tax = \$100/year. The lump-sum tax will not change the shape of the short-run AVC curve or the shape of the short-run MC curve. This is because the lump-sum tax works like a one-time increase in fixed costs. It can only shift up the ATC and AFC curves. A unit tax, however, will cause AVC and MC curves to shift up.

6. False. The short-run MC curve is not necessarily monotonically increasing because at the earlier stages of production, the marginal product of labor might increase. Hence, the short-run MC curve could fall initially and increase later on as the benefits of the division of labor from hiring the last person outweigh his or her MP_L.

7.

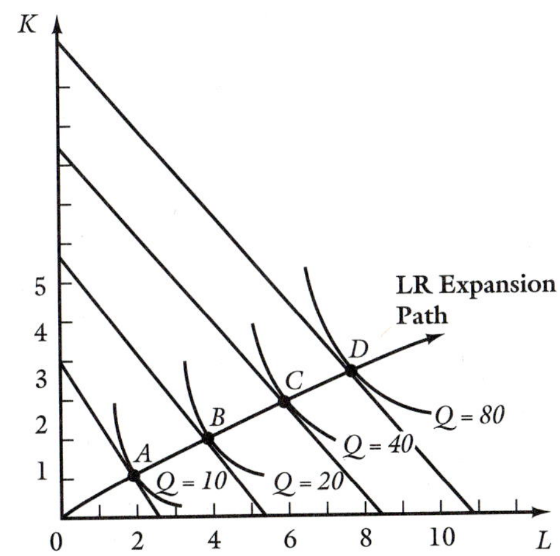

$Q = F(K, L = 2K)$

8. The statement is false because the small-scale gardening service will not disappear. Instead, it can operate side by side with the large-scale firm. The reason is that economies of scale prevail only when the firm produces at a higher level of output. Because many gardens are so small, it might not be profitable (because of higher cost) for the large firm to operate at a lower level of output. Alternatively, one can consider the services they provide to be different. For example, the large gardening firms provide services to universities while the small firms provide services to households.
9. In addition to the production information, the manager needs to know the following information: wage rate of the workers and rental rate of the capital.
10. Given $Q = 500K^{.5}L^{.5}$, $w = \$10$ and $r = \$20$.
    a. $Q = 10{,}000$; then the optimal solution is $K = 5$ and $L = 20$.
    b. If $Q = 25{,}000$ is the profit-maximizing solution, then $K = 12.5$ and $L = 50$.
    c. Given that $K = 10$, the cost-minimizing amount of labor the firm will hire to produce output $Q = 25{,}000$ is $L = 250$.
11. ATC = $1{,}000/Q + 10Q - .2C_Q$, where C_Q is the learning effect on ATC.
    a. There is a positive learning effect for this firm because cumulative output will reduce the firm's ATC by $0.2C_Q$.
    b. When there is no learning effect, ATC = $1{,}000/Q + 10Q$; TC = $10Q^2 + 1{,}000Q$; MC = $20Q$, so we find the minimum point of ATC by solving ATC = MC, which gives $Q = 10$.
    c. Given $C_Q = 200 + Q$, then ATC = $1{,}000/Q + 9.8Q - 40$; TC = $1{,}000 + 9.8Q^2 - 40Q$; MC = $19.6Q - 80$, so using ATC = MC, we have $9.8Q^2 - 40Q - 1{,}000 = 0$, which is a quadratic equation. The per unit output rate is approximately 2 times higher with the learning effect than without it.
12. Given that $MC_1 = \$10$ and $MC_2 = MC_3 = \$8$ for the current output level of Q, the firm is not minimizing cost. To minimize costs, the firm should solve $MC_1 = MC_2 = MC_3$. Thus, plants 2 and 3 should increase their output rates. This rule applies regardless of whether all sales of the firm occur at plant 1. The only difference is that transportation cost may add to the marginal cost of production at plants 1 and 2.
13. Pizza stores will not allow consumers to switch toppings because they have preset proportions to achieve a specific unit cost. If customers change these proportions, they are likely to increase the firm's unit costs. The pizza firm allows choice for a higher price, but not at the price paid for the specials.

14. 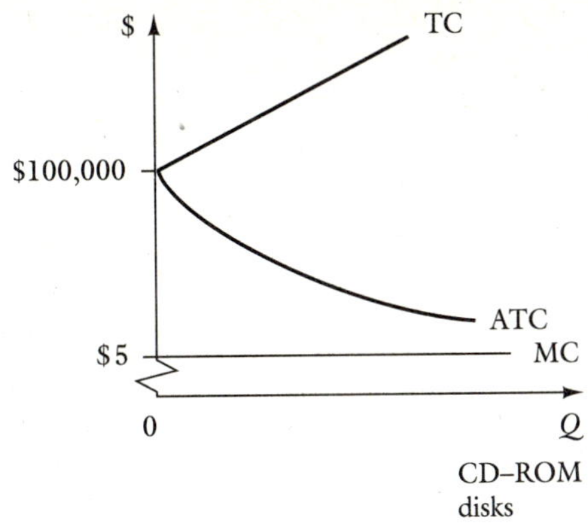

Fixed costs are \$100,000 and variable costs are \$5 per CD-ROM disk. Thus, TC = 100,000 + 5Q; ATC = 100,000/Q + 5; and MC = 5.

Chapter 10

LEARNING EXERCISES

10.1 The cross-price elasticity of demand between two firms that produce goods that are perfect substitutes is equal to infinity.

10.2 a. −10

b. 20 percent

c. −.1

10.3 It produces at MR = MC, since for a perfectly competitive firm P = MR, 30 = 10 + 2Q or Q^* = 10.

10.4 When P < \$35.

Q	AVC
0	0
1	50
2	40
3	35
4	40
5	45

10.5 Self-test question.

10.6 It will shift up the MC and AVC curves of a typical firm. In the short run, a typical firm's supply curve will shift to the left.

10.7 It becomes more elastic.

10.8 a. Fixed cost equals $142,350.

b. Annual profits are ($4 – $3) × 600 × 365 = $219,000.

c. $ATC_{500} = AVC_{500} + FC/500 = \$2.25 + \$.78 = \$3.03$.

10.9 If demand decreases, the number of firms in the industry decreases to reduce total output. The output rate of all remaining firms stays the same.

10.10 No change with constant-factor-cost industries; entry price increases (decreases) with increasing-or-decreasing-factor-cost industries, with just the reverse for exit prices.

10.11 The argument is the same as with Figure 10.14 except that both the firm and consumer can gain (not lose) if one more unit is produced.

10.12 No.

10.13 Not likely, unless instructors can benefit in some way by assigning a lower-cost textbook to students.

PRICE THEORY PROBLEMS

1. When firms shut down in the short run they must pay the fixed cost, which equals their losses. Thus, there is no reason to believe that firms on average earn positive profits.
2. True. In a perfectly competitive industry, there is a free entry and exit.
3. –10; –5
4. Setting $P = MC$ gives $Q = 16$. To find out whether the firm will shut down, we need to know the minimum point of AVC. Using MC = AVC at the minimum of the AVC we can solve for the minimum point of AVC: $Q_{min} = 20$; AVC = $324. In the short run, firms will shut down because $P <$ AVC. The minimum market price at which the firm will operate is the minimum point of AVC, which is $324. The minimum output that will keep firms in operation in the short run is $Q_{min} = 20$.
5. a. In a perfectly competitive market, a trade embargo on Japanese imports (55 percent share) will not affect a domestic firm's MC and AC curves. However, it will raise the market price in the short run as fewer Japanese computers are available in the market. As a result, the existing firms will have positive economic profits. Free entry will assure that the price falls to its previous level in the long run as other companies replace the Japanese imports.

   b. A decrease in input prices shifts down the MC and AC curves. With lower costs, existing firms will produce more and receive positive economic profits in the short run. In the long run, as new firms are attracted into the industry, the market price falls until the zero-economic-profits condition holds.

c. A new software program will increase the incentive for buying IBM-compatible computers. An increase in demand raises the market price. As a result, the existing firms in this industry will enjoy positive economic profits. However, in the long run, other brand name computers, such as Apple Macintosh, will offer similar software. The availability of substitutes then reduces the price of IBM-compatible computers.

6. Assuming a constant-cost industry, an increase in population overnight shifts the demand curve to the right, leaving each firm's MC and AC curves unchanged. Price increases along the short-run supply curve and economic profits are positive. As new firms enter, the short-run supply curve shifts to the right until the economic profits are zero. In a constant-cost industry, price returns to its original level.

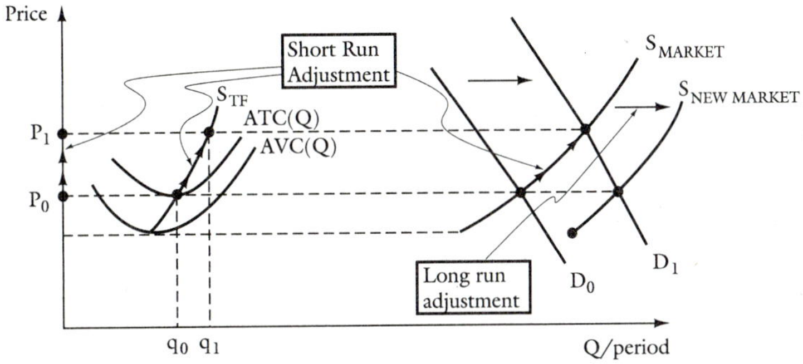

7. In the long run, P = LATC and MC = LATC. Find LRMC from TC (TC = LATC × Q): LRMC = $\Delta TC/\Delta Q = 2Q + 12$ or $1{,}000{,}000/Q + Q + 12 = 2Q + 12$, which can be used to solve for the long-run output level of a typical firm: $Q_{LR} = 1{,}000$; $P_{LR} = \$2{,}012$. With 50 manufacturers of cellular phones, the market output is $50Q$ or 50,000 units.

8. True, because it will still produce at the lowest point of its AC curve in the long run. Industry output decreases because there are fewer firms.

9. If the industry is in long-run equilibrium, then the introduction of a license fee causes some firms to shut down, which reduces industry output and raises market price. Some firms shutdown because the higher price expands output of the typical firm, but decreases output sold in the market.

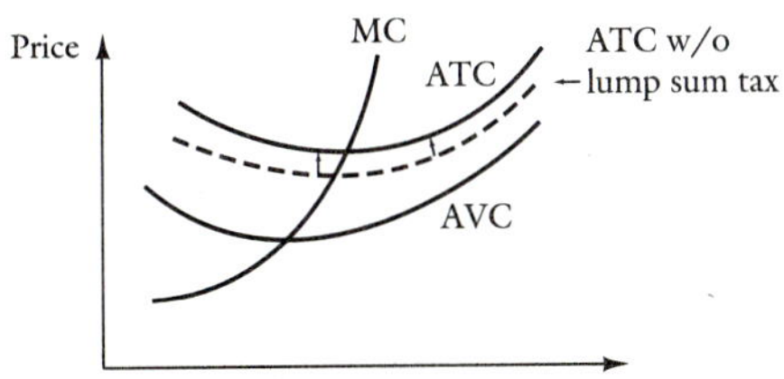

The lump-sum tax causes the ATC curve to shift up, which increases the breakeven price for a typical firm.

10. a. Set P = MC to solve: $Q_{mkt} = 50$; $P = \$100$.
    b. Each firm sells 10 packages of business cards.
    c. $P_{new} = \$110$; $Q_{new} = 100 - 0.5(110) = 45$ cards.
    d. The deadweight loss is equal to $[10 \times (50 - 45)]/2 = \$25$. The loss is from consumers' surplus.
11. a. In long-run equilibrium, $P = \text{LATC}_{min}$ and $\text{LATC}_{min} = \text{MC}$, which implies $Q_{min} = 4$, so each firm produces 4 units; $P = \text{LATC}_{min} = \$5$.
    b. At $P = \$5$, $Q_{market} = 40$, so the total market surplus equals consumers' plus producers' surplus. Producers' surplus is zero and consumers' surplus equals the area under the market demand curve above price, so total market surplus equals $1,600.
    c. Without entry, $P = \$10$ and $Q_{market} = 80$. After entry there are 20 firms.
12. Given the cost equations, we have

$$\text{LATC}_H = F_H/Q_H + \beta_H Q_H \text{ and } \text{LMC}_H = 2\beta_H Q_H$$

$$\text{LATC}_L = F_L/Q_L + \beta_L Q_L \text{ and } \text{LMC}_L = 2\beta_L Q_L$$

Solve for Q_H and Q_C as functions of P^*: $Q_H = P^*/2\beta_H$ and $Q_C = P^*/2\beta_L$, which are substituted into the two long-run average cost equations to make each equation a function of P^*. Using these new expressions in equation (10.5) and rearranging terms gives the required result.

CHAPTER 11

LEARNING EXERCISES

11.1

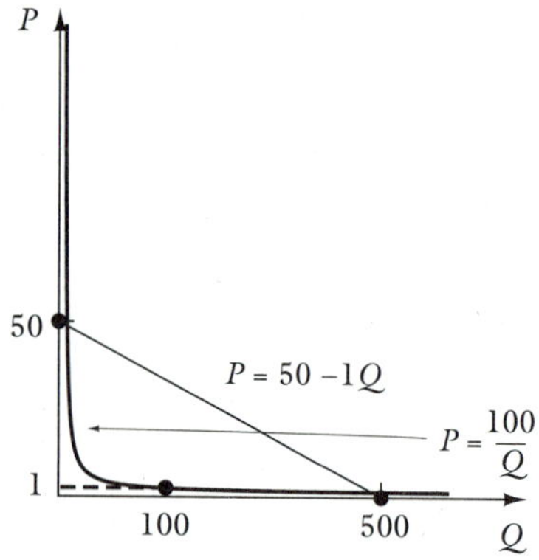

$P = 50 - .1Q$, price falls by \$1; $P = 100/Q$, price falls by 9 cents.

11.2

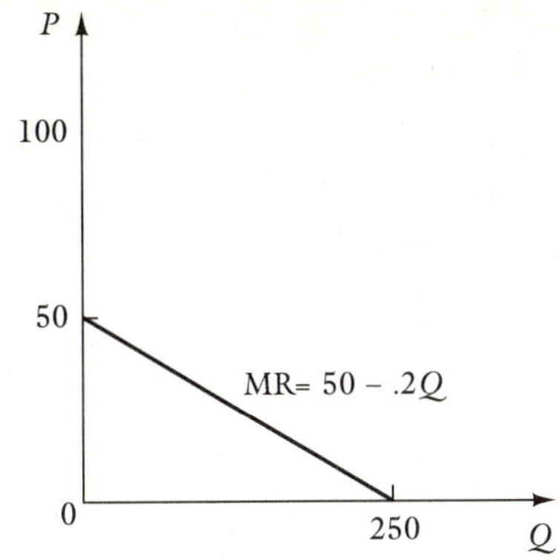

MR = 50 – .2Q; MR = 100.

11.3 MC = 80 + .02Q and MR = 200 – .02Q. MR = MC at Q = 3,000; P = \$170; profits equal –\$20,000 if the firm operates.

11.4 SMC = 60 + .02Q; Q = 3,500; P = \$165; profits equal -\$5,000 if the firm operates, a decrease of \$75,000 per year; tax revenues equal \$70,000.

11.5 Other currencies can become substitutes for most transactions, except tax payments.

11.6 Applications are expected to increase (greater rewards) and challenges decrease (more to lose). The price of a new car will increase slightly.

11.7 a. Tacit collusion if its purpose is to divide up the market.

b. Most likely competitive behavior.

c. May or may not be collusive, depending on the price agreed to in the exchange.

d. Not collusive.

11.8 The number of conversations is likely to decrease, and the content is expected to be brief and guarded.

11.9 P = SMC(4 firms) at the competitive solution, so Q = 30,000; MR = SMC(4 firms) at the monopoly solution, so Q = 18,000. If fixed cost is zero, then profit equals \$562,500 for *each* competitive firm and \$1,012,500 for each cartel firm.

11.10 Demand is expected to be less elastic during Passover and Valentine's Day.

11.11 Yes, if their marginal cost is greater than marginal revenue at the optimal output rate. The other firms do not have to pay a less efficient firm if the monopoly price is too low to cause this firm to enter.

11.12 The deadweight loss due to monopoly is computed in the same manner as in Figure 11.11 except that the long-run cost curves are used.

11.13 If $L > 1$, the market price is in the inelastic range (-because L = $1/\eta$), which is evidence against market power if the product or service is sold for a single price to all customers. If the firm sells at different prices, however, this evidence is less clear.

11.14 Before the merger, HHI = 3,000; after the merger, HHI = 4,200.

11.15 With no merger, HHI = 875. Any two small firms can merge, and a big and small firm can merge.

PRICE THEORY PROBLEMS

1. False; consumers will drop out of the market as price increases.
2. No, it depends on where the new marginal revenue curve intersects the old marginal cost curve.
3. There is no simple answer to this question. Firms with market power make excess profits and attract entry. The Lerner and Herfindahl indices are guides. A cross-price elasticity of zero is an indication of potential market power. We could test for a low cross-price elasticity, but there are many factors we must control for in our analysis. Without controls, our conclusions are only preliminary and conditional.
4. No, the existing monopoly is expected to capitalize the value of the monopoly profits in the sales price.
5. The existing liquor stores may gain if entry is restricted by regulation.
6. The answer depends on the shape of the average and marginal cost curves. If the average cost curve decreases over the entire range of output, then MC < ATC and the statement is correct.
7. Generally, the price increase will be less for the monopolist.
8.

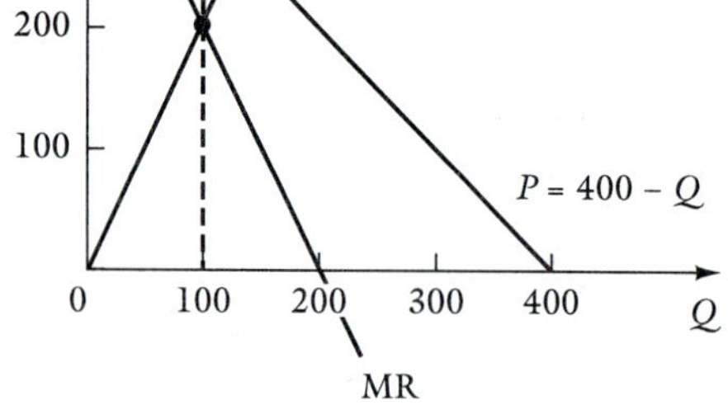

$Q = 100$; $P = 300$.

9. a. $Q = 400$; $P = \$6$.

   b. $Q = 375$; $P = \$6.25$. Tax revenue = \$187.50.

10. Producers' surplus = \$1,600; consumers' surplus = \$800.

   a. $Q = 800$; $P = \$2$.

   b. Producers' surplus = 0; consumers' surplus = \$3,200; deadweight loss = \$800.

11. a.

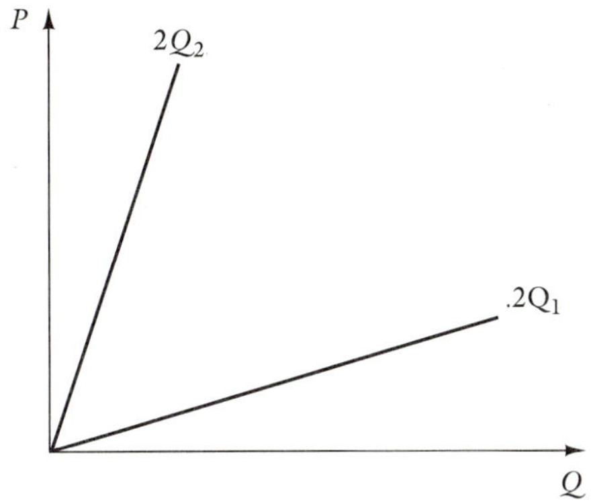

Plant 1.

   b. $Q = 98$, $Q_1 = 89$, $Q_2 = 9$, $P = \$510$.

   c. $Q = 94$, $Q_1 = 63$, $Q_2 = 31$. Yes, plant 2 produces relatively more output.

12. If each Q represents one player, then the competitive structure yields $P = \$62.50$, $T = \$57.50$ per player, and $Q = 11.5$ players. (Note: Set P = MC, where MC = 5 + T, and solve for Q as a function of T and maximize $T \times Q$) For the monopoly, set MR = MC, then solve and maximize. The monopoly solution yields the same result. The city officials are indifferent.

CHAPTER 12

LEARNING EXERCISES

12.1 Consumers' surplus has increased relative to the monopoly solution and the deadweight loss has decreased because the firm is producing more.

12.2 Increasing the cost of arbitrage will prolong the two-price equilibrium. Production increased from old oil wells.

12.3 The individual purchases at most Q_3 kwh per month.

12.4 RealPure sets MR = MC in each market to maximize profits. Different marginal costs imply different prices, so the firm is not practicing pure price discrimination.

12.5 Yes. The maximum each firm is willing to pay is $590,000.

12.6 Single-price strategy: P_1 = $75, P_2 = $50; profits = $300.

Pure bundling strategy: P_B = $85; profits = $340.

The mixed bundling strategy is no better than the pure bundling strategy.

12.7 If it lowers price, the gain in T^* is less than the increase in revenues; if it raises price, there is some consumers' surplus remaining above the LMC curve that the firm has not extracted, so profits are reduced.

12.8 If the demand by the high-demand group is sufficiently large that the area under this demand curve (above LMC) exceeds the profits when the low-demand group is included, then the firm will set T^* to exclude the low-demand group. A small number of low-demand group members may create this result.

12.9 If they anticipate long lines, then consumers are willing to pay less for GuestPasses; this decreases ride utilization.

12.10 No, the amount is expected to exceed (by a small margin) the maximum that the second-highest bidder is willing to pay.

12.11 Higher.

PRICE THEORY PROBLEMS

1. a. If discriminatory, then volume is an indicator of price elasticity. If not, then higher volume reflects lower production costs.
   b. Coffee is costly to produce, so the lunch price must reflect the combined cost of the product or it is a form of bundling to extract consumers' surplus.
   c. Florida residents live closer to Disney World in Orlando, which gives them greater discretion over when to visit the theme park. More discretion is expected to imply a more elastic demand curve. On the cost side, Disney may offer discounts only during off-peak periods to increase utilization and lower its average cost.
   d. This mechanism sorts customers according to whether they spend time collecting coupons, a signal of the value of their time. A manufacturer may offer coupons to reduce inventories, which reduces costs.
   e. Those attending one week might have only bought a single-game ticket. The discount may induce them to attend a second game. Season ticket holders will not be affected. In contrast, distributing discounts at a football game has a lower cost than mailing or advertising because the intended recipients are all in one place.
2. This may be price discrimination using bundling or it may reflect cost differences because some luxury items and options take longer to sell.

3. This is a tying or bundling arrangement, which may be discriminatory depending on the price Kellogg charges for toy and cereal products. If toys are less expensive than in the retail store and the retail store's cost of selling toys is no different than Kellogg's, it is discriminatory. If costs of selling are different, it is unclear. If the toys are not available at retail, then Kellogg may be acting competitively or as a monopolist.

4. a. $Q = 400$; $P = \$600$; profits = \$160,000.
   b. $Q = 800$; $P = \$200$; profits = \$320,000.
   c. Profits = \$245,000, so continue to price-discriminate.

5. a. Find the output at which $MR_{NY} = MR_{CA} = MC$; $Q_{NY} = 9$, $Q_{CA} = 4$, so $P_{NY} = \$11$, and $P_{CA} = \$6$; $\text{profits}_{NY} = \$26$ and $\text{profits}_{CA} = \$16$.
   b. Deadweight loss in New York equals \$40.50 and in California it equals \$8.

6. a. Find the output at which $MR_{early} = MR_{late} = MC$; $Q_{early} = 2$, $Q_{late} = 3$, so $P_{early} = \$4$, and $P_{late} = \$5$; $\text{profits}_{early} = \$4$ and $\text{profits}_{late} = \$9$.
   b. The theater charges \$2 per movie viewed. The early admission charge or tariff equals \$8; the late admission charge equals \$18; $\text{profits}_{early} = \$8$ and $\text{profits}_{late} = \$18$.

7. a. Single-price strategy: $P_A = \$50$, $P_B = \$50$, profits = \$200.

   Pure bundle strategy: $P_{bundle} = \$100$, profits = \$300.

   The mixed bundle strategy is no better than the pure bundle strategy.

   b. Single-price strategy: $P_A = \$50$, $P_B = \$50$, profits = \$90.

   Pure bundle strategy: $P_{bundle} = \$100$, profits = \$135.

   Mixed bundle strategy: $P_A = \$50$, $P_B = \$50$, $P_{bundle} = \$100$, profits = \$135.

   The mixed bundle strategy is no better than the pure bundle strategy.

8. a. Single-price strategy: $P_A = \$15$, $P_B = \$15$, profits = \$75.

   Pure bundle strategy: $P_{bundle} = \$25$, profits = \$75.

   Mixed bundle strategy: $P_A = \$20$, $P_B = \$20$, $P_{bundle} = \$30$, profits = \$100.

   b. Total consumers' surplus equals \$115. Subtracting profits leaves \$15.

9. a. Set MR = MC to solve for Q: $Q = 50$, $P = \$150$, profits = \$2,750.
   b. Set P = MC to solve for the usage fee: $Q = 75$, $P = \$125$. With $Q = 75$, the access fee equals \$2,812.50 and profits equal \$4,625.

10. Firms may offer these options to discriminate between high- and low-usage customers. Low-usage customers (less than 150 minutes per month) would likely prefer the first option and high-usage customers (more than 150 minutes per month) would likely prefer the second option. A person who expects to use 150 minutes would be indifferent between the two options. Companies may also find that their costs are different for low- and high-usage customers, which may justify the two pricing schemes.

11.

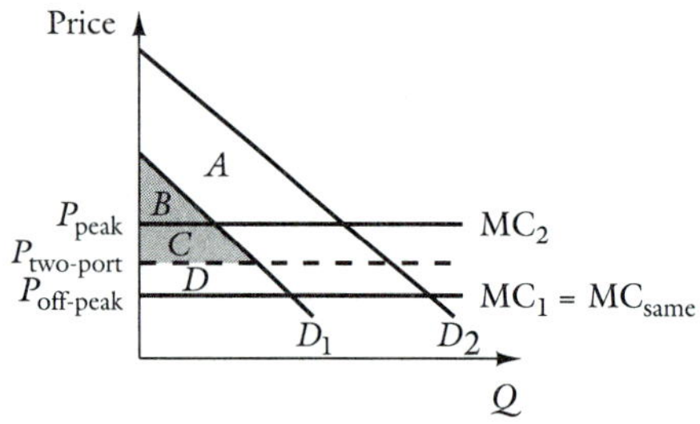

With a constant marginal cost initially, $MC_1 = MC_{same}$, the optimal two-parts structure is a usage fee equal to $P_{two\text{-}part}$ and an access fee equal to areas $B + C$. With marginal cost different between periods, the optimal pricing structure is to set P_{peak} for the usage fee during the peak demand (D_2), charge a peak access fee equal to areas $A + B$, set the usage fee equal to $P_{off\text{-}peak}$ during the off-peak periods, and charge an off-peak access fee of $B + C + D$.

12.

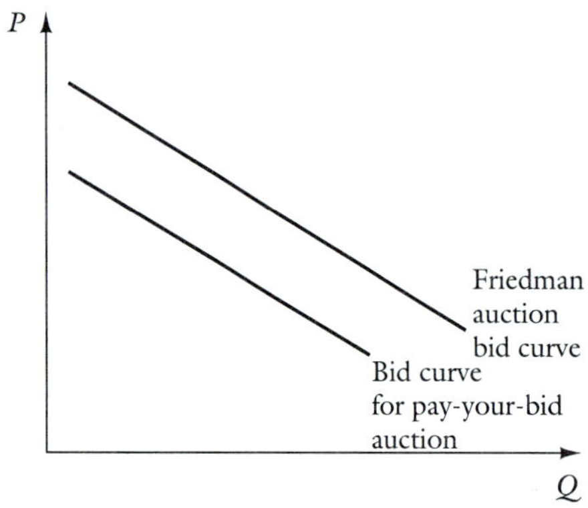

CHAPTER 13

LEARNING EXERCISES

13.1 Its demand would then be the market demand curve, which lies further to the right than D_{SR}.

13.2 Efficient allocation requires that price equal marginal cost, but this holds in both cases because the marginal cost curve intersects the minimum of the long-run average cost curve.

13.3 The full price expression is $(N/L)FC + m + 2t(^1/_4N)$, where $N = 5$, $t =$ \$8, $m = 4$, FC = 100, and $L = 1{,}000$, so the full price equals \$5.30.

13.4 Monopoly profits equal \$1,620,000; Cournot-Nash profits equal \$1,440,000; competitive profits equal \$0.

13.5 As the difference between in the slopes of the two linear demand curves increases, the difference between the two linear marginal revenue curves increases.

13.6 Firms may adopt such clauses in response to customers' concerns that they are paying the lowest price offered for the product or service. Without such guarantees, the firm would not make the sale, compared to a firm that will offer the most-favored-customer guarantee.

13.7 The price leader's inverse demand curve is $P = 0$ if $P_{market} \geq \$62.50$; $P = \$62.50 - Q/2$ if $\$25 \leq P_{market} < \$62.50$; and $P = 100 - Q$ if $P_{market} < \$25$. The optimal output rate for the price leader equals 37.5 units, $P_{market} = \$43.75$, and $Q_{small} = 18.75$ units.

13.8 Add "Retreat to Washington, D.C." as the third option.

13.9 No; *Newsweek* will prefer to run the AIDS hospital story if *Time* chooses to run the AIDS hospital on its cover.

13.10 *Time*'s first move is to choose the AIDS story for its cover. *Newsweek* is indifferent on its first move.

13.11 The similarity is that competitors almost always match price decreases, but they match price increases less often.

13.12 Sam does not really care because any sentence given is a life sentence. Thus, Carlos is unsure of Sam's optimal strategy. The likely outcome is indeterminate.

PRICE THEORY PROBLEMS

1. Firms in monopolistically competitive markets have some (limited) market power, whereas perfect competitors have no market power. Both models allow entry and this results in zero profits in the long run.
2. The perfect competitor produces at the minimum of the long-run average cost curve in equilibrium, but the monopolistic competitor produces a lower output rate at a higher long-run average cost.
3. Advertising that their fuel additives make car engines last longer, emit less pollutants, and increase combustion efficiency as measured by miles per gallon.
4. The marginal revenue of the ad campaign is \$3,000 (40 × \$75). To determine if profits have risen, we need to know the firm's cost structure and its advertising expenditures. If profits rise, increasing advertising expenditures is a good strategy. Competitors will likely advertise, too.
5. Differentiated products, such as Chiquita bananas, give firms limited market power. It makes sense to expend resources to differentiate a product if the resulting market power increases profits. Advertising is popular in oligopolistic industries for many reasons, including information distribution to customers, sending quality signals, and as a response to competitors' actions.

6. This result occurs when these changes take place within the kinked part of the demand curve. The model is inefficient in the usual sense if MB $\neq$ MC at the market equilibrium, which is generally the case.
7. a. There is no dominant strategy for either firm.
   b. There are two Nash equilibria: Mrs. Sweet chooses "crunchy" and Tasty Bakery chooses "soft 'n chewy" or Mrs. Sweet chooses "soft 'n chewy" and Tasty Bakery chooses "crunchy."
   c. Tasty Bakery is indifferent between "crunchy" and "soft 'n chewy" on the first move because they both yield \$1,400 if Mrs. Sweet responds optimally. But if Tasty Bakery chooses "soft 'n chewy" then Mrs. Sweet receives \$1,200 by choosing "crunchy," which is the best possible result for Mrs. Sweet.
8. a. There is no dominant strategy for either firm.
   b. There are two Nash equilibria: Fastread, Inc., chooses the romance series and Paperbook, Inc., chooses the mystery series, or Fastread chooses the mystery series and Paperbook chooses the romance series.
   c. The cooperative outcome is for Paperbook, Inc. to choose the mystery series and Fastread to choose the romance series.
   d. Fastread gains the most because it gains \$4,000 more than with its next-best alternative. Fastread must offer Paperbook at least \$1,000 to cooperate because Paperbook will prefer to publish the romance series for which it earns \$4,000 instead of \$3,000.
9. Cooperation will tend to break down either immediately or systematically over time as the final day approaches. Each vendor can work backwards from the last day to determine the gains from violating the cooperative agreement. Thus, the agreement will be unstable from the beginning.
10. a. The United States chooses the low tax no matter what Japan does.
    b. There are two Nash equilibria: Japan chooses the high tax and the United States chooses the low tax, or Japan chooses the low tax and the United States chooses the low tax.
    c. On the first move, Japan is indifferent between choosing a high or low tax policy.
11. Monopoly: $P = \$7$, $Q_1 = 2.5$; $Q_2 = 2.5$; total profits = \$25, split equally.
    Cournot-Nash: $P = \$5.33$, $Q_1 = 3.33$; $Q_2 = 3.33$; total profits = \$22.23, split equally.
    Perfect competition: $P = \$2$, $Q_1 = 5$, $Q_2 = 5$; total profits = \$0.
12. The dominant firm assumes that the other firms will let it set its output rate first, and they will then serve the residual demand. A low-cost firm can run other firms out of the market if it sets price below the average variable cost of all other firms. If it does this with the idea of raising price later to a monopoly level, it will gain only if new entry is restricted. If entry is not restricted, firms will enter and the firm will find itself back in the same situation as before. Thus, it generally gains only if reentry is restricted or costly.

CHAPTER 14

LEARNING EXERCISES

14.1 They would work for the same network if the second star offered a marginal revenue product that exceeded the star's opportunity cost.

14.2 If wages increase, quantity demanded of labor decreases. If output price increases at the same time, this has the effect of shifting the derived demand for labor to the right, which may fully or partially offset the decline in quantity demanded due to the wage increase.

14.3 Growth in demand for the output of lawyers (say) encourages lawyers to specialize and encourages division of labor, which paraprofessionals represent. A contraction in demand will reverse these effects.

14.4

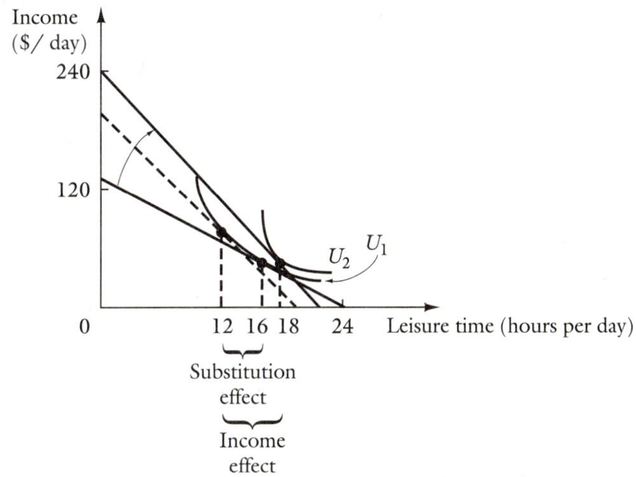

14.5 From 1940 to 1945, arc-supply elasticity equals .41, and between 1945 and 1950, arc-supply elasticity equals 5.3. Real wages increased significantly in the first period, but wartime activities resulted in only a small change in average weekly hours worked; that is, many workers were in the military and thus not available for work. After the war, real wages fell, mainly because soldiers reentered the workforce; thus, average hours worked declined only slightly.

14.6 Madonna's economic rent equals $r_2 - r_1$.

14.7 Eventually, these companies matched Ford's wage; otherwise, they would have lost their best workers to Ford.

14.8 The only difference is that MRP_L is used instead of VMP_L, which is shown in Figure 14.14. Because marginal revenue is less than price, the monoponist employs less labor if it has market power in its output market.

14.9 With the union, players receive $w - H$ in net wages if they work and

$- H$ if they don't work. Without the union, each player receives w_C in wages and all players are employed. For the union to survive, it must set H such that $w - H$ exceeds w_C for 50 percent plus 1 players.

14.10 The highest-ranked station will lose $2 million in advertising revenue if Connie Hennings leaves, so its managers should be willing to match the offer by the second-highest-ranked station. If the station falls to number three in the rankings, what it will offer depends on how much this drop in the ratings reduces profits.

14.11 $w^* = 3 - 12.65 = \$17.35$. There is likely to be less search because the lower reservation wage makes it more likely you will find a job on any given search.

PRICE THEORY PROBLEMS

1. Disney has the property rights to the use of the Mickey Mouse character, which gives it market power. Because the individual who plays Mickey Mouse is anonymous when in costume, there is no attachment of the character to the individual actor, so Disney is operating in a competitive labor market.
2. Row 2: 180; Row 3: 40; row 4: 240; row 5: 4; row 6: 246.
   a. 6 hourly workers.
   b. Reduces to 5 hourly workers; yes, because only one worker is put out of work.
3. On average it looks like a backward-bending labor supply curve, but there may be other factors that explain these changes. For example, salaries may have increased because of bonuses tied to performance in previous years; thus, the connection between current hours worked and current salaries may be imperfect.
4. The value of the marginal product for a college professor can increase when new technology—television and video—allows more students access to a lecture and when other activities, such as grant writing, produce income for a university. These activities act to increase wages. The "winner take all" characteristic is present in research, because the first to discover and develop a new idea generally receives the greatest credit and reward for the effort.
5. If salary information is known, it encourages comparisons between workers. Such comparisons may lead to dissatisfaction and lower productivity, so employers try to limit access to salary information. Unions reveal salary schedules because they are responsible to the majority of workers, not the owners of the firm. The majority of workers can judge the success of the union over time if they know the salary schedule.
6. If the perfectly competitive firm discriminates, it increases its cost above that of its competitors and must sell its product for a higher price. A higher price, however, will cause customers to switch to other firms. The switching will drive the discriminating firm out of business

eventually. A monopoly also minimizes costs, so it loses profits if it discriminates, but there are no competitors, so it is not driven out of business.

7. a. Equating MRP_L to MFC gives $w = \$26.66$ and $L = 6.67$. (The .67 is a part-time worker.)
   b. We would use the VMP_L instead of the MRP_L to compute the demand curve.
   c. Wage demand is $w = \$53.33$ for 6.67 workers.
8. To attract the same number of soldiers, the military had to raise wages and benefits. The effect on quality is ambiguous. It would reduce the number of high-marginal-product workers drafted, but those who volunteer may be more motivated to perform. Specifically, even if a high-marginal-product person is drafted, there is no guarantee that the individual will provide high productivity at the low wage paid during the draft. Thus, the volunteer army may be more productive. Training programs and other benefits increased.
9. Solve $[(30 - w^*)/2] \times [(30 - w^*)/15] = \$3$ for w^*. This gives $w^* = \$20.51$. The probability of finding an acceptable offer on the first search is $(30 - 20.51)/30$ or .32.
10. Yes, if they planned to study the same subject and pay the same costs. Obviously, if income and/or tuition costs differ for the two individuals, they may make different choices.

Chapter 15

Learning Exercises

15.1 Assuming that your personal discount rate equals 15 percent, you should pay the tuition now ($\$5{,}000 \le \$5{,}217$).

15.2 $75,934

15.3

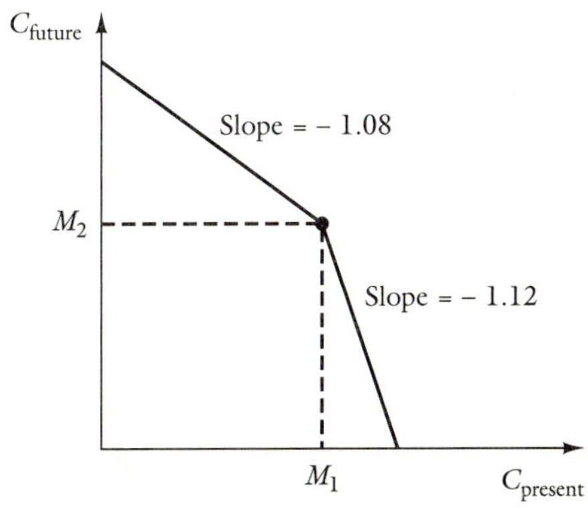

15.4

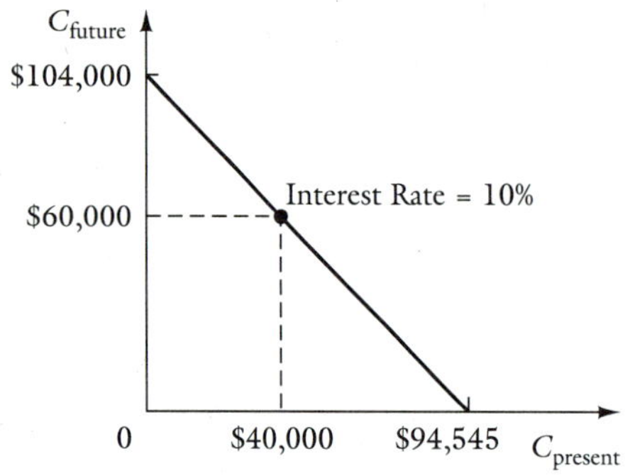

15.5 The loss in wealth will reduce both present and future consumption as individuals save more to replace the wealth losses.

15.6 Self-test question.

15.7 The risk of default helps explain why corporate bonds offer higher average returns.

15.8 Speculators can profit if they accurately forecast that there is an imbalance between supply and demand in the future and current futures prices.

15.9 Mike is risk averse, Judy is risk neutral or a mild risk lover, and Henry is a risk lover.

PRICE THEORY PROBLEMS

1. a.

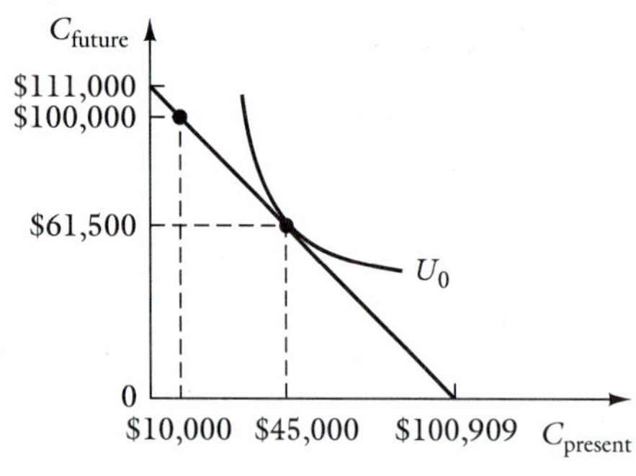

b. 1.10

c. Worse off.

2.

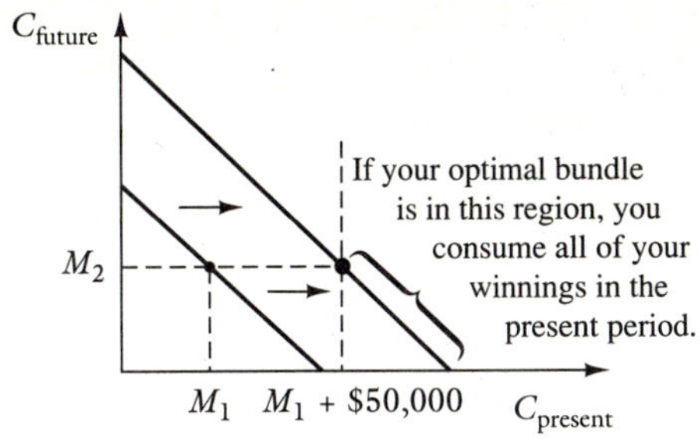

3. $1,000; $1035.66

4.

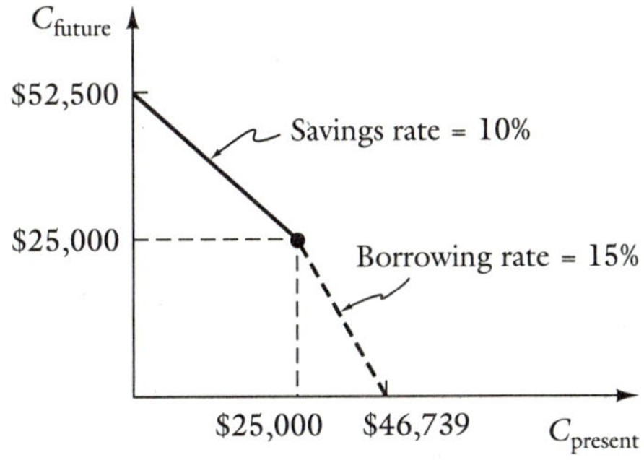

5. The possible solutions are that you consume only in the present, you consume only in the future, or that you are indifferent across all bundles on the intertemporal budget constraint. If you consume only in the present, then MRTP > 1 + r.

6. The expected value of your uncertain stream is $125 (.5 × $200 + .5 × $50). To hedge this stream, bet $75 that the team will lose at every game. If they win, your net is $200 – $75 = $125; if they lose, your net is $50 + $75 = $125.

7. Expected cost equals 15 × $8,000 or $120,000, which requires a premium of $120 from each of the 1,000 women. Moral hazard may be a problem: once insured, some women may find it advantageous to try to get pregnant.

8. You buy in present value the rights to all future assets distributions (dividends) and any capital appreciation of the assets. If past performance is correlated with dividends and capital appreciation, then it will affect what you are willing to pay for these rights.

9. Weather changes affect the supply of crops that the speculator may have bought or sold in a futures market. The speculator should acquire information until marginal benefit equals its marginal cost. An in-house weather service may be useful to speculators who take large positions and can therefore justify the cost of the service.

10. You would want suppliers to maintain a certain minimum inventory level of these items in case you run out during a "rush" job.

11. No. As the price increases, the net expected gain from a given policy decreases. Thus, individuals are expected to reduce their consumption of insurance, which they do by lowering its face value.

12.

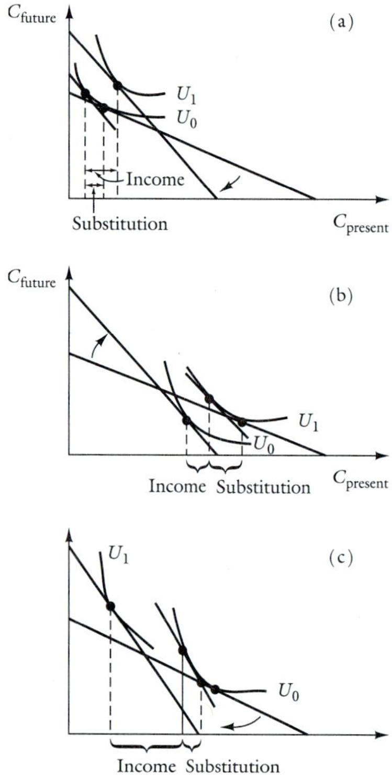

Chapter 16

Learning Exercises

16.1

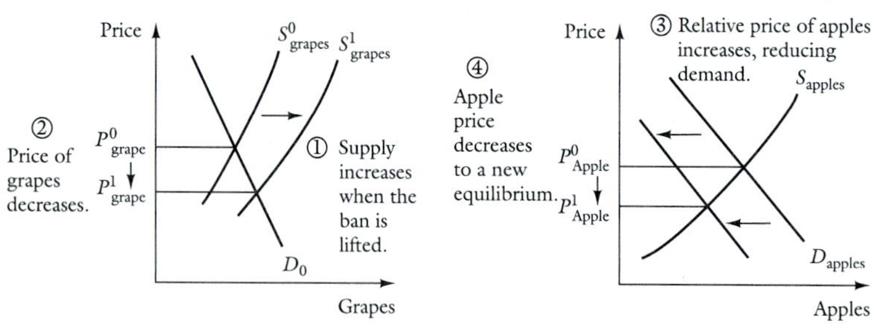

16.2 A nonzero cross-price elasticity indicates that demand in one market is affected by price changes in another market. Thus, feedback effects are linked directly to cross-price effects.

16.3 The MRS is one measure of the degree of substitution between two goods. If two goods are perfect substitutes, the MRS is a constant and indifference curves are straight lines. The region of mutual advantage vanishes with perfect substitutes. Accordingly, as goods become more complementary, the size of the region of mutual advantage increases.

16.4 The Divider will be worse off if this split is not the optimal one from the Divider's viewpoint. The Chooser may be better or worse off.

16.5 Yes, a free trade agreement with a third country opens the United States to imports from this country transshipped through Mexico and opens that country to exports from the United States transshipped through Mexico. The United States and other countries control for this problem by requiring labels that indicate the country of origin. The third country avoids this by placing Mexican labels on its goods.

16.6 The PPF expands outward along the food axis but does not change its intersection point along the clothing axis.

16.7 Parents can make tied investments in a child's education that cannot be traded between children. For example, parents may pay tuition directly instead of giving cash to a son or daughter for this purpose.

16.8 Produce more clothing and less food.

PRICE THEORY PROBLEMS

1. The essential difference here is that when the relative price of grapes increases, the demand for apples decreases (shifts to the left) instead of increasing. Thus, the price of apples decreases.
2. The analysis is the same, but the use of the tax receipts can affect demand and supply if the funds are directed to consumers of apples or grapes, or to producers of these products. A subsidy to apple consumers will result in higher prices for producers (consumers' price plus the subsidy) and a larger quantity sold in equilibrium, but a lower consumer price.
3. False. For perfect substitutes many individuals will choose to consume only one good. In the market, there will be a continuum of individuals along the demand curve. After the tax causes price to change, some individuals will substitute to the other commodity, which increases its demand and changes relative price, causing feedback effects. The partial equilibrium approach does not take into account the feedback effects.
4. a. $P_E = \$8,979.59$ and $P_R = \$9,795.92$.

b. Partial equilibrium: $P_R = \$10,795.92$
c. General equilibrium: $P_E = \$9,081.63$ and $P_R = \$10,816.33$.

5. a. There is no incentive to trade.
   b. The analysis is the same as in the text except that the indifference curves form right angles. Thus, efficient trade occurs when the apex of these curves meet at the same bundle or when either the vertical or horizontal segments of these curves overlap so that one individual cannot gain without making the other individuals worse off.
   c. Efficient exchange occurs when the linear indifference curve intersects the apex of the right-angled indifference curve.

6. a.

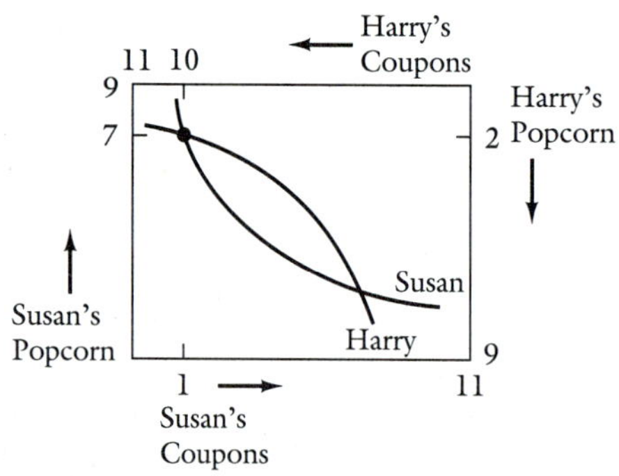

   b. The endowment is not efficient; Susan will consume more video coupons and less popcorn and Harry will consume more popcorn and fewer video coupons at the efficient solution.

7. The mix is not technically efficient. The food industry should use more labor and less capital, and the clothing industry should use less labor and more capital.

8. The production possibilities curve is linear. No, output efficiency requires that MRT = MRS for all individuals.

Chapter 17

LEARNING EXERCISES

17.1 The new solution produces more clothing and less food than the competitive solution shown in Figure 17.1.

17.2 Marginal cost may be zero, but it must cost some resources to produce. The optimal output is zero in a private market if there is no way to make individuals pay for the good. With lump-sum taxation used to pay, the optimal is where marginal benefit equals zero.

17.3 Many county sheriff departments receive per diem payments for prisoners. These budgets would decrease if the sheriffs did not run the jails.

17.4 The United States could auction the fishing rights, but they are of lower value if there is no mechanism for enforcing the winner's exclusive right to harvest a particular catch. High monitoring and enforcement costs make this solution impractical.

17.5

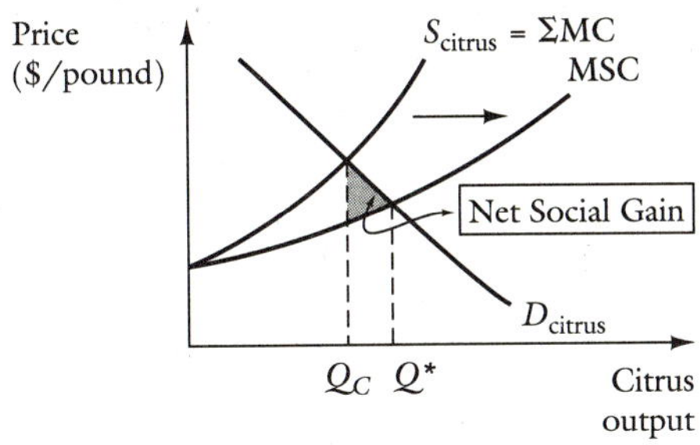

17.6 Air pollution is a bad. Generally, its economic cost is measured by the amount of income needed to provide you with the satisfaction you would have without air pollution.

17.7 The area between the new (higher) marginal cost curve and the old marginal cost curve places a bound on what the fishing industry is willing to pay the citrus farmers.

17.8 Yes, the price of new cars will increase.

17.9 By issuing allotments, the government can limit the output of negative externality producing goods.

17.10 The number of writers attempting to produce biographies will decrease, thus shifting supply to the left and increasing price. The cost of producing software code will also increase, thus increasing its market price.

PRICE THEORY PROBLEMS

1. Public goods can be produced privately if the cost of exclusion is not too high. Public authorities must be able to impose mandatory taxation on consumers in order to pay for the provision of public goods. Privatization is a method whereby the private sector produces public goods, but the public sector raises funds (taxes) to pay for their production.
2. a. Within the neighborhood, nonrival and nonexclusive.
   b. If safety is the good produced, nonrival and nonexclusive.
   c. Rival and exclusive.
   d. Nonrival and exclusive (it affects a certain area).
   e. If you own a television set, nonrival and nonexclusive.
   f. Rival and exclusive.

g. Rival and nonexclusive.
h. If you buy it, rival and exclusive.
i. Rival and exclusive, although others may enjoy its appearance.
j. Rival and nonexclusive.
k. Rival and exclusive.
l. When in your possession, rival and exclusive.

3. If the existing location of these rare plants could be documented, then one scheme would be to give farmers a share of the profits generated from any new drugs. This gives farmers an incentive to perserve the species variety found on their land. If the rare plants are found in multiple locations, a given farmer has less incentive to perserve the species because any new drugs can be developed from another source.
4. Flowers planted in the front yard provide a positive externality to neighbors and drivers passing by. Flowers planted in the backyard are usually seen only by the homeowner. Thus, flowers in the backyard are private goods. Given your valuation of flowers in the front yard, the number planted is optimal, but including the valuation of the neighbors, the number planted is too little (assuming that the Coase theorem does not apply). If you don't like your neighbors, you may plant even fewer flowers in the front yard.
5. Both approaches can cause firms to produce the socially optimal output rate if the policies are implemented correctly. The main difference is that the output restriction leaves firms with more producers' surplus than the tax policy. With the tax policy, the use of the tax revenues can affect the demand or supply curves, depending on how the funds are spent. If demand is highly variable, the tax approach allows output to adjust, so it is preferred.
6. With a positive externality, the output restriction must be in the form that the firm produces *no less* than a given output rate. Price controls will not cause firms to produce the socially optimal output rate.
7. The number of transplants would increase because it would be less costly to find (and pay) a donor for an organ. The cost of developing a black market in organs will drop significantly if only blood type matters for a match. The Coase theorem suggests that with zero transaction costs the socially optimal transplant rate will arise. But there are penalties if organs are bought and sold; thus, transaction costs are not zero.
8. The transaction costs of bribing patrons to stop smoking are high relative to the benefits received. Addiction to smoking lowers the expected return to bargaining because addicted patrons will ask for a larger bribe.

Credits

Table 4.1. From "The Allocation of Time: Empirical Findings, Behavioral Models, and Problems of Measurement" by F. Thomas Juster and Frank P. Stafford in JOURNAL OF ECONOMIC LITERATURE, 29 (June 1991). Reprinted by permission of the American Economic Association.

Table 7.2. Data for Table, "Merger Activity Involving Domestic Buyers and/or Sellers, 1970–1990" is collected by Merrill Lynch Business Advisory Services and reprinted by permission of Merrill Lynch.

Table 7.2. "Shareholder Proposal on Rights Plan for Colgate Palmolive, Co., 1987 Proxy Statement." Reprinted by permission of the California State Teachers' Retirement System.

Figure 15.7. From THE WALL STREET JOURNAL, September 18, 1992. Reprinted by permission of The Wall Street Journal, © 1992 Dow Jones & Company, Inc. All Rights Reserved Worldwide.

Index